THE NEW CAMBRIDGE HISTORY OF

ENGLISH LITERATURE

The New Cambridge History of English Literature is a programme
of reference works designed to offer a broad synthesis and
contextual survey of the history of English literature through
the major periods of its development. The organization of each
volume reflects the particular characteristics of the period
covered, within a general commitment to providing an accessible
narrative history through a linked sequence of essays by inter-
nationally renowned scholars. The History is designed to accommodate the range of insights and fresh perspectives brought by
new approaches to the subject, without losing sight of the need
for essential exposition and information. The volumes include
valuable reference features, in the form of a chronology of
literary and political events, extensive primary and secondary
bibliographies, and a full index.

The Cambridge History of Medieval English Literature
EDITED BY DAVID WALLACE

The Cambridge History of Early Modern English Literature
EDITED BY DAVID LOEWENSTEIN AND JANEL MUELLER

The Cambridge History of English Literature, 1660–1780
EDITED BY JOHN RICHETTI

The Cambridge History of English Romantic Literature
EDITED BY JAMES CHANDLER

The Cambridge History of Victorian Literature
EDITED BY KATE FLINT

The Cambridge History of Twentieth-Century English Literature
EDITED BY LAURA MARCUS AND PETER NICHOLLS

THE CAMBRIDGE
HISTORY OF
VICTORIAN LITERATURE

*

Edited by
KATE FLINT

CAMBRIDGE
UNIVERSITY PRESS

CAMBRIDGE
UNIVERSITY PRESS

University Printing House, Cambridge CB2 8BS, United Kingdom

Cambridge University Press is part of the University of Cambridge.

It furthers the University's mission by disseminating knowledge in the pursuit of education, learning and research at the highest international levels of excellence.

www.cambridge.org
Information on this title: www.cambridge.org/9781316606131

© Cambridge University Press 2012

First published 2012
5th printing 2015
First paperback edition 2016

Printed in the United Kingdom by Clays, St Ives plc.

A catalogue record for this publication is available from the British Library

Library of Congress Cataloguing-in-Publication Data

The Cambridge History of Victorian Literature / edited by Kate Flint.
p. cm. – (The new cambridge history of English literature) ISBN 978-0-521-84625-7 (Hardback)
1. English literature–19th century–History and criticism.   2. Literature and society–Great Britain–History–19th century.   I. Flint, Kate.   II. Title.   III. Series.
PR461.C36 2012
820.9′008–dc23
2011024207

ISBN 978-0-521-84625-7 Hardback
ISBN 978-1-316-60613-1 Paperback

Contents

Notes on contributors   *xi*

Introduction   *1*
KATE FLINT

PART I
AUTHORS, READERS, AND PUBLISHERS

1 · Publishing and the materiality of the book   *15*
DAVID FINKELSTEIN

2 · Victorian reading   *34*
LEAH PRICE

3 · Periodicals and reviewing   *56*
HILARY FRASER

PART II
WRITING VICTORIA'S ENGLAND

4 · The expansion of Britain   *79*
DAVID AMIGONI

5 · High Victorianism   *102*
JANICE CARLISLE

6 · The *fin de siècle*   *124*
STEPHEN ARATA

vii

Contents

PART III
MODES OF WRITING

7 · Lyric and the lyrical   151
ANGELA LEIGHTON

8 · Epic   172
HERBERT F. TUCKER

9 · Melodrama   193
CAROLYN WILLIAMS

10 · Sensation   220
KATE FLINT

11 · Autobiography   243
LINDA H. PETERSON

12 · Comic and satirical   265
JOHN BOWEN

13 · Innovation and experiment   288
JEROME MCGANN

14 · Writing for children   311
CLAUDIA NELSON

PART IV
MATTERS OF DEBATE

15 · Education   331
DINAH BIRCH

16 · Spirituality   350
ELISABETH JAY

17 · Material   370
ELAINE FREEDGOOD

Contents

18 · Economics and finance   *388*
MARY POOVEY

19 · History   *405*
ANDREW SANDERS

20 · Sexuality   *422*
SHARON MARCUS

21 · Aesthetics   *444*
ELIZABETH HELSINGER

22 · Science and literature   *466*
GILLIAN BEER

23 · Subjectivity, psychology, and the imagination   *487*
HELEN SMALL

24 · Cityscapes   *510*
DEBORAH EPSTEIN NORD

25 · The rural scene: Victorian literature and the natural world   *532*
FRANCIS O'GORMAN

26 · 'The annihilation of space and time': literature and technology   *550*
CLARE PETTITT

PART V

SPACES OF WRITING

27 · Spaces of the nineteenth-century novel   *575*
ISOBEL ARMSTRONG

28 · National and regional literatures   *598*
SARA L. MAURER

29 · Britain and Europe   *622*
NICHOLAS DAMES

Contents

30 · Victorian empire   641
PABLO MUKHERJEE

31 · Writing about America   662
DEIRDRE DAVID

PART VI
VICTORIAN AFTERLIVES

32 · 1900 and the *début de siècle*: poetry, drama, fiction   685
JOSEPH BRISTOW

33 · The future of Victorian literature   712
JAY CLAYTON

Select bibliography   730
Index   759

Notes on contributors

DAVID AMIGONI is Professor of Victorian Literature at Keele University. He is the author of *Victorian Biography* (1993), *Colonies, Cults and Evolution: Literature, Science and Culture in Nineteenth-Century Writing* (2007), and editor of *Life Writing and Victorian Culture* (2006). He edited the *Journal of Victorian Culture* between 2005 and 2008. He is completing a critical guide to Victorian literature (forthcoming 2011).

STEPHEN ARATA is Associate Professor of English at the University of Virginia and the author of *Fictions of Loss in the Victorian Fin de Siècle* (1996) as well as numerous essays on nineteenth- and twentieth-century English literature and culture.

ISOBEL ARMSTRONG is Emeritus Professor of English and Fellow of Birkbeck College, University of London. She has taught in the universities of Leicester and Southampton and at Harvard and Johns Hopkins University. She has written widely on nineteenth-century literature and poetry: *Victorian Poetry: Poetry, Poetics and Politics* (1993), *The Oxford Anthology of Nineteenth-Century Women's Poetry* (1996); and on the aesthetic: *The Radical Aesthetic* (2000). Her latest book is *Victorian Glassworlds. Glass Culture and the Imagination 1830–80* (2008). Her long poem, *Desert Collages*, was published in 2007.

DAME GILLIAN BEER is King Edward VII Professor Emeritus at the University of Cambridge. Among her books are *Arguing with the Past: Essays in Narrative from Woolf to Sidney* (1989), *Open Fields: Science in Cultural Encounter* (1996), and *Darwin's Plots* (3rd edition, 2009). She has been President of the British Society for Literature and Science and of the British Comparative Literature Association. She is at present finishing a study of Lewis Carroll's 'Alice' books and is editing Carroll's complete poems.

DINAH BIRCH is Professor of English Literature at the University of Liverpool. Her research interests focus on nineteenth-century literature, with particular reference to the work of John Ruskin and to women's writing. Her most recent monograph is *Our Victorian Education* (2007), and she is the general editor of the seventh edition of the *Oxford Companion to English Literature* (2009).

JOHN BOWEN is Professor of Nineteenth-Century Literature at the University of York and a Fellow of the English Association. He has written widely on nineteenth-century fiction and is the author of *Other Dickens: Pickwick to Chuzzlewit* (2000) and has edited Dickens's *Barnaby Rudge* and *Palgrave Advances in Charles Dickens Studies* (with Robert L. Patten).

JOSEPH BRISTOW is Professor of English at the University of California, Los Angeles. His recent books include *Oscar Wilde and Modern Culture: The Making of a Legend* (2008). He is international editor of the *Journal of Victorian Culture* (Routledge) and series editor of Palgrave Studies in Nineteenth-Century Writing and Culture.

JANICE CARLISLE has been Professor of English at Yale University since 2004. She has published books and articles on Victorian fiction and autobiography, as well as a study of the works of John Stuart Mill. A book analysing the First and Second Reform Acts from the perspectives of Victorian illustrated journalism and painting is forthcoming.

JAY CLAYTON is William R. Kenan, Jr. Professor and Chair of the English department at Vanderbilt University. He is the author of *Romantic Vision and the Novel* (1987), *The Pleasures of Babel: Contemporary American Literature and Theory* (1993) and *Charles Dickens in Cyberspace: The Afterlife of the Nineteenth Century in Postmodern Culture* (2003).

NICHOLAS DAMES is Theodore Kahan Professor in the Humanities and Professor of English and Comparative Literature at Columbia University. He is the author of *Amnesiac Selves: Nostalgia, Forgetting, and British Fiction, 1810–1870* (2001), and *The Physiology of the Novel: Reading, Neural Science, and the Form of Victorian Fiction* (2007).

DEIRDRE DAVID is the author, most recently, of *Fanny Kemble: A Performed Life* (2007). Among her other publications are *Fictions of Resolution in Three Victorian Novels* (1981), *Intellectual Women and Victorian Patriarchy: Harriet Martineau, Elizabeth Barrett Browning and George Eliot* (1987), and *Rule Britannia: Women, Empire, and Victorian Writing* (1996). In 2001, she edited *The Cambridge Companion to the Victorian Novel* (soon to be re-issued in a revised edition), and in 2008, co-edited (with Eileen Gillooly) *Contemporary Dickens*. She is Professor Emerita of English, Temple University, Philadelphia, and is currently working on a biography of Olivia Manning, the mid twentieth-century English novelist.

DAVID FINKELSTEIN is Dean of the School of Humanities, University of Dundee. His publications include *The House of Blackwood: Author–Publisher Relations in the Victorian Era* (2002), the co-authored *An Introduction to Book History* (2005), and the edited *Print Culture and the Blackwood Tradition, 1805–1930* (2006). Other co-edited works include *The Book History Reader* (2001, 2006).

KATE FLINT is Provost Professor of English and Art History at the University of Southern California. She is the author of *The Woman Reader, 1837–1914* (1993), *The Victorians and the Visual Imagination* (2000), and *The Transatlantic Indian, 1776–1930* (2009), as well as many essays on Victorian and twentieth-century literary, cultural, and visual history. Her current work is on flash photography and surprising illumination.

HILARY FRASER holds the Geoffrey Tillotson Chair of Nineteenth-Century Studies at Birkbeck College, University of London, where she is also Dean of Arts. She has written monographs on aesthetics and religion in Victorian writing, the Victorians and Renaissance Italy, nineteenth-century non-fiction prose, and gender and the Victorian periodical. She is currently working on women's writing about art in the nineteenth century.

ELAINE FREEDGOOD is Professor of English at New York University and the author of *Victorian Writing about Risk: Imagining a Safe England in a Dangerous World* (2000) and *The Ideas in Things: Fugitive Meaning in the Victorian Novel* (2006), and the editor of *Factory Production in Nineteenth-Century Britain* (2003).

ELIZABETH HELSINGER is the John Matthews Manly Distinguished Service Professor of English, Art History and Visual Arts at the University of Chicago. Her publications include *Ruskin and the Art of the Beholder* (1982), *Rural Scenes and National Representation* (1997), *Poetry and the Pre-Raphaelite Arts* (2008), and numerous articles on Victorian literature and the arts. An editor of *Critical Inquiry* and long-time member of the Governing Board of the Smart Museum of Art at the University of Chicago, she has also served as Chair of both English and Visual Arts departments at Chicago.

ELISABETH JAY is Director of the Institute for Historical and Cultural Research, Associate Head of School, and Professor of English at Oxford Brookes University. She has written widely on nineteenth-century literature, and in particular on women's writing, and literature and theology of the Victorian period.

ANGELA LEIGHTON is Professor of English and Senior Research Fellow at Trinity College, Cambridge. Her books include: *Shelley and the Sublime* (1984), *Elizabeth Barrett Browning* (1986), *Victorian Women Poets: Writing Against the Heart* (1992) and *On Form: Poetry, Aestheticism, and the Legacy of a Word* (2007). In addition to many essays on nineteenth and twentieth-century literature, she has also published two volumes of poetry: *A Cold Spell* and *Sea Level*. She is currently working on a book on music and literature.

SHARON MARCUS is Orlando Harriman Professor of English and Comparative Literature at Columbia University. She is the author of *Apartment Stories: City and Home in Nineteenth-Century Paris and London* (1999) and *Between Women: Friendship, Desire and Marriage in Victorian England* (2007).

SARA L. MAURER is Assistant Professor of English at the University of Notre Dame, where she specializes in nineteenth-century British and Irish literature. Her book *The Dispossessed State: Britain, Ireland, and Narratives of Ownership in the Nineteenth Century* (2011) argues that Ireland played a major role in how nineteenth-century British literature imagined the British state.

JEROME McGANN is the John Stewart Bryan University Professor, University of Virginia. His most recent publications are *Byron's Manfred* (2009) and *Are the Humanities Inconsequent?* (2009).

PABLO MUKHERJEE was educated in Kolkata, Oxford and Cambridge. He is currently Associate Professor in the English and Comparative Literary Studies department at Warwick University. He is the author of *Crime Fiction and Empire* (2003) and *Postcolonial Environments* (2010), as well as a wide range of essays and edited collections.

CLAUDIA NELSON is Professor of English at Texas A&M University. She has co-edited three anthologies of critical essays and is the author of *Boys Will Be Girls: The Feminine Ethic and British Children's Fiction, 1857–1917* (1991), *Invisible Men: Fatherhood in Victorian Periodicals, 1850–1910* (1995), *Little Strangers: Portrayals of Adoption and Foster Care in America, 1851–1929* (2003), and *Family Ties in Victorian England* (2007). *Precocious Children and Childish Adults: Age Inversion in Victorian Literature* will appear in 2012.

DEBORAH EPSTEIN NORD is Professor of English at Princeton University, where she also teaches in the Program in the Study of Women and Gender. She is the author of *The Apprenticeship of Beatrice Webb* (1985), *Walking the Victorian Streets: Women, Representation, and the City* (1995), and *Gypsies and the British Imagination, 1807–1930* (2008), and the editor of John Ruskin's *Sesame and Lilies* (2002).

FRANCIS O'GORMAN is Professor of Victorian Literature at the University of Leeds. Recent publications include an edition of Conan Doyle's *The Hound of the Baskervilles*, the edited collections *Victorian Literature and Finance* (2007) and *The Cambridge Companion to Victorian Culture* (2010), and essays on Coleridge, Wordsworth, and Tennyson. His *Anxious Ruskin* and his edition of Ruskin's *Praeterita* will both appear in 2012.

LINDA H. PETERSON is Niel Gray, Jr. Professor of English at Yale University. She has published two scholarly studies of Victorian autobiography, and edited *The Life of Charlotte Brontë* (2006) and *Harriet Martineau's Autobiography* (2007). Her most recent book is *Becoming a Woman of Letters: Myths of Authorship, Facts of the Victorian Market* (2009).

CLARE PETTITT is Professor of Victorian Literature and Culture at King's College, London. Her publications include *Patent Inventions: Intellectual Property and the Victorian Novel* (2004) and *'Dr. Livingstone I Presume?': Missionaries, Journalists, Explorers and Empire* (2007). She is currently writing a book entitled *Distant Contemporaries: The Invention of a Shared Present*.

MARY POOVEY is the author, most recently, of *Genres of the Credit Economy: Mediating Value in Eighteenth- and Nineteenth-Century Britain* (2008) and *A History of the Modern Fact: Problems of Knowledge in the Sciences of Wealth and Society* (1998). She is Samuel Rudin University Professor in the Humanities and Professor of English at New York University.

LEAH PRICE is Professor of English at Harvard University. Her books include *The Anthology and the Rise of the Novel* (2000) and *Literary Secretaries/Secretarial Culture* (co-ed. 2005); she co-edited a special issue of PMLA on *The History of the Book and the Idea of Literature. How to do Things with Books in Victorian Britain* is forthcoming in 2012.

ANDREW SANDERS is Professor Emeritus of English at the University of Durham. His books include *The Victorian Historical Novel* (1978), *Charles Dickens: Resurrectionist* (1982), *Anthony Trollope* (1998), *Dickens and the Spirit of the Age* (1999), *Charles Dickens* (2003), and *The Short Oxford History of English Literature* (1994). In addition to his work as an editor of Victorian fiction he has written widely on nineteenth-century culture.

HELEN SMALL is Fellow in English at Pembroke College, Oxford. She is the author of *The Long Life* (winner of the Truman Capote Award for literary criticism, 2008). She has written widely on nineteenth-century literature, including *Love's Madness: Medicine, the Novel, and Female Insanity, 1800–1865* (1996). She is currently writing a book about the value of the humanities.

HERBERT F. TUCKER teaches English as the John C. Coleman Professor at the University of Virginia, where he also serves as associate editor for *New Literary History* and co-editor for the Victorian series of the University Press. He has published *Browning's Beginnings: The Art of Disclosure* (1980), *Tennyson and the Doom of Romanticism* (1988), and *Epic: Britain's Heroic Muse 1790–1910* (2008), and has edited *Victorian Literature 1830–1900* (2001), *Critical Essays on Alfred Lord Tennyson* (1993), *Under Criticism* (1998), and *A Companion to Victorian Literature and Culture* (1999).

CAROLYN WILLIAMS is Professor of English at Rutgers University, New Brunswick. Author of *Transfigured World: Walter Pater's Aesthetic Historicism* (1989) and *Gilbert and Sullivan: Gender, Genre, Parody* (2011), she is currently working on nineteenth-century English melodrama, under the working title *The Aesthetics of Melodramatic Form*.

Introduction

KATE FLINT

Alone of all the volumes in the *New Cambridge History of English Literature*, this one is named after the reign of a monarch. To identify a literary period in this way is necessarily problematic, and the utility of the label 'Victorian' has long been contested.[1] On the other hand, it has endured – albeit with shifting sets of connotations. Not least among the reasons for this endurance is the apparent precision offered by the bounding dates of the Queen's reign (1837–1901), with the latter of these years more or less coinciding, conveniently, with the end of a century. Yet even before Queen Victoria's demise, her long tenure of the throne had encouraged many commentators to look backwards, thus accentuating the notion of her reign as marking a distinctly defined era. Both her Golden and Diamond Jubilees stimulated evaluative retrospectives – such as Alfred Russel Wallace's *The Wonderful Century. Its Successes and Failures* (1898) – of all that had been achieved (the emphasis was almost invariably teleologically framed) over the preceding decades, whether in politics or industrial invention, the physical sciences or the field of culture.

The sense that Victoria's accession marked a very useful, clearly defined starting point was, of course, in many ways constructed in hindsight, a product of the lengthy reign of a monarch who had attracted a good deal of attention right from her accession, due to the combination of her youth and the fact of her being a woman. This was accentuated as a result of an expanding popular press that exploited these circumstances, then her marriage to Prince Albert of Saxe-Coburg and Gotha in 1840, and then her rapidly growing family.[2] But other, less monarchically centered factors allowed late

---

1 An extensive discussion of these debates, as well as some compelling arguments for the period label 'Victorian' to be retained, is offered by Martin Hewitt, 'Why the Notion of Victorian Britain Does Make Sense', *Victorian Studies* 48:3 (2006), pp. 395–438.
2 See John Plunkett, *Queen Victoria. First Media Monarch* (Oxford and New York: Oxford University Press, 2003). For more on the cultural and literary impact of Queen Victoria, see also Margaret Homans, *Royal Representations: Queen Victoria and British Culture,*

Victorians to look at the decade of her coming to the throne as a starting point, whether they considered the beginnings of the railway system (which was to make a yet greater sociological and economic impact on the country in the 1840s); or the impact of the 1832 Reform Act, and the questions it raised concerning democracy and suffrage; or the ideological and material repercussions of the passing of the 1834 Poor Law Amendment Act. In terms of literature itself – to take just three examples – the publication of Tennyson's *Poems, Chiefly Lyrical* (1830), signalled the emergence of a writer who, whilst clearly building on the works of the second-generation Romantics who had preceded and pre-deceased him, was perceived over the decades to come as giving voice to many of the period's most pressing private and public concerns. The writings of Thomas Carlyle (*Sartor Resartus* (1833–4); *The French Revolution* (1837–48); *Past and Present* (1843)), similarly, incorporate elements from German Romantic philosophy in his experimental ways of addressing the relationship of the visible and invisible, the material and spiritual worlds, and in reconceptualizing both the interrelations of earlier and contemporary times, and the problems of historical perspective. The appearance of Dickens's *Sketches by Boz* (1836) and *Pickwick Papers* (1837) could, likewise, be seen as indicating not just a new voice in prose writing, but as pointing towards new modes of interaction with a rapidly expanding reading public, whether through prose that simultaneously commemorated and critiqued contemporary society (the transformation of the occasional essay into investigative journalism), or through the creation and commercialization of new habits of reading.

At the other end of Victoria's reign, 1901 provided a strong sense of a break for many commentators of the time, even if the relatively arbitrary cross-over point between 'Victorian' and 'modern' cultural formations has subsequently been repositioned in various ways, with the emphasis increasingly falling – as in this volume – on a whole period of transition, rather than on some neat date. The new generation of writers were keen to emphasize their dramatic rupture with the previous century, and their own attempts to provide a symbolic date for the end of the Victorian era have fed into the periodization of literary history – none more strongly than Virginia Woolf's well-worn formulation concerning the change in 'human character' that allegedly took place at the end of 1910, the year that saw the death of Edward VII, whose brief reign marked what historian G. M. Young called the Victorian period's 'flash Edwardian epilogue'. Yet even when one

1837–1876 (University of Chicago Press, 1999), and Adrienne Auslander Munich, *Queen Victoria's Secrets* (New York: Columbia University Press, 2006).

considers the social impact of the suffrage movement, the shock to the artistic system offered by the first Post-Impressionist Exhibition at the Grafton Galleries in December 1910, or the importance of the issues behind the constitutional crises that provoked the two General Elections of that year, each of these areas may be seen as a culmination of trends as well as a decisive severance with what had preceded them.[3] And the rupture was by no means absolute: others have preferred to see the social watershed of the First World War as signifying the true end of the period.

Yet the social and stylistic volatility of the late nineteenth century has led some critics and historians to see the transition away from 'Victorianism' as occurring somewhat earlier. One obvious point of comparison and contrast with this *Cambridge History* volume is Philip Davis's impressively thorough and immensely readable *The Victorians*, volume VIII of the new Oxford English Literary History (2002). Davis ends at 1880. But however reasoned this concluding point (whether determined by the author's own arguments concerning religion or literary form, or by the over-arching decision of his series editor), to cut off one's definition of what constitutes the Victorian period at this point is to miss many opportunities, not least to see the later Victorians chafing against the earlier decades of the century in formal, as well as ideological terms.

The 1916 *Cambridge History* – this volume's ancestor – solved the problem of how to construct a period divide by confining its definition of a Victorian writer to include only those who were already dead. Henry James passed away just in time to be included in the bibliographies, if not in the main body of the text, but his literary career, to take but one example, is suggestive of many of the themes and stylistic challenges that were explored in the later years of Victoria's reign: the indeterminacy of language and, indeed, of literary interpretation; concerns with internationalism and national identity; issues of sexual identity, freedom of expression, repression and control; the relationship between the aesthetic and the commercial; the ability of narrative prose to capture the life of the mind, with all its contradictions; the continual interchange between immediate sensory perception, memory, and

---

3 G. M. Young, *Portrait of an Age. Victorian England* (1949; Oxford University Press, 1977), p. 184. For 1910, see Peter Stansky, *On or About December 1910: Early Bloomsbury and its Intimate World* (Cambridge, MA: Harvard University Press, 1996). Virginia Woolf's comment that 'on or about December 1910 human character changed' can be found in her 1924 essay 'Character in Fiction' (later revised and reprinted as 'Mr Bennett and Mrs Brown'), in *The Essays of Virginia Woolf*, ed. Andrew McNeillie, vol. III (San Diego, New York, London: Harcourt Brace Jovanovich, 1988), p. 421.

the workings of the unconscious, and so on. The final two decades of Victoria's reign can now be seen as bearing a peculiarly close relationship to late twentieth-century theoretical concerns – with performance and style; with the politics of the imperial and the global; with anxiety about the nature of democracy and representation; with eugenics and genetics; with new and rapidly developing technologies in the media. This fact was doubtless in part responsible for the proliferation of work on the cultural history of this later part of Victoria's reign during the late twentieth century – scholarship that, in turn, helped to complete the scholarly rehabilitation of Victorian literature, and that rendered our understanding of what constituted 'the Victorian' considerably more complex.

In other words, although this volume retains the label 'Victorian', it does so in the full and alert awareness that it is a label of convenience – as well as a term that carried some very precise connotations for those who were its immediate successors, and who could use it as an aesthetic rallying call for all that they wished to be seen as standing against. Yet the chapters that follow seek to break down – as has been the case with much recent scholarship – any sense of reductionism in the term. They emphasize, rather, the way in which these sixty-four years, with their dramatically shifting and expanding markets for print, were a crucible for literary experimentation – stylistic and thematic – as writers sought to give expression to major changes within society. Many chapters point, too, to the impossibility of drawing strict cut-off points – whether at the beginning or end of the supposed period – when it comes to the topics and writers whom they are treating.

Porosity, indeed, is a significant characteristic of literary scholarship when it comes to addressing the Victorian period. The emergence of cultural studies as a significant force within university English departments over the past couple of decades – something which has called into question what may be said to constitute the boundaries of literary history themselves – has been particularly noticeable in relation to Victorian literature. A number of factors are responsible for this: they range from the abundance of source materials to the continued existence of a very large number of physical objects and edifices as well as institutional practices, and perhaps, above all, our fascination with an age still so relatively close to our own, which, despite its significant differences, seems to have shared – or at least been responsible for producing – so many of our cultural preoccupations. Jay Clayton discusses these admirably in *Charles Dickens in Cyberspace* (2003), his examples ranging from evolution/genetics to the relationship of the human to the machine. Clayton reminds one, moreover, that the twentieth century's disciplinary division between the two cultures of arts and science was one which only slowly gained currency within the nineteenth century, and has been disrupted again by today's digital age. If the Victorians were responsible for the growth of the archive, and the consolidation of a whole range of classificatory schemes; if the period saw the development of a range of discreet disciplinary and audience-determined discourses, they were simultaneously amassing a huge, humanly inexhaustible amount of textual and material evidence. The relative accessibility (both archivally and linguistically) of this evidence has allowed not just for extensive documentation of research, but for the tracing of discursive patterns across disparate fields. Such cultural exploration has therefore been in a symbiotic relationship with those approaches that have emphasized discourse theory rather than biography or individual intentionality, and that have foregrounded that critical Holy Trinity of class, gender, and race. Nor is that an arbitrary order of categories, but one that corresponds to the successive, if rightly overlapping waves of emphasis in Victorian literary studies over the last four decades of the twentieth century: decades that did so much to establish the terms in which Victorian studies became popular, even fashionable. Moreover, the breadth and variety of print culture in the period has enabled the contextualization of the 'literary' within the growth of consumerism, and within the growth of those very institutions (whether of literary criticism and reviewing, or of academic study), that have enabled and demanded the consideration of what constitutes the 'literary' in the first place.

There is, however, nothing very new in the association of interdisciplinarity with Victorian literary studies. In his Introduction to *The Dickens World* (1941), Humphry House noted that

> For some years past, criticism – and more particularly what is called 'Literary History' – has been becoming more sociological . . . The emphasis of literary history has shifted from 'influences' traced as a kind of genealogical descent from one major writer to another, to biography which seeks out sources of creation in the psychological details of each writer's life; and it is shifting now again to the sociological and economic environment in which particular works have been produced.[4]

He illustrates this with reference to Bonamy Dobrée and Edith Batho's *Introductions to English Literature*, and in particular to their volume *The Victorians and After* (1938). What one might say has shifted again is the fact that psychology has re-entered Victorian studies, whether in relation to questions of gender, or,

---

4 Humphry House, *The Dickens World* (Oxford University Press, 1941), p. 15.

more broadly, in company, say, with the dynamics of desire and repression; and that scholars have begun to re-assess the importance of life-writing, incorporating both biography and autobiography into getting a stronger purchase on the Victorians' understanding of themselves, and on the narratives which they constructed in order to make sense of their lives and times.

Yet in foregrounding the cultural emphasis of literary studies of the Victorian period over the past couple of decades, this volume will also respond to the amount, and to the type, of attention that has, nonetheless, been paid to individual authors. Those critical emphases on class, on gender, and on race have, indeed, led to a significant re-appraisal of the Victorian canon: to far greater attention being paid, above all, to women writers, but also to working-class male authors (such as Chartist poets), and to the voices of writers from the regions and from the colonies. Beyond this, the significant editorial work which has been performed during the past forty or so years on authors already regarded as major, and the publication of their letters, of journalistic pieces and occasional writings, and other forms of archival work have added to, and in some cases challenged our understanding of these writers. This volume brings out the relationship of literary figures to one another, whether that relationship be one of personal friendship, of shared literary circles, or one of intertextuality.

The daunting amount of material that could potentially be covered by this volume is indicated by the fact that two of the three nineteenth-century volumes of the original Cambridge History – each amounting to 600+ pages – are devoted to the Victorians. The first of these volumes is very definitely biographical in its organization. In dividing up its chapters to deal, in rough chronological order, with Carlyle; the Tennysons (Charles and Frederick, as well as the Poet Laureate); Robert Browning and Elizabeth Barrett Browning; Matthew Arnold, Arthur Hugh Clough, James Thomson; the Rossettis, William Morris, Swinburne; lesser poets of the middle and later nineteenth century; the prosody of the nineteenth century (from *Ossian* and Percy's *Reliques*, through Blake, the Romantics, and theorists of prosody); nineteenth-century drama; Thackeray; Dickens; the political and social novel (Disraeli, Charles Kingsley, Mrs Gaskell, 'George Eliot'); the Brontës; lesser novelists (including Bulwer Lytton, Trollope, Mrs Oliphant, Wilkie Collins); and George Meredith, Samuel Butler, George Gissing, it brings out the importance that earlier scholars placed on literary biography, on the ways in which individuals, rather than social or intellectual or cultural movements, defined the literary taste and production of a period. Although the chapter headings in the second of the two Victorian volumes suggest a more generalizing approach (they range from 'Philosophers', and 'Historians, Biographers and Political Orators', through 'Caricature and the Literature of Sport' and 'The Literature of Travel, 1700–1900'), the internal structure of each of these chapters almost invariably becomes a chronological, author-based survey. By contrast, this volume places its emphasis firmly on ideas, on themes, and on connections. Like its 1916 predecessor, it considers 'literature' as a very wide category. It is premised on the belief that the intellectual and cultural movements of the Victorian period are particularly well suited to modes of approach that foreground not just interdisciplinarity, but that trace the importance and impact of these movements across, as well as within, particular genres, and that closely examine the links (and divergences) between different linguistic, rhetorical, and formal modes of treating analogous subjects.

The volume falls into six sections. The first, 'Authors, Readers, and Publishers', sets up the contexts in which writing was produced, disseminated, and consumed, for, as with any period, the history of literature in this period is inseparably bound in with the histories of publication and readership. To look at the history of the book – as this sub-discipline has come to be known – is to be reminded of the material reality involved in the production and consumption of books. It involves considering such issues as the development of new and cheaper technologies of printing and paper manufacturing; the growth and characteristics of publishing houses and their particular specialties (books for overseas markets, for drawing-room display, for railway bookstalls); the reasons lying behind different modes of volume publication, including three-decker novels, series, reprints, anthologies, and abridgements; the ways in which books were advertised and sold, and the actual appearance of texts and what they feel like to hold and touch.

But the materiality of texts is only part of the picture. The proliferation of printed material in the Victorian period must be understood side by side with the expansion of the reading public, and the growth of particular 'niche' markets. It has to be seen in relation to the conditions of authorship: the different pressures faced by female and male writers; questions of anonymity and pseudonymity, lionization and fame; financial pressures; the mental and physical demands of serialization; and the degree to which it was possible (and often necessary) to combine writing with other occupations – in other words, the rewards and the tensions associated with publication, or with attempting to get published. Necessarily, authors are continually in dialogue with their readership, or projected readers: to understand this relationship means considering how books were encountered (in libraries – whether private, including the phenomenon of the circulating library, or public and as private possessions); where and how they were read (aloud within a family group; in solitude; greedily; dutifully; as part of formalized or self-directed education; passed from one person to another in a workplace); and exploring the concerns about reading that were publicly expressed, whether such concerns involved the possibility that print would corrupt morals, or would inflame readers politically.

Not all printed material was consumed in book form, by any means. The periodical exercised an enormous influence over Victorian literary and cultural life: as an outlet for writers (of both non-fictional prose and imaginative works); as a format for the circulation of new developments in science, philosophy, history, politics, economics, and other emerging disciplines; as a means of disseminating all kinds of information (whether at the level of 'useful knowledge', in publications aimed at artisans and members of the lower middle classes, or in the form of travel writing); and as a forum for reviews. Whilst the period saw the growth and emergence of a number of intellectually influential publications, such as *Blackwood's Edinburgh Magazine*, the *Fortnightly*, and the *Westminster Review*, it was also important for the development of more widely circulating magazines which relied above all on the appeal of the fiction that they included, such as *Household Words*, *All the Year Round*, *Temple Bar*, the *Cornhill*, and *Longman's Magazine*. Weekly publications were important and influential, too, in terms of the literary reviews and advertisements that they contained (especially the *Spectator*, the *Saturday Review*, and the *Athenaeum*), and the period also witnessed the emergence of general scientific and anthropological journals, satiric periodicals (not just *Punch*, but such publications as *Fun* and *Judy*); and publications aimed at specific audiences (whether *The Girl's Own Paper* or the relatively radical *Shafts*, the *Magazine of Art*, or *Cycling*). The expanding outlets for print were supported, moreover, by technologies that led to the inclusion of an increasing number of illustrations. The implications of having text, picture, and non-editorial material such as advertisements in potential dialogue with one another is just one of the many areas in which we see the History of the Book intersecting with developments within visual culture.

Without the material presence of books and periodicals, and readers to buy, borrow, and consume them, there would be no literary history, which is why the volume gives precedence to this material. The second section, 'Writing Victoria's England', offers a more traditional approach to Victorian literary history. It breaks down the long period into three sections. Running through each of these is the theme of literature and national identity, something that is of crucial importance to the volume as a whole. They set up the question of what might be the relationship of literary writing with England's – and Britain's – perception of itself, and its relationship to the rest of the world, including its expanding colonial possessions. These broad-based accounts provide a set of contexts alongside which the later chapters may be read.

The next category, 'Modes of Writing', is the most radically conceived section of this volume. Without doubt, the Victorian period saw the significant growth and development of various genres and sub-genres. Discreet genres were used to group texts for the purposes of both reviewing and advertising, and these distinctions have often been maintained by sub-categories of the discipline of literary study throughout the twentieth century. But these chapters explore the idea that modes of writing – lyrically, or epically, or melodramatically – very often function across generic boundaries, and that acknowledging this fact opens up new practices of understanding what is peculiarly Victorian about the ways in which these writers thought about their material, intellectual, and spiritual environments. Their preoccupations are here openly linked to both conventionality and experimentalism in language and in form, as a means of investigating how ideas spill over and are transformed, between one genre and another.

This section is followed by one – 'Matters of Debate' – that highlights some of the most controversial and contested areas of Victorian life and thought, whether these involved spiritual beliefs or sexual conduct, economics, education, or aesthetics. An emphasis on *why* these specific topics should have mattered so much, and what was at stake – and for whom – when it came to the energy that was invested in debating them links these thematic concerns to the literary forms that gave them imaginative currency. The contexts in which these discussions took place, however, were not just cerebral ones, and the idea of the Victorian environment and its topographies is developed in the next section, 'Spaces of Writing'. Building on the idea that there are correspondences between mental space and social space – whether the latter is figured in terms of room, or streets, or fields, or countries – this part of the volume examines the ways in which spaces, both literal and figurative, are constructed within literature. The chapters not only look at the importance of urban, rural, and regional locations to Victorian literature, but they set out to place Victorian writing in relation to the wider world.

'Spaces of Writing' is organized like a series of circles that radiate ever outwards from the organizing idea of spatiality, and it necessarily raises the issue of what constitutes the 'English literature' of the *Cambridge History*'s title. Whereas some of the earlier chapters draw readily on examples from the whole of the British Isles, it is also important to distinguish what is distinct about Scottish, Welsh, and Irish writing in this period, as well as writing from different English regions. Colonial writing presents a more complex question, particularly at a time when national literatures in English were starting to develop in Britain's possessions, with a greater or lesser degree of reaction against – or homage to – the seat of empire. The earlier *Cambridge History* contained discreet chapters on Anglo-Irish literature; Anglo-Indian literature; English–Canadian literature, the literature of Australia and New Zealand, and South African poetry. Each of these is still an extraordinarily useful bibliographic resource: indeed, the tendency of every chapter in this volume's predecessor to aim for a condensed package of factual information ensures that both the chapters themselves, and the attendant bibliographies, are still exceptionally good starting places for research. Yet given how much could be said, in fact, about the literature produced within these different countries, it was a reluctant editorial decision to retain an Anglocentric position. Even if spillage in the contents and discussion of these chapters towards works that were written outside Britain's shores was both inevitable and desirable – demonstrating how writers and books themselves travelled and returned – the emphasis falls on texts that were written by those primarily domiciled within the United Kingdom and Ireland. This is an emphasis that has allowed, too, for due weight to be given to literature's involvement, during the period, with both American and European concerns.

The final section examines what may be called – following the inspiration of John Kucich and Dianne Sadoff's 2000 volume, *Victorian Afterlife* – 'Victorian Afterlives'. The Victorian volumes of the previous *Cambridge History* offer an intriguing set of glimpses into how the Victorian period came to be evaluated by its inheritors. Whilst many of the sections in the two volumes are relatively reverential, one also encounters value judgments that explicitly pit a self-conscious sense of modernity, in form as well as in content, against the writings of the previous century. Thus we are told, for example, that 'Relying, in the Victorian manner, upon variety rather than upon concentration of interest, Collins's books have a ponderous air (some of his shorter tales excepted) as compared with the economical technique of Poe, or with modern forms of the detective tale which turn upon quick deductions from meticulous detail, discard lumber and aim at a consistent psychology.'[5] As has been frequently noted, the twentieth century witnessed a deliberate, self-conscious reaction against its social and literary predecessors, a 'growing tendency to disparagement and even ridicule of all men and things, and aspects of things, which can be defined as "Victorian"', remarked on by Edmund Gosse in his 1918 article about 'the agony of the Victorian Age'.[6] The tendency to typify this through the stylized satire of Lytton Strachey's *Eminent Victorians*, or the manifestos to be found in *Blast*, or by calling on the preposterous Christmas tree of the Albert Memorial and the over-stuffed interiors of grey, rain-soaked London, as Virginia Woolf does in *Orlando* (1928) when she wanted to characterize (or caricature) the Victorian period, has often served to obscure the lines of continuity as well as of rupture that one finds between nineteenth- and twentieth-century culture.[7]

Within literature itself, those writers who emerged into prominence in the decade following Victoria's death were aware, to be sure, that they were chronicling a changing society – but in both style and subject matter, a novelist like E. M. Forster is marked by a tension between Victorian conventions as well as by his sympathy for change. Like several of his contemporaries, including writers as diverse as Woolf, D. H. Lawrence, and John Galsworthy, his fiction often follows a recursive pattern, unable to move away from Victorian interiors (whether of rooms or of consciousnesses), if only to be able to record and understand the cultural and material environments that formed characters and readers alike. Such formation is deliberately addressed, of course, in novels such as Forster's *A Room with a View* (1908) and *Howards End* (1910), Arnold Bennett's *Clayhanger* (1910), and D. H. Lawrence's *The Rainbow* (1915), which interrogate the legacies of Victorian Britain; it provides the nostalgia for rural England that underpins the lyric prose of Edward Thomas or George Sturt; it is necessarily inseparable from those memoirs that establish particularly vivid portrayals of Victorian lives and childhoods, whether Edmund Gosse's *Father and Son* (1907) or – for the formative impress of Victorian life on the memory endured a long time – Flora Thompson's *Lark Rise to Candleford* trilogy (1939–43).

---

5 Sir A. W. Ward and A. R. Waller (eds.), *The Cambridge History of English Literature*, vol. XIII, *The Nineteenth Century* (Cambridge University Press, 1917), p. 487.
6 Edmund Gosse, 'The Agony of the Victorian Age', *Edinburgh Review* 228 (1918), p. 276.
7 Such an approach is being increasingly challenged, however. See, by way of an excellent example, Steve Ellis, *Virginia Woolf and the Victorians* (Cambridge University Press, 2007).

This concluding section, therefore, sets out to question any lingering belief that the boundary set up by the end of Victoria's reign, just one year after the turn of the century, was a particularly solid one. Yet at the same time that the Victorian period experienced a considerable surge in popularity as an academic subject of study during the last quarter of the twentieth century, so it increasingly seized the imagination of a wider public. The profusion of works that deal with Victorian themes and, at the same time, play with, exploit, and explore Victorian fictional and poetic conventions – to mention a brief sample, A. S. Byatt's *Possession* (1990) and *Angels and Insects* (1992); John Fowles's *The French Lieutenant's Woman* (1969), and Sarah Waters's first three novels, *Tipping the Velvet* (1998), *Affinity* (1999), and *Fingersmith* (2002) – taken together with consumer nostalgia (whether in interior furnishings or replica sepia-tinted photographs), fascination with Victorian sexuality and scientific inquiry (especially in relation to the natural world) all point to a strong fascination with the *idea* of Victorianism. This leads us to ponder what, in other words, might be the nature of the relationship that the later twentieth century and beyond has forged between the Victorians, nostalgia, and post-modernity, and how, indeed, literature from the Victorian period – whether interpreted through criticism or through new creative works – may continue into the future.

PART I

*

AUTHORS, READERS, AND PUBLISHERS

Publishing and the materiality of the book

DAVID FINKELSTEIN

On 29 November 1814, a printing revolution shook the world of British printing and publishing. After months of secret work, the owners of *The Times* of London used imported Koenig presses, steam-powered, flat-bed cylinder machines to issue overnight that morning's edition. Churning out material at 1,000 impressions an hour, they produced an entire run of 4,000 copies and delivered them to readers at an unrivalled speed. The *Times* editorial announced its triumphant entry into the industrial age with typical hyperbole. 'Our journal of this day', it intoned, 'presents to the public the practical result of the greatest improvement connected with printing since the discovery of the art itself.'[1] Further refinements by Augustus Applegarth and Edward Cowper in the 1820s led to wholesale adoption of more efficient presses by the industry, so that by the late 1830s its use was ubiquitous throughout Britain. The steam press, which replaced the hand-operated, metal Stanhope press, joined innovations such as the Fourdrinier papermaking machine in mechanizing the process and lowering the cost by which texts reached the market, so powering print to its key place in Victorian cultural life, and thus conjoining steam in the public mind with print activity. As James Secord notes, 'The steam-powered printing machine, machine-made paper, public libraries, cheap woodcuts, stereotyping, religious tracts, secular education, the postal system, telegraphy, and railway distribution played key parts in opening the floodgates to an increased reading public.'[2]

Steam proved to be the defining symbol of progress throughout the century, a metaphor for changes wrought by British innovation and adaptation. It joined other visible examples of evolving communication and

---

1 *The Times*, 29 November 1814.
2 James A. Secord, *Victorian Sensation: The Extraordinary Publication, Reception, and Secret Authorship of Vestiges of the Natural History of Creation* (University of Chicago Press, 2000), p. 30.

transportation systems, including national and international postal systems, telegraph lines, and powerful and swift metal ships and railways carrying passengers eager for reading material to inform and entertain. Nature itself, Karl Marx exclaimed in the 1840s, was now challenged by human intervention: 'Nature builds no machines, no locomotives, railways, electric telegraphs . . . These are products of human industry: natural materials transformed into instruments of the human will.'[3] Such transformation was captured and fed back to readers in popular print form, ranging from novels, illustrated newspapers, and literary journals, through to street advertising, pamphlets, and plays. The result was that 'print culture, reporting on itself, occupied a central place in public awareness of industrial revolution'.[4]

The path to efficiency was not always smooth. The start of the century was marked by a period of high costs, high book prices, and extensive government taxation on paper and periodicals in an effort to suppress and control mass access to potentially subversive literature. By the end of the century, though, technology and social change had advanced to the stage where the breakthrough achievement of the *Times* no longer dazzled; in 1896, the US newspaper tycoon J. Pulitzer could boast of his newly installed Hoe rotary presses, capable of printing and folding 96,000 eight-page copies of the *New York World* in one hour from stereotype plates and on rolls of pulp paper rushing by at over thirty miles per hour.[5] Such technical wizardry produced enough copies overnight to cater for a readership of over 1,500,000, dramatizing the scale of change wrought in international print circles in less than eighty years. This compression of action and expansion in production was replicated in British book-trade activity. In 1821, it cost thirty-one shillings and sixpence to buy a best-selling three-volume novel by Walter Scott; more than the average weekly wage of most. By 1894, three-volume first editions had disappeared in favour of more affordable, one-volume cloth-bound editions retailing at six shillings, which would be followed a few months later by a reprint edition costing two shillings and sixpence, and then reprinted in paperback at sixpence.[6] Between 1846 and 1916, British publishers quadrupled their production rates while at the same

3 Quoted in Asa Briggs and Peter Burke, *A Social History of the Media, from Gutenberg to the Internet* (London: Polity Press, 2002), p. III.
4 Secord, *Victorian Sensation*, p. 30.
5 James Wald, 'Periodicals and Periodicity', in Simon Eliot and Jonathan Rose (eds.), *A Companion to the History of the Book* (Oxford and New York: Blackwell Publishing, 2007), p. 426.
6 Simon Eliot, 'From Few and Expensive to Many and Cheap: The British Book Market 1800–1890', in Eliot and Rose, *History of the Book*, pp. 291–2.

time halving their book prices.[7] Library practices and commercial distribution systems also played their part in production considerations. As noted later in this chapter, the distribution of texts across Victorian Britain became more sophisticated and far-reaching as networks of libraries and commercial outlets sprang up to service a range of readers and reading interests. As readership expanded, publishers experimented with different formats and prices to reach different audiences, until in 1900 the Net Book Agreement was brought in to harmonize prices across the UK market.

Technical advances were not limited to textual production. The nineteenth century witnessed a revolution in British visual representation, marked by four distinctive phases of development. The first involved the advent of wood engraving, pioneered in particular by the Newcastle-based engraver Thomas Bewick in the 1790s. His technique of wood-block carving would be a significant feature of books and journals in the first half of the nineteenth century, reaching its apogee in the visually arresting layouts and illustrations of the weekly *Illustrated London News*, launched in 1842 with an initial editorial that made clear the link between illustration and literary production. 'Art', it declared, 'as now fostered, and redundant in the peculiar and facile department of wood engraving – has, in fact, become the bride of literature.'[8]

Literature would gain further illustrative benefits from the commercial introduction in 1819 of steel engraving by the London-based Charles Heath, which allowed artists to etch prints on to steel plates through an acid process. Lithography, a process of printing images from stone surfaces, invented in 1798 but refined in the 1820s (and developed with even greater success in the 1850s through the introduction of the transfer lithography cylinder machine), joined steel in furnishing literary miscellanies and gift annuals of the 1820s and 1830s with suitable illustrations to garnish and accompany the poetry and fiction in their pages. Their use was particularly prevalent in literary annuals and gift books published in the 1820s, designed for sale during the Christmas season and marketed for a female readership. These lavishly illustrated works, the best known of which included *Forget Me Not*, *The Literary Souvenir*, and *The Keepsake*, explicitly linked illustrations to poetry, and dominated the market between 1825 and 1835. Their ubiquity led many to account them responsible for a decline in poetry publications.

---

7 Alexis Weedon, *Victorian Publishing: The Economics of Book Production for a Mass Market 1836–1916* (Aldershot: Ashgate Publishing Ltd, 2003), p. 158.
8 *Illustrated London News*, 14 May 1842.

As Southey would remark in 1828, 'the Annuals are now the only books bought for presents to young ladies, in which way poems formerly had their chief vent'.[9] Later publishers would continue this link between poetry and illustration, most notably Edward Moxon in the 1830s and 1840s with his illustrated collections of Browning, Shelley, and Tennyson, and Macmillan in the later years of the century with Arnold and Tennyson.

The use of lithography in books and journals persisted through to the 1880s, when half-tone and photogravure processes enabled publishers to begin mass-producing photographic illustrations with greater clarity. The illustrative art of the book culminated in the Arts and Crafts movement led by William Morris, who between 1891 and 1898 brought his vision of craftsmanship to the production of illustrated works at his Kelmscott Press. In those seven years he produced fifty-three books whose visual, typographic, and textual design and clarity set a standard admired, imitated, but rarely achieved in future years by subsequent private presses and printers.

Thus the reign of Queen Victoria saw an important shift in the relationship between text and image: images in books became central to shaping the Victorian cultural imagination, embellishing, illuminating, and expanding storylines and themes. Illustrators and authors were acutely aware of the impact of visual accompaniments on the reception of fiction, working closely together in certain circumstances to create linked material. As Michael Steig notes, the Victorian illustrator fulfilled three functions in literary production throughout the century, acting as 'collaborator, attempting to express the author's intention visually; interpreter, offering his own comments on the meaning of the work; and perhaps even an *artist*, sometimes creating independently valuable works of art'.[10] In the case of Charles Dickens, for example, as Robert L. Patten has elaborated in fine case studies of his literary collaborations with key illustrators throughout his life,[11] text and images interacted powerfully to influence the development of plot and theme. Thus George Cruikshank's masterly images for the serialization of *Oliver Twist* in

9 Robert Southey to Grosvenor C. Bedford, 8 December 1828, in Charles Cuthbert Southey (ed.), *The Life and Correspondence of the late Robert Southey in Six Volumes: Volume 5* (London: Longman, Brown, Green and Longmans, 1850), p. 336.
10 Quoted in Robert L. Patten, 'Serial Illustration and Storytelling in *David Copperfield*', in Richard Maxwell (ed.), *The Victorian Illustrated Book* (Charlottesville and London: University Press of Virginia, 2002), p. 123.
11 See Robert L. Patten, *Charles Dickens and His Publishers* (Oxford University Press, 1978); Patten, 'Dickens as Serial Author: A Case of Multiple Identities', in Laurel Brake, Bill Bell, and David Finkelstein (eds.), *Nineteenth-Century Media and the Construction of Identities* (Basingstoke: Palgrave, 2000), pp. 137–53; Patten, 'Serial Illustration', pp. 91–128.

Bentley's Miscellany in 1838, say, guided Dickens in his writing more than his official biographer John Forster cared to admit, a fact his literary contemporary Samuel Warren commented on in 1842: 'thus the writer follows the caricaturist, instead of the caricaturist following the writer'.[12]

Illustrated books and illustrated journals provided spaces for readers to populate with their imagination and in which to discover and contextualize their cultural understanding of contemporary society. As the *Illustrated London News* suggested in self-congratulatory tones eight months after its launch, its own success was proof of the interlinked power of image and text: 'We discovered and opened up the world of Illustration as connected with News, and the quick-sighted and sound-judging British public peopled it at once.'[13] Further developments over the next half-century ensured a continuing discovery of the possibilities of the illustrative world.

As print technology evolved, authors drew their own conclusions about the merits of its features, and in particular about those of the ultimate symbol of progress, the steam press. 'I am persuaded', James Brewster commented to Byron, 'that you must write by steam', recognizing how the poet could accrue valuable cultural capital and financial profit from harnessing this new power.[14] The quickening in pace of printing times, the increasing visual richness of surrounding material, and the lowering of costs enabled publishers to turn the words of authors rapidly and attractively from manuscript to print, while expanding transportation links ensured the results reached further and more quickly across physical borders than ever before.

Such industrialization of printing and publishing systems was part of a larger industrialization of business across Britain and then Western Europe. Mechanization enlarged market potential, shifting power in the book trade at the same time. As Roger Escarpit notes, 'Faced with a developing market, printing and bookselling underwent a major change, as nascent capitalist industry took charge of the book. The publisher appeared as the responsible entrepreneur relegating the printer and bookseller to a minor role. As a side effect, the literary profession began to organize.'[15]

---

12 Samuel Warren, [Q.Q.Q., pseudonym] 'Dickens's American Notes for General Circulation', *Blackwood's Magazine* 52 (1842), p. 785.

13 *Illustrated London News*, 6 January 1843.

14 Tom Mole, 'Byron's "Ode to the Framers of the Frame Bill": The Embarrassment of Industrial Culture', *Keats–Shelley Journal* 52 (2003), pp. 111–29.

15 Roger Escarpit, *The Book Revolution* (London and Paris: George G. Harrap & Co. Ltd. and UNESCO, 1966), pp. 22–3.

British printers and publishers were among the first to transform their structures and print products to acknowledge such changes, with many moving from small, locally and regionally focused organisations to large, predominantly family-run corporate enterprises. Family firms that weathered the economic crash of 1826 that had brought down the likes of Constable (publisher of Scott) would emerge as significant power brokers in the field of literary production. These included Macmillans, William Blackwood & Sons, John Murray, William Chambers, Smith, Elder & Co, and William Longman, almost all founded within the first twenty years of the century. Their national dominance would translate into international success as they expanded into the colonial markets that emerged from the 1870s onwards, and that are discussed later in this chapter.

The rise of the novel as a cultural signifier during the nineteenth century was closely linked to technological and commercial innovations of the period. The number of titles produced and quantity of print runs rose sequentially throughout the century, particularly as a massive growth in readership spurred on by improved educational provision was nurtured and supported by public and commercial sources, ranging from working mens' clubs and institutes to circulating libraries, bookshops, and railway bookstalls. It is estimated that the number of general book titles published per decade rose roughly from 14,550 in the 1800s to around 60,812 in the 1890s; predominant were non-fiction, educational, and reference titles. Nevertheless, at the peak of book production, Victorian fiction accounted for about a third of the titles listed in contemporary book-trade journals.[16]

Popular titles could achieve substantial sales in their own right. While a best-selling novel of the 1800s might have had a combined print run and sales of up to 12,000, by the 1890s popular titles were achieving print runs and sales of 100,000 in various editions within the first five years of publication.[17] Mass consumption of fiction was not discriminatory, regardless of what contemporary cultural commentators hoped for or feared: as one critic observed, the Victorian novel was not fussy in its thematic reach – as a medium of high popularization it was 'at its loftiest a conveyor of culture and the arts, at its most frivolous a purveyor of gossip'.[18] The popular appetite for fiction was fed in various ways. Among innovations tried were

---

16 Eliot, 'From Few and Expensive', pp. 294, 299.   17 *Ibid.*, p. 294.
18 Robert Colby, review of Richard D. Altick, *Presence of the Present, Nineteenth-Century Literature*, 46:4 (1992), p. 546.

serializations of fiction and non-fiction, used to boost newspaper and journal sales and act as advertising for publishers' wares. Serialized fiction was consumed by all classes, though in different formats, ranging from high-quality monthlies (*Blackwood's Magazine* and the *London Magazine*), mid-century middle-class literary publications (*Cornhill Magazine*, *Temple Bar*, and *Macmillan's Magazine*), late-century 'illustrated' magazines (*The Strand*, *Scribner's Magazine*), mass-circulation weeklies and monthlies (*Household Words*, *Chambers's Edinburgh Journal*, *Tit-Bits*), and also through syndication by intermediaries such as Tillotson's Fiction Bureau in metropolitan, regional, and provincial newspapers. From the 1840s through to the 1890s, serialization and syndication were standard fare for literary periodical and newspaper sources, a process whereby fiction was inserted into almost all forms of mass textual consumption. In newspaper and periodical spaces, Victorian readers encountered poetry and fiction in conjunction with fashion, news, opinion, and reportage, a cornucopia that also functioned as a method of engaging and satisfying general reading expectations, as Leah Price discusses in the next chapter.

Part-publication serials also grew in popularity after Charles Dickens's success with *The Pickwick Papers* (1836–1837), and throughout the century authors such as Anthony Trollope, George Eliot, and Edward Bulwer Lytton experimented with monthly publication formats as a way of deviating from the central format of the three-volume or 'three decker' novel that dominated Victorian production between 1836 and 1895. The three-volume novel (or 'three-decker', so nicknamed in honour of the venerable and imposing three-gun decks of contemporary British warships) was for most of the Victorian period the central method of circulating new fiction in book form, 'the most important single development in the history of the nineteenth century'.[19] Archibald Constable was one of the first to issue fiction in this particular format, charging ten shillings and sixpence per volume for his three-volume editions of Walter Scott's historical romances in the 1820s. Following the collapse of Constable's business in 1826, the London bookseller Henry Colburn adopted the formula, publishing 'silver fork' novels in the 1830s by Benjamin Disraeli, Bulwer Lytton, and G. P. R. James at Constable's old prices of a guinea and a half (thirty-one shillings and sixpence) for a full three-volume set. This process in turn was copied by Richard Bentley, one-time partner of Colburn, and then by the publisher Hurst and Blackett. Others followed, until it became the de facto first-edition format for the

19 John Sutherland, *Victorian Novelists and Publishers* (London: Athlone Press, 1976), p. 12.

remainder of the century, bolstered in part by commanding sales guaranteed by C. E. Mudie's network of circulating libraries and W. H. Smith's and John Menzies' railway stall outlets between the 1840s and 1890s.

But novels were not the only creative works consumed by nineteenth-century audiences. Poetry collections were extremely popular in the first quarter of the century, with annual numbers of titles published rising from 1,121 in 1815 to an estimated 1,377 in 1828.[20] The English poetry market peaked in the 1820s, declining afterwards as a result of the rise in popularity of the illustrated gift book and literary Annual, and a market demand and preference for prose and fiction. By the 1830s almost all publishers ceased publishing individual works of poetry, with some exceptions, namely Edward Moxon from 1830 to 1858, and Macmillan from the 1880s to the early twentieth century. Where publishers did venture into poetry, they either expected poets to subsidize the publication costs, thus limiting the range of titles and individuals featured in this fashion, or sought better returns through poetry collections, general anthologies, or reprints aimed at the educational market. Sales figures for best-sellers in the latter categories attested to a market demand for 'easy, versified narrative and sentimental melodrama'.[21] The sentimentalized form of Richard Barham's *Ingoldsby Legends*, which originally appeared in *Bentley's Miscellany* from 1837 to 1839 and was republished by Bentley in one-volume form, sold 425,000 copies between 1857 and 1895; Palgrave's more general poetry anthology, the *Golden Treasury*, published by Macmillan in 1861, would sell 61,000 copies by 1884.[22] Not until the twentieth century would poetry regain a foothold through niche-marketing lists of entrepreneurial publishers such as Faber and Faber.

Distributing texts

Charles Mudie, W. H. Smith, and John Menzies were central distributors of fiction and general works in the nineteenth century. Long-standing critical tradition has it that the circulating library system begun by C. E. Mudie in London in 1842 monopolized and dictated terms by which Victorian fiction in particular was produced and distributed for the next fifty years.[23] But

---

20 Lee Erickson, *The Economy of Literary Form: English Literature and the Industrialization of Publishing, 1800–1850* (Baltimore and London: Johns Hopkins University Press, 1996), p. 26.
21 *Ibid.*, pp. 37–8.
22 *Ibid.*, p. 37; John Feather, *A History of British Publishing*, 2nd edn (London and New York: Routledge, 2006), p. 130.
23 Guinevere L. Griest, *Mudie's Circulating Library and the Victorian Novel* (Bloomington and London: Indiana University Press, 1970).

Mudie's supposed power over the type of novels published over the second half of the century was more mythical than actual, for British publishers would complicate the scenario through an intertwining of business interests from 1864 onwards after a secret network of firms supplied Mudie with funds necessary to save his circulating library from bankruptcy.[24]

In 1848 the newspaper and railway bookstall network pioneer W. H. Smith began selling books at his railway news stalls. By 1862 he had moved from being the leading newspaper agent of Britain to monopolizing bookstall operations in almost all of the English railway stations. Competition north of the border came with the entrance in the Scottish market in 1857 of the Edinburgh bookseller John Menzies, who by his death in 1879 was running a vast network of book and newspaper concessions at all major Scottish railway stations. Between these three distribution points, texts were disseminated on a vaster scale than ever before.

From the 1830s onwards, authors and publishers followed a general formula for fiction, poetry, and linked prose: first serialization in literary periodicals, followed by first hard cover and then cheap reprint publication. Anthony Trollope, George Eliot, Mary Elizabeth Braddon, and Charles Dickens were among many novelists who produced works with an eye to the rhythm and cadence of periodical serialization, issuing material in three-chapter sequences over a period of several months, then publishing the full (sometimes further revised) version in three volumes in the month following appearance of the concluding chapters. This would be supplemented a year or so later by a six-shilling reprint. The result was a planned issuing of interdependent expensive and cheap formats serving an expanding and fiction-seeking readership.[25]

Thus commercial imperatives and an expanding readership played their part in shaping nineteenth-century publishing approaches to literary production. William Hazlitt highlighted this fusion of mass markets and mass audiences, and in particular the role of British literary periodicals in negotiating between the two, in 'The Periodical Press', his well-known 1823 contribution to the *Edinburgh Review*. 'Literary immortality is now let on short leases', he declared, 'and we must be contented to succeed by rotation.' He continued,

---

24 David Finkelstein, '"The Secret": British Publishers and Mudie's Struggle for Economic Survival 1861–64', *Publishing History* 34 (1993), pp. 21–50.
25 Sutherland, *Victorian Publishers*, p. 20.

We exist in the bustle of the world, and cannot escape from the notice of our contemporaries. We must please to live, and therefore should live to please. We must look to the public for support. Instead of solemn testimonies from the learned, we require the smiles of the fair and the polite. If princes scowl upon us, the broad shining face of the people may turn to us with a favourable aspect. Is not this life (too) sweet? Would we change it for the former if we could? But the great point is, that *we cannot*! Therefore, let Reviews flourish – let Magazines increase and multiply – let the Daily and Weekly Newspapers live forever![26]

Running parallel to this accelerating and enlarging publishing industry was a shifting focus for writing and marketing: from pleasing patrons and elite opinion-makers to pleasing a mass audience. Negotiating a fit between format, writers, and readers preoccupied many publishers and editors seeking to navigate the literary currents of the nineteenth century. As educational opportunities, real income, and leisure increased throughout the century, readership expanded. Publishers had to invent a range of subjects and marketing strategies to satisfy new audiences.[27] Many publishers turned to producing branded literary periodicals, often eponymously named, to promote the authors linked to their 'house' and earn valuable cultural capital in the process. *Blackwood's Magazine* (founded in 1817), *Bentley's Miscellany* (founded in 1837), *Macmillan's Magazine* (founded in 1859), *Cornhill Magazine* (founded in 1860), and *Longman's Magazine* (founded in 1882) were just some of the journals that acted in such capacity. Reasons for so doing, as William Tinsley declared on finding his losses for *Tinsley's Magazine* (launched in 1867) running at around £25 a month, were quite plain: 'What cheaper advertisement can I have for twenty-five pounds a month? It advertises my name and publications; and it keeps my authors together.'[28]

From the mid nineteenth century, publishers seeking to break away from the three-volume straitjacket began issuing popular series of cheap works, 'Literature for the Millions' and 'yellowback' fiction published at low prices and intended for mass consumption through accessible venues such as railway bookstalls. Around 1,300 titles were published in George Routledge's 'Railway Library' of novels priced at one shilling each, well within the range

---

26 William Hazlitt, 'The Periodical Press', in *The Complete Works*, ed. P. P. Howe, 21 vols. (London: Dent, 1930–4), vol. XVI, p. 220.

27 David Finkelstein and Robert L. Patten, 'Editing *Blackwood's*; or, What Do Editors Do?' in David Finkelstein (ed.), *Print Culture and the Blackwood Tradition* (University of Toronto Press, 2006), p. 150.

28 David Finkelstein, 'Introduction', *ibid.*, p. 12.

of most pockets. The railway bookstall pioneer W. H. Smith also ventured into the publishing market, issuing in conjunction with Chapman and Hall from 1854 onwards inexpensive, two-shilling paperback novels for sale specifically at railway stations (dubbed yellowbacks on account of the yellow tint of the paper covers).[29] Many of these series were reprints, made cheaper by the fact that the titles had gone out of copyright and no royalties had to be paid.

Exporting books overseas

For British publishers, some of the most lucrative areas for book distribution from 1890 to 1920 were the overseas colonial markets of Canada, Australia, New Zealand, India, and other British-dominated territories. As one commentator notes, 'without the colonial edition the export market to the colonies might have been lost altogether to British publishers by the end of the nineteenth century'.[30] While a variety of London-based houses had experimented with specially produced, one-volume 'colonial editions' of popular fiction and non-fiction from 1843 onwards, it was not until Macmillan's successful launch of its Macmillan's Colonial Library in 1886 that colonial export sales really took off. Colonial editions were British books produced for the colonies, either initially as separate publications or as cloth and paperbound versions of cheap-edition sheets printed for the British market.

The increasing importance of the colonial market to British publishers led, for example, to the founding of the British Publishers' Association in 1896. (One of its main aims was to work to protect publishing interests in the 'colonial fiction' market.) By 1900, seventeen British-based publishers were running 'colonial' series, and 60 per cent of all exported books were being sold to British possessions. Of these, 27 per cent were accounted for by Australian sales alone, worth over £390,000 per annum, making it the single largest overseas consumer of British-produced books. Indeed, Australia would prove one of the largest markets for British book exports from 1889 to 1953, thus making it an ideal venue for British fiction.[31]

---

29 David Finkelstein and Alistair McCleery, *An Introduction to Book History* (London and New York: Routledge, 2005), p. 89.
30 Graeme Johanson, *Colonial Editions in Australia, 1843–1972* (Wellington, NZ: Elibank Press, 2000), p. 105.
31 *Ibid.*, pp. 257–8; Martyn Lyons, 'Britain's Largest Export Market', in Martyn Lyons and John Arnold (eds.), *A History of the Book in Australia, 1891–1945* (St Lucia, Queensland: University of Queensland Press, 2001), pp. 19–26.

In India, British novels and historical romances were among a significant number of literary texts popular in nineteenth-century colonialist and Indian circles alike, part of an influx of English-language texts into Indian markets after the enactment of the English Education Acts of 1835. The acts, a result of initiatives by Thomas Babington (Lord Macaulay) and other reformers bent on establishing the primacy of English education in India, created new market opportunities for British publishers, and imports of British books and printed matter into India rose as a result. John Murray was among the first to attempt publishing initiatives specific to India, issuing reprints of his best-selling titles under the Murray Colonial and Home Library series that ran between 1843 and 1849. As noted earlier, in 1886 Macmillan would reposition itself with its Colonial Library Series, drawing on Murray's past experiment as well as on Richard Bentley's short-lived Bentley's Empire Library (which published sixteen titles between 1878 and 1881). Kegan Paul started up its own Indian and Colonial Library Series in 1887 in an attempt to compete with Macmillan, but the venture proved unsuccessful and was terminated in 1889.[32]

The types of texts shipped to Indian shores were multifarious, including grammar and general textbooks, biographies, poetry, histories, plays, novels, and literary periodicals. Priya Joshi notes that the British novel, particularly that which held to 'serious standards', was a dominant textual form imported into India in the nineteenth century, brought in as a means of supporting and legitimating Englishness in the colony. 'Yet the fiction consumed most voraciously', she argues, 'discussed, copied, translated, and "adapted" most avidly into Indian languages, and eventually into the Indian novel – was not the novel of "serious standards" but the work of what are often considered minor British novelists whose fortunes soared for several generations among enthusiastic and loyal Indian readers long after they had already waned in Britain.'[33]

The publisher's reader

The increasing value ascribed to literary property created space for new intermediaries such as publishers' readers and literary agents to filter and promote the 'raw' material prepared for mass consumption. The publisher's

32 See Priya Joshi, *In Another Country: Colonialism, Culture, and the Development of the English Novel in India* (New York: Columbia University Press, 2002), pp. 93–138; Johanson, *Colonial Editions*, throughout.
33 See Priya Joshi, 'Culture and Consumption: Fiction, the Reading Public, and the British Novel in Colonial India', *Book History* 1 (1998), p. 197.

reader was one interesting role that evolved as publishers were inundated by unsolicited manuscripts from aspiring authors. The publisher's reader was not a new phenomenon: literary advisers to publishers or their predecessors (booksellers) had often been utilized and invoked when judgment was required on particular submissions. Arthur Waugh highlighted the apocryphal figure such informal readers represented in mid-century literary circles when he wrote that 'the literary adviser of the mid-Victorian era was ... a sort of mysterious soothsayer, imprisoned in some secret back room, and referred to cryptically as "our reader".'[34] Late nineteenth-century publishers' readers were, with few exceptions, recruited from a network of elite educated 'men of letters', such as John Forster, John Morley, Andrew Lang, Edward Garnett, and George Meredith, though there were powerful women advisers who managed to break through the gender barrier in this arena, including Margaret Oliphant, Elizabeth Rigby, and Geraldine Jewsbury.

As the nature of author–publisher relations changed to accommodate the increasingly complex nature of copyright and serialization negotiations, the role of the publisher's reader assumed an important mediating position. Readers were hired to seek out new material, to encourage new prospects to join particular publishing lists, and to act as expert evaluators of literary texts passed on by editors and publishers. Much like the literary agent who later would usurp some of these roles, the reader not only drew on established contacts but advised both authors and publishers on literary material. Edward Garnett, for example, advised Jonathan Cape on new writers who might join his lists while also undertaking thorough readings of submissions. As one source noted, 'He revised manuscripts but often the kinds of advising he did went below the surface to touch upon the theme, motivation and structure of a novel.'[35] Geraldine Jewsbury, reader for Bentley's, was employed in a different manner, dealing not with individual authors but solely with their texts, advising on suitability for publishing, rating, approving or recommending rejection of what fitted her conception of Bentley's lists. 'Her services were primarily on behalf of the publisher', the historian Fritschner notes, 'only secondarily on behalf of the authors, and least of all on behalf of literature. She tried to uphold literary standards within the category of literature as an

---

34 Arthur Waugh, *A Hundred Years of Publishing* (London: Chapman and Hall, 1930), p. 139.
35 Linda Marie Fritschner, 'Publishers' Readers, Publishers, and their Authors', *Publishing History* 7 (1980), p. 94.

entertainment or a diversion. Generally her acceptance or rejection of a manuscript depended upon her evaluation of the commercial potential of the manuscript.'[36]

Such tasks were increasingly required from such 'expert' evaluators as more individuals sought entry into the literary profession. As one US example demonstrates, the volume of manuscripts received by journal editors did not recede as the century progressed, but increased exponentially: editors of the leading US monthly magazine of the nineteenth century, the *Century* (with a peak circulation in 1897 of 250,000 copies), for example, saw a doubling of submissions, moving from 1,700 manuscripts in 1873, to 2,000 in 1874, 2,400 in 1875, and finally 3,200 by 1876.[37] It should be noted, incidentally, that a number of American periodicals, including the *Century, Scribner's*, and *Harper's Monthly* enjoyed a wide circulation within Britain. The number of titles issued annually in Britain reflected similar exponential growth in the market over much of the nineteenth century, rising from an average 580 in the 1820s, to 2,600 in the 1850s and 6,044 in 1901.[38] The readers' place in such activity involved a fine balance between satisfying commercial needs and encouraging aesthetic development, so playing a crucial role in shaping policies within publishing firms and influencing the formulation of a 'branded' set of literary outputs from particular 'list' publishers. As the movement of literary agents into the publishing system expanded, and they began assuming many of the functions previously undertaken by the publisher's reader, the reader ceased to play a significant role as a securer of literary talent, becoming restricted to a subsidiary position as a hired evaluator of literary texts.

Authors and copyright

The rise of a mass reading public in the nineteenth century (with interest in and ability to pay for printed works) created changes in the economic fortunes of authors, generating an audience from whom authors could earn money if successful in capturing their imagination. Crucially it was the development of copyright as a legal concept that led to

36 *Ibid.*
37 Matthew Schneirov, *The Dream of a New Social Order: Popular Magazines in America, 1893–1914* (New York: Columbia University Press, 1994), pp. 11, 66.
38 Raymond Williams, *The Long Revolution* (Harmondsworth: Penguin, 1965), pp. 185, 187, 191–2.

an economic revolution, a result of political battles and legal refinements over the majority of the century.

Interpretations of who owned the results of an author's efforts would be clarified in 1774 following a landmark legal case in London between a Scottish and English bookseller. Donaldson vs. Becket established the legal precedents and concepts of individual copyright ownership that was to shape international interpretations of copyright in the century that followed. Initially authors or interested parties purchasing a copyright were granted sole reproduction rights for fourteen years; in 1814 this was extended to twenty-eight years. The 1842 Copyright Act, a result of a five-year Parliamentary struggle initiated by Thomas Telfourd in 1837, allowed literary copyright to be extended to include an author's life plus seven years, or forty-two years, whichever was the greater. It also included provisions protecting copyright across the British colonies for works first published in Britain.

Copyright value was keenly observed and managed by the more astute novelists of the Victorian period. Their assiduity in establishing literary worth emerged from a fundamental re-appraisal of the nature of literary property and of the individuals responsible for it. As Catherine Seville points out, the most remarked-on transformation of literary activity in the nineteenth century was the shift from regarding authors as imitators of nature to perceiving them as creators, a perception 'that found its strongest expression in the Romantic vision of the author as a central, unique and essentially solitary figure, providing privileged access to the meaning of the text'.[39]

Many realized soon enough that conceptualizing the author as a creator required the same author to act as a business person. Copyright was the key to managing this transition. As Trollope noted in his posthumously published autobiography, without copyright there was little incentive for the modern author to continue in this profession: 'Take away from English authors their copyright, and you would very soon take away also from England her authors.'[40] Such blithe assessment of literary power applied to just a few of the high earners, underneath whom toiled a large band of hopefuls whose earning power were less certain and yet who persisted in the profession. As census records reveal, over the last quarter of the nineteenth century the number of individuals who classed themselves as working in

---

39 Catherine Seville, *The Internationalisation of Copyright Law: Books, Buccaneers and the Black Flag in the Nineteenth Century* (Cambridge University Press, 2006), p. 14.
40 Anthony Trollope, *Autobiography* (Oxford University Press, 1980), p. 107.

the literary profession, either as authors, editors, journalists, or reporters almost doubled, rising from 6,000 in 1881, to 8,000 in 1891, to 11,000 in 1901. And this may have been a considerable understatement, for another estimate claimed 14,000 men and women in 1888 scribbling in London alone, though such numbers probably included those who dabbled rather than depended exclusively on literary work for a living.[41] Another authority, Walter Besant, founder in 1884 of the Society of Authors and major crusader for the rights of authors, more cautiously estimated in 1901 that from those numbers, about 1,300 could be adjudged active novelists, of whom a small proportion (sixty) made £1,000 or more a year, another 150 enjoyed a passable income, and 'the rest of the one thousand three hundred made little or nothing'.[42]

Turning literature into profit depended on systems for rewarding authors that were refined over the Victorian period as the market value and cultural positioning of writers changed. A standard approach dating back to the early period of printing involved the purchase at a fixed price of an author's copyright, sometimes outright, sometimes for a fixed number of years or editions. Under this system, authors were paid up front but did not share in any subsequent profits from sales until such time as they were able to purchase back or regain ownership in their texts. Much early- to mid-century fiction was produced and sold in this way, and publishers paid lump sums according to their estimation of the potential success of the manuscript under scrutiny. Best-selling authors of the period frequently commanded a premium: in 1862, for example, George Smith successfully wooed George Eliot away from her Edinburgh publishers William Black-wood with a staggering offer of £10,000 for the copyright and serialization rights of her novel *Romola*; in 1873 Trollope made do with £3,000 for *The Way We Live Now*, while Disraeli relinquished copyright in 1880 to Longman for £10,000 for his final work *Endymion*. As one critic astutely notes, such extreme examples merely underscored the general market economy structures that entwined publishers and authors: 'The novelist provided the middle-class reading public with an agreeable work, which until the death of the three-decker in 1895 was close to being a standard commodity; and the price was a measure of how well the task of literary production had been achieved.'[43]

41 Peter Morton, *'The Busiest Man in England': Grant Allen and the Writing Trade, 1875–1900* (Basingstoke: Palgrave Macmillan, 2005), p. 61.
42 Quoted *ibid.*, p. 112.
43 Paul Delany, *Literature, Money and the Market: From Trollope to Amis* (Basingstoke: Palgrave, 2002), p. 147.

The literary agent

In the late 1880s, possibly as a result of the publicity and attention paid to forceful arguments expounded by the US publisher George Haven Putnam in his *Authors and Publishers: A Manual of Suggestions for Beginners in Literature* (1883) and *The Grievances between Authors and Publishers* (1887), British publishers began adopting the system of royalty payments that effectively underpins publishing terms to this day. The royalty system provided payments to authors based on an agreed, sliding-scale percentage of the retail price of every copy of their work sold. Royalty payments would play a significant part in author–publisher relations from the latter quarter of the century onwards, particularly following the entrance of literary agents as mediators and negotiators of literary worth.

The rise of the professional literary agent from the late nineteenth century onwards has been described in detail in several important works.[44] Individuals had frequently acted on behalf of friends and colleagues in such a capacity throughout the century. Notable examples included John Forster, mediating contracts and business arrangements for acquaintances and close colleagues such as Charles Dickens, Tennyson, Thomas Carlyle, and Robert Browning between the 1830s and the 1860s. Thackeray praised Forster as the ultimate negotiator: 'Whenever anybody is in a scrape we all fly to him for refuge', he wrote, 'he is omniscient and works miracles.'[45] Others supporting authors in such ways included George Henry Lewes for George Eliot from the 1850s to 1870s, Theodore Watts-Dunton for Algernon Swinburne in the 1880s and 1890s, and Thomas Aspinwall, who as US consul in London from 1827 to 1854 negotiated British publishing deals for Washington Irving and James Fenimore Cooper.[46]

By 1900, such informal support had been superseded by what was available from the professional literary agent. One of the first known, if least distinguished, British agents to emerge was A. M. Burghes in 1882, later charged in court with defrauding his clients. A more reliable pioneer was the Scots-born Alexander Pollock Watt, who began advertising commercially as a literary

---

44 Mary Ann Gillies, *The Professional Literary Agent in Britain, 1880–1920* (University of Toronto Press, 2007); James Hepburn, *The Author's Empty Purse and the Rise of the Literary Agent* (London: Oxford University Press, 1968); James L. W. West III, *American Authors and the Literary Marketplace since 1900* (University Park: Pennsylvania State University Press, 1985).

45 Hepburn, *Author's Empty Purse*, p. 26.

46 James J. and Patience B. Barnes, 'Thomas Aspinwall: First Transatlantic Literary Agent', *The Papers of the Bibliographical Society of America* 78:3 (1984), pp. 321–32.

agent in 1881. It is to Watt that credit is due for laying down the ground rules for the profession, establishing the standard commission fee (10 per cent) for successful representation, and presenting himself as an intermediary, the scout who acted for both publisher and author. His skill lay in recognizing and perfecting the mediating role of the literary agent as arbiter and evaluator of literary property, or more precisely, as one commentator noted, in 'participating in, and in fact becoming the source of, the valuation of copyright'.[47] Watt specialized in expanding the scope and reach of established authors such as Rider Haggard, Rudyard Kipling, Wilkie Collins, and Arthur Conan Doyle.

A rival would appear in 1896 in the form of James Brand Pinker, who aimed his energies at promoting newly emerging Modernist authors such as Joseph Conrad, Stephen Crane, Ford Madox Ford, D. H. Lawrence, James Joyce, and H. G. Wells. Until his death in 1922, he served as a prominent and imposing negotiator of literary property, a man of patience who, Conrad wrote, 'has treated not only my moods but even my fancies with the greatest consideration'.[48] Other agents who gathered in London at the turn of the twentieth century included the American agent Curtis Brown, and C. F. Cazenove and G. H. Perris, who would found the influential Literary Agency in 1899.[49]

The activities of these intermediaries were strongly resisted by publishers, who viewed them as unnecessary and predatory destroyers of author–publisher relations. As William Heinemann virulently exclaimed: 'My theory is that when once an author gets into the claws of a typical agent, he is lost to decency. He generally adopts the moral outlook of the trickster, which the agent inoculates with all rapidity, and the virus is so poisonous that the publisher had better disinfect himself and avoid contagion.'[50] At the end of the First World War, however, the process instigated by the insertion of such intermediaries was irrevocably part of publishing and literary publishing. In 1894 there were six agents registered in the London *Post Office Directory*. By 1914 there were more than thirty agencies and syndicates advertising literary services in trade journals.[51]

47 Mary Ann Gillies, 'A. P. Watt, Literary Agent', *Publishing Research Quarterly* 9 (1993), p. 22.
48 Hepburn, *Author's Empty Purse*, p. 58.
49 Robert Gomme, 'Edward Thomas and the Literary Agency of London', *Book Collector* 47:1 (1998), pp. 67–78.
50 Frederick Whyte, *William Heinemann, a Memoir* (London: Jonathan Cape, 1928), p. 124.
51 David Finkelstein, *The House of Blackwood: Author–Publisher Relations in the Victorian Era* (University Park: Pennsylvania State University Press, 2002), p. 129.

The professionalization of literary sales was just one of several shifts that took place in the organization of the literary and publishing professions. By 1900, almost all areas of the profession were represented by specific associations; these included the Society of Authors (founded by Walter Besant in 1884), the Publishers Association (founded in 1896), and the Associated Booksellers of Great Britain and Ireland (founded in 1895). The shift exemplified a move away from 'personal' relations, a misty-eyed, genteel publishing approach that favoured courtesy and cordial links with authors (at the same time as it disguised a publishing model tilted in favour of publishers' interests), towards a more commercial, profit-driven structure coping with a multiplicity of media outlets for printed products. List publishers who had relied on the certainty and stability of nineteenth-century publishing models found themselves facing new challenges and giving ground to younger, more entrepreneurial entrants. Likewise, literary stars of the late century would give way to their Modernist literary successors. But the Modernists, for all their radical literary positions, nevertheless became participants in a market economy they inherited from the previous generation, dependent on a commercial publishing system that had successfully exported British literary culture and publishing models around the English-speaking world.

2

Victorian reading

LEAH PRICE

In 1847, Sir Arthur Helps began an essay on reading with the dutiful observation that 'It appears to me remarkable that this subject should have been so little touched upon', but one sometimes feels that the Victorians touched on little else.[1] Literacy was credited for reducing criminality and blamed for encouraging sexual licence; the topic fuelled both visual and verbal media, writing and speech. When twenty-first-century scholars gain access to nineteenth-century clichés about reading, they do so via print; but the Victorians themselves used the spoken word to praise writing. Sermons remained the traditional venue for arguments about the benefits and dangers of the printed word, but by the 1830s they faced secular competition from after-dinner speeches of benevolent organizations, lectures at the opening of mechanics' institutes, and public addresses like Ruskin's *Sesame and Lilies* – not to mention Parliamentary debates, themselves transcribed in shorthand and read by many more people than those who had heard them. To read that record now is to remember how many of the policies over which Victorian MPs argued related, directly, or indirectly, to literacy. Schools, libraries, copyright law, postal rates, and above all the taxes that determined the pricing of printed matter: the institutions that the Victorians established, reformed, and attacked were centrally concerned with reading.

This is not to say, of course, that they were concerned specifically with the reading of what we now call 'Victorian literature'. On the one hand, many of the texts composed in this period have had long afterlives, continuing to be reprinted and reread at other times and places. (Until the USA ratified international copyright in 1885, much of the audience for British texts was American – if only because the ability to reprint texts originally published in Britain without paying the content provider made them

---

1 Sir Arthur Helps, *Friends in Council*, 2 vols. (New York: Thomas R. Knox, 1847), vol. I, p. 1225.

a bargain.) On the other, much of what the Victorians themselves read was written – though less often printed – in earlier centuries. Because copyright priced new texts out of many readers' reach, the steadiest sellers were reference books, reprints, and above all devotional literature.[2] Even in book form, the British and Foreign Bible Society (jointly founded by Evangelicals and Nonconformists in 1804) was one of the biggest Victorian publishers, while the Society for Promoting Christian Knowledge (its High Church predecessor) was capable of distributing eight million tracts in 1867 alone.[3] At the end of a secularizing century, the *Publisher's Circular* was still listing more theological works than any other class: 975 religious books in 1880 against 580 novels and 187 books of poetry and drama.[4] This is not to say that demand corresponded to supply: an 1839 survey of 151 peasant families in Kent found that eighty-six owned a Bible or other religious book, while only eight owned a secular book,[5] but by the end of the century, fewer than 1 per cent of loans from public libraries were classified under 'religion'.[6] This chapter, then, will not focus on the reception of the texts discussed elsewhere in this volume. Rather, it will explore the Victorian theory and practice of reading. What was read in this period, and by whom? What hopes and fears did writers attach to reading (their own and others'), and what vocabulary did they develop to describe – endlessly, ambivalently – those textual encounters?

At mid-century, Matthew Arnold declared that 'the main effort, for now many years, has been a critical effort';[7] decades later, Oscar Wilde aphorized that 'the highest Criticism deals with art not as expressive but as impressive purely'.[8] Both spoke for a culture in which consumption was upstaging production. (This was not just true for literature: Regenia Gagnier and Paul Saint-Amour have argued that the marginal revolution in economics

---

2 See William St Clair, 'The Political Economy of Reading', *The John Coffin Memorial Lecture in the History of the Book* (London: Institute of English Studies, 2005).

3 Richard Altick, *The English Common Reader: A Social History of the Mass Reading Public, 1800–1900* (University of Chicago Press, 1957), pp. 100–3.

4 *Ibid.*, p. 108. Similarly, the *London Catalogue, 1816–1851* lists 10,300 works of divinity against 3,500 of fiction. Charles Knight, *The Old Printer and the Modern Press* (London: J. Murray, 1854), p. 262.

5 David Mitch, *The Rise of Popular Literacy in Victorian England* (Philadelphia: University of Pennsylvania Press, 1992), pp. 44–5.

6 Robert Darnton, 'First Steps toward a History of Reading', in *The Kiss of Lamourette: Reflections in Cultural History* (New York: Norton, 1990), p. 161.

7 Matthew Arnold, *Complete Prose Works*, ed. R. H. Super 11 vols. (Ann Arbor: University of Michigan Press, 1960–77), volume III, p. 258.

8 Oscar Wilde, 'The Critic as Artist', in *Plays, Prose Writings and Poems*, ed. Isobel Murray (London: J. M. Dent, 1975), p. 26.

provided a model for a new critical interest in the demand side of culture.[9])
A century earlier, debates about class crystallized around autodidactic
writers like Stephen Duck or Hannah Yearsley; by the time of Victoria's
death, in contrast, working-class *reading* had become a greater subject of
concern. Indeed, one might argue that what frightened social thinkers about
the expansion of the reading public was precisely the divorce of reading
from writing – the growth of a class imagined as passive recipients rather
than responsible participants. In the words of the Shakespearean critic
Edward Dowden, 'Our caterers nowadays provide us with a mincemeat
that needs no chewing, and the teeth of a man may in due time become as
obsolete as those which can still be perceived in the foetal whale.'[10]

That fear may help explain the emphasis in prescriptive literature on the
strenuousness of reading, and in particular on the need to link textual
consumption to some form of production. Thus Arnold Bennett wrote that
real reading required 'more resolution, more pertinacity, and more expenditure of brain-tissue ... It means, in fact, "work" ... I do not think that the
literary taste can be satisfactorily formed unless one is prepared to put one's
back into the affair.'[11] Such advice applied particularly well to women:
assumed to be naturally more passive than men, they needed to fight the
association of reading with idleness by copying down quotations, indexing
favourite passages, summarizing arguments, and (by the end of the century)
even taking notes on books to practice their shorthand.[12] When Lucy
Soulsby declared 'I have no faith in reading that is compatible with an
arm-chair',[13] she was privileging those kinds of reading that required a
writing-desk over those that manifested neither bodily nor moral backbone.

These debates about women's reading make visible concerns that applied,
even if more subtly, to men's as well. One set of values which could be
described as 'muscular' – reading instrumentally, generating durable traces
of an evanescent activity, marking up the book – constantly clashed with an
equally strong desire for receptivity: being absorbed, carried away, marked

9 Regenia Gagnier, *The Insatiability of Human Wants: Economics and Aesthetics in Market Society* (University of Chicago Press, 2000), p. 41; Paul K. Saint-Amour, *The Copy-wrights: Intellectual Property and the Literary Imagination* (Ithaca, NY: Cornell University Press, 2003), p. 36.
10 Edward Dowden, 'Hopes and Fears for Literature', *Fortnightly Review* n.s. 45 (1889), pp. 169–70.
11 Arnold Bennett, *Literary Taste: How to Form It* (London: Hodder and Stoughton, 1909), p. 61.
12 Kate Flint, *The Woman Reader, 1837–1914* (Oxford: Clarendon Press, 1993), p. 95.
13 Lucy H. M. Soulsby, *Stray Thoughts on Reading* (London: Longmans Green and Co., 1898), p. 6.

for life by one's reading. What was most often expressed as a difference among audiences (men study, women skim) could also be mapped on to genre: a few standard devotional books were reread 'intensively' (and republished, forming the most profitable part of the backlist), while secular literature in general and novels in particular were read 'extensively'.[14] (Thus, a speech given at the opening of the Kilburn public library – once again, an oral paean to silent reading – pointed out that it was neither 'possible [nor] necessary to read *The Proverbs of Solomon* and *King Solomon's Mines* the same way'.[15]) As we have seen, the short shelf-life of fiction both caused and reflected the fact that it was rented rather than bought. But the very disposability that made the fortune of circulating libraries worried moralists: could a book that did not stand up to rereading be worth reading at all? According to Herbert Maxwell in 1893, 'Unless the recollection of what is read is ensured by notes, reading is a task as fruitless as that of the daughters of Danaus; it serves to spend our limited capital in time without enriching the ever-diminishing store of future.'[16] How could reading (by definition a fleeting experience) continue to yield dividends (in the form of tangible objects)?

The Victorian struggle between active and passive reading has a more concrete consequence for scholars today. Marginalia, valued earlier in the century as proof that reading involved strenuous production rather than idle consumption, was embargoed by the new public libraries, which saw readers' hands as wandering, dirty, or even capable of spreading disease. A side effect was an impoverishment of the evidence available to modern scholars trying to trace the reception of particular texts: since free public libraries tended to order books directly from the publisher rather than inheriting or buying them from an individual collector, and since they so strongly discouraged their own patrons from writing in books, this record of reader response becomes increasingly thin.[17]

---

14 As David Vincent reminds us, intensive and extensive reading inhered in genres more than in individual readers: 'The same reader might now skim a newspaper on his way to work and spend an evening on a single paragraph of a precious book.' David Vincent, *The Rise of Mass Literacy: Reading and Writing in Modern Europe* (Cambridge: Polity Press, 2000), p. 103.

15 J. E. C. Weldon, 'The Art of Reading Books', *National Review* (April 1894), pp. 213–18, p. 217.

16 Herbert Maxwell, 'The Craving for Fiction', *Nineteenth Century* (June 1893), pp. 1046–61, p. 1060.

17 See H. J. Jackson, *Marginalia: Readers Writing in Books* (New Haven, CT: Yale University Press, 2001).

Rules against writing in library books addressed the question of voluntary defacement, but not of involuntary contamination. The second half of the century saw a spate of 'book disinfecting apparatuses', 'metal fumigators', and other inventions designed to disinfect library books after use. Surprisingly, our fullest description of these devices comes from an advocate of free libraries, Thomas Greenwood, who elsewhere urged wealthy collectors to bequeath their books to the public, on the grounds that 'books, like coins, are only performing their right function when they are in circulation'.[18] Just as the marginalia which middle-class men saw as a bulwark against passive reading could look like defacement when practised by women or lower-middle-class library patrons, so the hope that circulation of books would transcend social differences was always haunted by the fear that exchange could contaminate.[19] As the traditional fear that texts could poison their readers was literalized by the worry that book-objects could spread disease, older concerns about the relation of the reader to a text gave way to newer ones about the relation of one reader to another.

To think about reading, in other words, meant to think about difference – between classes, sexes, ages, eras. In Britain, as elsewhere in nineteenth-century Europe, literacy came to serve as a kind of litmus test for social progress; signatures on marriage registers, statistics about educational level, and examination results of schoolchildren, were all tabulated and correlated with other measures of economic, moral, and medical well-being. (Ironically, as David Vincent points out, statisticians gave far more attention to literacy than they did to the numeracy that made their own enterprise possible.[20]) English reformers like G. R. Porter tried in vain to refute the French statistician A. M. Guerry's 1833 claim that a rising literacy rate correlated with a rise in crime. The economist W. R. Greg, however, could show only that although high education levels seemed to correlate with a high rate of property crimes, the opposite was true for crimes of violence.[21] The historian David Vincent has noted the paradox underpinning the foundation of secular national school systems in the nineteenth century: 'If organized religion was the

---

18 Thomas Greenwood, *Public Libraries: A History of the Movement and a Manual for the Organization and Management of Rate-Supported Libraries* (London: Simpkin Marshall, 1890), p. 5.
19 See Lewis C. Roberts, 'Disciplining and Disinfecting Working-Class Readers in the Victorian Public Library', *Victorian Literature and Culture* 26:1 (1998), pp. 105–32; Greenwood, *Public Libraries*, pp. 494–5.
20 Vincent, *Rise of Mass Literacy*, p. 5.
21 Patrick Brantlinger, *The Reading Lesson: The Threat of Mass Literacy in Nineteenth-Century Britain* (Bloomington: Indiana University Press, 1998), p. 74.

intended victim of many literacy campaigns, it managed, at the very least, to bequeath to the secular education process its vocabulary of spiritual reconstruction.'[22]

Modern scholars are blessed (and cursed) by the Victorians' own obsession with literacy statistics. Recent estimates lend some support to their triumphalist narrative, charting a jagged climb from a 50 per cent adult literacy rate in 1750 to 95 per cent by 1900.[23] The overall rise is all the more striking given a temporary dip at the end of the eighteenth century: as the factory system raised the opportunity cost of schooling for children, and as the establishment of new churches and schools failed to keep pace with families migrating to new industrial cities, literacy rates temporarily dropped off. The Industrial Revolution, once seen as the fruit of Enlightenment literacy and numeracy, looked in the short term like their greatest enemy.[24] Yet in the long run, regional differences in literacy began to flatten – though in the last quarter of the nineteenth century the London area, the far north, and the Channel coast were still more heavily literate.[25] Gender difference levelled out as well. In 1850, 70 per cent of men were measured as literate, against 55 per cent of women;[26] by the end of the century, though, female literacy rates actually surpassed men's in the rural South and East, where girls were less likely than boys to be withdrawn from school for farm labour.[27] As literacy became universal, however, it also ceased to become a distinction; literacy made possible geographical mobility from country to city, but social mobility proved more elusive. Biographies and autobiographies represent literacy as the cause of an individual's prosperity, but in hindsight it more often looks like an effect of family income.[28] The inequalities that literacy was expected to overcome were often ultimately reinforced by it.[29]

The statistics are further complicated by changing measures of what it meant to be literate – including, most basically, whether literacy meant the ability to produce text or to consume it. At the beginning of the century, more people could read than could write – in Webb's estimate, twice or

22 Vincent, *Rise of Mass Literacy*, p. 22.
23 Mitch, *Rise of Popular Literacy*, p. xvii; Altick, *Common Reader*, p. 171.
24 Vincent, *Rise of Mass Literacy*, pp. 67–8.   25 *Ibid.*, p. 13.
26 Martyn Lyons, 'New Readers in the Nineteenth Century: Women, Children, Workers', in Guglielmo Cavallo and Roger Chartier (eds.), *A History of Reading in the West*, (Cambridge: Polity Press, 1999), pp. 313–44: p. 313.
27 Vincent, *Rise of Mass Literacy*, p. 12.   28 *Ibid.*, p. 66.   29 *Ibid.*, p. 25.

three times as many. Even at mid-century, many working-class homes contained printed matter but no writing materials.[30] But the gap between those skills steadily narrowed, in part because the Revised Code of 1862 stipulated that writing be taught from the beginning, rather than waiting until the child already knew how to read.[31]

Where observers both then and now agree in registering a steady increase in literacy rates, its causes remain more contentious. The growth of a literate population was clearly related – both as effect and as cause – to the steady cheapening of printed matter (always with the exception of the novel): as David Vincent points out, a penny would buy a 250-word broadside in the 1840s, a 7,000-word songbook by the 1860s, a 20,000-word novelette by the 1880s, and by the 1890s an unabridged version of a classic text.[32] The Victorians themselves made grand claims for the effects of infrastructures and institutions, like National Schools, public libraries, and the penny post. Recent historians, however, have discounted the importance of successive state interventions in formal education – first subsidies to (1833) and inspections of (1846) church schools, then legislation making elementary education universal (1870), compulsory (1880), and free (1886).[33] (One reason is that as late as the 1850s those schools educated only a minority of pupils; when the Education Act passed in 1870, 44,000 London children were still attending dame, private, or ragged schools that received neither subsidy nor inspection.[34]) Instead they stress the practical uses that literacy acquired in economic life – or, put the other way around, the rising opportunity cost of *not* knowing how to read. The ability to fill out printed forms became increasingly crucial to finding (and, though less universally, performing) work. So did the ability to scan printed matter: post-1850 accounts of public libraries suggest that the want ads were among the most heavily used sections of the newspaper. Other historians, however, have stressed that the occupational value of reading deflated as literacy became more universal: in David Vincent's words, 'a determined programme of reading and writing was usually an escape from, rather than an encounter with [people's] struggle to maintain their family economies'.[35]

In the last generation before the advent of the radio, leisure, too, was increasingly structured by printed matter. Lyons observes that the first

30 David Vincent, *Literacy and Popular Culture: England 1750–1914* (Cambridge University Press, 1989), p. 10.
31 Mitch, *Rise of Popular Literacy*, pp. 60–1.
32 See Vincent, *Literacy and Popular Culture*.   33 Vincent, *Rise of Mass Literacy*, p. 31.
34 *Ibid.*, p. 34.   35 *Ibid.*, p. 147.

generation to accede to mass literacy 'was also the last to see the book unchallenged as a communications medium'.[36] David Mitch traces popular literacy to the growth of a national sport network made possible in turn by the growth of railways and telegraphs. Betting spurred on interest in sporting news and sales of newspapers: 'Many a man made the breakthrough to literacy by studying the pages of the One O' Clock [a sporting paper].'[37] The question of what exactly counted as 'reading' made visible tensions between a rhetoric of moral, economic, or intellectual self-improvement and a reality in which literacy was put to more mundane uses. Thus, Florence Bell remarks that among factory workers, 'About a quarter of the men do not read at all: that is to say, if there is anything coming off in the way of sport that they are interested in, they buy a paper to see the result. That hardly comes under the head of reading.'[38]

Periodicals aroused particular anxiety, as a society which ranked books among luxury goods gave way to one in which newspapers came to exemplify both the benefits and the dangers of mass consumption. Opposition to the 'taxes on knowledge' instituted in 1819 became one of the mainstays of both radical and Liberal politics; in fact, for the early Victorians, questions about the distribution of printed matter were arguably as central to political debate as were longer-lived issues like suffrage and free trade. On the one hand, the hard-won abolition of advertising duties on newspapers (1837), stamp tax (1855), and paper duty (1861) led to the creation of cheap mass-circulation dailies in place of a split between expensive stamped newspapers and the cheap underground publications produced during the 'war of the unstamped' that lasted between 1819 and 1836. The result was the rise in the 1870s of the New Journalism, which culminated in the first half-penny paper (the *Daily Mail*, 1896) and tabloid (the *Daily Mirror*, 1903), both founded by Alfred Harmsworth, Lord Northcliffe.

The New Journalism revolutionized mass reading on both sides of the Atlantic: it addressed a new 'half-educated' public by shortening the average article (*Tit-Bits*, founded in 1881, was often blamed for fragmenting readers' attention spans); stressing human interest (the demise of the guaranteed audience provided by the circulating libraries forced publishers to direct attention to literary authors' private lives, often via the new genre of the

36 Lyons, 'New Readers', p. 313.
37 Quoted in Robert Roberts, *The Classic Slum: Salford Life in the First Quarter of the Century* (Harmondsworth: Penguin, 1973), p. 164.
38 Florence Eveleen Olliffe Bell, *At the Works: A Study of a Manufacturing Town* (London: Thomas Nelson, 1911), p. 207.

interview);[39] encouraging first-person reports (thus, James Greenwood's *Night in a Workhouse* (1866) recounted the journalist's own undercover experience, as did W. T. Stead's exposé of child prostitution in the *Pall Mall Gazette* of 1885, 'The Maiden Tribute of Modern Babylon'); and incorporating reader participation. *Tit-Bits* was especially ingenious, pioneering correspondence columns, treasure hunts, prizes for amateur contributions, and even a life insurance scheme that promised to compensate the next of kin of any commuter found in a railway wreckage with copies of the current week's issue on his person.[40]

The New Journalism partly reflected changes in the technologies by which the news was produced: in the second half of the nineteenth century, the speed with which data was transmitted and the media in which it was represented were transformed by inventions like the electric telegraph, the telephone, the typewriter, the phonograph, the photograph itself, and later the halftone block for photo reproduction.[41] Less tangible, but equally transformative, were the new price structures enabled by the end of the taxes on knowledge, and new cultural assumptions about the relation of reading to other forms of consumption. As Evelyn March Phillipps complained in 1895, 'before long, we shall not be surprised to find even the Times giving away the equivalent for a screw of tea or tobacco with every copy sold'.[42] The New Journalism substituted bodies for text, in two senses: not only in upstaging reviews of literary works by descriptions of their authors' clothes, homes, and appearance, but also in combining reading with other consumer needs.

The eighteenth century bequeathed to the Victorians an association of mass literacy either with universal enlightenment or with mob rule. On the one hand, the Society for the Diffusion of Useful Knowledge founded by Henry, Lord Brougham in 1826 developed new distribution systems for publishing cheap books – and, in commissioning content for publications like Charles Knight's *Penny Magazine*, to challenge the trickle-down model that for over a century had made cheap books a repository for outdated text

---

39 'Behind every speech and act there is a man', T. P. O'Connor, 'The New Journalism', *New Review* 1 (1889), p. 428. On the interview, see Rosemary Van Arsdel, 'Women's Periodicals and the New Journalism: The Personal Interview', in Joel Weiner (ed.), *Papers for the Millions: The New Journalism in Britain* (Westport, CT: Greenwood, 1988), p. 245.

40 Peter D. McDonald, *British Literary Culture and Publishing Practice, 1880–1914* (Cambridge Studies in Publishing and Printing History Index, Cambridge and New York: Cambridge University Press, 1997), pp. 146–9.

41 Joel Wiener, Introduction, *Papers for the Millions*, p. xii.

42 Evelyn March Phillipps, 'The New Journalism', *New Review* 1 (1895), pp. 182–9: p. 182.

that happened to be in public domain. For early Victorian radicals and reformers, literacy formed at once the cause and the measure of social progress: Bentham was only the most famous author to propose literacy as a criterion for suffrage. According to John Stuart Mill, 'So complete was my father's reliance on the influence of reason over the minds of mankind, whenever it is allowed to teach them, that he felt as if all would be gained if the whole population were taught to read.'[43] As late as 1902, Lord Avebury could still revive those pieties in his address to the annual meeting of the National Home Reading Union – an organization that encouraged people without much formal education to form reading circles to improve their taste: 'If people realised the intense enjoyment of reading, there would be very little pauperism, extravagance, drunkenness, and crime.'[44] Here again, reading could be praised most effusively in a speech.

On the other hand, the fear of mass literacy remained acute even as its targets shifted, from the Newgate novels of the 1830s to the New Journalism of the 1890s. In 1807 Samuel Whitbread's bill guaranteeing two years of free education to poor children was defeated on the grounds that educating the poor would 'teach them to despise their lot in life' by 'enabl[ing] them to read seditious pamphlets, vicious books, and publications against Christianity'.[45] In *New Grub Street* (1891), George Gissing still worried that literary production was now catering to the 'quarter-educated'. Between those two moments, the imitative theory of the dangers of reading may be best exemplified by Harrison Ainsworth's Newgate novel *Jack Sheppard* (1839), whose highwayman hero was widely blamed for corrupting its readers.

Put simply, literacy provoked ambivalence. Even staunch Liberals could use ambiguous language, like the double entendre in G. M. Trevelyan's remark that 'Since we have given everyone the key to the house of knowledge, we must show them the door.'[46] And as Patrick Brantlinger has shown, a contrast between virtuous illiterates like Joe Gargery or Mr Boffin and treacherous upwardly mobile readers like Bradley Headstone, Silas Wegg, or Pip directly contradicts Dickens's oft-stated faith in the moral value of education. Victorian ambivalence about reading makes it crucial not to

---

43 John Stuart Mill, *Autobiography* (Oxford University Press, 1924), p. 89.
44 Lord Avebury (Sir John Lubbock) at a meeting of the Home Reading Union, 27 February 1902, quoted in Frank Herbert Hayward, *The Reform of Moral and Biblical Education* (London: S. Sonnenschein, 1902), p. 143.
45 J. L. Hammond, Barbara Bradby Hammond, and John Christopher Lovell, *The Town Labourer* (London and New York: Longman, 1978), p. 49.
46 G. M. Trevelyan, 'The White Peril', *The Nineteenth Century and After* 50 (1901), pp. 1043–55: p. 1052.

flatten out the different venues in which quotable remarks for or against it appeared. Kate Flint shows, for example, that women's reading was cele-brated in particular genres (autobiography, for example) at the very moment when concern was being expressed about it in others (medical manuals and conduct literature).[47]

Conservative critics attacked not just popular literacy itself, but the faith of middle-class intellectuals like Lord Avebury in the mechanical act of running one's eyes along the page. Francis Hitchman was hardly exagger-ating when he observed in 1890 that

> There are not a few good people in whose eyes in a book is a species of Fetish, and who look upon printed paper with as much reverence as do the Maho-metans. To all such the boy who, in their own phrase, 'never has a book out of his hands', is worthy of respect and even of admiration. Unfortunately, however, the lad of this type revels in a literature which is not precisely of the kind of which Cobbett and Franklin hoarded their pence.[48]

Hitchman may have been right to charge that reformers confused the means with the end. By equating (free-thinking?) idealists who saw reading as a panacea with (Mahometan) materialists who worship paper, he satirized the formalism that made reading a good in itself. Similarly, Florence Bell stresses that

> learning to read does not necessarily lead to the enjoyment of literature. It is, no doubt, an absolutely necessary step in that direction, but I cannot help thinking, on looking at the results all around, and not only among the workmen, that all knowledge and practice of reading make nearly as often for waste of time as for edification ... The spread of education has a broad back. It is made to bear the burden of many unrealized, if not unrealizable projects.[49]

What commentators disagreed about was not simply the moral conse-quences of working-class reading, but also how closely they resembled the effects of reading within the social class to which those commentators themselves belonged. Reading was credited (and blamed) with the power both to divide and to unite. When Trollope wrote that 'Novels are in the hands of us all; from the Prime Minister down to the last-appointed scullery-maid', he was celebrating the same fact that Alfred Austin deplored when he wrote

---

47 Patrick Brantlinger, *The Reading Lesson: The Threat of Mass Literacy in Nineteenth-Century Britain* (Bloomington: Indiana University Press, 1998), p. 5. Flint, *Woman Reader*, throughout.
48 Francis Hitchman, 'Penny Fiction', *Quarterly Review* 171 (1890), pp. 150–71, p. 151.
49 Bell, *At the Works*, p. 204.

in 1870 that 'unhappily, the sensation novel is that one touch of anything but nature that makes the kitchen and the drawing-room kin'.[50] In theory, shared books cut across social class – whether for good or for evil, as when an 1868 cartoon in *Punch* showed a maid borrowing a lodger's sensation novel.[51] In practice, as later historians have stressed, a single text could be read in widely differing material forms (circulating-library triple-decker, cheap reprint, pirated abridgment) and adopted by equally divergent interpretive schemes.

In fact, even the same copy of a book could mean different things depending on where it was read – schoolroom or church, parlour or bedroom, pub or railway carriage – and how it was read: silently or aloud, communally or privately. The two don't always align in this period: railways (unlike coaches) enabled silent reading in public spaces, and indeed it was precisely when crammed together with strangers that individuals hid behind unfurled newspapers and absorbing books. While writers and illustrators continued to idealize the image of a father reading a Bible to his family around the hearth, less traditional models of reading aloud were coming to compete: the Chartist declaiming a newspaper in a pub, or – in a riposte to the trope of the selfless daughter reading to the aged and infirm – Rhoda Broughton's satirical representation of a rakish father forcing his daughter to read Parisian *feuilletons* to him.[52] The growing opposition between books marketed for collective reading at home and for individual use in public – on the one hand, the 'Railway Libraries' founded in the 1840s and the Tauchnitz series of English-language books marketed to travellers on the continent; on the other, series with names like 'Parlour Library' and magazines called *Household Words* or *Family Paper* – simplified a reality in which members of the same family might read different books side by side in the parlour, while the same newspapers that commuters used to carve out privacy were sold by the cries of newsboys, read aloud and passed around from hand to hand.[53]

The Victorians imagined themselves – whether for good or ill – to be more thickly enmeshed in communication at a distance than any previous

50 Anthony Trollope, 'The Higher Education of Women', in Morris L. Parrish (ed.), *Four Lectures*, (London: Constable and Co., 1938), p. 108; [Alfred Austin], 'Our Novels: The Sensational School', *Temple Bar* (July 1870), pp. 410–24: p. 424.
51 Flint, *Woman Reader*, p. 279.
52 Rhoda Broughton, *Second Thoughts*, 2 vols. (London: Richard Bentley, 1880), vol. 1, pp. 95–8.
53 Tony Davies, 'Transports of Pleasure: Fiction and Its Audiences in the Later Nineteenth Century', in *Formations of Pleasure* (London and Boston: Routledge & Kegan Paul, 1983), p. 49.

era: together, literacy rates and communications infrastructures defined their modernity. Thus, Thomas Hardy set *Far from the Madding Crowd* in 'a modern Wessex of railways, the penny post ... labourers who could read and write, and National school children'[54] and Disraeli summed the nineteenth century up as an age of 'railroads, telegraphs, penny posts and penny newspapers'.[55] Indeed, *The Times* fiction reviewer E. S. Dallas refused to grant the invention of printing any more cultural importance than recent communications technologies: 'the railway and the steamship, the telegraph and the penny postage ... have enormously increased the number of readers, have of themselves created a literature'.[56] And comparisons could range across place as well as time: although Britain still lagged behind the Scandinavian countries in literacy rates, for example, its postal system handled more letters per capita than any country in Europe. Between 1876 and 1913, the British postal system processed more items per capita than any other country in Europe.[57]

This emphasis on material infrastructures should not seem entirely foreign to literary critics today, because nineteenth-century Britain incubated many of the institutions and technologies that now structure our own reading. We inherit its inventions (the mass-circulation daily newspaper, the advertising circular, the index card); our own content flows through the distribution channels that the Victorians created, from the most utopian (the public library) to the most mundane (the pillar box) – 'libraries' and 'mail boxes' being terms that have readily been borrowed for the virtual capacities of the internet.

What died with the Victorians, however, was a sense that those last two categories were interconnected: that the humblest material contingencies of governing the circulation of ideas could themselves embody political idealism. In 1834, on reading a *Times* report of a speech given in Edinburgh the night before, Lord Cockburn remained silent about the content of Brougham's oratory. Instead, his diary pointed out the purely external fact that the newspaper postdated the speech by only twelve hours: 'post-horses, macadam roads, shorthand and steam-printing never did more'.[58] Like the

---

54 Thomas Hardy, Preface to 1912 Wessex edition, *Far from the Madding Crowd* (London: Penguin, 2003), p. 392.
55 Altick, *Common Reader*, p. 210.
56 E. S. Dallas, *The Gay Science*, 2 vols. (London: Chapman and Hall, 1866), vol. II, p. 312.
57 Vincent, *Rise of Mass Literacy*, p. 19.
58 *Journal of Henry, Lord Cockburn, 1831–42*, 2 vols. (Edinburgh: Edmonston and Douglas, 1874), vol. I, p. 68.

'lucifer matches' that Hardy used to symbolize enlightenment, macadam roads emblematized the march of mind, not just of horses: even a worker at the Fernside Paper Mills could remark in a prize essay that 'Cheap literature' has 'opened, and as it were, macadamized a people's road to learning'.[59] In Matthew Arnold's satire of this logic

> Your middle-class man thinks it the highest pitch of development and civilisation when his letters are carried twelve times a day from Islington to Camberwell, and from Camberwell to Islington, and if railway-trains run to and fro between them every quarter of an hour. He thinks it nothing that the trains only carry him from an illiberal, dismal life at Islington to an illiberal, dismal life at Camberwell; and the letters only tell him that such is the life there.[60]

Arnold was right to point to the gap between the lofty claims made for the act of reading and the vulgar practicality of most of what was being read. In any history of literature, it is worth remembering how small a place those texts that we would now call literary occupied in the Victorian printed output. Simon Eliot has calculated that according to the 1907 Census of Production in Britain,

> books were worth some 14% of the total value of print production (and that included manuscript books and ledgers). The two areas of largest value were ... jobbing printing and periodical printing. The most common reading experience, by the mid-nineteenth century at latest, would most likely be the advertising poster, all the tickets, handbills and forms generated by an industrial society, and the daily or weekly paper.[61]

One reason for this is that new commercial genres – the advertising circular, the bulk mailing – were created in response to the expansion and streamlining of the postal system, beginning with the establishment of the penny post in 1840. Early Victorian reformers like Rowland Hill denounced a society in which postage rates sundered families, deadened trade, and silenced ideas; in which correspondence was prohibitively expensive for the masses (who therefore had less incentive to learn writing) but free for those few who had personal connections to a MP willing to abuse the privilege of franking (that

---

59 Andrew King and John Plunkett (eds.), *Popular Print Media, 1820–1900*, 3 vols. (London; New York: Routledge, 2004), vol. III, p. 4.
60 Arnold, *Complete Prose Works*, vol. V, pp. 21–2.
61 Simon Eliot, 'The Reading Experience Database; or, What Are We to Do About the History of Reading?' online document, *The Reading Experience Database 1450–1945*, www.open.ac.uk/Arts/RED/redback.htm, accessed 15 June 2010.

is, sending letters for free); in which postage on letters had to be paid by the recipient, while prepayment was available only for printed matter. The government stamp that newspapers required until 1855 constituted a form at once of taxation, of censorship (since it priced political news too high for working-class readers), and of prepayment: for the flat fee incorporated into the original purchase price, it entitled newspapers to be circulated and recirculated without charge to the recipient. In 1838, the Select Committee on Postage drew attention to the frauds encouraged by the gap between the high price of sending personal letters and the free circulation of stamped newspapers: 'the present existing practice of corresponding through the medium of newspapers, viz. by means of conventional forms in the address, marks under the print, concealed writing on the margin or wrapper, and other contrivances, to which the high rates of postage have given birth'.[62] Another unintended consequence of the stamp tax was that inflated prices forced workers to club together to buy newspapers: reading thus came to look like an occasion for oral debate and collective action.

Today, we take for granted two of the basic features of the postal system established from 1839 onwards: prepayment by the sender and rates standardized for anywhere within the nation, regardless of distance. The reformers didn't simply standardize across distances, however, but also across classes: in the process, they destroyed the monopoly on free postage held by MPs – who had routinely lent their franking privileges as part of an economy of favours. When Harriet Martineau exulted that 'tradesmen's and artizans' families can at last write to one another as if they were all MPs', she equated correspondence with political power. The result was a shift (in one scholar's words) from the post conceived as 'a taxable privilege giving access to the public sphere' to the post as 'a public service for private individuals'.[63]

Some of the postal reformers' hopes proved justified. With the introduction of prepaid penny postage, later followed by the adhesive stamp and the pillar box, the volume of letters sent through the post increased dramatically. Although much of this expansion took the form of commercial correspondence and advertising, radicals tended to emphasize instead the moral benefits of personal letters: most commonly invoked was the *Pamela*-esque scenario

---

62 'A Report of the Select Committee on Postage', *Fraser's Magazine* 18 (1838), pp. 250–2: p. 252.
63 Mary Favret, *Romantic Correspondence: Women, Politics, and the Fiction of Letters* (Cambridge University Press, 1993), p. 204.

of a child in service in London being rescued from vice by the letters of a parent in their village. Thus, Rowland Hill's pamphlet *Post Office Reform: Its Importance and Practicality* (1837) quotes letters by middle-class observers that describe labourers spurred by cheap postage to learn to write – though not, strikingly, the labourers' letters themselves. Rowland Hill quoted evidence that 'The consequence of high rates, in preventing the working-class from having intercourse by letter, is, that those who learned at school to write a copy have lost their ability to do so.'[64] Literacy figured in his writings not simply as an end in itself, however, but also as a means to morality more generally. Thus, Hill quoted an employer testifying that 'I have seen much of the evils resulting from want of communication between parents and their children among the young persons in our estab-lishment; I find the want of communication with their parents by letter has led, in some instances, to vice and profligacy which might have been otherwise prevented.'[65] Meanwhile, a member of the Statistical Department of the Board of Trade speculated that 'many young persons of both sexes, who are continually drawn to this metropolis from distant parts of the kingdom, and are thenceforth cut off from communication with their early guardians, might under different circumstances, be kept from entering on vicious courses'.[66] Yet cheap postage was thought to encourage labour mobility as well: one petition for repeal of the stamp tax argued that cheap newspapers would allow workers to 'know when and where our labour is likely to bear a fair price ... If compelled to leave the country of our birth, we wd fain know in what land our labour is in demand, and not, as too many have done, strew with our bones an inhospitable soil.'[67] The Select Committee on Postage heard 'evidence to show that the difficulty of commu-nication aggravated "The remarkable pertinacity of the poor to continue in their own parish, rather than remove to another where their condition would be bettered"'.[68] The new labour force, then, was imagined as physically portable but morally anchored by family correspondences.

Where printed books are concerned, however, the most important Victorian innovation was probably not the postal system but the circulating

---

64 Rowland Hill and George Birkbeck Norman Hill, *The Life of Sir Rowland Hill ... And the History of Penny Postage*, 2 vols. (London: Thos. De La Rue, 1880), vol. I, p. 309.

65 *Ibid.*, p. 308.

66 Sir Rowland Hill, *Post Office Reform, Its Importance and Practicability* (London: C. Knight and Co., 1837), p. 78.

67 Dobson Collet, *History of the Taxes on Knowledge*, 2 vols. (London: T. Fisher Unwin, 1899), vol. I, p. 84.

68 Hill, *Life*, vol. I, p. 309.

library. While some genres (such as reference books and devotional books) were bought more often than borrowed, others (notably the novel) found their most reliable distribution channel not through the bookseller but through the library. The Public Libraries Act of 1850 spurred the foundation of free lending libraries in many towns, but equally important was the foundation eight years earlier of Mudie's Circulating Library. Private lending libraries had been common enough in the eighteenth century, when recent fiction already made up most of their stock, but the circulating library became even more attractive after price increases in the 1810s placed the novel – now almost invariably published in three volumes at a guinea and a half – out of reach of most individual buyers. Not only was the new novel more expensive both than reprints of older fiction and than poetry (at about a fifth of the price), it was also the most ephemeral of genres, dominated by best-sellers that quickly faded from view rather than by a durable backlist. It therefore made cultural as well as economic sense to borrow novels rather than buying them: on the one hand, Mudie's yearly fee was less than the cost of a single novel; on the other, novels appeared to have more in common with newspapers – to be read on first appearance and then forgotten – than with either poetry (made for rereading and display) or steady sellers (Bibles, cookbooks, reference works). To its defenders, the novel looked timely and topical; to its critics, ephemeral and modish. Both perceptions formed at once the cause and the effect of a cycle in which a successful novel would trickle down a series of formats: serialization in a magazine or independent part issue, usually running for a year and a half; library-issue triple-decker at a guinea and a half; a six-shilling one-volume reprint a few years later; and eventual oblivion, sometimes pulping.

Everywhere, the novel's ephemerality made its users unwilling to pay higher prices; but where in the United States the result was disposable books, cheaply produced for a single reading, in Britain novels were expensively produced in order to stand up to multiple borrowings. It is worth remembering that the Victorians leased many kinds of objects, not just novels: even furniture was commonly rented in the age before instalment plans, credit cards, and widely diffused mortgage lending.[69] But Charles Edward Mudie was the first bookseller to take this principle to its logical conclusion. From New Oxford Street, he delivered throughout London by

---

69 Simon Eliot, 'The Business of Victorian Publishing', in Deirdre David (ed.), *The Cambridge Companion to the Victorian Novel* (Cambridge University Press, 2001), pp. 37–60: p. 39.

van and throughout Britain by rail, eventually devising a system for shipping books abroad in tin boxes. By 1863 Mudie's offered a million volumes, leading one writer in the *Spectator* to miscalculate that it was 'larger than the Bodleian or the Vatican library'.[70] The only real competition came from the railway circulating libraries established in 1860 by W. H. Smith, the booksellers who pioneered the distribution of printed matter along the fifteen thousand miles of track laid between 1840 and 1870 – first by channelling newspapers and other periodicals outward from London, then by opening bookstalls in railway stations (starting in 1848 and rising to over a thousand branches by the turn of the century), and in 1860 by opening a rival to Mudie's consisting of circulating library branches set up in railway stations.

Smith's shared Mudie's double function: a distribution network, but also a gatekeeper. Mudie took the adjective in 'Select Library' very literally, refusing to stock books that struck him as irreligious, immoral, or even simply indelicate. Since the circulating libraries provided both dependable and substantial sales (half the first edition of *Great Expectations*, for example, was bought by Mudie's, as were half of the 4,000 novels published by Bentley in 1864) they shaped not just the consumption but also the production of novels, determining what publishers would accept and, indirectly, what novelists would submit.[71]

While this influence has usually been framed in negative terms – and Mudie's certainly did create a kind of self-censorship – it should also be acknowledged that the existence of a stable market for new fiction was part of what drove the great flowering of the Victorian novel in general, and of domestic fiction in particular. Wyndham Lewis may have had a point when he credited Mudie's, tongue in cheek, with instilling in 'the British middle-class mind those few ideas it possesses'.[72] In particular, because young girls were considered at once the largest and most susceptible segment of the novel-reading public, a hypothetical girl became the lowest common denominator against whose supposed sensitivities every new publication was measured. As Dickens complained in *Our Mutual Friend*,

> The question about everything was, would it bring a blush into the cheek of the young person? And the inconvenience of the young person was that ... she seemed always liable to burst into blushes when there was no need at

70 Guinevere Griest, *Mudie's Circulating Library and the Victorian Novel* (Bloomington: Indiana University Press, 1970), p. 28.
71 John Sutherland, *Victorian Fiction: Writers, Publishers, Readers* (Basingstoke: Palgrave, 2006).
72 Griest, *Mudie's Circulating Library*, p. 223.

all ... There appeared to be no line of demarcation between the young person's excessive innocence, and another person's guiltiest knowledge ... The soberest tints of drab, white, lilac, and grey, were all flaming red to this troublesome Bull of a young person.[73]

When Eliza Lynn Linton argued that every house should contain a 'locked bookcase', or when Thomas Hardy speculated that the demise of the circulating library would make books 'naturally resolve themselves into classes instead of being, as now, made to wear a common livery in style and subject',[74] both were protesting the unintended consequences of a century-old rehabilitation campaign. Hardy was responding in part to Mudie's refusal to stock *Jude the Obscure*; similarly, Mudie's rejection of George Moore's *A Modern Lover* (1883) inspired Moore's *Literature at Nurse, or Circulating Morals* (1885), which called the 'British matron' Mudie's nom de plume. Such polemics, however, had little effect on the power of circulating libraries. Rather, Mudie's and W. H. Smith committed commercial suicide when in 1894 they informed publishers that they would now pay a maximum of four shillings per volume. In the wake of that decision, a single six-shilling volume became the standard format for new fiction, and buying replaced borrowing.

The Victorians associated modernity not just with an excess of readers, but also with an excess of print. In fact, the statistics about the number of new readers mirrored equally oft-cited calculations about the number of new books. For decades, alarmists continued to reprint a chart showing that as many books were published in 1868 alone as in the first half of the eighteenth century.[75] The same held true for raw material: paper production went from 2500 tons in 1715 to 75000 tons in 1851; measured per person, production shot up from two and a half pounds per year in 1800 to eight and a half in 1860. In 1893, Herbert Maxwell contrasted 'the number of books that a single bookworm' could consume (9,000, in his estimate) with the number produced (20,000 annually added 'to the shelves of the British Museum').[76]

Part of the problem was that newspapers proliferated after abolition of the taxes on knowledge. Ephemeral forms were blamed for crowding

---

73 Charles Dickens, *Our Mutual Friend* (1864–5; Oxford University Press, 2009), chapter 11, pp. 129–30.
74 Eliza Lynn Linton, 'Candour in English Fiction', *New Review* 2 (1890), pp. 10–14: p. 13; Thomas Hardy, 'Candour in English Fiction', *New Review* 2 (1890), pp. 15–21: p. 21.
75 Joseph Ackland, 'Elementary Education and the Decay of Literature', *Nineteenth Century* 35 (1894), pp. 416–18.
76 Herbert Maxwell, 'The Craving for Fiction', *Nineteenth Century* 33 (1893), pp. 1046–61.

out more durable classics: 'at the end of the year [*The Times*] is comprised in a book larger than all the classics and all the standard histories of the world put together'.[77] Yet the problem became recursive, since newspapers and magazines themselves were padded out with hackneyed statistics about the number of newspapers and magazines. As a journalist observed in 1862,

> There are persons who will count up the number of acres which a single number of the *Times* would cover if all the copies were spread out flat, or illustrate the number of copies by telling us how long the same weight of coal would serve an ordinary household ... Every morning, it is said, a mass of print, containing as much matter as a thick octavo volume, is laid on our breakfast-tables.[78]

Indeed, the *Pall Mall Gazette* proposed marking Victoria's Jubilee by a year in which 'the literary soil should be allowed to lie fallow', with an embargo on the production of new literature – except, of course, for newspapers.[79]

Readers had to cope not only with new material, however, but also with the survival of older books and the reprinting of older texts. In the Malthusian reasoning of one reviewer, 'the fire-proof inventions of the present day' had the unintended consequence of ensuring that 'there is no epidemic among books ... no law of mortality by which the number of books is regulated like that of animals'.[80] The result, as Frederic Harrison saw it, was that 'the first intellectual task of our age is rightly to order and make serviceable the vast realm of printed material which four centuries have swept across our path'.[81] And his contemporaries did in fact rise to that task, in the form of collective projects like the *Oxford English Dictionary* and the *Dictionary of National Biography*. The most characteristic genre of the nineteenth century may not, in the end, be the novel or even the newspaper so much as the reference book.

The Victorians, in short, were discovering information overload. Maria Jane Jewsbury described hers as 'an age of books! Of book making! Book

77 Unsigned review, 'Journalism', *Cornhill Magazine* 31 (1862), pp. 52–63.
78 *Ibid.*, p. 60.
79 *Pall Mall Gazette* (12 January 1886), p. 4; Kelly J. Mays, 'The Disease of Reading and Victorian Periodicals', in John O. Jordan and Robert L. Patten (eds.), *Literature in the Marketplace: Nineteenth-Century British Reading and Publishing Practices* (Cambridge University Press, 1995), pp. 165–94: p. 189.
80 Unsigned review, 'The Encyclopedia Britannica', *Quarterly Review* 70 (1842), pp. 44–72.
81 Frederic Harrison, *The Choice of Books, and Other Literary Pieces* (London: Macmillan, 1886), p. 18.

reading! Book reviewing! And book forgetting.'[82] 'The difficulty of finding
something to read in an age when half the world is engaged in writing books
for the other half to read is not one of quantity', noted one journalist in 1893,
'so that the question, "What shall I read?" inevitably suggests the parallel
query, "What shall I not read?"'[83] In *The Choice of Books*, Harrison, too,
presented the problem in negative terms: 'the most useful help to reading is
to know what we should not read, what we can keep out from that small
cleared spot in the overgrown jungle of "information"'.[84]

On the one hand, there was the hope that the spread of literacy would
perfect civilization; on the other, the fear that the spread of print would
destroy it. As George Craik remarked in his classic compendium of exemplary biographies, *The Pursuit of Knowledge Under Difficulties*, 'If one mind
be in danger of starving for want of books, another may be surfeited by too
many.'[85] A decade later, an article in the *Victoria Magazine* presented these
problems as mirror images: 'Of the underfed, in these days of education of
women, education of ploughboys, education of curates, we are sure to hear
enough, but of the sufferings of their scarcely less pitiable antipodes, whose
complaint is overfeeding, we are not so likely to be well informed.'[86]

Printed attacks on printed matter always risk self-referentiality, if not
quixotism. 'We find the "Quarterly Review" anathematising circulating
libraries with great force', notes an 1871 article on 'Circulating Libraries',
but 'this is very hard on libraries now-a-days, especially as no inconsiderable
number of the "Quarterly Review" is taken in by Mr Mudie'.[87] Conduct-
books remarked that trashy reading took time away from outdoor activity,
but neglected to count the hours eaten up by their own perusal. Some
genres circumvented this problem by distinguishing the readers discussed
from the readers addressed: thus, men were instructed on how to control
their daughters' reading, or middle-class philanthropists informed about the
reading habits of mechanics. In obscenity trials, too, middle-class male jurors
were asked to speculate about the effects of a book on their housemaid.

82 Lucy Newlyn, *Reading, Writing, and Romanticism: The Anxiety of Reception* (Oxford
University Press, 2000), p. 3.
83 Unsigned article, 'A Few Words About Reading', *Chamber's Journal of Popular Literature, Science, and Arts* 70 (1893), pp. 225–7.
84 Harrison, *Choice of Books*, p. 3.
85 George L. Craik, *The Pursuit of Knowledge under Difficulties*, new edn, 2 vols. (London:
J. Murray, 1858), vol. I, p. 22.
86 C. H. Butterworth, 'Reading, Overfeeding', *Victoria Magazine* 14 (1869–70), pp. 500–4:
p. 500.
87 Hain Friswell, 'Circulating Libraries', *London Society* 20 (1871), pp. 515–24: p. 519.

But even the addressee of a proto-sociological tract rarely maintained complete distance from the styles of reading under discussion. When Florence Bell set out to survey the reading habits of a manufacturing town in 1911, she ended up turning her sociological gaze back on her own readers: 'On finding what were the results of the inquiry made respecting reading among the workmen, a similar investigation was attempted among people who were better off, and the result of this inquiry among those whom we may call "drawing-room readers" is curiously instructive.'[88] If reading (in Austin's words) made kitchen and drawing-room kin, so did discourses *about* reading. The fears and fantasies that Victorian intellectuals attached to literacy refracted their own entanglement in the world of print.

---

88 Bell, *At the Works*, p. 250.

3

Periodicals and reviewing

HILARY FRASER

> Journalism will, no doubt, occupy the first or one of the first
> places in any future literary history of the present times, for it is the most
> characteristic of all their productions.[1]

Fitzjames Stephen's predictive remark on the prominent place that will be occupied by journalism and the periodical press in an imagined literary history of the future is borne out by the positioning of this chapter, which foregrounds their status as among the most important and exemplary of the literary forms of the Victorian age. The nineteenth century saw the beginnings of the modern mass media. Tens of thousands of serial titles were published in the course of the century, encompassing a vast range from intellectually heavyweight quarterlies to popular penny weeklies, fashionable magazines, and esoteric specialist journals, and touching the lives and minds of every Victorian citizen. As a medium for the circulation of new ideas and discoveries and forum for reviews, the periodical press, it is generally agreed by Victorian and modern commentators alike, provided a dynamic context for lively argument during a period of unprecedented, unresolved, and irresolvable speculation and debate. It played a critical role in defining nineteenth-century literary and political culture. However, although the convenient fact that both the Victorians and ourselves regard periodical literature as a pre-eminent sign of the times may seem to confirm that the cultural prominence of the periodical press at this historical moment has always been a self-evident truth, the fact that for many decades, with a few honourable exceptions,[2] journalism was virtually invisible in

---

1 Fitzjames Stephen, 'Journalism', *Cornhill Magazine* 6 (1862), pp. 52–63: p. 52.
2 See Richard D. Altick, *The English Common Reader: A Social History of the Mass Reading Public, 1800–1900* (University of Chicago Press, 1957; 2nd edn, Columbus: Ohio State University Press, 1998); Isobel Armstrong, *Victorian Scrutinies* (London: Athlone Press, 1972); Louis James, *Fiction for the Working Man, 1830–1850* (1963; Harmondsworth: Penguin, 1974); Michael Wolff, 'Charting the Golden Stream: Thoughts on a Directory of Victorian Periodicals', *Victorian Periodicals Newsletter* 13 (1971), pp. 23–8. The Research

twentieth-century literary studies of the Victorians, other than as a 'background' to the canonical forms of the novel, poetry, and drama, suggests otherwise. The last *Cambridge History* of Victorian literature, commissioned a hundred years ago as the 'long' nineteenth century was making way for the Moderns, does laudably include two chapters on journalism, but they are placed in the middle of the second volume devoted to the period. As Joanne Shattock and Michael Wolff note in the Introduction to their collection of essays *The Victorian Periodical Press: Samplings and Soundings*, whilst periodicals are widely referred to in scholarship on the Victorians, they had never before then been the subject of extensive study in their own right.[3] This serves to remind us that modern views of what was 'characteristic' of the Victorians are inescapably shaped by the cultural and critical world we ourselves inhabit, and by the institutional and commercial practices that form the contexts from which our histories of an earlier age are produced. Furthermore, even where we do agree with the Victorians that journalism is one of the most characteristic of Victorian literary forms, do we understand precisely the same thing when we speak of the quintessential period features that writing for the serials in the nineteenth century ostensibly displays? It is, I suggest, in the robust dialogue between nineteenth-century and early twenty-first-century perceptions of what it is that is so characteristically Victorian about journalism and reviewing that we may find a focus for mapping the literary historical journey that critical scholarship on the press has taken over the century and a half that separates Stephen's observations from our own time, and for determining the significance of the periodical press as a locus of Victorian cultural formation.

The sheer scale of the press in the nineteenth century is astounding. *The Waterloo Directory of English Newspapers and Periodicals, 1800–1900* lists more than 50,000 newspapers and periodicals, and within that vast number there is a staggering range.[4] Victorian directories, most notably *Mitchell's Newspaper Press Directory* (which was first issued in 1846, and appeared annually from

Society for Victorian Periodicals was founded in 1968, and with it the *Victorian Periodicals Newsletter* (1968–78), which later became *Victorian Periodicals Review* (1979–). *The Wellesley Index to Victorian Periodicals 1824–1900*, 5 vols. (1966–89) and *The Waterloo Directory of Victorian Periodicals, 1824–1900* (1976) provided valuable research tools for these pioneering researchers into the Victorian periodical press, complementing *Poole's Index to Periodical Literature 1802–1906*, 7 vols. (1882–1906).

3 Joanne Shattock and Michael Wolff (eds.), *The Victorian Periodical Press: Samplings and Soundings* (Leicester University Press, 1982), pp. xiii–xv.

4 See Laurel Brake and Marysa Demoor (eds.), *Dictionary of Nineteenth-Century Journalism in Great Britain and Ireland* (Gent: Academia Press; London: The British Library, 2009), p. 663 on the *Waterloo Directory*. Both the *Waterloo Directory* and the *DNCJ* are invaluable resources for periodicals research.

1856) and *May's British and Irish Press Guide* (from 1871), give the modern student of the nineteenth-century press not only a rich sense of local variations and specializations in serial publication, but also insights into the velocity of growth in the periodical market. We learn from the former, for example, that, in 1864, 1,764 periodical titles are in production; by 1887, 3,597 were listed.[5] Circulation figures are similarly astonishing. The *Cornhill Magazine* (1860–75), for example, according to Richard Altick sold 120,000 copies of its first number – impressive given its price at a shilling; while the penny illustrated fiction weekly *London Journal* (1845–1928) achieved sales of over half a million copies per issue in the early 1850s.[6]

As both nineteenth-century and modern commentators have understood, periodicals in the nineteenth century were at once defined by and constitutive of modernity. At a material level, modern technological advances had a huge impact on the production, the cost, the appearance, and the distribution of periodical publications. For example, the period saw great changes in the techniques, quality, and cost of graphic reproduction. The revival of wood engraving in the 1820s and 1830s enabled a profusion of cheap illustrated publications, and was particularly favourable to the development of the early Victorian radical graphic press and illustrated miscellanies, whilst photography played an increasingly important role in the expansion of illustrated periodical publication in the 1880s and 1890s. The coming of the railway transformed distribution networks, and produced a new kind of reader on the move. At the same time, as Gilles Deleuze reminds us, 'A society is defined by its amalgamations, not by its tools', and so the importance of such technical innovations lies in what he terms 'the interminglings they make possible or that make them possible'.[7] It is, then, in the particular constellations and dialectical exchanges at different historical junctures between new technologies and other social, economic, and cultural forces – such as the labour market and employment legislation, urbanization and demographic change, the legal regulation and taxation of the media, education and literacy, feminism, and imperialism – that we must look for the definitively Victorian characteristics of the periodical press as genre.

5 Simon Eliot, *Some Patterns and Trends in British Publishing, 1800–1919* (London: Bibliographical Society, 1993), p. 148.
6 Altick, *English Common Reader*, 2nd edn, p. 359; Andrew King, *The London Journal, 1845–83: Periodicals, Production and Gender* (Aldershot: Ashgate, 2004), pp. 82–9, 243–4.
7 Gilles Deleuze and Felix Guattari, *A Thousand Plateaus: Capitalism and Schizophrenia*, trans. Brian Massumi (Minneapolis: University of Minnesota Press, 1987), p. 90.

The Victorian periodical is imbricated in political, material, and institutional histories, and detailed analyses of these form an important branch
of modern studies of nineteenth-century print media.[8] This double role,
producing and being produced by changing forms of knowledge and practice, is something that Victorian commentators themselves acknowledged
and critiqued, often, self-reflexively, in the pages of the very publications
that are invoked. They were seemingly intrigued by periodical writing
and its broader cultural meanings, in particular its entanglement with and
its articulation of the modern. Thomas Carlyle, for instance, identified
reviewing for the periodical press as the paradigmatic cultural form of what
was, in his view, a morbidly self-obsessed age. In his *Characteristics* (1831),
which itself began life as a review in the leading periodical the *Edinburgh
Review* (1802–1929), the first of the nineteenth-century quarterlies, he observed,
not without an ironic sense of his own implication, that 'Reviewing spreads
with strange vigour', predicting that 'By and by it will be found that all
Literature has become one boundless self-devouring Review ... Thus does
Literature ... like a sick thing, superabundantly "listen to itself." ' Reviewing is
regarded as symptomatic of 'the diseased self-conscious state' not only of
literature, but of modern life. 'What', he asks, 'is all this that we hear, for the
last generation or two, about the Improvement of the Age, the Spirit of the
Age, Destruction of Prejudice, Progress of the Species, and the March of
Intellect, but an unhealthy state of self-sentence, self-survey; the precursor and
prognostic of still worse health?' Contemporary culture is relentlessly patho-
logized; the periodical press at once its most diseased organ, the agent of
quackery, and the medium through which contagion is spread:

> all things must be probed into, the whole working of man's world be
> anatomically studied. Alas, anatomically studied, that it may be medically
> studied, that it may be medically aided! Till at length indeed, we have come
> to such a pass, that except in this same *medicine*, with its artifices and
> appliances, few can so much as imagine any strength or hope to remain
> for us. The whole Life of Society must now be carried on by drugs: doctor

8 See, for example, Laurel Brake, Bill Bell, and David Finkelstein (eds.), *Nineteenth-
Century Media and the Construction of Identities* (Basingstoke: Palgrave, 2000); Laurel
Brake and Julie F. Codell (eds.), *Encounters in the Victorian Press: Editors, Authors, Readers*
(Basingstoke: Palgrave Macmillan, 2005); Marysa Demoor, *Their Fair Share: Women,
Power and Criticism in the Athenaeum, from Millicent Garrett Fawcett to Katherine Mans-
field, 1870–1920* (Aldershot: Ashgate, 2000); Margaret Beetham, *A Magazine of Her Own?
Domesticity and Desire in the Woman's Magazine, 1800–1914* (London and New York:
Routledge, 1996); Hilary Fraser, Stephanie Green, and Judith Johnston, *Gender and the
Victorian Periodical* (Cambridge University Press, 2003).

after doctor appears with his nostrum, of Coöperative Societies, Universal Suffrage, Cottage-and-Cow systems, Repression of Population, Vote by ballot. To such height has the dyspepsia of Society reached: as indeed the constant grinding internal pain, or from time to time the mad spasmodic throes, of all Society do otherwise too mournfully indicate.[9]

Uncannily anticipating Jean Baudrillard's post-modernist concept of 'the precession of simulacra' whereby representation precedes reality,[10] Carlyle critiques the 'artifices and appliances' – or what he elsewhere referred to as the 'machinery' of modern life – of which the review, at a remove from the authenticity of real literature, is for him so symptomatic. His very deployment of the extended metaphor of disease and diagnostic treatment itself seems to exemplify that retreat from the real of which he writes. At the same time such rich metaphorical language conveys the cultural embeddedness of the periodical, its 'interminglings' with broader intellectual and discursive fields.

The metaphorical resonances of journalistic genres and practices sprang naturally to mind for many other writers of the period too. Writing several decades after Coleridge, the journalist Walter Bagehot finds in the press the quintessential modern urban form. 'London is like a newspaper', he writes in an article for the *National Review* (1855–64) on 'Charles Dickens' in 1858:

Everything is there, and everything is disconnected. There is every kind of person in some houses but there is no more connection between the houses than between the neighbours in the lists of 'births, marriages, and deaths.' As we change from the broad leader to the squalid police report we pass a corner and we are in a changed world.

Dickens's own journalistic experience equips him admirably to represent this modern metropolis in his fiction, according to Walter Bagehot, for 'He describes London like a special correspondent for posterity.'[11] In Bagehot's phrase, writing that is definitively live and of the moment, eyewitness news, is envisaged as nonetheless preserved for readers who are yet to come. Dickens writes the present for the future. The trope of journalism expands to encompass both the Victorian novelist-reporter and the modern reader thumbing through the newspaper of the past. In another article of this

---

9 Thomas Carlyle, 'Characteristics', *Critical and Miscellaneous Essays*, 3 vols. (London: 1887), vol. III, pp. 191–227: pp. 218, 208.
10 Jean Baudrillard, 'The Precession of Simulacra', in *Simulacra and Simulation*, trans. Sheila Faria Glaser (1981; Ann Arbor: University of Michigan Press, 1994), p. 161.
11 [Walter Bagehot], 'Charles Dickens', *National Review* 7 (1858), pp. 458–86: p. 468.

period, 'The First Edinburgh Reviewers' (1855), Bagehot contrasts the older early nineteenth-century model of journalism typified by the *Edinburgh Review* with the modern style. He identifies 'the review-like essay and the essay-like review' not, like Carlyle, as symptomatic of the cultural malaise at the heart of modern life, but as 'the very model of our modern writing', something to be welcomed and celebrated as meeting the new needs of the times. He comments on the 'casual character of modern literature', of which he notes 'everything about it is temporary and fragmentary ... The race has made up its mind to be fugitive, as well as minute.'[12] Such remarks point up the expendability of periodicals within commodity culture: the periodical, as Margaret Beetham notes, is decidedly an 'ephemeral form', whose 'claims to truth and importance are always contingent'; it is 'designed to be thrown away'.[13] Bagehot's emphasis on the temporary and the fragmentary is taken up again by Charles Baudelaire, who similarly sees journalism as the key cultural medium of modern life. In 'The Painter of Modern Life' (1863), he identifies the magazine fashion-plate as the art form that most effectively registers the nuances of modernity, by which he means 'the ephemeral, the fugitive, the contingent', and he proposes Constantin Guys (1802–92), a graphic artist who was for some years at mid-century on the staff of the *Illustrated London News* (1842–1989), as his representative modern artist. By the final decade of the century, Oscar Wilde, himself a writer for the periodical press and one-time editor of the magazine the *Woman's World* (1887–90), can at once complain 'We are dominated by Journalism', and celebrate the modern cultural values that journalism had come to enshrine, such as the elevation of the 'Critic' to 'Artist' and 'The Truth of Masks'.[14]

This is the kind of contemporary writing about nineteenth-century journalism that appeals to modern critics, who frequently see themselves as inhabiting a 'society of the spectacle' in which, according to Guy Debord, 'all that once was directly lived has become mere representation'.[15] We are drawn to a cultural form whose fragmentary, contingent characteristics mark it out as an intrinsically modern medium suited to the disaggregated experience of individuals within an emergent consumer society. Interest in

---

12 [Walter Bagehot], 'The First Edinburgh Reviewers', *National Review* 1 (1855), pp. 253–84: pp. 54–55.
13 Beetham, *A Magazine of Her Own?*, p. 9.
14 Charles Baudelaire, *The Painter of Modern Life and Other Essays* (New York: Da Capo, 1964), p. 13; Oscar Wilde, 'The Soul of Man Under Socialism', *Fortnightly Review* o.s. 55, n.s. 49 (February 1891), pp. 292–319: p. 309.
15 Guy Debord, *The Society of the Spectacle*, trans. Donald Nicholson-Smith (New York: Zone Books, 1994), p. 12.

popular and ephemeral forms, in criticism and theory as a distinct field of study, and in the fertile cross-connections between different disciplinary fields, deriving from late twentieth- and twenty-first-century developments in new historicism, film theory, gender, and cultural studies, has drawn modern scholars to look more attentively at the periodical press as a product of its time and, further, as signifying the new consciousness of time that accompanied modernity. This consciousness appears exemplified by the rhythms and periodicities of this genre's publication, by its quarterly, monthly, weekly, or daily chromatic regularity, by journalism's simultaneous engagement with being of the moment, and with duration and seriality.[16]

For literary and cultural historians today, the Victorian periodical press is in considerable part of interest because it seems such an index of the contemporary; appearing to bring us closer to an understanding of both the condition of modernity and the everyday lives and preoccupations of ordinary people. It does seem to offer us an experience of the Victorian present, and of Victorian presentism, what Richard Altick calls the 'presence of the present'.[17] There was indeed an urgent awareness of the historical moment of the present but, given the sense of the acceleration of time, of its contingency as well; and so alongside the valorization of instantaneity and the instant there was a contradictory desire to arrest and store ephemera and, effectively, time itself. This was manifested in the development of new kinds of interest in archival processes and technologies. For the nineteenth century was also the great age of the museum (with the opening of the National Gallery in 1824, Sir John Soane's house-museum in 1837, the South Kensington complex in 1857, the National Portrait Gallery in 1859, the Natural History Museum in 1881, and the Tate Gallery in 1897) and, as well as being agents and engines of the present day, periodicals both reflected and participated in the general passion for collecting, preserving, classification, and display that characterized Victorian museum culture.

It is not unusual, of course, for particular cultural obsessions to derive from their opposites, and visual theorists have identified other, and related, contradictory dynamics that are characteristic of this moment of modernity. Writing of the mid–late 1800s, Jonathan Crary, for example, observes that, at the very moment when perception seems to be 'characterized by

---

16 See James Mussell, *Science, Time and Space in the Late Nineteenth-Century Periodical Press* (Aldershot: Ashgate, 2007).
17 Richard D. Altick, *The Presence of the Present: Topics of the Day in the Victorian Novel* (Columbus: Ohio State University Press, 1991).

experiences of fragmentation, shock, and dispersal' – to be defined, in short, by distraction – reciprocally and paradoxically a disciplinary regime of attentiveness was inaugurated.[18] Similarly, Mary Ann Doane considers how the new sense of the divisibility of time that emerged in the late nineteenth century posed a challenge to traditional ideas of time as the ultimate continuum. She identifies the 'dilemma of discontinuity and continuity' as the 'epistemological conundrum that structures the debates about the representability of time at the turn of the century'.[19]

Such oppositional categories can help frame our thinking about the Victorian press, which notably exemplifies, in relation to both its form and its content, at once distraction and attention, continuity and, equally, discontinuity – for example, in the juxtaposition of diachronic narration and synchronic images, or the contiguity of attention-grabbing headlines and advertisements with discursive text. It also participated in the ironic cultural project of archiving the present whereby, as Doane argues in relation to early film, 'what is archived is not so much a material object as an experience – an experience of the present'.[20] The contradictory imperatives of currency and storage are enshrined in the very titles of some nineteenth-century serials, from the early *Lady's Monthly Museum* (1798–1828) and *Monthly Repository* (1806–37) to later journals such as the *Monthly Record* (1869–91). Interestingly, both aspects of periodicalism, its presentism as well as its archival recording function, intensified in the later part of the century. The sense of journalistic immediacy was vastly enhanced by the use of illustration, and publications such as the *Illustrated London News* (1842–1989) and the *Penny Illustrated Paper* (1861–1913) led the way in featuring large numbers of sometimes crude yet often vividly effective pictures that powerfully evoke the immediacy of newsworthy contemporary events, even though early on, as Peter Sinnema points out in relation to the *ILN*, the scene of production was often at a distance from the actual events portrayed, with 'the lion's share of drawings' in the 1840s and 1850s, 'astonishingly, produced in the immediate vicinity of the publishing house, based on news already reported in the daily press'.[21] As periodical illustration became more and more lavish from the mid-1880s, with

---

18 Jonathan Crary, *Suspensions of Perception: Attention, Spectacle, and Modern Culture* (Cambridge, MA and London: MIT Press, 2000), p. 1.
19 Mary Ann Doane, *The Emergence of Cinematic Time: Modernity, Contingency, the Archive* (Cambridge, MA and London: Harvard University Press, 2002), p. 9.
20 *Ibid.*, p. 82.
21 Peter W. Sinnema, *Dynamics of the Pictured Page: Representing the Nation in the Illustrated London News* (Aldershot: Ashgate, 1998), p. 70.

the development of new reproductive technologies and the dedication of more space to pictures and illustrated advertisements and supplements, and as, increasingly, woodcut engravings were superseded by photographic images, the press's capacity to capture the moment of the present became ever more convincing. The world becomes, in such illustrated news periodicals, and in the more ephemeral fashion magazines that proliferated at the turn of the century, in Siegfried Kracauer's phrase, a 'photographable present'.[22] But this is precisely where the dilemma of the drive to capture the ephemeral present is most evident. Roland Barthes memorably finds in the photograph a curious conjunction of the 'here' and 'then',[23] and this formulation seems particularly apt when we think about the early use of photographs in news stories, at a time when communication was sometimes slow and uneven. Indeed, this was still to be the case in 1912, when pictures of the intact *Titanic*, the indexical sign of its unsinkability, appeared on the front pages of the press immediately following the disaster, with headlines reporting 'Everyone safe' (the *Daily Mirror* (16 April 1912)), 'No lives lost' (the *Daily Mail* (16 April 1912)). Such stories became, immediately, a part of the Titanic archive.

This last example reminds us that of course we experience time in a different way now than it was experienced a hundred years ago and more. But, as Doane points out, 'The ideologies of instantaneity, of temporal compression, of the lure of the present moment that emerge in this period have not disappeared; they confront us now in the form of digital technologies',[24] so-called 'time-based' media not least, and this is another lens through which, as twenty-first-century critics, we view nineteenth-century periodicals. If the development of digital technologies and the cultural phenomenon of the Internet have encouraged modern readers to think about the temporal properties of the Victorian press in new ways, the growth of electronic media has also contributed to changes in the ways we think about authorship, about texts, and about literature and the public sphere, complementing the important theoretical work in these fields that dominated the final decades of the twentieth century. Again, we can see why it is that modern scholars are attracted to Victorian periodicalism, because in all its different forms, from elite highbrow journals such as the

---

22 Siegfried Kracauer, 'Photography'. in *The Mass Ornament: Weimar Essays*, ed. and trans. Thomas Y. Levin (Cambridge, MA and London: Harvard University Press, 1995), p. 59.

23 Roland Barthes, *Camera Lucida: Reflections on Photography*, ed. and trans. Richard Howard (New York: Hill and Wang, 1981), p. 77.

24 Doane, *Cinematic Time*, p. 20.

Westminster Review (1824–1914) to magazines for women and girls, such as the *Englishwoman's Domestic Magazine* (1852–79) and the *Girls' Own Paper* (1880–1956), it is a medium that destabilizes and complicates ideas about authorship and authorial voice, about the integrity of the text, about what we understand by the literary, about the public sphere. Periodicals, like the Internet, unsettle the boundaries between writers and readers, between the verbal and the visual, and between the cultural, the counter-cultural and the commercial. They likewise offer not a discrete, homogeneous, single-authored text but an open-ended dynamic debate in process, a dialogue between contributors offering different points of view, between text, illustration, and advertisement, between different forms of communication (what we now think of as multimedia experience). The popular Victorian magazine, especially, represents miscellaneity, fragmentation, polyphony, anonymity, and the democratization of knowledge, but, more interestingly perhaps than its post-modern counterparts, it does so within, and as the mouthpiece for, a culture that ostensibly valorized integrity, singularity, identity, authenticity, and elitism.

This tension is perhaps nowhere more apparent than in the case of the Author, who may be said to have come into being as a professional entity only a century or so before Roland Barthes controversially announced his death in 1967.[25] The Victorian era saw the rise of the celebrity author and also the establishment of professional associations such as the Guild of Literature and Art, promoted by Dickens and Bulwer Lytton in 1850, and the Society of Authors, founded in 1884. Being a writer in the nineteenth century, equally for major authors and minor players and hacks, generally involved engaging in a number of different kinds of writing practice, not least because of the influence of periodicalism, the expansion of which in the first half of the nineteenth century was the major catalyst for the professionalization of authorship. The main forum for the debates that emerged at mid-century around the dignity of the author and the calling of literature was, of course, the periodical press. Yet ironically, except in those periodicals specifically designed to showcase celebrity writers (such as Dickens's *Household Words* (1850–9) and *All the Year Round* (1859–95), the *Cornhill* (1860–1975) under Thackeray's editorship, or *Belgravia* (1867–99) with its promotion of Mary Braddon's sensation fiction), the Author was typically

---

25 Roland Barthes, 'Death of the Author', first published in the American journal *Aspen*, reprinted in *Image–Music–Text*, ed. and trans. Stephen Heath (New York: Hill and Wang, 1977).

invisible in this the fastest growing sector of the literary marketplace. For the prevailing convention in the monthly and quarterly periodicals was to publish articles and reviews anonymously or pseudonymously, rather than over the signatures of individual contributors, and this was a practice that was widespread until the 1860s, when it began to come increasingly under attack.[26] Furthermore, the preferred 'house style' of some nineteenth-century journals tended to flatten out the personal and the idiosyncratic, the individual voice of the author, rendering their own work sometimes unrecognizable to writers when they looked back at their early work. Leslie Stephen, for example, reading his youthful contributions to the *Saturday Review* (1855–1938) many years later, was startled to discover that he 'could rarely distinguish them by internal evidence', and had evidently 'unconsciously adopted the tone of [his] colleagues, and, like some inferior organisms, taken the colour of [his] "environment"'. 'The contributor', he concludes from this, 'occasionally assimilates: he sinks his own individuality and is a small wheel in a big machine.'[27] And writers' work was shaped by the medium in other ways that undermined the idea of the authority of the Author: they had to write to strict deadlines and word limits; they were ideologically constrained to conform to the political line of the journal to which they contributed; they had to share the publication space with other authors; often their role was to be responsive to an editor's initiative, or reactive to another piece of writing, rather than independently creative; and as reviewers they were expected to 'puff' books published by the publishing house that owned the very magazine for which they wrote.[28]

In his 1969 essay, 'What Is an Author?', Michel Foucault argues that works of literature are collective cultural products and do not arise from singular, individual beings, and this seems a particularly apt model for the nineteenth-century periodical.[29] Whilst novelists often published their fiction in serials as well as writing critical articles and reviews for the periodical press, the 'author function' of the journalist, as distinct from the novelist, was

---

26 The *Wellesley Index to Victorian Periodicals*, first published in five volumes (1965–88) is an immensely valuable research tool in this regard, attributing authorship to anonymously published articles in forty-five key monthly and quarterly journals, and providing a list of pseudonyms for British periodicals.

27 Leslie Stephen, 'Some Early Impressions – Journalism', *National Review* 43 (1903), pp. 420–36: p. 432.

28 See William St Clair, *The Reading Nation in the Romantic Period* (Cambridge University Press, 2004), p. 187.

29 Michel Foucault, 'What is an Author?' in *Language, Counter-Memory, Practice*, trans. Donald F. Bouchard and Sherry Simon (Ithaca, NY: Cornell University Press, 1977), pp. 124–7.

predicated upon a less personal relationship between writer and text, and between writer and reader. Both the convention of anonymity and the practice of stylistic assimilation made the genre and discourse of journalism more collaborative and inclusive than forms of writing, like the novel, in which authorship was – at least for men – more commonly singular and announced (women were more likely to make the strategic decision to publish under a pseudonym). The practice of anonymity interestingly did not lead to the erasure of gender in the discourse of journalism. On the contrary, the periodical press played a key role in the formulation and circulation of Victorian gender ideologies, and the gender of both reader and author was a primary category in reviewing.[30] Anonymity, indeed, gave unprecedented opportunities for authorial performativity and masquerade, for posturing and playfulness: for example, it comes as a surprise that the gentleman crackling the *Times* (1785–) and leaving 'the "ladies" to discuss their own matters' in an article of 1854 in the *Westminster Review* (1824–1914) was in fact George Eliot; that the author of the most vituperatively mis-ogynistic of the 'Girl of the Period' articles in the *Saturday Review* (1855–1938) in the 1860s was Eliza Lynn Linton; and equally that 'Barbara', who presided over the column 'Chats about Books' in *Woman* (1890–1912) in the 1890s, was Arnold Bennett.

Periodical publication at the beginning of the century had been dominated by the great mandarin reviews – the Whig *Edinburgh Review* (1802–1929), the Tory *Quarterly Review* (1809–1967), and the monthly *Blackwood's Edinburgh Magazine* (1817–1980) – and these were the authorial preserve of educated middle-class men of letters. But the opportunities for self-concealment, dis-guise, and cross-dressing afforded by the convention of anonymity, together with the prospect of regular remuneration, opened up journalism as a profes-sion to women and to men of more modest social backgrounds, especially after the launch of the Radical quarterly, the *Westminster Review* (1824–1914). According to Barbara Onslow, 'The numbers of women in journalism almost certainly increased over the century', as entry to the profession became more democratic.[31] Journalism was increasingly identified as an open profession to which anyone could apply themselves, rather than a closed shop that was the

---

30 See Fraser *et al.*, *Gender and the Victorian Periodical*; Laurel Brake, *Subjugated Knowledges: Journalism, Gender and Literature in the Nineteenth Century* (Basingstoke: Macmillan, 1994); and Nicola Diane Thompson, *Reviewing Sex: Gender and the Reception of Victorian Novels* (London: Macmillan, 1996).

31 Barbara Onslow, *Women of the Press in Nineteenth-Century Britain* (Basingstoke: Macmillan, 2000), p. 15.

exclusive preserve of an educated male coterie. This was a regrettable development for some, such as the hostile reviewer of 'Modern Periodical Literature' in
the *Dublin Review* (1836–1968) of 1862, who blames the 'reward of money' for
having 'tended to reduce the public writer to the level of a tradesman', and
having brought about a situation where, of the battalions of journalists
now writing, 'a vast number, we may fairly say the majority, were never
meant for authors'.[32] But it was an inevitable consequence of the press's
particular role in the popularization of specialist knowledges for the general
reading public, which, as the periodical market expanded, demanded of journalists that they be able to turn their hands to any area of general knowledge
that might present itself.

Furthermore, the traditional hierarchy of author and reader changed in
the nineteenth century as a direct consequence of periodical and newspaper
publishing practices. As Walter Benjamin was to write in 'The Work of Art
in the Age of Mechanical Reproduction' (1936):

> For centuries a small number of writers were confronted by many thou-
> sands of readers. This changed toward the end of the last century. With the
> increasing extension of the press, which kept placing new political, religious,
> scientific, professional, and local organs before the readers, an increasing
> number of readers became writers – at first, occasional ones. It began with
> the daily press opening to its readers space for 'letters to the editor'.

He predicts that with the development of this practice, which may be said to
have begun in the UK with the 'Letters to the Editor' page of *The Times*
under Thomas Barnes's editorship of the paper from 1817 to 1841 and became
a particularly popular feature of Sunday papers from the 1850s, 'the distinction between author and public is about to lose its basic character. The
difference becomes merely functional; it may vary from case to case. At any
moment the reader is ready to turn into a writer.' The modern situation
(which has only become more pronounced since Benjamin's time, with the
development of the new electronic media and the possibilities of hypertext),
whereby 'Literary license is now founded on polytechnic rather than specialized training and thus becomes common property', was inaugurated in
the nineteenth-century press.[33]

32 [Thomas Donnelly], 'Modern Periodical Literature', *Dublin Review* 51 (1862), pp. 275–308:
   pp. 276, 305.
33 Walter Benjamin, 'The Work of Art in the Age of Mechanical Reproduction', in
   Illuminations: Essays and Reflections, trans. H. Zohn (New York: Schocken, 1968), pp. 217–52:
   pp. 231, 232, 232.

The text of the periodical itself became an increasingly democratized literary form during this period, one that participated in a network of cultural production and consumption, and was characterized by plurality rather than singularity. In this new age of mechanical reproduction, such plurality was experienced in the Victorian periodical in multiple ways: some weekly serials, such as the *Northern Star* (1837–52) and the *Leader* (1850–60), were issued in multiple, often slightly different regional editions in order to reach readers at a geographical distance from the place of publication at the same time as local readers; intellectual property was flagrantly stolen and cheaply reproduced (copyright was legislated for in 1842, reported on by a Royal Commission in 1878, flouted and fought over throughout the period); articles were collected and republished, novels were serialized and reprinted in volume form, and writing of all kinds was sampled, or re-presented in the form of a popular synopsis or a review, in the pages of periodicals. The Victorian periodical text is also characterized internally by its plurality, its multivocality, and its multivalency, by its dialogic and heteroglossic energy, that is, by the dynamic interplay of competing and sometimes conflicting discourses that comprise it. It is a collection of voices and images that speak to each other within each issue as well as serially and intertextually, their meanings shaped by their relation to other periodical texts as well as to the world to which they refer.

The plurality of the periodical text and the periodical author was intimately bound up with an equivalently radical plurality of readership, which again puts us in mind of the contemporary democratization of knowledge experienced by the Internet generation, and provides an imaginative connection between our own conceptualization of the mass media and that of the Victorians. Then as now, a congruence of technological advances, population growth, rising living standards, political and cultural change, and legal and fiscal reform provided the catalyst and the mechanism for this revolution. Tom Standage draws similar parallels with the Internet age in his study of the nineteenth-century telegraph in *The Victorian Internet*.[34] Such cultural and technological resonances are suggestive, but of course it is important not to erase important differences between forms of technology, publication, and communication in the two periods.

The Reform Acts of 1832 and 1867 and the Education Act of 1870 triggered far-reaching social and economic changes, the most significant of which for the democratization of the press were the vastly increased literacy rates

---

34 Tom Standage, *The Victorian Internet: The Remarkable Story of the Telegraph and the Nineteenth Century's Online Pioneers* (London: Weidenfeld and Nicolson, 1998).

among all classes, which made possible a huge expansion in readership, and the new sense of political agency and class identity engendered among those hitherto excluded from the political process. New developments in printing technology, such as the introduction of steam-powered rotary presses from about 1815 to the 1830s, and typesetting machines, such as Robert Hattersley's in 1857, Alexander Mackie's steam-driven model ten years later, and Frederick Wick's rotary casting machine patented in 1881, lowered the cost yet improved the quality of periodical publishing, and the rapid expansion of the railways and shipping lines enabled more efficient distribution networks. Economic reforms such as the removal of the so-called 'tax on knowledge', through the reduction of Stamp Duty on newspapers to 1d in 1836 and its eventual abolition in 1855, and the removal of tax on paper in 1861, significantly affected the production costs of journals. Furthermore, as Andrew King and John Plunkett point out in the introduction to their valuable reader on *Victorian Print Media*, the very nature of the printing process meant there was an economic logic driving the expansion of the low-cost popular market in print media, for '[i]ncreasing numbers of readers created economies of scale for publishers, which overall favoured lower prices and more production, which attracted more readers, and so on and so forth in a continuously widening gyre'.[35] Added to this there were other incentives to the expansion of the reading public that were the result of changes in the material conditions of reading: the removal of the window tax in 1851, which enabled bigger windows and brought more natural light into the houses of the poor; new and cheaper forms of domestic lighting, brought about by developments in candle technology (the discovery of paraffin wax in the mid nineteenth century, the development of better wicks, the industrialization of candle production in 1834 when Joseph Morgan invented a machine to manufacture 1,500 per hour, which meant that even the poorest people were able to afford candles) and, for the wealthier classes, by the introduction of gas lighting and, in 1879, the incandescent electric lamp; an increase in the availability of public reading spaces in the form of public libraries, mechanics' institutes, coffee houses, and railway carriages.

This was the context for the massive explosion of popular print media forms in the middle of the nineteenth century.[36] An article of 1849, quoting

---

35 Andrew King and John Plunkett (eds.), *Victorian Print Media: A Reader* (Oxford and New York: Oxford University Press, 2005), p. 5.

36 See *ibid.*, pp. 165–236, for a fruitful discussion of the ambiguities for both Victorian and modern commentators of the term 'popular', which 'emerges as always political and always ready for tactical redefinition' (p. 165).

from another published in *Blackwood's* twenty years earlier, in a way that testifies to the prolonged and continuing escalation of this new mass reading culture, reiterates its claim that, 'A great revolution there has been, from nobody's reading anything, to every body's reading all things.'[37] Beginning with the 'improving' *Penny* and *Saturday Magazines* (1832–45 and 1832–44) and the first serialized fiction launched in the 1830s, the popular market came into its own with the serialized publication of Dickens's *Pickwick* in 1836–7 and Edward Lloyd's 'Penny Dreadfuls'. In the 1840s and 1850s, numbers of penny fiction magazines were produced for family reading, the most successful of which were the *Family Herald* (1842–1940), the *London Journal* (1845–1928), *Reynolds Miscellany* (1846–69), and *Cassell's Illustrated Family Paper* (1853–67). These were widely circulating magazines relying on the serialized fiction they included, described by Wilkie Collins (anonymously) in 1858 as 'a new species of literary production', the reading matter of '*a public of three millions* – a public unknown to the literary world; unknown, as disciples, to the whole body of professed critics; unknown, as customers, at the great libraries and the great publishing houses; unknown, as an audience, to the distinguished English writers of our own time'; as an 'unknown public', in short, which lies right 'out of the pale of literary civilisation'.[38] Notwithstanding the sensationalizing and racializing tones of Collins's article, which recalls the language of nineteenth-century social investigators on the 'unknown country' of 'darkest England', it draws attention to a class of periodical literature that has only recently been brought back in the pale of literary history.

Collins's article was published in Dickens's journal *Household Words* (1850–9), and it is journals such as this – *All the Year Round* (which replaced it in 1859, and ran till 1895), *Temple Bar* (1860–1906), the *Cornhill* (1860–1975) and *Longman's Magazine* (1882–1905) – widely circulating magazines that published the serialized fiction, reviews, and social reportage of writers who have become part of the Victorian canon – that are most familiar to modern readers. But an increasing amount of critical attention has been given to investigating the full breadth and variety of print culture in the period. Alongside the mass-market publication aimed at the vast middle ground, and these more elevated literary magazines, as well as those devoted to investigative journalism and the influential high-cultural journals such as *Blackwood's Edinburgh Magazine* (1817–1980), the *Fortnightly* (1865–1954), and

---

37 *Eliza Cook's Journal* 1 (1849), p. 182, quoting [John Wilson], 'Monologue, or Soliloquy on the Annuals', *Blackwood's Magazine* 29 (1829), p. 950.
38 [Wilkie Collins], 'The Unknown Public', *Household Words* 18 (21 August 1858), pp. 217–22.

the *Westminster Review* (1824–1914) for which the intellectual critic wrote, were a proliferating number of periodicals aimed at specialist interests, and targeting niche readerships. There were magazines for men, for women, for boys and for girls, for servants, for colonials; for Chartists, for Christians, for cyclists; for conservatives and for radicals, for travellers and for home-makers. There were quarterlies, monthlies, and, increasingly importantly, weeklies, such as the influential *Athenaeum* (1828–1921), the *Spectator* (1828–), and the *Saturday Review* (1855–1938) – which ensured that publications in volume form were reviewed right after their publication date, and that theatrical productions and art exhibitions were also covered extensively and while they were still open. These periodicals ranged from the morally and intellectually serious to the satirical and the slapstick (*Punch* was launched in 1841, remaining in print till 2002, *Judy* in 1867, running till 1910), from the uncompromisingly highbrow to the middlebrow to the definitively lowbrow. The period saw the establishment of specialist art publications, such as the *Art Journal* (1839–1912) and the *Magazine of Art* (1878–1904) and general scientific journals such as *Nature* (1869–) and *Mind* (1876–), while both the more intellectually inclined general journals and specialized periodicals enabled the circulation of new ideas in science, philosophy, history, politics, economics, sociology, anthropology, and other emerging disciplines.

Not least, the periodical press was the main public forum for literary criticism in the nineteenth century, and provided the context within which the emerging discipline of English was forged and defined. Literary reviewing evolved over the decades, broadly speaking, from an illustrative model depending on lengthy quotation and paraphrase, to more analytical, and often more judgmental (or overtly laudatory) pieces. Reviewing practices expanded to include more autonomous disquisitions on some aspect of the central theme of a literary work that sometimes seemed only tenuously related to the book under review. Gladstone's monumental twenty-two-page review of Mrs Humphry Ward's novel *Robert Elsmere* (1888) in the *Nineteenth Century* (1877–1901), for example, which was reprinted in pamphlet form and very widely read, is not so much a detailed literary analysis of the novel as a vigorous refutation of the hero's (and author's) religious position.[39] While in the early nineteenth century the critical essay depended for its existence upon the books it reviewed, as the century progressed the contrary increasingly became the case, with books emerging as collections

---

39 William E. Gladstone, '*Robert Elsmere* and the Battle of Belief', *Nineteenth Century* 23 (1888), pp. 766–88.

of review essays which had first appeared in periodicals. Mark Pattison observed, indeed, in 1877 that 'books are now largely made up of republished review articles'.[40]

In the course of the nineteenth century the critic achieved recognition as an intellectual and creative phenomenon with an equivalent cultural capital to the artist. Criticism and imaginative literature had always, of course, been closely intertwined; for example, what Jerome McGann has identified as 'the Romantic ideology' was formulated in the critical essays and creative manifestos of the writers whose poetry exemplified it.[41] This tendency was continued and elaborated by Victorian writers: George Eliot honed her writerly skills as a periodical reviewer for the *Westminster Review* (1824–1914), and critically redefined what a 'lady novelist' was capable of before publishing her first work of fiction;[42] the Pre-Raphaelite poets and artists launched their own journal, the *Germ* (1850), in which to publish a critical manifesto for their creative work; and Oscar Wilde first articulated the aestheticism that was to define his literary identity in his critical journalism.

But additionally, and growing out of the more independently critical journalism of early nineteenth-century writers like William Hazlitt and James Leigh Hunt, Victorian journalists such as G. H. Lewes, R. H. Hutton, and Alfred Austin exercised considerable influence as literary and cultural critics for the periodicals. Furthermore, the practice and purpose of criticism itself as an intellectual discipline and a cultural tool began to be articulated and theorized in the Victorian period, in the writings of figures such as Matthew Arnold, John Ruskin, Walter Pater, and Oscar Wilde. Arnold's seminal essay 'The Function of Criticism at the Present Time' (1865), for example, emphasizes the crucial role of the critic in the modern world, his principal task being in a dispassionate and non-partisan way 'to see the object as in itself it really is'.[43] According to this expanded definition, literary

---

40 Quoted by Walter E. Houghton, 'Periodical Literature and the Articulate Classes', in Joanne Shattock and Michael Wolff (eds.), *The Victorian Periodical Press: Samplings and Soundings* (London: Leicester University Press, 1982), pp. 3–27: p. 21. Joanne Shattock, in *Politics and Reviewers: The Edinburgh and The Quarterly in the Early Victorian Age* (London: Leicester University Press, 1989), p. 9, quotes Leslie Stephen's opinion that 'much of the most solid and original work of the time first appears in periodicals'.

41 Jerome J. McGann, *The Romantic Ideology* (University of Chicago Press, 1983).

42 See [George Eliot], 'Silly Novels by Lady Novelists', *Westminster Review* 66 (1856), pp. 442–61.

43 Matthew Arnold, 'The Function of Criticism at the Present Time', in *Essays in Criticism, The Complete Prose Works of Matthew Arnold*, ed. R. H. Super, 11 vols. (Ann Arbor: University of Michigan Press, 1960–77), vol. III, p. 258.

criticism is conceived as a particular application of a broader critical imperative to make '*a disinterested endeavour to learn and propagate the best that is known and thought in the world*'.[44] Arnold was Professor of Poetry at Oxford when he produced this and his other major critical works, and it was precisely for its ivory-tower elitism that R. H. Hutton criticized Arnold's definition of the function of criticism in his reviews of his work in the *Spectator* (1828–) in the 1860s: 'he regards the power of seeing things as they are as the monopoly of a class; and indeed, arrived at as he arrived at it, it must always be the monopoly of a class'. For a 'cut-and-dried man of culture' like Arnold, who in Hutton's view despises the populace, 'the only criticism which is really likely to be useful on the minor works of every-day literature is that which has been trained and disciplined in worthier studies', and 'no doubt it is a trial to men steeped in the culture of the noblest literature of the world, to appreciate fairly the ephemeral productions of a busy generation'. But according to Hutton, 'Unless he can enter into the wants of his generation, he has no business to pretend to direct its thoughts.' It is, instead, the critic reviewing for the press who responds to the real cultural needs of 'ordinary Englishmen', rather than the 'intellectual angel' who pontificates from on high, that in Hutton's view best serves the interests of British cultural life broadly conceived.[45]

Wilde, in a very different kind of work written a quarter of a century later but also in response to Arnold's essay, similarly recognizes the elitism of Arnold's critical stance. 'The Critic as Artist', first published in two parts in July and September 1890 under the title 'The True Function and Value in Criticism', is a witty commentary in dialogue form on the theories and practices of criticism in the nineteenth century. Wilde's celebration of 'criticism of the highest kind' as an art form in itself, in that 'It treats the work of art simply as a starting-point for a new creation', represents no single critic's theory, and indeed significantly modifies the individual views of writers such as Arnold, Ruskin, and Pater, and yet 'The Critic as Artist' provides an effective summation of what 'criticism' had come to mean by the end of the century.[46] Wilde's essay pays homage to these individuals

---

44 *Ibid.*, p. 283.
45 R. H. Hutton, 'Mr Grote on the Abuses of Newspaper Criticism,' in R. Tener and M. Woodfield (eds.), *A Victorian Spectator: Uncollected Writings of R. H. Hutton* (Bristol: Bristol Classical Press, 1989), pp. 39–43: pp. 42–3. See also Hutton, 'An Intellectual Angel', *Victorian Spectator*, pp. 111–16.
46 Oscar Wilde, 'The Critic as Artist', in *Complete Works of Oscar Wilde*, introduced by Vyvyan Holland (London: HarperCollins, 1966), p. 1028.

who had such a formative influence on the development of criticism in his century, but it also, like Hutton's review, recognizes the importance of the periodical press. He distinguishes between cultured critics of 'the higher class', who 'write for the sixpenny papers', and the 'ordinary journalist', who is described as 'giving us the opinions of the uneducated' and 'keeping us in touch with the ignorance of the community', reminding us that, just as Arnold's idea of 'Culture' was conceived as a response to the 'Anarchy' of political democracy, so, with the democratization of the press, criticism was necessary for the cultural control of the vast and expanding newly literate reading public. The exaggeratedly effete upper-class tones of Gilbert's sympathy for the 'poor reviewers' of second-rate three-volume novels, who are 'apparently reduced to be the reporters of the police-court of literature, the chroniclers of the doings of the habitual criminals of art', underline the imbrication of the literary review with the class dynamics of nineteenth-century society. It is significant that, although like Arnold he recognizes the crucial role of criticism in contemporary nineteenth-century life, Wilde's Gilbert envisages the critic as one who retreats from the demands of the 'real world', who detaches himself from history; he predicts, indeed, that 'as civilisation progresses and we become more highly organised, the elect spirits of each age, the critical and cultured spirits, will grow less and less interested in actual life, and *will seek to gain their impressions almost entirely from what Art has touched'.*[47]

Hutton's review and Wilde's essay, in their engagement with the question of the function and different modes of criticism, throw interesting light on the question of the unstable literary history of critical scholarship on the Victorian periodical press with which this chapter began. For all that he insisted upon the fact that art should not be conceived as something isolated from life, Arnold's critical position has continued to be identified as an elitist one that does just that. The convergence of the perceived functions of criticism and of the academy in his cultural programme has not gone unnoticed by modern critics and theorists, and he has been either hailed or condemned for what all agree was his crucial role in the institutionalization of literary studies within universities and in the development of 'English' as an academic discipline. When Wilde's Gilbert announces in 1890 that 'It is to criticism that the future belongs', and imagines an 'educational system' which would 'try and develop in the mind a more subtle quality of

47 *Ibid.*, pp. 1022–48.

apprehension and discernment',[48] it is as if he foresees the rise of English from its unsteady beginnings in the Mechanics' Institutes and Working Men's Colleges to its triumphant establishment in the Cambridge of the 1930s. Arnold's emphasis on criticism as a moral activity involving the transmission of fundamental human values was to be refined and elaborated by the Leavises, but the roots of their own critical practice are clearly to be found in Arnold's dogmatic assertions of 'correct literary opinion', of what is 'right and wrong', 'sound and unsound'; in his cultural 'touchstones'; and in his ranking of writers, and erection of a canonical 'great tradition'. For as long as qualities such as 'high seriousness' and 'the grand style' were the measure of what constitutes the 'literary' and the touchstones of academic English, journalism and the periodical press, purveyors of what Hutton referred to as 'the ephemeral productions of a busy generation', were (somewhat ironically, given their role in the development of literary criticism) not considered worthy of literary critical study. It is only under the very different critical and institutional conditions that prevail today, and from the more interdisciplinary perspective of Victorian Studies that recognizes the porosity of literary studies and its inflection by cultural history and by media and cultural studies, that 'the reporters of the police-court of literature, the chroniclers of the doing of the habitual criminals of art', pitied and dismissed so summarily by Wilde's Gilbert, are found to have an interest of their own, giving us a unique window on to an age that shared, and was perhaps responsible for forming, many of our own cultural preoccupations.

48 *Ibid.*, pp. 1054–5.

PART II

*

WRITING VICTORIA'S ENGLAND

4

The expansion of Britain

DAVID AMIGONI

In June 1829, a remarkable essay appeared in the *Edinburgh Review*. Entitled 'Signs of the Times' it prophesied, in an unusually energetic and compelling style, the crisis facing an industrializing – indeed mechanizing – society. Urban experience was in the ascendant and responding to an increasingly complex, rapidly expanding social machine. Exploring the ways in which traditionally constituted modes of inward reflection, such as religion, were fragmenting under the pressure of speculative and journalistic over-production, the essay feared that even 'literature' had been re-organized by the 'Genius of Mechanism.'[1] Thomas Carlyle's 'Signs of the Times' has long been regarded as a seminal work for appreciating the onset of the urban, industrial, and intellectual expansion that characterized the distinctive tensions organizing Victorian culture. It needs also to be seen as part of a wider challenge: how should one see, understand, and record the vast material expansion that was being experienced? One answer came in the form of the compendious *Official Descriptive and Illustrated Catalogue of the Great Exhibition of the Works of All Nations*, the catalogue which preserved for posterity the contents and layout of the great Crystal Palace in South Kensington in 1851. The three volumes might be seen as the triple-decker novel to end all triple-deckers, nothing less than a vast map of mid-Victorian 'things' and the machinery that produced them. But what could literature do in the face of this relentless productivity?

Henry Mayhew found a role for the literary as he looked for a commanding perspective on a scene at the centre of commercial expansion, the port and City of London in 1849. He sought it from the heights of St Paul's, 'the huge black dome, with its ball of gold looming through the smoke (apt emblem of the source of its riches!)'. Mayhew wrote in one of his first letters

---

1 [Thomas Carlyle], 'Signs of the Times', *Edinburgh Review* 98 (1829), pp. 439–59: pp. 443–4.

for the newspaper, the *Morning Chronicle*, that were to be the basis for his much more famous *London Labour and the London Poor*:

> In the hope of obtaining a bird's-eye view of the port, I went up to the Golden Gallery that is immediately below the ball of St Paul's. It was noon, and an exquisitely bright and clear spring day; but the view was smudgy and smeared with smoke. And yet the haze which hung like a curtain of shadow before and over everything increased rather than diminished the vast sublimity of the city that lay stretched out beneath. It was utterly unlike London as seen everyday below, in all its bricken and hard-featured reality; it was rather the phantasm – the spectral illusion, as it were, of the great metropolis – such as one might see in a dream, with here and there stately churches and palatial hospitals, shimmering like white marble their windows glittering in the sunshine like plates of burnished gold – while the rest of the scene was all hazy and indefinite. Even the outlines of the neighbouring streets, steeples, and towers were blurred in misty indistinctness. Clumps of buildings and snatches of parks looked through the clouds like dim islands rising out of the sea of smoke ... As you peeped down into the thoroughfares you could see streams of busy little men, like ants, continually hurrying along in opposite directions; while, what with carts, cabs, and omnibuses, the earth seemed all alive with tiny creeping things, as when one looks onto the grass on a summer's day.[2]

Mayhew reminds us that Victorian expansion was, in the first instance, urban expansion, led by London: 'every year, further house room has to be provided for twenty thousand persons – so that London increases annually by the addition of a new town of considerable size'.[3] The 1851 Census revealed that there were, for the first time, more urban than rural dwellers in Britain. In rapidly industrializing Wales, new and expanding towns were eating up the countryside; in 1801, Cardiff had a population of fewer than 2000: by 1891, it had expanded to 129,000.[4]

The literary texture of Mayhew's prose reveals complex processes of cultural and technological change. His bird's-eye view of London was achieved by ascent of a commanding visual platform of long standing. But its rhetoric clearly also owed something to the new vogue for balloon ascents; in the 1850s, Mayhew would view London in very similar terms

---

2 Henry Mayhew, from Letters I (19 October 1849) and XLVII (11 April 1850), *Morning Chronicle*, in E.P. Thompson and Eileen Yeo (eds.), *The Unknown Mayhew: Selections from the Morning Chronicle, 1849–50*, 1971 (Harmondsworth: Penguin, 1984), p. 114.
3 *Ibid.*, p. 113.
4 K. Theodore Hoppen, *The Mid-Victorian Generation: 1846–1886*, New Oxford History of England (Oxford University Press, 1998), p. 522.

from the basket of Charles Green's famous balloon 'Nassau'.[5] Mayhew's perspective also owes something to, while simultaneously swerving away from, a Romantic inheritance: Wordsworth's 1802 sonnet 'Upon Westminster Bridge' recorded a vision of a sunlit, sleeping cityscape ('towers, domes, theatres and temples lie / Open unto the fields') 'glittering in the smokeless air'. By contrast, the clarity of vision that the clear skies seem to promise to Mayhew is 'smeared' by 'smudgy' smoke. The 'smoke', signalling expanding industry, trade, and concentrated domestic urban life, is a new mediator of visual experience: it defamiliarizes the known, turning his vision away from 'bricken' reality and into a dream-like phantasm, which confirms 'a much more sublime and ideal effect from the very inability to grasp the whole of its literal reality'.[6] This passage thus owes much to the critical categories that were being elaborated by nineteenth-century novel criticism: a critical opposition between the 'real' and the 'ideal' organized evaluations of the burgeoning products of the fiction market in this period. A writer born of urban expansion, Charles Dickens, and one to whom Mayhew has been frequently compared, could not be exclusively located within either category of realism or imaginary idealism.

There are two other notable 'ways of seeing' in this passage. The reference to glimpses of buildings and parks, arising from the 'sea' of smoke as though they were islands in view uses as sources of comparison lands that lie beyond the metropolis, and indeed beyond England itself. The expansion of Britain in the nineteenth century involved population migrations to and from colonies: by 1880, England's population loss by emigration was 23 in 10,000 (Scotland's was as high as 58 in 10,000).[7] As Jean-Louis Comolli argues, colonial expansion joined forces with the technologies and languages of visualization, for the period witnessed 'something of a geographical extension of the field of the visible and the representable: by journeys, explorations, colonisations, the whole world becomes visible at the same time as it becomes appropriable'.[8] Accordingly, colonial expansion aided the pursuit of natural history, which is the second 'way of seeing' that Mayhew draws upon. Looking down on London's streets and reducing its scale – in effect inverting the power of a microscope, another newly popularized tool of

---

5 See Kate Flint, *The Victorians and the Visual Imagination* (Cambridge University Press, 2000), pp. 9–10.
6 Mayhew, *Unknown Mayhew*, p. 113.   7 Hoppen, *Mid-Victorian Generation*, p. 523.
8 Jean-Louis Comolli, 'Machines of the Visible', in Teresa de Lauretis and Stephen Heath (eds.), *The Cinematic Apparatus* (London and Basingstoke: Macmillan, 1980), pp. 122–3.

visual technology, while implicitly appealing to its effects – Mayhew sees people as though they are ants – notably colonist dwellers – and modes of transportation as though they are creatures creeping in the grass. In fact, sea-born transportation played a role in revolutionizing the very approach to natural history in the nineteenth century. The voyage of Charles Darwin on HMS *Beagle* (1831–6) did much to shape Darwin's famous vision of nature as a 'tangled bank' of interdependent evolving life forms.

Mayhew's view of a homogenized 'mass' of ant-like human creatures was symptomatic of an emerging challenge: how to disaggregate an expanding population into sub-groups and individual subjects, and yet hear their distinctive patterns of speech and individual voices. Mayhew's solution was to descend to the street level. Rather than looking down at the figures who worked the ships in the port of London, he interviewed them, and recorded their experience of working life. A fireman recorded the poor conditions in the engine room of a steam ship: the intense heat bred and sustained its own insect colony: 'I hardly knew what bugs were, in comparison on shore, but their head-quarters are in the engine-rooms of steamers.'[9] If poor conditions were the crushing norm, another sailor praised the philanthropy of the shipping master Richard Green of Poplar.[10] Another remarked on the voices he encountered during African travels, marked by a particular dialect of English expansion: 'There were some fine strong fellows among the natives; some had a few words of English; all that knew any English could swear; they soon pick that up; it's like their ABC among sailors.'[11] The expansion of Britain – both internal and overseas – was most often presented as a heroic story, as we shall see in the more formal, literary voices from the 1840s to the 1880s that presented and explored its effects. But there were in these voices from the earlier phase of the period – organized by the genres of historical writing, religious and scientific writing, poetry, and the novel – if not profanities, then certainly discordant notes.

Britain's place in the world: voices of history

The title of this chapter is pre-figured by J. R. Seeley's influential work of historiographical and geo-political polemic, *The Expansion of England* (1883). It is appropriate to begin this section with the emerging historiographical

---

9 Mayhew, Letter XLVI, 3 April 1850, in *Unknown Mayhew*, p. 386.
10 Mayhew, Letter XLII, 14 March 1850, in *ibid.*, p. 369.
11 Mayhew, Letter XLI, 11 March 1850, in *ibid.*, p. 369.

coverage of the nineteenth century: this was the genre of writing that, as the age elapsed moment by moment, inscribed the terms in which expansion would be understood, and received by later generations.

Harriet Martineau, in her important work of mid-Victorian historiography, *History of the Peace* (1849), observed that 'now we were at peace, there was leisure and energy disposable for projects of geographical discovery'.[12] Martineau's liberal history narrated events from Waterloo and the fall of Napoleon, to the repeal of the Corn Laws. The history included inventions (steam and factory technology) and the development of cotton manufacture; the rise of the country banks and increasing 'national' financial confidence; there were mentions of the heroic figures of Romantic science (William Herschel and Michael Faraday), and even the relatively raw new talent of Charles Dickens. Britain's colonial possessions figured substantially in Martineau's *History of the Peace*; the recent history of the East India Company was accounted for, and patterns of emigration (to Canada, Australia, and New Zealand) were noted, as well as colonial conflicts within 'the Peace': for example, the Canadian 'rebellion' that was in progress when the young Victoria acceded to the throne in 1837.

By establishing a clear narrative of progress (for instance, it loosely frames Dinah Mulock's influential 1857 novel of the rise of an impoverished but virtuous and ultimately successful character and his family, *John Halifax, Gentleman*), this work of popular history represented in itself another powerful building block in the post-Napoleonic expansion of Britain. Martineau's work – a pictorial history, which exploited the technology for the mass reproduction of wood engravings (its appearance is not unlike that of the *Illustrated London News*, founded 1842) – was itself a good example of the way in which a published format was assumed to contribute to the expansion of peace, knowledge, and virtue: it was originally conceived and initially executed by the popular publisher and author Charles Knight. Martineau took over from Knight, and the book was eventually published by W. and R. Chambers, publishers of popular scientific speculation, and the phenomenally popular *Chambers's Edinburgh Journal*, which began publication in 1832, and which squeezed Knight's comparable *Penny Magazine* out of the market. *History of the Peace* was published in an edition comparable to Chambers' People's Library editions: cheap paper, printed in double columns (a massive expanse of text, across 762 pages). The opening editorial of *Chambers's*

---

12 Harriet Martineau, *History of the Peace: A Pictorial History of England during the Thirty Years Peace 1816–1846* (Edinburgh: W. & R. Chambers, 1849), p. 214.

Edinburgh Journal claimed to satisfy 'the universal appetite for instruction' shared by 'every man in the British dominions'.[13] An important literary dimension of the expansion of Britain was enshrined in the relationship between colonial territories and cheap, but reliably produced, 'improving' reading.

Almost forty years later, history had achieved a stronger foothold in university teaching, and the Cambridge historian J. R. Seeley published *The Expansion of England* (1883). 'England' dominates in the title, so the Union between England, Scotland, and Ireland was subsumed within the name of the dominant imperial power. However, Seeley's work was really about the colonial formation of what he called 'greater Britain'. Seeley produced a powerful argument about the relationship between patterns of European colonization and the continuities of eighteenth-century history. He saw the conflicts between Britain, France, and Spain in the eighteenth century not as Eurocentric conflicts, but as conflicts that were precisely about attempts to expand 'greater' versions of these nation states into new world territories: for example, the Anglo-French conflicts over India and the North American territories (the Canadian rebellion that coincided with Victoria's accession to the throne was a hangover from the Anglo-French rivalries, still active in Canada), and Seeley's reading of Napoleon's Egyptian campaign presented it as the last French attempt to secure strategic routes to, and attain control of, India.

In Seeley's view, post-1816 really did mark a decisive break with the patterns of warfare and its motives that had characterized the eighteenth century, in so far as the English nationality, language, religion, and statehood had successfully imposed itself to become 'Greater Britain' in Canada, the Southern Hemisphere, and, with qualifications, India; this at the expense of 'greater France' or 'greater Spain'. Seeley also advanced the view, powerfully symbolized in the Great Exhibition of 1851, that distinctively nineteenth-century agencies of technological modernization – 'steam and electricity' – would create a situation in which 'distance is abolished by science', making the consolidation of 'greater Britain' possible.[14] Of course, 'improving' reading, mass-produced by the steam press, transported to colonial territories by steam ships, would play its

---

13 James A. Secord, *Victorian Sensation* (Chicago and London: Chicago University Press, 2000), pp. 67–8.
14 J. R. Seeley, *The Expansion of England: Two Courses of Lectures* (1883; London: Macmillan, 1895), p. 89.

role in expanding 'greater Britain'; Chambers's publishing house exemplified this aspiration. The second edition of Darwin's travel narrative, *Journal of Researches* (1845), was published in John Murray's Colonial and Home Library, a series that Murray expressly designed to exploit the Copyright Act of 1842, and take advantage of the market exclusivity that the act sought to reserve for British dominions and colonies in the effort to supply 'improving' reading.[15] Carlyle's dark forebodings about mechanization in 1829 had, by the time that Seeley published his work in 1883, become the key to the future.

Whereas Carlyle had seen history as the unleashed energies of 'Chaos', pitted against human heroism and the biographies of innumerable individuals, Seeley was clear that the object of history was the state, as 'individuals are important to history in proportion, not to their intrinsic merit, but to their relation to the State'.[16] He argued that 'there are in general three ties by which states are held together, community of race, community of religion, community of interest'.[17] If the story of 'race' community is a complex one that lies beyond the provenance of this chapter, the impact of expansion upon the communities of first, Anglicanism as the state church; and, secondly, the communities that grouped around different understandings of the 'national interest' were no less complex, and resonant in some of the conflicts and uncertainties at the heart of religious, scientific, poetical, and novelistic writing.

'Literature' itself is thus a further important dimension of Seeley's thesis: he had, in common with other nineteenth-century historians such as Macaulay, an acute understanding of the way in which metaphor and narrative shaped historical consciousness: for Seeley, his thesis about expansion 'binds together the past of England and her future, and leaves us, when we close the history of our country, not with minds fatigued and bewildered as though from reading a story that has been too much spun out, but enlightened and more deeply interested than ever, because partly prepared for what is to come next'.[18] Seeley encourages us to think about the role of narrative and discourse in 'the expansion of Britain', and its place in understanding the articulation of 'interest', without reductively arguing that either is exclusively a phenomenon of narrative and discourse.

---

15 David Amigoni, *Colonies, Cults and Evolution: Literature, Science and Culture in Nineteenth-Century Writing* (Cambridge University Press, 2007), pp. 84–5.
16 Seeley, *Expansion of England*, p. 8.   17 *Ibid.*, p. 13.   18 *Ibid.*, p. 358.

Religious and scientific voices

If English Protestant intellectuals and spiritual leaders such as Charles Kingsley sought to construct narratives in which Britain was *the* centre of the world, geographically and spiritually, other spiritual leaders, such as the Catholic convert J. H. Newman, diverged from this view. Newman critically presented spirituality as transcendent of the process of state consolidation and material expansion. This was an issue that produced deep conflict within the Anglican Church. Scientific writers, such as Charles Darwin and Alfred Russel Wallace, depended on colonial expansion, but produced a knowledge that unsettled traditional ideas of centrality and progress.

John Henry Newman's long and complex path from the Anglican Church to Roman Catholicism was an emotional as well as a theological journey. But it was, in no small part, also a critical reaction to the expansion of the post-1832 liberal British state, and its pursuit of 'interest' overseas, using the Anglican Church as its instrument. Of course, it is well known that hostility to liberalism was at the heart of Newman's Anglo-Catholic refutation of the claimed catholicity of the Anglican Church, which led him to Tract 90, his critical reading of the Church of England's foundational Thirty-Nine Articles, and the conversion to Rome. It is important also to register the role that imperial expansion played in shaping Newman's views in the late 1840s. In the *Apologia Pro Vita Sua*, Newman records that between 1839 and 1841, the Archbishop of Canterbury, government ministers, and the Prussian Ambassador launched a scheme for consecrating an Anglican Bishop for Jerusalem, thereby establishing for Protestantism (in its English and Prussian varieties) a foothold in the East.[19] If Newman protested more circumspectly in *The British Critic* of July 1841, in various letters he was clear about both the politics and the consequences. In a letter to the *Times* (1 November 1841), signed in Greek 'a private person', though not published, Newman identified imperial politics, and the mission to sustain power in India, as lying at the heart of the initiative: 'the main object was, and I believe is, to negotiate with the heretical Monophysites, especially of Mesopotamia. Mesopotamia is the way to the Euphrates. The Euphrates is the way to India. It is desirable to consolidate our empire.'[20] In an earlier letter to

---

19 J. H. Newman, *Apologia Pro Vita Sua*, ed. Martin J. Svaglic (Oxford: Clarendon Press, 1967), pp. 131–6.
20 *Letters and Diaries of John Henry Newman*, ed. Gerard Tracey, 31 vol., vol. VIII, *1841–Apil 1842* (Oxford: Clarendon Press, 2000), p. 299.

J. W. Bowden (October 1841), citing 'the fearful business of the Bishop of Jerusalem', Newman contended that 'if any such event should take place, I shall not be able to keep a single man from Rome. They will all be trooping off, sooner or later.'[21] Newman would quarrel publicly with Charles Kingsley over the aspersions cast against the Catholic convert's integrity, manliness, and Englishness, a quarrel that would lead to the publication of the *Apologia*: the differences between the two over the question of Britain's expansive role in the East were symptomatic of the religious differences between them, and the different understandings of British 'interest'.

The Reverend Charles Kingsley delivered his lectures on 'Alexandria and Her Schools', an account of Ptolemy's ancient-world Alexandria, to the Philosophical Institution, Edinburgh, in 1854. Kingsley informed his listeners that

> A glance at the map will show you what ... a centre of the world, this Alexandria is, and perhaps arouse in your minds, as it has often done in mine, a suspicion that it has not yet filled its whole destiny, but may become at any time a prize for contending nations, or the centre of some world empire to come.[22]

The immediate context of Kingsley's lectures was the Crimean War, the event that terminated Harriet Martineau's 'Thirty Years Peace', and which heightened concerns about the relations between Western and Eastern Europe, and East and West as expressed in a conflict between Islam and Christianity. In Carlylean mode, Kingsley observed in his concluding lecture, entitled 'The Cross and the Crescent', that 'the whirligig of time brings about its revenges. The stream of commerce is now rapidly turning back to its old channel; and British science bids fair to make Alexandria once more the inn of all the nations.'[23] England, for Kingsley, was the centre of the world, scientifically, militarily, commercially, and morally – but in order to command this position geographically, it would need to extend itself through the 'manly' endeavour of colonial expansion into the east, and the site of Alexandria in particular.

Kingsley's sense that 'science' would deliver this prize assumed a relationship between science, colonialism, and economic expansion. This was not a fanciful expectation. When the young Charles Darwin joined H.M.S. *Beagle* in 1831 as gentleman companion to Captain Robert FitzRoy, he took up his position as unofficial ship's naturalist. However, natural history was very

---

21 *Ibid.*, pp. 288–9.
22 Charles Kingsley, *Historical Lectures and Essays* (London: Macmillan, 1880), p. 18.
23 *Ibid.*, p. 129.

much a secondary occupation of the *Beagle*: above all, the ship was under-taking surveying work of the coast of the Southern America (one of the reasons why such a high proportion of Darwin's time was spent on land in that continent).[24] The survey was designed to provide Britain with strategic advantage in the exploitation of new South American trading opportunities. Alfred Russel Wallace, who independently arrived at a theory of evolution by natural selection, but from a less privileged social position than Darwin, found himself involved in a rather different form of surveying: he surveyed the land in South Wales to facilitate the railway building boom of the 1840s.[25] The money he earned was put towards travel to the Rio Negro and the Amazon, to collect natural specimens – a real example of how involvement in industrial expansion could facilitate both science and individual social mobility (a point that was to be influentially made, of course, by Samuel Smiles in his 1859 *Self-Help*). And when Wallace had established himself as a naturalist, he found that a powerful savant such as Sir Roderick Murchison, working through the scientific institution of the Royal Geographical Society, could work levers of power with the Admiralty to get him free passage aboard naval and civil vessels bound for Australia and the Malay Archipelago.[26]

However, if there was a close relationship between science and colonial expansion throughout the century, the relationship did not foreclose the often unsettling character of the knowledge that was generated. Darwin's *Journal of Researches* (1839) was one of the century's best-selling travel narratives, independently of any fame (and notoriety) Darwin would attain through the *Origin*. Darwin's *Journal* in fact made an eloquent case for the aesthetic dimension of natural history and the improvement of the person who studies it, especially as part of a programme of overseas travel, a kind of exotic Grand Tour for the naturalist.[27] And yet, if Darwin continued to work with the language of Romantic science and aesthetics, the emergent picture of evolving nature was one of massive productivity. In the first edition of the *Journal*, Darwin described the South American continent as 'the great

---

24 See Janet Browne, *Charles Darwin: Voyaging* (London: Jonathan Cape, 1995), p. 181.

25 For an account of this activity, see James R. Moore, 'Wallace's Malthusian Moment: the Common Context Revisited', in Bernard Lightman (ed.), *Victorian Science in Context* (Chicago and London: University of Chicago Press, 1997), pp. 290–311.

26 Peter Raby, *Alfred Russel Wallace: A Life* (London: Chatto and Windus, 2001), pp. 88–92.

27 Charles Darwin, *Journal and Remarks: 1832–1836*, in *Narrative of the surveying voyages of His Majesty's Ships Adventure and Beagle between the years 1826 and 1836, describing their examination of the southern shores of South America, and the Beagle's circumnavigation of the globe*, 3 vols. (London: Henry Colburn, 1839), vol. III, pp. 602–8.

workshop of nature'.[28] Alongside this sense of industrial fecundity and productivity was a profound sense of waste and destruction on which the business of natural selection depended, not just in the present, but throughout a sublime chronology which had left the earth littered with bones and fossils of extinct life forms. The historic loss was as significant as the profit of continuing speciation; indeed, the latter depended on the former. Darwin's theory imagined a massively expansive nature, without necessarily establishing clear lines of progress.

A similar problem haunted Kingsley's excavations of history, which sustained the tradition of Edward Gibbon's *History of the Decline and Fall of the Roman Empire* (1776–89): expansion in the present was built upon a past civilization which had already attained power, nobility, intellectual distinction, and coherence – and degenerated. There is no doubt that Kingsley's sense of the Alexandrian empire, its dusty urban centres and the intellectual 'schools' on which it was founded was imagined as a first, pagan iteration of the British empire. Kingsley invoked the poet Alfred Tennyson as the interpreter of the logic of historical mutability and destruction: Kingsley took his epigraph for 'Alexandria and Her Schools' from the Prologue to the great elegiac poem, *In Memoriam*, in 1854 still a recently published work:

> Our little systems have their day;
> They have their day and cease to be;
> They are but broken lights of Thee;
> And Thou, O Lord, art more than they.[29]

Poetical voices, creative and critical

Throughout the century, poetry was the field of literary art in which Victorian expansion was most conspicuously registered as both an informing and disabling phenomenon. Kingsley's lectures on Alexandria became oddly important because they provided Edmund Clarence Stedman, the first author to write a critical study entitled *Victorian Poets* (1875), with an image of Alexandria that helped him to contextualize the bucolic echoes of the Alexandrian poet Theocritus that many readers could hear in Tennyson's verse. Stedman condensed Kingsley's lectures on Alexandria, Ptolemy's court, and its ambition to create 'a literary age':

---

28 *Ibid.*, p. 204.
29 Alfred Tennyson, *In Memoriam* (Prologue, lines 17–20), in *The Poems of Tennyson in Three Volumes*, ed. Christopher Ricks (London: Longman, 1987), vol. II, p. 316.

Alexandria was the centre, the new Athens, of the civilised world. But the period, if not that of a decadence, was reflective, critical, scholarly, rather than creative ... In material growth, it was indeed a 'wondrous age', an era of inventions, travel and discovery; the period of Euclid and Archimedes; of Ptolemy with his astronomers; of Hiero with his galleys long as clipper-ships; of academies, museums, theatres, lecture-halls, gymnasia; of a hundred philosophies; of geographers, botanists, casuists, scholiasts, reformers and what not – all springing into existence and finding support in the luxurious, speculative, bustling, news-devouring hurly-burly of that strangely modern Alexandrian time.[30]

It is hard to ignore the nineteenth-century resonances, and important to remember that Stedman was an American journalist and financier – as well as poet and literary historian – who wrote his study during the decade (the 1870s) when Britain's economic expansion was slowing and America's accelerating. Alexandria with its schools of philosophers and scientists, its lecture halls, museums, theatres, and journalism was, like nineteenth-century Britain and America, a manufacturer and exporter of both things and information. Poetry had to struggle to maintain its position. In Stedman's characterization of the Alexandrian age as 'critical', rather than 'creative', there is an echo of the pessimistic assessment of the place of poetry in the nineteenth century that Matthew Arnold gives in his 1865 essay 'The Function of Criticism at the Present Time'. Written later in the century, these early critical works on Victorian poetry are instructive for the terms in which they conceptualized the poetical voice, and its surrounding contexts. For instance, Hugh Walker's *The Greater Victorian Poets* (1895) compared the 'realism' of Robert Browning's dramatic mono-logues to photography.[31] Walker held that Victorian poetry was shaped by democracy, the advance in material comfort, and science.[32] But Walker's contention that Victorian poetry was above all 'practical' was a less than satisfactory answer to a troubling question: how could a refined linguistic art contribute to and survive in a culture that venerated machines and things?

---

30 Edmund Clarence Stedman, *Victorian Poets* (Boston: Houghton Mifflin, 1887), p. 208. Stedman cites from Kingsley's essay 'Alexandria and Her Schools', pp. 205–6. Stedman is responsible for one of the first usages of 'Victorian' to be cited by the *OED*; it is from this phase of his argument – the comparison between Tennyson and Theocritus – that it appears.

31 Hugh Walker, *The Greater Victorian Poets: Tennyson, Browning, Arnold* (London: Swan Sonnenschein, 1895), p. 65.

32 *Ibid.*, pp. 1–2.

In fact, though the contexts identified by Walker did indeed exert shaping power, Victorian poetry was more critically reflective, and linguistically innovative, than its late Victorian critics recognized. It has taken the more recent work of Isobel Armstrong to demonstrate the way in which the competing aesthetics of Alfred Tennyson and Robert Browning were shaped by the watershed decade of the 1830s, with its turbulent sense of reform and national crisis. Armstrong's work persuasively reconstructs the way in which, on the one hand, Browning experimented with the dramatic voice precisely to represent the identities that were being shaped and challenged by such changes, while also exploring the possibilities of representation itself; on the other, Tennyson's lyric symbolism, especially as interpreted through the criticism and theory of Arthur Hallam, was a means of testing the way in which the poetic voice could respond to and challenge utilitarian conceptions of language.[33] Such reassessments of the dramatic monologue have done much to put into question Matthew Arnold's later lament about the 'unpoetical' character that, for him, pervaded the post-Romantic nineteenth century. In the later decades of the nineteenth century, there was a tendency to dismiss the work of Tennyson, seeing it as complicit with the drive for material comfort. In John Morley's 1891 critical essay on Robert Browning's *The Ring and the Book*, Morley described Tennyson's work as representing 'the ethics of the rectory parlour set to sweet music, the respectable aspirations of the sentimental curate married to exquisite verse'. *The Ring and the Book*, by contrast, was unafraid of 'black passions, hate, cruelty, greediness, lust [and] craft'.[34] There is little doubt that Browning's great serial poem of the late 1860s represented the peak of early and mid Victorian poetic experimentalism: its retelling of a story of murder, the exploitation of women, the machinations of civil and ecclesiastical law, through an inventive use of a variety of dramatic voices to represent character perspectives, positions it firmly in the decade of the sensation novel, initiated by Wilkie Collins's *The Woman in White* (1859–60). Although the poem recalls events in late seventeenth-century Rome, it could be read as casting a refracted light on contemporary society: the central conceit of the poem concerns the way in which events recorded in an old yellowing book have

---

33 Isobel Armstrong, *Victorian Poetry: Poetics and Politics* (London: Routledge, 1993); especially chapters 1 and 2.
34 John Morley, 'On "The Ring and the Book"', in *Studies in Literature* (London: Macmillan, 1891), p. 279.

to be remade in the present by artistic crafting (the symbol of the ring). Thus is the voice of the 'British public' gently satirized for its uncritical faith in spiritual and institutional progress, which cites the main public figures of English Roman Catholicism while playing with the ideals of manliness connoted by their names:

> It's not the custom of the country. Mend
> Your ways indeed and we may stretch a point:
> Go get you manned by Manning and new-manned
> By Newman and, mayhap, wise-manned to boot
> By Wiseman, and we'll see or else we won't!
> Thanks meantime for the story, long and strong,
> A pretty piece of narrative enough . . .[35]

Poetical engagements with the corruptions of the past haunt Victorian narratives of material expansion, and spiritual and moral progress: they consciously tarnish their 'prettiness'. But poetical art also interrogated mid Victorian confidence directly, without the alibi of history. If Morley was right about Browning, his criticism of Tennyson failed to acknowledge the darker aspects of the poet's own experiments with the dramatic voice. Tennyson's *Maud: A Monodrama* (1855) is a complex dramatization of resentment and madness. *Maud* also articulated a condemnation of Victorian commercial rapaciousness, issued from the break with the celebration of the 'Thirty Years Peace' marked by the Crimean conflict: 'Why do they prate of the blessings of Peace? We have made them a curse, / Pickpockets, each hand lusting for all that is not its own.'[36] And for the speaker of the poem, disinherited by his father's financial speculations, separated from contact with his love, Maud, by his lack of fortune, the rural village into which he was born is now fatally contaminated by a seething and speculative urban culture: 'Below me, there, is the village, and looks how quiet and small! / And yet bubbles oe'r like a city, with gossip, scandal and spite.'[37] Even the early 'Ulysses' (written 1833, published 1842) is spoken by a voice that yearns for a world beyond its allotted responsibility, governance of an island in which people will be 'subdued' to the good of civilization.

---

35 Robert Browning, *The Ring and the Book*, Book I, lines 441–8, in *The Poetical Works of Robert Browning*, vol. VII, *The Ring and the Book*, Books I–IV, ed. Stefan Hawlin and Tim Burnett (Oxford: Clarendon Press, 1998), pp. 29–30.
36 *Maud* Part I, I, vi, lines 21–2, in *The Poems of Tennyson*, vol. II, p. 520.
37 *Maud*, Part I, IV, ii, lines 107–8, *ibid.*, vol. II, pp. 528–9.

Fiction: finding the voice of 'realism'

In his *Autobiographic Memoirs* (1911), Frederic Harrison observed that the Victorian novel was a document of 'eternal modernity' conveyed by a 'photographical realism' that could present a 'literal transcript of the man in the street and the woman "with a morbid past"'.[38] It was fiction, above all, that was seen as having the credentials to 'document' Victorian expansion. If Henry Mayhew initially surveyed London's relentless growth from the heights of the dome of St Paul's, 'Boz', the persona that Dickens employed at the beginning of his career, provided Mayhew with a model of 'social investigation' to follow (in fact, the *Morning Chronicle* had employed Dickens as a journalist-sketch writer before Mayhew, and some of Boz's sketches appeared in the newspaper). Between 1833 and 1836, 'Boz' had already descended to street level, listening to voices and 'sketching' actions, pastimes, and the dense fabric of urban life into narratives that were published in newspapers and magazines. As the persona developed away from Boz, reporter of the comic exploits of Pickwick, and into Dickens the master-author of the serial novel, so his perspective expanded. By the time of *The Old Curiosity Shop* (1840–1), Dickens's narrative skills took hunted Nell Trent and her grandfather on a journey away from London, first into the country-side beyond, and then into the industrialized regions of the Black Country ('tall chimneys, crowding on each other, and presenting that endless repetition of the same dull, ugly, form, which is the horror of oppressive dreams') in which they encounter the horror of the social unrest that would mark the 'Hungry Forties', where 'maddened men, armed with swords and firebrand, spurning the tears and prayers of women who would restrain them, rushed forth on errands of terror and destruction'.[39] Yet, even within these night-marish representations of material deprivation, Dickens could imagine for his readers redemptive spaces, and the way in which the material power of productivity – the furnace fire in the factory – could be idealized by the mind as a source of meaning and emotional attachment. For instance, Nell's encounter with the furnace dweller shows the way in which he finds resources of hope in his bleak surroundings. Orphaned from a young age, the fire has become both hearth and memory: '"It's like a book to me", he said – "the only book I ever learned to read; and many an old story it tells

---

38 Frederic Harrison, *Autobiographic Memoirs* (London: Macmillan, 1911), p. 28.
39 Charles Dickens, *The Old Curiosity Shop* (Oxford: Oxford University Press, 1998), chapter 34, p. 338: pp. 340–1.

me ... It's my memory, that fire, and shows me all my life ... He [his father] died before it. I saw him fall down – just there, where those ashes are burning now ..."[40] For Dickens's furnace dweller, memory is kindled as the fire 'reminds' him, through ashes, of the 'household' ancestors who have fallen before, and are yet commemorated by, the fire's enduring energy. Of course, for Dickens's character, this is his book of life, and the means by which a form of literacy becomes a presence in his existence. But for Dickens, too, this was the positive function of literature for the urban middle class: the metaphoric substitution of the ashes for the place of the fallen father is the very means by which idealized sentiment and attachment would be activated and reclaimed for a life saturated by material possessions and financial pressures.

And yet, in the face of urban expansion and change, Dickens's fictional aesthetic was not completely accepted as a credible basis for realism in fiction and the arts. Indeed, there came to prominence in the 1840s and 1850s writers who adopted a subtly different approach to the question of truth within fictional art. Elizabeth Gaskell was one of these writers; she came to prominence in 1848 with the publication of *Mary Barton*, a novel of Manchester working-class life that exemplified some of the now recognizable strategies of realism. These can be summarized as a shared set of aesthetic contentions: that drama and romance were woven into the mundane fabric of everyday life; that desire for betterment and fulfilment were in constant conflict with obstructions such as poverty, hardship, or habit; characters, such as Mary Barton and her father John, moulded by familial inheritance and shared patterns of behaviour, and yet who offer the possibility (in this case, young Mary Barton herself) of moral transformation; and a narrator who can remain sympathetically poised between all of these tensions. Such a sympathetic narrator-observer, close to and knowledgeable about the time and place of the story, announces her presence in the 'Preface' to *Mary Barton*. That said, her very attempt to eschew the ways in which her art might challenge principles of political economy, or established narratives of social cohesiveness, paradoxically illustrated the offensive potentialities of realism. Dickens himself was troubled by these challenges. Though Gaskell was cultivated by Dickens through his editorship of *Household Words*, he was not comfortable with some of Gaskell's choice of material. For instance, her narration of the event that causes the

---

40 *Ibid.*, p. 337.

Hale family's departure to the industrial town of Milton in *North and South* (1855, serialized first in *Household Words*) was felt by Dickens to be 'a difficult and dangerous subject':[41] Mr Hale, an Anglican clergyman, discourses at length on his decision to leave the established Church because he can no longer defend its privileges. Clearly, different emphases over the question of 'interest' and belonging – Elizabeth Gaskell was the wife of a dissenting (Unitarian) minister in industrial Manchester – divided fiction writers as they came to select events and episodes that best 'reflected' situational realism, but which impinged on deeply ideological questions.

In Dickens's *The Old Curiosity Shop* social and moral otherness was embodied in Quilp, the grotesque dwarf-like creature of 'diversified . . . occupations' (rent collector, ship-breaker), but in any event sustained by exploiting the commercial energy around the Port of London.[42] By contrast, Gaskell's realism was more equitably human and grounded in, as Philip Davis has observed, a 'structural complexity'.[43] This complexity attempted to grasp but reconcile the differences between social classes, cultures of work, and indeed genders. Sympathy and expanded understanding were the goals. Another emerging writer of fiction sought to theorize, aesthetically and sociologically, what Gaskell practised. In the relaunched *Westminster Review* for 1856, an anonymous review article appeared surveying Wilhelm Riehl's sociological history of central European peasantries, *The Natural History of German Life*. Riehl's work was another example of the commitment to sociological investigation and taxonomy that Mayhew's writing pioneered in Britain. When *London Labour and the London Poor* appeared in 1861, Mayhew prefaced his work on the urban working classes through ethnological categories applied to 'tribal' societies from Africa and the South Seas. Central Europe, Africa, the South Seas: the expansion of Britain was also evident in the burgeoning intellectual horizons, and the cross-cultural borrowings, that were appealed to in seeking to explain Britain's new and increasingly divergent populations to itself. As well as opening up many areas of enquiry concerning the representation of the lives of ordinary people, Eliot's review was above all a manifesto for the power of art in spreading 'social sympathies'.[44]

41 Dickens to Mrs Gaskell, [15] 17 June 1854, *Pilgrim Edition of the Letters of Charles Dickens*, ed. Graham Storey, Kathleen Tillotson, and Angus Easson 12 vols. (Oxford: Clarendon Press, 1993), vol. VII [1853–5], pp. 355–6.
42 Dickens, *Old Curiosity Shop*, chapter 4, p. 34.
43 Philip Davis, *The Victorians: 1830–1880* (Oxford University Press, 2002), p. 50.
44 [George Eliot], 'The Natural History of German Life', *Westminster Review* 66 (1856), pp. 28–44.

The essay has become recognized as perhaps the most important statement on realist aesthetics published in English in the nineteenth century, and should be seen alongside, in the sphere of the visual arts, the realist tenets of the Pre-Raphaelite Brotherhood.[45] Both theories of realism were committed to detailed representations, drawn from ordinary life, that refused conventional idealisms. The author of the review 'The Natural History of German Life' was Marian Evans, sub-editor of the *Westminster Review*, and very much attuned to metropolitan and European intellectual debate, though born and brought up in rural Warwickshire. Deeply versed in radical intellectual culture, she was the English translator of German Biblical Criticism who went on to become 'George Eliot', the novelist. If the essay's criticism of Dickens's grotesque emphasis on exteriority, combined with his tendency to idealize morality, are well known, its opening is less frequently discussed. Yet its opening curiously parallels Mayhew's fragmentary, phantasmal grasping of the sublime greatness of London. Focusing on what it revealingly calls 'picture-writing of the mind', the essay begins by mediating on the necessarily fragmentary perspective that will be revealed in any use of the term 'railways'. The great symbol of modernity, railways might give rise in a certain speaker to 'expanded views as to the multiplication of railways in the abstract ... He may talk of a vast network of railways stretching over the globe, of future "lines" in Madagascar ... [though] his distinct conceptions of on the subject do not extend beyond his one station and his indefinite length of tram-road.'[46] A fragmentary limited perspective is ironically the product of sublime, expansive modernization: only art, verbal and visual, can intercede in efforts to fill the gap. Both Marian Evans and her partner George Henry Lewes exercised a keen interest in the emerging discipline of psychology, and it was psychology that assisted them in their elaboration of a new aesthetic of realism. Lewes's book, *The Physiology of Common Life* (1859–60), was an attempt to theorize the relation between sensation, verbal articulation, and the structures of everyday life. As I have suggested, Dickens's own practice as a narrative artist sought, implicitly, to trace and stimulate similar connections. But Dickens's resistance to theorizing this art left the field open to Marian Evans, or 'George Eliot', who practised fiction in line with an intellectually refined theory.

45 James Malpas, *Realism* (London: Tate Gallery, 1997), p. 13.
46 [Eliot], 'Natural History,' p. 29.

Eliot may have begun 'The Natural History of German Life' 'picture-writing' a railway, but in her fictional narratives, the challenge of modernization was seen in the context of a 'developmental hypothesis' that simultaneously borrowed from and contributed to evolutionary thought, and its sense of both growth and loss; the paradigm was expressed through a stock of naturalistic metaphors and backdrops.[47] Eliot's early fictions, *Adam Bede* (1859) and *The Mill on the Floss* (1860) were novels, at one level, of rural and historic nostalgia, set in a late eighteenth-century village (Hayslope) or a semi-rural provincial town in the late 1820s (St Oggs): but they were also stories about the contradictory forces of development, both social and personal. For instance, the eponymous Dorlcote Mill on the Floss is powered by water, a force of nature. But engineering work and competing ownership of the water (diverting the strong flow away from Dorlcote Mill), permitted by impersonal law, represents modernity's indifference to the fate of Mr Tulliver, miller, and a headstrong, superstitious peasant 'type' straight out of Eliot's reading of Wilhelm Riehl. Tulliver's desire to educate his son, Tom, to use literacy to elevate him socially and equip him for struggle with lawyers, overlooks the potential of an intellectually talented and curious daughter, Maggie.

Middlemarch (1871), the most remarkable example of realism in English in the Victorian period, is organized by the natural metaphor of the web. Set in a provincial town during the reform movement of the early 1830s, the narrative weaves together past and present, different sectors of traditional and progressive society, and different character fates shaped by gender, generation, and education. The real weaver of the web was of course Eliot's remarkable narrative voice, which could reach inner lives, and explain determined fates and contingencies in equal measure. Eliot's realism took 'structural complexity' to new levels, and in doing so contributed powerfully to a critical understanding of uneven historical development. As we have seen, the historian Seeley would write in 1833 about the historical expansion of Britain in ways that emphasized the capacity of narrative to capture interest in a clearly delineated moral story. However, Eliot's complex narrative about provincial life during the origins of the Victorian period in the 1830s, from the perspective of the 1870s – a decade in which writers started to write self-consciously about a 'Victorian' age – challenged readers of fictional realism into a more interrogative reflection on the progress that

---

47 See Gillian Beer, *Darwin's Plots: Evolutionary Narrative in Darwin, George Eliot and Nineteenth-Century Fiction*, 3rd edn (Cambridge University Press, 2009), see in particular chapter 5, 'George Eliot: *Middlemarch*'.

they had lived through; or indeed, had perhaps failed to achieve if they were, like Dorothea Brooke, the St Theresa type of *Middlemarch*, women.

Gender and fiction: the woman's voice

Realism, in the hands of both Gaskell and Eliot, was at the heart of fiction that was committed to the spread of social sympathy. The characters who were best able to embody and diffuse sympathy were generally women. In *North and South*, Margaret Hale mediates between the working-class Higginses, and the factory-owner Thornton. In *The Mill on the Floss* Maggie Tulliver mediates between the Tullivers and the middle-class professional Wakems, though in this instance, the consequences are tragic and cannot move beyond the social and, in particular, patriarchal restrictions that bear down on Maggie. But if realist fiction called for and imagined expanded horizons, the obstructive social, economic, legal, and educational restrictions experienced by Victorian middle-class women were in danger of excluding them from modernity's forward-moving settlement.

A focus on the single woman, and a submerged and tentative exploration of what feminists would later identify and name as 'patriarchy', produced a different, perhaps even awkward, fictional voice. Charlotte Brontë offers a particularly strong example of those writers – poets as well as novelists, men as well as women – who experimented powerfully with the first-person female voice in order to explore communities of 'interest' in an expanding, yet still constrictive, nation. Charlotte Brontë's *Villette* (1853) is a novel that is, in one sense, about the difficulty of binding one particular voice – that of Lucy Snowe, without family, single, in need of employment – into a 'greater Britain' that in practice denied her an active and meaningful sense of belonging outside of family and marriage.

When Lucy departs from England, she departs for the continent to 'Labassecour' (Belgium), and the town of 'Villette' (Brussels), where she becomes a schoolteacher. The chapter in which she becomes an export of 'Greater Britain' overseas is one of vocal complexity and contradiction. It provides us with another perspective on our starting point, Henry Mayhew atop St Paul's Cathedral, seeing a phantasmal vision of London, and glimpsing romantic visions of an expanding urban and colonial Britain beyond it. Lucy Snowe travels to London, which she first experiences as a Babylon. In the morning, though, she wakes, at her hotel in the City of London:

> The next day was the first of March, and when I awoke, rose and opened my curtain, I saw the risen sun struggling through fog. Above my head,

above the house-tops, co-elevate almost with the clouds, I saw a solemn, orbed mass, dark-blue and dim – THE DOME. While I looked, my inner self moved; my spirit shook its always-fettered wings half loose; I had a sudden feeling as if I, who had never yet truly lived, were at last to taste life; in that morning my soul grew as fast as Jonah's gourd.[48]

While Mayhew became animated and excited by the view of London from the heights of the dome of the cathedral, Lucy is moved by the vision of the dome itself, as it emerges from the mist and fog, set against the infinite promise of the sky. However, the Protestant Lucy Snowe, steeped in the Bible, would know that while her soul grew as fast as 'Jonah's gourd', God also made the worm that would wither the gourd the next day (Book of Jonah, 4:6, 8): in the same way in which Mayhew's descriptive powers appeal at once both to realism and romance, privileging the ideal and the romantic, Lucy Snowe's sense of 'imperial promise' is brought back to the earthy, the prosaic. The power of phantasmal visuality as it appropriates a territory is to be regarded suspiciously. This is Lucy as she voyages up the Thames Estuary and the English Channel in the steam packet, tellingly named *The Vivid*:

> Deep was the pleasure I drank in with the sea-breeze; divine the delight I drew from the heaving channel waves, from the sea-birds on the ridge, from the white sails on their dark distance, from the quiet, yet beclouded sky, overhanging all. In my reverie methought I saw the continent of Europe, like a wide dream-land, far away. Sunshine lay on it, making the long coast one line of gold; tiniest tracery of clustered town and snow-gleaming tower, of woods, deep-massed, of heights serrated, of smooth pasturage and veiny stream, embossed the metal-bright prospect. For background, spread a sky, solemn and dark-blue, and – grand with imperial promise, soft with tints of enchantment – strode from north to south a God-bent bow, the arch of hope.
>
> Cancel the whole of that, if you please, reader – or rather let it stand, and draw thence a moral – an alliterative, text-hand copy – 'Day-dreams are delusions of the demon'.
>
> Becoming excessively sick, I faltered down into the cabin.[49]

The woman novelist knows how the script might be written by more confident public voices, or perhaps, acknowledging the way the verbal intersected with the visual in Victorian culture, how the heroic scene should

---

48 Charlotte Brontë, *Villette* (London: Penguin Classics, 2004), chapter 6, p. 47.
49 *Ibid.*, pp. 62–3.

be visualized and painted ('For background, spread a sky, solemn and dark-blue'). But her voice jolts the reader into a reversal by breaking down into self-conscious self-censure: debilitating sea-sickness is the outcome of this voyage of self-discovery.

Conclusion: the expansion of literature

Three years before the publication of Lucy Snowe's fictionalized voyage to Belgium, the Belgian nation, along with many others, joined Britain's great celebration of world peace through trade, and displayed its arts and luxury goods at the Great Exhibition of 1851. *The Illustrated London News* carried an entire 'Supplement' on the Exhibition (6 March 1852) which included an illustration of the great variety of objects that Belgium displayed. The objects depicted ranged from 'Framed Mirrors' to 'Busts of [the] King and Queen of the Belgians', and 'Velvet Pile Carpet'. Britain, France, and Belgium: all these northern European states were expanding industrial nations and centres of middle-class economic power and consumption by 1851. Negatively, the Great Exhibition might be seen as a crushing realization of Carlyle's prophecy of 'literature' itself becoming a mechanism. The *Official Catalogue* of the Exhibition declared grandly that literature represented 'a species of industry . . . [that] carr[ies] the productions of the human mind over the whole world, and may be called the raw materials of every kind of science and art, and of all social improvement'.[50] Accordingly the Exhibition displayed raw materials, engines of production, and elaborately finished objects; steam presses, rolls of paper, the materials of bookbinding, and occasionally an aptly named, pious specimen book (such as *The Victoria Book of Common Prayer*). But literature as a complex mode of symbolizing culture nonetheless enacted an energetic and expansive capacity to take command of the base materials that comprised it, and mechanisms that produced and displayed it, converting them into 'voices' that could indeed be disseminated 'over the whole world'. The *Official Catalogue* displayed evidence of the fact. The second volume of the work carried, as an Appendix, not only the review of the *Catalogue* by the *Times* (13 September 1851) but a characteristically inventive review published in Dickens's *Household Words* (23 August 1851). The review endowed this compendious catalogue of abundant things with nothing less than a voice, dramatizing the relationship

---

50 *Official Descriptive and Illustrated Catalogue of the Great Exhibition of the Works of All Nations*, 3 vols. (London: Royal Commission, 1851), vol. II, p. 536.

between text and audience: 'I am a catalogue of the Great Exhibition. You are the public.' Having announced itself to 'the public' in this way, the voice of the sublimely compendious catalogue went on allusively, but also perhaps a little darkly, to acknowledge that it had always been in danger of becoming 'a monster like that chronicled in Frankenstein'.[51]

The 'public' was, of course, a heterogeneous entity by 1851; Dickens's magazine was one of the new popular publications that would seek to capture and organize middlebrow taste throughout the 1850s and 1860s (it would be succeeded by *All the Year Round*, *Cornhill*, and *Macmillan's*). One could moreover argue that the expanding society of Victorian Britain was, by 1851, in danger of revealing its own 'monstrous' embodiment: an uneasy union stitched together artificially from many different centres of class and ideological 'interest'. Middlebrow publications containing imaginative literature and entertaining 'instruction' had to jostle with writings that sought to address deep spiritual, political, intellectual, and gender differences. While the Great Exhibition opened to celebrate a world seemingly at one with itself over industrialism and free trade, the radical working-class call for Chartist democracy had been marginalized only a couple of years earlier. In 1851, a Woman's Suffrage petition was delivered to the House of Lords. Just two years later (1853) Thomas Carlyle would republish, as a precursor to his vitriolic 'Latter-day Pamphlets', his notorious 'Occasional Discourse on the Nigger Question', which dismissed liberal philanthropy and a mission of 'improvement' in the colonies; freed black slaves could not, by virtue of their 'nature', be reformed by a liberal, emancipationist ideology when they failed to acknowledge mastery and the harsher lessons of the 'Gospel of Work'.[52] Historians and literary critics from the 1870s onwards fashioned unified stories to explain both the expansion of Britain, and the way in which it conditioned a distinctively 'Victorian' literature. These built on modes of historiographical understanding that had taken shape as early as the 1840s. While these stories remain important reference points, the troubled creative energies that recast poetry and prose between 1830 and the late 1860s tell a more conflicted tale.

---

51 *Ibid.*, pp. 5–6.
52 The essay first appeared in *Fraser's Magazine* (1849); see Thomas Carlyle, *Critical and Miscellaneous Essays*, IV, in *Works: Centenary Edition*, ed. H. D. Traill, 30 vols. (London: Chapman and Hall, 1899), vol. XXXIX, pp. 348–83: p. 367.

5

High Victorianism

JANICE CARLISLE

One day late in November of 1859, Matthew Arnold decided to stay home for dinner. Doing so, he thought, would keep his 'cook's hand in', but Arnold had another reason for taking an early meal: that evening he was planning to participate in the drill exercises of his amateur rifle corps, the Queen's Volunteers, which met three times a week in Westminster Hall.[1] Like a number of his fellow writers – Thomas Hughes, William Morris, and Dante Gabriel Rossetti – Arnold was taking part in the volunteer movement, one of the most revealing oddities of high-Victorian culture. Although members of this force were sometimes mocked for their military incompetence and their vanity – the chance to wear fanciful uniforms was one of its many attractions – most contemporaries viewed the volunteers as a serious response to the threat to British security posed by the ambitions of Napoleon III and the eagerness of the French military to build a steam-powered, iron-clad fleet. Reacting to fears of a French invasion, Parliament moved quickly in May of 1859 to authorize the formation of units of volunteer riflemen who would be trained to defend the southern coast of England. By 1861, forty-eight members of Parliament had joined up, a figure that almost tripled between 1868 and 1880. The movement, however, was less remarkable for the noteworthy individuals whose efforts it engaged than for the numbers of otherwise ordinary men who chose to enlist. Enrolling approximately 100,000 men in its first year, this Victorian auxiliary army rose in strength to 200,000 by the 1870s.[2] It therefore virtually equaled in size and arguably exceeded in visibility the regular army, half of whose units were at any given time stationed overseas.

---

1 Matthew Arnold, *The Letters of Matthew Arnold*, ed. Cecil Y. Lang, 6 vols. (Charlottesville: University of Virginia Press, 1996–2001), vol. I, p. 507; p. 508, n.1.
2 Ian F. W. Beckett, *The Amateur Military Tradition 1558–1945* (Manchester University Press, 1991), p. 192; Hugh Cunningham, *The Volunteer Force: A Social and Political History 1859–1908* (London: Croom Helm, 1975), pp. 15, 2.

This episode in the annals of Victorian military and cultural life – perhaps more important to the latter than to the former – illustrates the need to recognize the difference between literary history and other varieties of historical inquiry. The appearances of the volunteer force in what have been traditionally defined as literary texts – fiction, poetry, non-fiction prose – are relatively fugitive and slight. Arnold reportedly composed 'Rugby Chapel' during drill practice,[3] but if that was the case, its concluding metaphor of life as a march is the only testament to the poem's origins. The volunteer movement is central to the plot of Charlotte Mary Yonge's *The Trial* (1864), the sequel to her better-known *The Daisy Chain* (1856); and the forming of the force occasioned one of Alfred, Lord Tennyson's minor, anonymous effusions, 'Riflemen Form!' in which he asks Englishmen to ready themselves for the coming battle against the French 'despot'.[4] Beyond a brief mention in Anthony Trollope's *Can You Forgive Her?* (1864–5) and two dismissive references in George Meredith's *Beauchamp's Career* (1874–5), however, the volunteer force hardly appears in the pages of canonical Victorian literature. In addition, the evidence about the movement in literary texts is generally misleading. *The Trial* is typical of the tendency to offer unreliable representations of the nature of this amateur army: by portraying membership in the volunteers as a distinctively genteel activity, Yonge largely ignores its most telling characteristic. Although the force was conceived initially as a middle-class institution, it quickly became evident that it could respond effectively to the feared massing of French troops on British shores only if men of the working classes enlisted in large numbers. Consequently, mill owners enrolled their factory operatives; landlords, their tenants and labourers. By 1862 in many areas of England and Scotland, members of the working classes constituted the majority of the volunteers.[5] Tennyson's poem seems to prophesy this development when it enjoins the men of England to take up arms:

> Let your reforms for a moment go!
> Look to your butts, and take good aims!
> Better a rotten borough or so
> Than a rotten fleet and a city in flames![6]

---

3 Park Honan, *Matthew Arnold* (New York: McGraw-Hill, 1981), p. 296. Although this poem is dated November 1857, it was probably written later since it seems to respond to an attack on Thomas Arnold that had not been published at that time; see Ian Hamilton, *A Gift Imprisoned: The Poetic Life of Matthew Arnold* (London: Bloomsbury, 1998), p. 199.
4 Alfred, Lord Tennyson, 'Riflemen Form!' in *The Poems of Tennyson*, ed. Christopher Ricks, 3 vols. (Harlow: Longman, 1987), vol. II, p. 603, line 11.
5 Cunningham, *The Volunteer Force*, p. 25.
6 Tennyson, *Poems*, vol. II, p. 603, lines 15–18.

When the poem asks its readers to attend to their 'butts', the embankments that were built for rifle practice, instead of promoting Parliamentary reform, Tennyson is offering a typically middle-class perspective on the volunteer force: devoting time to its activities, it was hoped, would distract workers from thinking about the need to extend the franchise or eliminate the 'rotten boroughs' that remained long after the passage of the Reform Act of 1832.

The distance between the nature as well as the number of the traces of the volunteer movement in literary texts and those in other contemporary records suggests that 'Mind the Gap', the iconic slogan of the London Tube, might well become the watchword for anyone writing literary history. The sense of potentially misleading divides is everywhere. Some of the more obvious are temporal or national in origin. The bathos of Tennyson's 'Riflemen Form!' is more evident now than it would have been in 1859 and still more so for some American readers than for most British. Disciplinary perspectives create other kinds of gaps, such as the one between literary-historical conceptions of nineteenth-century experience and accounts of so-called real Victorian phenomena. Yet in the case of the volunteers, the difference between past and present viewpoints remains arguably more significant: despite the fact that notices and illustrations of volunteer activities year after year filled the pages of both the *Illustrated London News* and *Punch*,[7] recent historians of Victorian Britain have been even more silent about the force than were most of Tennyson's fellow writers. In this discussion of the high-Victorian period, defined here as the time span between the late 1850s and the late 1870s, analysis of the canonical, largely middle-class literature that still represents the Victorian age to most readers can offer only a limited perspective on the historical realities of these decades, but it is, I think, a perspective that cannot be found elsewhere.

In making this argument, I am engaging in the kind of cultural analysis for which Raymond Williams set out an agenda in *The Long Revolution*. There he refers famously to the 'structure of feeling' to which both the 'documentary culture', such as literary texts, and the 'dominant social character' of a period can provide access. Although Williams's use of these terms shifts during the course of his discussion, he does not waver in his conviction that his approach allows one at least to begin to apprehend the patterns and the relationships between patterns that define a 'whole way of life'. Taking the

---

7 See Janice Carlisle, *Picturing Reform in Victorian Britain* (Cambridge University Press, 2012), ch. 3.

1840s as his exemplary object of inquiry, Williams identifies its 'dominant social character' as the ascendancy of the values championed by 'the industrial and commercial middle class' – among them, hard work, sobriety, and domesticity. Responding to a society defined by its devotion to 'success and money', the literature of the 1840s, according to Williams, witnessed to a quite different kind of reality: 'Man alone, afraid, a victim.'[8] The conjunction of these contradictory attitudes constitutes for Williams the structure of feeling typical of the 1840s.

A similarly distinctive form of affective response, what I call impersonal or cultural nostalgia, was repeatedly expressed by professional writers during the high-Victorian decades. In his role as a political commentator, Walter Bagehot remarked in 1872 that the English are 'so very miscellaneous a people' that whenever they agree on a matter, that consensus must be taken seriously.[9] British writers were no less 'miscellaneous' a group, with such different experiences, temperaments, and talents that it is hard to imagine that they could ever have seen the phenomena of their contemporaneous culture with anything like a single vision, but to a remarkable extent they did. Although this account, then, seems to ignore the eccentric and the bizarre by finding in diverse texts their commonalities, the fact that a pattern emerges so clearly is itself, like the volunteer force, a notable sign of high-Victorian times – a relatively large-scale movement of opinion and effort joined in a common, if uncoordinated, response to similar conditions. Examining how and why texts written in the 1860s and 1870s consistently evoked an anxious and paradoxically forward-looking regret identifies some of the sources of that 'structure of feeling' and specifies its relation to the 'dominant social character' of those decades. Although literature, as Williams recognized, cannot provide full access to what he called the 'felt sense of the quality of life at a particular place and time',[10] high-Victorian literary texts do let one, if not cross the divide between past and present, at least imagine what it might have felt like to inhabit the territory on its other side.

Most commentators, both then and now, have agreed that during the decade following the Great Exhibition of 1851, Victorian Britain, by one definition or another, came into its own. The note of self-congratulation that had accompanied accounts of the success of the spectacles housed in the

---

8 Raymond Williams, *The Long Revolution* (New York: Columbia University Press, 1961), pp. 48, 66, 46–7, 61, 68.
9 Walter Bagehot, 'Introduction to the Second Edition', in *The English Constitution*, intro. R. H. S. Crossman (Ithaca, NY: Cornell University Press, 1963), p. 280.
10 Williams, *The Long Revolution*, p. 47.

Crystal Palace was heard again in the following decades: *The Times*, for instance, announced in 1865 that the nation was enjoying 'an epoch of unbroken peace and unparalleled prosperity'.[11] To a large extent, the present seemed to deserve celebration simply because its conditions were not those of the recent past. The contrast between the Britain of the 1860s and 1870s and the country in the 1830s and 1840s and even the mid-1850s seemed an irrefutable argument for pride. The Hungry Forties, the political threats posed by Chartism, and the war in the Crimea were quickly becoming bad memories. Even outrage over the 1865 uprising at Morant Bay in Jamaica and its bloody aftermath did not compare with the horrified responses to the Indian Rebellion of 1857. Similarly, the unrest that attended the passage of the Second Reform Act in 1867, by no means negligible, was less widespread and violent than it had been when the various first reform bills were being debated, even though the later measure was considerably bolder, almost doubling the number of those enfranchised to a third of adult men, including virtually all the workers living in the boroughs of England and Wales. Equally persuasive was the contrast between Britain's present economic might and the inferiority of the rest of the world. Producing half the world's output of iron and more steel than all European countries combined, Britain dominated shipbuilding and shipping, originating a quarter of the world's trade by 1860. As historians now conclude, 'in a commercial sense . . . Britain was *the* world power'; 'so striking a "dominance" is unique in modern economic history'.[12]

If such perspectives on the high-Victorian period were gratifying to contemporaries, its status in relation to the future known only to descendants of the Victorians is perhaps even more flattering. To call the twenty or so years before the 1880s 'high' Victorian suggests a particular visual image, that of a peak, a mountain whose summit has been reached, from which only descent, in all directions, is possible. Historical hindsight justifies the use of the adjective 'high' in ways that revivify this dead metaphor. Signs of the coming decline are now routinely remarked upon by historians of this period. Despite its unimpeachable economic superiority, Britain's ability to influence political developments on the Continent was lessening; as early as

---

11 *The Times*, 19 October 1865, p. 7.

12 Eric Hobsbawm, *The Age of Capital 1848–1875* (New York: Vintage, 1996), p. 40; Keith Robbins, *The Eclipse of a Great Power: Modern Britain 1870–1992*, 2nd edn (London: Longman, 1994), p. 50; K. Theodore Hoppen, *The Mid-Victorian Generation 1846–1886* (Oxford: Clarendon Press, 1998), p. 155; Eric J. Evans, *The Forging of the Modern State: Early Industrial Britain 1783–1870*, 3rd edn (Harlow: Longman, 2001), p. 426.

1864, according to one account, it had 'ceased ... to be a great *European power* at all'.[13] Britain's loss of its industrial dominance at the end of the century was presaged in the 1860s by its relative lack of scientific experimentation and technical training, areas in which Germany and the United States already excelled.[14] Many historians also subscribe to the view that Britain reached not only its peak during this period, but also a point of stasis or balance. The argument of W. L. Burn's *The Age of Equipoise*, the most influential formulation of this characterization, is still being debated, yet historians often write of 'the "golden age" of paternal, dynastic European capitalism between 1850 and 1875' or a period of 'exceptionally peaceful class relations'.[15] The trials of the coming decades – a period when threats posed by Irish nationalism, working-class socialism, and an expanding empire evoked increasingly violent reprisals – make sense of the application of such glowing epithets to the conditions of the 1860s and 1870s. From the current, ever-increasingly distant retrospect that frequently sees this period through the lens of world wars and genocide and environmental disaster, high-Victorian Britain often appears more and more stable, more and more golden.

That was not the way it always seemed at the time, however, and literary texts offer a way of closing the gap between then and now by providing a more mobile and less aureate sense of the high-Victorian decades. If not all of Thomas Carlyle's contemporaries joined him in fearing that 'our poor old England' was rushing blindly toward 'malodorous quagmires' of political chaos and uninhibited freethinking, as he opined in the pamphlet *Shooting Niagara: And After?* (1867),[16] many of them describe the present as an era of bewildering change. 'Perplexed' is the adjective routinely used to identify

---

13 Evans, *The Forging of the Modern State*, pp. 419–28; on Britain as no longer a 'great power', see Hoppen, *The Mid-Victorian Generation*, p. 166.
14 For an influential, but widely debated thesis, see Martin J. Wiener, *English Culture and the Decline of the Industrial Spirit 1850–1980* (Cambridge University Press, 1981). See also Hoppen, *The Mid-Victorian Generation*, pp. 286–7, 307–10.
15 Patrick Joyce, *Work, Society and Politics: The Culture of the Factory in Late Victorian England* (Brighton: Harvester, 1980), pp. xiv, 136; Harold Perkin, *Origins of Modern English Society* (London: Routledge, 1969), p. 345. W. L. Burn's study *The Age of Equipoise: A Study of the Mid-Victorian Generation* (New York: Norton, 1965) is the classic statement of this position. See two collections of essays devoted to the question of whether Britain had attained stasis or balance by mid-century: Ian Inkster *et al.* (eds.), *The Golden Age: Essays in British Social and Economic History 1850–1870* (Aldershot and Burlington, VT: Ashgate, 2000); Martin Hewitt (ed.), *An Age of Equipoise? Reassessing Mid-Victorian Britain* (Aldershot: Ashgate, 2000).
16 Thomas Carlyle, *Shooting Niagara: And After?* (London: Chapman and Hall, 1867), pp. 22, 55.

both the times and those living in them. Looking back in 1872 on the previous decade, Bagehot wrote impressively of the 'change since 1865 [as] a change not in one point but in one thousand points ... a change not of particular details but of pervading spirit'; and he noted that any contemporary commentator on the British constitution 'who tries to paint what is before him is puzzled and perplexed: what he sees is changing daily'. Frances Power Cobbe, contemplating the justice that should obtain in relations between the strong and the weak, complained, 'we, in our day, are perplexed and well nigh overwhelmed with the difficulties presented to us'. From Walter Pater's perspective, 'gem-like flame[s]' were rare; more easily observed was 'the gaudy, perplexed light of modern life'. Such comments validate the view of contemporary life that Arnold offered in his first lecture as the Chair of poetry at Oxford, which he published in 1869: without the 'intellectual deliverance' so obviously required by it, the present could evoke only 'that impatient irritation of mind which we feel in the presence of an immense, moving, confused spectacle which, while it perpetually excites our curiosity, perpetually baffles our comprehension'.[17]

The sense of the present as a time of perplexing change suggests that the so-called age of equipoise was anything but. The 1860s and 1870s were marked by an economic, intellectual, political, and technological dynamism that was preparing the way for future developments at an astonishing speed, moving propulsively towards the feminism, Labour politics, and global conflicts that can be seen as its logical outcomes. Many of the elements of the modern world now taken for granted – from high-powered explosives and high-speed communications, department stores, national holidays, ready-made clothes, subways, and team sports, to party politics and corporate capitalism – had their origins in high-Victorian inventions and innovations. Everywhere one looked during those years, one could see ways in which political and economic and cultural life in all its varieties was being atomized, professionalized, centralized, codified, and commercialized. Even the volunteer movement reflects such developments. What began as relatively independent and locally based 'rifle clubs' of middle-class men, supported by private donations, soon became subject to the government control and oversight that went along with government funding. Rifles

---

17 Bagehot, *The English Constitution*, pp. 268, 276. Frances Power Cobbe, 'Criminals, Idiots, Women, and Minors', *Fraser's Magazine* 78 (1868), p. 778. Walter Pater, *The Renaissance: Studies in Art and Poetry*, ed. Donald L. Hill (Berkeley: University of California Press, 1980), pp. 189, 182; Matthew Arnold, 'On the Modern Element in Literature' (lecture delivered in 1857), *Macmillan's Magazine* 19 (1869), p. 305.

were issued to working-class participants, corps were organized into battalions and brigades, practices were supervised by paid drill sergeants from the regular army, and the efficiency of individual units was judged and rewarded by government inspectors – all these changes foretelling the time when defending the nation, both homeland and empire, would become a burden increasingly borne by reserve armies. Like similar developments in education, religion, transport, and communications, the dizzyingly rapid transformation of the present into the future, affecting both the sense of national destiny and the feel of everyday life, might well have seemed deeply perplexing.

Those living through and with such changes often managed to cope with them by looking to the past, by seeming to avert their gazes from what was, in Arnold's words, 'an immense, moving, confused spectacle'. If the structure of feeling characteristic of the high-Victorian period is built around a single emotion, nostalgia, the forms that such a longing takes are often, in appropriately Victorian fashion, ornate and even contradictory. As Svetlana Boym explains, nostalgia often predominates in post-revolutionary periods as a response to profoundly felt changes; and it became in the nineteenth century a 'historical emotion', an 'incurable disease' suffered by a culture rather than a 'treatable' illness of homesick individuals.[18] Much of the criticism dealing with the role of memory in Victorian literature has identified the source of its 'elegiac' spirit in recognitions of 'personal loss'.[19] Without doubt the high-Victorian period, like the larger historical era of which it is a part, was well populated with individuals who ached to recapture their personal pasts – autobiographies begun or published during the 1860s and 1870s by John Henry Newman, John Ruskin, and Margaret Oliphant speak to the power of that impulse. Yet the extent to which writers during these decades exhibited symptoms of nostalgia as a condition suffered by the culture as a whole demonstrates how quickly many of those in the high-Victorian period felt themselves to be hurtling towards the future, towards a time when nostalgia would take on a specifically postmodern valence, becoming, in Arjun Appadurai's terms, 'nostalgia without memory', a longing for a past of which one has had no personal experience. Such an emotion, as Appadurai theorizes, transforms the past into

---

18 Svetlana Boym, *The Future of Nostalgia* (New York: Basic Books, 2001), pp. xvi, 7.
19 John D. Rosenberg, *Elegy for an Age: The Presence of the Past in Victorian Literature* (London: Anthem Press, 2005), p. 4. After briefly treating the effects of the 'dizzying present', Rosenberg turns to 'the particularities of certain writers' lives' (pp. 2–3).

'a synchronic warehouse of cultural scenarios, a kind of temporal central casting, to which recourse can be had as appropriate'.[20] Victorian writers repeatedly turned to such a cultural storehouse of images, actions, and figures from a past that they knew only through their imaginations of it.

The patently nostalgic responses of high-Victorian literature are only rarely simple-minded or naively escapist, contrary to typically dismissive ways of thinking about this emotion. Charles Dickens's Jenny Wren, the impoverished dolls' dressmaker of *Our Mutual Friend* (1864–5), is the unlikely avatar of this form of cultural memory. By insisting that she can actually smell the aroma of 'all sorts of flowers that I was never among', she recreates a rural English countryside that evokes a simpler past that she has never experienced. Yet her imaginative recreation of a fantastical realm – a place where the fragrances of flowers that bloom in different seasons mingle impossibly with each other – offers her physical pleasures as she continues to 'work, work, work' in what she never forgets is 'not a flowery neighbourhood'.[21] Even the most gorgeous visions of former times do not ignore the divide between then and now. Morris famously tells the readers of *The Earthly Paradise* (1868–70) to leave behind the present:

> Forget six counties overhung with smoke,
> Forget the snorting steam and piston stroke,
> Forget the spreading of the hideous town;
> Think, rather, of the pack-horse on the down,
> And dream of London, small, and white, and clean,
> And the clear Thames bordered by its gardens green . . .

Yet the next nine lines of the poem go on to describe that simpler medieval England in palpably modern terms: it is the centre of global trade, with its imports of Levantine spices and Italian cloth; and Chaucer, its greatest poet, is a commercial clerk who composes, not immortal verse, but 'bills of lading'.[22] As this example suggests, the ache of longing for the past expressed in high-Victorian literature often establishes complex interrelations between past and present, thereby transforming nostalgia into an emotion that indirectly – but sometimes boldly – confronts the unknown and presumably

---

20 Arjun Appadurai, 'Disjuncture and Difference in the Global Economy', in Bruce Robbins (ed.), *The Phantom Public Sphere* (Minneapolis: University of Minnesota Press, 1993), pp. 272–3.
21 Charles Dickens, *Our Mutual Friend* (London: Penguin, 1997), Book the Second, chapter 2, pp. 237–8.
22 William Morris, 'Prologue', *The Earthly Paradise*, ed. Florence S. Boos, 2 vols. (New York: Routledge, 2002), vol. I, pp. 69–70, lines 1–6, 15.

more distressing demands of the future. This temporal interplay characterizes even those moments of backward longing most tinged with sadness
and most suffused by wish-fulfilment. When Arnold speaks in *Culture and
Anarchy* (1869) of 'the Oxford of the past' and of himself as one 'brought up
amidst the beauty and sweetness of that beautiful place', he describes a
university that he could not have known in the 1840s: when he was a student
and then a fellow there, internecine wars were being waged over Newman's
feared and then finally accomplished apostasy. Yet Arnold insists on speaking of Oxford in its current 'defeat . . . isolation . . . [and] want of hold on the
modern world' as an institution capable of 'prepar[ing] currents of feeling'
that will undermine liberalism and therefore 'ke[ep] up our own communications with the future'. Like Ruskin insisting in *Sesame and Lilies* (1865) that
heeding 'the words of the dead' allows one to move forward, to 'advance'
and 'become . . . increasingly' 'great in life', Arnold hopes that remembering
the Oxford of the past, even as the site of failure and defeated ambitions, is a
way of reaching out towards the future.[23]

How terrifying that future seemed to many high-Victorian writers is
revealed by one of the most extreme forms of a longing for the past in this
period, a structure of feeling that I call proleptic nostalgia: a temporal
inversion that involves imagining a time in the future, usually after one
has died, when the present will have become the past. What might appear to
be a highly personal perspective on the relation between time and consciousness actually becomes, by virtue of its typicality in high-Victorian
literature, a kind of cultural trope in which the future, drained of its
potential threats, becomes the locus of a sometimes anodyne contentment.
Examples of this variety of 'nostalgia without memory' abound: Jenny Wren
asks one of her companions to join her in an imagined post-mortal state by
calling out repeatedly, 'Come up and be dead!'; Charles Darwin writes his
autobiography in 1876 'as if I were a dead man in another world looking
back on my own life'; and Robert Browning's Pompilia, the young and
saintly heroine of *The Ring and the Book* (1868–9), tries to see her life 'by a
light / That's later than my life-time', from the viewpoint of her son when
he will have reached the age at which she dies. Similarly, in Christina
Rossetti's 'Song' ('When I am dead, my dearest') – as in several other lyrics

23 Matthew Arnold, *Culture and Anarchy*, ed. Samuel Lipman (New Haven, CT: Yale
   University Press, 1994), p. 42; John Ruskin, *Sesame and Lilies, The Collected Works of John
   Ruskin*, ed. E. T. Cook and Alexander Wedderburn, Library Edition, 39 vols. (London:
   George Allen, 1912), vol. xviii, pp. 98–9.

in her 1862 collection, *Goblin Market and Other Poems* – the speaker imagines a disembodied future in which it will not matter whether 'I shall' be remembered or forgotten. Such moments evoke the strong appeal of an imagined future peace, which Jenny Wren can convey only through an oxymoron: 'you feel as if you were dead ... and such a strange good sorrowful happiness comes upon you!'[24]

Paradoxically, however, proleptic nostalgia often emphasizes the present that it attempts to turn prematurely into the past. The famous conclusion to Pater's *The Renaissance* (1873), which first appeared as a review in 1868, invites its readers to see their current lives from the vantage point of their inevitable deaths: being able to imagine how the present will look from the perspective of a future insensibility becomes a way of encouraging 'a quickened, multiplied consciousness' in the here and now. Proleptic nostalgia can even open up the possibility of one's living a counterfactual present. The title character of Browning's poem 'James Lee's Wife' (1864) longs for a future in which she will have died of 'joy' because her husband has loved her: 'Could I fancy "As I feel, thus feels he"', the annihilating and loveless present, she speculates, will have been replaced by a past for the experience of which death is a small price to pay. To opposite effect, the speaker in Dante Gabriel Rossetti's *The House of Life* (1870) imagines the future in which 'after death' he will be able to view, as if they had material bodies, the 'lost days of my life': 'God knows I know the faces I shall see, / Each one a murdered self.'[25] He may dread a future in which his potential selves, 'murdered' by his actions or inactions, will haunt him. Yet this peculiar form of retrospection, possible only in a future that does not exist, makes the present a time of chilling certainty rather than harassing doubt: the speaker already knows what he will see after death, and, more important, he knows what God now knows.

---

24 Dickens, *Our Mutual Friend*, Book the Second, chapter 6, p. 280; Charles Darwin, *Autobiography*, in Charles Darwin and Thomas Henry Huxley, *Autobiographies* (Oxford University Press, 1983), p. 8; Robert Browning, *The Ring and the Book*, in *The Poetical Works of Robert Browning*, vol. VIII, ed. Stefan Hawlin and T. A. J. Burnett (Oxford: Clarendon Press, 2001), Book VII, p. 235, lines 634–5; Christina Rossetti, 'Song', *Poems and Prose* (Oxford University Press, 2008), pp. 21–2, line 9. Cf. Christina Rossetti, 'After Death' and 'Remember', pp. 26, 27–8. Dickens, *Our Mutual Friend*, Book the Second, chapter 6, p. 279.

25 Pater, *The Renaissance*, p. 190; Robert Browning, 'James Lee's Wife', in *Selected Poems* (London: Penguin, 2001), 'On Deck', p. 156, line 367; Dante Gabriel Rossetti, *The House of Life*, *Collected Writings*, ed. Jan Marsh (London: J. M. Dent, 1999), stanza LXXXVI, 'Lost Days', p. 318, lines 9, 1, 10–11.

Such instances of proleptic nostalgia, of imagining an emotion before one can have experienced it, suggest the extent to which other, more conventional forms of this affect involve an anxious consciousness of both the future over which one has no control and a recognition of the realities of the present. In high-Victorian literature a number of specific subjects tend to offer occasions for impersonal nostalgia. While the emotions evoked by the topics that I treat here – historic cultures, heroism, and workers – identify a distinctive 'felt sense of the quality of life' in the 1860s and 1870s, they also speak to the desire of high-Victorian writers to distance themselves and their work from the increasing commercialism of their times. To revert to the far away and long ago, even when doing so acknowledges the here and now, is to try to establish literature as a realm to which crass money-getting has relatively little relevance. That was, of course, precisely not the case in high-Victorian Britain. The historian K. Theodore Hoppen has described 'The Business of Culture' that characterized this period: publishing, painting, running theatres, and managing music halls were increasingly arenas of big business that at times paid very well. The book trade, requiring more and more capital investment, could yield higher and higher profits. Best-selling authors, including playwrights who learned from the 1860s onwards to negotiate for themselves a share of a production's profits, often amassed significant wealth.[26] When Tennyson could earn £8,000 in one year from the sales of *Enoch Arden, &c.* (1864) and when George Eliot was paid £7,000 for the publication and six-year copyright of *Romola* (1863)[27] – both works, significantly, telling stories set in the more or less distant past – literature was, if nothing else, a form of commerce. Those writers who most consistently shared with their readers their nostalgic longings, impersonal or otherwise, were, arguably, the most highly rewarded. For professional writers, 'nostalgia without memory' was appealing, at least in part, because it distinguished their work from the tawdry concerns of getting and spending even as it indirectly acknowledged the realities of a world in which money and the status that it bought could seem at times to be, as Karl Marx explained in the first volume of *Capital* (1867), all that mattered.

The Victorian taste for depictions and recreations of the past has been well and repeatedly documented, but Britons in the high-Victorian period tended to find particularly satisfying the imaginative act of looking back on

---

26 Hoppen, *The Mid-Victorian Generation*, chapter 11, especially pp. 382, 392.
27 Peter Levi, *Tennyson* (London: Macmillan, 1993), p. 257; Gordon S. Haight, *George Eliot: A Biography* (Oxford University Press, 1968), p. 356.

cultures that could be imagined as unified or unitary. In his major work of literary criticism, *The Gay Science* (1866), E. S. Dallas, searching for a theory of literature equal to the critical challenges that he currently faces, turns to 'the old creed, which has the prescription of about thirty centuries in its favour', because it, like the past, is so simple: according to that 'old creed', art has only one goal, and it can be summed up in three words, the 'cultivation of pleasure'. Arnold's sense of Hellenic values in *Culture and Anarchy* has a similar effect. 'The simple and attractive ideal' of Hellenism involves its conception of human beings as wholes: 'our best self' is 'one, and noble, and secure, and peaceful'. What ancient Greece is to Arnold, Italy during the Renaissance is to Pater, who describes its 'unity of culture' as a unity of 'spirit' in which art and thought, art and religion, mind and matter constitute 'one complete type of general culture'. Ruskin also consults ancient wisdom in *Unto This Last* (1860) when he follows out the etymologies of words in classical languages so that he can discover their 'simplest or radical' meanings. Latin and Greek, not English, allow one to reject the way that the term 'value' is defined in the nineteenth century by political economists: the Latin '*valor*, from *valere*, to be well or strong ... *in* life', proves that value is 'that which leads to life with its whole strength'. In one of the most stunning of the high-Victorian moments in which the past becomes a model for the present, Newman in the *Apologia pro Vita Sua* (1864) describes his recognition that in 1839 he had already been 'converted to Rome' by his study of the Monophysites, heretics of the fifth century CE: 'I saw my face in that mirror, and I was a Monophysite.' Although Newman here seems to focus intently on past divisions within the early Church, this episode of ancient history ultimately proves that Church's triumphant unity: because the Monophysites were condemned by both Pope Leo and the Council of Chalcedon, the Church of Rome, unlike the Church of England, retains its status as the 'One Fold of Christ', with which Newman himself must become one.[28]

Pater directly contrasts the 'unity of culture' that he finds in fifteenth-century Italy to the 'exhausting' and 'limiting' controversies of the present with their 'inflexibilities and antagonisms' and 'exclusions'. To a large extent, as Pater's analysis suggests, the nostalgic treatment of the distant

---

28 E. S. Dallas, *The Gay Science*, 2 vols. (London: Chapman and Hall, 1866), vol. I, p. 4; Arnold, *Culture and Anarchy*, pp. 90, 136; Pater, *The Renaissance*, pp. 20, xxiv; Ruskin, *Works*, vol. XVII, pp. 64, 84; John Henry, Cardinal Newman, *Apologia pro Vita Sua and Six Sermons*, ed. Frank M. Turner (New Haven, CT: Yale University Press, 2008), pp. 226, 317.

past so characteristic of high-Victorian texts constitutes a reaction against what Mary Poovey defines as the modernizing impulses of 'disaggregation', which predominated in the second half of the nineteenth century.[29] In the 1860s and 1870s, division was everywhere the rule – from politics, in which the distinctions formed around the labels 'liberal' and 'conservative' took on new meanings; to academic life, in which separate disciplines, particularly in the social sciences, were taking shape with the publication of their foundational texts; and to the professions, in which civil engineers or architects, for instance, differentiated themselves from older occupations through training, testing, and the forming of associations. Even the Church of England felt the impress of such developments, with clergymen becoming 'exclusively religious specialists' whose callings were announced for the first time in the 1860s by their wearing of the 'dog collar'. Also prominent was the tendency for people to gather in groups based on their particular and differentiating interests. Among intellectual elites, the X Club (1864) catered to the scientifically inclined; and the Metaphysical Club (1869), to those concerned with questions of belief. Beginning in the 1870s, church-sponsored groups, drawing on the middle and lower-middle ranks of society, proliferated; and friendly societies and cooperative organizations became an increasingly important constituent of working-class experience.[30] The volunteer movement was in this way, as in so many others, typical: different classes and occupational groups formed separate corps. Thomas Hughes drew the men in his unit from the students of the Working Men's College. The artist George Cruickshank enrolled workers in his corps of teetotallers; and men devoted to the fine arts – John Everett Millais and William Holman Hunt and Frederic Leighton, along with Morris and Rossetti – took their places in the more exclusive Artists' Rifles.

New forms of affiliation, by joining people together, suggested that they were to be valued less as individuals than as participants whose identities were subsumed in that of the group. Such an untoward outcome helps to identify the cultural logic behind the second category of the nostalgically rendered subjects that I am treating here, the exceptional person whose heroism is defined by his – almost always *his* – impulse towards self-sacrifice. Drawing heavily from the 'warehouse of cultural scenarios' in which images

29 Pater, *The Renaissance*, p. 20; Mary Poovey, *Making a Social Body: British Cultural Formation, 1830–1864* (University of Chicago Press, 1995), pp. 3–4.
30 Hoppen, *The Mid-Victorian Generation*, pp. 468, 488, 465; Evans, *The Forging of the Modern State*, p. 352.

of England's past glory were stored, depictions of heroism high-Victorian style often focus on ideals of bold leadership and courage in battle. More typically, however, self-sacrifice is deemed the epitome of heroism. When Tennyson in 1862 dedicated his *Idylls of the King* to the recently deceased Prince Consort, the poet calls him 'my king's ideal knight' because 'Albert the Good' gave himself so tirelessly to others: 'With . . . sublime repression of himself', he was 'Laborious for [England's] people and her poor'. The playwright Tom Robertson has fun with medieval ideals of high-born virtue when the aristocratic mother of *Caste* (1867) recalls at length the exploits of her son's ancestors as they have been recorded in 'the Chronicles of Froissart', but when she declares that 'his honour calls him' to leave his wife and serve in India, she is voicing a widely held belief in the sanctity of selfless military duty, a belief that is no laughing matter.[31]

Such heroism knows no boundaries of caste or even of species in high-Victorian representations. It is perhaps one of the ingredients of Tennyson's *Enoch Arden* that made that poem his most popular during the nineteenth century. Set in a small fishing village a hundred years before the present, this tale depicts its eponymous hero, a simple sailor, as the embodiment of determined renunciation. Returning more than ten years after he has departed to win a livelihood for his family, he discovers that his wife Annie, thinking him dead, has remarried. Arden, instead of asserting his rights, dies quietly, blessing his rival, but not before he arranges to have sent to his wife a token of his death. The emblem of proleptic nostalgia, this dying gift allows him to imagine in advance that the certain knowledge that he has died will finally liberate her to live in the present. Even the fallen world of contemporary life can foster such devotedness. Ruskin in *Unto This Last*, to the incredulous dismay of some of his readers, praises the professions of soldier, lawyer, and doctor because he assumes that such men put first something other than their own interests, unlike the merchant, whose motivations are always selfish. Heroic self-sacrifice is a motivation that often characterizes the gentry, landed or otherwise, in high-Victorian fiction as if it were a kind of birthright. Characters like the military man Alick Keith of Yonge's *The Clever Woman of the Family* (1865) and Roger Carbury in Trollope's *The Way We Live Now* (1874–5) are ready to give body parts and

---

31 Arjun Appadurai, *Modernity at Large: Cultural Dimensions of Globalization* (Minneapolis: University of Minnesota Press, 1996), p. 30; Tennyson, 'Dedication', *Idylls of the King*, in *Poems*, vol. III, pp. 264–5, lines 6, 42, 18, 34; Tom Robertson, *Caste*, *Plays by Tom Robertson*, ed. William Tydeman (Cambridge University Press, 1982), pp. 155, 158.

an estate, respectively, to redeem or enrich the lives of others. Roger, in particular, epitomizes the chivalric ideal of sacrifice for the object of unrequited love: 'What could be the devotion which men so often affect to feel if it did not tend to self-sacrifice on behalf of the beloved one.' Dorothea Brooke, as the narrator of George Eliot's *Middlemarch* (1871–2) so movingly concludes, lives in a world in which there is no place for the 'heroic' virtues of a St Theresa or an Antigone – 'the medium in which their ardent deeds took shape is for ever gone' – yet Dorothea, famously like a biblical quotation in a column of newsprint, is heroic in her ability to put others before herself. Although her gesture of self-sacrifice, her attempt to help Rosamond, results in Dorothea's ultimately being rewarded with the prize that she is ready to renounce, marriage to Will Ladislaw, her 'self-forgetful ardour' yields, in moral terms, the most impressive action that the novel has to offer. One high-Victorian text in which one might least expect to find instances of such deeds is Darwin's *The Descent of Man* (1872), but the subject of self-sacrifice becomes one of the many ways in which its author makes his case that human beings and animals have 'social instincts' and feelings in common. He famously concludes his proof that human beings are evolved from primates by declaring, 'For my own part I would as soon be descended from that heroic little monkey, who braved his dreaded enemy in order to save the life of his keeper ... as from a savage who delights to torture his enemies', a reference to a story told earlier about 'the sympathetic and heroic conduct' of 'a little American monkey' at the Zoological Gardens who rescued his 'warm friend', a keeper there, from an attack by a 'great' and 'fierce baboon'.[32] Darwin's own heroic boldness in declaring his proud sense of kinship with a monkey gains additional force when set against the competitive energies of a present that, as the narrator of *Middlemarch* laments, makes it less and less likely that his fellow men will rise to such a standard.

In *The Subjection of Women* (1869), John Stuart Mill provides another perspective on the characteristic high-Victorian investment in the heroic individual when he contrasts past and present after, surprisingly, praising medieval chivalry for promoting gender relations more admirable than those typical of the nineteenth century: the chivalric ideal encouraged

---

32 Ruskin, *Works*, vol. xvii, pp. 36–7; Anthony Trollope, *The Way We Live Now* (Oxford University Press, 2009), chapter 100, p. 468; George Eliot, *Middlemarch*, ed. David Carroll (Oxford: Clarendon Press, 1986), Finale, p. 825; chapter 81, p. 783; Charles Darwin, *The Descent of Man* (New York: Penguin, 2004), pp. 689, 126.

'gentleness, generosity, and self-abnegation' towards the weak because it flourished in a 'state of society in which everything depended for good or evil on individual prowess ... In modern societies, all things ... are decided, not by individual effort, but by the combined operations of numbers.'[33] Debates in the House of Commons in the lead-up to the passage of the Second Reform Act in 1867 often turned on the difference between the value of the single individual and the threat posed by numbers, the former supposedly the preserve of those middle-class and genteel men who already had the vote, and the latter, of those workers who hoped to be enfranchised. Carlyle makes that point in *Shooting Niagara* when he decries democracy as the political development that will turn 'the Count of Heads [into] the Divine Court of Appeals on every question and interest of mankind'. That outcome is, for Carlyle, just one instance of the widespread ascendancy of what he calls '*Swarmery*', the 'Gathering of Men in Swarms'.[34] Moreover, high-Victorian legislation, in theory if not always in practice, centralized and gave over to government many of the roles previously performed by individuals or by charitable organizations: in the decade of the 1870s alone, significant reforms in the court and prison systems, as well as public health acts, necessitated increases in the number of civil servants, whose positions from 1870 were open to genuinely competitive examination. The apparent reign of numbers and the new prominence of government action created conditions inimical to a 'social instinct' like self-sacrifice, conditions that prompted regretful backward glances towards the valour of the knight-errant or the instincts of an American monkey.

The destructive and impersonal tendencies of the present were also thought to be lessened by the efforts of two figures prominent in the literary texts of the high-Victorian period, the good woman and the good worker. A loving wife was thought capable of making whole a man wounded in body or spirit by solving what, in another context, Pater calls 'the problem of unity with ourselves' – or at least that is how the story goes in many novels written in the 1860s.[35] This narrative was in many ways retrograde. Middle-class women at the time were scoring some of the victories that would ultimately lead to full property rights, higher education, and the franchise. Yet working-class men had even more reason to think that the

33 John Stuart Mill, *The Subjection of Women*, *The Collected Works of John Stuart Mill*, vol. xxi, ed. John M. Robson, intro. Stefan Collini (University of Toronto Press, 1984), p. 328.
34 Carlyle, *Shooting Niagara*, pp. 1, 4.
35 Janice Carlisle, *Common Scents: Comparative Encounters in High-Victorian Fiction* (New York: Oxford University Press, 2004), chapters 2 and 3. Pater, *The Renaissance*, p. 182.

future would satisfy their demands for greater freedom, in this case freedom from middle-class control. Not only did the passing of the Second Reform Act foretell the further democratization of the country in 1884, when another reform bill became law, but the very processes that had led to the 1867 act demonstrated to workers that their trades unions could serve as effective political organizations. In a confined but significant way, 1874 saw progress towards self-representation when two workers were elected to sit in the House of Commons. Major legislation of the 1870s served workers' interests more obviously than had the factory acts of the first half of the century, though the passage in 1874 of another such measure reduced the work week to fifty-six and a half hours. In 1871 trades unions were finally legalized, and their funds protected by law. In 1875 the Employers and Workman Act limited the penalties for breach of contract, but perhaps more significantly it replaced the old terminology of 'master' and 'servant' with less out-of-date and less loaded, if not entirely neutral, language. When the Ballot Act became law in 1872, traditionalists complained that its secrecy was craven and unmanly, but its passage made official the recognition that workers might not feel free to declare in public their political allegiances, precisely because their interests might differ from those of the employers who were still in that year known as their masters. Writers of the high-Victorian period, drawing upon the storehouse of nostalgic images of the English past in their responses to such developments, had recourse again and again to the same figure, that of the English artisan. Contemplation of the so-called skilled worker or labour aristocrat invariably evoked feelings of pride and trust in the country that had fostered him. Although artisans played a significant role in the economy of the 1860s and 1870s, those depicted in literary texts tend to be located in a simpler world of rural life, if not actually in the past; and they almost invariably embody the values of self-reliant industry and contentment with one's lot.

Enoch Arden is, not surprisingly, one of the chief of such figures. Heroic in his self-denial, this 'brave, God-fearing man' is a superlatively gifted craftsman. After returning to his village, he makes a living by doing a number of tasks: 'Almost to all things could he turn his hand. / Cooper he was and carpenter, and wrought / To make the boatmen fishing-nets.'[36] Like Wemmick, the son of an artisan, in Dickens's *Great Expectations* (1860–1), Arden is a jack of all trades; and like the blacksmith Joe Gargery, he quietly

---

36 Tennyson, *Enoch Arden*, *Poems*, vol. II, p. 646, lines 809–11.

and passively accepts his lot. Unlike these figures, however, Arden is anything but a figure of fun. His depiction therefore resembles that of another character in high-Victorian fiction, Eliot's Caleb Garth, who is treated in *Middlemarch* with such pious respect that he can seem little more than a cardboard cutout. Garth has risen to the status of land manager, but his willingness to dirty his hands in the work that he does, his pride in his manual competence, and his inability to manage anything as tawdry as money align him with nostalgic conceptions of artisanal labour. Arden and Gargery and Garth, all located in the past of the mid-eighteenth or early nineteenth century, make sense of the backward-looking representation of a contemporary worker like Sam Gerridge in Robertson's *Caste*, a 'mechanic' unashamed of his paper cap. Gerridge believes that everyone should stay in the railway carriage in which he or she has started the journey in life, whether that carriage be first or second or third class; and he weeps for joy over the good fortune of his betters. Sam, like Garth and Arden, is evidently very good at what he does, so good that he is able at the end of the play to buy a business, becoming with its purchase a 'master tradesman'.[37]

Skill is one of the characteristics that apparently make such figures so attractive, with their handicraft setting itself in opposition to the effects of present-day crass commercialism. Even as Carlyle decries in *Shooting Niagara* the reign of Cheap and Nasty, the production of the shoddy goods that typify the present, he turns to images of artisanal labour to explain what 'poor old England' needs – 'the quiet old House' now requires, as never before, 'carpentering, chiselling, sawing, and hammering'. Even as Ruskin in the first volumes of *Fors Clavigera* (1871–84) offers one withering denunciation after another of the craftsmanship that is now wasted on 'the flimsy dresses, toys, metal work, and other rubbish, belonging to [the] accursed life' of Britain's urban populations, he turns to the image of the potter as the kind of worker he wants to see on the 'small piece of English ground, beautiful, peaceful, and fruitful', that he expects his Guild of St George to turn into a patch of paradise.[38] In every endeavour, the artisan becomes the model of work faithfully done, not only for Carlyle and Ruskin, but for writers as dissimilar as Mill and Dickens and Browning. Well might Dallas in *The Gay Science* conclude, 'Horny-hand is now a hero as much as any knight of old.'[39]

---

37 Robertson, *Caste*, pp. 146, 160.
38 Carlyle, *Shooting Niagara*, p. 20; Ruskin, *Works*, vol. xxviii, p. 136; vol. xxvii, p. 96.
39 Dallas, *The Gay Science*, vol. ii, p. 272.

All the nostalgically treated subjects that I have discussed – the supposedly unified cultures of the past, heroic self-sacrifice, and the idealized
worker – come together in Thomas Hardy's depiction of Gabriel Oak in
Far from the Madding Crowd (1874). His name identifies his iconic status:
Gabriel is the leader of Milton's angelic horde; and oak, the symbol of the
hardy shelter offered by England itself. Less a shepherd than he is artisan
and musician and veterinarian, this 'extraordinary good and clever man'
inhabits a rural setting in which 'Then' is 'Now', in which 'mediaevalism
and modernism' unite. In his 'grim fidelity' to Bathsheba Everdene, he is
willing to sacrifice himself by twice saving her hay ricks, first from fire,
then from water. This second act of heroism is cast in the nostalgic mould
of chivalric love: Oak tells himself, 'I will help to my last breath the
woman I have loved so dearly' as he feels descend upon him, as if he
were St George, the 'dragon' of the approaching storm.[40] For long
stretches of the plot, he wastes his many gifts when, in the role of a
forlorn lover, he remains on Bathsheba's farm, fulfilling the duties of a
bailiff without either a bailiff's pay or status. Oak is rewarded at the end of
the novel when the fatal result of another man's obsessive love for
Bathsheba frees her to marry her employee. Like Eliot's Felix Holt, Oak
is a worker who is not a worker; rather, he is a potential landowner who
wears the disguise of an agricultural labourer: he puts on a smock only to
have it literally burned off his body when he risks his life to save his lady's
property. This astonishingly contradictory figure is presented in *Far from
the Madding Crowd* as the object of the reader's admiration – a figure who
calls up all the emotions associated with the nostalgic structure of feeling
characteristic of high-Victorian literature, including the vicarious contentment that comes from witnessing the triumph of traditional virtues, as well
as the regretful pride that is evoked when a distinctively English past,
magically projected into its future, becomes a present the loss of which can
already be mourned.

The divide between Gabriel Oak as a nexus of backward-looking desire
and the volunteer movement with which I began may seem wide and even
unbridgeable, but both testify to the strength of the nostalgic impulses
behind their creations. As its chief twentieth-century historian notes, the
movement was suffused with an 'aura' of romance. The Enfield rifle, in
particular, was understood in the most nostalgic of terms: as the modern

---

40 Thomas Hardy, *Far from the Madding Crowd* (London: Penguin, 2003), chapter 15, p. 97;
chapter 21, pp. 127, 126; chapter 28, p. 169; chapter 51, p. 312; chapter 35, p. 215.

version of the English longbow,[41] it spoke of past victories at Crécy and Agincourt. During the first meeting at Wimbledon in 1860 of the British National Rifle Association, an organization founded to support the volunteers, the medals that were awarded (and are still being awarded yearly) were embossed with images of a modern rifleman and a medieval archer standing side by side. Ordinary men were praised for enlisting in the volunteers because they were demonstrating their willingness to sacrifice time and money, in the words of contemporary accounts, for 'something as noble as knight-errantry', for 'chivalry' undertaken to defend the weak and the vulnerable. That those needing protection were female went without saying, though it was quite frequently said. A reporter in 1860 declared – with an unconscious bathos that recalls Tennyson's 'Riflemen Form!' – that the sight of 'healthy, handsome muscular men' arrayed in a formation of volunteers evoked in 'the imagination' a 'beautiful picture' of a 'mother bending over her cradled babe, bidding the beloved infant to lie still and slumber, for God and the Volunteers were keeping guard'.[42] By the time that Hardy was publishing his portrait of Gabriel Oak, the men who, with their newly acquired military skills, were protecting British women and children were largely workers – factory labourers, farm hands, as well as artisans. Far from existing on opposites sides of a gap, whether between real life and literature or between one kind of historical account or another, high-Victorian texts and the volunteer movement brought into being remarkably similar imaginative worlds.

Those worlds – one textual, the other historical – are not, by most current standards, particularly attractive places: in them the nation becomes a union of like-minded defenders of its past and future glories, a polity in which almost everyone is expected to endorse the heterosexual compact, in which self-sacrificing heroism is the highest form of individual development and working-class men are valued for their grateful submission to their supposed betters. To readers of the twenty-first century, such a vision may appear merely regressive. Moreover, it seems unable to accommodate those strange moments in high-Victorian literature that continue to provide readers with occasions for delight: Pip's wild flights of verbal invention in *Great Expectations*, Eliot's frenzied description of the 'stupendous fragmentariness' of Rome in *Middlemarch*, or Ruskin's declaring himself

41 Cunningham, *The Volunteer Force*, p. 113.
42 Beckett, *The Amateur Military Tradition*, p. 169; Cunningham, *The Volunteer Force*, pp. 72–3.

'a Communist of the old school – reddest also of the red' in *Fors Clavigera*.[43] Yet it would be a mistake, I think, not to find impressive the world conjured up by high-Victorian cultural nostalgia. Like the kingdom that Tennyson created for King Arthur briefly to rule, this 'city ... built / To music' was erected, often knowingly, upon instabilities that ensured its inevitable obsolescence.[44] Imagining into verbal existence this particular structure of feeling required nothing less than a reconfiguring of the conventional notions of the relations of the past and the future to the perplexing present. That so many 'miscellaneous' writers, to use Bagehot's term, contributed to this collective achievement is itself wondrously strange.

43 Eliot, *Middlemarch*, chapter 20, p. 187; Ruskin, *Works*, vol. xxvii, p. 116.
44 Tennyson, 'Gareth and Lynette', *Idylls of the King*, in *Poems*, vol. iii, p. 289, lines 272–3.

6

The *fin de siècle*

STEPHEN ARATA

In the final decades of the nineteenth century, William Blake's work was rescued from its long obscurity by those, like Algernon Charles Swinburne and William Butler Yeats, who found within it the possibilities for a humanist aesthetic practice that could engage (and possibly transform) the world without being bound to it. Swinburne's seminal *William Blake: A Critical Essay* (1868) and Yeats's eclectic edition of *The Works of William Blake, Poetic, Symbolic, and Critical* (1893) are landmarks of *fin-de-siècle* literary culture. Together they provide an index to Blake's importance for late Victorian writers; they also afford insight into many of the period's characteristic preoccupations and concerns. 'To him all symbolic things were literal, all literal things symbolic', Swinburne writes, adding that Blake 'walked and laboured under other heavens, on another earth, than the earth and heaven of material life'.[1] As Swinburne makes clear, the crucial distinction is not between (material) earth and (immaterial) heaven but between a mind shackled to material life by the 'mechanical intellect' and a mind liberated from that life by what Yeats, referring to Blake, described as 'the visionary realism' of the imagination.[2] For these later poets, Blake's work was most compelling for its recreation of the world – all of heaven and of earth too – within the space of the imagination, a recreation that was also a redemption. Blake knew that 'imagination was the first emanation of divinity', writes Yeats, and that 'the imaginative arts were therefore the greatest of Divine revelations'.[3]

Much of the innovative artistic work of the *fin de siècle* sets itself in explicit opposition to the utilitarian and mechanistic cast of late Victorian society at

---

1 Algernon Charles Swinburne, *William Blake: A Critical Essay* (London: J. C. Hotten, 1868), pp. 40–1.
2 William Butler Yeats, 'William Blake and His Illustrations to the *Divine Comedy*' (1897), in *Essays and Introductions* (New York: Macmillan, 1961), p. 121.
3 Yeats, 'William Blake and the Imagination' (1897), in *Essays and Introductions*, p. 112.

large. Swinburne and Yeats were far from alone in deriving sustenance from Blake's disdain for instrumental reason and his belief in the imagination's transfiguring power. Sustaining, too, was Blake's pursuit of transcendence through the cultivation of beauty. Writing shortly after the death of Dante Gabriel Rossetti in 1881, F. W. H. Myers argued in Blakean terms that the modern 'Worship of Beauty' signalled the rebellion 'of Art against Materialism'. In Myers's view, Rossetti's work epitomized that rebellion. His poetry and painting embody a desire for transcendence – 'beauty spiritualized into a beatific dream' is the way Myers puts it – in a world that, taking its 'dominant tone' from science, each year 'grows more soulless and severe'. In making a religion of beauty and a sacrament of art, Rossetti 'stands on the side of those who see in material things a spiritual significance'.[4]

Yet Myers is also aware, as who is not, that Rossetti's is a sensual art. Its turn away from materialism is not a turn away from carnality, from the 'fleshliness' that discomfited so many readers. Recognizing that the beauty of human bodies is central to Rossetti's art, Myers nonetheless describes that art in terms of a perpetual overcoming of the flesh in the name of 'beauties impalpable'. A few years after Myers's essay, Walter Pater comes nearer the truth when he writes that for Rossetti flesh and spirit are one. In 'the vehement and impassioned heat of his conceptions', Pater writes, 'the material and the spiritual are fused and blent: if the spiritual attains the definite visibility of a crystal, what is material loses its earthiness and impurity'.[5] He notes that a similar fusion characterizes both the theology and the practice of the medieval Church, whose central representative was Dante; notes, too, that Rossetti, shorn of the religious faith that fortified Dante, sacralizes art in its stead.

The idea that poetry might fill the role left vacant by religion was a familiar one in the latter part of the century. Matthew Arnold outlines the normative view in *Literature and Dogma* (1871) and 'The Study of Poetry' (1880): genuine poetry both transmits and enacts the central values of Western culture. In an age of faltering faith, Arnold's great tradition of English poets constitutes a secular apostolic succession whose ministry still makes possible the ethical life, conceived in Christian terms, at the individual and the communal levels. By contrast, for the period's more radical writers the language of religion

---

4 Frederic W. H. Myers, 'Rossetti and the Religion of Beauty', in *Essays Modern* (London: Macmillan, 1885), pp. 330, 322.
5 *Ibid.*, p. 326; Walter Pater, 'Dante Gabriel Rossetti' (1889), in *Appreciations, with an Essay on Style* (London: Macmillan, 1911), p. 212.

served precisely to critique that tradition from within. Swinburne memorably describes Blake as one who 'was born and baptized into the church of rebels'.[6] The same could be said of another tutelary spirit of the *fin de siècle*, Charles Baudelaire. Swinburne prefaces his study of Blake with an epigram from Baudelaire, a figure as unknown to most English readers in 1868 as was Blake himself.[7] The two writers were important to Swinburne for many of the same reasons, not least for the way their profoundly religious sensibilities set them in opposition to dominant Christian ideologies and institutions. Belief in the divinity of the creative spirit led Blake 'to readjust all questions [of faith] by the light of art and law of imagination – to reduce all outlying provinces, and bring them under the governance of his own central empire – the "fourfold spiritual city" of his vision'.[8] For Blake and Baudelaire, as for Swinburne himself, 'all moral duty or religious necessity, were not so much abrogated or superseded as summed up, included and involved, by the one matter of art'.[9]

Like Baudelaire, Swinburne condemns the 'heresy of instruction' as the supreme artistic sin, but also like Baudelaire he contends that 'the spirit and mind of men' receive 'a certain exaltation and insight' from true art that has the effect of clarifying the moral sense.[10] 'Art for art's sake first of all': Swinburne's iteration of Théophile Gautier's famous dictum is primarily a call to excellence in execution, a reminder that 'the important thing [is] to have her [i.e., art's] work supremely well done'.[11] Art is a medium of beauty, Swinburne argues, and beauty inheres in form. The artist therefore strives for formal perfection in the work. The critic's business is to judge how well a particular artistic design has been executed, not simply to agree or disagree with whatever sentiments may be expressed in the work. Swinburne signals the decisive shift in emphasis from subject to treatment that characterizes critical writing in the last quarter of the century. Examples are everywhere. Pater argues that art is 'always striving ... to get rid of its responsibilities to its subject or material'. Yeats regrets that Tennyson and Wordsworth so often 'troubled the energies of their imaginative passions' by conceiving of poetry narrowly in terms of content. Henry James admonishes critics to 'apply the test of execution' if their goal is to 'estimate quality'. Oscar Wilde identifies the 'sense of form' as 'the basis of creative no less than of critical achievement'. Arnold Bennett notes in his journal that, in marked contrast to

---

6 Swinburne, *William Blake*, p. 3.
7 See Patricia Clements, *Baudelaire and the English Tradition* (Princeton University Press, 1985), pp. 10–76.
8 Swinburne, *William Blake*, p. 94.   9 *Ibid.*, p. 86.   10 *Ibid.*, p. 91.
11 *Ibid.*, pp. 91–92.

his own contemporaries, 'none of the (so-called) great masters of English nineteenth-century fiction had (if I am right) a deep artistic interest in form and treatment; they were absorbed in "subject"'. Robert Louis Stevenson counsels young writers to 'bow your head over technique. Think of technique when you rise and when you go to bed. Forget purposes in the meanwhile; get to love technical processes.'[12] By emphasizing their commitment to artistic technique, these writers sought among other things to distinguish themselves from 'Grub Street' hacks concerned only to cater to a debased popular taste. At the same time, as the above list suggests, a shared love for the 'technical processes' of art links writers who in other respects have little in common. Aesthetes, decadents, naturalists, romancers, social realists: all professed their allegiance to treatment ahead of subject. 'Form', Wilde's mouthpiece Gilbert in 'The Critic as Artist' sums up succinctly, 'is everything.'[13]

No one, not even Wilde, was willing quite to argue that literature is without moral effect, only that didacticism is no part of the writer's purpose. The morality of an artwork becomes a function of its artistry, of its being 'work supremely well done', and is therefore not extractable as content. Thus Swinburne can, with only seeming perversity, praise the 'distinct and vivid' morality of Baudelaire's poems in *Les Fleurs du Mal*, since he believes that 'perfect workmanship makes every subject admirable and respectable'.

> If any reader could extract from any poem a positive spiritual medicine – if he could swallow a sonnet like a moral prescription – then clearly the poet supplying these intellectual drugs would be a bad artist; indeed, no real artist but a huckster and vendor of miscellaneous wares. But those who will look for them may find moralities in plenty behind every poem of M. Baudelaire's.[14]

---

12 Pater, 'The School of Giorgione', in *The Renaissance: Studies in Art and Poetry*, ed. Donald L. Hill (1893; Berkeley: University of California Press, 1980), p. 138; Yeats, 'William Blake and the Imagination,' p. 113; Henry James, 'The Art of Fiction' (1884), in *Literary Criticism: Essays on Literature, American Writers, English Writers*, ed. Leon Edel (New York: Library of America, 1984), p. 50; Oscar Wilde, 'The Critic as Artist' (1891), in *The Artist as Critic: Critical Writings of Oscar Wilde*, ed. Richard Ellmann (University of Chicago Press, 1982), p. 398; Arnold Bennett, *The Journal of Arnold Bennett* (New York: Viking, 1933), entry for 1 January 1898; *The Letters of Robert Louis Stevenson*, ed. Bradford A. Booth and Ernest Mehew, 8 vols. (New Haven, CT: Yale University Press, 1994–5), vol. IV, pp. 140–1.

13 Wilde, 'The Critic as Artist,' p. 399.

14 Swinburne, 'Charles Baudelaire: *Les Fleurs du Mal*' (1862), in *Algernon Charles Swinburne: Major Poems and Selected Prose*, ed. Jerome McGann and Charles L. Sligh (New Haven, CT: Yale University Press, 2004), pp. 343, 346. For Swinburne's defence of *Poems and Ballads*, see *Notes on Poems and Reviews* (1866), in McGann and Sligh, pp. 348–59.

Swinburne defended his own *Poems and Ballads* in much the same terms.

The commitment to craft, to art for art's sake, was not a retreat from 'reality' but an effort to engage it critically through a momentary standing apart from the world. Indeed, the artist's desire to create beauty could be inseparable from a desire to change the world. The popular image of the late Victorian aesthete as self-regarding dilettante is repeatedly belied by the practices of those for whom the pursuit of beauty was also the pursuit of social and political transformation. In his short story 'The Tables of the Law' (1897), Yeats ascribes to his fictional alter ego Michael Robartes the belief that 'the beautiful arts were sent into the world to overthrow nations, and finally life herself, by sowing everywhere unlimited desires, like torches thrown into a burning city'.[15] Once awakened to the possibility of a life made beautiful in all its aspects, we are also awakened to the impoverishment of the world as it is and to a desire to change it. Such awakening is literalized in the case of William Guest, the protagonist of William Morris's *News from Nowhere* (1890), who rises one morning to find himself in a utopian future. In the England of Morris's imagining, the end of economic injustice releases women and men to pursue what Morris believes is the natural human desire to create beauty – not transcendent beauty but rather the beauty of everyday objects made by human hands: garments, utensils, tools, furnishings, dwellings. In turn, the quest for beauty (as opposed to profit or status or power) as the primary human activity ensures that social relations remain on a right footing. All utopias are lovely, but Morris's version is striking for its subordination of all possible human goods – wisdom, learning, justice, comfort, pleasure, even love – to the good arising from the cultivation of loveliness. For Guest, as (Morris hopes) for readers of his narrative, the vision of life in Nowhere pricks those limitless desires that can lead to the overthrow of nations. Beauty thus becomes a catalyst of revolution, aesthetics and politics making common cause in the service of human fulfilment.

Utopias momentarily estrange us from the real world by making it strange. They alter our frames of reference so that the structures of society begin to lose their aura of inevitability. The desire to disrupt accustomed responses and upset familiar forms of thought and perception is typical of much late-century writing, even writing that harbours no overt political designs upon its audience. Following Baudelaire, Pater maintains that

---

15 William Butler Yeats, *Short Fiction* (Harmondsworth: Penguin, 1995), p. 202.

'the addition of strangeness to beauty' defines the romantic as opposed to the classical element in art.[16] According to Pater, that element had come to dominate modern writing. It signifies a prevalent taste for the curious and the novel, but it also points towards a Blakean desire to cleanse the doors of perception so that reality – the reality hidden by the operations of the mechanical intellect – might fully reveal itself. To momentarily release us from normal modes of cognition is one office of great art, Pater argues. In 'the highest and most complete form of poetry ... the meaning reaches us through ways not strictly traceable by the understanding'. Pater offers as one example of such poetry 'some of most imaginative compositions of William Blake'.[17] For Swinburne, it was Blake who first recognized that 'the supreme works of verse and colour ... are not things of the understanding'. Instead, it is 'only by innate and irrational perception that we can apprehend and enjoy' them.[18] The productive estrangement from usual modes of thought and perception is central to the aesthetics of *fin-de-siècle* Symbolism, which drew extensively on the work of Baudelaire and Pater. It is of course central to religious practice too, as theorists of Symbolism such as Arthur Symons were well aware. That overlap helps explain the tendency of many *fin-de-siècle* writers to describe art in terms of ritual or ceremonial performance. When the not especially religious Joseph Conrad notes in a 1908 letter that 'a man who puts forth the secret of his imagination to the world accomplishes, as it were, a religious rite', he is at once underlining his oft shaken but never abandoned belief that art helps bind communities together and his conviction that art fundamentally alters our perceptions of the world. Like a religious ritual, it can even be a vehicle of transcendence.[19]

For Conrad as for many others, the idea of transcendence had long since come uncoupled from anything resembling Christian dogma. Yet a faith in the power of art to pierce the veil of the material world is just as central to the poetry of the Jesuit Gerard Manley Hopkins. Because almost all of his poems remained unpublished until 1918, and because his religious calling removed him from public life, Hopkins is often left out of accounts of late Victorian literature. Yet his practices and interests as an artist were of his time. For Hopkins, poetry begins in a preternaturally acute perception of the things of the world in their individuality. Believing that beauty inheres in

---

16 Pater, 'Postscript', in *Appreciations*, p. 246.
17 Pater, 'The School of Giorgione', in *The Renaissance*, p. 137.
18 Swinburne, *William Blake*, p. 35.
19 *The Collected Letters of Joseph Conrad, Vol. 4: 1908–11*, ed. Frederick Karl and Laurence Davies (Cambridge University Press, 1990), p. 137.

the particular, Hopkins shuns abstraction. His poetry is part of an accelerating century-long move away from the general categories that structured eighteenth-century thought. This shift is a legacy of Romanticism, transmitted to Hopkins – as to so many others – in no small part by John Ruskin. Also relevant for Hopkins was the increasing dominance of inductive models of inquiry in contemporary science. No Victorian poet had a keener interest in or a firmer grip on the consequences for art of the changes in methodology driving research in the natural sciences at mid-century.

Hopkins's poetry strives to convey the irreducible particularity of objects or experiences. The dedication of 'The Windhover' (1877) 'to Christ our Lord' alerts us to the hawk's symbolic role in the poem, but the poet's foremost concern is to describe *this* bird at *this* moment in its

> riding
> Of the rolling level underneath him steady air, and striding
> High there, how he rung upon the rein of a wimpling wing
> In his ecstasy! then off, off forth on swing,
> As a skate's heel sweeps smooth on a bow-bend: the hurl and gliding
> Rebuffed the big wind.

The windhover stands for Christ but is also uniquely itself. Its flight as Hopkins observes it comprises a single unrepeatable action. Communicating his experience of this action, however, requires the poet to bring together a series of discrete sense impressions into an image that conveys continuous motion (all those gerunds: 'riding', 'rolling', 'striding', 'wimpling', 'gliding') and completed gesture simultaneously. For Hopkins such an image derives from, and is thoroughly charged with, a creative energy that both fuses and productively deforms. 'Brute beauty and valour and act, oh, air, pride, plume, here / Buckle!' The six nouns that converge on the verb 'buckle' are subjected to a power by which they are at once strapped together (buckled) and forcibly distressed (buckled) into new shapes. And it is the very pressure of this fusion and deformation, union and destruction at once, that produces the 'fire that breaks from thee then, a billion / Times told lovelier'.[20]

The emphasis on parts at the expense of wholes was much commented upon as a general feature of *fin-de-siècle* writing. It was usually taken as the keynote of a decadent style. In *fin-de-siècle* England, the *locus classicus* for the

---

20 Gerard Manley Hopkins, 'The Windhover', in *The Poetical Works of Gerard Manley Hopkins*, ed. Norman H. Mackenzie (Oxford: Clarendon Press, 1990), p. 144, lines 2–7, 9–10, 10–11.

claim that decadent writing privileges the part is Havelock Ellis's 1889 essay 'A Note on Paul Bourget', which includes Ellis's translation of Bourget's contention that a 'style of decadence is one in which the unity of the book is decomposed to give place to the independence of the page, in which the page is decomposed to give place to the independence of the phrase, and the phrase to give place to the independence of the word'.[21] For Hopkins, by contrast, an attention to particulars is not atomizing but instead leads to an ever more acute awareness of form and pattern. Here again Ruskin's example was crucial. Hopkins's painstaking descriptions of the natural world in his journals take up the challenge Ruskin laid down in *Modern Painters* (1843) and *The Elements of Drawing* (1857) to recover 'the innocence of the eye' by recording without preconception the shape, colour, and texture of natural objects. To do so is necessarily to uncover the 'law' of their design. (A note in Hopkins's journal reads: 'I have now found the law of the oak leaves.'[22]) Hopkins coined the word 'inscape' to designate the dynamic pattern of attributes that makes a thing itself. The apprehension of inscape involves 'instress': the thrust of energy by which one grasps, at a level deeper than intellection, the distinctive being of some thing outside oneself. Hopkins at times describes instress as the power of the perceiving mind during moments of highest imaginative intensity, at other times as a force that holds together a particular object and emanates from it. In a letter of 1864, Hopkins writes that the 'highest poetry' originates in 'a mood of great, abnormal in fact, mental acuteness, either energetic or receptive, according as the thoughts which arise in it seem generated by a stress and action of the brain, or to strike into it unasked.'[23] Or, as a journal entry from 1871 succinctly puts it, 'What you look hard at seems to look hard at you.'[24] The fusion of mind and object through the act of instress produces a joy that is at once aesthetic and religious. For Hopkins, to apprehend inscape is to apprehend divinity. An object's inscape is the mark of God's creative power on it. The task of the poet is to reincarnate that divinity in the form of poetry. In realizing the inscape of its subject, the poem itself becomes a field of creative energy whose apprehension is a form of instress.

---

21 Havelock Ellis, *Views and Reviews: A Selection of Uncollected Articles 1884–1932* (Boston: Houghton Mifflin, 1932), p. 52.

22 *The Journals and Papers of Gerard Manley Hopkins*, ed. Humphry House and Graham Storey (London: Oxford University Press, 1969), p. 146.

23 *Further Letters of Gerard Manley Hopkins, Including his Correspondence with Coventry Patmore*, ed. C. C. Abbott (London: Oxford University Press, 1956), pp. 221–2.

24 Hopkins, *Journals and Papers*, p. 204.

The poem is more than an aggregate of its separate parts (and thus not decadent); at the same time its formal patterning helps sustain the integrity of each individual part.

'One of two kinds of clearness one should have' as a poet, Hopkins wrote in a letter to Robert Bridges, 'either the meaning to be felt without effort as fast as one reads or else, if dark at first reading, when once made out *to explode.*'[25] It is of course the second kind of 'clearness' that characterizes Hopkins's poetry, which puts a premium on moments of intensity. To seize and record the evanescent intervals of experience most fully charged with beauty: in the view of many, this is what art is best suited to do. The cultivation of intensity is likewise the business of the aesthetic critic whose procedures Pater begins to outline, and to demonstrate, in his essays of the 1860s and early 1870s. To 'be present always at the focus where the greatest number of vital forces unite in their purest energy', as Pater advises, is to be always in the presence of beauty, and thus to achieve a kind of secular salvation.[26] By century's end the yoking of beauty and intensity was a given, a point of departure for poets and critics alike. By 1902 Arthur Machen could assert, simply, that the definition of literature is 'ecstasy'.[27]

For Machen, the language of rapture evokes a transcendence that is no longer grounded in religious belief, as it was for Hopkins. Precisely because '[t]he world is charged with the grandeur of God,' to apprehend the inscape of any portion of that world is to be at the place where divinity 'will flame out'.[28] In an 1868 notebook entry Hopkins refers to the phenomenal world as 'the brink, limbus, lapping, run-and-mingle of two principles which meet in the scape of everything'.[29] To be 'at' the place where matter and divinity intersect, though, is to be anywhere at all. Like Pater, his one-time tutor at Oxford, Hopkins believed that the greatest number of vital forces will unite in their purest energy wherever the properly attentive observer happens to be. 'These things, these things were here and but the beholder / Wanting',[30] yet in the absence of the beholder, endowed with a mental acuteness at once energetic and receptive, the significance of 'things' necessarily remains unrealized. Hopkins's commitment to realizing objects in their irreducible

25 *Letters of Gerard Manley Hopkins to Robert Bridges*, ed. C. C. Abbott (London: Oxford University Press, 1955), p. 90.
26 Pater, 'Conclusion', in *The Renaissance*, p. 188.
27 Arthur Machen, *Hieroglyphics* (1902; London: Secker, 1926), p. 18.
28 Hopkins, 'God's Grandeur', *Poetical Works*, p. 139, lines 1–2.
29 Hopkins, *Journals and Papers*, p. 130.
30 Hopkins, 'Hurrahing in Harvest', *Poetical Works*, p. 149, lines 11–12.

particularity commits him too to the belief that even the most ordinary objects can lead one out of the material realm altogether.

Hopkins's religious faith led him to rule out purely materialist accounts of the world, but that faith paradoxically made his relation to contemporary science less fraught than that of other poets. As Gillian Beer has shown, the value Hopkins places on exact observation aligns him with scientists such as John Tyndall. Like Hopkins, Tyndall stresses the importance of what he calls 'the prepared imagination' as a precondition for deriving meaning from sensory perceptions.[31] Among other things, Tyndall is notable for his keen sense of the beauty of natural objects and processes, which for him was an inseparable part of a fully scientific understanding of the world. Hopkins's faith and Tyndall's firm conviction that religion and science should be kept separate derive from and feed back into the same habits of observation and sensual response. For Tyndall, religious faith occludes right observation by leading one to try to look *through* what should be looked *at*, whereas for Hopkins, scientific method stops short of what should be its final goal, which is to pull aside the veil of the world in order to make contact with the reality behind it.

Hopkins was nevertheless willing to grapple with issues raised by inquiries in the sciences. His late poem 'That Nature is a Heraclitean Fire and of the Comfort of the Resurrection' (1888) engages with the laws of thermodynamics, which reveal that the material world is governed not by simple change and process but instead by entropy leading to final disintegration. 'Million-fueled, nature's bonfire burns on' until the energy of the universe dissipates completely and 'death blots black out'. Poetically speaking, the comfort Hopkins takes in the promise of a final resurrection into an eternity immune to dissolution or decay is less interesting than the superb concluding image of the soul as 'immortal diamond'[32] – as, that is, a thing of surpassing and permanent beauty formed by the very forces of heat and pressure that elsewhere produce annihilating conflagration.

His active interest in scientific thought distinguishes Hopkins from the many late Victorian writers who dismissed science as irrelevant to their concerns. Yeats was famously contemptuous of the materialist outlook of thinkers such as Tyndall, Herbert Spencer, and Thomas Huxley, which, he

---

31 Gillian Beer, *Open Fields: Science in Cultural Encounter* (Oxford: Clarendon Press, 1996), pp. 242–72.
32 Hopkins, 'That Nature is a Heraclitean Fire and of the Comfort of the Resurrection', *Poetical Works*, p. 198, lines 9, 15.

contended, inevitably leads to woefully impoverished responses to the world: dull, drab, soul-destroying. One task of the Yeatsian artist is to restore, and perpetually to renew, the sense of the numinous of which science is said to have robbed us. To release the modern world from its bondage to fact is also the professed goal of popular novelists such as Rider Haggard and Hall Caine, who under the banner of an anti-mimetic 'romance' fiction sought to counteract what they considered the dreary and falsifying empiricism of the Realist novel. Sounding more Yeatsian than Yeats, Haggard in 1887 claimed that romance fiction (such as his own best-selling *King Solomon's Mines* (1886) and *She* (1887)) answers the desire of all men and women who 'long to be brought face to face with Beauty, and stretch out their arms towards that vision of the Perfect, which we only see in books and dreams'.[33]

That aesthetic and scientific ways of perceiving reality radically diverge was widely assumed in the period and was itself a radical divergence from earlier assumptions concerning the relation of art to science. To live in the realm of imagination, as Yeats at times proposed, is in some degree to abstract oneself from the sensual world. In his *fin-de-siècle* work Yeats seldom tries to produce the illusion that the world evoked in his poems exists prior to or even apart from our experiences of the poems themselves. Images drawn from nature recur, but they are counters of the imagination, not objects in the world. Yeats was capable of arguing (though he was hardly consistent on this point) that poetry grounded merely in 'the observations of the senses' was necessarily second-rate. Such poetry in fact 'binds us to mortality because it binds us to the senses' in contrast to the visionary realism of the genuine poetic imagination, which 'divides us from mortality by the immortality of beauty'.[34] The location of what Yeats would later call the artifice of eternity is not a realm beyond the world but the realm of poetry. Only there can the red rose of spiritual beauty be found. For Yeats, the beauty that is momentary in the mind (and in the flesh is mortal) is given permanence in art. The poet becomes like Swinburne's Proserpine, who 'gathers all things mortal / In cold immortal hands'.[35]

Other writers, such as Pater, were driven to seek provision within scientific paradigms themselves. No less urgently than his contemporaries, Pater defined beauty in terms of its incompatibility with an instrumental

---

33 Rider Haggard, 'About Fiction', *Contemporary Review* 51 (February 1887), p. 173.
34 Yeats, 'William Blake and the Imagination', p. 112.
35 Swinburne, 'The Garden of Proserpine', in *Major Poems*, p. 131.

reason he associated with scientific inquiry. Unlike others, though, Pater sought to bend scientific discourse to aesthetic uses. Jonathan Freedman notes that Pater begins from the assumption that 'the process of rational, analytic thought and its hyperactive step-child, scientific inquiry, has stripped us of our self-satisfied humanism'; he then seeks to discover whether 'one can discern principles within that process that one can turn against it'.[36] One of Pater's great achievements in *The Renaissance* is to recast Kantian aesthetics in the twin vocabularies of Victorian physics and physiology. He opens the 'Conclusion' to the volume by noting, as Hopkins does, the congruence of Heraclitean philosophy and modern physics. All things are in perpetual flux, say both Heraclitus and John Tyndall. Life, including human life, 'is but the concurrence, renewed from moment to moment, of forces parting sooner or later on their ways'. Pater pursues to their logical conclusions the implications of conceiving of the world in these terms. Beauty can never be other than transitory – immortal diamonds are in flux, too – and is perceived by a self that is no self but rather a confluence of ever-shifting energies. Under the scrutiny of science, both the self and the world are shown to be unstable: 'flickering' is a favoured term of Pater's. All experiences are defined by their evanescence, a truth that Pater uses to argue for the importance of seizing as they pass the most intense of these experiences. To do so is to engage in non-cognitive acts: moments of pure perception, beyond the bounds of reason or even conscious thought, analogous to the moment the body responds in 'delicious recoil from the flood of water in summer heat'. Such moments afford us a 'quickened sense of life', and they come most often in the form of 'the poetic passion, the desire for beauty, the love of art for its own sake'. The privileged place Pater claims for art is grounded in his belief that aesthetic responses are the most vital, the most fully human, experiences available to us.[37]

Like Hopkins, Pater insists on the particularity of each experience. The goal of aesthetics is to 'define beauty, not in the most abstract but in the most concrete terms possible' by finding 'the formula which expresses most adequately this or that special manifestation of it.'[38] 'Formula' fails to capture the performative quality of Pater's critical writings. Confronted by beauty, Pater shuns definition, tends sometimes even to shun description, in

---

36 Jonathan Freedman, *Professions of Taste: Henry James, Aestheticism, and Commodity Culture* (Stanford University Press, 1990), p. 66.
37 Pater, 'Conclusion', in *The Renaissance*, pp. 187, 186, 190.
38 Pater, 'Preface', in *The Renaissance*, p. xix.

favour of enacting a response. He is again like Hopkins in this regard. Where he parts company from his pupil is in his conviction that all knowledge and experience are relative. The pleasure Hopkins takes in the fleeting beauties of this world depends on his confidence that they emanate from a world of fixed and unchanging beauty.[39] For Pater, one consequence of modern thought is that we can no longer speak of the 'absolute'. 'To the modern spirit, nothing is, or can be rightly known' – or, as he goes on to show, rightly experienced – 'except relatively and under conditions'. We can place Hopkins's image of the soul as immortal diamond alongside Pater's famous image of aesthetic consciousness as 'a hard, gemlike flame'.[40] The flame is only gem*like*: we may perceive it as 'hard' or substantial but we know that it is in fact perpetually in motion, the concurrence, renewed from moment to moment, of forces parting sooner or later on their ways. Pater's defence of the value of fleeting, relative, situated knowledge and experience was perhaps his most fertile contribution to *fin-de-siècle* thought. His insight was taken up and further developed (without Pater's earnestness) by Oscar Wilde, just as Hopkins's yearning for the absolute was refigured (and stripped of its Christian theology) by Yeats before becoming a central component of high Modernism.

The idea that we are made – intellectually, emotionally, even physically – by the quality and intensity of our sensory impressions gained further traction from the rise of physiological aesthetics in the last decades of the century. Its theorists sought to put the study of aesthetics on a scientific basis by mapping the bodily changes produced by artistic stimuli. In *Physiological Aesthetics* (1877), Grant Allen defines the beautiful as, simply, that which gives the greatest amount of pleasurable sensory stimulation. Allen's formulation echoes Pater's description of aesthetic objects as 'powers or forces producing pleasurable sensations',[41] but Allen, unlike Pater, does not try to identify the particular attributes of objects that cause those pleasures. Instead he focuses on the metabolic changes that result from sensory stimulation, which were, he believed, in the long run the basis of individual growth. In much the same spirit, in the early 1890s Vernon Lee attempted to correlate aesthetic theory with biology by tracking the physical reactions of

---

39 At the same time, in poems such as 'Binsey Poplars' and 'Inversnaid' ('Let them be left / O let them be left, wildness and wet; / Long live the weeds and the wilderness yet' ('Inversnaid', *Poetical Works*, p. 168, lines 14–16)) Hopkins shows an acute awareness of how often the flight of beauty from the world is the result of human destructiveness.
40 Pater, 'Coleridge', in *Appreciations*, p. 66; 'Conclusion', in *The Renaissance*, p. 189.
41 Pater, 'Preface', in *The Renaissance*, p. xx.

her partner Kit Anstruther-Thomson to selected works of art. In their jointly authored essay 'Beauty and Ugliness' (1897), Lee and Anstruther-Thomson posit that the body responds to an artwork's formal beauty by unconsciously imitating that form, momentarily incorporating into itself the same balance and harmony of part to part that it finds in the artwork.[42]

Allen and Lee considered themselves disciples of Pater. Despite their avowed efforts to put Paterian aesthetics on a biological footing, however, arguably they were more interested in proving conclusively – that is, 'scientifically' – that genuine connoisseurship is ever only possible for the select few. If, Allen argued, aesthetic feelings originate in the firings of nerve-endings, the quality of those feelings is determined by the degree of 'fineness and discrimination in the nerves themselves.'[43] A sloppy social Darwinism underlies Allen's claim that hierarchies of taste and sensibility parallel hierarchies of class and race and gender because those higher up the scales are at more advanced stages of human evolution. As Allen's example suggests, much *fin-de-siècle* theorizing about the nature and practice of aesthetic appreciation is in implicit and often anxious reaction to rapid social changes occurring over the century's last decades: to the diversification of the reading public, for instance, or the increasing prominence of women in positions of cultural (and even on occasion of political) authority, or the accelerating spread of what would soon be known as mass culture. As critics such as Jonathan Freedman and Regenia Gagnier have pointed out, the *fin-de-siècle* witnessed the creation of a new social caste: the expert in aesthetic judgment, separated from the hoi polloi not just through his possession of esoteric knowledge but also through his more or less innate ability to feel intensely and discriminate finely.[44] That with few exceptions (Vernon Lee being one) members of this caste were male, university educated, and from the professional middle classes is at once highly relevant and utterly unsurprising.

In some circles, the ability to cultivate sensation was virtually the sole criterion of personal worth, a sign of distinction as well as the source of a certain amount of authority and prestige. In 1886 a sceptical George Meredith expressed 'amazement at the importance we attach to our hold of sensation',

---

42 Vernon Lee and Clementina Anstruther-Thomson, *Beauty and Ugliness and Other Studies in Psychological Aesthetics* (London: Bodley Head, 1912). The original essay was published in two parts in the *Contemporary Review* in October and November 1897.
43 Grant Allen, *Physiological Aesthetics* (London: King, 1877), p. 48.
44 Freedman, *Professions of Taste*; Regenia Gagnier, 'Productive Bodies, Pleasured Bodies: On Victorian Aesthetics', in Talia Schaffer and Kathy Alexis Psomiades (eds.), *Women and British Aestheticism* (Charlottesville: University Press of Virginia, 1999), pp. 270–89.

suggesting that it was at best a mixed blessing, since sensation disabled certain modes of consciousness.[45] Few followed Meredith's lead here, though many did worry that the rage for 'appreciation' could have an enervating rather than a stimulating effect on one's character. Of George Somerset, the aesthetically inclined protagonist of his 1881 novel *A Laodicean*, Thomas Hardy says that he 'suffered from the modern malady of unlimited appreciativeness'.[46] Somerset's assiduous self-cultivation results not in a sensibility of hard gem-like flame but instead in the 'lukewarmness' of the Laodiceans in the Book of Revelations. Unmoored and drifting, incapable of decisive action, Somerset suffers an 'ache of modernism' different from but sharp as the one afflicting Tess Durbeyfield.

In practice, cultivating sensation too often depended on the demeaning objectification of other people, mostly women or the poor. Diana Maltz has shown how efforts to help the poor became, for many a well-intentioned philanthropist or social worker, inseparable from 'the pursuit of squalor as an aesthetic experience'.[47] Consider this squirm-inducing reminiscence from Hugh Reginald Haweis, who for a time was curate of St Peter's in London's impoverished Bethnal Green:

> I know not what glamour in those days hung over the grimy and repulsive aspects of Bethnal Green life ... The reeking streets seemed beautiful to me in the evening sunshine; the unwashed and multitudinous children feeding on garbage in the gutter, filled me with infinite tenderness and pity, the more because they seemed so happy; the sick poor dying in back rooms, the work-house wards, the close factory houses packed with pale girls staring at straw bonnet work, etc. etc ... all these scenes of my daily life seemed to me then exquisitely pathetic, novel, interesting and exciting. I was not in the least depressed by the surrounding misery; I was not responsible for it ... I was strangely exhilarated by it.[48]

In less dramatic but no less oppressive ways, the fetishizing of female beauty – so prominent a feature of *fin-de-siècle* art and aesthetics – often went hand in hand with a desire to ward off incursions by actual women into traditional precincts of male privilege, including the privileges associated with artistic practice and aesthetic evaluation. To many, the phrase 'female aesthete' had a faintly oxymoronic ring to it. If not every man could quite bring himself

45 *The Letters of George Meredith*, ed. C. L. Cline (Oxford: Clarendon Press, 1970), p. 804.
46 Thomas Hardy, *A Laodicean: A Story of To-Day* (1881; Harmondsworth: Penguin, 1997), chapter 1, p. 7.
47 Diana Maltz, *British Aestheticism and the Urban Working Classes 1870–1900* (London: Palgrave, 2006), p. 89.
48 H. R. Haweis, *My Musical Life* (London, 1884), p. 115.

to assent to Havelock Ellis's claims concerning women's 'defective sense for purely aesthetic beauty', many were content to believe that 'the artistic impulse is vastly more spontaneous, more pronounced, and more widely spread among men than among women'.[49] As a result, women were consistently associated with 'lesser' aesthetic forms, mostly those aligned with popular culture or with journalistic writing. This resulted not just in a distorted view of the work of prominent writers such as Sarah Grand, Mona Caird, Lucas Malet, and Oliver Schreiner, but also in the neglect of experimental work by writers Talia Schaffer has called the 'forgotten female aesthetes': poets such as Alice Meynell, Graham R. Tomson, and Michael Field, critics and essayists such as Vernon Lee and Mary Haweis, and prose fiction writers such as Elizabeth von Armin, Ouida, George Egerton, and John Oliver Hobbes.[50] Working self-consciously within the discourses of male aestheticism, such writers offered some stringent critiques of those discourses. They also explored women's modes of consciousness and sensibility through, in part, an array of vigorous re-inventings of generic forms.

Female aesthetes explored with great subtlety the question of art's relation to the burgeoning commodity culture of the *fin de siècle*. In novels such as Amy Levy's *The Romance of a Shop* (1888), Ella Hepworth Dixon's *The Story of a Modern Woman* (1894), and Gertrude Dix's *The Image Breakers* (1900), aestheticism of the Wildean variety is consistently represented as being complicit with the marketplace it ostensibly rejects. Yet the entanglement of aesthetic practices with the practices of consumerism was a fraught topic for artists of all genders. What – if anything – distinguishes a 'genuine' work of art from a 'mere' consumer product? While assiduously cultivating our sensations, on what basis can we discriminate the sensations produced by commodities from those produced by art objects? If much serious art in this period sets itself explicitly in opposition to material culture, that is largely because the lines between the two had become so blurred. That blurring has led many critics, Theodor Adorno perhaps most powerfully, to dismiss *fin-de-siècle* aesthetics as little more than a cover for the triumph of consumerist ideology.[51] Such dismissals, though, underestimate the clarity with which late Victorian thinkers understood the issues at hand.

49 Havelock Ellis, *Man and Woman: A Study of Human Secondary Sexual Characters* (London: Walter Scott, 1894), pp. 326–7.
50 Talia Schaffer, *The Forgotten Female Aesthetes: Literary Culture in Late-Victorian England* (Charlottesville: University Press of Virginia, 2000).
51 Theodor Adorno, *Aesthetic Theory*, trans. C. Lenhardt (London: Routledge and Kegan Paul, 1984), pp. 337–43.

In his *History of Aesthetic* (1892), Bernard Bosanquet notes the significance of aesthetics in the development of economic theory in Britain during the eighteenth and nineteenth centuries, a situation unique among European nations.[52] For Bosanquet, as for many others, Ruskin's work was decisive in this context. Ruskin insisted – eloquently, repeatedly, in numerous venues over multiple decades – that the aesthetic value of any made object ultimately derives from the quality of the labour expended to produce it. Genuine aesthetic appreciation therefore requires an awareness of political economy. Ruskin insisted too on the importance of developing an ethics of consumption, one grounded in an understanding of the conditions in which commodities, including artworks, are produced. Central to Ruskin's position was his belief that the quality of the labour that goes into the making of an object will always be discernible in the finished product. Beauty is defined not abstractly but as, in part, a function of the social conditions in which the work of creation takes place. Ruskin, and after him Morris, deplored the fact that England was overrun with 'things', made badly and in abundance. Morris recognized that the engine of capitalism required that an 'immensity of work' be performed in 'the making of useless things'.[53] Here is the reverse side of the period's fixation on particularity: the rejection of mass production and mass consumption. Morris's and Ruskin's praise for the imperfection in the made object that marks it as the creation of a particular individual, Hopkins's search for the unique pattern that comprises inscape, Pater's valuing of the fleeting and unrepeatable experience – these analogous gestures are efforts to resist or undercut the dominance of industrial mass production.

Ruskin decried what he memorably called the 'illth' of contemporary life under capitalism.[54] The opposite of both health and wealth, illth also evokes, and is consonant with, the idea of filth. Implicit in Ruskin's social critique is the suggestion that economic and social inequities manifest themselves – become, as it were, tangible – as filth. This is not simply to say that poverty is ugly, but rather to posit that ugliness is the ultimate truth of the structures and processes of capitalism, which cannot in themselves be apprehended by the senses. Though Ruskin had little use for the French-inflected Realist fiction that began to appear in Britain in the 1870s and 1880s, that fiction

52 Bernard Bosanquet, *A History of Aesthetic* (London: Swan Sonnenschein, 1892), pp. 441–70.
53 William Morris, 'Art and Socialism' (1884), in *The Collected Works of William Morris*, ed. May Morris, 24 vols. (London: Longmans, Green, & Co., 1910–15), vol. XXIII, p. 198.
54 *Unto This Last* (1860), in *The Works of John Ruskin*, ed. E. T. Cook and Alexander Wedderburn, 39 vols. (London: George Allen, 1903–12), vol. XVII, p. 89.

often pursues the Ruskinian task of rendering economic abstractions in terms of tactile experience. The novels of George Gissing are a case in point. The typical Gissing protagonist – concisely described by Gissing himself as 'well educated, fairly bred, *but without money*' – experiences his economic oppression primarily as a form of aesthetic deprivation. Gissing sourly turned away from efforts to explain in systemic terms the plight of this 'class of young men distinctive of our time', focusing instead on the sensory starvation that comes to define their lived experiences of the world.[55] Beauty is a felt absence in these novels, which linger with masochistic relish over descriptions of the waste cityscapes and claustrophobic interiors of a modernity synonymous with ugliness. Gissing's characters often proceed as if beauty, could it only be found again, would be sufficient to alleviate social ills. '[N]othing in this world is more useful than the *beautiful*', says a character in *Workers in the Dawn* (1880), because 'nothing works so powerfully for the benefit of mankind'.[56] Gissing himself was nowhere near so optimistic. His novels tend to fetishize the hopeless anger that to him seemed the only legitimate response to the illth of modernity. He disliked Émile Zola's work and rejected comparisons to him, but he was perhaps the sole late Victorian novelist who took up the challenge Zola laid down in an 1891 journal article. 'Say shit to the century', Zola advised his fellow writers.[57]

Gissing frequently depicts 'the nether world' of abject urban poverty, but he is finally more interested in the lives of those on the border separating poverty from the lowest reaches of middle-class respectability. Gissing himself spent most of his adulthood on that border, and like many of his characters – Edwin Reardon in *New Grub Street* (1891) is the best-known example – he found on his occasional and usually brief ascents into the middle class that life there was more 'impoverished' in every sense except the economic. The spiritual and aesthetic aridity of middle-class life is a constant theme of *fin-de-siècle* literature. Gissing's novels have plenty of company in this regard. Chiding the philistines was a favoured pastime of late Victorian writers, who brought this particular form of jeremiad to

---

55 *The Collected Letters of George Gissing*, ed. Paul Mattheisen, Arthur C. Young, and Pierre Coustillas 9 vols. (Athens: Ohio University Press, 1990–7), vol. v, p. 296.

56 George Gissing, *Workers in the Dawn* (1880; Brighton: Harvester Press, 1985), chapter 38, p. 269. Italics are in the original.

57 Quoted in Neil Blackadder, '*Merde!* Performing Filth in the Bourgeois Public Sphere', in William A. Cohen and Ryan Johnson (eds.), *Filth: Dirt, Disgust, and Modern Life* (Minneapolis: University of Minnesota Press, 2005), p. 184.

a new level of perfection. Their critiques often focused on a new social space associated with petit bourgeois life and with the ethos of consumerism: the suburb. In the suburbs, critics saw the objective correlative of what T. W. H. Crosland in 1905 called the 'dead-level of dulness and weariness and meanness' of petit bourgeois ideology, the banality of petit bourgeois taste.[58] 'Nothing fine, nothing rare, nothing exquisite, it seemed, could exist in the weltering suburban sea', laments Lucian Taylor in Arthur Machen's *The Hills of Dreams* (1907). Suburbia, he thinks, is 'the only hell that a vulgar age could conceive or make, an inferno created not by Dante but by the jerry-builder'.[59] John Norton, Paterian dilettante and classicist in George Moore's *A Mere Accident* (1887), likewise cannot contemplate suburban life 'without a revulsion of feeling'. In the suburbs, he contends, 'there is no yearning for anything higher or better'.[60] Even *fin-de-siècle* writers who chronicled suburban life charitably, such as Arnold Bennett and H. G. Wells, or at least comically, as George Grossmith does in *Diary of a Nobody* (1892), saw it as by definition antithetical to the fine, the rare, and the exquisite.[61] While suburban life seems to lend itself most readily to the literary techniques of Realism or Naturalism, it is worth noting how often suburban landscapes become sites of the uncanny in *fin-de-siècle* Gothic fiction – as they were sites, too, for ghost stories from the mid-century onwards. The eponymous monster of Richard Marsh's *The Beetle* (1897) resides in a jerry-built house in Walham Green; the eponymous monster of Bram Stoker's *Dracula* (1897) buys property in Purfleet. The suburb's in-betweeness – a 'desolation that was neither town nor country', as Lucian Taylor puts it after moving to Shepherd's Bush[62] – could make it seem a liminal place, a border between the worlds of the supernatural and the extraordinarily mundane. All of Machen's outlandish tales are set wholly or in part in the suburbs.

Yet it was finally the suburban bourgeoisie who, as a class, most enthusiastically embraced the dictum that beauty enriches. Even Charles and Carrie Pooter, Grossmith's iconic figures of middlebrow vulgarity, believe implicitly in the power of beauty to make ordinary life better. The Aesthetic Movement of the 1870s and 1880s was primarily a middle-class affair, inseparable – as the

---

58 T. W. H. Crosland, *The Suburbans* (London: John Lane, 1905), p. 69.
59 Arthur Machen, *The Hill of Dreams* (New York: Alfred Knopf, 1923), pp. 242, 243. Though it was not published until 1907, Machen completed the novel in 1897.
60 George Moore, *A Mere Accident* (London: Vizetelly & Co., 1887), pp. 54, 55.
61 On suburbia in late Victorian and Edwardian fiction, see Kate Flint, 'Fictional Suburbia,' in Peter Humm, Paul Stigant, and Peter Widdowson (eds.), *Popular Fictions: Essays in Literature and History* (London: Methuen, 1986), pp. 111–26.
62 Machen, *Hills of Dreams*, p. 156.

Pooters' example makes plain – from the expanding opportunities for consumerism that the period offered. Whereas for Ruskin the cultivation of a healthy aesthetic sensibility served to make one fully aware of the corruption of sensibility produced by consumerism, in the culture at large a refinement of taste most often displayed itself by way of conspicuous consumption. The last decades of the century saw 'revolutions' in middle-class architecture, home furnishing, dress, and design, much of it indebted to the work of Morris and his followers. But while Morris had found in aestheticism the seeds of an utterly transfigured world, most proponents of the Aesthetic Movement were content simply to beautify the appurtenances of the world as it is. Radical and consumerist aestheticisms get oddly entangled in the period: Walter Hamilton's *The Aesthetic Movement in England* (1881), for instance, moves with breezy unselfconsciousness from accounts of avant-garde poetry to surveys of changes in home decoration.[63]

Middle-class faith in the restorative effects of beauty is nowhere more evident than in the efforts of philanthropists to rescue the destitute and the downtrodden with the aid of the aesthetic. From the 1870s onward the poorest districts of London's East End were overrun by 'missionary aesthetes' determined, in Diana Maltz's words, to remedy 'slum chaos and slum brutality through communal aesthetic revelation'.[64] Benefactors founded museums for the poor, such as the Whitechapel Art Gallery and the South London Art Gallery. In 1875, the Kyrle Society for the Diffusion of Beauty among the People commenced diffusing beauty among the people. (Modelled on the much older Society for the Diffusion of Useful Knowledge, the Kyrle Society in its very name signalled that the relation of *utile* to *dulce* in art was being refigured.) Such endeavours were often satirized. In his best-known novel, *A Child of the Jago* (1896), Arthur Morrison holds up for comic ridicule the efforts of the East End Elevation Mission and Pansophical Institute to 'manufacture . . . the Superior Person' by means of such 'radiant abstractions' as 'the Higher Life, the Greater Thought, and the Wider Humanity'. Such grandiosity is put in contrast to the hard-nosed and pragmatic efforts of the Reverend Henry Sturt, who by means of steadily

---

63 By contrast, Mary Haweis is considerably more attuned to the potential for cultural transformation latent in what would otherwise seem the frivolous pursuits of *The Art of Beauty* (1879), *The Art of Dress* (1880), or *The Art of Decoration* (1881).

64 Maltz, *British Aestheticism and the Urban Working Classes*, p. 1. See also Seth Koven's account of the politics and erotics of dirt in late Victorian philanthropy in *Slumming: Sexual and Social Politics in Victorian London* (Princeton University Press, 2004), especially pp. 183–227.

'working, alleviating, growing into the Jago life, [while] flinging scorn and ridicule on evil things' achieves what modest good can reasonably be expected among the poor, in Morrison's view.[65]

Roman Catholics and High Church Anglicans nevertheless frequently sought to relieve the sufferings of the poor through sacramental worship and Church ritual, practices in which spiritual renewal and aesthetic awakening were said to go hand in hand. In the case of the Anglican clergyman Stewart Headlam, belief in the transformative power of sacrament and ritual was combined with radical politics and a quasi-Decadent surrender to the ravishments of art. Headlam achieved a lasting notoriety not primarily for his defence of Ritualism, or for his controversial political gestures (he supported many of the reforms sponsored by the radical secularist Charles Bradlaugh, for instance, and in 1895 he posted bail for the disgraced Oscar Wilde), or for his conviction that the catechism was history's 'best manual of Socialism', or even for his belief that the beauties of sacramental observance would awaken the poor to the need for political revolution. He was instead best known for his passionate advocacy of dance, which he considered to be at once a form of worship and a potential instrument of social renewal. Criticized for his patronage of the ballet and – more scandalous still – the music hall, Headlam responded by celebrating dance in terms remarkably like those later used by Symons and Yeats: dance is embodied art, and true art is sacramental. Though the dancer may well be unconscious of the fact, Headlam writes, it is nonetheless true that 'the poetry of motion is the expression of unseen spiritual grace'.[66]

Unsurprisingly, even the sincerest efforts to disseminate beauty among the poor did little to alleviate the actual miseries of poverty. Missionary aestheticism was directed at individuals, leaving the systemic causes of suffering untouched. Wilde was not alone in arguing that altruism did not solve the problem of poverty but was instead 'an aggravation of the difficulty' because it distracted attention away from poverty's root causes. It is not enough to continue 'amusing the poor', he writes in 'The Soul of Man under Socialism' (1891). The goal instead must be to *reconstruct society on such a basis that poverty will be impossible*. Yet for Wilde too the ultimate goal

---

65 Arthur Morrison, *A Child of the Jago* (London: Ward, Lock, & Co., 1896), chapters 2, 14, pp. 21, 174. Morrison based Sturt on the Reverend A. Osborne Jay, Vicar of Holy Trinity, Shoreditch. Jay produced highly readable accounts of his own East End experiences in *Life in Darkest London* (1891) and *A Story of Shoreditch* (1896).

66 Stewart Headlam, *The Laws of Eternal Life, Being Studies in the Church Catechism* (London: Frederick Verinder, 1888), p. 43.

was the transformation of individuals. With characteristic flair, he argues that reconstructing society on *socialist* lines would allow for the flourishing of *individualism*, which he defines as 'the full development of Life to its highest mode of perfection' through the refinement of aesthetic sensibility.[67] Central to Wilde's position was his belief that the full development of Life is, under proper social conditions, open to all.

In 'The Soul of Man Under Socialism' Wilde goes even further, offering an unashamedly utopian vision of a world in which individuals not only develop to the full their aesthetic capabilities but also make their own lives and persons into works of art. Here Wilde shows himself to be the descendant not of Ruskin but of Baudelaire, whose figuration of the dandy as embodied artwork – 'the ultimate incarnation of the idea of beauty' in Baudelaire's phrase – was central to Wilde's self-fashioning.[68] Where Ruskinian aestheticism was grounded in the values associated with work – self-making through productive labour – the Baudelairean dandy held himself apart from those values, opting instead for an identity inseparable from the pleasures of consumption and spectatorship. For Ruskin and Morris, as for Marx, men and women come into possession of their humanity through life-affirming acts of *expression*: outward-directed actions that alter or leave a lasting mark on the physical world or on the minds of other men and women. For Baudelaire and those who followed him, self-making was tied up with *impression*: the self shaped by the action of forces from without. The Baudelairean dandy is of course not merely passive. A perpetual vigilance, comprised of continuous acts of will, judgment, taste, and discipline, ensures that the impress of the world's energies moulds the self in desired ways. But the focus is resolutely inward, the goal to give one's life the shape of art.

The scandal of the late-century Decadent movement, for which Baudelaire's life and writings were touchstones, lay largely in this rejection of productivity as a human ideal. French literature of the period provides multiple literary explorations of Decadent self-making, the best known being J.-K. Huysmans's *À rebours* (1885). In England, where the fetishizing of work remained strong throughout the century, such radical self-fashioning was most often explored under the auspices of the Gothic. In *fin-de-siècle* Gothic fiction, the idea of a life wholly devoted to and formed by consumption is

---

67 Wilde, 'The Soul of Man Under Socialism', in *The Artist as Critic*, pp. 256, 257. Italics are in the original.
68 Charles Baudelaire, 'Further Notes on Edgar Poe' (1857), in *Charles Baudelaire: Selected Writings on Art and Literature*, ed. and trans. P. E. Charvet (Harmondsworth: Penguin, 1992), p. 195.

literalized as a species of vampirism. Huysmans's Des Esseintes and Stoker's Count Dracula have this much in common: noblemen of good breeding and better 'taste', they exist largely in isolation from humanity but survive by feeding off other lives. A familiar figure in late Victorian Gothic is the creature who drains the vitality of others or whose preternatural beauty or goodness is linked to a hidden ugliness. Rider Haggard's queenly Ayesha in *She* (1887) lives largely upon the devotion of her enslaved suitors, while Robert Louis Stevenson's upright Henry Jekyll draws vicariously on the monstrous excesses of his alter ego Edward Hyde. Even Wilde's best-known exploration of Decadent self-fashioning, *The Picture of Dorian Gray* (1891), takes the form of a cautionary Gothic fable.

To give one's life the shape of art: the contours of this endeavour would soon be changed by a generation of writers whose aesthetic sensibilities were formed in the *fin-de-siècle* they alternately celebrated and satirized.

> He drew forth a phrase from his treasure and spoke it softly to himself.
> – A day of dappled seaborne clouds.

> The phrase and the day and the scene harmonized in a chord. Words. Was it their colours? He allowed them to glow and fade, hue after hue: sunrise gold, the russet and green of apple orchards, azure of waves, the greyfringed fleece of clouds. No, it was not their colours: it was the poise and balance of the period itself. Did he then love the rhythmic rise and fall of words better than their associations of legend and colour? Or was it that, being as weak of sight as he was shy of mind, he drew less pleasure from the reflection of the glowing sensible world through the prism of a language manycoloured and richly storied than from the contemplation of an inner world of individual emotions mirrored perfectly in a lucid supple periodic prose?[69]

In its own rhythms, its balance and poise and supple lucidity (not to mention its adjectival luxuriance), this passage from *A Portrait of the Artist as a Young Man* (1916) is a splendid example of *fin-de-siècle* aesthetic prose – unless, that is, we decide to take it as Joyce's parody of such prose, perhaps deciding at the same time to take Stephen Dedalus, at this stage of his life and linguistic self-fashioning, as his send-up of the late-century aesthete. As Stanislaus Joyce makes clear in his account of the voluminous if desultory reading his brother undertook during his time at University College, Dublin, Joyce himself was nothing if not a true child of the *fin-de-siècle*. Wilde was one point of orientation for him: as late as 1909, Joyce considered translating

---

69 James Joyce, *A Portrait of the Artist as a Young Man* (1916; New York: Penguin, 1992), pp. 180–1.

'The Soul of Man Under Socialism' into Italian. Another was Blake, whose combination of 'intellectual sharpness with mystic sentiment' and vision of a 'glorified humanity' never lost their appeal.[70] Yet Joyce transfigured his *fin-de-siècle* inheritance. In creating Stephen Dedalus he did not make himself a mask in Wilde's sense or even Yeats's. Stephen is a quite different thing, an aesthetic artefact Joyce made from his life. That is to say, Stephen's life takes on the shape of Joyce's art.

70 Stanislaus Joyce, *My Brother's Keeper: James Joyce's Early Years* (New York: Viking), p. 98. In 1909 Joyce wrote from Trieste to Robert Ross, Wilde's literary executor, asking permission to translate 'The Soul of Man Under Socialism' into Italian. Permission was granted, but Joyce never undertook the project. See Richard Ellmann, *James Joyce*, 2nd edn (New York: Oxford University Press, 1982), p. 274. The quotations concerning Blake are from Joyce's 1912 lecture on Blake. See James Joyce, *Occasional, Critical, and Political Writing* (Oxford University Press, 2000), pp. 180–1.

PART III

*

MODES OF WRITING

7

Lyric and the lyrical

ANGELA LEIGHTON

... the forms are often confused.[1]

'The Editor is acquainted with no strict and exhaustive definition of Lyrical Poetry',[2] wrote Francis Palgrave in the preface to the first of his immensely popular anthologies, *The Golden Treasury: Of the Best Songs and Lyrical Poems in the English Language* (1861). A crucial arbiter of poetic tastes in the nineteenth century, *The Golden Treasury* would go on to sell about ten thousand copies a year until the Second World War.[3] In 1860, Palgrave had written to Tennyson to ask advice about methods of selection: 'I hesitate whether *Elegies* such as Gray's, and *Sonnets* should properly be included. They are lyrical in structure, and sonnets have always ranked as lyrical; but their didactic tone appears to me not decisively lyrical.'[4] The problem of what is, and is not, lyrical would never be easily settled. At this time Palgrave decided to exclude both didactic poetry and 'all pieces markedly dramatic'.[5] However, by the time he came to the 1897 edition, he was forced to acknowledge not only 'a vast extension in length of our lyrics' but also their frequently 'dramatic character'.[6] The 'dramatic', which in 1861 seemed antipathetic to lyric, could no longer be categorically excluded. For much of the nineteenth and twentieth centuries, the term 'lyric' has eluded decisive definition, its relation to the 'dramatic' being one of the word's most difficult faultlines. As a term, it is both frustratingly unspecific yet powerfully enduring.

---

1 James Joyce, *A Portrait of the Artist as a Young Man* (Harmondsworth: Penguin, 2000), p. 232.
2 Francis Turner Palgrave, selected and arranged, *The Golden Treasury: Of the Best Songs and Lyrical Poems in the English Language* ed. Christopher Ricks (London: Penguin, 1991), p. 5. Thanks to Heather Glen for this example.
3 Christopher Ricks, in *ibid.*, p. 444.   4 Letter to Tennyson, quoted in *ibid.*, p. 439.
5 *Ibid.*, p. 5.   6 *Ibid.*, p. 461.

Certainly, since Palgrave, definitions have proved no easier. Unlike the sonnet or the ballad, the term does not apply to a specific verse form, nor does it, like the ode or the epic, identify a particular authorial stance or theme. Many kinds of shortish poem might be classed as lyric, whether in strict or free verse, whether personal or impersonal in theme. As for 'the lyrical', that term covers almost any poetic-sounding writing in verse or prose. No doubt the Romantics' tendency to experiment with mixed modes, William Wordsworth's *Lyrical Ballads* (1798), Mary Robinson's *Lyrical Tales* (1800), and Percy Bysshe Shelley's *Prometheus Unbound: A Lyrical Drama* (1820), for instance, helped muddy the issue. Palgrave's first attempt to separate the lyric from didactic, narrative, or dramatic poetry proved short-lived. By the time of the first *OED*'s definition (1928), the word is not much clearer: 'Of or pertaining to the lyre; adapted to the lyre, meant to be sung; pertaining to or characteristic of song. Now used as the name for short poems (whether or not intended to be sung), usually divided into stanzas and strophes, and directly expressing the poet's own thoughts and sentiments.'

This too proceeds with caution. 'Now used' does not spell out when exactly, or how it was used before, and 'usually divided' also means 'not always'. John Hollander helps to flesh out the chronology behind this statement when he points out that 'the fundamental separation between the lyric poem and the actual text for music [happened] in the seventeenth century'.[7] Before then, 'lyric' referred to the words of a text intended to be sung, as the term 'lyrics' still does. Nevertheless, even after the seventeenth century the etymology of 'lyric' as 'pertaining to the lyre' remains audible in the word, reminding us of its origins in music and song. Certainly, the lyre offers a metaphor for poetry long after any lyres were regularly played. 'Make me thy lyre, even as the forest is' (1819),[8] Shelley writes with no irony in 'Ode to the West Wind', though by the time Pound uses the figure, a century later, it is loaded with Modernist (and gender) distrust: 'If she with ivory fingers drive a tune through the lyre',[9] he writes in *Homage to Sextus Propertius* (1917). If the lyre as an image for poetry-making goes out of fashion in the twentieth century, the use of song as a synonym for verse

---

7 John Hollander, *Vision and Resonance: Two Senses of Poetic Form* (New Haven and London: Yale University Press, 1985), p. 188.

8 Percy Bysshe Shelley, *Poetical Works*, ed. Thomas Hutchinson, corr. G. M. Matthews (London: Oxford University Press, 1970), pp. 577–9: 579.

9 Ezra Pound, 'Homage to Sextus Propertius', in *Personae*, revised Lea Baechler and A. Walton Litz (London: Faber, 1990), pp. 203–25: p. 213.

remains familiar to the present day. Poetry has always found its natural home-metaphors in the vocabulary of music.

Thus lyric, 'pertaining to or characteristic of song', refers to a singable kind of verse, even if no longer verse set to music. However, the rest of the dictionary definition remains debatably open. Lyric may or may not be in 'stanzas and strophes', while the notion that it should 'directly [express] the poet's own thoughts and sentiments' depends on some unquestioned assumptions. How do we know they are the poet's? How do we know something is thought or felt? How direct is 'directly'? Like many definitions of lyric, this one begs as many questions as it answers.

The dictionary definition is largely driven by the unspoken assumption that lyric is opposed to drama. In lyric, supposedly, there is a direct correlation between the poet's sentiments and the words of the poem. Lyrical expression is neither strategic nor oblique, and the lyrical poet is a straight talker, who says what s(h)e feels. John Ruskin, defining the lyric in 1873, made precisely this point. Distinguishing lyric from dramatic and epic forms, he declares: 'Lyric poetry is the expression by the poet of his own feelings.'[10] The poet's 'own feelings' go into the lyric quickly and simply, without deliberation or deviation. The poet feels, and the poem expresses it. Some forty years before, John Stuart Mill had offered a powerfully influential account of the essential difference between poetry and eloquence (or dramatic speaking), when he wrote that: 'eloquence is *heard*, poetry is *over*heard'(1833). Thus separating all poetry from drama, and simplifying all types of poetry into the lyric, he explains that the 'symbols' of poetry 'are the nearest possible representations of the feeling in the exact shape in which it exists in the poet's mind'.[11] He, likewise, simplifies the journey from poet's mind to poem. An 'exact shape' is transferred from one to the other, without ironic or dramatic distance between them. Both Ruskin and Mill, then, describe the lyric as having a heartfelt, inner compulsiveness, a kind of simplicity of intention that reproduces and expresses nothing but 'feeling'. Lyric is a private, confessional mode, with no ulterior designs on its reader, and apparently without writerly labour. Behind all these accounts lies a Romantic notion of inspiration that is both swift and unaccountable.

10 John Ruskin, Letter xxxiv, *Fors Clavigera*, in *The Works of John Ruskin*, 39 vols., eds. E.T. Cook and Alexander Wedderburn (London: George Allen, 1903–12), vol. xxvii, p. 629.
11 John Stuart Mill, *Autobiography and Literary Essays*, 29 vols., ed. John M. Robson and Jack Stillinger (London: Routledge & Kegan Paul, 1981), vol. i, p. 348.

The opposition between lyric and drama resonates long after the end of the Victorian age. James Joyce, defining the lyric perhaps a little self-mockingly at the end of *A Portrait of the Artist as a Young Man* (1916), also distinguishes the lyric from epic and dramatic writing, asserting that: 'The lyrical form is in fact the simplest verbal vesture of an instant of emotion, a rhythmical cry.'[12] Joyce, through his hero, repeats the idea that the lyric expresses, easily and instantly, an 'emotion'. Such an 'emotion' is the pinprick which causes the lyric's 'rhythmical cry'. As late as 1977, the critic Barbara Hardy is continuing this long tradition of thought. 'The advantage of lyric poetry', she writes, 'comes from its undiluted attention to feeling and feeling alone.'[13] It may not be clear whose feeling is being attended to, whether the poet's, the reader's, or perhaps the poem's, but 'feeling' remains the main impulse of a poetry which, she explains, 'frequently cuts out history and character entirely'.[14] If that 'frequently' leaves a little chink for dispute, lyric nevertheless continues to be defined in opposition to drama, the genre of 'history and character'.

These examples attest to the enduring power of the Romantic version of lyric, stemming from Mill and Ruskin. There are, however, others. Perhaps the most powerful refutation of lyric as conveyor of the poet's feelings comes in T. S. Eliot's essay 'The Three Voices of Poetry' (1953). Eliot, like Joyce, is writing in reaction to the Victorians, as his echoes of Mill suggest. He proposes, for instance, that 'our enjoyment of great poetry is the enjoyment of *overhearing* words which are not addressed to us'.[15] He defines the first voice of poetry, the lyric voice, as 'the voice of the poet talking to himself – or to nobody'.[16] In spite of this audible tribute to Mill,[17] Eliot then offers an extended critique of the feeling lyric. First of all, worrying that the term 'lyric' 'cannot be satisfactorily defined',[18] he

---

12 Joyce, *Portrait of the Artist*, p. 214.
13 Barbara Hardy, *The Advantage of Lyric: Essays on Feeling in Poetry*, (London: Athlone Press, 1977), p. 2.
14 *Ibid.*, p. 54.
15 T. S. Eliot, 'The Three Voices of Poetry', in *On Poetry and Poets* (London: Faber and Faber, 1957), pp. 89–102: p. 100.
16 *Ibid.*, p. 97.
17 Geoffrey Hill suggests that Eliot's reference to Gottfried Benn at this point is 'inane', avoiding, as it does, Benn's sympathy with the Nazi party. But Hill also adds his own comment on the lyric. 'Of course', he writes, 'the lyric is addressed to no one.' 'A Postscript on Modernist Poetics', in Hill, *Collected Critical Writings*, ed. Kenneth Haynes (Oxford University Press, 2008), pp. 565–80: p. 573.
18 Eliot, 'Three Voices', p. 96.

proceeds to question the *OED*'s stress on shortness. 'How short does a poem have to be . . .?'[19] he quizzes. He then quibbles about how the lyric reflects 'the poet's own thoughts and sentiments'. By contrast, he writes: 'What you start from is nothing so definite as an emotion, in any ordinary sense; it is still more certainly not an idea.'[20] Dissociating the lyric from the poet's feelings, he hints that it originates in something much vaguer: there is 'nothing so definite as an emotion' behind a poem. Moreover, since the lyric does not express the poet's feelings or ideas, it is impossible to separate it from drama. Those three voices of poetry – the poet talking to himself, to an audience, or through a dramatic character – are, he suggests, 'most often found together', in particular 'the first and second'.[21] So Eliot, ultimately rebuffing the heritage of Mill, offers a definition of the lyric as essentially a mixed mode which cannot be tracked back to the poet's private feelings. In other words, if the lyric is 'the voice of the poet talking to himself – or to nobody', this is not incompatible with its being dramatic, and having half an eye to an audience.

Eliot's is a typically Modernist distrust of lyric as the voice of true feeling. A few years later, the critics Wimsatt and Brooks summarized the effects of such scepticism: 'once we have dissociated the speaker of the lyric from the personality of the poet, even the tiniest lyric reveals itself as drama'.[22] By detaching the lyric from the poet's feelings, it can be given a voice, a character, and a dramatic context of its own. Even 'the tiniest lyric' thus becomes a performance. Other poets at this time were rejecting the opposition to drama. Robert Frost, for instance, claimed in the Preface to his collection *A Way Out* (1929) that 'Everything written is as good as it is dramatic. It need not declare itself in form, but it is drama or nothing.' This is true, he insisted, even of the 'least lyric'. The reason is, not only that the poet's feelings have been removed from the debate, but that, as Frost puts it: 'A dramatic necessity goes deep into the nature of the sentence.'[23] Here, the old division of genres has completely broken down. There is no essential difference between lyric and dramatic forms because both are constructed in language.

---

19 *Ibid.*, p. 97.   20 *Ibid.*, p. 98.   21 *Ibid.*, p. 99.
22 William K. Wimsatt, Jr. and Cleanth Brooks, *Literary Criticism: A Short History*, 4 vols. (London: Routledge & Kegan Paul, 1970), vol. iv, p. 675.
23 Robert Frost, *The Collected Prose of Robert Frost*, ed. Mark Richardson (Cambridge, MA: Harvard University Press, 2007), p. 99.

What is clear, then, is that the lyric remains a subject of debate and disagreement, and that its definition involves some negotiation with drama. For Mill and Ruskin, the lyric is a speech from the heart, as opposed to a performed eloquence. For Eliot and Frost, there is no originating feeling to guarantee meaning, and therefore the lyric is only another form of drama. This might look like a disagreement between the Victorians and the Modernists, but in fact it is not. Palgrave himself changed his criteria of selection between 1861 and 1897, as he wrestled with the lyric's relation to drama. And there were other Victorians who recognized the difficulty of separating the two. One of the main reasons for this difficulty, as Palgrave himself recognized, was the emergence of a distinctive new genre which, long before the Modernists, helped confuse the whole issue: the dramatic monologue.

Mixed modes

> and the women sang
> Between the rougher voices of the men,
> Like linnets in the pauses of the wind:
> And here I give the story and the songs.[24]

As early as 1831, Arthur Hallam's review of Tennyson's *Poems, Chiefly Lyrical* (1830) announced that Tennyson's lyrics about women were 'summaries of mighty dramas', and that his verse in general offered 'a new species of poetry, a graft of the lyric on the dramatic'.[25] A century before Eliot and Frost, then, the lyric and the dramatic were elided. Tennyson's very title, *Poems, Chiefly Lyrical*, is a reminder that 'lyrical', the adjective, refers to qualities *within* poems rather than to a distinct type of poetry. These are not chiefly lyrics, but '*Chiefly Lyrical*' – the 'lyrical' being only one among other qualities.

'Mariana', for instance, might be read either as the summary of a drama or as a private lyric, as story or as song. On the one hand, this is a poem which yearns for action, and for explanations. Why is the house decayed? Why is Mariana weary? For whom does she wait? Will he or will he not come? Inevitably, the reader searches for clues as to what is going on, or

---

24 Alfred Tennyson, *The Princess*, in *The Poems of Tennyson*, ed. Christopher Ricks, 3 vols. (1969; London: Longmans, 1987), vol. II, pp. 185–296, lines 236–9.
25 Arthur Henry Hallam, 'On Some of the Characteristics of Modern Poetry, and on the Lyrical Poems of Alfred Tennyson', in *The Writings of Arthur Hallam*, ed. T. H. Vail Motter (London: Oxford University Press, 1943), pp. 182–98: p. 197.

explanations for nothing going on. For this, indeed, is a lyric poised on the edge of drama, casting for motivations, intentions, actions. When Mariana's refrain: 'I am aweary, aweary, / I would that I were dead!' alters, in the final stanza, to 'Oh God, that I were dead!'[26] it is as if some catastrophic knowledge has occurred, some change of heart or deepening of despair. That small verbal alteration alerts the reader to the drama of the speaking voice. This is not the poet 'directly expressing [his] own thoughts and sentiments', but a woman, trapped in some way, and either about to break out or to stay permanently in. In this monotonously static, circular poem, that tiny change in the refrain has the ring of a calamitous event.

'Mariana', then, seems to justify Hallam's point about the dramatic grafting of Tennyson's lyrics. Like many others, it recalls and expects action, even if action never comes. On the other hand, Herbert Tucker has recently tackled the argument from the opposite point of view, arguing that Tennyson 'relyricized' the dramatic monologue, 'stripping his speakers of personality in order to facilitate a lyric drive'.[27] While Hallam finds drama in the lyric, Tucker finds lyric in the drama. These are not, of course, incompatible points of view. Tennyson's great monologues – 'The Lotos-Eaters', 'Ulysses', 'Tithonus', 'Lucretius' – may be read either as drama or as lyric. They are dramas in the sense that theirs are named characters, known from other books, whose activities ripple outwards and affect the still moment of the poem. However, they are lyrics in the sense that action is curtailed, the voice loses its historical specificity, and the tone is somehow impersonal, generalized. Tennyson can make context fall away and motivation fail, so that we listen to a voice trapped, it seems, in the condition of its own speech.

In 'Mariana', this accompanying failure of drama is captured by the epigraph from Shakespeare's *Measure for Measure*: '*Mariana in the moated grange*'. This, Tennyson explained, 'was no particular grange, but one which rose to the music of Shakespeare's words'.[28] Just as the poem was inspired by the sound of a phrase, with its alliteration of m's and haunting long vowels, so there is a sense in which the poem too only insists on the music of its words. This is, after all, no 'particular grange' or particular Mariana. The poem circles back to the sound of its own refrain, with that increasingly

---

26 Tennyson, 'Mariana', in *Poems*, vol. 1, pp. 205–9, lines 11–12, 84.
27 Herbert F. Tucker, 'The Dramatic Monologue and the Overhearing of Lyric', in Chariva Hosek and Patricia Parker (eds.), *Lyric Poetry: Beyond New Criticism* (Ithaca, NY and London: Cornell University Press, 1985), pp. 226–43: p. 229.
28 Tennyson, *Poems*, vol. 1, p. 205.

meaningless repetition of 'aweary', as if Tennyson had become addicted to the stalemate of his own language. John Hollander has suggested, intriguingly, that 'refrains would seem to have the property of remembering' not only 'their own previous occurrence in the poem', but 'their distant ancestry in song and dance'.[29] Refrains are a reminder that poems are songs, haunted by the music and rhythm of other songs. They don't necessarily go anywhere or do anything; they merely come round again and again. So Tennyson remembers, not Shakespeare's character Mariana, but the tune of a phrase in his head, which then ancestors the tunes of his own poem. As we read 'Mariana', we, too, begin to wonder if our ideas are only rising on the music of its words.

It may be, then, that terms like 'lyric' and 'dramatic' involve the reader in a choice. With Tennyson it is possible to read dramatically, listening round the words for the story, for messages, feelings, hopes; or else to read lyrically, listening to the sound of a voice which somehow belongs to nothing except the language it speaks, having no body, no real history, and no future beyond those words. The lyric may be story or song, the one intriguing us by hints of action, the other sounding a meaningless tune, which lives on in the ears when reading is finished.

Robert Browning, the inventor and greatest practitioner of the dramatic monologue proper, is often contrasted to Tennyson in his greater concern for character and history. But even in Browning, the lyric–dramatic opposition is not always clear cut. He himself, as if to call attention to the link, titled one of his volumes *Dramatic Lyrics*. Oscar Wilde, a little playfully, once castigated Browning for not being a poet at all: 'it was but rarely that he could sing',[30] he complained; he merely used 'poetry as a medium for writing in prose'.[31] Certainly, Browning's interest in the complex motivations of character suggests that drama matters more to him than lyric. His speakers seem to speak more than sing. They engage in cannily self-justifying soliloquies, while keeping a wary eye on the audience. When the Duke of 'My Last Duchess' informs us: 'Then all smiles stopped together',[32] we read the intonations of his language, hearing the double meaning and

29 John Hollander, 'Breaking into Song: Some Notes on Refrain', in *Lyric Poetry: Beyond New Criticism*, pp. 73–89: p. 77.

30 Oscar Wilde, 'The Critic as Artist', in *Intentions* (London: Methuen, 1919), pp. 93–217: p. 102.

31 *Ibid.*, p. 104.

32 Robert Browning, 'My Last Duchess', in *The Poetical Works of Robert Browning*, 2 vols. (London: John Murray, 1924), vol. I, p. 384, line 46.

decoding its literal sense. It could also be argued, however, that the poem does not stop there. Once the storyline is understood, and the Duke's motives found out, the reader returns to the work to hear its voice, to listen to the repetitions, to catch something of that 'lyric drive' which sings through the story. There is always something over and above the dramatic situation in Browning's poetry, a sense of language not quite in the control of its speakers, but playing tunes beyond what they know.

In 'The Dramatic Monologue and the Overhearing of Lyric', Herbert Tucker argues, invoking Mill's word, that the reader constantly *overhears* lyric in the monologue. 'Lyric, in the dramatic monologue, is what you cannot have and what you cannot forget', he writes.[33] Even in Browning's murderers and cheats, fixers and spongers, there are would-be singers. Their ways with words are poetic and musical, sometimes in shocking contrast to their content. 'My first thought was, he lied in every word' is the first line of ' "Childe Roland to the Dark Tower Came" '. This poem is a reminder of the thin line between dramatic monologue and lyric. The lie at the start puts us on our guard, warning us that we must be lie detectors and not be taken in. Yet the poem never tells what the 'second thought' was, unless it is, indeed, the poem itself, agreeing to the lie, obeying it, or finding that there is nothing but the lie. So the speaker, after a long, absurd journey, arrives at the dark tower's 'round squat turret, blind as the fool's heart',[34] and finds no heroic revelation or reward. Even so, in a desperate gesture of purpose, he blows his horn at the end, and confirms the meaning of the title: that at least Childe Roland *came*. It may be, then, that this monologue, driven by one who 'lied in every word', is in fact a lyric, a song which, like all songs, is a kind of lie but with no possibility of detection.

Indeed, like Tennyson's 'Mariana', the title too is a quotation. It takes its bearings and inspiration from an old song in Shakespeare: '*Edgar's song in "Lear" '*. Song, then, is the issue, even for Browning. This mad song, like Edgar's original, is a snatch that defies history, story, purpose, and meaning. Its own ancestry in another song ensures that it defeats detection, interpretation, the sense of a moral solution. This second Childe Roland will fulfil his allotted fate, follow the advice of the liar and blow his horn at the end. He does nothing except make a kind of desperate, heroic music, which is also, finally, what the poem has made, against the odds that it lied.

---

33 Tucker, 'Dramatic Monologue and the Overhearing of Lyric', p. 235.
34 Browning, *Poetical Works*, vol. 1, pp. 435–38, lines 1,182.

Song, then, the lyric drive, inhabits the dramatic monologue like a wish, an alternative, something overheard that cannot be forgotten. These may be opposite modes, but they can exist together. Certainly, without song, the dramatic monologue is in danger of being *merely* a debate, merely a kind of legalistic drama of ideas and disclosures. Augusta Webster's 'A Castaway' is a fine, dramatic account of the prostitute's life, but it lacks that element of song which Christina Rossetti, for instance, brings to her own dramatic monologue about the fallen woman: 'The Convent Threshold'. The difference can be heard from the start. 'Poor little diary, with its simple thoughts, / Its good resolves, its "Studied French an hour," '[35] Webster writes, catching the speaking voice and never letting go of the twists and turns of its reasoning. But Rossetti begins:

> There's blood between us, love, my love,
> There's father's blood, there's brother's blood;
> And blood's a bar I cannot pass . . .[36]

and immediately we are aware of another register. Though both poems are technically dramatic monologues, in Rossetti's the speaking voice is overlaid by repetitions, echoes, by the rhythm of a song which sings through the matter of a specific voice. The repetition of the word 'blood', and its half-rhyme with 'love', suggests a refrain, an incantation already removed from the literal sound of the speaker's voice. Webster's poem is *merely* dramatic, its interest specific and local. Rossetti's, however, opens up beyond the intentions of its speaker, and gives us something like a tune, a frequency of language beyond the reach of reason.

The Victorians relished these mixed modes, as is suggested by the numbers of poems that exploit the closeness of lyric and drama. Browning's Fra Lippo Lippi speaks, but he also sings. He distracts his waylayers by falling into snatches of song intended to throw them, and the reader, offguard: '*Flower o' the broom, / Take away love, and our earth is a tomb!*'[37] Indeed, Browning might be defining lyric itself here, as a kind of distraction, intended to captivate or derail a follower. But he also lets us hear how lyric has method in its madness, relevance in its irrelevance. Against the friar's

---

35 Augusta Webster, 'A Castaway', in Angela Leighton and Margaret Reynolds (eds.), *Victorian Woman Poets: An Anthology* (Oxford: Blackwell, 2005), pp. 433–48: p. 433.

36 Christina Rossetti, 'The Convent Threshold', in *The Complete Poems of Christina Rossetti: A Variorum Edition*, 3 vols., ed. R. W. Crump (London & Baton Rouge: Louisiana State University Press, 1979–90), vol. I, pp. 61–5: p. 61, lines 1–3.

37 Browning, 'Fra Lippo Lippi', in *Poetical Works*, vol. I, pp. 517–23, lines 53–4.

spun-out excuses and deviations, Browning sets these songs that exonerate him, by telling a simple, general truth.

Tennyson, similarly, employs a mixed genre in *The Princess* (1847), which he pointedly subtitled 'A Medley'. The songs in it are sung by the women – a reminder that the lyric has always had a subtle inflection of femininity about it. Here, the songs change the tone, distract the story, and hint at other dimensions of thought which cannot be accommodated by the drama. So, for instance, the lovely lyric 'Tears, idle tears, I know not what they mean' suggests, after the busy-ness of events, that none of this matters, that it was all long ago, and that it was all, perhaps, *just* a play. The lyric reflects on what the drama is up to, but gives it an eerie unimportance, a distance which puts it in perspective: 'I know not what they mean.' While drama directs meaning, however subtly and complexly, there is a sense in which lyric gives up on meaning. Does it matter? Can it be known? Was it worth crying about? Those 'idle tears' are, after all, tears for no reason or tears that cannot help. They merely come round, again and again, like the refrain which takes us back to 'So sad, so strange, the days that are no more'.[38] Lyric opens up into a kind of no-time and no-place, where the sounds that language makes, in echo and alliteration, take over from the sense it should offer.

Throughout *The Princess*, lyrics like 'Sweet and low, sweet and low' or 'The splendour falls on castle walls' offer curiously oblique comments on the narrative, while opening up a hall of echoes in the ear. Both 'Fra Lippo Lippi' and *The Princess* are examples of forms that expose the differences between lyric and drama, while also suggesting that each may be read in terms of the other. After all, 'idle tears' may be precisely the reaction the storyline provokes, while in the drama itself, the Prince's strange fits and trances take him, dramatically, into the remote, self-absent register of the lyric.

In some cases, this mixing of drama and lyric may be only an accident of publishing history. The Brontës, for instance, wrote poems that are known as pure lyrics, but which were once part of those messy, experimental narratives, Angria and Gondal, that the four siblings wrote to pass the time and play out their fantasies. When Charlotte published Emily's lyrics, lifting them out of their containing story, she changed the angle of our reading. A poem, for instance, like 'Cold in the earth, and the deep snow piled above

---

38 Tennyson, *Poems*, vol. II, pp. 185–296, lines 21, 35.

thee' (1846) loses its dramatic voice, its history and context, and becomes an impersonal lament. Put back into the story line, its dramatic specificities and ironies reappear: such that the speaker, Rosina, probably *has* forgotten, after 'fifteen wild Decembers', her youthful lover Julius. There is a timescale, a gendering, and an irony in the original poem that are lost when it is reprinted in lyric isolation:

> Cold in the earth – and the deep snow piled above thee,
> Far, far, removed, cold in the dreary grave!
> Have I forgot, my only Love, to love thee,
> Severed at last by Time's all-severing wave?[39]

Read without its context, the repetitions of 'cold', 'far', 'love', and 'sever' not only give the poem an audible inner distance, but also suggest a haunting of sounds, as if remembering were a matter of hearing something. This work is almost a test-case of the differences between drama and lyric. As dramatic monologue, with Rosina as speaker, the pronouns 'I' and 'thee' are rooted in specific characters and a larger story, and the reader only borrows them, so to speak, as (s)he reads. But as lyric, the pronouns are uninhabited, shifting in and out of the reader's own I's and thee's, and touching on any number of presumed invisible presences. The history of lyric, Susan Stewart has suggested, is 'the history of a relation between pronouns'.[40] As drama, those pronouns have a fixed relation within the poem, one which is affected by context and story. As lyric, they cut free, becoming the voices of anyone or no one, thus breaking the poem's dependence on contingent actions.

The poetry of the Brontës is a reminder that the categories of dramatic monologue and lyric come quite close, and that definition may depend on accidents of reproduction as well as readerly choice. We can read any verse as drama, doing it in voices, swayed by the sense of character behind it; or we can read it as lyric, as a sound removed from action, motivation, and consequences, even, like Tennyson's tears, from meaning itself. In all these poems, the two modes come together, like a reminder of the thin line that divides them. The impersonality, dissociation, and contextlessness of the lyric may be dramatized, as in Mariana's lovelorn weariness or the Prince's absent-minded trances, or they may become the very linguistic

---

39 Emily Jane Brontë, 'Remembrance', in *The Complete Poems*, ed. Janet Gezari (London: Penguin, 1993), pp. 8–9: p. 8, lines 9, 1–4.
40 Susan Stewart, *Poetry and the Fate of the Senses* (Chicago and London: University of Chicago Press, 2002), p. 46.

atmosphere of the work, overriding cause and effect, paralysing action, and turning the verse towards music and song.

Song

'Song's our art.'[41]

'Song' must be one of the most overused words in English poetry. It appears in innumerable titles of short poems, it offers an old and ongoing metaphor for the poet's activities, and it points to the connections between poetry and music. The *OED* definition of lyric as 'pertaining to or characteristic of song' puts the idea of musical sound at the heart of this genre – a reminder that the lyre still plays in the word 'lyric'. This is not only an old figure of speech, but reflects that aspiration to make poetry singable. As Northrop Frye puts it in his chapter 'Approaching the Lyric': 'Lyric . . . often retreats from sense into sound, from reason into rhyme, from syntax into echo, assonance, refrain, even nonsense syllables.'[42] The lyric, more than any other genre, aims to make more music than sense, and it does so through foregrounding rhyme, echo, assonance, refrain. After the great experiments in dramatic monologue and other mixed modes in the first half of the nineteenth century, the second half sees a renewed emphasis on song. One reason for this is the rise of aestheticism from the 1860s onwards. Walter Pater's famous assertion in *The Renaissance* (1873) that '*All art constantly aspires towards the condition of music*'[43] helped reinstate the lyric as the most prized form of verse. The connection with music is the reason why, as Pater puts it, 'lyrical poetry, precisely because in it we are least able to detach the matter from the form . . . is, at least artistically, the highest and most complete form of poetry'.[44] Music has always provided the most apt metaphor for the poet's activities, but in the second half of the Victorian period the 'condition of music', the condition of pure aural appeal, is appealed to ever more insistently.

One of the most interesting aspects of this aesthetic musicalizing of literature is the way that Pater's actual prose aims for lyrical effects. His well-known passage about the Mona Lisa, for instance, works its magic

---

41 Browning, 'Transcendentalism', in *Poetical Works*, vol. I, p. 508.
42 Northrop Frye, 'Approaching the Lyric', in Hosek and Parker, *Lyric Poetry*, pp. 31–7: p. 34.
43 Walter Pater, *The Renaissance: Studies in Art and Poetry* (London: Macmillan, 1901), p. 135 (author's italics).
44 *Ibid.*, p. 137.

through the ear rather than the critical intelligence. Indeed, the whole paragraph 'retreats from sense into sound', becoming detached from its context and producing a kind of hallucinatory verbal trance:

> She is older than the rocks among which she sits; like the vampire, she has been dead many times, and learned the secrets of the grave; and has been a diver in deep seas, and keeps their fallen day about her; and trafficked for strange webs with Eastern merchants; and, as Leda, was the mother of Helen of Troy, and, as Saint Anne, the mother of Mary; and all this has been to her but as the sound of lyres and flutes . . .[45]

As a piece of critical analysis of Da Vinci's painting, this is indeed nearly nonsense. A diving vampire, who buys Eastern cloth, and is the mother of a succession of semi-mythical women is, if taken literally, a ridiculous figment of Pater's imagination. But if we let the passage speak to the ear, its power becomes audible. This has something to do with the rhythm, the careful punctuation, and that unstoppable, lulling copula 'and', which allows the most unlikely phrases to follow each other, unquestioned, till we get to 'and all this has been to her'. Here, suddenly, the object observed in a painting becomes the subject who listens – and who listens precisely to this description of herself. It is as if the pronoun 'she' were undergoing a transformation into something impersonal, universal, till she is no longer the Mona Lisa, but any figure of myth or history, in all times and places. This 'she' develops the open-endedness of the lyrical pronoun, no longer rooted in an identity but somehow encompassing anyone or no one. By the end she is also the reader, listening to 'all this'. Pater leads us by the ear, hypnotizing us by his incantatory rhythms, then letting us know that what we, and 'she', are hearing is indeed a kind of lyric: 'the sound of lyres and flutes'. That little etymological joke acknowledges what the passage has done: it has turned critical prose into lyric, into 'echo, assonance, refrain, even nonsense syllables'. This, perhaps, was recognized by Yeats, who versified the passage and placed it at the head of his 1936 *Oxford Book of Modern Verse*. Pater could not have offered a better example of the lyric impulse in action, as he turns the specifics of (art) history and story into nothing but 'the sound of lyres and flutes'.

The songfulness of lyric is its most decisive characteristic, and is apparent in the poetry written in the second half of the Victorian age. At the very end of the century, Arthur Symons, in *The Symbolist Movement in Literature* (1899),

---

45 *Ibid.*, p. 125.

looked back to French literature to summarize this trend. 'All the art of Verlaine', he wrote, 'is in bringing verse to a bird's song, the art of Mallarmé in bringing verse to the song of an orchestra.'[46] English poetry, no less than French, had long taken 'song' as a model for what poetry should be: a writing that speaks more to the ear than to the sense. Symons is writing in the aftermath of a great flourishing of song, as the Aesthetic movement denounced story, morality, and message in literature, and insisted, instead, on 'the condition of music'. One of the great lyric poets of this period is A. E. Housman. In his retrospective essay, 'The Name and Nature of Poetry' (1933), he offers a definition of lyric which, untouched by Modernism, recalls its roots in Aestheticism. The 'very summits of lyrical achievement', he claims, are in Shakespeare, who could write 'ravishing poetry' which is 'nonsense', and who could 'pour out his loveliest poetry in saying nothing'.[47] The lyric, then, may speak 'nonsense' and say 'nothing'. By removing the burden of sense and message, Housman lets the lyric sing its tune instead:

> From far, from eve and morning
>   And yon twelve-winded sky,
> The stuff of life to knit me
>   Blew hither: here am I.
>
> Now – for a breath I tarry
>   Nor yet disperse apart –
> Take my hand quick and tell me,
>   What have you in your heart.
>
> Speak now, and I will answer;
>   How shall I help you, say;
> Ere to the wind's twelve quarters
>   I take my endless way.[48]

This short lyric, which was set to music by Vaughan Williams in Housman's lifetime (thus fitting the earliest definition of lyric as a setting for music), emphasises the minimalism of song. The sentiment is pure Pater, a reworking of the epicurean Conclusion to *The Renaissance* with its sense of life's material coalescing and dispersing. This short, simple lyric, which plays off its feminine half-rhymes, 'tarry/tell me', 'answer/quarters', against masculine full rhymes, beautifully catches the sense of life's hurry in its

46 Arthur Symons, *The Symbolist Movement in Literature* (London: Heinemann, 1899), p. 14.
47 A. E. Housman, *Collected Poems and Selected Prose*, ed. Christopher Ricks (London: Penguin, 1988), p. 366.
48 *A Shropshire Lad* in *Ibid.*, Poem XXXII, p. 56.

shortness of line, and breath, while the vastness of time and space is warded off by the fleeting hold of a hand. The singing lilt of the poem keeps a kind of effortless, perfect, musical time.

Even here, however, a sense of drama can be felt. There is, after all, a situation, a story, a love story even, with two characters and an imaginary conversation between them. There is also that small ambiguity of pronunciation in the last stanza: 'Speak now' might be read in the colloquial sense of 'now then, speak' or with the emphasis, more urgently, on *'now'*. Similarly, in the following line, 'say', might mean 'for instance,' and be quickly passed over, or it might be a plea to 'say it!' Even while the lines trip off the tongue with the ease of a nursery rhyme, there are little warning signs of something more difficult, more specific, an accent of speech which suggests a speaker, hopefully or hopelessly pleading with another. Even this perfect little lyric carries the tiniest accent of drama.

Helen Vendler has written about the 'invisible listeners' of the lyric, those presences, whether heavenly or human, which distinguish it from the 'lyric of solitary meditation'.[49] Wherever there is a listener, and therefore a relationship between I and you, there is potential for drama. The lyric often trades on this doubleness, allowing us to read its pronouns in different ways, dramatically or lyrically. In T. S. Eliot's essay 'Poetry and Drama' (1951), he explains the role, in one of his own plays, of the 'lyrical duets' inserted into the dramatic action. The passage offers a tentative but memorable definition of lyric: 'These passages are in a sense "beyond character", the speakers have to be presented as falling into a kind of trance-like state in order to speak them. But they are so remote from the necessity of the action that they are hardly more than passages of poetry which might be spoken by anybody . . .'[50] The lyric gestures ' "beyond character" ' and action, to a place where the personal pronoun is no longer a human agent. That 'trance-like state' seems a good description of the tone of the lyric voice, which speaks as if in suspension from context. We listen differently to this voice, not just to find out what it means or what it is hiding (Housman's homosexual secrets, for instance), but in order to feel the entrancement of its sounds. The idea of 'poetry which might be spoken by anybody' suits the way that lyric slips in and out of dramatic voices – on the one hand, tied to character, even the character of the poet; on the other, catching the voice of no one or 'anybody'. There is a kind

---

49 Helen Vendler, *Invisible Listeners: Lyric Intimacy in Herbert, Whitman, and Ashbery* (Princeton and Oxford: Princeton University Press, 2005), p. 80.
50 Eliot, 'Poetry and Drama', in *On Poetry and Poets*, p. 83.

of open access about the lyric, which goes beyond drama, into ungrounded, uncharted regions, remote from person or event.

This impersonal direction is caught in a particular kind of lyric that develops in the nineteenth century: the lyric about being dead. Being dead is, after all, a way of speaking, not in one's own voice and from a place utterly 'remote from the necessity of action'. It is a genre that appeals almost exclusively to women poets, as if it reflected a death-in-lifeness which has biographical origins.

> When I am dead, my dearest,
>   Sing no sad songs for me;
> Plant thou no roses at my head,
>   Nor shady cypress tree:
> Be the green grass above me
>   With showers and dewdrops wet;
> And if thou wilt, remember,
>   And if thou wilt, forget.[51]

This poem, like many of Christina Rossetti's, is simply called 'Song'. If it were called 'Song of the Dying Woman', or 'Eliza's Song', it would have a rather different ring, disclosing a specific emotional agenda and a gendered speaker. But this 'Song' is ' "beyond character" ', and that is its power. It lends itself to transmission from voice to voice, from situation to situation. It might be read as a love letter or a letter of repudiation; it might be a call for pity or pitilessness; it might betray too much or too little feeling. Each of those emotional contexts would turn the poem into a kind of drama, spoken in someone's voice. But the poem, by itself, is intriguingly, openly habitable, throwing attention on to the 'how' of its language rather than the 'who' of a person or the 'why' of a situation. It hums along, on the swing of a tune, till the idea of who 'my dearest' is becomes unimportant, and we 'forget' even about forgetting. This process is helped along, not only by rhythm, rhyme, and refrain, but also by those intransitive verbs: 'And if thou wilt, remember, / And if thou wilt, forget.' Forget who, forget what? The poem has never supplied any object, so that remembering and forgetting become like empty gestures, waving in thin air. The lyric, withdrawing from messages, insists instead on the memorability of its own noises.

---

51 Rossetti, 'Song', in *Complete Poems*, vol. 1, p. 58, lines 1–8.

Rossetti's fondness for the condition of being dead, or nearly dead, or long dead, is certainly a way of looking ' "beyond character" '. When she begins her lyric 'At Home' with 'When I was dead', she instantly unhomes any sense of home. Who is 'I' if she *was* dead'? And when was that? And where are we now, if even death is in the past? What are the credentials of a speaker whose 'I' belongs to a time long after being 'dead'? So the lyric takes its stand outside any place where we might be 'at home' in time. Emily Dickinson plays similar tricks of perspective in poems which speak from beyond the grave. 'I heard a Fly buzz – when I died – '[52] she begins, thus letting the rest of the poem be spoken by an 'I' that has no historical place or time at all. The disappearance of the speaker in death allows the lyric voice to be heard all the more clearly and strangely, like the strangeness of that buzz which seems to go on and on through death itself. This is not the voice of a ghost, but the ghostly effect of a voice without body or being. The long tradition of women poets 'playing dead' runs from Rossetti and Dickinson, through Stevie Smith and Sylvia Plath, to a number of contemporaries.[53] It is a surprisingly distinct and continuous tradition, suggesting a need for women to disappear to themselves in order to speak in the lyric 'I'. From this tomb-like self-absence, the poet becomes anybody or nobody, and the song sings (almost) for its own sake.

So, from Mill's and Ruskin's understanding of the intimate, feeling presence of the poet, we have arrived at almost the opposite theory: that the lyric voice is impersonal, unfeeling, and self-distanced, housing any number of speakers. The 'highest lyric works', writes the twentieth-century theorist, Theodor Adorno, 'are those in which the subject, with no remaining trace of mere matter, sounds forth in language until language itself acquires a voice ... This is why the lyric reveals itself to be most deeply grounded in society when it does not chime in with society, when it communicates nothing.'[54] Once again, the idea of saying nothing, communicating nothing, is part of what releases the lyric's power as song. 'Sing no sad songs for me', Rossetti sings, enacting what she preaches. For this 'Song' is indeed not 'sad', nor is it, any longer, 'for me'. It is for anyone, or no one, or for 'nothing' at all.

52 Emily Dickinson, 'I heard a Fly buzz – when I died – ' in *The Complete Poems of Emily Dickinson*, ed. Thomas H. Johnson (London: Faber, 1970), pp. 223–4.

53 See Angela Leighton, *On Form: Poetry, Aestheticism, and the Legacy of a Word* (Oxford University Press, 2007), pp. 251–5.

54 Theodor Adorno, 'On Lyric Poetry and Society', in *Notes to Literature*, 2 vols., ed. Rolf Tiedemann, trans. Shierry Weber Nicholsen (New York: Columbia University Press, 1991–2), vol. I, p. 43.

The Victorian period, perhaps second only to the Renaissance, is the great age of the lyric. Women, in particular, Christina Rossetti, Mary Coleridge, Alice Meynell, Emily Dickinson, Mary F. Robinson, Michael Field, and many others, excel in a form which is short, tuneful, and offers a kind of poetic anonymity to its writers. In addition, Tennyson, Housman, Swinburne, Dowson, Johnson, Hardy and the early Yeats are great masters of song – of a lyricism which forces the reader to listen, not in order to hear something: a story, a drama, an emotion, but almost just for listening's sake. For the point of any song is that it is not essentially a form of communication, but a form of listening. The song pays attention to listening, and demands it. *Listen!* the singer seems to say, and the poem, the voice of 'language itself', then only serves to deepen the kind of listening we are prepared to give it. By listening, the reader comes to hear how the lyric, in Garrett Stewart's words, is 'Acoustically textured to the point of distraction'.[55] Such distraction is at least as important as condensation into sense. Lyric can set the echoes flying, as if in a huge hall of sound. It plays a verbal tune in our ears that is full of recollections of older, earlier tunes. Through rhyme, echo, rhythm, refrain, those tunes achieve their meaning precisely by distracting us from the other business of understanding what they are about.

Two other kinds of verse that become prominent at this time, but conform to the lyric, are nonsense poetry and the hymn. Nonsense, after all, specializes in a world where sound predominates over sense, aural memorability over meaning. *Laughable Lyrics* (1877) was the title of one of Edward Lear's collections. Both Lear and Carroll wrote poems, like 'Jabberwocky' or 'The Jumblies', which distract attention by the sheer, nonsensical power of their words. Their sounds speak to us, long before and long after we know what they are about. The hymn, too, is a form of lyric. Those great Victorian hymns, like Newman's 'Lead, kindly Light', Bridges's 'Thee will I love', and Christina Rossetti's 'In the bleak mid-Winter', all invoke an 'I' who is everyman, neither poet nor dramatic character, but a presence speaking for all and sundry. The words of the hymn, in stanzaic form, regular metre and easy rhyme, return the lyric to its original definition, as a poem made to be set to music.

One religious poet, however, whose work does not fit the simplicity of the hymn is Gerard Manley Hopkins. Hopkins's extraordinary experiments with rhythm seem to lift him out of the Victorian age altogether, while the

---

55 Garrett Stewart, *Reading Voices: Literature and the Phonotext* (Berkeley: University of California Press, 1990), p. 37.

sheer muscular contortions of his language seem too strenuous for the title of song. Yet Hopkins himself was probably the most insistent of all these poets that his work be read as music. 'I never did anything more musical',[56] he comments of one poem. Of another he insists: 'To do [it] any kind of justice you must not slovenly read it with the eyes but with your ears.'[57] Of the sonnet, 'Spelt from Sybil's Leaves', he explains that it 'should be almost sung: [being] most carefully timed in *tempo rubato*'.[58] Yet to hear the song in Hopkins's poetry requires an almost complete revision of the term:

> Earnest, earthless, equal, attuneable, vaulty, voluminous, . . . stupendous
> Evening strains to be time's vast, womb-of-all, home-of-all, hearse-of-all
> night.
> Her fond yellow hornlight wound to the west, her wild hollow hoarlight
> hung to the height
> Waste; her earliest stars, earlstars, stars principal, overbend us,
> Fire-featuring heaven.[59]

Even without Hopkins's peculiar stress-dynamics (which I have omitted), 'Spelt from Sybil's Leaves' has a slowness, a density of words, a difficulty of speech and timing which sometimes seem too obstreperously experimental to be called either lyric or song. He forces the conventions of religious verse – its simplicity, familiarity, generality – into an eccentric, difficult, tussling form which seems to break all the rules of metre, of line-endings, of what the sonnet form might sound like. That breath-taking ellipsis '. . .' brilliantly marks the pause before the exclamation of 'stupendous', while 'to the height', which ought to make a satisfying parallel rhyme with 'night', then topples, unexpectedly, into the unheavenly 'Waste', twisting, on the way, from noun to adjective. As for the dictionary-like lists, 'Earnest, earthless, equal', echoed in 'earliest' and 'earlstars', they begin to sound like a game of language rather than an exhortation of praise to the evening.

All this would seem about as far from song as it is possible to go. Yet, in spite of the extraordinary violence of its tone, the sheer, obstructive block of Hopkins's vocabulary, he himself advised a reader: 'but take breath and read it with the ears, as I always wish to be read, and my verse becomes all right'.[60]

---

56 Quoted in *The Poems of Gerard Manley Hopkins*, ed. W. H. Gardner and N. H. MacKenzie (London: Oxford University Press, 1970), p. 282.
57 *The Letters of Gerard Manley Hopkins to Robert Bridges*, ed. Claude Colleer Abbott (London: Oxford University Press, 1955), p. 51.
58 Quoted in *The Poems of Gerard Manley Hopkins*, p. 284.
59 *Ibid.*, pp. 97–8.   60 *Letters of Gerard Manley Hopkins*, p. 79.

To 'read with the ears' is to hear the music at work, to find the rhythm against our expectations, and to let that rhythm take the swing of it. It is to hear the syncopations of the metre, the lovely lilt of 'womb-of-all, home-of-all, hearse-of-all', and does it matter if, in the echoing rightness of 'fond yellow hornlight' and 'wild hollow hoarlight', we are not quite sure what we are looking at? But 'read with the ears' and the semi-matching sounds of 'yellow' and 'hollow', of 'horn' and 'hoar', will suggest something, something similar yet different, at once visible and audible, like the word 'horn' itself.

This is Hopkins at his most flamboyant, even, one might say, dramatically self-parading. But in the end, this too is more lyric than dramatic, more sound than event. It is the music of his words that remains, words riding one on the other, knocking against the ear like someone demanding entry, through them, to the brain. This, indeed, is poetry trying to make us 'attuneable', training the reader to think through listening, and doing so in a way that is more daringly, abrasively novel than anything else in the nineteenth century. Hopkins turns his anguished faith into a lyric mode that, indeed, 'sounds forth in language till language itself acquires a voice'. That voice, like all lyrics, ultimately just sings, even if, meanwhile, it teaches us to listen to a new kind of song.

***

'But . . . read it with the ears.' Hopkins's advice might, in the end, be the best description of both lyric and the lyrical. To some extent, the very meaning of those terms is in the ears of the listener. Even if simply defined as 'song', the lyric is a capacious form, ranging from Emily Brontë's quasi-dramatic monologues to Housman's minimal rhymes, from Christina Rossetti's limpid death verses to Hopkins's muscular experiments in the sonnet. The lyrical, meanwhile, is a quality that might be found in almost any literary genre. It refers to those moments when sound takes over from sense, and we hear, as it were, the lyre at work in the words. The various definitions given in this chapter are all of them attempts at trapping something which, while not essentially separate from other literary terms, like the dramatic, the epic, the narrative, keeps our ears fastened to what we read, marking its rhythms and following its tunes. Both lyric and the lyrical are reminders that poetry takes us into the sound tracts of words, where the tune's the thing. Listening carefully to lyrical poetry not only makes us hear differently, but also makes us think differently. At least, it makes us think 'with the ears', and that, perhaps, requires another account of what it means to think at all.

8

Epic

HERBERT F. TUCKER

Epic came to the Victorians trailing clouds of glory, and casting shadows of doubt correspondingly profound. Poets not besotted by ambition had to wonder whether that could still be the supreme muse's call they were hearing and, if it was, how it could possibly be meant for them. Their reluctance was only deepened by the genre's immediate prehistory. During an enthusiastic Romantic revival the fallen king of kings had been exhumed, stuffed, and reseated on its throne. Cross-dressed and class-slummed, radicalized and commodified, epic had declined far towards the categorical shorthand which mass culture has made it for us – bigness aspiring to grandeur – but which, for the Victorians, it had not yet become. Epic's abiding prestige kept it eligible for purposes of national promotion and imperial reassurance, even as Britannia's place at the top of a modernizing world entailed institutional and intellectual developments that seemed hardly compatible with the traditions of the genre. Accordingly this chapter grasps epic as something between a genre and a mode, whose formal conventions laboured under peculiar stress because the cultural functions they represented did too. Our core narrative will trace the historically unbroken if largely unacknowledged verse-epic tradition that connects the age of Byron to that of Pound, with collateral attention to an epic modality that emerged in prose narratives when they sought to bind Victoria's tribe by linking distant origins to present ends and common history to heroic values.

Forensic thirties: epic under reform

The coronation year 1837 witnessed two works that staked out options of generic conservation and convulsion between which Victorian epic would persistently veer. Southey's *Joan of Arc* came from a sitting poet laureate and serial epoist at the end of his inspiration, Carlyle's *The French Revolution* from a man of letters entering service as the nation's shadow laureate-in-fact. Each work anticipated a general Victorian habit of looking abroad for home truths; and in looking specifically to political crises in France each work took a position on the political spectrum that, running from revolution to reaction, coloured most nineteenth-century thought about the drift and meaning of history. Southey for his part offered an act of contrition. The 1837 *Joan* overhauled wholesale the impudent poem of 1796 that he had published in his twenties, and in wartime at that, starring a French heroine, English villains, and allegorical machinery bristling with Enlightenment. From these youthful indiscretions the revised epic performed a double recovery: into the flexible, moderate blank verse that Southey had helped refine to sweetness for the new century; and into a sage new serenity for his once militant heroine. The Maid of Orleans still drew realm-subduing certitude from sources beyond this world, yet now her vision fused divine authority with suave evolution and discerned a steadying providential hand in the reciprocation of betterment with continuity.

Carlyle, too, vested in historical process what explanatory power he could rally his punch-drunk epic to supply. But for him there was nothing gentle about that process, and he constructed *The French Revolution* to ensure that his reader would see things the same way. Jagged, random, peppered with tropes of flood, conflagration, and earthquake, the prose style of *The French Revolution* paraded its conviction of history's resistance to prediction, control, or even full comprehension in hindsight. When Carlyle held up to derision the futility of all controlling designs, he did not exempt his own. Exhausting the fixed genres much as the revolution had combusted the *ancien régime*, the book fed heroism, pathos, humour, and despair alike to the dark fire of a sovereign national energy that had erupted ungovernably in 1790s France – and might do again in 1840s Britain. The textual ensemble performed with antic glee a thesis in metahistory: no formula can render an epoch whose rule it was to swallow all formulas up.

The contrast between *Joan of Arc* and *The French Revolution* is stark, yet the two works disclose commonalities that define a Victorian threshold for epic. In each the plot transpires through individuals whose humanity is dwarfed by vast transpersonal force, and whose contingent heroism largely consists in their explicit recognition of that force. The history-making power that visits Joan from on high, and that surges up through the rioting sans-culottes to galvanize Mirabeau, Danton, and Napoleon in turn, derives in each case from the immediate prehistory of the epic genre. The 1820s had transported epic to the end of the world, most notably in Robert Pollok's best-seller

The Course of Time (1827) but also by typological proxy in an array of flood-and-thunder epics that had fortified the authority of their embattled genre by assuming a vantage that should be total because terminal, and infallible because divine. (If the genre-subverting irreverence of Byron's *Don Juan* (1819–24) was to blame for this compensatory rush to eschatology, its major beneficiary was Scott in the historical novel, where a modern retrospect across cultural formations doomed by their very pre-modernity garnered, at the end of the day, an authority not structurally distant from that claimed by Pollok and company.) At the same time, Southey and Carlyle were adapting to a new dispensation when, in place of the ultimate scenario of Judgment, they offered deliberative acts quickened by oratory and conducted within forensic venues. Thus Joan is a reluctant warrior but an avid persuader; *The French Revolution* swirls with the litter of paper instruments and discursive currencies, all of them subjected to Carlyle's irony even as they furnish the documentary substance of his book. These modifications bespeak a mission that was entailed on the first Victorian epoists by the Reform ethos of denominational toleration and franchise extension: to bestow stabilizing gravitas on a national order freshly keyed to ongoing change and constituted on secular terms of debate and compromise.

Hence the 1830s rapprochement between epic purpose and dramatic form. Biblical closet scripts that John Edmund Reade subtitled *An Epic Drama* (1830) and *A Drama in Twelve Scenes* (1839) frame the decade's preference for pondering matters of heroic moment within a forum virtually public. Dramas of ideas poised on historical crisis appeared from Henry Taylor (*Philip van Artevelde*, 1834), Thomas Noon Talfourd (*Ion*, 1835), and Robert Browning (*Paracelsus*, 1835; *Strafford*, 1836). While these plays were not epics, their reliance on conflict articulated in protracted dialogue, and their conscription of the reader into an imaginary theatre for judicious response, were features that properly epic poems displayed as well. A conspicuous case in point is the young Benjamin Disraeli's *Revolutionary Epick* of 1834, which let liberalism defeat reaction in a staged debate before the bar of public opinion but then exposed ideas to the embarrassment of history, by lobbing into the hygienic parliament of allegories a dirty bomb of real news: the alleged liberator Napoleon has just subjugated Italy. To similar purpose John Colin Dunlop's *Oliver Cromwell* (1829) put ideology to the test of action, punctuating long closet dialogues between the Lord Protector and his daughter with word of the notorious Piedmont massacres and then with the attack of an assassin; at each interruption Cromwell's reflexive leap to arms contradicts the tolerant words of his lips, and in the process dialogue itself is dialecticized.

A pair of more ambitious poems from the end of the decade exhaled the spirit of Reform back to the public in strikingly different forms, which met with diametrically opposite responses. Philip James Bailey launched in *Festus* (1839) at a modest 8,000 lines what proved to be but the first instalment of an increasingly corpulent text that by century's end was five times that size. A drama in format, as in its provenance from the *Faust* of Goethe, *Festus* grew with the years from a closet to an attic to a warehouse district, through the omnivorous ingestion that had been its raison d'être from the start. Since nothing human could be alien to Festus's reckless optimism, Bailey let him do and say whatever came to mind; the sublimely indiscriminate character of the poem's contents makes a perfect fit with its illimitable scope (scenes occur across town, over the rainbow, in 'Space', and 'Everywhere'), its institution of benevolent world government under the eponymous poet-king, and its ethos of unconditional universal forgiveness. The Broad Church could get no broader, nor could an epic's scope. Indeed, all Bailey's subsequent enlargement was a matter of building out the blank tracts claimed by his 1839 conception, and erecting bleachers from which yet another phalanx of interest groups might behold the spectacle of their togetherness.

Where this epic about a self-absorbed poet-politician sold steadily for decades, the one Browning brought out at the same time on a like theme, *Sordello* (1840), nearly wrecked a career of much greater promise. It is not hard to see why: taking more than one leaf from Carlyle's playbook – the street scenes, the feel for political history in its density, the curiosity about rhetoric as human science – Browning embedded thirteenth-century political intrigues within a performance of his own narratorial difficulties, which in turn reflected those of the Italian troubadour at the centre. With breathless syntax and severe insistence on the vanity of human wishes, *Sordello* lavished every dram of its optimism on Browning's fantasy of an elastically learned poetry audience that scarcely existed in 1840 and has not arisen since. Ironically, the vanguard elitism of *Sordello* sprang from the poet's wish to practise an art that should be democratically transparent and tribunally dedicated to the wretched of the earth. Sorely misguided tour de force though it was, the poem was also a genuine answer to the signal literary challenge of the 1830s: to acquaint the British imagination with its own imminent transition to democracy. Browning crashed and burned *Sordello*, then, for an avant-garde conviction epic in its breadth. His wager that a radically activated readership might become a self-governing citizenry draws out by contrast the undemanding reader-ingratiation that made Bailey's spectatorial poetic a success.

The early Victorian heir-apparent to epic standing, the novel, remained until the later 1840s on all fours. The novels of Scott, imparting world-historical momentum to ordinary lives closely observed, had made Britain's past and present mutually interpretive along a continuum that was to prove nineteenth-century Britain's most durable myth of itself. But with the death of the master, historical fiction descended to successors who inherited only portions of his art. W. H. Ainsworth and G. P. R. James purveyed in historical dress, and with an occasional glint of the silver fork, sequential adventures betraying less kinship with the Waverley novels than with Captain Marryat's books for boys. Literary adventurism on this order expressed an impulse to juvenilize epic that would engender Victorian epic translations by the dozen, especially of the *Odyssey*, into prose or easy verse. A complementary simplification attended Edward Bulwer Lytton's historical fiction, a species of *roman-à-clef* that projected the present on to the past in flat if exotic parables of contemporary concerns: *The Last Days of Pompeii* (1834) and *Rienzi* (1835) were the author's sociological *England and the English* (1833) by other means. Scott's balanced articulation of elder and current realities within a process of ongoing change eluded even Dickens, who in *Barnaby Rudge* (1841) found the sixty-years-since national past equivalent in interest to the present but not different enough to require an accounting of how the one brought forth the other. On the collective energies of city and crowd Dickens was already a riveting writer, yet an essentially synchronic genius for systems-analysis kept his imagination of national affairs panoramic and comprehensive, rather than diachronically epic, for another two decades. Meanwhile the former parliamentary reporter's inaugural novels imparted a forensic 1830s character to the picaresque by grounding *The Pickwick Papers* (1837) in the proceedings of a debating club, and keeping *Oliver Twist* (1838) within legal hail of Newgate.

Vagrant forties: export–import epic

Social conscience was an expensive habit for a nationalist genre, and the hungry 1840s could seldom afford it. The first Victorians had poised their epics on the Homeric–Miltonic topos of the great consult, partly in order to honour the institutional management of progress, but partly in order to acknowledge that the work of national reconstitution was far from complete. Recalling this unfinished business, or disguising it, became the epic burden of the 1840s. Back on the threshold of Reform the neglected working-class stake in Britain had given heroic dimension to Ebenezer

Elliott's indignant *Village Patriarch* (1829). Now prophetic populism rang out in a different key from the imprisoned Chartist poet Thomas Cooper. *The Purgatory of Suicides* (1845) both resumed the forensic mode of recent years – the poem chiefly comprises orations by figures driven to terminal despair – and exposed the futility of that mode from the standpoint of history's unregarded losers. As if to redress Cooper's cold comfort, the poet-engraver W. J. Linton produced in *Bob Thin, or the Poorhouse Fugitive* (1845) a brief graphic epic in the tradition of William Blake that followed its protagonist from Satanic mills into an agrarian workers' commune; that this escape plot savoured of fairy tales was part of the point. Glorification of work as such let R. H. Horne spread a wider tent in *Orion* (1843), a mythological epic first offered at a farthing per copy, which merged savoir-faire with laissez-faire under the banner of progressivism and made its giant hero a civil engineer, artisan, and navvy all at once. From the political right, Sarah Stickney Ellis's narrative of a family's commercial seduction in *The Sons of the Soil* (1840) showed that conservatives as well as radicals might deploy the epic vision of cultural wholeness for purposes of social critique.

In the meantime, occupants of the new ideological mainstream contrived to sidestep such critique through tactics of displacement and fragmentation. Where the undeniable disfranchisement of the working poor kept middle-class interest from masquerading, even to itself, as the national interest *tout court*, epic writing that catered to this majority audience had to resort elsewhere and do tricks with mirrors. Thus the chief accomplishment of the 1840s in large, conspective historiography concerned not British history but the *History of Greece* (1846). George Grote's twelve volumes attracted the polarizing notice they did because by long-practised transposition the classic tale they told was also the tale of Britain's emergent self-conception. At least in this respect the utilitarian republican Grote concurred with traditionalist adversaries like Thomas Arnold, or the rising and incorrigibly allegorical Homerist W. E. Gladstone, that the history of ancient Greece was all told more modern than not.

The major 1840s reconception of poetic epic took its principal form from the re-issue of ballad anthologies (Percy's *Reliques*, Scott's *Minstrelsy* among others) whose evocation of old Britain as a common denominator helped efface invidious contemporary divisions within the realm. This ballad revival was accompanied by a fresh creative departure along the lines of Grote's *History*: the traditions of an antique literary classicism were putatively broken up and broadcast as song, then repossessed in writing as British by adoption. In this latter mode William Maginn's serially issued *Homeric Ballads* (1838, 1850) set the fashion, while T. B. Macaulay's 1842 *Lays of Ancient Rome* hit the jackpot. Here an imperial readership-in-training got to look back millennia at classic Romans looking back centuries at the folk roots of their own *res publica*, savouring on the cusp of metropolitan empire a heartier day when Rome had been ancient indeed. Macaulay made this periscopic recollection tell by means of a bluff Saxon diction, set into vernacular ballad stanzas thumpingly paving the thoroughfare of nation-hood. It was a complex entertainment that divided to conquer: the assemblage of its component parts into an only just pre-imperial whole let readers participate freely in a community imagined at once by formal integration and by historical reach. The confident *Ballads* and triumphant *Lays* showed that a tune sufficiently Englished might pipe all cultural stuffs home to market, and at the same time that Britishness proved less troublesome when repatriated from abroad than when experienced at first hand.

An export–import trade in nationalism flourished even within epics of massively traditional gauge that featured manifestly British topics. John Fitchett's *King Alfred* (1841–2), at 130,000 lines the longest poem in the language, had begun life at the turn of the century as an invasion epic, when Britannia's defence rather than the projection of her power was at issue; as the poem supported its leviathan bulk over the years on every ingestible Fitchett could snatch, its growth kept pace with the national ambition. At the middle of the poem for sixteen very long books – a *Faerie Queene* and then some – Alfred holes up in a Wessex bunker and reviews detailed reconnaissance not just from his besieged shires but from every quarter of Europe, with Mesopotamia and India thrown in for good measure. In Fitchett's epic mind to expel the Dane no longer sufficed: a lasting domestic security had to be grounded in global intelligence, centrally coordinated.

So Bulwer Lytton discovered in producing *King Arthur* (1848), the first Arthurian epic the nineteenth century brought to term. Earlier in the decade Reginald Heber (1841) and then Tennyson (1842) had sampled the matter of Arthur for epic purposes, but each heroic fragment had drifted out of Britain, and history, into faery realms. Bulwer Lytton in contrast, tying a couplet to an extended ballad stanza, found an 1840s way to confer 'the completeness of epic narrative' upon 'the elements of national romance' (1849 preface), where 'completeness' denoted both formal coherence and referential inclusion. Completing Arthur's education called for a Continental grand tour heading ethnically upstream, across Scandinavia and Italy towards Indo-European origins that were epitomized, never mind how improbably, in a stranded Alpine community whose Etruscan tongue proved a version of Celtic Arthur's own. In the climactic wedding of Welsh prince to Saxon princess, genealogy mated etymology, race trumped politics, and Britain's national myth co-opted an Aryan unity conducive to empire.

The same topos of hierogamy appealed at this juncture to two better poets engaged in heavy flirtation with epic and seeking to bestow national significance on a rickety plot. Where Reform-era epic had been a constitutional concern, for the rising star Tennyson the genre had to do with reconstitution. Heroic virtue, long since dissolved into the legendary matrix of 'The Epic' and 'Morte d'Arthur' (1842), might come back redeemed in *The Princess* (1847) as a sexual drive cosmically endorsing class harmony under benevolent rule, social and scientific change without angst. (In *Idylls of the King* this same conjugation would be not the climax of the plot but its golden *donnée*, hallowing an ideal polity from which the tragic action fell away.) A year after *The Princess*, A. H. Clough's *The Bothie of Toper-na-fuosich* likewise crowned with comedy's marital knot an affirmation of union between Scottish and English, unspoiled and enlightened, pastoral and imperial interests – all outsourced to a New Zealand that forms Clough's antipodean counterpart to the dynastic neverland of Tennyson. Meanwhile each poem fingered a light mock-epic continuo in prosody: Tennyson's, subtitled *A Medley*, alternated versatile blank verse with lyric interludes; Clough's *Long-Vacation Pastoral* worked ingenious mischief with a ragtime update of the classic hexameter. Neither poem is an epic, yet the way their timbres, extended similes, and narrative apparatus keep telling us so keeps the heroism they disclaim a possibility ostentatiously unrealized.

In prose narrative, too, the hungry forties preferred heroism afar to the home-grown kind. Having draped the mantle of his *Hero-Worship* lectures (1841) on the native Abbot Samson of *Past and Present* (1843) and then on Cromwell (1845), Carlyle spied a gleam on the horizon and embarked on the long Prussian detour of *Frederick the Great* (1858–65). Even W. M. Thackeray's most sanguine reader had to concede that *Vanity Fair* (1847) was *A Novel Without a Hero* when the action quit tawdry England for the gallant chances of war with Napoleon and still found nothing great. Sheer contrariness took Thackeray's disciple Anthony Trollope to revolutionary France for *La Vendée* (1850), a historical novel that forsook the epicizing Scott tradition by uncoupling what gallantry it did exhibit from any enlarging sense that something of major importance had taken place in the 1790s. All these developments in prose have much in common with poetry's predilection for breaking the epic down into portable parts that travelled light, crossed borders with minimal interference, and incurred few of the duties that had been payable, once upon a time, in the currency of moral obligation or national commitment. Clough held up a mirror to this aspect of the age in the fastidiously deflated Homericism of *Amours de Voyage*, a post-nationalist, revolution-proof palinode set amid the rubbish of contemporary Rome that went unpublished till 1858 but belonged, as the sardonic title implies, to the touristic decade before.

Fat fifties: epic recentred

High Victorianism coalesced circa 1850 around two focal points, the celebrant self and the public extravaganza. The latter staged the Great Exhibition and Wellington's funeral, each an occasion for congratulation on Britain's having once again dodged the virus of insurgency. The former sponsored major fictions in autobiographical form with names like *Jane Eyre* (1847), *David Copperfield* (1849), and *Alton Locke* (1850), where the eponym was an author and authorship the badge of self-fashioning. These foci defined a new orbit for 1850s epic, which under the sign of poetic Spasmodism called home its foreign investments and exploited instead the heroic reaches of the modern self. The posthumous release of Wordsworth's autobiographical *Prelude* (1850) could not have been better timed to feed a heroic updraft that lesser living poets noisily exploited in a manner indebted less to Wordsworth than to Bailey's *Festus*. A rash of experimental dramas in form, bland narratives in fact, appeared in the early 1850s that made a poet their hero. Hyperbolically leveraging lyricism into the place of epic action, these works of the Spasmodist school strained towards a creative apotheosis that should assimilate not just the state but the very cosmos to dictates of a recrudescent Romanticism. Where the poet was king of infinite space, anything might turn up. Where plot went for nothing, the literary arena filled up instead with an inventory of images, grafting on to the epic simile the world-scouring comprehensiveness of an epic catalogue boasting Crystal Palace dimensions.

On the extended wings of self-authenticating impulse Alexander Smith's *A Life-Drama* (1852), J. Stanyan Bigg's *Night and the Soul*, and Sydney Dobell's *Balder* (both 1854) reconvened epic unity out of the previous decade's diaspora, but at constant risk of bathos and to the steady accompaniment of zealous reproof from custodians of the classical legacy. The critical career of Matthew Arnold took off in an anti-Spasmodist preface (*Poems*, 1853) recalling poetry to the dishonoured Aristotelian unities of fable and structure, which he immediately illustrated in the episodic torsos 'Sohrab and Rustum' (1853) and 'Balder Dead' (1855). And the minor balladeer and verse romancer W. E. Aytoun kindled into satiric brilliance with *Firmilian* (1854), a 'Spasmodic Tragedy' that tickled to an early death the movement whose facile moves it laid bare to ridicule by poker-facedly reproducing them.

Not that spasmody disappeared with Spasmodism; it went underground, and afield, to fertilize the most interesting poetry of the decade. Clough, who to his friend Arnold's vexation was an early champion of spasmodic verse, left unpublished at his death in *Dipsychus* (1850–4) a tormentedly clever songbook of self that bore clear traces of the movement. In America, where *Festus* enjoyed greatest popularity, a spasmodic throb surfaced in the tomtom of Longfellow's pastiche *Hiawatha* (1855), while a confluence like Bailey's of self-celebration with epic inventory irrigated Whitman's *Leaves of Grass*. *Maud* (1855) was not yet Tennyson's awaited epic, but its monodramatic format and obsessive versification show how attentively the new Laureate in taking office had taken the pulse of the moment. *Maud* also tapped epic potential in the recent military venture into the Crimea; and Russian scenery contributed to eponymous book-length poems as different as Thulia Henderson's *Olga*, Alfred Austin's *Randolph* (both 1855), Kinrahan Cornwallis's *Yarra Yarra* (1858), and *Lucile* (1860) by Owen Meredith (pen name of Bulwer Lytton the younger).

The last three of these works infused spasmodic thrills into a wanderlust that on one hand recalls the emigrant 1840s epic, on the other hand corresponds to contemporary developments in the historical novel of epic parts. For a Thackeray half reconciled to heroism in silhouette, the time travel of *Henry Esmond* (1852) evidently implied an ocean-crossing too in the sequel *Virginians* (1857–9). With a view to the Church establishment – since 1830 a hotly contested issue in national definition – Charles Kingsley and John Henry Newman traded blows for the faith in *Hypatia* (1853) and *Callista* (1856), novels *à clef* on the Bulwer Lytton model that revisited the emergence of Christianity and treated it as a formative cultural crisis still burningly pertinent. With *A Tale of Two Cities* (1859) even the homebody Dickens joined epic's world-historical pilgrimage, demoting London for once to second-city status beside the significance of what had transpired in revolutionary Paris, and in the process recouping at last the legacy of Scott. In slackened pursuit of a similar aim, Charles Reade spent the many volumes of *The Cloister and the Hearth* (1862) on the Continent, slowly making the late Middle Ages safe for the Reformation, humanism, and thereby England's ascendancy – an aim compassed the next year, with daunting research and austere concentration, when George Eliot's most ostentatiously historical novel *Romola* witnessed the birth of the modern in Quattrocento Florence. Concurrently in *Sylvia's Lovers* (1863) Elizabeth Gaskell combined several of the epicizing manoeuvres we have seen adopted by other mid-century novels: returning to modernity's Napoleonic crisis of sixty years since, she recruited the daily life of an English fishing town into an orbital sweep that, linking the North Sea to the Holy Land, and maritime power to commercial capitalization, palpably governed her hapless principals' lives.

All this fictional study abroad left the national hearth to be stoked by proper historians, who stood ready to meet the public's abiding appetite for narratives of group destiny integrated by moral force. J. M. Kemble's *The Saxons in England* (1849), while its narrative culminated with the catastrophe of Norman invasion, found cause nonetheless to felicitate the surviving kingdom on a balance between obedience and freedom that had preserved it the year before against revolution of a Continental kind. The same stance fortified Macaulay, whose *History of England from the Accession of James II* (1849–61) bestrode the mid-century like a colossal monument to the Reform mentality of his generation. By bracketing the tumultuous Commonwealth years and climaxing with the very different Glorious Revolution of 1688, Macaulay exalted the heroic compromises of political realism, an ethic whose affinity with fictional realism was manifest in his recourse to techniques taken from the novel. J. A. Froude's twelve-volume *History of England from the Fall of Wolsey to the Defeat of the Spanish Armada* (1856–70), scaled back like Macaulay's during the course of its serial publication from an initial plan compassing the death of Elizabeth, became thereby not less epically triumphant but more. Each retrenched *History of England* enlarged its reach by making the shaped events of an epoch prove pragmatism and liberty to be perennial national values.

In contrast to these patriot histories, the systematically philosophical historian H. T. Buckle's *History of Civilization in England* (1857–61) did not aggrandize England but put it in its place. Buckle's theme was just what the title said: English history happened to exemplify on a national level, with maximal clarity, laws universally at work within the development of (Western) civilization itself. Introductory exposition of these laws, with illustrations amply drawn from a diversity of national histories, occupied the only two volumes Buckle lived to complete. Yet from them emerges the vast totality of a conception that raised the encyclopaedic ambition of epic to a characteristic Victorian height: to make a science of history by basing history on science, and to educe the progress of ideas and institutions from considerations of climate, geography, and biology as human culture encounters and transforms them. Clasping national with cosmic modes of explanation had always been epic's affair; Buckle's heroic, impossible historiography undertook to do the job from a vantage as comprehensive as Herbert Spencer's and Charles Darwin's.

Or John Ruskin's. *The Stones of Venice* (1851–3), the most consecutively extended narrative Ruskin ever wrote, fetched its matter from overseas but brought its moral as smartly home to modern readers as did any 1850s history of England. That Ruskin's comparative valuation of medieval and modern orders emphatically inverted the national historians' shows how indifferent epic per se remained to the appeal of progressivism, even at the height of an age of improvement. What elevated Ruskin's history lesson in architectural civics to epic status was not the vector of its belief but its epiphanic incandescence. As Ruskin worked his art-historical matter up into a city-state's saga of rise and fall, what began as an antiquarian inventory of ornament flared into the discovery that architectural history was social history. With a horrified fascination that remains etched into the text, Ruskin recognized that the public form of Venetian architecture harboured a people's fatal story of ennobling common life corrupted by the very ambition that first excited it. He recognizes, further, that the debacle of his European story is precisely the triumph of that modernity within which England's self-fashioning, from Reformation on to Industrial Revolution, forms one long, stained sequel. *The Stones of Venice* hurled splendid reproach both at the national-epic historiography of its decade and at the pathetic fallacy of those puny Michelangelos of auteur poetics the Spasmodics.

Still, *auteur* poetics remained the new order of the day; and the Victorian conflict they expressed between the needs of unique individuality and collective belonging was most successfully negotiated in Elizabeth Barrett Browning's *Aurora Leigh* (1856). The fictive autobiography of an Anglo-Italian poet who forges her own identity in literature, earns her own bread in London, then learns her own heart on a long pilgrimage through Paris back to Florence, the poem transfigures leading epic themes of its decade. Awash in Victorian discourse of gender, class, and nationhood, Aurora's nine-book narrative conducts a sustained meditation on the modern writer's responsibility to and for public discourse, most pointedly when the structural fulcrum Book 5 balances a manifesto of epic's viability, as if to test it, against a glittering soirée scene that reads like Henry James in training. But while Barrett Browning skirted the novel, finally she did not embrace it: its conventions exacted too much of the freedom her poem spoke for. She meant to want it all – creative self-reliance, erotic fulfilment, and an active hand in public life – heroic goals whose incompatibility with the marriage-plotted norms of fiction may be seen from their laboriously partial accomplishment in her model *Jane Eyre*, or in the epos-haunted *Middlemarch*.

Nor were these goals compatible with the varieties of fixed narrative retrospect that those two novels represent, and that Barrett Browning rejected in favour of Aurora's vivid diaristic seriality, which repeatedly confronts the precocious heroine with the fallacy of her own snap judgments from an earlier instalment. *Aurora Leigh* thus suggests, what prevailing accounts of the genres do not prepare us to find, that epic poetry offered greater hospitality to Victorian narrative experiment than prose fiction did, particularly as the conventions of the latter hardened under the pressure of commercial success. Revolving the epic models available in her time, Barrett Browning not only borrowed spasmody's up-to-date version of the old Homeric immediacy of presentation but also subverted its trumpery certitude, by playing impulsiveness against itself. The resulting narrative took canny advantage, as male Spasmodism of the day could not, of a Victorian woman's privilege to identify the authentic with the spontaneous, deep instinct with promptings from above.

Mythic sixties: epic in high fidelity

To rehabilitate the divine was the definitive effort of high culture during the 1860s, and it was an effort that brought out the worst in Victorian epic and the best. What *Origin of Species* did to the Bible story in 1859, *Essays and Reviews* did the next year to the history of that story's reception; and, because the disputed ground was in each instance a question of narrative, those who arose either to refute the new learning or to restate it discovered themselves alike on epic terrain. Tennyson offers the richest case: the gradual composition and release of the *Idylls* let epic assert its claim on him in public, and in slow motion. Not only did the poem as completed in 1885 strike blows on both sides of the chief Victorian debate over cultural authority, but its epic rearmament was the work of a dozen years that spanned the 1860s. In 1859 the first *Idylls of the King* to be so called appeared as four linked tales of aborted love and marriage gone bad: these were pretty much the medieval charades that Swinburne derisively dubbed them, in effect domestic fiction in fancy dress. But a decade later with the *Holy Grail* volume (1869), Tennyson renewed the generic promise that 'The Epic' and

'Morte d'Arthur' had vouchsafed back in 1842. This recovery of civic momentum sprang from a conviction that Arthur's was a myth about myth, a story about the power of a story and a people to hold each other true. Furthermore, this change of focus was enabled by the centrality that mythology, in a modern comparatist sense, had acquired within 1860s thinking about cultural unity in its religious, political, and anthropological aspects. At the end of his own grail quest the laureate came to understand how the rise and fall of Camelot might figure the dream and nightmare of Victoria's empire in plotted detail, not just allegoric generality. The intellectual ferment of the decade that witnessed Henry Maine's *Ancient Law* (1861) and Walter Bagehot's *English Constitution* (1867) lit the way towards an analytic imagination of how sovereign power derives from the credit a nation vests in public images and circulating stories.

The best epic achievements of the late 1860s were penetrated by this insight, but there were plenty of aspirants on whom it left no dent. Among these was Trollope, who pursued mega-narrative across the decade in a direction opposite to Tennyson's. A reader of *The Warden* and *Barchester Towers* (1857) who knew that those books were to launch a six-novel series enmeshed in clerical lives might well have anticipated, as Anglicanism entered a fresh period of crisis, that the series would assume an epic character, pitting the new England against the old with Balzacian amplitude. From this possibility, however, Trollope turned aside: at the end of the line, *The Last Chronicle of Barset* (1867) gathers to a profundity that is tragically chastened, yet almost entirely personal in scope. It may be the Barset novels' abstention from national ambition that drew Trollope next into the Palliser series (1865–80), also six novels long, and now in busy touch with parliaments, elections, and cabals. Here, though, something about the substitution of statesman and aristocrat for churchman and bishop disabled the potential for national mythology that had slumbered in Barsetshire; perhaps the 1860s moment had simply passed. In any case the epic modality of Trollope's second *roman fleuve*, while it is genuine, belongs to the phase after this one: the vanished imaginative power of a Plantagenet ideal cashes out in the demythologized vulgarity of Lizzie Eustace's diamonds, while the fresh life derives from further afield than English town or county – from Ireland, Vienna, the global spoils of guano.

So imperial a prospect lay a few years in the future of the British epic; meanwhile it was time for mythic contest, as the shock administered by science and scholarship to Christianity sent the nearly moribund biblical epic once again marching as to war. The late Romantic battleaxe Edwin

Atherstone came out of retirement with catastrophe epics of Egypt (1861) and Nineveh (1868). The popular poet Jean Ingelow treated her readers to the same tune, with an antediluvian patriarchal setting, in *A Story of Doom* (1867). And the orthodox epic of the hour was the comprehensively titled *Yesterday, To-Day, and For Ever* (1866) by E. H. Bickersteth, Anglican cleric and bishop-to-be. As if to show once for all what the truth of myth comes down to, the poem takes permanent leave of this world in Book 1 with the protagonist's death, thus clearing eleven books more for an afterlife diversified by a résumé of Bible history, followed by Armageddon, the Millennium, and the rest. The poor jilted world has its revenge, all the same, by suffusing the whole chiliastic scenario with the smug prejudices of a Victorian paterfamilias.

In these straight-edge epics the multiple affirmation of patriarchal orthodoxy shored up established authority against the tremors set off by Darwinism, the Higher Criticism, and the political agitation preceding the second Reform Bill of 1867. Other and better writers greeted the changing times with epic works that held patriarchy up for examination rather than emulation. The strangest of these is George Eliot's neglected *Spanish Gypsy* (1868), a punitively stark fable of filial obedience to paternal exactions, in which the family romance becomes a mirror for scrutinizing the fatality of clan allegiance. Each of the plot's two 'Spanish Gypsies' is broken to the bitter yoke of a raced destiny – Fedalma the unwitting Zíncala princess who has been bred up a Spanish bride, Don Silva the Hidalgo suitor who for her sake elects a Zíncalo identity till the cry of blood summons him back – in a tragic equation of nobility with renunciation that is so heavily ethnicized as to make lovers of *Daniel Deronda* squirm. Browning founded *The Ring and the Book* (1868–9) on documents from a seventeenth-century case of wife-murder that put the law of the father, including papal authority, on kaleidoscopic trial. Even conservative Tennyson uncoupled his childless Arthur's right to rule from anything resembling paternal lineage and based it instead on something hard to distinguish from public opinion.

In different ways all three of these works made authority hinge on allegiance, not the other way round; their heroism was an elective belonging that shaped a tradition to live by. That is why all the protagonists were in effect not heirs by birth but adopted orphans, consciously declaring identity in terms not of family but of fellowship. And their willing subscription to the cultural mythology of a collectivity made each protagonist's belief a magnet for the belief of others: Silva's in Fedalma, the Round Table's in Arthur. The project of reconstituting faith unfolded most beautifully in Browning's epic, where the belief of Caponsacchi and Pompilia in one another as living avatars of a Holy Family became, in the eyes of the aged Pope no less, a proof of Christianity and not vice versa; while Guido, invoking a modern comparative-religionist perspective to claim evil as his pagan good, reinvented Satan in his own condemned person. If the heroism of collective conviction was a mere given for Ingelow and Bickersteth, in these mytho-poetic epics of the late 1860s it was a precious attainment.

The socially negotiated pluralism within which these poems produced modern heroism got built into their structure of narration as well. Correl-ation of formal with cultural unity is an old story in the epic tradition, but it became newly urgent as the second Parliamentary Reform Bill set about sharing power with a constituency unprecedentedly diverse. Browning's experiment was the most radical, a shattering of narrative perspective among a dozen witnesses whose nodes of congruence were the more impressively rare for the wilderness of prejudice and crossed purpose from which they arise. Eliot's principle of diversification arose at the level of format, where prose alternated with verse of lyrical as well as narrative kinds, and magisterial description with scripted drama. Comparable effects in *Idylls of the King*, encoded by the one-and-many title, proceeded from the patterns of correspondence and contrast that Tennyson arranged while shaping a twelve-book whole. Beside the more loosely anthological epic practice of the 1840s, and of the decades just ahead, the play of partition with control at the Victorian epic crest of 1868–9 was a high-stakes game. The works still crackle with the electricity of an expensive wager on the cohe-rence of their changing culture – something that their authors, unlike most successors in the next generation, were not content to take for granted.

These three climactic Victorian epoists were joined, in William Morris, by a rising giant in the genre. Morris grappled the power of myth to the heart of his calling, yet in such a way as to diffuse the urgency that animated his elder peers. *The Earthly Paradise* (1868–70), heralded by its spin-off *The Life and Death of Jason* (1867), was a tissue of myths: a library of tales drawn from the south and north of Europe as ceremoniously told, so the framing fiction runs, on some uncharted Bermuda settled long ago by Greek emigrants and now visited by Nordic refugees from the Middle Ages, grown old in fruitless quest of happiness. Exchanged between the two groups in monthly rites spaced over a year, these tales in one sense are all about the earthly paradise – which is to say, about desire in its vagary and contretemps – while in another sense they *are* that paradise, recognized at last in the consummate sweetness of melancholy disillusion. This resigned affect found a textural parallel in Morris's stanzaic and couplet prosody, slightly quaint yet relaxed and full of forward motion. It found a structural parallel in the totalizing symmetry of Morris's calendrical wheel, which denied privilege to any of the two dozen stories and distributed it instead among the ensemble. Where totality inheres not in narrative but in design, purpose gets swallowed in disposition; the heroism the constituent tales manifest is rather exhibited than endorsed. The brand of 1860s faith that *The Earthly Paradise* vested in myth, at the end of an empty day, was belief in nothing more than the honour due to the next yarn in a great, enfolding fabric.

Towards the *fin de siècle*: epic imperialized

What looked easy about the eclecticism of Morris's best-seller attracted into the market a crowd of imitators whose anthological wares clutter the final third of the century. Redactions and selections appeared of the *Eddas*, the *Tain*, the ancient epics of Chaldea and India; Morris alone made full-scale translations of *Beowulf*, Virgil, and Homer. There were an *Epic of Women* (Arthur O'shaughnessy, 1870), an *Epic of Hades* (Lewis Morris, 1877), an *Epic of Olympus* (C. R. Low, 1897). New book-length poems introduced readers to the life of the Buddha (Edwin Arnold, *The Light of Asia*, 1879), the life of Mazzini (Harriet King, *The Disciples*, 1873), Maori folkways (Alfred Domett, *Ranolf and Amohia*, 1872), Norse mythology (Robert Buchanan, *Balder the Beautiful*, 1878), the Catholic conquest in Ireland (Aubrey de Vere, *Legends of Saint Patrick*, 1872), the Mormon conquest in America (Hannah King, *An Epic Poem*, 1884). Matters widely familiar came to the genre for reinforcing accreditation as well: British history in outline (F. T. Palgrave, *The Visions of England*, 1881), British military history in detail (Low, *Britannia's Bulwarks*, 1895), Christian history (Thomas Cooper, *The Paradise of Martyrs*, 1873 sequel to his Chartist *Purgatory* of 1845), the life of Jesus (Arnold, *The Light of the World*, 1891, sequel to his Buddhist blockbuster of 1879).

These titles and many like them adapted epic's old *paideia* function to the purpose of glorified information delivery within emergent mass culture. They offered their consumer traditional generic dignity at a discount, and set a premium on readiness of access. Sub-sectioned, browsable, unprecedentedly bland, the *fin-de-siècle* epic stood to its Victorian forerunner somewhat as the novella did at the same time to the three-decker. The book might be long, but the attention span it presupposed was short, because its rationale was anthologically episodic. What rounded the late-Victorian collection of parts towards epic wholeness – and saved readers from vertigo within the emporium of world narratives – was the reassuring consistency with which epoists subscribed to one and the same masterplot: humankind's progress from antiquity to modernity, barbarism to civilization, outland to metropolis. Victoria's empire had long been an acknowledged fact but had lacked an explanatory ideology. Once this omission was addressed, circa 1870, by the doctrine of imperialism, each entry in the period's teeming epic bibliography became legible as an episode within the constant evolution of modern sophistication from primitive beginnings. The imperialist theorem of progress was understood to posit Western man as the crowning point to which all tended, and from which all should be judged.

While nothing in Britain answered fully to the *épopée humanitaire* of Victor Hugo (*La Légende des siècles*, 1859, *et seq.*), there was a fitful early start in Owen Meredith's *Chronicles and Characters* (1868), whose mix of poetic forms and tones found unity in the progressive meaning of history that these implied for a sequence of incidents from ancient Greece to revolutionary France. Towards the end of the day Buchanan in *The City of Dream* (1888) and Mathilde Blind in *The Ascent of Man* (1889) revived this medley mode, with less historical circumstance and more atmospheric zeitgeist, in homage respectively to Comtean and Darwinian principles. Flush with these works was the 1889 Jubilee Edition of Bailey's *Festus*, its now brontosaurian mass sustained by a steady diet of world histories and mythologies; the whiggish presentism which had focused that poem from the beginning took shape now as, in effect, a proto-imperialism with which the world had finally caught up.

Imperialism fully articulate turned up more regularly in other narrative genres. J. R. Green's not so very *Short History of the English People* (1874) evinced a characteristic mix of populist with racialist appeal: the people itself constituted the hero, breeding up leaders worthy of an innate collective genius for governance. For E. A. Freeman, too, in *The History of the Norman Conquest* (1870), England's power was rather born than made; where Kemble in 1849 had represented the Saxon commonwealth as a painstaking political achievement, Freeman invoked transpersonal cycles that swept across the race with an explanatory force like that of biblical typology. A similarly providential spirit animated William Stubbs's organic conception of *The Constitutional History of England* (1874–8), where the unwritten constitution was inscribed within the evolving body of a heroic state that stood a law unto itself. To project this historical dynamic on to a map of the world engrossed new branches of adventure fiction, which exposed the imperialist faith to challenge (albeit never to defeat), and in the process conferred on the sub-genre an epic resonance it had lacked half a century before. In globe-trotting plots Rider Haggard, Rudyard Kipling, and Joseph Conrad elaborated epic's definitive confrontation between the modern and the remote, while the mutual fungibility of temporal with spatial remoteness underwrote H. G. Wells's science-fiction thought experiments on a human species whose grounding norm remained firmly Victorian.

Nearly all these narratives in prose relied on the same over-arching postulate of progress as their verse counterparts. Where they indulged a dystopian imagination, the worst nightmare they envisioned – the horror Conrad shared with the myth-and-ritual historiographer J. G. Frazer in *The Golden Bough* (2 vols. 1890, 12 vols. 1915) – was not the irruption into civilization of the oppressed per se, but erasure of the progressivist premise in whose cleansing name oppression had taken place. History's numberless tragedies were tolerable for the *fin-de-siècle* epic imagination, as for post-Darwinian thought at large, because they were presumptively contained within a redemptive comedy. Clear recourse to this logic informed so late a condition-of-England novel as Mary Ward's *Robert Elsmere* (1888). It also grounded *Daniel Deronda* (1876), where the age's most epic-minded prose writer sheltered a tragedy of withering personal remorse within a rising action of collective triumph. The same ethnic hope that the epoist of *The Spanish Gypsy* had denied in north Africa, the novelist now credited in Zion – another country, to be sure, but also a brave new dispensation that caught a portion of its glow from the torch of empire.

Late Victorian progressivism thus made epic more manageable than ever for poets and readers alike. But a genre made facile was by the same token made cheap. Somewhat like the standard of prosodic mediocrity, which has seldom been higher than at the *fin de siècle* when anybody could sound rather good, the progressivist masterplot offered to aggrandize any myth or history a poet might plug in. A conspiracy of uplift so diffusive prompted a handful of dissenters to correlate the world-historical at narrative length with the world-weary; it also roused the best poets of the day to cry 'No' in epic thunder. Among the former rank neo-chivalric fantasists like John Payne (*The Romaunt of Sir Floris*, 1870), William Watson (*The Prince's Quest*, 1880), and Owen Meredith in his mock-epic curtain-call *King Poppy* (1892). R. W. Dixon bogged *Mano* (1883) deep in medieval obscurities, apparently for their own inconclusively historical sake, while future laureate Alfred Austin honed an increasingly contrarian anomie on successive versions of anticlimactic nineteenth-century action, fizzling out at last on the Communard barricades of Paris, in *The Human Tragedy* (1862, 1876, 1889).

Compelling human tragedy demanded not Austin's chilly indifferentism but a heroism that could burn through the temporary into the enduring. Morris conceived such heroism in the stubbornly original, because stubbornly traditional, *Sigurd the Volsung* (1876); so did A. C. Swinburne in *Tristram of Lyonesse* (1882), where operatic splendour welled up from the embraced certitude of loss. Here the epic principals, blinded by circumstance yet existentially true, advanced towards foreknown catastrophes that suffering taught them to embrace in affirmation of the human lot. The clash of invincible passion against implacable fate set the tragic joy of these poems a world apart from the consolatory programme of late Victorian epic as usual. To have earned a place in the unswerving tale one inhabited was the acme of heroic ambition for both poets, who took up a like relation themselves to the tradition of epic poetry. For Swinburne the doom of love within the legend of Tristram and Iseult figured his own submission to a world literary order in which the supersession of early by late entrants meant nothing; for Morris, more pointedly, the exactions of *Sigurd* marked a radical, perhaps penitential change from *The Earthly Paradise*, whose generous provision of narrative options had done much to foster the eclectic culture comfort against which the new epic threw all its weight. It was to Morris's example, as at last to his epic hexameter, that the young W. B. Yeats turned in *The Wanderings of Oisin* (1889) for lessons in a defiance that on one hand repudiated Anglo-Christian progress narrative as such, on the other hand politicized its repudiation in the name of an Ireland that remained unborn because it was still colonized by what that narrative stood for.

This nationalism of Yeats's struck a note that was almost inaudible in late Victorian epic, because the genre had dissolved it into the chord of implicitly anglophile cultural cosmopolitanism. Only in post-Victorian days, when rival empires thrust into the Great Game with an aggressiveness making for Great War, did an Edwardian epilogue to our story resettle British epic in Englishness. Having gone dark for a dozen years, the genre flamed out once more after 1905 in three full-blown epics of invasion and conquest: themes whose symbiotic balance both scripted and critiqued the propaganda that would soon nerve the nation to war in earnest. Alfred Noyes's *Drake: An English Epic* (1908) was altogether worthy of its name but not of much more, except to the student itemizing the generic conventions that its dozen books dutifully recapitulated. Charles M. Doughty in *The Dawn in Britain* (1906) made of the genre something altogether more original, especially in the sense of a return to Homeric radicals of presentation. A match for Browning's *Sordello* in the obscurity of its ancient-Briton matter and of its elliptical, idiolectal manner, as uncompromising in outlook as Morris's *Sigurd*, the poem can leave no reader who meets it halfway in any doubt as to the sincerity of its patriotism or the disillusioned view it takes of empire. In Thomas Hardy's masterpiece *The Dynasts* (1908) an author whose life had nearly spanned the period this chapter covers consummated our genre in a return to the century's precipitating crisis, the French wars and the ferment of thought behind them. Hardy's 'epic-drama' format anticipated effects suited to cinema and for that matter to digitized animation, even as the voiceover of his onlooking Spirits expressed a full gamut of response to horror, glory, and the irony and pathos of circumstance lying between. Bespeaking and incorporating the reader's experience of a history transformed to spectacular narrative, *The Dynasts* exfoliated from Napoleon's day through Hardy's into the future of its foreseen reception. In doing so it reclaimed the ancient epic involvement of audience with story, under the sign of an interactive textuality that advanced on – because Hardy had partially learned it from – narrative innovations to which Victorian epic had honourably played host.

9

Melodrama

CAROLYN WILLIAMS

From grand opera to soap opera, from Gothic and nautical to domestic, urban, and imperial, from stage to screen, melodrama has been a dominant shaping force of modernity for over two hundred and fifty years. We live, still, within its aesthetic regime in the twenty-first century. Ignored as bad drama until its rehabilitation began in the 1960s, melodrama is now both widely acknowledged as an important dramatic genre, with its own coherent set of conventions, and also understood more broadly as a mode of apprehension, behaviour, and social action.

In its most literal definition, melodrama consists of a combination of music and drama in which passages of music either alternate with passages of dramatic speech or subtend them almost continuously and in which speech and action are interrupted by moments of static pictorial composition, the tableaux. Thus melodrama is an organized audio-visual field, dialectically working back and forth between music and pictures, music and speech, movement and stasis, sound and silence. As Juliet John argues, 'the emotional economy of melodrama is best figured as a series of waves'; as Martin Meisel puts it, melodrama offers 'a style of punctuated discontinuity, visually marked'.[1] Music and tableaux provide punctual markers of the narrative structure as well as guides for the audience's affective response; they articulate its shifts in mood or tone as the drama moves between high and low plots, terror and comedy, complications and resolutions, absorption and shock. When Dickens characterized the old melodrama as a piece of 'streaky bacon' (in chapter 17 of *Oliver Twist*), it was this contrastive feature of its temporal form to which he alluded. Melodramatic music and tableaux serve to demarcate the streaks of the bacon.

---

1 Juliet John, *Dickens's Villains: Melodrama, Character, and Popular Culture* (Oxford University Press, 2003), p. 31; Martin Meisel, 'Scattered Chiaroscuro: Melodrama as a Matter of Seeing', in Jacky Bratton, Jim Cook, and Christine Gledhill (eds.), *Melodrama: Stage Picture Screen* (London: British Film Institute Publishing, 1994), p. 65.

Audiences experience melodramatic rhythm as periods of suspenseful absorption pierced by intensified moments of shock, terror, or sentiment. Of course, shock and sentiment are not Victorian discoveries, but they take novel forms within the context of melodrama; Matthew Buckley explains that melodramatic shock derives from the political modernity of the French Revolution and develops towards the perceptual modernity of cinema and other mass media.[2] The periodic shocks and wavelike rhythm are articulated through a pointed visual style. On the level of the acting body, sweeping gestures come to a point in the body's brief pose or 'attitude'. On the level of the dramatic action, static poses arrest the action, then dissolve into action again, then freeze into the next pose, rather like the dissolving views of the magic lantern. On the level of the play as a whole, dramatic action climaxes in the frozen moments of the tableaux. Melodramatic music supports and underscores this pointed visual style, stopping and starting to delineate passages of action or mood, sometimes blatantly punctuating the narrative development with interludic songs or crashing chords.

For the broadest definition of melodrama, we look through a modal lens. One view of melodrama as a mode, according to which any drama with musical accompaniment may be considered a melodrama, has the advantage of emphasizing the historical continuity between opera, stage melodrama, film, and television. A different sort of modal perspective yields 'the melodramatic imagination', which has the advantage of emphasizing connections between the stage genre and other genres (like the novel), discourses, and social practices (like political manifestations).[3] Yet another modal perspective focuses entirely on melodrama's familiar, persistent concerns, such as the triumph of virtue over villainy, or the central place of the suffering woman in the melodramatic plot.

A more specific definition of melodrama can be found by looking at it as a dramatic genre. This chapter will focus first on melodrama as a specific genre that reaches its high water mark in England during the first three-quarters of the nineteenth century. But in the end, the chapter will turn outward towards the most important modal extensions of the genre in realist fiction, psychoanalysis, and film. These closing thoughts will demonstrate why and how the term 'melodramatic' has come to mean so many

---

2 Matthew Buckley, 'Sensations of Celebrity: Jack Sheppard and the Mass Audience', *Victorian Studies*, 44:3 (Spring 2002), pp. 423–5.
3 See Peter Brooks, *The Melodramatic Imagination* (1976; 2nd edn New Haven, CT: Yale University Press, 1995) and Elaine Hadley, *Melodramatic Tactics: Theatricalized Dissent in the English Marketplace, 1800–1885* (Stanford University Press, 1995).

things in later usage: histrionic body language; radically inhibited or exaggerated expression; sudden revelations; highly compressed plots with improbably happy endings; elaborate spectacle and special effects; stock ensembles of character, almost always focused on the family; villains whose actions drive the plot; victimized women, around whom the plot turns; and blatant incitements to audience reaction – whether shock or sentiment, cheers, screams, hisses, or tears.

Melodrama replaces tragedy – not in the sense of the new driving out the old or the bad driving out the good, but in the much more powerful sense of a genre answering to new cultural and historical needs.[4] The novel possibility of seemingly tragic situations nevertheless issuing in a happy ending marked melodrama as a mixed genre, whose aim was to mediate new forms of social life in post-Enlightenment, post-Revolutionary modernity. The genre coalesces in the second half of the eighteenth century in France; but the genealogy of English melodrama encompasses native and German roots as well. Native roots include English ballad opera, most notably John Gay's *The Beggar's Opera* (1728); *pantomime dialogueés*, a precursor genre important in France, but originally an English form, invented when David Garrick, responding to the silent pantomimes of John Weaver and John Rich, added speech to his pantomimes; the tradition of bourgeois sentimental drama centring on the pathos and humour of ordinary people (Richard Steele's *The Conscious Lovers* (1722) and George Lillo's *The London Merchant* (1731), for example); sentimentalism in general, with its strong association of feeling with virtue; and Gothic drama, with its exploration of evil and its searching ambivalence about the relative status of the empirical and the supernatural.

German sentimental drama, already influenced by English practice, returns to influence English drama in the works of Friedrich von Kotzebue, whose scandalous vogue in England is registered when the denizens of Austen's *Mansfield Park* (1814) stage *Lover's Vows*, with unsettling results. (Kotzebue's *Das Kind der Liebe* (1780), literally 'The Love-Child', had been euphemistically adapted in plot as well as title by Elizabeth Inchbald (1798).) German Gothic influences its English counterpart as well. Finally, *Sturm und Drang* drama by Klinger, Lenz, Goethe, and the young Schiller was felt in England; Jane Eyre, for example, reads Schiller with Diana and Mary Rivers at Moor House. Though he later repudiated his early play, Schiller offers in

---

4 For a classic engagement of this debate see George Steiner, *The Death of Tragedy* (New York: Alfred A. Knopf, Inc., 1961); Peter Brooks answers Steiner in *The Melodramatic Imagination*, pp. 81, 96, 104, 107.

Die Räuber (1781) the classic formulation of the melodramatic plot of fraternal rivalry, in which a bad brother manipulates his father into disinheriting
the good son, who then becomes an exaggeratedly vicious criminal owing to
his father's bad treatment; of course, the two brothers triangulate around
the central figure of a virtuous, suffering woman.

The French influence on English melodrama, however, is the most
important, and it, too, involves a complex historical exchange with native
English sources. For example, the Parisian 'rescue operas', an immediately
post-Revolutionary phenomenon, were influential in London, where innumerable performances of the fall of the Bastille were popular in both musical
and non-musical forms. Stemming from Diderot, French sentimental drama
(*drame bourgeois*, like that of Beaumarchais and Sedaine) is the determining
influence on Guilbert de Pixérécourt, the father of classic French melodrama. James L. Smith stresses his importance, along with the marking date
of 1800, when he explains that with *Coelina, ou L'enfant du mystère* Pixérécourt 'established overnight the pattern of popular melodrama for the next
hundred years'.[5] Pixérécourt's famous statement that he wrote his plays for
people who could not read, while probably apocryphal, is legendary in
histories of melodrama, for the statement identifies its civic pedagogy and
its commitment to new forms of visual literacy. At the height of his
popularity (1800–20), Pixérécourt's works were widely adapted and produced in England, an example of the generally triangular culture of dramatic
adaptation (moving from France to England and thence to America) that
was a central dynamic of nineteenth-century theatre before the advent of
international dramatic copyright. (The chief turning point in that complex
history may be marked by the Berne Convention of 1886 and its many
subsequent revisions.) It is always important to remember that brilliant
adaptation is a form of dramatic authorship in the nineteenth century, and
that many English adaptations are strikingly different, and often better, than
their originals.

There are several different ways to conceptualize 'the first melodrama',
each of them useful for approaching an understanding of the genre. (In other
words, this is not an argument about the indeterminacy of origins, but an
argument about different angles of vision on a process of origination
that took at least half a century.) Usually denominated as the first
French melodrama, Boutet de Monvel's *Les Victimes cloîtrées* (1791) is a grisly

---

5 James L. Smith, *Melodrama* (London: Methuen & Co, 1973), p. 3.

anti-clerical play involving imprisonment of the heroine deep under a convent and of the hero deep under a monastery. This melodrama clearly illustrates post-Enlightenment, post-Revolutionary anti-clerical and anti-aristocratic fervour. From another point of view, Jean-Jacques Rousseau created the first French melodrama, *Pygmalion* (probably written in 1762, produced 1770 in Lyons and widely published by 1771). In Rousseau's play, Pygmalion assumes a series of attitudes while addressing passionate declamations to his statue of Galathée. Music announces the mood of each declamation, and then recedes into the background while Pygmalion speaks, as we have come to expect of melodramatic music in theatre and film. We can also see the melodramatic dynamic of stillness and movement, silence and speech or music, expressed in Rousseau's choice of subject matter. (The story of Pygmalion and Galatea exerts a continuing fascination across the Victorian period, in works by Browning, W. S. Gilbert, Burne-Jones, and Shaw.) Rousseau explained the novel form by pointing out that music announces and prepares for dramatic speech. Though he called his *Pygmalion* a 'scène lyrique', still reserving the term 'melodrame' for opera, we can recognize the rudiments of the genre of melodrama here.[6]

At about the same time (in the 1760s), Denis Diderot formulated a theory of the tableau in his writings about painting and drama. In both contexts, Diderot identifies the tableau as a pictorial form of dramatic condensation, a freeze-frame picturing a moment that suggests both past and future, held together in dramatic suspense. Diderot argued that the tableau should call to the beholder (*attirer*, *appeler*), arrest the beholder (*arrêter*), and enthrall (*attacher*) the beholder, who becomes fixated with absorption.[7] In other words, the pictorial arrest of time evokes stillness and absorption in the spectator. This aspect of Diderot's dramaturgy influenced Lessing's idea of the 'pregnant moment' in *Laokoön*, which itself exerted a powerful influence on discussions of the genres throughout the nineteenth century in England, and which, of course, like *Pygmalion*, is formulated through the contemplation of a statue that embodies an arrested moment in time.

The first English melodrama is almost always said to be Thomas Holcroft's *A Tale of Mystery* (Covent Garden, 1802), an adaptation of Pixérécourt's *Coelina*. Yet, although the first to use the term 'melo-drame' on its

---

6 See Peter Branscombe, 'Melodrama,' in *The New Grove Dictionary of Music and Musicians*, vol. XII, ed. Stanley Sadie (London: Macmillan, 1980), pp. 116–18.

7 Michael Fried, *Absorption and Theatricality: Painting and the Beholder in the Age of Diderot* (University of Chicago Press, 1980), pp. 91–3.

title page, *A Tale of Mystery* was not actually the work that inaugurated the genre, for melodramas were performed in both France and England throughout the 1790s. Still, it provides a convenient marker for a moment of transition and translation, the moment when classic French melodrama crosses the channel into England. Holcroft's changes to the original are indicative of some characteristics specific to English melodrama. He greatly elaborated the musical and stage directions, to indicate the performance of emotional reaction and its evocation in the audience. But Holcroft changed the political meaning of the plot as well. The Pixérécourt original is fiercely anti-aristocratic. Francisque, the mysterious, heroic mute figure, who is later revealed as Coelina's father, is 'a poor man', whereas in Holcroft's adaptation, Francisco is a nobleman. In Pixérécourt's version, the play resolves itself quite clearly through an appeal to the law; in Holcroft's version, the ending does not fully resolve the issues raised by the plot. In other words, the incendiary content of this play is captured in both French and English versions, but differently so. The French version emphasizes the virtues of the ordinary man and advances its faith in law as an effective replacement for the old order, while the English adaptation is both more reformist and yet more shocking in its refusal to resolve the plot at all; the fate of the villain is not clear, and the family is made the symbolic bearer of socio-political violence and corruption.

The uneven development of revolution is apparent to any student of the nineteenth century. England had already had her revolution, and, in the aftermath of the American and French Revolutions, was intent upon not having another. In the wake of 1789, state censorship and efforts to regulate the populace through the theatre were important to the formation of melodrama in both France and England. In the English setting, the relation of melodrama to state censorship has its prehistory in the Licensing Act of 1737 and the nineteenth-century after-effects of that act. The 1737 Act laid the groundwork for the reception of melodrama by restricting 'legitimate', or spoken, drama to the two Patent Theatres, Drury Lane and Covent Garden. All other theatrical productions were deemed 'illegitimate', and they could not be performed at all, unless they highlighted their difference from spoken drama. Many inventive ways were found to evade this restriction. Written banners and scrolls, puppets, dancing, dumb show or pantomime, and especially music enabled expression by means other than the spoken word, while these features announced, at the same time, that the play did not pretend to be legitimate drama. Pantomime and music are especially important in melodrama, both of them gesturing towards significance that cannot be evoked verbally. The very presence of music in the melodrama, then, testifies to its illegitimacy. It is no exaggeration to claim that the music is a sign of melodrama's struggle to challenge the law and to press beyond language, to express what is disallowed or cannot be said in words.

As Jane Moody has persuasively demonstrated, a rich and diverse 'illegit-imate culture' grew up in London around the East End and transpontine theatres that produced performances intent upon flying under the radar of this law. (Thus the geography of Victorian London, East against West, south against north, may be mapped according to dramatic genre.) Moody argues that the 1843 abolition of the distinction between legitimate and illegitimate theatre had a deleterious effect, since it exposed all theatre alike to the scrutiny of the Lord Chamberlain's Examiner of Plays. State surveillance in effect became more pervasive after the distinction was abolished. Her work powerfully details the anti-authoritarian nature of illegitimate culture.[8] For present purposes, the important points to keep in mind are that the distinction continues to have an effect, even after it is abolished, and that melodrama can evoke radical associations even after it becomes middle class and reformist in orientation.

So what kind of plays fall into the category of Victorian melodrama? Early in the nineteenth century, Gothic and nautical plays predominate. Gothic melodrama concentrates on ghosts, vampires, and other supernatural phenomena, posing a range of tantalizing questions about the extent to which a supernatural force remains at work in the modern world. Matthew 'Monk' Lewis's *The Castle Spectre* (1797) was followed by many adaptations of Mary Shelley's *Frankenstein* (1818) and various versions of the vampire legend, such as James Robinson Planché's *The Vampire, or the Bride of the Isles* (1820). Later in the Victorian period, this interest in the supernatural modulated towards the psychological, in plays that consider extrasensory perception and visionary experience, like Dion Boucicault's *The Corsican Brothers* (1852) and Leopold Lewis's *The Bells* (1871). Some melodramatists were adept at combining nautical elements with Gothic elements. Edward Fitzball, for example, explores the legend of a phantom ship in *The Flying Dutchman* (1826) and relates the world of smugglers to a fading Gothic family in *The Inchcape Bell, or the Dumb Sailor Boy* (1828).

---

8 Jane Moody, *Illegitimate Theatre in London, 1770–1840* (Cambridge University Press, 2000).

Nautical melodrama, a uniquely English form that flourished in the 1820s and 1830s, responds to the massive naval deployments necessitated by the Napoleonic wars and to the huge demographic shifts from country to city. Douglas Jerrold's *Black Ey'd Susan* (1829) and *The Mutiny at the Nore* (1830) focus on the plight of common sailors in thrall to unjust authority, while pirate melodramas such as Edward Fitzball's *The Red Rover* (1829) focus on lawlessness at sea. Nautical heroes – Long Tom Coffin in Fitzball's *The Pilot* (1825), William in *Black Ey'd Susan* (1829), and Harry Hallyard in J. T. Haines's *My Poll and My Partner Joe* (1835), for example – are famous for speech laden with nautical metaphors, which is sometimes interrupted by flights of impassioned romantic or patriotic eloquence. The patriotism of nautical melodrama has been effectively analyzed by Jacky Bratton, who points out that later nautical melodrama, written under the aegis of empire, is less radical than the early-century plays (especially by Jerrold) often were.[9]

From the late 1820s on, melodrama increasingly focuses on domestic themes, which were already implicit in Gothic and nautical melodrama as well. It is important to note that 'domestic melodrama' is a broad term indeed, encompassing plays dedicated variously to examining the family; gender, class, and racial struggles; delineations of life in both country and city; imagining the nation; and international relations within an imperial context. Some domestic melodrama focuses on the struggles of working people, such as J. B. Buckstone's *Luke the Labourer* (1826), John Walker's *The Factory Lad* (1832), and Jerrold's *The Rent Day* (1832). These plays often protest unfair conditions imposed by landlords or local magistrates. The many temperance melodramas – Jerrold's *Fifteen Years of a Drunkard's Life* (1828), H. W. Smith's *The Drunkard* (1844), or T. P. Taylor's *The Bottle* (1847), for example – highlighted one specific domestic problem, while seduction melodramas examined the gender-specific perils that beset women outside the domestic sphere. Some seduction plots focus sympathetically on the woman's situation within the sexual double standard (Kotzebue's plays, for example, were scandalous in England for this reason), while others, such as the many mid-Victorian versions of *Maria Marten, or Murder in the Red Barn*, focus on the criminal behaviour of the seducer. Upper-class criminals were by and large unsympathetic, but melodrama often glorifies a criminal hero

---

9 Jacky Bratton, 'British Heroism and the Structure of Melodrama', in J. S. Bratton, Richard Allen Cave, Breandan Gregory, Heidi J. Holder, and Michael Pickering (eds.), *Acts of Supremacy: The British Empire and the Stage, 1790–1930* (Manchester University Press, 1991), pp. 18–61.

of the working or middle classes. *Jack Sheppard*, the play by J. B. Buckstone (1839), followed publication of William Harrison Ainsworth's novel by only a few months, and its tableaux relied heavily on the Cruikshank illustrations to that novel. Wrongfully accused heroes, as in Tom Taylor's *The Ticket-of-Leave Man* (1863), served to show that the virtues of ordinary people are often misunderstood by society at large.

Some criminal melodramas were dramatizations of actual crimes, and here the alliance between popular journalism and melodrama may be keenly felt. Many of these plays are simply sensational and macabre: *The String of Pearls* (1847), a melodrama by George Dibdin Pitt, was an early version of the story of Sweeney Todd, the demon barber of Fleet Street, who murdered his patrons and allowed his accomplice to bake their flesh into pies; that play was staged even before the story on which it was based had finished its serial publication. In the 1860s, sensation melodramas were every bit as popular as sensation fiction. These plays specialized in the 'sensation scene', which displayed the rich proliferation of special effects in the stagecraft of Victorian theatres. Dion Boucicault's *The Poor of New York* (1857), staged in many places, first as *The Poor of Liverpool* (1863) and eventually as *The Streets of London* (1864), featured a house on fire, while *Under the Gaslight* (1867) by Augustin Daly, as well as Boucicault's imitative response, *After Dark* (1868), both featured a hero tied to the railroad tracks, while the heroine watches in agony, before he is freed just in the nick of time.

Melodrama also grappled with the relation of England to other parts of the world. Dion Boucicault is widely acknowledged as the first playwright to move beyond the buffoon-like stage Irishman towards a more sympathetic and realistic characterization, in plays like *The Colleen Bawn* (1860) and *Arragh-na-Pogue* (1864). He was also a transatlantic playwright, who spent a portion of his life producing plays in New York, where he first presented his anti-slavery melodrama, *The Octoroon* (1859). Active, too, in the imperial context, Boucicault contributed *Jessie Brown, or The Relief of Lucknow* (1858), which presented a version of the Indian Rebellion of the previous year.

The politics and poetics of English melodrama develop together over the course of the nineteenth century. Melodrama is devoted to the expansion of democracy, as well as to the exploration and construction of modern forms of social organization like class, gender, nationality, ethnicity, and race. Like the novel, melodrama helps to mediate the transition from a society based on inherited status to one based on social class. Within this framework, feminine virtue becomes an intensely conventional representation of domestic virtue in general, in both senses of the word 'domestic', both familial and national. The plight of 'the common man' is thus often represented by a woman, gender standing in for class. 'Helpless and unfriended', the endangered heroine also often represents the nation's vulnerability, gender standing in for nation. But the heroine is only the most central of melodrama's vulnerable and inarticulate figures, a group including orphans, mutes, and even animals. Without a voice, they literalize the suffering of the disenfranchised. This figural point may be taken in a sociological sense, as Martha Vicinus does, or in a philosophical and psychoanalytic sense, as Peter Brooks does, or both.[10] In either respect, melodrama metonymically highlights the suffering attendant upon an emerging new social order.

It is often argued that English melodrama loses its most trenchantly radical potential as it moves from the earlier forms of Gothic and nautical melodrama to the later forms of domestic melodrama. This argument is frequently correlated with the increasing return of middle-class audiences to the theatre, starting around mid-century. But the radical potential of melodrama subsists all along, depending, of course, on the particular intertwining of progressive and conservative elements in each individual play. Focusing on the poor and dispossessed can carry a radical significance even when the plot seems to inculcate fidelity to the state; the potential for incitement to rebellion circulates with the idea that virtue might go unrecognized or that crimes against the virtuous might go unpunished. In other words, the graphic depiction of social misery is itself incendiary.[11] As Peter Brooks argues, 'The *reward* of virtue ... is only a secondary manifestation of the *recognition* of virtue.'[12]

Socio-political issues are embodied in melodrama not only as content but also as form. For example: melodrama's obsession with social recognition often takes the form of the trial scene, such as the court martial at the end of *Black Ey'd Susan* (1829), the kangaroo court on 'the selvage of civilisation' in *The Octoroon* (1859),[13] or the dream-trial at the end of *The Bells* (1871). Trials present an occasion for producing chains of testimony, empirical evidence or documents, and networks of witnessing to be examined for their potential to achieve or thwart justice. Often they are found wanting. Then

10 Brooks, *The Melodramatic Imagination*; Martha Vicinus, ' "Helpless and Unfriended": Nineteenth-Century Domestic Melodrama', *New Literary History* 13:1 (1981), pp. 127–43.
11 Daniel Gerould, 'Melodrama and Revolution' in Bratton, Cook, and Gledhill, *Melodrama*, pp. 185, 188.
12 Brooks, *The Melodramatic Imagination*, p. 27, italics in original.
13 Dion Boucicault, *The Octoroon*, in *Selected Plays of Dion Boucicault*, ed. Andrew Parkin (Gerrards Cross, Bucks.: Colin Smythe, 1987), p. 180.

the last-minute revelation or rescue – one great hallmark of melodrama – will close the gap that has dangerously opened up between Justice and human law. Thus, too, the repetitive representation of claustral or carceral enclosures (convents and monasteries, Gothic dungeons, modern prisons and jails) alludes to corruption in the hierarchy of Church, state, and social order. But in a more general sense, the dynamic of confinement and release models the expressive dynamics of melodrama in general. In this respect, mute characters, strangled cries, pantomimic gestures, and, more generally, the silent tableau and the melodramatic music all indicate the desire for an expressiveness beyond the normal range of language or social existence. We should note that the hyper-expressionistic valence of melodrama actually serves to highlight the *difficulties* of expression in the modern world. Like wrongfully convicted prisoners, heroic criminals, or virtuous folk unjustly held back, expression *will* burst out somehow; that is its relentless logic. In other words, again, the chief formal features of melodrama – the music and the tableau – are not 'merely' formal, but are fully integrated with the social thematics of the genre.

Melodrama conveys its social significance in other ways as well. Critics often point out that the characters of melodrama are types. They are static for the most part, neither mixed in motive nor developing through experience in time. We should not dismiss this characteristic of melodrama as simplistic, however, but should instead focus on the aesthetic and political value of typification, for the type focuses attention specifically on abstract social function rather than on individuality. Significantly, the typical characters of melodrama fit together in a systematic ensemble, just as the 'stock character' is relative to the 'stock company' in the theatre. Ensemble playing was an economic structure, but considered in aesthetic terms, it supports the sense that an entire world is being encapsulated, condensed, and abstracted in the representations of the play. Thus melodrama offers a sort of emblem of society, usually conveyed through the vehicle of the family.

The central stock figures of melodrama are familiar: the virtuous, suffering heroine; the hero so earnest and dutiful that he often seems naive; and the villain, who is the active force driving the plot.[14] Because melodrama so blatantly personifies evil as a 'given', and as an individual figure, we can sense the fear that social corruption is systematic and ungraspable, incomprehensible and relentless. In the villain, in other words, the sense of

---

14 See Michael R. Booth, 'The Character of Melodrama', in *English Melodrama* (London: Herbert Jenkins, 1965), pp. 13–39.

overwhelming difficulty in the world at large is condensed into the figure of a person, who can then be defeated, punished, or expunged. So, too, the semiotic convention of physiognomic legibility – the idea that the villain may be easily recognized – fosters the confidence or hope that villainy might somehow be legible in real social situations. The 'black villain' (the most overt) sported a brow furrowed with cork lines, a black wig, and a dark complexion, while the 'gentlemanly villain' (popular from mid-century on) wore a top hat, frock coat, and fur-lined cape, and slapped his thigh with his kid gloves.

If the villain drives the plot, the heroine forms its focal point. Desired by many, preyed upon by many, she suffers extravagantly.[15] Though in one respect she is aligned with others whose powers of expression are severely limited, in another respect she is flagrantly and effectively expressive. Michael Booth points out that 'in cases of extreme grief and despair the acting of heroines was as physically intense as the bravery of heroes'.[16] The heroine's innocence is stipulated as given, yet she is often misunderstood. Thus the figure of the heroine is complex, sometimes working as an admonition, part of a cautionary tale enforcing gender norms, sometimes working as an unruly sign of gender norms in the process of change.[17]

The melodramatic hero is compounded of strength, bravery, and endurance, on the one hand, and great tenderness, on the other. One audible sign of the heroine's perfect virtue is her neutral and uncharacterized speech. In relation to the heroine's purity of speech, the hero is sometimes a mixed figure, as in nautical melodramas such as *Black Ey'd Susan*, where he usually speaks in a dense metaphorical jargon, showing that he is fully inhabited by his role as servant of the state, but under the stress and pressure of strong emotion, his speech will become a heightened form of manly eloquence, sometimes even rising into blank verse. Thus melodrama portrays the systematic and self-perpetuating structure of gender relations; in melodrama, both masculinity and femininity are shown to be in crisis. Either hero or heroine might be orphaned, emblematically stripped of parental protection, in which case their central representational value – as experimental test-cases of virtue under siege – is compounded by the social and

---

15 *Ibid.*, pp. 24–7, 37–8.   16 *Ibid.*, p. 200.
17 On the cultural significance of the heroine, see Vicinus, ' "Helpless and Unfriended," ' pp. 127–43, and Léon Mestayer, 'What the Heroine Taught, 1830–1870,' in Michael Hays and Anastasia Nicolopolou (eds.), *Melodrama: The Cultural Emergence of a Genre* (New York: St Martin's Press, 1996), pp. 235–44.

epistemological resonance of their positions as unmoored characters making their way in the world (just like orphans in the novel).

The central figures of melodrama are often accompanied by particular foils and doubles. For example, the villain might have an accomplice, who will, late in the plot, convert from bad to good, swinging the plot's resolution along with him. If the heroine lives in a gentry household, she might be attended by a cheeky female servant, the soubrette figure, whose suitor will be another servant or artisan. They will speak out clearly against authority and for common sense, though their comic malapropisms will make their lack of education audible. These are examples of the comic woman and the comic man, who form the lower half of the double plot characteristic of English melodrama. They set in relief and cast an ironic light on the high tensions of the main plot. Jacky Bratton helpfully calls these the 'contending discourses' of melodrama.[18] On the other hand, if the heroine lives in a humble cottage, she might have an old father and mother, the 'good old man' and the 'good old woman' of melodrama, one of whom (usually the father) will misunderstand her, doubt her virtue, and cast her out of the house.

Strife within and across the generations is represented through familial pairs, which also enable the representation of emergent historical change. So, for example, if orphaned, the heroine might have a parent-surrogate, most often an uncle, who will be either ineffectual or villainous (as he is in *A Tale of Mystery* and *Black Ey'd Susan*). The villainous, avuncular father-surrogate economically makes it possible for a plot to stress, simultaneously, both sibling rivalry in the older generation and the absence of parental authority for the younger generation. For similar reasons, in the younger generation, the virtuous hero might be paired with a bad brother who has deceived the father into disinheriting his virtuous son. This structure of inheritance gone awry emphasizes the failure of an older social order; that failure in the past continues in the present, within the younger generation, whose dangerous fraternal violence is provoked and permitted by the absence of a strong father. The vertical hierarchy of inherited status is giving way to the horizontal relations of democracy, but the transition is not an easy one. Melodrama both registers and hastens this transition, working, as the novel does, to mediate new concepts of class, gender, and nation through which modern social relations will be understood.

18 Jacky Bratton, 'The Contending Discourses of Melodrama', in Bratton, Cook, and Gledhill, *Melodrama*, pp. 38–49.

Because of the typified abstraction of the melodramatic ensemble, the absent or displaced father inexorably also suggests an absent Father. Peter Brooks has emphasized the nineteenth-century struggle to conceive of a modern world without Providential order. In his famous formulation, melodrama is charged with 'uncovering, demonstrating, and making operative the essential moral universe in a post-sacred era'.[19] His influential phrase, the 'moral occult', refers to the hope, or secularized faith, that a man-made order might be seen effectively to replace Providence. Thus melodrama asks: how might we hope that virtue will be recognized and justice prevail, since we can no longer rely on Providence? In practice, melodramas usually do not answer this question directly or decisively; instead, they launch debates, sometimes hedging all bets (both asserting and denying the operation of Providence, as in *The Corsican Brothers*), sometimes floating modern replacements for Providence (as the photograph is said to be the 'eye of God' in *The Octoroon*[20]), and sometimes simply focusing on the failure of social institutions to recognize virtue and providing a last-minute rescue or revelation instead.

The improbably happy endings so characteristic of melodrama deserve to be understood better. From a fully realistic, disenchanted point of view, the conventional melodramatic resolution may seem like the flimsiest fantasy. But it should be seen as wish-fulfilment of a special sort, the blunt assertion that even in a post-Providential world, justice can be done and common virtue can be recognized somehow. That 'somehow' is often quite strained, even nonsensical. But the suddenness, extremity, and improbability of the melodramatic resolution testify to the great difficulty of imagining the mechanism of any just resolution at all. To bolster its endings, melodrama extravagantly relies on various forms of evidence; in general, an older logic of evidence written on the body (scars, birthmarks) gives way to a logic based on documentary evidence (wills, letters, posters and playbills, photographs). The emerging problems of the new social order seem intractable; the impasse in the melodramatic plot testifies to this anxiety. Poetic justice stands in for a social justice that is in grave doubt. The melodramatic happy ending is not, in other words, a sign of naivety; it is a sign of the crisis in social signification that the genre seeks to assuage or work through.

The character-types of melodrama are recognizable at first sight and on first hearing, through their names, costumes, gestures, speech, and the

---

19 Brooks, *Melodramatic Imagination*, p. 15.   20 Boucicault, *The Octoroon*, p. 173.

music that accompanies them. In monologue, dialogue, and frequent 'asides' they will also repeatedly announce their identities, feelings, and intentions. In a general formal sense, too, melodrama famously depends on visual and aural data, on the principle of physiognomic legibility and sonic recognition, and on the externality of signs. As in the novel, so too in melodrama, the question of whether inner worth (or the lack of it) might be externally legible gives rise to both positive and sceptical answers. Melodrama is known for making these forms of recognition seem dependable, but the best English melodramas treat the genre's supposed faith in visual recognition as a given and then work to complicate or undermine it. For example, Raker, a good character in Douglas Jerrold's *Black Ey'd Susan* (1829), says: 'I must look a villain, and that's the truth. Well, there is no help for an ugly countenance; but if my face be ill-favoured, I'll take care to keep my heart of the right colour.'[21] As we can see, the principle of physiognomic legibility is self-consciously acknowledged as a generic convention and is explicitly parodied, even early on.

The high point of the genre's contemplation of physiognomic signs is achieved in Dion Boucicault's *The Octoroon* (1859), which braids several melodramatic threads very tightly together – female virtue under threat, illegitimacy in the family, property ownership and transfer, epistemological questions relating to visual evidence – and binds them all to the institution of slavery. Zoe (played originally by Boucicault's actress wife Agnes Robertson) is the perfect melodramatic heroine, desired by many and powerless within the web of her social setting. The melodramatic villain's conventional cry – 'you shall be mine, all mine!' – is quite literalized in this play, when he buys Zoe at a fully staged slave auction. Though relegated to the back story, the fact that Zoe is 'the natural daughter' of Judge Peyton and his quadroon slave twists melodrama's focus on illegitimacy in the family towards a new end; instead of being treated as an outcast, she is lovingly embraced as a member of the family, yet prohibited from marrying within its social network. Further, if the plantation were not encumbered, Zoe would be free through the will of the late Judge. Thus an absent, ineffectual, and profligate father has caused the legal, economic, and social chaos this melodrama works to restore to order: his property is controlled by a villainous overseer; his widow is threatened with loss of her home; and Zoe remains a slave, both a daughter and a piece of property, in this racially charged vision of status inconsistency.

---

21 Douglas Jerrold, *Black-Ey'd Susan*, in George Rowell (ed.), *Nineteenth-Century Plays* (Oxford University Press, 1953), p. 8.

The Octoroon grounds its critique of slavery and the colour line in its sceptical attitude towards physiognomic legibility. The hero, George Peyton, falls in love with Zoe without realizing that she is an octoroon. George knows nothing of anti-miscegenation laws, having come to Louisiana from cosmopolitan Paris, where such laws would seem utterly barbaric. Zoe's racial difference does not 'show', and he does not see it. She must point out to him the subtle blue tinge darkening her fingernails and the whites of her eyes. Thus the play provides both a prurient lesson in racism and a trenchant critique of it; working through both highly visible and audible minstrel stereotypes and also the near-invisibility of Zoe's racial identity according to law, it simultaneously offers a critique of physiognomic legibility and of race relations. At the same time, the play's use of a photograph as the form of legible evidence that finally exposes the villain updates and extends melodrama's politics of visuality with a new technology; and it mirrors, in theme and form, the melodramatic tableau.

Along with the physiognomic legibility of characters and the frequent recourse to pantomimic action, the master-convention of melodrama's visual semiotics is the tableau. Tableaux occur in many other theatrical genres as well, but they have a special significance within melodrama, whose visual conventions cohere around it. Tableaux typically mark the end of the acts, and sometimes also appear in their middle. Suddenly the dramatic action stops, and the acting bodies freeze into a static pictorial composition. Indeed, the technical term for the tableau, in the play texts of the period, is 'Picture'. Tableaux interrupt and segment the drama into readable passages; they also precipitate a shift in representational registers, calling the audience to an active rather than absorbed relation to the spectacle, asking them to read and interpret the composition. As a form of dramatic condensation, the tableaux look both before and after, summarizing the import of the action so far and suggesting plot development to come. Indeed, melodramatic narrative is literally suspended on these pictures, strung out like a wire between these points of condensed visual significance. The concluding tableau will attempt a summation, but will inevitably leave some issues unresolved.

In *Realizations*, Martin Meisel emphasizes the importance of the tableau while writing the history of relations between the painting, theatre, and illustrated novels of nineteenth-century England.[22] All three involve a punctuated narrative form, he argues, in which pictures interrupt and at the same

22 Martin Meisel, *Realizations: Narrative, Pictorial and Theatrical Arts in Nineteenth-Century England* (Princeton University Press, 1983).

time clarify the ongoing story. He calls this narrative form 'serial discontinuity', emphasizing both the interruptive nature of the form and its serial visualizations:

> [I]n the 19th century serial discontinuity was a common style, marking the dominant narrative, pictorial, and theatrical forms ... all these forms were both narrative and pictorial, but ... drama, indeed melodrama, was central, with its situational grammar, its punctuating crystallizations into a pictorial configuration with narrative import and accent: often an impasse, sometimes a resolution, typically followed by a cut (a curtain) or a dissolve. Motion in effect was movement to and away from pictures (or, more radically, was the succession of pictures) and even acting theory turned from a discourse based in rhetorical analysis to one that was fundamentally pictorial. It is the pictorialism, with its narrative functions, that now stands out when compared with earlier and later styles.[23]

The history of the stage in nineteenth-century England is a history of developing pictorialism as well. Gradually the wings and forestage shrink; managers from the 1830s to the 1880s experiment with the 'box set'; the 'fourth wall' develops, cutting a planar division between the audience and the performance. The pictorialism of the Victorian stage reaches its apogee in Squire and Marie Bancroft's management of the Haymarket Theatre, beginning in 1880, when they transformed the proscenium arch into a gigantic gilt picture frame, by extending it across the bottom as well as the sides and top; but their spectacular gesture merely made explicit a long nineteenth-century history, coalescing that development into a summary visual statement. The box set and the fourth wall form the basis for middle-class domestic realism in the 'cup-and-saucer' or 'drawing-room' comedies of T. W. Robertson (made famous by the Bancrofts during their earlier management of the Prince of Wales's). Melodrama, too, depends on these divisions, though not specifically on the box set. Melodramatic audiences feel their separation from the representation; they always know what the characters, entangled in the toils of the plot, do not know, and yet they enjoy violating the boundary between audience and representation, too, hissing and booing, screaming their warnings, as if the characters could hear them. My main point, for now, is simply that the tableau, with its planar orientation towards the audience, both prefigures and also stands as a microcosm of the general pictorialism of the Victorian stage.

---

23 Meisel, 'Scattered Chiaroscuro', p. 67.

Melodramatic tableaux are as infinitely variable as the plays themselves, but we can nevertheless isolate several general kinds. Frozen bodies locked in mutual stares of recognition might serve as the fundamental tableau situation, since each figure in the throes of recognizing the other is also fixed in the role of audience to the other. Their sudden pause is followed by their sudden starting away from one another in the typical form of the double-take reaction, movement followed by stasis followed by movement again. In another kind of tableau, sentimental domestic scenes allow the audience to deduce the characters' evolving relations to one another. But they also make their sentimental appeal to the audience, jerking tears or sighs. The opposite of the domestic tableau, the otherworldly 'vision scene' opens in the backstage, revealing another reality altogether. During the 1860s, 'sensation scenes' become popular, which often combined movement and enforced stillness (think of the hero tied to the railroad tracks in Daly's *Under the Gaslight* and Boucicault's *After Dark*). Finally, tableau 'realizations' imitate famous paintings and are recognized by the audience as a tour de force of melodramatic visuality. The most famous use of this convention occurs in *The Rent Day* by Douglas Jerrold (1832), which opens on a realization of the title painting by David Wilkie, while Act II opens on a realization of another, related, Wilkie painting, 'Distraining for Rent'. Tableau realizations offer an artful confusion of art and life; notably, they could not be effective were it not for the dramatic increase in the popular circulation of images from the 1830s on. Thus they show that the ability to recognize works of art was no longer an elite phenomenon, and they provide good evidence for the growth of new forms of visual literacy.

Again, this is by no means merely a formal matter. Social significance and argument coalesce in these visual points of the melodrama. In these pictures, ideological contradictions are often made clearly visible, as if the ongoing flux of history could be suddenly and artificially stopped, allowing for both aesthetic and political apprehension.

For example, Act II of *Black Ey'd Susan* ends with the nautical hero, William, defending his wife Susan against a man who is threatening her virtue. William (originally played by the great T. P. Cooke, who dominated the melodramatic stage in the 1820s and 1830s) strikes the would-be rapist down. Suddenly realizing that he has struck his own ship's Captain, William 'turns away horror-struck . . . [and] Susan falls on her knees', while the other sailors 'bend over the Captain'.[24] This tableau brings to a point the

---

24 Jerrold, *Black-Ey'd Susan*, p. 30.

masculine self-division of the nautical hero, whose public duty to national service absolutely conflicts with his private duty to his wife. William is court-martialled for striking his superior officer. At the end of the play, his innocence is restored when a document is discovered that shows he had been discharged from the Navy before he struck the Captain. Thus William is released from prison, from his crime, and from national service all at the same conclusive moment. He leaps from the platform where he was to have been hanged, and, accompanied by music, a concluding tableau features the Captain bringing Susan on stage and giving her back to William. Thus the concluding tableau registers the necessity for William to be legally processed back to private life. The state must grant him the right to return home.

Another good example of ideological complexity may be seen in the concluding tableau of *The Octoroon*, when a steamboat blows up in the background, while in the foreground the '*grand Tableau*' forms,[25] including all the characters – black and white, English, Irish, and native American. The curtain drops on this happy vision of class, gender, and racial plots, all melodramatically resolved. The steamship explosion in the background has rightly been called 'orgasmic', for it expresses an overcoming of law in the union of the lovers at last. (This is the English ending. The concluding tableau in the American version stresses the intractability of the colour line, depicting Zoe dead in the arms of her lover.) But it is also a tacit admission of the violence necessary (in the background) to secure the fantasy of a happily unified, multicultural nation (in the foreground). Since the play was first performed in New York four days after the hanging of John Brown for his abolitionist rebellion at Harper's Ferry, these associations are no doubt relevant. Given the fact that *The Octoroon* cites the photograph both as a modern, technological replacement for Providence ('the eye of God') and as a microcosmic form of the tableau, we can see that this play is dedicated to joining its trenchant cultural commentary to meta-generic wit.

Some melodramas focus metaphysical significance through the tableau. James Robinson Planché's *The Vampire; or, The Bride of the Isles* (1820) opens with a vision, in which the heroine dreams of the danger she will soon face in the ensuing play. Suddenly the Vampire appears – every bit like a melodramatic villain – to proclaim: 'She is mine!'[26] This melodrama then considers transmigration of spirit, for the Vampire appears to triumph over

---

25 Boucicault, *The Octoroon*, p. 190.

26 James Robinson Planché, *The Vampire; Or, The Bride of the Isles*, in *Plays by James Robinson Planché*, ed. Donald Roy (Cambridge University Press, 1986), p. 49.

space and time, life and death, and above all, over the limitations of personal identity that seem to be secured by the body. This kind of supernatural hypothesis is harnessed to social significance in Dion Boucicault's adaptation of *The Corsican Brothers* (1852), which takes up the premise that one 'identity' could be divided between two bodies and two places. The twin Corsican brothers share a form of extrasensory perception, through which one always knows when the other is in danger. The much-praised special effects used in this melodrama – the Corsican Trap and the device of Pepper's Ghost – enabled the realistic staging of an apparition, while Charles Kean played both brothers to great effect. However, from our point of view after more than a hundred years of cinematic melodrama, Boucicault's most important innovation is the representation of simultaneity in time. This is accomplished by means of the tableaux.

Act I and Act II end at the exact same moment – at exactly ten minutes past nine – when one twin dies in a duel in Paris while the other, at home in Corsica, feels that his brother is in danger and anxiously awaits news. In the concluding tableau to Act I, the Corsican scene is in the foreground, while the backstage opens to reveal a duel in Paris, in which the other brother has perished. Then the entirety of Act II is a flashback, showing what happened in Paris during the time span of Act I. Act II ends with the Act I double-tableau precisely reversed. The duel takes place in the fore-stage, *an exact reproduction of the tableau that terminated the first act*, after which '*the back of the scene opens slowly and discovers the chamber of the first act, the clock marking the hour, ten minutes after nine*'. In other words, the juxtaposition of the two pictures in each double-tableau, then their reversal, represents simultaneity in time. It is important to realize that melodrama had this montage-effect in its lexicon of conventions at least by mid-century.[27] The uncanny identification of the brothers suggests a Gothic pessimism about social progress; like simultaneity in time – and like the identification of the brothers – the primitive Corsican law of vendetta and the supposedly civilized law of Paris collapse into sameness. Remarks suggesting that the plot is directed by Providence give way in the end, and the horrible point of it all seems to be that there is no world elsewhere – neither a city where vendetta has been transcended through civil procedure, nor a Providential earthly order, nor an other world. However, the

---

27 See Meisel, 'Scattered Chiaroscuro', pp. 69–75, for another discussion of simultaneity in time in *The Corsican Brothers*.

melodramatic drive to push beyond the limits of the body has provided an important technique for the future of cinema.

In *The Bells* (1871) by Leopold Lewis, a critique of the socio-political underpinnings of middle-class comfort is conveyed through the mutual involvement of tableaux and music. This plot turns on the hidden guilt of its central character, Mathias, who murdered a Polish Jew in order to steal his gold, fifteen years before the play begins. Mathias's prosperous burgo-master's life is founded on this secret crime. (The role of Mathias was created by Henry Irving, in his first star turn.) At the end of Act I, left alone on stage, Mathias begins to hear sleigh-bells, like the bells on the sleigh of the murdered Jew. His increasing anxiety is expressed in the repetitive melodramatic 'Music with frequent chords'. Both the tableau and the music concentrate our attention on the idea that interiority can take external form, bursting out in the music or flashing back in a sudden stage picture. Since the audience can see that Mathias is alone on stage, what follows in the famous vision scene must be understood as a purely psychological effect, a projection of Mathias's memory and internal disquiet. At ten o'clock, the precise clock-time marking the anniversary of the murder, the music swells. A tableau is disclosed in the backstage, depicting the exact scene from the past, with the Jew in his sleigh, immediately before the murder. The stillness of the tableau is broken; the stage picture moves. The Jew suddenly turns his head and 'fixes his eyes sternly' on Mathias, who recoils, arching back-ward, 'utters a prolonged cry of terror and falls senseless' to the floor.[28] Thus, this vision scene is a recognition scene as well; the dead Jew figuratively comes to life momentarily, terrifying Mathias and the audience alike. The return of the repressed is like the return of the dead – and all this is conveyed through the stillness of the tableau breaking into dramatic action once again.

In Act III, Mathias dreams that he has been arrested, put on trial, convicted of murder, and sentenced to death by hanging. He awakes from this nightmare at the very end of the play, gasping for breath, struggling in his invisible bondage, and begging his family to 'take the rope from [his] neck!' However, since the rope is a figment of his guilty conscience, no one can save him. Mathias dies, to the crescendo accompaniment of the insist-ently thematic music of the bells, *fortissimo*. In other words, in *The Bells*, melodramatic music is both affective and effective. It guides audience affect, as melodramatic music always does, but as a representation of Mathias's

---

28 David Leopold Lewis, *The Bells*, in Rowell, *Nineteenth-Century Plays*, pp. 481, 482.

conscience, the music also seems to cause the death of the protagonist. No other character in the play knows what Mathias knows, sees what he sees, hears what he hears, or knows of his dream. Only the audience is privy to these audio and visual externalizations of Mathias's interiority. The music of the bells hovers everywhere, in the ambient space of the theatre, orchestrating audience suspense and enacting the vengeance of self-punishing guilt.

Like everything associated with theatrical production, the quality – and quantity – of melodramatic music depended on the budget. Lavish, large-scale productions would commission original music, composed by one authorial hand and played by a pit orchestra of twenty-five or thirty instruments. In cheaper productions, however, the number of musicians might be reduced to two or three – perhaps a couple of strings and a harmonium. These more or less ad hoc ensembles would play from a book of melodies, called 'melos' for short, that were arranged by type or mood. *Furiosos* – also called 'hurries' – were used to accompany chase scenes, or scenes of combat. The *agitatos*, or 'agits', were used to underscore storms and scenes of emotional distress. *Andantes* set off touching sentimental scenes of melancholy or romance. And, finally, *tremolos*, or *mysteriosos* – often called 'mysts' – accompanied 'scenes of apprehension, terror, the appearance of visions or ghosts', or any other suspenseful and uncanny episode.[29] (The ghost myst from *The Corsican Brothers* is surely the best example of these.) Melodramatic music, in other words, is mood music. It is blatantly thematic, as ostentatiously typified as the characters and situations it helps to characterize. But it is highly effective and has had an enormous influence – on Richard Wagner's development of the leitmotif, for example, and of course in the form of the cinematic soundtrack, where it still exerts its powerful emotional and aesthetic effect today.

Early in the nineteenth century in England, melodramatic music might be interruptive or interludic, as in ballad opera. But increasingly the music grew almost continuous, suppressing itself during passages of declamation and swelling between those passages of dramatic speech. Melodramatic declamation – a rhythmic, heightened oratorical style, characterized by the addition of extra syllables – is carefully produced in relation to the music.[30] Indeed, the articulation of speech in relation to the music makes it clear that speech itself is often a dimension of melodramatic music, and that melodrama often

---

29 David Mayer and Matthew Scott, '*Four Bars of Agit*': *Incidental Music for Victorian and Edwardian Melodrama* (London: Samuel French and the Theatre Museum, V&A, 1983), p. 2.
30 Booth, *English Melodrama*, 'Appendix: Melodramatic Acting', pp. 190–210.

purposefully blurs the boundaries between speech and song. Working around and behind the declamation, the music starts and stops, rises or falls, and themes repeat and vary, providing the melodrama with one important dimension of its temporal structure. Like the tableaux, music supplies the 'points' of the form (with chords or with separate songs), but unlike the tableaux, the music also provides the underscoring, the subtending arc of connection and development of the whole.

Peter Branscombe distinguishes English from French melodrama on the basis of its almost continuous music.[31] This was a historical development, the music becoming more and more continuous over the course of the nineteenth century, but we can see a sudden increase even in the first English melodrama, *A Tale of Mystery* (1802), where the music cues are much more frequent and explicit than those of *Coelina*, from which it was adapted. The music delineates and marks the shifting moods of the action: *'Hunting-music'*, *'Music to express pain and disorder'*, *'Confused music'*, *'Music of doubt and terror'*, *'Threatening music'*. For example, when Selina overhears the plotting of the villains, the music softens (*'expressing pain and alarm'*), pauses when she reveals the danger to Francisco, then swells and *'continues tremendous'* until the villain enters, when it *'suddenly stops'*. This play text is explicit in signalling not only the entrances, but also the stops: *'After which, sudden pause of music'*, *'Music ceases'*, *'Sweet and cheerful music, gradually dying away'*.[32]

When music cues are plentiful – or better still, when the music survives – we can analyse the overall musical form of a particular melodrama, as in David Mayer's edition of *The Bells*.[33] On the other hand, we can sometimes see, in the music, certain features of the history of melodrama as a genre. *Black Ey'd Susan*, for example, was founded on a popular ballad by John Gay, 'All in the Downs', or 'Sweet William's Farewell', which had appeared in *The Beggar's Opera*. The use of this music within *Black Ey'd Susan* illustrates the survival of the older native stock of ballad opera and broadside ballad circulation. Strains of this 'theme song' are distributed across the play. But in the dead centre of the play, the entire ballad is sung by Blue Peter, one of William's messmates, who says the song was 'made by Tom Splinter' as a true description of Susan and William's own

---

31 Branscombe, 'Melodrama', p. 116.

32 Thomas Holcroft, *A Tale of Mystery, a Melo-Drame; as Performed at the Theatre-Royal, Covent Garden* (London: Richard Phillips, 1802), pp. 3, 9, 15, 17, 19–20, 24.

33 David Mayer (ed.), *Henry Irving and 'The Bells': Irving's Personal Script of the Play* (Manchester University Press, 1980).

parting.[34] Thus the musical origins of the work – and of the genre to which it belongs – are embedded at its heart, and rationalized by the plot. Like tableau 'realizations', in other words, the music can also refer to a world outside the play; like the tableaux, melodramatic music can attain meta-generic significance, commenting on the form of melodrama as a genre, as it does in *Black Ey'd Susan* and *The Bells*.

During the nineteenth century, melodrama and the novel are inextricably intertwined, two titanic bourgeois genres dedicated to a similar set of social and representational problems. Not only do they develop in tandem, but they also symbiotically related, since melodramatizations of novels are a matter of common practice; for example, the sea tales of James Fenimore Cooper were immediately adapted in several versions, as were many of Dickens's novels, *Jane Eyre*, *East Lynne*, and *Uncle Tom's Cabin*. Moreover, all the great Victorian novelists write with an awareness of melodramatic technique. In Dickens the influence of the popular theatre is especially clear, and much good critical commentary has addressed this fact.[35] But even at the high point of English realism, in Eliot and James, the force of melodrama is also clearly felt. Eliot in particular is hyper-conscious of musical form and tableau-effects. And, as Brooks points out, James builds on melodrama to press beyond the realism of the great tradition; as he puts it, 'Melodrama's relation to realism is always oblique – it is tensed toward an exploitation of expression beyond.'[36]

Until the late twentieth century, studies of the Victorian period largely ignored melodrama except to dismiss or denigrate it. Repeatedly noting that there was no serious drama until Ibsen, Pinero, Wilde, and Shaw, earlier critics forgot that the separation of 'theatre' from 'drama' was a tangible Victorian after-effect of the Licensing Act and that the strong influence of the illegitimate genres lasted throughout the Victorian period, frequently shaping high drama as well. The return to drama usually identified with the advent of Ibsen, Pinero, Wilde, and Shaw owed as much to melodrama as to the developing stage realism of T. W. Robertson and his followers, who advanced the subdued 'natural acting' in a box set that eventually defines realism on the stage. Ibsen's plays in particular were

---

34 Jerrold, *Black-Ey'd Susan*, p. 25.
35 For example, Paul Schlicke, *Dickens and Popular Entertainment* (London: Unwin Hyman, 1985); Edwin M. Eigner, *The Dickens Pantomime* (Berkeley: University of California Press, 1989); John, *Dickens's Villains*; and Sally Ledger, *Dickens and the Popular Radical Imagination* (Cambridge University Press, 2007).
36 Brooks, *Melodramatic Imagination*, p. ix.

strongly inflected by melodrama, a debt that can be perceived in his ironic uses of the tableau[37] and his ostentatiously spare use of music. The 'rise of realism' on the stage famously lags behind the rise of Realism in the novel. J. Jeffrey Franklin is correct, however, when he argues that 'during this period each of these two cultural forms determined ... their formal properties and thematic territories *in direct reference to the other*.'[38] Much late nineteenth-century melodrama strives towards an explicitly documentary realism, as for example in the painstakingly exact replication of the Borough Market in Southwark on a Saturday night in George Robert Sims's *The Lights O' London* (1881). But melodrama was taken to be strikingly realistic even early on; compared to the conventions of the past, its use of prose dialogue, common language, and characters from ordinary life seemed radically realistic. The history of melodrama helps us to remember that realism is always relative, developing unevenly across genres, as well as within genres.

A serious look back at the history of the novel, starting from before realism became the standard, can remind us that melodrama works on similar fundamental questions of social, ethical, and epistemological recognition. The public externality of melodrama has often been contrasted with the privacy of novel reading, but it is imperative that we see the two together, both launching debates about civic virtue, both actively inculcating yet also pressing against normative social expectations, both conditioning and constructing elements of the public sphere. Like the novel, melodrama explores the range of attitudes – from credulity to scepticism – about whether outer, visible appearance can be interpreted correctly to reveal inner, psychological or ethical truth. The characters of melodrama are typified, whereas the characters of Victorian fiction are individualized; but those novelistic characters are individualized against the backdrop of social type (Jo, for example, in *Bleak House* represents all the other 'men and women ... dying thus around us every day',[39] while Dorothea in *Middlemarch* represents the difficulty of becoming a modern St Theresa). Formally, too, melodrama and the nineteenth-century novel work on similar problems. Illustrated novels employ an intermittent pictorialism, very much like the intermittent tableaux of melodrama, as Meisel has made clear

---

37 Toril Moi, *Henrik Ibsen and the Birth of Modernism: Art, Theater, Philosophy* (Oxford University Press, 2006), pp. 111–36.

38 J. Jeffrey Franklin, *Serious Play: The Cultural Formation of the Nineteenth-Century Realist Novel* (Philadelphia: University of Pennsylvania Press, 1999), p. 92, italics in original.

39 Charles Dickens, *Bleak House* (Oxford University Press, 2008), chapter 47, p. 677.

in *Realizations*.[40] Most profoundly, both the novel and melodrama develop bold technologies for switching back and forth between differing registers of representation or points of view, especially when it comes to shifting between internal and external perspectives. In this respect, free indirect discourse might be usefully compared to the operations of the tableau.

Psychoanalysis develops as an outgrowth of the same problems, forms, and insights that structure melodrama. Psychological melodramas in the later nineteenth century – like *The Bells* – dwell explicitly on memory, guilt, and ways the past repeats itself in the present. But in more general terms, some of the critical concepts of psychoanalysis are strikingly melodramatic. As Brooks puts it: 'Psychoanalysis can be read as a systematic realization of the melodramatic aesthetic.' To prove his point, he mentions 'the dynamics of repression and the return of the repressed' and 'the drama of recognition', but he gives even more attention to hysteria, the somatic expression of psychic conflict, 'the maximal conversion of psychic affect into somatic meaning – meaning enacted on the body itself'. Hysterical body language, then, is akin to melodrama's externalized semiotic system and its pressure to move expression beyond language. Because of its desire to be expressive beyond the realm of language, melodrama is 'an aesthetics of hysteria' and psychoanalysis is 'a kind of modern melodrama'.[41] Thus, as Brooks and others see it, melodrama encodes the same problems in representation that psychoanalysis was developed to theorize.

Many nineteenth-century technologies contributed to the development of cinema – periodical printing, panoramas and dioramas, all sorts of optical toys, the magic lantern with its serially dissolving views, other technologies of projection, and especially photography – so the histories of technology and aesthetics must be read in close conjunction with one another. One important point about the technology of film particularly displays its continuity with melodrama. For cinematic form also grows out of the longer history of serial pictorial narration, of which melodrama is the central manifestation. When a sequence of pictures is used to tell a story – from Hogarth's progresses to comic strips – the reader or spectator must imaginatively bridge the space between the pictures, in order to construct an implied narrative continuity. The film strip must be interpreted in this sense, with its sequence of still shots run in front of a light source at a precise speed to create the illusion of movement.

---

40 Meisel, *Realizations*, pp. 29–68.   41 Brooks, *Melodramatic Imagination*, pp. 201–2, xi.

The technology of cinematic moving pictures represents both the apotheosis and the negation of melodrama's dialectic of stillness and movement, pictures and music, silence and sound.[42] Whenever you see a freeze frame in a film or video, the melodramatic tableau hovers in the historical and aesthetic background.

42 Carolyn Williams, 'Moving Pictures: George Eliot and Melodrama', in Lauren Berlant (ed.), *Compassion: The Culture and Politics of an Emotion* (London: Routledge, 2004), pp. 105–44.

Sensation

KATE FLINT

On 13 November 1849, Charles Dickens witnessed the execution of Marie and Frederick Manning at the Horsemonger Road Goal in Southwark, South London. He had rented a flat with a good view for the purpose, he claimed, of observing the responses of the thirty thousand people who had gathered together to watch the occasion – and he described what he saw in a letter to *The Times* later that day:

> I believe that a sight so inconceivably awful as the wickedness and levity of the immense crowd collected at that execution this morning could be imagined by no man, and could be presented in no heathen land under the sun. The horrors of the gibbet and of the crime which brought the wretched murderers to it faded in my mind before the atrocious bearing, looks, and language of the assembled spectators.

He describes the 'screeching, and laughing, and yelling in strong chorus of parodies on negro melodies, with substitutions of "Mrs Manning" for "Susannah", and the like', and the 'fightings, faintings, whistlings, imitations of Punch, brutal jokes, tumultuous demonstrations of indecent delight when swooning women were dragged out of the crowd by the police, with their dresses disordered, [which] gave a new zest to the general entertainment'. He expressed his horror at the fact that

> when the two miserable creatures who attracted all this ghastly sight about them were turned quivering into the air, there was no more emotion, no more pity, no more thought that two immortal souls had gone to judgement, no more restraint in any of the previous obscenities, than if the name of Christ had never been heard in this world . . .[1]

---

[1] Charles Dickens, letter to the Editor of *The Times*, 13 November 1849, in *The Letters of Charles Dickens: The Pilgrim Edition*. 12 vols., 1965–2002, vol. v, 1847–9, ed. Graham Storey and Kenneth Fielding (Oxford University Press, 1981), pp. 644–5.

Dickens used his repulsion at the crowd's remorseless fascination with the hanging of this couple – convicted of murdering a friend for his money, an act followed by burying his body beneath their kitchen flagstones, and then trying to sell his possessions – as a weapon in his campaign against public executions. Both the letter itself, and the case of the Mannings and the publicity that it generated, have, however, a far broader significance because of the ways in which they point to the appeal of the sensational throughout the Victorian period. The sensational may be defined in terms of startling and novel sights that were made available to a mass spectatorship – from Julia Pastrana the Baboon Lady to Blondin the tight-rope walker; from panoramas through ventriloquists and magicians and dancing dogs to the early kinematographs; from exotic animals in zoos to the various appearances of Buffalo Bill's Wild West Show from 1887 onwards. Or the sensational may be understood as referring to the way in which criminal or illicit activity occurs within and disrupts a familiar social context, or the way in which the ordinary is broken into by the horrific or disquieting presence of the supernatural (whether a barely perceptible ghostly presence or the soft, sticky embrace of a monstrous beetle). This latter definition of the sensational – as that which burst disruptively or shockingly into the everyday – is the more common way of interpreting the term in a literary context, but the two definitions are closely linked. For like the sensation fiction that became popular in the early 1860s, and that prompted journalistic anxiety (whether real or feigned) about the effects of reading such material, especially on women, Dickens's account makes one consider the response of the audience as well as the actions of the protagonists in moral terms: what does it mean to be fascinated by, and to consume, the sensational – whether in person, through newspaper accounts, or through novels? The history of literary sensationalism in the Victorian period does not just involve the transgressive actions of fictional protagonists, described through twisting and often complex plots that are calculated to engage, shock, and sometimes sexually titillate the reader: it also demands that we pay attention to readerly responses, and think about the ways in which a reader's actual nerves and senses are played upon (or were believed to be played upon) by the sensational text.

The crime and execution of the Mannings were widely reported in the press. Mrs Manning, in particular, was a figure of fascination who prefigured some of the types that would later be found in sensation fiction: she was, apparently, the prime mover in the murder; she was a foreigner, having been born in Switzerland (Dickens is rumoured to have based both the murderous French maid, Hortense, in *Bleak House* (1852–3) and Madame Lafarge, in *A Tale of Two Cities* (1859) upon her);[2] she was sexually attractive – even when on the scaffold; having worked as a lady's maid to Lady Blantyre, daughter of the Duchess of Sutherland, she was familiar with an aristocratic as well as with a working-class lifestyle, and had come to appreciate luxurious things. But aspects of the case's coverage pointed backwards rather than forwards. The couple were popularized in broadside ballads, illustrated with woodcuts (sometime generic, rather than accurate records) and sold for a penny or a halfpenny – a form of publicity that was to disappear with the advent of cheaper newspapers that, in turn, brought criminal and sexual misconduct into literate homes through the reportage of incidents, police activity, and court cases. Marie and Frederick Manning were also transformed into the subjects of fictionalized memoirs: in one, Marie is on the point of entering a nunnery when she elopes with a bandit chief.[3] This particular fantasy suggests the legacy of Gothic fiction written by such practitioners as Ann Radcliffe and Matthew Lewis, with its romanticizing of European landscape as a dramatic backdrop for improbable drama.

Accounts of actual criminal activity lay behind the Newgate novels of the 1830s and 1840s: a genre that became increasingly controversial not just for its alleged glamorizing of criminal and low life, but for the way in which it often portrayed criminals not as inherently evil, but as the victims of society or of particular circumstances. Such apparent sympathy for wrongdoers was especially condemned by those who thought it all too easy to draw an inappropriate parallel between, say, Dick Turpin in William Harrison Ainsworth's *Rookwood* (1834) and political radicals in Britain or Europe. The genre's name – bestowed on it by critics rather than by the novelists themselves – came from the *Newgate Calendar*, named after the principal London prison, originally published in 1760 as a narrative of notable crimes committed since 1700, then issued in updated form around 1820, with a late flourish – the *New Newgate Calendar* – appearing from 1863 to 1865. Writers like Ainsworth, Edward Bulwer (from 1843, Bulwer Lytton) – author of *Paul Clifford* (1830) and *Eugene Aram* (1832), Thomas Gaspey (*Richmond*, 1827, and *The History of George Godfrey*, 1828), and T. P. Prest, *Newgate: A Romance* (1847) drew their subject matter from the *Calendar's* accounts of the lives,

---

2 See Sally Ledger, *Dickens and the Popular Radical Imagination* (Cambridge University Press, 2007), p. 43.
3 Robert Huish, *The Progress of Crime, or The Authentic Memoirs of Maria Manning* (London: no publisher, 1849).

exploits, and crimes of historical reprobates. As was so often to be the case with subsequent sensation fiction, these 'absolute drugs in the literary market'[4] (Thackeray's name for them – he was to publish a satirical anti-Newgate novel, *Catherine, A Story*, 1839) claimed the moral high ground, maintaining that they taught good conduct through counter-example – but their appeal for many lay in the details of scheming and violence that they contained. Yet Newgate novels also often followed in the more reformist and ethically questioning tradition of William Godwin's fiction, as displayed, say, in his *Caleb Williams* (1794). *Paul Clifford*, for example (a novel that begins with the notoriously parodiable phrase 'It was a dark and stormy night; the rain fell in torrents')[5] asks whether some crimes are less heinous than others. If a man can say that 'From the grinding of the poor, the habitual overreaching, or the systematic pilfering of my neighbours, my conscience is as free as it is from the charge of cruelty and bloodshed',[6] should he receive a less severe punishment than an out and out villain? Was the philologist Eugene Aram, who – as Bulwer has him put it – 'destroyed a man, noxious to the world'[7] in fact deserving of thanks, not punishment, for having killed the apparently noxious swindler who was also having an affair with his wife? (This crime fascinated the poet Thomas Hood, who published a ballad, 'The Dream of Eugene Aram', in 1831.)

Popular fiction has recurrently been accused of two particular things: that it corrupts the minds and morals of those who consume it, and that, reliant upon formulae, it lacks literary merit. Newgate fiction did not escape these charges. Thackeray complained – possibly inventively – of the stage version of *Jack Sheppard* that 'one or two young gentlemen have already confessed how much they were indebted to Jack Sheppard who gave them ideas of pocket-picking and thieving [that] they never would have had but for the play',[8] and *Punch*, in 1841, offered a 'Literary Recipe' for 'A STARTLING ROMANCE': 'Take a small boy, charity, factory, carpenter's apprentice, or otherwise, as occasion may serve – stew him down in vice – garnish largely with oaths and flash songs – Boil him in a cauldron of crime

4 William Makepeace Thackeray, 'Foreign Correspondence', Contributions to the *National Standard* (1833), in *The Complete Works of William Makepeace Thackeray*, 22 vols. (Boston and New York: Houghton, Mifflin and Co., 1889), vol. XXII, p. 8.
5 Edward Bulwer Lytton, *Paul Clifford*, 2 vols. (Boston: Little, Brown, and Company, 1893), vol. I, p. 1.
6 *Ibid.*, vol. II, p. 193.
7 Edward Bulwer Lytton, *Eugene Aram* (Leipzig: Bernhard Tauchnitz, 1842), p. 401.
8 Gordon Norton Ray (ed.), *The Letters and Private Papers of William Makepeace Thackeray*, 4 vols. (Cambridge, MA: Harvard University Press, 1946), vol. I, p. 395.

and improbabilities. Season equally with good and bad qualities ...' The author goes on to enumerate a whole lot of further ingredients that take the form of criminal activities, a mad mother, and bad associates, before offering the finishing touches: 'Serve up with a couple of murders – and season with a hanging-match. N.B. alter the ingredients to a beadle and a workhouse – the scenes may be the same, but the whole flavour of vice will be lost, and the boy will turn out a perfect pattern. – Strongly recommended for weak stomachs.'[9] This last reference is clearly to Dickens's *Oliver Twist* (1837–9), with its plot centring on juvenile crime and on a newly vibrant trade in stolen goods, with Oliver remaining apparently completely unaffected by his time spent among boy pickpockets and by his friendship with Nancy, the prostitute. But I would argue that the novel's most truly sensationalist elements are located not so much within the activities of the underworld community as within its description of London slums, especially the filthy squalor of Jacob's Island, the heavily polluted district of Bermondsey where Sykes meets his death. Social reportage of living and working conditions in London, in the cities of the industrial north, and among agricultural labourers consistently sought – especially from the 1840s onwards – to bring home the need for sanitary reform, for better and less crowded housing, and for safer mills and factories, by incorporating deliberately shocking details into their reports, articles, and published letters. In turn, these accounts of 'nauseous nests of plague and pestilence', as Henry Mayhew described this same district of Bermondsey,[10] or the graphic descriptions of children's mutilated limbs that Henry Morley gives in his 1854 article 'Ground in the Mill', published in Dickens's magazine *Household Words* (and referenced by him in a footnote to the serialized version of *Hard Times*) fed into fiction that foregrounded social issues and the need for extensive improvement. Whether we think of the sordid, insanitary condition of the Davenports' leaky cellar in Elizabeth Gaskell's *Mary Barton* (1849) or the riot scene in her *North and South* (1854), or of another, even more Gothically lit visit to Jacob's Island in Charles Kingsley's *Alton Locke* (1854), or the decaying tenements of Tom-all-Alone's in Dickens's *Bleak House*, which contain 'a crowd of foul existence that crawls in and out of gaps in walls and boards; and coils itself to sleep, in maggot numbers',[11] where Dickens's repellent cross-species

---

9 'Literary Recipes', *Punch*, 7 August 1841, p. 39.
10 [Henry Mayhew], 'A Visit to the Cholera Districts of Bermondsey', *Morning Chronicle*, 24 September 1849, p. 4.
11 Charles Dickens, *Bleak House* (Oxford University Press, 2008), chapter 16, p. 236.

metaphors ratchet up the sense of revulsion, these descriptions are without any doubt intended to shock the reader.

These novels of social protest are set firmly in the present day – or, at the very least, in very recent times. Charles Reade was ultimately best known for his historical novel *The Cloister and the Hearth* (1861),[12] but he came to believe that there was little demand for fiction set in the past:

> I write for the public, and the public don't care about the dead. They are much more interested in the living, and in the great tragic-comedy of humanity that is around and about them and environs them in every street, at every crossing, in every hole and corner. An aristocratic divorce suit, the last great social scandal, a sensational suicide from Waterloo Bridge, a woman murdered in Seven Dials, or a baby found strangled in a bonnet-box at Piccadilly Circus, interests them much more than Margaret's piety or Gerard's journey to Rome.[13]

Reade saw himself primarily as a dramatist, and began his career writing for the stage, but it was as a novelist that he made his name. His fiction – heavily dependent on material drawn from his copious collection of newspaper clippings, as well as on his practised manipulation of the melodramatic twist – tended to focus on particular issues and abuses: prison discipline and the treatment of criminals in *It's Never Too Late to Mend* (1856), private lunatic asylums in *Hard Cash* (1863), and trade unions in *Put Yourself in His Place* (1870). As these dates, and topics, suggest, there is a considerable similarity here (in theme – Reade's style is far more leaden) with Dickens's habit, in his later fiction, of composing his fiction around particular issues: the convoluted legal system in *Bleak House*; debt and investment in *Little Dorrit* (1855–7); waste and dust heaps in *Our Mutual Friend* (1864–5). The later novels by Dickens contain, too, plot elements that recur as staples of sensation fiction: illegitimate birth, concealed and changed identities, women of questionable sanity, fraud, spectacular rises and falls in personal fortune, drug use, incarceration, suicides, and corpses.

Whether atrocious social conditions are described through starkly descriptive prose or startling metaphors, these techniques are engaged in order to

---

12 Although set in the fifteenth century and purporting to tell the story of Erasmus's parents, *The Cloister and the Hearth*, nonetheless, contains many elements that would have been at home in more present-day fiction – such as sibling jealousy, a lying letter, and sublimated sexual desire.

13 Charles Reade, quoted in John Coleman, *Charles Reade As I Knew Him.* (London: Treherne & Co., 1903), p. 263. Margaret and Gerard are the central characters of *The Cloister and the Hearth*.

shock the reader into compassionate awareness, and beyond that – perhaps – into action. They display the overlap that existed between realism and sensationalism in the mid-century – something that is manifested through the direction that much sensational fiction was to take. Rather than drawing on historical sources, its authors – and not just those who wanted to prod their readers into reformist or charitable activity – as well as the critics stressed the contemporaneity of the work – containing what Henry James, considering Wilkie Collins's fiction, called 'those most mysterious of mysteries, the mysteries which are at our own doors'.[14] Despite the murders and the deceptions and the acts of arson, these novels, which became enormously popular in the early 1860s, are filled with the mundane – with the minutiae of railway timetables, the sending of telegrams, the evening promenades at seaside resorts, the details of a room's furnishings, the boredom of a woman's life with a work-preoccupied husband. George Levine has drawn our attention to how 'underneath the surface of every realist novel there is a "monster" waiting to get out'; arguing that under 'the valued domesticity there are desires and energies restrained by the conventions of Victorian realism and by the developing conventions of Victorian society'.[15] Sensation fiction makes explicit, in other words, the desires and violent drives that are more or less kept in check by realist fiction, but that nonetheless are present, simmering under the surface. Both forms of writing, after all, frequently share themes of deep tensions and power struggles between the rising middle classes and members of the old aristocracy, which reverberate around questions of class mobility, personal identity, the development of professional skills, and the importance of money.

So what – to borrow the title of Patrick Brantlinger's highly influential 1982 essay – was 'sensational' about the so-called sensation novel?[16] How might the novels that were discussed under this heading be distinguished from other fictions that pivot on similar dramatic plot components? Murder, pursuit, shipboard mutiny, and falsely claiming a love rival to have perished are, after all, to be found in Elizabeth Gaskell's writing; George Eliot introduces disinheritance, binding wills, a lurking former mistress, and a slightly suspicious yacht drowning to her later fiction.

14 [Henry James], 'Miss Braddon', *Nation* 9 (November 1865), p. 593.
15 George Levine, *How to Read the Victorian Novel* (Malden, MA, and Oxford: Blackwell Publishing, 2008), p. 102.
16 Patrick Brantlinger, 'What is "Sensational" about the "Sensation Novel"?' *Nineteenth-Century Fiction* 37:1 (1982), pp. 1–28.

To some extent, the sensationalism of sensation fiction was produced by the fact that the novels designated by this label – works by Wilkie Collins, Mary Braddon, Mrs Henry (Ellen) Wood, and Sheridan Le Fanu, above all – were seen as a scandalous eruption, and were themselves turned into a newsworthy, moral-panic-inducing phenomenon.[17] Their newsworthiness was heightened by their symbiotic relationship to actual news – to the growth of 'sensational' journalism in general (something enabled by the expansion of the press after the repeal of the stamp tax in 1855, and paper duty in 1860), and, in particular, to the attention paid to divorce cases (especially following the passing of the Matrimonial Causes Act in 1857, which gave women limited access to divorce) and bigamy trials – notably the Yelverton bigamy-divorce trial of 1861.[18] A number of novels, including Mary Braddon's *Lady Audley's Secret* (1862), *Aurora Floyd* (1863), and *John Marchmont's Legacy* (1863), Wilkie Collins's *Man and Wife* (1870, which exploits anomalies between Scottish and English marriage laws), J. R. O'Flanagan's *Gentle Blood, Or the Secret Marriage* (1861, which drew heavily on the trial papers), and Mrs Henry Wood's *East Lynne* (1861) all contain bigamous marriages.

More newspaper columns meant more space for detailed accounts of trials, and concomitant accusations and counter-accusations, which in turn led to the building up of cumulative narratives structured around competing versions of truth and falsehood. Like the sensation novels, many of these accounts dwelt on the body of the overly or inappropriately sexualized woman, at the centre of some form of scandal. 'The scandal plot is so persistent', writes William Cohen,

> because it provides a way of working out the novel's own double duty: the duty of telling stories composed centrally of incidents from private life and, simultaneously, of using these stories to teach widely applicable public lessons. Scandal motivates a type of moral pedagogy in the novel, genera-ting exemplary narratives that both school readers in acceptable behavior and enable them to experience vicariously the violation of norms. Novels

---

17 The argument that the concept of 'sensation fiction' was to some extent a media-created phenomenon is advanced by Ronald Thomas, 'The Sensation Novel', in John Richetti (ed.), *The Columbia History of the British Novel* (New York: Columbia University Press, 1994), pp. 479–507. In *The Making of the Victorian Novelist: Anxieties of Authorship in the Mass Market* (London: Routledge, 2003), pp. 59–90, Bradley Deane argues that the 'sensation novel' is entirely the product of a critical discourse seeking to police class boundaries.

18 See Jeanne Fahnestock, 'Bigamy: The Rise and Fall of a Convention', *Nineteenth-Century Fiction* 36:1 (1981), pp. 47–71.

toe the orthodox line in castigating sexual transgression by the same means that they occasion its pleasurable consumption.[19]

that is, by incorporating the dynamics of sexual desire into the plot structure. On occasion, the narrator will also step aside from recounting events and conversations and will make a portentous comment in their own voice – as when Wood has the narrator interrupt the plot line of *East Lynne*, just after Lady Isabel Vane (wrongly believing her husband to be unfaithful) runs off with the rakish Sir Francis Levinson, and demand, in anguished tones: 'Lady – wife – mother! should you ever be tempted to abandon your home, so will you awake! Whatever trials may be the lot of your married life, though they may magnify themselves to your crushed spirit as beyond the endurance of woman to bear, *resolve* to bear them ...'[20] A number of late twentieth-century critics have suggested – most influentially Elaine Showalter in *A Literature of Their Own* (1978) – that such pious moralism is in effect little more than window-dressing, offering a respectable cover to the pleasures that were to be had in reading of transgressive women. Sensation novels do, indeed, frequently offer women readers the possibility of identifying with these women's audacity in privileging their own emotional, and (as in Braddon's *Lady Audley's Secret*) material imperatives above all others, allowing for a vicarious repudiation of the conventional Victorian expectation that a woman exhibit selfless abnegation in the face of the demands of husband and/or family. Yet at the same time such women's self-seeking actions are not rewarded by the plot, and thus the reader's moral certainties are rarely rocked to the degree that the genre's detractors would have one believe – unless, that is, one were to consider it wrong for women to be reading about such issues in the first place. Certain critics claimed to detect the potential for damage not just because of the access to dangerous feelings that this fiction provides, but because the pace and eventfulness of the plot might render women dissatisfied with the 'dull, neutral tinted universe' of their own lives (the phrase is Mary Braddon's, describing, however, not the life of a bored woman, but that of Robert Audley before he finds real purpose in his life in tracking down what happened to his close friend George Talboys, the first husband of Lady Audley, whom she had dispatched for dead down a convenient well).[21]

19 William A. Cohen, *Sex Scandal: The Private Parts of Victorian Fiction* (Durham, NC: Duke University Press, 1996), p. 19.

20 Mrs Henry Wood, *East Lynne* (Oxford University Press, 2008), chapter 25, p. 283.

21 Mary Elizabeth Braddon, *Lady Audley's Secret* (Oxford University Press, 1987), vol. III, chapter 9, p. 441.

This association of the sensation novel with sexuality led to some works of fiction being grouped under the generic umbrella of 'sensation fiction' solely on the grounds of somewhat risqué activity on the part of their independently minded female protagonists – for example, early novels by Rhoda Broughton, such as *Not Wisely, But Too Well* (1867), *Cometh Up as a Flower* (1867), and *Goodbye Sweetheart!* (1872), in which the heroines have a tendency to find themselves alone, in potentially highly compromising situations, with often highly unsuitable young men, yet appear decidedly unfazed by their predicament. But although Broughton's fiction frequently relies on suspense, it lacks some of the further elements that distinguish sensation fiction proper from this new, racy type of romantic fiction that employs either the direct power of a breathless first-person narrator, or a third-person narration that assumes a chummily close relationship with the female reader (although Broughton certainly had her male fans as well). Novels by Wilkie Collins, Braddon, Wood, and others present sexualized women as disruptive forces, to be sure, but as in *Lady Audley's Secret*, or Collins's *Armadale* (1866), men are far more often shown as victims of physical desire than are those women who deploy their attractiveness for status, power, and wealth, laying bare male vulnerability. Woman's strength can demonstrate itself in less stereotypically seductive ways, however. In Collins's *The Woman in White* (1859–60), for example, the decidedly mannish Marion joins forces with Walter Hartwright, the artist-hero, to unmask the fraud that has been perpetrated in an attempt to defraud her half-sister Laura of both identity and inheritance.

The unmasking of secrets is one of the hallmarks of sensation fiction. Process rather than theme, it offers the reminder that the genre is characterized by more abstract features than the circumstantial components of murder, arson, bigamy, stolen identity, gambling, and suspect wills. Sensation fiction makes one consider the dynamics of exclusion and inclusion; of what constitutes knowledge, how it is obtained, and what might make it reliable or suspect. It is concerned with relativity of point of view (Collins, notably, in both *The Woman in White* and *The Moonstone* (1868) experiments with narratives told in different modes – letters, journal entries, court depositions – a technique that Bram Stoker would later adopt, in 1897, when writing *Dracula*). As Levine, again, has pointed out, the genre raises important questions of causation and agency: how much emphasis should be placed on human motivation (whether propelled by greed, or a desire for justice), and how much weight, in the workings through of what are often convoluted plots, should be given to the providential hand restoring order, or, for that matter, to the effects of chance and coincidence. It is no surprise, given these more formal aspects, that Thomas Hardy should have been drawn to the apparatus of the sensation genre for some of his earliest novels (such as *Desperate Remedies* (1871), and *A Pair of Blue Eyes* (1873)), and that its traces remain throughout his fictional career. Sensation fiction foregrounds, too, issues of identity in ways that reach far beyond impersonation and forgery. Jonathan Loesberg maintains that the genre tends to approach problems of identity 'in its legal and class aspects rather than in its psychological aspect',[22] but in fact, its frequent recourse to tropes of madness and hysteria and dreams (notably in *Armadale*) and to characters who are prey to alcoholism and drug abuse (most famously in *The Moonstone*) displays a concern with unstable borders, both of class (a common complaint against sensation fiction was that it made 'the literature of the kitchen the favourite reading of the Drawing-room'),[23] and of body and mind. If sensation fiction tends, as a genre, not to be especially concerned with subtleties of character, it still invites being analysed in the context of the developing concerns with what George Henry Lewes termed *The Physical Basis of Mind* (1877).

For women readers, in particular, were thought of as being susceptible – both to supposedly forbidden knowledge (of, for example, female protagonists who, as Margaret Oliphant sensationally put it, 'marry their grooms in fits of sensual passion; women who pray their lovers to carry them off from husbands and homes they hate; women, at the very least of it, who give and receive burning kisses and frantic embraces, and live in a voluptuous dream')[24] and because of their physiological make-up, which supposedly rendered them more vulnerable to the effects of reading than men. Lewes wrote in 1865 of how in certain 'feminine natures' there is an unusual direct connection between the brain and heart along the pneumo-gastric nerves that allows for the rapid transmission of shock and surprise;[25] Henry Maudsley's medical writings in the 1870s, whilst primarily directed towards defending different types of education for women and men, reinforced the idea that woman's innate tendency towards sympathy and identification, designed to make her bond readily with her children, could have dangerous

---

22 Jonathan Loesberg, 'The Ideology of Narrative Form in Sensation Fiction', *Representations* 13 (Winter 1986), p. 117.
23 [W. Fraser Rae], 'Sensation Novelists: Miss Braddon', *North British Review* 43 (1865), 204.
24 [Margaret Oliphant] 'Novels', *Blackwood's Edinburgh Magazine* 102 (1867), p. 259.
25 Editor [G. H. Lewes], 'The Heart and the Brain', *Fortnightly Review* 1 (1865), pp. 66–74. For medical, physiological, and psychoanalytic theories about Victorian women's modes of reading, see Kate Flint, *The Woman Reader 1837–1914* (Oxford University Press, 1993), pp. 53–70.

consequences when extended towards (over)identification with fictional heroines. This form of misreading was metafictionally addressed by Braddon herself in *The Doctor's Wife* (1863) which, in addition to focusing on an English Madame Bovary, led astray in her desires by the influence of novels, includes a sympathetic portrayal of the (male) hack writer of sensation fiction. More recently, D. A. Miller, in a 1986 piece, argued that reading sensation fiction encourages, still, a 'hysterical' form of consumption, in which our rational faculties play second fiddle to our susceptibility to the affect created by excitement and suspense.[26] This is little more than a reworking of H. L. Mansel's 1863 jibe that this genre is distinguished by 'preaching to the nerves instead of the judgment'.[27]

But thinking about the ways in which the sensation novel was believed to play upon the nervous system, thereby inducing physical responses in the reader – a quickened heartbeat, a more rapid circulation of the blood – is a means of alerting oneself to the role of the senses in reading generally – not just the way in which the reader's attention and absorption are played upon, but the degree to which sound, smell, and sight are all deployed, heightening one's awareness of what Lewes called the 'vast and powerful stream of sensation'.[28] In *Common Scents*, Janice Carlisle places her analysis of the role of smell in fiction of the 1860s (especially, but not exclusively, important both as an evoker of memory, and as a determinant of class and social taste) within contemporary theorization of 'a remarkably direct and simple connection between sensory experience and mental life'.[29] John Picker, in *Victorian Soundscapes*, writes of the Victorian period as an age alive with sound: 'alive with the screech and roar of the railway and the clang of industry, with the babble, bustle, and music of city streets, and with the crackle and squawk of acoustic vibrations on wires and wax'.[30] With these last mentions of new technologies of transmitting and recording sound, he also points towards the ways in which mysterious noises – strange tappings, and banging doors, and whooshing gusts of air, and vibrations that indicate something that the human ear cannot quite pick up – form a

---

26 D. A. Miller, 'Cage aux folles: Sensation and Gender in Wilkie Collins's *The Woman in White*', in Jeremy Hawthorn (ed.), *The Nineteenth-Century British Novel* (London: Edward Arnold, 1986), pp. 94–124.

27 H. L. Mansel, 'Sensation Novels', *Quarterly Review* 113 (1863), p. 482.

28 G. H. Lewes, *The Physiology of Common Life*, 2 vols. (New York: D. Appleton and Company, 1875), vol. II, p. 64.

29 Janice Carlisle, *Common Scents. Comparative Encounters in High-Victorian Fiction* (New York: Oxford University Press, 2004), p. 7.

30 John M. Picker, *Victorian Soundscapes* (New York: Oxford University Press, 2003), p. 4.

frequent part of the apparatus of ghost stories. Modern life, too, transformed the field of sight: to quote Jonathan Crary, whose theoretical work on vision, modernity, and spectatorship has been particularly influential, 'vision in the nineteenth century was inseparable from transience – that is, from the new temporalities, speeds, experiences of flux and obsolescence, a new density and sedimentation of the structure of visual memory'.[31]

Sensationalism, in other words, was indivisible from a wider interest in the workings of the human sensorum, in the collisions of this sensorium with rapid changes in both technology and social practices, and – as sensation fiction, especially in its serialized, magazine form, proliferated – from consumer demand for fictional novelty. This, in turn, made the sensation novel self-consciously aware of its own inbuilt obsolescence.[32] The search for the new sensation became a mark of the modern throughout the remainder of the century: it is fitting that Sue Brideshead, in Hardy's *Jude the Obscure* (1895), perversely visiting the church in which she is about to marry Phillotson with her cousin and soulmate Jude, should exclaim against her folly at taking him on such an upsetting excursion: ' "My curiosity to hunt up a new sensation always leads me into these scrapes. Forgive me!" '[33] To this end, the parameters of sensation fiction themselves shifted. In 1862, Margaret Oliphant remarked, approvingly, of Wilkie Collins as a writer 'who boldly takes in hand the common mechanism of daily life'; who creates characters who might very well be living in the society with which we are familiar, and by these means 'has accomplished a far greater success than he who effects the same results through supernatural agencies, or by means of the fantastic creations of lawless genius or violent horrors of crime'.[34] Yet the remainder of the Victorian period witnessed a resurgence in popularity of the ghost story, the development of detective fiction (full of all kinds of criminal activity), and the proliferation of all kinds of fantastic figures, from vampires to ageless white African queens. Although the ordinariness of settings remains a recurrent feature, the geographical

---

31 Jonathan Crary, *Techniques of the Observer. On Vision and Modernity in the 19th Century* (Cambridge, MA; MIT Press, 1990), pp. 20–1.

32 See Eva Badowska, 'On the Track of Things: Sensation and Modernity in Mary Elizabeth Braddon's *Lady Audley's Secret*', *Victorian Literature and Culture* 37 (2009), pp. 157–75. For serialization and the sensation novel, situating these works alongside the articles, illustrations, and advertisements to be found in periodicals, see Deborah Wynne, *The Sensation Novel and the Victorian Family Magazine* (Basingstoke: Palgrave, 2001).

33 Thomas Hardy, *Jude the Obscure* (London: Penguin, 1998), p. 173.

34 [Margaret Oliphant], 'Sensation Novels', *Blackwood's Edinburgh Magazine* 91 (1862), p. 566.

locations of sensational fiction broaden out, especially to the expanding territories of the British empire. New forms of tension are thus created between supernatural circumstances that, as in some of Kipling's short stories ('The Mark of the Beast,' 'At the End of the Passage') or B. M. Croker's 'The Dâk Bungalow at Dakor' (1893) seem to have been activated by contact with other cultures, and yet are witnessed by very matter of fact English women and men. Even in a story as preposterous as Rider Haggard's *She* (1886–7), the Cambridge don who travels to Africa and encounters the two-thousand-year-old Ayesha who has rendered herself immortal whilst she awaits the coming of her reincarnated lover through immersing herself in a pillar of eternal fire, keeps himself (and the reader) grounded through recurrent, faintly comedic references to potted tongue and the London Underground.

The long oral history of the ghost tale is strongly present in many Victorian ghost fictions, told to – as one of Le Fanu's narrators puts it – 'a circle of intelligent and eager faces, lighted up by a good after-dinner fire on a winter's evening, with a cold wind rising and wailing outside, and all snug and cosy within'.[35] In other words, it opens in a comfortable domestic sanctum, a microcosm of the apparently stable and unremarkable world that is about to be disrupted. This tradition lasts through the century, to the framing settings of Robert Louis Stevenson's 'The Body-Snatcher' (1884) and Henry James's 'The Turn of the Screw' (1898) – the last of these straddling, with irresoluble ambiguity, the uncertain borderline between supernatural revenants and psychological disturbance that characterized a very large number of these fictions. The Ghosts of Christmas Past, Present, and Future in Dickens's *A Christmas Carol* (1843) that Scrooge dreams up are so close to being palpable that they seem creatures of allegory rather than destabilizing hallucinations. But many other apparitions refuse to be pinned down through any logic. Cathy's ghost, in Emily Brontë's *Wuthering Heights* (1847), is produced somewhere in the haunted hinterland between Lockwood's dreaming, the projection of Heathcliff's desperate desire, and the folk repertoire of rural Yorkshire. Dickens's signal-man – the subject of his 1866 short story of the same name – is deeply unsettled by an apparition that has twice foretold death on his stretch of railway tracks, and that seems to be linked (even to the extent of somehow causing the signal-man's own death) to the narrator's gestures and language – but how? The ghosts that James's governess sees may or may not be products

---

35 [Sheridan Le Fanu], 'An Account of Some Strange Disturbances in an Old House in Aungier-Street', *Dublin University Magazine* 42 (1853), p. 721.

of her repressed sexuality, her loneliness, her fantasizing about her employer, or the endurance, somehow, of their troubled and possibly malevolent presences.

Like so many Victorian ghosts, these disquieting apparitions – and other manifestations that are not even visible, but exist, as Picker pointed out, as sudden blasts of cold air, or the low wail of a baby, or in the there-but-not-there-ness of a shadow without originary substance – are essentially textual products. They emanate not from detailed delineation, but from a refusal to describe fully or to explain. Their mystery, their capacity to unsettle, comes from the workings of the reader's imagination on textual gaps and silences. If, critically – and 'The Turn of the Screw,' in particular, has stimulated a large number of readings anxious to tease out James's figure in the carpet in this tale – there has often been a drive to explain away the mystery through recourse to Victorian, Freudian, or post-Freudian psychoanalytic theory (whether projection and desire is located in protagonists or in readers), or to an unearthing of source material, such readings often seem determined to flatten out, to explain away the enjoyable thrill of being unsettled upon which ghost stories rely. More useful, and ultimately more influential, has been the account that Freud gave in his paper on 'The Uncanny' (1919) of the quasi-pleasurable fear that results from the mingling of the imaginary with the real, the 'familiar and the unfamiliar' in settings that are *unheimlich* – literally, 'unhomely,' the German word customarily translated as 'uncanny'.

The temporary pleasures of destabilization are hard to sustain over a long fiction (Romantic Gothic fiction often relied upon a near-picaresque narrative form, setting its ghostly episodes within recurrent, but diverse peaks of suspense). It is no surprise, therefore, that many Victorian ghost story writers experimented with the short story, and the genre expanded as a result of the growing number of magazines that printed such fiction, such as *Belgravia*, *Temple Bar*, *Argosy*, and the *Cornhill*. Many of these writers were women (and there is a distinct overlap with some of the best-known sensation novelists): Amelia Edwards, Louisa Baldwin, Mary Elizabeth Braddon, Catherine Crowe, Rhoda Broughton, Lettice Galbraith, Elizabeth Gaskell, Vernon Lee, Rosa Mulholland, Edith Nesbit, Margaret Oliphant (notwithstanding her comments about the advantages of Collins eschewing the apparatus of the supernatural), and Charlotte Riddell. Very many of their stories – like sensation fiction – rely on the powers, whatever they are, that inhabit and disrupt the domestic setting – sometimes exposing, as Eve Lynch has put it, 'the secrets of the guilty house', often bringing to light 'a hidden social dilemma that "airs" itself in the public arena of its readership'.[36] Similarly, too, they have frequent recourse to the experiences of semi-outsiders to these locations: servants, governesses, guests. Yet even within the short story, a good deal of the impact depends on the pacing of the narrative, the establishment of the quotidian, and then the slow realization that things are not as they seem, that rumours of ghosts (a not infrequent starting point for a sceptical first-person narrator) may not be things to laugh off, that there is something ill defined and (almost invariably) malevolent around. This produces the realization for the reader that – apart from establishing, if effective, an aura of apprehension building up to terror – the narrative is simply not going to follow any predictable path. As M. R. James, who started publishing ghost stories in the 1890s, was to write:

> Two ingredients most valuable in the concocting of a ghost story are, to me, the atmosphere and the nicely managed crescendo ... Let us, then, be introduced to the actors in a placid way; let us see them going about their ordinary business, undisturbed by forebodings, pleased with their surroundings; and into this calm environment let the ominous thing put out its head, unobtrusively at first, and then more insistently, until it holds the stage.[37]

Unlike earlier Gothic fiction, and unlike the sensation fiction of the mid-century, Victorian ghost stories carry no guarantee that normalcy will be re-established in the fictional world through their conclusion: they often shock through the unresolved suddenness of their endings.

Victorian Gothic also holds out the promise of terrorizing the reader about his or her immediate world, offering, as Roger Luckhurst puts it, 'a continuum from the subtle terrors of the *psychological* Gothic to the body horrors of the *physiological* Gothic'.[38] At the psychological end of the scale, there is considerable overlap with the literature of hallucination, scary narratives offering a framework, a coherent code for, in Robert Miles's words, 'the representation of fragmented subjectivity'.[39] Miles is referring to the earlier part of the century: this representation becomes even more clearcut when informed by later developments in the study of the relationship

---

36 Eve M. Lynch, 'Spectral Politics: the Victorian Ghost Story and the Domestic Servant,' in Nicola Bown, Carolyn Burdett, and Pamela Thurschwell (eds.), *The Victorian Supernatural* (Cambridge University Press, 2004), pp. 67–86.

37 M. R. James, introduction to Vere H. Collins (ed.), *Ghosts and Marvel: A Selection of Uncanny Tales from Daniel Defoe to Algernon Blackwood* (Oxford University Press, 1924), p. vi.

38 Roger Luckhurst, introduction to *Late Victorian Gothic Tales* (Oxford University Press, 2005), p. xii.

39 Robert Miles, *Gothic Writing 1750–1820: A Genealogy* (London: Routledge, 1993), p. 2.

(or disconnect) between the conscious, rational self, and the working of the unconscious. This can be seen most clearly in Robert Louis Stevenson's *Dr Jekyll and Mr Hyde* (1886), which plays on the idea that someone may simultaneously possess a controlled, respectable side and an animalistic one driven by desires that are commonly repressed – and furthermore that this terrifying, unofficial self may eventually prove the stronger. This urban Gothic story predated the Jack the Ripper murders that took place in Whitechapel and surrounding areas of London in late 1888 (and possibly into 1891) and the sensationalist newspaper reporting that accompanied them, but taken together, they helped to consolidate a new sense of the capital as a site of unspeakable, unthinkable crime that might be prompted by no more definite purpose than a bestial desire to maim, assault, and kill. Oscar Wilde develops the theme more subtly in *The Picture of Dorian Gray* (1891), through deploying the device of a painted portrait that shows Dorian's physical decay even as the exquisitely beautiful young man appears, in real life, physically unaltered despite a career of dissipation, emotional callousness, and murder.[40] Wilde asks, through this, questions about whether or not it is possible to remain untainted by one's actions; what the ethical implications might be if one assumed that one *could* get away with what one liked; and – an issue with broad aesthetic as well as psychological implications – what the relationship may be between what the observer may see, and what might be going on beneath a surface.

When Jekyll/Hyde is lying in bed and looks down at his hands, he sees in horror that they are covered in dark fur. This physical manifestation of the bestial is important, since late nineteenth-century Gothic was undoubtedly informed by fears of human devolution, the imagined possible reversal of the evolutionary process that, some feared, would result in a human descent into the primitive. Cultural indications of such degeneration were spelled out by Max Nordau in *Degeneration* (translated into English in 1895, and symptomatic of the fact that this was a European, and not just a national fear) – the spottiness and indistinctness of Impressionism, and what he saw as the exaggerated hysteria of Symbolist art. Mapped on to imaginary

---

40 By the early nineties, the magic picture was a familiar trope in the domestic Gothic, and one that both overtly and by association was linked, too, to the contemporary practices of photography, and the alchemy of darkroom development of images. See Kerry Powell, 'Tom, Dick and Dorian Gray: Magic-Picture Mania in Late Victorian Fiction', *Philological Quarterly* 62 (1982), pp. 147–70, and Mary Warner Marien, *Photography and its Critics. A Cultural History, 1839–1900* (Cambridge University Press, 1997), pp. 13, 50–53.

bodies, these anxieties take the form of the beast-like, light-fearing, and violent Morlocks of H. G. Wells's *The Time Machine* (1895), and the Beast Folk of *The Island of Dr Moreau* (1896), products of dispassionate and sinister experimentation on animals who, through vivisection and re-piecing, are being manipulated so as to take on undesirable human characteristics – and then are found to revert into the worst aspects of animality. As with many other subjects of the Victorian Gothic, including mummies and werewolves, all kinds of borderlines are being challenged, referencing contemporary scientific theories and archaeological investigations in their disruption of certainties concerning individual and species identity. Questions are posed about whether it is possible to inhabit the present and the past simultaneously (or to engage in time-travel), and about the problems that can be involved – as is also the case with ghosts – when it comes to determining what is living, and what is dead.

No creature straddles this borderline more effectively than the vampire. By the time Bram Stoker published *Dracula* in 1897, a number of blood-sucking predators in enticing human form had appeared in nineteenth-century fiction, including *The Vampyre*, authored by Byron's physician, John Polidori (1819); James Malcolm Rymer's *Varney the Vampire*, which appeared in serialized, penny-dreadful form between 1845 and 1847 and then as an 868-page double columned novel; and Sheridan LeFanu's lesbian *Carmilla* (1872). Rymer's work established various elements that would subsequently be developed in vampire fiction, from the physical detail (Varney's long, pointy teeth), to his hypnotic powers, to the tradition of the internally tortured, sympathetic vampire figure who is the more frightening and alluring because of the claims that he makes on the reader's understanding and compassion. LeFanu's tale brings out – as does Stoker's – the erotic appeal in such a character: Laura, the narrator is simultaneously attracted and appalled by her friend's attentions: 'It was like the ardour of a lover; it embarrassed me; it was hateful and yet overpowering; and with gloating eyes she drew me to her, and her hot lips traveled along my cheek in kisses; and she would whisper, almost in sobs, "You are mine, you *shall* be mine, and you and I are one for ever."'[41] Stoker's Count Dracula, although seemingly heterosexual (even if he does grab at the throat of his prisoner, Jonathan Harker, after he cuts himself shaving) exercises, likewise, an erotic power over his victims. What is also notable about this

---

41 J. Sheridan LeFanu, 'Carmilla', in *In a Glass Darkly* (London: Richard Bentley, 1886), p. 391.

novel – written, like several of Collins's sensation fictions, as a piecemeal collection of evidentiary texts (in this case, journal entries, letters, log records, newspaper reports, and transcriptions of phonograph recordings) – is the emphasis on the imbrication of the traditional (Transylvanian count, peasant superstitions, mutation into werewolf, sea fog, or hordes of rats) and the modern. *Dracula* pivots not just on recording technology that preserves the human voice on wax cylinders, but on the use of typewriters and on discussions concerning the role of women; it references the recently invented and highly portable Kodak camera; and if the vampire himself transcends – like Ayesha – the normal temporal limits of mortality, the plot is fuelled by the urgency of telegrams, and the careful reading of railway timetables. This mixture of the mythic and the contemporary, too, has made Stoker's novel extremely attractive to a range of critical interpretations that have brought out some of the underlying social fears that can be detected within the novel: not just fears about women's sexual desires (or, for that matter, about men's desire to dominate them) but about racial invasion (especially in relation to Jewish immigration), imperial decline, the attractions of an expanding United States, and other issues of identity, both individual and national, that are readily referenced through the emotive trope of blood.

The melodramatic plot of *Dracula* culminates in a pursuit that is not just a race against the clock, but leads towards a showdown between good and evil. The fact that Dracula has penetrated Harker's wife Mina with his teeth, and sucked at her breast like a kitten lapping at a bowl of milk (Stoker's use of the appealingly domestic in both setting and simile adds to the novel's horror), means that the intermingling of their fluids ensures that the Manichaean struggle takes place on a psychic site as well as in the recognizable geographical terrain of London, Whitby, and the Carpathians. It is, ultimately, a struggle conceived of in metaphysical terms, unlike the forms of villainy, tracking, and unmasking that lie at the centre of much detective fiction. The tradition of detection within British fiction may be traced back to the American influence of Edgar Allan Poe, whose three short stories, 'The Murders in the Rue Morgue', (1841), 'The Mystery of Marie Roget' (1842), and 'The Purloined Letter' (1845), helped establish the type of the eccentric, brilliant, charismatic detective characterized by an ability to think laterally, and to attend to the importance of the overlooked detail.

British fictional detectives developed alongside the institutions that supported their real-life counterparts: Sir Robert Peel's Metropolitan Police Act of 1829 paved the way for the setting up, in 1842, of a special Criminal Investigation Department dedicated to detective work. The distinction between the real and fictitious was not always clear. Supposed memoirs (like William Russell's *Recollections of a Detective Police Officer*, 1856) were often works of fiction. Dickens, fascinated by detective work in London, published a number of articles in *Household Words* on the topic, including 'On Duty with Inspector Field', a man widely taken to be the model for Inspector Field in *Bleak House*, and probably for Inspector John Cutting, in R. D. Blackmore's *Clara Vaughan* (1864), in which a young girl tries to find out the truth about her father's killer. Sergeant Cuff, in Wilkie Collins's *The Moonstone*, may well have been based on Jack Whicher, in charge of the investigations into the notorious, and much debated, Road Hill House murders of 1860[42] ('the perfect detective', T. S. Eliot called Cuff, although others have pointed out that his subordination to his employers reinforces not just his class position, but the fact that he is not an independent restorer of law and order).[43] The involvement of Dickens and Collins in the growth of the detective character and plot reinforces the closeness of detective fiction to sensation novels, as does that of LeFanu, who, with 'The Murdered Cousin' (1851), and *A Lost Name* (1868 – expanded from an earlier short story), helped to inaugurate the sub-genre of the locked room mystery. The choice of the country house as location – that microcosmic unit that could be put under fictional threat by the presence, or suspected presence of an outsider, whether opium addict or Indian juggler or snake – was as useful a plot device in detective stories as it was in sensation novels or ghost tales.

Yet detective fiction came to exploit the potential offered by large cities, particularly London, for combining crime (whether practised by gang or individual) with anonymity and potential for disguise and disappearance, as well as for various forms of exchange of portable property. The urban setting of Fergus Hume's best-selling *The Mystery of a Hansom Cab* (1886 – British publication 1887) was not London, but Melbourne. 1887 was the year, however, that saw the publication of the first of Arthur Conan Doyle's Sherlock Holmes narratives, *A Study in Scarlet* in *Beeton's Christmas Annual*, followed by *The Sign of Four*, which appeared in *Lippincott's Monthly Magazine* in 1890. In the first of these, Holmes addresses his constant sidekick (a character role borrowed from Poe) and veteran of the Afghan wars (a foretelling, from the start, of the degree to which the activities of empire

---

42 See Kate Summerscale, *The Suspicions of Mr Whicher* (New York: Walker and Company, 2008), pp. 267–9.
43 [T. S. Eliot], 'Wilkie Collins and Dickens', *Times Literary Supplement*, 4 August 1927, pp. 525–6.

will figure in these tales) John H. Watson, M.D. He explains how his method relies on both 'observation' – of telling details that could readily be overlooked – and 'inference', often arriving at conclusions by the elimination of all other alternatives – with both being dependent upon 'knowledge'.[44] Conan Doyle, a physician, claimed that his protagonist was inspired by the surgeon Dr Joseph Bell, for whom he had worked at the Edinburgh Royal Infirmary. Though precise in his methods, Holmes is bohemian in lifestyle (frequently using cocaine, constantly taking stimulus from shag tobacco, and living, a bachelor, in a chaos of domestic clutter): he represents the replacement, in fiction, of the police detective with the professional amateur. This combination of objective method with personal individuality, coupled with the solid middle-class settings which the narratives shared with their readership, helped to fuel the popularity of the Sherlock Holmes stories, which started to appear in the newly launched *Strand* magazine from July 1891. At its peak, the publication sold half a million copies a month.

Sherlock Holmes was a formula figure, his readily identifiable character traits and utterances linking together what were otherwise self-contained stories. As Conan Doyle himself put it, 'his character admits of no light and shade. He is a calculating machine, and anything you add to that simply weakens the effect.'[45] The *Strand* attempted to build on the success of this formula with a series of stories by Arthur Morrison, starring Martin Hewitt (these followed what looked to be Holmes's fatal plunge into the Reichenbach Falls in 1893: Conan Doyle resurrected him in 1903). The detective short story became a staple of other late nineteenth-century magazines, many of these featuring detectives who appeared on repeated occasions. Within juvenile fiction, the first Sexton Blake story appeared in the *Halfpenny Marvel* in December 1893. The idea of a woman's perseverance and intelligence motivating the hunt for a criminal was present in the genre from early on (as with *Clara Vaughan*, or Collins's *The Law and the Lady* (1875)). Professional women detectives (rarely, however, feminist in their attitudes) appeared from at least 1864, in Andrew Forrester, Jr.'s *The Female Detective*: following the success of Sherlock Holmes, 'lady detectives' emerged in larger numbers, and included George Sims's Dorcas Dene, and Catherine Louisa Pirkis's Loveday Brooke, who exploited her talent for

---

44 Sir Arthur Conan Doyle, *A Study in Scarlet* (London: Penguin, 2001), pp. 21–2.
45 Sir Arthur Conan Doyle, 'The Truth about Sherlock Holmes,' in Peter Haining (ed.), *The Final Adventures of Sherlock Holmes* (New York: Barnes and Noble Books, 1993), p. 32.

impersonation while working for a detective agency. As a nursery governess looking for work, or a house decorator, she readily could blend into middle-class environments. As Ebenezer Dyer, her employer, put it:

> in the first place, she has the faculty – so rare among women – of carrying out orders to the very letter: in the second place, she has a clear, shrewd brain, unhampered by any hard-and-fast theories; thirdly, and the most important item of all, she has so much common sense that it amounts to genius – positively to genius.[46]

Writing in his autobiography, *Memories and Adventures* (1924), Conan Doyle spelt out his method:

> The first thing is to get your idea. Having got that key idea one's next task is to conceal it and lay emphasis upon everything which can make for a different explanation. Holmes, however, can see all the fallacies of the alternatives, and arrives more or less dramatically at the true solution by steps which he can describe and justify.[47]

Watson, perpetually impressed by Holmes's reasoning and methods, is in many ways a surrogate for the reader, and although he is present at some dangerous and suspenseful moments, his role is to underscore the detective's deductive brilliance, and to help celebrate rationality and the power of explanation. In detective fiction, as Michael Cox has pointed out, there is always the certitude that one *can* arrive at an understanding of what has appeared disruptive and unsettling. This contrasts with the Gothic form, that so often refuses to reassemble fractured subjectivities. The apparent restoration of moral and social order – at least in the kind of world assumed to be inhabited by the reader: Holmes, refreshingly, suggests the possibility of alternative lifestyles – ensures that the work of detective fiction has much in common with that of sensation novels, and puts it at odds with the form of the ghost story. 'In the opposing implications of the two genres', writes Cox, 'can be glimpsed the tension between a belief in human power and the consciousness of human dependence on some greater order that helped form the cultural temper of the Victorian age.'[48]

---

46 C[atherine] L[ouisa] Pirkis, *The Experiences of Loveday Brooke, Lady Detective* (London: Hutchinson, 1894), pp. 7–8.

47 Sir Arthur Conan Doyle, *Memories and Adventures* (London: Little, Brown, 1924), pp. 106–7.

48 Michael Cox, Introduction to *The Oxford Book of Victorian Detective Stories* (Oxford University Press, 2003), p. xxvi.

Yet what links all the types of fiction that may be thought of as sensational in the Victorian period, whether focusing on detectives, biga-mists, murderers, adulterers, revenants, or the Undead, is the degree to which its readers' affective responses were thought to be caught up in its consumption.[49] This emphasis on the audience is key. Dickens claimed to be horrified by the crowd's response to the execution of the Mannings, yet he himself was not immune to the transgressive sexual signals sent by Maria Manning's body, 'a fine shape, so elaborately corseted and artfully dressed, that it was quite unchanged in its trim appearance as it slowly swung from side to side'.[50] Similarly, reviewers might have sought to condemn sensationalism for the ways in which it over-excited its (female) readers, and unreasonably aroused their expectations about how life could be more interesting, whilst at the same time finding plenty of sensational substance in describing the responses of these same readers, stimulating their own morally and physiologically infused critical rhetoric. The lasting importance of the sensational within Victorian writing, therefore, lies not just within the groundwork that it established for future paradigms within popular fiction, but for the way in which it drew sustained attention to readerly response, located in both body and mind. More than this, the power of this affect could be shown as residing not in external stimuli, but in the workings of suspense and omission, coincidence and shock and surprise, as they occur within the pacing of a plot, the calculated omission or hiatus, the ambiguous term. Sensationalism goes far beyond the inclu-sion of certain types of subject matter: it inheres in the reader's response to their rhetorical manipulation by a text that has calculated designs upon them.

49 For a discussion of the reasons behind the recent critical interest in sensation novels, and the investment that late twentieth-century and early twenty-first-century readers have in this type of fiction, see Anna Maria Jones, *Problem Novels: Victorian Fiction Theorizes the Sensational Self* (Columbus: Ohio State University Press, 2007).
50 [Charles Dickens], 'Lying Awake', in *Household Words* 6 (30 October 1852), p. 146.

II

Autobiography

LINDA H. PETERSON

In *Sartor Resartus*, as Carlyle reconstructs the auto/biography of Diogenes Teufelsdröckh from the scraps and fragments of his subject's life, he pauses to wonder at 'these autobiographical times of ours'.[1] The phrase captures the expressivist turn of the early Victorian era and the explosion of writing in an autobiographical mode. As a word, 'autobiography' was virtually a neologism when *Sartor Resartus* was published in *Fraser's Magazine* in 1833–4. In 1797 it had appeared (negatively) in the *Monthly Review* as a 'pedantic' term; it reappeared (positively) in 1809 in the *Quarterly Review* when Robert Southey praised the life of the Portuguese painter Francisco Vieira as a 'very amusing and unique specimen of autobiography'.[2] By 1826 the publishers John Hunt and Cowden Clarke had launched a popular series, *Autobiography: A Collection of the Most Instructive and Amusing Lives Ever Published, Written by the Parties Themselves*, and by 1828 Carlyle was musing, 'What would we give for such an Autobiography of Shakspeare.'[3] The increasingly frequent use of the word 'autobiography' in the Victorian period is matched by the increasing number of periodical articles and reviews on the subject: 34 in the 1820s, 127 in the 1840s, 304 in the 1860s, and 433 in the first decade of the

---

1 Thomas Carlyle, *Sartor Resartus: The Life and Opinions of Herr Teufelsdröckh*, ed. Mark Engel and Rodger L. Tarr (Berkeley: University of California Press, 2000), p. 73.

2 *Oxford English Dictionary*, s.v. *autobiography*. In the *Monthly Review*, 2nd series 24 (1797), p. 375, the term 'autobiography' is proposed as a pedantic, but linguistically coherent alternative to the 'partly Saxon, partly Greek' term 'self-biography'; in the *Quarterly Review* 1 (1809), p. 283, Southey uses the term in a review article about *Extractos em Portuguez e em Inglez* (London: Wingrove, 1808).

3 *Autobiography: A Collection of the Most Instructive and Amusing Lives Ever Published, Written by the Parties Themselves*, 26 vols. (London: Hunt and Clarke, 1826–9); in 1829 Whittaker, Treacher & Arnot took over the series, publishing translations of European autobiographies and contemporary life-writing (vols. XXVII–XXXIV). Thomas Carlyle, 'Goethe' (1828), in Carlyle, *Essays on Goethe* (London: Cassell, 1905), p. 16.

twentieth century, according to the *Periodicals Index Online*.[4] Indeed, from the French perspective, even in 1866 'autobiography' was an English invention, 'still rare in France but conspicuously common across the Channel'.[5]

Autobiographical writing in the Western tradition goes back at least to the Greeks and Romans, as the classical scholar Georg Misch observed in *A History of Autobiography in Antiquity* (1949–69, trans. 1951).[6] But the dramatic rise of autobiographical modes of literature is a nineteenth-century phenomenon, linked to the expressivist turn that philosopher Charles Taylor has described in *Sources of the Self: The Making of Modern Identity* (1989). According to Taylor, the 'notion of an inner voice or impulse, the idea that we find the truth within us', is a key aspect of modern identity, as is the corollary role of the 'creative imagination' in modern art and literature, which turns from mimesis to self-expression and results in 'new forms which give articulation to [an individual's] vision'. Yet equally important for understanding the varieties of Victorian autobiography are two other 'moral ideas' that Taylor identifies as particularly Victorian: 'the significance of ordinary life and the ideal of universal benevolence'.[7] In most instances, Victorian autobiography derives not only, or even primarily, from a desire to express the self, but also from a belief in the writer's duty to publish a life history for the good of readers, who may profit from both the missteps and the achievements recorded in the autobiographical text.

The kinds of autobiographical literature surveyed in this chapter reflect these general concerns with the importance of the ordinary life, the instructive uses of life writing, and the need for self-expression. Yet Victorian autobiographies also emerge from specific social, religious, and political contexts and from a particular convergence of oral and print culture, and these contexts receive attention as well. Spiritual autobiographies of the period range from the testimonies of early nineteenth-century Evangelicals and Methodists, to the mid-century conversion narratives of the Oxford Movement, to the deconversion accounts of later Victorian intellectuals.

4 These statistics derive from a search of articles in *Periodical Index Online* http://pio.chadwyck.com/articles (accessed 8 January 2009) that include the word 'autobiography' in the title. The numbers of articles of or about autobiography in Victorian periodicals would actually be higher, given the limitations of the *PIO* database.
5 *Grand Dictionnaire Larousse*, 1866 edn; quoted in Jerome Hamilton Buckley, *Autobiography and the Subjective Impulse since 1800* (Cambridge, MA: Harvard University Press, 1984), p. 38.
6 Georg Misch, *A History of Autobiography in Antiquity*, trans. E. W. Dickes, 3rd edn (Cambridge, MA: Harvard University Press, 1951).
7 Charles Taylor, *Sources of the Self: The Making of Modern Identity* (Cambridge, MA: Harvard University Press, 1989), pp. 378–9, 395.

Political accounts include the testimonies and self-help narratives of working-class men and women, as well as the monumental 'life and letters' of famous Victorian politicians and statesmen. Artists' and authors' autobiographies lay claim to the power of the imagination but also reveal a broad effort to professionalize these fields and gain solid middle-class status; the accounts of women document their social and economic struggles (and successes) in entering the professions of arts and letters. And the experimental and increasingly common uses of autobiographical modes in fiction and periodical genres suggest the widespread rhetorical effectiveness of this mode in Victorian print culture.

Spiritual autobiography, secularization, and scientific models of life writing

Victorian writers inherited a well-established tradition of spiritual autobiography, descending from John Bunyan's *Grace Abounding* (1666) and George Fox's *Journals* (1694) and continuing with the Methodist and Evangelical conversion narratives of George Whitefield (1740), John Newton (1764), Thomas Scott (1799), William Cowper (1816), and others of the late eighteenth and early nineteenth centuries.[8] These autobiographies relied on both oral culture, in the public testimonies of believers, and print culture, in the cheap publication of exemplary lives or in collections such as *The Friends' Library* (1837–50).[9] As Joyce Quiring Erickson has pointed out, the reading, writing, and speaking of spiritual life narratives became a form of witness and welcome, inclusion and discipline, in early Methodist communities; following John Wesley's organizational pattern of small 'bands', larger 'classes', and even larger public preaching, Methodist societies 'mandated frequent discussion of personal spiritual affairs'.[10] From written and spoken accounts, ordinary men and women learned to shape their narratives of conversion and to analyse their life experiences within biblical patterns and

---

8 John Bunyan, *Grace Abounding to the Chief of Sinners*, ed. Roger Sharrock (Oxford: Clarendon Press, 1962); George Fox, *Journals* (London, 1694); John Newton, *An Authentic Narrative of Some Remarkable and Interesting Particulars in Life of [the Rev. Mr. John Newton]* (London, 1764); *Memoir of the Early Life of William Cowper* (London, 1816); George Whitefield, *Brief and general account of the first part of the life of the Reverend Mr. George Whitefield: from his birth to his entring [sic] into holy-orders, Written by himself* (Boston, 1740); Thomas Scott, *The Force of Truth: An Authentic Narrative* (London, 1779).
9 William Evans and Thomas Evans (eds.), *The Friends' Library*, 14 vols. (Philadelphia: Joseph Rakestraw, 1837–50).
10 Joyce Quiring Erickson, '"Perfect Love": Achieving Sanctification as a Pattern of Desire in the Life Writings of Early Methodist Women', *Prose Studies* 20 (1997), p. 73.

religious frameworks of interpretation. Similar practices of oral and written autobiography existed within other Protestant groups.

Spiritual autobiographies spread widely during the nineteenth century with the rise of tract societies, religious periodicals, and cheap books and pamphlets. The success of Hannah More's *Cheap Repository Tracts* (1795–8) triggered the proliferation of tract series, from the *Scotch Cheap Repository Tracts* (1808) and *Dublin Tracts* (1820–4) directly modelled on More's, to independent publishers' series such as Houston and Sons', which published exemplary life histories, fictional and factual. Not all tracts employed first-person narratives, but personal witness was a common and influential tract form. So, too, autobiographies were a staple of religious periodicals such as the *Wesleyan Methodist Magazine* (1822–1913), the *Baptist Magazine* (1809–56), and the *Church of England Magazine* (1836–75), which often placed them as the lead article. With the advent of cheap paper, innovations in printing, and increasing literacy, religious societies could also re-issue older spiritual autobiographies. John Newton's *Authentic Narrative* (1764), an account of his conversion from the slave trade to Evangelical Christianity, appeared in at least a dozen editions between 1764 and 1805, and was later appended to editions of his *Works*. Even a modest account, like *A Legacy, or Widow's Mite* (1723) by the Quaker Alice Hayes, went through multiple cheap editions, with the religious publisher Darton and Harvey issuing a small, tract-size volume in 1836 – thus sending the message that such spiritual narratives remained timely and relevant to Victorian readers.

Narrative conventions of the spiritual autobiography – a 'conviction of sin', a period of uncertainty or 'wandering in the wilderness', and a dramatic moment of conversion or 'seeing the light' – shaped the accounts of ordinary lives and literary texts as well. In his *Autobiography* (1873), for example, John Stuart Mill describes the crisis in his mental history as the state 'in which converts to Methodism usually are, when smitten by their first "conviction of sin"'; so, too, his discovery of Wordsworth's poetry and its healing power recalls the conversion episodes of Evangelical autobiography – even though Mill's is a thoroughly secular account of a Utilitarian philosopher and logician.[11] Similarly, Harriet Martineau's narrative of her loss of Unitarian faith and discovery of Comtian positivism repeats the pattern of religious conversion, even though she takes care to call the change a 'revolution' in her *Autobiography* (1877): 'I was like a new creature

---

11 John Stuart Mill, *Autobiography*, ed. Jack Stillinger (Boston: Houghton Mifflin, 1969), p. 81.

in the strength of a sound conviction', Martineau recalls; 'a new light spread through my mind, and I began to experience a steady growth in self-command, courage, and consequent disinterestedness.'[12] Beyond autobiographies per se, the narrative patterns of spiritual autobiography influenced the structure of many Victorian novels, as Barry Qualls has demonstrated in *The Secular Pilgrims of Victorian Fiction* for Charlotte Brontë's *Jane Eyre*, Charles Dickens's *Great Expectations*, George Eliot's *The Mill on the Floss*, and others that replicate a pattern of temptation, trial, and salvation (or loss).[13]

Autobiographical writing proliferated during periods of religious controversy, particularly during the Oxford Movement (1833–45) and in the aftermath of the controversial *Essays and Reviews* (1860). In the Oxford Movement, with its turn away from an Evangelical emphasis on personal conversion and a (re)turn to ecclesiastical authority and High Church doctrine, the Evangelical mode of interpreting personal experience became suspect. John Henry Newman's *Apologia pro vita sua* (1864) carefully avoids the pattern of Evangelical conversion and models itself instead on Augustine's *Confessions* (*c.* 400). Written to explain his decision to enter the Roman Catholic Church and to defend himself and the Church from charges of duplicity, Newman draws widely on his knowledge of Early Church history and saints' lives. Newman's *Loss and Gain* (1848), a novel, fictionalizes his own experience by depicting the increasing confusion of Charles Reading, an Oxford undergraduate, as he studies Anglican doctrine, finds it wanting, and eventually enters a Roman Catholic communion.

Of course, not all conversions went in the direction of Rome. Victorian autobiographies record movements to theism, agnosticism, and atheism. *Phases of Faith: Or, Passages from the History of My Creed* (1850) by Frances Newman, brother of John Henry, traces a movement away from Evangelical Calvinism to theism, beginning with his 'strivings after a more primitive Christianity'[14] and rejection of the Old Testament, continuing with his scepticism about the Gospels and Pauline epistles, and reaching a position that the Bible was unsuitable as a basis for morality, given its support of superstition, slavery, and the subordination of women. James Anthony Froude, brother of the Anglo-Catholic Richard Hurrell Froude and one-time associate of John Henry Newman, recorded his religious perplexities

---

12 Harriet Martineau, *Autobiography*, 3 vols. (London: Smith, Elder, 1877), vol. I, pp. 109–10.
13 See Barry Qualls, *The Secular Pilgrims of Victorian Fiction* (Cambridge University Press, 1982).
14 Francis William Newman, *Phases of Faith: or, Passages from the History of My Creed* (London: John Chapman, 1850), p. 26.

(and sexual frustrations) in an autobiographical novel, *The Nemesis of Faith* (1849). Narrated by a young Anglican clergyman who, like Froude, had doubts about his vocation, the novel was publicly burned by Froude's Oxford college (Exeter) and its author forced to resign his fellowship – despite the fact that Froude claimed he had, with the publication of *Nemesis*, exorcised his 'spiritual difficulties' and was 'done for ever with the subjective'.[15] These autobiographies, products of the Oxford Movement and its controversies, were followed in the 1860s and 1870s with accounts that revealed the intellectual challenges of the Higher Criticism in *Essays and Reviews* – including William White Hale's fictionalized *Autobiography of Mark Rutherford* (1881) and *Mark Rutherford's Deliverance* (1885) and Mary Humphry Ward's third-person novel, *Robert Elsmere* (1888), which recreates the spiritual ferment of Oxford in the era of Walter Pater, Mark Pattison, and T. H. Green.

As these examples attest, autobiography was written not just for the sake of introspection or private confession, but rather was used as a vehicle for public self-explanation, for self-positioning in religious controversies, and for advancing a cause. Newman's *Apologia* began when he answered an attack by Charles Kingsley in the pages of *Macmillan's Magazine* (January 1864): 'Truth, for its own sake', Kingsley had written, 'had never been a virtue with the Roman clergy. Father Newman informs us that it need not be.' Newman felt obliged to defend his veracity. His brother Francis Newman's *Phases of Faith* was expanded, and a ninth chapter added, 'Reply to the "Eclipse of Faith"', after a hostile fifty-five-page article appeared in the *British Quarterly Review* (August 1850) and an entire book, *The Eclipse of Faith* by Henry Rogers, was published to refute Newman's position. Brother against brother, one Oxford college against another, Evangelicals against Anglo-Catholics, Anglicans against theists – or 'tit for tat', as Newman put it in the *Apologia*.

Controversial autobiographies – or autobiographies that engage in religious and philosophical controversies – were not restricted to university men. Harriet Martineau's *Autobiography* (1877) traces her movement away from the Unitarianism of her youth, through what she terms a 'metaphysical fog', to the positivism of Auguste Comte and agnosticism of her adult life; this movement coincides with an acceptance of her physical disabilities, as

---

15 Letter from James Anthony Froude to Charles Kingsley, 27 February 1849, cited in Waldo Hilary Dunn, *James Anthony Froude: A Biography, 1818–1894*, 2 vols. (Oxford: Clarendon Press, 1961–3), vol. I, p. 134.

Martineau rejects a Christian 'worship of sorrow' and replaces it with a scientific approach to medical ailments which includes the controversial practice of mesmerism. Frances Power Cobbe's *Life* (1894) quietly sandwiches a chapter, 'Religion', about her loss of Anglican faith and embrace of Theism, between chapters on 'School and After' and 'My First Book'.[16] Annie Besant's *Autobiographical Sketches* (1885), first published serially in the periodical *Our Corner*, record her rebellion against a God who allows pain and suffering to 'torture' her young daughter. Besant's later *Autobiography* (1893) expands her spiritual quest to cover her movement from atheism and free-thought to her discovery of Theosophy, or, as she expresses it in her final chapter title, 'Through Storm to Peace'.[17] Besant's autobiographical text ends on what Carol MacKay calls 'the upbeat cry of the spiritual warrior':[18] 'Peace to all Beings.'

If some Victorians turned away from orthodox Christianity to embrace alternative philosophies, others adopted scientific theories to comprehend their life experiences. In his *Autobiography* (1876), written for 'my children and their children', Charles Darwin does not apply principles of 'Darwinian' evolution per se, but adopts a scientific perspective 'as objective and as detached' in his 'private-experiential' book, to quote James Olney, as in his 'public-scientific' work: 'I have attempted to write the following account of myself', Darwin explains, 'as if I were a dead man in another world looking back on my own life.'[19] Darwin also discussed the erosion of his religious beliefs in the wake of his scientific discoveries (though these comments were omitted by his son Francis, who edited and published the *Autobiography* after his father's death). Darwin's followers took his objective scientific stance further and analysed themselves as biological specimens. Herbert Spencer, for example, introduces his *Autobiography* (1904) as 'a natural history of myself' and analyses 'family traits' that are also 'displayed in other lines of descent'.[20] Darwin's cousin Francis Galton, in the 'Parentage' chapter of

16 Martineau, *Autobiography*, vol. I, p. 156; vol. II, p. 147; Frances Power Cobbe, *The Life of Frances Power Cobbe, by Herself*, 2 vols. (Boston: Houghton Mifflin, 1895).

17 Annie Besant, *Autobiographical Sketches* (London: Freethought Publishing Company, 1885), and Annie Besant, *An Autobiography* (London: T. Fisher Unwin, 1893).

18 Carol Hanbery MacKay, 'Introduction' to *Autobiographical Sketches* (Peterborough, Canada: Broadview Press, 2009), p. xv.

19 Charles Darwin, *The Autobiography of Charles Darwin, 1809–1882*, ed. Nora Barlow (New York: W.W. Norton, 1958), p. 21; James Olney, *Metaphors of Self: The Meaning of Autobiography* (Princeton University Press, 1972), p. 183.

20 Herbert Spencer, *An Autobiography*, 2 vols. (London: Williams and Norgate, 1904), vol. I, pp. vii, xi.

Memories of My Life (1908), analyses the 'six nearest progenitors, namely the two parents and four grandparents', who 'bequeathed very different combination of [traits] to their descendents' – including a physical debility from his grandfather Samuel Galton and a 'hereditary bent of mind' from his grandfather Erasmus Darwin.[21] The most rigorous (if at times fallacious) example of 'scientific' treatment occurs in Samuel Butler's autobiographical fiction, *The Way of All Flesh* (1903). Applying concepts from Lamarck, Erasmus Darwin, and his own writings on purposive evolution, Butler depicts the 'oneness of personality between parents and offspring' and the offspring's unconscious memory of 'certain actions which it did when in the person of its forefathers'.[22]

Autobiographical writing in the Victorian period reveals, predictably from our modern perspective, the growing conflict between religion and science and follows a trajectory commonly referred to as 'secularization'. The shift might also be seen as an aspect of 'the eclipse of biblical narrative', in Hans Frei's useful phrase,[23] in that autobiographical writing reveals a lessening of the power of biblical patterns to explain human experience and an increasing experimentation with other theories and models of self-interpretation. A powerful late Victorian example of this shift appears in *Father and Son* (1907) by Edmund Gosse – in 'the records of a struggle between two temperaments, two consciences and almost two epochs'.[24] While autobiographers continued to write accounts of their spiritual lives, sometimes in a traditional mode, many other Victorians turned to science, social science, and philosophy for their models.

Working-class and professional autobiographies

Autobiographical writing by workers and professionals appeared regularly during the period but more frequently during times of political crisis, just as spiritual autobiographies circulated during religious controversies. A famous example is *The Autobiography of a Working Man* (1848), written by Alexander Somerville or 'Somerville of the Scots Greys', as he was known. His *Autobiography* describes rural Scottish poverty, 'hard work and little wages',

---

21 Francis Galton, *Memories of My Life* (London: Methuen, 1908), pp. 1–12.
22 Samuel Butler, *The Way of All Flesh* (London: Grant Richards, 1903), p. 24.
23 Hans W. Frei, *The Eclipse of Biblical Narrative: A Study in Eighteenth and Nineteenth Century Hermeneutics* (New Haven, CT: Yale University Press, 1974).
24 Edmund Gosse, *Father and Son: A Study of Two Temperaments*, ed. James Hepburn (Oxford University Press, 1974), p. 5.

and coming to literacy and radicalism, but it focuses on his determination, during the political crisis of the first Reform Bill (1832), to resist orders to fire on demonstrators marching from Birmingham to London. Somerville wrote an anonymous letter to a newspaper in which he expressed a belief that his fellow soldiers would not follow the commands of the Duke of Wellington in resisting 'the national will as declared by the House of Commons'. Somerville's authorship was discovered; he was court-martialled, tried, and sentenced to 200 lashes (100 of which were given); and his case became a cause célèbre in the fight against violent and unjust punishment. He wrote his account, however, not only to explain his actions of 1832, but also to warn, in the era of the Chartist demonstrations of 1848, against 'the conspiracy of trades' unionists and political lunatics', whom he felt encouraged mob rule. Somerville saw his autobiography as providing 'reflections instructive to general readers'.[25]

Like Somerville, many working-class autobiographers turned to life writing for purposes beyond self-expression. In a broad sense, their accounts reflect the two 'moral ideas' that Charles Taylor identifies as particularly Victorian: 'the significance of ordinary life and the ideal of universal benevolence'.[26] In more specific ways, their accounts were meant to be instructive to their fellow men and useful in the fight for better working conditions and political reform. William Dodd, for example, wrote his *Narrative of the Experiences and Sufferings of William Dodd, A Factory Cripple* (1841) at the urging of Anthony Ashley Cooper, the sixth Earl of Shaftesbury, to detail the appalling conditions of textile workers and the harmful physical and mental effects of child labour; Lord Ashley used testimonies such as Dodd's in support of legislation that would restrict children's workdays to a maximum of ten hours. (Many such testimonies were published in the *Parliamentary Papers*, commonly referred to as Blue Books.)[27] Frank Forrest's *Chapters in the Life of a Dundee Factory Boy* (1850), similarly written in hopes of improving working conditions, details the dirty, low-roofed, ill-ventilated, ill-drained rooms that led to 'mill fever', 'a strong, heavy sickness that few escaped on first becoming factory workers'. Ellen Johnston's *Autobiography* (1867), the history of a 'factory girl', describes the appalling domestic life and

25 Alexander Somerville, 'Preface to the First Edition', in *The Autobiography of a Working Man*, ed. John Carswell (London: Turnstile Press, 1951), pp. xxiii–xxiv.
26 Taylor, *Sources of the Self*, p. 395.
27 For a discussion of this political use of working-class testimony, see Janice Carlisle, 'Introduction', in James R. Simmons, Jr. (ed.), *Factory Lives: Four Nineteenth-Century Working-Class Autobiographies* (Peterborough, Ontario: Broadview Press, 2007), pp. 24–6.

working conditions of the female Scottish labourer, even as it gives expression to working-class solidarity and hope for a better life.[28]

Although concerned with the progress of their class or artisanal group, working-class autobiographers often reached beyond class interest to improve relations between workers and employers – as in an article written for *The Nineteenth Century* by a butler who used his experience to identify causes of 'the servant problem' and offer solutions that would 'remove the obstacles which lie in the way of a servant's material well-being', give 'some opportunity for mental improvement', and thus improve domestic servants' performance.[29] The journalist Henry Mayhew similarly argued, in a newspaper article written before the publication of *London Labour and the London Poor*, that 'the labourer and the capitalist, the workman and employer, are to my mind partners ... so I do protest, in common honesty and justice, against the working-man being filched of his fair fame'.[30] Mayhew incorporated first-person narratives into his sketches of urban workers in the *Morning Chronicle* (1849–50) and later into his four-volume compilation, *London Labour and the London Poor* (1861–2), stating that his was 'the first attempt to publish the history of a people, from the lips of the people themselves – giving a literal description of their labour, their earnings, their trials, and their sufferings, in their own "unvarnished" language'.[31] The rhetorical power of Mayhew's sketches derives, in large part, from the first-person testimonies.

Mayhew, an impoverished journalist, profited financially from his collection of workers' lives. Workers themselves often published their life writings to earn extra money or to better their circumstances and raise their class status. After the birth of her daughter, Ellen Johnston began publishing as a 'duty' to 'turn the poetic gift that nature had given [her] to a useful and profitable account'.[32] Charles Manby Smith's *The Working Man's Way in the World: being the Autobiography of a Journeyman Printer* (1853) described the

28 James Myles [Frank Forrest], *Chapters in the Life of a Dundee Factory Boy; An Autobiography* (Dundee: James Myles, 1850), p. 16. These accounts are included in *Factory Lives*; Carlisle's introduction gives an extensive account of the origin and uses of such working-class autobiographies.

29 Excerpted in *The Annals of Labour: Autobiographies of British Working Class People, 1820–1920*, ed. John Burnett (Bloomington: Indiana University Press, 1978), pp. 208–9; the account was originally published as 'A Butler's View of Man-Service', in *The Nineteenth Century: A Monthly Review* 31 (1892).

30 Henry Mayhew, *Selections from London Labour and the London Poor*, ed. John L. Bradley (London: Oxford University Press, 1965), p. xxix.

31 *Ibid.*, p. xxxiv.

32 Ellen Johnston, *Autobiography, Poems and Songs of Ellen Johnston, the 'Factory Girl'* (Glasgow: William Love, 1847), pp. 6–7.

apprenticeship of a printer's 'devil' and the difficult conditions under which compositors laboured, but his account also proved a means of entry into a career as a journalist; published serially in *Tait's Edinburgh Magazine* (1851–2) and then as a book, the autobiography turned his hard life to ready profit. Smith continued to publish narratives of workers, fictional and factual, until 1868.[33] In his and many other working-class accounts, there is a tension between class solidarity and the Victorian belief in individual progress, notably in the form of 'self-help'. Indeed, Samuel Smiles's seminal biographies of workers who persevered and eventually made good reflect a mid-Victorian ethos that influenced many Victorian autobiographies. Smiles's *Self-Help, with Illustrations of Conduct and Perseverance* (1859), first given as lectures to young men in Leeds, later published as a book, models through its life histories the positive achievements of energy, cheerfulness, prudence, and industry – his four keywords.[34]

While some working-class authors used life-writing as a means of advancement, the autobiographies of authors, artists, and other rising professionals reflect, even more intensely, the function of autobiography to secure (or at least make a bid for) middle-class status. In her study *The Victorian Artist: Artists' Lifewritings in Britain, ca. 1870–1910*, Julie Codell demonstrates the pivotal role of life-writing in the achievement of professional status for Victorian artists. Public self-presentation in a wide range of autobiographical genres – not only full-length memoirs and posthumous life-and-letters, but also interviews and mini-biographies in periodicals or entries in biographical dictionaries – made a crucial difference in the Victorian artist's ability to distinguish himself (or herself) from less desirable stereotypes (the failed Romantic genius, the bohemian, the degenerate) and to reach equity with other professions. According to Codell, this meant presenting themselves as 'gentlemen and ladies whose material success and public appeal became representative of English cultural domination and superiority'.[35] This argument about artists' life-writing is bolstered by accounts of actors and actresses, who similarly presented themselves in terms of respectable middle-class domesticity and who, like Fanny Kemble in *Records of a Girlhood*

---

33 See Charles Manby Smith, *The Working Man's Way in the World*, ed. Ellis Howe (London: Printing Historical Society, 1967), esp. Appendix, 'C. M. Smith's Known Publications'.

34 Samuel Smiles, *Self-Help, with Illustrations of Conduct & Perseverance*, ed. Asa Briggs (London: John Murray, 1958).

35 Julie Codell, *The Victorian Artist: Artists' Lifewritings in Britain, ca. 1870–1910* (Cambridge University Press, 2003), p. 2.

(1879), Marie Bancroft in *On and Off the Stage* (1886), co-authored with her husband, and Ellen Terry in *The Story of My Life* (1908), projected a bourgeois subjectivity in an attempt to make theatrical careers respectable.[36] It is also supported by Trev Broughton's study of professional civil servants like Philip Meadows Taylor who used autobiography, in *The Story of My Life* (1877), to debate policies of Indian rule, secure a middle-class legacy for himself and his children, and create a new style of masculinity for the Indian civil servant, less 'the colonial adventurer living on his wits', and more the career-minded professional 'preoccupied with rank and advancement'.[37]

Autobiographies of authors reveal an especially intense concern with professional status, a concern that involves complex questions about earnings, income, and the literary marketplace on the one hand, and genius, inspiration, and lasting literary achievement on the other. In *On Heroes and Hero-Worship* (1841) Thomas Carlyle made the man of letters the modern exemplar of heroism: 'so long as the wondrous art of *Writing*, or of Ready-writing which we call *Printing*, subsists, he may be expected to continue, as one of the main forms of Heroism for all future ages'. Carlyle emphasized the author's struggle against the 'galling conditions' of the marketplace and the supreme achievement of artistic inspiration: ' "originality", "sincerity", "genius", the heroic quality we have no good name for'.[38] In the same decade, in an article for *Fraser's Magazine* on 'The Condition of Authors in England, Germany, and France', G. H. Lewes emphasized instead the English author's economic status and professional success, arguing that such success was well-deserved given the author's contribution to the nation: 'The man who has devoted his talents and energies to the laborious task of improving and amusing mankind, has done the State as much service as the man who has marched at the head of a regiment.'[39] Despite their different emphases on genius versus service, financial versus literary achievement, both Carlyle and Lewes express central concerns that emerge throughout the autobiographies of Victorian authors about their public roles.

36 For a discussion of these and other autobiographies of actors and actresses, see Mary Jean Corbett, *Representing Femininity: Middle-Class Subjectivity in Victorian and Edwardian Women's Autobiographies* (New York: Oxford University Press, 1992), chapters 4–5.

37 Trev Lynn Broughton, 'Promoting a Life: Patronage, Masculinity and Philip Meadows Taylor's *The Story of My Life*', in David Amigoni (ed.), *Life Writing and Victorian Culture* (Aldershot: Ashgate, 2006), p. 108.

38 Thomas Carlyle, *On Heroes, Hero-Worship and the Heroic in History*, ed. Michael K. Goldberg, Joel J. Brattin, and Mark Engel (Berkeley: University of California Press, 1993), pp. 133–4.

39 [G. H. Lewes], 'The Condition of Authors in England, Germany, and France', *Fraser's Magazine* 35 (1847), pp. 285–95.

In William Wordsworth's *The Prelude*, for instance, written in 1805 but published posthumously in 1850, the poet's inspiration in nature figures as a prominent theme, but so, too, does the poet's service to humankind:

> Prophets of Nature, we to them will speak
> A lasting inspiration, sanctified
> By reason, blest by faith: what we have loved
> Others will love, and we will teach them how,
> Instruct them how the mind of Man becomes
> A thousand times more beautiful than the earth
> On which he dwells[.][40]

In *Aurora Leigh* (1856), a novel-poem written in the first person and incorporating autobiographical elements, Elizabeth Barrett Browning similarly concludes with the social good produced by poetry and the poet:

> Loves filial, loves fraternal, neighbour-loves
> And civic – all fair petals, all good scents,
> All reddened, sweetened from one central Heart![41]

Harriet Martineau's *Autobiography* (1877), written in 1855 but reserved for publication until after her death, gives inspiration a less important role, but service to humankind is essential. Recalling her first important publication, the *Illustrations of Political Economy* (1832–4) that made her fame and fortune, Martineau emphasizes her readers' needs: 'I thought of the multitudes who needed it, – and especially of the poor, – to assist them in managing their own welfare ... The people wanted the book; and they should have it.'[42] Yet Martineau also acknowledges the financial circumstances that led her to become an author and the pleasure she felt in earning a steady, professional income – totalling approximately £10,000 during her lifetime. The greatest emphasis on financial success (and least on public service) appears in Anthony Trollope's *Autobiography* (1883), which scandalized Victorian readers with its discussions of tradesman-like work, bargains made with publishers, and complacent, even gloating satisfaction with earnings. Reviewers feared that Trollope had 'brutalized' the literary ideal with his vulgar materialism.[43]

---

40 William Wordsworth, *The Prelude, 1799, 1805, 1850*, ed. Jonathan Wordsworth, M. H. Abrams, and Stephen Gill (New York: W. W. Norton, 1979), 1850 edn, Book Fourteenth, p. 483, lines 446–52.

41 Elizabeth Barrett Browning, *Aurora Leigh*, ed. Margaret Reynolds (Athens: Ohio University Press, 1992), Book 9, p. 585, lines 888–90.

42 Martineau, *Autobiography*, vol. I, pp. 161, 171.

43 See, for example, the review in *Macmillan's Magazine* 44 (1883), pp. 47–56.

It may be more accurate to read this and other late Victorian authors' life-writing – including Walter Besant's *Autobiography* (1902), George Sala's *Life and Adventures, Written by Himself* (1895), and even Leslie Stephen's private *Mausoleum Book* – as part of a continuing and unresolved debate about the social roles that authors play, models of authorship that should be endorsed, and criteria that should be used for judging literary success.

For women writers, these issues were particularly acute. At the beginning of the Victorian era, women still suffered from a prejudice against scribbling females as déclassé. Early in her *Autobiography* Harriet Martineau recalls that

> Jane Austen herself, the Queen of novelists ... was compelled by the feelings of her family to cover up her manuscripts with a large piece of muslin work, kept on the table for the purpose, whenever any genteel people came in. So it was with other young ladies, for some time after Jane Austen was in her grave; and thus my first studies in philosophy were carried on with great care and reserve.

Martineau recalls, too, with bitterness, that her mother made her refuse an offer of professional literary work in London and sent 'peremptory orders to go home', adding 'I rather wonder that, being seven and twenty years old, I did not assert my independence, and refuse to return, – so clear as was, in my eyes, the injustice of remanding me to a position of helplessness and dependence, when a career of action and independence was opening before me.'[44] Margaret Oliphant experienced more support from her mother, but records, too, how her early writing took place at the family worktable and how, even in her widowhood when authorship became her 'profession and sole dependence', she wrote in a 'little second drawing-room' that looked out to 'the other drawing-room where all the (feminine) life of the house goes on'.[45]

The equation of domestic and literary work – or the extension of domestic work into the public sphere – was a strategy for authorizing women's careers. In her *Autobiography* (1899) Oliphant sets the originary scene of authorship at her mother's sickbed, where she writes as an alternative to doing needlework and to amuse her family. Mary Howitt treats authorship as a family venture, first undertaken with her sister, then with her husband William and later her daughters Anna Mary and Margaret; Howitt's *Autobiography* (1889) is collaborative memoir, incorporating an account of her

---

44 Martineau, *Autobiography*, vol. i, p. 149.
45 Margaret Oliphant, *Autobiography*, ed. Elisabeth Jay (Oxford University Press, 1990), pp. 30–1.

husband's life, drawings of family homes by Anna Mary, with the whole edited by Margaret. Charlotte Elizabeth Tonna speaks of writing, in her *Personal Recollections* (1841), as a 'literary avocation' or, in biblical terms, as a 'free-will offering'[46] – the former phrase refusing professional status, the latter suggesting that her writing is an extension of Christian good works.

Yet not all women authors chose to align writing and domesticity (or Christianity) in their memoirs. In a letter reprinted in the 'Memorials' volume of her *Autobiography*, Martineau asks her mother to treat her as 'a professional son'. Frances Power Cobbe asserts in her *Life* (1894) that her journalistic career 'proved, I hope, once for all, that a woman may be relied on as a journalist no less than a man', and Eliza Lynn Linton describes her work for the *Morning Chronicle* alongside of male journalists in *My Literary Life* (1899) and casts herself, in her autobiographical novel *The Autobiography of Christopher Kirkland* (1885), as a man.[47] In *The Life of Charlotte Brontë* Elizabeth Gaskell took a different tack: although she emphasizes the exemplary behaviour of her subject, Charlotte Brontë, as dutiful daughter, sister, friend, and wife, she emphasizes even more the exceptional genius of the novelist, Currer Bell.

Victorian autobiographies by workers and professionals, in other words, enabled their writers to engage larger issues of class and gender, domestic life and professional goals, and common assumptions about self-help, self-development, and individual or class progress. While autobiographers reflected on these issues as they pertained to their individual lives, they also, by the public nature of autobiography, were debating the issues in the contexts of contemporary essays, books, and novels that treated the same subjects.

The colonial and imperial experience: autobiographies of British subjects around the globe

Victorian autobiography includes an enormous body of texts, many now forgotten, written by British men and women who explored the globe, settled in colonial territories, and carried out the work of the British empire.

---

46 Charlotte Elizabeth Tonna, *Personal Recollections*, 4th edn (London: Seeley, Jackson and Halliday, 1854), pp. 221, 136.
47 Martineau, *Autobiography*, vol. III, p. 91; Cobbe, *Life*, vol. II, p. 392; Eliza Lynn Linton, *My Literary Life* (London: Hodder and Stoughton, 1899), and *The Autobiography of Christopher Kirkland* (London: Richard Bentley and Son, 1885).

A few – like Catherine Parr Traill's *The Backwoods of Canada* (1836) and Susannah Moodie's *Roughing It in the Bush* (1852) and *Life in the Clearings* (1853) – have become founding texts of a new national literature. Undertaken to provide an accurate account of settler life in British North America, these women's memoirs, along with their brother Samuel Strickland's *Twenty-Seven Years in Canada* (1853), record the hardships of the colonial experience, as well as the advantages that emigration offered to middle-class British subjects. Traill, Moodie, and Strickland write against periodical articles and memoirs by sportsmen and adventurers – like the *Emigrant and Sportsman in Canada, . . . with Sketches of Canadian Life, Sporting Adventures, and Observations of Forests and Fauna* by John J. Rowan (1876) – and instead record their search for a better life for their families, their attempt to transplant British values on to colonial soil, and their adaptations of old world ways to new world challenges. In this last purpose, they represent a fundamental colonial compromise between old and new, past and future, European and North American.

Other British subjects recorded lives and experiences at the outposts of empire. Some autobiographers depict home life abroad in terms familiar to British readers; the semi-fictional, semi-autobiographical *The Rose and the Lotus; or, Home in England and Home in India* (1859), for instance, describes a young woman's education and social life on the Indian subcontinent and back in London amidst other Anglo-Indians within middle-class norms.[48] Other writers emphasize the exotic aspects of their lives abroad. Fanny Parkes, wife of a customs collector for the East India Company, wrote *Wanderings of a Pilgrim in Search of the Picturesque* (1850) about her river travels in her own yacht, manned by native seadogs, from Allahabad to Agra to see the Taj Majal; using the popular aesthetic category of the picturesque, Parkes frames exotic Indian sights within a mode familiar to her British readers. Another resident in India, Emily Eden, wrote of both domestic and exotic in *Up the Country* (1866), a memoir compiled from letters composed while she was living with her brother George, the governor-general of India, from 1835 to 1842. Still other autobiographers, most notably missionaries to India, China, Africa, and the Caribbean, testify to their efforts to spread Christian beliefs around the globe and, often, to their conflicts with British administrators who disagreed with their efforts and wished to suppress their influence on native peoples. Such conflicts between opposing sets of British

48 [Elizabeth Johnston], *The Rose and the Lotus; or, Home in England and Home in India by the Wife of a Bengal Civilian* (London: Bell and Daldy, 1859).

values emerge in seminal accounts of missionary literature, such as the *Journal and Letters of the Rev. Henry Martyn ... Chaplain to the East India Company* (1837) and *The Life of Mrs Sherwood* (1854). Conflicting sets of values, reflecting ethnic, racial, and class perspectives, emerge also in the memoirs of Crimean war nurses, *The Autobiography of Elizabeth Davis: A Balaclava Nurse* (1857) and the *Wonderful Adventures of Mrs. Seacole in Many Lands* (1857), the first written by a Welshwoman who severely critiques the inept administration of the British War Office and Florence Nightingale, the second by a Jamaican-born Creole nurse who, rejected by the War Office, the Crimean Fund, and then Florence Nightingale, went to the Crimea using her own resources and established a convalescent hotel for wounded soldiers and officers.[49]

One bitter conflict – the opposition to slavery by missionaries and colonial abolitionists – helped to initiate an important nineteenth-century form of life-writing: the slave narrative. For instance, the Canadian writer Susannah Strickland Moodie had been active in the Anti-Slavery League before her emigration, and served as amanuensis for *The History of Mary Prince, a West Indian Slave, related by Herself* (1831) and *Negro Slavery Described by a Negro, Being the Narrative of Ashton Warner, a Native of St Vincent's* (1831).[50] The former, which describes Prince's sufferings as a Caribbean slave and her journey to London in 1828 with her abusive owner, is the first narrative of a black woman published in Britain; the latter, the life story of a male Caribbean slave, attempts to establish Warner's right to freedom once on British soil. These autobiographies drew attention to the continued practice of slavery in British colonies, despite the official end of the slave trade in 1807, and furthered the abolitionist cause in their depictions of brutal practices and abuse of human rights. Other British abolitionists embedded negative scenes of slavery – and arguments for its abolition – in their personal memoirs. Mary Howitt's *Our Cousins in Ohio* (1849), a compilation of her sister Anna's American letters from Cincinnati, includes tales of slavery in the states south of the Ohio River and more hopeful chapters about freed blacks in Ohio.

---

49 *The Autobiography of Elizabeth Davis: A Balaclava Nurse*, ed. Jane Williams (London: Hurst & Blackett, 1857), and *Wonderful Adventures of Mrs Seacole in Many Lands* (London: James Blackwood, 1857).

50 *The History of Mary Prince, a West Indian Slave, related by Herself* (London: F. Westley and A. H. Davis, 1831), and *Negro Slavery Described by a Negro, Being the Narrative of Ashton Warner, a Native of St Vincent's; With an Appendix Containing the Testimony of Four Christian Ministers, Recently Returned from the Colonies, on the System of Slavery as It Now Exists* (London: Samuel Maunder, 1831).

Explorers, adventurers, and sportsmen contributed autobiographical memoirs to the growing literature of colonial and imperial experience. Charles Darwin's *Voyage of the Beagle* (1839), written during his first foreign travel as a geologist and natural historian, famously documents the geology of Patagonia and the fauna of the Galapagos Islands – research preliminary to the evolutionary theory of his *On the Origin of Species* (1859) – but Darwin also gives accounts of British settlements in New Zealand and Australia. Mary Kingsley, niece of Charles Kingsley and a distinguished ichthyologist in her own right, travelled to West Africa to collect specimens and wrote two books about her experiences, *Travels in West Africa* (1897) and *West African Studies* (1899); the first was a best-seller, but both provided English readers with a record of native African cultures and a strong case against the Christianization of native peoples. The Victorian explorer, Richard Burton, published over forty volumes, including his *Personal Narrative of a Pilgrimage to El-Medinah and Meccah* (1855–6), for which he disguised himself as a Muslim, and *The Lake Regions of Central Africa* (1860), which describes his explorations with John Speke for the source of the Nile. (Speke gave his own account in 1863 in *The Journal of the Discovery of the Source of the Nile*.) In the life-writing of sportsmen, among the most famous is Henry Courteney Selous's *A Hunter's Wanderings in Africa: Being a Narrative of Nine Years Spent Amongst the Game of the Far Interior of South Africa* (1881), an account of his long life as a big-game hunter in an era when ivory was the principal trade commodity from the African interior; like other hunting memoirs from Africa, India, and the Americas, it includes important details about fauna and natural history.

Although a British reader might have bought or borrowed these books for their exciting or exotic travelogues, they also provided information about non-Western cultures and became, in some cases, seminal texts of newly emerging disciplines. Darwin's exclamation at Sydney Cove, Australia – 'My first feeling was to congratulate myself that I was born an Englishman' – was a common response in foreign travel, but not all autobiographers concluded with the superiority of English culture. Even Darwin, in a moment of cultural comparison, was able to see the pleasures of life in Tahiti and admit his admiration for the tattooed Tahitian body.[51] Burton was de facto a comparative anthropologist, particularly fascinated by the sexual practices

---

51 Charles Darwin, *The Voyage of the Beagle: Journal of Researches into the Natural History and Geology of the Countries Visited during the Voyage of H.M.S. Beagle Round the World* (New York: Modern Library, 2001), pp. 360–1, 385.

of non-Westerners. Mary Kingsley travelled to Africa because of her deep unhappiness with life as a single, middle-class Englishwoman. Harriet Martineau documented the appeal (as well as the drawbacks) of the American way of life in *Society in America* (1837) and *Retrospect of Western Travel* (1839). What runs through these autobiographical travelogues are comparisons of life abroad with British life at home – and in these comparisons emerge the techniques and practices not only of the autobiographer, but also of the sociologist and anthropologist.

Literary autobiography and autobiographical fiction

This account of Victorian autobiography has emphasized expressive and purposive life-writing, especially on religious, political, social, and professional issues. Yet often the purpose in writing autobiography was pleasure – the pleasure of remembering the past, of recording family history for descendants, of memorializing an 'old England' that was passing away. Many privately printed memoirs articulate this motive in their titles or prefaces, as in *Memoirs of a Gentlewoman of the Old School, by a Lady* (1830), *Aunt Janet's Legacy to Her Nieces: Recollections of a Humble Life in Yarrow at the Beginning of the Century* (1894), or the *Autobiography of Thomas Wright, of Birkenshaw* (1864), written 'for the instruction and amusement of his children and descendants'.[52] Canonical Victorian autobiographies also emerge from personal pleasure or aesthetic desire. John Ruskin insists, in the preface to *Praeterita* (1885), that he has written his sketches of the past 'frankly, garrulously, and at ease; speaking of what it gives me joy to remember at any length I like ... and passing in total silence things which I have no pleasure in reviewing'.[53] And, indeed, readers have enjoyed and admired Ruskin's descriptions of his childhood in 'Herne Hill Almond Blossoms', his visits to Scotland in 'The Banks of the Tay' and 'Roslyn Chapel', and his accounts of European travels in the later chapters.

Yet Ruskin's disclaimer also reminds us that he, like many other Victorians, used autobiography to work through difficult personal experiences and

---

52 *Memoirs of a Gentlewoman of the Old School, by a Lady* (London: Hurst, Chance, 1830); *Aunt Janet's Legacy to her Nieces: Recollections of a Humble Life in Yarrow at the Beginning of the Century* (Selkirk: George Lewes & Son, 1894); *Autobiography of Thomas Wright, of Birkenshaw*, ed. by his grandson, Thomas Wright (London: John Russell Smith, 1864).

53 John Ruskin, *Praeterita*, in *The Works of John Ruskin*, ed. E. T. Cook and Alexander Wedderburn, 39 vols. (London: George Allen, 1903–12), vol. xxxv, p. 11.

traumatic past events. Ruskin omits, for example, all mention of Effie Gray, the wife who abandoned him for John Millais and had their marriage annulled for non-consumption. Ruskin alludes to, but barely discusses, his unrequited love for the young Rose la Touche. And it is arguable that the second volume of *Praeterita*, which covers the years in which Ruskin cast off his Evangelical faith, attempts to prove to himself that he had not disappointed his parents (who had, in fact, been dismayed by his deconversion). Ruskin's final sentence in the preface to *Praeterita* – that 'an old man's recreation in gathering visionary flowers in fields of youth, has taken, as I wrote, the nobler aspect of a dutiful offering at the grave of parents who trained my childhood to all the good it could attain'[54] – suggests that transforming the difficult and disturbing aspects of his life was a key purpose in composing an autobiography.

Ruskin was not alone among Victorian writers in this transformative gesture. In *Confessions of an English Opium Eater*, published in the *London Magazine* in 1822, expanded with *Suspiria de Profundis* to become a book (1856), Thomas DeQuincey observes that 'guilt and misery shrink, by a natural instinct, from public notice' and that English readers (as opposed to French) revolt against a writer who 'obtrud[es] on our notice his moral ulcers or scars'. Yet DeQuincey chose to write about his opium addiction, in part, to work through its pains and to achieve 'future hours of tranquility'; he notes that he turned to opium 'as a resource for healing' the consequences of 'some early events in my life'.[55] (His biographers have suggested that he never resolved the underlying personal maladjustment that led to his addiction.[56])

Among novelists, Charles Dickens frequently turned his childhood fears and unhappiness into autobiographical fiction – from the opening chapters of *Dombey and Son* (1847–8) at Mrs Pipchin's establishment to the startling account of London life as a child labourer in *David Copperfield* (1849–50) to the depiction of debtors' prison in *Little Dorrit* (1855–7). Dickens privately gave John Forster, his friend and later biographer, an autobiographical fragment about his father's bankruptcy and his employment at Warren's blacking factory as a twelve-year-old boy – an episode that Dickens never revealed to his wife or family and that plunged him into shame, misery, and

54 *Ibid.*, p. 12.
55 Thomas DeQuincey, *Confessions of an English Opium Eater, Being an Extract from the Life of a Scholar*, ed. Aileen Ward (New York: New American Library, 1966), pp. 107, 115.
56 See Ward's 'Foreword', pp. x–xi, *ibid.*, for modern judgments about DeQuincey's addiction.

desolation: 'No words can express the secret agony of my soul, as I sunk into this companionship ... and felt my early hopes of growing up to be a learned and distinguished man, crushed in my breast.'[57] As Robert Patten points out, 'Every word of his confession reveals the destructive cost to the self of this nodal past', even as, in writing the autobiographical *David Copperfield*, Dickens 'learns to make his reality through language ... and becomes adequate through fictions of his adequacy'.[58] A similar assessment might be made of Charlotte Brontë's process in writing autobiographical fiction. Consciously and unconsciously, Brontë used her novels to revisit the childhood trauma of her sisters' deaths in a cholera epidemic at Cowan Bridge School (the Lowood School of *Jane Eyre: An Autobiography*, 1847) and to rework her experience as a student in love with her Brussels professor (in *Villette*, 1857). Though less triumphant than Dickens's *David Copperfield*, Brontë's fiction enabled the construction of a self that could survive and even succeed. (This heroic self is reproduced in *The Life of Charlotte Brontë* (1857), where Gaskell credits Brontë with possessing the 'heart of Robert Bruce within her'.[59])

For Victorian novelists the list of autobiographical fiction (in both origin and form) might be expanded significantly: Anne Brontë's experience as a governess in *Agnes Grey* (1847), John Henry Newman's conversion to Roman Catholicism in *Loss and Gain* (1848), Margaret Oliphant's unhappy marriage to a cousin and 'arranged' husband in *The Days of My Life: An Autobiography* (1857), Marian Evans's childhood with her brother, introduced with a scene of self-reflection, in *The Mill on the Floss* (1860), William White Hale's religious crises in the *Autobiography of Mark Rutherford* (1881), and Eliza Lynn Linton's intellectual development and professional career in *The Autobiography of Christopher Kirkland* (1885). As a form, autobiography allows, virtually requires, the creation of a personal myth, an act of self-interpretation, an analysis of the past in light of the present. This myth-making impulse, or hermeneutic imperative, became important generically for Victorian novelists as two key modern forms emerged during the century: the *bildungsroman* and the *kunstlerroman*.

57 John Forster, *The Life of Charles Dickens*, 3 vols. (London: Chapman and Hall, 1872–4), vol. I, p. 53.
58 Robert L. Patten, 'Autobiography into Autobiography: The Evolution of *David Copperfield*', in George P. Landow (ed.), *Approaches to Victorian Autobiography* (Athens: Ohio University Press, 1979), pp. 278, 286.
59 Elizabeth Gaskell, *The Life of Charlotte Brontë*, 2 vols. (London: Smith, Elder, 1857), vol. II, p. 7.

These fictional forms of life-writing developed in tandem with autobiography itself. From the early decades of the nineteenth century, when autobiography appeared as a pleasing if egotistical innovation, to the middle decades, when the form expanded to include ordinary men, women, and workers, to the end of the period, when it seemed as if every writer and artist, politician and public servant, produced a personal memoir – the writing of autobiography became a Victorian expression of the importance of the individual self. It reflected a confidence in the availability of viable modes of self-analysis, whether religious, philosophical, or scientific, and a belief that an individual life, rightly understood, could be instructive to others as well as oneself.

Comic and satirical

JOHN BOWEN

The Victorian period is one rich in comic writing. Indeed, a high proportion of its major literary achievements and much of its most innovative work, from Dickens through Carroll to Wilde, are comic in one form or another. Within that pattern, however, there is a wide range of kinds of writing and significant changes in their nature as the century proceeds. Victorian comic verse is relatively weak in satire but strong in formal invention, deploying parody, pastiche, and grotesque verbal facility in often unsettling ways. The dominant kinds of novel that the Victorians inherited from their major eighteenth- and early nineteenth-century precursors – Fielding, Smollett, Sterne, Burney, and Austen – were essentially comic ones, both in mode and plotting, but novelists found the essentially providential assumptions that had underpinned those authors' comic resolutions increasingly unsustainable as the century went on. Victorian readers were also much less happy than their Augustan and Romantic precursors with satire, whether in prose or verse, and the cruelty and vulgarity that often accompanied it.

The 1820s have with reason been seen as marking something of a 'watershed' in the English comic imagination, separating the frank and bawdy satirical world of Gilray and Rowlandson from the more seemly and genially humorous comic landscape of the Victorians.[1] Bums, farts, and extra-marital sex would have no place in *Punch; or the London Charivari* (1841–2002), the most enduring and significant home of graphic humour in the period. There were, indeed, strongly anti-comic forces in Victorian society – Thomas Carlyle characteristically inscribed the words 'Ernst is das Leben' ('Life is in Earnest') on the title page of his influential *Past and Present* (1843) – and the manly, aristocratic codes of eighteenth-century satire were increasingly marginalized by the forces of respectability and

---

1 Vic Gatrell, *City of Laughter: Sex and Satire in Eighteenth-Century London* (London: Atlantic, 2006), p. 19.

the perceived need to write for a family audience. Many distrusted satire in its most blatant, non-fictional forms and the aggression that underlies it was increasingly repudiated or disavowed as 'humour itself was beginning to be taught good manners'.[2] There was no English political writing of the period to match the satiric transformations wreaked on the French Emperor Louis Napoleon Bonaparte by Karl Marx in *The Eighteenth Brumaire*.[3] The strength of the break, however, should not be overemphasized, for the battle between the forces of solemnity and laughter was neither simple nor short. Victorian domestic virtue (or cant) may have clipped satire's sharper claws and veiled its ruder parts but, as it did so, it created magnificent satirical targets, as such monuments of humbuggery as Dickens's Chadband (in *Bleak House*, 1853) and Pecksniff (in *Martin Chuzzlewit*, 1843–4), Samuel Butler's Theobald Pontifex (in *The Way of All Flesh*, 1903), and the sublime Lady Bracknell in Wilde's *The Importance of Being Earnest* (1895) show.

Indeed, if there is a watershed in Victorian comic writing, it may come after all not in the 1820s or 1830s (for we see much of the vigour of eighteenth-century comedy continuing in such texts as Dickens's *Pickwick Papers* (1837) and Thackeray's *The Luck of Barry Lyndon* (1844)), but the 1850s. There is a sharp, indeed epochal, contrast to be drawn between the major fiction before the mid-century (as represented by the earlier Dickens and Thackeray) and after (in their later work, and that of George Eliot (1819–80), Wilkie Collins (1824–89), George Meredith (1828–1909), George Gissing (1857–1903), and Thomas Hardy (1840–1928)). The second half of the century's fiction is notably darker, more pessimistic, and less funny. The reasons for this complex and uneven pattern of change are many but include, at minimum, the failure of the 1848 revolutions and the consequent divisions of class-based politics and culture, the impact of evolutionary theory, and the loss or crisis of religious faith experienced by many later-nineteenth century writers.[4] In English fiction and theory, George Meredith (1828–1909), author of the most significant theoretical statement on the comedy of the period, 'On the idea of comedy and the uses of the

---

2 *Ibid.*, p. 547.
3 Karl Marx, *The Eighteenth Brumaire of Louis Napoleon Bonaparte*, in *Surveys from Exile: Political Writings Volume Two* (Harmondsworth: Penguin, 1973), pp. 143–250.
4 For different but related arguments about the scale and significance of changes in fictional form at the mid-century, see Georg Lukács, *The Historical Novel* (Harmondsworth: Penguin, 1969) and Elizabeth Deeds Ermarth, *The English Novel in History 1840–1895* (London: Routledge, 1997).

comic spirit' (1877), is in many ways the pivotal figure in his simultaneous sophistication and narrowing of the nature and scope of the comic imagination.[5] This is not to say that comic writing ended at the mid-century. The opposite is true in many ways, for the later decades saw the remarkable and inventive flourishing represented by Lewis Carroll's *Alice* books (1865; 1871), Jerome K. Jerome's (1859–1927) *Three Men in a Boat* (1889), the works of Gilbert and Sullivan, George and Weedon Grossmith's *The Diary of a Nobody* (1892), Samuel Butler's and Max Beerbohm's writings, and the transcendent wit of Oscar Wilde. Much of the best Victorian comic writing is in prose, but it also produced significant comic verse, from the works of Thomas Hood (1799–1845) and Winthrop Mack-reth Praed (1802–39) earlier in the century to W. S. Gilbert's *The 'Bab' Ballads* (1868) and the work of Rudyard Kipling (1865–1936). After the mid-century, the most inventive comic imaginings were created not within the dominant form of the three-decker novel but within what appeared to be minor or marginal modes.

Although verse satire was not a major Victorian form, the radically new cultural and temporal perspectives created by scientific discovery and rapid social change created regular satiric opportunities, as we see in such poems as Dickens's 'The Fine Old English Gentleman' (1841), May Kendall's (1861–1943) 'The Lay of the Trilobite' (1887) and Arthur Hugh Clough's (1819–61) 'The Latest Decalogue' (1862),

> Thou shalt have one God only; who
> Would be at the expense of two?[6]

Radical political satire is best represented by the chartist leader Ernest Jones's (1819–1869) 'Song of the Low' (1859):

> We're low – we're low – we're very very low,
> As low as low can be;
> The rich are high – for we make them so –
> And a miserable lot are we!
> And a miserable lot are we! are we!
> And a miserable lot are we![7]

5 George Meredith, 'An Essay on Comedy', in Wylie Sypher (ed.), *Comedy* (Baltimore: Johns Hopkins University Press, 1980).
6 A. H. Clough, 'The Latest Decalogue', in *Poems*, ed. F. L. Mulhauser (Oxford: Clarendon Press, 1974), p. 205.
7 Ernest Jones, 'The Song of the Low', in *Notes to the People* (London: J. Pavey, 1851), p. 953.

It is Amy Levy's 'The ballad of religion and marriage' (c. 1889, not published until 1915), though, that most effectively captures that 'unique combination of acumen and pathos' that is the distinguishing mark of comic verse of the period:[8]

> Monogamous, still at our post,
> > Reluctantly we undergo
> Domestic round of boiled and roast,
> > Yet deem the whole proceeding slow.
> Daily the secret murmurs grow;
> > We are no more content to plod
> Along the beaten paths – and so
> > Marriage must go the way of God.[9]

The major poets of the mid-century have their occasional comic flourishes, in Alfred Tennyson's (1809–92) 'Northern Farmer: New Style' and 'Hendecasyllabics', Robert Browning's (1812–89) 'Soliloquy of the Spanish Cloister', and, most exquisitely and succinctly, 'Rhyme for a Child Viewing a Naked Venus in a Painting of "The Judgement of Paris"':

> He gazed and gazed and gazed
> Amazed, amazed, amazed, amazed.[10]

Literary genres from tragedy and epic to diary and travel-journal were fertile sources for parody, and the literary comedy of the period is recurrently enriched by a culture constantly irrigated by the performance arts of parody and pastiche. Both Tennyson's and Browning's idioms ripely invite parody, most brilliantly accomplished in C. S. Calverley's (1831–84) 'The Cock and Bull', a version of Browning's 'The Ring and the Book' in clotted, self-conscious splutter:

> You see this pebble-stone? It's a thing I bought
> Of a bit of a chit of a boy i' the mid o' the day –
> I like to dock the smaller parts-o'-speech,
> As we curtail the already cur-tail'd cur
> (You catch the paronomasia, play 'po' words?)
> Did, rather, i' the pre-Landseerian days.[11]

---

8 *The New Oxford Book of Victorian Verse*, p. xxix.

9 Amy Levy, *The Complete Novels and Selected Writings of Amy Levy, 1861–1889*, ed. Melvyn New (Gainesville: University Press of Florida, 1993), p. 405.

10 Robert Browning, *The Poems: vol. II*, ed. John Pettigrew and Thomas J. Collins (Harmondsworth: Penguin, 1981), p. 958.

11 C. S. Calverley, *The Complete Works* (London: George Bell and Sons, 1901), p. 110.

One of Theodore Martin's (1816–1909) *Bon Gaultier Ballads* (1845) grafts Tennyson's voice and manner on to the low-life charmer Dick Swiveller of Dickens's *The Old Curiosity Shop* (1840) to lament his beloved's marriage to another man, by imagining the peculiar horrors of her marital bed:

> Louder than the loudest trumpet, harsh as harshest ophicleide,
> Nasal respirations answer the endearments of the bride.[12]

An 'ophicleide' is a loud brass instrument. Striking at the heart of the earnest doubt of much mid-Victorianism is A. C. Swinburne's (1837–1909) parody of Tennyson's 'The Higher Pantheism' in 'The Higher Pantheism in a Nutshell' (1880):

> Doubt is faith in the main: but faith, on the whole, is doubt:
> We cannot believe by proof: but could we believe without?
>
> . . .
>
> God, whom we see not, is: and God, who is not, we see:
> Fiddle, we know, is diddle: and diddle, we take it is dee.[13]

Much Victorian theorizing about comedy is driven and vexed by three issues: the relation of wit to humour; the nature of different national characters as seen in their comic writing; and the relation of comedy to ethical design or morality. George Eliot's (1819–1880) essay on 'German Wit: Heinrich Heine' is characteristic of the period in its wish to distinguish wit from humour, and to align them with both mental and national characteristics: 'perhaps the nearest approach Nature has given us to a complete analysis, in which wit is as thoroughly exhausted as possible, and humour as bare as possible of wit, is in the typical Frenchman and the typical German'.[14] The significance of such ideas was not particularly their analytic force but the strong distrust of wit that they show, for wit was 'for the mid-Victorians . . . a deeply suspect commodity as tending towards "heartlessness", amorality – even blasphemy'.[15] Although Eliot sees humour as Germanic, it was more common to think of it as a characteristically English middle way between the wit of France and buffoonery of Germany.[16]

---

12 Theodore Martin, 'The Lay of the Lovelorn', in *The Book of Ballads* edited by 'Bon Gaultier' (Edinburgh and London: Blackwood, 1868) p. 105.
13 Algernon Charles Swinburne, *Collected Poetical Works*, 2 vols. (London: William Heinemann, 1924), vol. II, pp. 787–8.
14 George Eliot, 'German Wit: Heinrich Heine', in *Selected Critical Writings*, ed. Rosemary Ashton (Oxford: World's Classics, 1992), p. 196.
15 Michael Slater, *Douglas Jerrold 1803–1857* (London: Duckworth, 2002), p. 224.
16 *Ibid*.

Thomas Carlyle (1795–1881), like Eliot an important channel through which German Romantic theorization of humour entered English intellectual life, argued that humour is:

> properly the exponent of low things; that which first renders them poetical to the mind. The essence of humour is sensibility, warm tender fellow-feeling with all forms of existence. True humour springs no more from the head than from the heart; it is not contempt, its essence is love; it issues not in laughter, but in smiles which lie far deeper. It is a sort of *inverse sublimity*; exalting, as it were, into our affections what is below us, while sublimity draws down into our affections what is above us.[17]

They are seminal remarks. Although Carlyle himself could be a satirist of great force and invention, most notably in *Sartor Resartus* (1833), he, like his contemporaries such as Dickens, saw humour as having a higher calling, because of the essentially ethical nature of the pleasure that it gives, its necessary link to human sympathy and thus to forms of insight both beyond and superior to those of mere reason.

Although it began serial publication before Victoria became Queen, Dickens's *Pickwick Papers* (1836–7) properly begins the history of Victorian comic writing. *Pickwick* does not simply enact the transformation of a brilliantly talented journalist and sketch writer into the defining novelist of his era, it also marks a key moment in the hegemony of prose fiction over poetry within English literature, of verbal over visual comedy, and – in the increasingly sympathetic treatment of its main character – of the humorous over the satirical. Dickens was originally required simply to provide the letterpress to accompany the illustrations of Robert Seymour (1798–1836) but, following the latter's suicide, he transformed the entire nature of the project and in consequence the trajectory of the English novel. Dickens had already changed the publishers' original plan of a tale of Cockney sportsmen, a popular sub-genre of the period, best represented by Robert Smith Surtees's (1803–64) ebullient *Jorrocks' Jaunts and Jollities* (1838). Determining 'to take my own way, with a freer range of English scenes and people',[18] Dickens shaped an essentially episodic or magazine-like form into something that had the breadth and scale of what his great predecessor Henry Fielding

---

17 Thomas Carlyle, 'Jean Paul Friedrich Richter', in *Critical and Miscellaneous Essays Volume One* (London: Chapman and Hall, 1872), p. 17 (emphasis added).
18 Charles Dickens, 'Preface to the Charles Dickens edition 1867', in *The Pickwick Papers*, ed. Mark Wormald (Harmondsworth: Penguin, 1999), p. 763.

(1707–54) called 'a comic epic-poem in prose'.[19] The early serial instalments of the novel were not a great success and it was only with the introduction of Sam Weller, Mr Pickwick's servant, that it took wing, both aesthetically and commercially. Class difference is a central part of the Victorian comic imaginary but the witty, ebullient, and streetwise Weller is at the end, rather than the beginning, of a tradition, the last major comic servant in English writing until P. G. Wodehouse's Jeeves, nearly a century later. There are, of course, many important servant scenes in nineteenth-century novels and in the magnificent lambasting of Mr Dombey by Susan Nipper ('I may not be Meethosalem, but I am not a child in arms') in *Dombey and Son* (1848) lies some of its best and most moving comedy, but it says much about Victorian class relations that, after Pickwick and Weller, neither Dickens nor his rivals and successors were able to create a master and servant couple of such resonant, exemplary force.[20]

Pickwick, for all its eminence, does not stand alone in the comic annals of the 1830s and 1840s. Frances Trollope (1779–1863), now unfairly better known as the mother of Anthony Trollope (1815–82) than as a novelist in her own right, was the author not just of the highly influential and often comic *Manners and Customs of the Americans* (1832), but also the *Widow Barnaby* series of novels (*The Widow Barnaby* (1839), *The Widow Married* (1840), and *The Barnabys in America* (1843)), that chart the adventures of her social-climbing heroine, narrated with a frankness and energy akin to that of Frances Burney's fiction of earlier in the century. Equally vulgar and busy are Surtees's hunting novels, from *Jorrocks' Jaunts and Jollities* (1838) and *Handley Cross* (1843) to *Mr Facey's Romford Hounds* (1865), which have a prime place within nineteenth-century sporting fiction, an important sub-genre of the period. Indeed when the predecessor to this volume was published in 1911, the equivalent chapter to this one was entitled 'Caricature and the Literature of Sport. Punch.'[21] Surtees is one of sporting literature's more attractive practitioners, who uses the freedom given by monthly publication to generate as many social and sporting scrapes for his hero as possible in a world pushy for wealth, good society, and pleasure. Like Frances Trollope, Surtees draws a highly mobile society, in which country, city, and spa town

---

19 Charles Dickens, 'Preface to the Cheap Edition, 1847', in *The Pickwick Papers*, p. 761. Henry Fielding, *Joseph Andrews* (1742; Harmondsworth: Penguin, 1977), 'Preface', p. 25.
20 Charles Dickens, *Dombey and Son* (Oxford: Clarendon Press, 1974), chapter 44, p. 588.
21 'Caricature and the Literature of Sport. Punch.', chapter 6 of A. W. Ward and A. R. Waller (eds.), *The Cambridge History of English and American Literature: Volume XIV. The Victorian Age*, Part Two, (Cambridge University Press, 1907), pp. 212–39.

alike create endless opportunities for clever (or not-so-clever) performances of the self. The Widow Barnaby is the relict of a provincial draper who passes herself off as something much grander, Soapey Sponge (in *Mr Sponge's Sporting Tour*, 1853), by good horsemanship, attention to dress, and barefaced cheek shows, as Thackeray famously puts it in *Vanity Fair* (1847–8), 'How to live well on nothing a year'.[22] Each hunt for Soapey is a deeply theatrical performance, requiring the correct costume, jargon, and physical dexterity. When things go right, the ten-pound horse is sold for three hundred guineas; when they go wrong, the hired brave hunter turns out to be a nag with a filthy temper and Soapey is pitched through a milliner's plate-glass window. The pleasures and pains of fox-hunting (particularly in the work of Anthony Trollope (1815–82), himself a keen huntsman and author of no fewer than seventeen different hunting scenes in his fiction) remain a staple of Victorian comic fiction, a dramatic, largely masculine world that defines itself against urban sophistication, industry, and display and yet is constantly infiltrated and threatened by them.

The episodic nature of such novels succours mobile, self-inventive prot-agonists, whose social being is essentially performative. Dickens's *Nicholas Nickleby* (1838–9) is probably the richest and most ambivalent exploration of this world, in which almost all social relations are theatrical and self-advertising in nature, a constant provocation to improvised self-reinvention.[23] The provincial theatre scenes, when Nicholas joins Vincent Crummles's touring theatre company, are among the great set-pieces of English comic writing, not least when Nicholas leaves the company and Crummles makes his final bow. They capture well Dickens's and the Victorians' ambivalent embrace of (and by) the performing self:

> As they hurried up to the coach, which was now in the open street and all ready for starting, Nicholas was not a little astonished to find himself suddenly clutched in a close and violent embrace, which nearly took him off his legs; nor was his amazement at all lessened by hearing the voice of Mr Crummles exclaim, 'It is he – my friend, my friend! . . . Farewell, my noble, my lion-hearted boy!'
>
> In fact, Mr Crummles, who could never lose any opportunity for professional display, had turned out for the express purpose of taking a public farewell of Nicholas; and to render it the more imposing, he was now, to

22 William Makepeace Thackeray, *Vanity Fair: a Novel without a Hero* (Harmondsworth: Penguin, 1968), chapter 36, p. 426.

23 See John Bowen, 'Performing Business, Training Ghosts', in *Other Dickens: Pickwick to Chuzzlewit* (Oxford University Press, 2000), pp. 107–31.

that young gentleman's most profound annoyance, inflicting upon him a rapid succession of stage embraces, which, as everybody knows, are performed by the embracer's laying his or her chin on the shoulder of the object of affection, and looking over it. This Mr Crummles did in the highest style of melodrama, pouring forth at the same time all the most dismal forms of farewell he could think of, out of the stock pieces.[24]

Dickens also made some significant contributions to thinking about comedy, most notably in an important self-justifying passage in *Oliver Twist* (1837–8). The need to make a rapid transition between scenes in that novel brings out an important declaration of method: Dickens compares his own work to stage melodrama, in which the tragic and comic scenes are presented 'in as regular alternation as the layers of red and white in a side of streaky bacon':

> We behold, with throbbing bosoms, the heroine in the grasp of a proud and ruthless baron; drawing forth her dagger to preserve the one at the cost of the other; and just as our expectations are wrought up to the highest pitch, a whistle is heard, and we are straightway transported to the great hall of the castle; where a grey-headed seneschal sings a funny chorus with a funnier body of vassals.[25]

It is a moment of bathos – 'absurd', says Dickens – but such changes, he continues, 'are not so unnatural as they would seem at first sight. The transitions in real life from well-spread boards to death-beds, and from mourning weeds to holiday garments, are not a whit less startling.' As Dickens sharpens the contrast between terror and humour, he also points to their deep affinity. They are both, he writes, 'abrupt impulses of passion or feeling', immediate and emotive experiences, which seem to fill the mind to the exclusion of all else.[26] The realist claim that the passage makes is equally significant: comedy is necessary because mixed modes are life-like. We cannot preserve the integrity of genres in our lives, which are necessarily profoundly mixed experiences, and so should not try to do so in fiction. Vulgar and popular literary forms, despite their apparent surface absurdity, are for Dickens more truthful to the world than more unified and elevated ones, and this is consistently reflected in his writing. Even in his least funny novel, *A Tale of Two Cities* (1859), it is necessary to the structure and form of the work that Sydney Carton's sublime self-sacrifice should be anticipated

24 Charles Dickens, *Nicholas Nickleby* (Harmondsworth: Penguin, 1999), chapter 30, p. 381.
25 Charles Dickens, *Oliver Twist* (Oxford: World's Classics, 1982), chapter 17, p. 102.
26 *Ibid.*

and accompanied by a parallel conversion of the ineffably 'low' Jerry Cruncher, grave-robber and resurrection-man, who finally succumbs to his wife's prayers (or, as he calls it, 'flopping') and reforms.

Oliver Twist was illustrated, as was the earlier *Sketches by Boz* (1836) by George Cruikshank (1792–1878), the finest graphic satirist of the age and great inheritor of the eighteenth-century satirical tradition. His long career demonstrates both strong continuity with Regency satire and its transformation into a less bawdy but more psychologically intense art.[27] Dickens is characteristically Victorian in his eschewing of the comedy of the lower bodily stratum, the shitting, pissing, and illicit sex that are integral to the tradition of Menippean satire and the work of his eighteenth-century and Romantic forebears, such as Tobias Smollett (1721–71) and Laurence Sterne (1713–68). But, like Thomas Love Peacock (1785–1866) (who after nearly a quarter of a century of fictional silence, produced the remarkable satiric and comic novel of ideas, *Gryll Grange* in 1860), Dickens is still fascinated by bodily processes, particularly eating and drinking. In *Bleak House* (1853), Mr Chadband, 'a large yellow man with a fat smile and a general appearance of having a good deal of train oil in his system' is, like so many of Dickens's great hypocrites, also very greedy:

> in beginning to eat and drink, he may be described as always becoming a kind of considerable Oil Mills or other large factory for the production of that article on a wholesale scale. On the present evening of the long vacation, in Cook's Court, Cursitor Street, he does such a powerful stroke of business that the warehouse appears to be quite full when the works cease.[28]

Here, Victorian propriety incites in Dickens a brilliantly creative metaphor: the food that Chadband ingests turns not into shit but oil, with which he greases the world around him, buttering up his victims, exuding an unctuous, refined excretion.[29]

Victorian comic verse often got a bad press in the twentieth century. For Philip Larkin, 'the facetious Victorian waggery ... the whimsical Elia stuff about your old pipe and your old college and "the ladies", the mock-heroic odes to collar studs and versified Pooterisms about the "funny side of

---

27 Robert L. Patten, *George Cruikshank: His Life, Times and Art*, 2 vols. (Cambridge: Lutterworth, 1992 and 1996).
28 Charles Dickens, *Bleak House* (Harmondsworth: Penguin, 1996), chapter 19, pp. 304–5.
29 On Chadband, see Steven Connor, *The Book of Skin* (Ithaca, NY: Cornell University Press, 2004), pp. 207–8.

life" ' was simply contemptible.[30] It is true that, in contrast to the 'satire boom' of the Romantic period, Victorian readers were much less comfortable with the kind of overt social and political aggression that marks, say, Byron's work or Shelley's 'The Mask of Anarchy'.[31] But Thomas Hood (1799–1845) displays in verse many of the same energies that animated his friend Dickens's earlier work. Just as *The Old Curiosity Shop* (1840–1) reclaims a near-Baroque capacity to sport with death, so Hood enlists himself in a disconcertingly witty jousting with mutilation, mortality, and prosthesis. His best poem, 'Miss Kilmansegg and her Precious Leg' (1840–1) is in one way a satire on wealth, but its gleeful linguistic energy takes it into much stranger psychic spaces:

> A Leg of Gold – solid gold throughout,
> Nothing else, whether slim or stout,
> Should ever support her, God willing!
> She must – she could – she would have her whim,
> Her father, she turn'd a deaf ear to him –
> He might kill her – she didn't mind killing!
> He was welcome to cut off her other limb –
> He might cut her all off with a shilling![32]

There is a ghastly, hilarious energy in Hood's punning, which seems to insert death's heads into the process of signification in an almost allegorical way. It has been argued that from the 1820s, the pun was dissociated from 'the truth-telling of satire' and that Hood's verse – and Victorian punning more generally – was essentially trivial because it 'uses puns to back away from the echoes and implications of words, to distract your attention by insisting on his ingenuity, so that you can escape from sinking into the meaning'.[33] But, as William Empson, who made the latter charge, also recognized, Hood's lyricism is also 'strong' and 'brave', a vision of both

---

30 Philip Larkin, *Further Requirements: Interviews, Broadcasts, Statements and Book Reviews 1952–1985*, ed. Anthony Thwaite (London: Faber and Faber, 2001), p. 292.

31 On romantic satire, see John Strachan (ed.), *British Satire 1785–1840*, 4 vols. (London: Pickering and Chatto, 2003), Gary Dyer, *British Satire and the Politics of Style 1789–1832* (Cambridge University Press, 1997), and Geoffrey Grigson (ed.), *The Oxford Book of Satirical Verse* (Oxford University Press, 1980).

32 Thomas Hood, 'Miss Kilmansegg and her Precious Leg', in *The Works*, ed. Thomas Hood, Junior and Frances Freeling Broderip, 11 vols. (London: Ward, Lock, 1882–4), vol. VII, p. 394.

33 Gatrell, *City of Laughter*, p. 429; William Empson, *Seven Types of Ambiguity* (1930; Harmondsworth: Penguin, 1972), p. 137.

war and the pursuit of wealth as essentially mutilatory activities, in which our vulnerable, hilarious human bodies pun themselves to death.[34]

One of Hood's most moving and radical poems, 'The Song of the Shirt', appeared, perhaps surprisingly to modern readers, in the Christmas 1842 number of *Punch*. It was by some distance the most important comic journal of the period, ensuring the consolidation of more domestically oriented graphic satire and humour, while providing a major outlet both for Thackeray and the unfairly neglected Douglas Jerrold (1803–57). Thackeray described Jerrold as 'the only rival whom he feared',[35] although his work, with one or two exceptions, has not fared nearly so well with later readers. But in his greatest prose success – the comic monologues *Mrs Caudle's Curtain Lectures* (1845) – he achieved something funny, strange, and lasting. A man and woman lie in bed late at night, as she takes her silent partner to task for coming back late, for bringing home friends, or for lending five pounds. Behind the unvarying scenario lies a characteristic-ally Jerroldian (and sexist) set of assumptions: beyond the home lies the happy, innocent, world of male sociability. These monologues were an ideal form for Jerrold, keeping him close to popular speech, curbing his wordiness, controlling and ironizing his aggression. They resemble, as Michael Slater points out, Browning's dramatic monologues but, in their unsettling intimacy and fascination with the humdrum dislocations of little suburban lives, they also achieve something distinctive and new, and pave the way for the later comedy of Jerome K. Jerome and the Grossmiths' *Diary of a Nobody*.[36] Besides *Mrs Caudle*, many minor classics of nineteenth-century humour (Gilbert à Beckett's (1811–56) *Comic History of England* (1847), Thackeray's *Punch's Prize Novelists* (1847), and, above all, the Grossmiths' *The Diary of a Nobody* (1888–9)), appeared first in *Punch*'s pages. But *Punch* was only one of many comic and humorous publications of the period, preceded by *Figaro in London* (1831–9) and many comic annuals, most notably Hood's *Comic Annual* (1830–9) and George Cruikshank's long-lasting *Comic Almanac* (1835–53), and accompanied by *Judy; or the London Serio-Comic Journal* (1867–1907), *Fun* (1861–1901), in which W. S. Gilbert published his 'Bab' Ballads, *The Tomahawk* (1867–70), and *Moonshine* (1879–1902). *Punch*'s success rested on its address to a family audience and comparatively genial

---

34 Empson, *Seven Types*, pp. 136–7.
35 Recorded by Douglas Jerrold's grandson, Walter Jerrold, *Douglas Jerrold and 'Punch'* (London: Macmillan and Co., 1910), p. 27.
36 Slater, *Douglas Jerrold*, p. 215.

tone, which became more marked after the death of Jerrold, its radical and satiric conscience. Its geniality and radicalism had its limits, however, as can be seen in its recurrent anti-Catholicism and 'schizophrenic racism as regards the Irish'.[37]

It is Thackeray, however, who has proved the most important and enduring of the *Punch* writers and the major satiric counter-example to Dickens. His fiction, like his earlier journalism in such series as *The Snobs of England* (1846–7), creates worlds of unfulfilled and futile desires, desires often simply for what others desire. As his masterpiece *Vanity Fair: A Novel without a Hero* (1848) concludes: 'Which of us is happy in this world? Which of us has our desire? Or, having it, is satisfied?'[38] In contrast to Dickens's broadly affirmative comic vision, Thackeray's is marked by a characteristically negative irony, what he himself called a 'cut-throat melancholy'.[39] Thackeray's work, at its strongest in *Vanity Fair*, allies a brilliantly inventive wit to a deeply discomforting and disillusioned satiric vision that in its closeness to nihilism often seems deeply at odds with the society in which he wrote. Snobbery, that 'mean desire for what is mean', is at the centre of modern life and conduct for Thackeray, a force that 'rules, and often ruins, the lives of those who concentrate all their energies on admiration and imitation'.[40] The sense of elation that comes from Thackeray's writing stems from the lifting of inhibition – both of the reader and the novel's characters – that follows his willingness to create characters held back by no internal or external restraint. He described them as 'a set of people living without God in the world' but then added, in a characteristically self-cancelling way '(only that is a cant phrase)'.[41] The plots of the earlier novels are driven by the roistering ambition of Barry Lyndon and the mould-breaking transgressions of Becky Sharp but their freedom exposes and mortifies both them and the worlds in which they flourish: Barry is a rapist, Becky in all probability a murderer. It is a satiric aesthetic and novelistic practice that simultaneously looks back to eighteenth-century precursors such as Fielding and Jonathan Swift and forward to Oscar Wilde and Evelyn Waugh: 'pathos', writes Thackeray, 'should be very occasional

---

37 *Ibid.*   38 Thackeray, *Vanity Fair*, chapter 67, p. 797.
39 William Makepeace Thackeray, *Letters and Private Papers*, ed. Gordon N. Ray 4 vols. (London: Oxford University Press, 1945–6), vol. III, p. 91.
40 Catherine Peters, *Thackeray: A Writer's Life* (Stroud: Sutton, 1999), p. 128.
41 Thackeray, *Letters and Private Papers*, vol. II, p. 309.

in humorous writing and indicated rather than expressed or expressed very rarely'.[42] Nowhere is the ambivalence of the Victorians' relation to their comic forbears better seen than in Thackeray's work, both in his lectures *The English Humourists of the Eighteenth Century* (1853) and his fiction, which repeatedly returns to the more uninhibited subject matter and moral codes of the eighteenth century, entranced by its satiric and erotic energy and his own melancholy, insuperable distance from it. Thackeray's novels are saturated by the seemingly infinite possibilities of a world of commodification, in which all people and things can be bought and sold for money. Yet loss and emptiness of every sort – death and bankruptcy most spectacularly – are the perpetual partners of this elation, losses from which neither reader nor author can remain immune: 'I want to leave everybody dissatisfied and unhappy at the end of the story – we ought all to be with our own and all other stories.'[43]

After the mid-century, comedy retains its force as a mode but the movement to the comic resolution of plots – in the classic forms of marriage, inheritance, social integration, and good fortune – becomes increasingly hard to sustain, resting as it does on faith-based, providential underpinnings. Comedy in fiction becomes more localized and endings become increasingly mixed or dark, as fiction gains a stronger sense of moral purpose and the claims of realism temper its wish-fulfilling impulses. Dickens's *Dombey and Son* (1848), for example, ends with a spectacular five weddings; his *Little Dorrit* (1857), a solitary one. Even Thackeray, so brilliantly and maturely disillusioned in his earlier work, compared himself to a clergyman, seeing 'his role as a writer as correlative with "the parson's own", much as George Eliot was to see serious fiction as a secular substitute for religion'.[44] Nevertheless, the 1840s and 1850s are one of the great periods of fictional expansion and literary achievement, and the incompatibility between the new modes of social and subjective experience and inherited frameworks of knowledge or belief can lead to superb comic undercuttings, as in the clash between Lockwood's genteelly Austenian assumptions about women and families and the very different domestic economy he encounters at Wuthering Heights: '"Ah, your favourites are among these!" I continued, turning to an obscure cushion full of something like cats. "A strange choice of favourites!" she observed scornfully. Unluckily, it was a heap of dead rabbits.'[45] Charlotte Brontë's *Villette*, in a way that seems to

42 *Ibid.*, p. 424.   43 *Ibid.*, p. 423.   44 Peters, *Thackeray: A Writer's Life*, p. 144.
45 Emily Brontë, *Wuthering Heights* (Harmondsworth: Penguin, 1965), chapter 2, p. 52.

intensify rather than diminish its emotional power, also contains what one can only call a kind of unacknowledged clowning:

> In my reverie, methought I saw the continent of Europe, like a wide dreamland, far away. Sunshine lay on it, making the long coast one line of gold; tiniest tracery of clustered town and snow-gleaming tower, of woods deep-massed, of heights serrated, of smooth pasturage and veiny stream, embossed the metal-bright prospect. For background, spread a sky, solemn and dark-blue, and – grand with imperial promise, soft with tints of enchantment – strode from north to south a God-bent bow, an arch of hope.
>
> Cancel the whole of that, if you please, reader – or rather, let it stand, and draw thence a moral – an alliterative text-hand copy –
>
> Day-dreams are delusions of the demon.
>
> Becoming excessively sick, I faltered down into the cabin.[46]

The novel's ability to play off the human will to idealize against the vulnerability and limitations of the physical body is a sign of its ability to master and subvert the modes and material of more dignified or idealizing genres. It becomes one of the century's richest sources of comedy, supremely so in Jerome K. Jerome's (1859–1927) *Three Men in a Boat* (1889).

There is a good deal of irony in George Eliot's (1819–80) fiction, particularly when she draws on childhood memory in the earlier scenes of *The Mill on the Floss* (1860), but comedy is too monopathic a response for Eliot and is usually embedded within acts of ethical sympathy. Casaubon, the old scholarly bat of *Middlemarch* (1872), has great comic potential, as when, on becoming engaged to the much younger Dorothea, he

> determined to abandon himself to the stream of feeling, and perhaps was surprised to find what an exceedingly shallow rill it was. As in droughty regions baptism by immersion could only be performed symbolically, so Mr Casaubon found that sprinkling was the utmost approach to a plunge which his stream would afford him; and he concluded that poets had much exaggerated the masculine passion.[47]

More often Eliot's undoubted comic gifts are subordinated to a moral imperative of sympathetic engagement that forestalls a fully comic response and embraces even a Casaubon: 'For my part I am very sorry for him. It is an uneasy lot at best, to be what we call highly taught and yet not to

---

46 Charlotte Brontë, *Villette* (Harmondsworth: Penguin, 1979), chapter 6, pp. 117–18.
47 George Eliot, *Middlemarch* (Harmondsworth: Penguin, 1994), chapter 7, p. 63.

enjoy . . .'[48] Eliot ends her career with the darkly satirical *Impressions of Theophrastus Such* (1879) but it is Elizabeth Gaskell (1810–65) who writes the most significant comic fiction of the mid-century in the brilliant linked tales that form *Cranford* (1853), which together tell the story of a provincial domestic world 'in possession of the Amazons'.[49] One of the best-loved, if most uncharacteristic, mid-Victorian fictions, *Cranford* is a memory piece for the most part, with much of its significant action set in the past, its narration closer to the free-wheeling anecdotes and ironies of family letter-writing than the grander structures of the typical Victorian three-decker. Free from the effort of plot, *Cranford* wins its effects through the consciously small scale of its actions and the pathos of the lives it conjures up. The subtlety and equanimity of its comic tone makes *Cranford* a very distinctive and pleasurable reading experience, its reflective irony able to smile even in the face of insuperable loss.

It is Anthony Trollope (1815–82) who provides the most substantial continuation of comic plotting and creates the most successful body of comic fiction after the mid-century, most notably in the Barsetshire novels (1855–67). James Kincaid has said that 'One could easily illustrate a textbook on comedy using nothing but the novels of Anthony Trollope, so widely does he range over various forms and techniques.'[50] The comic modes displayed in his forty-seven novels are remarkably varied and include some suggestive, if unsatisfactory, satire in *The New Zealander* (1855–6 but unpublished until 1972) and *The Fixed Period* (1882), his late novel set one hundred years ahead in the fictional island of Britannula. But it is in his contemporary realist social comedies, or comedies of manners, particularly the five Barsetshire novels – *The Warden* (1855), *Barchester Towers* (1857), *Dr Thorne* (1858), *Framley Parsonage* (1861), *The Small House at Allington* (1864) and *The Last Chronicle of Barset* (1867) – that Trollope's comic vision is most assured. The tension between his realist impulses and satirical self-consciousness fuels these dextrously deflationary fictions and in Mrs Proudie and Dr Slope creates two of the great comic monsters of the century. Whereas these works are close to Victorian norms in their ideological allegiances and quotidian realism, the period also saw the production of some remarkably anti-normative writing in Edward Lear's (1812–88) *A Book of Nonsense*

---

48 *Ibid.*, chapter 29, p. 280.
49 Elizabeth Gaskell, *Cranford* (Oxford: World's Classics, 1998), chapter 1, p. 1.
50 James Kincaid, 'Comedy in Trollope's Works', in R.C. Terry (ed.), *Oxford Reader's Companion to Trollope* (Oxford University Press, 1999), p. 111.

(1846) and *The Owl and the Pussycat* and Lewis Carroll's (1832–98) *Alice in Wonderland* (1865), *Through the Looking Glass* (1872), and 'The Hunting of the Snark' (1876). Carroll was both a fertile source of parody for later writers and a brilliant parodist himself, of Isaac Watts ('How doth the shining crocodile') and Wordsworth ('You are old Father William') in the *Alice* books and, at greater length, of Longfellow's *Hiawatha* in 'Hiawatha's photographing':

> First the Governor, the Father:
> He suggested velvet curtains
> Looped about a massy pillar;
> And the corner of a table,
> Of a rosewood dining-table.
> He would hold a scroll of something,
> Hold it firmly in his left-hand;
> He would keep his right-hand buried
> (Like Napoleon) in his waistcoat;
> He would contemplate the distance
> With a look of pensive meaning,
> As of ducks that die in tempests.
>
> Grand, heroic was the notion:
> Yet the picture failed entirely:
> Failed, because he moved a little,
> Moved, because he couldn't help it.[51]

Parody, like almost everything else that the *Alice* books lay their hands on, from evolutionary theory to mock turtle soup, is set to work in formally inventive ways, fuelling the curious affective dissonance of these works, repeatedly invoking a psychological depth that can never be attained. Reading these books of quarrelling and tetchy pedantry can be a disturbing experience, which lifts the reader into surreal, uncharted realms of verbal and semantic creativity and inversion. Fascinated by the rule-making and rule-breaking that underpin social, bodily, and linguistic life, Carroll creates 'two of the most original, experimental works of literary fiction in the nineteenth-century', and some of the most perversely comic explorations of the constraints and liberations from which they are made.[52]

George Meredith (1828–1909) in some ways resembles his father-in-law Thomas Love Peacock in his distinctively intellectual and satirical

---

51 Lewis Carroll, *Works*, ed. R.L. Green, (London: Hamlyn, 1965), p. 783.
52 Lewis Carroll, *Alice in Wonderland and Through the Looking Glass* (Harmondsworth: Penguin, 1998), p. xii.

conception of comedy. He is the most self-conscious and distinctive of nineteenth-century comedians, with a coherent theory of comedy and a set of complex fictional explorations of it. Distinguishing comedy from both satire and humour, Meredith often works to confound our expectations, divorcing the comic, for example, both from bodily experience and from laughter. For him, comedy is an essentially intellectual affair, built around the vagaries of human desire, in societies in which women have certain kinds of formal equality and freedom but lack true equality. In class terms, Meredith's is a drastically reduced idea of the comic, which for him can only fully be at play among the leisured few: 'the laughter of comedy is impersonal and of unrivalled politeness, nearer a smile – often no more than a smile'.[53] His own comic vision is seen at its best in *The Egoist: A Comedy in Narrative* (1879), which immediately follows the *Essay on Comedy* and in some ways revises its essential terms.[54] In his fascination with the impermeability of self to other, most sharply seen in the very different perceptions of two people who think themselves in love, his comedy is one deeply allied to shame and humiliation. Indeed, for Meredith comedy is very close to masochism, a way of gaining pleasure from the infliction or receiving of pain.

Where Meredith takes the high road to comic invention, the two great classics of English comic writing of this period, Jerome K. Jerome's (1859–1927) *Three Men in a Boat (to say nothing of the dog)* (1889) and George (1847–1912) and Weedon (1854–1919) Grossmiths' *The Diary of a Nobody* (1894) took the low. Jerome, unlike the Grossmiths, did not come out of the *Punch* stable, which consistently guyed him as the vulgar comedian "'Arry K. 'Arry'. His work, now often seen as archetypal English comedy, was thought to be that of a 'new humourist', full of 'colloquialisms, slang and vulgarity', tainted by vulgar American influence.[55] But the book's fame is entirely deserved. The journey up the Thames becomes idyllic precisely through its lack of idyll (rain, collapsing tents, things and people falling in the river, terrible food, lack of sleep, idleness, quarrelsomeness, exhaustion). The material of modern life – both its objects and psychic states (hypochondria, depression, anomie, greed, and work-avoidance) – is constantly contrasted with another, impossibly ideal, life of sea-bathing, romanticism, and healthy

53 Meredith, 'An Essay on Comedy', p. 47.
54 See Gillian Beer, 'Meredith's Idea of Comedy: 1876–1880', *Nineteenth-Century Fiction* 20:2 (1965), pp. 165–76.
55 Jerome K. Jerome, *Three Men in a Boat and Three Men on the Bummel* (Oxford University Press, 1998), p. xix.

outdoor pursuits. Playing on the absurd power of objects, commodities and things to trip people up, the book constantly holds out the prospect of an appropriate and happy relationship between the human and the material world and repeatedly finds the impossibility of ever achieving it. Like much Victorian humour, Jerome's is a deeply homosocial world, of men getting away from women, a state the texts both satirize and endorse, but there is also a tender lyric and Romantic impulse in his work: one that is often sent up, but sometimes surprisingly affirmed.

Victorian comedy often concerns clerks and office-boys, from Dickens onwards. The Grossmith brothers' *The Diary of a Nobody* brilliantly captures the comic banality of a suburban clerk's life and in the comic diary format creates an important and still-vigorous comic sub-genre. Much of the pleasure of *Diary* is its guying of the more banal end of Victorian waggery in Pooter's execrable puns: 'Carrie brought down some of my shirts . . . She said: "The fronts and cuffs are much frayed." I said without a moment's hesitation "I'm 'FRAYED they are." Lor! how we roared. I thought we should never stop laughing.' But it is a prickly, harassed little world at Brickfield Terrace:

> August 20. I am glad our last day at the seaside was fine, though clouded overhead. We went over to Cummings' (at Margate) in the evening, and as it was cold, we stayed in and played games; Gowing, as usual, overstepping the mark. He suggested we should play 'cutlets', a game we never heard of. He sat on a chair, and asked Carrie to sit on his lap, an invitation which dear Carrie rightly declined.
>
> After some species of wrangling, *I* sat on Gowing's knees and Carrie sat on the edge of mine. Lupin sat on the edge of Carrie's lap, then Cummings on Lupin's and Mrs Cummings on her husband's. We looked very ridiculous, and laughed a good deal.
>
> Gowing then said: 'Are you a believer in the Great Mogul?' We had to answer all together: 'Yes – oh, yes!' (three times). Gowing said: 'So am I,' and suddenly got up. The result of this stupid joke was that we all fell on the ground and poor Carrie banged her head against the corner of the fender. Mrs Cummings put some vinegar on; but through this we missed the last train, and had to drive back to Broadstairs, which cost me seven-and-sixpence.[56]

George Grossmith was for many years a leading performer with the Savoy Operas, playing many roles in the comic operas of W. S. Gilbert

---

56 George and Weedon Grossmith, *The Diary of a Nobody* (Oxford University Press, 1998), pp. 33, 103.

(1836–1911) and Arthur Sullivan (1842–1900). Gilbert had a long and productive career, first as a satirist in verse and prose, making a name for himself with *The 'Bab' Ballads* (1869) which first appeared in *Fun*, as did the germ of *Trial by Jury* (1875), his first collaboration with the composer Sullivan. To these works, Gilbert brought the skills of a theatre critic, a fluently inventive writer of light verse and parodies, and long experience of both serious and comic drama, to create some of the most enduring successes of nineteenth-century theatre. As in the *Alice* books, there is a fascination with the ways in which the power of the law and social convention is built on institutions and structures – legal, social, linguistic – that are inherently absurd and nonsensical. The threat of death, however ironized, is never far away in Gilbert's best work, as when the jailer and torturer Wilfrid Shadbolt in *The Yeomen of the Guard* tries to persuade the jester Jack Point to teach him his craft:

> POINT. (*bitterly*) I am a salaried wit; and is there aught in nature more ridiculous? A poor, dull, heart-broken man, who must needs be merry, or he will be whipped; who must rejoice, lest he starve; who must jest you, jibe you, quip you, crank you, wrack you, riddle you, from hour to hour, from day to day, from year to year, lest he dwindle, perish, starve, pine, and die! Why, when there's naught else to laugh at, I laugh at myself till I ache for it!
>
> WILFRED. Yet I have often thought that a jester's calling would suit me to a hair.
>
> POINT. Thee? Would suit *thee*, thou death's head and cross-bones?
>
> WILFRED. Aye, I have a pretty wit – a light, airy, joysome wit, spiced with anecdotes of prison cells and the torture chamber. Oh, a very delicate wit! I have tried it on many a prisoner, and there have been some who smiled. Now it is not easy to make a prisoner smile.[57]

It is a comic inversion (Gilbert loved to turn worlds upside-down) but one invested with a Hood-like poignancy; the opera ends with the lovers, Fairfax and Elsie, joyfully united but with the jilted jester Point, having sung his 'song of a merryman, moping mum', falling insensible at their feet.[58]

Samuel Butler (1835–1902) wrote two of the most original and strange fictions of the period. *Erewhon* (1870) is a satire, with flashes of brilliant invention such as the 'Hospital for Incurable Bores', but it is *The Way of All*

---

57 W. S. Gilbert and Arthur Sullivan, *The Yeomen of the Guard*, in *The Complete Annotated Gilbert and Sullivan*, ed. Ian Bradley (Oxford University Press, 2001), p. 815.

58 *Ibid.*, p. 857.

Flesh (written in the 1870s and 1880s but only published posthumously in 1902) in which Butler is at his most disturbing and hilarious, creating the only serious rival to *Vanity Fair* as the greatest satirical novel of the century. *The Way of All Flesh* has rightly been described as 'a devastating denunciation of the Victorian family' but even that is too limiting a description, for the story begins in the 1750s and the roots of the insufferable childhood that Ernest Pontifex undergoes lie in his grandfather's pre-Victorian Evangelical hypocrisy.[59] There is a clarity and glee in Butler's dissection of moral ideals and a courageous inversion of much Victorian wishful thinking, exemplified by the recurrent malice that parents show towards their children in the book. Satire often leans to an abstraction from the density of human life but Butler successfully marries satiric aggression to novelistic particularity, ensuring an intimacy and psychological acuteness to the writing that give it a wide reach.

The Way of All Flesh's realism and density of motive make one think of the fiction of Gustave Flaubert (1821–80) but its narrative voice also has the confidence to address its reader directly, to sometimes devastating effect:

> O schoolmasters – if any of you read this book – bear in mind when any particularly timid drivelling urchin is brought by his papa into your study, and you treat him with the contempt which he deserves, and afterwards make his life a burden to him for years – bear in mind that it is exactly in the disguise of such a boy as this that your future chronicler will appear. Never see a wretched little heavy-eyed mite sitting on the edge of a chair against your study wall without saying to yourselves, 'perhaps this boy is he who, if I am not careful, will one day tell the world what manner of man I was.' If even two or three schoolmasters learn this lesson and remember it, the preceding chapters will not have been written in vain.[60]

There is a rare example of a 'New Woman' author using an essentially comic form in Ella Hepworth Dixon's (1857–1932) *My Flirtations* (1892). However, the greatest explorer of the comedy of sexual identity of the *fin-de-siècle* is Oscar Wilde (1854–1900). His work, in its wit, lack of earnestness, and fascination with sexual and social transgression, encapsulates how much Victorian comic writing had changed over the course of the century and is the culmination of the changes of the preceding three decades. Like Meredith (whose style he described as 'chaos illuminated by flashes of

---

59 John Sutherland, *The Longman Companion to Victorian Fiction* (London: Longman, 1988), p. 663.
60 Samuel Butler, *The Way of All Flesh* (Harmondsworth: Penguin, 1966), chapter 28, p. 148.

lightning'[61]), the core of his work lies in sexual difference and transgression among the leisured classes; like Carroll, he took verbal wit to the edge of vertigo. Earlier in the century there had been a flourishing tradition of 'Irish' humour, most notably Samuel Lover's (1797–1868) *Handy Andy* (1842) and the many novels of Charles Lever (1806–72), revived in a spirited reworking of the hunting novel *Some Experiences of an Irish R.M.* (1899) by Edith Somerville (1858–1949) and Martin Ross (the pseudonym of Violet Martin, 1862–1915) but Wilde's Irish otherness was much less easily contained within such stereotypes. His aestheticism was already being caricatured in Gilbert and Sullivan's *Patience* (1881) – indeed their partner Richard D'Oyly Carte (1844–1901) sponsored Wilde's first lecture-tour of the USA – and his understanding (or performance) of the essentially performative nature of the self is as central to the characterization of his plays as it is to his biography. In 'The Decay of Lying' (1889, rev. 1891), he created what has been described as 'the truly revolutionary document of comedy during the century ... the manifesto of the liberation of comedy from the inhibitions of English Puritanism', outfacing and subverting as it does the aesthetic and ethical norms that had dominated the century's taste.[62] *The Importance of Being Earnest: A Trivial Comedy for Serious People* (1895), the most important stage comedy for two centuries, in many ways defies criticism, so effortlessly does it seem to move from paradox to paradox, as it spins sexual, social, and legal identities out of and into a web of lost identities, cucumber sandwiches, and nothingness. His most important comic follower is Max Beerbohm (1872–1956) 'the incomparable Max', who at twenty-four had insouciantly published some seven essays, most notably 'The Pervasion of Rouge' or 'In Defence of Cosmetics', as *The Works of Max Beerbohm with a Bibliography by John Lane* (1896).

The pyrotechnics of Wilde's work mark one fitting end to this account of Victorian comic writing but it may be more appropriate to conclude with a very different Irish author, whose first novel was published in the year that Wilde was released from prison, and who can stand for the many nineteenth-century writers who did not intend to be funny but who nevertheless succeeded. Described by John Sutherland as the 'leading candidate for the worst Victorian novelist ever published',[63] Amanda M. Ros's *Irene Iddlesleigh* (1897) and *Delina Delaney* (1898) can reach sublime heights of absurdity:

---

61 Oscar Wilde, 'The Decay of Lying: an Observation', in *De Profundis and Other Writings* (Harmondsworth: Penguin, 1973), p. 65.

62 Roger B. Henkle, *Comedy and Culture: England 1820–1900* (Princeton University Press, 1980), p. 303.

63 Sutherland, *Longman Companion to Victorian Fiction*, pp. 544–5.

' "Speak! Irene! Wife! Woman! Do not sit in silence and allow the blood that now boils in my veins to ooze through cavities of unrestrained passion and trickle down to drench me with its crimson hue!" '[64] Ros attempted sublime and tragic emotions, to absurd and bathetic effect. More properly characteristic of the end of the century, however, is the work of the most important novelist of the period, Thomas Hardy (1840–1928) who created a profoundly dark, indeed properly tragic, imaginative vision in his novels. Yet Hardy's works, unlike those of Ros, have a complex inward understanding both of comic irony (his 1894 collection of stories was entitled *Life's Little Ironies*) and the possibility of essentially comic resolutions of his characters' fates. His novels shake to the core the kinds of providential plot-structure that had underpinned so many of his precursors' works, as they constantly hold out the possibility of happiness and comic fulfilment and yet repeatedly withhold or frustrate those hopes. Reflecting a profoundly anti-comic sense of the novelist's task, Hardy ended *Tess of the D'Urbervilles* (1891), with the famous words, ' "Justice" was done, and the President of the Immortals, in the Aeschylean phrase, had ended his sport with Tess.'[65] It is a terrible and moving moment, but too pessimistic a place to end. For an equally powerful and unillusioned counter-affirmation, we must turn to Hardy's great contemporary, Friedrich Nietzsche (1844–1900), author of the century's most radical philosophical revaluation of comedy's significance. For Nietzsche had, just a few years before *Tess*'s composition, also cited Aeschylus, but to very different purpose and effect. His words from *The Gay Science* convey just how joyful and long-reaching the nineteenth century can be in its understanding of, and affiliation to, the power of laughter and stand in exemplary contrast to those of Hardy:

> There is no denying that *in the long run* each of these great teachers of a purpose was vanquished by laughter, reason and nature: the brief tragedy always changed and returned into the eternal comedy of existence, and the 'waves of uncountable laughter' – to cite Aeschylus – must in the end also come crashing down on the greatest of these tragedians.[66]

64 Amanda McKittrick Ros, *Irene Iddlesleigh: a Novel* (Belfast: W. and G. Baird, 1897).
65 Thomas Hardy, *Tess of the D'Urbervilles* (Harmondsworth: Penguin, 1978), chapter 59, p. 489.
66 Friedrich Nietzsche, *The Gay Science*, ed. Bernard Williams (Cambridge University Press, 2001), p. 29.

13

Innovation and experiment

JEROME MCGANN

Viewed in a perspective of innovation and experiment, few cultural periods have been more inadequately represented by twentieth-century critics and scholars than the age of Victoria. A nation of shopkeepers ruled by a dismal science and proud of its vulgar spirit of commonplace proprieties: the word 'Victorian' still carries such overtones, and not without reason. So how could one expect any adventurous aesthetic practices to emerge from such a world?

That question, that situation, was a central preoccupation for the Victorians themselves, and their responses produced one of the most fruitful periods of aesthetic innovation in British history. If Victorian commercial enterprise underwrote many of these innovations, as it did, many others emerged as acts of critical response to the age's prevalent complacencies.

Between the death of Lord Byron (1824) and the death of Algernon Swinburne (1909) – two of England's greatest literary innovators – a spirit of practical invention powered every part of the British empire, not least of all those sectors devoted to literature. This was an age of great publishing entrepreneurs. Aided partly by innovative business methods and partly by remarkable advances in papermaking, printing, the graphic arts, and communication networks, the many new commercial schemes and projects forced writers to rethink and re-invent their writing practices, often in very direct ways. The system of serial publication and the three-decker novel; the explosion of the venue of the literary gift book and annual; the breakthrough advances in the graphic arts; the massive proliferation of newspaper and periodical publication: these are only the most famous examples where the forces of material production utterly transformed the practice of 'literature'.

Fiction

Two of the period's earliest ventures in literary experimentation would prove to be two of the most important as well, exerting influences that would go out far and in deep. Carlyle's *Sartor Resartus* (1833–4) and Dickens's *The Posthumous Papers of the Pickwick Club* (1836–7) are key points of experimental departure that would not even begin to exhaust their resources until the death of Pater and the imprisonment of Wilde. I shall comment at length on Carlyle's *Sartor* because its production and reception define, in certain key respects, a long and pervasive Victorian scene of writing.

Like Browning's *Sordello* (1840), *Sartor Resartus* is one of the most wonderful and exasperating works of the nineteenth century. In each case a major writing innovation is achieved through a bold experiment in style and method. Carlyle's case is in many ways the more fascinating – see the analogous history of L. E. L. below – because it emerges directly out of his conflicted involvement with the material culture of his period – what he called the 'Dog's-meat Bazaar' of contemporary periodical publication that was inaugurated in 1817 by *Blackwood's Edinburgh Magazine*. Taking an eclectic approach to editorial content and graphic design, *Blackwood's* created an environment that spurred remarkable innovations in literary style and genre. The situation exasperated and challenged Carlyle himself. If writers are 'sadly off with these Magazine-vehicles', he observed, they are 'once for all our element in these days' and so we must 'work in it'.[1] *Sartor Resartus* was first printed by *Fraser's Magazine* – a conscious *Blackwood's* clone – in instalments in 1833–4.

With one exception (Ralph Waldo Emerson), the little notice *Sartor* attracted at that point was equivocal at best. When John Stuart Mill censured Carlyle in 1833 for the strange prose style his friend was cultivating in *Sartor*, with its unsettling swings from sarcasm and jest to earnest, idealistic flights, Carlyle did not disagree. 'You are right about my style', he wrote, for I

> *see* only that I cannot yet see. Irony is a sharp instrument; but ill to handle without cutting *yourself*. I cannot justify, yet can too well explain what sets me on it so often of late: it is my singularly anomalous position in the world . . . I never know or can even guess what or who my audience is, or whether I have any audience: thus too naturally I adjust myself on the DEVIL-may-care principle.

1 *The Letters of Thomas Carlyle to John Stewart Mill, John Sterling, and Robert Browning*, ed. Alexander Carlyle (New York: Frederick A. Stokes and Co., 1923), pp. 92, 42–3.

Sartor is transcendental Dog's-meat, nor does Carlyle, either in his letters or in the work itself, want to balance or reconcile that contradiction. Emerson's transcendentalist admiration and the anonymous *Sun* reviewer's loathing (a 'heap of clotted nonsense'[2]) are equally just characterizations. Neither *Sartor* nor its author rise above the subjects taken up, nor do they escape – or even try to escape – their Dog's-meat element. The work becomes then what Carlyle always wanted his writing to be: an act of historical revelation carried out, in this case, through the only means at his disposal. And Carlyle's unknown, wildly diverse audiences are themselves caught by and revealed through that writing.

This paradox of style is matched by *Sartor*'s paradoxical method. The work is a transparent hoax spun out of a parody of the *Bildungsroman*, on one hand, and from the magazine review-essay on the other. At bottom it develops a root and branch critique of the tradition of Realist fiction that would dominate the Victorian age as well as the theory of fiction on which such writing is based. Carlyle regarded the verisimilitudes sought through Realist representations as deceptions. His 1832 essay 'Biography' makes this point in a procedural turn of wit that epitomizes his method in *Sartor*. Discussing the relation of fiction to reality, Carlyle invents and then quotes extensively from the *Aesthetische Springwurzeln* of his fictive Professor Gottfried Sauerteig. The purport of the fictional professor's ideas is that 'Fiction, while the feigner of it knows that he is feigning, partakes, more than we suspect, of the nature of lying.'[3] The remarkable character of this sentence literally *demonstrates* how one can use the deceptions of fictional form to escape the limitations of those forms. For while the German professor states that feigners who know that they are feigning are thereby uttering lies, Carlyle is also intimating that another class of self-aware feigners exist, of which he is one. These feigners are not liars, they are revelators. *Sartor Resartus* is a prophetic revelation of its age uttered by a man in and of that age.

In the letter to Mill where he speaks of periodical publication as a 'Dog's-meat Bazaar', he also set down a shrewd analysis of why these popular venues were useful to writers, like himself, who wanted most of all to speak the truth. Carlyle applauds Mill for his new project, to launch yet another

---

2 *Letters to Mill, Sterling, Browning*, p. 74; quoted in the Appendix to *Sartor Resartus, The Works of Thomas Carlyle*, 30 vols., vol. I (London: Chapman and Hall, 1896), p. 242.

3 Thomas Carlyle, *Critical and Miscellaneous Essays*, Centenary Edition, 30 vols. (New York: Charles Scribner's Sons, 1899), vol. XXVII, p. 49.

periodical (in this case, the short-lived *London Review*). 'I approve greatly of your purpose to discard Cant and Falsehood of all kinds.' For better and for worse, the periodical is, like the gift book and annual, a means of expression that the age demanded. Carlyle then reflects on what it makes possible:

> There is a kind of Fiction which is not Falsehood, and has more effect in addressing men than many a Radical is aware of. This has struck me much of late years in considering *Blackwood* and *Fraser*; both these are furnished as it were with a kind of theatrical costume, with orchestra and stage lights, and thereby alone have a wonderful advantage; perhaps almost their only advantage. For nothing was ever truer than this: *Ubi homines sunt modi sunt*; a maxim which grows with me in significance the longer I meditate it.[4]

This is a proto-Brechtian view of the procedural opportunities opened by the new regime of serial publication. Edgar Allan Poe in America, coming to a similar understanding at exactly this time, would compose 'How to Write a *Blackwood's* Article' in order to argue the same point – or rather, like *Sartor*, to demonstrate the point by a performative writing move. One writes periodical fictions like 'Von Kempelen and His Discovery' or *Sartor Resartus* 'to instruct by deceiving unsuccessfully',[5] by baring the devices of one's own writing and the social scene in which the writing participates.

A bit earlier, in his essay on 'Goethe' (1826), Carlyle argued that 'the fiction of the poet is not falsehood' only if he 'address[es] us on interests that *are*, not that *were* ours; and in a dialect which finds a response, and not a contradiction, within our bosoms'.[6] Thinking then in Coleridgean terms, he imagined for 'us' in the present an ideal dialect and audience. As that Romantic illusion faded for Carlyle in the next few years, the possibility – perhaps the necessity – of *Sartor Resartus* was born. What emerged was a sympathetic exchange *in* the contradictions and diversities of Carlyle's diverse audiences. The famous and contradictory 'Testimonies of Authors' that Carlyle himself printed at the head of the first (1838) book publication of his work show how well aware he was of the unusual discourse field with which his work was involved.

Another of Carlyle's friends, the young radical John Sterling, also wrote a strong critique of *Sartor* in a letter full of both admiration and dismay. On

---

4 Carlyle, *Letters to Mill, Sterling, Browning*, p. 93.
5 Carlisle Moore, 'Thomas Carlyle and Fiction: 1822–1834', in Herbert Davis, William C. DeVane, and R. C. Bald (eds.), *Nineteenth-Century Studies* (Ithaca, NY: Cornell University Press, 1940), pp. 131–78: p. 152.
6 Carlyle, *Critical and Miscellaneous Essays*, vol. xxvi, p. 251.

the one hand *Sartor* 'resembles some of the master-works of human invention', on the other it is a 'lawless oddity' replete with 'strange heterogeneous
combination[s] and allusion[s]'.[7] As Sterling's response seems to catch fire
from the contradictions of Carlyle's great work, Carlyle's response, like his
response to Mill, draws flame from his friend's: 'Your objections ... have
good grounds to stand on ... Surely ... too much evil cannot be said of
[*Sartor*].' Nonetheless, Carlyle goes on to defend *Sartor*'s 'coal-marks' in these
startlingly acute terms: 'But finally, do you reckon this really a time for
Purism of style ...? I do not. The whole ragged battalions of Scott's-novel
Scotch, with Irish, German, French, and even Newspaper Cockney (when
Literature is little other than a Newspaper) storming in on us ...' *Sartor*,
Carlyle adds, 'issued thro' one of the main *cloacas* of Periodical Literature
[i.e., *Fraser's Magazine*]' and as such is properly taken as a 'wretched far-
rago'.[8] This clarity of mind about his own work defines its innovative
greatness. It produced *Sartor*'s own internal contradictions – those innumerable passages where *Sartor* reflects parodistically on itself and its resolutely
hoaxing impurities; it induced Carlyle to multiply those contradictions in the
book version's 'Testimonies of Authors', and – finally – it licensed its early
readers to deal with the work in kind. It is only later academics who fail to
see that A. H. Everett's notorious early critique in the *North American Review*
is a kind of parody review, a *faux naïf* revelation that *Sartor* is ... nothing but
a hoax! A parody aiming to match Carlyle's own.

Sartor Resartus is a prescient forecast of the opportunities made possible
by signal changes in material culture. From Thackeray through the Pre-
Raphaelite circle and on through the Aesthetic nineties, writers would
innovate on Carlyle's innovation. D. G. Rossetti's 'Hand and Soul' was read
as a non-fiction report exactly because it exploited the miscegenated body of
materials in *The Germ*, where it was published (1850). And in a certain sense
it *is* non-fiction since it involves a serious argument on a central topic of
art history. The story proposes nothing less than a complete revisionist
understanding of the aesthetic and historical meaning of the art of the
Renaissance and the late Middle Ages. Thereafter Swinburne, Morris, Pater,
Vernon Lee, Whistler, Beerbohm, and many others – whether in earnest or
in jest – would test the non-fictional capacities of parodic fictions.

Swinburne's work in this mode is less well known than it should be, not
least because only a few of these works were published in his lifetime.

---

7 Thomas Carlyle, *The Life of John Sterling* (New York: Charles Scribner's Sons, 1900), p. 110.
8 Carlyle, *Letters to Mill, Sterling, Browning*, p. 192.

But '"The Monomaniac's Tragedy", by Ernest Wheldrake' (published in *Undergraduate Papers* in 1858), 'A Criminal Case', 'Dead Love' (published in *Once a Week* in 1862), 'A Portrait', 'Les Abimes, par Ernest Clouet', and his uncompleted parody *The Chronicle of Tebaldeo Tebaldei* signal the body of writing that made possible his parodic masterpiece *Notes on Poems and Reviews* (1866) – a serious, tongue-in-cheek (not to say 'cheeky') manifesto for the new poetry he had unleashed a few months earlier in *Poems and Ballads*.

Better known are Pater's very different, wholly serious works that run their fine lines between fiction and non-fiction. The 'Giordano Bruno' essay that Pater published in 1889 in the *Fortnightly Review* is a section culled from his unfinished novel *Gaston de Latour*. 'Hyppolytus Veiled' was published as an essay in cultural criticism in *Macmillan's* (also in 1889), but in fact Pater regarded it as that innovative fictional form he stamped with his name, though he did not invent it: an imaginary portrait (as he told Arthur Symons in December 1888).[9] But much of Pater's critical non-fiction, not least of all his *Studies in the History of the Renaissance* (1873), can be read as fictional narrative. *Pari passu*, the imaginary portraits are clearly written as critical and interpretive works in the field of what we would call literary and cultural studies.

If we turn back to the 1830s of Carlyle, the figure of Dickens looms as large as Carlyle. When that innovative masterpiece *The Pickwick Papers* appeared, Carlyle scorned its good-natured sentimentalities. 'Thinner wash … was never offered to the human palate' he told Sterling in the summer of 1837 as he was still reading the serial parts.[10] Yet in many respects *Pickwick* replicates the possibilities revealed earlier by Carlyle. It too is a hodge-podge of various materials and mixed styles. On the other hand, if its fiction that the work is an editorial compilation recalls *Sartor*, Dickens handles that device in the most perfunctory way. Unlike Carlyle, Dickens would not even try to reinvigorate the old eighteenth-century literary convention that both of these works invoke. What he did do, however – and here he went well beyond Carlyle, whose *Sartor* was complete when its serial run began – was to exploit the seriality of his work in extraordinary ways.

The first paragraph of the opening chapter alludes directly to the opening illustration by Robert Seymour, where the Pickwick Club is assembled

---

9 Walter Pater, *The Letters of Walter Pater*, ed. Lawrence Evans (Oxford: Clarendon Press, 1970), p. 90.
10 Thomas Carlyle to John Sterling, *The Collected Letters of Thomas and Jane Welsh Carlyle*, vol. IX July 1836–December 1837 (Durham, NC: Duke University Press, 1981), p. 268.

listening to Mr Pickwick. This textual event is an emblem of the scene of writing and reading that Dickens is undertaking with *Pickwick*, for his readers are what the decorated title page calls them: the 'Corresponding Members' of the social group being created by *Pickwick* itself, whose 'Sporting Transactions' are our own acts of reading. The last instalment – twenty monthly parts and nearly two years later – returns to that initial self-reflexive textual event. Once again the Pickwick Club is convened at its table, this time to experience the moment when – as the title of the last chapter puts it – 'The Pickwick Club is finally dissolved.' 'I shall never regret', Mr Pickwick tells his listeners, 'having devoted the greater part of two years to mixing with different varieties and shades of human character, frivolous as my pursuit of novelty may have appeared to many.'[11] The remark – Mr Pickwick's entire last oration – is nothing less than Dickens's farewell salute to his readers.

A perhaps even more remarkable feature of Dickens's serial text is the four 'Addresses' to the reader that appear in numbers II, III, X, and XV of the monthly instalments. These documents break into the novel's purely fictional space and place it firmly in the world of the getting and spending public. These texts make different kinds of reports to the reader about facticities relevant to the unfolding work: the death of the book's illustrator Robert Seymour (who in fact proposed the idea of the work in the first place); plans to alter the physical design of *Pickwick*; letters and communications from readers; and even a report from the author explaining why a 'severe domestic affliction of no ordinary kind' interrupted the serial publication.[12]

These kinds of move may well recall similar moves made earlier by Sterne and, most important for Dickens, Scott. But the invasions of imaginative space in Dickens are newly inflected since they admit authorial agencies other than the nominal author himself. The first part of the second of these addresses was written by Dickens's publisher, who also added in later numbers various publisher's announcements about *Pickwick*. The 'Corresponding Members' of the Pickwick Club are thus quite various and include both in-house and public persons, and anything they might think to contribute seems potentially relevant to the ongoing work. So in the second Address to the reader Dickens himself discusses a communication he

---

11 Charles Dickens, *The Pickwick Papers* (Oxford University Press, 2008), chapter 57, p. 714.
12 Address by Charles Dickens, printed in Part xv of the serial publication of *The Pickwick Papers* (30 June 1837), reprinted in Dickens, *The Pickwick Papers* (New York and Boston: Books, Inc, 1868), p. xiii.

received from a 'correspondent', who sent a critique of the author along with a newspaper clipping relevant to 'the Cabman's description of his Horse' in chapter 2 of the first numbered instalment. A 'Notice to Correspondents' was printed late in the series – whether by Dickens or not we don't know – which referred to the 'immense number of communications purporting to be "suggestions" for the Pickwick Papers'. 'It is wholly out of our power to make use of such hints', these correspondents are told, 'as we really have no time to peruse anonymous letters.'[13] But the truth is that Dickens was usually writing his serial instalments only just in time to meet his deadlines. Always unfolding *in medias res*, therefore, his fictions would in fact regularly 'make use of such hints' as came to him randomly from external events, responses, and other 'correspondent' suggestions that intersected with his writing. Dickens's readers were to be active agents in Dickens's writing process, as much a part of the Dickensian world as Sam Weller or Mr Pickwick.

Poetry

This Dickensian example of innovation born from a serious alliance with print technology recalls the earliest state of post-Romantic verse, whose later Victorian career remained closely bound to the emergence of the gift books and annuals, the popular venue/genre so dear to the Victorians and so disdained by neo-classical Modernists. The astonishing Wilde/Beardsley *Salome* (1894), often judged a Modernist precursor, in fact emerges from an imaginative refiguring of the graphical tradition, begun in the 1820s, that made L. E. L. a central Victorian presence and that passed through the critical hands and eyes of key later figures like D. G. Rossetti and William Morris.

The shape of post-Romantic poetry, not least through its Victorian variations, is clearly forecast by the analysis of Wordsworth's poetry in *Biographia Literaria*. Acknowledging the watershed that Wordsworth's poetry represents, Coleridge nonetheless criticizes his theory of poetic diction and its underlying myth of benevolent natural reciprocities. Against Wordsworth's (basically associationist) idea that we 'half-create, / And what perceive'[14] our experience (and thence the representations of our

---

13 *Ibid.*, p. xiv.
14 William Wordsworth, 'Lines Written a Few Miles Above Tintern Abbey,' in *The Major Works including The Prelude*. ed. Stephen Gill, revised edn (Oxford and New York: Oxford University Press, 2008), p. 134, lines 107–8.

experience), Coleridge follows a more humanist line: 'We receive but what we give, / And in our life alone does Nature live.'[15]

In the Victorian period, Wordsworthian benevolence would be translated from a poetic method to a cultural ideology, as we see most clearly in the criticism of both Arnold and Pater. Given the extreme social and cultural tensions of the Victorian age, the Wordsworth recreated by Arnold became the English Goethe, source of sweetness and light.

While Coleridge's ideas would themselves be worked into that line of thinking, they represent a very different and much less coherent philosophical and aesthetic position. In that incoherence lies the importance and strength of Coleridge's critique of Wordsworth, which involved as well a self-critique. A long and distinguished line of aesthetics begins with Arthur Henry Hallam, reaches its supreme expression in Poe and Swinburne, and plays itself out in Pater and Oscar Wilde. It is not a straight line but more like a complex river system, with various tributaries breaking away to fertilize a topographical area of great diversity. Not all of this work is particularly innovative, least of all experimental. It is, however, notably various, like the cultural period itself.

Innovation, including poetic innovation, can only come when rules are broken, decorum breached. Wordsworth's epochal declaration that there neither is nor should be any real difference between poetry and prose clearly made a signal breach with tradition. Swerves usually come in highly deliberated, even programmatic ways, in which case we speak of the work as 'experimental' or – to adopt a later terminology – avant-garde. But they may also emerge by force of circumstance. John Clare's work, for example, is highly innovative when it feeds upon its alienations, most especially in its madhouse environment. Indeed, so unusual is Clare's poetry of 1841 that it would (it could) only gain a proper hearing in another century. By contrast, the breakthrough Browning consciously achieved with *Sordello* (1840) did register its presence – negatively, as we know. It would take the celebrity and the enthusiasm of the next half-generation – D. G. Rossetti and Swinburne in particular – to make that work safe for the democracy of letters.

Carlyle was much interested in *Sordello* and indeed in everything that Browning was trying to do. This is entirely understandable, for Browning quite grasped the import of Carlyle's aggressive question to John Sterling: 'do you reckon this really a time for Purism of style?'[16] *Sordello* is

---

15 Samuel Taylor Coleridge, 'Dejection: An Ode,' in *Poetical Works*. ed. Ernest Hartley Coleridge (London, Oxford, New York: Oxford University Press, 1969), p. 365, lines 47–8.
16 Carlyle to Sterling, *Collected Letters*, vol. IX, p. 135.

programmatically impure and difficult in exactly the same way that *Sartor* is. But like *Lyrical Ballads* (1798), which does not consciously exploit its material means, *Sordello* confines its innovations to language and rhetoric, making no effort to exploit – as both Carlyle and Dickens did – the expressive potential of the printed book. Browning's innovations are important and astonishing enough, of course, as are the innovations of *Lyrical Ballads*. But we want to be clear about their precise character.

While innovation and experiment are both frequent in the Victorian period, Browning's example seems to have licensed a series of experimental poetries and poetics that carry through the end of the century and set the groundwork for the aggressive experimental work of the Modernists. Two movements dominate, and a third phenomenon – one can scarcely call it a movement, programmatic or otherwise – is important. All three, as will be clear, exhibit overlaps as they feed and reflect upon each other.

The first is the Pre-Raphaelite programme, which would mutate into a number of distinctive, and distinct, types and forms. The second is non-programmatic and located in the late nineteenth-century's interest in prosody and versification. The circle of the PRB – in particular Christina and D. G. Rossetti, Swinburne, and George Meredith – are key figures in investigating the technical resources so dramatically present in the work of Browning and Arthur Hugh Clough. Coventry Patmore's 'Essay on English Metrical Law' (1857) is pivotal for nearly everyone, but especially for D. G. Rossetti – whose own early experiments it confirmed – and for G. M. Hopkins, who used it as a point of departure for those verse experiments that would so interest the twentieth-century academy.

One other important phenomenon of Victorian poetry and poetics is relevant: nonsense and its kissing cousin, pastiche. Not really experimental in the sense defined above, this kind of work nonetheless produced some of the period's most startlingly inventive verse. The tradition of children's poetry plays a major role in its development.

In this context, and given our historical vantage, we can see the remarkable prescience of Hallam's early review of Tennyson's poetry. Tennyson epitomizes Hallam's 'poetry of sensation' because 'He sees all the forms of nature with the "eruditus oculus", and his ear has a fairy fineness.' As that remark suggests, the two sensational forms that Hallam locates are visual and phonetic, and he illustrates these forms out of two poems in particular: the 'Recollections of the Arabian Nights' and 'Oriana'. The first is important because it is 'a perfect gallery of pictures', and the second because, like Dante and Petrarch, 'it produce[s] two-thirds of [its] effect by sound' alone and the medium of its prosodic 'phras[ing]' and 'music'. When Hallam writes that 'Sound conveys [these poets'] meaning where words would not', the radical status of his 'sensational' poetics is clear. 'Where words would not': for Hallam, poetic 'words' die of their referential significance, their logopoeia (as Ezra Pound would call it). What he looks for is a poetics of visible language, on one hand, and a poetry that aspires to the condition of music on the other.[17]

L. E. L. and gift book writing

Letitia Elizabeth Landon ('L. E. L.') is an important innovative, but not an experimental, poet. Emerging at the deliquescence of the Romantic period, she became an immediate sensation and remained a virtually mythic figure until the end of the century. Where *Sordello* cultivates prosodic difficulties, however, L. E. L. discovers them. Her breaches of verse decorum emerge from her arresting, superficial style, which gets built before our eyes (and in our ears) out of a studied imitation of the most mannered writing of the previous period, from the Della Cruscans to Byron. Her great subject – the decadence of a culture of sincerity and its palaces of art – comes most immediately from Byron and gets passed directly along to Tennyson, whose early 'lady poems', so much praised by Hallam, were all written at the poetical feet of L. E. L, and whose masterpiece, *In Memoriam* is, as Herbert Tucker has shrewdly observed, a signature period piece because it is an epic of cliché. Nor did the influence end there. Both of Tennyson's most innovative works, *The Princess* and *Maud*, descend from the medley form that L. E. L. virtually invented in her collections *The Improvisatrice*, *The Troubador*, and especially *The Golden Violet*.

Think about these verses:

> And my own heart is as the lute
> I now am waking;
> Wound to too fine and high a pitch
> They both are breaking.[18]

17 Arthur Hallam, 'On Some of the Characteristics of Modern Poetry, and on the Lyrical Poems of Alfred Tennyson', (1831), in *The Poems of Arthur Henry Hallam, together with his Essay on the Lyrical Poems of Alfred Tennyson*. ed. Richard Le Gallienne (London: Elkin Mathews, 1893), pp. 107, 118, 122.
18 Herbert Tucker, *Tennyson and the Doom of Romanticism* (Cambridge, MA: Harvard University Press, 1988), p. 378; L. E. L., 'Song', in *Selected Writings*, ed. Jerome McGann and Daniel Riess (Peterborough, Ontario: Broadview Press, 1997), p. 100, lines 17–20.

From one perspective this is clumsy and injudicious, as if L. E. L. had no ear for verse proprieties. 'Wound to too fine and high a pitch' is not only torturous, it puts into circulation a word play ('Wound') that seems relevant at the thematic level but unintegrated at the prosodic. A kind of technical anarchy hovers around all of L. E. L.'s verse. 'I now am waking'? As in 'I am now waking up, becoming conscious', or as in the poetical cliché about 'waking the lute'? The latter seems the primary referent, but it is so weak and undesirable that the reader's mind drifts towards the other. And suddenly we begin to register the possibility of a relation between the two, though the verse appears not to have sought out the relation but to have stumbled upon it randomly. (That 'seeming', that poetic illusion, is the crucial effect, so that it makes no difference, so far as the reader is concerned, whether it was deliberated or not.) One observes the same kind of event in the final line with the word 'breaking'. Is this a transitive or intransitive expression? 'Intransitive', we initially decide, but because a clear poetic debility comes with that choice, the other possibility, awkward but more interesting, rises to our view.

Does the poem itself, as it were, work for these effects, or make anything of their relations? It's difficult to say. Even if these effects appear accidental, as they do, that very accidentality only lends them greater force. Elizabeth Barrett (later Barrett Browning) said as much in 1841 when Mary Russell Mitford contrasted L. E. L.'s with Felicia Hemans's technical procedures. If Hemans is the better craftsperson, as Mitford argued (and Barrett agreed), L. E. L. is the more interesting poet: 'more elastic, more various & of a stronger web'.[19]

Poems like 'The Lady of Shalott' and 'The Palace of Art' sketch a cultural crisis – 'the doom of romanticism', as Herbert Tucker calls it in the title of his study of Tennyson – that pervades the nineteenth-century.[20] This is L. E. L.'s central, recurrent subject, and Hallam's essay analyses Tennyson's significance in exactly those terms. The 'melancholy [that] characterizes the spirit of modern poetry', he observes – anticipating Arnold's 'Preface' to his 1853 *Poems* – stems from the 'return of the mind upon itself' in face of widespread social tensions and disfunctions.[21] Tennyson's aestheticism is for Hallam a clear index of this social state of affairs.

19 Mary Russell Mitford to Elizabeth Barrett, *The Brownings' Correspondence. Vol. V. January 1841–May 1842*, ed. Philip Kelley, Ronald Hudson, and Scott Lewis (Winfield, KS: Wedgestone Press, 1987), p. 75.
20 Herbert F. Tucker, *Tennyson and the Doom of Romanticism* (Cambridge, MA: Harvard University Press, 1988).
21 Hallam, 'Characteristics of Modern Poetry', p. 91.

Relevant here is L. E. L.'s characteristic medium of expression. We think of the dramatic monologue as the Victorian period's most distinctive poetic genre, and in one sense it is. But until mid-century its most distinctive poetic venue – poetry's most distinctive social form and vehicle of expression – was the gift book and annual, launched into its Victorian ubiquity in 1823 with the first volume of the *Forget-Me-Not*. The vast majority of L. E. L.'s poems were first printed in such books or in related periodicals like *The Literary Gazette*. The innovative character of L. E. L.'s work is bound up in the form of these books and periodicals, which consciously package their materials as art objects. Elaborately decorated and built around their signature steel engravings, these works set their poems, stories, and non-fictions in an explicit relation to the commerce of fashionable art. The venue appalled Wordsworth and others like him, who saw it (correctly) as the very epitome of a world of 'getting and spending'.[22] To have fashioned a genuine aesthetic out of these kitsch materials, however, was one of the great experiments, and achievements, of the period.

'Give a man a mask and he will tell you the truth.'[23] Wilde's comment applies when forms of sincerity cannot be trusted, as – in the wake of Byron – they were not trusted by either L. E. L. or Hallam. Landon's female heroines – Erinna, Corinne, L. E. L. herself – are masks for Landon's self-expression. 'L. E. L.' is the mask she dons in order to enter and explore from within the factitious worlds of early Victorian society and its poetical mirrors, where 'none among us dares to say / What none will choose to hear.'[24] L. E. L.'s is thus a special kind of bad poetry, recognized as such by herself and by her readers, including those who admired her work, like Barrett Browning. 'Thy life is false and feverish, / It is like a masque of thee':[25] reading L. E. L.'s verse in 1839, Maria Jane Jewsbury can say that, and mean it for the highest praise, because she reads in the same spirit that the author writ: 'I live among the cold, the false, / And I must seem like them.'[26] In this case, to seem is to be, what is false is what is true.

22 William Wordsworth, 'The World is Too Much with Us', in *The Major Works*, p. 270, line 2.
23 Oscar Wilde, *The Picture of Dorian Gray* (1891), in *Oscar Wilde: The Major Works*, ed. Isobel Murray (Oxford University Press, 2008), p. 213.
24 L. E. L., 'Lines of Life,' *Selected Writings*, p. 112, lines 43–4.
25 Maria Jane Jewsbury, quoted in an unsigned review of Laman Blanchard, *The Life and Literary Remains of L. E. L.*, *Tait's Edinburgh Magazine* 8 (1841), p. 449.
26 L. E. L., 'Lines of Life,' in *Selected Writings*, p. 111, lines 9–10.

The lives of the dramatic monologue

This exemplary Victorian sub-genre descends from two Romantic forms. The first source is the poetry of sincerity, so-called: poems of dramatic self-expression like 'Frost at Midnight' and 'The Solitary Reaper'; Robert Langbaum's classic study of *The Poetry of Experience* tracks Browning's non-subjective dramatic monologues to these highly personal and subjective poems. A convention of immediacy turns the reader into a spectator and overhearer of a particular person's particular act of expression. In its Romantic mode, the fiction is that we overhear the thoughts of the poet *in propria persona*: for instance, Wordsworth musing a few miles above Tintern Abbey in July 1798. In Browning, however, the poet – Browning *in propria persona* – disappears and his famous 'Men and Women' step out, speaking like characters in a drama.

The other source, unobserved by Langbaum, is important because it allows us to see how this signal innovation developed and mutated both before and after Browning. Two key works are Byron's 'The Lament of Tasso' and 'The Prophecy of Dante'. In these cases the poetic fiction – that we are reading a poem spoken by a known historical character – comes to us in a staged form. The whole force of such poems depends upon their double-voiced condition, upon our awareness of Byron's ventriloquism. Byron's translation of the Paolo and Francesca episode in Dante is probably his supreme achievement in this mode.

Poets like L. E. L. and Hemans cultivate this Byronic form, but the first poet to stamp it with greatness is Tennyson in his 1830 and 1832 volumes. 'Ulysses', 'Mariana', 'Tiresias': Tennyson's haunted and haunting voice permeates these poems and lifts them – as Browning's dramatic monologues are never lifted – to a palatial aesthetic world. Like L. E. L.'s poems, Tennyson's leak melancholia, the residue of the diseased beauties they discover and recreate.

Oscar Wilde's astonishing commentary on Browning in 'The Critic as Artist' explains the difference he made from the monologues that went before. Wilde's argument is that Browning fashioned his Shakespearean creatures by turning poetic language into 'ignoble clay', translating forms of verse into prose, what Wilde calls Browning's 'monstrous music'. He is 'great ... not as a poet [but] as a writer of fiction ... He used poetry as a medium for writing in prose.'[27] This is witty but more than witty, it is acute

---

27 Oscar Wilde, 'The Critic as Artist – Part I' (1888), in *Major Works*, p. 245.

to a degree. Browning's prose poetry, so to say, descends directly from Wordsworth's famous 'Preface' to *Lyrical Ballads* where he argues that there is no essential difference between prose and poetry. Browning's monologues are an explication, at once theoretical and practical, of what Wordsworth's idea might mean. So when Wilde says that 'Meredith is a prose Browning, and so is Browning'[28] he is completing an elliptical history of an important nineteenth-century stylistic development. Meredith's notorious, wonderful – and difficult – prose makes a poetic drama of its own resources and resourcefulness. His fictions exist to service his style, not the other way round. Seeing this, Wilde uses Meredith to expose how Browning's dramatic monologues create a vehicle for what Wilde calls 'the mechanism of mind'.[29] Browning simulates that mechanism by eliminating lyrical resources from his writing. In Wilde's view, this move makes possible the 'poetic prose' of Meredith.

In constructing these mental mechanisms Browning works hard to appear an invisible, disinterested reporter. If we look carefully, of course, we can see his hand tilting the ideological scales of the monologues. In the signature piece 'My Last Duchess', for example, Browning uses his monologue to argue that sincerity is a higher value – even a higher aesthetic value – than artifice – even though his poem is itself an act of supreme artifice, as the artfully disguised rhymes testify. The point of this kind of procedure, however, is to distract us from inquiring about the poem's ideology, to suggest that Browning's views need have no relevance for our judgments of the poetic work. What Arnold says of Shakespeare in his sonnet on the bard is just the aesthetic condition Browning pursues with his dramatic monologue: 'Others abide our question, thou art free.'[30]

All that would change with the work of the next half-generation, as we see in the brilliant innovations of Meredith's 'Modern Love' and – the exemplary case – D. G. Rossetti's 'Jenny'. In a sense Rossetti has simply recovered the ventriloquizing manner of Byron and L. E. L., using the voice of his 'young and thoughtful man of the world' – as he described the speaker of the 'Jenny' monologue – to serve as a mask for himself. As the poet's views and attitudes are worked back into the substance of this kind of poem, however, they are laid out for the reader's critical reflection and judgment.

---

28 *Ibid.*   29 *Ibid.* p. 244.
30 Matthew Arnold, 'Shakespeare' (1844), in *The Poems of Matthew Arnold*, ed. Kenneth Allott (London: Longmans, 1965), p. 49, line 1.

These monologues are deliberately written so that the poetry solicits the reader's questions, which will be searching and troubled given (1) the volatile character of their subjects (adultery in one case, prostitution in the other) and (2) the speakers' culpable involvement in the enacted scenes. Unlike the self-expressive monologues of L. E. L. or Tennyson, however, where the poet's complicity produces the melancholy tone discussed by Hallam, both 'Jenny' and 'Modern Love' cultivate an objectivity they learned from Browning. The effect is stunning.

Rossetti called this aesthetic procedure the art of the 'inner standing-point'.[31] He came to it by two assiduous practices: poetic imitation and pastiche, on the one hand – poems like 'Ave' or 'The Blessed Damozel' – and on the other his translations of a varied group of early Italian poets, from the *stil novo* of Dante to the bawdy verse of Cecco Angiolieri.

Translation, pastiche, nonsense, and pure poetry

In certain respects, D. G. Rossetti's 1861 volume of translations *The Early Italian Poets* is clearly a more significant cultural event than his books of so-called original verse (1870, 1881). From a technical vantage point, this early book was a training exercise, carried out over a period of some fifteen years, to discover the new style of writing that Pater would celebrate and analyse: 'At a time when poetic originality in England might seem to have had its utmost play, here was certainly one new poet ... with a structure and music of verse, a vocabulary, an accent, unmistakably novel.' Pater traces the innovations in Rossetti's *Poems* (1870) and *Ballads and Sonnets* (1881), but everything about those two famous books, both in style and method, was discovered by Rossetti through his translation work. The writing pressed urgently towards extreme technical artifice – what a later poet who wrote out of the same tradition called 'supreme fiction'.[32]

The other innovation in this translation work is the peculiar way Rossetti torques his Italian originals for a clear contemporary relevance. The translation of Dante's *Vita Nuova* illustrates his intention in the clearest way. Rossetti makes Dante's *Bildungsgedicht* not only a personal manifesto – Rossetti changed his name from Gabriel to Dante Gabriel while he was

---

31 Dante Gabriel Rossetti, unpublished note to 'Ave' (1847–48): see *Collected Poetry and Prose*, ed. Jerome J. McGann (New Haven and London: Yale University Press, 2002), p. xxvi.
32 Walter Pater, *Appreciations: with an Essay on Style* (London: Macmillan and Co., 1889), p. 229; Wallace Stevens, *Notes Toward a Supreme Fiction* (Cummington, MA: The Cummington Press, 1942).

engaged in the work – but a call to his culture at large, that it undertake the pursuit of a *New Life*. For Rossetti, as for Arnold and so many other Victorians, this meant a cultural turnabout: in Rossetti's case, replacing the spirit of commerce with a practice of art. The idea is hardly new, and Rossetti draws particular inspiration from Poe, Blake, and Shelley. But the strange 'music', the startling 'vocabulary', the entire 'accent', as Pater observed, is indeed 'unmistakably novel'.

Writers from William Morris to William Butler Yeats, Pound, and Wallace Stevens studied Rossetti's innovations in their various ways. Of the Victorians, Swinburne learned the most, partly because – like the later Moderns – he broke so sharply away. Only briefly, in the late 1850s and early 1860s, does Swinburne put himself to a Rossettian and a Pre-Raphaelite schooling. The imagist and scriptural work that the Rossettis and Morris developed can be seen in poems like 'A Match' and 'Laus Veneris', but with 'Dolores' and the 'Anactoria' reworked in 1865, Swinburne had launched himself along an entirely new course.

In the 1860s Rossetti and Swinburne planned to produce a joint translation of Villon, but the project never came to fruition, and one can see why. Both were remarkably innovative translators because, like Dryden and Pope, both erased the distinction between translated and original work. But consider the differences between the opening of these two translations:

> Tell me now in what hidden way is
>   Lady Flora the lovely Roman?
> Where's Hipparchia, and where is Thais,
>   Neither of them the fairer woman?
>   Where is Echo, beheld of no man,
> Only heard on river and mere, –
>   She whose beauty was more than human? . . .
> But where are the snows of yester-year?
>
>   ('A Ballad of Dead Ladies')[33]

> What though the beauty that I love and serve be cheap,
>   Ought you to take me for a beast or fool?
> All things a man could wish are in her keep;
>   For her I turn swashbuckler in love's school.
>   When folks drop in, I take my pot and stool,
> And fall to drinking with no more ado.
> I fetch them bread, fruit, cheese, and water too;

---

33 Rossetti, 'A Ballad of Dead Ladies' (1870), in *Collected Poetry and Prose*, p. 119, lines 1–8.

I say all's right so long as I'm well paid;
'Look in again when your flesh troubles you,
    Inside this brothel where we drive our trade.'
                            ('The Ballad of Villon and Fat Madge')[34]

Rossetti's translation is a work for the printed page and the eyes of the mind, which is why it made such an impression on Pound. By contrast, what Swinburne called 'song' is his great commitment. His translation begs to fill the mouth, begs to be recited. As a result, and quite unlike Rossetti, his verse, while thoroughly Romantic in its intensity of style, grows increasingly impersonal. This commitment is a distinct form of what has been called 'art for art's sake'. In a certain, very important sense the verse is not 'about' anything except its own action, as T. S. Eliot once lamented. The poetry thus develops a clear and serious parody of the biblical 'I am that I am', with that 'I' merging in the 'voice' of the verse. Poems like 'The Garden of Proserpine' or 'Hertha' lose their nominal authorship in their textual unfolding.

I am that which began,
    Out of me the years roll,
Out of me God and man;
    I am equal and whole;
God changes, and man, and the form of them bodily; I am the soul.[35]

These verses establish the poem's Lucretian argument. 'Hertha' is one of the (historical) names assumed by the 'I' of the poem, the name naming an impersonal process – autopoietic, self-engendering, and self-sustaining – mapped by various sciences and mimetically revealed – mirrored – in art. Swinburne's program of 'art for art's sake' is both a manifesto and a demonstration of this material and world-historical process.

Poetry that aspires to the condition of music, like Swinburne's, seems peculiarly apt for a poetic mimesis of this kind. The late nineteenth century's remarkable explorations of prosody and versification, both in theory and practice, represent a general effort to come to terms with the ideas that Swinburne's poetry so dramatically exhibits. Especially pertinent here is Patmore's important essay of 1857, 'Essay on English Metrical Law', which confirmed, if it did not actually stimulate, the famous poetical experiments

---

34 A. C. Swinburne, 'The Ballad of Villon and Fat Madge' (c. 1862–3), in *Major Poems and Selected Prose*. ed. Jerome McGann and Charles L. Sligh (New Haven and London: Yale University Press, 2004), p. 411, lines 1–10.
35 Swinburne, 'Hertha' (1871), in *Major Poems and Selected Prose*, p. 144, lines 1–5.

that Hopkins would pursue and that Robert Bridges would call 'the new prosody'. Patmore's ideas about English poetry's 'dipodic' and isochronous structure reflect his view that the laws of poetry are based in how lines of verse are spoken. Although Patmore did not fully develop his theory until 1857, his ideas were well developed much earlier, as we see in his 1850 review of Tennyson's *In Memoriam*: 'each line, however many syllables it may contain, ought to occupy the same time in reading, according to the analogy of bars in music'.[36]

Hopkins's ideas about 'sprung rhythm' and 'running rhythm' would gain much celebrity in the twentieth century. As Hopkins was himself aware, he was exploring metrical innovations that Swinburne had long been involved with. Swinburne's 1858 translation of the 'Dies Irae' and his pastiche border ballads were his first forays into isochronous versification, quite possibly under the direct influence of Patmore's ideas. The full emergence of this work would not come until 'Anactoria' and *Tristram of Lyonesse*, both of which were written, he said, on a 'scheme of modulation and movement' that was 'original in structure and combination'.[37] As with Hopkins, the originality comes from a kind of metrical miscegenation whereby non-dipodic verse forms (like sonnets) are forced to carry dipodic metrical units. In each case, heavy alliteration marks the presence of the isochronous structures.

In Swinburne's 'Sapphics' and 'Anactoria', Patmore's *The Unknown Eros*, and Hopkins's 'The Wreck of the Deutschland' or 'Spelt from Sibyl's Leaves', verse innovation comes marked with Arnoldian high seriousness. Some of the most outstanding metrical innovations of the period, however, were made in poetry's lower rooms. Christina Rossetti's 'Goblin Market' is the touchstone here precisely because its serious religious message unfolds as light dipodic verse – 'de-doggerelised Skeltonic', in Saintsbury's brilliant formulation.[38] The line of nonsense that runs through the period, immortalized in the work of Lewis Carroll and Edward Lear, represents exactly the same drive towards a *poésie pure* and art for art's sake. One has only to read Swinburne's 'Dolores' or his incomparable self-parody 'Poeta Loquitur' to see the relation clearly – performatively – defined.

---

36 [Coventry Patmore], 'In Memoriam', *North British Review* 13 (1850), p. 542.
37 Cecil Y. Lang (ed.), *The Swinburne Letters*. 6 vols. (New Haven: Yale University Press, 1959–62), vol. II, p. 74.
38 George Saintsbury, *A History of English Prosody*, 3 vols., *Volume III, From Blake to Mr Swinburne* (London: Macmillan and Co. Ltd., 1910), p. 353.

What Hallam praised in Tennyson's 'Oriana' – poetry aspiring to the condition of music – becomes widely realized and explored in children's literature (so-called) and in verse born from Pre-Raphaelite and Arts and Craft sensibilities. The connection between these two modes of late Victorian cultural writing was brilliantly exposed in 1978 by Veronica Forrest-Thomson's critical study of *Poetic Artifice*. Setting Lear's 'The Akond of Swat' next to Swinburne's 'Faustine', Forrest-Thomson demonstrates the aesthetic commitments shared by these two comic works. The 'high seriousness' that Arnold demanded for poetry and literature gets weighed and found wanting in Carroll and Lear, the Rossettis and Swinburne (to name only the most obvious cases).

The importance of this late Victorian movement towards what the twentieth-century would call 'the word as such' can scarcely be overestimated. Gertrude Stein and Stevens, James Joyce and Flann O'Brien, Hugh MacDiarmid and Louis Zukofsky: all went to nonsense school, on one hand, and to music lessons on the other. Here are some texts that explain – not by precept, but by example – why one should listen to those Victorian voices:

> Down the glen tramp little men.
> One hauls a basket,
> One bears a plate,
> One lugs a golden dish
> Of many pounds' weight.
> How fair the vine must grow
> Whose grapes are so luscious;
> How warm the wind must blow
> Through those fruit bushes.[39]

> Beautiful Soup! Who cares for fish,
> Game, or any other dish?
> Who would not give all else for two p
> ennyworth only of Beautiful Soup?
> Pennyworth only of beautiful Soup?[40]

> Out and in and out the sharp straits wander,
>   In and out and in the wild way strives,
> Starred and paved and lined with flowers that squander

39 Christina Rossetti, 'Goblin Market' (1862), in *The Complete Poems of Christina Rossetti*, ed. R. W. Crump (Baton Rouge and London: Louisiana State University Press, 1979), p. 12, lines 55–63.
40 Lewis Carroll, 'Beautiful Soup', in *Alice in Wonderland*, ed. Donald J. Gray 2nd edn (New York, London: W. W. Norton & Co., 1992), p. 85, lines 10–14.

Gold as golden as the gold of hives,
Salt and moist and multiform: but yonder
See, what sign of life or death survives?[41]

'Lady Jingly! Lady Jingly!
  'Sitting where the pumpkins blow,
  'Will you come and be my wife?'
Said the Yonghy-Bonghy-Bò.
'I am tired of living singly, –
'On this coast so wild and shingly, –
  'I'm a-weary of my life:
  'If you'll come and be my wife,
  'Quite serene would be my life!' –
Said the Yonghy-Bonghy-Bò,
Said the Yonghy-Bonghy-Bò.[42]

Hollow heaven and the hurricane
And hurry of the heavy rain.

Hurried clouds in the hollow heaven
And a heavy rain hard-driven.

The heavy rain it hurries amain
And heaven and the hurricane.

Hurrying wind o'er the heaven's hollow
And the heavy rain to follow.[43]

In place of verse constructed out of ideas about language and textuality –
the 'poetry of experience' from Wordsworth to Browning – we have here
verse constructed from musical imperatives. The great theorist (and practitioner) of this approach in England was Swinburne, who argued repeatedly
that the basis of poetry should not be any 'language really used by men',
but what he called 'song' – verse in which the figure of the poet disappears
into the music of the work, becoming 'now no more a singer, but a
song'.[44]

---

41 Swinburne, 'By the North Sea', in *Major Poems and Selected Prose*, pp. 193–4, lines 181–6.
42 Edward Lear, 'The Courtship of the Yonghy-Bonghy-Bò' (1871), in *The Complete Verse
  and Other Nonsense*, ed. Vivien Noakes (New York and London: Penguin Books, 2002),
  p. 325, lines 23–33.
43 Dante Gabriel Rossetti, 'Chimes' (1878), in *The Complete Writings and Pictures of Dante
  Gabriel Rossetti. A Hypermedia Research Archive*, ed. Jerome McGann: www.rossettiarchive.
  org/docs/2–1881.1stedn.rad.html#p275, lines 49–56.
44 A. C. Swinburne, 'Thalassius' (1880), in *Selected Poetry and Prose*, ed. John
  D. Rosenberg (New York: The Modern Library, 1968), p. 248, line 474.

Coda: the fiction of George Meredith

Reflecting on 'The Novels of George Meredith' in an essay she published in 1928 (the centenary of Meredith's birth), Virginia Woolf underscored the 'experimental' character of his work: it came to overthrow 'the conventional form of the novel. He makes no attempt to preserve the sober reality of Trollope and Jane Austen; he has destroyed all the usual staircases by which we have learnt to climb. And what is done so deliberately is done with a purpose.'[45] As the French critic Abel Chevalley put the matter in his 1921 study of the relation of English fiction to the Modernist movement, with the publication of *The Ordeal of Richard Feverel*, Meredith's writing had 'advanced by at least fifty years' beyond what Victorian novelists of the period were attempting to do with their work.[46] Had fiction 'remained what it was to Jane Austen and Trollope', Woolf went on to say, 'fiction would by this time be dead. Thus Meredith deserves our gratitude and excites our interest as a great innovator.'[47]

As everyone knows, Meredith's remarkable 'style' focuses the issue. It is a style that covets odd, even shocking, moves of various kinds. Sentence by sentence, often phrase by phrase, the writing arrests and challenges a reader's attention, building from its many small disjunctions its daring architectonics. To a certain sensibility – clearly not Woolf's – the writing can seem carelessly constructed, a mélange of incommensurable elements – good and bad writing, even. At once a comedy and a tragedy, *Feverel* is the test and exemplary case.

Meredith's innovation – what he has 'so deliberately done ... with a purpose'[48] – is very like what we recognize in Joyce's *Ulysses*. It is a purpose that emerged with the innovations that began in *Blackwood's* and that achieved their strange early perfection in *Sartor Resartus*. Carlyle was a great influence on Meredith, whose fiction, and *Feverel* in particular, shifts attention from plot and character to the stylistic forms and conventions by which the recreated world becomes known to us. His prose fashions its human dramas by a pastiche of the styles that are taken to define the social and ideological preoccupations of his world. This is a new kind of 'realist' fiction, a realism of the life illusions that underpin social order and drive human

---

45 Virginia Woolf, 'The Novels of George Meredith' (1928), in *The Second Common Reader* (New York: Harcourt Brace: New York, 1932), p. 228.
46 'Il avait ... pris le devants par au moins cinquante années.' Abel Chevalley, *Le roman anglais de notre temps* (London: Humphry Milford, 1921), p. 55.
47 Woolf, 'Meredith,' p. 234.   48 *Ibid.*, p. 228.

action. More than this, Meredith 'deliberately' includes his own writing, his own 'novels', within the critical horizon that the writing develops.

From a vantage point we can take because we stand beyond the horizon of a certain kind of Modernism, Meredith's work acquires an even greater interest and importance. Next to *Feverel*, a book like *Ulysses* can seem in many respects a purely formal achievement, the perfection of an art for art's sake forecast not by Baudelaire or Swinburne, but by Pater and James. In this respect Meredith's innovations expose the limits of an aesthetic temperament. His formal innovations not only anticipate the Modernism of Woolf and Joyce, they make common cause with later writers like Rushdie, DeLillo, and Pynchon. James deplored Meredith's 'fantastic and mannered' procedures and the social and political purposes they served: 'the artist was nothing to the good citizen and liberalized bourgeois'.[49] But history turns James's criticism into an explanation of Meredith's importance – the privilege of Meredith's historical backwardness. For all his evident commitment to art and artifice, Meredith's Victorian temper shared with Ruskin the belief that 'THERE IS NO WEALTH BUT LIFE',[50] and he discovered for us the unusual aesthetic resources that lay concealed in that belief.

---

49 Henry James, letter to Edmund Gosse, 15 October 1912, quoted in Ioan Williams (ed.), *George Meredith: The Critical Heritage* (London: Routledge, 1995), p. 406.
50 John Ruskin, 'Unto this Last' (1860), in *The Works of John Ruskin*, ed. E. T. Cook and Alexander Wedderburn, 39 vols. (London: George Allen, 1903–12), vol. XXII, p. 105.

14

Writing for children

CLAUDIA NELSON

During Victoria's reign, works written primarily for children became both more numerous and more heterogeneous. As printing technology continued to improve and to lower production costs for books and magazines, and as younger and poorer segments of the population became literate, authors, publishers, and purchasers were increasingly likely to define children as a distinct audience. Or, more accurately, one might say that they constituted increasingly significant multiple audiences, delineated not only by age but also by gender, social class, and religion. The ever-expanding number of print texts available to the young, and the growing belief among producers and purchasers that a precise sense of one's audience was important to success, led to the creation of a remarkably diverse – and often innovative and sophisticated – body of writing for children. The extraordinary range in tone, content, physical format, and stylistic and narrative characteristics reveals a culture that took childhood unusually seriously and saw children and their needs in many different ways.

The polyphony of children's literature

Victorian children's texts emerged from the clash between two ways of understanding childhood: the concept that children are adults' moral inferiors, in need of substantial guidance if they are to mature into productive and virtuous citizenship, and the concept that civilization is corrupt and that children, not yet implicated in its inexorable sullying of humankind, are superior to adults in their innocence, enjoyment of simple pleasures, and willingness to imagine and trust. At the turn of the nineteenth century, the former view was associated both with the Evangelical heirs of the Puritans, such as Mary Martha Sherwood, whose *The Fairchild Family* (1818–47) was a best-seller, and with the rational moralists, secular writers such as Thomas Day and Maria Edgeworth. The contrasting tendency to idealize childhood as a state of prelapsarian bliss was popularized by the Romantics, most famously William Wordsworth in poems for adults such as 'Ode. Intimations of Immortality from Recollections of Early Childhood' (1807), which asserts that 'Not in entire forgetfulness, / And not in utter nakedness, / But trailing clouds of glory do we come / From God, who is our home; / Heaven lies about us in our infancy!'[1]

The debate between proponents of these two outlooks, and the rise of a compromise position that appreciated the virtues of childhood while simultaneously noting the drawbacks of inexperience, is reflected in countless Victorian works for the young. One of the best-known examples of a text that draws upon all three stances is *Alice's Adventures in Wonderland*, published in 1865 by Lewis Carroll (Charles Lutwidge Dodgson). Before reaching Wonderland, Alice has endured the minatory upbringing experienced by most middle-class girls of her generation; for instance, she has been required to commit to memory the didactic verse of Isaac Watts. Dodgson, however, believed that young girls' appeal was natural, inherent, and considerably greater than that of adults, and *Alice* accordingly teems with attacks on the adult urge, personified in such figures as the Queen of Hearts, to control and hector children. While the narrator is not above having fun at Alice's expense and establishes that she is far from the angel-child common in Victorian sentimental fiction, both *Alice* and its 1872 sequel, *Through the Looking-Glass*, sometimes imply that childhood is precious and fleeting, a state that should move adults to nostalgia rather than to domination.

Poetry, too, reveals conflicting adult stances on childhood. As Alice's familiarity with Watts's moral verse suggests, rhyme was often used as a training tool, one that might be used either in secular education as a way to assist memorization of the alphabet and other educational building blocks (Sara Coleridge's 1834 *Pretty Lessons in Verse for Small Children*, written for her own offspring, introduces Latin, geography, and history, among other subjects) or in character education as children were set to learn hymns or exemplary ballads. Pre-Victorian moral verse such as Felicia Hemans's 'Casabianca' (1826), which presents blind obedience to parents as heroic, remained popular fodder for recitation by children in school or at home. In addition, didactic adult poetry transferred well to the children's market;

---

1 William Wordsworth, 'Ode. Intimations of Immortality from Recollections of Early Childhood' (published 1815, composed 1802–4), in *'Poems, in Two Volumes, and Other Poems', 1800–1807*, ed. Jared Curtis (Ithaca, NY, and London: Cornell University Press, 1983), p. 273.

critic Lorraine Janzen Kooistra notes that an 1859 illustrated edition of Alfred, Lord Tennyson's *The Princess* was a top seller in the Christmas gift-book market for a decade, and that lushly produced volumes of poetry formed an important segment of this market throughout the mid-Victorian years.

Yet much Victorian children's verse evacuates moral content other than the celebration of innocence, while some hints at subversion. Consider the following from Kate Greenaway's collection *Marigold Garden* (1885): 'When we went out with Grandmamma–/Mamma said for a treat– / Oh, dear, how stiff we had to walk / As we went down the street. / . . . She told us – oh, so often – /How little girls and boys, / In the good days when she was young, / Never made any noise.'[2] Young Susan's disdain for adult rules is clear. Similarly, 'Aunt Effie' (Jane Euphemia Browne), a popular children's poet of the 1850s, also sympathetically adopts the stance of the child oppressed by grown-up mores. In 'Little Rain-drops', the speaker remarks wistfully, 'They say I'm very naughty, / But I've nothing else to do, / But sit here at the window; / I should like to play with you. / The little rain-drops cannot speak, / But "pitter, pitter pat"/ Means, "We can play on *this* side, / Why can't you play on that?"[3] Even poets who ostentatiously adopt an authoritarian tone may, like Hilaire Belloc in his introduction to *The Bad Child's Book of Beasts* (1896), undermine this endeavour through deft overstatement: 'I call you bad, my little child, / Upon the title page, / Because a manner rude and wild / Is common at your age. / The moral of this priceless work / (If rightly understood) / Will make you – from a little Turk – / Unnaturally good.'[4]

It comes as no surprise, then, that even collections of Victorian verse by a single author may reveal shifting and contradictory attitudes towards childhood. Greenaway's *Marigold Garden* contains rebellious lyrics such as the one quoted above, but it also includes poems that seem to validate the adultist preference for good behaviour, as well as poems that ignore conduct altogether. Christina Rossetti's *Sing-Song* (1872) juxtaposes rhymes focusing on the information that forms the curriculum for the small child (the alphabet, basic sums) with ethical messages ('Hurt no living thing'), gentle pastorals, and, according to some late twentieth-century critics, covert

2 Kate Greenaway, *Marigold Garden* (London and New York: Frederick Warne, 1885), p. 16.
3 ['Aunt Effie'], 'Little Rain-drops', in John W. S. Hows, *Hows' Primary Ladies' Reader: A Choice and Varied Collection of Prose and Poetry, Adapted to the Capacities of Young Children* (Philadelphia: E. H. Butler & Co., 1865), p. 83.
4 Hilaire Belloc, *The Bad Child's Book of Beasts* (1896), reprinted as *Hilaire Belloc's Cautionary Verses* (New York: Alfred A. Knopf, 1941), p. 157.

discussions of sexuality and challenges to the patriarchal world view.[5] The simplicity of the best Victorian poetry for children is deceptive.

The literary advocacy of childhood as special, together with the condemnation of adults who fail to appreciate the young, was connected to a larger social effort during the Victorian period to segregate children from adults. Upper- and middle-class boys, and toward the end of the era girls as well, increasingly attended boarding school, so that many affluent children were raised primarily in environments in which peer relationships predominated over adult–child ties. Meanwhile, reformers sought to rescue working-class children from the darker branches of adult-centred employment (for instance, from work as factory hands, chimney sweeps, miners, or prostitutes) and, as historian Hugh Cunningham chronicles, to extend to them some of the benefits of middle-class childhood by removing them from the streets and, if possible, educating them. Separate reformatories were established for juvenile offenders, on the theory that children were more readily salvaged than their elders; workhouses sought to keep young inmates apart from the old. Increasingly, children of all classes were expected to herd with their contemporaries.

The boom in a 'children's literature' as distinct from that for adults is as closely related to this segregationist desire as it is to increased literacy and cheaper print technology. And if many reformist texts that advocated the appreciation and protection of childhood as a vulnerable or quasi-sacred state were aimed primarily at adults, others addressed younger readers. Although most readers of Charles Dickens's *Oliver Twist* (1837–8), say, would have been fully grown, texts including the *Alice* books and John Ruskin's *The King of the Golden River* (written 1841, published 1851), which exempts the child hero from the dishonest rapacity of the grown-up brutes who are his brothers and foster-fathers, were originally created to please specific children.

The glorification of childhood may be found in any number of genres, from domestic fiction to school stories to poetry to waif tales to animal stories – Anna Sewell's 1877 *Black Beauty*, for instance, may be read not only as a plea for kindness to horses, but also as a parable in which the relationship of the anthropomorphic title character to his various masters comments on the styles of authority that adults assumed towards children. Some neo-Romantic children's literature, such as Mary Louisa Molesworth's *Carrots*

---

5 Christina G. Rossetti, *Sing-Song: A Nursery Rhyme Book* (London: Macmillan, 1893), p. 105.

(1876), focuses primarily upon glorifying childish naivety for its own sake, but at its most characteristic, the mode depicts childish innocence's reforming effect upon adults. Thus the best-selling tract *Jessica's First Prayer*, written by 'Hesba Stretton' (Sarah Smith) and first published in the religious family magazine *Sunday at Home* in 1866, casts the title character, a street child, as unwitting evangelist, since her awakening faith and natural unselfconsciousness bring to Christ a man who has ignored his minister's sermons. Juliana Ewing's *The Story of a Short Life* (1882), by a writer who influenced Rudyard Kipling and Frances Hodgson Burnett, tells of a little boy's affecting and protracted death, one designed to bring his admirers (whether inside or outside the story) to accept whatever Providence may visit upon them. While Ewing and Stretton seek to make their protagonists plausible through down-to-earth, humorous touches, the inspirational and sentimental are uppermost.

Evidence from memoirs and autobiographical fiction suggests that responses to this insistence on ideal childhood's exemplary nature varied. Some Victorian children delighted in the literature of moral childhood, while others – E. Nesbit, for example, who ridiculed virtuous fictions such as Maria Louisa Charlesworth's *Ministering Children* (1854) in her stories about the enterprising Bastable family – found pleasure and empowerment rather in scorning this mode. Nevertheless, moral texts circulated widely, even if most of these books (like much Victorian children's literature) would have been acquired as presents or prizes instead of being purchased by young readers themselves.

The Romantic tendency to idealize childhood, and the realist effort to acknowledge childhood as different from adulthood if not necessarily superior to it, also contributed to a renaissance in literary genres that had come to be associated with the young. Foremost among these genres was the fairy tale. Members of the first generation of Victorians, including Dickens, W. M. Thackeray, and Charlotte Brontë, looked back upon their childhood consumption of fairy tales with pleasure, often because fairy tales – imported into England by late eighteenth- and early nineteenth-century publishers as examples of the exotic rather than of the morally useful – were the least didactic and most imaginatively stimulating works that had been available to them. In addition to incorporating fairy-tale motifs into their novels for adults, a number of these authors produced literary fairy tales for children, in which instructive elements are counter-balanced by fantasy. Dickens, for instance, included a playful fairy tale narrated by a child in *A Holiday Romance* (1868); wrote nostalgically of his childhood pleasure in reading (fairy tales were a favourite); hosted

Hans Christian Andersen when the Danish writer visited England; and, in his 1853 essay 'Frauds on the Fairies', attacked his former friend and illustrator George Cruikshank for inserting temperance messages into retellings of classic fairy tales, thus steering them towards instruction at the expense of delight.

Hence, while Victorian fairy tales are certainly not devoid of moral content, this content often exalts 'childlike' attributes such as innocence over qualities or issues associated with adulthood. Dickens, Thackeray, Ruskin, Thomas Hood, and others used the fairy tale to criticize what they identified as the greed, injustice, and (for Ruskin in particular) environmental irresponsibility of the Industrial Revolution. Rossetti used it to warn against appetite, including sexual appetite, in works such as 'Goblin Market' (1859) and *Speaking Likenesses* (1874). George MacDonald, who described himself as writing not for children but 'for the childlike' of any age, used it to extol the traits that he considered childlike in the best sense of the word, such as faith, trust, perception, and a lack of concern for shibboleths, especially those relating to social class. Such adapting of serious messages to the fairy-tale form illustrates both the belief, common to much Victorian children's literature, that reform may best be accomplished by persuading the young to retain or adopt a reformist viewpoint, and the complementary position that adults may be cleansed by becoming 'as little children'.

Simultaneously, we see Victorians taking pleasure in the fairy tale for its own sake. In adult circles, Andrew Lang propounded the anthropological approach to folklore, which viewed traditional tales as sources of data about the origins of human society. Still, he did not limit himself to writing learned articles in the *Fortnightly Review* and the *Encyclopaedia Britannica*. Between 1889 and 1910, he also edited twelve collections of fairy tales named for colours (*The Blue Fairy Book*, *The Red Fairy Book*, and so on), aimed not at educating children but at entertaining them. Lang's bifurcated publication record on folklore is another manifestation of the growing conviction in Victorian Britain that even when children and adults share an interest in a body of works, they are likely to read these works for different reasons and in different ways.

In other words, while some authors consciously encourage adults to adopt a childlike stance (Florence Montgomery prefaces her best-selling 1869 novel *Misunderstood*, 'The following is not a child's story. It is intended . . . for those who are willing to stoop to view life as it appears to a child',[6] and Hannah

---

6 Florence Montgomery, *Misunderstood* (London: Richard Bentley, 1869), p. v.

Mary Rathbone invites readers of her 1841 poetry anthology *Childhood* to examine 'the expression of the feelings excited by the contemplation of children'[7]), and others, such as Dickens, wrote for adults in a manner readily accessible to older children, fairy tales were frequently directed towards an age-differentiated dual audience presumed to have different tastes and needs. Literary fairy tales such as Lang's comic *Prince Prigio* (1889) and its sequels could contain a significant amount of material aimed over children's heads; thus Lang's *Prince Ricardo of Pantouflia* (1893) offers a satirical look at Max Müller's theory that Indian solar mythology is connected to all myths worldwide. Similarly, Oscar Wilde's fairy tales, written shortly after the author had become a father, speak to young readers but also incorporate the occasional homoerotic subtext. 'The Fisherman and His Soul' (1891), for instance, features a devil whose 'face was strangely pale, but [whose] lips were like a proud red flower', whose 'delicate white hands were gemmed with rings', and who has a strange effect on the title character: 'The young Fisherman watched him, as one snared in a spell. At last their eyes met, and wherever he danced it seemed to him that the eyes of the man were upon him.'[8]

Gender roles and children's literature

In the most strongly neo-Romantic Victorian children's works, a category that includes many literary fairy tales and other fantasies, the idealized protagonists' enactment of gender roles tends to stress the feminine. Nominally male, figures such as Gluck in Ruskin's *The King of the Golden River* and Diamond in MacDonald's *At the Back of the North Wind* (1871) display the same sweetness, beauty, concern for others, and lack of aggression that also typify the good Victorian heroine, and indeed they may have been intended as models for girls at least as much as for boys. Ruskin created his fairy tale to amuse his future wife, Effie Gray, and MacDonald's story originally ran as a serial in *Good Words for the Young*, a magazine aimed at children of both sexes. Yet with the exception of a limited number of genres including fantasy, some tract literature and poetry, novelty publications such as pop-up and pull-tab books, and works for the very young, most imaginative writing

---

7 H. M. R. [Hannah Mary Rathbone], *Childhood, Illustrated in a Selection from the Poets* (London: Harvey and Darton, 1841), p. v.

8 Oscar Wilde, 'The Fisherman and His Soul', in *The Complete Short Stories* (New York: Oxford University Press, 2010), pp. 178–9.

for Victorian children primarily targeted either boys or girls. Thus, although many works had crossover appeal for individuals of the 'wrong' sex or age (letters from correspondents printed in certain boys' magazines, for instance, indicate that a small but significant segment of their audience was female), a major function of much Victorian children's literature was to help readers identify and develop traits considered appropriate in adult men and women. Understandably, the genres associated principally with girlhood, such as domestic fiction and girls' historical novels, focused most closely on offering instruction in femininity, while those associated with boyhood, such as adventure fiction and boys' school stories, focused on masculinity – though authors might differ in their understandings of what constituted the ideal form of each, especially since gender roles were by no means static over the period.

The popular and prolific Tractarian novelist Charlotte Mary Yonge affords useful insight into the socialization of well-to-do Victorian girls. No neo-Romantic, Yonge believed rather that a child's natural impulses might need to be curbed or redirected by wise adults (it was an article of faith with her that adult wisdom required a sincere and strong Christianity, preferably Anglican in expression) so that he or she could develop into a useful member of society. At the same time, she was fully aware, having experienced the process herself, of the frustration that a bright girl might endure over the restrictions that the Victorian world placed on female endeavour. Her fiction, then, often recognizes that people may not initially welcome discipline; she invokes faith and the desirability of pleasing authority figures as a way of inviting readers to accept the bridle and bit.

Countess Kate is a case in point. In this 1862 novel, the protagonist unexpectedly inherits a title and is sent into the care of two spinster aunts. Used to living in a large and lively adoptive family, Kate chafes at the decorum of a childless household. Though not a bad child, she repeatedly gets into trouble for unladylike behaviour: tearing and dirtying her clothes, failing to moderate her voice, forgetting her manners, drawing attention to herself in public in undesirable ways such as jumping into a fountain in a panic during a thunderstorm. Never successful, the placement with the aunts culminates in Kate's underhandedly concealing her disobedience, and finally in her running away from home, an act that the narrative identifies as inexcusable in a gently reared girl. The happy ending puts Kate in the care of yet another set of guardians, who will be able to provide the guidance and control that she needs in order to be able to fulfil the responsibilities of her station.

Countess Kate's exceptionally detailed account of its protagonist's interior life models for readers traits that its author, and many of her contemporaries, considered indispensable to productive womanhood. That the narrative pays so much attention to the moral timbre of Kate's actions suggests that girls need to examine every aspect of their behaviour and must work constantly to improve. Nor should their efforts be confined to enthusiasm about churchgoing. Yonge emphasizes that Christian precepts must be embraced in secular settings as well – that duty to neighbour encompasses not only glamorous and dramatic gestures such as becoming a missionary, but also behaving considerately towards one's governess, restraining natural exuberance so as not to disturb an invalid aunt, and accepting the authority of elders even when they seem unjust. (Yonge's willingness to acknowledge the flaws of parents or surrogate parents, apparent also in works such as *The Castle Builders* (1854), helps to differentiate her from some of her predecessors.) Again and again, Kate finds herself in situations where self-control is essential. That she generally fails to measure up suggests simultaneously that ideal femininity does not come easily, that indiscipline tends to expose girls to humiliation, and that maturing entails not a single brief high-stakes struggle but an interminable series of tiny battles, many of which may be lost.

Victorian boys' stories sometimes make a strikingly similar set of points, even while their authors note that boys' behaviour *looks* different from girls'. Consider a widely read Evangelical school story, Frederic Farrar's *Eric, or Little by Little* (1858). Eric's spiritual drama is played out at school rather than at home, and his action is less circumscribed than Kate's; for instance, although he too runs away, he ships out as a cabin boy rather than seeking out family members as Kate does. Moreover, while except for her flight from her aunts Kate's wrongdoing consists largely of overly boister-ous play and some unauthorized shopping (done in the company of her maid, who has tempted her into this disobedience), Eric's involves swear-ing, drunkenness, and stealing, all activities that middle-class Victorians associated with the rabble. Kate's conduct puts her at risk of being labelled a hoyden; Eric's threatens him with a slide into the proletariat. Yet in Farrar's novel as in Yonge's we encounter the idea of incremental misdoing, the warning that one apparently trivial error will lead to another more serious, so that both boy and girl readers are directed to watch themselves and to cultivate self-control, respect for authority, forethought, and piety.

Other canonical works emphasizing the development of ideal masculinity seek to have things both ways. A novel contemporaneous with *Eric*, Thomas

Hughes's *Tom Brown's Schooldays* (1857), celebrates both a hearty, secular manliness and something more androgynous and Christian. Through a series of set-pieces focusing on athletic encounters between men – an exhibition backsword bout at a county fair, a football game, a fistfight, a cricket match – Hughes establishes the importance of strength, skill, and masculine competition. Simultaneously, he indicates that physical prowess is not enough; the sturdy title character must also accept the guidance provided by a smaller, weaker, and more feminine boy, George Arthur, who brings prayer and soul-searching into Rugby dormitories. Even less overtly earnest works such as Kipling's *Stalky & Co.* (1899), which examines the connection between the apparent lawlessness of three schoolboys and the military exploits that such boys may perform in later life, indicate that what looks like unregenerate wildness masks its own brand of morality.

Middle-class Victorian children's fiction does not take a unitary viewpoint on the conduct and outlook considered suitable for girls and boys. For instance, later Victorian writers such as Nesbit, as well as Anglo-Irish writers such as Annie Keary and Flora Shaw, tend to be readier than their predecessors to accept tomboyish behaviour in girls, and the girls' school story of the end of the century, by such practitioners as L. T. Meade, Evelyn Sharp, and Mrs George de Horne Vaizey, also places a premium upon liveliness absent from early examples of the genre. Similarly, the difference in affect as we move from *Eric* to *Stalky* is symptomatic of authors' changing views on the desirability of expressing or repressing strong emotion (the 'stiff upper lip' modality dominated English masculinity towards the end of the century). Individual variations aside, however, the fascination with gender that this body of fiction displays has much to tell later generations about Victorian understandings of sex roles and of reading's place in the socialization of children. These stories work by engaging their readers' interest in the actions and consciousnesses of other children, much more than in the instructive voice of an adult narrator. Although narrators frequently comment on the errors or achievements of the youthful players, the process through which gender is explained assumes that children learn best if their negative and positive role models are peers rather than parents.

Domesticity and exoticism

Indeed, much Victorian children's fiction excludes parents altogether, thus giving the child more scope to act – or, from the viewpoint of the reader, to imagine acting. Influential Victorian commentators both male and female, from Ruskin to advice-givers such as Sarah Stickney Ellis and Isabella Beeton, often positioned the home as the cornerstone of English society. Yet the growth of empire created a widespread understanding that the world was not limited either to home or to England, and children's texts repeatedly examine issues such as the loss of parents, the departure from home, the attempt to reconstitute home in an alien setting, and even the joyful repudiation of home in favour of an anti-domestic freedom. Mirroring the variety noticeable elsewhere in the juvenile literature of this period, any given work following the child outside the home may differ drastically in outlook from its neighbour.

On one end of the scale, we might place novels such as Burnett's *Little Lord Fauntleroy* (1886), which separates little Cedric from his native United States and his mother only so that he can import his democratic stance and filial love to his new home in England with his grandfather. The inevitable happy ending permits Cedric to form a blended household that incorporates representatives of both the old life and the new, effectively extending the boundaries and values of 'home' across the Atlantic: a colonization by domesticity. On the other end might be works such as the eighty-one historical novels for adolescent boys produced by G. A. Henty from 1871 to 1902. These works adhere to a formula in which the teenaged hero, often an orphan, leaves home early in the proceedings, becomes involved in military action, and, after making his fortune and advancing the interests of his country, settles down in the final chapter to his reward, a suitable marriage. Characterization is slight; from century to century and nation to nation, the Henty protagonist is a type rather than an individual, and the devotee's attention is directed instead towards historical detail. If the latter, as critics have pointed out, was not invariably accurate, it nonetheless permitted the books to assert their wholesomeness by virtue of their patriotism and focus on information.

Between these poles lies a wide variety of travel and/or adventure writing for children. Some works resemble *Little Lord Fauntleroy* in emphasizing feminine and domestic values; many of these narratives are strongly Christian. Thus Anne Bowman's *The Boy Voyagers; or, The Pirates of the East* (1859) bears a dashing and secular title and conveys its title characters from England to Africa to Asia, yet its focus is not only on exoticism but also on conversion, presented as a necessary prerequisite to reunion with a parent. Similarly, the popular Evangelical children's author Charlotte Tucker, who wrote under the pen name A.L.O.E. ('A Lady of England'), produced works such as *The Light in the Robbers' Cave* (1862), whose protagonist must be rescued not only from a band of Italian robbers, but also from the arrogance that causes 'his manner, even to his mother, [to be] petulant and imperious'. At the end of the process, he understands that 'his first post of duty must be home'.[9] Yet the children's literature of the exotic also includes many novels that focus on the secular and that celebrate masculine experience in nondomestic settings, even while happy endings typically involve a return to home and family.

Robert Louis Stevenson's *Treasure Island* (1883) illustrates the idiosyncratic way in which Victorian adventure stories might explore the counterpoint of home and not-home, the familiar and the strange. Inspired by a map that Stevenson created in conjunction with his young stepson, and initially read as a work-in-progress in nightly instalments to family and friends, this novel both sends its narrator on a voyage that seems to undermine the very idea of home and hints that domesticity may serve to disguise men's most sinister impulses. Just as Jim Hawkins's family's inn is simultaneously his home and the bolt hole of a pirate hoping to evade his erstwhile shipmates, the apparently kindly old cook John Silver turns out to be the most terrifying member of a fearsome crew once Jim has left inn and mother behind and set off to make the family fortunes. What makes Silver particularly dangerous is his ability to dissemble, to move easily between murder and nurturing the young or deferring to his social superiors. In the context of a Britain that was not only maintaining a vast empire overseas but was also experiencing an influx of foreigners into capital and seaports, Silver's nightmarish shifting between the familiar and the unfamiliar, his skill at duping those who deem themselves respectable, is an uncanny warning about the permeability of the borders of the dominant society.

Victorian children's magazines

Before being published in book form, *Treasure Island* was serialized in *Young Folks*, and this fact reminds us that in the second half of the century, boys' magazines were the major venue for the mingling of the domestic and the exotic – if not necessarily within a given serial, certainly within a given number. Periodicals such as the *Boy's Own Paper*, *Chums*, the *Captain*, and dozens more (critic Diana Dixon has counted 160 magazines for children marketed in 1900 alone) sought to maximize audience appeal by featuring

9 'A. L. O. E.', *The Light in the Robber's Cave* (London: T. Nelson and Sons, 1862), pp. 8, 171.

multiple genres and viewpoints. Thus adventure stories jostled school stories, historical romances, how-to articles addressing boys living at home, advice columns, contests, and more. Their counterparts for girls, similarly, ran domestic stories, historical sagas (generally less martial than those offered to boys), music, poetry, instructions for handicraft projects, and letters, to name only a few typical features. As compendia of different kinds of literary productions, magazines assisted in forming young readers' tastes by acquainting them with multiple genres and, often, with other readers' responses to particular works or ideas.

They thus enjoyed a symbiotic relationship to book publishing; serials by well-known authors helped to sell magazines, but simultaneously advertised the hardcover publication that frequently followed a text's initial appearance. Hence periodicals for children provided a forum for writers both experienced and inexperienced. The comparatively low production costs and built-in audience of established magazines lowered the risk inherent in showcasing new authors or works; alongside major stories by famous names appeared countless works by the obscure, some of whom became prominent in turn. Similarly, some important children's writers, among them Yonge, Henty, and adventure novelist W. H. G. Kingston, edited magazines after achieving fame as authors, seeing this work as a way of encouraging younger colleagues and maintaining a special relationship with readers. Magazine editing was often perceived as a way of helping children to develop desirable traits such as patriotism or piety, or to instil a love of handicrafts or poetry – although if letters printed in correspondence columns are any indication, subscribers took much more interest in the serial of the moment than in the sentimental verses that showed up in magazines with a middle-class female readership.

Also worthy of note is the extent to which work for children penetrated magazines aimed predominantly at adults. In 1883, for instance, one of Yonge's historical novels was the inaugural serial in the *English Illustrated Magazine*, which was also to serve as a venue for such important late Victorian children's illustrators as Greenaway and Walter Crane. Nesbit's first really successful literary productions, the Bastable stories, were first printed at the end of the 1890s, predominantly in adult periodicals – the *Illustrated London News* and the *Pall Mall* and *Windsor* magazines – although she also sold some work to children's venues, among them *Nister's Holiday Annual* and the *Girl's Own Paper*, which serialized her memoir 'My School-Days' from October 1896 to September 1897. Nesbit's children's fantasies (with illustrations by H. R. Millar) were a mainstay of the *Strand* from 1899 until shortly before the First World War; Kipling's *Stalky & Co.* first appeared in the *Windsor* in 1898–9.

English-language periodical publishing for children began in 1751, when publisher and bookseller John Newbery launched a magazine with the Brobdingnagian subtitle *The Young Gentleman & Lady's Golden Library, Being an Attempt to Mend the World, to Render the Society of Man More Amiable, and to Establish the Plainness, Simplicity, Virtue & Wisdom of the Golden Age, So Much Celebrated by the Poets and Historians.* While Newbery's magazine lasted only three issues, the idea behind it proved more durable. Eighteenth-century England boasted a mere eleven children's magazines, but the nineteenth century, which witnessed a corresponding boom in adult periodicals as literacy rates and print technology improved, saw several hundred titles appear (and, usually, disappear). Despite wide variations in outlook and ideology, certain themes recur, notably the tension between commercialism and what Newbery's subtitle calls 'mend[ing] the world'.

Magazines associated with religious denominations were particularly numerous in the nineteenth century, and appropriately, the first Christian-themed magazine for the young, the *Youth's Magazine; or, Evangelical Miscellany*, was founded in 1805 by a teenager, William Lloyd. Like many of the titles that followed it, the *Youth's Magazine* was associated with a more powerful umbrella organization, in this case the Sunday School Union, which helped assure readership; Lloyd's brainchild survived to merge with the *Bible Class Magazine* in 1867. Nineteenth-century church papers benefited from other factors also, including their suitability as 'rewards' commemorating diligence or attendance in schools and widespread acceptance of Sabbatarian principles, which forbade light reading on Sundays but permitted the perusal of religious material.

Some Christian magazines were more overtly religious than others. At one extreme were titles such as the *Children's Friend* (1824–1930, founded by the same Reverend W. Carus Wilson who inspired *Jane Eyre*'s rigid Mr Brocklehurst), whose graphic descriptions of human sacrifice and other 'heathen' barbarisms helped create support for the cultural and political imperialism that promised, implicitly and explicitly, to end un-Christian atrocities. Less overtly Christian, if equally imperialist, were the Religious Tract Society's *The Boy's Own Paper* and its sister organ, *The Girl's Own Paper* (1879–1967 and 1880–1956 respectively). Designed as healthy-minded alternatives to the growing number of sensational story papers for the young, these weeklies so successfully navigated the marketplace that the RTS worried that their profitability might mean that their tendency was to corrupt rather than to improve. The emphasis here was not on the pleasures of Sunday school but on more generalized forms of character building. One may find any number of children's periodicals with no religious slant that shared this commitment to uplift. In a secular version of the affiliation of Sunday titles to particular religious organizations, various reform movements, from temperance to vegetarianism, sponsored magazines to ensure that youngsters growing up in these movements might have reading material that affirmed their principles.

Victorian commentators on juvenile magazines expressed anxiety about the less morally oriented aspects of the field – the areas driven not by high-mindedness but by profit. While commercialism has been crucial in children's periodical publishing from Newbery onwards, it seemed particularly evident in the mushrooming of Victorian titles that aimed principally at the newly literate children of the working classes. Not necessarily of weaker literary quality than the exhaustingly didactic early religious periodicals, the hack papers that flourished from the mid nineteenth century through the 1940s horrified critics because of their violent and/or slapstick content, their willingness to curry favour with young consumers by pandering to their baser instincts.

The social effects of such publications were often presumed to be negative. Like Congressional investigations of American comic books in the 1950s, the criticism aimed at 'penny dreadfuls' and other mass-market story papers focused on their potential to improperly socialize the child consumer by liberating his (for the at-risk reader is usually figured as male) violent instincts, acquainting him prematurely with sexual situations, and encouraging disrespect towards elders or class superiors. Nevertheless, such periodicals arguably had a positive influence upon children's literature, not only because they helped to inspire beloved works of later periods, but also because the outcry against them heightened adult commitment to the production of children's literature that would please as well as preach.

Text and image

If the success of children's magazines depended partly upon social developments such as the establishment of an efficient delivery system to convey the product to customers beyond London, the creation of a large literate audience who valued children's reading enough to purchase it, and refinements in technology so that large print runs could be produced cheaply, the boom in *illustrated* texts for children required all these developments and more. Until the mid nineteenth century mass-produced illustrations were typically monochrome wood engravings. The wood whose grain is best suited to the production of the latter is boxwood, but because box trees have a comparatively narrow girth, the engraving blocks are limited in size, restricting the scope of images that may be produced with any single block (though an image may be spread across multiple blocks, a technique that poses its own difficulties). Moreover, the process of engraving is painstaking and time-consuming, requiring substantial skill. All these factors resulted in a tendency for early Victorian illustrations to be small and generic, since publishers often economized by recycling – even stealing – images from existing texts.

Advances in photography in the late 1830s, however, made possible advances in illustration as well. Initially, photography expedited engraving because the image to be reproduced no longer had to be drawn by hand on to the wooden blocks for the engraver to cut; photographs of the image could now be used as guides, permitting more accurate renditions. In the 1880s, the development of the halftone photo-engraving process, in which acid rather than an engraving tool is used to cut the lines, substantially increased precision, and the invention of three-colour photographic reproduction on to glazed paper facilitated the production of illustrations with real claims to beauty. Especially after the establishment of copyright laws that covered images as well as text, illustration became newly profitable for publishers and artists alike, and the elaborately produced illustrated 'gift book' for children became a Christmas staple.

It was in the 1850s and 1860s that the mass-marketed British children's book began to become more self-consciously attractive on a visual level, largely through the efforts of publisher Edmund Evans. Evans's contributions were not limited to making improvements in the printing of children's books, for example by spearheading the development of the eight-page chapbook-style 'toy book' of the 1830s from an insignificant pamphlet-sized rendition of a traditional tale, characterized by minimal production values, into a form that combined low cost with sophisticated design. He also had a gift for spotting talented young illustrators such as Walter Crane (the first of the successful illustrators to use colour), Greenaway, and Randolph Caldecott, all born in the mid-1840s but already productive in the mid to late 1860s.

Like their counterparts in the world of children's text, the best Victorian children's illustrators created distinctive and varied styles and works. Crane's adaptations of Pre-Raphaelite, Renaissance, Greek, and Japanese principles are readily distinguishable from Greenaway's trademark images of children in high-waisted dresses and velvet suits, Caldecott's apparently spontaneous and lively sketches, and, later, the equally individual work of Arthur Rackham and Beatrix Potter, among the most notable proponents of what is sometimes termed the 'golden age of children's book illustration'. The illustrated children's books of the Victorian era profited from the confluence of an adult art world fascinated by literary texts and by the narrative potential of the visual; the assumption that illustrated books were particularly stimulating to the imagination (and that imagination should be encouraged); and the desire of publishers that their products stand out in an increasingly crowded market. The idiosyncratic flourished in this environment. The extraordinary range of Victorian illustration, from the drawings that Edward Lear created from the 1840s through the 1870s to accompany his nonsense verse to the late Victorian work of the versatile W. Heath Robinson, testifies to the premium placed upon the new. And the quality of the images helps to demonstrate how seriously illustrated children's books were taken, as the level of excellence achieved implies that the consumer is meant to pore over and treasure the result.

Conclusion

During the Victorian period, the development of new conceptions of children and of children's reading practices resulted in the production of an extraordinarily rich variety of works for this expanding market. Building upon existing forms, the era saw radical departures from the past in any number of genres. Poetry moved from Wattsian didacticism to nonsense verse (Carroll, Lear, Belloc), evocations of the child's sensibility (Stevenson in *A Child's Garden of Verses*), and fantastic narrative (Rossetti, Robert Browning in 'The Pied Piper of Hamelin'). Domestic fiction widened beyond the straightforward presentation of positive and negative role models to encompass instances such as the 'pickle' story, *à la* Catherine Sinclair's *Holiday House* (1839), which celebrated childish naughtiness as endearing; the sentimental tale; and the family saga – simultaneously shifting from an emphasis on stereotypical or homiletic characters to a naturalistic style designed to provide insight into the child mind. Fairy tales no longer had to be imported from the Continent, although some foreign material continued to circulate widely: the fairy tales of Andersen, the Brothers Grimm, and the Norwegians Peter Christen Asbjørnsen and Jørgen Moe; Heinrich Hoffman's verse collection *Der Struwwelpeter* (1845, trans.

1848); American texts such as *The Adventures of Tom Sawyer* (1876; published in England six months before it appeared in the United States), *Little Women* (1868), and Susan Coolidge's *Katy* books; and a pioneering Australian work for children, Ethel Turner's *Seven Little Australians* (1894), among many other popular texts. The very end of the period saw the inauguration of the modern picture book (as opposed to illustrated works dominated by text) with Potter's *The Tale of Peter Rabbit* (1901), presaged a few decades earlier by Caldecott's illustrations for traditional rhymes. In kind as in number, far more juvenile works were available in Victoria's reign than ever before, and they addressed a wider range of children.

They also sought to shape both the child reader and adult perceptions of childhood. Through devices from pictures to pathos, reader identification with characters to narrators' homilies, authors and illustrators sought to provide guidance and pleasure; instil good principles and the behaviour appropriate to the imagined reader's class, nation, age, and gender; further adult sympathy with the young; cultivate their audience's imagination; and accomplish all this in new and potentially profitable ways. From the finished products, we may derive both entertainment and information about the beliefs and inner workings of the culture that created them. Since, after all, the Victorians saw children's literature as invaluable to the socialization of the young, the genre was an efficient and lucid conveyor of cultural values, couched in a form designed with a dual purpose: instruction and delight.

PART IV

*

MATTERS OF DEBATE

Education

DINAH BIRCH

Education is the process underlying the production, transmission, and interpretation of all texts, and as such it is the bedrock of literary culture. Its purposes and methods were debated with particular intensity during the nineteenth century. What was at stake was the means to power and self-determination. Some saw its development as a necessary social control; for others, it could provide a way of escaping constraint. The politics and practice of schooling were often a central theme for Victorian writers. But literature could also be in itself a vehicle for teaching, and many saw it in these terms. Conflicting definitions of the pedagogies of writing shape the most prominent features of the literary landscape, defining the fundamental premises which were extending the scope of every genre, whether fiction, poetry, drama, journalism, or criticism.

Education and reform

Numerous campaigns throughout the nineteenth century drove a wholesale transformation of schools, colleges, and universities, and the consequences were far-reaching. By 1901, the entangled and often chaotic condition of education in England and Wales that had characterized the early 1830s had developed into a more heavily regulated system, supported and supervised by the state.[1] In the early decades of the nineteenth century, educational provision at all levels was still heavily dominated by religious institutions, as it had been for centuries. The role of organized religion was particularly crucial in supplying elementary education for the poor. For children from working families, many of whom would themselves be at work during the

---

1 The provision of a broadly based system of public education has a much longer history in Scotland, and in Ireland too the development of education in the nineteenth century follows a separate and different pattern.

week, Sunday schools run on a voluntary and charitable basis often offered the only accessible means of education. The more ambitious Sunday schools would also provide tuition for adults. In 1833, the government began to involve itself in the teaching of needy children, granting small annual sums of money to fund the construction of schools to provide elementary education. This move did not break the link between religion and education, for the schools in question were governed by churches and chapels, but it proved to be the first step in the slow and piecemeal movement towards the secularization of education.

Though literacy levels rose through the mid-Victorian period, uneasiness about uneven and inadequate educational systems also grew, exacerbated by political anxieties arising from the expanded electorate created by the Reform Acts of 1832 and 1867, and a growing awareness of the commercial competition represented by better-trained workers in continental Europe and North America. William Forster's Elementary Education Act of 1870 represented the first real acceleration in the slow movement towards a national system of education. Forster's Act established board schools, partly funded by the state, to provide elementary education in areas where existing provision was inadequate. These schools remained fee-paying, and attendance was not obligatory. But with the Elementary Education Act of 1880 basic schooling became free (for both boys and girls, from the ages of five to ten) and, for the first time, compulsory. Board schools became, for thousands of children, the way to a disciplined and competent education. Arthur Conan Doyle's detective Sherlock Holmes – that fictional embodiment of rational thought – spoke for many when he pointed out the newly built board schools to Watson, as their train approached Clapham Junction:

> 'It's a very cheery thing to come into London by any of these lines which run high, and allow you to look down upon the houses like this.'
> I thought he was joking, for the view was sordid enough, but he soon explained himself.
> 'Look at those big, isolated clumps of building rising up above the slates, like brick islands in a lead-colored sea.'
> 'The Boardschools.'
> 'Lighthouses, my boy! Beacons of the future! Capsules with hundreds of bright little seeds in each, out of which will spring the wiser, better England of the future.'[2]

2 Arthur Conan Doyle, 'The Naval Treaty', in *The Memoirs of Sherlock Holmes* (1893), ed. Christopher Roden (Oxford University Press, 1993), pp. 228–9.

Access to formal education gradually became almost universal, and the appetite for printed material which followed revolutionized the production and consumption of books and periodicals of every description. But it would be a mistake to see this as a smooth progress towards a wholly co-ordinated system, more effective in every way than the disorder it had replaced. Educational practices continued to be deeply divided along lines of class, region, gender, and religion. The reluctance of the Anglican church and rival Dissenting bodies to hand over control of the schools they sponsored and ran was a major obstacle to nationalized reform. So too were the obdurate divisions of class, for despite the increasing involvement of the state, affluent middle-class families persisted in their custom of educating their children privately, using fee-paying schools and home teachers of widely varying levels of aspiration and competence. This was a major difference between schooling in England and on the Continent, where state involvement in the provision of education was much more readily accepted, and indeed welcomed. In England, such intervention was frequently viewed as an example of the kind of tyranny that it was the duty of every free-born Briton to resist – an attitude that lingered right through the nineteenth century, and beyond. Nevertheless, it became widely acknowledged that the inconsistent and inefficient organization of schools and colleges, many of them offering narrow and badly taught courses of study, was a significant barrier to national progress. Inadequate education was not simply a problem for the poor. The Taunton Commission (1864–8), a major Schools Enquiry Commission charged with the investigation of endowed secondary and proprietary schools supplying teaching for middle-class children, uncovered a disturbingly patchy and confused picture. Originally planned to look only at the education of boys, as a result of protest from female educational reformers it extended its remit to cover the provision of schooling for girls. Partly as a result of the Commission's findings, definitions of what might be prescribed as useful learning for both boys and girls, once the fundamentals of literacy, numeracy, and religious knowledge had been acquired, were significantly extended.

This expansion continued a pattern of growth that was already marked in Victorian schools and colleges. Ambitious programmes of learning were not invented in the nineteenth century – it is worth remembering that the great Dissenting academies founded in the eighteenth century had established a remarkable tradition of teaching in science, English literature, modern languages, history, geography, political theory, and economics. These had, however, taught relatively small numbers, and their sectarian affiliations meant that they drew on a limited pool of pupils. Throughout the nine-teenth century, teaching comparable with that pioneered by the Dissenting academies became more widespread. Elite institutions traditionally dedi-cated to the study of classics, theology, and mathematics for boys, and those which had emphasized social accomplishments, including music, fine needlework, and drawing for girls, enlarged their curricula. Grammar schools also began to diversify their teaching. Originally established to provide teaching in the classics, they had become hampered by the rigid terms of their foundations. The Grammar Schools Act of 1840 developed the range of subjects that could be taught in these schools to include science and literature. In 1871, the requirement that grammar school masters must be Anglican ministers, licensed by their bishops, was removed. Practical training for poorer sections of society was supported by the work of Mechanics' Institutes, the product of a movement established in the 1820s to provide scientific and vocational education for working men. These institutes, increasingly dominated by the middle classes, sometimes developed into eminent and influential institutions of higher education. The University of Manchester Institute of Science and Technology (UMIST), and Birkbeck College in London, were both originally Mechanics' Institutes. On a smaller scale, mutual improvement societies, run with varying degrees of regulation and success, sprang up among groups of working men hungry for a better level of education. Often short-lived and poorly funded, they nevertheless offered access to teaching, and to collections of books, that would otherwise have been beyond the reach of men without the resources for travel or formal instruction. Alternative models for loosely organized, informal groups of readers flourished, for working-class readers were not wholly dependent on middle-class educational initiatives.[3] As Jonathan Rose has pointed out, 'From the beginning of the industrial revolution, the British working class enjoyed a reputation for self-education.'[4] Here, the Public Libraries Act of 1850, which laid the foundations for a comprehensive system of freely accessible and publicly funded libraries in England and Wales (the provisions of the Act were extended to Scotland and Ireland in 1853), had a lasting impact. Many children, and adults too, found their own way to education in these 'universities of the street corner'.

3 See Jonathan Rose, *The Intellectual Life of the British Working Classes* (New Haven and London: Yale University Press, 2001), for a comprehensive account of the diverse means by which working-class children and adults were able to educate themselves, often to a remarkably sophisticated level.
4 *Ibid.*, p. 187.

For many such readers, the paths to learning were solitary. Determined and sometimes isolated efforts for self-improvement amongst both men and women were important throughout the period. The persistent popularity of Samuel Smiles's *Self-Help: With Illustrations of Conduct and Perseverance* (1859) is instructive. Here too a tradition which might seem quintessentially Victorian can be seen to have older roots, as Smiles is eager to confirm – quoting, for instance, the eighteenth-century historian Edward Gibbon: 'Every person has two educations, one which he receives from others, and one, more important, which he gives to himself.'[5] Poverty should be seen as no obstacle to learning, as Smiles understands the matter, and his arguments serve to bolster the self-respect of his labouring readers. They have, after all, been taught to work:

> This is an advantage which the working classes, strictly so called, certainly possess over the leisure classes, – that they are in early life under the necessity of applying themselves laboriously to some mechanical pursuit or other, – thus acquiring manual dexterity and the use of their physical powers. The chief disadvantage attached to the calling of the laborious classes is, not that they are employed in physical work, but that they are too exclusively so employed, often to the neglect of their moral and intellectual faculties. While the youths of the leisure classes, having been taught to associate labour with servility, have shunned it, and been allowed to grow up practically ignorant, the poorer classes, confining themselves within the circle of their laborious callings, have been allowed to grow up in a large proportion of cases absolutely illiterate. It seems possible, however, to avoid both these evils by combining physical training or physical work with intellectual culture: and there are various signs abroad which seem to mark the gradual adoption of this healthier system of education.[6]

Smiles was right to claim that models for education at all levels were increasingly inclined to incorporate what he calls 'physical training or physical work', and that this impulse took a variety of forms. A growing emphasis on physical culture in schools and universities was one symptom of this shift, and competitive sport acquired a higher profile in many schools and colleges.

Step by step, as opportunities for higher education became more varied and widely available, practical or vocational curricula to cater for the needs and aspirations of students destined for commercial rather than clerical careers multiplied. In 1826, the foundation of University College in London

5 Samuel Smiles, *Self-Help: With Illustrations of Conduct and Perseverance* (Oxford University Press, 2002), p. 261.
6 *Ibid.*, p. 264.

initiated a movement to provide opportunities for a serious higher education for students barred from the exclusively Anglican older universities. In 1831, King's College London was founded, as an Anglican foundation, and in 1836 University College and King's College combined to create the University of London. It was joined by other colleges and new universities, many based in the rapidly expanding industrial cities of the Midlands and the North, offering wider choices of specialization, and recruiting students (notably Nonconformists) who had previously been excluded from a university education. Owens College, which later became the Victoria University of Manchester, dates from 1851; Mason College, later the University of Birmingham, was founded in 1880; University College Liverpool followed in 1881. George Gissing, who attended Owens College, gives a vigorous picture of life in the early days of these institutions in his account of 'Whitelaw College' in *Born in Exile* (1892).

The universities of Oxford and Cambridge remained powerful and prestigious, but they began to move away from their long-established primary functions of providing service, training, and support for the Church of England. John Henry Newman's quasi-autobiographical novel, *Loss and Gain* (1848), reflects the intensity of religious experience that could accompany a university education for young men of his generation, though the clergyman Edward Bradley (writing as Cuthbert Bede) gives a comic account of life in Oxford, *The Adventures of Mr Verdant Green* (1853–7), that reminds his readers that some undergraduates were not inclined to take their spiritual responsibilities quite as seriously. Responding to the recommendations of the Royal Commission of 1850, Oxford and Cambridge introduced and examined new subjects, including natural sciences and law, history, medieval and modern (European) languages and literatures, and engineering. From the 1870s onwards, Oxford and Cambridge followed other institutions of higher education in opening their doors to non-Anglicans, and to women. In a slow and fragmented fashion, the education of women throughout the Victorian period grew more thorough and rigorous, in terms of access to the privileged bodies of knowledge represented by science and the classics, and leading eventually to training for professions previously reserved for young men.

Education and religion

These changes were comprehensive, but they were not harmonious. There was little consensus as to the proper objectives of education, nor was there any widely shared agreement as to what systems would best serve its aims.

The gradual secularization of pedagogic values was controversial, and bitterly contested. The link between religious instruction and institutions dedicated to the provision of formal education remained strong. In 1900, most elementary schools in England and Wales still had a denominational affiliation. Throughout the early and middle decades of the period, all students and fellows of colleges in Oxford and Cambridge were obliged to be members of the Anglican Church, a stipulation only abolished with the University Tests Acts 1871. Schoolmasters were often also ordained ministers. The reform of boys' public schools[7] in the middle decades of the nineteenth century was often religiously motivated, and widely read school stories like F. W. Farrar's *Eric, or Little by Little* (1858), or Talbot Baines Reed's later *Fifth Form at St Dominic's* (1891–7), reflect the centrality of religious purpose in much educational reform. The tone of girls' schools was equally devout, and this too is reflected in the stories they generated, like Elizabeth Meade's vivid *A World of Girls: The Story of a School* (1896). Those most closely involved with teaching commonly believed that the dissociation of education and religion would have dangerous and destructive results.

Progressive reformers were not always eager to sever this link. Many saw such work as a religious duty. The foundation of the Ragged School Union in 1846, with the purpose of providing, free of charge, something better than the uncertain teaching of dame schools for poor children, focused on reading, writing, arithmetic, and Bible study. The philanthropic Lord Shaftesbury, for many years the President of the Union, saw the work of the ragged schools as an expression of his Evangelical religious faith, and he stoutly resisted later attempts to dilute their assertively Christian tone. Charles Dickens, an active supporter of ragged schools, put the matter with characteristic fervour in a letter to the *Daily News* (1852), describing the ragged school movement as he encountered it in a visit to London's Field Lane as an attempt

> to introduce among the most miserable and neglected outcasts in London, some knowledge of the commonest principles of morality and religion; to commence their recognition as immortal human creatures, before the Gaol Chaplain becomes their only schoolmaster; to suggest to Society that its duty to this wretched throng, foredoomed to crime and punishment,

---

7 Elite fee-paying schools in England are known as 'public schools', though they cater only for the wealthy.

rightfully begins at some distance from the Police-office; and that the careless maintenance from year to year, in this capital city of the world, of a vast hopeless nursery of ignorance, misery and vice; a breeding place for the hulks and gaols: is horrible to contemplate.[8]

Dickens's polemic here is uncompromising. He speaks of the need to inculcate in the children the principles of morality and religion, in acknowledgment of their immortality. Thoughts of literacy and numeracy take second place. In *Bleak House* (1852–3), which began publication in the same year as his letter to the *Daily News*, the hungry and ignorant figure of Jo the crossing-sweeper represents the 'wretched throng' that Dickens describes. No ragged school rescues Jo, but it is not an accident that his one formal lesson, as he lies dying, comes when he follows the charitable doctor Allan Woodcourt in a recitation of the Lord's Prayer.

Those who wanted to animate middle-class education would also often define their purpose in terms of their Christian calling. Dr Thomas Arnold, the celebrated headmaster of Rugby School, is a telling example. Arnold transformed Rugby into one of the most disciplined and influential public schools for boys in England. His pupils, drawn from the prospering landed or middle classes, stood in no need of redemption from the degradations of poverty. But his deepest motives as an educationalist, like those of Lord Shaftesbury, were neither academic nor social; they were religious. An ordained Anglican minister, he wanted to shape Rugby into a school that would turn boys into thoughtful Christian gentlemen. This mattered more than their intellectual or social progress, though it was intimately bound up with both. Like many educationalists of his generation, he did not see childhood as a condition that was to be valued for its own sake. In *The Christian Life: Its Course, Its Hindrances, and Its Helps* (1841), published shortly before his death, Arnold argued that childhood was a stage that should be passed through as quickly as possible, for its unformed characteristics were incompatible with the development of faith:

> It is quite clear, that if the change from childhood to manhood can be hastened safely, it ought to be hastened; and that it is a sin in every one not to try to hasten it: because, to retain the imperfections of childhood when you can get rid of them, is in itself to forfeit the innocence of childhood; to exchange the condition of the innocent infant whom Christ blessed, for that of the unprofitable servant whom Christ condemned. For with the growth

8 Charles Dickens, *The Daily News*, 4 February 1846.

of our bodies evil will grow in us unavoidably; and then, if we are not positively good, we are, of necessity, positively sinners.[9]

This was clearly not a policy calculated to promote the exuberance of youth. Though the disciplines of sport came to figure largely in the moral training offered at Rugby, Thomas Hughes's popular novel *Tom Brown's Schooldays* (1857), which vividly recalls Hughes's years as a pupil at Rugby and fixed the image of public school education in the minds of its numerous readers, is inclined to exaggerate the role of games in the boys' lives. No matter how sporting their inclinations, Arnold's pupils were not encouraged to be sportive. They were taught to take themselves, their responsibilities, and the growth of their Christian identity, with the utmost seriousness. A successful education was not, for Arnold, primarily a matter of acquiring social, vocational, or intellectual skills. It demanded the rigorous instruction of the individual as a whole, in which the development of moral and spiritual qualities mattered more than the nurturing of academic prowess. It was a model that attracted many followers and imitators. Tom Brown's father muses on the advice he should give his son:

> 'I won't tell him to read his Bible, and love and serve God; if he don't do that for his mother's sake and teaching, he won't for mine. Shall I go into the sort of temptations he'll meet with? No, I can't do that. Never do for an old fellow to go into such things with a boy. He won't understand me. Do him more harm than good, ten to one. Shall I tell him to mind his work, and say he's sent to school to make himself a good scholar? Well, but he isn't sent to school for that – at any rate, not for that mainly. I don't care a straw for Greek particles, or the digamma; no more does his mother. What is he sent to school for? Well, partly because he wanted so to go. If he'll only turn out a brave, helpful, truth-telling Englishman, and a gentleman, and a Christian, that's all I want,' thought the Squire.[10]

Hughes's account of Tom Brown's education continued in *Tom Brown at Oxford* (1861), a lesser-known sequel to his celebrated school story. Universities were shifting from their earlier dedication to religious service, but Hughes is at pains to emphasize that the sporting rather than intellectual interests that continue to dominate Tom's life are primarily Christian in

---

9 Thomas Arnold, *The Christian Life, its Courses, Hindrances and Helps* (London: B. Fellowes, 1841), pp. 19–20.
10 Thomas Hughes, *Tom Brown's Schooldays* (Oxford University Press, 1989), pp. 73–4.

their nature. Tom will not become a clergyman; instead, he becomes a 'muscular Christian': 'the least of the muscular Christians has hold of the old chivalrous and Christian belief, that a man's body is given him to be trained and brought into subjection, and then used for the protection of the weak, the advancement of all righteous causes, and the subduing of the earth which God has given to the children of men'.[11]

Other Christians, less muscular, were equally vigorous in their defence of universities as religious institutions. John Henry Newman was the most influential figure in the Oxford Movement, which from the 1840s onwards mounted a vigorous rearguard action in its opposition to any separation between the religious, social, and intellectual functions of a university. Compelled to leave Oxford after his conversion to the Roman Catholic church in 1845, in 1854 Newman became the rector of the new Catholic university in Dublin. Newman defended the concept of a university as a place where the mind would be formed and cultivated for its own sake, rather than with the aim of communicating practically useful knowledge. His religion was profoundly at odds with that of Thomas Arnold, who had been a leading member of the Anglican liberal broad church movement, but he too saw the highest objective of education to be the formation of a Christian gentleman:

> All that goes to constitute a gentleman, – the carriage, gait, address, gestures, voice; the ease, the self-possession, the courtesy, the power of conversing, the talent of not offending; the lofty principle, the delicacy of thought, the happiness of expression, the taste and propriety, the generosity and forbearance, the candour and consideration, the openness of hand; – these qualities, some of them come by nature, some of them may be found in any rank, some of them are a direct precept of Christianity; but the full assemblage of them, bound up in the unity of an individual character, do we expect they can be learned from books?[12]

To be identified as a gentleman was unquestionably a matter of much practical utility for any young man, but for Thomas Arnold, Thomas Hughes, John Henry Newman, and many who thought like them, its social advantages were not the point. Learning to be a gentleman was a matter of moral and spiritual training, and this represented its deepest value.

---

11 Thomas Hughes, *Tom Brown at Oxford* (London: Macmillan, 1861), p. 99.
12 John Henry Newman, 'The Rise and Progress of Universities', in *Historical Sketches*, 3 vols. (London: Longmans, Green & Co, 1909); vol. III, p. 10.

Education and gender

Squire Brown's confidence that the example and teaching of Tom's mother would provide the primary foundation of Tom's religious education is representative of his generation and class. Women were habitually identified as the natural guardians of religious faith, and it was generally expected that girls' schools would communicate a Christian identity to their pupils. Informally, middle-class girls would often become teachers in their own right, for the Sunday Schools for the poor that flourished in the early and middle decades of the period would customarily draw on the charitable work of unmarried young women in well-heeled families. Such schools would combine basic literacy with religious instruction. For some young women, the experience of teaching in Sunday Schools, or in other charitable schools for the poor, was an onerous obligation; for others, it proved to be a valuable experience of a wider social world, coupled with a welcome opportunity to exercise authority outside the home.

Across all social classes, gender defined an individual's experience of education. The diverse experiences of the Clough family serves as an illuminating demonstration of the depth of the divisions it imposed.[13] Among Thomas Arnold's pupils at Rugby was the poet Arthur Hugh Clough, whose introspective but successful years as a schoolboy left him with lifelong anxieties about his spiritual and social responsibilities. Clough went up to Oxford in 1837, and became, like Newman, a fellow of Oriel, at that date the most intellectually challenging of the Oxford colleges. The religious turbulence then prevailing in Oxford, and in Oriel particularly, led to Clough's resigning his fellowship in 1848, and taking up a post at University Hall, a hostel for students attending University College London. Work as an examiner in the Education Office followed, before Clough's short though brilliantly creative life came to a premature end in 1861. Arthur Clough's sister, Anne Jemima Clough, also worked in education throughout her life, but her career necessarily took a very different direction. Her first experience of teaching poor children in charitable schools in Liverpool fired a lifelong enthusiasm for the role. Young women who had been brought up as ladies, and took up the teaching profession as a means of earning a living, would often do so out of economic necessity, and the

---

13 Gillian Sutherland gives a perceptive and detailed account of the family's literary and educational history in *Faith, Duty, and the Power of Mind: The Cloughs and their Circle, 1820–1960* (Cambridge University Press, 2006).

dismal plight of teachers and governesses forced to support themselves in this way became a topic of frequent comment, in both literary and polemical terms. In the earlier decades of the nineteenth century, novels intended to highlight the suffering of governesses appeared in significant numbers, including Julia Buckley's *Emily: The Governess* (1836), or Marguerite Blessington's *The Governess* (1839). The foundation of the Governesses' Benevolent Institution, in 1843, designed to improve the position of the governess, generated a handful of novels written to raise funds for the foundation's work, including Dinah Mulock Craik's forthright *Bread Upon the Waters: A Governess's Life* (1852), and Anna Maria Hall's *Stories of the Governess* (1852). Many early readers of the most celebrated Victorian governess novel, Charlotte Brontë's *Jane Eyre* (1847), would have seen the novel in this context.[14]

Not every woman who taught was driven by financial need. Some women made a free and positive choice to take up the profession, and this was the case with Annie Clough. With little support from her family, she was soon running her own school in Ambleside, where she acquired invaluable experience, in both pedagogic and administrative terms. In making this move, she became part of a large and self-sufficient group of women who, in the middle decades of the nineteenth century, took advantage of the lack of formal regulation with regard to girls' education, and sought financial and personal independence by founding and organizing their own schools. The more successful of these schools provided women with an invaluable opportunity to acquire an income and a source of rewarding work without losing their social status as ladies, which would otherwise be threatened by their accepting paid employment. Their curricula varied widely, not least because they were not, as was the case with boys' schools, compelled to drill their pupils in Latin and Greek, though in fact many girls' schools did provide teaching in classical languages. More commonly, the teaching focused on basic literacy and numeracy, with additional subjects including French, German, or (more rarely) Italian, music, drawing, geography, Bible studies, needlework, and sometimes a modicum of natural science. In practice, the head of such a school would provide what her resources, and the expectations of fee-paying parents, would allow. The schools would usually be small, with pupils varying in age, and the model would be domestic, with the aim of replicating the

---

14 Cecilia Wadsö Lecaros describes the development of this fictional sub-genre in *The Victorian Governess Novel* (Lund University Press, 2001).

disciplines and support provided by a family. Such schools could provide both teachers and their pupils with a freedom that their more expensively and intensively educated brothers were denied.

Annie Clough profited significantly from her years in Ambleside, as did her pupils (including the tempestuous young Mary Arnold, the niece of Matthew Arnold, who later became celebrated as the novelist Mrs Humphry Ward). But, like many women teachers of her generation, she came to see the limitations of smaller schools for girls organized on the domestic model. She was among the women who gave evidence to the Taunton Commission on secondary education, suggesting that larger and better resourced institutions would have much to offer the education of girls. These views led to her participation in the fledgling movement to establish colleges of higher education in Oxford and Cambridge. At first simply in charge of a modest hostel for a small group of young women wishing to attend lectures in Cambridge, Annie Clough later became the first Principal of Newnham College, founded in 1871 to enable girls to pursue disciplined courses of study at the university. Newnham College was among the earliest examples of a growing number of institutions established to provide young women with wider opportunities to qualify for paid employment outside the home, not only as teachers, but in the closing decades of the nineteenth century in a growing variety of occupations – including work as typists, telegraphists, secretaries, doctors, lawyers, or journalists.

It was within the energetic new colleges and universities, founded to meet demands and needs that could not be supplied within established practices of higher education, that the study of English literature began to take its place in formal syllabuses, alongside the traditional specialization in Latin and Greek that had long been identified as the proper focus of a gentlemanly interest in the humanities. Young women, and working men, were much less likely to have had access to the intensive preparatory training necessary for success in a classics-based degree, and had less to gain, professionally and socially, from acquiring such skills. The movement to diversify the study of literature began in the recently founded University of London in the 1830s. John Ruskin and Robert Browning were among the first to hear university lectures on English literature, delivered by the Evangelical Reverend Thomas Dale (1797–1870) in King's College London, where Dale, who had previously served in University College London as the first professor of English language and literature in England, lectured from 1836 until 1840. Dale's lectures, which began with Anglo Saxon poetry and included a consideration of the English language,[15] emphasized the role of the study of both English language and literature in the construction of a national identity. This concern became characteristic of early courses in the study of English literature, as they began to develop in an expanding range of institutions for higher education. A developed sense of national pride was seen as a legitimate goal for the literary study of both male and female students, and the study of English literature, or indeed the literatures of other modern European languages, was often identified as particularly appropriate for a rising generation of students. The need to support the practical and ideological demands of the expanding British empire contributed to these developments. The empire called for teachers, and missionaries – male and female – and those who left Britain to fill those roles were often supported by a strong conviction of national identity and obligation derived from their own education. Rudyard Kipling's schoolboys in *Stalky & Co.* (1899), rebellious and subversive, show that the assimilation of those ideals was more than a matter of crude brow-beating; the ideals of national honour had entered 'the secret places of their soul'.[16]

Working and travelling overseas often provided new opportunities for ambitious young people. But in England, deep-rooted obstacles and prejudices did not simply evaporate as these fresh prospects began to expand. Fictional accounts of education in the latter half of the nineteenth century often provide eloquent reminders of their persistence. George Eliot's account of the ill-considered distinctions between the education of Maggie and Tom Tulliver in *The Mill on the Floss* (1860) reflect the experiences of an earlier generation, but Mr Tulliver's remarks on the economic futility of intelligence in women embody assumptions that proved painfully slow to change: ' "She's twice as 'cute as Tom. Too 'cute for a woman, I'm afraid," continued Mr Tulliver, turning his head dubiously first on one side and then on the other. "It's no mischief much while she's a little un; but an over-'cute woman's no better nor a long-tailed sheep, – she'll fetch none the bigger price for that." '[17] Like many of those who comment on Victorian education, in novels or elsewhere, George Eliot reminds her readers of connections

15 See Franklin E. Court, 'The Social and Historical Significance of the First English Literature Professorship in England', *PMLA* 103:5 (1988), pp. 796–807, for an account of Dale's career, and the nature of his teaching. Chris Baldick gives an illuminating account of the rise of the academic study of English in *The Social Mission of English Criticism 1848–1932* (Oxford University Press, 1983).

16 Rudyard Kipling, 'The Flag of Their Country', in *Stalky & Co.* (Oxford University Press, 1999), pp. 218–19.

17 George Eliot, *The Mill on the Floss* (Oxford University Press, 1980), chapter 2, p. 12.

between education and money. It was commonly believed that the expenditure of resources on education was primarily vindicated by the status and wealth that learning would make possible, and for parents this was often the justification for investing in the education of boys rather than girls – as Mr Tulliver assumes, in planning the education of his son, Tom: ' "What I want, you know," said Mr Tulliver, "– what I want is to give Tom a good eddication; an eddication as'll be a bread to him." '[18] Tom is sent away to school, though the education he receives at the hands of Mr Stelling, his complacent clergyman teacher, is dreary and unfruitful. Maggie is educated, with equally unsatisfactory results, at home. This reflects a common (though not universal) pattern among the Victorian middle classes, and one which drew much critical comment from a variety of novelists. Little Paul Dombey, thoughtful but fragile, cannot cope with the demands of Dr Blimber's academy in Dickens's *Dombey and Son* (1848). The education of his sister Florence is neglected, though she is seen to be more robust in every way. Ethel May, the spirited heroine of Charlotte Yonge's *The Daisy Chain* (1856), is oppressed by her exclusion from the ambitious schooling provided for her brother Norman. But she finds scope for action in her own work as a teacher, and finally Norman's education, rigorous and exacting, is seen as an insufficient preparation for the complex demands of adult life.

A generation later, Thomas Hardy gives a sombre account of the closed minds and locked gates of Christminster, a fictionalized reflection of Oxford, in his final novel, *Jude the Obscure* (1895). Jude's motives in his thwarted wish to become an undergraduate are mixed – partly idealistic, but also grounded in his wish for social and financial advancement:

> And then he continued to dream, and thought he might become even a bishop by leading a pure, energetic, wise, Christian life. And what an example he would set! If his income were £5000 a year, he would give away £4500 in one form and another, and live sumptuously (for him) on the remainder. Well, on second thoughts, a bishop was absurd. He would draw the line at an archdeacon. Perhaps a man could be as good and as learned and as useful in the capacity of archdeacon as in that of bishop. Yet he thought of the bishop again.[19]

Sue Bridehead, Jude's doomed lover, is equally frustrated in her hope of enriching her life through advancing her education. Her ambition to join a new generation of female teachers is more realistic than Jude's hopes of

18 *Ibid.*, chapter 2, p. 9.
19 Thomas Hardy, *Jude the Obscure* (Oxford University Press, 1985), vol. 1, chapter 6, p. 34.

matriculating at Christminster, and suggests the growth of vocational possibilities for women. Yet the novel represents her vocational training as a confinement rather than expansion, transforming her into 'a woman clipped and pruned by severe discipline'.[20] Her intimacy with Jude eventually leads to her expulsion from the training-school. The novel's thinking on education amounts to a scathing condemnation of the narrow-mindedness and snobbery that Hardy had encountered in his youth. But it is not an accurate reflection of a contemporary social problem. In 1895, opportunities for talented and ambitious working-class boys were not restricted to futile attempts to gain admission to an ecclesiastically inclined Christminster, and many girls of Sue's spirited disposition found a professional qualification as a teacher to be an effective way to independence, rather than the source of further disappointment.

Writing and teaching

Writing and teaching were not mutually exclusive occupations. In many cases, those working in education were also active authors, writing for many reasons and in a diverse range of genres, literary or otherwise. Their motives were often partly financial, for both writing and teaching enabled those without the resources of inherited wealth to earn a living without losing middle-class status. This was equally true for men and women. When Arthur Clough's religious difficulties made it impossible for him to follow the conventional career path that went with an Oxford fellowship, alternatives were available in the rapidly diversifying field of opportunities for employment in education. Clough's sceptically questioning intelligence as a poet is bound up with this work, where he continued to contend with the established connection between education and religion that had complicated his own early career: 'All education is in England, and I think in America, so mixed up with religious matters, that it is a great difficulty.'[21]

Matthew Arnold, the son of Dr Thomas Arnold and a friend of Clough, also found that his religious doubts made it impossible for him to retain his fellowship at Oriel College in Oxford. Like Clough, Arnold turned to professional work in education, earning an arduous living as an inspector of schools for thirty-five years. Arnold's cultural criticism, and his poetry, is

---

20 *Ibid.*, vol. 3, chapter 1, p. 136.
21 Letter to R. W. Emerson, 10 June 1854, in *The Poems and Prose Remains of Arthur Hugh Clough*, ed. Blanche Clough, 2 vols. (London: Macmillan, 1869), vol. 1, p. 218.

deeply concerned with the faltering authority of religion as the spiritual foundation for modern life. The resources of literature might provide an alternative way of enabling his troubled generation to find a way through their perplexities, which were, as Arnold defined them, both intellectual and emotional. Literature could carry responsibilities that had once been the work of religion – it could connect ethics with feeling. This was a central reason for his professional insistence that serious literary study should figure in any national scheme for education. But his sense that contemporary writing – including his own – lacked the assurance and depth of what had gone before was debilitatingly persistent:

> But where will Europe's latter hour
> Again find Wordsworth's healing power?
> Others will teach us how to dare,
> And against fear our breast to steel;
> Others will strengthen us to bear –
> But who, ah! who, will make us feel?[22]

This sense of belated inadequacy led to his abandoning poetry for his activities as a critic and inspector. Literature could educate, but the alienated writing of his own generation was not capable of teaching what its readers needed to learn.

Other writers were more confident that their work could continue the educational work of religion. Anthony Trollope, brisk and businesslike in his self-definitions as a novelist, is surprisingly explicit on the matter:

> The writer of stories must please, or he will be nothing. And he must teach whether he wish to teach or no. How shall he teach lessons of virtue and at the same time make himself a delight to his readers? That sermons are not in themselves often thought to be agreeable we all know. Nor are disquisitions on moral philosophy supposed to be pleasant light reading for our idle hours. But the novelist, if he have a conscience, must preach his sermons with the same purpose as the clergyman, and must have his own system of ethics.[23]

Such convictions were not confined to male writers. Elizabeth Missing Sewell was, like Annie Clough, the sister of men who had access to the traditional resources of higher education that her sex denied to her. Richard Clarke Sewell became fellow and vice-president of Magdalen College in

---

22 Matthew Arnold, 'Memorial Verses: April 1850' (44), in *The Poems of Matthew Arnold*, ed. Kenneth Allott (London: Longmans, Green & Co., 1965), p. 229.
23 Anthony Trollope, *An Autobiography* (Oxford University Press, 1980), chapter 12, p. 222.

Oxford, and later reader in law at Melbourne University in Australia; Henry
Sewell became a politician in New Zealand, and eventually its first premier;
James Edwardes Sewell was a fellow of New College Oxford and vice-
chancellor of the university, while the impulsive William Sewell, the brother
that Elizabeth was closest to and the one who gave her most trouble, was a
fellow of Exeter College Oxford, and one of the founders of the public
school Radley College. This did not prevent her achieving remarkable
success as both writer and teacher, publishing a series of enduringly popular
novels, while running two ambitious and highly regarded schools. Sewell
did not doubt that her novels, which often debate educational policy and
practice, should be didactic. But she does not share Trollope's confidence in
any 'system of ethics', of whatever kind. 'A system, indeed, even supposing
it to be good for one, cannot possibly be good for all.'[24] One of the things
her fiction has to teach is that the influence of any instruction, whether
imparted in schools or through novels, will be uncertain. No teacher should
hope to produce a fixed and measurable outcome. Mrs Anstruther, one of
her teaching heroines, muses ruefully on the outcome of her labours:

> as I look around, and see the many influences which have united in forming
> the characters of the children, whom I once fancied I was training according
> to my own theories, I almost begin to question whether, in fact, I have
> laboured at all. Certainly I have not done what I intended to do, and the
> result has not been what I expected. Not one of my children has realised my
> ideal – and yet I do not say that this ideal would have been better than
> reality; for I never supposed they would be perfect; I never imagined them
> gifted with wonderful talents; but I fancied I understood the materials with
> which I had to deal, and that, by working upon them in certain ways,
> I should assuredly produce a foreseen and definite result.[25]

Sewell's fiction warns of the unmanageable contingencies of life, in which
teaching must be as dynamic as the minds and imaginations of those who
learn: 'I only know that I seem always to be in a process of formation;
always, as it were, receiving into and amalgamating with myself, the
residuum of the moral experiments which I am unconsciously making.'[26]
Fiction can share in these fluid energies, and Sewell saw no contradiction in
the pedagogic ambitions of her parallel careers as teacher and writer.

---

24 Elizabeth Sewell, *Principles of Education*, 2 vols. (London: Longman, 1865), vol. I, p. 30.
25 Elizabeth Sewell, *After Life* (London: Longmans, Green & Co., 1868), p. 471.
26 Elizabeth Sewell, *The Journal of a Home Life*, 2 vols. (London: Longmans, Green & Co.,
    1867), vol. I, p. 30.

Seen in this light, the didactic purposes of a writer might not be a matter of communicating a specific agenda, whether moral or practical, though the proliferation of self-help manuals offering specific advice and information is a reminder of the scale of popular appetite for direct instruction. The strategies of imaginative literature would sometimes be equally forthright – as when Ellen Wood, author of the astonishingly successful sensation novel *East Lynne* (1861), concludes her colourful book with a blunt exhortation: 'Never forget that the only way to ensure peace in the end is to strive always to be doing right, unselfishly, under God.'[27] Other writers developed more indirect or even ambiguous approaches. This did not mean that they were uninterested in the pedagogic potential of literature. The learned George Eliot had much to say about the need for solid educational principles, and she always saw herself as a teacher: 'I think "Live and teach" should be a proverb as well as "Live and Learn".'[28] But what her subtle and complex novels teach is that education must be more than a matter of externally imposed regimes of study. The learning that mattered most would develop the whole personality of the pupil. 'He was ceasing to care for knowledge – he had no ambition for practice – unless they could both be gathered up into one current with his emotions,'[29] George Eliot observes of the young Daniel Deronda, as he moves towards a deeper understanding of his conflicting experiences. In a period deeply engaged with the expansion of learning at every level, this vision of wholeness persists as a powerful model for the proper goals of an educated society.

27 Ellen Wood, *East Lynne* (Oxford University Press, 2005), chapter 47, p. 625.
28 George Eliot, letter to Sara Hennell, 27 November 1847, in *The George Eliot Letters*, ed. Gordon S. Haight, 9 vols. (New Haven and London: Yale University Press, 1954–78), vol. I, p. 242.
29 George Eliot, *Daniel Deronda* (Oxford: Clarendon Press, 1984), chapter 32, p. 336.

16

Spirituality

ELISABETH JAY

'What is the question now placed before society with a glib assurance the most astounding? The question is this – Is man an ape or an angel? My Lord, I am on the side of the angels.'[1] It was with this pithy, reductive summary that Benjamin Disraeli characterized the popular conception of the challenge that evolutionary explanations of man's origin and descent offered to Victorian religion. Tennyson put the matter rather more bluntly: 'We shall all turn into pigs if we lose Christianity and God.'[2] Darwin's hypotheses appeared to challenge man's claim to be more than the sum of his physical and rational parts, raising questions as to where to locate humanity's inclinations to the mystical, ethical, moral, and aesthetic. Disraeli's quip reveals the clarity of an assimilated Anglican Jew's recognition that mid nineteenth-century Britain's religion was both a very public concern, central to the sense of national culture, and a matter of highly individualized belief.

'Spirituality' is nowadays employed as an inclusive term for indicating metaphysical longing, or a sense of the transcendent not easily aligned with, or confined within, particular histories of institutionalized affiliation. Confronted with aeons of geological change, the theory of natural selection, imperial encounters with alternative cultures, and technological advances that challenged previous conceptions of the possible, the Victorian age also witnessed movement away from the orthodoxies of Bible, Church tradition, and shared liturgy, and towards privatized belief systems. Even grudging concessions like that of the poet Arthur Hugh Clough's, 'That there are powers above us, I admit',[3] raised questions as to the nature of such praeter-, or

---

1 W. F. Monypenny and G. E. Buckle, *The Life of Benjamin Disraeli*, 6 vols. (London: John Murray, 1910–20), vol. IV, p. 374.

2 Lucy Masterman (ed.), *Mary Gladstone (Mrs Drew): Her Diaries and Letters*, (London: Methuen, 1930), p. 157.

3 Arthur Hugh Clough, *Arthur Hugh Clough: The Poems*, ed. F. L. Mulhauser, 2nd edn. (Oxford: Clarendon Press, 1974), p. 373.

super-natural 'powers', whether they might eventually prove susceptible to scientific interpretation, and what channels of communication they might afford to human beings. The mesmeric experiments, widely current between the 1830s and 1860s, which seemed to offer evidence that such powers could be brought to bear by one person on the human body or psyche of another, were symptomatic of traditional theology's weakening grip, and of a concomitant need to explore and test the resulting chaos of interpretive systems thus unleashed.[4] Speculation about the powers, spaces, and channels to which mediums bore witness ranged from the avowedly 'rational' testimony of Harriet Martineau,[5] through the Society for Psychical Research,[6] to séances fuelled by varying combinations of genuine yearning for communion with the souls of the dear departed and cynical opportunism. Those who attended often scarcely knew in which camp to place themselves, nor did they necessarily find dabbling with the occult incompatible with their regular church worship. Margaret Oliphant, who counted prominent clergymen among her friends, was dismissive of the spiritualist soirées hosted in the 1850s, 'half as entertainment and half as consolation', by John and Mary Howitt and Dinah Mulock, supporters of that most famous of Victorian mediums, Daniel D. Home.[7] Yet she was happy for her household to indulge in 'table-rapping' as an amusement, and also confessed that she derived 'great comfort' from the 'momentary contact' she felt she had been permitted with her eldest son after his death, even while acknowledging that it might have been 'only some trick of the mind'. Consequently her writings reflected a full spectrum from Christmas ghost stories, through haunting tales of the supernatural, to 'The Little Pilgrim' series, designed to provide Christian consolation for the bereaved.[8]

The question of the part played by the human mind raised the vexed question of literature's role in revealing and mediating the spiritual. For a poet as interested as Robert Browning was in 'the dangerous edge'[9] between the material and the spiritual experienced in those liminal moments

4 For a comprehensive account see Alison Winter, Mesmerized: Powers of Mind in Victorian Britain (Chicago and London: University of Chicago Press, 1998).
5 Harriet Martineau, Letters on Mesmerism (London: Edward Moxon, 1845).
6 See Janet Oppenheim, The Other World: Spiritualism and Psychical Research in England, 1850–1914 (Cambridge University Press, 1985), pp. 57, 135–47, and 245.
7 See Peter Lamont, The First Psychic: The Peculiar Mystery of a Notorious Victorian Wizard (London: Little, Brown, 2005).
8 All references to be found in Elisabeth Jay, Mrs Oliphant: 'A Fiction to Herself': A Literary Life (Oxford: Clarendon Press, 1995), pp. 139–91.
9 Robert Browning, The Complete Works of Robert Browning, ed. Roma A. King Jr et al., 16 vols. (Athens: Ohio University Press), vol. v, p. 307.

between life and death, his habit of ventriloquizing the voices of the dead seemed at times uncomfortably close to necromancy, and at others to claiming prophetic inspiration. Indeed Browning's furious denunciation of opportunist trickery in 'Mr Sludge, the Medium', it has been argued, stemmed from anxiety about such proximities rather than from antipathy to Elizabeth Barrett Browning's spiritualist interests.[10] Even if the poet 'makes' rather than 'fakes' these ghostly voices, this presented the problem, raised by Browning's casuistical Bishop Blougram, that a sense of the transcendent may indeed be no more than an effect triggered by 'a sunset touch, / A fancy from a flower-bell, someone's death, / A chorus ending from Euripides'.[11] In other poems Browning pursued the doubts that had been raised in the mid-century mind as to the continuing efficacy of Nature ('Caliban upon Setebos') and the Word ('Death in the Desert') as the traditionally accepted means of God's self-revelation to humanity. Blougram's appeal to Euripides rather than the gospels hints at the way in which the link between the secular and the sacred was being challenged or collapsed.

The study of classical languages had long formed the basis of the university education received by Anglican clergy. As the Rev. John Keble, Oxford Professor of Poetry, expressed it, 'a close and constant study of the writings of classic poets, philosophers and historians: who may all be considered as poets, so far at least as they are wont to elevate the mind',[12] could be presumed to inculcate the ability to read 'language in general, and especially the languages of Holy Scripture, and the human style of its several writers, as fit *media* through which His supernatural glories and dealings might be discerned'.[13] To Matthew Arnold, Keble's godson and successor as Oxford Professor of Poetry, who had experienced the erosion of belief in the unique status of the Bible brought about by German comparative criticism,[14] and saw increasing evidence to doubt the existence of a providential God operating through his creation, it seemed obvious enough that it was time

---

10 Adam Roberts, 'Browning, the Dramatic Monologue and the Resuscitation of the Dead', in Nicola Bown, Carolyn Burdett, and Pamela Thurschwell (eds.), *The Victorian Supernatural* (Cambridge University Press, 2004), pp. 109–27.

11 Browning, *Works*. vol. v, p. 299.

12 John Keble, *Keble's Lectures on Poetry 1832–1841*, trans. E. K. Francis, 2 vols. (Oxford: Clarendon Press, 1912), vol. II, p. 477.

13 John Keble, *Tract No 89: On the Mysticism attributed to the Early Fathers of the Church* (London: J. G. F. and J. Rivington, 1840), p. 171.

14 See Matthew Arnold, *Literature and Dogma: an Essay towards a better apprehension of the Bible* (London: Smith, Elder, 1873); and *God and the Bible: A Review of Objections to 'Literature and Dogma'* (London: Smith, Elder, 1875).

to decouple literature's power to affect from matters of religious belief. 'More and more', he asserted, 'mankind will find that we have to turn to poetry to interpret life for us, to console us, to sustain us. Without poetry, our science will appear incomplete; and most of what now passes with us for religion and philosophy will be replaced by poetry.'[15]

Charting the ways in which religious belief and practice inflected Victorian literature, therefore, inevitably involves incorporating understandings which varied from Keble's sense of literature as a handmaiden to revealed religion to Thomas Carlyle's assertion that 'in this confused time' there were many who 'have no other method of worship' than that provided by the new priestly order of writers producing 'Newspapers, Pamphlets, Poems, Books', so as 'in any way [to show] us better than we knew before'.[16] Carlyle and Arnold's sense that 'poetry', understood as covering various genres of imaginative literature, was gaining ground on religious publications would seem, on the face of it, to be borne out by the available statistics. Whereas in the mid-century publications of literature, broadly interpreted, were on a par with religious output, in the period between 1870 and 1880 literature attained 29.8 per cent of the whole, while religious works slipped to 15.6 per cent of the whole, and then to below 10 per cent in the final decade. Yet changing categorizations over a period that saw a marked increase in non-sectarian, non-dogmatic devotional texts, and advances in cheap publishing methods that favoured an absolute increase in both religious and secular texts, make it difficult to calibrate these trends. According to *Mitchell's Newspaper Press Directory* for the years 1864–77, titles 'of a decidedly religious character' still formed a third of the periodical and magazine output.[17]

Reading the Victorian spiritual condition through literary evidence is likely to produce a far less stable and coherent picture than that offered by histories which rely on the trajectories of religious movements and institutions to structure their narrative. The latter approach, however, runs the double risk of allowing highly individual and subjective accounts to stand proxy for wider currents of thought, and of underrating the fluidity of religious allegiance that was so notable a feature of the early Victorian period. To contemporaries the political, religious, and literary landscapes

15 Matthew Arnold, *The Complete Prose Works of Matthew Arnold*, ed. R. H. Super, 11 vols. (Ann Arbor: University of Michigan Press), vol. IX, pp. 161–2.

16 Thomas Carlyle, *The Works of Thomas Carlyle*, 30 vols. (London: Chapman and Hall, 1896–9), vol. V, pp. 162–3.

17 Simon Eliot, *Some Patterns and Trends in British Publishing 1800–1919* (London: The Bibliographical Society, 1994), pp. 46–50, 86–7.

of the late 1820s to 1840s seemed sufficiently apocalyptic to justify searching for 'signs of the times' that might variously, indicate an imminent millennium, legitimate flocking to the sermons of fashionable new prophets such as the Rev. Edward Irving, or justify seceding from the Established Church in search of greater apostolic purity. Three works written in this period convey a rather different picture from the magisterial account of the Oxford Movement's rise and fall subsequently composed by John Henry Newman in *Apologia Pro Vita Sua* (1864). Newman wrote *The Essay on the Development of Christian Doctrine* (1845) and his satirical novel, *Loss and Gain* (1848), in the throes of detaching himself from the Anglican Church. His brother Francis William Newman's *Phases of Faith, or, Passages from the History of My Creed* (1850) records a pilgrimage that, after the Evangelical youth and Oxford education the brothers shared, diverged to pursue Bible Christianity and periods of worship with the Plymouth Brethren, the Baptists, and the Unitarians, before settling for theism. These texts convey the charged religious atmosphere of a period when it seemed reasonable and essential to both brothers to find a path to salvation, whatever the cost in terms of former loyalties. In the elder brother's case this led – after a bout of mental wrestling which he subsequently shaped into the autobiography's account of providentially led evolutionary progress – to seeking spiritual safety in Rome's authority, and, in the younger's, to embracing the supremacy of individual judgment his sibling so deplored.

The obsessive devotion to setting forth a highly individual spiritual stall as though it had been arrived at by logical process is so pronounced in the Newman brothers as to seem a family trait, yet a sense of isolation consequent upon conscientiously examining and discarding the orthodoxies of family and faith communities is characteristic of many spiritual autobiographies of the period. John Ruskin's *Praeterita* (1885–9), for instance, suggests that this intensely sociable man conceived of himself as solitary and alienated. After being uprooted from the comfortable austerities of wealthy Dissenting Evangelicalism to the heart of the Establishment as a gentleman-commoner at Christchurch, Oxford, Ruskin experienced repeated ruptures in the process of sifting out from the biblically based teaching of his youth a residual Christian ethics and sense of the mystery of creation. The consciousness of having trodden a lonely but virtuous path served to animate harsh judgments of those whose religion seemed little more than unexamined sentiment: of Charles Dickens, Ruskin wrote that 'He knew nothing of the nobler power of superstition – was essentially a stage manager, and used everything for effect on the pit. His Christmas meant mistletoe and pudding – neither resurrection from dead, nor rising of new stars, nor teaching of wise men, nor shepherds.'[18]

Spirituality is rooted within a world of stubbornly individual integrity, but is experienced in relation to constantly changing cultural anxieties: this makes literary texts particularly illuminating sources in a variety of ways. For one thing, they reveal the way in which the particularities of individual circumstance map on to wider class, gender, and regional preoccupations. A series of revivalist and liturgical campaigns, which might have been expected to produce greater uniformity throughout the four constituent parts of the kingdom, failed to erase the distinctive nuance provided by local arrangements and identities. The writing and reading of texts and tales also played their own part in transforming lives. The haunting memory of Calvinist-inspired tales of eternal damnation, the receipt of a religious tract, the solitary devouring of a spiritual autobiography, a systematic course of sceptical reading, and, above all, contemplating the status of the Bible as a sacred text, were to prove as likely a first step on the road to various kinds of conversion as any revivalist meeting. The writers of the high Victorian period relied upon their readership's acquaintance with a small core of works of religious literature that was likely to include John Milton's *Paradise Lost* (1667) and John Bunyan's *The Pilgrim's Progress* (1678–84), and might encompass Mrs Henry Sherwood's *The History of the Fairchild Family* (1818–47) or John Keble's *The Christian Year* (1827).[19] This shared inheritance, besides providing a shorthand of key symbolic moments, introduced readers to many important skills, such as how to read allegorically and typologi-cally[20] and how to interpret the classical world through a Christian lens, and, in some, developed the art of enjoying the medium without swallowing the message. Anglophone writers from the American Louisa May Alcott to the South African Olive Schreiner tapped into this British Christian discourse. Alcott's appropriation of Charlotte Yonge's recent best-seller *The Heir of Redclyffe* (1853) and her rereading of *The Pilgrim's Progress*, itself a text coloured by the aftermath of civil conflict, made the remote domestic sufferings of Civil War America, depicted in *Little Women* (1868), sympathetic to transatlantic readers. The Boer Protestantism depicted in Schreiner's *The*

18 John Ruskin, *The Works of John Ruskin*, ed. E. T. Cook and A. Wedderburn, 39 vols. (London and New York: George Allen, 1903–12), vol. xxxvii, p. 7.

19 See F. Elizabeth Gray, ' "Syren Strains", Victorian Women's Devotional Poetry and John Keble's *The Christian Year*', *Victorian Poetry* 44 (2006), pp. 61–76.

20 George P. Landow, *Victorian Types, Victorian Shadows, Biblical Typology in Victorian Literature, Art, and Thought* (Boston: Routledge & Kegan Paul, 1980).

Story of an African Farm (1883) was accessible because it relied on a common repertoire of the Bible, Bunyan, and hymns by Isaac Watts and John Wesley. It could be argued that writing in the shadow of this master discourse helped to mask divergence at the same time as further exoticizing non-Anglocentric spiritual traditions. Such a politicized reading would privilege Alcott and Schreiner's debts to Emersonian Transcendentalism and thus align them with those British women who found in the 'One Life' spiritual cocktail, proffered by Madame Blavatsky and the Theosophical Society (founded in 1879), an arena where they could articulate their desire for spiritual and political enfranchisement from the old orthodoxies.[21]

When the American William James came to define the concept of 'religion' he spoke of it as *the feelings, acts, and experiences of individual men in their solitude, so far as they apprehend themselves to stand in relation to whatever they may consider the divine*.[22] Although some historians have argued that the privatization of religion was becoming a marked feature of English life by the end of the Victorian period,[23] James's definition, which reflects America's conscious efforts to depoliticize the competing faiths of its immigrant communities, would seriously have misrepresented mid-Victorian England's sense of its religion as hard-wired into the constitution, playing a determining role in many educational and welfare issues and frequently inflecting social and cultural assumptions. In such an environment it was logical to understand personal beliefs as having public outcomes, and to search, sometimes using fiction's powers of imaginative resolution, for systems and communities that seemed most capable of realizing personal convictions. The plethora of Victorian religious hypocrites that stalk the pages of Victorian literature form one measure of the seriousness with which Victorians took the link or tussle between private spirituality and its public expression.

Carlyle diagnosed this difficulty in disentangling 'the Spiritual, eternal Essence of Man, and of Mankind', from the 'wrappages' of its cultural expression as peculiarly English. He had required the combined forces of German Romanticism, and a move from Lowland Scotland to literary

---

21 Joy Dixon, *Divine Feminine: Theosophy and Feminism in England* (Baltimore and London: Johns Hopkins University Press, 2001).

22 William James, *The Varieties of Religious Experience: A Study in Human Nature, Gifford Lectures delivered at Edinburgh University* (London, New York, Toronto: Longmans & Green, 1929), p. 31.

23 Sarah C. Williams, 'Victorian Religion: a Matter of Class or Culture', *Nineteenth Century Studies* 17 (2003), pp. 8–9, 13–17, provides a useful analysis of the debate and the terms in which it has been constructed.

London, to shake off some of the Calvinist shackles of his childhood and to alert him to the importance and the near impossibility of obtaining 'a foothold outside time' from which to critique nationally rooted beliefs. Through the defamiliarizing device of the whimsical German Idealist in *Sartor Resartus* (1833–4), Professor Teufelsdröckh, Carlyle hoped to waken a nation, naturally disposed to regard the speculative and the visionary as inherently foreign, to the parochialism of its preoccupation with the 'din and frenzy of Catholic Emancipations, and Rotten Boroughs'.[24] We can most clearly discern the way in which the British sense of the spiritual was bound up in the traditions of a community connecting individuals to both their familial and national inheritance in writers whose loss of orthodox faith threatened these markers of continuous identity. Tennyson's residual faith was frequently cast in tones as mistily transcendentalist as Carlyle's Teufelsdröckh's:

> Moreover, something is or seems,
> That touches me with mystic gleams,
> Like glimpses of forgotten dreams –
>
> Of something felt, like something here;
> Of something done, I know not where;
> Such as no language may declare.[25]

Yet this poem, 'The Two Voices', in which the speaker wrestles with the scientific materialism that had similarly depressed Carlyle, is resolved in a localized blessing that cannot help but remind us that Tennyson's upbringing, however unhappy and eccentric, had taken place in an Anglican rectory.

> On to God's house the people prest:
> Passing the place where each must rest,
> Each entered like a welcome guest.[26]

The metaphysical uncertainties voiced in the poet's gradually evolved elegy, *In Memoriam A. H.*, were also to find a resting place in the continuities affirmed by the church celebration of a wedding where the bride is imagined, 'Her feet, my darling, on the dead; / Their pensive tablets round her head' and the couple's signatures in the parish register which promise to be read as 'Mute symbols of a joyful morn, / By village eyes as yet

---

24 Carlyle, *Works*, vol. 1, pp. 213 and 3.
25 Alfred Tennyson, 'The Two Voices', in *The Poems of Tennyson*, ed. Christopher Ricks, 3 vols. (Harlow: Longman, 1987), vol. 1, pp. 390–1, lines 379–84.
26 *Ibid.*, lines 409–11.

unborn'.[27] The Anglican burial service, 'with its interchange of beseeching cries for help, with outbursts of faith and praise – its recurrent responses and the familiar rhythm of its collects', so George Eliot told readers of *Adam Bede*, maintained 'a channel' for blending 'a certain consciousness of our entire past and our imagined future' with 'all our moments of keen sensibility'.[28] Despite Thomas Hardy's rational conviction that the dead are 'gone for good', the accumulated wisdom of the past speaks from the resurrected voices of those buried in Mellstock churchyard.[29] It may well have been their longing for a community shaped by shared worship that attracted renegade Anglicans such as Eliot and Hardy to the liturgical ritual developed by the Positivists.[30]

The lingering potency of the myth of a Christian nation where personal spirituality found its natural expression in a national system of parochial worship was exposed as a matter for debate by the deductions drawn from the 1851 Religious Census. Horace Mann's commentary, issued in January 1854, drew a stark binary divide between the religious fidelity of country congregations and the spiritual imperviousness of a radicalized city populace. Fiction, with its already well-developed capacity to travel back and forth between the inner life, the domestic and the public spheres, offered an ideal site for testing the various parts of Mann's proposition. Novels such as Charles Dickens's *Bleak House* (1852), Elizabeth Gaskell's *North and South* (1855), and George Eliot's *Adam Bede* (1859) have often been cited as contributing confirmatory evidence for Mann's analysis, yet the varied pictures they present need to be read as part of a highly politicized debate no less than the 'industrial novels' of the previous decade. The brickmaker and Jo in *Bleak House* respectively ratify a picture of the urban poor as either hostile to, or untouched by, organized religion, but the bourgeois and the upper-class characters offer less conveniently packaged evidence of religious alignment. The title, *North and South*, alerted readers to the novel's intention of investigating the clichéd dichotomies of contemporary analysis: urban or agricultural, Anglican or Dissenting, enthusiast or sceptic, pacifist or bellicose. The Anglican parson, whose doubts over the rights of an Established Church have reluctantly persuaded him into the ranks of educated Dissent,

27 Tennyson, *In Memoriam*, in *Poems*, vol. II, p. 454.
28 George Eliot, *Adam Bede* (Oxford: Clarendon Press, 2001), p. 186.
29 'Friends Beyond', in *The Complete Poetical Works of Thomas Hardy*, ed. S. Hynes 5 vols. (Oxford: Clarendon Press, 1982–95), vol. I, pp. 78–9.
30 See T. R. Wright, *The Religion of Humanity: the Impact of Comtean Positivism on Victorian Britain* (Cambridge University Press, 1986), pp. 176 and 96.

immediately assumes that a distraught northern working man wanting audience with him will prove to be 'a drunken infidel weaver', never dreaming that the one person in the novel to entertain a glimpse of a universe devoid of meaning is his staunchly Anglican daughter.[31] Another Midlands-born novelist who had migrated to the city, was equally sceptical of bald contrasts between the stony terrain of urban spirituality and the receptive fields of 'Loamshire', and was thought to produce pictures of contemporary piety so realistic that they could only be those of a clergyman. It suited George Eliot's particular brand of evolutionary meliorism to represent the pastoral care exercised in agrarian communities, reminiscent of the institutionalized mutual obligation depicted in Carlyle's *Past and Present* (1843), as untested by advances in scholarship, unaware of approaching bitter doctrinal warfare, and hopelessly ill equipped for combatting the urban godlessness her contemporary readership had been taught to fear. The goodness of bachelor clergy like Irwine (in *Adam Bede*) and Farebrother (in *Middlemarch*) partly consists in their silent acquiescence in their own obsolescence.

Narratives of Victorian religion and its literature have continued to be ideologically inflected. Successive waves of literary criticism, inflected by Marxist attention to class struggle, New Historicism's desire to locate representational practice within its given period, gender theory's models of differentiation, and post-colonial scholarship, have found themselves, like John Henry Newman when studying the Monophyites,[32] inspecting Victorian religious debates and practices only to find their own reflection. Jerome McGann's claim in 1983 that 'If Hopkins had never existed, the New Criticism would have had to invent him' scarcely conceals his own ploy of identifying the then 'unfashionable' Christina Rossetti as a suitable case for resurrection by New Historicism.[33] The studies of the literary output and representation of particular religious institutions and sects which began to appear in the mid 1960s were often stimulated as much by a nostalgic desire to record a fast-vanishing inheritance as by a reaction against the notion of the autonomy of the text. Although sometimes methodologically naive, they did valuable work in mapping a territory by then mainly known at second-hand through biased accounts, such as Samuel Butler's *The Way*

---

31 Elizabeth Gaskell, *North and South* (Oxford University Press, 2008), pp. 223, 42.

32 John Henry, Cardinal Newman, *Apologia pro Vita Sua* (Oxford: Clarendon Press, 1967), p. 108.

33 Jerome J. McGann, 'The Religious Poetry of Christina Rossetti' (1983), in Joseph Bristow (ed.), *Victorian Women Poets* (Basingstoke: Macmillan Press, 1995), pp. 167–88: p. 170.

of All Flesh (1903), Lytton Strachey's *Eminent Victorians* (1918), or Edmund Gosse's *Father and Son* (1907).

The Dissenting world in particular had remained *terra incognita*.[34] The diversity produced by its championship of the rights of the individual conscience meant that while it embraced political radicalism and quietism, smug philistinism and a thirst for education, its critics could tar all sects with the same brush. Dissent as a trope for provincialism was particularly attractive to those, like J. A. Froude or Matthew Arnold, who considered themselves to occupy the intellectual and cultural heartlands of Britain and were anxious to put distance between their own unorthodoxy and the taint of Nonconformity.[35] The material expression of Nonconformity's proliferating history was a gift for 'condition of England' fiction: in Dickens's industrial Coketown, 'eighteen religious persuasions' had each erected 'a pious warehouse of red brick', while in older settlements the classical designs of eighteenth-century Quaker, Baptist, and Independent meeting-places, were supplemented by chapels in backstreets or on the village margins, invariably depicted as 'ugly', 'mean', or 'squalid' in keeping with the congregations they attracted.[36] Although he had experienced the best education afforded by cultured metropolitan Dissent, Robert Browning knew something of invincible Anglican prejudice: the Rev. Charles Kingsley wrote of him as 'born and bred a Dissenter . . . nothing will take the smell of tallow and brown sugar out of him. He cannot help being coarse and vulgar.'[37] In his poem, 'Christmas Eve' (1850), Browning got to the spiritual nub of the matter. Presenting a congregation afflicted by poverty, ignorance, and disease, and a pastor whose genuine zeal is let down by his false biblical exegesis, the poem's speaker asks of Dissent as a spiritual conduit, 'But the main thing is, does it hold good measure?' The teachings of the German higher critics are intellectually attractive, but when death approaches, the speaker concludes, man 'gropes for something more substantial / Than a fable, myth or personification'. The educated speaker's decision to remain

---

34 Valentine Cunningham, *Everywhere Spoken Against: Dissent in the Victorian Novel* (Oxford: Clarendon Press, 1975) remains the most comprehensive guide.

35 Newly exiled from Oxford, J. A. Froude wrote 'We hate Manchester – Manchester in any form – Unitarian Manchester most of all.' Waldo Hilary Dunn, *James Anthony Froude: A Biography*, 2 vols. (Oxford: Clarendon Press, 1961–3), vol. I, p. 167.

36 Charles Dickens, *Hard Times* (Oxford University Press, 1989), Book the First, chapter 5, p. 29; Cf. William Hale White, *Revolution in Tanner's Lane* (London: Oxford University Press, 1936), pp. 158–60.

37 Quoted in M.F.Thorp, *Charles Kingsley, 1819–1875* (Princeton University Press, 1937), p. 95.

within the Dissenting fold is spelt out in a pun on the work of salvation: 'The giving out of the hymn reclaims me.'[38] It is the Dissenting chapel tradition of hymn-singing that recalls the speaker to the familiar rhythms that in their corporate expression offer an inclusive salvation to the disparate individuals gathered there.

Despite hymn-singing's Dissenting associations, in 1861 the Anglican Church felt able to give the benefit of its inclusive imprimatur to *Hymns Ancient and Modern*, whose title proclaimed its desire to accommodate those who venerated the liturgy of the Early Church, together with those who preferred the Protestantism of German Lutheranism, and those who saw in the metrical diversity of the hymn the chance to moralize, dogmatize, or, in the case of female authors, an opportunity, legitimated by the service of God, to put words in others' mouths.[39] While earlier phases of feminist criticism, especially those with a Marxist underpinning, were inclined to dismiss religion as Victorian patriarchy's chief prop, more recent analysis has come to see the market it created for devotional and improving literature for both adult and juvenile readers as opening up a field of semi-professional activity subtly at odds with the notion of domestic 'silent self-sacrifice' preached in many a pulpit.[40]

By Victoria's accession, the Evangelical mission was in its third generation: it had preached humanity's inherited inability to follow Christianity's moral teachings and the necessity of personally laying hold upon Christ's sacrifice as the sole route to salvation. It had also instigated considerable moral and philanthropic reform. The question as to whether its propaganda machine and numerical growth were in inverse proportion to its spiritual efficacy is raised in acute form by the concluding chapter of Thackeray's *Vanity Fair* (1848) which suggests that administrative flair and worldly ambition had found their perfect expression in the Victorian charity industry. Always quick to grasp social codes, Becky Sharp has read her way to the heart of the Evangelical system: 'She has her enemies. Who has not? Her life is her answer to them.' Becky's 'works of piety' might be interpreted as outward evidence of Becky's eleventh hour conversion, but by leaving her

38 Browning, *Works*, vol. v, pp. 95–6.
39 See J. R. Watson, *The English Hymn: A Critical and Historical Study* (Oxford: Clarendon Press, 1997), pp. 335–460.
40 See Anne Hogan and Andrew Bradstock (eds.), *Women of Faith in Victorian Culture: Reassessing the Angel in the House* (London: Macmillan, 1998); Elisabeth Jay, 'Women Writers and Religion', in Joanne Shattock (ed.), *Women and Literature in Britain 1800–1900* (Cambridge University Press, 2001), pp. 251–74.

inner state decipherable only by her and her c/Creator, Thackeray neatly exploits Evangelicalism's dogmatic separation between faith and works, and gestures to the way in which a newly redeemed Becky might refashion her history to the demands of a religious biography.[41]

The doctrinal emphasis might fall differently upon misspent youth or uncanny premonitions of saintliness, missionary endeavour or miraculous feats, but religious biography and autobiography, sometimes abbreviated for inexperienced readers, came to form part of the staple diet of Victorian readers. Newman's extraordinary effect upon his generation, judged Margaret Oliphant, was in large part achieved by his *Apologia*, 'the story of a struggle through difficulties with which the common mind could have little sympathy, which was as engrossing as any novel'.[42] George Eliot made this connection when she arrogated the genre's morally educative potential for her first fictional collection, *Scenes of Clerical Life* (1857).

Although Evangelicalism was not the sole agent in the increasingly widespread literacy of the Victorian period, its insistence on the absolute authority of the Word of God, interpreted by the inner light of the Holy Spirit, as the route to personal salvation, placed a premium upon unmediated access to the Bible, and on the imperative of the individual conscience. This inheritance emerges nowhere more strongly than in the works of the Brontë sisters, where Emily's poetic declaration, 'No coward soul is mine',[43] is matched by Jane Eyre, Lucy Snowe (in *Villette*), or Helen Huntingdon's reliance, in *The Tenant of Wildfell Hall*, upon 'that still small voice which interprets the dictates of conscience'[44] as the one sure resource enabling spiritual survival for even the most oppressed of women making their way through a fallen society in which male power is materially undergirded and psychologically encoded.

It was the way in which Evangelical preaching of the Word of God had too often become attenuated to repeating a few 'simple' truths, and was untrammeled by the regulatory function of the Church as an authority and well-spring of doctrine, that troubled a small group of Oxford clergy in the summer of 1833. In the attempt to rally fellow clergy to the threat posed by

41 William Makepeace Thackeray, *Vanity Fair: a Novel without a Hero* (Oxford University Press, 1991), chapter 67, p. 877. See also Elisabeth Jay, *The Religion of the Heart: Anglican Evangelicalism and the Nineteenth-Century Novel* (Oxford: Clarendon Press, 1978).

42 M. O. W. Oliphant and F. R. Oliphant, *The Victorian Age of English Literature*, 2 vols. (London: Percival, 1892), vol. II, p. 7.

43 D. Roper and E. Chitham (eds.), *The Poems of Emily Brontë* (Oxford: Clarendon Press, 1995), p. 183.

44 Charlotte Brontë, *Jane Eyre* (Oxford: Clarendon Press, 1969), chapter 19, p. 252.

rationalist thought and liberal politics, they issued a series of ninety Tracts (1833–41), designed to remind Anglicans of a patristic inheritance, derived from the Early Church and available as a bulwark against the excesses of the Protestant Reformation and contemporary reformers. The fragility of the proposed equilibrium between Anglicanism and Catholic dogma was exposed when Newman, unable to continue his reconciliation of the two, was admitted into the Roman Catholic Church in 1845. Perhaps the only true literary successor to the original spirit of the Oxford Movement was Charlotte Yonge, whose prodigious output of fiction and history was eagerly consumed in the upper middle-class households she sought to educate. Yonge ensured this purity by sequestering herself in her Hampshire birth-place and setting up her father, together with that Oxford émigré, the Rev. John Keble, as her twin lodestars. Her best-known novel, *The Heir of Redclyffe* (1853), disseminated their teaching to a readership that included Dante Gabriel Rossetti, William Morris, and Mary Arnold (Mrs Humphry Ward), but later works offered a rather fossilized impression of the Movement. Christina Rossetti, whose urban, artistic, and political milieu was very different from Yonge's, met Tractarianism in post-Newman mode, through a priest whose interests in millennial prophecy were to colour her own preoccupation with the Book of Revelations.[45] For Gerard Manley Hopkins, the Tractarianism he encountered courtesy of Edward Bouverie Pusey and Henry Parry Liddon formed an undergraduate phase, en route to admission by the Jesuit order in 1866; moreover any debt to Keble's sacramental understanding of nature was complicated by his reading in John Ruskin.

Mid-century defections to Roman Catholicism served to reactivate old political suspicions, and to reawaken an interest in the political uses of history and historical fiction. The period of the Early Church Fathers or late Tudor England served as well as the contemporary scene as a battle-ground for debating origins, dogma, and moral priorities.[46] Dismayed by Tractarianism's anti-liberal traits, and Evangelicalism's assertion of man's essential depravity, Charles Kingsley and his fellow Christian Socialists sought to effect a bloodless revolution by making Christ's kingdom on earth available to all, through harnessing scientific progress to social reform and

45 See Christina Rossetti, *The Face of the Deep: a Devotional Commentary on the Apocalypse* (London and New York: SPCK, 1892). See also Diane D'Amico and David A. Kent, 'Rossetti and the Tractarians', *Victorian Poetry*, 44 (2006), pp. 93–104.

46 Michael Wheeler, *The Old Enemies: Catholic and Protestant in Nineteenth-Century English Culture* (Cambridge University Press, 2006), contextualizes a slew of such historical novels.

offering literary prototypes of effective Christian manliness to vie with Tractarianism's ascetic saints or Evangelicalism's inward-looking heroes.[47]

The face of Roman Catholicism changed swiftly in the early Victorian period when the limited numbers of English gentry, continuing their quiet practice of the old faith, were swelled by a vast influx of poor and largely uneducated Irish seeking escape from famine in the new work provided by the coming of the railways and swift industrialization. The unobtrusive observances of the former were caricatured as a sinister mission to wavering Tractarians, while the Papist adornments of the newly arrived priests who ministered to their flocks in urban ghettoes marked them out as dangerously 'foreign'. The cultural shock sustained by J. H. Newman and Hopkins, as they found themselves in a new world, whose centre was Rome and whose language was Latin, it has been argued, helped to produce a new corpus of English Catholic writing.[48]

The Jewish experience in England shared some of these characteristics: the emancipatory acts, permitting Roman Catholics (1829) and Jews (1858) to enter Parliament, in effect decoupled the question of national allegiance from other elements of the faith. Moreover, the comparatively small number of Jews (35,000) living in England and Wales at the time of the 1851 census was suddenly augmented, in the 1880s, by a wave of impoverished immigrants fleeing persecution in Eastern Europe (c. 150,000 between 1881 and 1914), again making visible a division between the indigenized and those whose way of life and worship was noticeably 'alien'. Racial stereotyping of morbidly nervous intellectuals, wealthy cosmopolitan bankers, and working-class denizens of London's East End was further complicated by a Christian interpretive framework that saw the Jews both as tribal precursors and ripe for the conversion and restoration to the Promised Land that would herald Christ's Second Coming. Recent scholarship on Victorian Jewish self-representation has emphasized the ambivalent meanings located in the word 'Jew' and the 'double vision' through which Anglo-Jewish writers viewed their world.[49]

---

47 For a detailed treatment of Charles Kingsley and Thomas Hughes's output see Norman Vance, *The Sinews of the Spirit: the Ideal of Christian Manliness in Victorian Literature and Religious Thought* (Cambridge University Press, 1985).

48 See Elisabeth Jay, 'Newman's Mid-Victorian Dream', in David Nicholls and Fergus Kerr (eds.), *John Henry Newman, Reason, Rhetoric and Romanticism* (Bristol: Bristol Press, 1991), pp. 214–32 and Ian Ker, *The Catholic Revival in English Literature, 1845–1961* (University of Notre Dame Press, 2003).

49 Nadia Valman, '"A Fresh-Made Garment of Citizenship": Representing Jewish Identities in Victorian Britain', *Nineteenth Century Studies*, 17 (2003), pp. 10–11, 35–45, offers a succinct survey and bibliography.

The most persistently teleological interpretation of nineteenth-century spirituality originated with the Victorians and was actively promoted by their immediate successors, who, following an evolutionary model, claimed that the nineteenth century had witnessed the slow but triumphant progress of secularization. Then as now, however, there were dissentient voices: the theologian manqué, R. H. Hutton, who was variously attracted by the Unitarianism of Francis Newman and A. H. Clough, the inclusive vision of F. D. Maurice's Broad Church, and John Henry Newman's battle with the rationalist temper of the times, was well equipped to detect false notes in representations of contemporary religion. The interrogation of biblical texts characterizing the agricultural labourers' conversation in Thomas Hardy's *Far From the Madding Crowd* (1874), he suggested, smacked more of the author than of a poor and ill-educated peasantry.[50]

The literature of Victorian heterodoxy ranged from fiercely moral blasphemy,[51] to more measured consideration of advances in biblical scholarship and scientific discoveries. Over the years of Victoria's reign scepticism slowly entered mainstream publications, initially often more by way of passages easily intelligible to fellow travellers but sufficiently indirect to avoid antagonizing more orthodox readers. George Eliot's painstaking translations of works by Strauss (*The Life of Jesus*, 1846) and Feuerbach (*The Essence of Christianity*, 1854) were never likely to attract audiences beyond freethinking circles, while her translations of Spinoza's *Tractatus* (1849) and *Ethics* (1854) remained unpublished in her own lifetime. In her fiction, however, the desire to reach a far wider readership led her to encode her message in terms broadly compatible with liberal interpretations of Judaeo-Christian teaching. The social ostracism, educational disadvantage, or financial loss that had loomed as a certain consequence of expressing doubt or disbelief mid-century was partly mitigated by the removal of religious tests, but legislation reflected rather than produced change. In practice the degree of scandal aroused by the public declaration of 'religious difficulties' depended upon the status of the writer, the style and tone in which they were expressed, and their intended audience. The outrage aroused by James Anthony Froude's novel *The Nemesis of Faith* (1849) derived not so much from the moral reservations expressed concerning ordination and Anglican dogma, as from the protagonist's febrile imaginings of his

---

50 R. H. Hutton, *Spectator*, 19 December 1874, pp. 1597–9.
51 See Joss Marsh, *Word Crimes: Blasphemy, Culture, and Literature in Nineteenth-Century England* (Chicago and London: Chicago University Press, 1998).

subsequent descent into immorality and despair, and the all-important fact that the author, fellow of an Oxford college, was already in deacon's orders. By contrast, Tennyson's poetic meditation upon the difficulties of sustaining faith in a providential Creator or belief in personal immortality, published the following year as *In Memoriam*, became the acceptable face of 'honest doubt' both because the poem as a whole could be read as a plea to 'faintly trust the larger hope' and because its author was not ordained.[52] Arthur Hugh Clough, like Froude, renounced his Oxford fellowship, but reserved his bitterest expressions of betrayal and loss for private circulation, perhaps because he knew that his bleakest moments alternated with intimations of residual spiritual truths. His 'Easter Day, Naples 1849', with its blasphemous antiphon, 'Christ is not risen', offers a direct challenge to Christianity's central claim in rhythms and phrases that simultaneously recall and deny time-hallowed Christian liturgy.[53]

Where Clough presents the epicureanism all too obviously practised in 'the great sinful streets of Naples' as Christianity's immoral counterpoint,[54] Edward Fitzgerald's 'Rubáiyát of Omar Khayyám'(1859) presents it as a sybaritic, private substitute for Eucharistic communion:

> Here with a Loaf of bread beneath the Bough,
> A Flask of Wine, a Book of Verse – and Thou
> Beside me singing in the Wilderness –
> And Wilderness is Paradise enow.[55]

Fitzgerald's flirtation with sensual pleasure, like his religious doubt, was ostensibly distanced from mid nineteenth-century concerns by being couched as the unorthodox philosophy of a twelfth-century Persian astronomer-poet and was quietly launched with an antiquarian bookseller. Nevertheless the very act of refashioning an ancient oriental text raised issues that could not have been more germane to the late 1850s.

> It is better to be Orientally obscure than Europeanly clear ... I always refer back to the Bible ... keeping so close to almost unintelligible idioms both of Country and Era. Well – it is done: and ... *has prepared all Englishmen at least for the reception of other Oriental works under the same forms*: both of *words* and *grammar*.[56]

52 Tennyson, *In Memoriam*, in *Poems*, vol. II, p. 372, line 20 and p. 415, line 11.
53 Clough, *Poems*, pp. 199–203.   54 *Ibid.*, p. 199.
55 Decker, C., ed., *Rubáiyát of Omar Khayyám: A Critical Edition* (Charlottesville and London: University Press of Virginia, 1997), p. 11.
56 A. M. Terhune and A. B. Terhune (eds.), *The Letters of Edward Fitzgerald*, 4 vols. (Princeton University Press, 1980), vol. II, p. 164.

Small wonder, then, that it was Benjamin Jowett's clever but wayward pupil, Algernon Charles Swinburne, who, when he read the poem in 1861, recognised its truly subversive potential. Jowett, Regius Professor of Greek, had argued the case for bringing to the Bible the same standards of historical and textual scholarship applied to other ancient texts in *Essays and Reviews* (1860). The substance of these essays had long been debated among theologians, but the fact that six out of the seven contributors were, and intended to remain, Anglican clergymen, raised a furore. Moving the theological debate from an academy, hitherto largely controlled by the Church, into the periodicals run by the literary circles of London and Edinburgh, occasioned a further shift in the slow divorce between religious sensibility and Christian dogma, provided a more accessible forum for women, and, increasingly drove the laity to form their own conclusions. Nevertheless, neither the decline in authoritative teaching, lamented by Trollope in the *Pall Mall Gazette*,[57] nor the 'alternations of Hebraism and Hellenism, of a man's intellectual and moral impulses, of the effort to see things as they really are, and the effort to win peace by self-conquest' recommended by Matthew Arnold as a panacea for England's troubled state in 1869,[58] entirely prepared the broader swathes of England's middle classes for the brazen iconoclasm of Swinburne's *Poems and Ballads* (1866). Swinburne's nervous publisher, Moxon, moved swiftly to withdraw the offending volume at the first hostile review. Swinburne had compounded the sin of representing Christianity as a projection of man's lust for suffering, by parodic allusions to biblical texts and by openly celebrating, in its stead, a version of Hellenism fuelled by the eroticism of the gods of Olympus rather than by the philosophical tradition foregrounded in Arnold's account of Greece. By the same token, Swinburne's use of the dramatic monologue to emphasize the uniformity of a universe in which man is always the victim of a greater sadistic force, deliberately perverted Browning's development of the form to demonstrate that the concept of historically situated religious revelation might render individual insight particular and partial, but also infinitely extended the world's wonder and complexity.

James Thomson (B.V.)'s choice of the weekly magazine, *The National Reformer* – run by atheist and republican Charles Bradlaugh – as an outlet for *The City of Dreadful Night* (1874), his terrifying vision of urban oppression and despair, ensured that the energetic metrics of his black apocalypse won

---

57 Ruth apRoberts (ed.), *Clergymen of the Church of England* (1866; Leicester University Press, 1974), p. 128.
58 Arnold, *Prose Works*, vol. v, pp. 171–2.

attention from unorthodox literati such as Dante Gabriel Rossetti and George Meredith rather than a wider public. George Eliot and Walter Pater were more to the general taste of the 1870s and 1880s. Though they doubted religion's claims to unique and absolute truth, they remained convinced of humanity's need for outlets for idealistic 'ardour' and 'spiritual grandeur'.[59] In *Daniel Deronda* (1876) Eliot strove to dramatize this thesis by killing off the increasingly blind, separatist Jewish visionary, Mordecai, so that his mission could be reconfigured by a multicultural hero whose job it is, in the teeth of contemporary prejudice, to sift and take forward the cultural, political, and ethical elements of Judaism. Mrs Humphry Ward fleshed out Pater's concept of spirituality in *Robert Elsmere* (1888), the fictional biography of an Anglican rector who, having renounced the supernatural element of Christianity, reconceives 'the spirit that spread the Church ... the spirit of devotion, through a man, to an idea'. The heart of this best-selling novel's attraction, however, lay in the unresolved dramatic tension between Elsmere's investment in his idealistic city mission to working-men, 'The New Brotherhood of Christ', and his love for his staunchly orthodox wife. Even his deathbed utterance, immensely significant to 'all persons of the older Christian type',[60] leaves open the question of personal immortality and the hope of reunion. Gladstone judged the novel that he recognized as 'eminently an offspring of its time' worthy of a weighty review.[61]

Turn-of-the-century fiction proves that the ideological debate over man's essential nature was far from over, that airing personal scepticism in public could offend both the sensibilities of immediate family and the family-friendly values of Mudie's circulating library, and that matters of chronology remained significant. George Du Maurier's sensational best-seller *Trilby* (1894) immediately preceded Hardy's *Jude the Obscure* (1895) in the pages of the American *Harper's Magazine*. Whereas Hardy's near-blind seer, Clym Yeobright, hero of *The Return of the Native* (1878), could have joined human-ist cause with Elsmere or Eliot's heroes in retaining his rural 'vocation in the career of an itinerant open-air preacher and lecturer on morally unimpeach-able subjects',[62] the apostate Jude's urban deathbed, unrelieved by the

---

59 George Eliot, *Middlemarch* (Oxford: Clarendon Press, 1992), Prelude, p. 3.

60 Mrs Humphry Ward, *Robert Elsmere* (Lincoln: University of Nebraska Press, 1967), chapters 49 and 51, pp. 577, 599.

61 W. E. Gladstone, 'Robert Elsmere and the Battle of Belief', *Nineteenth Century* 23 (1888), pp. 766–88.

62 Thomas Hardy, *The Return of the Native* (Oxford University Press, 2005), Book 6: chapter IV, p. 389.

consolations of theism, had more affinity with Thomson than with their tempered optimism. A heroine who deliberately quoted Shelley and Swinburne and survived adultery was less easy to forgive than simple Tess Durbeyfield, who atoned for her sins by dying. W. H. Smith's were persuaded by the Bishop of Wakefield to withdraw *Jude* from their library.[63] Meanwhile, the bright promise held out, in the Bishop's most famous hymn, of 'the golden evening' and 'yet more glorious day' reserved 'For all the saints ... Who thee by faith before the world confessed',[64] is best appreciated when set against the drab suicidal gloom of *Jude the Obscure's* world where moral struggle is waged without hope of reward.

Compared with Jude and Sue, Trilby and her admirer, Little Billee, are safely remote 'innocents abroad'; moreover, Trilby dies in expiation for her various deviations from womanly behaviour. Although the novel fed contemporary preoccupations with the European Jew and with mesmerism, Du Maurier followed his master Thackeray's ploy in keeping a mocking narrative distance from Little Billee's inner life: this allowed him to denounce the Anglican clergy's wilful blindness to Darwinian thought, while implying that such issues belonged to the naive 1850s rather than the maturity of *fin-de-siècle* debate.

By their use of the quasi-biographical fictional format, Samuel Butler – whose *The Way of All Flesh* lay dormant for thirty years before its publication in 1903 – and James Joyce, who started work on *Stephen Hero* between 1901 and 1906, contrived to suggest that the Anglican Evangelicalism and Roman Catholicism of their respective childhoods were spent historical forces; but their passionate explorations of religion's tentacular reach into every aspect of Victorian public and private life tell another story. Although the Modernist Hero might wish to confine his 'sudden spiritual manifestations' or glimpses of meaning he called 'epiphanies'[65] to mental or physical origins, he found himself, like Butler, contemptuous of the 'vulgar' scientific materialism emanating from 'the High Priests of Science'.[66] The coarse profanities emanating from Joyce's ironically named medical student Temple seem to continue to provide reluctant corroboration for Tennyson's contention that, without a sense of the spiritual, man would indeed turn into a pig.

63 Frederick Douglas How, *Bishop Walsham How: a Memoir* (London: Isbister, 1898), p. 344.
64 [William How, Bishop of Wakefield], Hymn 20, 'For all the Saints', in *Hymns Ancient and Modern*, new edn (London: William Clowes & Sons, 1868), p. 358.
65 John J. Slocum and Herbert Cahoon (eds.), *Stephen Hero* (St Albans: Panther, 1977), pp. 188–9.
66 Originally named as Thomas Huxley and John Tyndall. Samuel Butler, *The Way of All Flesh* (Harmondsworth: Penguin, 1971), pp. 405, 443.

Material

ELAINE FREEDGOOD

Manufactured calico, tea cups, dresses, pins, and forks flowing from the factories and workshops of the 'great' towns; imported sugar, coffee, tea, Madeira, silk, and diamonds arriving from the colonies and zones of 'free trade'; handmade crafts fashioned by middle-class women and by William Morris; souvenir postcards and plates returning home from Blackpool, Skye, and the Alps; collections of butterflies, ferns, and cacti lovingly bought, gathered, and displayed by amateur and professional naturalists; rubbish and 'dust' piling up uncomfortably and often dangerously in streets and alleys: the material world of the Victorian period and its literature delights and daunts us in its variety and vastness. How do we read and interpret this array of stuff when we encounter it in the varied genres of Victorian literature? This chapter will enlarge on the possibilities that inhere in these questions, both as they pertain to modes of Victorian writing and to the way we read them now.

'Even the humblest material artefact, which is the product and symbol of a particular civilization, is an emissary of the culture out of which it comes', T. S. Eliot writes in *Notes towards the Definition of Culture.*[1] This is one of the epigraphs of the historian Asa Briggs's monumental *Victorian Things* and might be its credo as well. Briggs takes us on an incomparable tour of the Victorian object world: daguerreotypes, spectacles, matches, needles, bonnets, Staffordshire figures, medals, souvenir heads, hankies, penny postage stamps, and cookery books connect us to the people who made and bought and used them, to wars, laws, strikes, fashion, and gender roles, to ideas about home and hearth, many of which were invented by the Victorians and are still practised by us. They connect us to people, things, and places with which we might not otherwise make contact.

---

1 T. S. Eliot, *Notes Towards the Definition of Culture* (London: Faber & Faber, 1948), p. 11.

When literary critics encounter these and other remarkable and unremarkable things in novels and poems, we do not think about them as emissaries. In literature, we analyse subjects, plots, themes, forms, and structures, but we tend to leave curtains, buttons, tables, top hats, and tobacco more or less alone. We have a powerful theoretical justification for doing so: the extremely influential and convincing idea of the 'reality effect' as theorized by Roland Barthes, (who was, paradoxically, also a great theorist of things in many of his other writings).[2] The theory of the reality effect attempts to account for the presence of so many apparently non-symbolic objects in the Realist novel: what are all these things doing in the novel? Barthes asks. What is their function? His answer: to gesture at a generic real; to reassure readers that the novel is taking place in a realized, or realistic, world. We need take no particular interpretive note of such items as the barometer in the living room of Madame Aubain in Flaubert's story 'A Simple Heart', Barthes explains: it simply signifies that we are 'in' a real(istic) bourgeois home of the place and period, in which barometers were commonplace possessions.

How then do we decide which objects are symbolic, and which are simply reality effects? This question should actually be phrased: how have we decided which objects are symbolic and which are reality effects? The interpretability of a given novelistic or poetic thing depends upon the critical method we are using, and literary critical methods change considerably over time. In the New Criticism of the 1950s, for example, objects in literature received attention largely when they rose to the stature of metaphors. So the tree that splits apart (but not all the way to the roots) in *Jane Eyre* when Jane must leave Rochester (but not for ever) is important for us to explicate, but the (literal) furniture of the novel is not. The tree is a metaphor; the chairs and tables are just and only things.

In New Historicism, a practice that began the 1980s, we can take more notice of things: they may be parts of a historical allegory that we must read beyond the 'givens' of the text. We can notice, for example, Jane's references to her material condition as a governess and relate them to the material conditions of governesses in the mid-nineteenth century.[3] In postcolonial

2 Roland Barthes, 'The Reality Effect', in *The Rustle of Language*, trans. Richard Howard (Berkeley: University of California Press, 1989), pp. 141–8. For what have become canonical discussions of objects see Roland Barthes, *Mythologies*, trans. Annette Lavers (New York: Noonday Press, 1972).

3 See Mary Poovey, 'The Anathematized Race: The Governess and Jane Eyre', in *Uneven Developments: The Ideological Work of Gender in Mid-Victorian England* (University of Chicago Press, 1988), pp. 126–63.

criticism, we would become able to 'read' Jane's numerous references to slavery. We could then interpret them, materially, in terms of the inevitable involvement of the novel in British slavery, in the Caribbean origins of certain objects that figure prominently in the novel, and their meaning in relation to the novel's geography and history as well as to its treatment of race, culture, and power.[4] In a feminist version of such criticism, Jane's frequent references to seraglios and harems can be treated as meaningful in terms of Britain's empire-building in the 'Orient', and its literal and figurative arrangements of gender and power, their impact on the novel, and the novel's implications in this history.[5] Different critical methods, in short, determine which novelistic 'material' seems interpretable.

If we do interpret literary objects, we usually perform what I have described elsewhere as 'weak metonymic readings':[6] readings that are limited by the immediate context in which we find particular objects. In Elizabeth Gaskell's industrial novel, *Mary Barton* (1848), for example, the narrator carefully catalogues the objects in the Barton family parlour: plates and dishes, cups and saucers, a dresser, a deal table covered with a 'gay-colored oilcloth', a japanned tea tray, and a crimson tea caddy, 'also of japan ware'.[7] If we read these objects according to the metonymic procedures of recent modes of literary criticism, we might understand them as indicating the domesticity of this family, their wish to emulate the middle-class parlours of the same period, in which small decorations and window coverings are the crucial accoutrements of a private sphere, a space of 'homeliness' and 'cosiness' that is under construction inside and outside of the novel in this period.

But if we take one of these apparently 'domestic' objects literally for a moment, and trace its origins, manufacture, distribution, and consumption, we escape the confines of metonymic reading as it is usually practised when interpreting literary objects. We might, for example, trace the making of 'japan ware' in Britain. Such a research gambit would include inquiring into

4 See Susan Meyer, *Imperialism at Home: Race and Victorian Women's Fiction* (Ithaca, NY: Cornell University Press, 1996) and Jenny Sharpe, *Allegories of empire: the Figure of Woman in the Colonial Text* (Minneapolis: University of Minnesota Press, 1993).

5 See Sue Thomas, 'The Tropical Extravagance of Bertha Mason', *Victorian Literature and Culture* 27:1 (1999), pp. 1–17; and Joyce Zonana, 'The Sultan and the Slave: Feminist Orientalism and the Structures of *Jane Eyre*', *Signs: Journal of Women in Culture and Society* 18 (1993), pp. 592–617.

6 See Elaine Freedgood, *The Ideas in Things: Fugitive Meaning in the Victorian Novel* (University of Chicago Press, 2006), pp. 2, 11, 12.

7 Elizabeth Gaskell, *Mary Barton: A Tale of Manchester Life.* ed. Shirley Foster (Oxford University Press, 2006), p. 15.

the history of the importation and the imitation of 'Oriental' lacquer ware, as well as a more theoretical consideration of the history and meanings of 'Japan' and japanoiserie in Britain in the mid nineteenth century. We would find out about lacquer production as a small scale 'sweated' trade in Britain (that is, piecework done by hand, and at home), and about the toxic materials women and girls used in the attempt to create the effect of the original hard, shiny surface of the Asian variety, and we would read the accounts of Victorian travellers to Japan, and Japanese travellers to Victorian Britain. Such research might cause the Japan ware in *Mary Barton* to resonate with the novel's plots and characters in unforeseen ways. It might allow us to find histories of domination and regimes of knowledge that were perhaps in many ways present to the original readers of *Mary Barton* but are lost to us now because our habits of reading do not allow us to venture very far in the investigation and interpretation of novelistic things like tea trays.

Such research depends in part on a massive Victorian literature of things. Composed in part of works that are not often read now, this literature includes tales of factory tourism with minute accounts of manufacturing processes; 'biographies' of objects like buttons and screws; detailed histories of particular industries like cotton and brass; 'it-narratives' – tales narrated by dolls, shillings, feathers, and other usually inanimate objects; catalogues of the Great Exhibition and other large displays, and other works that Victorians read to learn about the objects by which they were surrounded and intrigued. In George Dodd's *Days at the Factories* (1843), for example, the making of vinegar, soap, clocks, and pianos is chronicled in the kind of abundant detail we routinely associate with the Victorian novel and that we often dismiss (and sometimes ignore) as amusing or even annoying. Consider this painstaking account of the making of a cigar:

> The cigar-maker is seated on a low stool in front of a low work-bench, provided with raised legs on three of its sides, but open at the side next the workman. He takes a leaf of tobacco, spreads it out smoothly before him on the bench, and cuts it to form a shape somewhat like that of one of the gores or stripes of a balloon. He then takes up a few fragments of tobacco-leaf, consisting of various small cuttings, lays them on the spread leaf, and rolls them up into a form nearly resembling that of a cigar. He next places this cigar against a gauge or guide, formed of a piece of iron, and cuts it to a given length. Finally, he lays a narrow strip of leaf on the bench, and rolls the cigar spirally in it, twisting one end to prevent the leaf from becoming loosened.[8]

8 George Dodd, *Days at the Factories* (London: Charles Knight, 1843), p. 130.

It seems worth pondering the fact that Dodd had a large audience for writing of this kind: other visits detail the 'mashing-machine' of a distillery, the splitting of sheepskins in a tannery for making book bindings and hat-linings, the measurements of a 'ripping-bed' for cutting marble slabs, and how, if in a printing factory the 'vacuities of the [letters] "a" and "e" have become filled up with little globules of metal, they have to be cleaned or picked out'.[9] Victorians, it seems, wanted to know how things were made – to the point, apparently, of desiring a set of virtual directions. Books like *Days at the Factories* were common: factory tourism featuring minute descriptions of production processes is a significant nineteenth-century genre. It suggests that Victorians may have read their 'material' world – in novels, in shops, at exhibitions, in poetry, at home – differently from the way we now read the things of our world. They could often bring to bear on such objects a knowledge of raw materials and production that is well beyond the grasp of most consumers now: Dodd, for example, does not hesitate to include details of slave labour, or the international and often imperial provenance of the raw materials, from animal skins to sugar, on which the workshops of the world depend.

Was there a 'manufacturing culture' in which culture and industry were not opposed in the way they are now? For writers who enthusiastically defended factory production in the 1830s and 1840s like Edward Baines, a historian of the cotton industry, and Andrew Ure, a political economist, industry was an organic development, a 'natural product of English ingenuity'.[10] For Charles Babbage, another defender of industry, the machines of the industrial revolution possessed a mechanical beauty: the possibility of mass reproduction offered the boon of precision and the wider distribution of useful and beautiful things.[11] The division of labour made for labour-saving machines and practices and ever more perfect products. Culture and industry, art and machines are not at odds in the work of these once influential but now little-read pro-industrial writers: they work in complex complementarity, advancing one another's best interests.

There was also a significant anti-manufacturing culture, led by John Ruskin, who believed profoundly in the value of the handmade, and abhorred the factory system, the division of labour, and the replacement

9 *Ibid.*, pp. 345–6.
10 See Joseph Bizup, *Manufacturing Culture: Vindications of Early Victorian Industry* (Charlottesville: University of Virginia Press, 2003), p. 19.
11 *Ibid.*, pp. 51–83.

of any human labour by machines. His work precipitated a Gothic revival in Victorian Britain and a renewed interest in medievalism. In *The Stones of Venice* (1853) he exhorted his readers to

> look round this English room of yours, about which you have been proud so often, because the work of it was so good and strong, and the ornaments of it so finished. Examine again all those accurate mouldings, and perfect polishings, and unerring adjustments of the seasoned wood and tempered steel . . . Alas! if read rightly these perfectnesses are signs of a slavery in our England a thousand times more bitter and more degrading than that of the scourged African, or helot Greek.[12]

The flaw is the sign of the handmade, and therefore we should not value 'perfectnesses': they can only be produced by machine, in factories which misuse human bodies and minds. Ruskin joins many militant labouring-class writers in comparing the factory worker to the slave. Although his answers are deeply and literally conservative – he wishes to preserve a pre-capitalist culture and mode of production and consumption, Ruskin prefigures the socialism of William Morris, about whom more below.

An event that pivotally shaped the way Victorians experienced the things of their world, the Great Exhibition of the Products of Industry at the Crystal Palace in 1851, put objects on display in an unprecedentedly massive and inclusive manner. The display was organized by nation, and in the largest display, that of Great Britain, by type of object: 'Carriages, Railway and Marine Mechanism', 'Tapestry, Floor Cloths, Lace and Embroidery', 'Mining and Mineral Products', 'Philosophical, Musical, Horological, and Surgical Instruments', 'Vegetable and Animal Substances used in Manufactures', 'Woollen and Worsted'.[13] The actual displays in these categories now have a wonderfully quirky quality: 'Specimens of hair watch guards', 'pins and needles', 'anchovy and other sauces', 'net for keeping fish alive', and 'artificial flower-plant, formed of beads'. It would be difficult today to find any of these items at an exhibition comparable to the Great Exhibition, let alone in the same category – 'Miscellaneous Manufactures and Small Wares'. We are not so generous, so inclusive, or so careful when it comes to the more humble aspects of our material worlds. As Charlotte Brontë wrote, the Exhibition's 'grandeur does not consist in one thing', 'but in the unique

---

12 John Ruskin, *Complete Works*, ed. E. T. Cook and A. Wedderburn, 39 vols. (London: George Allen, 1903), vol. x, p. 193.
13 *Official Catalogue of the Great Exhibition of the Works of Industry of all National* (London: Spicer Brothers, 1851), pp. 14, 27, 30, 60, 77, 97, 142, 144, 145, 147.

assemblage of all things'.[14] The Exhibition achieved a previously unimaginable comprehensiveness: it did not seem like a sample of the products of world industry; it seemed to offer at least one of everything – or so it amazingly appeared.

The Great Exhibition has, accordingly, been analysed by many contemporary scholars of Victorian culture as a key moment in the history of commodity culture, as perhaps *the* moment of its consolidation. The splendour of the Crystal Palace display inaugurated a specular and a spectacular system, one scholar argues: a system in which *looking at objects on display* becomes a central activity of consumers.[15] The literature that accompanies the advent of this system is often haunted by an anxiety that the 'social and moral world was being reduced to a warehouse of goods and commodities'.[16] And yet, although many of the writers of the period were critical of what we now call commodity culture, the massive cataloguing and detailing of things in their works has meant that Victorian literature in general and the Victorian novel in particular helped guarantee the commodity's rise to ascendancy: 'our sense of the commodity's invasiveness may owe its largest debt neither to the eloquence of social prophecy ... nor the elaborations of social theory but rather to the Victorian novel and its narrative heirs'.[17] Writers like Dickens and Thackeray, who were profoundly critical of the depredations of industrialization, including its massive output of stuff, tend to pile things up in their prose. Thackeray, for example, introduces Jos Sedley in *Vanity Fair* (1848) as a 'very stout, puffy man, in buckskins and Hessian boots, with several immense neckcloths, that rose almost to his nose, with a red-striped waistcoat and an apple-green coat with steel buttons almost as large as crown pieces (it was the morning costume of a dandy or a blood of those days) ...'[18] The problem with excessive and ostentatious clothing is that cataloguing it, however satirically, repeats the excess and ostentation. Thackeray becomes an exhibitor of the very goods he disparages; his fiction prefigures the function of the department store

---

14 Charlotte Brontë, *Letters of Charlotte Brontë*, ed. Margaret Smith (Oxford University Press, 2007), p. 190.
15 Thomas Richards, *The Commodity Culture of Victorian England: Advertising and Spectacle, 1851–1914* (Stanford University Press, 1990), p. 3.
16 Andrew H. Miller, *Novels behind Glass: Commodity Culture and Victorian Narrative* (Cambridge University Press, 1995), p. 6.
17 Jeff Nunokawa, *The Afterlife of Property: Domestic Security and the Victorian Novel* (Princeton University Press, 1994), p. 4.
18 William Makepeace Thackeray, *Vanity Fair* (Oxford University Press, 1983), chapter 3, p. 26.

window. I take this idea from a book that is titled, fittingly, *Novels behind Glass*.[19] Realistic novels and department stores share large stocks of commodities; their methods of display are skilful and seductive.

Now let us consider how we 'read' Jos's unfortunate outfit. We know that these clothes are not metaphors: hessian boots are not put into a comparison with something else; rather they, along with the rest of Jos's outfit, are metonymic indicators of his character. Even if we are not knowledgeable about the fashion of the period we understand that wearing 'several immense neckcloths' indicates absurd excess, especially given that said cloths are widely outflanking the anatomical area for which they are intended. We understand that Jos is vain and ridiculous, a would-be dandy who is instead a clown. Novels teach us to read the possessions of their characters in this way (partly through various cues from the narrator: in this case tone is obviously a crucial guide); metonymic realism works by such contiguities between characters and their belongings.

In a Dickens novel we are also often introduced to characters by way of their clothing. We meet Miss Tox, in *Dombey and Son*, through learning that she has a problem with 'all her collars, frills, tuckers, wristbands, and other gossamer articles – indeed of everything she wore which had two ends to it intended to unite – that the two ends were never on good terms, and wouldn't quite meet without a struggle'.[20] Miss Tox cannot make ends meet literally or figuratively, we understand: we understand it because Dickens has her enact it for us in the loose ends of her excess garments. In this case her clothing is brilliantly and comically both metonym and metaphor, and in this case a metaphor of another metaphor: Tox's tatters enact the metaphor of being unable to make ends meet financially; she performs her having-come-down-in-the-world condition (at one time she could afford gossamer embellishments), which turns out to be in keeping with her cloying, dependent character.

Many of the garments listed above were the products of the immense mechanization and steady improvement of textile production that formed a large part of the industrial revolution. Beginning in the eighteenth century, better and better machines were invented for the spinning and weaving of cotton, silk, linen, and wool. The result is that Britons could have British-made cottons that were indeed 'gossamer': previously such high-quality fabric came only from India, Egypt, or China, where handlooming was, for centuries, far superior to anything made in Britain.

19 Miller, *Novels behind Glass*, pp. 14–49.
20 Charles Dickens, *Dombey and Son* (Oxford University Press, 2008), chapter 1, p. 4.

The technological innovations of the nineteenth century include not only power looms and spinning jennies, but also massive improvements in the manufacture of iron and steel, the 'Vulcanizing' of rubber by Goodyear, the invention of the misspelled mackintosh by MacIntosh, the invention of materials like linoleum and celluloid, the gramophone, telephone, and typewriter, improved lenses for eyeglasses, telescopes, and microscopes, improvements in printing and papermaking – each of these inventions or improvements altered – sometimes radically – some aspect of the material world of Victorian Britain. They make their way into literary form and content: as printing processes improved, for example, authors could correct their manuscripts far more extensively than earlier in the century when type had to 'stand' in chases, waiting for reprinting, and any changes were laborious and expensive.

What about the representation of labour? Asa Briggs points out that 'the title of Annie Carey's "Autobiography of a Lump of Coal" was more characteristic of the period than such a title as "The Autobiography of a Miner". The great 'distance between the literature of things and the literature of people' must be noted: people and the things they make are separated in representation as they are in the market.[21] And the literature of things is larger, although now much less read, than is the literature of the people who cultivated and mined and made them.

There are notable exceptions: Thomas Hood's 'The Song of the Shirt' tripled the circulation of the magazine *Punch* after it appeared in 1843. In it, Hood implores his readers to think about the suffering that the production of their clothing causes:

> Oh! men with sisters dear,
> Oh! men with mothers and wives,
> It is not linen you're wearing out,
> But human creatures' lives.[22]

Hood restores some of the social relations of production to the shirt in this very popular poem, which was 'dramatized, set to music, and even printed on handkerchiefs'.[23] The seamstress became an object of pity in Victorian art and literature; as Lynn Alexander has argued, she often 'stood'

---

21 Asa Briggs, *Victorian Things* (Bury St Edmunds: Folio Society, 1996), p. 272.

22 Thomas Hood, 'Song of the Shirt' (lines 24–7), in *Punch, or the London Charivari*, 16 December 1843.

23 Lynn M. Alexander, *Women, Work, and Representation: Needlewomen in Victorian Art and Literature* (Athens: Ohio State University Press, 2003), p. 52.

in, symbolically speaking, for other less attractive, less sympathetic members of the labouring class whose lives were also being 'worn out' in commodity production.[24]

What of things that are not commodities, or not always commodities? The heirloom, for example, is precisely the kind of thing that must be kept out of circulation – at least ideally. The eponymous Eustace diamonds motor the plot of Anthony Trollope's 1872 novel because it is not clear, given the ambiguities surrounding the laws on the subject of heirlooms, if Lizzie Greystock Eustace, the not particularly grieving widow of Florian Eustace, actually has a right to her dead husband's diamonds. Are they an heirloom, or a wife's paraphernalia, or marital property? Real property was the most significant form of wealth in nineteenth-century Britain and it was largely stabilized through the laws of primogeniture as an heirloom – as inalienable from the family line. Portable property, like diamonds, on the other hand, represented a much less stable category of objects: Lizzie literally carries these diamonds around with her and robberies of them, real and staged, finally obscure even their 'physical' place. Indeed, the issue of her right to the diamonds becomes a national debate, with Lizzieites and anti-Lizzieites lining up with learned opinions on the question of where the law stands. The instability of the meaning of these diamonds, and their legal status, suggests a greater instability in the Victorian object world: the identities and the values of things are always in flux, even things, like heirlooms, that seem beyond the fluctuations and depredations of the market – a force that could not seem to stay put in the public sphere.

In detective fiction, a genre invented in the Victorian period, the clue is usually an object that speaks volumes. Or it is the impress of an object on a subject. Sherlock Holmes tells Dr Watson that his 'first glance' is always at a woman's sleeve, which will tell of the use of typewriters and sewing machines. Dints in a nose bespeak a pince-nez; an inky thumb means that a letter has been written lately.[25] The material world incriminates the human world in detective fiction: meaning so much of which has become interior in Victorian fiction, remains insistently exterior in the matter of the clue. The reach of the British empire and newly accessible areas of 'free trade' made foreign goods available on an unprecedented scale in the Victorian period. Paradoxically, it is often just such imports that form the

24 Ibid., p. 1–94.
25 Arthur Conan Doyle, 'A Case of Identity', in The Adventures of Sherlock Holmes (Oxford University Press, 2008), pp. 30–48.

379

key accessories of the Victorian construction that has now become naturalized as 'home' – always both a place and an idea. In a household guide called *The Drawing Room* (1878), Lucy Orrinsmith recommends the following decorative objects to adorn a set of shelves in that room: Venetian bottles, old Delft vases, old Nankin cups, a Persian tile, an Algerian flower-pot, an old Flemish cup, an Icelandic spoon, a Japanese cabinet, and a Chinese fan.[26] The outside world is welcomed in, in very small doses, domesticated, tamed, and put into the service of Britain in the decorative schemes of middle-class women whose work it is to indemnify the safety and security – however symbolic – of this sphere. But these cabinets and cups, fans and spoons also change the space they inhabit and alter the culture they come to decorate and enrich: the colours and patterns of Persia and Venice and Algeria do not remain on tiles and bottles and flower-pots; they necessarily infect and inflect the designs and hues they find in British parlors.

The profusion of goods in the Victorian period also created – because of the preponderance of the machine-made object – a longing for the 'hand-made' object. Middle-class women made crafts of myriad kinds, filling their parlours with embroidered footstools and fire screens, Berlin wool-work rugs, crocheted doilies, paper fans and wax flowers, shell sculptures, and cucumber seed collages.[27] These objects were part of the cosiness that families like the Bartons may have tried to emulate (or that their creator, Elizabeth Gaskell, may have wished them to wish to emulate). The domestic sphere as such was a relatively new construction in the mid nineteenth century: it was made necessary by the separation of home and work the factory system necessitated. The rise of the suburb, for example, created the idea, realized with marvelous literalism by Wemmick in *Great Expectations*, that any man's home should be his castle. Accordingly, Wemmick outfits his tiny villa in the seedy suburb of Walworth with a small moat and a drawbridge.[28]

With or without the help of household management guides, furniture moves around quite a bit in the Victorian novel: it is often being moved in or out, or rearranged, with significant economic and/or psychological meaning.[29] In *Middlemarch*, Lydgate's furniture is traumatically and

---

26 Lucy Orrinsmith, *The Drawing Room: Its Decoration and Furnishing* (London: MacMillan and Co., 1878), p. 133.
27 See Talia Schaffer, 'Craft, Authorial Anxiety, and *Cranford*', *Victorian Periodical Review* 38:2 (2005), pp. 222–39.
28 Charles Dickens, *Great Expectations* (Oxford University Press, 2008), Chapter 37, pp. 267–8.
29 Thad Logan, *The Victorian Parlour* (Cambridge University Press, 2001), pp. 202–31.

dramatically removed when he fails to pay his debts. Jane Eyre buys mahogany furniture with crimson upholstery for her cousins when she inherits her uncle's fortune. The eponymous Miss Marjoribanks fulfills what her creator Margaret Oliphant describes as a 'fundamental duty of women': she 'harmonizes' the drawing-room of her father's house when she moves into it, 'by the simple method of rearranging half the chairs and covering the tables with trifles of her own'.[30] Lydgate loses his home, and nearly loses his disheartened wife along with it; Jane Eyre becomes an heiress and can repay the generosity of cousins with some tasteful new furniture; Lucilla Marjoribanks is beginning to assume her authority as the woman in charge of her father's house: control or loss of control of furniture signifies mightily in the Victorian novel.

The Arts and Crafts Movement, founded by William Morris, had as one of its goals the reformation of the 'bad' taste of the nineteenth century, the kind of taste that Tertius Lydgate, Jane Eyre, and Lucilla Marjoribanks might all have been accused by him of having (although there is much about certain William Morris wallpaper, for example, given its propensity for birds and flowers in what we may now experience as a riotous profusion, that seems as hyper-ornamental now as the busiest Victorian middle-class parlour may have once seemed to him). Nonetheless, Morris led a group of artisans who wished to save Britain from the ugliness of the industrially made thing, and from the alienation of the industrial toil required to produce it. From John Ruskin, Morris developed his devotion to the artistic, thoughtful labour that goes into handwork. From Marx, Morris developed a hope for a society based on economic equality, in which labour would be unalienated, and difficult and unpleasant labour would be kept to a minimum and divided fairly. In his 'Utopian Romance', *News from Nowhere* (1890), Morris describes an ideal society in which all

> work which would be irksome to do by hand is done by immensely improved machinery; and in all work which it is a pleasure to do by hand machinery is done without. There is no difficulty in finding work which suits the special turn of mind of everybody; so that no man is sacrificed to the wants of another.[31]

A poet and novelist as well as a maker of furniture and wallpaper, Morris is emblematic of the combined strains of the critique of industrialization in late

---

30 Margaret Oliphant, *Miss Marjoribanks* (Oxford University Press, 1998), p. 62.
31 William Morris, *News from Nowhere and Other Writings* (Oxford University Press, 2009), p. 84.

nineteenth-century British socialism: a wish for a certain quality of life and an imagined quality of goods that would necessarily accompany that life.

Although the commodity fetish as such is not discussed in Britain until the very end of the Victorian period (Marx is not translated into English until 1886), the idea is often invoked in twentieth- and twenty-first-century analyses of Victorian culture. For Marx, in a system of alienated and abstracted exchange we lose sight of 'the social relations of production'. We think only of money value at the moment of exchange, but 'later on' we wonder about the mystery of that value. Where does it come from? How does an object acquire its money value? Our objects become 'social hieroglyphics', Marx claims: we want to read or translate them; we understand they have meanings we do not comprehend, but we cannot properly fathom their value.[32] Marx's assignment of the term 'fetish' to the commodity suggests derision given the lowly rank of animistic cultures in the mid nineteenth century: he is critiquing that which is 'irrational' in capitalist economics – exchange value – and suggesting the ways in which it haunts those of us who must participate in it.

The idea of fetishism derives from the reports of early travellers to Africa and then from anthropology, a body of knowledge and then a university discipline that begins to become organized as such in the Victorian period. In *Primitive Culture* (1871), E. B. Tylor defines fetishism as the 'doctrine of spirits embodied in, or attaching to, or conveying influence through, certain material objects'.[33] Tylor, the first Briton to accord 'primitive' peoples the possibility of 'culture', concludes his discussion of fetishism among the 'lower races' with the following observation: 'I will venture to assert that the scientific conceptions current in my own schoolboy days, of heat and electricity as invisible fluids passing in and out of solid bodies, are ideas which reproduce with extreme closeness the special doctrine of Fetishism.'[34] Thus fetishism, although attributed by Tylor and other early anthropologists to Africans and indigenous peoples of the Americas who believed in the spiritual inhabitation of inanimate objects, is also put into close analogy with the scientific thought of Britain extant in Tylor's own lifetime.

Fetishism – investing objects with an energy, spirit, or power by people at one moment or place that these same objects are not thought to possess by

---

32 Karl Marx and Friedrich Engels, *Capital: A Critique of Political Economy*, vol. 1 (New York: International Publishers, 1967), p. 74.
33 E. B. Tylor, *Primitive Culture*, 2 vols., (London: John Murray, 1871), vol. II, p. 144.
34 *Ibid.*, p. 160.

other people at another time or place – becomes a powerful concept in the late nineteenth century and remains so in the twentieth and early twenty-first. Marx uses it to describe our relationship to commodities when we accept their exchange value as natural; Freud uses it to describe our relationship to objects that become sexually charged that are not actually genital. Object relations that are deviant in some way acquire this label, yet early on Tylor admits the prevalence of fetishism, or something very like it, as a common mode of human understanding and explanation of the mysteries of the object world. The explorer and proto-ethnographer Mary Kingsley proclaimed herself an animist and declared that 'there must be a common-sense element in fetish customs that enables them to survive in the strange way they do'.[35] Fetishism was not especially strange to Tylor or Kingsley; they also were two major participants in one of the disciplines – anthropology – that arrives in the nineteenth century to decode it. This discipline also gives us the category of material culture as an area of study: perhaps a close relative of fetishism itself. The concept of the fetish, in all of its utility and conceptual fecundity, is essentially a spoil of empire: one of the many cultural riches some raw material of which was perhaps extracted from Africa and then enduring attributed to certain African cultures by Europe.

Literature was itself an important commodity in the Victorian period. Writers were typically making a living from their writing, and they kept an eye on sales, actively participating in the design and marketing of their texts. George Eliot, for example, specifically wanted the individual 'numbers' of *Middlemarch*, which came out in serialized form over eighteen months in 1871–2, to be produced such that each one looked like a complete novel in and of itself. As a result, *Middlemarch*, unlike many monthly serials of the same period, is the size of the mass market paperback novel of today and did not appear in the large, magazine-like format of other novels serialized in the same period. This 'look' would increase sales, Eliot thought, because readers would not have to worry about missing an instalment: they would feel that any particular volume was complete in itself.

With the advent of the collecting of modern first editions and special or limited editions in the 1880s, the book becomes a kind of hyper-commodity in that it remains a commodity after purchase: collectors begin to buy books with the idea of reselling them; a volatile book market, based on rarity and singularity, is born. '[A] distinct trade has sprung up', writes J. H. Slater in

35 Mary Kingsley, *Travels in West Africa* (London: MacMillan and Co, 1897), p. 490.

1894, 'not only for the purposes of ministering to the exigencies of the demand, but also to extend its scope.'[36] New kinds of 'value' are invented and attached to books in the late nineteenth century 'to extend [the] scope' of the book trade, as Slater frankly admits here: collectors of books, like those of stamps and coins, peruse catalogues and look for certain 'points' – bindings, end papers, and so on – often invented as significant points of value by the authors of the catalogues themselves.[37]

The materiality of the document within Victorian literature also bears remarking upon. J. Hillis Miller famously called *Bleak House* 'a document about the interpretation of documents'.[38] Daniel Hack has, more recently, described it as a 'document about the materiality of documents and the interpretation of that materiality'.[39] And materiality yields information in the novel: handwriting has much to say about its authors in the novel, revealing their identities at crucial moments. In a reversal of Pip's situation in *Great Expectations*, in which he tries to get an idea of what his parents looked like from the style of the writing on their gravestones, the 'matter' of the text speaks volumes in *Bleak House*: 'the meaningful materiality of documents'[40] suggests that novels and novelists do more than symbolic work in the world. Their texts are physical items with physical properties and effects.

Is the labour of the writer restored to the product of his labour with this insistence on the materiality of the letters of his text? In a postscript to *Our Mutual Friend*, Dickens refers to his rescue of the manuscript of that novel after a train accident in another instance of bringing the material of the text to our attention:

> On Friday the Ninth of June in the present year, Mr and Mrs Boffin (in their manuscript dress of receiving Mr and Mrs Lammle at breakfast) were on the South Eastern Railway with me, in a terribly destructive accident. When I had done what I could to help others, I climbed back into my carriage – nearly turned over a viaduct, and caught aslant upon the turn – to extricate the worthy couple. They were much soiled, but otherwise unhurt.[41]

36 J. H. Slater, *Early Editions* (London: K. Paul, Trank, Treubner, 1894), p. 2.
37 See N. N. Feltes, *Literary Capital and the Late Victorian Novel* (Madison: University of Wisconsin Press, 1993), pp. 35–64.
38 J. Hillis Miller, Introduction, Charles Dickens, *Bleak House* (Harmondsworth: Penguin, 1971), p. 11.
39 Daniel Hack, *The Material Interests of the Victorian Novel* (Charlottesville: University of Virginia Press, 2005), p. 38.
40 *Ibid.*, p. 61.
41 Charles Dickens, *Our Mutual Friend* (Oxford University Press, 2009), p. 822.

Before mechanical reproduction, there is one writer and one text: both can and could be lost to us. Yet looked at another way, in materializing text and author, this account of the train accident de-materializes character: they 'live' only on paper, we are harshly reminded.

And this reminder comes as a shock at the end of a novel in which the materiality of the body, and all that it uses, discards, and excretes, is dramatized with a vengeance. The most famous substance of this novel is waste. A fortune has been made from 'dust' heaps: garbage is turned to gold in a dream that was enacted quite literally, if unsuccessfully, in many Victorian experiments in sewage farming. Dead bodies are also sources of profit: they are pulled out of the Thames and stripped of any money and valuables still in their pockets. There is a debate in the novel about whether or not these bodies can own anything given that they are dead and therefore not capable of the kind of self-possession expected of the nineteenth-century individual, let alone the possession of other kinds of property. But in a twisted reversal of this problem, certifiably alive individuals have difficulty hanging on to their body parts: a character called Silas Wegg tries to buy back his amputated leg from Mr Venus, a taxidermist who has bought it (illegally) from a hospital. Silas Wegg wishes 'to collect himself'.[42] The body is a material object, or a set of articulated parts, that is not necessarily entirely possessed by the person to whom it belongs.[43]

The land and landscape are also crucial materials of Victorian literature. So real are the landscapes of the Brontës' Yorkshire and Hardy's 'Wessex' that whole tourist industries have sprung up to accommodate devoted readers who wish to tread the earth that seem so truly to have 'felt' the feet of Jane and Heathcliff and Jude. This strange geographical literalism means that the landscape of these two parts of Britain is seen 'through' the novels that made them desirable as vacation spots. Similarly, there is a London that belongs to Dickens: walks and tours visit the streets and markets and courts that we have 'visited' in his novels: reality follows fiction in these cases; the material world of the novel is powerful enough to make the material world outside it attractive and compelling in new ways.

The land, the very earth became better known in the Victorian period, and not always with happy results. In his *Principles of Geology* (1833), Charles

---

42 *Ibid.*, p. 82.
43 For an important reading of this novel and its 'bioeconomics', see Catherine Gallagher, *The Body Economic: Life, Death, and Sensation in Political Economy and the Victorian Novel* (Princeton University Press, 2006), chapter 4.

Lyell makes clear one of the more shocking findings of nineteenth-century science: the extinction of species. Alfred, Lord Tennyson 'translates' this devastating information into some harsh questions for nature in *In Memoriam*: 'From scarped cliff and quarried stone / She cries, "A thousand types are gone; I care for nothing all shall go." '[44] The poet asks if humanity will eventually be 'blown about the desert dust, / Or seal'd within the iron hills?'[45] In addition to mourning his intimate friend Arthur Hallam, Tennyson mourns a very particular Victorian fall into a difficult knowledge of nature, a nature seemingly at odds with the varieties of Christianity that most Victorians practised.

The Origin of Species of course confirms this finding a generation later, but Darwin offers consolation in the beauty of natural selection, which he 'proves' from massively detailed, often beautifully written observations of the natural world:

> It is interesting to contemplate an entangled bank, clothed with many plants of many kinds, with birds singing on the bushes, with various insects flitting about, and with worms crawling through the damp earth, and to reflect that these elaborately constructed forms, so different from each other, and dependent on each other in so complex a manner, have all been produced by laws acting around us.[46]

Darwin's love of nature was shared by many Victorian collectors of all kinds of flora and fauna: people who watched birds, collected sedges, and caught bugs to pin them down in endless display cases like those of the lovelorn Reverend Farebrother in *Middlemarch*. Such collecting is often posited in Victorian novels as a benign if slightly daffy hobby: one that is clearly preferable to Chartism or gambling or other dangerous behaviours that it may be replacing.

The inevitably humic materiality of the human body is evoked powerfully in the opening lines of Amy Levy's 'Epitaph (On a Commonplace Person who Died in Bed)':

> This is the end of him, here he lies:
> The dust in his throat, the worm in his eyes,
> The mould in his mouth, the turf on his breast;
> This is the end of him, this is best.[47]

---

44 Alfred Lord Tennyson, *Poems*, ed. Christopher Ricks, 3 vols. (Harlow: Longman, 1987), vol. II, p. 129, section 56, lines 2–4.
45 *Ibid.*, p. 129, section 56, lines 19, 20.
46 Charles Darwin, *The Origin of Species*, ed. Jim Endersby (Cambridge University Press, 2009), p. 376.
47 Amy Levy, *A Minor Poet and Other Verse* (London: T. Fisher and Unwin, 1884), p. 88.

The corpse is put before our eyes – 'here he lies': the language and the broken-up, end-stopped lines insist on the finality of death and the break-down of the body. The dust, worms, mould, and turf already enter, mingle with and cover this dead body with the substance with which it will soon become one. 'This is the end of him' the poem insists: accept these physical facts; picture him this way, here, before you, this is how dust goes back to dust – with the help of worms, and mould, and a covering of turf. 'Commonplace people who die in bed' must suffer this indignity, but they also present for us, or allow the poet to represent for us, the truth of our fragile material condition. This condition was much better known to the Victorians than it is to us: people died at home, and were often mourned at home, frequently with the coffin lying on the dining-room table.

The elaborate Victorian culture of death produced a wealth of material objects: mourning clothes, which were prescribed for women and men in various amounts and combinations and for various periods of time depending on their relationship to the deceased. If you pick up one of the serial instal-ments of *Dombey and Son* or *Can You Forgive Her?*, the advertising pages that enclose the text at its beginning and end are crowded with notices from retail warehouses of mourning clothes, often promising twenty-four hour service. Mourning jewelry was made out of the braided hair of the dead; a locket with a photograph of the dead might be set into a bracelet of such material, thus the hair and photograph – the presence and the representation of the dead – could be kept together and worn by the bereaved survivor as a kind of simultaneous acknowledgment and refusal of loss.[48] The power of such a small example of the 'material' in Victorian culture suggests that the object relations of that period were substantially different from those of our own: the ideas that could be invested in things were perhaps not only more powerful; things themselves were perhaps able to bear more meaning. It is possible that there was a 'thing culture' that has yet to be explored in the Victorian period, a material culture that held meanings that we, given the state of our own object relations, will have to struggle to imagine. Fortunately we have the help of the extensive archive of Victorian thing culture, texts that help us listen to the emissaries and to what they can tell us about the culture they inhabited, and about the one we inhabit now.

---

48 Geoffrey Batchen, *Forget Me Not: Photography and Remembrance* (New York: Princeton Architectural Press, 2004), pp. 70–1.

Economics and finance

MARY POOVEY

The years of Queen Victoria's reign witnessed rapid and dramatic changes in Britain's financial infrastructure, its own economic well-being and its place in the global economy, and the way that economic developments were conceptualized, by experts and ordinary Britons alike. Various kinds of writing – from economic treatises to financial journalism to imaginative literature – contributed to these changes in several ways, not least in making 'the economy' imaginable as one of the invisible, but inescapable, forces influencing nearly every aspect of nineteenth-century life.

By the time Victoria assumed the throne in 1837, London had become the financial capital of the world, having surpassed Paris and Amsterdam, which occupied this position at the end of the eighteenth century. Almost all foreign and domestic bills of exchange flowed through the London bill broking houses centred around Lombard Street; the great merchant bankers who routed English capital overseas had their offices in the narrow streets near Caple Court; and the principal institutions of British finance – the Bank of England, the London Stock Exchange, and the Royal Exchange (which burned in 1838 and was rebuilt in the 1840s) – clustered in the district known as the City, near the Bank's home on Threadneedle Street. In addition to facilitating overseas investment, these institutions also formed the hub of what was just beginning to be a trunk-and-branch system of English banking. In this system, which was modelled on its much more extensive counterpart in Scotland, the Bank of England stood at the centre of a network that extended credit, through the bill broking houses, London agency banks, and affiliated private and joint-stock banks, to farmers, industrialists, and country gentlemen far from London. By means of this credit system, which was progressively refined and regulated during the century, the surplus capital generated each year in the agricultural districts was funnelled to other parts of the country, where money was needed to finance industry and business; and the interest paid for the use of this money flowed back to the farmlands in time for the new year's planting. Because of this elaborate financial system, English men and women were able to purchase the spoils of empire that regularly arrived on the ships that English investors also financed, and whose transit was eased by the end of hostilities with France. The prosperity of the 1850s and 1860s, and the rise of a global commercial society that accompanied it, rested upon this infrastructure of banks, bill broking houses, and investment facilities, the most visible signs of which were the varieties of paper credit by which the alchemy of writing and temporal deferral amplified the power of England's scant gold reserve.

By 1837, however, it had also become clear that Britain's aggressive role in the global economy did not simply or inevitably increase national and individual wealth. The year that Victoria took the throne also marked the beginning of an economic downturn whose seeds had been laid the previous year, in a rash of speculative investments in American cotton and finance houses. Exacerbated by poor harvests at home and abroad, the economic depression sparked by the 1837 panic dragged on into the next decade. Even before the Hungry Forties, the events of 1836–7 caused alarm because the speculation and panic of these years repeated a similar sequence that had occurred a decade before, when unbridled speculation and the panic that followed caused so many banks to fail that England was brought to the verge of barter. The repetition of these events raised the ominous possibility that such seizures, far from being anomalies, were regular features of Britain's economy. When these episodes continued to occur, as they did with startling regularity – in 1846–7, 1856–7, 1866, 1878, and 1890 – contemporaries tried desperately to explain them and to neutralize the threat they seemed to pose. Some financial journalists, like Walter Bagehot, argued that crises were simply regrettable phases of economic expansion, while at least one economic theorist, W. Stanley Jevons, tried to naturalize them by correlating panics to eruptions of sun spots.

The repeated financial crises, along with Britain's increasingly elaborate financial infrastructure, signalled the beginning of the financialization of British culture. By this I mean two things: the increased impact of money being used *as money* (to generate interest) in Britain's overall economic growth; and the proliferation of representations of speculation – along with attempts to distinguish between investment and speculation – in the writing of the period. I call this development the financialization of *culture* because the imaginative fallout of the riches and greed contemporaries associated with speculation, as well as the losses and fear that panics invariably caused, began to inform the period's cultural products, just as the movement of capital was beginning to supplement labour as a source of the nation's wealth. This began in earnest after the collapse of the 1846 railway mania, when the parliamentary commissions convened to investigate the industry began to expose the intricate schemes criminals had devised to swindle investors. Even though financialization did not dominate the British economy or its culture until the late twentieth century, in the wake of the railway mania, writers began to find financial topics nearly irresistible, and much of the writing that seems most characteristically Victorian grappled with the way that the invisible movement of capital was already beginning to transform the distribution of political and economic power, both within Great Britain and across the globe, by challenging the way value was conceptualized and circulated.

The gradual financialization of Victorian culture needs to be understood in relation to another distinctively nineteenth-century development: the establishment and codification of differences among kinds of writing. By the end of the century, distinct kinds of writing were generally associated with specific academic disciplines or professions, but, for most of the century, before disciplines and professions assumed their modern forms, writers struggled to identify what was unique about the genres they produced. Because financialization was beginning to affect British culture in general, and because so many writers tried to help readers negotiate the resulting transformation of value, identifying what was distinctive about the various genres that dealt with this subject was particularly challenging. With the benefit of hindsight, we can identify three kinds of writing that dealt with economics and finance in this period, but it is important to recognize that the generic distinctions I use here were still being negotiated in the Victorian period. At the end of this chapter I discuss how the campaign to distinguish among kinds of writing was played out in relation to literary writing in particular, but first I want briefly to describe the three genres that now seem so distinct. The first is political economy theory, which was extremely influential – if not exactly popular – during the entire nineteenth century; in the 1890s, political economy was subsumed into the academic discipline of economics. The second genre, financial journalism, took many forms in this period and overlapped, in significant ways, with literary writing. Unlike literary writers, however, financial journalists generally sought to explain economic and financial events so that readers would be able to understand the increasingly complex transactions occurring in the City; financial journalism thus belongs to the large category of informational writing that, by the end of the century, was associated with many of the modern disciplines. The third genre, novelistic, dramatic, and poetic engagements with economic and financial subjects, contains a wide variety of works, but two of their most characteristic features are the tendency to translate these topics into ethical terms and a preference for the connotative, as opposed to referential, capacity of language. As we will see, these features helped imaginative writers identify what was distinctive about literary writing – especially prose fiction, which, in both form and content, so closely resembled other engagements with economic and financial matters and which never attained a secure place in any discipline or profession.

Political economic theory

Victorian political economic theory can be grouped into four general categories. The first, classical political economy, carried over both Adam Smith's concern with the social factors that underwrote economic forces and his argument that the combination of unregulated trade (laissez-faire) and increased specialization (the division of labour) would gradually distribute the world's riches to its neediest inhabitants. In the early nineteenth century, an optimistic version of Smith's doctrine was most forcefully articulated by David Ricardo, while a more cautious, even pessimistic, version was promulgated by Thomas Robert Malthus, whose work on population led him to worry that need would always outstrip supply unless the poor exercised sexual restraint. In the first decades of the Victorian period, the Smithian version of classical political economy was promulgated by J. R. McCulloch, who tirelessly promoted laissez-faire, and John Stuart Mill, one of the century's most respected followers of Smith. In 1832–3, Harriet Martineau cast these theories into the more accessible form of stories, which, as *Illustrations of Political Economy*, enjoyed a degree of popularity the theorists never attained. In the first decades of the century, a second variant of political economy appeared, this one a version of Malthusian economics that emphasized the spiritual dimension of economic behaviour. Often called Evangelical political economy, the doctrines advanced by the Scotsman Rev. Thomas Chalmers and Richard Whatley insisted that the market could produce spiritual benefits by chastening ambition and rewarding self-restraint. Evangelical political economy enjoyed considerable influence until Parliament began to pass limited liability legislation in the 1850s, for in making corporations, not individual investors, legally responsible for companies' actions, these laws diminished the role that individual moral rectitude could play in ensuring that businesses pursued spiritual ends.

A third, more radical strain of political economic theory was less influential than either classical or Evangelical political economy, but some version of this theory was almost always present in the Victorian period. Some radicals, like William Cobbett and John Wade, tried to challenge the basic assumptions of classical political economy by insisting that labour was the only basis of value and that vested interests had to be overthrown in favour of a more equitable distribution of wealth. Others, like John Bray, the radical printer from Leeds, and John Ruskin, the respected art critic, sought to extend the tenets of classical political economy to their logical conclusions in order to reveal the injustices of an unregulated system of competition. Other important economic radicals included Samuel Bailey, Robert Owen, and the late-century socialist H. M. Hyndman. The major work of the century's greatest radical political economist, Karl Marx's *Das Capital*, was composed in London in the 1850s and translated into English in 1887.

The fourth variant of economic theory marked an important shift within mainstream writing on this subject. Often called marginalist economics, this variant is associated in England with W. Stanley Jevons, whose *Theory of Political Economy* appeared in 1871. Jevons replaced Smith's labour theory of value with an account of economic behaviour that emphasized prices and the subjective determinants that dictated demand. In a period of economic abundance, Jevons argued, a nation's economy is driven not by problems of production and distribution or by an invisible hand that mysteriously adjusts the overall system, but by individual consumers' rational assessments of what they are willing to pay for what they actually want. Jevons's theoretical insights were elaborated late in the century by Alfred Marshall, who, from his position as Professor of Political Economy at Cambridge, helped transform political economy into the modern discipline of economics.

Financial journalism

British newspapers had long carried information about shipping, trade, and international rates of exchange, but it was only in 1826 that the London *Times* inaugurated a regular 'City column' containing stock prices and City news. In the 1840s, partly in response to the railway mania, sufficient numbers of periodicals began to publish articles about finance for us to identify a distinctive genre of financial journalism. The essays that belong to this genre range from the relatively technical discussions of political economic principles that appeared in the pages of the *Edinburgh Review* to the humorous, anecdotal accounts of 'Change Alley supplied to *Blackwood's* and *All the Year Round* by writers like David Morier Evans and Malcolm Ronald Meason. Walter Bagehot, editor of the influential *Economist*, was the period's most prominent financial journalist, but W. H. Mills, Dickens's sub-editor for *Household Words*, Thomas Massa Alsanger, City reporter for the *Times*, and the travel writer Laurence Oliphant can also be included in this category. Financial journalists often drew upon the theories developed by political economists, but, by and large, most financial journalists sought to present portraits of the City that would make its idiosyncratic culture entertaining. As they did so, and even when they cautioned readers about the dangers of speculation or fraudulent companies, financial journalists provided information about financialization and helped neutralize the anxieties it produced by naturalizing the institutions that enabled financial opportunities to multiply.

Economics and finance in literature

We can find economic themes and representations of finance in every literary form published in the Victorian period. Theatrical performances of Charles Reade's *Gold* ran in London in 1853, for example, and poems like Tennyson's *Maud* traced the impact of a father's suicide, caused by a failed speculation, on its deranged narrator. Of all the period's literary forms, however, it was the novel that most fully engaged economics and finance as explicit themes, as sources for characters and plots, and in their language, style, and form. There are several ways to explain the link between Victorian novels and finance. First, despite the continued prestige of poetry, after the 1820s novels were potentially the most profitable form of literary production, and, if the reactions of Dickens, Trollope, and Margaret Oliphant are representative, this fostered in novelists an avid interest in taking full advantage of the market for prose fiction. Second, even though novel-writing was not a speculative venture for most writers – because publishers typically purchased copyrights outright instead of asking the novelist to share costs, risks, and potential profits – a Victorian reader's engagement with a novel did require the habits of mind intrinsic to financial investing. Victorian novels published before the 1890s tended to be very long – either because circulating libraries like Mudie's encouraged triple-decker novels or because the format with which some novelists tried to sidestep the libraries' influence, serialization, also dictated complex plots and numerous characters. In order to enjoy such lengthy works, a Victorian reader had to invest emotion in the characters, attention to the distended plots, and time in the act of reading; she had to take risks and be willing to defer gratification; and she could assume that such risks would yield abundant returns – in the friendships cultivated with fictional characters, the gratification supplied by a happy ending, or the simple satisfaction of having completed a novel of such length. Arguably, such reading habits helped make the mental attitudes crucial to investing seem as natural to nineteenth-century Britons as memorization, the mental counterpart to hoarding, had seemed to their ancestors.

Even if we limit our survey to Victorian novels, there are still many ways to understand the relationship between these texts and economic and financial issues. Some critics have described structural homologies between an aspect of the economic domain and the features of Victorian novels. Scholars like Claudia Klaver and Christina Crosby, for example, have identified a logic of capitalism or of the money form of value in the plots of Victorian novels; and others, like Marc Shell, have drawn a metaphorical equation between money and language itself. Others, like Catherine Gallagher and Regenia Gagnier, have identified thematic or structural counterparts to political economists' ideas in aesthetic theory or individual novels. Gagnier highlights the formalism implicit in both late nineteenth-century aesthetic theory and marginalist economics, for example; and Gallagher stresses the difference between Dickens's adoption of the classical labour theory of value in *Hard Times* and George Eliot's thematic adoption of the marginalists' focus on the 'final increment' in *Daniel Deronda*.[1] In addition to identifying such structural and thematic homologies, literary critics like Patrick Brantlinger have emphasized the prominence that representations of financial and economic themes play in the period's fiction; and scholars like John Sutherland and David Finkelstein have helped recover the economics of Victorian publishing itself, as one of the conditions that made all literary production possible.

By placing Victorian novels alongside the other two genres I have discussed, we can also see that, precisely because of their structural similarities and shared social function, nineteenth-century novelists also wanted to distinguish between the writing they produced and that of economic theorists and journalists. In retrospect, the difference between literary writing and other genres seems obvious: literary works did not primarily explain or justify economic and financial developments, as political economic theory and financial journalism aspired to do. Instead, despite the avid interest they

---

1 Catherine Gallagher, *The Body Economic: Life, Death, and Sensation in Political Economy and the Victorian Novel* (Princeton University Press, 2006), p. 138.

privately expressed towards their own earnings, most Victorian novelists assumed a critical stance toward Britain's credit economy. At the time, however, the distinction between imaginative and informational writing seemed difficult to define, and we can see that some of the aesthetic choices novelists made were dictated by a desire to stabilize this distinction. To understand this, it is helpful to trace the way a few representative novelists treated financial topics.

The three novels I consider represent a spectrum of Victorian engagements with finance. The first, Dickens's *Little Dorrit* (1855–7), deploys what I take to be the Victorian novel's most common device for invoking and managing economic and financial themes, a gestural aesthetic that alludes to specific events or historical figures but then marginalizes these references in winding up the novel. The second, George Eliot's *Silas Marner* (1861), is unusual in the degree to which it depends not upon an allusive aesthetic but on symbolism and metaphor. In using a character's attitude towards money as an index to moral worth, however, *Silas Marner* is completely representative, and, as we will see, the elaboration of tropes is one device by which writers like Dickens marginalized what look like literal references to financial events. My third example, Anthony Trollope's *Can You Forgive Her?* (1864–5), is also unusual in one sense: to a degree rare among Victorian novels, the first work in the Palliser series provides explicit information about how particular financial instruments worked. As in the majority of nineteenth-century novels, however, this informational agenda is consistently subordinated to the ethical project that governs the novel as a whole, for Trollope repeatedly presents money as the means by which one character can 'save' another from potentially ruinous weaknesses.

It would have been easy for Dickens's contemporaries to identify the real-life referents of Mr Merdle, the fictional financier whose activities ensnare so many of the characters in *Little Dorrit*, for contemporary newspapers were filled with accounts of the two crimes that inspired this character. The first was exposed in June 1855, as Dickens was writing the first chapters of *Little Dorrit*, when the directors of the Strahan, Paul, and Bates Bank absconded with their investors' money. Meanwhile, in Ireland, another bank was being plundered from within, this time by the MP John Sadlier, who managed to forge £150,000 worth of shares before the Tipperary Bank collapsed. When the magnitude of his crimes was disclosed, in February 1856, Sadlier committed suicide. Two days later, Dickens began the sixth number of *Little Dorrit*, in which he introduced Mr Merdle.

While Dickens clearly wanted to capitalize on readers' interest in these figures, he does not seem to have been particularly interested in exploring the details of their crimes or motives. In the novel itself, the Merdle plot figures only briefly, the details of Merdle's activities remain vague, and the effects of the speculation he inspires are registered in a moral vocabulary that obscures his actual crimes. Even though Merdle's criminal activities lead to the collapse of the partnership formed by Clennam and Doyce, moreover, it is Arthur Clennam's insistence that he publicly take responsibility for the firm's debts that makes his creditors act; this, in turn, leads to Clennam's incarceration in debtors' prison; and it is this imprisonment that paves the way for his reunion with Amy Dorrit. This reunion culminates in marriage, of course, but it also enables Clennam to be spiritually reborn; and when Doyce returns from the continent, pays Clennam's debts, and frees him from the Marshalsea, the novel dispenses with the entire subject of financial speculation. Merdle's transgression thus functions primarily as a blocking agent in the romance plot that centres on Clennam and Amy Dorrit and in the *bildung* chronicle of Clennam's reform. Because Clennam never blames Merdle for the failure of the firm and because Dickens only presents Merdle's crimes as abstractions ('Forgery and Robbery'), the narrative forgoes a sustained exploration of the intricacies of the financial crimes with which contemporary news accounts were filled.

Dickens does use the speculative mania Merdle's activities spawn to link two plots that otherwise barely overlap: his highly mannered treatment of high society, which is populated by stereotypical characters like the Barnacles, and the more detailed Bleeding Heart Yard plot, where individuated characters like Mrs Plornish and her father appear. Rumours of riches to be made from investing in Merdle's ventures flow from the first plot, where the Barnacles could afford to – but do not explicitly – speculate, to the second, where the rent-agent Pancks spreads the 'contagion' to Clennam, even though both must borrow to invest. In Dickens's characterization of Clennam, the desire to speculate becomes a psychological disorder, a monomania that must be cured before Clennam can merit Little Dorrit. While the character's ethical reform is crucial to the resolution of the novel, the precise nature of Clennam's moral affliction is less important than that it be amenable to cure – not by an explanation that might enable readers to discriminate between a sound investment and irrational speculation, but simply through the moral transformation that Amy inspires.

As the narrative focus is increasingly trained on Clennam, Merdle is relegated to ever-more marginal positions. He is briefly addressed in an elaborate apostrophe that satirically elevates him to astral heights ('Merdle! O ye suns, moon, and stars, the great man!');[2] then he rapidly descends, reappearing only as a shadowy presence in his stepson's apartment, then as an unidentified body, then as a series of words, which dwindle into an adjective already demoted to a cliché ('the Merdle lot').[3] Once Merdle disappears, Clennam takes responsibility for his company's debts, in a substitution that suggests that being in debt is equivalent to Merdle's forgeries and theft – even though the former, unlike the latter, can be redeemed by the rehabilitation Clennam has already begun to undergo.

Dickens's vague gestures towards actual financial crimes typify the way that many mid-century novelists capitalized on the financial transgressions that financial journalists and Parliamentary commissions exposed. *Hard Times* also invokes a bank crime (embezzlement) to test a character's moral worth; Margaret Oliphant's *Hester* uses securities fraud to reveal the fatal flaw in Edward Vernon's character; in George Eliot's *Middlemarch*, the banker Bulstrode falls both because he lied about the legacy his first wife left her daughter and because he has secretly invested in a manufacturer of toxic dye; and in *The Way We Live Now*, Trollope gestures towards another shadowy financier, who draws young men too foolish for their own good into a speculative web as ruinous – and almost as imprecisely detailed – as Merdle's speculative ventures. While these thematic appropriations reveal how rich the vein of finance was for novelists looking to entertain readers, they also show how little interest most Victorian novelists had in helping readers understand why financial crime was so common in the period or in exploring the details of the crimes themselves. Eager to borrow from financial journalists, most Victorian novelists were also content to limit their criticism of financial crimes to individuals, in relation to whom such transgressions could be psychologized, moralized, and subordinated to the ethical issues with which novelists were primarily concerned.

George Eliot's *Silas Marner* chronicles the life of an early nineteenth-century linen-weaver, whose excommunication from a narrow religious community has driven him to the outskirts of Raveloe, a small village as obscure as the weaver himself. Cut off from his previous community, unwilling to think about his past or future, Marner gradually 'reduce[s] his

---

2 Charles Dickens, *Little Dorrit* (Oxford University Press, 2008), Book II, chapter 16, p. 514.
3 *Ibid.*, Book II, chapter 32, p. 667.

life to the unquestioning activity of a spinning insect',[4] until one day a neighbour pays the weaver in gold. His first 'five bright guineas' soon grow into a hoard, and Silas comes to love the 'bright faces' of the coins,[5] to imagine that they are 'conscious of him', and to consider them 'his familiars'.[6] The narrative depicts the weaver's obsession with the gold as a parody of a human relationship, in which an arid simulacrum of love barely sustains, but emphatically is not, the genuine article:

> His life had reduced itself to the functions of weaving and hoarding, without any contemplation of an ends towards which the functions tended ... He loved the guineas best ... He spread them out in heaps and bathed his hands in them; then he counted them and set them up in regular piles, and felt their rounded outline between his thumb and fingers, and thought fondly of the guineas that were only half earned by the work in his loom, as if they had been unborn children.[7]

Marner's golden reverie is soon exploded by a thief, who makes off with the weaver's hoard, leaving Marner devastated. But Eliot uses the loss of the beloved gold to make space for another 'treasure' that can truly fill the 'casket' of Marner's heart.[8] Her mother having frozen in the snow, a little blonde child makes her way to Marner's door, and the old weaver, momentarily mistaking her for the gold he has lost, gradually opens to the love she offers, gives her a name, and adopts her as his own. As love for Eppie replaces the love he had once lavished on the gold, Marner ceases to miss his money, ceases to care about the wages he now earns, and begins to manifest the human sympathies the gold had barely kept alive.

> The disposition to hoard had been utterly crushed at the very first by the loss of his long-stored gold: the coins he earned afterwards seemed as irrelevant as stones brought to complete a house suddenly buried by an earthquake ... And now something had come to replace his hoard which gave a growing purpose to the earnings, drawing his hope and joy continually onward beyond the money.[9]

Eliot makes Marner's initial hoard a poor symbol of the child who takes its place in order to imply that the value of the former can be surpassed by the value of the love the child elicits and confers. Thus, substituting the child for the gold enables Eliot to transform the lust for money, which was

---

4 George Eliot, *Silas Marner* (Oxford University Press, 2008), Part I, chapter 2, p. 16.
5 *Ibid.*   6 *Ibid.*, Part I, chapter 2, p. 18.   7 *Ibid.*, Part I, chapter 2, pp. 19, 20.
8 *Ibid.*, Part I, chapter 10, p. 79.   9 *Ibid.*, Part I, chapter 14, p. 129.

preserving, but also contracting, the weaver's sympathies, into the generosity of spirit that leads Marner to allow Eppie to choose whether she will return to her real father (the wealthy brother of the man who absconded with Marner's gold) or remain with the weaver and marry a local youth. When Eppie elects the latter, the narrator leaves no doubt that the 'treasure' Eppie has brought Silas Marner has dignified both characters and elevated the value of their actions above worldly measure. 'Perfect love has a breath of poetry which can exalt the relations of the least-instructed human beings', the narrator declares.[10] Even her disappointed father, the landowner Godfrey Cass, ultimately has to accept that the logic of money has been transcended by the love whose value Marner and Eppie have demonstrated. ' "There's debts we can't pay like money debts, by paying extra for the years that have slipped by" ', Cass admits as he relinquishes all claim to Eppie.[11]

Silas Marner provides a particularly clear example of the way that Victorian novels subjected economic themes – in this case, the value of gold – to the alchemy of a moral lesson by emphasizing the connotative capacity of language – that is, the elevation of figuration and suggestion over denotation and reference. Marner initially mistakes Eppie for actual gold because he thinks that her blonde hair is literal 'gold on the floor',[12] but when the young girl is called a 'treasure',[13] metaphor trumps such literalness. When Eppie chooses her adopted 'father' Marner over her literal father, she repeats this logic: what a linguistic figure can be made to mean, through imaginative elaboration and the power of connotation, is more valuable than what reference, denotation, or quantification can convey. Eliot's preference for language's ability to transfigure and ennoble over its referential capacity also helps explain why the historical inaccuracies of this tale and the textual contradictions it contains do not matter to the ethical lesson it confers: in the first decades of the nineteenth century, when the events of *Silas Marner* are explicitly set, a weaver would have been far more likely to be paid in some kind of paper money than in gold; and, in the novel itself, Eppie's 'auburn' hair inexplicably metaphorizes into 'gold' again at the end of the novel.[14]

Eliot's promotion of connotation, figuration, and symbolism over reference, denotation, and the literal is echoed in countless other Victorian novels. When, at the end of Dickens's *Our Mutual Friend*, Bella Wilfer

---

10 *Ibid.*, Part II, chapter 16, p. 142.   11 *Ibid.*, Part II, chapter 20, p. 169.
12 *Ibid.*, Part II, chapter 16, p. 132.   13 *Ibid.*, Part II, chapter 19, p. 166.
14 *Ibid.*, Part II, chapter 16, p. 133; Conclusion, p. 184.

becomes 'the true golden gold' embodied in female virtue,[15] Dickens also implies that metaphor can trump reference because moral values have the power to surmount the exchange value of literal gold – at least in the realm of imaginative fiction. When Dorothea Brooke relinquishes Casaubon's wealth in order to marry Will Ladislaw in *Middlemarch*, Eliot provides a narrative version of this linguistic principle: in all of these novels, a character's attitude towards money is an index to his or her moral worth – a value the novelists also convey by emphasizing the moral connotations of monetary terms like 'treasure', 'worth', 'value', and 'gold'.

Trollope's *Can You Forgive Her?* contains one of the period's most complex novelistic engagements with financial issues. On the one hand, the novel provides unusually detailed accounts of particular financial instruments: in chapter 60, for example, when George Vavasour wants to obtain the money that his cousin Alice has promised him, Trollope provides a letter instructing Alice where and how to sign the bill, a dialogue explaining the relationships among cheques, ready money, and a bill due in fourteen days, and a dramatic enactment of the difficulty George faces in cashing the bills Alice signs – as well as an exact account of the fee he must pay to do so. (He exchanges a £500 bill of exchange for £200, but has to pay the broker £40 and leave another £500 bill as security.) On the other hand, and despite the central role money plays in nearly every aspect of all three of the plots, the novel repeatedly uses monetary transactions to convey ethical lessons, primarily about the relationships among money, desire, and 'salvation'. Because Trollope genders the relationship between money and salvation, moreover, the ethical lessons are also lessons in gender propriety. Women like Glencora Palliser and Alice Vavasour must be saved from the social independence their inherited money confers upon them – and from the attendant ability to choose unsuitable lovers; men like Burgo Fitzgerald and George Vavasour, the inappropriate suitors in question, must be saved from their desire for money. This is accomplished when some of the money that once belonged to the women is transferred to the rejected men by the husbands who have displaced them.

This elaborate transfer of money from relatively wealthy female characters to insolvent, unworthy males through the intermediaries of legitimate husbands belongs to a larger pattern by which Trollope divests money of its

---

15 Charles Dickens, *Our Mutual Friend* (Oxford University Press, 2008), Book IV, chapter 13, p. 772.

value as a medium of exchange and a measure of market worth in the process of elevating other forms of value. Thus, money seems to be of most (ethical) worth when it ceases to function as money: it loses this function when a character gives the money away without considering its (worldly) value (as Alice does when she promises her money to George, as Mr Grey does when he actually gives money to George, and as Plantagenet Palliser does when he gives money to Burgo) or when a character has so much money that actual amounts do not matter (as with Glencora's fortune, the monetary sum of which is never revealed). The clearest example of Trollope's tendency to value money most when it cancels its market function appears at the end of the novel when Mr Grey is able to 'pay himself' by marrying Alice.[16] Because, unbeknownst to Alice, Mr Grey has been substituting his own money for the money she has been giving George, Mr Grey has effectively been loaning money to Alice every time George borrows it from her; but because Alice's money becomes Mr Grey's when they marry, he pays himself – that is, he cancels her debts and his credits – in consummating his love.

In the novel's two principal plots, then, one character can save another with money – but only when a male character who has earned the right to do so (Mr Palliser, Mr Grey) takes the money from a wealthy woman who is too independent (Glencora, Alice) and gives it to another man; this man, the recipient of the laundered gift (Burgo, George), is thus saved from his own worst tendencies, which Trollope depicts as emanating from an agonizing craving for money to spend. If a man's lack of money is the source of his moral failings, then receiving money – from the husband who has displaced him – cures him of his lack; or, more precisely, in *Can You Forgive Her?*, the receipt of money exiles the flawed suitors from the novel, which closes with pragmatic summaries of the way money can transform a litany of woes into domestic peace. The only plot that deviates from the pattern I have just described – Mrs Greenow's comic courtship by two suitors, Captain Bellfield and the farmer Cheesacre – ends with the wealthy widow spending her money as she likes. She chooses the impecunious Captain over the well-to-do farmer because her money can transform the Captain into a better man, whose merit can be expressed in a familiar metaphor: ' "He's as good as gold" ', Mrs Greenow explains to Alice.[17] Then, reflecting on the fate of her

<hr>

16 Anthony Trollope, *Can You Forgive Her?* (Oxford University Press, 2008), chapter 77, p. 384.
17 *Ibid.*, chapter 78, p. 390.

other, more solvent suitor, Mrs Greenow dismisses the 'sentimentality' of others' professed indifference to money: ' "I always think that worldliness and sentimentality are like brandy-and-water. I don't like either of them separately, but taken together they make a very nice drink." '[18] This pragmatism is echoed in the novel's penultimate chapter, when Alice, contemplating her wedding gifts, professes not to distinguish between the garnets Lady Midlothian has given her and the diamonds presented by the Marchioness. In response, Glencora Palliser, whose passionate entanglement with Burgo Fitzgerald has provided so much of the novel's interest, dismisses such 'romantic' frivolities: ' "Diamonds are diamonds, and garnets are garnets" ', she remarks sharply; ' "and I am not so romantic but what I know the difference." '[19]

At most, such pragmatism supplements the negation of monetary value promoted by the novel as a whole; as part of an ethical lesson, Trollope's endorsement of 'worldliness' has already been qualified by the 'punishment' he inflicts on characters who misuse money.[20] Like Dickens and Eliot, Trollope emphasized ethical ideals over the monetary information he incidentally included. In so doing, all of these novelists implicitly promoted literary writing as a generic alternative to the work of economic theorists and financial journalists – despite the overlap in content and form that modern critics have identified.

Establishing this generic differentiation belonged to a campaign to identify distinctive qualities in a kind of writing that formally resembled its informational counterpart (in being prose) and that some critics still associated with escapism or self-indulgence. This campaign was articulated most explicitly by Thomas de Quincey when he distinguished between 'literature of knowledge' and 'literature of power' and cast the latter as more valuable than the former because it cultivated the human capacity for sympathy. 'The first speaks to the *mere* discursive understanding; the second speaks ultimately it may happen to the higher understanding or reason, but always *through* affections of pleasure and sympathy.'[21] It proved quite difficult for novelists to draw sharp distinctions between these two kinds of 'literature', however, especially when so much contemporary fiction resembled informational writing in so many ways. In the 1860s and 1870s, the campaign to identify distinctively literary qualities in novels came to a head over the

---

18 *Ibid.*, chapter 78, p. 393.   19 *Ibid.*, chapter 79, p. 411.   20 *Ibid.*
21 Thomas De Quincey, 'The Works of Alexander Pope', *North British Review*, 9 (1848), p. 302.

novels of Charles Reade. Following the example of the French novelist Victor Hugo, Reade had developed an aesthetic practice that transformed newspaper stories into thinly veiled fictions. Even though Reade wanted to use this documentary realism to teach the same kind of ethical lessons for which his contemporaries used more explicitly imaginative means, Reade's novels provoked sharp criticism because they threatened to obliterate the distinction between 'truth' and 'fact'. This, in any case, was the charge Margaret Oliphant levied against Reade, as she tried to police the boundaries of what counted as literary 'art'.

> Fact is no guide at all to art . . . Truth is one thing and fact is another. Truth is that grand general rule of humanity, the harmonious law which runs through everything, which tempers the wind, and varies the circumstances at once of good and evil, and makes it possible for a man to keep steadily along the path of his life, rarely driven to utter desperation by the combinations against him. Fact is the exceptional and contradictory, which breaks rudely into the sweet breadth of use and wont . . . A man who follows fact in art at the expense of truth, is accordingly taking the lawless instead of the harmonious, the exceptional instead of the natural – a mistake which is fatal to a hundred novices . . . who are amazed to find that portraits of actual people, and stories 'founded on fact', are not accepted by any audience as true to nature.[22]

Oliphant's specific target in this passage – the 'hundred novices' who, like Reade, mistakenly based their fictions on 'fact' – marked the boundary between true 'art' and other kinds of writing. Like De Quincey, Oliphant struggled to define this boundary. When she links 'lawless', 'exceptional', and 'contradictory' to 'fact' and 'harmonious', 'natural', and 'use and wont' to 'truth', she offers distinctions that are just as metaphorical – and just as imprecise – as De Quincey's categories. 'All the steps of knowledge, from first to last, carry you farther on the same plane, but could never raise you one foot above your ancient level of earth: whereas, the very first step in power is a flight – is an ascending into another element where earth is forgotten.'[23]

It is not surprising that literary writers' attempts to define the unique contributions their works made to the mediation of value deployed the figurative language their works elevated over mere reference. As an alternative model of value – or a kind of value remodelled by linguistic

22 Margaret Oliphant, 'New Books', *Blackwood's Edinburgh Magazine* 108 (1870), p. 185.
23 De Quincey, 'Pope', p. 303.

elaboration – literary writing implicitly distanced itself from the market model of value, just as most Victorian writers insisted that novels and poems and plays were superior to the dry tomes of economic theory and the merely informational contributions of journalists. What they did not typically emphasize is what many modern literary critics point out: the ability to generate something out of nothing is the capacity shared by the literary understanding of language and the financial use of money.

History

ANDREW SANDERS

The first Victorian generation witnessed what many of them recognized as unprecedented change in the physical and political world about them. It was a sentiment famously described by Thackeray in his 'Roundabout Paper' of October 1860 entitled *De Juventute*. For Thackeray, the coming of the railways in the 1830s seemed to demarcate one age from another and not just his own youth from his middle age:

> We who have lived before the railways were made to belong to another world. In how many hours could the Prince of Wales drive from London to Brighton, with a light carriage built expressly, and relays of horses longing to gallop the next stage? . . . It was only yesterday, but what a gulf between now and then! *Then* it was the old world. Stage-coaches, more or less swift, riding-horses, pack-horses, highwaymen, knights in armour, Norman invaders, Roman legions. Druids, Ancient Britons painted blue, and so forth – all these belong to the old period. I will concede a halt in the midst of it, and allow that gunpowder and printing tended to modernise the world. But your railroad starts a new era, and we of a certain age belong to the new time and the old one. We are of the time of chivalry as well as the Black Prince or Sir Walter Manny. We are of the age of steam.[1]

For Thackeray the railway seems to have accelerated the passage of time even more so than the inventions of gunpowder and the printing-press, speeding the modern world away from that of the Prince Regent and his post-chaise as much as from those of the Druids and the Ancient Britons. In a sense the Prince Regent, Thackeray's contemporary, can now be equated both with the Black Prince and, even more abstrusely, a Druid.

What Thackeray is also implying in his *De Juventute* is that, rather than finding themselves *déraciné*, his contemporaries felt a deep need to explore

---

1 W. M. Thackeray, *De Juventute* (1860), in *The Works of William Makepeace Thackeray*, 26 vols. (London: John Murray, 1910–19), vol. xx, p. 72.

and establish roots. To many Victorians, however, the past was decidedly *not* another country. It was an intensely various country, generally European in its constitution, its traditions and its geography, but it was a familiar one. It appeared to be readily visitable, and it seemed to be self-evidently contiguous with the present. The past stood out boldly before readers of history and historical novels and dramas as monitory, for it offered both examples and warnings to the present. Victorian readers knew, of course, that in the past men and women did things differently, but what the Ancient Romans, or the Plantagenets, or Renaissance Florentines, or Scottish Covenanters did, and how and why they did it, was a matter both of fascination and of vital modern concern – or so historians, historical novelists and historical dramatists aspired to believe.

Nineteenth-century readers may have spurred an urgency in knowing from whence they had come, but the roots examined by Victorian historians were neither exclusively racial nor national in their pursuit of knowledge. Patriotism was self-evidently not enough. As a perusal of any of his novels suggests, Thackeray for one remained fascinated by the history of British influence in the country of his birth, India. The professional historians who were his contemporaries would have readily acknowledged their debts to the recent German renovators of their discipline, Niebuhr, Müller, and Ranke, and to those French historians whose analyses of the disjunctures of modern civilization and politics were to prove so influential (Michelet, Guizot, and Thiers). It should not be forgotten that the most provocative, but nonetheless seductive, study of the racial, social, and cultural consequences of the Norman invasion of England was the work of a Frenchman, Augustin Thierry, whose *Histoire de la conquête d'Angleterre par les Normands, de ses causes, et ses suites* was published in Paris in 1825.[2] Thierry's work helped develop the myth, fostered by Sir Walter Scott in *Ivanhoe*, of the Norman influx as the *fons et origo* of the modern class system.[3] In their various ways British historians of the nineteenth century were both to counter old myths and to foster new ones in equal measure.[4] Although an undertow of

---

2 Augustin Thierry, *The History of the Conquest of England by the Normans*, trans. William Hazlitt, 2 vols. (London: David Bogue, 1847).

3 For a further discussion of this issue see Andrew Sanders, ' "Utter Indifference"? The Anglo Saxons in the Nineteenth-Century Novel', in Donald Scragg and Carole Weinberg (eds.), *Literary Appropriations of the Anglo-Saxons from the Thirteenth to the Twentieth Century* (Cambridge Studies in Anglo-Saxon England 29: Cambridge University Press, 2000), pp. 157–73.

4 For general discussions of historical myth-making and the 'invention of tradition' see Eric Hobsbawm and Terence Ranger (eds.), *The Invention of Tradition* (Cambridge

Protestant nationalism might strike latter-day readers as a constant feature of British history writing, and although that writing might now be viewed as emphatically 'eurocentric' in its world view, the enterprise of many prominent and once respected Victorian historians was very far from insular. Notable British historians of the period were severally to publish substantial studies of Jewish history from Old Testament times to the Napoleonic era (Henry Hart Milman, 1830), of Greece (Connop Thirwall, 1835–44; George Grote, 1845–56), of Rome (Thomas Arnold, 1838), of medieval Christianity (Henry Hart Milman, 1840, 1855), of the Papacy (Mandell Creighton, 1882–94), of the rise and influence of rationalism in Europe (W. E. H. Lecky, 1865), of the French Revolution (Thomas Carlyle, 1837), and of the life of Frederick the Great (Thomas Carlyle, 1858–65).[5] If we add to this list John Ruskin's expansive study of the history, the art, and the architecture of Venice, *The Stones of Venice* (1851–3), it can be seen how variously intelligent British readers were drawn into an intellectual participation in a European-wide debate about the unsteady development of Judaeo-Christian civilization. Perhaps more significantly, these readers were also bidden to respond to the ever-present challenges presented to them by the very idea of progressive development. As Jerome H. Buckley has noted of the perception of time in the Victorian period: 'Whatever the historian's effort to achieve objectivity, public change could seldom for long be contemplated with a calm detachment; it called for evaluation as advance or decline, change for the better or change for the worse.'[6]

There was, however, a great deal of contemporary stress laid on the special conditions which had given rise to the constitutional distinction of Britain and to the social and geographical circumstances which were deemed to have given Britons an advantageous edge in developing their empire, their commerce, and their industry. No Victorian historian was more influential, or persuasive about the nature of Britain's *mission civilisatrice* than Thomas Babington Macaulay (1800–59, created first Baron Macaulay in 1857). Macaulay's biographer, his nephew the historian Sir George Otto Trevelyan, recognized the breadth of his uncle's achievement

University Press, 1983); J. B. Bullen, *The Myth of the Renaissance in Nineteenth-Century Writing* (Oxford: Clarendon Press, 1994), and Hilary Fraser, *The Victorians and Renaissance Italy* (Oxford: Blackwell Publishing, 1992).

5 For what remains the most useful general survey of nineteenth-century historians see G. P. Gooch, *History and Historians in the Nineteenth Century* (London: Longmans, Green & Co., 1913).

6 Jerome H. Buckley, 'The Four Faces of Victorian Time', in C. A. Patrides (ed.), *Aspects of Time* (Manchester University Press, 1976), p. 64.

as 'a man of letters ... a statesman, a jurist and a brilliant ornament of society' but he added that there were also tens of thousands of readers 'whose interest in history and literature he has awakened and informed by his pen'.[7] In his own day Macaulay was perhaps best known for his enduringly popular poems *The Lays of Ancient Rome* (1842) and for his much-reprinted *Essays* (written for the *Edinburgh Review* from 1825 and first collected in 1843). Given his insistent reiterations of Protestant England's providential progress, it is strange to recall that in his review of Leopold von Ranke's *History of the Popes* (1840) Macaulay archly prophesied that the Papacy might 'still exist in undiminished vigour when some traveller from New Zealand shall, in the midst of vast solitude, take his stand of a broken arch of London Bridge to sketch the ruins of St Paul's'.[8] It was an apocalyptic idea, not of Papal durability, but of British vulnerability, which appears to have haunted the Victorian imagination.[9] The suggestion that London might one day share the fate of ancient Rome and become a curiosity in the eyes of its former colonials does not, however, form the keynote of Macaulay's masterpiece, *The History of England* (five volumes, 1848–61). The book is centred instead on the idea of possessive political development. Macaulay's title is effectively a misnomer, for he was determined to focus his historical attention on the late seventeenth-century 'Glorious Revolution' and to describe not just the complex fortunes of England in the period, but also those of Scotland, Ireland and, by extension, the American colonies. Each is shown to be vitally bound up with the burgeoning prosperity and constitutional development of the United Kingdom.

Macaulay's great innovation as a writer of history was to describe social patterns which lay beyond political and military ones. He stated his intention with an opening declaration:

> It will be my endeavour to relate the history of the people as well as the history of the government, to trace the progress of useful and ornamental arts, to describe the rise of religious sects and the changes of literary taste, to portray the manners of successive generations, and not to pass by with neglect even the revolutions which have taken place in dress, furniture,

---

7 Sir Otto Trevelyan, *The Life and Letters of Lord Macaulay* (1876; London: Longman, Green & Co., 1893), p. 2.

8 T. B. Macaulay, review of Leopold von Ranke's *The Ecclesiastical and Political History of the Popes During the Sixteenth and Seventeenth Centuries*, trans. S. Austin, *Edinburgh Review* 72 (1840), p. 258.

9 Anthony Trollope was to give the title *The New Zealander* to a collection of essays written in 1855–6 (but not published until 1972), and the last plate of Gustave Doré's *London* (1872) shows the New Zealander at work amidst the ruins.

repasts, and public amusements. I shall cheerfully bear the reproach of having descended below the dignity of history, if I can succeed in placing before the English of the nineteenth century a true picture of the life of their ancestors.[10]

Macaulay conspicuously, and very effectively, drew on sources and influences, notably literary sources, which lay beyond the customary archival or documentary domain of historians. Macaulay had in one of his earlier essays accredited his innovatory method to the influence of the novels of Sir Walter Scott. Despite his evident admiration of the Waverley novels, Macaulay the historian seems to take brief exception to Scott's act of intelligent trespass:

> To make the past present, to bring the distance near, to place us in the society of a great man or on the eminence which overlooks the field of a mighty battle ... to call up our ancestors before us with all their peculiarities of language, manners, and garb, to show us over their houses, to seat us at their tables, to rummage their old-fashioned wardrobes, to explain the uses of their ponderous furniture, these parts of the duty which properly belongs to the historian have been appropriated by the historical novelist.[11]

Macaulay was, in fact, re-appropriating what he felt properly belonged to the historian, but he was doing so by adopting something of the method and the narrative technique of Scott and his imitators. Where he believed he differed was in his determination to 'draw from the occurrences of former times general lessons of moral and political wisdom'. Where, in telling a story, the novelist merely 'showed', the scrupulous historian was obliged to pause to analyse, to interpret, and to teach.[12]

Macaulay's great 'set-pieces' (his analysis of the condition of England in 1685, say, or his accounts of the landing of William of Orange or the Battle of the Boyne) are therefore integrally linked to his grand intellectual theme, again first expressed in the *Essays*, that 'the history of England is emphatically the history of progress'. It was 'the history of a constant movement of the public mind, of a constant change in the institutions of a great society'.[13]

---

10 Thomas Babington Macaulay, *The History of England: from the Accession of James the Second*, 5 vols. (London: Longman, Brown, Green, and Longmans, 1849), vol. I, p. 3.

11 Thomas Babington Macaulay, 'Hallam' (1828), in *Critical and Historical Essays*, 8th edn, 3 vols. (London: Longman, Brown, Green & Longmans, 1864), vol. I, pp. 113–14.

12 *Ibid.*, p. 114.

13 Macaulay, 'Sir James Mackintosh' (1835), in *Critical and Historical Essays*, vol. II, p. 226. For a general summary of this 'Whig Interpretation' see Hugh Trevor Roper, Introduction to Lord Macaulay, *The History of England* (Harmondsworth: Penguin Books, 1979), p. 39. See also J. W. Burrow's fine account of Macaulay's influence in *A Liberal Descent: Victorian Historians and the English Past* (Cambridge University Press, 1981).

This insistent argument, articulated with the recent passage of the Reform Bill in 1832 and the reforming deal of the post-Reform Whig government in mind, stands as one of the central pillars of Macaulay's own political agenda. The study of the past, and the analytical interpretation of selected data, provide the present with a firm justification for its espousal of gradual development. The struggles between Crown and Parliament in the middle of the seventeenth century, and the effective triumph of Parliament over a re-assertive, and potentially tyrannical, Crown in the reign of James II, had set an agenda for the steady and 'constant' change in the political and social institutions of Great Britain. Macaulay's articulation of the idea of the organic development of the constitution and of society alike was the founding principle of what was subsequently dubbed the 'Whig Interpretation of History'. Macaulay, raised to the peerage by a grateful Lord Palmerston and buried in Poets' Corner in Westminster Abbey after his untimely death, did not live to finish his *History* as he had initially aspired to do. He was unable to extend his survey of the consequences of what victorious Whigs had styled the 'Glorious Revolution' into the eighteenth century and to observe its impact on such phenomena as the Act of Union with Scotland, on Jacobitism and on the American Revolution. Significantly enough it was a novelist, Thackeray, the author of *Henry Esmond* and *The Virginians*, who at his publisher's suggestion, toyed with the idea of assuming Macaulay's historical mantle until he too was defeated by death.[14]

Thomas Carlyle, caricatured by Anthony Trollope as 'Dr Pessimist Anticant', was a historian of a very different stamp from Macaulay. For Carlyle the observation of contemporary society suggested far less evidence of happy and enlightened progress; the study of history too demanded not so much a consideration of the state of England in 1685 as a desperate attempt to diagnose the ills of England in the mid nineteenth century by placing those ills in an unflattering perspective. Where Macaulay sought to congratulate the English on their political achievement, Carlyle took pleasure in disconcerting them. There was little love lost between the two men, Carlyle glibly dismissing his rival as 'the sublime of commonplace'.[15] Seemingly appropriately, Macaulay the man struck him as having little of the physically heroic about

---

14 See Gordon N. Ray, *Thackeray: The Age of Wisdom 1847–1863* (London: Oxford University Press, 1958), p. 372.
15 See Fred Kaplan, *Thomas Carlyle: A Biography* (Cambridge University Press, 1983), p. 382.

him, largely because Macaulay the historian had failed to recognize what Carlyle saw as the dynamic of history: heroism itself.

Like his rival, Carlyle had first established his reputation, and had first outlined the principles on which he was to work, in a series of essays in contemporary journals. Amongst the most influential of these are 'Signs of the Times' (*Edinburgh Magazine*, June 1829) and 'On History' (*Fraser's Magazine*, 1830). The former, with its self-consciously apocalyptic title, reflects on the then current fascination with millenarianism before crucially defining the modern age as 'The Mechanical Age' and 'The Age of Machinery'. Carlyle sees this defining mechanical principle as evident in all aspects of national life from its economics to its theology, from its aesthetics and its literature to its politics and its morals:

> Men are grown mechanical in head and in heart, as well as in hand. They have lost faith in individual endeavour, and in natural force, of any kind. Not for internal perfection, but for external combinations and arrangements, for institutions, constitutions, – for Mechanism of one sort or another, do they hope and struggle. Their whole efforts, attachments, opinions, turn on mechanism, and are of a mechanical character.[16]

Carlyle is not dispraising either science or technology, but he is observing a society losing its old bearings and failing to embrace the moral and intellectual consequences of the new. To balance this dystopic vision of the present he suggests in the essay 'On History' that the study of the past may offer both examples and lessons. 'Before Philosophy can teach by Experience', he argues, 'the Philosophy has to be in readiness, the Experience must be gathered and intelligibly recorded.' What he means here by 'experience' is history, and history he insists is 'the essence of innumerable Biographies'.[17] This 'biographical' bias was to shape all of Carlyle's historical enterprise.

The significance of biography as a means of exploring historical experience is very much evident in Carlyle's series of public lectures, delivered in May 1840 and published in the following year under the title *On Heroes, Hero-Worship and the Heroic in History*. The lectures deal with male heroism as a variously historical, religious, aesthetic, and social phenomenon (gods, prophets, poets, priests, writers, and leaders). His 'heroes' have all 'shaped themselves in the world's history' as 'the modellers, patterns, and in a wide sense creators, of whatsoever the general mass of men contrived to do or to

---

16 Thomas Carlyle, 'Signs of the Times' (1829), in *Works of Thomas Carlyle*, 30 vols. (London: Chapman and Hall, 1896–9), vol. xxvii, pp. 62–3.
17 Carlyle, 'On History' (1830), in *Works*, vol. xxvii, p. 86.

attain'.[18] Carlyle's last two lectures ('The Hero as Man of Letters' and 'The Hero as King') most directly address the social and political issues of his own day. His men of letters (Dr Johnson, Jean-Jacques Rousseau, and Robert Burns) are all 'new' men, all of them of humble origin who rose to eminence through intellectual effort and without the benefit of patronage. His 'kings' (Cromwell and Napoleon) are equally self-made breakers of moulds. A king, for Carlyle, is the *Ableman*, a proto-Nietzschean *Übermensch*, who sweeps away tired conventions by dint of his inspired will. Thus the taciturn Cromwell 'drives towards the practical and the practicable ... a man with his whole soul *seeing*, and struggling to see' while that 'far inferior sort', Napoleon, possessed 'a certain instinctive ineradicable feeling for reality' until an equally instinctive 'fatal charlatan-element' got the upper hand.[19] A strong anti-democratic, or at least anti-populist, bias runs through the lectures as it does through *Past and Present* (1843), a work very much directed at the problems besetting what Carlyle himself termed the 'Condition of England'. The work is divided into four parts: a singularly provocative 'Proem' which attacks modern economic and social complacency; an extended study of the twelfth-century 'heroic' Abbot Samson of St Edmundsbury; a various view of work and the 'modern worker', and, finally, a 'Horoscope' which attempts to disturb the present day with dire warnings of a collapse into moral anarchy. In one sense *Past and Present* seeks to challenge those amongst Carlyle's contemporaries (such as the Catholic architect and cultural polemicist, A. W. N. Pugin) who sought to portray the state of art and society in the Middle Ages as infinitely tidier and happier than in the Godless present. For Carlyle, the past is neither a lost Golden Age nor a monitory prologue; it is simply history, vivid, resonant, but essentially retrievable. Having rejected any nostalgia for the past, the book consistently sets out to disconcert the present by offering a series of pithy diagnoses of its multiple social ills and shortcomings.

Carlyle's historical method is essentially that of a zealous preacher obsessed with failed vocations in the past, present woes, and a pending Armageddon. His complex, often extremely experimental language echoes that of the Old Testament prophets, the Reformation divines, and Roman orators. He does not rant (though some readers find him repugnant), but he calls steadily and aggressively for repentance, renewal, and a restored sense

---

18 Thomas Carlyle, *On Heroes, Hero-Worship and the Heroic in History* (1841), in *Works*, vol. v, p. 1.
19 *Ibid.*, pp. 215, 218, 237, 239, 241.

of mission. His complex masterpiece, *The French Revolution* (1837), had a considerable impact on his times (Charles Dickens, for one, rashly claimed in 1851 to have read it five hundred times!).[20] Something of that impact was undoubtedly the consequence of the nineteenth century's troubled fascination with the events of the Revolution, its political innovation as much as its prolific blood-letting, but Carlyle offered much more than an account of those events: his narrative is at once compellingly dramatic, intricately detailed, and decidedly *epic* in its sweep.[21] In an important way *The French Revolution* is the true fulfilment of what Carlyle had earlier aspired to: history as the 'essence of innumerable Biographies' built as it is around a series of portraits of major Revolutionary figures and drawing on fragments of eye-witness accounts, letters, journals, pamphlets, memoirs, and autobiographies. This great history of the Revolution is a multi-voiced narrative, held together and urged forward by the insistent, authoritative, but completely individual, voice of Carlyle himself. Its exploitation of multiple historical perspectives and points of view was to have a profound effect both on popular historiography and on subsequent historical fiction. Nevertheless, what tends to stick in the memory are the *History*'s great set-pieces, the accounts of the fall of the Bastille, the Royal Family's enforced journey to Paris in 1789, the Flight to Varennes, the storming of the Tuileries in 1792, the execution of Louis XVI, or the demise of Robespierre (whom Carlyle had famously dubbed the 'seagreen Incorruptible').[22] Nothing in Carlyle's later achievement as a historian, whether as editor of Cromwell's letters and speeches or as the biographer of Frederick the Great, really rivals the innovative narrative genius of *The French Revolution*.

Carlyle's often pessimistic prognostications about the decline and fall of civilizations are to some degree echoed in John Ruskin's superbly and elegantly digressive *The Stones of Venice* (3 volumes, 1851–3). Ruskin was inclined to refer to Carlyle simply as his 'master', remarking to J. A. Froude on one occasion that he felt that this 'master' had, like some classical god,

---

20 Charles Dickens to John Forster, summer 1851, in *The Letters of Charles Dickens*, vol. VI, 1850–2, ed. Graham Storey, Kathleen Tillotson, and Nina Burgis (Oxford: Clarendon Press, 1988), p. 452.

21 For a fine analysis of Carlyle's achievement see John Clubbe, 'Carlyle as Epic Historian', in James R. Kincaid and Albert J. Kuhn (eds.), *Victorian Literature and Society: Essays Presented to Richard D. Altick* (Columbus: Ohio State University Press, 1994), pp. 119–45.

22 Thomas Carlyle, *The French Revolution. A History*, 3 vols. (London: Chapman and Hall, 1896), vol. II, p. 168.

been 'born in the clouds and struck by the lightning'.[23] *The Stones of Venice* is a study not simply of the surviving monuments of painting, sculpture, architecture, and design created by Venice at the height of its power, but of its steady decline (Ruskin first saw the city nearly forty years after it had lost its independence and when its decayed buildings were languishing under Austrian rule). Ruskin's extended 'essay', as he modestly describes it, is neither pure history nor pure art history (though the latter discipline barely existed in his time). It is a novel form of social and cultural archaeology assembled by scrupulous and meditative observation. As Ruskin insists in his Preface, when it came to studying the architecture of Venice 'every date in question was determinable only by internal evidence', obliging him to examine not just 'every one of the older palaces, stone by stone, but every fragment throughout the city which afforded any clue to the formation of its styles'.[24] Its celebrated opening paragraph, however, disconcertingly interrelates past, present, and future and links history to prophecy:

> Since first the dominion of men was asserted over the ocean, three thrones, of mark beyond all others, have been set upon its sands: the thrones of Tyre, Venice and England. Of the First of these great powers only the memory remains; of the Second, the ruin; the Third, which inherits their greatness, if it forget their example, may be led through prouder eminence to less pitied destruction.[25]

This is as much Jonah preaching to Nineveh as a future New Zealander seeking out the evidence of Venetian decay in London rather than broken Roman arches. Ruskin inherently aspires to *read* buildings as the truest indicators of the quality of a civilization. As an interpreter he variously interweaves history and politics, aesthetics and economics, theology and geology. His stylistic effects can be both disconcerting and dazzling, for as one early reader, Charlotte Brontë, found there is an earnestness in *The Stones of Venice* which was likely to make Unitarians (and, we presume, some historians) 'fume and fret over his deep, serious, and (as *they* will think) fanatical reverence for Art'.[26] This 'reverence' may lead Ruskin into inflating

23 E. T. Cook, *The Life of John Ruskin*, 2 vols. (London: George Allen & Co., 1911), vol. I, pp. 475–6. See also Tim Hilton, *John Ruskin: The Early Years 1819–1859* (New Haven, CT and London: Yale University Press, 1985), pp. 150–1.
24 John Ruskin, *The Stones of Venice* (1851–53), in *The Works of John Ruskin*, ed. E. T. Cook and Alexander Wedderburn, 39 vols. (London: George Allen, 1903–12), vol. IX, p. 4.
25 *Ibid.*, p. 17.
26 Charlotte Brontë to George Smith, 7 January 1851, in *The Letters of Charlotte Brontë: With a Selection of Letters by Family and Friends. Volume II: 1848–1851*, ed. Margaret Smith (Oxford University Press, 2000), p. 546.

certain *idées fixes* into universal truths (he is insistent, for example, that the inception of Venice's moral and imperial decay coincides with its first flirtation with the Renaissance). As the shrewd George Eliot remarked, despite the 'stupendous specimens of arrogant absurdity' in his work Ruskin's 'grand doctrines of truth and sincerity in art, and the nobleness and solemnity of our human life, which he teaches with the inspiration of a Hebrew prophet, must be stirring up young minds in a promising way'.[27] The very intensity of his vision was to inspire generations of these young minds to use their eyes, as much as their intellects, in articulating their relationship to the past.

Ruskin's work obliged his vast number of Victorian disciples to respond to a semi-exotic aesthetic and to a faded imperial dream, both of which lay beyond their immediate and insular experience. To many responsive readers, however, it was the past of their own nation which impinged most readily and vividly on their perception of their present condition and on their future destinies. For J. A. Burrow, the thirty years between 1848 and 1878 were marked by 'a remarkable flowering of English narrative history' and by an 'elaboration in the interpretation of what arguably had been the three great crises in the history of the English as a nation'. These three crises were the Norman Conquest, the Reformation, and the Revolution of 1688.[28] In relation to these critical periods Burrow discusses Macaulay's *History*, William Stubbs's *The Constitutional History of England in its Origin and Development* (3 volumes, 1873–8), Edward Augustus Freeman's *The History of the Norman Conquest* (4 volumes, 1867–79), and James Anthony Froude's *The History of England from the Fall of Wolsey to the Defeat of the Spanish Armada* (12 volumes, 1856–70). Burrow is well aware that his chosen historians have distinctive historical, philosophical, and, to some degree, religious (i.e. liberal Protestant) agendas. All four were also determined to correct popular misconceptions (Freeman, for example, set out to undermine Augustin Thierry's idea of a continuing class conflict between aristocratic Normans and plebeian Saxons). All also sought to re-map and recolonize territory which had all too often been occupied by ill-informed, romantically inclined poets or unscholarly writers of literary fiction. For Macaulay, as we

---

27 George Eliot was initially addressing her comments about Ruskin's 'absurdity' to his *Political Economy of Art*. George Eliot to Sara Hennell, 17 January 1858, in *The George Eliot Letters: 1852–1858: Volume 2*, ed. Gordon S. Haight (New Haven, CT: Yale University Press, 1978), p. 422.

28 J. A. Burrow, *A Liberal Descent: Victorian Historians and the English Past* (1981; Cambridge University Press, 1983), p. 1.

have seen, the prime villain remained the enduringly popular Sir Walter Scott and the 'Wizard of the North' had fostered a remarkable literary progeny. As one Victorian critic remarked, Scott's work began 'from the full light of his own days' and had gone back 'century after century . . . [and] had, in all, a range of about eight centuries through which he roamed, as in his proper domain'.[29] Scott had dealt with issues pertaining to the Norman Conquest (in *Ivanhoe* of 1820 and *Count Robert of Paris* of 1832), Reformation Scotland (in *The Monastery* and *The Abbot*, both 1820), Elizabethan England (in *Kenilworth* of 1821), and Puritan England (in *Woodstock* of 1826), and with the prelude to and the consequences of the Glorious Revolution in Scotland and England in a whole succession of novels (*Waverley* of 1814, *Old Mortality* of 1816, *Rob Roy* of 1817, *Peveril of the Peak* of 1823).

Scott's Victorian successors and imitators maintained a rivalry with the historians, knowing that there was a ready and receptive audience for their work. History seemed to be the proper province of novelists determined to show off their intellectual credentials. Historical fiction was, as one critic remarked, capable of uniting 'the learning of the historian with the fancy of the poet', but, equally persuasively, it could judiciously edit, discarding 'from human annals their years of tedium' while bringing prominently forward 'their eras of interest'.[30] It was not therefore only the modern poet-dramatist who could aspire to inherit Shakespeare's mantle as the imaginative delineator of national history: so too might the nineteenth-century novelist. The Victorian sense of intimacy with the past was in part the result of a sentiment that readers of historical fiction were able to participate imaginatively in the experience of their ancestors.

The work of Burrow's mid-century historians can be readily paralleled in that of their novelist and dramatist contemporaries. The Norman Conquest was variously dealt with in Edward Bulwer Lytton's *Harold, the Last of the Saxon Kings* (1848), in Charles Kingsley's *Hereward the Wake* (1866), in Tennyson's verse-drama *Harold* (1876), and, somewhat less memorably, in General Sir Charles Napier's historical romance, *William the Conqueror* (published posthumously in 1858 in an edition by the military historian Sir William Napier). William Harrison Ainsworth's sensationalist Gothic dabblings in Reformation history (such as *The Tower of London* of 1841 and

29 David Masson, *British Novelists and their Styles: Being a Critical Sketch of the History of British Prose Fiction* (Cambridge: Macmillan & Co., 1859), p. 167.
30 Archibald Allison, 'The Historical Romance', *Blackwood's Edinburgh Magazine* 58 (1845), p. 341.

Windsor Castle of 1843) were to be outclassed in terms of verisimilitude by two works notably influenced by J. A. Froude, Kingsley's swashbucklingly Protestant diatribe *Westward Ho!* (1855) and Tennyson's drama *Queen Mary* (1875). The continental origins of Reformation thought were also explored in Charles Reade's fictional study of Erasmus's immediate forebears, *The Cloister and the Hearth* (1861), while the intrigues related to the captivity of Mary, Queen of Scots (and to the Queen's 'unknown' daughter) figure in the prolific Charlotte M. Yonge's *Unknown to History* (1882). Although the Glorious Revolution itself proved less of a draw to English novelists, events anterior to it figure in R. D. Blackmore's *Lorna Doone* (1869) and Arthur Conan Doyle's *Micah Clarke* (1887) (both set at the time of the Monmouth rebellion) and its immediate consequences are explored in Thackeray's *The History of Henry Esmond, Esq. A Colonel in the Service of Her Majesty Queen Anne* (1852).[31]

It would be wrong, however, to suppose that these were the only critical moments in national history to have inspired Victorian writers. For many poets history did not even have to be *real* history. Tennyson's epic recycling of Arthurian legend in his *Idylls of the King* (1842–91) may have become the most ambitious literary reconstruction of the world of Camelot, but its subject matter was far from unique. The revitalization of the medieval notion of chivalry, often loosely associated with Arthur's court, came to haunt many Victorian imaginations and has even been seen by some commentators as instrumental in fostering the gentlemanly ideals which shaped Britain's imperial ambitions.[32] Although the great moulder of the morals of Rugby School, and the historian of Rome, Dr Thomas Arnold, would have had little truck with such dreamy fantasies, his son Matthew was to include the dialogue romance 'Tristram and Iseult' in his *Poems* of 1852. In the original edition the three sections of the poem were given titles printed in Gothic script. William Morris's *The Defence of Guinevere and Other Poems* was published in 1858 and Robert Stephen Hawker's extraordinary blank verse *Quest of the Sangraal* in 1864. Tennyson was to turn to documented history in his second, and, in its time, most popular historical drama, *Becket* (1884), the martyred Archbishop proving to be one of

31 For these and other historical novels of the period see Andrew Sanders, *The Victorian Historical Novel 1840–1880* (London: Macmillan, 1978), and Avrom Fleishman, *The English Historical Novel: Walter Scott to Virginia Woolf* (Baltimore and London: Johns Hopkins University Press, 1971).
32 See Mark Girouard, *The Return to Camelot: Chivalry and the English Gentleman* (New Haven, CT and London: Yale University Press, 1981).

Sir Henry Irving's most admired roles. The spiritual certainties, and the rich architectural and visual culture of the later Middle Ages had, since the late eighteenth century, increasingly assumed the character of a lost golden age. To some nineteenth-century commentators, notably William Cobbett and A. W. N. Pugin, the Reformation ruptured more than religious continuities: it marked a watershed which was at once social and aesthetic. As Pugin wrote in the preface to the expanded second edition of his *Contrasts* in 1841, 'the real origin of both the revived Pagan and Protestant principles is to be traced to the decayed state of faith throughout Europe in the fifteenth century which led men to dislike, and ultimately forsake, the principles and architecture which originated in the *self-denying Catholic principle, and admire and adopt the luxurious styles of ancient Paganism.'* Paganism and Protestantism, Renaissance and Reformation were all of them 'monsters.'[33] Pugin brought his point home through a series of devastating satirical plates contrasting sturdy medieval churches with paltry, gimcrack modern ones. One of his most bitingly successful plates shows a great, but idealized fifteenth-century almshouse (based on St Cross near Winchester) juxtaposed with a Benthamite panopticon workhouse. Another shows two 'contrasted' pictures of towns. The 'Catholic' town of 1440 is a model of piety, the towers and spires of its parish churches and monasteries piercing the sky; the same blighted town in 1840 has broken spires, the neglected ruins of an abbey, and a skyline now dominated by factory chimneys; where there was once an open space there is now a penitentiary, where there was once a stone bridge and a chapel, there is now an iron toll-bridge. The decay of the happy old order is meant to be self-evident. A similar nostalgia for a lost age also informs Benjamin Disraeli's otherwise forward-looking political novels of the 1840s. In *Sybil* of 1845, for example, the ruins of Marley Abbey proclaim

> a place where all the rights of hospitality were practised; where the travel-ler, from the proud baron to the lonely pilgrim, asked the shelter and the succour that were never denied, and at whose gate, called the Portal of the Poor, the peasants on the Abbey lands, if in want, might appeal each morn and night for raiment and for food.[34]

33 A. W. Pugin, *Contrasts: or A Parallel between the Noble Edifices of the Middle Ages, and Corresponding Buildings of the Present Day: Shewing the Present Decay* (London: Charles Dolman, 1841), p. iii (italics in original). For general studies of Victorian medievalism see Alice Chandler, *A Dream of Order: The Medieval Ideal in Nineteenth-Century Literature* (London: Routledge & Kegan Paul, 1971), and Girouard, *Return to Camelot*.

34 Benjamin Disraeli, *Sybil; Or, The Two Nations* (1845; Oxford University Press, 2009), chapter 4, p. 57.

No need, therefore, for grudgingly given poor relief and for union work-houses. For some Victorian writers the England of the later Plantagenets, as much as the England of Arthur, was a dreamy land of chivalric gestures, noble piety, and knightly bounty; for others, more crucially, pre-Reformation England was a land blessedly free of machines and applied Utilitarianism. William Morris, who began his artistic career dreaming medieval dreams, was never to lose his vision of a pre-industrial earthly paradise. When this vision was shot through with the socialist principles he had imbibed from reading Marx, as it is in *News from Nowhere* of 1891, Morris lovingly explores a post-industrial future in which society has been transformed by a return to self-sufficient artistic communities in which swords have been beaten into beautifully crafted ploughshares.

Certain raw wounds of the more recent past had an evident currency in the social and constitutional debates associated with the Reform Acts of 1832, 1867, and 1884. The political and religious divisions of the English Civil War were, for example, to figure significantly in C. W. Cope's murals in the peers' corridor in the newly completed Palace of Westminster (commissioned 1853 and completed 1867).[35] The period of the 'English Revolution' was to prove equally stimulating to writers. In the reformist 1830s Robert Browning felt that the subject of his historical tragedy *Strafford* (1837), the struggle between autocracy and representative government, was very much 'in the air'.[36] An alternative, and partisan picture of loyalty to Church and King is explored in Frederick Marryat's *The Children of the New Forest* of 1847, while writers influenced by the Oxford Movement, such as J. H. Shorthouse in his *John Inglesant* (1880), were drawn to a period in which the soul and culture of the Church of England were tested to the extreme. For the greatest Scottish writer of the last third of the nineteenth century, Robert Louis Stevenson, the three highly esteemed adventure stories, *Kidnapped* (1886), its sequel *Catriona* (1893), and *The Master of Ballantrae* (1889) reveal a deep fascination with the fissures in Scots culture produced by the extended period of Jacobite unrest that had earlier so preoccupied Sir Walter Scott.

The influence of contemporary historiography on the historical novel was not, of course, confined to fiction that dealt exclusively with 'the matter of

35 For these murals, see Maurice Bond (ed.), *Works of Art in the House of Lords* (London: Her Majesty's Stationery Office, 1980), pp. 92–101.
36 Cited by Mrs Sutherland Orr, *Life and Letters of Robert Browning* (London: Smith, Elder & Co., 1891), p. 88.

Britain'. The long shadow of Edward Gibbon's provocative and often contentious *The Decline and Fall of the Roman Empire* falls over the work of Victorian sceptics and Christian apologists alike. The history of the declining Roman empire was read both in terms of loss and gain, of ends and beginnings. It is the small body of fleeing Christians who represent the emergent future at the end of Bulwer Lytton's widely admired *The Last Days of Pompeii* (1834) while the persecution of the early Church forms the subject of Cardinal Wiseman's *Fabiola: A Tale of the Catacombs* (1854) and of John Henry (later Cardinal) Newman's *Callista: A Sketch of the Third Century* (1856). Wilkie Collins's first published novel, *Antonina, Or the Fall of Rome* (1850), has a Christian heroine beset by pagan Romans and pagan Goths alike. Far less sympathetic pictures of primitive Christianity are offered in Kingsley's assertively Protestant *Hypatia, Or Old Foes with a New Face* (1853: the faces of the 'old foes' being those of Victorian Catholics and Tractarian divines) and in Walter Pater's infinitely more ambiguous philosophical romance *Marius the Epicurean* (1885). The national aspirations and the anti-Papal struggles of the Italian Risorgimento were inspiring to both Bulwer Lytton's *Rienzi: The Last of the Tribunes* (1835) and George Eliot's intensely scholarly *Romola* (1863).[37] The latter story, set in the politically tangled Florence of Savonarola, has a Positivist historical perspective which allowed Eliot to express a greater frankness about the loss of religious faith and the independence of a central woman character than she felt able to do in her novels set in the nineteenth century. To the chagrin of some latter-day historians and of twentieth-century Marxian critics the most enduringly popular, and influential, of Victorian historical novels remains Dickens's *A Tale of Two Cities* (1859). Dickens's debt to Carlyle is evident throughout the narrative, but the distinctiveness of the novel lies largely in the fact that the few *actual* historical personalities who appear in the novel figure only glancingly. What Dickens seeks to represent is not revolution as a creative act but as a supremely disruptive element in the experience of fictional characters who are caught up in an intensely plotted moral drama. These characters are also haunted, even more weightily than Scrooge is, by the ghosts of the past, the present, and the yet-to-come. Public and private histories are interlinked. Time does not necessarily heal: it catches characters out and it is they who are obliged to work out a process of reconciliation for themselves.

---

37 For *Romola*, see Caroline Levine and Mark Turner (eds.), *From Author to Text: Re-Reading George Eliot's Romola* (Aldershot: Ashgate, 1998).

In *Waverley* Scott had famously presented his readers with a story set 'sixty years since'. His perspective remained (and remains) useful in the sense that the gap of two generations allows for some detachment from disruptive historical experience. Some Victorian writers (George Eliot in *Adam Bede* of 1859, for example, or Elizabeth Gaskell in *Sylvia's Lovers* of 1863) readily adopted Scott's perspective. Others, particularly those who explored aspects of their own lives in fiction, found themselves obliged to cross back from the railway era in which they were writing to that 'other world' – the age of the stagecoach. In these latter cases, however, a private history (such as David Copperfield's) rarely seems to take on the weight of 'history' proper. When Thackeray spoke in 1860 of the 'gulf between now and then' his readers would still primarily have celebrated him as the author of *Vanity Fair* of 1847–8. *Vanity Fair* is not autobiographical but its setting in the raffish England of George IV does, almost dangerously, impinge on the earlier Victorian decades. Much of what Thackeray describes was still living memory to readers of the generation of the novelist's own parents. There is certainly a good deal of detachment in the narrative, an achievement enhanced by the novel's narrator's decidedly quizzical irony, but the 'then' and the 'now' are in fact far less distinguished from one another than they are, say, in *Esmond* or *The Virginians*. Nevertheless, *Vanity Fair* seems emphatically to be set in another world. It seems to deny the continuities which many of its first readers must readily have recognized (an aspect of the novel reinforced by the fact that Thackeray's illustrations show his characters in early Victorian rather than Regency dress). The advances of the railway age may have appeared to accelerate the passage of time but Thackeray was also well aware of the fact that he was animating what the writer Alan Bennett has almost disarmingly described as 'that remotest of periods, the recent past'.[38]

38 Alan Bennett, 'Bad John' (1994), reprinted in *Writing Home* (London: Faber & Faber, 1998), p. 497.

Sexuality

SHARON MARCUS

To take 'sexuality' as a rubric for understanding Victorian literature may seem a bit odd, since few words better illustrate the gulf between how the Victorians saw themselves and how we see them. 'To have sex' was not a common locution until the early twentieth century, and it was only in that century's final decades that feminist and queer theorists began to insist on distinctions among 'sexuality', 'sex', and 'gender'. Sexuality came to denote a complex of desires, affects, sensations, identifications, and acts; sex, to mean the biological characteristics that identify individuals as male or female, though those physical differences increasingly came to seem culturally constructed and physically manipulable; and gender, to refer to an individual's sense of identity as masculine or feminine, as well as to social demarcations of masculine and feminine qualities and roles. In the nineteenth century, to be sexual meant to be sexed male or female; in the twentieth, sexuality became shorthand for sexual orientation. And though two Victorian men, Havelock Ellis and John Symonds, helped initiate that change in usage, even they thought of the sexual in Victorian terms, as referring primarily to male or female sex. Thus, when they coined the phrase 'sexual inversion' in the 1890s, they used it to label men who felt like women and women who felt like men, not men who desired men and women who desired women.

Before the 1890s, sexuality was a biological term whose primary meaning indicated a type of reproduction in plants and animals. For most of the Victorian period, sex meant the quality of being male or female, not the act of sexual intercourse. Women are 'the fair sex' in *The Pickwick Papers*, men 'the sterner sex' in *Shirley*. Sex was not something one did; it described who one was. Sex served as a principle of classification that defined individuals and conferred collective identity; each person had a sex and belonged to one. The word thus often appears in Victorian literature modified by a possessive pronoun. Elizabeth Gaskell in *Wives and Daughters* writes of a woman who can charm not only men but also 'her own sex', and Miss Betsey Trotwood in *David Copperfield* is 'the best of her sex'.[1] To have a sex was both to embody certain qualities as a person and to merge with a group. Women, routinely seen as less individualized than men, were thus often called 'the sex'; describing three dairymaids in the throes of desire for the same man, Thomas Hardy calls 'each . . . but portion of one organism called sex'.[2] Elizabeth Barrett Browning was one of the few writers to anticipate the twentieth-century sense of the word, when, in Book 5 of her epic poem *Aurora Leigh*, she refers to 'sexual passion', but she also uses the word in the sense more usual for her time when she alludes to 'sexual prejudice', by which she means male prejudice against women. Even Thomas Hardy, often in tension with his generation's ways of speaking about desire, saw the erotic energies of the sexual as inseparable from the division of male and female into two sexes. Sue Bridehead is 'cold-natured, – sexless' because she lacks physical interest in men.[3]

Since variants on the word 'sex' meant something so different to the Victorians than to us, a nominalist who believes that names create reality might suggest that, because the Victorians lacked a word for what we now call sexuality, they also had no experience of the agglomeration of desires, acts, and identity to which that word came to refer. Conversely, a wilful universalist, for whom all eras resemble our own, might insist that our predecessors experienced sexuality exactly as we do, but merely called it something different. Ever since Lytton Strachey published *Eminent Victorians* in 1918, we have mocked the Victorians for not being as sexually knowing as we are; in the wake of Michel Foucault's introduction to the *History of Sexuality* (1976), we have mocked ourselves for being, like the Victorians, obsessed with talking and writing and thinking about sex. Brilliant as both texts are, each takes too unitary a view of contemporary and past beliefs. This chapter opts instead to explore the topic of Victorian sexuality by building philosophical debate into the concept of sexuality itself and by adopting a dual temporal perspective. The first section explores how we might align the modern understanding of sex as a form of power with Victorian ways of using sex to define boundaries. The second section takes an equally modern idea, that sex defies power, and asks to what extent

---

1 Elizabeth Gaskell, *Wives and Daughters* (Harmondsworth: Penguin, 1969), chapter 19, p. 254; Charles Dickens, *David Copperfield* (London: Penguin, 1996), chapter 24, p. 337.
2 Thomas Hardy, *Tess of the D'Urbervilles* (London: Penguin, 1998), chapter 23, p. 147.
3 Thomas Hardy, *Jude the Obscure* (Oxford University Press, 2009), Part Third, chapter 4, p. 143.

Victorians thought of erotic desire as breaking boundaries. The final section reverses course and compares a Victorian presence to a modern absence by taking seriously the Victorian equation of sex and love, which subsequent generations have derided as either cloying sentimentality or a ruse of power.

Making boundaries: sexuality as alliance and power

In *The History of Sexuality*, Michel Foucault contrasts sexuality to alliance. Alliance, an aristocratic strategy for maintaining bloodlines and consolidating property, prevailed up through the eighteenth century and presumed a separation between sexual reproduction and sexual desire. In a regime of alliance, few equated love and marriage; hence the sense in courtly love that the ideal lover was never a husband, or the acceptance of extra-marital affairs among the aristocracy. Sexuality, as Foucault defines it, refers to the ways that sexual desire and knowledge became essential to a sense of self and to a form of middle-class power. Though Foucault traces that equation of sex and subjectivity to medieval practices of confession, he argues that it developed fully only in the nineteenth century. Well before Foucault, Peter Cominos influentially argued that the middle class used the notion of sexual respectability to define itself against both workers and elites, newly defined as licentious.[4] Following Foucault, Nancy Armstrong highlighted the political stakes of sexuality: by making respectability and self-control a new basis for political power, the middle class argued that only those who could govern themselves had a right to govern others.[5] Reformers appointed themselves arbiters of sexual morality and, as such, sought to prevent children from masturbating, consenting male adults from having sex with other male adults, and working-class men and women from mingling in factories. Keenly alive to the ways that sex became an instrument of exploitation as well as of corruption, they declared themselves protectors of the weak and sought to prevent aristocratic men from buying sex with young girls.

The conceptual and chronological distinctions between alliance and sexuality should not obscure the many ways that alliance survived into the nineteenth century. Sexual interactions and unions continued to serve the purpose of alliance: to demarcate boundaries between races, classes, nations,

---

4 Peter Cominos, 'Late-Victorian Sexual Respectability and the Social System', *International Review of Social History* 8 (1963), pp. 18–48, 216–50.
5 See Nancy Armstrong, *Desire and Domestic Fiction: A Political History of the Novel* (Oxford University Press, 1987).

and especially between men and women. That sexuality was one of the key traits differentiating the civilized from the savage was considered common sense during an imperial era. Even the most liberal ideologues of empire considered non-Europeans to lack the sexual self-control they attributed to British men and women, despite evidence to the contrary. British men in the colonies had sex with native men, hired native women as prostitutes, lived with them as mistresses, and even married them, but the delusion that natives were more sexually permissive than their rulers remained intact among most British people.[6] In popular entertainment, Sarah Bartmann, the African woman exhibited in 1810 as the 'Venus Hottentot', notorious for her large buttocks and genitalia, had been considered visible proof of the excessive sexuality of African women.[7] In 1857, the British responded with violent outrage to reports that Indian men had raped British women during a military uprising.[8] Throughout the period, novelists reinforced the belief that British Christians were uniquely able to restrain sexual desire by associating figures marked as racial and religious outsiders with sexual predation: Fagin in *Oliver Twist*, Heathcliff in *Wuthering Heights*, and Ferdinand Lopez in *The Prime Minister*.

Marriage played a special role in regulating empire. The British sought to influence marriage laws and customs in countries they took over, for example by changing age-of-consent laws or challenging the treatment of widows. Many British writers contrasted a Christian ideal of monogamous marriage between equal souls to the polygamous treatment of women as inferior objects. John Stuart Mill was more critical of marriage but similarly contrasted progress to savagery by calling the subjection of women an instance of 'the primitive state of slavery lasting on' and obstructing 'the progress of civilization'. Responding to the common objection that Christianity enjoins wives to obey their husbands, he invidiously compared Eastern religions to Christianity: 'To pretend that Christianity was intended to stereotype existing forms of government and society, and protect them against change, is to reduce it to the level of Islamism or of Brahminism.'[9]

---

6 See Philippa Levine, 'Sexuality, Gender, and Empire', in Philippa Levine (ed.), *Gender and Empire* (Oxford University Press, 2004), pp. 134–55.

7 See Anne Fausto-Sterling, 'Gender, Race, and Nation: The Comparative Anatomy of "Hottentot" Women in Europe, 1815–1817', in Jennifer Terry and Jacqueline Urla (eds.), *Deviant Bodies* (Bloomington: Indiana University Press, 1995), pp. 19–48.

8 See Jenny Sharpe, *Allegories of Empire: The Figure of Woman in the Colonial Text* (Minneapolis: University of Minnesota Press, 1993), pp. 57–82.

9 John Stuart Mill, 'The Subjection of Women', in John Stuart Mill and Harriet Taylor Mill, *Essays on Sex Equality*, ed. Alice S. Rossi (University of Chicago Press, 1970), pp. 130, 131, 177.

It was the rare author who dared to suggest that imperial rulers often failed to rule themselves, as George Eliot did in a dinner party scene in *Daniel Deronda* (1876), when one of the guests discussing a recent outbreak of violence in Jamaica remarks that 'the blacks would be manageable enough if it were not for the half-breeds'. Only Daniel, who at this point in the novel believes he is illegitimate and is thus keenly aware of his tenuous hold on the status of British gentleman, reminds the company that 'the whites had to thank themselves for the half-breeds'.[10]

Sexuality also cemented solidarity among middle-class Britons by demarcating them from other European nationalities. Here the sharpest border marked by sexual stereotypes was the one with France, which juxtaposed the stolid Northern European and the passionate, theatrical Mediterranean. British literary critics denounced French authors for depicting sexual practices such as adultery, homosexuality, incest, bestiality, and necrophilia.[11] The few British novelists who hinted at such topics in turn tended to associate them with France. In *Little Dorrit*, it is in France that Miss Wade hands Arthur Clennam the 'History of a Self-Tormentor', which explains her perverse attachment to another woman; in *Dombey and Son*, it is in a French apartment that Edith Dombey appears to be on the verge of adultery; and in *Vanity Fair*, the seductive Becky Sharp has a French mother and speaks excellent French. Perverse and predatory men typed as foreign include Rigaud/Blandois in *Little Dorrit*, Count Fosco in *The Woman in White*, and Dracula in the novel that bears his name. In *Trilby*, George Du Maurier describes Svengali as a combination of Frenchman, Jew, and Eastern European, noting that his 'vicious imaginations ... which look so tame in English print, sounded much more ghastly in French, pronounced with a Hebrew-German accent, and uttered in his hoarse, rasping, nasal, throaty rook's caw, his big yellow teeth baring themselves in a mongrel canine snarl, his heavy upper eyelids drooping over his insolent black eyes'.[12] The press coverage of the Jack the Ripper murders and Oscar Wilde's trials towards the end of the century further linked sexuality with nationhood by associating the sex murderer and the sodomite with foreign bodies.[13]

10 George Eliot, *Daniel Deronda* (London: Penguin, 1995), chapter 29, p. 331.
11 See Sharon Marcus, 'Comparative Sapphism', in Margaret Cohen and Carolyn Dever (eds.), *The Literary Channel: The Inter-National Invention of the Novel* (Princeton University Press, 2002), pp. 251–85.
12 George Du Maurier, *Trilby* (Oxford: Oxford World's Classics, 1998), Part Third, p. 92.
13 See Sander Gilman, *The Jew's Body* (New York: Routledge, 1991), pp. 104–27; Judith Walkowitz, *City of Dreadful Delight: Narratives of Sexual Danger in Late-Victorian London* (University of Chicago Press, 1992), pp. 191–228; Ed Cohen, *Talk on the Wilde Side* (New York: Routledge, 1992).

In Victorian literature, sexuality defined class alliance in two key ways. First, sexual self-control defined membership in the middle class; second, fictional narratives aimed at middle-class readers rarely depicted happy marriages across class lines. Charlotte Brontë's *Jane Eyre* exemplifies both ways of cementing sex and class. Jane resists her desire to become Rochester's mistress and thus demonstrates the self-discipline celebrated by Samuel Smiles in his best-selling work *Self-Help* and John Stuart Mill in his essay *On Liberty*.[14] Even before she discovers that Rochester is married, but believes that he is on the verge of becoming engaged to Blanche Ingram, she declares to him, ' "I am a free human being with an independent will; which I now exert to leave you." ' After discovering Rochester's marriage to Bertha Mason (another sexually threatening figure coded as a racial outsider), Jane reiterates to herself her determination to 'keep the law given by God; sanctioned by man' although 'body and soul rise in mutiny against their rigour'.[15] By the time Jane ultimately marries Rochester, the social and economic gaps between them have narrowed. No longer the lowly governess overcome by the Byronic employer whose power she resists throughout their courtship, the married Jane is a woman of wealth in her own right, while Rochester has lost his grand house to fire, though he still possesses a manor house where he and Jane live after marrying.

In *Jane Eyre*, the social proximity of spouses at novel's end allegorizes a feminist belief in sexual equality as much as it does a bourgeois allegiance to ideas of social caste, but most Victorian literature expressed more simply the idea that sexuality should maintain class lines by uniting in marriage only people belonging to the same class. The prevalence of cousin marriages in Victorian fiction reflects the common belief that marriage should reproduce the existing social order and keep property within families. Even apparent exceptions only prove the rule. In *Middlemarch*, Will Ladislaw is poor and Dorothea Brooke is rich, but both are equally cultivated, and Dorothea gives up an estate when she marries Will, which minimizes their economic inequality. In *The Woman in White*, Walter Hartright hesitates to tell Laura Fairlie of his love for her, not only because she is engaged to be married, but also because she is his superior in birth and wealth. Walter and Laura do ultimately wed, but only after Laura has been so physically, legally, and

---

14 Jeffrey Nunokawa, in an essay on 'Sexuality' for Deirdre David (ed.), *The Cambridge Companion to the Victorian Novel* (Cambridge University Press, 2001), notes that Victorian novels teach readers to discipline desire and defer its gratification, p. 126.
15 Charlotte Brontë, *Jane Eyre* (London: Penguin, 1996), chapters 23, 27, pp. 284, 356.

financially diminished that she owes her few resources to Walter's heroic efforts. When, towards century's end, Sydney Grundy featured a cross-class marriage in his play *The New Woman*, he did so to make the polemical point that because feminists had denatured upper-class men and women, a man could find a real wife only among the poor. Gerald, the main character, finally accepts that his wife may never be a lady because he comes to appreciate her willingness to be 'Only a woman'.[16]

Victorian ideas about sexuality also created a division between pure women, who had sex only with their husbands, and fallen women, who were disqualified from ever marrying. Although in reality prostitution was often a phase for working-class women who then became wives and mothers, most Victorian poetry and fiction tended to caution that once fallen, always fallen.[17] The speaker in Augusta Webster's poem 'A Castaway' (1870), a woman of middle-class birth, who is now mistress to various wealthy men, verbally scourges herself as 'the thing / Of shame and rottenness ... / Who should not dare to take the name of wife / On my polluted lips'.[18] Similarly, the male speaker in Mathilde Blind's poem 'The Russian Student's Tale' instantly recoils from the woman he loves when he learns of the sexual past that makes her a 'social leper': 'I hear tell with cheek aflame / Her ineradicable shame – / ... Oh, loved and lost beyond recall!'.[19] *Tess of the D'Urbervilles*, Esther in Elizabeth Gaskell's *Mary Barton*, Little Em'ly in Charles Dickens's *David Copperfield*, and Hetty Sorel in George Eliot's *Adam Bede*, all dead or exiled by the end of the novels in which they appear, suggest that Victorian fiction gave fallen women no future.

A final border patrolled by sexuality, policed even more strictly than that between pure and impure women, was the line dividing men and women into distinct classes with different relationships to labour, capital, money, and property. Then as now, wives and daughters received no pay for doing household work or managing household servants. Though wives had the right to financial support from their husbands and could incur debts in their husbands' names, for most of Victoria's reign they had no rights to their own property or income (except for special provisions under the law of equity). Nor did a wife have any rights to her children or her own person;

---

16 Sydney Grundy, *The New Woman* (London: Chiswick Press, 1894), p. 104.
17 On the social reality of prostitution, see Judith Walkowitz, *Prostitution and Victorian Society: Women, Class, and the State* (Cambridge University Press, 1980).
18 Augusta Webster, *Portraits* (London: Macmillan, 1870), p. 52, lines 393–7.
19 *The Poetical Works of Mathilde Blind*, ed. Arthur Symons (London: T. Fisher Unwin, 1900), pp. 226–7, 228, lines 127, 83–6.

only fathers had legal custody over offspring and there was no legal concept of marital rape. Caroline Norton sought to change those laws in publications that included *English Laws for Women in the Nineteenth Century* (1854), as did the women who founded and wrote for the feminist periodical the *English Woman's Journal*. In *He Knew He Was Right* (1868–9), Anthony Trollope dramatized the damage done by a husband who takes marital law literally and decides he will no longer give his spouse 'the privileges of his wife, if she refused to render him the obedience which was his privilege'. The imperious Trevelyan's obsession with his wife Emily's purported infidelity tips into madness when he demands that she confess to adultery she has not committed, simply to demonstrate her 'submission' to him. Gradually, other characters begin to perceive him less as a wronged husband with a legitimate complaint and more as a 'tyrant' who above all else loves 'his power as a man' and thus 'misuses [his] power grossly and cruelly'. Although both the narrator and various characters deem Trevelyan insane, they also note that even when he abducts his young son from his wife, he acts within the law; he is a tyrant 'because he had the power to tyrannise'.[20] Only towards the end of the century did reformers and authors begin successfully to challenge the power that husbands legally exercised over wives. An article on 'Wife Torture', first published in the *Contemporary Review* in 1878, by journalist and reformer Frances Power Cobbe, inspired lawmakers to make it easier for working women to press charges against violent husbands, while Sarah Grand's novel *The Heavenly Twins* (1893), about a woman who contracts a venereal disease from her husband, challenged the rectitude of women's sexual submission in marriage.

The economic division between women and men that obtained even for the unmarried further secured the differences between the sexes. For much of the nineteenth century, middle-class women had limited educational and economic options. The governess and the seamstress were, despite their gentility, often portrayed as objects of pity or scorn in fiction and non-fiction. The entry of middle- and upper-class women into universities and office work after the 1870s seemed revolutionary enough to justify the neologism 'New Women' to refer to those who supported themselves and lived without supervision. For working-class women, the difficulty of earning a living or family wage enforced dependence on male providers, and

---

20 Anthony Trollope, *He Knew He Was Right* (London: Oxford University Press, 1963), chapter 5, p. 44; chapter 11, p. 99; chapter 62, p. 591; chapter 79, p. 742; chapter 98, p. 919; chapter 62, p. 591.

the sense that proper ladies did not earn their own bread was so entrenched that labouring women were often considered either unsexed or oversexed.[21]

Though marriage was the only legitimate sphere for middle-class women for much of the century, it was rarely acknowledged as a form of work. More commonly, authors romanticized the wifely role. In *He Knew He Was Right*, the narrator pities the 'old maids who are born and live and die without that vital interest in the affairs of life which nothing but family duties, the care of children, or at least of a husband, will give to a woman'. Yet in the same novel, a series of characters acknowledge that women marry to survive – that 'in that matter of falling in love it was absolutely necessary that bread and cheese should be considered'. Other novelists dramatized more starkly that many women married because it was their only means of support. As a delightfully blunt secondary character in Margaret Oliphant's novel *Hester* describes it, courtship is 'of course . . . a matter of business . . . and very important business too. What can be so important for a girl as settling?'[22]

Because men were patrons, and women their dependants, another line emerged separating men as sexual subjects and actors from women as sexual objects or reactors. Consider the many moments in Victorian literature when men speak of women as captives or treat them as objects of exchange. In Robert Browning's dramatic monologue 'My Last Duchess' (1842), the poem's speaker is an aristocratic husband whose sense of sexual ownership in his wife takes the extreme form of killing her because 'she liked whate'er / She looked on, and her looks went everywhere'. The jealous duke destroys his wife – 'I gave commands; / Then all smiles stopped together'. The duke's power reduces his wife to an image he can fully possess, 'my last duchess painted on the wall, / Looking as if she were alive'.[23] Though the duke's reaction to his wife's flirtatiousness is extreme, the strictures on even oblique forms of female sexual agency made the coquette an object of opprobrium in

21 On the economic bases of the supposedly natural divisions between men and women, see Mary Poovey, *Uneven Developments: The Ideological Work of Gender in Mid-Victorian England* (University of Chicago Press, 1988). On the working-class politics that awarded family wages to men alone, see Anna Clark, *The Struggle for the Breeches: Gender and the Making of the English Working Class* (Berkeley: University of California Press, 1995). On the sexual difference between middle-class and working-class women, see Nancy Armstrong, 'Gender and the Victorian Novel', in David, *Cambridge Companion to the Victorian Novel*, pp. 97–100.

22 Trollope, *He Knew He Was Right*, chapter 51, p. 483; chapter 4, p. 30; Margaret Oliphant, *Hester: A Story of Contemporary Life*, 3 vols. (London: Macmillan, 1883), vol. III, chapter 1, p. 2.

23 Robert Browning, *The Major Works*, ed. Adam Roberts (Oxford University Press, 2005), p. 102, lines 23–4, 45–6; p. 101, lines 1–2.

many other works. In Charlotte Bronte's *Villette*, narrator Lucy Snowe dismisses Ginevra Fanshawe as 'preposterously vain' (Chapter 14, p. 214); Eliza Lynn Linton ranted against the 'slang, bold talk, and fastness' of 'The Girl of the Period' in an 1868 *Saturday Review* essay; and critics such as Geraldine Jewsbury were disgusted by Rhoda Broughton's novel *Cometh Up as a Flower* (1867) because of the 'very ardent terms' and 'sensual sentimentality' the young woman who narrates the novel uses to describe her male lover and her response to him.[24]

The protocols of courtship recorded in Victorian marriage plots reinforced a sexual politics in which men led and women followed. In *Hester*, the eponymous protagonist chafes at the 'degrading suspense' she must endure until the man she thinks she loves decides to propose yet still feels that to 'know exactly how he regarded her would much help her in deciding ... how she regarded him. ... She was half ashamed to feel that [her sentiments] depended on his. Was this a confession of feminine inferiority?'. Oliphant, writing in the 1880s, allows her heroine to defy the limits placed on female agency by having her perform a 'heroic deed'; even more daringly, Oliphant gives Hester 'two men whom she may choose between', while leaving it an open question whether she will marry at all. New Woman literature attacked the double standard even more boldly. Where Trollope had asserted that a man who is 'false' to his wife 'does not disgrace her ... [b]ut the slightest rumor on a woman's name is a load of infamy on her husband's shoulders', New Woman writers argued for a single sexual standard that would either require men to be sexually pure or allow women to be sexually free.[25] By the 1890s, the prostitute no longer symbolized the dangers women faced if they strayed outside marriage but had become an emblem of sexual hypocrisy. As a dying prostitute in Mathilde Blind's poem 'The Message' (1891) angrily puts it, 'Was she a wicked girl? What then? / She didn't care a pin! / She was not worse than all those men / Who looked so shocked in public, when / They made and

---

24 Charlotte Brontë, *Villette* (London: Penguin, 2004), chapter 14, p. 159; unsigned article [Eliza Lynn Linton], 'The Girl of the Period', *Saturday Review* (4 March 1868), p. 339; Geraldine Jewsbury, review of *Cometh Up as A Flower*, in the *Athenaeum* 2060 (20 April 1867), pp. 514, 515.

25 Oliphant, *Hester*, vol. II, chapter 13, p. 221, chapter 12, p. 197, chapter 14, p. 250; vol. III, chapter 15, p. 264; Trollope, *He Knew He Was Right*, chapter 5, p. 43. See Ann Ardis, *New Women, New Novels: Feminism and Early Modernism* (New Brunswick, NJ: Rutgers University Press, 1990); Sally Ledger, *The New Woman: Fiction and Feminism at the Fin de Siècle* (Manchester University Press, 1997); and Elaine Showalter, *Sexual Anarchy: Gender and Culture at the Fin de Siècle* (New York: Viking Penguin, 1990).

shared her sin.'[26] As the nineteenth century ended, sexuality was increasingly perceived as a force more likely to overturn the borders between men and women than to secure them.

Breaking barriers

Even before the end of the century, however, Victorian literature represented sexuality as an uncontainable force with the power to shatter the self and society. The 1860s were a key turning point. The staunchly conservative Miss Stanbury sums up that decade's sexual upheaval in *He Knew He Was Right* when she sputters about 'divorce bills, and woman's rights, and penny papers, and false hair, and married women being just like giggling girls, and giggling girls knowing just as much as married women'. Even before that, the boundary between fallen and respectable women could seem surprisingly porous. On the one hand, the distance between pure and impure women was seen as absolute, because fallen women could never be restored to purity. On the other hand, the distinction was highly tenuous, because female innocence was deemed so fragile that a woman risked corruption from mere proximity to a fallen woman. In *David Copperfield* (1850), Mr Wickfield prevents his daughter Agnes from giving Annie Strong a goodnight kiss because he suspects Annie of adultery. In Dante Gabriel Rossetti's poem 'Jenny' (1870), the male speaker notices Jenny's similarity to his 'cousin Nell' even as he chastises himself for comparing them: 'So pure, – so fall'n! How dare to think / Of the first common kindred link?'. He does dare to think of it, however, and the dash he places between the parallel phrases 'so pure' and 'so fall'n' links the two women as much as it separates them, as do the generically female weaknesses he thinks they share – love of pleasure, dress, and novelty. Even a novel like *Trilby*, whose hero Little Billee manages to discount his beloved Trilby's sexual experience when he declares that 'love levels all' (Part Fourth, p. 134), belies its character's radical vision by assigning Trilby the fallen woman's usual literary lot of death without marriage.[27]

The prostitute thus became a figure for contagion, for the insidious spread of disease from one person to another in ways that defied the

---

26 Blind, *Poetical Works*, p. 245, lines 66–70.
27 Trollope, *He Knew He Was Right*, chapter 15, p. 400; Dante Gabriel Rossetti, *The Works of Dante Gabriel Rossetti*, ed. W. M. Rossetti (London: Ellis, 1911), p. 89, lines 207–8; Du Maurier, *Trilby*, Part Fourth, p. 134.

apparent separation of bodies, genders, and classes. In 'The Message', Blind wrote that 'The fallen woman, in her despair, is / ... a thing to fear / Like fever-tainted air' (line 153, p. 248). Literally associated with contagion in debates about how to curb venereal disease, the prostitute also became a figure for a more pervasive anxiety about men's ability to determine their fates in an era that celebrated the power of a strong, autonomous will.[28] In 'Jenny,' a male speaker watches the woman of the title sleep: 'Yet Jenny, looking long at you, / The woman almost fades from view. / A cipher of man's changeless sum / Of lust, past, present, and to come / Is left'. As a 'cipher' of male 'lust,' Jenny represents the uncontrollable, disruptive desires men feel unable to master. As Leslie Minot has shown, the prostitute also became a figure for the blurring of temporal borders as the possessor of an aberrant memory, irrevocably separated from her innocent past and com-pelled to erase consciousness of a shameful present.[29] As the speaker in 'Jenny' asks himself, 'is there hue or shape defin'd / In Jenny's desecrated mind, / Where all contagious currents meet, / A Lethe of the middle street?' His answer is no, because, as the reference to Lethe implies, Jenny's mind retains no memories: 'as they coil those eddies clot, / And night and day remember not'. Rossetti's Jenny never wakes to express any desires of her own, but in literature that emphasized the prostitute's wish to redeem herself, memory plays a key role. In Dickens's baroque Christmas tale 'The Haunted Man' (1848), a man who has obtained the power to erase all painful memories confronts the limits of that gift when he encounters a fallen woman and realizes that her 'awakened recollection' of a past wrong can restore 'the first trace of her old humanity' to her ravaged face.[30] In Blind's poem 'The Message', a memory of her mother similarly transfigures and redeems a dying prostitute. Ironically, the ability of memory to undo temporal boundaries by allowing the past to surge into the present helps restore a modicum of selfhood to the fallen woman so often accused of undoing all order.

The sense that passion could disrupt self and society went well beyond debates about prostitution. Desire as a dangerous, anti-social force storms

---

28 Blind, *Poetical Works*, p. 248, line 153. See Amanda Anderson, *Tainted Souls and Painted Faces: The Rhetoric of Fallenness in Victorian Culture* (Ithaca, NY: Cornell University Press, 1993).

29 Rossetti, *Works*, p. 43, lines 276–80; Leslie Minot, 'Remembering Sex: Prostitution, Memory, and History in Nineteenth-century French and British Literature', PhD thesis, University of California Berkeley, 1998.

30 Rossetti, *Works*, p. 41, lines 163–6, 169–70; Charles Dickens, 'The Haunted Man', in *The Christmas Books*, vol. II (Harmondsworth: Penguin, 1971), p. 312.

through Victorian poetry and fiction, with metaphors of passion as flood and fire abounding. In *The Mill on the Floss*, soon after Maggie Tulliver drifts down a river with Stephen Guest and becomes a social outcast, she dies in a flood. Fires and storms erupt at key moments in *Jane Eyre*; in Christina Rossetti's *Goblin Market*, one sister's craving for forbidden fruit is matched in strength only by her sister's self-sacrificing love. Elizabeth Siddal, model to the Pre-Raphaelites and herself a poet, described love as an exhausting force in 'Worn Out' (1856): 'I cannot give to thee the love / I gave so long ago – / The love that turned and struck me down / Amid the blinding snow'.[31] In 'The Defence of Guenevere' (1858), William Morris has the adulterous queen describe her passion as both a burning that leaves her 'white with flame' and as an oceanic merger in which she and Lancelot slide 'Until one surely reached the sea at last, / And felt strange new joy'.[32]

The poets lambasted as 'the Fleshly School' of the 1860s revelled in desire's corrosive ability to shatter the self. In 'The Blessed Damozel' (1850), Dante Gabriel Rossetti wrote of love overcoming temporal and metaphysical barriers between past and present, life and death, earth and heaven, body and soul. Writing of the blessed damozel, dead for ten years, the poetic speaker momentarily experiences her physical presence: 'Yet now, and in this place, / Surely she leaned o'er me – her hair / Fell all about my face.'[33] Algernon Swinburne turned to pagan antiquity to author-ize his vision of blissfully punishing love. The spurned lover in 'The Triumph of Time' (1866) glories in his thwarted, self-sacrificing passion – 'To have died if you cared I should die for you, clung / To my life if you bade me' – and imagines the apex of love as a shared death: 'I wish we were dead together to-day, / Lost sight of, hidden away out of sight, / Clasped and clothed in the cloven clay, / Out of the world's way, out of the light, / ... / Made one with death, filled full of the night'. Unable to merge with the beloved in a mutually annihilating embrace, he redirects his addresses to the sea, an alternative to the living woman not because she assuages his wounds but because she inflicts them more completely: 'Thy sweet hard kisses are strong like wine, / Thy large embraces are keen like pain'.[34]

31 Elizabeth Siddal, 'Worn Out', in Thomas J. Collins and Vivienne Rundle (eds.), *The Broadview Anthology of Victorian Poetry and Poetic Theory: Concise Edition* (Ontario: Broadview Press, 2000), p. 410, lines 9–12.

32 William Morris, 'The Defence of Guenevere', in Collins and Rundle, *Broadview Anthology*, pp. 439, 440, lines 70, 98–9.

33 Rossetti, *Works*, p. 3, lines 21–2.

34 Algernon Charles Swinburne, *Poems and Ballads, First Series: The Poems of Algernon Charles Swinburne*, 6 vols. (London: Chatto, 1904), vol. I, pp. 37–8, lines 105–6, 113–20, 268–9.

In form as well as content, Victorian writers linked desire to imaginative writing's ability to overcome the separation between persons and the physical boundaries of space and time. In 'Anactoria' (1866), for example, Swinburne assumes the voice of Sappho and speaks of her desire for the woman of the title: 'That I could drink thy veins as wine, and eat / Thy breasts like honey! That from face to feet / Thy body were abolished and consumed, / And in my flesh thy very flesh entombed!'.[35] Swinburne's impersonation of the lesbian lyric poet confounds the differences between antiquity and modernity, male and female desire, life and death. Though Swinburne was uniquely extravagant in his identification with a lesbian poet, his use of a fictional voice to cross gender borders was quite common. In *Bleak House*, Charles Dickens alternated between a magisterial third-person narrator and the first-person voice of Esther Summerson. Though Dickens's impersonation of Esther, who rarely expresses desire directly, raised fewer eyebrows than Swinburne's ventriloquism of Sappho, in both cases a male author used the mimetic qualities of fiction to inhabit a female persona. Linguistic cross-dressing was also quite common in sensation fiction and may have contributed to the criticisms levelled against it. Wilkie Collins wrote a substantial section of *The Woman in White* in the voice of Marian Halcombe, who herself combines masculine and feminine traits. Poet Amy Levy often wrote either as a man addressing a female beloved ('Ralph to Mary') or as an unmarked 'I' addressing an equally unmarked 'you' ('Love in Exile', 'Haunted Streets'). In other poems, Levy wrote as a neutral 'I' openly celebrating a female beloved ('Sinfonia Eroica: To Sylvia', 'London in July', and 'At a Dinner Party').[36] The poems articulate multiple possibilities: the female adoption of a male voice; the articulation of a love that floats free of gender; and the use of the gender-neutral first and second persons to suggest lyric love between women.

The power of fiction to conjure personhood made words themselves a vehicle for shuttling readers back and forth across the fences separating adult from child or male from female. The linguistic playfulness of a work like Lewis Carroll's *Alice in Wonderland* (1865) allows male adult and female child to trade places.[37]

---

35 *Ibid.*, p. 60, lines 111–14.
36 See Amy Levy, *Xantippe and Other Verse* (Cambridge: E. Johnson and Co., 1881); *A Minor Poet and Other Verse* (London: T. Fisher Unwin, 1884); *A London Plane Tree and Other Verse* (London: T. Fisher Unwin, 1889).
37 See James Kincaid, *Child-Loving: The Erotic Child and Victorian Culture* (New York: Routledge, 1992), and Catherine Robson, *Men in Wonderland: The Lost Girlhood of the Victorian Gentleman* (Princeton University Press, 2001).

Fiction's ability to move readers made literature itself a focus of both erotic excitement and sexual policing. Thomas Laqueur has noted that those who deplored masturbation associated it with the power of imagination to free individuals from their dependence on others to fulfill their needs and pleasures.[38] Conversely, fiction was often seen as a dangerous goad to masturbation, not only because its content could arouse readers but also because it had the formal power to promote fantasy by allowing them to occupy multiple positions in a given story or scene. Even plain-spoken Realists were subject to chastisement if they got carried away by fiction's transporting powers. When Anthony Trollope wrote 'A Ride across Palestine' (1861), in which a man falls in love with his younger male traveling companion, an editor expressed anxiety about publishing it, although the tale ultimately reveals the young man to be a young woman in disguise. The story's setting in a region where religions mingle, and remnants of the past define the contemporary landscape, allegorizes fiction's power to carry readers across time and space and into the skins of others. Bram Stoker's Dracula represents the same powers of fiction in a more Gothic mode. Dracula literally gets under his victims' skins to create a type of being, the undead, that resembles the simultaneously real and unreal status of fictional characters themselves.

Fiction's capacity to blur boundaries led critics to brand various sub-genres as threats to society. Henry Mansel compared sensation fiction to an addictive drug, a contagious disease, and decaying garbage because it allegedly overexcited readers and exposed lurid aspects of everyday life.[39] By focusing on what Henry James called 'the mysteries which are at our own doors ... the terrors of the cheerful country-house and the busy London lodgings', sensation fiction levelled the barriers between public and private, high and low entertainment, and middle- and working-class audiences.[40] The Obscene Publications Act of 1857 sought to limit the access of women and young people to sexually explicit literature, while others called for censorship of newspaper coverage of divorce trials, even as sensation novelists made bigamy a favourite plot device.[41] The imagined border between French immorality and British propriety was upheld when,

38 Thomas W. Laqueur, *Solitary Sex: A Cultural History of Masturbation* (New York: Zone Books, 2003), pp. 247–358.
39 Henry Mansel, 'Sensation Fiction', *Quarterly Review* 113 (1863), pp. 481–514.
40 Henry James, 'Miss Braddon', *The Nation* (9 November 1865), p. 593.
41 See Barbara Leckie, *Culture and Adultery: The Novel, The Newspaper, and the Law 1857–1914* (Philadelphia: University of Pennsylvania Press, 1999).

in 1889, the state indicted and convicted Henry Vizetelly for publishing translations of novels by Emile Zola and other French novelists who depicted adultery, rape, prostitution, and homosexuality. In an article cuttingly entitled 'Tommyrotics' (1895), Hugh Stutfield dismissed the 'diseased imaginings' of what he called 'erotomaniac fiction' in which female authors wrote about pleasure and rebellion.[42]

Critics like Mansel and Stutfield fought a losing battle, however, for print culture made it as difficult to control representations of sexuality as to control sexual acts themselves. In the 1880s and 1890s, a series of scandals and trials, along with the innovations of New Woman fiction, put paid to the mid-Victorian consensus that sexuality existed primarily in the service of alliance. In 1886, newspapers published detailed accounts of a divorce trial in which Virginia Crawford claimed that liberal MP Charles Dilke had been her lover and had persuaded her to try such French perversities as sex with another woman. The Cleveland Street scandals of 1889 revealed the existence of a ring of telegraph boys who provided prominent men with sexual services. The press reaction to such revelations was censorious but itself uncensored, making sex between men a matter of public knowledge and discussion. When Charles Whibley reviewed Oscar Wilde's novel *The Picture of Dorian Gray* for the *Scots Observer* in 1890, he could count on readers understanding what he meant when he lambasted Wilde for writing for 'outlawed noblemen and perverted telegraph-boys'.[43] Wilde's play *The Importance of Being Earnest* (1895) delighted West End theatre audiences with its farcical courtship plot and its paean to a realm of pleasure outside marriage, which Algernon calls Bunburying, after the fictional friend he pretends to visit whenever he needs to get away. As Algernon puts it, 'A man who marries without knowing Bunbury has a very tedious time of it.'[44] As the testimony at his trials suggested, Wilde himself paid little heed to the distinctions between respectable married life and a sexual underworld. Men who later blackmailed Wilde or testified against him had spent time with him in his Chelsea home, at the Savoy hotel, while on vacation with his wife and children, and in London lodgings where heavy curtains, strong perfumes, and women's costumes turned a man's rented rooms into a British fantasy of an Oriental seraglio. As the 1890s unfolded, writers began

42 Hugh E. M. Stutfield, 'Tommyrotics', *Blackwood's Magazine* 57: 956 (1895), p. 837.
43 Cited in Appendix H, Oscar Wilde, *The Picture of Dorian Gray*, ed. Norman Page (Peterborough: Broadview Press, 1998), p. 274.
44 Oscar Wilde, *The Importance of Being Earnest*, in *The Major Works*, ed. Isobel Murray (Oxford University Press, 2000), p. 487.

to assert, rather than merely hint, that women, like men, could experience sexual desire outside wedlock. In an influential essay on 'Marriage' (1888), Mona Caird claimed that women were not naturally chaste, and George Egerton, Victoria Cross, and Netta Syrett published short stories in which female characters experience their greatest erotic pleasure with men who are not their husbands. Anti-feminist reaction flourished, and the state sentenced Wilde to two years of prison and hard labour, but the last decade of the century was the golden age of Bunburying in Victorian literature.

Love

In the twentieth century, the concept of sexuality attracted thinkers who wanted to purge adult discourse of mawkishness. Freudians replaced what they considered sentimental idealizations of love with an aggressive desiring libido; the conflict of Eros and Thanatos; and anal, oral, and genital phases. Foucauldians classified sexuality as an offshoot of power, as the discourses, institutions, and norms that informed people's relationships to bodily comportment and personal identity. As we have seen, the Victorians themselves already understood sexual desires and acts as forces that could make and break persons and classes, but they also associated those desires and acts with deep and sincere emotion, with the 'abandonment', 'rapture', and 'feeling' that Virginia Woolf wrote of finding in Christina Rossetti and Alfred Tennyson but in none of the poets writing after World War I.[45] In a 1957 account of The Victorian Frame of Mind that remains definitive, Walter Houghton subsumed all discussion of sex under the rubric of 'love'. What may seem a timid circumlocution, designed to avoid naming sex, also cannily expresses a peculiarly Victorian directness with regard to feeling. Though reticent about, even embarrassed by sex, many Victorians openly embraced the intensely positive emotions that can accompany it.

Two genres that highlight the Victorian ease with deep feeling are poetry and life-writing. In both, one finds authors surrendering to the belief that sexual love can make two people into a single being. In 'Monna Innominata' (1881), a sonnet sequence that imagines a female beloved, on the model of Dante's Beatrice, speaking for herself, Christina Rossetti wrote of 'the love which makes us one': 'For verily love knows not "mine" or "thine"; / With separate "I" and "thou" free love has done, / For one is both and both are

---

45 Virginia Woolf, A Room of One's Own (New York: Harcourt, Brace & World, 1979), pp. 14, 15.

one in love'.[46] Poet couples who wrote of love's power to meld two into one performed the transformation they described in the very act of writing about it. In 'Sonnets from the Portuguese', Elizabeth Barrett Browning wrote, 'I think of thee! – my thoughts do twine and bud / About thee, as wild vines, about a tree . . . / Yet, O my palm-tree, be it understood / I will not have my thoughts instead of thee / Who art dearer, better!' Preferring the beloved to thoughts of the beloved, immersion in the other to anything generated by the self, the speaker then asks the beloved to shake off the 'bands of greenery' that represent those autonomous thoughts, for 'in this deep joy to see and hear thee . . . / I do not think of thee – I am too near thee'.[47] Barrett Browning's complex image, itself so hard to disentangle into its component parts, figures love as a delicate balance of coalescence and distance. Just as love shifts between similarity and difference, the poem's first and last lines both echo and negate each other: 'I think of thee' – 'I do not think of thee'. As the poem unfolds, each of those clauses comes to mean its apparent inverse: 'I think of thee' here implies too much distance, 'I do not think of thee' now paradoxically signifies perfect union. In 'By the Fire-Side', Barrett Browning's husband Robert, usually the more ornate poet, wrote straightforwardly of 'our one soul': 'At first, 'twas something our two souls should mix as mists do; each is sucked / In each now'. Like his wife, Robert Browning celebrates that interdependence: 'Oh I must feel your brain prompt mine, / Your heart anticipate my heart, / You must be just before, in fine, / See and make me see, for your part, / New depths of the divine!'.[48] Later in the century, Katharine Bradley and Edith Cooper, an aunt and niece who became lovers and co-authored plays and poetry under the name Michael Field, wrote a poem entitled 'Ah, Eros doth not always smite' (1893) in which they linked love to a 'friendship' that 'rises without pain'. In 'It was deep April, and the morn', a poem that celebrates the vows they took on Shakespeare's birthday, they speak as both one and two, jointly memorializing the day on which 'My Love and I took hands and swore, / Against the world, to be / Poets and lovers evermore'.[49]

---

46 Christina Rossetti, *The Complete Poems*, ed. R. W. Crump (London: Penguin, 2001), p. 296, Sonnet 4, lines 9–11.
47 Elizabeth Barrett Browning, *The Complete Poetical Works of Elizabeth Barrett Browning*, ed. Harriet Waters Preston (Cambridge: Riverside Press, 1900), p. 220, Sonnet 29, lines 1–2, 5–7, 10, 12, 14.
48 Robert Browning, *Major Works*, p. 169, lines 127–9, 131, 136–40.
49 Michael Field, *Underneath the Bough: A Book of Verses* (London: George Bell and Sons, 1903), p. 7, line 11; p. 100, lines 3–5.

Life-writing (memoirs, biography, diaries) was another key literary site
for elaborating sexuality as an intersubjective bond. Lovers used the act of
writing a biography to merge with a beloved by telling his or her story,
often disappearing into a narrative voice whose only distinguishing trait was
intimate knowledge of the beloved biographical subject. In her biography of
her lover Charlotte Cushman, Emma Stebbins rarely used the first person
singular, inserting herself into the narrative directly only to say that 'It was
in the winter of 1856–57 that the compiler of these memoirs first made
Miss Cushman's acquaintance, and from that time the current of their two
lives ran, with rare exceptions, side by side.'[50] Like many Victorian
biographers writing about lovers, spouses, or family members, Stebbins
presented those parallel currents as so perfectly merged that she could write
about Cushman with all the authority and invisibility of an omniscient
narrator, describing Cushman's household, impressions, and experiences
as though she and her subject were one person. Others used life-writing
to give form to an egalitarian ideal of love as perfect reciprocity. In his
Autobiography, for example, John Stuart Mill wrote of his relationship with
Harriet Taylor as 'the friendship which has been the honour and chief
blessing of my existence, as well as the source of a great part of all that
I have attempted to do ... for human improvement'. By granting so much
to a woman whom many found unremarkable, Mill incurred a great deal
of mockery, but his decision to tell the story of his own life as in large part
the path towards 'complete companionship' with a beloved expressed a
widely held Victorian ideal.[51]

Intense emotions could also lead to a heightened sense of distance and
difference between lover and beloved that coexisted in febrile tension with
desires for erotic merger. Labour activist and literary critic Edith Simcox
recorded her self-abnegating worship of George Eliot in a secret diary; since
Eliot enjoyed Simcox's attention but did not return her passion, the diary
itself became the site where Simcox experienced the thrill of worshipping
the woman she called 'my goddess'.[52] No clear line divided erotic bonds
based on mutuality from those based on hierarchy. In a diary that she began

50 Emma Stebbins, *Charlotte Cushman: Her Letters and Memories of Her Life* (Boston: Houghton, Osgood, 1879), p. 100.
51 John Stuart Mill, *Autobiography* (1873; New York: The Liberal Arts Press, 1957), pp. 119, 121.
52 Constance M. Fulmer, Margaret E. Barfield (eds.), *A Monument to the Memory of George Eliot: Edith J. Simcox's Autobiography of a Shirtmaker* (New York: Garland Publishing, Inc. 1998), p. 26. Simcox kept her diary from the 1870s through the 1890s but it was not published in complete form until the late twentieth century.

at her lover's request, working woman Hannah Cullwick recorded sexual scenes in which her submission to the genteel Arthur Munby, her lover and later husband, mingled with displays of her superior physical strength, which he was aroused by and admired. As John Addington Symonds noted in his autobiography, British public schools practically institutionalized the sexual servitude of younger boys to older ones: 'Every boy of good looks had a female name, and was recognized either as a public prostitute or as some bigger fellow's "bitch." '[53] Yet the youthful diary of John Russell, later Lord Amberley (and father of philosopher Bertrand Russell) shows that public schools also fostered intensely sentimental erotic bonds among male peers. While at Harrow, Russell wrote at length in 1859 about his love for a schoolmate, remembering a time when 'we were – *almost* friends. *Almost*; I dare not say quite. Perhaps I deceived myself; perhaps my own vain, foolish heart flattered me & made me think I was loved even as I loved.'[54] The same school that Symonds described as obscene and brutal was for Russell a site of fervent, eroticized hero worship.

The wish to merge with a beloved other also existed in relationships that were not defined by sex, such as friendship. Alfred Tennyson's love for Arthur Hallam, a university friend who died young, made his elegy *In Memoriam* as intense a record of love as anything penned by spouses or lovers. *Goblin Market* depicted absolute, self-sacrificing love between sisters; other poems by Christina Rossetti, such as 'A Better Resurrection', and the work of Gerard Manley Hopkins depicted an engulfing erotic link between human beings and Jesus. For aesthetes such as Walter Pater, Oscar Wilde, and Vernon Lee, works of art became the vehicle for fantasies of coalescence with a beloved person or object. In poems celebrating fellow poets, such as Letitia Landon's 'Stanzas on the Death of Mrs Hemans', Christina Rossetti's poem about Landon, 'L. E. L.', and Matthew Arnold's elegy for Arthur Clough, 'Thyrsis', authors separated by death used writing itself to unite themselves with other writers.

The negative feelings that often result from sexual desire and exist alongside love were more difficult for Victorian writers to represent. While writers and readers were passionately interested in elegy and mourning, and readily expressed feelings of loss for loved ones who were dead, they had

---

53 Phyllis Grosskurth (ed.), *The Memoirs of John Addington Symonds* (University of Chicago Press, 1984), p. 94.
54 Bertrand Russell and Patricia Russell (eds.), *The Amberley Papers* (London: George Allen & Unwin, 1966), p. 180.

little tolerance for mixed emotions, directed either at beloveds who were living, or at life itself. Jealousy, so often a component of deep love, often appears in Victorian fiction as a form of stigma, disfiguration, even madness. Anthony Trollope's *He Knew He Was Right* equates jealousy with insanity. In *Little Dorrit*, Charles Dickens depicts Miss Wade as a 'self-tormentor', whose jealous love of a man drives her to seduce his wife's maid into sharing both her home and her fierce resentment of family, friends, and society. Readers were outraged by the rejection, anger, and depression with which Charlotte Brontë's heroines, Jane Eyre and Lucy Snowe, respond to loneliness and unrequited love; one review of *Villette* excoriated its heroine for her 'bitterness' and 'needlessly tragical apostrophes'. Critics of George Meredith's *Modern Love* (1862), a sonnet sequence concerning marital jealousy and breakdown, similarly dismissed his subject matter as unhealthy and 'morbid'.[55] The testiness and embarrassment which characterized the reception of works that paraded ugly feelings may explain why some writers went to the other extreme, suppressing any hint of resentment altogether, or expressing it only through silences and erasures. Emma Stebbins, for example, in her memoir of Charlotte Cushman, gave voice to her dislike of Cushman's other lovers only indirectly – by effacing any mention of them from her story. The national stereotype of the phlegmatic Englishman is inaccurate, given the readiness and earnestness with which Victorian fiction represented strong, deep, positive emotions. The discomfort with bad feeling, however, is undeniable if one compares nineteenth-century English fiction to its Russian counterpart, whose tragic bent illuminates the essentially comic boundaries of the English literary field.

Conclusion

What we now call sexuality includes aspects of physical, emotional, social, and political existence so multifarious that no single essay could cover them all. Important aspects of sexuality that have received little attention here include state efforts to control sexuality through police, courts, prisons, and schools; the medical construction of women's minds and bodies as naturally inferior and deviant; and the reproductive aspects of sexuality that preoccupied nineteenth-century followers of Malthus such as Darwin and the eugenicists. All of these elements were linked to the modes of sexuality

---

55 Unsigned review of *Villette* in *Littell's Living Age* 36 (1853), p. 589; unsigned review of *Modern Love* in *The Athenaeum* (31 May 1862), pp. 718–19.

addressed here: the use of sexuality to make categories, and to break them; to divide individuals and groups, and to unite them.

The diverse meanings of marriage in Victorian literature offer a final glimpse of the multifariousness of nineteenth-century sexuality. Marriage, the chief institution of sexuality at the time, could signify the autonomy of children relative to adults, of individuals relative to society, even of women relative to men, as it does in the many novels of courtship that ratify a woman's right to marry for love. Marriage also meant the enslavement of human beings to convention, the subordination of women to men, and the promulgation of heterosexual lifelong monogamous unions as superior to other forms of desire. Finally, by the end of the century, marriage and sexuality came to represent an ideal of similarity rather than difference, as when the man who loves the female narrator of Grant Allen's *The Type-Writer Girl* (1897) tells her he wants 'a thinking woman, with heart, soul, brain, courage ... a comrade and a help, meet for me'.[56]

The story of the nineteenth century was not a simple one of progress from one form of sexuality to another; Allen's novel, for example, ultimately impedes the marriage of true minds. The very concept of sexuality, born as the nineteenth century closed, preserved many of that epoch's hierarchies and boundaries. At the same time, many of the later developments that claimed to break utterly with the Victorian past merely extended demands for equality and diversity already registered in nineteenth-century literature. The contradictory emotions, impulses, and actions that twentieth-century thinkers grouped under the rubric of sexuality found such ample expression in Victorian literature because both sexuality and literature embody the tensions between sameness and difference, justice and power, order and destruction, that thrive during periods of technological innovation and imperial expansion. In this respect, as in many others, those who come after the Victorians will probably continue for many decades to register the great distance separating them from these predecessors, while simultaneously discovering their surprising proximity.

56 Grant Allen, *The Type-Writer Girl* (Peterborough: Broadview Press, 2004), p. 119.

Aesthetics

ELIZABETH HELSINGER

Derived from the Greek *aesthesis*, for English-speakers at the beginning of Victoria's reign 'aesthetics' was a largely technical, not yet anglicized term for 'the science which treats of the conditions of sensuous perception'. First used in 1750 by Alexander Baumgarten in something like the modern sense ('the philosophy or theory of taste, or of the beautiful in nature and art', *OED*), 'aesthetik' was embraced by both Schiller and Hegel. Coleridge attempted unsuccessfully to introduce it into English as an unfamiliar but useful term to designate a convergence of form, feeling, and intellect, but it was not widely adopted to denote the study of beauty in nature or the visual arts until the 1850s, and was not common in discussions of literature or music before the 1870s. The term's slow anglicization was due in part to its association with German metaphysicians regarded, in Britain, with suspicion. The work of the systematic German philosophers (Kant and Hegel) and their interest in the place of aesthetic pleasure in a theory of mind had few serious students in Britain between Coleridge and Pater. By 1875, James Sully, author of the Encyclopedia Britannica's first entry on aesthetics, gives due place to Kant, Hegel, and other German philosophers.

Most Victorian aesthetic speculation took place not through formal philosophical investigation but through literature and criticism. It was driven by the need to make sense of a perceived abundance of art and literature (from both past and present) and to defend the arts under conditions felt as increasingly hostile: industrialization, worship of the 'Goddess of Getting On', and dependence on a market of under-educated middle and aspiring-middle classes. Major questions of Victorian aesthetics are addressed in, and as, literary form itself: in peculiarly reflexive and self-conscious forms of poetry such as the dramatic monologue, the frame poem, and the translation; in the Realist novel's experiments with framing, description, and point of view; and in the fantasies of Realism's constantly generated others, romance, Gothic, sensation, and detective fiction. Many of these fantasies belong to the literature of art, small-scale forms that dramatize aesthetic problems, including short fictions by Dante Gabriel Rossetti and Christina Rossetti, Walter Pater, Henry James, Vernon Lee (Violet Paget), and Oscar Wilde; Alfred, Lord Tennyson's poetic fables; Robert Browning's dramatic monologues on art and artists or (less often) music and musicians; and Rossetti's Sonnets on Pictures. Throughout the century, literature and criticism were particularly concerned with the psychological experience of beauty – the pleasure derived from sensuous form and sensuous perception – debating optimal conditions for assuring that experience while worrying constantly about its social and ethical effects. Although music had been prominent in German idealist philosophical thinking, Victorian writing on aesthetics takes its terms more frequently from the visual arts. This chapter first examines aesthetic matters as discussed in Victorian criticism, then reviews briefly the overlapping high and vernacular cultures of art that gave particular impetus to aesthetic speculation. A third section considers Victorian ideas about the beautiful and its permissible or prohibited others. The conclusion sketches the contours of a Victorian literature of art.

Aesthetics and criticism

Victorians turned to national traditions when they wrote about the matter of aesthetics. John Ruskin, whose brilliant, passionate, and many-sided writings on art and society from 1838 to the early 1880s were widely influential, was not simply being perverse when, in *Modern Painters* II (1846), he refused the term. Ruskin wanted a word which did not 'degrade' the 'perception and appreciation of ideas of beauty' to 'a mere operation of sense, or perhaps worse, of custom', as *aesthesis*, he thought, might imply.[1] Believing, at least through the early 1850s, that divine design sustained a continued interest in the beauty of natural things and the arts that imaginatively reproduced them, he never fully embraced the shift from an object-based to a perception-based aesthetics. (Like the Jesuit poet Gerard Manley Hopkins, Ruskin could affirm: 'These things, these things were here and but the beholder / Wanting'.[2]) Ruskin addressed an explicitly British audience, setting aside German aesthetics to direct his arguments against inherited

---

1 John Ruskin, *The Works of John Ruskin*, ed. E. T. Cook and Alexander Wedderburn, 39 vols. (London: George Allen, 1903–12), vol. IV, pp. 35–6.
2 Gerard Manley Hopkins, 'Hurrahing in Harvest', in *The Major Works* (Oxford: Oxford University Press, 1986, 2002), p. 134, lines 11–12.

eighteenth-century English neo-classical ideas of generalized beauty and contemporary Utilitarian dismissals of art and beauty as useless. His impassioned defence of the arts was minutely grounded in visual experience but continually insisted on the moral and transcendental reach of perception activated by beauty in nature or art, as in perhaps his most widely quoted formulation: 'To see clearly is poetry, prophecy and religion all in one.'[3] Ruskin proposed 'theoretic' as a better term than 'aesthetic', insisting that perception in his full and demanding sense is the starting point for both the 'contemplative' and 'penetrative' imaginations of artists and beholders. (He derived his preferred term from the Greek *theorein*, Plato's word for philosophical contemplation, adapted from an earlier use denoting the religious and civic spectatorship of those attending performances at the dramatic festivals in Athens.) For readers like Charlotte Brontë (who wrote of *Modern Painters* I 'this book seems to give me eyes'[4]), Ruskin's prose demonstrated an unparalleled visual and verbal attentiveness of a kind that she sought in vain from readers and critics. At the same time (beginning with *The Stones of Venice*, particularly its central chapter, 'The Nature of Gothic', 1853), Ruskin insisted on art's expressive relation both to the social conditions under which it is made and to those under which it is perceived. Building on Thomas Carlyle as well as Augustus Welby Pugin, he attacked the rationalized division of labour, the preoccupation with profits, and the widening gap between rich and poor for their hostility to art in modern Britain. Ruskin's aesthetic theories drew on English empiricism, associationism, and Scottish moral philosophy (Bacon, Hobbes, Locke, and Hume; Alison and Hartley; Shaftesbury, Hutcheson and Adam Smith), while his language continually modulated into the inspired figurative rhetoric of the King James Bible. But it was his example more than his theories that taught writers as different as Brontë and George Eliot, William Morris, Pater, Lee, and Wilde the power of intensely attentive perception for critically engaging both life and art.

Ruskin's concerns (though not his Evangelical religious views) were central to heated but productive debates about the relation of art to social conditions and moral practice throughout the period. The desire of almost all critics before the mid 1860s to discover a convergence between aesthetic and moral perception placed on literature and the arts a heavy burden of

3 Ruskin, *Works*, vol. v, p. 333.
4 Charlotte Brontë, letter to W. S. Williams, published in *Macmillan's Magazine* 64 (1891), p. 280.

responsibility. The arts were asked to create the grounds for social cohesiveness while constructing intelligible narratives of personal development
and social progress, connecting a confusing present with both a usable past
and a confidently better future. Religion, undermined by the geologists'
hammers in the earlier part of the period and Darwin's apes in the latter,
could no longer provide the ethical and social underpinnings of a cohesive
civil society, whose need was more deeply felt in the face of political
tensions and social incoherence perceived to be the consequences of an
expanding, urbanizing, industrializing, democratizing nineteenth-century
Britain. Ruskin's national orientation was widely shared among writers
and critics of literature, as was his sense of the urgency of calling on 'the
moral energies of the nation' not only to 'elevate [art] to its healthy and
beneficial operation' but to cultivate through art those moral energies in the
first place.[5] The key to art's 'healthy and beneficial operation', for Ruskin
and for a majority of his contemporaries, lay in the intertwined operations
of sense perception and imaginative feeling – especially when identified as
sympathy, a favourite Victorian term. 'Moral perception', in the characteristic Victorian expansion of *aesthesis* (building on eighteenth-century moral
philosophers from Shaftesbury through Adam Smith), works together with
imagination to make possible poetic sight and insight – perception that is
potentially both moral (a ground of ethical values and practices) and visionary
(to the extent that it allows the mind access to that which it does not or
cannot literally see, including past and future). Feeling (especially as sympathy, or feeling binding us to others) was thought to be important both
for artist or writer and reader or beholder. When Arthur Hallam praises
Tennyson's early work as poetry of sensation, not reflection, he specifies that
sensory particulars of the external world are held 'fused . . . in a medium of
strong emotion'.[6] Hallam, like W. J. Fox, a more radical reviewer, welcomed
Tennyson's poetry of particulars fused in a medium of emotion as an expansion of self and society. Sympathy becomes the capacity to imagine what
is different. In Robert Browning's version the artist can cross boundaries of
both history and culture, 'Lending our minds out' to inhabit other selves.[7]

---

5 Ruskin, *Works*, vol. IV, p. 28.
6 Arthur Henry Hallam, 'On Some of the Characteristics of Modern Poetry, and on the
Lyrical Poems of Alfred Tennyson', repr. from *Englishman's Magazine* I (August 1831), in
*The Poems of Arthur Henry Hallam together with his Essay on the Lyrical Poems of Alfred
Tennyson*, ed. Richard Le Gallienne (London: Elkin Matthews and John Lane, 1893), p. 109.
7 Robert Browning, 'Fra Lippo Lippi', in *The Poems*, ed. John Pettigrew and Thomas
J. Collins (London: Penguin, 1981), vol. I, p. 547, line 306.

For most critics, however, art properly took not strange but familiar sights and common ('home') feelings as its province, awaking sympathy through what the artist and her subjects shared with readers.[8] 'The poet is doing his noblest work in resuscitating moral truths from the inert conditions of truisms and conferring upon them a perennial bloom and power' (Coventry Patmore), or, as Matthew Arnold put it (resisting the pressures to focus on modern life, however), the poet should select actions 'which most powerfully appeal to the great primary human affections: to those elementary feelings which subsist permanently in the race, and which are independent of time'.[9]

For many Victorians, the art that worked most directly on the emotions to produce sympathy was music. Building on Romantic theories, Herbert Spencer (in 'The Origin and Function of Music', 1857) praised music as the natural language of the emotions developed from intonational patterns of speech. What most appealed to Victorians, including George Eliot, were the potential moral effects of the sympathetic feelings music might elicit. Hugh Haweis's *Music and Morals*, 1871, reiterating a by then familiar view, went through twelve editions in as many years despite incisive objections from Eduouard Hanslick in Germany and Edmund Gurney in England to any claims that music, independent of verbal language, could do more than suggest mood or create generalized states of arousal. Hanslick, whose formalist approach to meaning in music in his 1854 *Vom Musikalisch-Schönen* was ultimately immensely influential, and Heinrich Helmholtz, whose important study of harmonic overtones (1863) was translated into English in 1875 (and eagerly read by George Eliot) as *On the Sensations of Tone as a Physiological Basis for the Theory of Music*, sought instead to ground claims for music's effects in a better understanding of tonal systems and musical form.

Arnold also expressed a dissenting scepticism about the primacy of sensation and emotion (and of the lyric poetry that had been its special home), preferring that poetry address the anxieties of an age of rapid change and uncertain direction by returning to the stabilities of classical forms built

8 Critics referred to opposed schools of poetry variously named the 'Idyllic' or 'National' (poems of English contemporary life arousing 'homebred sympathies') and the 'Ideal' or 'Psychological' ('the abstractedly great or ideally beautiful'); cf. [Aubrey de Vere], *Edinburgh Review* 90 (1849), p. 409; and [H.B. Forman], *London Quarterly Review* 32 (1869), p. 330.

9 Coventry Patmore, *Edinburgh Review* 114 (1856), p. 339; Matthew Arnold, *The Complete Prose Works of Matthew Arnold*, ed. R. H. Super, 6 vols. (Ann Arbor: University of Michigan Press, 1960, 1962), vol. I, p. 4 (Preface to *Poems*, 1853).

around great actions and ideas. Perception is central to the possibility of creative work, but, according to Arnold, it is the province of criticism, not art, and a product of the 'free play of the mind', not of the heart and the senses. Criticism is that 'endeavour, in all branches of knowledge, theology, philosophy, history, art, science, to see the object as in itself it really is' and to make what it sees known (to put ideas in circulation in an act both intellectual and social).[10] Arnold's 'to see the object as in itself it really is' thus differs on two counts from Browning's psychologically oriented realism or Ruskin's science of aspects (of 'the aspects of things ... [as] they produce such and such an effect upon the eye or heart'[11]). Arnoldian criticism provides for the creative imagination 'ideas; the best ideas' about what is external to the mind.[12] For Arnold, what is most missing in Romantic and contemporary British aesthetic activity is such an atmosphere of 'fresh thought, intelligent and alive'.[13] Despite what may seem Arnold's too-ready belief that a truly 'disinterested' Culture – where the free play of mind is at work – can be promoted by an equally disinterested State (beyond party factions, class loyalties, or religious anti-intellectualism, as he argued in *Culture and Anarchy*, 1869), his effort to turn aesthetics away from its emphasis on sympathy and 'home affections' marks an important intervention. The practical criticism that followed from Arnold's emphasis on ideas, however, led away from close engagements with the particularities of language and form while it retained his contemporaries' emphasis on the social and ethical responsibilities of both art and criticism.

It is against this burden of responsibility that we should understand the interventions made by the aesthetic and social experiments of the 1850s and 1860s. In poetry and the arts these experiments initially reworked medieval and early Renaissance art and craft practices. The group of young painters who provocatively exhibited their strange-looking works under the initials 'PRB' (Pre-Raphaelite Brotherhood) in 1849 and published a short-lived journal of criticism, poetry, and fiction, *The Germ*, 1850, provided no formal manifesto. Instead, contributions, notably Dante Gabriel Rossetti's – a prose tale, a group of sonnets, and a longer poem, 'The Blessed Damozel' – enact criticism as literature reflecting on itself through

---

10 Arnold, *Complete Prose Works*, vol. I, p. 140 (*On Translating Homer*, 1861); also quoted by Arnold in 'The Function of Criticism at the Present Time', 1863, *Complete Prose Works* vol. III, p. 258.
11 Ruskin, *Works*, vol. v, p. 387 (*Modern Painters* III, 1856).
12 Arnold, *Complete Prose Works*, vol. III, p. 260 ('The Function of Criticism').
13 *Ibid.*, vol. III, p. 263.

another art. Rossetti and his PRB companions, followed shortly by Morris, Pater, and Algernon Charles Swinburne, drew possibilities for moving out of an unsatisfactory present into an as yet uncertain future from unexpected encounters with arts and practices of the past. Morris's early prose tales and first published volume of poetry, *The Defence of Guenevere*, 1858, elaborate the spare, visually vivid, intensely focused, and psychologically disturbed art (literary and pictorial) of a beauty highly patterned yet verging on the grotesque of the Pre-Raphaelite and medieval work that excited him, while taking up Ruskin's arguments for the grotesque as an aesthetics of social criticism, a sign of imaginative energy warped in its expression by repressive social and cultural conditions. Morris was the organizing spirit for the briefly utopian community of artist-artisans and the more lasting decorative arts business begun in the early 1860s; his later commitments to art as craft and to socialism – a different but no less hopeful vision of the future, product not of gradual progress but of revolution – are most forcefully argued in a series of lectures and prose fictions from the 1870s and 1880s (especially 'The Lesser Arts', 'Useful Work and Useless Toil', 'A Dream of John Ball', and *News from Nowhere*, 1890). Morris's interest in pattern and repetition, rhythmic and historical, corresponds with Rossetti's formally inventive visual and poetic work of the 1850s, but for Morris these formal practices were an antidote to the degradation of sensory capacities that accompanied modern life. Pre-Raphaelite efforts to interrupt conventional assumptions and practices by attending to craft and formal design contributed both to Aestheticism's insistence on 'art for art's sake' and to socially utopian Arts and Crafts movements at the end of the century.

Beginning in the 1860s, Swinburne and James McNeill Whistler (American by birth, continental by upbringing, but making his career as an artist, decorator, and polemicist in London) with Pater and Wilde took up the first of these possibilities, arguing that good art must first of all obey its own laws while criticism concerns itself with the formal means by which the arts and literature achieve their effects. When Swinburne, borrowing from Théophile Gautier (whose source was Victor Cousin) introduced the phrase 'art for art's sake' to Victorian aesthetics in his 1868 essay on William Blake, he was making room for the reception of a neglected but passionately political poet whose ideas and behaviour, like his poetry, were perceived as radically unconventional – at best eccentric or mad. Swinburne's defence of Blake, like that which he had made of his own work two years earlier (in *Notes on Poems and Reviews*), asserted the rights of 'work done for the work's sake, the simple laws of ... art'.[14] In the case of neither Blake nor himself (at least after 1870) could Swinburne argue for the divorce of art from political or ethical passion, however. He reserved his greatest praise for those like Sappho, Blake, Percy Shelley, Walt Whitman, Victor Hugo, and Emily Brontë whose work achieves intensity through (Blake) 'violent belief'; (Blake and Whitman) 'pity and passion'; or (Emily Brontë) an 'essentially tragic' genius which can wholly immerse itself in a 'love which devours life itself'.[15] In his 1872 essay on Hugo, Swinburne qualified the misunderstood phrase:

> the worth of a poem has properly nothing to do with its moral meaning or design ... but on the other hand we refuse to admit that art of the highest kind may not ally itself with moral or religious passion, with the ethics or politics of a nation or an age ... In a word, the doctrine of art for art is true in the positive sense, false in the negative; sound as an affirmation, unsound as a prohibition.[16]

Although Pater, James, Lee, and Wilde were not, like Swinburne, equally committed to a radical Shelleyan or Blakean imaginative literature promoting liberation (sexual, theological, and political), their dedications to the form and craft of art 'done for the work's sake, the simple laws of ... art' were less a retreat from art's engagements with the world than an attempt to make space in art, against repressively invoked orthodoxies, for an alternatively moral perception (especially in matters of sexuality). Aesthetic criticism counters restrictions on subject matter by returning to the more radical implications of Hallam's and Fox's praise for Tennyson's early poetry.

It is only in the work of late-century author-critics who emphasize form and style like Pater, James, Lee, and Wilde that it becomes common to write about literature as aesthetic activity. Earlier Victorian speculative criticism had focused on poetics (e.g., J. S. Mill's 'What Is Poetry' of 1833, E. S. Dallas's *Poetics* of 1852) and did not develop an extensive vocabulary for formal analysis of aesthetic effects, with the partial exception of metrical theory (e.g., Coventry Patmore's 'Essay on English Metrical Law', 1855, and many others), though literary criticism is strikingly filled with terms drawn from painting: 'colouring', 'scene', 'canvas', 'landscape', 'picturesque'). The 'aesthetic criticism' practised by late-century writers fittingly acquires its

---

14 Algernon Charles Swinburne, *Major Poems and Selected Prose*, ed. Jerome McGann and Charles L. Sligh (New Haven: Yale University Press, 2004), p. 359.
15 *Ibid.*, pp. 376, 383, 402, 405.　　16 *Ibid.*, pp. 386, 387.

name in the preface to a book which discusses both literary and visual work, Pater's 1873 *Studies in the History of the Renaissance*. Pater's aesthetic critic 'regards . . . all works of art and the fairer forms of nature and human life, as powers or forces, producing pleasurable sensations, each of a more or less peculiar and unique kind. This influence [the aesthetic critic] feels and wishes to explain, analyzing it, and reducing it to its elements.'[17] The social and moral horizons toward which Ruskin's 'theoretic' sight aspired are apparently foreclosed (though Pater's later work, including his novel, *Marius the Epicurean*, 1885, reintroduces some of these considerations). What Pater, radically revising Arnold, proposes as the method of a new criticism ('the first step towards seeing one's object as it really is, is to know one's own impression as it really is'[18]), was extended by James, Lee, and Pater himself to investigation of the material and formal means for producing those impressions in fiction, prose, and the visual arts. (For Lee, at least for a time, this led to investigations of the physiological or embodied nature of the beholder's responses to form.) In *The Renaissance*, Pater famously countered Hegel's developmental hierarchies by making music – for him a fusion of intellectually apprehended form with the nuances of imaginatively grasped sensation and feeling – the impossible object of every art's desire: 'For while in all other kinds of art it is possible to distinguish the matter from the form, and the understanding can always make this distinction, yet it is the constant effort of art to obliterate it.'[19] Music most nearly approaches this goal: not, *pace* Hegel, replacing material with spiritual apprehension but fusing the two. In gestures of affiliation with the anti-realist desires that music represented for the visual arts, Whistler called his paintings 'symphonies' and 'nocturnes', while both Pater and Lee produced compelling fictions of an elusive, sensuous, and dangerous beauty whose purest form was music.[20]

A habit of conflating the aesthetics of literature with the particular ideas and practice (often in caricatured form) of the Aestheticism of the 1870s, 1880s, and 1890s has had the unfortunate effect of obscuring the subtleties of that space-clearing turn in criticism and aesthetics, eliding both its radical re-posing of the nature of aesthetic encounters and its continuities with the longer intertwined histories of Victorian literature and the arts. In critical

---

17 Walter Pater, *Studies in the History of the Renaissance* (Oxford University Press, 2010), p. 4.
18 *Ibid.*, p. 3.   19 *Ibid.*, p. 124.
20 For example, Pater's 'Denys L'Auxerrois' in *Imaginary Portraits* (1887); Lee's 'A Wicked Voice' in *Hauntings* (1890).

and literary practice, if not in terminology, the attention to literary making (*poesis*) was displaced by that directed to perceiving (*aesthesis*) well before Pater. Victorians were throughout the period concerned with how the arts, including literature, affect readers and beholders. The language of visual perception and the example of visual arts strongly inflect discussions of literature's action on its audiences from at least the 1830s. Yet the Aesthetic Movement, though it did not initiate the concern with aesthetic matters in Victorian England, did reorient the critical discussion in two historically significant ways. First, it challenged the practice of reading art and literature primarily as occasions for the exercise of moral energies through sympathetic perception, and second, it modelled an alternative: engaging with works of art as peculiarly intense perceptual experiences, mediations of the real that were often divorced from narrative content and instead were created through languages as conscious constructs, deliberately patterned repetitions – less disengagements from, than slant engagements with, 'life' or 'the real'. Some aesthetic critics' attention to analysing art's formal means and effects helped to change the nature of criticism itself: to bring about that shift from a Victorian emphasis on summary, quotation, and judgment (where a primary responsibility of the critic is to select and classify, in the face of confusing excess in literary and artistic production) to what would become the Modernist (and Post-modernist) practices of attending closely to textual and sensory detail, taking pleasure in the self-conscious play of words, figures, and forms to multiply meanings in text and image. Such criticism, when skilful, aimed to amplify, complicate, and intensify where earlier Victorian criticism had hoped to simplify and order aesthetic encounters with works of art.

The cultures of art

The adoption of the terms 'aesthetics' and 'aesthetic' around mid century coincides with the dawning of an extraordinary period when, as a contemporary critic observed, 'there began to be a great talking about Art'.[21] Poetry, music, and visual art were more accessible across the classes in Victorian England than ever before (in large part thanks to print capitalism) and occupied a greater share of public attention. Reviews, essays, novels, and poems extended into print the conversations among passers-by at

---

21 [Reverend John Eagles], 'The Fine Arts and Public Taste in 1853', *Blackwood's Magazine* 74 (1853), p. 92.

print-shop or photographic studio window; visitors to the popular annual exhibitions, new museums, and artists' open-studio days; at Parliamentary hearings looking into national museums and art education; or in the lecture halls of universities, Schools of Art, Working Men's and Women's Colleges, crafts guilds, and Mechanics Institutes. As we know from the fiction of the period, the talking about art reached from the streets and galleries into the parlours and drawing-rooms of the upper, middle, and aspiring-to-be-middle classes. Rochester reads Jane's character through her watercolour drawings in their first extended conversation; Lucy Snowe asserts to a shocked European M. Paul her Englishwoman's right to look at (and criticize) a Rubens nude. In *Bleak House* (1852–3) Mrs Bayham Badger discourses on her portraits to her dinner guests while Guppy and Jobling debate the merits of prints from *British Beauties* in a dingy furnished room above Krook's rag and bottle shop. Margaret Hale and her father talk despairingly of the wallpaper at their new lodgings in industrial Milton. Lydgate and Rosamond conduct their provincial courtship over the illustrations of the latest literary annual while poor Dorothea Brooke – judged sadly ignorant of the most important subjects by her sister – can think of nothing to say about the redecoration of her sitting-room or the art treasures of Rome. The highly visible cultures of art provide the occasions and the matter for much of the most interesting critical and theoretical discussion, not only of the arts (especially visual) but also of literature as one of the arts.

Victorian musical culture was also extending its social reach. Performances of European music for both private and concert audiences proliferated; these audiences were newly learning to listen in silence but were also increasingly helped to identify musical themes and structures by programme notes and reviews. As much fiction (and the private letters and diaries of women in particular) attests, pianos, singing, and sheet music held a central place in middle-class domestic life, at times competing with less welcome music from insistent street musicians outside. From the 1840s choral singing attracted thousands of working-class and Dissenting participants instructed through sol-fa methods of teaching sight-singing. Ballads (often old tunes fitted with new words) and instrumental music persisted among both rural and urban working classes, with new music halls already on the rise. For some poets and novelists music and the susceptibility to its effects represent the purest (least mediated) experience of the sensations and emotions the arts can arouse (in *Middlemarch*, Caleb Garth lacks his wife and daughter's interest in literature but is deeply moved by oratorios). Music's effects are productively invoked in cross-arts comparisons, often to criticize aesthetic ideas derived too exclusively from literature and the visual arts, especially Realist fiction and painting (Eliot, Tennyson, Swinburne, Rossetti, Pater).

We can also link discussions of aesthetic matters to rising anxiety over the social, political, and commercial implications of arts both accessible and popular. The foundation of the National Gallery in 1824 exposed rifts between those who saw the new national art museum as a continuation of an older aristocratic tradition of collecting and viewing, and those who envisioned a national middle-class institution, whose principles of collecting and exhibiting would be both more organized (historical survey, national treasure-house) and less exclusive than visits to private collections. Parliamentary commissions revisited policies of admissions and conditions of collecting and display several times throughout the century, concerned not only with the National Gallery but, from the 1850s, with the new museum at South Kensington (the future Victoria and Albert Museum). The latter was designed to give greater access to the 'respectable' working classes (introducing gas lighting, longer hours, Saturday and eventually Sunday opening days, and refreshment rooms) – largely because its major focus was not painting but the decorative arts, whose health depended on the aesthetic education of those who would make these objects as well as those who would buy them.

Beginning in the late 1830s, Victorians engaged in a long debate about the value of musical and arts education and museum access for the working classes. Such education, particularly if focused on religious music or the production of better design (patterns for textiles, shapes and designs for a variety of luxury and everyday objects) would, it was argued, raise the moral tone of the lower classes in the post-Reform Bill era of exploding literacy and potential universal suffrage, while (in the case of design education) keeping Britain commercially competitive with long-time rivals like France and newer ones like Germany and the USA. Where music was thought to offer moral improvement by working directly on the emotions of the less educated, visual arts education was to shape a more contented, better informed, productive, and compliant populace while enhancing national commercial competitiveness. Both were opposed by those who feared they would only increase working-class discontent and be a waste of money. Despite these fears, Parliament in the late 1830s authorized the municipal construction of new museums in provincial cities and similarly dispersed state schools of practical art, though what was taught and who could use the museums continued to be debated for decades.

While Romantic fascination with the artist as an expressive genius of unique imaginative powers did not disappear, the Victorians were more preoccupied with art as experienced by ordinary people and embodied in material artefacts with which they could live. Art in everyday life might indeed mean reproductions (visual or musical) of works of 'fine' art, but it might also mean the design, decoration, advertising, and home use of more ordinary objects – including those mass-produced, relatively inexpensive, and widely available items of furnishing, clothing, and entertainment that new industrial materials and techniques made possible. This vernacular culture of art, which included books, prints, and music aimed at a mass audience but also the 'lesser arts', as William Morris was to call them, of dress, décor, and household objects, crossed the boundaries of class. It provided means for establishing and displaying taste that could distinguish between educated, that is middle-class, and uneducated ('vulgar' or 'common') working-class tastes. Yet it also challenged the distinctions between high and low, fine and popular, art and commodity, that many were attempting to establish. Writers and critics questioned how 'Art' was perceived, made, used, and how – or if – it might be said to differ from other commodities in a world of proliferating objects with which to adorn and domesticate living spaces.

The Great Exhibition of 1851 famously stimulated not only the commercial production but the consumption of colourful and increasingly inexpensive household and personal goods, by working-class as well as middle-class buyers. In its wake followed a proliferating discourse of advertisement, criticism, and advice for domestic consumers. Literature and the 'fine' arts benefited from aroused consumer desires, but the expanded markets in paintings, prints, illustrated books and magazines, pianos, and sheet music for domestic use, promoted and catered to by enterprising dealers and publishers and spreading, in its inexpensive forms, to cottages as well as bourgeois drawing-rooms, also troubled definitions of 'art' and the 'aesthetic'. In succeeding decades some of the most contentious discourse centred not on the fine but on the decorative arts – or even, most woundingly for those who maintained their idealism about the detached disinterestedness of the fine arts, on paintings as another species of 'room furniture', with the artist no different from the hack parlour-song writer as manufacturers of commodities for sale. The domain of the aesthetic expanded from that of art as a special mode of imaginative perception to the aesthetic as a way of living. Professional taste-setters and advice-givers guided eager participants from the middle and lower-middle classes, competing with artists to define aesthetic values. The extravagant gestures and polemical ripostes of Whistler (*The Gentle Art of Making Enemies*, 1890) – after he was sued by his patron, Frederick Leyland, for unauthorized decorative creativity in the Peacock Dining Room and in turn took Ruskin to court (in 1877) when that critic unwisely referred to his painting as wilful imposture – betray the artist's increasing need to reassert aesthetic authority in a newly fluid world of fine and vernacular arts.

Contributing to a general rethinking of inherited aesthetics were the considerable scientific and technological advances in understanding and modelling perception. The stereoscope, the photographic camera, and the phonograph are only three of the best-known, distinctively Victorian devices which made newly available certain aspects of seeing and hearing that conventions of representation and habits of observation and listening had previously occluded – most notably, for visual perception, one-point perspective, and the editing of detail (stereoscopy modelled ordinary binocular vision better while photography revealed a world of the unnoticed). These devices were available in popular forms as both tools and toys. At the same time, empirical investigations into the physiology and psychology of vision and hearing, discussed for lay audiences in contemporary journals and showing up in fiction and poetry, often focused on aberrations and distortions built into human perception. (The camera and phonograph also helped to reveal some of the gaps between embodied and mechanical perception.) Artists and writers on art were alerted to the potential of precisely those aspects of perception that photography and phonography in their early stages could not replicate: shades and tones of the unselfconscious voice, colour and the visibility of the medium, light (and its refractions and reflections) in air and water, and perhaps still more significantly for literature, the reach of the imagination to vision or audition that exceeded embodied or mechanical perception, from the microscopic or macroscopic to the frankly visionary. Novelists and poets were also stimulated to experiment with the effects of framing, differences in perspective or point of view, and the wealth of detail modelled by photography, while they pushed still further Victorian explorations of psychological and physiological distortions of perception. Criticism of literature in turn drew heavily on the experiences and the language of photography, painting, and psychology.

Beauty and its others

Beauty – that which is in the first instance pleasing to behold in eye or ear or imagination – remains a central term of approbation for works of art and for poetry. But what has long been said remains true: aesthetic questions were for the Victorians closely entwined with both socio-political and moral concerns. Keats's overwhelming passion for Beauty deeply troubled Arnold, who early in his critical career (in the 1853 Preface to his *Poems*) believed it made that poet a bad model for contemporary writers. While art and literature (like music) were not usually asked to be explicitly didactic, their capacity to instruct by example of their content as well as through the emotions made visual and literary art especially the focus of an often-anxious rhetoric. Though the beautiful was often shown to be neither good nor true, novels and poems, like pictures, were expected to aspire to representations of a beauty coincident with both. For much of the period, Realism bore the heaviest burden of readers' and viewers' expectations and fears: detailed information about contemporary (or historical) life, in representational fictions verbal or visual as in reports and statistics, histories and natural histories, was to be the source of truth and the demonstration of progress. Much pressure was exerted on writers to take contemporary life as subject matter and to represent it accurately. Realist fiction and poetry of contemporary life were alike praised for their ability to create what Raymond Williams was to call 'knowable communities' by representing, and arousing, 'home' affections embedded in familiar scenes – as we find in Tennyson's 'English Idyls' as well as in most domestic fiction.[22] 'Beauty', in these representations of the familiar, resided in the emotions that such representations depicted and aroused in readers. 'Home' affections generally excluded ugly feelings (disgust, envy, spite, discontent, despair, boredom) or insisted on their eventual correction, containment, or expulsion.

Much early twentieth-century energy was expended to dissociate Modernism from what was almost universally regarded as the unhealthy conjunction of Victorian aesthetics with the morality of a timid, conventional art. The late twentieth century shifted the grounds of the objection to the unacknowledged entanglements of aesthetics with a liberal bourgeois society's political, social, and economic agendas. (This line of criticism has particularly emphasized the ideological functions of the Victorian novel, enacting complex connections binding an ultimately coherent social body, and managing the tensions between its demands and an individuated, psychologically complex personhood solicited by authoritative narrators in their relations with readers.) Even forms as various as the Victorian novel exerted pressures invisible to their

---

22 Raymond William, *The Country and the City* (New York: Oxford University Press, 1973), p. 165.

users. Yet it should also be noted that this criticism in part takes its cue from Victorian novels themselves. Realism used the moral authority accorded it by Victorian readers to question the possibilities of arriving at 'truth' (even while formally it aspired to represent unified social and individual bodies), repeatedly dramatizing its characters' failures to see clearly. As imagined and presented in fiction, poetry, and even painting, psychological needs or social, religious, and political conditions are depicted in such a way that individual responses to the beautiful distort already elusive norms, as they do ethical and social judgments.

While this may be most obvious as a feature of novels (*Middlemarch*), it is also characteristic of poems. Browning's Duke ('My Last Duchess') or the speakers of 'Porphyria's Lover', 'Pictor Ignotus', 'Fra Lippo Lippi' or 'Andrea del Sarto' – connoisseur, lover, and artists alike – achieve their brief lyrical moments by weaving a tissue of illusion and self-delusion which the dramatic monologue, that special invention of Victorians uncomfortable with Romantic lyricism, invites us to observe. Often the speaker is already self-questioning though unable or unwilling to give up beloved habits of mind and body that affect aesthetic judgment (Andrea or the speaker in 'Bishop Bloughram's Apology', or the unnamed young man of Rossetti's 'Jenny'). At other times the speaker is mad or criminal (or both), as are the speakers in Tennyson's 'Maud' or 'Simeon Stylites', or, again, those in Browning's 'Porphyria's Lover' and 'My Last Duchess'. Morris's Guenevere ('The Defence of Guenevere') or the old men in his 'Concerning Sir Geoffray Teste Noir' and 'The Wind' call up memories warped by unacknowledged passions. In almost every case faith in the purity of lyric expressiveness or an inspired imaginative grasp of 'beauty' is undermined by the poet's staging of it as pathologically distorted (in ways that the poems present to us as socially or culturally symptomatic) and rhetorically motivated: eloquence, not 'poetry', in Mill's sense, because uttered by a speaker with one eye on a real or imagined audience in need of persuasion.[23] As readers we witness the speaker's only partly successful efforts to transcend ideological, material, or psychological limits to the perception of 'beauty'. Frame poems (Tennyson's 'The Princess' or those he wrote for his 'Morte D'Arthur' and 'The Gardener's Daughter') are another way in which poets registered the need to distance themselves from endorsing an idealistic claim

23 See John Stuart Mill, 'What is Poetry' (1833), rev. and repr. as 'Thoughts on Poetry and its Varieties' in *Dissertations and Discussions Political, Philosophical and Historical* (London: John W. Parker and Son, 1859), p. 71, for this distinction.

to poetry's power by specifying the limiting human conditions of 'beauty's' perception or creation. Key texts for understanding this distinctively Victorian staging of the rhetorical and embodied character of beauty are Tennyson's early lyric, 'The Lady of Shalott', 1832, 1842, Arnold's Preface to his *Poems*, 1853, and Browning's *The Ring and the Book*, 1868, with its vivid demonstration of the poet's distrust of language – legal argument, historical document, public discussion, private defence, or lyric poetic expression – to arrive at the 'truth' of its beautiful heroine. Tennyson's fable has a particularly productive afterlife. The Lady is doubly an artist, weaving into tapestry what she sees through her mirror's reflection of the world that passes by her windowed tower while she sings a pure, content-less song recalling Shelley's skylark, heard as enchanting melody from an unseen source by listeners beneath her tower. The poem's focus, however, is on the fragility and dependence of all kinds of art, poetic or musical or visual, and on the mediations of unreliable reflection and perception. Not only do mirror and tower render the Lady's artistic representations 'shadows' of life even to herself. Her art is also subject to incomprehension and distortion from its beholders, whether as music (her work song and her later swan song) or picture (the tapestry is destroyed and only the body of the singer and her name, which is also the title of the poem, survive to stand for artistic 'beauty' for a bewildered audience in Camelot). The poem's reflections on its own conditions of creation and reception live on most memorably in repeated paintings and designs after it, especially among the Pre-Raphaelites (in works by D. G. Rossetti, W. Holman Hunt, J. E. Millais, and Elizabeth Siddall). Such stagings of the problematic nature of the beautiful use mixed forms and media to incorporate analysis and self-consciousness (the stance of the aesthetic critic-to-be) into their representations of the beautiful.

Beauty readily generates its others, testing and extending the boundaries of what is admissible as art. Produced by the visions of the mad or criminal, embodied by unreliable or confused perceivers, representing the maimed senses of the socially and physically marginal, the beautiful often appears as the grotesque. The Victorian grotesque (whose roots are in Roman and Renaissance fantastic decorative arts, while it became associated with medieval art in the eighteenth century) is always on the verge of becoming the unbearably ugly, the merely painfully deformed. It is often equated with the low, common, or vulgar, which for some readers and viewers have no place in art. This is the realm of the difficult-to-look-at, the unsightly which is also the *unheimlich*, the uncannily and disturbingly strange which may either be the foreign or, worse, a transformation of the familiar. Ruskin develops the notion of the grotesque into an aesthetic expression of difficult social conditions, a form of play that becomes forced, bitter, and imaginatively cramped (though it can rise to terrible but broken vision). His examples range from caricature and satire through fantasy to the symbolism of prophecy (in *The Stones of Venice* III and *Modern Painters* III). With or without Ruskin's gloss, the grotesque has considerable explanatory power; it is the most frequent other to both realism and beauty. The grotesque carvings above the door of Wuthering Heights which warn off visitors; the grotesque performance of Vashti, the great actress who enthralls Lucy Snowe and repels the conventional John Bretton; the grotesque Pre-Raphaelite portrait in *Lady Audley's Secret* that points to the sensation heroine's criminal past and mental pathology: each marks the eruption of the unsightly or the *unheimlich*, an unseemly excess of feeling represented by bodily distortion. Visual grotesques accurately signal Gothic, sensation, or uncanny elements in each novel (and so warn us of ugly feelings, from bigotry and greed to uncontrolled sexual desire, indexing social conditions disturbing to contemplate). When Walter Bagehot characterizes Browning's poetry as grotesque, he condemns Browning's stylistic distortions and interest in criminal and pathological characters on implicitly moral no less than literary grounds.[24] Some grotesque distortion is more acceptable than others: Thackeray (who published much of his art criticism as Michael Angelo Titmarsh, a grotesquely comic pseudonym yoking the sublime with the ridiculous) warmly praises the grotesque caricatural art of George Cruikshank, redeemed by its pervasive good humour and affectionate views of human nature despite the satirical thrust of his cartoons (e.g., 'An Essay on the Genius of George Cruikshank', 1840). Thackeray's characterization applies well to his own satires in the text and illustrations for *Vanity Fair*, to Dickens's art of comic caricature (and that of his illustrators), and to much of *Punch*.

The picturesque, though often invoked, is less contested and less meaningful for Victorian criticism. For most literary critics it simply means 'like a picture' or 'worthy of being painted'. Ruskin is wary of the picturesque as mere unthinking attraction to quaint subjects and rough textures, visual pleasures that rely on the divorce of sympathy from sight and ignore the often miserable conditions that produce picturesque effects in impoverished

---

24 Walter Bagehot, 'Wordsworth, Tennyson and Browning; or Pure, Ornate and Grotesque Art in English Poetry', in Richard Holt Hutton (ed.), *Literary Studies* (London: Longman's Green, 1879), vol. II, pp. 338–90, esp. pp. 375–88.

rural or urban subjects (see particularly his condemnations in *Modern Painters* IV). The sublime, a third aesthetic possibility (with a much longer history back to the late classical Longinus, revived and elaborated in the eighteenth century), almost disappears from critical discourse. Compatible neither with Realism and the domestic novel nor with poetry of 'home feelings' and idyllic English life, nor yet with the genial comic satire of Thackeray or early Dickens, sublimity (the experience first of annihilation and then of exaltation in the presence of the grand and the terrible) was not the spirit of the new age. It demanded greater openness both to humiliation and to transcendence than most Victorian arts displayed. Thackeray had little tolerance for the serious sublimities of Turner. Ruskin (his sensibilities formed by the Romantic aspirations of an earlier age) was deeply moved by them, but even in Turner he read modern deformations that he called the terrible grotesque. Sublimity persists in some urban fiction and poetry, as occasional moments crossed with the grotesque in Dickens's later novels, for example. It re-emerges in the 1860s and 1870s as a Shelleyan, politicized aesthetics in the work of Swinburne and James (B. V.) Thompson ('The City of Dreadful Night'), another instructive troubling of the aspirations to containment which invocations of beauty could mask.

One might finally note the important place in Victorian aesthetics of both 'interest' (in the Kantian sense of a least-possible degree of aesthetic pleasure that still engages critic or reader) and Arnoldian 'disinterest' (willed suspension or attempted transcendence of partisan or personal political, religious, or social views before a work of art or literature). Both interest and disinterest serve to qualify or counterbalance the emphasis on perception, feeling, or the social and ethical responsibilities of art that mark so much Victorian thinking.

The literature of art

The talking about art provoked a very considerable literature. Artists and pictures, particularly portraits (and less often, music and musicians), make many appearances in novels and poems, as one might expect from the importance of the high and vernacular contemporary cultures of art. For the most part, these representations depict artists as hardworking professionals, not distraught geniuses, and eventually reward them with both material and romantic success. Dinah Mulock Craik's *Olive*, 1850, includes an extensive account of her heroine's progress from a woman apparently excluded from marriage plots by physical deformity to successful if pragmatically professional artist (Craik gives a devastating portrait of the condescension of male artists and their institutions along the way). Amy Levy's *The Romance of a Shop*, 1888, makes her new women sister-heroines the proprietors of a photography studio, and Wilkie Collins's modest hero, Walter Hartwright (*The Woman in White*, 1860) is an artist who makes his living as a drawing instructor. But even respectable art-professionals like Hartwright or the Lorimer sisters attract to themselves sensational (especially sexually transgressive) plots and characters – mysterious, beautiful women, doubled identities, secrets of birth, alien others, the sexually suspect, and the mad. In some novels the artist-figure is herself half Gothic, half sensation: Anne Brontë's Helen Grahame (*The Tenant of Wildfell Hall*, 1847) and Mary Elizabeth Braddon's Lucy Audley, who, like Craik's Olive, struggled to survive by her art before she turned to murder and matrimony. Lady Audley's similarities to the much more acceptable Olive (whose eventual marriage effectively removes art from the novel) are perhaps greater than her differences. Even when the pictures created by these artists are not described, portraits of exotic and sensuous beauties recollected from contemporary painting might be said to haunt the novels' plots. Lady Audley's perfectly English beauty is belied by the 'beautiful demon' of her painted Pre-Raphaelite image; Levy's Gertrude Lorimer is sent to photograph the beautiful but emaciated corpse of her later suitor's adulterous wife; and portraits real and imagined fascinate their viewers and ultimately offer clues to detection of hidden secrets in *Bleak House* and *The Mystery of Edwin Drood*, 1870. The sculptor protagonist of Thomas Hardy's *The Well-Beloved*, 1892 (revised 1897, 1903, and 1912), whose professional career and history of repeated short love affairs are governed by his constant pursuit of ideal beauty as it flits from one human embodiment to another, is, like Hardy's novel itself, haunted by imaginary portraits. The imagined beautiful drives the novel itself beyond Hardy's usual territory (the morally and sexually unconventional) into realms of the visionary and fantastic that he ordinarily confined to his short stories. Just as interesting, perhaps, are the numerous representations of visual and musical arts as domestic practices, never as safe as might be supposed: Maggie Tulliver's attraction to forbidden love is played out in duets at a parlour piano, as is Rosamond Lydgate's dalliance with Will Ladislaw. The tone-deaf eponymous heroine of George Du Maurier's *Trilby*, 1894, is transformed into a sexually fascinating musical diva when hypnotized by the sinister foreign (and Jewish) musician, Svengali. Victorian fiction and poetry supply endless further examples of art's evident capacity to disrupt homely feelings and domestic realism by introducing forms of the beautiful as the unseen but imagined or the unsightly and *unheimlich*, the foreign, the beautiful grotesque.

The cultures of art also stimulate several kinds of writing that focus more particularly on art's forms and powers. Victorian aesthetic criticism is often the site of formal and stylistic experimentation. Ruskin begins the practice of using language to evoke works he will analyse from a double perspective: following and even moving into the imagined presence of a work of art or nature while he steps back to comment on it. Swinburne and Pater take up and expand his use of prose to recreate the experience of art as a necessary part of the analytic endeavour. Criticism of this sort may migrate to more purely 'literary' genres: Swinburne's 'Notes on Designs of the Old Masters at Florence' (1868) includes the prototype for Pater's evocation of Leonardo's *Mona Lisa*, later lineated and published by William Butler Yeats as the first poem in an anthology of modern poetry. Poetry or fiction may also be the site of aesthetic double consciousness, half creatively imaginative, half analytic. Rossetti's Sonnets for Pictures, his prose fictions, and his poems (like 'The Blessed Damozel') incorporate what he calls an 'inner standing point' but also reflect, in form as well as content, the distance that separates the modern poet or reader from the art she strives imaginatively to enter. Some of Pater's best criticism is to be found in his 'Imaginary Portraits', short fictions and novellas about artists, writers, and works of art. Lee's philosophical dialogues (e.g. *Baldwin*), parodies (*Miss Brown*), and ghost stories ('Amour Dure', 'Dionea', 'Oke of Okehurst'), supplement her more Paterian essays and studies, while Wilde's criticism is by turns fiction (*The Picture of Dorian Gray*, 1890, 1891; 'The Portrait of Mr W. H.', 1889), parody, pastiche, and witty conversation (in plays and essay-dialogues like 'The Critic as Artist', 1890) – virtuoso performance, in and out of print. As Wilde, deftly summarizing (and turning on its head) Victorian aesthetics from Ruskin and Arnold through Pater, proposes with characteristic perversity, criticism is more generative of new forms than art itself. Criticism has become the superior art: it will give us the object as in itself it really is *not*, but as it appears to an attentive, imaginative beholder, the only kind of aesthetic truth, Wilde maintains, that matters ('The Decay of Lying', 'The Critic as Artist'). Wilde's essays, which incorporate through allusion, quotation, and explicit discussion much of the writing discussed in this chapter, perfectly grasp a defining feature of British aesthetics in the preceding half-century: not that poems and novels are less imaginative than prose criticism, but that criticism and imaginative literature borrow each other's forms and strategies to explore the determining conditions, the perceptual problems, and the changing forms of the aesthetic in nineteenth-century Britain. In the intercalary or intermediate forms of the literature of art, Victorians make perhaps their most distinctive contributions to aesthetics.

22

Science and literature

GILLIAN BEER

H. G. Wells opens his satirical, visionary novel *The Food of the Gods*, published at the turn of the twentieth century in 1904, with a backward glance at a singular novelty that has emerged in the previous fifty years:

> In the middle years of the nineteenth century there first became abundant in this strange world of ours a class of men, men tending for the most part to become elderly, who are called, and who, though they dislike it extremely, are very properly called 'Scientists'. They dislike the word so much that from the columns of *Nature*, which was from the first their distinctive and characteristic paper, it is as carefully excluded as if it were – that other word which is the basis of all really bad language in this country.[1]

Wells nips at the heels of this new class of 'men', so unworldly, but so insistent on each his own achievement that they dislike being classed in the gross – and, with a sly refusal to name it, he imports his own gross allusion to that 'other word' that asserts the body. Scientists, he suggests, see themselves as all intellect, but are trapped in their shuffling mediocre bodies and their anxious self-assertion.

Yet their achievements are enormous.

> To witness some queer, shy, misshapen, grey-headed, self-important little discoverer of great discoveries . . . or to read the anguish of *Nature* at the 'neglect of science' when the angel of the birthday honours passes the Royal Society by, or to listen to one indefatigable lichenologist commenting on the work of another indefatigable lichenologist, such things force one to realise the unfaltering littleness of men.
>
> And withal the reef of science that these little 'scientists' built and are yet building is so wonderful, so portentous, so full of mysterious half-shapen promises for the mighty future of man![2]

---

1 H. G. Wells, *The Food of the Gods* (London: William Collins, 1969) p. 3.
2 *Ibid.*, pp. 6–7.

Wells turns to the metaphor of the coral reef, with its growth produced by the impacted remains of small creatures. The coral reef was Darwin's initial metaphor in his Notebooks for the evolutionary process, one for which he later in the *Origin* substituted the tree diagram. So Wells embeds the work of scientists in natural process while mocking the 'unfaltering littleness' of the individual ego striving for recognition.

During the Victorian period the new professionalism of the sciences went alongside more traditional explorations in natural history and work in private laboratories. Even at the universities in the earlier part of the period, while mathematics and Euclid were fundamental to higher education, other scientific work was scanted and classical learning still held the highest prestige. That mixed economy of new and old methods, and the uncertainty of public appreciation, opened scientific endeavour out quite readily into the wider culture. Indeed, it often needed to bolster its claims by recourse to allusions from classical literature and the great English poets, such as Milton. By the end of the nineteenth century scientific work had gained its place in higher education, in the public realm, and in research laboratories funded by the universities. I shall return to that process later in this chapter.

It is striking that the story Wells goes on to tell in *The Food of the Gods*, like that of *The Island of Dr Moreau* a few years earlier (1896), shows a distrust and horror at the possible outcomes of scientific enquiry and particularly of scientific experimentation. This dread of large-scale scientific experiment uncontrollable in its human consequences is new in the nineteenth century. It is particularly intense in the later years and it is still reverberating strongly in our own time. It takes much of its force from the close ties between the human and other animal forms of life revealed in the arguments of Darwin and, indeed, of his predecessors. It has an immediate relevance in the arguments for and against vivisection that became so troubling to many late Victorian people. These discussions stretched across into Europe and drew on scientific and literary writing there as well.

The publication of Claude Bernard's *Introduction à l'étude de la médicine expérimentale (Introduction to the Study of Experimental Medicine,* 1865) brought newly into the light the necessary association between experiment on still-living beings, rather than residues, and the advance of medical knowledge. Bernard argued that only by the study and comparison of *live* organisms (and by the intervention of vivisection) could the processes of health and disease be understood. He also established the concept of the controlled experiment, where a single factor only is changed: the control group undergoes all the same experiences as the experimental group save for the salient single variation. Zola praised, and claimed to apply, Bernard's method in his essay *Le roman expérimentale* (*The Experimental Novel*, 1880). Here, following Bernard, he uses the term 'experiment' not as an open-ended spontaneous composition (as twentieth-century usage in the arts would have it) but rather as a severely controlled process of sorting evidence by varying conditions one by one. Zola's twenty novels studying the Rougon-Macquart family (the Rougons legitimate, the Macquarts illegitimate) responded quite directly to Bernard's text: the novels insisted on recognizing the animal nature of humankind and the affinity with other animals' behaviour and appetites. They demonstrated the shaping force of inherited conditions and of fundamental survival needs: hunger, in *Germinal*, drives the characters to act in ways not fully under the control of their individualities. Zola's novels insisted too, through their study of family generations, on reducing the number of factors at play in order to be able to pinpoint elements in behaviour and inheritance. Bernard was chary of any move to equate science and the arts, but Zola seized the opportunity of Bernard's theories to argue for the close equality between them.

These bold 'scientific' characteristics of Naturalism caused considerable shock among British critics and readers; and indeed the brutality of the struggle to survive among the characters can still appal. The publication in English translation of *La terre* (*The Earth*, 1885) was one of the most hostile moments in the relations of science, literature, and society in the later nineteenth century. The scene that then most troubled opinion was one that showed collaboration across species: the young woman helps the bull insert his pizzle in the cow in order to mate. Now, the scene where an old man is set on fire to wipe out his witnessing might cause greater distress. But the grinding 'bestial' poverty of the whole milieu remains grim indeed. The publication of this and other Zola novels resulted in two trials for obscenity and the imprisoning for three months in 1889 of the publisher, Henry Vizetelly, then already over seventy years old.

So as this example shows, the relations between science and literature, and their bearing on social mores, were often heated in this period, and not only in relation to evolutionary theory. As Wells makes clear in the passage I quote above from *The Food of the Gods*, the professionalization of the 'scientist' was still underway throughout the later nineteenth century, with a range of practice. But by the time Wells was writing, private laboratories and scientific demonstrations as paid entertainment were giving place to institutional laboratories, such as the Cavendish laboratory in Cambridge under the guidance of the great physicist James Clerk Maxwell. Wells himself was trained as a scientist at the Normal School of Science, South Kensington (later part of Imperial College) on a government scholarship from 1884. Here he was taught by T. H. Huxley and his first book, published two years before *The Time Machine* (1895), was a *Textbook of Biology* (1893).

Literature as a resource for scientists

Scientific ideas enter the more general culture at various speeds. Those drawing on anatomy and what we now call biology tend to move rapidly out of the laboratory and into ordinary discourse. On the face of it, mathematical and physical work might be expected to move more slowly because they require knowledge of advanced mathematics. But even here, in the Victorian period, the presence of major workers like Faraday made for broad access to current scientific insights. Faraday pursued major physical and chemical enquiries without deep mathematical knowledge, and communicated with much broader publics through lectures and demonstrations. This accessibility resulted in rapid, if loose, assimilation of new ideas. For example, words like 'force' and 'race' that bore very specific meanings within the context of their professional usage also bore social implications that could unreel beyond the control of scientists. Moreover, as the website *Sciper* now makes available for us to discover, the idea of 'science' was appropriated, shifted, used to legitimize or to challenge assumptions, in a great array of periodicals of the time, by no means all of them journals of high culture.[3]

Indeed, a glance at the early volumes of *Nature* from its inception in 1869 will show how soft were the boundaries between professional scientists and intelligent amateurs in the Victorian period, and how much anxiety surrounded the issue – among scientists in particular. The Editor's opening letter 'To Our Readers' in volume 2 of *Nature*, after the first six months of publication, makes satirical use of the advice he has received for making the journal a success (though any success has already been deemed impossible by his advisors):

> 'Science is so small, her victories so few,' said some, 'that a weekly account of them is altogether beside the question – the well would run dry.' Others said: 'Science is large, it is true, but her followers are not numerous. You

---

3 www.sciper.org The free website draws on sixteen general periodicals and allows the researcher to discover references to science not only in reviews but in short stories, travelogues, and poems.

may perhaps number your readers by hundreds, if you take care to appeal to scientific men only; but as far as the outside world, they care nothing for science.' On the other hand it was held that a popular scientific weekly journal would be a certain success under certain conditions – some such as these: in the first place, the articles were to be as light as air; each fact was to be clothed in a delicate atmosphere of adjective and imagery; next, each page was to be studded with beautiful pictures, correctness both in text and illustration giving way to a certain more or less subdued sensationalism; and lastly, and above all, every care was to be taken to spare the reader the least trouble in the matter of thinking.[4]

Popular fiction is the joke model for the journal that *Nature* is determined *not* to be, but literature nevertheless remains a point of departure and of confirmation for scientific writers at that time. The epigraph to all the early volumes of *Nature* emphasizes the degree to which scientists sought a confluence between imagination, observation, and theory validated in the work of poets, as well as through the opinions of their peers. At the front of every issue, beneath a picture of the globe emerging from clouds, we find:

> 'To the solid ground
> Of Nature trusts the mind that builds for aye.' – Wordsworth

'Ground' in this new context implies both earth and argument; 'Nature' is the eternal and the testable world. Wordsworth's lines are invoked to secure the alliance between Science and Nature.

The recourse to poetry for affirmation is a strikingly frequent move by scientists in the Victorian period. In part it derives from the priorities of formal upper-class education at the time. To be able to write Greek verse was lauded more highly than any skill in chemistry. Scientific education had very little presence in the values of public school enquiry. Faraday and Tyndall were both self-made men whose path had led them through practical work into scientific issues. Other major workers like James Clerk Maxwell had been through the Scottish system, which paid more regard to a broad-based intellectual training. For the physical scientist, the demonstration of familiarity with literature was a badge of authority that could reinforce his communication with a wide audience. It was also very frequently a statement of what endures, a statement that went some way to assuage the anxieties felt in the face of the New. This anxiety is

---

4 *Nature. A Weekly Illustrated Journal of Science* 2 (Thursday 5 May 1870), p. 1.

the counter-track to the association of science with progress, expansion, and improvement in the Victorian age.

For the pioneering 1870s mathematician W. K. Clifford, husband of the novelist Lucy Clifford, creativity is invested in the capacity to change and respond, both for individuals and for societies. He suggests that there 'are actually two new senses, the scientific and the artistic, which the mind is now in the process of forming for itself'. Even 'the Spirit of the Age' is not 'a thing absolutely fixed, permanent, free from fluctuations ... the entire history of humanity ... tells how there were great waves of change which spread from country to country, and swept over whole continents, and passed away'.[5]

John Tyndall in chemistry, like Thomas Henry Huxley in biology, was uninhibited in his willingness to relate scientific work to the activities of ordinary life. In the Introduction to his book *On Light*, based on lectures delivered in the USA in 1872–3, he characterizes his language as 'plain' and his aim as being 'to develop and deepen sympathy between science and the world outside science': 'I agreed with thoughtful men who deemed it good for neither world to be isolated from the other, or unsympathetic towards the other, and, to lessen this isolation, at least in one department of science, I swerved aside from those original researches that had previously been the pursuit and pleasure of my life.'[6] Tyndall represents himself as being drawn away from primary research by the need to communicate to non-scientists. He is both enthusiast and missionary. He is also conscious of the difficulties that occur when writing must be put in place of demonstration: 'During their delivery, the experimental facts were before the audience, forming visible links in the logic of each discourse. Here, by the use of plain language, I have endeavoured to reproduce distinct images of these facts, and to show them in their proper relations.'[7] This suggestive passage brings out the work that must be done in the symbolic activity of *writing* to substitute for the direct engagement of the senses in experiment, both for practitioner and audience. Tyndall, like Faraday, could produce extraordinary public spectacle as part of his scientific practice: for example, he produced a blue sky in the darkened Senate House at Cambridge. He also persuaded instruments to sing at a distance and in one public experiment

5 William Kingdon Clifford, *Lectures and Essays*, 2 vols. (London: Macmillan, 1901), vol. 1, p. 84.
6 John Tyndall, *Six Lectures on Light*, 2nd edn (London: Longmans, Green, and Co., 1875), pp. 1–2.
7 *Ibid.*, p. v.

watched a 'sensitive naked flame' respond in a graphic dance of the vowels, as he recited Edmund Spenser to it across the room:

> Her ivory forehead full of bounty brave,
> Like a broad table did itself dispread:
> For love his lofty battles to engrave
> And write the battles of his great godhead.[8]

Tyndall's acoustic investigation in this case concerns pitch and tone quality. His material performance of the experiment draws on literature, partly for its pleasurable authority, but also for its experimental immediacy, here realized as the voice. The Spenser also makes for economy, despite its voluptuous content: its vocalization gathers a wide array of vowels and consonants close together, allowing the witnesses to watch the variety of pitch appear as wavering marks on the wall, all within these four lines. So aesthetic pleasure and function combine.

Great physicist and skilled poet, James Clerk Maxwell took a somewhat tart view of Tyndall's efforts at popularization. Among his original light verse was 'A Tyndallic Ode', written in satire and appreciation of Tyndall (Pindaric Odes as a genre gave wing to licensed madness). Many of Maxwell's stanzas engage with one or other of Tyndall's demonstrations, experiments, and inventions, such as the clean Tyndall Box, the properties of ice, the singing flame, and the blue of the sky. The scheme and metre of Maxwell's poem is a pastiche of Tennyson's 'The Brook'. Tennyson's poem opens:

> I come from haunts of coot and hern,
> I make a sudden sally,
> And sparkle out among the fern,
> To bicker down a valley.

Maxwell responds:

> I come from fields of fractured ice,
> Whose wounds are cured by squeezing,
> Get warm again by freezing.
> Here, in the frosty air, the sprays
> With fern-like hoar-frost bristle,
> There, liquid stars their watery rays
> Shoot through the solid crystal.[9]

---

8 Quoted in John Tyndall, *Sound: A Course of Lectures Delivered at the Royal Institution*, 3rd edn (London: Longmans, Green & Co., 1875), p. 238.

9 Alfred Tennyson, 'The Brook', in *The Poems of Tennyson*, ed. Christopher Ricks, 3 vols. (1969; London: Longmans, 1987), vol. II, p. 502; Lewis Campbell and William Garrett,

Among themselves scientists enjoyed playing with literature and trying out the intricacies of classical metre as an intellectual discipline.

Although the education offered to boys in public school was so largely concerned with classical literatures and so little with the sciences, it would be a mistake to imagine that literate Victorian people did not have easy access to descriptions of science and scientific materials. There was an immense industry producing popular books for the education of children both male and female. The standards assumed may come as a salutary surprise to modern readers. For example, the Reverend Jeremiah Joyce began publishing his scientific dialogues for children long before Victoria came to the throne but they went through many editions in her reign. There are three children, Charles, James, and Emma, in *Scientific Dialogues; intended for the instruction and entertainment of young people: in which the first principles of Natural and Experimental Philosophy are explained by the Rev. J. Joyce.* The young people put often taxing questions to their father, or a tutor, on mechanics, astronomy, optics, magnetism, pneumatics, hydrostatics, electricity, and galvanism. The typical flavour of the questions runs like this: 'Emma: You said just now, papa, that all the mechanical powers were reducible either to the lever or inclined plane; how can the screw be referred to either?'[10] That takes their father thirteen lines to answer. Such works flavour Lewis Carroll's Alice, with her rational questioning in the face of the importunate adults she encounters.

The Royal Institution also opened science out to much wider audiences in London, often in a form that enchanted people in much the same way that conjuring does. So did the annual meetings of the British Association for the Advancement of Science, to which the public were admitted and which took place in a variety of cities across the country. When we think about the access of Victorian people to current scientific ideas we need to recognize the popularity of the public scientific lecture and demonstration. Large crowds attended Faraday's lectures, as they also did those of Huxley and Tyndall. It was through this public means, as much as through reading, that women could gain insight into current scientific controversies, alongside men. Walt Whitman in a poem of 1865 evokes the crowded scene and public applause for scientific lectures (here, in the United States)

The Life of James Clerk Maxwell with Selections from his Correspondence and Occasional Writings (London: Macmillan, 1884) p. 412.

10 Jeremiah Joyce, *Scientific Dialogues* (London: Thomas Allman [n.d., c. 1854] 'New edition, complete in one volume, with 185 wood cuts'), p. 67.

even as he distances himself from the kinds of knowledge being produced and turns to nature for fulfilment.

> When I heard the learn'd astronomer;
> When the proofs, the figures, were ranged in columns before me;
> When I was shown the charts and diagrams, to add, divide, and measure them;
> When I, sitting, heard the astronomer, where he lectured with much applause in the lecture-room,
> How soon, unaccountable, I became sick and tired;
> Till rising and gliding out, I wander'd off by myself,
> In the mystical moist night-air, and from time to time,
> Look'd up in perfect silence at the stars.[11]

The stars might seem to offer permanence and perfection, but a creeping awareness that the universe is subject to cataclysm, change, and disorder – indeed, that disorder might be the fundamental nature of things – began to breed anxieties in the wake of the second law of thermodynamics. The idea of entropy, first enunciated by Helmholtz in 1847, presented a universe in the process of running down, its energy irretrievable, and its end-state a calm without discrimination. The cooling of the sun seemed to threaten if not imminent, yet inevitable, disaster.[12] And the variety of the world might collapse into mere waste. Indeed, that dread is confronted by Gerard Manley Hopkins in the opening of 'Spelt from Sibyl's Leaves' where words like 'equal' and 'waste' carry a charge from the thermodynamics that so fascinated Hopkins: 'earth her being has unbound; her dapple is at an end'.[13] Thomas Henry Huxley probed the idea that 'evolution signifies a constant tendency to increased perfection' by combining evolutionary and thermodynamic theory:

> If what the physical philosophers tell us, that our globe has been in a state of fusion, and like the sun, is gradually cooling down, is true; then the time must come when evolution must mean adaptation to an universal winter, and all forms of life will die out, except such low and simple organisms as the Diatom of the arctic and antarctic ice and the Protococcus of the red snow.[14]

---

11 Walt Whitman, *Leaves of Grass and Selected Prose* (London: J. M. Dent, 1993), p. 238.
12 For fuller discussion see my '"The Death of the Sun": Victorian Solar Optics and Solar Myth' and 'Helmholtz, Tyndall, Gerard Manley Hopkins: Leaps of the Prepared Imagination', in Gillian Beer, *Open Fields: Science in Cultural Encounter* (Oxford: University Press, 1996), pp. 219–72.
13 Gerard Manley Hopkins, 'Spelt from Sibyl's Leaves', in *The Poetical Works of Gerard Manley Hopkins*, ed. Norman H. Mackenzie (Oxford: Clarendon Press, 1990), p. 191.
14 T. H. Huxley, 'The Struggle for Existence in Human Society' (1888), *Collected Essays*, 9 vols. (London: Macmillan, 1906), vol. IX, p. 199.

The extreme and final visit forward through time of Wells's *The Time Machine* (1895) confronts the traveller with exactly that dark, bleak shore:

> The darkness grew apace; a cold wind began to blow in freshening gusts from the east, and the showering white flakes in the air increased in number. From the edge of the sea came a ripple and whisper. Beyond these lifeless sounds the world was silent. Silent? It would be hard to convey the stillness of it. All the sounds of man, the bleating of sheep, the cries of birds, the hum of insects, the stir that makes the background of our lives – all that was over.[15]

And in his monumental work of myth-systems, *The Golden Bough*, of which the first volume appeared in 1890 and the twelfth in 1915, James Frazer foresees inexorable decline and death in the universe (though he struggles to equate these dire predictions with the unstable dreams through which our minds haunt themselves and comforts himself with Prospero's renunciation). 'In the ages to come man may be able to predict, perhaps even to control the wayward courses of the winds and clouds, but hardly will his puny hands have strength to speed afresh our slackening planet in its orbit or rekindle the dying fire of the sun.'[16]

The changing nature of Nature

Whitman turned to the natural world and the universe of stars for self-confirmation. Yet the question of Nature's nature – and of its shifting relationship to the human – became a besetting one for many more than scientists. In the 1860s T. H. Huxley's challenging title *Man's Place in Nature* suggests one fundamental issue: how entirely is the human a part of the material order of living things? In *Vestiges of the Natural History of Creation*, published anonymously by Robert Chambers in 1844 and an astounding popular success, that problem had already been addressed. Chambers positioned the human as 'the type of all types', the acme and summation of life: 'Man, then, considered zoologically, and without regard to the distinct character assigned to him by theology, simply takes his place as the type of all types of the animal kingdom, the true and unmistakable head of animated nature upon this earth.'[17] Man remains at the head of creation

15 H. G. Wells, *The Time Machine* (London: J. M. Dent, 1993), p. 86.
16 James Frazer, *The Golden Bough*, 12 vols. (London: Macmillan, 1890–1915), vol. XI (1913), pp. 306–7.
17 Robert Chambers, *Vestiges of the Natural History of Creation and Other Evolutionary Works*, ed. James Secord (University of Chicago Press, 1994), pp. 272–3.

but Chambers argues for 'creation by law' rather than by 'special exercise'. He is careful to make this an argument that preserves God's dignity:

> Is it conceivable, as a fitting mode of exercise for creative intelligence, that it should be constantly moving from one sphere to another, to form and plant the various species which may be required in each situation at particular times? Is such an idea accordant with our general conception of the dignity, not to speak of the power, of the great Author?[18]

Existing hierarchies are maintained in Chambers's argument, but nevertheless his work challenged and perturbed many of his readers, as well as producing humorous rebuttals. Disraeli in *Tancred* (1847) renames *Vestiges* 'The Revelations of Chaos'. Lady Constance, deeply impressed by the work, tells Tancred:

> You know, all is development. The principle is perpetually going on. First, there was nothing, then there was something; then – I forget the next – I think there were shells, then fishes; then we came – let me see – did we come next? Never mind that; we came at last. And the next change will be something very superior to us – something with wings.[19]

More piercing was the later insight of Emily Pfeiffer in her sonnets 'Evolution' and 'To Nature'. Evolution is

> Hunger, that strivest in the restless arms
> Of the sea-flower, that drivest rooted things
> To break their moorings, that unfoldest wings
> In creatures to be wrapt above thy harms.[20]

And she addresses Nature thus, in the octave of her sonnet:

> Dread Force, in whom of old we loved to see
> A nursing mother, clothing with her life
> The seeds of Love divine,– with what sore strife
> We hold or yield our thoughts of Love and thee!
> Thou art not 'calm', but restless as the ocean,
> Filling with aimless toil the endless years –
> Stumbling on thought, and throwing off the spheres,
> Churning the universe with mindless motion.[21]

---

18 *Ibid.*, p. 161.
19 Benjamin Disraeli, *Tancred: or, The New Crusade*, 2 vols. (Leipzig: Bernhard Tauchnitz, 1847), vol. I, p. 124.
20 Emily Pfeiffer, 'Evolution', in *Sonnets* (London: Field and Tuer, 1886), p. 51.
21 *Ibid.*, 'To Nature. II', *Sonnets*, p. 30.

Instead of a maternal being, nature becomes part of the world of 'force', aimlessly 'churning the universe with mindless motion', 'cold motor of our fervid faith and song' as she writes in the sestet.

Mindless, yet generating mind and love; machinate, yet impinging on 'soul': the paradoxes gathered in the concept 'nature' were discomfiting. No longer could nature be understood securely as the expression of God's munificence and order, as had been the argument in the Bridgwater Treatises. Indeed, the human understanding of nature began to be comprehended as possibly a process of self-description, rather than as an authoritative reading informed by stable evidence and referring to a world designed by God. Oscar Wilde argues in 1891 in 'The Decay of Lying' that 'Nature is no great mother who has borne us. She is our creation. It is in our brain that she quickens to life. Things are because we see them, and what we see, and how we see it, depends on the Arts that have influenced us.'[22]

Nature and evolution

Although Darwin is now the dominant name in discussions of Victorian natural history, much literary response to evolutionary ideas precedes the publication of the *Origin*. Moreover the sciences of geology and of astronomy fascinated a broad public. When we turn to the major poem of the earlier part of our period, Tennyson's *In Memoriam*, we find the grieving poet rebuked by imagined speakers for singing 'private sorrow's barren song' in the face of the growing power of the people and the opening of the universe to exploration by astronomers:

> When Science reaches forth her arms
> To feel from world to world, and charms
> Her secret from the latest moon...[23]

The most enduringly famous single line (part-line) in Tennyson's poem, 'Nature, red in tooth and claw', gives voice already to the dismay that evolutionary theory (and in particular Herbert Spencer's formulation of 'the survival of the fittest') would later arouse.[24] But that poem (LVI) is more

---

22 *Oscar Wilde: The Major Works*, ed. Isobel Murray (Oxford University Press), pp. 232–3.
23 Tennyson, 'In Memoriam A.H.H', *Poems*, vol. II, p. 340.
24 *Ibid.*, section LVI, *Poems*, vol. II, p. 372.

preoccupied with geological evidence of how things pass away than with the
process by which things come to dominate:

> 'So careful of the type?' but no.
> From scarped cliff and quarried stone
> She cries, 'A thousand types are gone:
> I care for nothing, all shall go.

Nature cannot be trusted to grant either permanence or order; even
'Man, her last work',

> Who trusted God was love indeed
> And love Creation's final law
> Though Nature, red in tooth and claw
> With ravine, shrieked against his creed-

> – man will be extinguished, 'blown about the desert dust.'[25]

Tennyson is responding to Lyell's *Principles of Geology* with its emphasis
on inexorable though gradual change. As many have noted, Lyell's epigraph
from John Playfair at the start of the second volume of *Principles* sets the tone for
his argument and makes it clear that extinction is a necessary and fundamental
process in nature: 'The inhabitants of the globe, like all the other parts of it, are
subject to change. It is not only the individual that perishes, but whole species.'[26]

Charles Darwin thought of himself initially as a geologist and, like
Tennyson, was deeply affected by Lyell's argument for endless change
throughout the materials of the earth over an enormous time span. Lyell
emphasized gradual rather than spasmodic transformation but his work
made clear how irretrievable was any idea of permanence. That emphasis
on constant change was a crucial element in Darwin's coming to the idea of
Natural Selection. Implicit in the phrase 'natural selection' is its assumed
contrary and companion, 'artificial selection': 'artifice' as the work of man
husbanding and selecting for his own advantage regardless of others' good.
Darwin suggests through that contrary between natural and artificial that
the work of 'natural' selection is more truthful, even more benign, though
intransigent in its dealings with organic beings struggling to survive.

Darwin struggled, too, on a lofty yet intimate scale with his own
fears and doubts about the implications of his new concept; at a semantic

---

25 *Ibid.*, section LVI, *Poems*, p. 373.
26 Charles Lyell, *Principles of Geology Being an Attempt to Explain the Former Change of the Earth's Surface by Reference to Causes now in Operation*, 2nd edn (London: John Murray, 1833).

level – which is always also at the level of philosophy – he struggled with the misprision, as he saw it, that accompanied his use of the words Nature and Natural Selection. In later editions of the *Origin* he repeatedly returns to the problems of agency and identity located in these terms. In the third edition he tackles these problems head on:

> It has been said that I speak of natural selection as an active power or Deity: but who objects to an author speaking of the attraction of gravity as ruling the movements of the planets? Every one knows what is meant and is implied by such metaphorical expressions; and they are almost necessary for brevity. So again it is difficult to avoid personifying the word Nature; but I mean by Nature, only the aggregate action and product of many natural laws, and by laws the sequence of events as ascertained by us. With a little familiarity such superficial objections will be forgotten.[27]

And so, with a little familiarity, the objections largely were forgotten, but they lurk in the undergrowth of response: the problem of intent and agency never vanishes from human discourse (gravity 'rules', nature 'selects'). And it is not quite the case, despite his assertion, that by 'Nature' Darwin means '*only* [my italics] the aggregate action and product of many natural laws'. Personification remains powerful.

For these reasons, as well as because the theory was itself so all-embracing and strenuous, the upheavals brought about by Darwin's ideas have many conflicted meanings in the literature of the later century. George Eliot was right to say, when she first read the *Origin*: 'it makes an epoch'[28] – although at that time she did not yet perceive what was original in Darwin's theory. Indeed, her fuller understanding of its significance comes in the later 1860s, along with her life companion G. H. Lewes's great fascination with Darwin's ideas. Even then, it is at the level of structure, rather than direct reference, that we can trace the full impact of his meaning for her. *Middlemarch*, in particular, questions the obsession with origins shown in the research of both Casaubon and Lydgate, and insists on the element of variability as the most fruitful to explore. Fates that look alike, and people who seem of a piece, are subtly varied in ways that determine which survives, which falls.

Within the idea of 'natural selection' elements are in tension: natural selection requires variability and hyper-production (both elements emphasizing liberal profusion) while the more frugal principle of selection controls their outpourings

27 Charles Darwin, *The Origin of Species By Charles Darwin: a Variorum Text*, ed. Morse Peckham (Philadelphia: University of Pennsylvania Press, 1959), p. 165.
28 George Eliot, letter to Barbara Bodichon, 5 December 1859, in *The George Eliot Letters*, ed. Gordon S. Haight, 7 vols. (New Haven and London: Yale University Press, 1954–5), vol. III, p. 227.

of possibility: 'Can we doubt (remembering that many more individuals are born than can possibly survive) that individuals having any advantage, however slight, over others, would have the best chance of surviving and of procreating their kind?'[29] The word 'individuals', twice repeated in this sentence, reminds us also that evolution for Darwin occurs through the life of the individual organism, spent, and surviving in progeny that carry several variations that may happen to advantage one – or some – of their number and not others.

That implacable story rears up in many places in later Victorian fiction: in particular, in Hardy's *Tess of the D'Urbervilles* where Tess, 'an almost standard woman' in the sense that she carries the qualities of womanhood, is destroyed by re-claiming her descent from a clapped-out aristocratic line, as well as being caught between the values of a society that equates purity with sexual ignorance and nature that urges onwards to procreation. Nature itself for Hardy always includes the warped and marred along with the fruitful. Tess walks at evening in the fecund uncultivated garden:

> She went stealthily as a cat through this profusion of growth, gathering cuckoo-spittle on her skirts, cracking snails that were underfoot, staining her hands with thistle-milk and slug-slime, and rubbing off upon her naked arms sticky blights which, though snow-white on the apple-tree trunks, made madder stains on her skin; thus she drew quite near to Clare, still unobserved of him.[30]

This viscous elemental world lies close to Darwin's vision of nature as both bountiful and indefatigably destructive: 'We behold the face of nature bright with gladness, we often see superabundance of food; we do not see, or we forget, that the birds which are idly singing round us mostly live on insects or seeds, and are thus constantly destroying life.'[31] The struggle of the individual takes a less glamorous form in George Gissing's fiction, with its insistence on lost opportunities and mediocre lives.[32] Here, Social Darwinism and Spencer's idea (adopted by Darwin in later editions of the *Origin*), 'the survival of the fittest', comes into prominence, as it does in George Moore's novels also.[33] Ordinary lives with their tender shoots of feeling and

---

29 Darwin, *Origin*, p. 164.
30 Thomas Hardy, *Tess of the D'Urbervilles. A Pure Woman Faithfully Presented*. The New Wessex Edition (London: Macmillan, 1975), p. 150. 'Madder' here is a dye of a dark crimson colour: compare the 'Maddermarket' in the old city centre of Norwich.
31 Charles Darwin, *On the Origin of Species* (Oxford University Press, 2008), p. 52–3.
32 For example, *New Grub Street* (1891), *The Nether World* (1889), *The Odd Women* (1893).
33 For example, *A Mummer's Wife* (1885) and *Esther Waters* (1894). Moore's novels were published by Henry Vizetelly, and he remained loyal to him when Vizetelly was imprisoned.

desire are, in these books, shown to be endlessly worsted by the large machinery of social life and by the ill mix of social life with the passions.

Science, fantasy, and satire

Some scientists, like the distinguished natural historian Philip Henry Gosse, sought a poetics of description for the natural world that would combine the approach of the field-observer with that of the poet. Rejecting 'Dryasdust' statistics he nevertheless relishes the disciplines of fieldwork:

> There is the field-observer's way: the careful and conscientious accumulation and record of facts bearing on the life-history of the creatures; statistics as fresh and bright as the forest or meadow where they are gathered in the dewy morning. And there is the poet's way; who looks at nature through a glass peculiarly his own; the aesthetic aspect, which deals, not with statistics, but with the emotions of the human mind, – surprise, wonder, terror, revulsion, admiration, love, desire, and so forth, – which are made energetic by the contemplation of the creatures round him.[34]

Gosse is concerned with affect, especially with wonder, and he is writing directly in the tradition of natural theology, demonstrating the workings of God's presence through natural history. He organises the chapter titles of his work through contrasts of scale – The Vast, The Minute – and through contrasts of effect – Harmonies, Discrepancies – and through extremes of all kinds – The Wild, The Terrible, The Unknown, The Great Unknown. Halfway through the work, he ends the chapter on 'The Vast' by a direct rebuttal of Darwin, unnamed, and of Darwin's insistence on 'laws': 'All these are the mighty works of an Almighty God; not self-produced, as some would fain assure us, by the operation of what are called eternal "laws", but designed by a Personal Intelligence, created by a Living Word, and upheld by an Active Power.'[35] The capitalized initial letters are not only for emphasis but to enforce the quintessential nature of these qualities.

Philip Gosse lives now most acutely in the work of his son Edmund Gosse, whose *Father and Son* (1907) explores the painful dilemma in which his father Philip found himself even before the publication of the *Origin*. How to justify the *ways* of God had changed into a yet more extreme question: how to justify *God*. Philip Gosse believed in the literal truth of the

---

34 Philip Henry Gosse, *The Romance of Natural History* (London: James Nisbet and Co., 1860), p. v.
35 *Ibid.*, pp. 146–7.

Bible account of creation. If God was not needed in order to explain the presence of life on earth, where was He? If he was not immanent in Nature, if Nature was to be understood as a process of production without intent or design, God had been usurped. Gosse saw his task as asserting the presence of God, active, intelligent, and alive in creation.

Gosse was well aware that there was a contradiction between current geological knowledge and the account given in Genesis. That was what led to his claim in *Omphalos* (1857) that at the moment of the adult Adam's creation a past had been invented or induced by God. This gave rings within the trunks of trees, a navel to the unborn creation Adam, and callouses on feet that had never yet walked. Gosse distinguished 'diachronic' time (which proceeds through history) and what he called 'prochronic' time (an originating time, and one beyond the calendar). The theory was not well received. Some saw it as suggesting that God lied. Yet it is a brilliantly tight-knit reconciliation of impossible counter-explanations. Perhaps it even haunts some of the time-plays in Lewis Carroll's *Alice* books where pasts are composed out of events that have not yet taken place and 'memory works both ways':

> 'I'm sure *mine* only works one way,' Alice remarked. 'I can't remember things before they happen.'
> 'It's a poor sort of memory that only works backwards,' the Queen remarked.
> 'What sort of things do you remember best?' Alice ventured to ask.
> 'Oh, things that happened the week after next,' the Queen replied in a careless tone.[36]

Much later on Gosse's idea greatly appealed to that connoisseur of impossible worlds, Jorge Luis Borges.[37] But the idea of the past as a back-formation did not catch on in Victorian fantasy in the way that the invented future was to do. We can see the amalgamation of future and past at its most fascinating in William Morris's *News from Nowhere, or, An Epoch of Rest* (1890), where after a great revolution a restored civilization much like that of the Middle Ages, but tinctured with socialism, has established itself. A fiercer version of that same idea of a past returning as the future is present in Richard Jefferies, *After London: or, Wild England* (1885), where a change in the

---

36 Lewis Carroll, *Through the Looking-Glass and what Alice Found There*. The Centenary Edition, ed. Hugh Haughton (London: Penguin, 1998), p. 172.
37 Jorge Luis Borges, 'The Creation and P. H. Gosse', in *Other Inquisitions 1937–1952*, trans. R. Simms (Austin: University of Texas Press, 1964), p. 23–5.

tilt of the earth has produced vast migrations of people, leaving a depopulated England ravaged by brutal possessors and fertile with only a few dominant species of plants and creatures: a kind of evolution in reverse has taken place.

Charles Kingsley's *The Water-Babies: a Fairy Tale for a Land Baby* (1863) lies closest to its own present day with its story of the rebirth and re-education of the drowned little chimney sweep, Tom. Tom goes again through an evolutionary process, physical and ethical, under the sea, moralizing then current recapitulation theory. Kingsley's tale imagines the plight of children in brutal employment now, as well as expanding its satiric reach across questions of belief and disbelief, creation and evolution. Strikingly, Kingsley was one of Darwin's early allies after the publication of the *Origin*, acknowledging in a letter to him that 'it is just as noble a conception of Deity, to believe that he created a few primal forms capable of self development into all forms needful pro tempore & pro loco, as to believe that He required a fresh act of intervention to supply the lacunas which he himself had made.'[38] Victorian fantasy informed by science tends to place itself more often in the far future as in *After London* or at the far ends of the earth, as in Samuel Butler's *Erewhon*, set in New Zealand and then in a 'nowhere' [erewhon] country. Bulwer Lytton's *The Coming Race* (1871) was, like Butler's *Erewhon*, issued anonymously, and there were even suggestions that Lytton was the author of *Erewhon*, denied in the Preface to the second (1872) edition of *Erewhon*. Butler's work is one of the first and most creative direct responses to Darwin's ideas. Perhaps now, the 'Book of the Machines' has most zest for us, with its extraordinarily prescient discussion of the power of machines, their capacity for reproduction, their intelligence, their way of ruling those they serve, and their coming miniaturization. But the satire in the final chapters, on 'The Rights of Animals' and 'The Rights of Vegetables' is now coming into its own as well. Man, the writer argues, is: 'Such a hive and swarm of parasites that it is doubtful whether his body is not more theirs than his, and whether he is anything but another kind of ant-heap after all. May not man himself become a sort of parasite upon the machines? An affectionate machine-tickling aphid?'[39] The language of technology begins to appear as something more than metaphor in much *fin-de-siècle*

---

38 *The Correspondence of Charles Darwin*, vol. VII, 1858–9, ed. Frederick Burkhardt and Sydney Smith (Cambridge University Press, 1991), p. 380. Darwin includes a simplified version of this letter in the Conclusion to the second edition of the *Origin: Variorum Text*, p. 388.

39 Samuel Butler, *Erewhon: or over the range* (London: Penguin, 1970), pp. 205–6.

writing. Take for example Richard Jefferies's description of the city in *The Story of My Heart* (1883). Here ideas of force and electricity are used to suggest a dynamic action in human society that is homologous with the action of tides and clouds: the city and its crowd

> rushes and pushes, the atoms tritivate and grind, and eagerly thrusting by, pursue their separate ends ... driving, pushing, carried on in a stress of feverish force like a bullet, dynamic force apart from reason and will, like the force that lifts the tides and sends the clouds onwards. The friction of a thousand interests evolves a condition of electricity in which men are moved to and fro without considering their steps.[40]

Eliza Lynn Linton in a novel published posthumously in 1900 tells in first person the experience of an old woman in her seventies who grows gradually young again. The sardonic tale is given verisimilitude by an appeal to new discoveries in science and technology: 'With the spectroscope and the phonograph, the germinative force of formic acid, the liquefaction of air, the Röntgen rays, and the new telegraphy, how can we say that any marvel in molecular rearrangement is impossible?'[41] In many of these works the 'wonder' of science is a starting point for imagining another quite different way of being. But that imagined difference depends on a fresh realization of the physical and dynamic mysteries out of which daily life issues, and of which it is composed. In 'The Decay of Lying' Vivian, Oscar Wilde's spokesman, remarks on what he claims to be the dependence of both life and nature on art: 'Scientifically speaking, the basis of life – the energy of life, as Aristotle would call it – is simply the desire for expression, and Art is always presenting various forms through which expression can be attained.'[42] Wilde's deliberately topsy-turvy argument plays into the fundamental truth at the basis of evolutionary thinking about diversification: 'the basis of life ... is ...the desire for expression'. The language looks far forward to now current genetic discourse: that process called 'gene expression'.

Satire, science, society

Scientific thinking was for the Victorians a source of joke and satire as well as a profound shaking of current assumptions. Indeed, many of those who

---

40 Richard Jefferies, *The Story of My Heart: An Autobiography* (London: Eyre and Spottiswoode, 1949), pp. 87–8.
41 Eliza Lynn Linton, *The Second Youth of Theodora Desanges* (London: Hutchinson, 1900), pp. 1–2.
42 Oscar Wilde, 'The Decay of Lying', in *Major Works*, p. 232.

responded to Darwin and the aftermath of Darwin's theories picked up and resisted the social implications of the emphasis on fitness. Mathilde Blind in *The Ascent of Man* presented the plight of those humans abandoned by the competitive insistence of evolutionary progress; Grant Allen in *The Evolutionist at Large* (1881) frames his essays at the start with 'A Ballade of Evolution'. The first verse runs:

> In the mud of the Cambrian main
> Did our earliest ancestor dive:
> From a shapeless albuminous grain
> We mortals our being derive.
> He could split himself up into five,
> Or roll himself round like a ball;
> For the fittest will always survive,
> While the weakliest go to the wall.

That last line, 'The weakliest go to the wall' is a running if varying refrain throughout the poem: 'the ugliest went to the wall', 'the weakliest went to the wall', 'the needier go to the wall'.[43]

The demand that the reader accept as inevitable the grim social implications of 'fitness' roused healthy resistance. Constance Naden, for example, herself well educated scientifically, spotted the degree to which science was itself becoming a form of religion as the explanatory power of religion faded. In a teasing poem, 'The New Orthodoxy', she mixes class politics (her middle-class Girton girl student has an upper-class suitor) with a broad sweep of scorn. The girl is dismayed by her suitor's back-sliding, not from religious belief but from scientific orthodoxy. Perhaps there is a suggestion too that evolutionary ideas, which rely on change, are more acceptable to the rising middle classes than to the established aristocracy. Resistance to the Victorian sages such as Carlyle and Ruskin would be just about tolerable, it seems, but there are worse rumours. Two verses from the middle of the poem give the flavour; the girl is writing to her suitor:

> Oh, the wicked tales I hear!
> Not that you at Ruskin jeer,
> Nor that at Carlyle you sneer,
> With his growls dyspeptic:
> But that, having read in vain
> Huxley, Tyndall, Clifford, Bain,

---

43 Grant Allen, *The Evolutionist at Large* (London: Chatto and Windus, 1881), p. xiii.

All the scientific train –
You're hardened sceptic!

Things with fin, and claw, and hoof
Join to give us perfect proof
That our being's warp and woof
    We from near and far win;
Yet your flippant doubts you vaunt,
And – to please a maiden aunt –
You've been heard to say you can't
    Pin your faith to Darwin![44]

The jaunty rhymes mock their own congruities. Things do not agree in argument simply because they rhyme, but the poem's flair supports the young woman. It is pointless to resist scientific knowledge; but literature must keep asking questions about the orthodoxies that can settle on science too. The Victorian tradition of light verse and satire keeps its readers alert to anomaly, and it challenges any premature resolution. In its often pugnacious way, it keeps the implications of scientific work visible and in question.

---

44 Constance C. W. Naden, 'The New Orthodoxy', in *A Modern Apostle; The Elixir of Life; The Story of Clarice, and Other Poems* (London: Kegan, Paul, Trench, & Co., 1887), pp. 140–1.

23

Subjectivity, psychology, and the imagination

HELEN SMALL

... let me ask myself one question – Which is better? – To have surrendered to temptation; listened to passion; made no painful effort – no struggle; – but to have sunk down in the silken snare; fallen asleep on the flowers covering it; wakened in a southern clime, amongst the luxuries of a pleasure-villa: to have been now living in France, Mr Rochester's mistress; delirious with his love half my time – for he would – oh, yes, he would have loved me well for a while. He *did* love me – no one will ever love me so again. I shall never more know the sweet homage given to beauty, youth, and grace – for never to any one else shall I seem to possess these charms. He was fond and proud of me – it is what no man besides will ever be. – But where am I wandering, and what am I saying, and above all, feeling? Whether is it better, I ask, to be a slave in a fool's paradise at Marseilles – fevered with delusive bliss one hour – suffocating with the bitterest tears of remorse and shame the next – or to be a village-schoolmistress, free and honest, in a breezy mountain nook in the healthy heart of England?

Yes; I feel now that I was right when I adhered to principle and law, and scorned and crushed the insane promptings of a frenzied moment. God directed me to a correct choice: I thank His providence for the guidance!

Having brought my eventide musings to this point, I rose, went to my door, and looked at the sunset of the harvest-day, and at the quiet fields before my cottage ...

While I looked, I thought myself happy, and was surprised to find myself erelong weeping – and why? For the doom which had reft me from adhesion to my master: for him I was no more to see ... (*Jane Eyre*, 1847)[1]

Impossible for Gwendolen not to feel some triumph in a tribute to her power at a time when she was first tasting the bitterness of insignificance: again she seemed to be getting a sort of empire over her own life. But how to use it? Here came the terror. Quick, quick, like pictures in a

---

1 Charlotte Brontë, *Jane Eyre*, ed. Ian Jack and Margaret Smith (Oxford: Clarendon Press, 1975), vol. III, chapter 5 (chapter 31), pp. 459–60.

book beaten open with a sense of hurry, came back vividly, yet in fragments, all that she had gone through in relation to Grandcourt – the allurements, the vacillations, the resolve to accede, the final repulsion; the incisive face of that dark-eyed lady with the lovely boy; her own pledge (was it a pledge not to marry him?) – the new disbelief in the worth of men and things for which that scene of disclosure had become a symbol. That unalterable experience made a vision at which in the first agitated moment, before tempering reflections could suggest themselves, her native terror shrank.

Where was the good of choice coming again? What did she wish? Anything different? No! and yet in the dark seed-growths of consciousness a new wish was forming itself – 'I wish I had never known it!' Something, anything she wished for that would have saved her from the dread to let Grandcourt come.

. . . 'you don't feel able to decide?' said Mrs Davilow, sympathizingly.

'I *must* decide,' said Gwendolen, walking to the writing-table and seating herself. All the while there was a busy undercurrent in her, like the thought of a man who keeps up a dialogue while he is considering how he can slip away. (*Daniel Deronda*, 1876)[2]

Each of these extracts depicts a woman in acute distress of mind. Jane Eyre and Gwendolen Harleth both struggle with the emotional and moral consequences of a choice (to marry or not to marry) that in neither case feels simply like a choice. For Jane Eyre, the decision not to marry Mr Rochester has been made for her by the discovery that he has a wife already living; the determination then to leave him was a reassertion of independence – but how incompletely achieved, and at what emotional price, she strives to make explicit. The second passage describes the ongoing mental turmoil associated with Gwendolen's need to decide whether or not she will marry the autocratic Grandcourt. Her recent announcement that she intends to accept him has been driven more by revulsion from the threat of poverty, and with it the loss of the power of 'doing as she liked', than by positive attraction to the man. The inner recoil that accompanied the declaration has just now taken added force from the discovery that (like Rochester) he has a pre-existing moral obligation to another woman, and to a child.

The differences in the depiction of psychology between these two passages are in part the result of differences in narrative perspective, prose style,

---

2 George Eliot, *Daniel Deronda*, ed. Graham Handley (Oxford: Clarendon Press, 1984), Book III, chapter 26, pp. 271–2.

and proximate literary influences. *Daniel Deronda* is no more the typical voice of 1876 than *Jane Eyre* was the typical voice of 1847. Nevertheless, in the vocabularies they have available to them for thinking about psychology, the prioritization afforded to those vocabularies, and the pressure placed upon them, they offer a starting point for charting the developments in thinking about subjectivity, knowledge of the mind, and the role of imagination that took place across the middle decades of the nineteenth century – developments that helped to shape, and were themselves shaped in part by, the period's imaginative literature.

Modern although it seemed to many of its first readers, radical though it was in its impassioned defence of the desires of a woman without financial independence or social position, *Jane Eyre* was in other respects a conservative text – more exactly, a text in which a strong moral conservatism is in tension with a fiercely iconoclastic individualism, and in which discernibly modern kinds of thinking about psychology are combined with much older models. Its depiction of the workings of the mind draws primarily on two psychological vocabularies which would have been familiar to eighteenth-century readers: faculty psychology and, not fully distinct from it, a Christian (high Anglican) vocabulary of soul-guidance. Both are employed in ways that attempt to reconcile a Romantic validation of free personal expression of desire with a felt need for stern self-restraint and grateful trust in God's providence.

Faculty psychology had its formal roots in sixteenth-century philosophy of mind, but the version early Victorian British writers inherited was fed by three main philosophical tributaries: the Scottish 'Common Sense' tradition of Thomas Reid and Dugald Stewart; the writings of Coleridge; and (though debates about its interpretation were fierce and ongoing) Kant's Third Critique.[3] The language of faculty psychology was also, importantly, an 'informal and everyday' language, 'connected with ordinary people's views about human capacities for affection, will, and the expression of what is beautiful'.[4] According to this view of the psyche, the mind was the seat of innate powers and capacities, including the will, reason, memory, and the passions – all of which were understood to be unified at a higher level in a transcendent consciousness. Some quasi-physiological support came, in the early nineteenth century, from phrenology (referenced at several points in

---

3 See Rick Rylance, *Victorian Psychology and British Culture 1850–1880* (Oxford University Press, 2000), p. 54.
4 Roger Smith, *The Fontana History of the Human Sciences* (London: Fontana, 1997), p. 203.

Jane Eyre), with its detailed mapping of the 'animal, moral and intellectual powers' of the mind on to the surface lumps and bumps of the skull.[5] Faculty psychology was also not incompatible with the theory and practice of mesmerism, or animal magnetism, in which subjects were placed in a trance-like state, during which the body was freed from the control of the will. (Mesmeric language seems especially strong at those moments in *Jane Eyre* when Jane experiences supernatural communications of God's or Mother Nature's will.)

When allied, as in Brontë's writing and the writings of Coleridge, to an explicitly Christian discourse of the soul, faculty psychology was (for all its hospitability to empiricist confirmation) a metaphysical model of mind, tending to intellectual and political conservatism. Like most nineteenth-century adherents, Brontë ranks the faculties hierarchically, with passion at the bottom, reason and its directive power, the will, at the top. The soul is made the arena of a strenuous psychomachia – a drama of opposing powers: reason/passion, will/weakness. But to that long-established structural model Brontë adds a much more recent set of ideas about psychic conflict, drawing (as Sally Shuttleworth has shown) on a familiarity with the psychological literature she encountered in *Blackwood's Edinburgh Magazine*, the Leeds periodical press, and the Haworth and Keighley Mechanics' Institutes, as well as various psychological and medical works in her father's library.

Jane Eyre's pervasive emphasis, for example, on the necessity of repressing passion and egoism ('scorn[ing] and crush[ing] the insane promptings of a frenzied moment'), and its description of normal functioning selfhood as a condition of self-concealment or masking, aligns closely with French psychiatry and German Romantic psychology of the period. Brontë may have read at first hand the writings of the French alienist Etienne Esquirol, whose *Treatise on Insanity* (the Keighley Mechanics' Institute Library held the 1845 English edition) pursued just such an account of the disjunction between inner impulses and socially sanctioned behaviour.[6] Her understanding of psychology seems even closer, in many respects, to the work of James

---

5 George Combe, *The Constitution of Man Considered in Relation to External Objects* (1828), 5th edn revd. (Edinburgh: J. Anderson jun., 1835), quoted in Sally Shuttleworth and Jenny Bourne Taylor (eds.), *Embodied Selves: An Anthology of Psychological Texts 1830–1890* (Oxford: Clarendon Press, 1998), p. 31.

6 See Sally Shuttleworth, *Charlotte Brontë and Victorian Psychology* (Cambridge University Press, 2004), p. 26.

Ferrier, which she is likely to have encountered in *Blackwood's*.[7] Ferrier was a controversial Scottish philosopher, who spent his professional life teaching in Edinburgh and St Andrew's universities. His ambition was to compel the school of Thomas Reid (then the orthodoxy in Edinburgh) into an accommodation with the arguments of German idealism. He had read Kant, Hegel, and Fichte in the original German, and considered them grossly misrepresented both by Coleridge and by Ferrier's own mentor, Sir William Hamilton. In the 'Introduction to the Philosophy of Consciousness', published in *Blackwood's* between 1838 and 1839, Ferrier argues that the defining quality of the human mind lies in the fact that 'there is generally something over and above the change [or sensory stimulus]' described by the empiricists. This 'unabsorbed something is the fact of consciousness, the notion and the reality of himself as the person experiencing the change.'[8] Consciousness comes into being, Ferrier claims, 'not through sensation, but by and through an act of discrimination, or virtual negation'.[9] Our minds are not the passive recipients of sensory experience, because it is the office of consciousness 'to combat, to weaken, or to destroy' the energetic forces of sensation.[10]

The Romantic notes in this forced marriage of common sense to idealism come out strongly in Ferrier's claims that man 'brings himself into existence, not indeed as a being, but as a *human* being; not as an existence, but as an existence *calling itself* "I," by an act of absolute and essential freedom'.[11] But this is also, perhaps surprisingly, an explicitly Christian philosophy. Ferrier concludes that morality is the product of the deep antagonism he has described between consciousness and our nature, and he ties the historical emergence of our consciousness to the biblical stories of the Fall and the Redemption.[12] These are precisely the notes of embattled but proud independence, allied with an explicit commitment to the Christian framework of original sin meeting with God's forgiveness, that one hears in *Jane Eyre*.

The sense found in both Esquirol and Ferrier of the necessarily fraught and contestatory nature of ordinary consciousness marked a significant shift

---

7 Shuttleworth, *ibid.*, pp. 174–5 notes Brontë's possible familiarity with Ferrier, and sees connections with his emphasis on normal consciousness as a condition of masking.
8 James Ferrier, 'An Introduction to the Philosophy of Consciousness', Part I, *Blackwood's Edinburgh Magazine* 43 (1838), pp. 186–201, 437–52, 784–91; 44 (1838), pp. 234–44, 539–52; 45 (1839), pp. 201–11, 419–30: Part II, *Blackwood's* 43 (1838), pp. 437–52: p. 447.
9 *Ibid.*, Part V, *Blackwood's* 44 (1838), pp. 539–52: p. 548.
10 *Ibid.*, Part II, *Blackwood's* 43 (1838), p. 449.   11 *Ibid.*
12 *Ibid.*, Part VII, *Blackwood's* 45 (1839), pp. 419–30.

from the eighteenth century's emphasis on sanity and insanity as conditions particular to the individual. In its place came an understanding that the powers and pathologies of the mind are formed largely through its inter-action with the world and with other people. The nationalist twist given to that more social and cultural view of psychology in *Jane Eyre* marks a prejudice on Brontë's part, though a common one in the period. Reason, for Jane Eyre, is a 'healthy' English attribute, holding the insanity of French passion defiantly at bay. She also adds a firmly doctrinaire moral and religious turn. 'Principle' and 'law' demand that she live not as a French mistress, 'slave in a fool's paradise', weakly deluding herself that Rochester's love will last, but make her way as an independent English schoolteacher, free from 'remorse' and 'shame'. Adherence to 'principle' and 'law' is supported – perhaps only made possible (there is some ambiguity) – by God's providence. Behind this driven, self-regulatory internal dialogue of self and soul, the ongoing literary influence of Bunyan's *Pilgrim's Progress* is plainly audible, pitted against the more Byronic elements in a kind of literary analogue to the war of the faculties.

The surprise in the passage comes with Jane's summary of this ferocious internal struggle as 'eventide musings'. Where a less calm word might be expected, Charlotte Brontë seems to invoke the Anglican service of *Evening Prayer*, with its injunctions to take stock of God's goodness at the close of the day. That, at least, is the superficial mood evoked. The emotional reach of the scene goes far deeper because the narrative voice is so evidently unpersuaded by its own rational determinations. Even before Jane's admis-sion that the certainty that she was right did not give her happiness, and that she wept rather than rejoiced in her proud isolation, the sentences strain to say something more than reason and self-control permit. The ultimate appeal is not to reason but to 'feeling', which resists rational and moral redirection and fights against concealment. Though the narrative perspec-tive is of long hindsight, the struggle against temptation seems not over but ongoing, discernible in the hyperbolic cast of the opposing choices on offer ('fevered with delusive bliss ... suffocating with the bitterest tears'), the heavy alliterativeness akin to verbal underscoring ('sunk down in the silken snare'), and the tensed syntax, evocative of the passion of the writing moment.

If the extract from *Daniel Deronda* feels to twenty-first century readers the more intimate and more recognizably modern portrait of psychological distress, this is not because George Eliot attempts to compete with Brontë in conveying the sheer intensity of desire. Written in the third person, rather than the first, the account of Gwendolen's psyche is less demonstratively emotional, but it is intimate with pained confusion of feeling and with the idiosyncracies of its heroine's psychology in a way that Brontë's updated psychomachia cannot quite be. *Daniel Deronda*'s psychological realism owes much to Eliot's quiet but extensive use of free indirect style, which permits ironic demurral from Gwendolen's self-perception, but which as often (and increasingly, across the novel) produces sympathetic immanence of description: 'Impossible for Gwendolen not to feel', 'Here came the terror', 'Quick, quick ...' If subjectivity is an internal drama of opposing forces in early Brontë, for late Eliot it is something less theatrical. The greater privacy, but also the greater loss of certainty about one's own mental processes – loss, indeed, of confident ownership of those processes – is captured in the readerly, rather than dramatic, image of 'pictures in a book beaten open with a sense of hurry'. Who owns the book, whose hand manipulates it, is unclear.

Often Eliot offers metaphors for psychological events which, though rendered in visual terms, are not strongly imagistic or scenic but which rather foreground the difficulty of insight into and knowledge of oneself. There is no Bunyanesque sinking down in snares or crushing of opposing forces. The pictures of Gwendolen's mind are more remote, less easily described. They come 'vividly, yet in fragments'; her encounter with Grand-court's former mistress has already become 'symbolic' – event turning abstract as it enters memory, 'unalterable experience' assuming the frighteningly static quality of a 'vision' (a revelation, as it seems to Gwendolen, of a moral 'truth' – that men and things are worthless). Such vision is too quick for conscious thought, resistant to 'tempering reflections'.

It is important then to note how firmly faculty psychology retains a place in Eliot's vocabulary. That it does so is less surprising when one considers how tenacious its hold is even now in our popular psychological vocabulary. Its stubborn persistence in the English language, though its scientific basis had by the 1860s been called into question, can be seen in the references to Gwendolen 'getting a sort of empire over her own life', and to apparently inborn powers and qualities of mental experience: resolve, repulsion, disbe-lief, 'native terror'. But whereas for Brontë those powers and qualities tend to be dramatically hypostatized (often capitalized, sometimes more amply personified), in Eliot they are subdued to a narrative which seems, like Gwendolen herself, unpersuaded of the accuracy of the available terms of psychological description. The account of what, and how, Gwendolen thinks is continually revised, partly because her mind is constantly changing (thought, for Eliot, is a complex and evolving process, not a drama of opposing forces), and partly because the existing vocabulary for the operations of the mind seems falsely crystallizing. What 'sort of empire' over oneself is it possible to have? Is 'resolve' a power within, or a posture to be aspired to? How does one access 'choice' or find a right focus for a 'wish'?

Part of Eliot's resistance to the mental taxonomies of faculty psychology can be explained in terms of her intellectual engagement with those opposing, and increasingly influential, strains in nineteenth-century psychological theory known collectively as 'the school of Locke' or 'the associationist school', critically developed by David Hartley in the 1740s and most famously but variously represented in the mid-Victorian period by James Mill, Alexander Bain, and Herbert Spencer. Even as firm a believer in God-given faculties as Brontë can be seen to have owed much to Lockean empiricism, with its view of the psyche as a blank slate, taking form and accruing ideas through perceptual and sensory experience. (It surely affects her sense of the formative power of childhood events.) But the years between early Brontë and late Eliot saw associationism shifting towards physiological psychology and then into the beginnings of evolutionary psychology. They witnessed important advances in the anatomical understanding of the brain as the organ of mind, and in the physiological basis of what we would now call neurology – including the localization of cerebral functions. ('Cerebrocentrism' took a surprisingly long time to become an established notion – as opposed to the notion of mind as more physically distributed, spatially extended. It only took firm hold by the 1830s through the work of materialist, necessitarian associationists, who tended to be on the Unitarian-to-atheist end of the religious spectrum – hence in part the opposition the idea encountered.[13]) The third quarter of the nineteenth century also saw a crucial turning of attention to the hereditary components of mental functioning and mental health, both in terms of family histories and (after Darwin's *The Expression of the Emotions in Man and Animals* (1872)) of much longer-evolved characteristics of the species.

Alexander Bain was probably more influential than any other one author in broadening public acceptance of the new physiological psychology. His

---

13 See Roger Smith, 'The Background of Physiological Psychology in Natural Philosophy', *History of Science* II:2 (1973), pp. 75–123 (esp. pp. 81–8); Robert M. Young, *Mind, Brain and Adaptation in the Nineteenth Century: Cerebral Localization and its Biological Context from Gall to Ferrier* (Oxford: Clarendon Press, 1970), esp. pp. 101–221; Rylance, *Victorian Psychology*, pp. 9–10. My thanks to Elfed Huw Price for the information on cerebrocentrism.

major works (*The Senses and the Intellect* (1855, 3rd revd edn 1868), *The Emotions and the Will* (1859, 3rd revd edn 1875), *Mind and Body: The Theories of their Relation* (1873)) extended the theoretical anatomical base of associationism, while also putting strict associationism under strain by recognizing 'a more active element, or spontaneity, in the mind itself'. (The summary is from J. S. Mill, one of Bain's staunchest supporters.[14]) Herbert Spencer's evolutionary developmental model of mind, pursued through two editions of *The Principles of Psychology* (1855 and 1870–2), marked, even more than Bain's, the culmination and the end point of the associationist model. Spencer abandoned the conventional terrain of psychology, in which the external findings of observation were brought into attempted correlation with the subjective reports of introspection (always a forced correlation, in Spencer's view). He argued that the only basis for a scientific psychology was comparative biology. The emotions had 'evolved through the various grades of the animal kingdom', and reached various stages of sophistication in the 'lower' and 'higher' human races. The will (for most psychologists the crucial factor in preserving individual agency and holding reductionist accounts of mind at bay), was to be seen, along with other higher so-called 'faculties' such as reason, memory, and the aesthetic sense, as a late outcome of natural selection – an advantageous superaddition on an otherwise incoherent complexity of mental responses.[15]

For many readers these developments greatly enhanced the threat that the workings of the mind would come to be seen as little more than automatism. Resistance to associationist and later physiological and evolutionary models of mind runs deep in the work of many – perhaps the majority of – literary writers in the period, including Brontë, A. H. Hallam, Tennyson, Dickens, Carlyle, Arnold, Thackeray. Associationism, Carlyle wrote, 'is not a philosophy of the mind; it is a mere ... genetic history of what we see *in* the mind'. To accept its tenets was to risk enslavement to the automatist culture of the machine age.[16] 'Who forged that other influence', Tennyson protests, 'That heat of inward evidence, / By which

---

14 J. S. Mill, 'Bain's Psychology', *Edinburgh Review* 110 (1859), pp. 287–321: p. 301. See Smith, 'The background', pp. 95–6; Young, *Mind, Brain and Adaptation*, pp. 150–96.

15 See Rylance, *Victorian Psychology*, pp. 215–16. For Bain's psychology and its contribution to theories of cerebral localization, see Young, *Mind, Brain and Adaptation*, pp. 101–33.

16 'Signs of the Times' (1829), in *The Works of Thomas Carlyle*, 30 vols. (London: Chapman and Hall, 1899), vol. XXVII, pp. 56–82: p. 64. Discussed in Anne Harrington, ' "Other ways of knowing": the Politics of Knowledge in Interwar German Brain Science', in Harrington (ed.), *So Human a Brain: Knowledge and Value in the Neurosciences* (Boston: Birkhaüser/Dibner Institute, 1992), p. 231.

[man] doubts against the sense?' And more pugnaciously: 'I think we are not wholly brain, / Magnetic mockeries . . .'[17]

Several elements in George Eliot's account of Gwendolen indicate, by contrast, a very early receptiveness towards physiological psychology. The description, for example, of a new wish, and a new moral sense, forming in Gwendolen implies something more than the banal observation that the mind is affected by experience: it speaks to a perception that the psyche is substantially *shaped* by experience. So, the unlooked-for encounter with another woman already deceived by Grandcourt operates as a direct catalyst of change in Gwendolen's mind. It enters into the 'dark seed-growths of consciousness', bringing into being a desire not to possess this knowledge and introducing a frightening new sense of moral despair. Eliot also appears (above all in those passages depicting Gwendolen in trance states of terror) to admit the more radical possibility that the mind has no innate faculties of resistance but only those powers developed in the course of a person's life. That possibility is countered, repeatedly in *Daniel Deronda*, by a moralizing emphasis on the potential strength of the will and (in keeping with the collective and altruistic strains in evolutionary psychology[18]) on the power of others to educate and assist that will, but the associationist inclinations of Eliot's language still put her at a long distance from the many more intellectually conservative, or simply less up-to-date, writers who continued to rely upon the concept of inborn faculties, granted and supported by God. The destabilizing of the old psychological surety brings terror to Gwendolen at this point in her life; with harder experience behind her, she will come to see it as offering the hope of genuine growth towards greater individual and collective good.

The single most telling sign for twenty-first century readers of Eliot's psychological modernity must be that reference to 'dark seed-growths of consciousness'. Eliot has a vocabulary for mobility and also layeredness of consciousness which – though earlier writers would have had little trouble understanding it – reflects familiarity with recent medical and philosophical writing about aspects of mental functioning not available to

---

17 'The two voices' (published 1842, dated 1833), lines 283–5 and *In Memoriam* (1850), section cxx, in *The Poems of Tennyson*, ed. Christopher Ricks, 3 vols., 2nd edn (Harlow: Longman, 1987), vol. I, p. 585; vol. II, p. 440.
18 Eliot's thinking about altruism was largely influenced by other (not primarily psychological) kinds of philosophical and sociological writing. On Eliot and social organicism more broadly conceived, see Sally Shuttleworth, *George Eliot and Nineteenth-Century Science: The Make-Believe of a Beginning* (Cambridge University Press, 1984).

rational self-reflection. Writers such as William Benjamin Carpenter, Eneas Sweetland Dallas, and Frances Power Cobbe, as well as Eliot's partner the philosopher and self-taught physiologist George Henry Lewes, had all written about the mind in ways that complicated or directly contested the 'tabula rasa' model and sought to replace it with the idea of complex strata of consciousness, only some of which are accessible to subjective scrutiny.[19] The notion of 'dark seed-growths of consciousness' is a subtler development of what had always been there in Eliot's writings: an awareness of the changing content and quality of consciousness as experience assists or thwarts the individual's moral development. *The Mill on the Floss*, for example, speaks of Maggie Tulliver 'adjusting her consciousness to [a] new idea', and of her having 'a keen, vibrating consciousness' of new possibilities in life, 'a new consciousness'.[20] *Middlemarch*, too, refers to 'begetting new consciousness'.[21] But *Daniel Deronda* offers a more particularized vocabulary for the individual's experience of such psychological changes – the felt obscurity of their sources and mechanisms, the difficulty of conveying the experience in the current languages of mental and moral development.

The reference to a 'busy undercurrent' in Gwendolen might have struck some few of Eliot's early readers as an echo from Lewes, who not long before had coined the term 'stream of consciousness', subsequently made famous by William James. Lewes uses the phrase in *The Physiology of Common Life* (1859–60) to describe the mind's movement between conscious and unconscious states, and between voluntary and involuntary responses to sensory stimuli. He writes also of 'the general stream of Sensation which constitutes [the reader's] feeling of existence – the consciousness of himself as a sensitive being'.[22] (The breadth of Lewes's literary uptake is evidenced by a direct reference to this book in the early pages of Dostoyevsky's *Crime*

19 William Benjamin Carpenter, *Principles of Mental Physiology* (1874), 2nd edn (London: Henry S. King, 1875); Eneas Sweetland Dallas, *The Gay Science*, 2 vols. (London: Chapman and Hall, 1866); Frances Power Cobbe, 'Unconscious Cerebration', in *Darwinism in Morals, and Other Essays* (London: William and Norgate, 1872); George Henry Lewes, *The Physiology of Common Life*, 2 vols. (Edinburgh: William Blackwood and Sons, 1859–60). Key extracts from these and other relevant texts are reprinted in Shuttleworth and Taylor (eds.), *Embodied Selves*, pp. 65–95.
20 George Eliot, *The Mill on the Floss*, ed. Gordon S. Haight (Oxford: Clarendon Press, 1980), pp. 264, 387, 388 (Book 5, chapter 1; Book 6, chapter 10, Book 6, chapter 10).
21 George Eliot, *Middlemarch*, ed. David Carroll (Oxford: Clarendon Press, 1986), p. 93 (Book 1, chapter 11).
22 Lewes, *The Physiology of Common Life*, 2 vols. (Edinburgh: William Blackwood and Sons, 1859–60), vol. ii, pp. 63, 66.

and Punishment.[23]) Eliot is not, or not often, interested in registering that fluidity of consciousness in the form and texture of her prose, as many subsequent writers would be, but she does convey the density and, crucially, the simultaneity of mental events and responses in ways that come through as a kind of pressure on the language – not least prepositionally and conjunctively: 'Again ... Here ... Yet ... and yet ... all the while'.

Above all, Eliot shares with Lewes an alertness to the linguistic and literary challenges incurred in attempting to render the life of the mind in words. Like him, she foregrounds the necessarily metaphoric character of all psychological descriptions: 'the stream of consciousness', the 'busy under-current ... like the thought of a man, who keeps up a dialogue while he is considering how he can slip away' (almost certainly a reference to the dualistic state of mind that contemporary medical writers called 'double consciousness'[24]). In common with Lewes, Eliot emphasizes the degree to which psychology must remain an art rather than a science.[25] 'Feeling is purely subjective', Lewes warns towards the end of *The Physiology*, summarizing what remains one of the great problems of psychology: 'That others feel, as we feel, is to us a matter of positive conviction, but can never be a matter of demonstration. We conclude that other men feel as we feel, because they act as we act ... we have no *proof*, rigorously speaking.'[26] Eliot stages both the 'positive conviction' and how incomplete and inexact this awareness of another person's interiority must remain (the 'equivalent centre of self', as she famously put it in *Middlemarch*,[27] is at once the same and irreducibly different): '"[Y]ou don't feel able to decide?"' Mrs Davilow says 'sympathizingly', rather than with validated sympathy. '"I *must* decide,"'

---

23 Fyodor Dostoyevsky, *Crime and Punishment*, trans. with an introduction and notes by David McDuff (London: Penguin, 2003), p. 22.
24 See esp. Robert Macnish, *The Philosophy of Sleep* (1830), 3rd edn (Glasgow: W. R. M'Phun, 1836); Arthur Ladbroke Wigan, *A New View of Insanity: The Duality of the Mind Proved by the Structure, Function and Diseases of the Brain, and by the Phenomena of Mental Derangement, and Shewn to be Essential to Moral Responsibility* (London: Longman, Brown, Green and Longman, 1844); Henry Holland, *Chapters on Mental Physiology* (London: Longman, Brown, Green and Longman, 1852). Extracts from these and other key works are reprinted in Shuttleworth and Taylor, *Embodied Selves*, pp. 123–40.
25 They are not exceptional in this. See, for example, Ferrier, 'Introduction', p. 192, claiming that we find psychology in Shakespeare, not 'on the dissecting table of Dr Brown'. And see Smith, 'The Background', on the persistent problem of consciousness in physiological accounts of psychology: much modern physiological psychology, as he notes, 'is concerned with debating whether such a science is possible in the first place' (p. 79).
26 Lewes, *Physiology*, vol. II, p. 237.   27 Eliot, *Middlemarch*, chapter 21, p. 198.

replies Gwendolen, acting with apparent decision, while the 'busy undercurrent' of psychological resistance flows on.

Brontë and Eliot are prominent and important examples of writers who engaged actively with contemporary psychological theories in their fiction and poetry. Many other literary figures were similarly well informed about developments in psychology and psychiatric medicine through the periodical press and the general intellectual arguments of the day. Robert Browning, Alfred Tennyson, Wilkie Collins, Edward Bulwer Lytton, William Makepeace Thackeray, Elizabeth Gaskell, and, later in the period, George Meredith, Walter Pater, Oscar Wilde, have all attracted close attention from critics interested in their specific intellectual debts and their responses to contemporary debate. To consider some of them comparatively, however, is to find very different orders and extents of engagement.

The most striking instance of literature responding directly and in a reformist spirit to contemporary developments in psychology is the vogue for sensation fiction in the early 1860s. When H. L. Mansel (Oxford philosopher, and later Dean of St Paul's) remarked that Wilkie Collins, Mary Elizabeth Braddon, Sheridan Lefanu, and Mrs Henry Wood were 'preaching to the nerves instead of the judgment',[28] he was of course disparaging sensationalism's stimulation and exploitation of its readers' anxieties. For critics now, sensation fiction's expressly neuro-physiological conception of the reading process is reason to value the genre anew. Novels such as *The Woman in White* (1860), *Lady Audley's Secret* (1862), and *Uncle Silas* (1864) drew closely on debates in this decade about nervous pathology – also about the definition of sanity and insanity, about latent insanity, moral insanity, hysteria, amnesia, double consciousness and other pathological or intensified states of mind. Some works, including Charles Reade's *Hard Cash* (1863) and various articles published in Dickens's periodicals *Household Words* and *All the Year Round*, had a declared intention to produce change in the asylum laws. Many demonstrated an interest in testing specific psychological theories. Collins, for instance, made intensive use, in *The Moonstone* (1868), of contemporary medical theories of amnesia, including W. B. Carpenter's work on unconscious and recovered memories and John Elliotson's 'wilder' model of the unconscious as revealed through mesmerism.[29]

28 Unattributed remark, quoted in unsigned review article [H.L. Mansel], 'Sensation Novels', *Quarterly Review* 113 (1863), p. 481.
29 William B. Carpenter, *Principles of Mental Physiology, with their Applications to the Training and Discipline of the Mind, and the Study of Its Morbid Conditions* (London: H. S. King and Co., 1874); John Elliotson, *Human Physiology* (1840), 5th edn (London:

Sensation fiction was exceptional in its topicality and, often, its avowedly social agendas. In the main the modes of engagement between literature and psychology (including psychiatry) are quieter, taking place at various literary levels – not only the content of the plot, but literary forms, and implicit assumptions about how the minds of characters and, indeed, of readers operate. For Robert Louis Stevenson, one of the keenest late-century respondents to evolutionary psychology, the primary literary interest of psychological theory lay in what it could teach a modern, civilized culture about 'the persistence of precivilized states of consciousness ... in the guise of romance, oral narratives, childhood make-believe, and the literary imagination'.[30] Degeneration theory, most influentially promulgated in this period, by Max Nordau and Cesare Lombroso, held that the civilized (European) human races were declining in biological fitness, and that insanity, criminality, and moral decadence were on the increase. It had widespread impact on late nineteenth-century psychology, as well as on the social and anthropological sciences more broadly. Stevenson's classic story, 'The Strange Case of Dr Jekyll and Mr Hyde', is reminiscent of sensation fiction in the way it plays on such fears of biological and psychological atavism: 'with ape-like fury, [Mr Hyde] was trampling his victim under foot and hailing down a storm of blows ...' The less well-remembered short story, 'Olalla' (1885), is still more explicit in its references to science as it describes the hereditary insanity, idiocy, and debauchery that have brought a once great Spanish family 'to the brink of destitution'.[31] But if these and Stevenson's other fictions lean towards heavy-handedness in dramatizing degeneration theory,[32] Stevenson was capable of considerable subtlety in the psychological explanations he offered for popular fiction's appeal to its readers:

> novels begin to touch not the fine *dilettanti* but the gross mass of mankind, when they leave off to speak of parlours and shades of manner and still-born niceties of motive, and begin to deal with fighting, sailoring, adventure,

Longman, Orme, Brown, Green, and Longmans, 1840). Discussed in Jenny Bourne Taylor, *In the Secret Theatre of Home: Wilkie Collins, Sensation Narrative, and Nineteenth-Century Psychology* (London: Routledge, 1988), p. 177. See especially her Introduction, pp. 57–63, and chapter 6. See also Ian Hacking, *Rewriting the Soul: Multiple Personality and the Sciences of Memory* (Princeton University Press, 1995), on the importance of the study of memory to securing psychology's status as a science from the 1860s onwards.

30 Julia Reid, *Robert Louis Stevenson, Science, and the Fin de Siècle* (Basingstoke: Palgrave Macmillan, 2006), p. 15.

31 Robert Louis Stevenson, *Dr Jekyll and Mr Hyde, The Merry Men, and Other Tales* (London: J. M. Dent, 1925), pp. 157–93: p. 157.

32 See Daniel Pick, *Faces of Degeneration: A European Disorder, c. 1848–c. 1918* (Cambridge University Press, 1989).

death or child-birth; and thus ancient outdoor crafts and occupations ... lift romance into a near neighbourhood with epic. These aged things have on them the dew of man's morning; they lie near, not so much to us, the semi-artificial flowerets, as to the trunk and aboriginal taproot of the race.[33]

The increased receptiveness to the new psychology, by the 1870s, extended to writers less fully persuaded of its explanatory power than Stevenson. Thomas Hardy's fiction, for example, was extensively influenced by Spencer's evolutionary developmentalism (as well as by Darwin, Haeckel, and many others). He may also have had some familiarity with the Spencerian concept of organic memory (popularized by Samuel Butler), according to which the experiences of our ancestors are recorded in our bodies as physiological and mental habits or intuitions. But Hardy was, characteristically, non-dogmatic. He depicted characters whose physical appearance is ambiguously at once representative and exceptional, and whose behaviour is seen to be determined by their biological inheritance and yet prone to sudden assertions of agency that disrupt the impression of determinism. So, in Clym Yeobright's face can be 'dimly seen the typical countenance of the future ... The view of life as a thing to be put up with, replacing that zest for existence which was so intense in early civilizations, must ultimately enter so thoroughly into the constitution of the advanced races that its facial expression will become accepted as a new artistic departure'.[34] Tess of the d'Urbervilles is 'an almost standard woman, but for the slight incautiousness of character inherited from her race'; the occasional flaring into violence that culminates in her murder of her seducer is, undecidably, the mental aberration of a moment, or the predictable expression of an inherited moral flaw (some 'obscure strain in the d'Urberville blood'), and thus a kind of physiological determinism at work in her, or perhaps the flaring out of an exceptional, individualistic romantic passion (Angel wonders at the 'strength of her affection for himself; and at the strangeness of its quality, which had apparently extinguished her moral sense altogether').[35]

However keen and however critical or otherwise a writer's engagement with contemporary sciences of the mind, the representation of psychology in literature necessarily takes its inspiration and its vocabulary from much

---

33 Robert Louis Stevenson, 'Pastoral' (1887), in *Memories and Portraits* (London: Chatto and Windus, 1904), pp. 90–105: pp. 102–3. Discussed in Reid, *Robert Louis Stevenson*, pp. 19–20.

34 Thomas Hardy, *The Return of the Native* (Oxford University Press, 2005), p. 165 (Book 3, chapter 1).

35 Thomas Hardy, *Tess of the d'Urbervilles*, ed. Juliet Grindel and Simon Gatrell (Oxford: Clarendon Press, 1983), pp. 128, 524, 524 (chapter 14, chapter 57, chapter 57).

further afield – historically as well as intellectually. Tennyson was an informed respondent to many branches of contemporary science, including early evolutionary thought and Victorian geology and astronomy. He had a special interest in psychiatry (unhappily so, given the history of insanity in his immediate family), but there were gaps in his knowledge and limits to his interest in the new psychology. His complimentary copy of Spencer is tellingly uncut after the first few pages.[36] An inveterate opponent of materialist theories of physiology and psychology, he gave the culture some of its most haunted expressions of those ideas ('all experience past became / Consolidate in mind and frame'; "Tis the blot upon the brain / That *will* show itself without'[37]). But the spurs to his thinking were always broader and more various than contemporary writings alone. Like many scientists, he was prompted to poetic argument with materialism by reading Lucretius on atomism as well as by reading his contemporaries, Lyell and Buckland. His portrayal of mental breakdown, in the monodrama *Maud* (1855), is in dialogue with Shakespeare, William Cowper, and Walter Scott, as much as with modern psychiatry. It owes a nearer debt to the work of the Spasmodic poets, briefly in vogue in the late 1840s and 1850s. Alexander Smith and Sydney Dobell, particularly, influenced his choice of the verse drama form as a vehicle for exploring psychological instability; also his experimental use of metre and rhythm to imitate the mental 'spasms' of insanity – though he brought a much higher order of technical control to the genre. *Maud's* reception was mixed. Its extended concentration on 'a morbid, poetic soul, under the blighting influence of a recklessly speculative age',[38] and its speaker's immoderate passion for war (toned down in later printings), drew hostile reactions from several readers, but it found some prominent admirers, including John Bucknill, one of the most famous alienists, or mad-doctors, of the day.[39]

> Dead, long dead,
> Long dead!
> And my heart is a handful of dust,
> And the wheels go over my head,

---

36 My thanks to Gregory Tate for this information.
37 Tennyson, 'The Two Voices', lines 365–6; *Maud* (1855), lines 247–8; 'Oh! That 'Twere Possible' (1837), lines 69–70; in *Poems*, vol. I, p. 589; vol. II, p. 577; vol. II, p. 23.
38 Hallam Lord Tennyson, *Alfred Lord Tennyson: A Memoir*, 2 vols. (London: Macmillan and Co., 1897), vol. I, p. 396.
39 Tennyson, *Maud*, *Poems*, vol. II, pp. 247–8; and see Edgar F. Shannon, Jr, 'The Critical Reception of Tennyson's *Maud*', *PMLA* 68:3 (1953), pp. 397–417, especially pp. 404–5.

> And my bones are shaken with pain,
> For into a shallow grave they are thrust,
> Only a yard beneath the street,
> And the hoofs of the horses beat,
> Beat into my scalp and my brain . . .[40]

Metre is here made to emulate the feverish pulsing of blood in the temples, repetitions (of words, sounds, syntax) become the index of a terrifying entrapment in one's own mind, where brain and body have come to seem a living grave. Instead of form containing or constraining thought, form is dictated by the perceiving mind, the lines finding their length from the pressure of the metrical 'beat/ Beat'.

Browning's case again raises the vexed question of how wide a range of influences may be pertinent to a historical understanding of psychology in literature. He seems to have derived his ideas about psychology as much from pre-Victorian writers as from his contemporaries. He acknowledged as his 'literary godfather' the radical Unitarian preacher William Johnson Fox, who advocated associationist psychology as the intellectual basis for a new poetry that would analyse the modern mind and impress itself directly upon that mind.[41] But in practice Browning's poetry was more profoundly indebted to Romantic (especially Shelleyan and Coleridgean) ideas of the transcendent power of the creative imagination and the decisive force of the individual will. His fascination with pathologies of mind (the dramatic monologue portraits of homicidal jealousy, or of egoism carried even to solipsism), and his interest, more widely, in the embodied conditions of the psyche had less to do with reading in the new sciences than with a mytho-poetic interest in the specific character of the poet's mind. The ingrained habit of dualistic thinking (the 'objective' versus the 'subjective' Poet, 'head' versus 'heart', 'will' versus 'conformity'), that marks his most influential expression in that vein, the 'Essay on Shelley' (1852), struck even his contemporaries as more a peculiarity of his intellect than typical of the period.[42]

Matthew Arnold's interest in contemporary psychological debates appears to have been still more narrowly cultivated. He can be presumed to have had at least a nodding acquaintance with developments in the

---

40 Tennyson, *Maud*, lines 240–8, in *Poems*, vol. II, p. 577.
41 Isobel Armstrong, *Victorian Poetry: Poetry, Poetics and Politics* (London: Routledge, 1993), pp. 32–3.
42 See Richard S. Kennedy and Donald S. Hair, *The Dramatic Imagination of Robert Browning: A Literary Life* (Columbia: University of Missouri Press, 2007), p. 59.

psychological sciences, as reported in the periodical literature, but his more sustained reading was in philosophy. In the mid-1840s he pursued some reading in the borderland between philosophy of mind and psychology, attacking Kant's separation of mental processes and Bishop Butler's more recent Kantian division of mental faculties, but it is not clear even then that he ventured much beyond Herder's *Metakritik* (1799).[43] His famous (though hardly, for him, typical) 'anti-psychological' polemic in the preface to his *Poems* (1853) was, like Browning's efforts to typologize two kinds of poetic psyche, primarily literary and philosophical rather than 'scientific' in inspiration. Its immediate prompt was a review of E. S. Dallas's *Poetics* (1852) and Alexander Smith's *A Life-Drama* (1852) in which David Masson (writing anonymously) claimed that 'perhaps the highest thing that one can attempt in the way of fictitious art' was 'a true allegory of the state of one's own mind in a representative history'.[44] 'No great poetical work has ever been produced' on that basis, Arnold protested. The poet is 'most fortunate, when he most entirely succeeds in effacing himself.'[45] The ideal model therefore should be not Shakespeare (or Wordsworth, or Keats), but Sophocles, and 'not so much [for] his contributions to psychology & the anatomy of sentiment, as [for] the grand moral effects produced by *style*'.[46]

Some histories of Victorian poetry have taken this redirection of Arnold's aims in poetry as definitive of mid-Victorian poetry – a turn away from Romantic and/or Epicurean inwardness towards a revitalized Aristotelian emphasis on action. But, as Ekbert Faas remarks, it is not even fully representative of Arnold's own poetic productions from 1853: 'Most of his greatest poems are cast in the mode of the great Romantic lyric. His one major drama, *Empedocles on Etna*, is clearly an allegory of Arnold's own mind in a representative history for which Byron's *Manfred* offers a precedent, and Spasmodic drama the immediate though poetically inferior contemporary context.'[47] In general, accounts of Victorian literature that rest on strong contrasts with Romantic literary inwardness are notoriously difficult to

---

43 My thanks to Nicholas Shrimpton for this information. Herder's *Metakritik* was on Arnold's reading list for 1845. It is not clear that he read it.

44 [David Masson], 'Theories of Poetry and a New Poet', *North British Review* 19 (1853), 297–338: p. 338.

45 'Preface to the first edition of *Poems* (1853)', in *Matthew Arnold*, ed. Miriam Allott and Robert H. Super (Oxford University Press, 1986), pp. 172–83: p. 177.

46 Letter to Arthur Hugh Clough, *c.* 1 March 1849, in *The Letters of Matthew Arnold*, ed. Cecil Y. Lang, 6 vols. (Charlottesville: University Press of Virginia, 1996–2001), vol. 1, p. 133. Quoted and discussed in Ekbert Faas, *Retreat into the Mind: Victorian Poetry and the Rise of Psychiatry* (Princeton University Press, 1988), pp. 122–5.

47 Faas, *Retreat into the Mind*, p. 123.

sustain. There are several locally defining moments in the literary critical polemics of the period which reveal how profoundly the Romantic validation of subjectivity and the creative power of the imagination continued to shape later nineteenth-century expectations for poetry, positively as much as negatively. John Stuart Mill's advocacy of literature as a protected space from the exhaustive demands of analytic reason, Swinburne's mischievous blurring of the distinction between 'dramatic' poetry and confessional 'lyric', Pater's and Wilde's revival of literary Epicureanism as a central element in aestheticism, are among the obvious countervoices to the Arnold of the 1853 Preface. But all such declarations of support for, or hostility to, psychological inwardness in poetry need to be read as polemical – self-consciously extreme and rhetorically motivated in the stance they take.

If there is any consistently 'Victorian' feature of these polemics, it is the underlying sense that the psychological interest of any literary work should be weighed in the writer's own mind and in the process of reception against more outward-looking, moralistic criteria for literature. The most distinctively 'Victorian' aspect, for example, of Ruskin's reworking of Romantic models of imagination, in volume ii of *Modern Painters* (1843), is the modifying appeal to conscience. There is, for Ruskin, a 'reciprocal action between the intensity of moral feeling and the power of imagination'. '[A]ll egotism, and selfish care, or regard are ... destructive' of that power. Though he is ready to concede that many 'daring and inventive conception[s]' result from nervous temperaments, especially in states of 'dreaming, fever, insanity, and other morbid conditions of mind', he declines to rank these productions with the 'right creations' of Imagination and its lesser companion, Fancy. In Ruskin's case, too, the most important influences are not scientific. He starts his analysis of the 'Imagination' with Dugald Stewart's description of combined processes of conception, abstraction, and aesthetic judgment, but finds Stewart's a 'meagre definition', which misses 'the very point and purpose' of the inquiry: namely, to account for the 'power of prophecy' that is 'the very essence' of imagination. Rejecting 'metaphysics' thereafter, he draws instead on the literary examples of Milton, Shakespeare, and Leigh Hunt's extended essay *Imagination and Fancy* (1844), and (quietly but pervasively) on his own immersion since childhood in the language of Evangelical theology.[48]

However close or remote Victorian literary writers' engagement with the psychological sciences, it is important to recognize that to talk of 'psychology'

---

48 John Ruskin, *Modern Painters* ii, in *The Works of John Ruskin*, ed. E. T. Cook and Alexander Wedderburn, 39 vols. (London: George Allen, 1903), vol. ii, pp. 257, 287, 298–9.

in this period is to beg a number of questions. Strictly speaking, its use to denote 'the science of mind' is a little premature and misleadingly narrowing. If the *OED* is correct, the word entered the English language in 1654 via S. Partlitz's translation of Nicholas Culpeper's *New Method of Physick*: 'Psychologie is the knowledg of the Soul [*Scientia de anima Ψυχολογια dicitur*]'. Its recalibration to mean 'the examination of the human mind' was an early eighteenth-century development, closely associated with Enlightenment attempts to bring the study of mental life within the domain of empiricist philosophy, but it retained the primary meaning of 'soul discourse' well into Victoria's reign. Even for later Victorian readers, 'philosophy of mind' would have been as natural a synonym as 'science of the mind'. Dugald Stewart's great categorical invention, 'philosophy of mind' was formulated very precisely to exclude the medico-materialist accounts of French atheists and Rational Dissenters. Those British writers who preferred the term, even late in the nineteenth century, can be regarded as recreating or renovating that larger discursive space – not necessarily out of hostility to the medical sciences, but wanting to include non-physicalist speculations about the nature and operations of the mind. When George Croome Robertson wrote the inaugural editorial for the journal *Mind* in 1876, he depicted psychology and philosophy as twinned enterprises. All natural science, including science of the mind, he claimed, 'must have an expression in terms of thought or subjective experience', so that 'Psychology may be shown to pass inevitably into philosophy'. He was, of course, making a territorial claim for philosophy (advocating a return to the 'unity' that until recently 'belonged to human knowledge under the name of Philosophy', and resisting the 'narrowing influences of modern [scientific] specialism') but he thought British philosophy should be in a position to benefit from advances in mental science, and believed it should be the adjudicator on just how 'scientific' they were. One of the purposes of the journal was thus 'to procure a decision on the scientific standing of psychology'.[49]

For the greater part of Victoria's reign, then, 'psychology' is best described as a set of loosely overlapping discourses on the mind: philosophy, sociology, medicine, anthropology, religion, and various common or 'folk' traditions. Literature is one of those discourses, but it also stands potentially outside them all – in a position to reflect upon all and any of them. At times it took the lead, as when, late in the century, James Sully

---

49 George Croome Robertson, 'Prefatory Words', *Mind: A Quarterly Review of Psychology and Philosophy* 1 (1876), pp. 1–6: pp. 4, 2, 3.

proposed to study the writings of Stevenson, Dickens, and others in order to measure 'the progress of our knowledge' of child psychology.[50] But while a contest for priority with the positive sciences is one way of conceiving the literary history of psychology in this period, it is not always the most relevant or enlightening. As Karen Chase rightly observes in *Eros and Psyche* (1984), the fundamental contribution literary writers made to Victorian psychology was in 'identify[ing] the experience that any science must explain'.[51]

By way of opening up the formal aspects of this question, Chase examines some of the means by which 'Realist fiction' gave imaginative structure to emotion, memory, and other aspects of mind. Those means include the psycho-geographical description of space in Brontë's romance narratives: her expression of her heroine's emotions through the contrasting dangers of exposure and confinement as experienced in architecture and landscape. They also include the interplay of different linguistic encodings of personality in *Pickwick Papers*, whereby the disjunctive, dangerous forces expressed in Jingle's speech patterns ('other day – five children – mother – tall lady, eating sandwiches – forgot the arch – crash – knock – children look round – mother's head off – sandwich in her hand – no mouth to put it in – head of a family off – shocking shocking') find an antidote in Sam Weller's reparative, exuberantly connective way with analogies ('That's what I call a self-evident proposition, as the dog's-meat man said, when the house-maid told him he warn't a gentleman').[52]

Matthew Arnold's opposing of 'style' and 'psychology' is, from this wider literary perspective a false distinction – as is George Eliot's equally famous distinction between exterior and interior descriptions of character in her *Westminster Review* article 'The Natural History of German Life' (1856).

> We have one great novelist who is gifted with the utmost power of rendering the external traits of our town population; and if he could give us their psychological character – their conceptions of life, and their emotions – with

---

50 James Sully, 'The New Study of Children', *Fortnightly Review* 58 (1895), p. 723, and 'The Child in Recent English Literature', *Fortnightly Review* 61 (1897), p. 218. See also Sally Shuttleworth, *The Mind of the Child: Child Development in Literature, Science, and Medicine, 1840–1900* (Oxford University Press, 2010).

51 Karen Chase, *Eros and Psyche: The Representation of Personality in Charlotte Brontë, Charles Dickens, and George Eliot* (New York: Methuen, 1984), p. 4.

52 Charles Dickens, *The Pickwick Papers*, ed. James Kinsley (Oxford: Clarendon Press, 1986), pp. 14, 327–8 (chapter 2, chapter 22).

the same truth as their idiom and manners, his books would be the greatest contribution Art has ever made to the awakening of social sympathies.[53]

This criticism – clearly of Dickens's early fiction, though she does not name him – represents George Eliot in the process of defining, by opposition, her own psychological realism: a realism tied to the conviction that fiction should take for its moral purpose the education of the reader through imaginative identification with the feelings and sufferings of others. It is unjust to Dickens and an inadequate description of Eliot's own subsequent practice in so far as it appears to set up a false polarity between inside and outside, 'life' and mere 'manners'. The plausibility of such oppositions rested, in part, on their likeness to that other commonplace Victorian distinction between 'objective' drama and 'subjective' lyric. Yet, as Eliot knew, there can be no direct or trustworthy access to the 'psychological character' of others except through complex combined processes of external observation of their physiology and behaviour, imaginative identification with their circumstances, and reliance on a common but historically always evolving vocabulary for subjective experience.

The importance of conceiving of literary psychology in terms of literary forms as well as content is that it allows for such engagement with indirect as well as direct forms of representing inner life. It also helpfully broadens the question of psychology beyond the analysis of the mental life of characters and/or writers to treat literary psychology as a product of the whole work – the psychic structures evoked by its handling of style, genre, thematics, rhetoric, plot. Thackeray wrote with no visible interest in the science or philosophy of psychology, yet his complex plotting of memory and forgetting is pertinent to a consideration of Victorian memory in its implicit resistance to the more fractured models of psychology then current.[54] Eliot herself understood emotion to be at least as much a literary effect as a product of a writer's intellectual ideas about psychology. In 'Notes on Form in Art' (1868), her most direct statement on this subject, she writes

53 [George Eliot], 'The Natural History of German Life', *Westminster Review* 66 (1856), pp. 51–79; reprinted in *Essays of George Eliot*, ed. Thomas Pinney (New York University Press, 1963), pp. 266–99: p. 271.
54 See Nicholas Dames, *Amnesiac Selves: Nostalgia, Forgetting, and British Fiction 1810–1870* (Oxford University Press, 2001). Dames argues that Thackeray shared with the associationism of Mill, Bentham, and Bain a desire to downplay the dispersive complexity of memory and to emphasize instead the coherence and durability of our most important memories. The argument rests on the contemporaneity of ideas, not direct influence.

of the value, sometimes, of 'suspend[ing] one's attention to revered authorities' in order to look at literary form as 'an element of human experience'. 'Feeling', she concludes, is the key constituent of any literature worth the name ('poetry' was her preferred term). And the language of feeling in literature, as she describes it, is 'the choice of rhythms & images', perhaps above all the structuring repetitions – 'the recurrence of [the formal] elements in adjustment with certain given conditions of sound, language, action, or environment'.[55] The psychology of the passage from *Jane Eyre*, to this way of thinking, lies above all in the press of interrogatives, the jagged self-contradictions, the heaping of simile upon simile; and the psychology of the passage from *Daniel Deronda* is to be found most tellingly in the compressed syntax, the continual and rapid shifting between narrative report and implied dialogue, the trailing of thoughts beyond the limits of sentences. The risk, if these less explicit means of representing subjectivity, psychology, and imagination are ignored, is that a historicist literary criticism will give too much weight to ideas (how the novelist, poet, dramatist would have articulated, with ideal fullness, if asked, his or her understanding of the mind and its workings). It may correspondingly underestimate how far most writers' understanding of psychology remained in the Victorian period, as now, only in part a matter of intellectual apprehensions, much more a heterogeneous mix of received ideas, intuited beliefs, literary conventions, imagination, and experiential report.

55 George Eliot, 'Notes on Form in Art', in *Essays*, pp. 431–6: pp. 432, 434, 435.

24

Cityscapes

DEBORAH EPSTEIN NORD

During the Victorian period the landscape of Britain was utterly transformed by unprecedented urban expansion, the movement of populations away from rural areas, and the proliferation of new industrial cities in the north of England. By the middle of the nineteenth century, for the first time in any country in human history, over half the population resided in towns or cities, tipping the balance away from a rural nation. For those Britons used to an agricultural economy and cottage industry, migrating from country to city meant learning how to subsist in a wholly new environment, in which traditional modes of working, dwelling, and even eating were all dramatically altered. Urban dwellers confronted overcrowding, strange and often dangerous working conditions, primitive and filthy living arrangements, polluted water and air, and rapidly spreading epidemic diseases. Factory work meant getting accustomed to new machines, new spaces and rhythms of labour, and reliance on inadequate wages. The configuration of the family changed as women and older children were hired more readily than their more highly paid husbands and fathers and left the home to work. Wives suffered the humiliation of demeaning work conditions, husbands faced unemployment, and, with mothers working outside the home, babies were farmed out to minders. Industrial production created new classes of employers and workers – 'masters' and 'men' as they were called – and London witnessed the growth of sweated industries and, especially in the last decades of the century, casual labour. Beginning in the late 1820s, the construction of the railroads recalibrated time and space, linking Manchester to Liverpool and Birmingham to London, and remapped the cities themselves, destroying old neighbourhoods and rendering unrecognizable the ones that remained.

The literature of the Victorian city registered these radical changes and the sensibilities of the mainly middle-class observers and urban dwellers who experienced them. Writers, critics, and reformers tried to absorb and make comprehensible the enormous material and social changes within the metropolis and the new industrial towns by representing in literary form the spaces, structures, and types of the urban scene. They exploited the setting of labyrinthine streets to create plots of mystery and detection, lamented the alienation of lives overwhelmed by soul-destroying labour and poverty, and celebrated the variety and idiosyncrasy of character observable on city streets. Both haunted and repelled by the spectre of suffering in previously unimaginable conditions, novelists and poets sought to inspire sympathy and indignation in their readers. Disturbed by hostile relations between social classes made manifest in unions, strikes, and expressions of outrage on the part of workers, they attempted to uncover and illustrate the causes of class antagonism and to enact the means for class reconciliation in their fictions. 'There are the facts of the new society', Raymond Williams remarked in *Culture and Society*, 'and there is this structure of feeling.'[1] It is the structure of feeling – fear, shock, repulsion, sympathy, delight, and bewilderment at the facts of the new society – that the novels, poems, and commentaries of the period reveal.

City dwellers lived in closer proximity to both neighbours and strangers than ever before, but they were also increasingly ignorant of those among whom they lived. This combination of intense, largely unsolicited intimacy and disturbing estrangement produced a dialectic that haunted nineteenth-century urban evocations throughout the century. This oscillation between connection and alienation, between insistent relationship and chilling indifference, began with the Romantics. Thomas De Quincey, searching the 'mighty labyrinths of London' unsuccessfully for the young prostitute Ann, his saviour and fellow peripatetic in *Confessions of an English Opium Eater* (1821), laments that he will doubtless be separated from her 'for eternity', even though she might be walking within a few feet of him on a neighbouring city street.[2] In 'Residence in London', the seventh book of Wordsworth's *Prelude* (1850), the poet marvels at 'how men lived / Even next-door neighbours, as we say, yet still / Strangers, nor knowing each other's name'.[3] The observation of this phenomenon – of being close but distant, near but hopelessly out of reach – recurs with startling frequency in works of the

1 Raymond Williams, *Culture and Society, 1780–1950* (London: Chatto and Windus, 1958), p. 99.
2 Thomas De Quincey, *Confessions of an English Opium-Eater* (Oxford and New York: Oxford University Press, 1998), p. 34.
3 William Wordsworth, *The Fourteen-Book 'Prelude'*, ed. W. J. B. Owen (Ithaca, NY and London: Cornell University Press, 1985), p. 139.

Victorian period. At times it appears as an expression of painful alienation and disorientation. At others it is used as an admonition to shame middle-class readers into noticing the poor who lived in the next district of London but remained as unknown as the denizens of Africa. The estrangement was registered, then, on both the personal and collective levels: individuals were ignorant of their neighbours but so were entire classes ignorant of one another. The environment of the city seemed to hinder, perhaps make impossible, human interchange and sympathy.

Out of this enduring sense of radical separateness emerged a countervailing insistence on both the reality and the desirability of connection. Isolation was an illusion, a form of self-deception, the product of ignorance and indifference. Blake imagined the web of urban connection in the 'London' poem of *Songs of Experience* (1793) in a formulation that had lasting power and influence. He locates the connections between disparate institutions, classes, and individuals in oppression, violence, and disease: the agony of the chimney-sweep shames established religion, the spilled blood of the soldier stains the walls of the king's abode, and the venereal disease of the street-walker spreads to the marriage bed of respectable men and women and renders their offspring blind. The 'mind-forg'd manacles', though invisible they may be, can be heard clanking on every limb and reverberating in every voice.[4] Blake conjures a circuit of cause and effect and of relationship and culpability that overrides the estrangement experienced by individuals on city streets. The most trenchant of urban observers throughout the Victorian period continued to expose the links, correspondences, and parallels between otherwise unrelated people living as strangers in the great agglomeration of the Victorian city.

Sketches

In the first decade of Victoria's reign the sketch form and its presiding spirit, the lone male walker, dominated literary renderings of London. Descendants of Pierce Egan's Tom and Jerry, the inquisitive swells who travelled the streets of the capital in the tremendously popular *Life in London: or, The Day and Night Scenes of Jerry Hawthorne, Esq. and his Elegant Friend Corinthian Tom in their Rambles and Sprees through the Metropolis* (1821), early Victorian literary spectators sampled high and low life, London entertainments and

---

4 William Blake, *The Complete Writings of William Blake*, ed. Geoffrey Keynes (London: Oxford University Press, 1966), p. 216.

low dives, early morning jaunts and late night revelries, scenes of incarceration and labour, and neighbourhoods both elegant and seedy. For Tom and Jerry the city appears as a cornucopia or, as Egan puts it, a 'complete CYCLOPEDIA' of experience, knowledge, and pleasure but rarely a source of lasting moral distress or narrative drama.[5] The episodic content and structure of the sketch mimicked the experience of urban encounters: brief, fleeting, and anonymous. Egan's swells keep their distance when encountering urban miseries or delights and remain as detached from those they observe as an audience from performers on stage.

Leigh Hunt, George Sala, and William Thackeray all followed in Egan's wake as urban sketch writers, but Tom and Jerry's best-known heir was Boz, the alter ego Dickens created in the 1830s for the pieces on London he published in a variety of newspapers, among them the *Morning Chronicle* and *Bell's Life in London*. At the very start of the Victorian era he collected the articles as *Sketches by Boz; Illustrative of Every-day Life and Every-day People* (1836–7), with memorable illustrations by George Cruikshank, who had also been one of Egan's illustrators. Boz rambles from the popular London entertainments of Greenwich Fair and Vauxhall Gardens to celebrations of yearly festivals and from the slums of Seven Dials to the Houses of Parliament. He records the comings and goings of daytime streets, as the sellers at Covent Garden prepare and hawk their wares, and nighttime streets, as after-theatre revellers feast on oysters and poor women sing ballads for a few pence from the crowd.

Passionate explorer of shops and modes of transportation, Boz is haunted by change: shops that open and then disappear, neighbourhoods razed for the sake of urban improvements, coaches and cabs replaced by omnibuses. He reads the signs of individual change in the clothes that hang in a second-hand shop in 'Meditations in Monmouth Street', in visits to a pawnshop by a series of women in 'The Pawnbroker's Shop', or in the freshly dyed suit of a man in the Reading Room of the British Museum in 'Shabby-Genteel People'. The sketches often begin with the rambler's fleeting glimpse of a person or building and gradually unfold as a narrative or hidden drama in Boz's thoughts. The walker on the street begins to turn novelist as his brief encounters become tales and as he eschews snapshot images for a closer and longer look behind facades and into private histories. 'A Visit to Newgate'

---

5 Pierce Egan, *Life in London: or, The Day and Night Scenes of Jerry Hawthorne, Esq. and his Elegant Friend Corinthian Tom in their Rambles and Sprees through the Metropolis* (London: John Camden Hotten, 1821), p. 51.

looks forward to Dickens's first novels, to *Pickwick Papers* (1836–7), which takes Samuel Pickwick out of his pre-lapsarian innocence into the gloomy confines of the Fleet Prison, and to *Oliver Twist* (1837–8), with its interest in crime and its evocation of Fagin's incarceration and execution in Newgate. Dickens's fascination with urban institutions, prisons chief among them, begins in his earliest work, as does his sentimental attraction to debased femininity. The fallen woman singing for pennies after hours in 'The Streets – Night' and the prostitute who has been beaten by her pickpocket lover in 'The Hospital Patient' set the stage for another feature of *Oliver Twist*: the benevolent streetwalker Nancy, victim of her murderous lover and pimp, Bill Sikes.

The low-life elements of Egan's *Life in London* reappear in the Newgate novel, of which *Oliver Twist* was a version and Edward Bulwer Lytton and William Ainsworth were practitioners, and in the underworld crime narratives of G. W. M. Reynolds's *Mysteries of London*, a popular weekly serial that debuted in 1844. The high-life strains found their way into what has been called the 'silver fork' novel, which focused on fashionable London, aristocratic intrigue, and the favoured spots of leisure and influence of the wealthy and powerful. Benjamin Disraeli's early works, like *Vivian Grey* (1826) and *The Young Duke* (1831), conform to this mode, and even his later 'condition-of-England' novels begin with dandified aristocratic heroes and high-society dinners before shifting to less elegant locales and more serious social matters. Thackeray's London sketches, written for *Punch* in the 1840s, offer glimpses of the well-to-do male spectator's domain – clubs, city dinners, gala parties, and other night pleasures – but his rambling alter ego 'Spec' has a tamed, bourgeois aspect as well. He claims a 'Mrs Spec' and frequents children's parties as well as bachelors' banquets. The world of upper-class, though not necessarily aristocratic, London figures prominently in Thackeray's fiction, whether the Russell Square home of Amelia Sedley's stockbroker father in *Vanity Fair* (1847–8), the grander realms of Sir Pitt Crawley to which Becky Sharp aspires in that same novel, or the Inns of Courts where the hero of *Pendennis* (1848–50) reluctantly sets out to read for the bar. Thackeray set his London novels in pre-Victorian decades and took a satiric view of the ethos of silver fork fiction, but the London settings and characters he favoured had more in common with Egan's high-life world than with the rookeries and pickpockets of Seven Dials or Jacob's Island.

Dickens and Thackeray both emerged out of the world of journalism, the venue for their urban sketches and some of their fiction. So, too, did Henry

Mayhew, co-founder of *Punch*, whose accounts of proletarian Londoners and their modes of work owed much to the forms of newspaper sketches, tales, and vignettes. Indeed, Mayhew's inquiry into how Londoners earned their livings, which ultimately became the four-volume *London Labour and the London Poor* (1851), began as an assignment from the *Morning Chronicle*. In the wake of the second major cholera epidemic to strike Britain in the nineteenth century, the paper appointed him to cover London as metropolitan correspondent. The subtitle of his collected pieces, 'Cyclopedia of the Conditions and Earnings of Those that *Will* Work, Those that *Cannot* Work, and Those that *Will Not* Work', suggests not only that he was entering into debates about the so-called deserving and undeserving poor but that his inventory of city labourers was the handiwork of an urban spectator who collected and catalogued London types and scenes, much like Egan's ramblers and Dickens's Boz.

Mayhew interviewed and wrote about the kinds of apparently unskilled workers whose labour often remained invisible to middle-class Londoners. He offered accounts of scavengers – river-dredgers, mudlarks, and pure-finders (collectors of dogs' dung, used for curing leather) – and those who sold all manner of things on the streets, from baked potatoes and periwinkles to sheet music. He surveyed Irish and Jewish neighbourhoods and, with his colleague Bracebridge Hemyng, devoted almost an entire volume of the collected articles to prostitution. Street entertainers, coal-heavers, chimney-sweeps, and sewer builders appeared in his columns, sometimes represented by lengthy monologues. His experience as a journalist enabled him to record with surprising proficiency the words of his interlocutors, so that his sketches include the language and opinions of his subjects. Readers came to know individual figures he wrote about: a young watercress girl who managed to resist Mayhew's insistent lines of inquiry and an umbrella seller whose melancholy circumstances prompted people to send in donations for his support. In addition to allowing the London street-folk to speak in their own voices, Mayhew conveyed a keen sense of the practical realities and economic conditions of their lives, often by including relevant statistics and tables. He was also alert to the culture, customs, and beliefs that attached to any given group of labourers. Mayhew's work is an extraordinary resource with a rich anthropological texture and the beginnings of a canny economic analysis of poverty.

If, as Raymond Williams suggested, the new aspects of the modern city had always been associated with a man walking alone, the female subject's role in urban representation was more equivocal.[6] She figured prominently as demi-mondaine, the object of male ramblers' desires, the fallen woman who inspired his pity, and the prostitute who became the object of his sociological interest. As free agent, stroller, and spectator, however, she is all but absent in literary texts of the first decades of the period. We think of the difficulties encountered by the Frenchwoman Flora Tristan, recorded in her *Promenades dans Londres* (1842), when she tried to walk freely around England's capital, and of the fleeting sojourn there of Charlotte Brontë's Lucy Snowe, the narrator of *Villette* (1853). Brontë's orphan protagonist finds herself in London without friend, protector, or destination. The intense elation she feels, precisely because she navigates alone, 'dar[ing] the perils' of the city, are dramatically short-lived.[7] Within a page of Lucy's recorded delight in urban rambling, she leaves England abruptly, voyaging out to the fictional Labassecour and its Gothic capital, Villette. Among the tiny sorority of female sketch writers, Harriet Martineau stands as an interesting case. Her vignettes of industrial life appeared not as sketches but as *Illustrations of Political Economy* (1832), mildly didactic tales demonstrating principles of taxation and the deleterious effects of strikes, and as a series of artful accounts of processes of manufacture, from button making to the production of pistols, appearing in Dickens's journal *Household Words* in 1851–2.

Industry

The fiction, poetry, and social criticism that emerged out of the experience of northern industrial cities in the 1840s and 1850s shifted the focus of urban representation to factory labour, machinery, class conflict, and the dynamics of a new economy. Manchester, sometimes named but at other times thinly disguised as a fictional town (Coketown in Dickens's *Hard Times* (1854) and Milton Northern in Elizabeth Gaskell's *North and South* (1855)), took on the identity of a 'shock city', the favoured location for exemplifying the traumatic changes in British society that industrialization had wrought. This body of literature had a number of aims: to enlighten southern Britons about a way of life that was unknown to them, to expose the miserable living and working conditions of industrial labourers, to imagine forms of reconciliation between social groups that seemed dangerously at odds, and, at times, to celebrate the inventiveness of the British spirit.

6 Raymond Williams, *The Country and the City* (London: Chatto and Windus, 1973), p. 233.
7 Charlotte Brontë, *Villette* (Oxford: Clarendon Press, 1984), p. 66.

Reactions to the industrial towns were invariably bound up with discussions of the economic and political philosophies – laissez-faire, utilitarianism, political economy – that seemed to underpin industrialism. In *Chartism* (1839) Thomas Carlyle offered a synthetic vision that brought together suffrage politics, economic theory, mechanical invention, transatlantic trade, statistics, the new Poor Law, and the industrial city itself in a mythical rendering of the phases of British history. Manchester, with its 'cotton-fuzz, its smoke and dust, its tumult and contentious squalor', had been produced by innovations of the eighteenth century – the steam engine and the spinning jenny – and in turn had produced new types and classes of men with new political demands. 'Ideas produce revolutions', Carlyle writes, 'and truly so they do; not spiritual ideas only, but even mechanical.'[8] Whatever his reservations about the ugliness of the mill towns and working-class agitation for the vote, he saw industrialization as a stage in the evolution of British society. Lancashire towns were not mere accidents but the crucial site of Carlyle's creation myth: 'Fish fled thereupon from the Mersey River ... England ... dug out her bitumen-fire, and bade it work: towns rose, and steeple-chimneys; – Chartisms also, and Parliaments they named Reformed!'[9] In a different key, but with the same sense of historical moment, Disraeli judged Manchester a 'human exploit' as great as Athens, guided not by the spirit of Art but by the 'distinctive faculty' of Science.[10]

Critics of industrialism despaired nonetheless, lamenting that towns and their environs had been defiled and the souls of industrial manufacturers and labourers crushed. Augustus Welby Pugin, Gothic revivalist and devout Catholic, published *Contrasts: or, a Parallel between the Noble Edifices of the Middle Ages and Corresponding Buildings of the Present Day; Shewing the Present Decay of Taste* in 1841. On a page that displayed woodcuts of the same town in two historical epochs – 1440 and 1840 – Pugin supplied the imaginative pivot for a full-scale critique of the industrial scene. His medieval town features numerous graceful church spires, an abbey, a guild hall, trees, and an open bridge. By contrast, the Victorian town claims myriad smoke stacks, massive factories, gas works, iron works, a prison complete with panopticon, a 'Socialist Hall of Science', and a toll bridge. The decay of taste and belief as embodied in the industrial city also figured in John Ruskin's

8 Thomas Carlyle, 'Chartism', in *Critical and Miscellaneous Essays*, 5 vols. (London: Chapman and Hall, 1899), vol. IV, pp. 181, 184.
9 *Ibid.*, p. 185.
10 Benjamin Disraeli, *Coningsby or, The New Generation*, 3 vols. (London: Henry Colburn, 1844), vol. II, p. 2.

enthusiasm for the Gothic style. In 'The Nature of Gothic', from the second volume of *The Stones of Venice* (1853), Ruskin declares that the 'great cry that rises from our manufacturing cities' reminds us that 'we manufacture everything there except men'. With mass production and division of labour we can 'blanch cotton, and strengthen steel', 'refine sugar, and shape pottery', but, Ruskin scolds, we cannot produce or enlarge a human spirit.[11]

Taking a cue from Carlyle's *Chartism*, as well as from empirical studies like James Kay's *The Moral and Physical Condition of the Working Classes Employed in the Cotton Manufacture in Manchester* (1832) and Edwin Chadwick's *Report on the Sanitary Condition of the Labouring Population of Great Britain* (1842), novelists of the 1840s and 1850s began to write narratives set in the cities of the north that came to be known as 'industrial novels'.[12] In *Hard Times*, appropriately dedicated to Thomas Carlyle, Dickens invented the visually memorable city of Coketown, with its black canals and ill-smelling rivers running purple with dye from textile mills and the pistons of its steam engines moving 'monotonously up and down like the head of an elephant in a state of melancholy madness'.[13] Benjamin Disraeli's *Sybil* (1845), with its haunting declaration that England consisted of two separate nations, rich and poor, and Elizabeth Gaskell's *Mary Barton* (1848), with its wrenching depictions of starvation among Manchester's unemployed, preceded *Hard Times*, and Gaskell's *North and South* and George Eliot's *Felix Holt, the Radical* (1866) followed. Charlotte Brontë's *Shirley* (1849), set in Yorkshire during the Luddite riots, also shares certain elements with the form. Women writers were drawn to the industrial novel in their desire to use fiction to awaken the conscience of the nation.

The earliest industrial novels emerged in a period of agricultural depression known as the 'hungry forties', which adversely affected rural and urban areas alike, and, particularly in Gaskell's case, arose from concern about social and political revolutions on the Continent. Given the suffering and discontent among the poor and working class, could the revolutions taking place in France and Germany be reproduced on British soil? The emotional texture and narrative shape of many industrial fictions reflect a distinct

11 John Ruskin, 'The Nature of Gothic,' chapter 6 of *The Stones of Venice*, vol. ii, in *The Works of John Ruskin*, 39 vols., ed. E. T. Cook and Alexander Wedderburn (London: George Allen, 1904), vol. x, p. 196.

12 Raymond Williams coined the phrase and defined the genre in *Culture and Society*, p. 99.

13 Charles Dickens, *Hard Times* (Oxford and New York: Oxford University Press, 1989), Part i, chapter 5, p. 28.

combination of sympathy for the suffering of the urban poor and fear of the potential power of aggrieved workers. Novelists looked at working-class mobilization, whether in the form of trade unions or Chartist campaigning, with suspicion. The union organizer, Slackbridge, in *Hard Times* is demagogic and self-serving. Induction into the trade union in *Sybil* resembles a pagan rite, complete with dark cloaks and black masks. Felix Holt's 'address to working men' advocates the power of knowledge and tradition over that of suffrage. The unemployed working man John Barton, in Gaskell's first industrial novel, assassinates the son of a mill owner on behalf of his union. Unemployed union men in *North and South*, angered by the importation of scab labourers, riot and hurl rocks at the home of their boss, John Thornton, and accidentally wound the novel's heroine, Margaret Hale. Novelists expressed middle-class anxieties about working-class unrest by exaggerating threats to social stability and by including these largely uncharacteristic acts of violence in their narratives of industrial life.

In the interest of promoting class reconciliation rather than class conflict, authors of industrial novels disparaged working-class politics, condemned violence, and strove to educate middle-class readers about the plight of poor workers. They aimed to surmount class antagonism by showing both the virtue and the documented misery of the poor and both the unfairness and the potential nobility of the manufacturing classes. Thornton, the object of workers' rage in *North and South*, and Carson, the father of John Barton's victim in *Mary Barton*, become agents of benevolence by learning to consider the needs of their 'men'. Ignorance is understood to be as serious an impediment to social justice as greed or cruelty. Industrial plots also imagined reconciliation through the mechanism of cross-class marriage. Thornton marries Margaret Hale, the genteel clergyman's daughter from the south of England who had previously scorned his callous treatment of workers. Egremont, an aristocrat who has been educated by his experiences in the industrial north, marries Sybil, a 'daughter of the people' in Disraeli's eponymous novel.[14] Two nations might become one and social revolution avoided, the novels suggest, through individual enlightenment, sympathy, and the rejection of unchecked self-interest. Of course, Disraeli's cross-class marriage turns out to be less convincing – and less radical – than it might at first seem after the novel reveals that Sybil also has aristocratic blood flowing in her veins.

---

14 Benjamin Disraeli, *Sybil: or The Two Nations* (1845; Oxford University Press, 2008), Book 5, chapter 4, p. 302.

Connections

The volatile 1840s gave way to a period of relative stability and prosperity in the 1850s and 1860s. The Great Exhibition, the first world's fair, held in the Crystal Palace in London in 1851, stood as a symbol of Britain's industrial and imperial power. The extraordinary iconic glass and iron structure of the Palace was itself a marvel of technological skill and inventive engineering. People came to the Exhibition from all parts of the British Isles and the globe to witness a display of international goods and artefacts and to pay homage to the enlightened, modern spirit of Britain. Challenging this image of a buoyant England and its radiant capital city were the monumental London novels of Dickens's late period: *Bleak House* (1853), *Little Dorrit* (1857), and *Our Mutual Friend* (1865). Dickens's principle mode of puncturing British pride and complacency was to remind his readers of the existence of the poor and neglected in their midst and, even more crucially, of their own role in perpetuating urban suffering. High life and low life, still features of his fiction, no longer existed side by side in alternating but unrelated scenes but intersected and paralleled one another in deep and troubling ways. In the tradition of Blake, Dickens insisted on the hidden connections of city life.

He devised a series of overarching metaphors in the late novels to give coherence to his vast panoramas of British life and to illustrate the web of connection that, in an invisible and subterranean way, united all characters and classes. The Court of Chancery in *Bleak House*, the prison and the Circumlocution Office in *Little Dorrit*, and the river Thames in *Our Mutual Friend* serve to suggest that no individual is beyond the reach of oppression or social misery. The early chapters of *Our Mutual Friend* alternate between discrete low-life scenes of Gaffer Hexam's riverside scavenging and high-life scenes of the Veneerings and their society friends, who idly discuss the heir to a great fortune who has been found drowned. Gradually, the narrative collapses the separation between these two worlds, using tropes of drowning, death, and baptism that reverberate until the very end of the novel. The opening of *Bleak House* makes similar use of the natural – or perhaps unnatural – imagery of fog, mud, and gas, grim antitheses to the sparkling glass and iron of the recently constructed Crystal Palace. There is nowhere in all the British landscape that fog cannot penetrate, from the polluted docksides of London and the slums of Tom-All-Alone's to the High Court of Chancery and even to the aristocratic domain of Chesney Wold in Lincolnshire.

When the third-person narrator of *Bleak House* famously asks what connection there can be between the 'place in Lincolnshire' and the 'where-abouts of Jo the outlaw with the broom', he sets the stage for the mystery of the novel and its unravelling.[15] The city-grown connections of disease, secret sexual and familial relationships, and ancient lawsuits link the likes of Jo, a virtually nameless crossing-sweeper of the sort described by Henry Mayhew, with Nemo, a penniless law copier, Lady Dedlock, an aristocrat's wife, Esther Summerson, an illegitimate orphan and narrator of half the novel, and the famous case of Jarndyce and Jarndyce. Smallpox, which stands in for a myriad of other diseases, both epidemic and venereal, in the novel, ravages high and low alike and threads together characters from all classes and all urban locales. The ultimate mystery of birth – who are the parents of Esther Summerson? – is played out in a search through labyrinthine London with Inspector Bucket, arguably the first important detective figure in English fiction, leading Esther around the city at night to find her mother. Although Esther already knows the identity of her mother, and although an actual murder has been committed in the novel, this nocturnal journey is at the heart of the novel's proposition that the fundamental mystery of the city is the secret of hidden affiliation. To discover the connections that exist but are obscured in the metropolis is the novelist's – and the detective's – task. 'The original social content of the detective story', writes the German critic Walter Benjamin, thinking of Edgar Allan Poe, 'was the obliteration of the individual's traces in the big-city crowd.'[16]

Just as the case of Jarndyce and Jarndyce joins together disparate strangers in *Bleak House*, so also financial scandal in *Little Dorrit* and the high capitalist economy of shareholding in *Our Mutual Friend* serve Dickens as metaphors for the web of modern urban connection. Mr Merdle, a man whose origins and actual business activities are unknown, attracts investment from the richest down to the poorest of society in *Little Dorrit*. The novel's narrator tellingly compares Merdle mania to an epidemic: 'a moral infection . . . a disease that will spread with the malignity and rapidity of the Plague'.[17] The source of Merdle's wealth, which turns out to be 'Forgery and Robbery', leads to the ruin of the 'multitude he had deluded' and confirms his role as a communicable poison and not the second coming, the 'shining wonder',

---

15 Charles Dickens, *Bleak House* (Oxford and New York: Oxford University Press, 1996), chapter 16, p. 235.
16 Walter Benjamin, *Charles Baudelaire: A Lyric Poet in the Era of High Capitalism*, trans. Harry Zohn (London: New Left Books, 1973), p. 43.
17 Charles Dickens, *Little Dorrit* (Oxford: Clarendon Press, 1979), chapter 13, p. 553.

worshipped by all.[18] Dickens's critique of a corrupt metropolitan elite influenced Anthony Trollope's *The Way We Live Now* (1873), a London novel of the 1870s. Trollope's Merdle-like financier, Augustus Melmotte, attracts power, influence, and investments through the appearance of enormous wealth and success. Like Merdle, he is both a mystery and a sham, and his life, like Merdle's, ends in suicide.

Dickens challenges the complacency of mid-century society by questioning the efficacy and morality of modern institutions and also by collapsing the apparent distinction between the modern and the primitive. In the first paragraph of *Bleak House* the narrator imagines a Megalosaurus, the most primitive of beasts, trudging up Holborn Hill in the primordial ooze of modern London, as if the society he describes has barely advanced from the moment of creation. The dinosaur inhabits the same universe as that most elevated citizen of the civilized world, the 'Lord High Chancellor in his High Court of Chancery', and wallows in the mud that fills the streets and accumulates 'at compound interest'.[19] In a similar gesture, the novel satirizes the ostensibly enlightened practices of modern philanthropy as it lampoons Mrs Pardiggle's and Mrs Jellyby's devotion to the 'foreign-grown savages' – Tockahoopo Indians and the natives of Borrioboola-Gha – while ignoring the 'home-made article', Jo the crossing-sweeper.[20] Where is the real savagery, Dickens asks, and what constitutes real charity? Who is primitive and who civilized? What is the status of Christian charity when Londoners are blind to the benighted in their midst and mothers like Mrs Jellyby ignore the suffering of their own children?

As the example of *Bleak House* suggests, Dickens also contemplated London's connection to empire and the world throughout his fiction, especially in his late novels. *Little Dorrit*, a work powerfully about London itself and yet also deeply and extensively concerned with places beyond Britain's borders, begins in Marseilles. It contains the scandal of Merdle, who is of 'world wide renown', the villain-without-a-country, Blandois, and the politically powerful Barnacles, who could be found stuck to public posts 'wherever there was a square yard of ground in British occupation under the sun or moon'.[21] The novel satirizes the touring habits of the British through the Meagles family, with its house full of knick-knacks from abroad that miniaturize and render innocuous the great monuments of foreign civilizations. Mr Meagles dotes on these tiny reproductions but asserts with pride that

18 *Ibid.*, chapter 61, pp. 690–1.   19 Dickens, *Bleak House*, chapter 1, p. 11.
20 *Ibid.*, chapter 47, p. 669.   21 Dickens, *Little Dorrit*, chapter 34, p. 390.

there is no 'allonging and marshonging' in his Twickenham home, no revolutionary zeal or alien cultural enthusiasms to disturb his domestic peace.[22] Just as Dickens collapses the distinction between high and low, aristocrat and chimney-sweep, so too, however, does he erase the distance between London and Paris or Rome in this novel. Mr Dorrit, the 'father of the Marshalsea', addresses his travelling party at a banquet in Italy after he has come into money and escaped English prison walls. Unable to escape the psychologically crippling imprisonment of so many decades of his life, he exemplifies the novel's internationalism in a haunting manner, by forgetting where he is. 'The broad stairs of his Roman palace', the narrator comments, 'were contracted in his failing sight to the narrow stairs of his London prison.'[23] The mind, formed and trapped by social institutions and psychic wounds, knows no distinction between England and other parts of the globe.

In the 1870s, other writers shared Dickens's insistence on human connectedness, both within the metropolis and between London and the rest of the world. Although the financial schemes of Trollope's Melmotte do not attract and unite all parts of English society, they do reach all the way to San Francisco and China. George Eliot's final novel, *Daniel Deronda* (1876), follows *Little Dorrit* in beginning outside of Britain, in the Continental spa of Leubronn, where Gwendolen Harleth is gambling on holiday. The opening of the novel echoes Dickens's fiction by setting the keynote of speculation, sounded again in the novel with reference to Gwendolen's grandfather's West Indian earnings and the collapse of her mother's fortunes through investment in a failed company. *Deronda* includes the cosmopolitan Klesmer, an artist and citizen of the world, and takes its male protagonist Daniel Deronda to the Continent in search of the truth of his origins. More than any other work by Eliot, it is a novel about London, and it navigates a metropolitan geography of different classes and ethnicities. It is also, however, a novel about the world, and it ends with its Jewish hero and his new bride on a boat headed for the Levant. In these late mid-century texts, London is both a variegated community and a place of transit on the world map.

Fin de siècle

Four separate but linked currents in urban representation are discernible in the writing of the century's final decades: a preoccupation with poverty, especially in the East End of London; narratives of mystery and detection;

22 *Ibid.*, chapter 16, p. 187.   23 *Ibid.*, chapter 55, p. 629.

fin-de-siècle Decadence and Aestheticism; and utopian, dystopian, and apocalyptic strains. The conjoined sociological and literary impulses of mid-century novels became increasingly separate in these decades, with the development of empirical sociology on one side and the deepening aesthetic and psychological dimensions of fiction on the other. The walker in the city took on new guises, from sociologist and detective to nocturnal stroller and aesthete.

The final completed novels of both Dickens and George Eliot offer glimpses of the part of London – the East End – that would come to dominate late-century writing about poverty, slum life, and working-class unrest. Limehouse, the dockside quarter of east London, is the site of the Six Jolly Fellowship Porters and the Hexams' home in *Our Mutual Friend*. In Eliot's novel, Daniel Deronda takes to 'rambling in those parts of London which are most inhabited by common Jews', among them Whitechapel, the East End district that was to be associated not only with poor Jews and Jewish immigration at the end of the century but with the Jack the Ripper murders.[24] Another period of economic depression, this time in the 1880s, together with a series of strikes and new statistical studies that revealed the extent of poverty in England's capital, led to what has been called a 'rediscovery of poverty'. The East End was at the centre of this rediscovery, and it took on symbolic significance in the imaginative representation of the city, much as the industrial north of England had done in the 1840s.

In 1883 the Reverend Andrew Mearns produced a penny pamphlet, called *The Bitter Cry of Outcast London, An Enquiry into the Condition of the Abject Poor*, that exposed to public view the dismal circumstances in which the London poor were living. Walter Besant, novelist and reformer, wrote *All Sorts and Conditions of Men* (1882) to awaken the interest of middle-class readers in the need to bring pleasure and enlightenment to the benighted citizens of the East End. At around the same time, George Gissing began to publish a series of novels in a Naturalist mode, among them *The Unclassed* (1884), *Demos* (1886), *Thyrza* (1887), and *The Nether World* (1889), about impoverished and often utterly hopeless slum dwellers. In the 1890s Arthur Morrison brought to light more violent aspects of working-class life in *Tales of Mean Streets* (1894) and *A Child of the Jago* (1896). Morrison's works, which intensified and rendered more extreme the Naturalism of Gissing,

---

24 George Eliot, *Daniel Deronda* (London: Penguin, 1995), chapter 33, p. 380.

represented criminal enclaves in the East End, sexual violence, gruesome neglect of children, and unemployed husbands ready to send their wives on to the streets and into lives of prostitution. These writers contributed to the idea of a semi-savage urban underclass, inhabitants of a subterranean world below the horizon of civilized life. Following on Gissing's 'nether world', titles referred to the 'deeps' and, over and over again, to the 'abyss' populated by the poor. H. G. Wells's *The Time Machine* (1895), with its worker class, the Morlocks, living below ground, owes something to this way of imagining the contemporary city, despite its setting in England's distant future.

Claims about the extent and depth of poverty in the 1880s, some of which grew out of the fiction of the period and some out of socialist critiques of the state, inspired the Liverpool shipping magnate Charles Booth to undertake an empirical study of the economic state of the inhabitants of London. He began his investigation with the East End in 1889 and, by 1903, had produced seventeen volumes of research, which he called *Life and Labour of the People in London*. With its echoes of Mayhew's title of the 1850s, Booth's monumental study became the late-century touchstone for understanding the types, patterns, and causes of unemployment and poverty in the metropolis. Using information about individual families and their incomes, he was able to determine and then to map varying degrees of poverty from street to street. Booth's maps, with a colour spectrum signifying the 'class' of people living in any given locale, have a lasting dramatic visual power. They illustrate, among other things, the patterns of spatial separation between classes that developed in the geography of the city. Booth's methodology, which combined participatory observation and statistical analysis, amounted to a new way of seeing, analysing, and describing the urban mass.[25]

The sociological imagination present in embryonic form in mid-century fiction found fuller expression in the work of Charles Booth. In similar fashion, the impulse towards plots of crime and mystery of earlier works like *Bleak House* emerged full blown at the *fin de siècle* in the urban detective fictions of Robert Louis Stevenson and Arthur Conan Doyle. In *The Strange Case of Dr Jekyll and Mr Hyde* (1886), the characters Utterson and Enfield,

25 The London School of Economics' *Charles Booth Online Archive* (http://booth.lse.ac. uk) is an invaluable source of information about Booth's inquiry into the life and labour of London and includes the poverty maps, Booth family papers, and his original survey notebooks.

when on one of their 'rambles' in a 'busy quarter of London', discover the strange abode of the divided protagonist on a 'sinister block of buildings'. Drenched in fog, a nocturnal city dotted with street lamps, Stevenson's London is a surreal 'city in a nightmare'.[26] The murders perpetrated by the demonic alter ego of the respectable Dr Jekyll eerily prefigure the very real Ripper murders that occurred two years later and also look forward to the morbid crimes of Count Dracula, who circulates among the 'teeming millions' of London, a vampiric but outwardly familiar metropolitan stroller looking for prey in Bram Stoker's novel (1897). Jekyll and the Count both change bodily shape to execute their crimes and both are implicated, like the Ripper, in transgressions that have a powerful psycho-sexual dimension. While Stevenson's London is a dreamscape, Stoker's is a cosmopolitan centre with great geographic precision.

The London of Sherlock Holmes, launched by Arthur Conan Doyle with 'A Study in Scarlet' in 1887, is also both an international capital and a metropolis shrouded in obscurity. At the beginning of Dr Watson's first narrative, he speaks of London as 'that great cesspool into which all the loungers and idlers of the empire are irresistibly drawn'.[27] Peopled by murderers, thieves, and criminal masterminds, Holmes's London is the late-century culmination of De Quincey's labyrinthine mystery, now to be solved only through the ratiocination of the great detective. Holmes, Inspector Bucket's most important descendant, emerges as the man who can not only navigate the maze of city streets and decode their mysteries but also solve the very riddles of modern life, for which urban crime stands as a potent emblem.

The nocturnal city of Stevenson's story and the ubiquitous fog in the detective tales of Conan Doyle appear as dominant elements in the works of poets and fiction writers associated with the Decadent and Aesthetic movements of the 1890s. Their favoured milieu is night-time London, a city of shadows, muted but mesmerizing colour, one-night stands, fleeting but poignant encounters, profane pleasures, and women of the demi-monde. Influenced to varying degrees by Baudelaire, Rimbaud, Verlaine, Impressionism, French Symbolism, and the Thames paintings of James McNeill Whistler, poets like W. E. Henley, Arthur Symons, Richard Le Gallienne,

---

26 Robert Louis Stevenson, *Dr Jekyll and Mr Hyde and Other Stories* (London: Penguin, 1979), chapter 4, p. 48.
27 Sir Arthur Conan Doyle, 'A Study in Scarlet', in *Sherlock Holmes: The Complete Novels and Stories*, 2 vols. (New York: Bantam, 1986), vol. I, p. 4.

and Oscar Wilde revel in the city that remains unseen by daytime ramblers and in the artificiality of its nocturnal form. In 'A Ballad of London', Le Gallienne apostrophizes the metropolis as a 'Great flower that opens but at night' and compares street lamps to lilies and hansom cabs to dragonflies.[28] The natural world becomes a perverse point of reference for evoking the man-made city of night. In 'Symphony in Yellow', Wilde sees an omnibus crawling 'like a yellow butterfly', but he also compares barges filled with hay to 'a yellow silken scarf' and the Thames to a 'rod of rippled jade', making use of the inanimate and aesthetically seductive trappings of dandyism to evoke the natural world.[29] At night the city becomes unrecognizable, the natural and unnatural inverted and disguised. In Wilde's 'Impressions du Matin' the 'yellow fog' converts the walls of houses to shadows and St Paul's to a bubble that looms over the town. Like Wordsworth's 'Composed Upon Westminster Bridge' (1802), Wilde's 'Impressions' describes the city's disorienting transition to morning. The latter poem, however, does not conjure the clear, pristine, unpeopled morning of Wordsworth's sonnet but rather the lurid final gasp of night, in which a lone prostitute stands illuminated by both the coming daylight and the 'flare' of the gas lamps. In 'Westminster Bridge', nature overwhelms the man-made town. In 'Impressions', unnatural femininity – 'lips of flame and heart of stone' – accentuates the artifice of the urban scene.[30]

The distinctive colours, fallen female sexuality, and fleeting encounters in Wilde's 'Impressions du Matin' also mark the urban nocturnes of Arthur Symons. In volumes of poetry titled *Silhouettes* (1892) and *London Nights* (1895), he creates a persona who haunts the operas, music-halls, and night-time streets of the city, where women's faces are revealed and yet distorted by lamplights and footlights. In 'Maquillage' the 'creamy white and rose' of his lover's face are the products of rouge and 'pearl-powder', artificial enhancements of the dark that fade as the hour of noon approaches.[31] Women of the stage, in 'Impression' and 'On the Stage', adorned with wigs, tights, make-up, and the 'pink and black of silk and lace', stand in a swirl of colours: 'From indigo to amethyst, / A whirling mist of multi-coloured

28 Richard Le Gallienne, 'A Ballad of London', in *Robert Louis Stevenson, an Elegy, and Other Poems Mainly Personal* (Boston: Copeland and Day, 1895), p. 26.
29 Oscar Wilde, 'Symphony in Yellow', in *Poems and Poems in Prose*, ed. Bobby Fong and Karl Beckson, vol. 1 of *The Complete Poems of Oscar Wilde*, ed. Russell Jackson and Ian Small, 3 vols. (Oxford and New York: Oxford University Press, 2000), p. 168.
30 Wilde, 'Impressions du Matin', in *Poems and Poems in Prose*, p. 153.
31 Arthur Symons, 'Maquillage', in *Silhouettes* (London: Leonard Smithers, 1896), p. 14.

lights'.[32] All women, whether prostitutes, actresses, dancers, or lost lovers are disguised, ultimately unknown and unknowable, and come and go with the night. In 'Nocturne', the speaker of the poem rides along the Embankment with his love in a cab, delighting in the 'magic and the mystery that are night's, / And human love without the pain'.[33] Although he hopes the nocturnal ride will last for ever, it ends abruptly, his vision of lasting love just a dream. Even when a woman's presence lingers, as in the case of 'Stella Maris', she is like all the others, encountered 'in random wayfare, as one meets / The chance romance of the streets'.[34]

Charlotte Mew, female contemporary of Wilde and Symons, also recorded the experiences of urban rambling and chance encounters in both poetry and prose. Her story 'Passed' appeared in the second volume of *The Yellow Book* in 1894 and offers an interesting gloss on the urban vision of male Decadents. Taking a colour from the aesthete's palette, Mew begins her story with the narrator's walking out in London's 'hour of pink twilight'. The unnamed woman relishes the 'first delirium of enchanting motion' as she ventures forth into the frosty evening. The accidental meeting that initiates this narrator's story is not, however, a romantic or sexual one but rather her discovery of a distraught young woman in a Catholic church. The woman's sister has been seduced and abandoned by an upper-class man and now lies dying. The narrator is drawn into the sisters' drama and then retreats to her own comfortable family, only to be wracked with guilt. She returns to the church in search of the miserable sister and does not find her but, in a second chance encounter a few months later, passes the young woman on a 'notorious thoroughfare in the western part of this glorious and guilty city'.[35] The woman, now also fallen from respectability, strolls arm in arm with her dead sister's seducer, a man who sports violets in his lapel and ushers his companion to a waiting carriage. Mew's narrator observes this couple, a kind so frequently evoked by Arthur Symons from the perspective of the upper-class male partner, from the vantage point of the female spectator. She begins as a free-spirited urban rambler and ends as a pained chronicler of women of the streets and their unscrupulous male companions.

---

32 Symons, 'Impression,' in *Silhouettes*, p. 15, and 'On the Stage', *London Nights* (London: Leonard Smithers, 1895), p. 15.
33 Symons, 'Nocturne,' in *Silhouettes*, p. 63.
34 Symons, 'Stella Maris,' in *London Nights*, pp. 40–2.
35 Charlotte Mew, 'Passed', in *Charlotte Mew: Collected Poems and Prose*, ed. Val Warner (Manchester: Carcanet Press, 1981), p. 70.

For Amy Levy, born in the same decade as Mew and also connected to Oscar Wilde, in this instance through her writing for his magazine *Women's World*, London was a source of inspiration and locus of freedom. Her favoured vantage point as poet and, to some extent as novelist, remained, however, not the street but the window above the street, either in a London flat or an omnibus. In *The Romance of a Shop* (1889), a novel in which four orphaned sisters set up a photography business in Baker Street, Gertrude Lorimer gazes longingly at the street from her flat, harbouring a 'secret, childish love for the gas-lit street, for the sight of the hurrying people, the lamps, the hansom cabs, flickering in and out of the yellow haze, like so many fire-flies'.[36] She enjoys the privileges of the hidden spectator, her potential vulnerability or unwanted involvement protected by the ability to see without being seen. In her poem, 'Ballade of an Omnibus', which appeared in the volume *A London Plane Tree and Other Poems* (1889), the speaker muses on various types of conveyance, only to come back in her refrain to 'An omnibus suffices me'. She does not mount a steed but rather the steps of the bus, choosing the 'topmost summit' for her observation of the 'city pageant'.[37] In *A Room of One's Own* (1929) Virginia Woolf wrote famously that Jane Austen had not been able to ride through London alone in an omnibus, thereby registering such a journey as a rite of passage for the emancipated modern woman. Levy, whose fiction looks forward to both George Gissing's *Odd Women* (1893) and Woolf's own 'Pargiters' section of *The Years* (1937), writes the urban woman's romance of London streets from a perch above the fray, able to travel alone, unlike Austen, but wary still of plunging into the crowd.

Fin-de-siècle writing also exhibited strains of dystopic, utopic, and even apocalyptic thinking about the city. Gissing's novels exuded a profound sense of social pessimism. Certainly his proletarian fictions communicated a vision of gloomy possibilities for progress or any emergence from the abyss of poverty. Even *New Grub Street* (1891), Gissing's novel about the profession of writing in the metropolis, offers a bleak and cynical view of the writer's life and the tyranny of the marketplace, as well as of relations between the sexes in the modern city. Arthur Morrison's *Child of the Jago*, a slum novel that also focuses, like the works of Conan Doyle and Stevenson, on crime, imagines the slum dweller as a being capable of the savagery popularly associated with

36 Amy Levy, *The Romance of a Shop*, in *The Complete Novels and Selected Writings of Amy Levy*, ed. Melvyn New (Gainesville: University of Florida Press, 1993), p. 110.
37 Amy Levy, 'Ballade of an Omnibus', in *The Complete Novels and Poems*, p. 386.

the 'dark continent'. Civilization no longer seems to embody redemptive structures of reform, charity, and progress, and the metropole can no longer boast of reassuring levels of refinement and human restraint.

One response to the perceived bleakness of London at the century's end came in the form of a utopia. In *News from Nowhere* (1891) the socialist, poet, and crafts designer William Morris imagined a futuristic metropolis that would eliminate both the oppression of capitalism and the pollutions of industrialism. The time-travelling protagonist of Morris's work returns home to Chiswick on the London underground after a late meeting of the Socialist League and contemplates with discontent and discomfort the means of traversing the city that 'civilization has forced upon us like a habit'.[38] He falls asleep that night and awakens in a sunny, fresh-aired, pre-industrial city, where the Thames runs clear and is once again teeming with fish. The 'smoke-vomiting chimneys' of the soap-works are gone, and the stone bridges over the river are now more beautiful than the Ponte Vecchio.[39] Dressed in a spotless blue tunic, Morris's late-nineteenth century man discovers that the style and aesthetics of the fourteenth century have been revived in the twenty-first. London has become decentralized and labour almost wholly agrarian. Like Carlyle, Ruskin, and Pugin, Morris's critique of the nineteenth-century city is rooted in enthusiasm for certain aesthetic and moral aspects of medievalism, yet he combines this with a socialist vision that grew out of the unrest and political aspirations of the late nineteenth century.

Although James Thomson's major poetic work on the city, *The City of Dreadful Night* (1874), is a work of the 1870s, it looks forward not only to the nocturnes and dystopic strains of the *fin de siècle* but to twentieth-century renderings of London in the work of, among others, T. S. Eliot. Thomson's pessimism about the human condition, concentrated in this poem around the alienating and moribund modern city, resembles that of Gissing. He imagines the city as a symbolic landscape presided over by the spirit of Melancholia.[40] A profound psychic suffering – loss of purpose, depression, faithlessness, suicidal despair – colours the metropolis and makes it into a place of living death, a wasteland. Poised somewhere between the 'suburban Sahara'

---

38 William Morris, *News From Nowhere; or An Epoch of Rest* (London: Routledge & Kegan Paul, 1970), chapter 1, p. 1.

39 *Ibid.*, chapter 2, p. 5.

40 Thomson uses a print of Albrecht Dürer's 'Melancholia' as the frontispiece for his poem. See James Thomson, *The City of Dreadful Night, and Other Poems* (London: Reeves and Turner, 1880).

of Dickens's *Our Mutual Friend*[41] and the wasteland of Eliot's 1922 poem, Thomson's dreadful city is a projection of anguished modern consciousness. Like Morris's London, which disappears overnight, Thomson's physical city disintegrates and is reborn as a kind of phantasm. The man walking in the city has become a man dreaming, and the Victorian city, with its factories, labyrinthine streets, and class strife, has vanished into thin air.

41 Charles Dickens, *Our Mutual Friend* (Oxford University Press, 2009), chapter 4, p. 33.

The rural scene: Victorian literature and the natural world

FRANCIS O'GORMAN

In one of John Ruskin's most celebrated passages of elegy, he recalled the pleasures of Croxted Lane, Dulwich. 'In my young days', he said, in Part 1 of *Fiction, Fair and Foul* (1880):

> Croxted Lane was a green bye-road traversable for some distance by carts; but rarely so traversed, and, for the most part, little else than a narrow strip of untilled field, separated by blackberry hedges from the better-cared-for meadows on each side of it: growing more weeds, therefore, than they, and perhaps in spring a primrose or two – white archangel-daisies plenty, and purple thistles in autumn. A slender rivulet, boasting little of its brightness, for there are no springs at Dulwich, yet fed purely enough by the rain and morning dew, here trickled – there loitered – through the long grass beneath the hedges, and expanded itself, where it might, into moderately clear and deep pools, in which, under their veils of duck-weed, a fresh-water shell or two, sundry curious little skipping shrimps, any quantity of tadpoles in their time, and even sometimes a tittlebat, offered themselves to my boyhood's pleasured, and not inaccurate, observation.[1]

But revisiting Croxted Lane in 1880, he claimed to find it entirely changed. He walked, he wrote, through the same place but

> no existing terms of language known to me are enough to describe the forms of filth, the modes of ruin, that varied themselves along the course of Croxted Lane. The fields on each side of it are now mostly dug up for building, or cut through into gaunt corners and nooks of blind ground by the wild crossings and concurrencies of three railroads. Half a dozen handfuls of new cottages, with Doric doors, are dropped about here and there among the gashed ground: the lane itself, now entirely grassless, is a deep-rutted, heavy-hillocked cart road, diverging gatelessly into various brickfields or pieces of waste; and bordered on each side by heaps

---

1 *The Library Edition of the Complete Works of John Ruskin*, ed. E. T. Cook and Alexander Wedderburn, 39 vols. (London: Allen, 1903–12), vol. XXXIV, pp. 265–6.

of – Hades only knows what! – mixed dust of every unclean thing that can crumble in drought, and mildew of every unclean thing that can rot or rust in damp: ashes and rags, beer-bottles and old shoes, battered pans, smashed crockery, shreds of nameless clothes, door-sweepings, floor-sweepings, kitchen garbage, back-garden sewage, old iron, rotten timbers, jagged with out-torn nails, cigar-ends, pipe-bowls, cinders, bones, and ordure, indescribable; and, variously kneaded into, sticking to, or fluttering foully here and there over all these, remnants, broadcast, of every manner of newspaper, advertisement or big-lettered bill, festering and flaunting out their last publicity in the pits of stinking dust and moral slime.[2]

Ruskin's loss was a personal one, a childhood place – once like Proust's *le côté de Méséglise-la-Vineuse* or *de Guermantes* – now contaminated. But it was national too.[3] Although the clutter of the new Croxted Lane gave to Ruskin's adjectival plenitude the energy of Dickensian grotesque, it was idleness – national indifference – that was visible in the mess.[4] That disorder was a legible emblem of the coldness of ordinary urban men and women, Ruskin invited his reader to deduce, towards a natural world given by God for human instruction and delight. One notable point about the old Croxted Lane was that it was not, looked at neutrally, particularly special. An ordinary rural scene made precious by memory, the lane's occasional primrose, odd stickleback, and small stream did not make for exceptionality. But even the familiarity of this kind of regular natural scene was endangered by the sooty skirts of the modern.[5]

Placing the rural world in relation to urban life formed a repeatedly tempting opposition for writers contemplating modernity in its industrial and technological manifestations in Victorian England. The putative Latin origin of 'country' from 'contra' was peculiarly apt for those troping the natural world against new urban spaces. Wordsworth had felt such a contrast; Coleridge, William Cobbett, and William Hazlitt too. But for

---

2 *Ibid.*, pp. 266–7.
3 On English rural scenes and nationality see, most recently, Elizabeth K. Helsinger, *Rural Scenes and National Representation: Britain, 1815–1850* (Princeton University Press, 1997) and Roger Ebbatson, *An Imaginary England: Nation, Landscape and Literature, 1840–1920* (Aldershot: Ashgate, 2004).
4 On broader associations between mess and modernity, see David Trotter, *Cooking with Mud: The Idea of Mess in Nineteenth-century Art and Fiction* (Oxford University Press, 2000), including Ruskin's commentary on Turner, pp. 57–9.
5 The unattributed photograph of Croxted Lane *c.*1880 in James S. Dearden, *John Ruskin's Camberwell* (St Albans: Brentham, 1999), p. 38, suggests that a good portion of the lane had not, by the time of *Fiction, Fair and Foul*, in fact been lost. It is now a main south London highway, the A2199.

Victorian writers, particularly at the beginning of the period, imagining the rural world as freighted with nostalgia for a pre-industrial past became a well-exploited trope for expressing, managing, and verbally controlling the disorientating experience of the new with its sharply altering class relations. That figure also solved, or at least temporarily suspended, other conceptual problems at the heart of the Victorian experience of the natural world. An idea of the rural as a way of charting the emergence of new social relations or of figuring the new identity of industrial England relocated anxiety away from the perceptional challenge created in part by the withdrawing authority of what might be given, *faute de mieux*, the shorthand name of Romantic convictions – richly contested themselves – about divine presence in land-scape.[6] That challenge was also sustained by the weakening of natural theology which, at the beginning of the nineteenth century, had been most prominently manifested in William Paley's *Natural Theology or, Evidences of the Existence and Attributes of the Deity, Collected from the Appearances of Nature* (1802). Natural history's heritage was long but the most conspicuous challenge to its interpretive credibility was Victorian evolutionary theory.[7] Responding to profound shifts in the interpretation of nature, and to the imperatives of interpreting industrial modernity and a changing sense of what England was, with all its dangerous political implications, the oppositional trope was a usefully flexible one. It was there in the plot of Dickens's *The Old Curiosity Shop* (1841), which made of Nell and her grandfather's final arrival in the small village a (temporary) imaginary consolation for the journey through the furnaces of the Midlands. Elizabeth Gaskell, in *North and South* (1854–5), took similar contrasts as a principal theme. The Hale family moved from 'lovely beloved Helstone' in the south, with its parsonage 'half-covered with China-roses and pyracanthus',[8] to the northern town of Milton, figured in starkly oppositional terms as an industrial workyard, covered with a 'deep lead-coloured cloud' and a 'faint taste and smell of smoke'[9] detectable from afar. Milton's association with narratives of hell was not accidental. But Gaskell's point was, in part, to undo the opposition between north and south: she settled a morally grown-up Margaret in due

---

6 The most obvious Romantic period texts to define difficulties with comprehending nature's significance are Coleridge's 'Dejection: An Ode' (1802) and Shelley's 'Mont Blanc' (1817).

7 On the pre-Victorian history of natural theology, see Colin Jager, *The Book of God: Secularization and Design in the Romantic Era* (Philadelphia: University of Pennsylvania Press, 2006).

8 Elizabeth Gaskell, *North and South* (Oxford University Press, 1982), chapter 6, p. 56.

9 *Ibid.*, chapter 7, p. 59.

course there as the wife of Thornton, the mill owner (though he carries Helstone roses in sign of his love for her). And Margaret herself presents to Nicholas Higgins an unappealing account of work in the rural south. 'They labour on, from day to day,' she says, applying a vocabulary familiar to northern factory work to agriculture, 'in the great solitude of steaming fields – never speaking or lifting up their poor, bent, downcast heads. The hard spade-work robs their brain of life; the sameness of their toil deadens their imagination.'[10] But the notion of the rural south against the industrial north, with all its suggestions of the modern urban world jeopardizing rural happiness and innocence, proved, beyond the opening pages of *Mary Barton* (1848) and the plot of *North and South*, an association hard to dislodge in imaginary maps of industrial England. It was glimpsed even in George Gissing's fiction, the most urban of late-century writers, who offered a rural episode contrasting with the slums of Clerkenwell in the sombre narrative of *The Nether World* (1889).

Fondness for an agrarian England, with its implicit mistrust of industrial modernity, sustained George Eliot's novels before her embrace of European themes in *Daniel Deronda* (1876) and her ironizing reflections on the business of writing in *Impressions of Theophrastus Such* (1879). *Adam Bede* (1859), *The Mill on the Floss* (1860), and *Silas Marner* (1861) found a suggestive environment for fictions of the new realism in rural life (though that did not exclude their use of a rich symbolic system, particularly in *Silas*). The landscapes of these novels, and of *Middlemarch* (1871–2), were represented with clarity and, especially in the story of Maggie's childhood in *The Mill*, bound together with pleasures. But that is not to say Eliot's rural lands were innocent ideals. Imagining countrysides rich in human discontent, Eliot declined to offer mere political nostalgia for an alluring pre-industrial rurality. Marner's primitive, pre-industrial life as a handloom weaver was, symptomatically, not held out as an admirable model for modern labour. And his very business hinted at broader historical themes of altering ways of living. The plight of English handloom weavers in the face of the mechanical inventions of, among others, Hargreaves and Arkwright in the previous century, had become notorious by the 1820s. Even Tennyson's 'The Lady of Shalott' (1832) registered a plot obliquely suggesting the extinction of the weaver which was not politically innocent. When Eliot depicted her first scene of Marner's rural work, she described him in terms of his harmony with his

10 *Ibid.*, chapter 37, p. 306.

surroundings, labouring 'at his vocation in a stone cottage that stood among the nutty hedgerows near the village of Raveloe'. The fact that this gentle scene was already in jeopardy, albeit only from village boys, quietly bespoke a fact about its cultural moment:

> The questionable sound of Silas's loom, so unlike the natural cheerful trotting of the winnowing-machine, or the simpler rhythm of the flail, had a half-fearful fascination for the Raveloe boys, who would often leave off their nutting or birds'-nesting to peep in at the window of the stone cottage, counterbalancing a certain awe at the mysterious action of the loom, by a pleasant sense of scornful superiority.[11]

At once a plain account of masculine curiosity, this sentence also represents a moment of hidden politics, an oblique anxiety about disruption and intrusion. That 'scornful superiority' was a pointed anticipation of a different kind of rejection of the handlooms which would, after the period in which *Silas Marner* was set, become a startling episode in the dramatic shift between countryside and city.

Croxted Lane, even in the freshness of its unpolluted state, was traversed by carts; Marner's work was hard. And agriculture itself was recurrently understood, in tension with Gaskell's apparent trope of opposition between rural and city, a matter of severe labour. An echo of Virgil's *Georgics* (29 BCE) with its pessimistic sense in Book 1 that all things in nature revert to uncontrolled states – 'Sic omnia fatis / In peius ruere, ac retro sublapsa referri'[12] – lingered in these Victorian contemplations of the work land relentlessly needed. For Charles Kingsley in *Yeast: A Problem* (1851), rural labour was as much part of the condition-of-England question as the factory hands. In the fields were labourers who lived wretched lives, who

> tumble into bed at eight o'clock, hardly waiting to take your clothes off, knowing that you must turn up again at five o'clock the next morning to get a breakfast of bread, and, perhaps, a dab of the squire's dripping, and then back to work again; and so on, day after day . . . week after week, year after year, without a hope or a chance of being anything but what you are, and only too thankful if you can get work to break your back, and catch the rheumatism over.[13]

---

11 George Eliot, *Silas Marner* (London: Blackwood, 1861), chapter 1, pp. 3–4.
12 Virgil, *Georgicon*, in *P. Vergili Maronis Opera*, ed. John Conington, revised by Henry Nettleship, 4th edn, 3 vols. (London: Whitaker, 1881–3), vol. 1., Lib. 1, pp. 180–1, lines 199–200: 'So all things by fate hasten towards the worst, and slipping away fall back.'
13 Charles Kingsley, *Yeast: A Problem* (London: Parker, 1851), chapter 13, p. 230.

Kingsley's representations drew on public documents about the rural poor, including from Sidney Godolphin Osborne's 'S.G.O.' letters to *The Times* from 1844 and Parliamentary 'Blue Book' inquiries. Emily Brontë's *Wuthering Heights* (1847) hinted, off-stage, at the strain of farm work with its relentless demands (even if it is never quite clear what Heathcliff is doing). Later in the century, the plain physical labour of rural life provided Thomas Hardy – searching out situations of human defeat by circumstances – with narratives of suffering which dispiritingly affirmed the ubiquity of unrewarded travail. *The Return of the Native* (1878), *The Mayor of Casterbridge* (1886), *The Woodlanders* (1887), *Tess of the D'Urbervilles* (1891), and *Jude the Obscure* (1895) contemplated labour – turf cutting, cattle keeping, spar making, bird scaring – that was back-breaking, mechanical, precarious, or merely dull. Work, Thomas Carlyle had said, would redeem: it could be, in *Sartor Resartus* (1833), an everlasting Yea. Hardy found no such optimism in a philosophy of agrarian labour. He had affection for the passing customs of the countryside, ways of life that modern England was making away with, but in Wessex, with its unruly and barely manageable lands, agrarian work was not ennobling.

The condition of nature, understood as an index of human moral identity, seemed to some the defining sign of Victorian England's moral jeopardy written on the landscape. Their convictions, influential in their own time, seem uncomfortably to prefigure the increasingly apocalyptic accounts of the deleterious effects of human beings on the environment in the present day. In Richard Jefferies's fantasy *After London, or Wild England* (1885), set in an undated future, London has sunk beneath the weight of its own vice. Surviving social structures, human beings, and animals have reverted to primitive and untamed states; most of history has been forgotten and nearly all books lost. In this hostile territory, the defaced natural world that survives over the sunken city of London bears the marks of the capital's symptomatic foulness where 'the earth was poison, the water poison, the air poison, the very light of heaven, falling through such an atmosphere, poison ... it was the very essence of corruption'.[14] As throughout the long tradition of utopian writing, the relationship between the narrated and the experienced, between what was read and the condition of life outside the page, gave the dystopic *After London* its torsion. Prophecy saturated representations of its natural world as, conversely, an optimistic anticipation of

14 Richard Jefferies, *After London* (Oxford University Press, 1980), p. 206.

national rejuvenation was present in the lush and biddable natural world of William Morris's *News from Nowhere, or, An Epoch of Rest* (1890), which had recovered from the ordeal of industrialization.

Ruskin, the most charismatic observer of nature's pollution, could not find a language to narrate the significance of what he observed. *After London*, Edward Carpenter in *Civilization: Its Cause and Cure* (1889), and John Graham in *The Destruction of Daylight: A Study in the Smoke Problem* (1907) perceived the condition of nature, in particular the air, as emblematic of the state of modern England. Delivering his two lectures on *The Storm-cloud of the Nineteenth Century* (1884), Ruskin thought so intensely. Insisting that he was speaking only of facts, Ruskin identified a sickness in the natural world, a faltering in the quality of its breathing which pointed to national ill health. Something like palsy infected cloud patterns and weather cycles, winds and light in present-day England. 'Blanched Sun, – blighted grass – blinded man': modern beliefs had no language to explain this disease, Ruskin said. But, he continued:

> I can tell you what meaning it would have borne to the men of old time. Remember, for the last twenty years, England, and all foreign nations, either tempting her, or following her, have blasphemed the name of God deliberately and openly; and have done iniquity by proclamation, every man doing as much injustice to his brother as it is in his power to do so. Of states in such moral gloom every seer of old predicted the physical gloom, saying, 'The light shall be darkened in the heavens thereof, and the stars shall withdraw their shining.'[15]

The relationship between that apocalyptic language – in the distinct biblical sense of the term – and the poisoned nature of the modern was strategically left open: Ruskin's conclusion that was not a conclusion invited his listeners to ponder unsettling connections between the discourses of the past and the meaning of the disrupted present. The relevance of Old Testament prophecy became all the more disturbing for not being directly proposed.[16]

Other writers linked the natural world to values or pleasures which had not lasted. Ruskin had remembered Croxted Lane as part of his 'young days', by which he meant the time of the early volumes of *Modern Painters*

---

15 Ruskin, *Complete Works*, vol. xxxiv, p. 40.
16 For an argument comparing Ruskin to Solomon and Old Testament prophetic writing, see Michael Wheeler, *Ruskin's God* (Cambridge University Press, 1999), especially chapters 1, 6, and 7. On Ruskin and environmental concerns, see the essays collected in Michael Wheeler (ed.), *Ruskin and Environment: The Storm Cloud of the Nineteenth Century* (Manchester University Press, 1995).

(1843–60). A significant strand of writing across the period maintained more extensive associations between pleasing rural landscapes and the passing of time from youth to age. The conception of hopefulness against maturation was present in *North and South* but, there as elsewhere, it was an uneasy association and accounts of the changing perceptions of the natural world were habitually about loss. Sometimes, there were the quietest regrets. Matthew Arnold's recollection of Oxfordshire and Berkshire, known as an undergraduate, in 'The Scholar-Gipsy' (1853) was framed with sorrow that the lands were rarely visited now. Tennyson's remembered locations were marked with a greater sense of personal loss in his youth – the death of his friend Arthur Henry Hallam – so that the rolling sound of the sea's waves became a bitter reminder that the 'tender grace of a day that is dead / Will never come back to me'.[17] At the end of the century, A. E. Housman's Shropshire was an imagined county of youth tinged with Decadent regret, learned of Tennyson, for the 'happy highways where I went / And cannot come again'.[18] This was nostalgia for an imagined past, but also part of a wider reluctance across the period to represent accessible Edenic or passionately admired landscapes which were experienceable now. It was a matter glimpsed in Emily Brontë. Recounting the deepest of youth's attachments to Yorkshire wilderness, *Wuthering Heights* could barely describe the landscape it cherished, and lent the moors the mysterious allure that only near absence could create. More darkly, Jefferies punctured his prolonged narration of the association between charmed youth and nature with a gloomy afterthought. His curiously absorbing plot-less account of boyhood in the outdoors, *Bevis* (1882), possessed its grim counter-narrative in the natural catastrophes of *After London*.

Shifts in nature's meaning came in part from the mid-century intervention of evolutionary science into humans' relations with their environment. Technology changed the way men and women literally saw the natural world and how they physically related to it and worked on it.[19] But biological science altered how many understood it at a conceptual or imaginative level. Charles Darwin, towards the end of his life, admitted in

---

17 Alfred Tennyson, 'Break, break, break' (1842), in *The Poems of Tennyson*, ed. Christopher Ricks, 3 vols. (Harlow: Longman, 1987), vol. II, p. 24, lines 15–16.
18 A. E. Housman, 'XL', in *A Shropshire Lad* (1896), from *The Collected Poems of A. E. Housman* (London: Cape, 1939), p. 42, lines 7–8.
19 On changing conceptions of vision see, for instance, Jonathan Crary, *Techniques of the Observer: On Vision and Modernity in the Nineteenth Century* (Cambridge, MA: MIT Press, 1990) and Kate Flint, *The Victorians and the Visual Imagination* (Cambridge University Press, 2000).

his *Autobiography* (1887) that he now had little aesthetic capacity left: his mind had become merely 'a kind of machine for grinding general laws out of large collections of facts'.[20] Art in any form failed to engage – and nature was not much better. 'I retain', he said, 'some taste for fine scenery, but it does not cause me the exquisite delight which it formerly did.'[21] That might have struck some as an all-sufficing emblem of modern science's relation with the natural world. Would that Oxford dons, Ruskin remarked in *Praeterita* (1885–9), had told him, when an undergraduate at Christ Church, that fritillaries grew in Iffley Meadow. But it was at least better that they did not tell him rather than informing him, 'as nowadays [they] would, that the painting on them was only to amuse the midges'.[22] This was directly a rebuke to Darwin, especially for *On the Various Contrivances by which British and Foreign Orchids are Fertilised by Insects* (1862), and to Sir John Lubbock, especially for *On British Wild Flowers Considered in Relation to Insects* (1875). Ruskin's words, more generally, were a knowingly wasted sigh about the failure of natural theology and the replacement, by the grimy narratives of sexual selection, of the assumption that the natural world was given for human instruction and gladness. Charles Kingsley's *The Water-Babies* (1862–3) described a subaqueous environment as seen through the lens of Darwinian natural selection. That world, in its deepest identity, was remorselessly vicious, its violent competition no less unsettling because it happened under water. H. G. Wells's *The Island of Dr Moreau* (1896) would satirize Darwinian evolutionism on a fantasy island by having men attempting brutally to change the direction of natural selection by surgery. Pain was inextricable from nature. By the time H. Rider Haggard depicted African big game hunts in the last decades of the century – the violent slaughter of men and elephants in *King Solomon's Mines* (1885) – the conception of life in wild nature, wherever it was, as a state of unceasing aggression, of violence, suffering, and death, was commonplace.

Haggard's hunts seemed refractions of the new view of the natural world as ferocious. But the hunting scenes, Darwin aside, were also representations of – hunting. One of the distinctive Victorian sub-genres of writing about the natural world was that which enthusiastically recorded its destruction. Nature, in such texts, was consistently the subject of human will: it was a ready-made offering against which men could test their strength, moral

20 Charles Darwin, *The Autobiography of Charles Darwin 1809–1882*, ed. Nora Barlow, (London: Collins, 1958), p. 139.
21 *Ibid.*, p. 138.   22 Ruskin, *Complete Works*, vol. xxxv, p. 261.

and physical. The literature of Victorian Alpine climbing – Leslie Stephen, John Tyndall, Edward Whymper – caught something of this, but not with the same bloodiness. Anthony Trollope, a committed fox-hunter, gave place throughout his fiction for sporting men and women; he published *Hunting Sketches* in 1865. Robert Surtees made a literary career, if not a very successful one, from writing tales of the chase – *Jorrocks' Jaunts and Jollities* (1838) and *Handley Cross, or, The Spa Hunt* (1843) among them – which identified the rural scene as an arena for human amusement. It was a male world, but not exclusively. Edith Somerville, of Somerville and Ross, hunted from her youth at the end of the century and was proud to be the first woman master of foxhounds in Ireland by 1903. Jefferies's Bevis, when he is not endeavouring to kill domestic cats for eating fish, or beating donkeys for being reticent, hunts wild fowl and otters. Writers of empire – R. M. Ballantyne, George Henty – found new domains for hunting overseas and there was a substantial body of non-fiction: Henry Faulkner in *Elephant Haunts* (1868) wrote a 'sportsman's narrative of the search for Doctor Livingstone';[23] Julius Barras wrote of *India and Tiger-Hunting* (1883). The literature of pursuit framed the natural world as a place for raw human entertainment, as a possession for men to do with as they wished. An attitude towards nature's availability to human desires, Anne Brontë certainly thought, could be learned at a poisonously young age. When, in *Agnes Grey* (1847), the narrator interferes to stop Tom, the boy in her charge, from torturing to death a nest of birds, his mother archly reprimands her: 'You seemed to have forgotten . . . that the creatures were all created for our convenience.'[24] It was an extreme opinion. But a version of Mrs Broomfield's view lay behind many representations of wild animal hunting, formal or informal, across the age. As Captain Nemo examines the bottom of the ocean in Jules Verne's *Vingt mille lieues sous les mers* (*Twenty Thousand Leagues under the Sea[s]*, 1869), he points out a prodigious pile of pearl oysters: 'et', says the narrator 'je compris que cette mine était véritablement inépuisable, car la force créatrice de la nature l'emporte sur l'instinct destructif de l'homme'.[25] It

---

23 From the subtitle to Henry Faulkner, *Elephant Haunts: Being a Sportsman's Narrative of the Search for Doctor Livingstone, with Sketches of Elephant, Buffalo, and Hippopotamus Hunting* (London: Hurst and Blackett, 1868).

24 Anne Brontë, *Agnes Grey* (Harmondsworth: Penguin, 1988), chapter 5, p. 105.

25 Jules Verne, *Vingt mille lieues sous les mers* (Paris: Livre du poche, 1995), Part 2, chapter 3, p. 183. 'And I understood that this source was truly inexhaustible, because the creative power of nature supersedes man's destructive instinct.'

was hard for many to look at the fecundity of the natural world in the period without a version of that conviction.

Gerard Manley Hopkins took an assumption like Verne's and transformed the natural world's seemingly perpetual regeneration into a gift from God, fathering forth beauty in male–female doubleness.[26] It was a vulnerable beauty, and, for Hopkins, as for a number of others, the human destruction of nature appeared, as recorded in literary writing, an act touched not with the heroic confidence of masculine self-expression or with the discourses of appetite and acquisition, but with the bitterness of bereavement. 'How to keep ... / Back beauty, keep it, beauty, beauty, beauty, ... from vanishing away?'[27] was Hopkins's inquiry in 'The Leaden Echo and the Golden Echo', primarily questioning the endless cycle of nature's decay and rebirth, but also implicitly condemning human ruination of precious scenes. The form of the question was disquieting, for Hopkins's words diminished in echoes like the beauty they tried to save. Croxted Lane had been Ruskin's regret and beyond that an emblem of national loss. Eugene and Annie Lee-Hamilton saluted instead the durability of a forest, far out-living the span of human life – 'there is nothing in eternal Nature, / Save Ocean, half so thrilling as the forest', they wrote, 'So full of charm to fleeting generations; / Outliving life, outliving death.'[28] But Hopkins, with acute eye and acuter emotional sensitivities, wrote of the opposite, of trees failing to outlive death in the most literal sense. 'Binsey Poplars' found only in poetry a way of preserving the destroyed lines of aspens at Oxford. In 'All felled, felled, are all felled',[29] the upright 'll's tease the reader with what was not true of the trees. Discerning the divine in his affection for a highly visualizable nature, Hopkins, who had admired the Dorset rural poet William Barnes, grieved over the demolition of a 'Sweet especial rural scene',[30] and that last word, 'scene', echoed with its homophone, confirming both the preciousness of sight in Hopkins's experience and the sorrowful past tense which was the elegy's temper concerning what had been *seen*.

Hopkins's relationship with the natural world drifted above many of the century's troubles with nature's relationship with God (though that is not to

26 See Gerard Manley Hopkins, 'Pied Beauty' (1877), in *The Poems of Gerard Manley Hopkins*, ed. W. H. Gardner and N. H. MacKenzie, 4th edn (Oxford University Press, 1970), p. 70, line 10.

27 *Ibid.*, p. 91, lines 1–2, ellipsis original.

28 Eugene and Annie Lee-Hamilton, 'To the Forest', in *Forest Notes* (London: Grant Richards, 1899), p. 8, lines 31–4.

29 'Binsey Poplars' (1879), in Hopkins, *Poems*, p. 78, line 3.   30 *Ibid.*, p. 79, line 25.

say that Hopkins's faith as a whole was untroubled). Hopkins's nature, perceived under high pressure, was always strange and personalized; it was fantastic, pictured in unsettling hyperboles, startling colours, and language and grammar shaken into new configurations of squeezed sense. Creatures combusted and exploded; kingfishers caught fire; the windhover buckled into flame; dragonflies became incendiary; seeds dropped like burning cinders; nature blazed with an electric current, 'like shining from shook foil';[31] thrushes sang 'like lightnings';[32] the stars seemed to be people sitting in the air; trees to be cages; the earth vertiginously tumbling: all things were 'counter, original, spare, strange'.[33] Hopkins's natural world was, in this respect, like Hopkins himself, the strange original, variously on the margins. His language, deeply informed by modern science, especially John Tyndall's physics, with its vocabulary of electricity and molecular change, added to that compound sense of Hopkins's poetic freshness and transformative surprise. He was set aside from the English mainstream by his Catholicism and from mainstream Catholicism by being a Jesuit and, like his natural world, he knew himself unusual, with severe self-dissatisfactions, dissonant sexuality, and sense of isolation as a peculiar writer among the Victorian poets. Yet in his eyes, God created the world as exceptionally varied, and that *pied* beauty was both celebratory and privately reassuring.

Divinity, for this Jesuit poet, was met in the experience of nature. Others could obtain little or nothing of Hopkins's underlying sense of nature's intimate, revelatory relationship with God. Perhaps the most disquieting conceptions of nature's meaning in the Victorian period were those among writers who struggled to find significances at all. For some, a new Cartesian division loomed as, contemplating the natural world, they wondered if nature was primarily otherness, simply the not-human. Attempting to express a relationship with that seemingly alien materiality was baffling, a problematic contemplation of what resisted being brought into significant connection with the human mind or heart. Photography, developing in the period, could distance a viewer further from natural scenes: regarding a representation of what was anyway separated from the human was easy perceivable as double alienation. Photography could also, at the same time, provide a new means, like the microscope, for revealing the beauties and harmonies of the natural world. Pre-Raphaelitism and its followers – especially William Holman Hunt

---

31 'God's Grandeur' (1877), in Hopkins, *Poems*, p. 66, line 2.
32 'Spring' (1877), in Hopkins, *Poems*, p. 67, line 5.
33 'Pied Beauty', in Hopkins, *Poems*, p. 70, line 7.

(1827–1910), John Brett (1830–1902), Charles Allston Collins (1828–73), Arthur Hughes (1832–1915) – found the best chance of meaning in a photographically Realist representation of nature through symbolism. Collins's *Convent Thoughts* (1850–1), now hanging in the Ashmolean Museum, Oxford, offered a nun contemplating a passion flower, meditating, the viewer is invited to assume, on the Passion of Jesus, which the flower's curious form traditionally suggests. In her reading of the flower's symbolic meaning, the nun was a model for one ambition of one sort of Pre-Raphaelite artist: the natural world is distinctly present to her as a material actuality and, in the absence of any other kind of connection, symbolism makes it signify. But the picture reveals the problems with that form of reading. *Convent Thoughts* is replete with distinctly realized nature in a multiplicity of forms – grasses, flowers, foliage, aquatic life – which, despite many possibilities for interpretation, cannot shake off the primacy of simple material actuality. Representation of the natural world here is about presence more than purpose. The draining of meaning from depictions of nature and the stalling of the possibilities of emotion evident in some Pre-Raphaelite canvases were problems for poets too. Victorian poetic discourse could represent actuality with clarity – but what then?

Ruskin had told artists in one of his most frequently misunderstood statements in *Modern Painters* I (1843) to 'Go to Nature in all singleness of heart, and walk with her laboriously and trustingly, having no other thought but how best to penetrate her meaning, rejecting nothing, selecting nothing, and scorning nothing.'[34] But it was certainly not all Ruskin thought an artist should do. Mere accurate representation was only one step: great art, while retaining a form of verisimilitude, presented nature through the understanding and affections of a great mind. And that mind – J. M. W. Turner (1775–1851) was the central example of *Modern Painters* (1843–60) – comprehended nature as the work of God, instructing humankind through natural form. D. G. Rossetti, Pre-Raphaelite poet, painter, and friend of Ruskin, opened up with peculiar lucidity the difficulty of following only the first part of Ruskin's instruction. In sonnets from *The House of Life* (1870/81) including 'Love's Last Gift' and 'Ardour and Memory', Rossetti found meanings in the natural world through analogies and comparison. 'The Hill Summit' offered an account of the sun setting which was, however, disinclined to propose a communicable significance for the event.[35] More conspicuously, the song 'The Woodspurge', present in the 1870

34 Ruskin, *Complete Works*, vol. III, p. 624.
35 See Dante Gabriel Rossetti, *Collected Poetry and Prose*, ed. Jerome McGann (New Haven: Yale University Press, 2003), p. 158.

version of *The House of Life*, provided the most conspicuous opportunity for the reader to probe Rossetti's version of Collins's problem. The poem described a moment of sorrowful *ennui* in which the speaker notices the seemingly insignificant foliage before him:

> ... My eyes, wide open, had the run
> Of some ten weeds to fix upon;
> Among those few, out of the sun,
> The woodspurge flowers, three cups in one.
>
> From perfect grief there need not be
> Wisdom or even memory:
> One thing then learnt remains to me,
> The woodspurge has a cup of three.[36]

The song offers that knowledge as something won, at least, from experience. Whatever has happened to the singer, there is some consolation in knowing a minor fact of botany. And yet what *is* that consolation exactly? And can that mere fact of nature bear enough significance to be meaningful to anyone else? Nature is not decisively symbolic in 'The Woodspurge'; there is no Wordsworthian revelation; no consolation from natural theology; no suggestion of the human mind reflected back through nature; no mapping of Englishness or historical change; no glimpse of scientific laws at work; no Ruskinian movement through accuracy towards interpretation. There is not even a bigger picture. This is no rural scene – but a tiny item from a rural scene. Rossetti's poem seemed to propose a faith in the simple empirical existence of the natural world. But where could such faith take modern art?

In aesthetics, there was an unexpected consequence of this strand of Victorian thought, with its heightened consciousness concerning the material presence of the natural world. Out of a Victorian problem with nature's meaning came a new understanding of the self-sufficiency of the visual image in poetry. The beginnings of Imagism as a literary practice, with its proffering of intensely realized features of the natural world (among other things) as mysteriously adequate were to be discerned here. The crisp visual image became a familiar part of the repertoire of Modernism – T. E. Hulme, H.D., Ezra Pound. But, before those, Katharine Bradley (1846–1914) and Edith Cooper (1862–1913), writing as Michael Field, took their Victorian

---

36 *Ibid.*, p. 177, lines 9–16.

literary inheritance of doubtfulness about nature's capacity to be more than its material self and reconfigured it as poetry on its way to Imagism:

> They are terribly white:
> There is snow on the ground,
> And a moon on the snow at night;
> The sky is cut by the winter light;
> Yet I, who have all these things in ken,
> Am struck to the heart by the chiselled white
> Of this handful of cyclamen.[37]

The white flowers of 'Cyclamen', first published in *Underneath the Bough* (1893), moved the poets and it was enough for their text to say that. What the well-delineated image of Michael Field's imagination suggested was the intensity of human feeling towards vividly perceived nature – and the poem's right not to have to explain that experience further.

Fragments of the natural scene were, for some, more manageable than a response to the significance of the natural world as a whole. It was no surprise that, across the age, a number of writers should have turned away from those problems to the figuration of natural scenes that were fantastic rather than experienceable, imagined rather than actual. Natural landscapes made alien or enchanted with spells possessed their own appeal. Alien landscapes, of course, did not *have* to be fantasized. The growth of the empire, the extension of international trade and travel, and the multitude of army campaigns brought new natural scenes into the repertoire of Victorian writers. *Snowflakes and Sunbeams, or, The Young Fur Traders* (1856) and *The Coral Island: A Tale of the Pacific Ocean* (1858) were but two of R. M. Ballantyne's adventure fictions which offered the British reader imaginative access to new settings overseas (the first promised to 'Plunge the reader into the middle of an artic winter');[38] Rudyard Kipling's contributions included India in *Kim* (1902) and the jungle in the *Jungle Books* (1894 and 1895); African terrains, both real and fantastic, appealed to Rider Haggard; Robert Louis Stevenson's *Travels with a Donkey* (1879) brought the Cévennes before readers; Olive Schreiner's *The Story of an African Farm* (1883), the South African Karoo; Joseph Conrad's *Almayer's Folly* (1895), Malaya. More locally, the Celtic lands of Great Britain were not omitted: Stevenson's *Kidnapped* (1886) was the most celebrated Victorian narrative to have challenged Scott's imaginative domination of rural Scotland;

---

37 Michael Field, 'Cyclamen', in *Underneath the Bough: A Book of Verses* (London: Bell, 1893), p. 108.
38 R. M. Ballantyne, *The Young Fur Traders* (London: Nelson, 1856), p. iii.

George Borrow's *Wild Wales* (1862) and Theodore Watts-Dunton's *Aylwin* (1898) were two popular books about Wales. Landscapes could be absorbing in their difference from England – though that was not to say that England had only one landscape. Rural writing from around the country from William Barnes (1801–86) in Dorset to Kingsley's *Westward Ho!* (1855) to Whitby in Elizabeth Gaskell's *Sylvia's Lovers* (1863) to R. D. Blackmore's *Lorna Doone: A Romance of Exmoor* (1869) to Hardy's Wessex emphasized that point.[39] But more ample considerations of fantastic scenes were to be found among writers who tested the limits of their imaginations in escaping from the knowable world of visible nature. They envisaged nature's hidden sides or they left the terrestrial behind altogether.

The bottom of the sea was alluring. Geologists' accounts of fossil marine creatures propelled an interest in the unreality of what was still unvisitable. With the laying of the transatlantic cable (the first functioning one was in 1858) human words were literally present at the bottom of the ocean. The imagination had reached there before. Tennyson's 'The Kraken' (1830) fantasized the home of the sea monster with hyperbolized natural forms, 'Huge sponges of millennial growth and height', 'unnumbered and enormous polypi'.[40] In France, later, Jules Verne's popular fantasy novels registered the same interests in *Vingt mille lieues sous les mers* and they travelled to the world beneath water and air in *Voyage au centre de la terre* (*Voyage to the Centre of the Earth*, 1864). Kingsley's *The Water Babies* and Ballantyne's *Under the Waves: Diving in Deep Waters* (1876) took the reader into imaginative sub-aqueous terrains while H. G. Wells, widely interested in the way science changed what it was possible to experience, removed the reader from the earth altogether in *The First Men in the Moon* (1901): Robert Cromie's *A Plunge into Space* (1890) had already fantasized what Mars was like ('sloping hills and pleasant vales'),[41] as had Percy Greg's *Across the Zodiac* (1880). Wells's Martian novel was *War of the Worlds* (1897). Tennyson, at the end of his career, speculated about all the planetary systems, the

> vast sun-clusters' gathered blaze,
> World-isles in lonely skies,
> Whole heavens within themselves.[42]

---

39 For more on this topic, see Keith D. M. Snell (ed.), *The Regional Novel in Britain and Ireland 1800–1990* (Cambridge University Press, 1999) and *The Bibliography of Regional Fiction in Britain and Ireland, 1800–2000* (Aldershot: Ashgate, 2002).
40 Tennyson, *Poems*, vol. I, pp. 269–70, lines 6, 9.
41 Robert Cromie, *A Plunge into Space* (London: Warne, 1890), p. 185.
42 Tennyson, *Poems*, vol. III, p. 97, lines 53–5.

Edwin Abbott's *Flatland* (1884) imagined another foreign and severely mathematical place, where, if there were tree trunks, there was no sun or other heavenly bodies perceivable in the sky and only an arid hierarchical society of two dimensions (women were lines; professional men and gentlemen squares or pentagons). Looking at the fractals of nature was impossible. Mathematics and biological science encouraged new imaginations of worlds, different landscapes, different forms of what was the 'natural' scene. Darwin's *The Origin of Species* (1859) had, before that, along with Charles Lyell and the New Geology, included an implicit invitation to speculate on the history of the known natural world on earth, to muse on the strange beings that lived here long before there were human witnesses. Even the age's best-remembered naturalist W. H. Hudson (1841–1922) had been tempted, from 'a sense of dissatisfaction with the existing order of things',[43] to imagine a world not his own in *A Crystal Age* (1887).

Fantasized natural scenes, from the futuristic texts of Wells to *News from Nowhere*'s tranquil rural life to Swinburne's meditation on nature taken out of time in 'A Forsaken Garden' (1878), made the natural world afresh: extraordinary, risky, bewitched, or strange. Yet thinking through the challenges of the experienceable world remained, and utopian or science fiction dreams of *voyages extraordinaires* declined to recompense, other than in imaginative pleasure, the Victorian writers who struggled with the human connections to the non-human environment. In Charles Kingsley's novel *Two Years Ago* (1857), Stangrave and Claude, his principal characters, muse idly on the way fish do not seem to learn – contrary to the apparent implications of Darwinism – how to avoid hooks. Stangrave makes from that resistance to change a majestic point: ' "[Is] it not a grand thought",' he asks, ' – "the silence and permanence of nature amid the perpetual flux and noise of human life? – a grand thought that one generation goeth and another cometh, and the earth abideth for ever?" '[44] Stangrave thought nature stayed the same. But in the context of the age, it was an ironic comment. The easy passage from observing the natural world to an implicitly moral truism about the dispensation of a divinely governed, permanently ordered earth was, apart from anything else, the kind of movement that was profoundly challenged in the period. In a diversity of forms, Victorian writers celebrated, mourned, and trampled the fertile land in which they lived: they thought about human connections with it, and they imagined

---

43 W. H. Hudson, 'Preface' to the second edition (1906) of *A Crystal Age* (London: Duckworth, 1927), p. [v].
44 Charles Kingsley, *Two Years Ago* (London: Cassell, 1909), p. 23 ('Introductory').

ways of getting out of it. They thought that nature was indestructibly permanent and they regarded its vulnerability to change. They remembered the preciousness, as Ruskin did at Croxted Lane, of private relationships with natural scenes, and they read public statements about the condition of England in the exposure of the natural world to the modern. 'What have those lonely mountains worth revealing?' a poem, perhaps by Emily Brontë, inquired.[45] The Brontë sisters were not, as none could be, representatives of the whole age. But that question, with its anxiety about nature's significance to the human mind and its hope of affective connection, was, all the same, asked in plural forms across the changeful literary landscape of the whole period.

45 Emily Jane Brontë, *The Complete Poems* (Harmondsworth: Penguin, 1992), p. [198]. For a summary of the arguments about the poem's authorship, see *ibid.*, pp. 284–5n.

26

'The annihilation of space and time': literature and technology

CLARE PETTITT

I am an old woman now, and things are very different to
what they were in my youth. Then we, who travelled, travelled in coaches,
carrying six inside, and making a two days' journey out of what people
now go over in a couple of hours with a whizz and a flash, and a
screaming whistle, enough to deafen one. Then letters came in but
three times a week: indeed, in some places in Scotland where I have stayed
when I was a girl, the post came in but once a month; – but letters were
letters then; and we made great prizes of them, and read them and
studied them like books. Now the post comes rattling in twice a
day, bringing short jerky notes, some without beginning or end,
but just a little, sharp sentence, which well-bred folk would think too
abrupt to be spoken.
(Elizabeth Gaskell, 'My Lady Ludlow' (March 1859)[1])

The narrator of Elizabeth Gaskell's 1859 story, 'My Lady Ludlow' is rattled and deafened by her accelerated entry into a technological age. Railway speed shrinks both distance and time and two days contract into two hours. She is baffled by a synaesthetic overload of speed, sound, and light: 'a whizz and a flash, and a screaming whistle': the history of technology is symbiotically linked to the history of perception. In her retrospect, the new technologies have affected the very way in which people communicate – letters have become 'short jerky notes ... without beginning or end'. If 'time–space compression'[2] changed the written style of letters, what stylistic effects might it have had on Victorian literature?

---

1 Elizabeth Gaskell, 'My Lady Ludlow', in *My Lady Ludlow and Other Stories* (Oxford: World's Classics, 1989), p. 1.
2 David Harvey, *The Condition of Postmodernity: An Enquiry into the Origins of Cultural Change* (Oxford: Blackwell, 1990). Although Marx is often quoted as the originator of the phrase 'the annihilation of space by time', the 'annihilation of space and time' is already being quoted as a common phrase by *The Times* in 1821.

The growth of a technologically embedded culture is both visibly and invisibly at work in the literature of the period. It is at its most visible in the railway trains and tracks that criss-cross Victorian literary writing from the 'ringing grooves of change' of Alfred Tennyson's *Locksley Hall* (1830/1842)[3] to the 'deep pits and trenches dug in the ground' to accommodate the new railway at Camden Town in Charles Dickens's *Dombey and Son* (1847) to 'the infant struggles of the railway system' in George Eliot's *Middlemarch* (1872), to William Morris's 'vapour-bath of hurried and discontented humanity, a carriage of the underground railway' in *News from Nowhere* (1891).[4] In the literature of the Victorian period, technology – or more precisely the machine culture of industrialized modernity – often provides a model of futurity and progress.

But literary train-spotting only gets us so far: the many new technologies of the nineteenth century also set about reassembling literary writing from within, forcing authors to write and think differently about the world around them. John Ruskin, up early on the morning of 4 July 1872 in his rooms in Venice, was trying to write contemplatively on a biblical verse, Isaiah 35:6, but found himself constantly interrupted by the steam whistles of the modern ships outside his window: 'Whistle fourth ... this time at high pressure, going through my head like a knife': altogether he incorporates seven such whistles into his text so that 'you will be able to form, from this page, an accurate idea of the intervals of time in modern music'.[5] Different forms of literary writing reshaped themselves in different ways to incorporate this 'modern music', but this chapter will show how technology is not only represented in Victorian texts: it also transforms them.

Technology, of course, has been around for as long as we have. Tools, clothing, weapons, writing: all provide means of organizing and protecting human existence. Literature itself is a technology, indeed one of the oldest technologies. It is a technology for producing narrative meaning: Nicholas

---

3 Alfred Tennyson, 'Locksley Hall', in *The Poems of Tennyson*, ed. Christopher Ricks 3 vols. (Harlow: Longman, 1987), vol. II, pp. 118–30: p. 130. Tennyson remembered '[w]hen I went by the first train from Liverpool to Manchester (1830), I thought that the wheels ran in a groove. It was black night and there was such a vast crowd round the train at the station that we could not see the wheels. Then I made this line.' Note to 'Locksley Hall', *Ibid.*, n. 181, p. 130.

4 Charles Dickens, *Dombey and Son* (London: Penguin, 2002), chapter 6, p. 79; George Eliot, *Middlemarch: A Study in Provincial Life* (Oxford University Press, 1988), chapter 56, p. 519; William Morris, *News from Nowhere*, in *News from Nowhere and Other Writings* (London: Penguin, 1998), chapter 1, p. 43.

5 John Ruskin, 'Letter 20: Benediction (Venice 3 July 1872)', *Fors Clavigera*, in *The Complete Works of John Ruskin* ed. E.T. Cook and Alexander Wedderburn, 39 vols. (London: George Allen, 1903–12) vol. XXVII, pp. 334–51: p. 342 and p. 341.

Dames suggests that 'the novel is a machine constructed to make its reader feel through an only slightly variable, and possibly perfectable, order of events'.[6] And Benedict Anderson long ago remarked that '[i]n a rather special sense, the book was the first modern-style mass-produced industrial commodity'.[7] While this chapter will return to the question of the special status of literature as 'technology', it starts by identifying three easily distinguishable ways in which the industrial technology of the nineteenth century has a determinative effect on literature: first, through technological progress in the production of text and illustration in the steam age; second, through technology within the content of the texts; and third, through the ways in which technology reorganizes narrative. These categories are never mutually exclusive, nor, as the chapter concludes, are they in any way sufficient to explain the relationship of a culture to a text. Indeed, the relationship of literature to technology in the nineteenth century offers a rich test case for exploring both the opportunities and the limits of historical criticism.

Printing technologies

Steam, if not the great leveller, is the great master of the ceremonies, who is daily introducing the various classes and ranks of society to one another, and making them better acquainted in common. (1852)[8]

It was steam that revolutionized both manufacturing and transport in the 1840s. After the introduction of the steam press, '[p]rinting is now a manufacture. The printing office is a factory.'[9] But it was not just the steam press, nor mechanized paper production, binding machinery, nor the new composing machines introduced in the 1840s, nor the steam railways that put nationwide delivery networks in place for the first time, nor the abolition of the paper tax in 1860, but the timely combination of all these technological developments which changed the way people read and wrote literature in the nineteenth century. Not only were Victorians jostling one another on the railway platform as we see in William Powell Frith's 1862 painting, *The Railway*

---

6 Nicholas Dames, *The Physiology of the Novel: Reading, Neural Science, and the Form of Victorian Fiction* (Oxford University Press, 2007), pp. 57–8.

7 Benedict Anderson, *Imagined Communities: Reflections on the Origin and Spread of Nationalism* (London and New York: Verso, 2006), p. 34.

8 Michael Angelo Garvey, *The Silent Revolution, or the Future Effects of Steam and Electricity upon the Condition of Mankind* (London: William and Frederick G. Cash, 1852), p. 134.

9 William and Robert Chambers (eds.), *Chambers' Information for the People* (Edinburgh: William and Robert Chambers, 1849), p. 720.

Station, they were also introduced to one another through the printed word in the periodicals, books, part-works, and newspapers that proliferated from the 1840s onwards. For example, Elizabeth Gaskell was sitting on an omnibus in Manchester in 1855: 'in the 'bus I sate next to somebody . . . he read "Little-Dorrit" and I read it over his shoulder. Oh *Polly*! He was such a slow reader – *you*'ll sympathize, Meta won't, my impatience at his *never* getting to the end of the page.'[10] Her complaint to her daughters about how little she was able to glean of the first part of Dickens's new serial as she craned her neck to read her neighbour's copy reveals the urgent 'news' value of the serialized novel. Periodical serialization and serialization in parts made fiction and poetry not only more affordable, but also more portable – reading was now comfortable on buses and trains and so the 'private' act of reading became absorbed into public space – particularly public urban space. In Gaskell's *Cranford*, Captain Brown is immersed in Dickens's *Pickwick Papers* on a railway platform: '[t]he Captain was a-reading some new book as he was deep in, a-waiting for the down train'.[11] Reading on a train or a bus creates a double narrative – the narrative of the plot and the narrative of the journey: the eye moving across the page as the locomotive or the bus moves across the landscape. In Dickens's own 'Mugby Junction: Barbox Brothers' (1866), the plot *is* the journey, or the seven possible journeys signified by the seven railway lines out of Mugby Junction with seven different possible termini.

Steam, according to one contemporary enthusiast, 'has broken down the boundaries which time and space had set to human enterprise; it has emancipated the genius of our race from local restrictions, made the wonders wrought in any one place the common property of mankind, and combined the material interests of all nations'.[12] Surely the single most important effect of technology on literature in the nineteenth century was this: that more reading matter – old and new – became more available to more people in more places. But this, of course, did not mean that everybody was reading the same things at the same time, even if the more ham-fisted accounts of the growth of mass readership in Victorian Britain sometimes seem to imply just this. Rather, diverse communities of readers

---

10 Elizabeth Gaskell to Marianne and Margaret Emily Gaskell [? late 1855], in *The Letters of Mrs Gaskell*, ed. J. A. V. Chapple and Arthur Pollard (Manchester University Press, 1997), p. 373.
11 Elizabeth Gaskell, *Cranford*, in *Cranford and Cousin Phillis* (London: Penguin, 1976), chapter 2, p. 55.
12 Garvey, *Silent Revolution*, p. 6.

developed over the nineteenth century and complex intersections developed between different reading constituencies.

By 1890 there were an estimated 10,000 print compositors in London alone, but it was not only type that proliferated. Technological developments changed the illustrations in texts too. The poverty of images available to the ordinary person at the beginning of the nineteenth century is difficult to imagine from our hyper-visual 'society of spectacle'. But by the end of the century, Walter Benjamin's 'Age of Mechanical Reproduction' was in full swing and the walls of the poorest cottage were embellished with printed ephemera, cards, and engravings. Over the century, technologies of wood engraving developed into steel-plate engraving, lithography, chromo-lithography, daguerreotypes, cyanotypes, wet collodion prints, and finally colour photography: although, as with all technologies, it is important to remember the uneven development of these media – wood engraving was still common in the last decades of the century, and it took a long time after the invention of photography to develop a way of incorporating photographs into printed text. In Flaubert's *Madame Bovary* (1856), Emma Bovary admires the engravings in a literary annual:

> She trembled as she blew back the tissue paper over the engraving and saw it folded in two and fall gently against the page … [revealing] pale landscapes of dithyrambic lands, that often show us at once palm trees and firs, tigers on the right, a lion to the left, Tartar minarets on the horizon; the whole framed by a very neat virgin forest, and with a great perpendicular sunbeam trembling in the water, where, standing out in relief like white excoriations on a steel-grey ground, swans are swimming about.[13]

In reminding us of the productive technique of steel engraving – 'white excoriations on a steel-grey ground' – Flaubert slyly deflates Emma's infatuation with the improbable romantic *mélange* of the image. But the scene also reminds us how delicious such visual novelties were in this period – particularly to a bored young woman living a long way from any city.

Steam dreams and the 'Mechanical Age'

Charles Mackay's 'The Days that are Gone', a poem published in the *Daily News* in 1846, is typical of the utopian rhetoric of mechanization at mid-century:

---

13 Gustave Flaubert, *Madame Bovary: Provincial Manners*, trans. Eleanor Marx Aveling (London: Vizetelly & Co., 1886), chapter 6, pp. 41–2.

> But thanks to the *Press*, and the *progress of mind*,
> And thanks to the *rail*, we have left them behind.
> Slow coaches, old Tories, dear postage – ye're gone;
> And war and oppression shall follow anon.![14]

For all its steam-triumphalism, though, the *Daily News*, a newspaper largely funded by railway money, also carried almost daily reports of railway accidents and boiler explosions – 'railways to blow you to pieces right and left' as Mrs Waule in *Middlemarch* says – reminding its readers of the risks and violence of the industrializing culture around them, as well as its benefits.[15] While narratives of machines and technology were often co-opted to a politics of progress and triumphalism, a strong counter-culture to the 'Mechanical Age' developed with Thomas Carlyle as its symbolic leader, joined later by John Ruskin, excoriating the effects of 'machinery' upon men. In Carlyle's words, this was the

> Age of Machinery, in every outward and inward sense of that word; the age which, with its whole undivided might, forwards, teaches and practises the great art of adapting means to ends ... Our old modes of exertion are all discredited, and thrown aside. On every hand, the living artisan is driven from his workshop, to make room for a speedier, inanimate one. The shuttle drops from the fingers of the weaver, and falls into iron fingers that ply it faster. The sailor furls his sail, and lays down his oar; and bids a strong, unwearied servant, on vaporous wings, bear him through the waters. Men have crossed oceans by steam; the Birmingham Fire-king has visited the fabulous East.[16]

But Carlyle's denunciations of the mechanical age are always complicated by the ambivalence of the fairy-tale language he uses. The steamship, for example, is here given 'vaporous wings'. On the one hand this is a diabolic fairyland, peopled by tyrants and goblins, as in Dickens's *Hard Times* (1854) in which the factories 'burst into illumination, before pale morning showed the monstrous serpents of smoke trailing themselves over Coketown'.[17] But on the other hand, the magical language of fairyland, a diction inherited from Romantic visions of industrialism, aestheticized processes of production so that the same factories in *Hard Times* are also 'fairy palaces'.[18]

14 Charles Mackay, 'The Days that are Gone', in *Voices from the Crowd, Daily News*, Wednesday, 28 January 1846, p. 5.
15 Eliot, *Middlemarch*, chapter 56, p. 520.
16 Thomas Carlyle, 'Signs of the Times', *Edinburgh Review* 49 (1829), pp. 439–59: p. 442.
17 Charles Dickens, *Hard Times* (Oxford University Press, 1989), chapter 11, p. 91.
18 *Ibid.*

This is especially striking in the 'thing' narratives published in Dickens's *Household Words* (1850–9), which smoothed, for example, the story of the production of glass, or of the manufacture of paper from rags in the paper mill, into a narrative of magical transformation, wonder and delight.

But the environmental costs of industrialization were becoming clear, too, even early in the century. The machine might be 'the universal servant of man, ready to relieve him of all drudgery, and to supplement his limited ability in carrying out the intentions of his will',[19] and steam might be the vaporous medium of the future, but it produced a dark twin: smoke. '[T]he torrents of black smoke that issue from the manufactory chimneys' were already seen as an environmental threat in the 1840s, and in the gardens of northern towns it was reported that 'none but deciduous shrubs can be kept alive'.[20] In Margaret Oliphant's *John Drayton*: '[t]he skies are lurid, and the land burned up by those roaring furnaces: everywhere the air seems choked by fiery dust'.[21] By the 1880s, Ruskin was prophesying environmental doom as a result of industrialization: 'Blanched Sun, – blighted grass, – blinded man'.[22]

Over the span of the nineteenth century, technology became conventionalized more and more as the 'opposite' of nature. Ulrich Beck has claimed that 'the concept of the classical industrial society is based on the antithesis between nature and society (in the nineteenth-century sense), [whereas] the concept of the (industrial) risk society proceeds from "nature" as integrated by culture'.[23] In fact, Victorian literary texts very early began to grapple with the problem of the boundary between technology and nature and there is plenty of literary writing in the nineteenth century that throws Beck's broad-brush characterization of nineteenth-century thinking into question. There is, after all, a gulf of difference between serious literary writing and the questionable verse that poured out in celebration of steam culture, such as 'To the Steam Press' (1845) by Charles Timperley:

19 Garvey, *Silent Revolution*, pp. 4–5.
20 *Report to Her Majesty's Principal Secretary of State for the Home Department, from the Poor Law Commissioners, on an Inquiry into the Sanitary Condition of the Labouring Population of Great Britain* (1842), p. 297. Derby is the place where the plants do not grow.
21 [Margaret Oliphant], *John Drayton; Being A History of the Early Life and Development of a Liverpool Engineer*, 2 vols. (London: Richard Bentley, 1851), vol. II, p. 113.
22 Ruskin, 'Lecture One February 4, 1884', *The Storm Cloud of the Nineteenth Century*, in *Complete Works*, vol. XXXIV, pp. 9–41: p. 40.
23 Ulrich Beck, *Risk Society: Towards a New Modernity*, trans. Mark Ritter (London: Sage, 1992), p. 81.

Now let the iron despot pause and tremble
Let him behold this *Steam Automaton,*
By ingenious man compelled to move
As if endowed by life and being –[24]

Serious literary writing takes up and measures the cultural complexities of the moment. Elizabeth Gaskell, for example, realized very early that the limits of technology were falsely imposed, and that, in truth, 'technology' knew no boundaries and had become the fabric and medium of modern living. In *Cousin Phillis* (1864), Gaskell makes no distinction between (safe) nature and (risky) technology, and this novella articulates a sharp warning about the risks involved in attempting to maintain such a conservative division in the face of oncoming modernity. Gaskell understands with a clarity that is remarkable so early in the process of industrial modernization, that technology *is* the new nature, and she foresees the catastrophe that will ensue if traditional ideas of what is 'natural' are not urgently reconsidered.

So, as the age of steam gathered speed in the middle decades of the nineteenth century, not only did it have a transformative effect on the ways in which texts were produced and distributed, but also on how those texts themselves represented and reformulated the modern world.

The machine in the text

This section tracks technology *within* narrative through three sub-genres of the Victorian novel – sub-genres which are broadly sequential in their relationship to one another. Through the development of the industrial novel, the sensation novel and the detective novel, between 1840 and 1890, we can see the gradual absorption of technology into the culture of modernity. In the late 1840s and early 1850s, what has come to be known as the 'industrial novel' was – according to one of its most accomplished critics, Catherine Gallagher – developing a narrative form in response to the challenge of new manufacturing technologies. If genre responded directly to the pressure of the steam age, what is striking from a survey of these novels is the way in which technology obtrudes into the narrative in an oddly awkward and obdurately 'thing-like' way. The machines stand out like monstrous anomalies – and become the locus of much of the tension and anxiety in the novel:

24 Charles Henry Timperley, *Songs of the Press and Other Poems Relative to the Art of Printers and Printing* (London: Fisher, Son, & Co., 1845), pp. 39–40: p. 40.

It went on again, beginning to move slowly up and down, like the strong right arm of some automaton giant. Greater and lesser cog-wheels caught up the motive power, revolving slowly and majestically, and with steady, regular rotation, or whirling round so fast, you could hardly see that they stirred at all. Of a sudden a soul had been put into that wonderful creature of man's making, that inert mass of wood and metal, mysteriously combined. The monster was alive![25]

In the relatively early days of machine technology, there was a lack of ready language to describe the new, and what has since become known as 'the industrial sublime' developed in an attempt to absorb machinery into the tradition of writing about the environment and natural, non-human world. Gaskell's description of the mill in *North and South* (1854) – 'the ceaseless roar and mighty beat, and dizzying whirl of machinery' – could almost be a description of a waterfall or cataract.[26] But the industrial sublime was never a stable representative strategy and often collapsed, as in this famous passage from Dickens's 1854 novel *Hard Times*:

It was a town of machinery and tall chimneys, out of which interminable serpents of smoke trailed themselves for ever and ever, and never got uncoiled. It had a black canal in it, and a river that ran purple with ill-smelling dye, and vast piles of building full of windows where there was a rattling and a trembling all day long, and where the piston of the steam-engine worked monotonously up and down, like the head of an elephant in a state of melancholy madness.[27]

Words such as 'vast', 'full', and 'trembling' all signal an effort towards the sublime, but the description breaks down into one of Dickens's oddest and weakest similes which moves it far from the 'natural': this elephant – already so out of place in Coketown – is no longer in a state of nature, but 'mad'. In fact, 'the analogical relay between local inhabitant and local nature breaks down here' as the machine ruptures the sense of 'locality'.[28] Stephen Blackpool's disappearance later in the novel becomes 'as monotonous a wonder as any piece of machinery in Coketown',

---

25 [Dinah Maria Craik (Miss Mulock)], *John Halifax, Gentleman*, 3 vols. (London: Hurst and Blackett, 1856), vol. II, chapter 12, p. 299.
26 Elizabeth Gaskell, *North and South* (London: Penguin, 1995), chapter 50, p. 407.
27 Dickens, *Hard Times*, chapter 5, p. 28.
28 Bill Brown, *A Sense of Things: The Object Matter of American Literature* (University of Chicago Press, 2003), p. 98. Brown is discussing Sarah Orne Jewett's *The Country of the Pointed Firs* (1896). See also Tamara Ketabgian, '"Melancholy Mad Elephants": Affect and Animal Machine in *Hard Times*', *Victorian Studies* 45 (2003), pp. 649–76.

which points exactly to the problem: *modern* wonder is based, not on the singular and unique sublimity of surging heights or gaping profundities but on monotonous repetitive power. A steam engine that worked monotonously up and down was like – well, like what? Machines, after all, are '[u]naffected by place, time or climate, incapable of fatigue, untouched by passions or infirmities':[29] they push analogy up against a new limit. The category confusion pivoted on the question of 'being': the machines seemed to claim a powerful presence, and even agency, but they belonged to no extant category of being. Dickens, aware of this, approximated with an elephant. These 'modern wonders'[30] are in fact often described as animate: 'a soul had been put into that wonderful creature of man's making'; '[t]he machine had become ... a living creature;'[31] and 'some real and living thing ... imprisoned in the dead wood and metal.'[32] But the human body does not function as a satisfactory analogue for the machine which both falls short of and exceeds the human. Much of the problematic of industrial fiction is invested in the boundary mapping between 'the machinery, human and metal' and it is this anxious dichotomizing that produces the effect of the machines standing obdurate and apart – unassimilable and difficult – in these texts.[33]

This boundary-policing between the human and the mechanical emerges in the industrial fiction of the 1840s and 1850s and modulates into a major theme of the literature of the later century. A strong frisson of the uncanny is produced by personifications of machines, which speaks to the simultaneous threat and potential of automata: an unease which creeps in early in the century and becomes most powerfully explicit in the emerging genre of science fiction of the end of the century – in the work of H. G. Wells, for example. Mechanical bodies, without fatigue and without conscience, can do the work of the human and so are able to threaten fundamentally the individual and unique sense of self that had emerged in the European

29 Garvey, *Silent Revolution*, pp. 4–5.
30 Bernhardt Rieger, *Technology and the Culture of Modernity in Britain and Germany, 1890–1945* (Cambridge University Press, 2005), pp. 20–50.
31 Geraldine Jewsbury, *Marian Withers*, 3 vols. (London: Colburn & Co., 1851), vol. I, chapter 2, p. 27. *Marian Withers* was commissioned by the *Manchester Examiner and Times* in the year of the Great Exhibition.
32 John Saunders, *Abel Drake's Wife. A Novel* (London: Lockwood & Co., 1862), chapter 11, p. 164.
33 Elizabeth Gaskell, *Mary Barton: A Tale of Manchester Life* (London: Penguin, 2003), chapter 6, p. 57.

philosophy of the eighteenth century and was becoming hegemonic in the liberal free-market society of the nineteenth century.

'He's found out summut about a crank or tank, I forget rightly which it is', says old Alice about Jem Wilson in Elizabeth Gaskell's 1848 *Mary Barton*.[34] However imperfectly described, the thing that Jem has invented makes this brief but important appearance in the text. But the cranks and tanks have more or less disappeared by the 1860s. This may, of course, be an innocent reflection of the increasing invisibility of technology in everyday life, after all '[t]he electric telegraph is now a familiar object; we look upon it with a careless eye, we pass onward, and forget if we ever considered its miraculous properties'.[35] But then again, perhaps it is not as innocent as it seems. If we think of literature less as historically mimetic and more as a particular way of thinking, then the sensation fiction fashionable in the 1860s might represent a way of thinking about some of the problems of speed, simultaneity, publicity, globalization, and social mechanism that machine culture was generating at this juncture. Over the century, the solitary quiddity of machines in the earlier industrial novels gives way to a world in which humans and machines move more closely together. In the description of Tess working 'on the platform of the [threshing] machine' in Thomas Hardy's *Tess of the D'Urbervilles* (1891), Tess's body becomes part of the mechanical process '[i]t was the ceaselessness of the work which tried her so severely ... for Tess there was no respite; for, as the drum never stopped, the man who fed it could not stop, and she, who had to supply the man with untied sheaves, could not stop either'.[36] A clear shift is visible here from both the utopian and pessimistic strains of writing about technology earlier in the century which either celebrated or feared the new 'freedom from work' engendered by machine culture. Hardy's late-century and proto-Modernist version focuses more on the directly dehumanizing threat of enslavement to machinery, with an explicit emphasis on the fragmentation of subjectivity.

The incidents of sensation plots were typically inspired by genuine crimes and scandals – the famous Yelverton–Longworth bigamy trial, the trials of Madeleine Smith, Constance Kent, and Rachel Leverson for murder, and the numerous well-publicized cases of false incarceration in asylums. In January 1845, John Tawell murdered his lover and fled by rail

---

34 *Ibid.*, chapter 10, p. 121.   35 Garvey, *Silent Revolution*, p. 7.
36 Thomas Hardy, *Tess of the D'Urbervilles* (Oxford University Press, 2005), p. 347.

to London disguised as a Quaker, but a telegraphic message reached Paddington station before he did, and he was duly arrested. He was hanged on 28 March 1845. The closeness of sensation fiction to the topical – to news – is made explicit by Mary Elizabeth Braddon in *Lady Audley's Secret* (1862): '[w]e hear every day of murders committed in the country. Brutal and treacherous murders; slow, protracted agonies from poisons administered by some kindred hand; sudden and violent deaths by cruel blows.'[37] Sensation fiction was, quite literally, a literature born out of the growing network of national newspapers in the 1850s and it worked through an unease about anonymity, identity, and 'character' in this newly mobile society of representation.

So by the time these stories that were often literally taken from the newspaper headlines began to catch on with the rapidity and tenacity of a virus in the 1860s, technology was already less conspicuous as a part of modern life. It could be said that sensation fiction merely uses the new technologies to repackage the melodramatic plots that had proliferated on the stage since the beginning of the period. But now the process of unmasking and the climactic recognition scenes are speeded up by the penny post, the railway, and the telegraph. In Mary Elizabeth Braddon's sensation classic *Lady Audley's Secret*, for example, it is by the recent invention of the telegraph that Clara is able to communicate the name of the seaside town in which Helen/Lucy met George Talboys – a key to the mystery. Indeed, theatrical melodrama used technology in a similar way: in Augustin Daly's *Under the Gaslight* (1867), Laura only just manages to free a man tied to the railway tracks as a train approaches 'Victory! Saved! Hooray!' he cries, '(LAURA *leans exhausted against switch*) And these are the women who ain't to have a vote! (As LAURA *takes his head from the track, the train of cars rushes past with a roar and a whistle from* L. *to* R.)'[38] In Dion Boucicault's *After Dark; A Tale of London Life* (1868), a full-sized model steam train ran across the stage on rails and stopped inches short of crushing a character: a stark dramatization of the perilous line between human flesh and the metal of machinery. Jonathan Crary has linked the modernization of subjectivity to the growth in popularity of optical devices like the stereoscope that 'operate directly on the body

---

37 Mary Elizabeth Braddon, *Lady Audley's Secret*, 3 vols. (London: Tinsley Brothers, 1862) vol. 1, chapter 7, p. 108.
38 Augustin Daly, *Under the Gaslight: or, Life and Love in These Times. An Original Drama*, Lacy's Acting Edition (London: Thomas Hailes Lacy, 1870), Act 3, Scene 3, p. 54.

of the individual'.[39] Sensation fiction explored the idea of the body as it was newly mediated by technology.

Sensation fiction even produces a machinery of plot that threatens to work mechanically upon its reader. *The Sensation Times and Chronicle of Excitement* was introduced in 1863 by *Punch*: 'This Journal will be devoted chiefly to the following objects; namely, Harrowing the Mind, Making the Flesh Creep, Causing the Hair to Stand on End, Giving Shocks to the Nervous System, Destroying Conventional Moralities, and generally unfitting the Public for the Prosaic Avocations of Life.'[40] *Punch* is making fun of the sensation craze here, of course, but the idea of this genre working upon its reader in predictable and monotonously replicable ways makes the 'machinery of plot' seem newly sinister. The 1860s sees a panic about the vacuity of the reader who, overwhelmed by the speed and intensity of modern narratives, was in danger of losing all judgment, all taste, and ultimately all identity. And these vulnerable readers were often imagined as female and/or working class: 'the literature of the kitchen' was becoming 'the favourite reading of the drawing room' as one critic complained.[41] If sensation fiction was characterized as a technology which called out mechanical responses in its readers – responses that were universally replicable regardless of the gender or status of the reader – it must be significant that in terms of its content, its authorship, and its publication, the sensation novel was dominated by women. The figures of the female detective, the actress, the governess, and the wicked, adulterous, duplicitous wife stalk the pages of many of these texts, and the prevalence of female authors and editors in the sensation field is striking. Mary Braddon wrote seventeen sensation novels; Ellen Wood twelve; Charlotte Riddell six; Florence Marryat seven; Annie Edwardes eight; and Matilda Houstoun eight. Could this be evidence of the early stages of the now long-standing relationship between information technology and women's struggle for visibility and agency in the modern world?

But technology is not only speeding up, in these narratives: it is also linking up. We see in the sensation fiction of the 1860s the emergence of a concept of a technological network: a network that is both potentially

---

39 Jonathan Crary, *Techniques of the Observer: On Vision and Modernity in the Nineteenth Century* (Cambridge, MA and London: MIT Press, 1990), p. 7. See especially chapter 4, 'Techniques of the Observer', pp. 97–136.

40 'Prospectus of a New Journal: *The Sensation Times and Chronicle of Excitement*', *Punch* (9 May 1863), p. 193.

41 [Fraser Rae], 'Lady Audley's Secret', *North British Review* 43:85 (1865), pp. 180–204: p. 204.

utopian and also deeply threatening to the human. So what is different in the treatment of technology in the sensation novels of the 1860s and the detective fiction at the end of the century? The Sherlock Holmes stories were first published in George Newnes's *Strand Magazine*: one of a new generation of middlebrow magazines illustrated with black and white photographs. The cover sports an engraving of the busy midday bustle in the Strand in the West End of London with the words 'The Strand Magazine' picked out in suspended electric lights over the street – a new phenomenon in 1892. The Electric Lighting Act of 1882 had opened up competition for municipal electrical lighting companies but it took some time before electric lighting took over from gas in London. Ubiquitous city lighting was one of the disciplinary strategies along with an ever more bureaucratized system of policing that led to a city of detection. A city that is lit, is – obviously – more legible, more penetrable by the eye in night and day.

When Sherlock Holmes looks down from the window of his rooms at the beginning of one of the earlier stories, 'A Case of Identity' (1891), he sees the 'dull, neutral-tinted London street'.[42] So when Watson says to Holmes at the beginning of this story that 'the cases which come to light in the papers, are, as a rule, bald enough, and vulgar enough. We have in our police realism pushed to extreme limits, and yet the result is, it must be confessed, neither fascinating nor artistic', he is referring in part to a world which is standardized, and highly lit – in which even secrets are obvious and clear as the light of day.[43] Holmes's great power, of course, is to make the well-lit and modern world of London in 1892 look murky and mysterious once more before throwing his own peculiar light upon the secrets of its inhabitants.

So, in Conan Doyle's stories technology becomes a means of enlightenment – but only a means. 'A Case of Identity' rests upon the evidence of a typewriter, in this case the machine, rather than the typist Mary Sutherland – although the machines and those that worked upon them were both called 'typewriters' in this period. This nomenclature was as revealing as it was confusing, pointing to the crisis of agency that the typewriter created. The idea of machine writing was of course an odd one when it was first introduced, separating, as it does, the hand from the text, and complicating and obscuring ideas of authorship. Friedrich Kittler has argued that the

---

42 Arthur Conan Doyle, 'A Case of Identity', in *The Complete Sherlock Holmes*, 2 vols. (New York: Barnes and Noble, 2003), vol. II, pp. 225–38: p. 226.
43 *Ibid.*, p. 225.

typewriter represents and has helped to effect a fundamental shift in the conception of persons and their relationship to language, manifesting the Modernist recognition of language as the cause, rather than the effect, of human agency.[44]

Yet Holmes seems intent on drawing out the character of this typewriter: 'A typewriter has really quite as much individuality as a man's handwriting', says Holmes – giving a mere machine the identity which, it shortly turns out, Hosmer Angel does not actually possess.[45] One of the first forensic science manuals ever published was Albert S. Osborn's *Questioned Documents* (1910), in which the typewriter is embodied as if it were animate: '[t]he identification of a typewritten document in many cases is exactly parallel to the identification of an individual who exactly answers a general description as to features, complexion, size etc., and *in addition* matches a detailed list of scars, birthmarks, deformities, and individual peculiarities'.[46] Here once again the machine is identified with the human body, but in this case – importantly – with the deformed human body. Holmes's job is to find the deviant and the undisciplined lurking in the interstices of the standardized machine-made world.

Along with electric lighting, the last quarter of the nineteenth century was also important for other kinds of electronic inventions – particularly communications technologies: the telephone, the phonograph, the wireless, and cinema. Disembodied voices began to join the already enormous archive of disembodied 'hands', or writing. In Bram Stoker's *Dracula* (1897) Dr Seward's diary is '(Kept in phonograph)':

> 18 September. – Just off train to London. The arrival of Van Helsing's telegram filled me with dismay. A whole night lost, and I know by bitter experience what may happen in a night. Of course it is possible that all may be well, but what may have happened . . . I shall take this cylinder with me, and then I can complete my entry on Lucy's phonograph.[47]

The phonograph record proves of doubtful durability, though, as all the wax cylinders are later destroyed in a fire and Seward's diary only survives in Mina Harker's typewritten transcript. In fact in both *Dracula* and in the

---

44 Friedrich Kittler, 'Technological Media', in *Discourse Networks, 1800/1900*, trans. Michael Metteer and Chris Cullens (Stanford University Press, 1990), pp. 229–64.

45 Doyle, 'A Case of Identity', p. 235.

46 Albert S. Osborn, *Questioned Documents: A Study of Questioned Documents with an Outline of Methods by which the Facts May be Discovered and Shown* (London: Sweet & Maxwell, 1929), p. 589. Emphasis original.

47 Bram Stoker, *Dracula* (Oxford University Press, 1996), p. 142.

Sherlock Holmes stories it is the information and distribution networks supported by machines, and not the machines themselves that pose the threat. The 'number of great wooden boxes filled with mould' imported into England by Count Dracula and distributed around London by the 'Great Northern Railway [through the] goods station King's Cross' represent a very modern plan executed 'systematically and with precision'.[48] Van Helsing, Jonathan and Mina Harker; and Sherlock Holmes have to find a way to short the circuit in order to stop the mechanism of the plot.

So in the forty years between 1850 and 1890, the representation of machines in literature shifts from making them the problematic object of enquiry to making them the medium of enquiry itself. While Margaret Oliphant's John Drayton first appears as a youth going out excitedly to see a telegraph machine working, Sherlock Holmes has to look beyond and through technologies to solve his cases. And by 1895 in H. G. Wells's *Time Machine* we witness the beginning of the miniaturization that will become a prevalent trope of modern technological development: 'The thing the Time Traveller held in his hand was a glittering metallic framework, scarcely larger than a small clock, and very delicately made. There was ivory in it, and some transparent crystalline substance.'[49] The Time Traveller's model machine is prophetic of the move from the macro to the micro – machines will grow small, they will become more and more prosthetic as nano-technologies in bio, molecular, and micro engineering transform the relationship between 'natural' and 'unnatural' until, as Donna Haraway has famously put it: 'we are all chimeras, theorized and fabricated hybrids of machine and organism; in short, we are cyborgs'.[50] In the next section, I want to suggest that the Victorians were cyborgs too, and that the subtlest ways in which literature and technology overlap in the nineteenth century are perhaps the most important.

Technology as reorganizing narrative

Thomas Carlyle in 'Signs of the Times' in 1829 warned that 'Men are grown mechanical in head and in heart, as well as in hand.'[51] Technology reorders narrative all the way through the nineteenth century from the inside as well

---

48 *Ibid.*, pp. 80, 96, and 226.
49 H. G. Wells, *The Time Machine* (London: Penguin, 2005), p. 8.
50 Donna J. Haraway, 'A Manifesto for Cyborgs: Science, Technology and Socialist Feminism in the 1980s', *Socialist Review* 80 (April 1985), pp. 65–107: p. 66. See also Haraway, *Simians, Cyborgs, and Women: The Reinvention of Nature* (New York: Routledge, 1991), p. 1.
51 Thomas Carlyle, 'Signs of the Times', *Edinburgh Review* 49 (1829), pp. 439–59: p. 444.

as the outside and becomes part of the politics of form of the wider work in which they are embedded.

The rhythm of Elizabeth Barrett Browning's powerfully sentimental protest poem about child-labour in the factories, 'The Cry of the Children' (*Blackwood's Magazine* 1843), uses the repetitive turning of machinery to create what is not exactly an argument, but a rhythm of ceaseless operation and overlong lines which override the 'natural' rhythm of the human heartbeat:

> For, all day, the wheels are droning, turning, –
> Their wind comes in our faces, –
> Till our hearts turn, – our head, with pulses burning,
> And the walls turn in their places –
> Turns the sky in the high window blank and reeling –
> Turns the long light that droppeth down the wall –
> Turn the black flies that crawl along the ceiling –
> All are turning, all the day, and we with all. –
> And, all day, the iron wheels are droning;
> And sometimes we could pray,
> 'O ye wheels,' (breaking out in a mad moaning)
> 'Stop! be silent for to-day!'

The point is that while this is a poem *about* machines in one sense, in a more important sense it is a poem which is written from inside and not outside; partly spoken in the voices of the children, it posits, through its very form, the way in which 'this cold metallic motion'[52] is inside them, and how machines have colonized their bodies so that they moan; their hearts are turning, their pulses are burning. Elizabeth Barrett Browning consulted the Government 'Blue Books' when she was writing her poem – the official reports urging legislative reform and the betterment of the condition of the workers – and she clearly saw her literary work as part of the same movement of factory reform. A similar effect is produced by Thomas Hood in his 'Song of the Shirt', first published in the Christmas number of *Punch* in December 1843:

> Work – work – work!
> From weary chime to chime,
> Work – work – work,
> As prisoners work for crime!

---

52 Elizabeth Barrett Browning, 'The Cry of the Children', in *Poems by Elizabeth Barrett Browning*, 2 vols. (London: Chapman & Hall, 1853), vol. II, pp. 142–9: p. 145, lines 77–88, 93.

> Band, gusset, and seam,
> Seam, gusset, and band!
> Till the heart is sick, and the brain benumbed,
> As well as the weary hand.[53]

The seamstress piece-worker is forced to fall into the repetitive rhythm of a clock-bound machine, and the wry re-ordering of the 'band, gusset, and seam' into 'seam, gusset, and band' within two lines resists repetition while admitting its ultimate powerlessness to do so. But the penultimate line succeeds in breaking the rhythm, stuttering against the regular beat and refusing it, only to collapse with the exhausted cadence of the 'weary hand' with which the stanza ends. The sensory experience of the new factory technologies creeps into the literary representation of the industrializing world.

But other technologies had profound effects upon writing too. Photography, for example, which was becoming more and more familiar as an optical technology at mid-century, began both to be referenced in nineteenth-century writing, and to enter into a dialogue with the written word in more complex ways. By the late century, plots had begun to evolve around photographs: Thomas Hardy's *A Laodicean* (1881), Amy Levy's *The Romance of a Shop* (1888), and Conan Doyle's 'A Scandal in Bohemia' (1891) all pivot upon photographs and photography in explicit ways. It has been argued that photography created a new index of 'reality' which writing was obliged to emulate, so that 'fiction and photography authorized each other in the name of realism'.[54] But photography itself was, in fact, associated with the unreal, with the imaginary and the phantom throughout the nineteenth century, which complicates a symmetrical alignment of 'photography' and 'literature' under the sign of 'realism'.[55] Indeed, even in texts which explicitly use photographs, the fraught relationship between the real and the represented is often suggested. In Hardy's *A Laodicean*, for example, a photograph lies: 'by a device known in photography the operator, though contriving to produce what seemed to be a perfect likeness, had given it the distorted features and wild attitude of a man advanced in intoxication'.[56] This is

---

53 Thomas Hood, 'The Song of the Shirt', in *Poems by Thomas Hood*, 2 vols. (London: Edward Moxon, 1846), vol. i, pp. 70–4: p. 72.

54 Nancy Armstrong, *Fiction in the Age of Photography: The Legacy of British Realism* (Cambridge, MA: Harvard University Press, 1999), p. 28.

55 See Daniel A. Novak, *Realism, Photography, and Nineteenth-Century Fiction* (Cambridge University Press, 2008), throughout.

56 Thomas Hardy, *A Laodicean, or, The Castle of the De Stancys* (London: Penguin, 1997), Book the Fifth, Chapter 4, p. 281.

explicit enough, but at the more abstract level of form photography is not faithful to the 'world' either: 'photography . . . fragmented the world into disconnected pieces, and also made those pieces interchangeable and abstract'.[57] Photography influences nineteenth-century formal literary experimentation in ways both deep and spectral. Indeed, the complexities of the relationship of photography to literary writing in this period provide a test case in the multiple and various ways in which literature and technology both form one another, and join together in their ceaseless work of unravelling and re-ravelling the category of the 'real'.

Not only photography but other Victorian optical technologies created new illusions and other ways of seeing: the magic lantern, the Phenakistiscope, the Praxinoscope, the Zoetrope (or the 'wheel of life'), the panorama, the diorama, the dissolving view, and the stereoscope are just a few examples. Much has been written about the effects of this visual revolution on the literature and culture of the Victorian period and its connection to Victorian narrative, both in terms of the scopic obsession of 'Realist' writing, and in terms of a newly moralized concept of seeing such as that championed by Ruskin who believed that 'close seeing' could 'mean . . . reading deeply into the object, recognizing the comprehensiveness of its self-expression, as it demonstrates its energies, displays the formal laws of its being, and sums up its past and its potential simply by the impact of its visual presence'.[58] It is no accident, of course, that Ruskin is formulating his theory of moralized or 'whole' seeing just as the technology of microscopy was becoming available to more and more people at mid-century. Tennyson, in his 1854 poem *Maud: A Monodrama*, performs this kind of microscopic seeing as a part of the poem's anxious enquiry in the relationship of perception and the material world:

> See what a lovely shell,
> Small and pure as a pearl,
> Lying close to my foot,
> Frail, but a work divine,
> Made so fairly well
> With delicate spire and whorl,
> How exquisitely minute,
> A miracle of design![59]

57 Novak, *Realism*, p. 7.
58 Patricia Ball, *The Science of Aspects: The Changing Role of Fact in the Work of Coleridge, Ruskin and Hopkins* (London: Athlone Press, 1971), p. 69.
59 Alfred Tennyson, *Maud: A Monodrama*, *Poems*, vol. ii, section ii, pp. 513–84: p. 568.

The 'exquisitely minute' is also a feature of Elizabeth Gaskell's last, great, undervalued, and unfinished novel, *Wives and Daughters. An Every-day Story*, published in parts in the *Cornhill Magazine* from August 1864 to January 1866. Paying close attention and seeing properly are both the method and message of the narrative. For example, when Roger Hamley the Darwin-like scientist-hero of the novel comes upon Molly crying over the shock of the news of her father's remarriage, he attempts to cheer her up:

> If Roger was not tender in words, he was in deeds. Unreasonable, and possibly exaggerated, as Molly's grief had appeared to him, it was real suffering to her; and he took some pains to lighten it, in his own way, which was characteristic enough. That evening he adjusted his microscope, and put the treasures he had collected in his morning's ramble on a little table; and then he asked his mother to come and admire. Of course Molly came too, and this was what he had intended.[60]

Roger has to adjust his sympathy to Molly, because her grief appears 'unreasonable and ... exaggerated' to him, but, a good observer and scientist in his negation of self, he makes the sympathetic adjustment – 'it was real suffering to her' – and accordingly attempts to alleviate it by adjusting his microscope and diverting her attention. The close proximity of the processes of Roger's sympathy and of his microscopy in this passage suggest that Gaskell is self-consciously drawing a parallel between the two kinds of 'seeing': the delicate adjustments of the microscope and the delicate adjustments of human sympathy. She later tells us that 'Roger had deep interest in the subject; much acquired knowledge, and at the same time, great natural powers of comparison and classification of facts; he had shown himself to be an observer of a fine and accurate kind.'[61] It is in fact the conventionally feminine qualities of patience, close observation, and self-negation which make him such an outstanding technician.

If *Hard Times* reveals Dickens's own struggle with finding explicit idioms for machine culture, more generally his literary style persistently 'queers' boundaries between things and people. It has been often noticed that Dickens's writing routinely transmutes the animate into the inanimate and back again, and in this his writing conflicts with any model of modern developmental psychology or secularity that posits a sharp break between the world of subjects and that of objects. Bruno Latour has argued that

60 Elizabeth Gaskell, *Wives and Daughters: An Everyday Story* (London: Smith, Elder & Co., 1867), chapter 10, p. 106.
61 *Ibid.*, chapter 33, p. 330.

modernity has created an artificial ontological distinction between inanimate objects and human subjects, whereas in fact the world is full of 'quasi-objects' and 'quasi-subjects'. What could seem like an archaic form of 'magical thinking' becomes in Dickens an imaginative cure for the modern industrial world of thing-proliferation in which he lives.[62] Instead of anxiously policing the boundary between the thing (or machine) and the human, he blurs it, and in this he reveals his hyper-modern cyborg credentials. In *Great Expectations* Mr Wemmick is half-man half-postbox; Peggotty's forefinger is a pocket nutmeg-grater in *David Copperfield*; in 'The Mudfog Papers' Dickens imagines 'an entirely new police force, composed exclusively of automaton figures'; in *Little Dorrit* Pancks becomes a '[t]ug . . . . puffing away into the distance'.[63]

In the first chapter of Henry James's *The Portrait of a Lady* (serialized in the *Atlantic Monthly* and *Macmillan's Magazine* in 1880–1) Ralph Touchett is in England while his mother is in America:

> 'My mother has not gone into details. She chiefly communicates with us by means of telegrams and her telegrams are rather inscrutable. They say women don't know how to write them, but my mother has thoroughly mastered the art of condensation . . . "Changed hotel, very bad, impudent clerk, address here. Taken sister's girl, died last year, go to Europe, two sisters, quite independent." Over that my father and I have scarcely stopped puzzling; it seems to admit of so many interpretations.'[64]

Ralph is still musing on whether it is the impudent clerk who has died when Isabel Archer and his mother appear in his garden. This is a very Jamesian joke, of course, on telegraphese and how open it is to multiple misinterpretations, but the fact that the novel opens with the difficulty and inefficiency of transatlantic communication is more than just a joke: it launches the whole network of badly received and mangled messages and inscrutabilities upon which the rest of the novel depends. Years later, James took up the same theme and used it more literally in his novella, 'In the Cage' (1898), in which a telegraph girl infers and even intervenes in a clandestine love affair being conducted across the wire. But it is in *The Portrait of a Lady* that James

---

62 Bruno Latour, *We Have Never Been Modern*, trans. Catherine Porter (Cambridge, MA: Harvard University Press, 1993), pp. 10–11. 'Quasi-objects' and 'quasi-subjects' are terms Latour borrows from Michel Serres's *Statues* (Paris: Francois Bourin, 1987).

63 Charles Dickens, 'Report of the Second Meeting of the Mudfog Association', in *The Mudfog Papers etc. Now First Collected* (London: Richard Bentley and Son, 1880), p. 136 and Charles Dickens, *Little Dorrit* (London: Penguin, 1998), chapter 13, p. 177.

64 Henry James, *The Portrait of a Lady* (Oxford: World's Classics, 2009), chapter 1, p. 26.

is most subtle in suggesting that railways, transatlantic steamships, and telegraphs may have shrunk space and folded up time, but human communication remains a thoroughly perilous undertaking.

If technology is a tool for the organization of process and for production, then literature is a tool for the organization of the experience of human life, and for the invention of meaning. Undoubtedly, this sounds somewhat Gradgrindian, and as a definition of literature it does little to account for the particular aesthetic pleasures or radicalisms therein, but it may be a necessary retrenchment in the face of such statements as: 'The abstraction of space and time as a material independent of actuality, and its re-engineering into new configurations, was *eventually perfected* in the cinema' [my emphasis].[65] This techno-evolutionary narrative suggests that one technical innovation leads tidily on to the next in a progressive sequence: each more complicated and powerful than the last. We know this is not the case. It is possible to argue, for example, that the possibilities unleashed by the telegraph in the nineteenth century are only beginning to be actualized in the twenty-first century on the world-wide web, after a period in which non-interactive technologies such as the television took precedence.[66] Similarly it is only at the turn of the twentieth and twenty-first centuries that e-mail has overtaken the immense connectivity of the Victorian postal service after the penny-post reforms of 1840 which made more than five postal deliveries a day in large cities. And the unevenness and diversity of technological spread across continents and cultures – if we start to look beyond the British Isles – makes any such teleological simplification not only impossible, but also dangerous.

Yet there is no doubt that technology was important to literature in the nineteenth century, both in purely instrumental ways, and in more far-reaching ones. The growth of a mass readership over the period was one of the most important developments of a modern society. Nineteenth-century literature did much to grapple, albeit sometimes in semi-unconscious ways, with the immense ethical and philosophical problems posed by a rapidly developing machine culture. It also created new imaginary places and spaces within society for that machine culture, which helped along the absorption

---

65 David B. Clark and Marcus B. Doel, 'Engineering Space and Time: Moving Pictures and Motionless Trips', *Journal of Historical Geography* 31:1 (2005), pp. 41–60.

66 Jay Clayton has argued that the telegraph is 'the precursor to the Internet'. *Dickens in Cyberspace: The Afterlife of the Nineteenth Century in Postmodern Culture* (Oxford University Press, 2003), p. 51. See chapter 2, 'The Voice in the Machine: Hazlitt, Hardy, and Dickens', pp. 50–80.

of the networks of modern life. So literature neither trails behind, nor runs in front of technological innovation: they rather conduct a complicated kind of dance with one another. We need to read the history of technology, as well as that of books, differently and to recognize the huge imaginative energy unleashed by Victorian machines, if we want to make visible the ways in which literary writing and the technological revolution in this period were constantly remaking the category of the human.

PART V

*

SPACES OF WRITING

Spaces of the nineteenth-century novel

ISOBEL ARMSTRONG

Everyday life takes the space of our three-dimensional world for granted. Length, breadth, and depth, as the elements of our spatial consciousness and the medium of social experience, are so much a part of existence that they can be ignored. When they are encountered in the novel, they can also be passed over as one of the necessary and relatively unimportant obligations of realism. Yet in a novel, as Bakhtin realized, 'Time, as it were, thickens, takes on flesh, becomes artistically visible; likewise, space becomes charged and responsive to the movements of time, plot and history.'[1] How then does a writer convince us through the abstractions of language that spatial experience created in a text is, by an extraordinary transposition, recognizable, vivid, a *lived experience*? How, in other words, does the novelist effect a mimesis of the a priori of space? This is the problem I address here. With the category of space uppermost, the 'thickening' of space in the novel, and the ways that it creates inter-spatial consciousness and social interaction, can be opened up.

Subtract the element of space from the nineteenth-century novel and it would be hard to say what is left. Most models of the novel, though, while they admit the indivisibility of space and time, begin with time. The criticism of Mikhail Bakhtin and Paul Ricoeur offers outstanding examples of this.[2] To begin with space: this would mean reversing the historical poetics of the chronotope, Bakhtin's term for narrative elements where time and space mutually intensify and become dynamic. In the chronotope history becomes visible as space, and the 'when' of the novel and the 'where' of the novel, as Franco Moretti elegantly puts it, come together in a unique

---

1 M. M. Bakhtin, *The Dialogic Imagination. Four Essays*, ed. Michael Holquist, trans. Michael Holquist and Caryl Emerson (Austin: University of Texas Press, 1982), p. 84.
2 See *ibid.*; Paul Ricouer, *Time and Narrative*, trans. Kathleen Blamey and David Pellauer, 3 vols. (Chicago and London: Chicago University Press, 1984–8).

convergence, one that could only occur at this juncture in the narrative and at this historical moment.[3] Making narrative space a priority would mean stressing that the 'where it happens' of narrative generates 'what happens' at least as much as the 'when' of temporality.

I begin with Immanuel Kant's philosophical reading of space because it illuminates the category of space and its social meaning in the Victorian novel. Space, Kant said in the *Critique of Pure Reason*, is the form of external experience as time is the form of internal experience. So a novel needs not simply to evoke space, as it would a smell or the taste and sight of a madeleine (famously in Proust) or a jam puff (in George Eliot's *The Mill on the Floss*). It has to make space a constitutive element, to *produce* it. Narrative is of necessity made temporal through the very act of reading. To some extent the work of creating time in a novel is effected by the linearity of narrative. Not so with space. The simple recapitulation of items in space (dressers, pictures, chairs, fireplaces) every time the same environment reappears in the narrative, so that repetition makes them take on representational force, is insufficient in itself to create spatial depths and relationships.

Space, Kant says repeatedly, is the condition of the possibility of the perception of phenomena and not an empirical conception. He makes four propositions that restate this fundamental premise. Space is external, it is 'outside me', understood as relational, and there is the presupposition of space in all external perception, in which things are in different places. The 'representation of space must be presupposed' in positing things side by side and in relation to one another, because without this it would not be possible to posit relations at all.[4] Second, we cannot think space away. Though we can think of it as 'empty of objects', space itself doesn't go away. Third, space is single. Though we may think in terms of a plurality of spaces, division and partition, space is not put together from segmented units after these are grasped as divided. It begins as a totality, 'essentially one' and is grasped as such. This is what allows us to work out the logical relations of geometry, without recourse to empirical sense data. Finally, space is infinite, all its parts coexisting ad infinitum: it contains us, not us it. For Kant, to be enslaved by the empirical would mean that the mind would be incapable of generating new knowledge. Furthermore, though space is an experience of

---

3 Franco Moretti, *Atlas of the European Novel 1800–1900* (London: Verso, 1998), p. 70.
4 Immanuel Kant, *Critique of Pure Reason*, trans. Norman Kemp Smith, 2nd edn (London: Macmillan, 1933), p. 68.

an individual consciousness, and no certainty of what we see can be guaranteed or shared, this solipsism is paradoxically a social, collective experience. *Without* human consciousness space and the things in it would be meaningless. Making sense of space, the spatial self, is something human beings share irreducibly. And space is the structuring element of all social relationships, from the infant at the breast to the configuration of chairs in a salon or drawing room. (The chronotope of the salon was for Bakhtin one that dominated the nineteenth-century novel.) The *First Critique* was published in 1781, the period when the novel was entering its second great phase. And when a spatial and inter-spatial subject emerges in it. Though post-modern readings of space, from those of Gilles Deleuze to Michel Serres, have challenged Enlightenment accounts such as Kant's, I will begin with descri-bing 'classical' inter-spatial consciousness. Even when this inter-spatial relation is under strain, challenged, or interrupted, it never disappears.

To start with, then, the inter-spatial subject is my theme. But first another step in Kant's thought needs to be filled in. Kant added a further element to his spatial thought, the body. Indeed, he began with it in an essay of 1768 on orientation in space, following this up with two more essays, in 1783 and 1786, published in between the first (1781) and second (1787) editions of the *Critique*.[5] Objects only take on directionality, he maintains, through their relation to the double-sided but unsymmetrical human body. Relatedness is not inherent in objects but is organized by the body alone. The pre-given corporeal ground of orientation in space depends on our physical bifurcation into 'incongruent counterparts', left-handed and right-handedness. This gives us the power to distinguish one side from another – left, right, up, down, front, back, over there, beyond, behind. Spatial differentiation and the intersecting vertical and horizontal planes of three-dimensional experi-ence projected from the body follow from this crucial capacity to match and not match. It is this capacity that enables us to occupy a concrete, fully inhabited world, the world of place as well as space. Even in a dark room such orientation occurs. In the world of fiction this inhabited space shares the sensory animation that Elaine Scarry attributes to visual experience and sense data in the novel. She describes strategies of writing that achieve this sensory belief. Her work has prompted me to think of parallel strategies for

---

5 Kant's theory of orientation in space is discussed in Edward S. Casey, *The Fate of Place. A Philosophical History* (Berkeley and Los Angeles: University of California Press), pp. 205–10. Kant's three essays on orientation are: 'Ultimate ground of the differentiation of regions of space' (1768), 'Prolegomena to any future metaphysics' (1783), 'What does it mean to orientate oneself in thought?' (1786).

realizing space in the novel. But these must be different because with space we are dealing with the intangibles of breadth and depth.[6]

The novelist needs not only to produce a mimesis of the a prioris of space – boundaries and horizons, windows and walls – but to create the concrete fully inhabited world of the situating body. It is a double task: it has to be done for the fictional consciousnesses in the text, and for the reader mediating the experience through print. Through language alone the fictional character must be orientated in space. But whereas the fictional character is fixed along a trajectory of moves by the author, the reader can be granted a mobile situatedness, sometimes identifying with the fictional character's spatial experience and perspective, sometimes external to it, looking *at* rather than *with* them. The mentalism of Kant's four principles help us to understand the ways this mimesis can happen in abstract terms. But these principles are more fully understood when we supplement them with his notion that the orientating corporeal agency of the body is crucial. In this way *space* 'thickens, takes on flesh', as it were, and time becomes charged with meaning. I begin with the way the novel realizes Kant's four founding principles, since they underlie the many imagined social spaces – houses, hovels, streets, alleyways, domestic rooms, ballrooms, shops, stairs, roads, fields, heath, marshes – of the nineteenth-century novel, and enable the novelist – and by extension the reader – to question how they come into being and what happens to the inter-spatial subject in them.

The way a novelist can *produce* space in language is by alternately negating and confirming the four principles that make spatial experience possible. Take away the body, reintroduce it; empty space of objects, restore objects; obliterate partitioned space, reinstate division; all of these are procedures that can be reversed or combined with one another. We are prompted into intensified spatial imagining when the novelist signals a change in spatial relations. (In a parallel argument Elaine Scarry shows how sensory awareness in the novel is cognitively intensified if an existing scene is overlaid with a transparent medium, which is then manipulated or removed. The scene takes on a paradoxical solidity when we are reminded that its sensory substantiveness has been made to disappear.)

To show how this works in practice, I want to take two moments of traumatic spatial disorientation, in each case experienced by a child who is subjected to the sudden and violent shock of physical assault and is seized

---

6 See Elaine Scarry, *Dreaming by the Book* (New York: Farrar, Straus and Giroux), 1999.

with horror. Space is first put under erasure, an obliteration which is then followed by the violent kinaesthetic reinstatement of it. We are shocked into space.

'Troutham had seized his [Jude's] left hand with his own left, and swinging his slim frame round him at arm's length, again struck Jude.' The 'whirling child', under 'the centrifugal tendency of his person', beheld 'the hill, the rick, the plantation, the path and the rooks going round and round him in an amazing circular race'.[7]

> The man, after looking at me for a moment, turned me upside-down and emptied my pockets. There was nothing in them but a piece of bread. When the church came to itself – for he was so sudden and strong that he made it go head over heels before me, and I saw the steeple under my feet – when the church came to itself, I say, I was seated on a high tombstone, trembling, while he ate the bread ravenously.[8]

The textual eye generally presupposes a reader who occupies a consciousness that is rendered stable through sharing the narrator's perspective, implicitly sharing the left/right orientation of a frontal gaze wherever that eye is positioned and directed – in the 'vast concave' of the field's 'brown surface' that stretched to the sky 'all round', or the 'dark flat wilderness beyond the churchyard, intersected with dykes and mounds and gates'.[9] But here the reader's gaze is disrupted along with the child's as each child is surprised into space after thinking it away, either as 'wilderness' or as a uniformly ploughed 'expanse' deprived of the gradation of contour and history. (In the *Jude* passage, moreover, the normally incongruent limb when it comes to the body's self-orientation, the left hand, is forced out of its function both for reader and child as it, and the sense of placement that it carries with it, is violated through the act of rotation.) The prior existence of an element where things are disrupted by violent movement – the rotating ricks and rooks on earth and in the sky, the inverted steeple 'under my feet' – becomes suddenly known or re-recognized as the condition of experience. An inherent, formative spatial order that was always there asserts itself through disorder. The coincidence of unlike tenses that refuse a clear temporal sequence to the coming into awareness of space means that, in both episodes, the simultaneous presence of a spatial world and the things in it is inescapable. *'[A]ll at once he became conscious . . . Troutham had seized his*

---

7 Thomas Hardy, *Jude the Obscure* (London: Penguin Books, 1998), chapter 2, p. 15.
8 Charles Dickens, *Great Expectations* (Oxford University Press, 2008), chapter 1, p. 4.
9 Hardy, *Jude the Obscure*, chapter 2, p. 14; Dickens, *Great Expectations*, chapter 1, p. 3.

left hand.' The 'trembling' child seated on a tombstone reaches back to earlier present participles: '*I found out* for certain . . . that the small bundle of shivers *growing afraid* of it all and *beginning* to cry, *was* Pip.'[10] Past and past perfect, past, present participle and imperfect, happen simultaneously. Indeed, the discovery that *was* Pip seems to be simultaneous with the seizure.

The 'identity of things', as Pip calls them,[11] means ambiguously both the inseparability of objects and space and the co-presence of the isolated self with them. Simply through the setting in motion of things round the body, through the optical illusion that exchanges the world's movement for the eye's, both novelists assert that relational experience is predicated on the precondition of external space, that one cannot think space away, that space is at once infinite and containing. And these are both cognitive and lived experiences, taking the reader into the spatial being of the text. They are also the conditions of an ontological crisis – a crisis of identity, a crisis of being – for the child. With the advent of the avenging or predatory adult, space triangulates. A third element intervenes between the dyad of child and external world as space becomes shockingly, suddenly, social, and an inter-spatial world is violently born. For some critics these experiences of inversion and rotation can signify the birthing of identity. But though the latent contrary suggestions of rape are muted ones, residing in the unconscious of the language, the sense both of exile, in the brown concave, in the marshes, and of violent power relations if not sexual crisis, is pressingly evident in the experience of these pre-adolescent boys – the steeple between the legs, the clacker repeatedly striking the child's rear. Pip's world is inverted; 'I'm turned away', Jude says to his aunt.[12] It is less that these spatial terms prefigure metaphorically what is to happen subsequently: rather they are interrogations of the multiple inter-spatial possibilities of these expressions in a mediated world as well as of the very terms themselves. What is 'the right way up' for Pip in a triangulated world? *Is* there a right way up? What is it to be erect? We can speak in terms of social mobility, ethics, and sexual relations through the notion of what is upright, all questioned in this novel. 'I'm turned away': the child labourer poignantly uses the strangely adult phrase for peremptory dismissal, invoking the

---

10 Hardy, *Jude the Obscure*, chapter 2, p. 15; Dickens, *Great Expectations*, chapter 1, p. 4; italics author's own.
11 Dickens, *Great Expectations*, chapter 1, p. 3.
12 Hardy, *Jude the Obscure*, chapter 2, p. 17.

arbitrary unemployment and economic destitution of the rural male worker. He *has* been turned away, whirled anti-clockwise and sacked by his employer, but his phrase also addresses the existential *condition* of being 'turned away', to suffer displacement, and the rest of the novel questions what this means. To be deflected, to be rejected, even to be captured by the 'turn' of symbolic meaning, as Jude is by the idealized towers of Christminster (his longing for these immediately follows his spatial displacement, and is itself a displacement), this is a major preoccupation of the novel. In a triangulated social world, what weight should be given to the passive voice of 'I'm turned'? What form of agency is granted in the 'ache of modernism'[13] – to borrow a phrase from Hardy's *Tess of the D'Urbervilles* – a pain that begins for Jude with his violent beating?

The following two passages work in opposite ways when it comes to setting out the segmentation and division of space – the theme of the third major Kantian premise. They also demonstrate his final principle, space as container. 'We made ourselves as snug as our means allowed in the arch of the dresser. I had just fastened our pinafores together, and hung them up for a curtain' when Joseph 'tears down my handywork'.[14] 'I rushed out of the room . . . I threw myself on my bed in my clothes . . . He held up the curtain of the bed . . . but I escaped and rushed downstairs. I took refuge in the courtyard . . . where I remained during the rest of the night.'[15] The single-ness of space is established paradoxically by demonstrating the perilousness of its partition. A fabricated partition made of pinafores to enable the children to retreat into a small world of their own, is quickly annihilated in Emily Brontë's novel. The children are exposed to the gaze of the perpetrator of this destruction, Joseph, and in addition Lockwood, the voyeuristic reader of Cathy's childhood journal long after it was written, and the reader. In Frankenstein's case, exposed to the monster he has made, space is subject to successive multiple divisions in the act of flight – bedroom, bed, curtain, stairs, courtyard – and though it is always progressively enclosed, the dividing barriers are all artificial and are of no avail. They mimic an artificial womb that parallels Frankenstein's usurpation of biological reproduction. Space is frighteningly single as Frankenstein seeks protection. He is trapped all night in the locked womb of the courtyard.

13 Thomas Hardy, *Tess of the D'Urbervilles* (London: Penguin Books, 2003), chapter 19, p. 124.
14 Emily Brontë, *Wuthering Heights* (London: Penguin Books, 2000), chapter 3, p. 21.
15 Mary Shelley, *Frankenstein or the Modern Prometheus* (London: Penguin Books, 2003), vol. 1, chapter 3, pp. 58–9.

As was the case with Hardy and Dickens, Emily Brontë and Mary Shelley do not remain content with the simple, immediate construction of space. Heathcliff ultimately barricades himself into Wuthering Heights (the series of obstacles to entering the house that Lockwood first encounters, beginning with the unopened gate, parallel the reader's experience with the obstacles of the framed narratives). Just as the huge dresser and its enclosed spaces in the main room reappears insistently, Heathcliff becomes obsessed with the small, enclosed spaces that make him inseparable from Catherine – the panelled box bed usurped by Lockwood, where he and Cathy slept with one another until they were twelve, the open-sided coffins that will unite them in death. 'Nelly, I *am* Heathcliff.'[16] As multiple variations, combined and recombined, of the same family names suggest, this is a group that cannot understand separation, Heathcliff the exile least of all. Inside Wuthering Heights the stone-flagged main room is elided with the entrance hall, Lockwood, ethnographer of provincial custom, notes. It is and is not a kitchen (the 'real' kitchen, signified by chatter and clatter, is vaguely 'within'). The room comprises indeterminate recesses and cavities where an unknown number of dogs, in symbiosis with their owner, lurk. The unstable categories of space reduplicate the unstable categories of kinship networks that seem to be activated by Heathcliff, the outsider, dark 'lazar' or gypsy boy, from Liverpool.

Usually read as disruption by a racial other, the uncertainty of the category and divisions of kinship also poses questions about the way a group or family regenerates – or not – its social and biological continuity. Heathcliff is the resistant, unassimilable outsider from whom Catherine nevertheless fails to separate, so that he is both incestuous sibling and lover. Through him Brontë explores what elements are and are not eligible for assimilation in a kinship group, and in so doing the novel questions the very constitution of family and kinship as a category. This is important because it is through the ambiguous legitimacy of bloodline and its transgressions that the nineteenth-century narrative explores those inclusions and exclusions that would make for a more (or less) equitable civil society. In nineteenth-century narrative texts the order of family, class, outsiders and insiders, the barrier and the border, are paramount. Some commentators, including Franco Moretti, Homi Bhabha, and Patrick Parrinder, connect the formation of the novel with the formation of the nation state. But the novels that

---

16 Brontë, *Wuthering Heights*, p. 82.

I discuss here are less about the nation state than about the way civil society can be made possible, and what strategies of inclusion and exclusion operate. Lockwood's dream of the sermon by the Rev. Jabes, infinitely divided into rhetorical parts, is a frantic dreamwork attempt to establish limits, separate categories, to create a finite hierarchical order.

On another scale altogether, it is through spatial values that *Frankenstein* questions whether the monster can belong to the category of the 'family' of man. It is never clear how far from or near he is to the human species. Though he asks for a mate of his own kind, suggesting he forms a race apart, the monster claims human rationality. It is no accident that he accosts Frankenstein in the sublime landscape of Mont Blanc, for the sublime, for both Burke and Kant, was the testing ground for achieving rationality and human masculinity. And the monster comes into consciousness through the a priori category of space, another prerequisite of the human. The definition of shape and form and the distinction between light and dark comes into being through a power of orientation that the monster always already possesses. Though his early experience is of a 'strange multiplicity of sensations' in which I 'saw, felt, heard, and smelt at the same time',[17] space exists, nevertheless, prior to this synaesthesic state, and his perception is spatial. He begins to perceive 'forms' 'with greater accuracy'.[18] But though the sensations become clearer they do not alter fundamental relationships. Well before the monster achieves an understanding of light and shade, bodily space is known to him: 'dark and opaque bodies had surrounded me, impervious to my touch or sight'.[19]

The monster's spatial education is unrealistically rapid, but it marks him with a defining human characteristic. Nevertheless, human spatial categories are themselves under strain, and this crisis is portrayed with a similar lack of realism that becomes functional in the text. The global reach of this novel, stretching to the pole and localizing itself among the proliferating place names of Europe, and taking the European tour to its very limits, makes no bid for realism. Its almost perfunctory one-dimensionality gives it an affinity with the Greek adventure stories and accounts of the road or journey that Bakhtin identified as strangely empty of space/time specificity.[20] But, though *Frankenstein* echoes the ancient

---

17 Shelley, *Frankenstein*, vol. 1, chapter 10, p. 105.   18 *Ibid.*, p. 106.   19 *Ibid.*, p. 105.
20 Bakhtin, *Dialogic Imagination*, pp. 100–1.

adventure tale, the thinness of the road experience is that of the nine-teenth-century tourism that was beginning to supersede the grand tour. The novel sets up an opposition between the humanly made landscape of European space and the wild. Yet the sketchiness of the antithesis betrays its arbitrary nature. For 'wild' is a humanly made category also, and cultivated and uncultivated territory alike belong to human experience. Frankenstein the man is trapped in European binary definitions of the human and the civilized that are at breaking point, ready to implode. This is why the verges of European culture (Ireland, Scotland, Russia) fray into the desolation of ice and snow.

Frankenstein is an intensely metaphysical novel. It combines the great Enlightenment tradition of the philosophical 'Inquiry' with the poetics of the sublime. Often the narrative produces only so much spatial detail as will grant credibility to the action. It maps space rather than producing it as a living context. But this simplicity enables it to pose its questions starkly: what makes a 'human' community and what are its boundaries? Why are the norms of eligibility, themselves humanly made, so narrow? Definitively post-revolutionary, the Victorian novel takes up these questions. But the outsider belongs to a space that 'thickens' in a more complex way.

Favourite chronotopes of the Victorian novel

Here I chart some of the dominant chronotopes of the period as a preface to looking more closely at two novels that respectively negotiate country and urban environments, George Eliot's *The Mill on the Floss* (1860) and Charles Dickens's *Dombey and Son* (1848).[21] My argument is that the dominant chronotopes of the novel at this time both create and are the product of a complex inter-spatial subject, or rather, the more open term I prefer, an inter-spatial consciousness.

The proliferation of new wants and needs that came with speed and mobility, both physical and social, and that accompanied the new forms of work and pleasure generated by industrial capitalism, charged the environ-ments of nineteenth-century fiction with a special particularity. The huge variety of spaces and places available to narrative created an extraordinary sensory glut as mass public space emerged in forms never previously witnessed. The takeup of nervous energy that Georg Simmel famously

21 George Eliot, *The Mill on the Floss* (London: Penguin Books, 1985); Charles Dickens, *Dombey and Son* (London: Penguin Books, 2001).

saw as the characteristic of an urban environment is palpable.[22] The rhythm of self-subsisting country estate, and the multi-class inn on the road, mediating town life, with its sharp antithesis between low and aristocratic life, that once characterized earlier eighteenth-century narratives, has disappeared. Horse-drawn coaches and private carriages now coexist with the steam engine and the railway station, steam vessels and ports. The slower pulse of rural life repeatedly appears as the antithesis of city spaces. But it is less a living alternative than a curious double or extension of the city, where febrile energy has become etiolated and exhausted. Dickens's *Bleak House* (1853) and Elizabeth Gaskell's *North and South* (1855) instance this enfeeblement. Lady Dedlock's '"place" in Lincolnshire',[23] a space of enervation and despair, links semantically with the law courts of Lincoln's Inn. The pastoral village of Helstone has its derelict squatters' cottages as Milton has its slums: it is not sealed off from the trading 'shoppy'[24] people that Margaret wants to exclude from its pastoral idyll and whom she finds again in the north; above all it is *not* a 'hale' or healthy culture; Mr Hale's religious doubt breeds in its environment. The elision of hale/hel may be accidental but it creates a subliminal disquiet about the pastoral environment.

Perhaps the most significant organizing opposition of the period is that between the highly specialized urban environment, London in particular, and the domestic house. The Victorian novelist charts a city that has become territorialized, partitioned into a series of specific settlements, enclaves, and zones, whose frontiers and borders denote particular groups, occupations, and class habitats.[25] In *Vanity Fair* (1848) Thackeray unerringly puts the man grown rich on trade, George Osborne's father, in Russell Square, interviewing the terrified Amelia in an imposing room where a clock decorated with a scene of the sacrifice of Iphigenia ticks on the mantelpiece. Henry James places Hyacinth, in *The Princess Casamassima* (1886), in the East End dressmaker's house, half workplace and half home, with its snippings of material, the remains of respectability denoted by its 'cheffonier', and a dingy sweet shop selling popular romances opposite. These environments are highly differentiated. Chop houses, churches, boulevards, alleys, mansion houses, slums, the offices of commerce and law (places of writing and calculation),

22 Georg Simmel, 'The Metropolis and Mental Life' (1903), in *Georg Simmel: On Individuality and Social Forms*, ed. Donald Levine (University of Chicago Press, 1971), p. 325.
23 Charles Dickens, *Bleak House* (London: Penguin Books, 1996), chapter 2, p. 20.
24 Elizabeth Gaskell, *North and South* (Oxford University Press), chapter 2, p. 19.
25 Moretti, *Atlas*, p. 92. See also David Harvey, *Spaces of Capital: Towards a Critical Geography* (London: Routledge, 2001).

wharves, warehouses, clubs, theatres, shops and parks, suburbs and stations – some or all of these places are guaranteed to be present in almost any novel of the period. The nuances of zoning and the hierarchy of class areas do not preclude the constant mix and mêlée of people on streets and in places of work and leisure. London's rich and poor neighbourhoods, it has been pointed out, were juxtaposed one against the other in a series of geographically discrete but small areas that meant a patchwork of rich and poor dwellings throughout the city. Dickens's Jo the crossing-sweeper in *Bleak House* is literally at the junction of the 'crossings' of groups in the novel. Work, particularly factory work, is generally excluded from the anthology of Victorian environments portrayed in fiction. Nonetheless, the novel is predicated on work. What it portrays is the infrastructure of urban capital, a nascent commodity culture, and a growing body of services generating and administering a bureaucracy that has the power to exclude and include people as members of civil society.

The domestic dwelling, the bourgeois family house, and even the minimal houses of the poor, appear to mark a retreat from the storm of affect in the city street, the transitory sights, smells, sounds, bill boards and advertisement hoardings (the frescoes of the city, Ruskin called them),[26] the cries of vendors, children, the drumming of hooves and wheels, the smells of food, coal smoke, and fetid city decay. 'For our house is our corner of the world', Gaston Bachelard characterized the house lyrically in *The Poetics of Space*.[27] It is the primal space, the 'original shell' of a vital space that fuses consciousness and the body with its physical container: the house is a kind of secretion from dreams, reverie, and memory as well as a material casing. It generates images and protects the unconscious. The oneiric possibilities of the house are such that our birth house is 'physically inscribed' in us,[28] so much so that not only can we 'read' a room, but others can 'read' this reading. Such reading he termed 'topoanalysis'.

Bachelard's celebration of the European house, and even of what is termed bourgeois interiority, lays him open to criticism. But his great insight, that space, even dreamed space, connects us with the world, and

---

26 John Ruskin, 'Mornings in Florence' (1877), in *The Works of John Ruskin*, ed. E. T. Cook and Alexander Wedderburn, 39 vols. (London: George Allen, 1903–12), vol. XXIII, p. 329.

27 Gaston Bachelard, *The Poetics of Space* (1958), trans. Maria Jolas (Boston: Beacon Press, 1969), p. 4. For a spatial study of the nineteenth-century novel see Robert L. Patten, 'From House to Square to Street', in Helena Michie and Ronald R. Thomas (eds.), *Nineteenth-century Geographies* (New Brunswick, NJ: Rutgers University Press, 2002), pp. 191–206.

28 Bachelard, *Poetics of Space*, p. 14.

that we can 'read' spaces, is of lasting importance. Often, though, characters are deprived of the 'original shell' of the oneiric house. Jane Eyre, Oliver Twist, David Copperfield, Pip in *Great Expectations*, all lack, and all long for, that primal space. Though Dickens is well aware that the domestic ideology that sets up a division between public and private, work and leisure, is suspect, he puts intense value upon the home. Nevertheless in the novel at this time the house comes under sustained critique. Far from being the retreat it seems it is often the place where power relations are played out. It can engender the wrong expectations, as the luxury of Thrushcross Grange fosters social ambition in Cathy after the primitive space and decor of Wuthering Heights. The difference between a home and an establishment is Thackeray's constant theme in *Vanity Fair*. The house can be overprotective, fostering a kind of infantilism that makes people refuse mature choices, as it does for Lily in Trollope's *The Small House at Allington* (1864). She prefers to memorialize the space of a past love rather than to encounter new ones. The house can become a prison, as it is for Marion and Laura, caught up in the power relations of inheritance, in Wilkie Collins's *The Woman in White* (1860).

But above all, the house is penetrable. Its cherished dreaming subject is always vulnerable. It can be invaded, as in *Dracula* (1897), when a bedroom window is shattered by the vampire in the shape of a monstrous hound. In Sarah Grand's *The Heavenly Twins* (1893) a girl disguised as a boy always enters the house of the tenor (who loves 'him'), perversely, by the window, a seduction that throws out all the norms of space and gender. It is through the paradoxical trope of the window, marking the physical and psychological limits of the house, that its porousness is evident. The window is the marker of longing and desire. The woman at the window, from *Jane Eyre* (1847) to *The Turn of the Screw* (1898), is one of the commonest chronotopes of the novel. Through the window the house generates a desire that it cannot contain. The window becomes an expressive outlet. Desire and domestic space are in constant dialectical tension.[29] The very safety, or seeming safety, of the house produces its antithesis, the longing to be somewhere else.

Less evident than the lyrical space of the window, but as important, is the chronotope of the bedroom. It is remarkable that this most intimate of

---

29 See, for a disciplinary account of domestic space, Nancy Armstrong, *Desire and Domestic Fiction. A Political History of the Novel* (New York, and Oxford: Oxford University Press, 1987).

spaces, with its flagrant reminder of sexuality, though often encountered under the alias of the sick room, should occur so insistently in the fiction of an age known for its *pudeur*. Foucault's hypothesis that the more it appears to be repressed the more sexuality asserts itself seems to be confirmed here.[30] From Becky Sharp's German garret, where a brandy bottle and a plate of cold sausage hidden in her bed betray their presence by clinking as she throws herself upon it in mock histrionic grief for the benefit of Jos Sedley, to Jane Eyre's bedchamber, where she wakes to see her wedding veil torn by Rochester's first wife, the bedroom hints of transgression. Its connotations often invade other spaces. Trollope's sexually disruptive but maimed Madame Neroni in *Barchester Towers* (1856) has her sickroom carried around with her in the shape of the portable sofa on which she reclines, transported into ballrooms, salons, and drawing-rooms. *Villette's* (1853) bedrooms, from a steamer's cabin to a girls' dormitory, outnumber all the other rooms mentioned in the text, including the schoolrooms of Madame Beck's establishment. Spaces become bedrooms by virtue of figures who sleep or rest in them. First laid in the Brettons' living-room after her collapse, Lucy's illness temporarily converts it into a sickroom before she inhabits a literal bedroom in the house. The famous reclining 'Cleopatra' painting converts the art gallery into a bedroom and, almost, according to Monsieur Paul's reading, into a bordello. The bedroom is the space of the innumerable illnesses and deaths of the Victorian novel. It is also the place where the flesh creeps and its occupants start awake with hypersensitive nervous intensity. Or it is the setting for existential and passional crisis, as it is for Dorothea in *Middlemarch* (1872) sleeping on the bare floor of her room after Will's betrayal.

In the bedrooms of the Victorian novel people die, give birth, weep, sleep, pray, and dream. It is the space where conscious and unconscious life comes together. Sexuality, though bracketed, is, as has been said, all the more insistent for that. An isolated self appears in the iconography of the bedroom, yet the bedroom is a deeply inter-spatial realm. Quite apart from the communal rituals round birth and death (rituals that are simultaneous at the beginning of Dickens's *Dombey and Son* (1848)), it is the space where attendance, nursing, and comforting take place, where, in recognizing loneliness, consciousness is not set over and against a public world but

---

30 Michel Foucault's critique of the 'repressive theory' occupies the first volume of *The History of Sexuality*, 3 vols., 1976–84, trans. Robert Hurley, vol. I, *Introduction* (London: Allen Lane, 1979).

defined as a social entity with social needs, the need for another. The city, rather than the bedroom, isolates because the needs it satisfies are not primal but the artificial creations of an economic order.

Though the comfort of the house often beckons in a way that suggests an unthinking celebration of the integrated Bachelardian self, it is always vulnerable. The threat of destitution, selling up, and dispersion, hangs over the house, from *The Mill on the Floss* (1860) to *Jude the Obscure* (1895). It is there in a painting like Robert Martineau's *The Last Day in the Old Home* (1862). The house, like its occupants, is never a stable entity. The inter-spatial subject is always under threat.

Something else permeates the spatial order. It is the presence of colonial space. There is not a single Victorian novel without its intimation of colonial space. Country, city, village, town, are permeable. Colonial space enters the heart of English territory. How this comes about we will see through readings of *The Mill on the Floss* and *Dombey and Son*. I begin with *The Mill*, despite its later date of publication, because it so clearly explores the 'classical' Kantian subject in space, followed by a novel that, though committed to the inter-spatial world, uses the spatial order differently, to combat dominated space.

Space and consciousness in two novels: *The Mill on the Floss*, *Dombey and Son*

The Mill on the Floss

'Ah, my arms are really benumbed. I have been pressing my elbows on the arms of my chair and dreaming that I was standing on the bridge in front of Dorlcote Mill ...'[31] The novel's very first sentence – 'A wide plain, where the broadening Floss hurries on',[32] itself hurries on without a main verb, in the impressionistic syntax of reverie and remembered space. This is a syntax of current and flow, the metaphors that persistently represent affect throughout the narrative. 'I remember ... I remember the stone bridge':[33] the images of river, sea, St Ogg's, and pastures, are not mapped as a prospect but overlap organically, organized like the generative psychology of the daydream, as the autumn-sown corn overlaps the last year's ricks, and as the masts of the ships mingle with the branches of the ash trees. Colours – black,

---

31 Eliot, *The Mill on the Floss*, Book 1, chapter 1, p. 55.
32 *Ibid.*, p. 53.   33 *Ibid.*

red, purple, green, gold, red-brown, red – possess an intensity in this palimpsestic landscape of memory that occurs nowhere else in the novel. The very same landscape recurs at the end of the novel, as Maggie navigates her way back to her brother, Tom, at the Mill. But this time it is black and colourless in the darkness of the flood. (George Eliot was possibly thinking of the different aesthetic effects of a landscape painting and the comparatively new technology of the shadowy black photograph – it is, after all, machinery that kills Tom and Maggie in the end.) It, too, is a landscape of memory, but less the layered lyrical memory of affective recall than an exercise in the association-ist psychology, worked out through spatial connections, that fascinated Eliot. Maggie connects the topographical marks of the submerged landscape through a creative act of relationship and orientation. Indeed, this is a journey back to the past, a second chance to rework the past. The detour over the fields from Tofton, the place fatally overshot by Stephen and Maggie on their illicit boat trip, the tips of the Scotch pines she recognizes near the Mill, scene of her forbidden meetings with Philip in the Red Deeps, are landmarks that now lead her back to Tom. Though 'Memory was excluded' on the boat trip,[34] and though for a moment 'the threads of ordinary association were broken'[35] when the flood strikes, just as the bridge, she finds, is broken, she is able to repair the connections and find her way. The thread or fibre of memory, physiological, textural, and symbolic, is almost as strong a narrative metaphor for emotional ties as water is for emotional currents. Orientating herself in the dark, Maggie is a quintessential Kantian consciousness.

Throughout, the bridge that initiates the novel, where the narrator crosses from her (or his) present into a felt and imagined past, is an insistent presence – so much so that, 'pressing my elbows on the arms of my chair', the whole body is committed to a corporeal memory of it. The idea of crossing is suggested not only by references to Bunyan's *Pilgrim's Progress*, with its biblical allusion, but also to the invented anthropology and mytho-graphy of the St Ogg's legend. It intimates an almost Heideggerian reading of the bridge as inwardness and connection, where the body does not stand over and against space but is *in it*, and where 'earth and sky', 'divinities and mortals', come together, crossing one another.[36] The bridge and the thread of connection are markers of associationist space and social connection.

---

34 *Ibid.*, Book 6, chapter 13, p. 589.   35 *Ibid.*, Book 7, chapter 5, p. 651.
36 Martin Heidegger, *Poetry, Language, Thought*, trans. Albert Hofstadter (New York: Harper and Row, 1975), p. 153.

Yet this spatial model is not unproblematic. Crossing also indicates the restless migrations of modernity. Tulliver's first lawsuit was lost over the bridge's right of way. The novel's great feat is to bring three kinds of space together, sometimes superimposing one on the other, but they are not always compatible. In *The Mill on the Floss* space is geologically layered. The Bridgewater treatise on geology by which Stephen Guest begins to seduce Maggie is not simply a historically correct gesture to the 1830s.[37] In Maggie's time these theologically conservative and controversial Treatises responded to modern developments in geology that challenged the biblical account of the date of creation. The reference points up Maggie's intellectual unconventionality as well as her longing for moral security. Nor is the defunct quarry of the Red Deeps, a geological terrain joined with industrial archaeology, where the love scenes between Philip and Maggie occur, simply a setting. Its being is the product of memory, of desire, and of law and economics: each, as in the upheaval of geological movement, disrupts the other. The space of memory, history, and anthropology, generally the province of the authorial voice, the rural idyll of childhood, and the new world of what Henri Lefebvre terms 'dominated space', constitute the three forms of space in the novel.[38] Kantian spatial consciousness enters into psychological and emotional space, as well as into the physical landscapes created by law and technology.

The authorial voice charts and celebrates the spaces of the past, continuing the affect-laden persona of the first chapter. It is the bearer of the St Ogg's history, from its account of the town buildings that incorporate earlier structures, making the town seem an organic 'outgrowth of nature',[39] to the myth of a heart's desire fulfilled – 'it is enough that thy heart needs it',[40] Beorl tells the crone who wants to cross the river, a message absolutely at odds with the punitive culture of the Gleggs and Tullivers. The narrator, almost at the midway point of the novel, invokes the antithetical geographies of the Rhine and the Rhone, ideological spatial fantasies of the poetically romantic and squalidly prosaic, aristocracy and peasant, that create a false dichotomy against which we are meant to see the rural petty bourgeoisie of the Dodsons and Tullivers. It is the heart's

---

37 The sixth Bridgewater Treatise (nine volumes of Treatises were published between 1833 and 1840), by William Buckland, *Geology and Mineralogy Considered with Reference to Natural Theology*, was published in 1836.
38 Henri Lefebvre, *The Production of Space*, trans. Donald Nicholson-Smith (Oxford: Blackwell, 1991), pp. 164–8.
39 Eliot, *The Mill on the Floss*, Book 1, chapter 12, p. 181. 40 *Ibid.*, p. 182.

desire of the narrator, despite the narrowness and mean denial of this society, to assimilate it to the lyrical space of remembered childhood and the deep continuities of the past. But this space is never intact. The familiar 'home scene', the 'mother tongue of the imagination', created by a well-known wood in May, 'thrill' the speaker: 'what grove of tropic palms, what strange ferns or splendid broad-petalled blossoms, could ever' possess the same intensity as speedwell and ground ivy?'[41] At the very moment of cherished territorial memory, colonial space invades the Bachelardian 'home scene' here. The one calls up the other, and the exclusiveness of home depends on a colonial outside. In a more aware moment, the narrator later calls up Tulliver's historical memory of the Mill, in contrast to the fashion for travel 'to the tropics', 'at home with palms and banyans'.[42] Yet the Zambesi intrudes upon the Floss. Significantly, Maggie's doll becomes a fetish, just as Mrs Tulliver describes her as a 'mulatter'.[43] She is constructed in terms of a dangerous passional otherness, a dark ethnicity, the source of her adolescent attempts to repress desire in her phase of cruel asceticism.

With consummate understanding, George Eliot produces through the narrator's voice a subtle conflict between the represented primal space of home and what Lefebvre calls the space of representation, the material conditions that are the context of representation.[44] This happens also in the rural idyll of childhood, the 'original shell' of oneiric primal space that the children grant to the Mill. 'If the past is not to bind us [threads again], where can duty lie?'[45] Maggie says to Stephen in the crisis of their 'elopement'. Her earliest memory is of Tom holding her hand by the river. Maggie's early spaces may belong to false or screen memory, but Eliot's point is that they have an imaginative hold on her. The space of representation, on the other hand, is quite different from her represented spaces: she is a cultural outcast in a narrow and hubristic provincial community: the countryside is not a 'pure' rural environment. The country is a place where boys kill stray cats for fun, rat catchers operate spectacles, fights occur. Maggie's fantasizing of her outcast state that motivates her retreat to the gypsies meets a half-understood space of representation. Here labourers jeer at the protected little girl. The gypsies huddle squalidly in a lane, not on her idealized common, steal her silver thimble, and contemplate abducting her.

41 *Ibid.*, Book 1, chapter 5, p. 94. 42 *Ibid.*, Book 3, chapter 9, p. 352.
43 *Ibid.*, Book 1, chapter 2, p. 60. 44 Lefebvre, *Production of Space*, p. 33.
45 Eliot, *The Mill on the Floss*, Book 6, chapter 13, p. 602.

These two structures of representation are necessarily superimposed on one another. Eliot repeatedly manoeuvres the narrative to bring them into ironic crossings where they deconstruct one another. The third form of space in the novel is the space of a whole new economic order of industrial capital in alliance with the scientific management of resources and technology. The Gleggs, Tullivers, and even its apostles, the Deanes, who are business partners with the entrepreneurial Guests and their oil mills, fail, in their proud narrowness, to understand it. For Eliot the grounds of fundamental change lie elsewhere than in political protest. Yet this is no Riehl-like 'organic' society in which slow change attends peasant communities.[46] What interests Eliot is that the affluent Dodsons are the class with the least power of analysis available to counter a new dominated space that accomplishes a total transformation of social space. Pivart's irrigation schemes reconfigure the geological terrain of the past. They are changing the space of representation through administered efficiency. This attacks Tulliver's very identity, bound up as it is with an atavistic belief in traditional rights confirmed by history. For Tulliver, tautologically, water was water –'You can't pick it up with a pitchfork.'[47] It is another conflict between represented space and the space of representation. Tulliver's primitive individualism and psychic geography are outmoded by plans for dominated space that see water simply as commodity and a form of exchange. Or, as in later plans for installing steam in the Mill indicate, power. (It is no accident that the Guest fortune is to finance Stephen's career as a Member of Parliament.) Technology is efficient, too. The irony of the lawsuit is that the water to the Mill appears to flow unimpeded when Tulliver works it under Wakem.

Tom and Maggie are killed, in literal terms, by a piece of machinery from the wharves, a component of the new space of technology. But they are also killed as a result of their own relations to space, emerging from their imaginative readings of primal space. It is quite clear that if they had remained in the higher part of the Mill, they would not have died. Taking to the boat was the problem, another of Maggie's impulses. It is also quite clear that it was *only* in death, or just before it, that they were not divided. That we do *not* read the novel in this bitterly ironic way testifies to Eliot's

46 Eliot's essay on the organic society described by Wilhelm Riehl through a study of German peasantry bears a complex relation to her work: 'The Natural History of German Life', *Westminster Review* n.s. 11, (1856), pp. 51–79.
47 Eliot, *The Mill on the Floss*, Book 2, chapter 2, p. 226.

astonishing ability to commit the reader to the vital space of the past and to create tragedy from its power. One can die for memory and desire.

Dickens's spatial strategy differs in every way from George Eliot's, but it is still committed to the inter-spatial consciousness. Her geological spaces, from surface to depth and vice versa, are alien to him. His novels generate a rapid serial succession of different surfaces and a restless transit from one to the other. The repeated upheaval of the urban landscape, at its greatest in the railway's depredations of Staggs Gardens, its 'chaos of carts' and 'Babel towers of chimneys',[48] but ever present in the kaleidoscope of street performers, fighting boys, cries of 'Mad Bull', dock workers, beggars, horsemen, foot passengers, omnibuses, drays, and wagons, means that represented space is always changing and never static. It changes according to the psychological state of the observer. 'Houses and shops were different from what they used to be'[49] in the same street when Walter knows about Sol's debt. In the same way, the same surface can undergo generic change. Satirically inflected as a mausoleum, with its bronze bust of Pitt and dusty urns in the library, Dombey's house becomes a lyrical folkloric space to portray neglected Florence's lonely mourning. It is a sleeping beauty environment – mirrors 'dim as with the breath of years', the 'tarnished paws of gilded lions' protruding from covers, 'the accidental tinklings among the pendant lustres'.[50] When Edith occupies the house the genre changes from folklore to melodrama and the surfaces of the interior literally reflect an eroticized commodity culture. The 'voluptuous glitter' of mirrors and jewels in her boudoir give back virtual images of her 'repeated, and presented all around him [Dombey], as in so many fragments of a mirror'.[51] The depthlessness of the virtual image recurs in the overlay of intrusive, one-dimensional footprints on the stairs that madden Dombey in his suicidal solitude after his firm's financial crash and sale of the household effects. These discontinuous readings evoke the 'striated' space and other terms for non-homogeneous spatial experience with which Deleuze and other post-modern theorists have sought to replace the monolithic categories of Lefebvre.[52]

Colonial space is on the surface, too, and permeates every environment of *Dombey and Son*. In Eliot's novel it is secreted into the text, a colonial

<hr />

48 Dickens, *Dombey and Son*, chapter 6, p. 79.   49 *Ibid.*, chapter 9, p. 136.
50 *Ibid.*, chapter 23, p. 351.   51 *Ibid.*, chapter 40, p. 612.
52 Gilles Deleuze and Felix Guattari, *A Thousand Plateaus. Capitalism and Schizophrenia*, trans. Brian Massumi (London and New York: Continuum, 1988), pp. 490–7.

unconscious. Nevertheless, if there is one thing that connects the discontinuous, metonymic spaces of Dickens's text it is the continual, overt reference to the dominated spaces of the East and West Indies and (to a lesser
extent) Australia. These references are flagrantly and consciously present in
the extravaganza of Dickens's peculiar blend of simplifying farce and piercing detail. This, unlike the rapidly shuffled representations of space in city
and town house alike, is the insistent, formative, space of representation. It
is not simply that the empirical details of the plot ensure that Walter is sent
to Barbados and that Alice returns from her convict life in Australia, or that
the Dombey offices are near those of the East India Company, that events
take us to the port of London, that Major Bagstock, whose sadism is
unleashed on his anonymous servant, the 'Native', and the unfortunate
Blitherstone, have had lives in Bengal (the Major also claims to have served
in the West Indies), that the great figures of the East India Company pay
court to Dombey's new wife. Right from the start AD stands for 'anno
Dombei': 'The earth was made for Dombey and Son to trade in ... rivers
and seas were formed to float their ships.'[53] The seafaring myths of heroism
in which mariners chant 'Rule Britannia', and that are nurtured in Sol Gill's
shop are the ideological complement of this global capitalism. We hear that
the sun never sets on the British empire. Servitude evokes images of slavery
and abjection, for Susan Nipper, 'being a black slave and a mulotter',[54] and
in the case of Withers, who is reduced to butting the heavy Skewton invalid
chair as elephants do in India. Leamington Spa and India become thus
incongruously yoked, despite Mrs Skewton's repudiation of the Major's
vulgar colonial status: 'you smell of the sun. You are absolutely tropical.'[55]

Dickens creates this insistent colonial space in two ways. First, his discrepant
spaces are assimilated to the urban glasshouse and the conservatory, that site of
plundered flora and fauna forced from the tropical to a temperate environment.
The forlorn conservatory where Polly displays Paul to Dombey, Pipchin's
exotic cacti, Miss Tox's window of indoor plants, Dr Blimber's school, avowedly a hothouse for forcing young boys' minds, the grass growing on the roof
and the vegetation sprouting on the window sills of Florence's sleeping beauty
house, all quote the glasshouse. Carker owns one. At the disastrous house-
warming a guest is reduced to sketching his pinery.[56] Dombey's offices, with

---

53 Dickens, *Dombey and Son*, chapter 1, p. 12.   54 *Ibid.*, chapter 5, p. 66.
55 *Ibid.*, chapter 26, p. 402.
56 For the importance of the conservatory space at this time see Isobel Armstrong,
Victorian Glassworlds. Glass Culture and the Imagination 1830–1880 (Oxford University
Press, 2008), pp. 167–203.

their glass dome, and hints of predatory sea creatures, become an aquarium, near relation of the conservatory. Through this Dickens links the 'House' of business to the domestic house and founds both on the capture of the exotic. At the same time the fragility of this structure is apparent.

Secondly, the black presence is literally taken into the bloodstream, because it presides over digestion and at meals. Sol's special Madeira has been 'to the East Indies and back'[57] in kegs used as ballast while the wine matured. The incessant smoking of tobacco in this household takes colonial produce into the lungs. This produce reaches the womb and the stomach: Perch begs Walter for some Barbados ginger to palliate his wife's pregnancy. The Major's Native stands ready at meals to galvanize his digestion with an assortment of strange, hot spices. As Dombey broods after dinner in Brook Street the night before his wedding, gazing into 'the cold depths of the dead sea of mahogany on which the fruit dishes and decanters lay at anchor',[58] 'two exhausted negroes' hold up the candelabra of the sideboard. This is less a levelling of all things to the digestive tract than a recognition that bodily space itself is changed by the products of the other. This corporeal ingestion means that all share in this process without distinction.

Distinction itself is annulled. But, in an era of property and capital, as Hume was the first to recognize, identity depends on 'Distinction'.[59] It is founded on those external possessions that are the mark of wealth and power and depends on the approbation and even envy of others to confirm its being. This is why Dombey is a distorted spatial subject. His internal emptiness comes about because his selfhood is created from what is outside him. At the same time he is unable to separate these possessions from himself, taking them for his essence (his literal-mindedness is a symptom of this state). Dombey only relates to things. Stairs in the Dombey residence (as opposed to Eliot's bridge), chronotope of the grand public transit space of the town house, perversely give up their two-way passage and become one-way conduits only. The ascent of the stairs, by the doctors, by Florence as she toils up them with her brother in her arms, by the sick Paul, or the crawling descent of Edith in her flight, negate interchange. 'Pride'/Distinction and envy work dialectically together. It is no surprise that Dombey and Carker share paranoid space, where the external world turns against them

---

57 Dickens, *Dombey and Son*, chapter 4, p. 7.   58 *Ibid.*, chapter 30, p. 469.
59 David Hume, *A Treatise of Human Nature*, ed. L. A. Selby-Bigge (Oxford: Clarendon Press, 1888), pp. 277–9, 309–16. For a discussion of envy in a Benthamite context that throws light on pride and distinction, see Frances Ferguson, 'Envy Rising', *English Literary History* 69 (2002), pp. 889–905.

and distinguishing marks blur or elide – the flip side of a world that serves omniscience. Dombey's train ride is paralleled by Carker's mad, horse-driven journey through France. 'Objects flitting past, merging into one another'; 'the past, present, and future all floated confusedly before him.'[60] The optical culture of the dissolving view here provides a model for this spatial experience.

Conclusion

The Victorian novel is heavily invested in exploring boundaries, which are the sites of power, status, and exclusion, as well as the taboos on transgressing barriers, whether of class, or morals. Maggie, outsider by virtue of gender and reject of the St Ogg's society, literally proves her navigational powers and, one might say, comes into Kantian spatial subjecthood in the process of renegotiating the landscape of the past. But this is a pyrrhic redemption which endorses the pessimistic aspects of Kant's spatial readings. She can never enter the collective life of St Ogg's even though that collective life is held up to critique. Dombey's contempt for the whole Cuttle/Sol network of 'low' nautical acquaintances means that he sees them as unfit for membership of the money society. He is outraged that Toodles should have 'community' with him in mourning. Sol's overlooked and unbought instruments of navigation seem to confirm his view. Yet these characters, like Walter, carry out by proxy overseas the tasks of the owners of capital, as Dickens is ironically aware. 'We must marry 'em [inferiors]' says the church Beadle, to provide fodder for national schools and standing armies, 'and keep the country going'.[61] Using the prosthetic aids of train and horse, Dombey and Carker prove themselves spatially disabled. The skills to traverse the high seas and the London streets belong to their inferiors.

I have used the categories provided by Kant, Bakhtin, Bachelard, and Lefebvre to explore the novel's reading of space. In reality none of these will quite do because there is no single consistent mimesis of space in these texts, just as there is no consistent mimesis of time. On the other hand, to think of space in a state of permanent post-modern discontinuity is also inappropriate. Heterotopia is not the condition of these texts. When space 'thickens' in the nineteenth-century novel, as it almost always does in moments of crisis, inter-spatial consciousness comes into being for characters and readers alike.

---

60 Dickens, *Dombey and Son*, chapter 55, pp. 831, 841.   61 *Ibid.*, chapter 57, p. 868.

28

National and regional literatures

SARA L. MAURER

While national and regional literatures are hardly the same thing, no distinct line separates them in the nineteenth-century British Isles. Regional literature documented small pockets of culture it treated as truly national in its characteristics. Thus Wordsworth's vision of the natural beauty of the Lake District promises readers a locality from which their English love of liberty might be revived, free of corrupting urban (or French) influences. Almost a century later, J. M. Synge's documentation of the life of Aran Islanders on the westernmost reaches of Ireland holds out a similar promise for Ireland, detailing the cultural peculiarities of the islands where he imagined that an essential Irishness remained intact. But these examples also expose the contradiction inherent in a literature that treats a specific region as authentically national: what makes a region recognizable as national is the alien element it contains, be it the sublimity of Wordsworth's wild landscapes or the musical inflections through which Synge apprehends a Gaelic he neither understood nor spoke.

The dynamic between region and nation in the British Isles was further vexed by the multi-national state that was the nineteenth-century United Kingdom. In this configuration, England, Wales, and Scotland, in their corporate identity as Great Britain, were united with Ireland under one Crown and one Parliament although each were to retain the distinct cultures that made them – nominally at least – separate nations. The multi-national composition of the British state complicates almost everything we might otherwise assume about the relationship between literature and national identity. Benedict Anderson's much-cited theory that novels contribute to a sense of nationality by creating a sense of a shared national 'meanwhile' explains the multi-plot ambitions of both the Scottish novels of Walter Scott and the English novels of Charles Dickens.[1] But Ian Baucom's

---

1 See Benedict Anderson, *Imagined Communities: Reflections on the Origin and Spread of Nationalism* (London: Verso, 1991), especially chapter 3.

assertion that as the territory under one rule expands, the 'territory of affect' contracts accounts for the narrow focus on a limited region found in Anthony Trollope's Barsetshire novels and Scotland's late-century Kailyard school.[2] Neither a theory of nation as the shared time of 'meanwhile' nor the theory of nation as preserved in the metonymic space of the region exhausts the possible relations to national identity put forward by the literature of the British Isles.

Thus, in the United Kingdom of Great Britain and Ireland regional literature too, mixed the terms of time and space. When it collaborates in creating a national identity, a literary region preserves in a small space the archaic and obsolete – Wordsworth's ruined cottages, Hardy's rural Wessex – while the rest of the nation joins a more homogenized modernity. In this way, regional literature helps a nation occupy two times at once. It also creates a situation in which an era – such as modernity – can be understood as the opposite of a space – such as a region. But this regional time scheme never takes on an orderly chronology in the British Isles. When imagined from the urban heart of London, the Celtic peripheries of the British Isles are the time zones from which a British modernity had already emerged. At the same time, Celtic authors imagined similar zones – the west of Ireland, the Highlands of Scotland – from which their own specifically non-English identities had emerged. Added to this mix was the century-long literary tradition of treating the small rural village in the south of England as more representative of England than its urban centres. Precisely what might count as whose archaic space, or what geographies or populations might be granted full participation in modernity, was never a settled question.

Culture and multi-national state

At the opening of the nineteenth century, all of the Celtic regions had many conditions in common. Each had a majority population embracing a faith outside of the Church of England. Each had a native language spoken by the rural lower classes, the use of which sharply decreased over the course of the century. Each featured an upper class who identified with an Anglicized culture and often absented themselves from their properties to live in the urban centre of London. But beyond that, each had a very different

2 See Ian Baucom, *Out of Place: Englishness, Empire, and the Locations of Identity* (Princeton University Press, 1999), p. 12.

relationship to the metropolitan core of England, relationships that in turn influenced how they understood their connections to one another.

Of the four nations, Wales – first conquered by England in the thirteenth century – was most literally the site of what came to be understood as British heritage. In the fifteenth century, Henry Tudor became Henry VII while styling himself as the new Arthur, the Welsh hero who would rule all of Britain. The unifying signifier of 'British' gained force from this originally Welsh Arthurian myth that an ancient 'Briton' would unite the island under one crown. But beyond myth, what emerged from the historical union was a corporate identity officially known as 'England and Wales' – which was often pronounced 'England' with the 'Wales' silent. Welsh writing in the nineteenth century referred to Wales as 'the Principality', a term of sovereign separateness anachronistic to the nation state. Non-Welsh British writing rarely named Wales as any abstract political unit at all. Wales was simultaneously too complicated and too much of an afterthought to fall into any particular category.

In the late eighteenth century, the modern preservation of a specifically Welsh culture became the concern of a population of wealthy Welsh expatriates living in London. Inspired by what they understood to be traditional Bardic culture, these gentlemen antiquarians revived the Welsh tradition of the Eisteddfod, a competitive recital of music and poetry. That these Eisteddfodau were first organized in London, and only later transferred back to Wales with generous funding from the metropole suggests the extent to which a Welsh-English economic web underwrote Welsh tradition. It was in London that Iolo Morganwg began his very influential popularization of the Welsh bardic tradition as originating in the ancient order of Druids. His wholesale creation of Druidic ritual and lore outlived him in the posthumous publication of his *The Secrets of the Bards of the Isle of Britain* (1829), and enforced a long-term association between druidic culture and Stonehenge, an association endowing Wales with a stronger connection to England's past than even the English had.[3]

Yet the dominant identity within nineteenth-century Wales, while rooted in the Welsh language, was far removed from the bards and Druids popularized by the cosmopolitan Welsh. The population's espousal of Methodism and Dissent meant that when Welsh was read, what was consumed was

---

3 See Prys Morgan, 'From a Death to a View: The Hunt for the Welsh Past in the Romantic Period', in Eric Hobsbawm and Terence Ranger (eds.), *The Invention of Tradition* (Cambridge University Press, 1983), pp. 43–100.

not the stuff of legend but sermons, scripture, and religious tracts. As the century wore on, Wales's identity within Britain was understood as a product both of its religious inclinations and its industrial development. Chartists in the increasingly industrialized south of Wales cemented both British perceptions of the Welsh as unruly radicals, and Welsh perception of Wales as unified in a liberal politics sympathetic to the working classes. The Welsh press called the imprisoned leaders of working-class unrest not 'Chartists' but 'the Welsh patriots'. In this identity, the Welsh were not England's ancient past, but an incarnation of political progress for which England was too conservative.

Scotland's integration into nineteenth-century Great Britain was taken for granted. Like England's earlier union with Wales, Scotland's 1707 Parliamentary unification with England was framed as the logical next step for nations that had already been united under one crown. Scottish rebellion in the years following union contested the legitimacy of the monarch, as the Scottish attempted to restore the deposed Jacobite line to the throne. The most convincing uprising came in 1745 when Bonnie Prince Charlie, backed by Scottish Highland chiefs, came within 120 miles of London. After their defeat, English retaliation included the systematic dismantling of the clan system in the Highlands, while the economic integration of the more urban lowlands proceeded. Only fifty years later, Walter Scott would romanticize the now defunct Highlands culture as politically harmless but culturally available to both Scottish and English alike.

The perceived success of the Scottish union made it the prototype for the Irish union with Great Britain in 1801. But in an age of waning monarchical powers, the logic of union did not work the same. The deep divide between Anglicized Protestant landowners and their Catholic, often Irish-speaking tenantry, kept open the question of who could legitimately determine the future of the Irish nation. In the eighteenth century, the brief convocation of an independent Irish Parliament made up entirely of Protestant landlords suggested that such men might head the country. The non-sectarian agenda of the 1798 United Irishmen uprising – one which aspired to join Catholic to Protestant in a common Irishness – was largely only an aspiration. By the time of the union the Catholic underclass had some reason to believe that Parliamentary rule from Westminster might better guard their interests than would an 'Irish' Parliament of landlords. Their hopes were short-lived, however, and the strongest of the subsequent popular movements against the British government tended to rely heavily on the mobilization of Ireland's rural Catholic lower classes, an identity that even the nationalist urban middle class and their Protestant allies among landowners came to treat as characteristically Irish.

Ireland also constituted the single largest challenge to Great Britain's conception of itself as a culture characterized by a love of liberty, respect for autonomy, and cautious gradualism. The incorporation of Ireland into Great Britain struck a blow at the Protestant identity that unified England, Wales, and Scotland when the 1829 Catholic Relief Act allowed Roman Catholics to be seated in Parliament. The catastrophic mid-century Irish famine also shook the British sense of itself as ushering the Irish into a new era of modern civilization. The debate that followed famine, about the British laissez-faire economic policy that exacerbated food scarcity in Ireland, permanently changed the economic assumptions that underpinned state intervention in crises.[4] By the second half of the century, the increasing possibility of a successful Irish Home Rule Bill contested even the idea of the English metropole. Scottish activists insisted that if Ireland was granted Home Rule, Scotland too should have Home Rule. The subsequent call for 'Home Rule all around' imagined either a tripartite system of government (with the British Isles divided into Ireland, Scotland, and a combined England and Wales) or a pentarchy (Ireland, Northern Ireland, Scotland, Wales, and England) who would unite in one Imperial Parliament, but otherwise govern separately.[5]

As this plan indicates, despite their differences, the Scottish, Welsh, and Irish alike understood themselves as sharing stewardship over the British empire. This identification was rife with contradictions, especially in Ireland, which – in its subordination to a British Lord Lieutenant and in its subjection to British troops posted on its own territory – was administered much like a British colony, and not a partner nation. Yet overseas empire provided the opportunity for even the Irish to see themselves as British. Bleak economic conditions prompted far more emigration from the Celtic regions than from England, so that Scottish, Welsh, and Irish subjects were more likely than the English to fill the ranks of citizens in the white-dominated settler colonies of the empire – Canada, Australia, and

---

4 See Gordon Bigelow, *Fiction, Famine, and the Rise of Economics in Victorian Britain and Ireland* (Cambridge University Press, 2003), especially chapter 4.
5 See for instance W. Scott Dalgleish, 'Scotland's Version of Home Rule', *Nineteenth Century* 13 (1883), pp. 14–26; William Mitchell, 'Article VI – Scotland and Home Rule', *Scottish Review* 11 (1888), pp. 323–46; W. Wallace, 'Article VI. – Nationality and Home Rule, Irish and Scottish', *Scottish Review* 12 (1888), pp. 171–87.

New Zealand – and in the military ranks of the other outposts of empire – most prominently India. And even though the term 'British' never applied to people living in Ireland, its emigrants and colonial administrators were seen as British while abroad.

However, unlike the Welsh or Scottish, the Irish also had the option of refusing the British label, as they increasingly did in the second half of the century, choosing to remain Irish patriots who amassed both money and arms to support the cause of Irish independence. Rudyard Kipling's fiction suggests that even this chameleon-like Irishness might be an asset for empire. In *Kim* (1901), the young army-orphan protagonist is half-Irish, half-English, and 'burned as black as any native', a combination which allows him to navigate Punjabi street culture, elite English schools, Tibetan spirituality, and ultimately a Russian spy enclave, as he aids the British espionage efforts to gain dominance in central Asia.[6] But Irish attitudes towards literature that played up the imperial qualities of Irishness were ambivalent at best. One of the best-selling novelists of the nineteenth century, the Anglo-Irish Charles Lever, established his reputation with his early military novels, *The Confessions of Harry Lorrequer* (1839) and *Charles O'Malley, the Irish Dragoon* (1840). Lever's main characters were rash, robust, and recklessly athletic Irish soldiers whose military prowess gained popularity everywhere but with Irish readers. Still, Lever's late novels focus on Irish figures whose love of masquerade serves them well in diplomatic service. These and his own columns in *Blackwood's Magazine* on continental affairs written in the voice of the improvident expatriate Cornelius O'Dowd might be considered an antecedent for *Kim's* Irish cosmopolitanism.

This overview of the Celtic regions of the United Kingdom leaves England for last, and in doing so risks falsely implying that those involved in the United Kingdom knew precisely what counted as 'England' and 'English'. But as has often been noted, English hegemony over the Celtic regions – a hegemony that was by the nineteenth century often described as 'British' – rendered 'English' an ill-defined term. 'British' could describe what was specifically English, or what partook of the corporate identity of England, Scotland, and Wales. If the term 'British' signified England's loss of individual identity in the union with Scotland, this loss of identity was only writ larger with every territorial expansion. The Britishness with which

---

6 Rudyard Kipling, *Kim* (Oxford University Press, 2008), chapter 1, p. 1.

Englishness was interchangeable signalled an England whose identity lay in the effortless absorption of other national identities – an identity so invested in assimilation as to be no clear identity at all.

This uncertainty was compounded by constant reference to England's intrinsic modernity. The improvements that the English press imagined England to bring both to the Celtic regions and to empire were ones that Wales, Scotland, and Ireland all saw as English technologies displacing a more local, indigenous way of life. Even literature within England treated these developments as similarly threatening to English social coherence. One need only read John Clare's poetry or William Cobbett's polemics to recognize the same laments about English life being destroyed by the modern spirit of improvement. If modernity was synonymous with Englishness, then Englishness represented a force which dissolved national identities – perhaps first and foremost its own.

Beyond national labels, the radical revision of the role of the state in modern culture vexed how even a 'British' identity might be determined. At the dawn of the nineteenth century, both Britain and Ireland were governed primarily by local institutions, uncoordinated by any national centre. However, the Victorian state grew increasingly centralized, bureaucratized, and involved in regulating the lives of those who had no part in the governing process. Women, children, the poor, and even the migrant workforce all came into increased contact with the state apparatus, giving ever larger numbers of people concrete experiences of themselves as subjects of the state, an experience that in the Victorian era was not legally distinct from membership in a nation.

The gradual but deeply contested expansion of citizens' rights and state responsibilities meant that in the British Isles, the national question had two components. One involved the question of what political incorporation meant, and to whom it could be extended. The other involved the question of whether one could identify with a cultural nation while integrating into a supranational political entity. The expansion of the British state did not automatically make citizens more prone to identify with the English centre. In the case of Wales, state involvement proved unwittingly instrumental in the formation of an oppositional Welsh national identity. The 1847 reports produced by the Westminster-appointed Welsh Education Commission connected Welsh-speaking and a lack of English literacy to conspiracy and moral degradation. Welsh indignation at the report's insulting tone galvanized a Welsh sense that their language and culture needed to be preserved.

Dominant liberal definitions of state membership emphasized education, communication, and rational consent as important in training citizens for participation in government, but even these theories reserved a place of primary importance for the community of irreducible loyalties into which one is born. 'Free institutions are next to impossible in a country made up of different nationalities', John Stuart Mill dictates in *On Liberty* (1867), defining a strong nationality as requiring common 'political antecedents; the possession of a national history, and consequent community of recollections'.[7] While Mill concedes that such extra-national government is possible – for most of his life he held out hope that Ireland could be more fully assimilated into the United Kingdom – he nonetheless treats an originary community of feeling as the preferred training ground which made possible wider affiliations. Much like the familial 'little platoons' that Edmund Burke argues are 'the first link in the series by which we proceed towards a love to our country, and to mankind', Mill sees the nation as providing a ready-made community which will train a citizen in an affectionate attachment that can later be applied more broadly.[8]

Burke's metaphor for primordial attachment as first happening in 'little platoons' loses its connotations of mobility when adapted by Victorian writers. George Eliot, mourning the peripatetic youth of her heroine Gwendolen Harleth, opines in *Daniel Deronda* (1876) that 'A human life, I think, should be well rooted in some spot of a native land, where it may get the love of tender kinship for the face of earth ... At five years old, mortals are not prepared to be citizens of the world, to be stimulated by abstract nouns, to soar above preference into impartiality.'[9] Eliot is far from alone in advocating the morally restorative power of affections exercised towards specific and limited areas. John Galt's tales of the small Scottish village (for instance, *The Annals of the Parish* (1821) and *The Provost* (1822)), Mary Russell Mitford's sketches of rural English life in *Our Village* (1832), John and Michael Banim's Irish series of *Tales of the O'Hara Family* (1825–6) and even the rough Yorkshire moors of Emily Brontë's and Charlotte Brontë's fiction all offer the reader intimate experiences of territorially bound communities, reiterating the importance of knowing where one comes from.

---

7 John Stuart Mill, *On Liberty* (1867), in *On Liberty and Other Essays*, ed. John Grey (Oxford University Press, 1991), p. 427.
8 Edmund Burke, *Reflections on the Revolution in France* (Oxford University Press, 1993), p. 47.
9 George Eliot, *Daniel Deronda* (Oxford University Press, 1984), chapter 3, p. 16.

From national tale to regional novel

It would be difficult to overestimate Walter Scott's influence on the position of Scotland in the nineteenth-century British literary imagination. His historical novels established past hostilities between Scotland and England as chronologically long gone, but also romantically present as British heritage. His spatialization of historical plots also contributed to the literary sense that time was place. In *Waverley* (1814), the hero's foray into the culture of primitive clan warfare is marked as a trip into the past by his northward trajectory into the Highlands. Conversely, in *The Heart of Midlothian* (1818) Jeanie Deans's encounter with modern law and the state come about as she travels south into the heart of London, to gain a pardon for her condemned sister. In making what is modern and not modern a matter of geography, Scott imagined both history and region to operate as all-pervasive ecosystems, whose dialect, dress, religious beliefs, folklore, and social relations both determined a character's mindset and guaranteed a novel's fidelity to the particularity of the situation it reported.

Yet it *would* be possible to over-state Scott's originality in crafting a literature that documents a national culture at the moment of its integration into an English-dominated political sphere. In writing *Waverley* he explicitly relied on the model of Maria Edgeworth's Irish fictions. In the preface to her 1801 *Castle Rackrent*, a narrative that comically records three generations on an Anglo-Irish estate, Edgeworth announces her intention in writing to be preservative: 'When Ireland loses her identity by an union with Great Britain ... she will look back with a smile of good-humoured complacency' at the cultural habits that once characterized Ireland.[10] Scott announced his own novelistic account of the Jacobite rebellion to be motivated by a similar hope 'of preserving some idea of the ancient manners of which I have witnessed the almost total extinction'.[11] At the beginning of the nineteenth century, to write an Irish national tale or a Scottish historical novel was to record the persistence of regional particularity after the fact of political subordination. Their mutual influence on one another reveals, as Katie Trumpener has

---

10 Maria Edgeworth, *Castle Rackrent* (Oxford University Press, 1995), Preface, p. 5.
11 Sir Walter Scott, 'Postscript Which Should Have Been a Preface,' *Waverley* (London: Penguin Books, 1981), pp. 492–3.

famously argued, the existence of a trans-Celtic public sphere, one in which literary Irishness and Scottishness emerge in conversation with one another, not just in conversation with England.[12]

Their trans-Celtic nature can be seen in their formal similarities. The tales were written either as strangers' encounters with the Celtic regions, or, less commonly, as Celtic journeys to a metropolitan centre. Their lengthy expositions on the difference between Celtic regions and English society address readers deficient in a sympathetic understanding of Celtic cultures. The accidental nature of most of these encounters – and the pre-existing ties they often reveal – imbue the connection of England and its Celtic regions with a sense of familial connection that can never be consciously willed nor entirely escaped. For instance, in Scott's *Redgauntlet* (1824) the lowlander Darsie Latimer is abducted to the Highlands, where he discovers that he is actually heir to the Jacobite laird Redgauntlet. The revelation of a character's hidden identity – one at odds with their own national allegiances – is standard in national tales both in Scotland and Ireland, a plot twist which delivers the shock of sudden union with people traditionally considered as foreign. The Anglo-Irish absentee landlord of Maria Edgeworth's *Ennui* (1809) discovers that he was actually born to an Irish peasant, and switched as a baby with the real heir to the estate. In Susan Ferrier's *Marriage* (1818), a trip to Bath leaves the virtuous and Scotland-bred Mary Douglas astonished at meeting the frivolous and shallow English mother and twin sister she has never known.

The inevitable marriage plot that structures almost all national tales mutes the effects of English conquest by uniting dispossessed and conqueror in an affectionately shared future. The plot of unknown identity and the marriage plot joining Celtic and English characters (both often present in the same book) open up the possibility of dual national allegiances. If family is the first unit through which a character learns to identify with the nation, then a family of mixed nationalities is the instrument through which one learns to identify with more than one nation. If one must be loyal to the nation of one's birth, then union is morally required in the hidden identity plot, where characters suddenly find themselves with a surplus of homelands. In addition to detailing the history and terrain of Scotland or Ireland, and offering dialogue in which

---

12 See Katie Trumpener, *Bardic Nationalism: The Romantic Novel and the British Empire* (Princeton University Press, 1997), see especially pp. 15–34.

characters argue for the dignity of those nations, the genre of the national tale improvises a host of configurations in which the rule of one nationality per person simply can not apply.[13]

When responding to the social upheavals of the British 1830s and 1840s, English novels turn to their Celtic predecessors for models of how to narrate a nation torn. Classified as 'condition-of-England' novels, these books use the strategies of the national tales to craft fiction that might adequately record and address the problem of class conflict. Benjamin Disraeli's *Sybil: or The Two Nations* (1845) implies in its title that only a solution analogous to union might keep the one nation of England together. Instructed by the exotic and peasant-identified Sybil, the aristocratic protagonist, Disraeli's landlord figure, Egremont, learns that the rich and poor are two nations 'between whom there is no intercourse and no sympathy; who are as ignorant of each other's habits and thoughts, and feelings, as if they were dwellers in different zones'.[14] In Disraeli's scheme of two nations estranged, the working classes who plan strikes and ultimately violence against the upper class see their plight not in terms of access to fair wages, the right to organize, or political enfranchisement, but rather – like the unassimilated Irish and Scottish characters of the national tale – in terms of an unfair territorial conquest. Comparing their position to the Saxons after the Norman invasion, Sybil anticipates that a restoration of the people's rights will involve a restoration of title to literal land. This racialized scheme draws in no small part on the tensions Scott popularizes in *Ivanhoe* (1819), his tale of medieval England.[15] The restoration Sybil anticipates unfolds in a plot also echoing the Irish national tale, when long-suppressed documents emerge that prove Sybil to be heiress to the local estate, whereupon she marries the dispossessed owner, turning theft into shared possession.

Elizabeth Gaskell's industrial novels also manage the Chartist clash through a regionalizing of class difference. She portrays the older members of her Manchester working class in *Mary Barton* (1848) as vessels of a Lancashire folk memory, still retaining local knowledge of herbal remedies,

---

13 For further discussion of the uses to which family metaphors are put in figuring English and Irish union, see Mary Jean Corbett, *Allegories of Union in Irish and English Writing, 1790–1870* (Cambridge University Press, 2000).

14 Benjamin Disraeli, *Sybil, or The Two Nations* (Oxford University Press, 1981), p. 65.

15 Christopher Hill lays out the long English tradition of using the Norman and Saxon clash as a metaphor for contemporary political struggle in 'The Norman Yoke', in John Saville (ed.), *Democracy and the Labour Movement* (London: Lawrence & Wishart, 1954), pp. 11–66.

folk songs, and insect life, and a dialect so broad that she provides footnotes to decipher it. In *North and South* (1855) her heroine Margaret moves to the industrialized north of England, a shift of location that proves as dizzying and identity-changing as any faced by Walter Scott's protagonists. Like the national tale protagonists before them, these heroines, in their naive navigation of new territory, unintentionally stumble into violence, rioting crowds, and accusations of criminal activity.

The condition-of-England novels' dependence on a genre started in the Celtic regions shows the extent to which union with Scotland and Ireland helped to constitute a subsequent literary Englishness. Representations of Scotland in both English and Scottish literature continued to define Englishness throughout the century, in a way that often emphasized Scotland's supply of what England lacked. William Scrope's much reprinted *The Art of Deer-Stalking* (1838) and *Days and Nights of Salmon Fishing in the Tweed* (1843) posited Scotland as the source of a revitalized masculinity, but one that was specifically *not* English. Only by standing in the river Tweed, the dividing line between England and Scotland, or by submitting to a native Highlands deer-hunting guide could Scrope's reader reclaim an authentic sporting experience that, as he often reiterated, simply was not available in England. Even the royal family endorsed this notion with their adoption of the Balmoral Estate as their summer vacation home. Queen Victoria's publication of journal extracts from summers at Balmoral, *Leaves from the Journal of Our Life in the Highlands* (1868), offer scene after scene of Prince Albert returned from the hunt, stag in hand.[16]

British literature written by both Scottish and English-born authors looked to the Highlands as a space which could morally orient characters towards British interests, even as they looked outward to empire. Arthur Hugh Clough's long poem, 'The Bothie of Tober-Na-Vuolich' (1848), recounts such a morally orienting expedition to the Highlands. His Oxford students, on holiday before exams, trek to the Highlands with their tutor. While there, radical student and Chartist poet Philip Hewson falls for the Highlands peasant girl Elspie Mackaye. Their subsequent marriage does not yield yet another union narrative, in which two cultures might unite their territories in an increased mutuality. Instead, Elspie anchors Philip's abstract radical ideals, providing him with that 'spot of native land' from which he can responsibly undertake geographically broader enterprises. After finishing

16 See Maureen M. Martin, *The Mighty Scot: Nation, Gender, and the Nineteenth-Century Mystique of Scottish Masculinity* (Albany: State University of New York Press, 2009).

his university exams, Philip returns to his new wife's home, to 'study the handling of the hoe and the hatchet' and to prepare for their subsequent emigration to New Zealand, a ground where his energies might be more effectively put to use.[17]

In this paradoxical function – as the home to which one turned in order to leave home – all of Scotland became a space disrupted by the presence of empire. An emblem of this disruption might be found in Robert Louis Stevenson's *Kidnapped* (1886), when the orphaned David Balfour travels to Edinburgh to claim a relationship with his newly discovered uncle. Sent up the winding stairs of the tower of the House of Shaw, David discovers in the darkness that the stair leads to nowhere. For the Lowlands David, a return to the Scottish family estate is no return at all, but only a free-fall that will end either in his death or – according to his homicidal uncle's back-up plan – in deportation to the Carolinas to end his days in slavery. Unlike the Waverley heroes who are unable to avoid a trip into the Highlands, David has to exert great effort simply to be marooned in the Highlands and remain on Scottish ground, rather than being abducted across the Atlantic.

Long haunted by what G. Gordon Smith first termed 'Caledonian Anti-syzygy', nineteenth-century Scottish literature was split between hard-headed realism and flights of absolute fancy. Tom Nairn suggests that this split was intrinsic to the situation of a thriving Scotland, which had no need to marry its surplus of fanciful national character to an uncompromising movement for political independence.[18] That Scotland's split personality was never quite at home on Scottish soil might be read in Stevenson's tales of dual consciousness, either as it is experienced across the global terrain of the Durie brothers' sibling rivalry in *The Master of Ballantrae* (1889) or as it is brought home to the heart of London in *The Strange Case of Dr Jekyll and Mr. Hyde* (1886).

As Scottishness took on more global properties, literary Englishness began to take shape more as a set of particular national characteristics than the abstract quality of being modern. In the following decades, as historian Martin Wiener argues, England embraced an image of itself as a small community 'rooted in time and space, bound together by tradition and by

---

17 Arthur Clough, 'The Bothie of Tober-Na-Vuolich' (1848), in *Poems. Selections* (Oxford: Clarendon Press, 1986), p. 160.
18 See Tom Nairn, *The Break-Up of Britain: Crisis and Neo-Nationalism* (London: New Left Books, 1977), especially pp. 38–150.

stable local ties'.[19] Literature that reflected this spirit presented Englishness as requiring a certain amount of ethnographical exposition, just as Scottishness and Irishness did in early century fiction.[20] Unlike the national tale or the condition-of-England novel, this English fiction defines English boundaries in plots of an uneventful daily life uninterrupted by abrupt historical shifts. Ian Duncan classifies these later century fictions as provincial, not regional. He argues that rather than imagining a region as a space apart from history, these fictions draw on the region as a barrier of everydayness through which the effects of those changes might be muffled.[21] Even a readerly entry into English regions was cushioned by a narratorial stance based not on introducing readers to a new terrain, but on providing small reminders of what the reader already knows.

Margaret Oliphant offers perhaps the most vivid illustration of how this stance could be both barrier to the upheavals of history, but also an invitation to identification for readers far outside provincial England. While the Scottish-born Oliphant wrote several novels of Scottish country life in her early career, she met with much more success in mid-career in her exhaustive documentation of the English Carlingford – 'a pretty place – mild, sheltered' with 'no alien activities to disturb the place – no manufactures and not much trade'.[22] Oliphant's Carlingford – much like the Scottish-born Carlyle's prophetic exhortations on the English condition – demonstrate that Scottish subjects might remain Scottish while wholly identifying not just with British concerns, but with English ones. But Carlingford also signals a paradoxical inclusiveness offered in the experience of reading an English provincial novel. By gently reminding readers of what they are politely sure the readers already know about the settings and

---

19 Martin Wiener, *English Culture and The Decline of the Industrial Spirit, 1850–1980* (2nd edn, Cambridge University Press, 2004), pp. 41, 42. For a review of the rise of England as a limited region after mid-century, see Krishan Kumar, *The Making of English National Identity* (Cambridge University Press, 2003). See also Raphael Samuel (ed.), *Patriotism: the Making and Unmaking of British National Identity.* Vol. III, *National Fictions* (London: Routledge, 1989), as well as Baucom, *Out of Place*, especially the first chapter, pp. 7–36.

20 For the auto-ethnographic impulses of British fiction – and its roots in early century national tales, see James Buzard, *Disorienting Fiction: the Autoethnographic Work of Nineteenth-Century British Novels* (Princeton University Press, 2005).

21 Ian Duncan, 'The Provincial or Regional Novel', in Patrick Brantlinger and William B. Thesing (eds.), *A Companion to the Victorian Novel* (New York: Blackwell, 2005), pp. 18–335.

22 Margaret Oliphant, *The Rector* and *The Doctor's Family*, facsimile edition (New York: Garland Publishing, 1975), chapter I, p. I. The Chronicles of Carlingford first ran as serial fiction before their publication as individual books between 1863 and 1876.

social scene of their tales, novels of this sort usher all comers into the common memories and habits of England.

Not coincidentally, the minute calibration of such tales gain popularity at the same time that George Henry Lewes undertook the recuperation of Jane Austen's literary prestige, praising her 'exquisite picture of English life' for 'representation of human nature in its familiar aspects, moving amid everyday scenes'.[23] But deep history troubles the Victorian rural novel's privileging of the small scale much more than it ever did in Austen's ideal of three or four families in a country village. The Victorian regional novel inherits from its Celtic predecessors a sense that local history and landscape irreducibly shape inhabitants. In this sense, George Eliot's *The Mill on the Floss* (1860) might be read as the triumph of regional historical particularity over a merely provincial insulation of daily habits. Eliot's St Ogg's is 'one of those old, old towns which impress one as a continuation and outgrowth of nature ... a town which carries the traces of its long growth and history like a millennial tree'.[24] The visible traces comprise a record of astonishing upheaval – floods, Roman and Saxon invasions, English civil wars – whose accumulation in one place renders each disturbance so small as to lull inhabitants into believing that they live in a present 'when men had done with change'.[25] While its description of disruptive history neutralized by a gradual sedimentation in one place articulates what other English provincial novels assume about the insulating powers of place, the book's cataclysmic ending gives the lie to such a complacent belief. Even as a provincial literary Englishness gained ascendancy in Anthony Trollope's Barsetshire novels (1855–67), Margaret Oliphant's chronicles of Carlingford (1863–76), and Eliot's own *Middlemarch* (1872), there persisted the sense that an animate landscape and a never-dead history might always rise up to unsettle the familiar.

George Borrow's hybrid travelogue-cum-novels – *Lavengro* (1851), *The Romany Rye* (1857), and *Wild Wales* (1862) – might be seen as laying bare the alien qualities at the root of Englishness. In all of these books Borrow exuberantly documented both the Welsh and Gypsies within Britain neither as coherent culture in their own right, nor as alien systems separate from England. Instead, the philological obsession with which he dwells on the

---

23 George Henry Lewes, 'The Novels of Jane Austen', *Blackwood's Edinburgh Magazine* 86 (1859), pp. 99–113.
24 George Eliot, *The Mill on the Floss* (London: Penguin, 1994), chapter 12, p. 123.
25 *Ibid.*, p. 127.

hybrid nature of the Welsh, the Romani, and the English languages partakes of an Austenian attention to detail – only one that delivers a sense of England's strangeness on a molecular level.[26]

This was a strangeness that was increasingly localized in the last third of the century. R. D. Blackmoor's popular *Lorna Doone: A Romance of Exmoor* (1869) married historical narrative to local specificity, a formula he followed in novels such as *Kit and Kitty: A Story of West Middlesex* (1889) and *Mary Anerley: A Yorkshire Tale* (1880). Blackmoor's literary vivisection of England was contemporary with the crippling depression that gutted what was left of English agriculture as a way of life. The decline inspired a sense of millennial decadence and a nostalgia both trained on the rural and regional. This was the era in which Thomas Hardy's Wessex emerged, as did the simultaneous mysticism (*The Story of My Heart* (1883)) and comic ethnography (*Hodge and His Masters* (1880)) of Richard Jefferies's countryside writing.

In Scotland intensely regional novels – commonly seen as comprising the 'Kailyard school' of novels – gained popularity throughout Britain in the last decade of the century. Extravagantly sentimental and given to religious fervour, novels such as Samuel Crockett's *The Stickit Minister* (1893), J. M. Barrie's *The Little Minister* (1898), and Ian McLaren's *Beside the Bonnie Brier Bush* (1896) were popular throughout Britain. The Kailyard school presented a highly reassuring picture of communal country life to which one could always return, but it was also a life almost opaque to the majority of those who consumed the narratives. Thick with dialect, the novels also featured an emotional excess that was more of a spectacle than an occasion for sympathetic identification. If the Kailyard school was preserving a disappearing rural life for its British readers, it was a rural life ambivalently exotic and familiar.

In this, Kailyard novels are not so far removed from their more pessimistic counterparts, who wrote the countryside as the location of alien ancient forces, forces whose concentrated local character count for more than their larger national provenance. The poison of the ancient past creeps into Thomas Hardy's *Tess of the D'Urbervilles* (1892), a tragedy that begins when the heroine discovers her family's ancient Norman roots. The discovery leaves her at the mercy of the man whose family has adopted the nomenclature for its own and ends when she murders her seducer and takes refuge

---

26 For more on Borrow see Ian Duncan, 'Wild England: George Borrow's Nomadology', *Victorian Studies* 41:3 (1998), pp. 381–403, and George Hyde, 'Traveling Across Cultures: George Borrow's Wild Wales', *Cambridge Quarterly* 33:4 (2004), pp. 331–43.

for one last night of freedom at the Druidic altar of Stonehenge. The vampires of Anglo-Irish fiction, such as Sheridan Le Fanu's 'Carmilla' (1872) and Bram Stoker's *Dracula* (1897), are often read as fictionally unleashing the horror of an Irish history long repressed in England. But their vampirically soil-bound habits also join them to British fiction that imagines history as anchored in specific localities, from which its destructive forces can always re-emerge.

And while no Gothic doom lurked behind either the founding of the Manx Language Society in 1899 and the first Cornish Language Society in 1903, their emergence at the end of the century suggests a turn towards the intensely local that retreats from larger national narratives. Even as Douglas Hyde proposed that the propagation of the Irish language was a necessary first step towards the ultimate political independence of Ireland, these societies treated Cornish and Manx only as a way of connecting with a disappeared local history whose political age was long over.

Ireland and the question of national literature

The characterization of the British Isles as shaped by a past it can barely remember owes much to Matthew Arnold's popularization of national character as the sum of irreducible racial traits. His *On the Study of Celtic Literature* (1867) at once attacks the insular English refusal to acknowledge virtues in non-English cultures, and champions racialist models of cultural difference. Arnold's influential essay is equal parts naked contempt for what he sees as an essentially flawed Celtic national character and firm conviction that such a character can be found in the formative racial mix that gives rise to Englishness. Arnold's description of 'the Celtic genius' partakes of vicious imperial stereotyping that attributes childish deficiencies to the indigenous 'races' of the British colonies. The Celt, Arnold reports, has been 'ineffectual' in both 'material civilization' and politics.[27] Arnold's opinion of the Celtic literature he defends is equally low: 'The Celtic genius, with its chafing against the despotism of fact, its perpetual straining after mere emotion, has accomplished nothing.'[28]

At the same time, Arnold's indictment of the Celtic genius can never be separated from his focus on its long connection to the English nation. When he examines the history of English poetry he discovers a 'turn for style' that

27 Matthew Arnold, *The Study of Celtic Literature* (London: John Murray, 1867), pp. 88, 89.
28 *Ibid.*, p. 86.

is 'the genuine poetical gift of the [English] race'.[29] Yet Arnold, after a survey of England's racial heritage, suggests that English poetry might 'plausibly derive ... from the root of the poetical Celtic nature in us'.[30] Celtic literature, when studied, reveals itself as already present within English literature. While Arnold concedes that politics might motivate some to study Celtic character, his aim is not primarily a desire for more effective control of Ireland. Instead, it is a call for facing the strangeness at the root of all Englishness, a strangeness that is also a harbinger of an English identity ever under the threat of dissolving.

Arnold's long meditation on this strangeness is prompted by his visit to the Welsh national Eisteddfod, an event favourable to the mixing of Celt and Saxon. Understood as an occasion during which those from England and Scotland might enjoy the Welsh countryside and the Welsh might pocket the money of tourists, the festivals became increasingly English-language friendly. The Eisteddfod's touristic transformation encapsulates the uneven cultural relationships among the nations of the British Isles, as well as the way that national cultures were preserved under those conditions. Wales might have the opportunity to attract attention to Welsh heritage, but only by presenting that heritage as a commodity amenable to outside tastes. Like Wales, Scotland, too, enthusiastically fashioned itself as the scene of consumption for tourists. It had the additional advantage of offering its culture as an exportable good, with Walter Scott's novels blazing the trail to the larger reading public in England. Scotland's economic and industrial development allowed for a commodifiable and profitable Scottish cultural identity, one that Nairn calls the 'boundless realm of shortcake tins, plaid socks, kilted statuettes and whisky-labels'.[31] But the profits from this commodification of national identity did not always go exclusively into Scottish pockets. The Edinburgh publishing industry also waned over the course of the nineteenth century, so that almost all of the so-called Kailyard school of novels were published in London, and often serialized in London magazines.

The situation in Ireland was even more dire. Ireland was never a site for tourism in the nineteenth century, and always the site for the exportation of raw materials whose profits accumulated elsewhere. In an Ireland rapidly losing its population – and losing the once widespread Irish language along with it – Irish culture was a resource whose exportation could only result in

---

29 *Ibid.*, p. 116.   30 *Ibid.*, p. 127.   31 Nairn, *The Break-Up of Britain*, p. 156.

impoverishment. Even Irish-authored books that sold well in Great Britain might be viewed with Irish suspicion as commodities that similarly depleted the country. Indeed, the Act of Union significantly weakened a once-thriving publishing industry. Extending English copyright laws to Ireland, Union killed the trade in pirated editions of British books, and no trade in original Irish-authored works succeeded it. The economic crisis of the famine years effectively wiped out what remained of Dublin publishers. While James Hogg, John Galt, and Walter Scott all published their works in Edinburgh, Maria Edgeworth, Charles Maturin, Emily Lawless, and George Moore all published their first works from London.

Even the gesture of trying to gain a hearing for Ireland within the British Isles carried with it threats of Irish culture's surrender to offshore ownership. Edgeworth included in her Irish fictions parodies of the travel writer whose books generalize from Irish anecdote with wild inaccuracy. Such figures reassure Edgeworth's audience that Edgeworth knows better. They also install a sense of an Ireland not entirely knowable by – and thus inalienable to – the outsider. The second and third decades of Irish tales further closed ranks by refraining from direct address to the British public who nonetheless continued to form its main readership. Instead, Catholic middle-class authors such as Gerald Griffin and John and Michael Banim, spun tales clearly aimed at someone unfamiliar with rural Irish life, but whose exact position they never specify. Unlike Edgeworth and Owensen, and unlike the Scottish Romantic writers, these Irish authors eschewed games with text and authorship played through layers of prefaces, footnotes, and mimicry of epistolary and journal forms. Instead, they hewed closely to a single narrative voice, as if vigilant to avoid the impression of including anything that might be left entirely up to non-Irish interpretation.

But that voice inevitably delivered contents which undermined notions of sincerity or even unified intention. Gerald Griffin's *The Collegians* (1829) features a murder advantageous to a member of the Irish gentry and yet committed without his knowledge by his peasant foster-brother. In the 1835 preface to the first English edition of *Traits and Stories of the Irish Peasantry* (published in Ireland in 1830), William Carleton announces his hope to dispel British prejudice through his stories. He calls particular attention to his characters' dialogue, offering it as a more faithful rendition of Irish than the stage brogue perpetuated in English music-halls. At the same time, his sketches include 'Going to Maynooth', recounting the adventures of young Patrick, whose father's ambition is to make of him 'the boy that can rattle off the high English, and the larned Latin, just as if he was born wid an English Dixonary in one cheek, a Latin Neksuggawn in the other, an' Doctor Gallagher's Irish Sermons nately on the top of his tongue between the two'.[32] Unable to harness the prestige of pure English for himself, and caught between a familial Irish dialect he disdains and a smattering of priestly Latin he cannot master, Carleton's hero drives home the point that occasion, audience, and the materiality of language might count for far more than intention or content.

Carleton's sketch shares with much Irish literature the sense that Ireland could not be represented to itself without England listening in. Nowhere were these tensions more apparent than in drama. Comic theatre from the seventeenth century onwards featured 'the stage Irishman' as a stock character, an impulsive, pugnacious, and big-hearted personage whose comic mangling of the English language provided much ambient humour. While the stage Irishman appeared in Dublin theatres as well as London, his success abroad met with the most suspicion at home. Samuel Lover, a playwright, novelist, and stage comedian whose musical review *Irish Evenings* (1844) proved sensationally popular in England and America, was criticized by the *Cork Magazine* editor Joseph Brenan for having produced a piece 'as characteristic of Ireland as Timbuctoo' and 'pander[ing] to English prejudice by taking the stage Irishman as his hero'.[33]

But any dramatic role is available for reinterpretation, and the stage Irishman was no exception. This was proven by Dion Boucicault, who, after thirty years away from Ireland, began to write melodramas centred on this figure. In a published volume of his melodramas, *The Colleen Bawn* (1860), *Arrah-na-Pogue* (1867), and *The Shaughran* (1874), full of the merry jigs, sworn enemies, and broad brogues familiar to stage Irishmen, Boucicault claimed it was his mission to abolish the stereotype. While it seems implausible that abolition was his straightforward intent, Boucicault did succeed in crafting vivid and well-loved Irish characters next to whom his honourable but stiff British characters dulled. Blithely ignoring any distinction between insulting stereotype and accurate representation, Boucicault himself called to Prime Minister Benjamin Disraeli's attention the public's taste for his plays, suggesting it pointed towards a popular

---

32 William Carleton, *Traits and Stories of the Irish Peasantry*, 5 vols. (London: Baldwin & Cradock, 1836), vol. v, p. 7.
33 Joseph Brenan, 'A National Literature For Ireland', *Cork Magazine* 1 (1847), p. 2.

support for Irish Home Rule.[34] Exactly whom Boucicault was really addressing in this declaration – Irish patriots, British playgoers, or a prime minister who knew little of Ireland – is difficult to determine. And it was this indeterminacy that was thrown out with the stereotype when, in their founding statement for a national Irish theatre, William Butler Yeats, Augusta Gregory, and Edward Martyn declared that 'we will show that Ireland is not the home of buffoonery and easy sentiment, as it has been represented'.[35]

The fear of British eavesdropping and appropriation and the ironic reappropriation of stereotypes placed expressions of Irish nationalism outside the codes of sincerity that dominated British novels in the nineteenth century. The mid-century famine also placed representations of Irish life outside of the Realist preference for historical gradualism. In representing a national calamity that, within the space of six years, resulted in the death or migration of almost a quarter of Ireland's population, there was little room for attention to the mundane rituals of daily life or to the orderly progress of civilization. Instead, when novels dealt with the famine, they often questioned the very assumptions of inevitable progress towards modernity on which the British novel was premised. Annie Keary's *Castle Daly* (1875) offers the courtship between the Irish-identified Ellen Daly and the economically pragmatic English John Thornley, who comes to manage her father's failing estate. The romance that overcomes their grave ideological differences on the causes and solutions for the famine only proceeds at the expense both of her Young Ireland brother, who is exiled for his rebellion, and his stern but faithful sister, the ironically named Bride, who remains with John, unmarried and in exile in Ireland. Too psychologically textured to leave these disappointed lives unnoticed, Keary's novel silently gestures towards the enormity of the famine, damage it also cannot repair.

While Realist conventions provided a way for those in the decades after the famine to take stock of how it had impacted their belief in progress, representations of the famine as it was unfolding did not have the certainty of outcome necessary to conduct such a discussion. When William Carleton began writing his novel *The Black Prophet* at the beginning of 1847, he could not have known that the year's crop failures would result in famine. But his

---

34 Elizabeth Butler Cullingford, 'National Identities in Performance: The Stage Englishman of Boucicault's Irish Drama', *Theatre Journal* 49:3 (1997), p. 287. See also Declan Kiberd's 'The Fall of the Stage Irishman', in Ronald Schleifer (ed.), *The Genres of the Irish Literary Revival* (Dublin: Wolfhound Press, 1979), pp. 39–60.
35 Augusta, Lady Gregory, *Our Irish Theatre: A Chapter of Autobiography* (Gerards Cross: Colin Smythe, 1972), p. 20.

novel, with its intended backdrop of the 1817 Irish famine, took on a prophetic quality. Young Ireland poet James Clarence Mangan also wrote of the famine in a register of messianic time that often mixed disaster with revolution. His call to political rebellion in 'Soul and Country' imagines a world in which the simultaneity of portent and fulfilment derange chronology: 'The signs are flaming in the skies; / a struggling world would yet be free, / . . . /The earthquake hath not yet been born / That soon shall rock the lands around.'[36] His mid-1847 exhortation on the occasion of famine, 'The Warning Voice', is no different: 'A day is at hand / Of trial and trouble', he begins, describing the 'blasted and sterile' land as a sign that 'False bands shall be broken / Dead systems will crumble.'[37] Even the conservative Anglo-Irish Aubrey De Vere wrote of famine as a return of cyclical history. Organizing his 'The Year of Sorrow: Ireland 1849' by season, De Vere greets spring as a return – 'Once more the cuckoo's call I hear' – and then greets famine as a similarly familiar occasion: 'Again the breath / Of proved Destruction o'er thee blows.'[38]

Both before and after famine the poetic forms of the ballad and the epic presented themselves as models of national literature less indeterminate in their Irish loyalties than drama or novels. Drawing on the same romantic antiquarianism that led Scott and Percy to collect the folksongs of their respective nations, Young Ireland's non-sectarian newspaper, *The Nation*, offered weekly ballads designed to enhance a sense of national identity among its readers. These ballads were collected in the oft-revised and expanded collection, *The Spirit of the Nation*, which was published first in 1843 and remained in print for the next fifty years. But where the idea of capturing the already obsolete past for a modern audience determined the meaning of the romantic ballad collection, in Ireland the ballad thrived because of its associations with a mobile national identity, one which – when put to music – would circulate ineffably, as if on air. This mobility proved especially forceful in an Irish nationalist movement that derived the bulk of its financial support from Irish emigrants in America, Canada, and Australia.

In the last third of the century, writers looked to ancient Celtic myths to provide materials for a national epic. This flowering came at the same time

36 James Clarence Mangan, *Poems, with Biographical Introduction by J. Mitchel* (New York: P. M. Haverty, 1859), p. 430.
37 *Ibid.*, p. 438.
38 Aubrey De Vere, *Selections from the Poems of Aubrey De Vere*, ed. George Edward Woodberry (New York: Macmillan, 1894), pp. 220, 222.

that English poet laureate Alfred Lord Tennyson announced the genre as obsolete in his episodic *Idylls of the King* (1859–72). Preoccupied with the problem of national epic in the age of empire, Tennyson's Arthurian kingdom's disintegration begins almost at its inception. Almost simultaneous with Tennyson's elegiac disidentification with the genre, the Irish Protestant Samuel Ferguson was scouring ancient documents for the source material for his epic, *Congal* (1872), the first composition in a series of publications by Irish writers that reworked the myths of Cuchalain in the name of national consciousness. Ferguson's epic established Ireland as possessing the same forms of literary heritage as did Great Britain, and perhaps excelling the British at their own game now that British poets no longer believed English epic to even be possible. Ferguson's version of the Cuchalain epic influenced the *fin-de-siècle* project of a Celtic revival, finding its way into Yeats's poetry and plays performed by the Abbey Theatre, before they were translated once again in Augusta Gregory's popular if somewhat sanitized translations.

Literary nationalism in the century's last third also looked to the Irish west as the land which preserved an uncorrupted Irish culture. Unlike the decadence and disintegration of the British literary local, in Ireland the spectre of an ancient rural past promised an Irish heritage intact from the days long before Saxon interference. Yet in unearthing this past, writers of the Celtic revival tended to treat regional inhabitants as mere vessels of culture, not active agents of political change. William Butler Yeats's *Celtic Twilight* (1893) insisted on the continuing existence of a pure Celtic spirit in the west of Ireland. Yeats suggests that this spirit was contained in the stories unreflectively repeated by inhabitants of the west, but could only be accessed by someone more learned in Irish history and literature. John Synge's ethnographic travelogue of the far-west *Aran Islands* (1907) similarly collapsed inhabitants and terrain into one category, both requiring interpretation from the outside.

The creation of an independent, predominantly Catholic state of Ireland in the twentieth century creates a teleology which inclines scholars to see 'true' Irish literature as always aligned with rejecting British cultural dominance and political control. But the range of options posited for solving the so-called 'Irish Problem' over the course of the nineteenth century meant that many of those writing to create an Irish literary identity were not committed only to movements and attitudes that would end British cultural dominance and give rise to Irish national autonomy. Many of the writers in the second half of the century – from the Young Ireland writers to Samuel

Ferguson to Augusta Gregory – revised their political positions on the Irish nation over the course of their lives, without drastically altering their literary strategies. Irish literature from the Victorian era teaches us to be alert to the nascent national stories that cannot be easily mapped on to twentieth-century outcomes. Anthony Trollope offers us just such a casual glimpse in *Phineas Redux* (1874) when Phineas Finn, the Irish born and raised former MP, receives an invitation from his Liberal friends in London to run again for Parliament. Finn is eager to return to parliamentary politics but unsure of giving up the easy life he leads in Dublin. Arguing the option with himself he asks, 'Did he not owe himself to his country?'[39] Not mentioning precisely to which country he is in debt, nor having settled on whether he will run for an Irish or English Parliamentary seat, Phineas nonetheless is drawn to Parliament's glamorous promise to imbue its members with the 'feeling that such duties were done in the face of the country'.[40] It is this indeterminism – coupled with the absolute urgency of patriotic feelings – which is the state of national literature during the British Isles's Victorian era.

---

39 Anthony Trollope, *Phineas Redux* (London: Penguin Classics, 1973), chapter 1, p. 10.
40 *Ibid.*, p. 7.

29

Britain and Europe

NICHOLAS DAMES

Crossing the Channel for the first time, Lucy Snowe, the autobiographical voice of Charlotte Brontë's 1853 *Villette*, beholds a vision:

> In my reverie, methought I saw the continent of Europe, like a wide dreamland, far away. Sunshine lay on it, making the long coast one line of gold; tiniest tracery of clustered town and snow-gleaming tower, of woods deep-massed, of heights serrated, of smooth pasturage and veiny stream, embossed the metal-bright prospect. For background, spread a sky, solemn and dark-blue, and – grand with imperial promise, soft with tints of enchantment – strode from north to south a God-bent bow, an arch of hope.[1]

Brontë's description of Europe imagined, or seen, for the first time by a rootless, adventuresome British woman has often been taken as emblematic of the Victorian experience of the Continent: a quasi-Gothic, quasi-Romantic land offering pleasures both *gemütlich* and 'imperial', pleasures that promise a release from British social strictures. It accords well with our experience of a large number of Victorian writers, from the Brownings to George Meredith, Walter Pater, and Oscar Wilde, to name only a few, for whom 'Europe' represented both inspiration and refuge, whether that Europe be Bohemian Paris or the Italy of the Risorgimento. The passage does not end on such a rainbow-tinged note, however. Characteristically, Lucy Snowe retracts: 'Cancel the whole of that, if you please, reader – or rather let it stand, and draw thence a moral – an alliterative, text-hand copy – "Day-dreams are delusions of the demon." Becoming excessively sick, I faltered down into the cabin.'[2] The Victorian experience of Europe: *la vie en rose*, or nausea?

Both were of course possible responses, and to the list of Europhilic Victorian writers one might all too easily counterpose an equally lengthy,

---

1 Charlotte Brontë, *Villette* (Harmondsworth: Penguin, 2004), chapter 6, pp. 62–3.
2 *Ibid.*, p. 63.

and equally influential, list of Victorian Europhobes, for whom the Continent was a morass of political instability, moral insensibility, and religious iniquity. More commonly, individual writers were capable of holding without undue distress both attitudes. Charles Dickens himself could be as adept at ridiculing British xenophobia as he was skilled at evoking its usual disgusts. *Little Dorrit* (1855–7) portrays a full range of British provincialism abroad, from the haughty Dorrits on tour through southern Europe to the rather more agreeable Mr Meagles, whose opinion of the French is that 'these people are always howling. Never happy otherwise.'[3] Yet one of its central villains is a theatrically French rogue, and its depictions of Italy – a land of 'beggars of all sorts everywhere', with 'swarms of priests' and 'swarms of spies' – recoils with a positively Meaglesesque shudder.[4] The contradictory attitudes that Victorian writers held towards Europe is not particularly a matter for surprise; what cultural attitudes are ever straightforward? What is remarkable about the Victorian experience of Europe, to the extent it can be generalized, is its sharp sense of *difference*, demonstrated by the polarized possibilities – ecstatic hope, or sickened disgust – that oscillate so frequently in the period's literary imagination. The Channel that Lucy Snowe crosses so uneasily had never before seemed so decisive a cultural, and political, barrier.

'How England became an island': Fernand Braudel's memorable formulation, describing the political and economic events of the early sixteenth century, might with equal justice be applied to the literary world of Victorian Britain.[5] As numerous studies by book historians and literary geographers have demonstrated, what had been a fluid market of trade and translation in the sphere of literary culture between Britain and Europe (primarily France) in the eighteenth century suddenly, and dramatically, became a nationally closed market. Franco Moretti's work on 'narrative markets' of the mid nineteenth century offers striking evidence that the presence of European novels in British circulating libraries declined steeply in the first half of the nineteenth century, reaching the remarkably xenophobic figure of 5 per cent by 1850; more anecdotally, Moretti cites the 1869 New Oxford Street catalogue of Mudie's library, which contained no works by such figures as Voltaire, Diderot, Pushkin, or Balzac.[6] A gap of twenty or

---

3 Charles Dickens, *Little Dorrit* (Oxford: Clarendon Press, 1979), Book 1, chapter 2, p. 12.
4 *Ibid.*, Book 2, chapter 3, pp. 389.
5 Fernand Braudel, *The Perspective of the World, Civilization and Capitalism, 15th–18th Century*, trans. Siân Reynolds, 3 vols. (Berkeley: University of California Press, 1992), vol. III, p. 353.
6 Franco Moretti, *Atlas of the European Novel, 1800–1900* (London: Verso, 1998), p. 157.

thirty years often separated French publication from British translation; Gustave Flaubert's 1857 *Madame Bovary*, for instance, appeared in English only in 1886 in a version by Karl Marx's daughter Eleanor. More notoriously, the publisher Henry Vizetelly's conviction for obscenity in 1889 as a result of his series of anonymous translations of Emile Zola's Rougon-Macquart novels functioned as an extreme instance of the British caution towards French literary work, even if more radical British Realists, such as George Moore and George Gissing, took Zola and Maupassant as models.[7] Beyond Western Europe, literary infiltration into Britain was even rarer. The novels of Ivan Turgenev, perhaps the most well-known Russian writer in Victorian Britain, were most usually read in English translations of French versions; not until the 1890s work of Constance Garnett and Isabel Hapgood were direct translations from the Russian easily available. For the student of the Victorian literary scene, it is often necessary to remember that this was not always the case. As James Raven has demonstrated, French writers were a staple of the British reading diet between 1750 and 1770, representing roughly a third of the most popular titles.[8]

Statistics and anecdotes of market protectionism are only half the story. As Moretti emphasizes, the rapid decline of British interest in European literature helped form the exceptionalism of the Victorian novel, which resisted the themes and plot dynamics of European fiction. The novel of ideas, the adultery plot, the development of quasi-scientific realism and naturalism: these essential ingredients of the European novel of the nineteenth century are sedulously avoided by British novelists, and ignored by the agents of British publishing and translation. The case of Goethe is particularly instructive: while *Wilhelm Meisters Lehrjahre* (1824–7), the paradigmatic *Bildungsroman*, had been translated often by the 1830s (including by Thomas Carlyle), the 1809 *Die Wahlverwandtschaften* – the century's first novel of adultery – was only translated in 1854, as *Elective Affinities*, by Carlyle's disciple J. A. Froude. Censorship, that is, could take the form of delay, and the criteria for selection was often generic. The novel of formation was acceptable – in fact, Victorian fiction would devote itself to elaborating this genre – while the adultery novel was ignored and marginalized. The great novelistic genres of the eighteenth century, such as sentimental fiction, were

---

7 For further detail, see the essays of Peter France ('French', p. 230–45) and David Constantine ('German,' p. 211–29) in Peter France and Kenneth Haynes (eds.), *The Oxford History of Literary Translation in English*, vol. IV (Oxford University Press, 2006).

8 James Raven, *British Fiction 1750–1770* (Newark: Delaware University Press, 1987), p. 21.

prominently transnational; works such as Samuel Richardson's *Pamela* (1740) shared a common literary space with Rousseau's *Julie, ou la Nouvelle Héloïse* (1761) and Goethe's *Die Leiden des jungen Werthers* (1774). Forms such as epistolary fiction traversed national boundaries with relative ease.[9] By the nineteenth century, Britain increasingly had developed a 'national' manner of literary production, in no small measure as a reaction against the tendencies of European literature.

What is implicit in the exclusions of the publishing world became explicit in the newly nationalist shape of literary history in the Victorian period. The novel, for instance, is increasingly treated as a form with its own distinctive development in Britain rather than a genre of European breadth; Clara Reeve's 1785 *The Progress of Romance*, which traced the form to Arabic and ancient Greek models, looks decidedly different from David Masson's 1859 *British Novelists and their Styles*, which despite a passing nod to Goethe looks largely to Scott as the origin of contemporary British fiction. By promoting an 'internal' literary space, one less and less interested in foreign modes or models, the joint operations of the marketplace and critics such as Masson ensured a corresponding lack of visibility for British writers abroad. Whereas Richardson and Byron had been European sensations, only Dickens, among Victorian writers, achieved any significant continental impact. Despite the fact that the novel is the most easily translated genre of literary production, most of the other major novelists (the Brontës, Eliot, Trollope, Hardy) are comparatively invisible to a Western European audience.

The geo-politics of this peculiar situation have long been understood as deeply, even constitutively, paradoxical. After the French Revolution and the final defeat of Bonapartist imperial ambition at Waterloo, British policy towards Europe was marked by cautious distrust and immense self-confidence; the upheavals of 1848 and 1870 played out without any British involvement, and increasingly the island kingdom seemed, for better and worse, immune to continental developments. In the distant memory of some Victorian adults, Europe was the land of battle and violence, such as the Waterloo described in W. M. Thackeray's *Vanity Fair* (1847–8) or the Terror of Dickens's *Tale of Two Cities* (1859); in the present, however, it was the land of tourism, visited by figures such as Mr Meagles, who asserts complacently that 'we know what Marseilles is. It sent the most insurrectionary tune into the

---

9 For further detail on the pervasive exchanges of British and French literary cultures in the eighteenth century, see Margaret Cohen and Carolyn Dever (eds.), *The Literary Channel: The Inter-National Invention of the Novel* (Princeton University Press, 2002).

world that was ever composed. It couldn't exist without allonging and marshonging to something or other – victory or death, or blazes, or something.'[10] To use the language of contemporary globalization theory, Britain was both core and periphery in nineteenth-century Europe: the Continent's major power, and also an isolated protectorate.

That paradox helps illuminate the literary relations between Britain and Europe in the Victorian period. Cosmopolitanism and xenophobia become two sides of the same coin in nineteenth-century Britain, since they are both ways of negotiating the ambiguous position of a nation that was at once core and periphery, metropole and province. Pascale Casanova has argued for the central role of Paris in modern literary space, but London – and Britain by extension – was not simply a 'province' of Western European literature.[11] In one way provincial by Parisian standards, London was also the centre of a far-flung network of Anglophone literature, far too politically confident and literarily self-sufficient to be just a province. As a result, British literary work increasingly expressed the centring, grounding force of provincialism – or, put another way, the provincialism of the centre: paradoxical forms of self-understanding, in which Britain could be peripheral, embattled, young, a minority (a Protestant enclave, an Anglo-Saxon bastion, a Roman province), and yet also central, imperial, dominant, and rooted (the land of the pound, the empire, the ancient privileges of Magna Carta and constitution). Literary intellectuals engaged with cosmopolitan forms of knowledge and technique, yet then applied those forms in strikingly nativist ways; the example of George Eliot, as I will later claim, best illustrates the phenomenon of transmuting the material of a European cultural 'core' into the finished products of British literary work.

Exceptionalism as a way of belonging: few expressed the paradox as consistently as Anthony Trollope, who in *Doctor Thorne* (1858) openly complains about the Napoleonic jibe that Britain is merely a commercial nation:

> England is not yet a commercial country in the sense in which that epithet is used for her; and let us still hope that she will not soon become so . . . If in western civilized Europe there does exist a nation among whom there are high signors, and with whom the owners of the land are the true aristocracy, the aristocracy that is trusted as being best and fittest to rule, that

---

10 Dickens, *Little Dorrit*, Book I, chapter 2, p. 12.
11 See Pascale Casanova, *The World Republic of Letters*, trans. M. B. DeBevoise (Cambridge, MA: Harvard University Press, 2004).

nation is the English. Choose out the ten leading men of each great European people. Choose them in France, in Austria, Sardinia, Prussia, Russia, Sweden, Denmark, Spain (?), and then select the ten in England whose names are best known as those of leading statesmen; the result will show in which country there still exists the closest attachment to, the sincerest trust in, the old feudal and now so-called landed interests.

England a commercial country! Yes; as Venice was.[12]

The closest reader of Trollope's passage will find it difficult to decide if Trollope's England is a member of Europe or a land apart – or if it is European only in the sense of the Venetian empire as Ruskin had recently described it, an island enclave with its back turned to the continent it dominates. The defence of 'feudal' England is Trollope's, but the logic of periphery as core is common to his period. Tracing the contortions such logic demanded will be the focus of this chapter.

As an acknowledgment of how varied such contortions could be, this chapter will proceed not in any rigorously conceptual path, but rather through the different European 'zones' that British writers most frequently responded to and negotiated. Three different Europes emerge from the welter of depictions, influences, and imaginary encounters scattered throughout Victorian literary work: Catholic Europe, particularly France; the tourist havens of Mitteleuropa, particularly Germany and Switzerland; and southern Europe, the Europe of the classical and imperial past, primarily located in Italy. Each zone posed different geo-political, cultural, and philosophical questions for the British writer, and each produced in turn a different imagination of Britain (and British literature) in response.

Catholic Europe; or, the meaning of Protestantism

Over a century's conflict with France ended with the Congress of Vienna in 1814–15. The Continent fully reopened to British travellers who had spent two decades barred from France, their nearest neighbour. It also brought to a close what was, by the middle decades of the nineteenth century, viewed as a heroic period in British history. As the increasingly dominant Whig historiography had it, from the defeat of the Spanish Armada to Waterloo, British liberties had been gradually won by repeated repulses of aggressive Catholic despotisms, including the native Catholic despotism of the Stuarts. It was no small irony, then, that shortly after what had seemed like the final

---

12 Anthony Trollope, *Doctor Thorne* (Oxford University Press, 2000), chapter 1, p. 12.

repulse of French power, Catholicism returned, in subtler forms, to the centre of British politics. Catholic Emancipation in 1829, the conversions of John Henry Newman and several other members of the Oxford Movement in the 1840s, and the installation of Cardinal Wiseman as Archbishop of Westminster in 1850 – the first British Catholic Archbishop since prior to Shakespeare's time – reinvigorated a strain of anti-Catholicism that had been almost made irrelevant by prolonged victory. If the anti-Catholicism of the Victorian period seems in retrospect needlessly paranoid compared to that of the sixteenth and seventeenth centuries, that paranoia gave it its force: it expressed the anxiety, and confusion, of a culture that was at once politically triumphant and yet still, at least in religious terms, peculiar: apart from the mainstream of Western European life.

Brontë's *Villette*, and her posthumously published *The Professor* (1857) are two of the most compelling examples of what might be called mid-Victorian Protestant paranoia. They are all the odder because of their foreign setting: in each, a sternly anti-Catholic narrator ventures to Belgium (called 'Labassecour' in *Villette*) to forge a career path that is blocked in socially restrictive Britain. Each narrator makes their way as an instructor of the English language, but must continually contend with a Catholic culture that is presented as inescapably Other. 'A subtle essence of Romanism pervaded every arrangement', Lucy Snowe relates of her school: 'large sensual indulgence (so to speak) was permitted by way of counterpoise to jealous spiritual restraint'.[13] The oldest, most traditional Anglican libels are dusted off by Brontë – Belgian Catholics are fleshy, self-indulgent, mildly depraved sensualists ruled by Jesuitical spies – and added to newer criticisms, such as the anti-individualism and anti-modernity of the Church; as Lucy adds, 'the CHURCH strove to bring up her children robust in body, feeble in soul, fat, ruddy, hale, joyous, ignorant, unthinking, unquestioning'.[14]

The interest in what might otherwise seem like pure xenophobia lies in the implicit alternative Brontë offers. Rather than making the contest between Catholicism and Anglican Protestantism a theological one, or even a cultural one, it becomes in both *Villette* and *The Professor* a difference in psychological tone. The Catholic character is physical, thoroughly embodied, and uncritical; the Protestant character, exemplified by Brontë's stern, prickly narrative voices, is instead in a continual state of self-examination and critique. Put more simply, the Catholics of these novels accept; the Protestant voices of

---

13 Brontë, *Villette*, chapter 14, pp. 140–1.   14 *Ibid.*, p. 141.

these novels reject. They reject the subtle traps of their Catholic employers; they reject the allure of Catholicism itself (in a notable scene, Lucy Snowe enters a confessional, only to insist, 'Mon père, je suis Protestante'); they even reject any of the conventional ways in which narrative voices ingratiate themselves with readers.[15] To be a Protestant, in Brontë, is not to adhere to any particular doctrinal formula, but instead to be a particular type of individual: the modern, isolated, self-questioning sceptic. Thus the odd narrative of these novels, in which a British individual must make a life in Catholic Europe while remaining untouched by its culture. As if returning the word to its literal roots, the Brontëan Protestant protests.

Protestantism as resistance, individual self-reliance, protestation: it is a social-psychological profile only, no longer a theological one. Not even particularly well-defined in sectarian terms – note that Lucy does not say 'je suis Anglicaine' – the Protestantism of Brontë's foreign novels is situated in the midst of a milieu (Catholic Belgium) that it must resist. The heroically isolated British figure holding off the unthinking Catholic hordes (or, in the case of Brontë's narrators, resisting the culture of their adopted home) is, of course, an archetype that pre-dates Brontë by centuries, but in her hands it becomes the means to develop an image of what modern individualism is, and how modern individualism, with all its anxious solitudes and refusals, is nonetheless more prized than the allegedly mindless obedience and sensual enjoyments of its Catholic counterpart. Brontë is not alone in this, although her anti-Catholicism is far more legible and unashamed than other writers of her stature; but throughout the mid-Victorian narrative tradition, strong selfhood is equated to a vague kind of Protestantism, while protean characters (sensualists, tricksters, the ambitious) are tainted in various ways by their proto-Catholicism or their Francophilia. One of the surest signs of moral alarm in the Victorian novel is a character's affection for French novels. More blatantly still, Thackeray dressed his anti-heroine Becky Sharp as Napoleon in one of his illustrations for *Vanity Fair*, with telescope in hand, peering out toward the chalk cliffs of Britain.

Even in the spate of historical novels situated at the time of the French Revolution, such as *A Tale of Two Cities* or Trollope's *La Vendée* (1850), specifically political or theological differences between Protestant Britain and Catholic France are far less important than psychological tendencies that derive from a vaguely defined Protestant culture. In one way, this

---

15 *Ibid.*, chapter 16, p. 178.

construction of a Protestant 'self' is clearly a displacement or evasion of the fissures within British Protestantism itself; transferring difference abroad, novels like Brontë's make the fractious quality of British religious life in the nineteenth century less visible. But this Protestant selfhood also helps answer one of the ur-questions of Victorian thought, which lingered in countless ways in the period's imaginative literature: how, or why, did revolution not happen in Britain? How, or why, are 'we' different from the French – in what ways might the British historical path be distinct? For twentieth-century British leftists this question would get turned around and asked in the tone of despair, as when Perry Anderson, in 1980, lamented 'the failure of British society to generate any mass socialist movement or significant revolutionary party in the twentieth century – alone among major nations in Europe'.[16] Common to both late twentieth-century leftists and Victorian conservatives like Trollope is a deeply felt exceptionalism generated by the British success, or failure, in avoiding their own revolution. Brontëan Protestant selfhood is one answer as to why this avoidance might have occurred: the resolute scepticism of British personality cannot be made amenable to any 'mass' movement of the kind Anderson describes.

Masses themselves – crowds, large groups, mobs, unified social elements – are by their nature deeply feared in Victorian narrative, and the frisson of French Revolutionary historical fiction is often to be located in the threatening ways crowds of all kinds are depicted. The Manette family of *A Tale of Two Cities*, safe in their London refuge, are nonetheless vulnerable to a peculiar sound heard by Lucie Manette: the sound of continual footsteps, a 'great crowd of people with its rush and roar', feet that are 'headlong, mad, and dangerous' – a ghostly premonition of the Terror, here imagined as nothing more or less than a mob.[17] The small domestic gathering, and the mob outside, across the Channel: such are the opposed units of Dickens's novel. This is, one might say, but a politicized and historicized version of Brontë's Protestant–Catholic opposition. It touches on another of the various aspects that opposition took, the aspect of the Singular (the family, the interior, the self) versus the Many (the faceless, onrushing masses). For much of the Victorian period, France in particular, and Catholic Europe in general, was imagined as the land of the Mass, in both senses of that term. Fear of native masses, such as Chartist rallies, had of course no small part to play in

---

16 Perry Anderson, *Arguments Within English Marxism* (London: Verso, 1980), p. 149.
17 Charles Dickens, *A Tale of Two Cities* (Oxford University Press, 1988), chapters 6, 21, pp. 122, 269.

this pervasive anxiety, but such fear was for the most part successfully displaced on to the continental terrain that was supposed to be the real home of mass action.

This opposition between British and French socio-psychological attitudes was so pivotal that it could even colour scenes and themes that were not explicitly set in Europe or openly referable to European matters. Take, for instance, a small scene of potential conflict from Eliot's *Middlemarch* (1871–2), between the landowner Brooke and his tenant Dagley. Brooke approaches Dagley to mention that Dagley's son Jacob has been caught poaching, and diffidently requests that his tenant 'just look after him, and give him a reprimand, you know?' Dagley instead loudly refuses, his words strengthened by drink: 'I'll be dee'd if I'll leather my boy to please you or anybody else, not if you was twenty landlords istid o'one, and that a bad un.'[18] Rather than exercise any of his rights, Brooke is shocked at his tenant's words – both embarrassed by Dagley's drunkenness and wounded in his *amour-propre* – and hastily retreats. The scene is rife with the potential to become open class conflict, yet the refusal of the landlord to own his legal power in the situation defuses conflict and turns it instead into social discomfort. What Dickens in *A Tale of Two Cities* had imagined, in France, as a relation of mutual ruthlessness and political action – the Marquis St Evrémonde's carriage runs over a young child, leading to his assassination by the child's enraged father – is in Eliot's Midlands locale imagined as a scene of *shame*: Brooke's embarrassment not only at his own potential authority, but at his misuse of that authority (he has just been described, in the local press, as an inattentive landlord). Self-critique, that is, triumphs over any assertion of exterior rights. The scene could be read as a small parable of English difference, of the inability of class warfare to gain any real traction in a British setting.

Of course not all British literary relations with France in the period were marked by this self-congratulatory sense of difference. In other realms, France represented a definition of 'culture' that could be usefully counter-poised to British empiricism and materialism. John Stuart Mill's 1834 essay 'The English National Character' is typical in this regard, and its enthusiasm for François Guizot's definition of 'civilization' would be influential through-out the century. In Britain, Mill writes,

---

18 George Eliot, *Middlemarch: A Study of Provincial Life* (Oxford University Press, 1988), chapter 39, p. 324.

such a phenomenon is scarcely known, as a man who prefers his liberty to a little more money, who, like so many thousands in France, can sit down contented with a small patrimony, affording him the necessaries and comforts of life, but nothing for ostentation, and devote himself to literature, politics, science, art, or even the mere enjoyment of quiet leisure.[19]

'Culture' could, however, cut different ways. The late century 'Decadent' movement in poetry, stemming from Swinburne's enthusiastic reception and translation of Baudelaire's *Fleurs du Mal* in the early 1860s, understood French 'Culture' as a revulsion from 'culture' in its normative, bourgeois senses: as a refusal of optimism, a thorough scepticism, an attraction to the sensual and the morbidly psychological. Late century poets like Ernest Dowson and Arthur Symons borrowed directly from a Baudelairean poetics, which were interpreted as the expression of an inward-turned sensibility hostile to social norms. Whether the France in question was the France of free inquiry and philosophical speculation, as it was for Mill, or the France of anti-bourgeois poetry, as for Swinburne, the shared sentiment was that – as far as the still cognate terms 'culture' or 'civilization' was concerned – they ordered these matters better in France.

Here the Brontëan refusal of Catholic claims of universalism in favour of Protestant particularism is reversed, as it would be in various ways by cultural commentators throughout the century. While not in any way admiring of Catholicism itself, the implied universalism of Catholic Europe – its hearkening back to the Roman imperium, to a Europe united – appealed to writers for whom 'culture' only made sense in a transnational context. Whether that was the transnationalism of philosophy, ethics, political thought (as in Mill or Matthew Arnold) or of aesthetics (as in Swinburne, or Wilde), French culture often was used as identical with Culture per se, as a riposte to provincialism of any kind. This logic did not, however, contest the exceptionalism that gave the Victorian period its flavour; whether for better or worse, France and the Western Europe of Catholicism functioned as inherently Other throughout the nineteenth century. The age when Diderot could extravagantly praise Richardson without excessive emphasis on the difference of language, national characteristics, or political culture was gone; in relation to all matters French, Victorian writers encountered the question of their own exceptionality.

---

19 John Stuart Mill, 'The English National Character', in *The Collected Works of John Stuart Mill*, ed. Ann Robson and John Robson, 33 vols. (University of Toronto Press, 1991), vol. XXIII, p. 721.

Mitteleuropa; or, the land of tourism

The middle decades of the nineteenth century were a heyday for British travel literature, particularly those books and sketches devoted to the reopened and tamed Continent, such as Frances Trollope's *Paris and the Parisians* (1836), Thackeray's *Paris Sketchbook* (1840), or Dickens's *Pictures from Italy* (1846). Notably, the interior of the Continent was now to receive as much attention as the comparatively swaddled worlds of France or Italy: John Tyndall's *The Glaciers of the Alps* (1860) and Leslie Stephen's *The Playground of Europe* (1871) explored a Swiss landscape that would become a gathering point of British tourism. As James Buzard has persuasively demonstrated, these new accounts of European travel are written against the very phenomenon – organized, mass tourism – that enabled their popularity; the writers of such books are anxious to present themselves as independent, even deracinated, agents of pure exploration.[20] While France and Italy were of course standard reference points, it was increasingly the German-speaking areas of Europe which were the sites for the tension between the urge for differentiation, or escape from British identity and culture, and the dismaying rediscovery of Britain abroad. More than any other European locale, Mitteleuropa often was the stage for the comedy of British tourism.

The later instalments of *Vanity Fair* offer a standard example of such comedy. For no particularly well-motivated reason, almost the entire cast of the novel relocates to the fictional principality of Pumpernickel, a thinly veiled version of Weimar, where Thackeray had spent time in the early 1830s, meeting the aged Goethe, like many of his compatriots. Thackeray provides a carefully delineated cross-section of the tourist classes of his time, those Britons who 'carry the national Goddem into every city of the Continent':

> There were jaunty young Cambridge men travelling with their tutor, and going for a reading excursion to Nonnenwerth or Königswinter: there were Irish gentlemen, with the most dashing whiskers and jewellery, talking about horses incessantly, and prodigiously polite to the young ladies on board, whom, on the contrary, the Cambridge lads and their pale-faced tutor avoided with maiden coyness: there were old Pall Mall loungers bound for Ems and Wiesbaden, and a course of waters to clear off the dinners of the season, and a little roulette and *trente-et-quarante* to keep the excitement going: there was old Methuselah, who had married his young

---

20 See James Buzard, *The Beaten Track: European Tourism, Literature, and the Ways to 'Culture', 1800–1918* (Oxford University Press, 1993).

wife, with Captain Papillon of the Guards holding her parasol and guide books: there was young May who was carrying off his bride on a pleasure tour (Mrs. Winter that was, and who had been at school with May's grandmother); there was Sir John and my lady with a dozen children, and corresponding nursemaids; and the great grandee Bareacres family that sat by themselves near the wheel, stared at everybody, and spoke to no one.[21]

And so on. Tourist Britannia is little different from Britannia at home, save for the more cramped quarters, which enforces the pleasures and discomforts of unexpected class mixing. Throughout his description of Pumpernickel and its British visitors, Thackeray is anxious to describe the comic effect of British travellers fancying themselves free of their national forms of behaviour, only in order to display those behaviours all the more openly and naively. (Naively enough that Thackeray even introduces his narrative voice as a character visiting Pumpernickel, as if his unselfconscious characters, on holiday, cannot even notice the presence of their narrator.) As for Pumpernickel itself, like many of the German principalities visited by Victorian narratives, it is a comic-opera setting, all diminutive charm and harmless diversion, its very safety functioning to starkly set off British norms. Like the Basel of Trollope's *Can You Forgive Her?* (1864), or the Dresden of *Phineas Finn* (1869) and *Phineas Redux* (1874), or the Rhenish scenery of Thackeray's own 'The Kickleburys on the Rhine' (1850), Pumpernickel is nothing more than a tourist haven: amusing to recall but fundamentally without independent existence or weight – a stage, like all tourist havens, for acting out innocent narcissisms. That the current Consort, Prince Albert, had come from the similarly miniature duchy of Saxe-Coburg and Gotha was surely relevant; German culture could be domesticated in mid-Victorian life not only because of its political and literal minorness, but also because of royal sanctions.

The tourist locales of central Europe were not always so charmingly inoffensive to Victorian writers. One need only think of Leubronn, the central European gambling den in which Eliot's *Daniel Deronda* (1876) begins, with its central character Gwendolen Harleth at the roulette table. Leubronn is the *reductio ad absurdum* of transnational tourism, the place where countless races, nationalities, and classes mix in order to drug themselves into a stupor of meaningless activity, the endless and joyless shuffle of money. Eliot notes Gwendolen's surroundings with distaste:

---

21 William Makepeace Thackeray, *Vanity Fair* (Oxford University Press, 1983), chapter 62, pp. 783–4.

'Those who were taking their pleasure at a higher strength, and were absorbed in play, showed very distinct varieties of European type: Livonian and Spanish, Graeco-Italian and miscellaneous German, English aristocratic and English plebeian. Here certainly was a striking admission of human equality.'[22] The shared experience of tourist gambling creates both an uncomfortable deracination – the 'varieties' engaged in identical pursuits – and a strange counter-racializing, in which even class distinctions, such as 'aristocratic' and 'plebeian,' become physically distinct, as if Norman and Celtic blood were suddenly, when juxtaposed in a central European milieu, starkly visible. It is a vision of Mitteleuropa as a site for rootless money-hunting: tourism at its least charming, nationality at its weakest. It is also the sort of place to which *Deronda* seeks an antidote.

That the antidote would in no small degree be located in central Europe as well – stemming from Daniel's mystical encounter with his own unknown Judaism in a Frankfurt synagogue – is part of the irony of Eliot's dyspeptic account of the nineteenth-century pleasure resort. Eliot and her partner G. H. Lewes spent much of 1854 in Weimar collecting material for Lewes's biography of Goethe, in the process of which they mingled with figures such as Liszt, Rubinstein, and Wagner, receiving an education in the musical and poetic avant-garde that even highly aware British composers lacked. In her subsequent reports on the trip, published in parts in 1855 issues of *Fraser's Magazine*, Eliot describes a sort of anti-Leubronn: a cosmopolitan site for artistic experimentation, protected by a small, civilized court, a bias-free and aesthetically curious society (Eliot notes the freedoms women enjoyed in Weimar), and a relative lack of financial motive occasioned by the small scale of the state. Within Eliot's own career, so much of it motivated by an engagement with German art and social theory, the image of central Europe oscillated uneasily between the virtues of cosmopolitanism and the vices of cultural indistinctness.

In most literary or fictional British accounts of central Europe in the period, the place of Britain within this emergent, competing world of multi-national mixture was as yet undecided. Whether imagining it as a neutral backdrop against which the comedy of Britishness emerges clearly, or a vision of what Europe as a whole was coming to – for better or for worse – central Europe, for Victorian writers, was intimately bound up with the rise of mass tourism, and the kinds of social and artistic life tourism could create.

---

22 George Eliot, *Daniel Deronda* (Harmondsworth: Penguin, 1995), chapter 1, p. 8.

Behind that multi-national life of central Europe was also a threat: the threat of British obsolescence, which emerged most clearly in a genre of 'invasion fiction' that proliferated at the end of the century. From William Le Queux's *The Great War in England in 1897* (1892) to Bram Stoker's *Dracula* (1897) and H. G. Wells's *The War of the Worlds* (1898), the threat from abroad – whether from Germany, Transylvania, or Mars – emerges from lands much like the mixed-race Mitteleuropean den of Leubronn.

Southern Europe; or, confrontations with history

In the Victorian present, Italy was the land of heroic, resurgent nationalism. The Risorgimento was occasion for widespread admiration and celebration across Victorian literary culture, as witness A. H. Clough's epistolary novel in verse *Amours de Voyage* (1858), an account of an Englishman caught up in the drama of Giuseppe Mazzini's Roman Republic in 1849, and George Meredith's *Vittoria* (1866), about the events of 1848 in northern Italy. Not all the fictional references to Italian national liberation were belated or imaginary; Elizabeth Barrett Browning's *Casa Guidi Windows* (1851) is a personal account of the birth, and demise, of the revolutionary hope of Florentines as witnessed by Barrett Browning herself, and Florence reappears as a central setting in *Aurora Leigh* (1856). Italian unification neatly combined the resurgent cultural interest in Italian art and culture with the dislike of a large, Catholic, central European empire, and as such sympathy for the Risorgimento was a dominant strain in the work of writers who felt a connection to European politics.

So much for the Victorian present; from our perspective, as compelling as such invocations as Browning's to '*bella libertà*' might be, the central Victorian imaginative response to Italy and southern Europe in this period was a reaction to its immense past. That past was pervasively mined in every Victorian genre: the Roman past in historical fiction like Bulwer Lytton's *The Last Days of Pompeii* (1834) and *Rienzi* (1835), or Walter Pater's *Marius the Epicurean* (1885); the early Italian Renaissance of Robert Browning's dramatic monologues or Pater's remarkably influential study *The Renaissance* (1873); the later Florentine empire of Eliot's *Romola* (1862–3); and the Venetian Republic of John Ruskin's *Stones of Venice* (1851–3). This is only the most partial of lists; any complete rendering of the use of Italian or southern European historical places, events, or motifs in Victorian literary culture would necessitate a study of its own. One way of summarizing the immense importance of the image of southern Europe (rather than its political actuality) is to note how much of this image is simply an image of pastness: a historical depth that is both endlessly complicated, boundlessly impressive, and relentlessly demoralizing. The Victorian writer, confronted with Italian or Greek history – and to a large extent, southern Europe *was* its history to Victorian writers – was confronted as well with the question of what, exactly, the 'history' of Britain itself was, or what kinds of 'history' Britain, and the individual British subject, owned.

Ruskin, with characteristic grandeur and bluntness, announced as much at the opening of *The Stones of Venice*.

> Since first the dominion of men was asserted over the ocean, three thrones, of mark beyond all others, have been set upon its sands: the thrones of Tyre, Venice, and England. Of the First of these great powers only the memory remains; of the Second, the ruin; the Third, which inherits their greatness, if it forget their example, may be led through prouder eminence to less pitied destruction.[23]

Confronted with Venetian decay, the British observer is forced to experience their own present as history, as the prelude to an unknown future. The image of Thomas Macaulay's New Zealander, the future observer of London in ruins, became a mid-Victorian commonplace for precisely this reason: the British observer of European decay can be re-imagined as a self-observer. The Victorian encounter with Italy thus often risks the charge of solipsism, but it is a risk of which most Victorian writers were well aware, and it factors, as we shall see in one example, into much of their thinking about their experiences of antiquity. Ruskin's intensely particular account of Venetian architecture, and the sweep of his theory of architecture's social function, largely exonerates him from the charge of solipsism – and as the example of Marcel Proust demonstrates, Ruskin's work had impact beyond British contexts – but the suspicion remains: when confronted with something so vast and alien – the many-layered pasts of southern Europe – what can one do but fall back on the tools of subjectivity, such as analogy (this is what Britain might be) or self-pity (how small I seem in comparison)?

Or, perhaps, refuge. The 'Hellenism' of Matthew Arnold's *Culture and Anarchy* (1867–8) is an antidote to the ills of British spiritual and cultural life, to its rigidities, its materialism, its self-righteousness; it is also an antidote with distinct class markers, as Hellenic culture was the unique fiefdom of

---

23 John Ruskin, *The Stones of Venice*, in *The Works of John Ruskin*, ed. E. T. Cook and Alexander Wedderburn, 39 vols. (London: George Allen, 1903–12), vol. XI, p. 17.

elite male secondary and post-secondary education. To be Greek was, in multiple ways, to be male and somehow alien, both central to and an antagonist of the culture at large. By the end of the century, Hellenism was more and more of an impossible refuge, comic and poignant alike. The struggling writers of George Gissing's *New Grub Street* (1891) only achieve some measure of happiness when they are pondering Greek metrics; in one bleak scene, Gissing imagines his two most indigent writers, Edwin Reardon and Harold Biffen, snatching a moment away from money worries:

> Then Biffen drew from the pocket of his venerable overcoat the volume of Euripides he had brought, and their talk turned once more to the land of the sun. Only when the coffee-shop was closed did they go forth again into the foggy street, and at the top of Pentonville Hill they stood for ten minutes debating a metrical effect in one of the Fragments.[24]

Reardon has, we learn, not only absorbed the usual Greek and Latin at school, but has spent time in Italy and Greece, unfitting him for the modern novel and modern commerce while providing him with an ideal that sustains his worst moments. There is nothing marketable, useful, or practical in this ideal. If anything, it represents (in its inaccessibility) the absolute distance that separates Victorian Britain from 'the land of the sun'.

Not that other, real British writers were unable to find uses for classical material. While Reardon and Biffen seem disempowered by their weight of Greek metrics, others fashioned a poetics out of encounters with the classics; as Isobel Hurst has shown, female writers of the period made constant use of classical learning, particularly as a way of addressing questions of female education. For accomplished classicists like Barrett Browning or Eliot, classical learning was a means to shape narrative rather than a disability. A more specific instance is the Victorian discovery of Sappho as a poet in, and of, fragments; Yopie Prins has argued for the importance of fragmentary Sapphic poetics in the careers of many female poets of the period, particularly the aunt-and-niece couple who wrote together under the pseudonym 'Michael Field'. For writers who, by virtue of gender or lack of formal education, came from cultural margins, the classics were often the route to a voice. For others, like Gissing's Reardon, who sought success in the mainstream of literary life, it could only be a handicap.

At its weakest, then, the image of southern Europe functions as a distant or purely internal refuge, or a wished-for transformation of British culture.

---

24 George Gissing, *New Grub Street* (Harmondsworth: Penguin, 1976), chapter 27, p. 412.

At its strongest – which is also, importantly, at its most potentially solipsistic – it is a provocation: the encounter of the self with the alien otherness of history. In this sense, Rome often functioned for Victorian authors as the most extremely European of cities: the place that condensed European culture in its entirety, and that challenged any British observer to feel at home. Thus Dorothea Brooke, from *Middlemarch*, left alone on her honeymoon to contemplate the incommensurability of self and history:

> To those who have looked at Rome with the quickening power of a knowledge which breathes a growing soul into all historic shapes, and traces out the suppressed transitions which unite all contrasts, Rome may still be the spiritual centre and interpreter of the world. But let them conceive one more historical contrast: the gigantic broken revelations of that Imperial and Papal city thrust abruptly on the notions of a girl who had been brought up in English and Swiss Puritanism, fed on meagre Protestant histories and on art chiefly of the hand-screen sort; a girl whose ardent nature turned all her small allowance of knowledge into principles, fusing her actions into their mould, and whose quick emotions gave the most abstract things the quality of a pleasure or a pain; a girl who had lately become a wife, and from the enthusiastic acceptance of untried duty found herself plunged in tumultuous preoccupation with her personal lot. The weight of unintelligible Rome might lie easily on bright nymphs to whom it formed a background for the brilliant picnic of Anglo-foreign society; but Dorothea had no such defence against deep impressions. Ruins and basilicas, palaces and colossi, set in the midst of a sordid present, where all that was living and warm-blooded seemed sunk in the deep degeneracy of a superstition divorced from reverence; the dimmer but yet eager Titanic life gazing and struggling on walls and ceilings; the long vistas of white forms whose marble eyes seemed to hold the monotonous light of an alien world: all this vast wreck of ambitious ideals, sensuous and spiritual, mixed confusedly with the signs of breathing forgetfulness and degradation, at first jarred her as with an electric shock, and then urged themselves on her with that ache belonging to a glut of confused ideas which check the flow of emotion.[25]

This is, importantly, both the confused lamentation of a young woman enduring sexual and affective disappointment and the whiplash sensation of horizons broadened too suddenly. It can be, and has been, read as a projection of Dorothea's disillusionment, but it is also much more. The thinness of British education and experience – its 'meagre' historical sense,

---

25 Eliot, *Middlemarch*, chapter 20, p. 193.

its narrowed range – is juxtaposed to a succession of incomprehensibly large historical tragedies, both Roman and Catholic. Here Whig history is effectively shattered; here British exceptionalism becomes a crippling illusion rather than a saving grace. 'Europe' here, as represented by Rome, is an idea of history as tragic accumulation, much like Walter Benjamin's Angel of History, which looks backward to see the rubble of the past accumulating at its feet. The power of the vision is its undoing: faced with such a vista of ruin, the only possible response is to flee, back to Britain, back to isolation.

Such a flight would possibly feel like a loss, but it might also come as a relief. Britain as a 'new' country, as yet bereft of the kind of tragic knowledge possessed by failed empires and vanished civilizations: the idea is as comforting as it is wounding to Victorian dignity. Few Victorian writers come as close as Eliot to touching the *mise en abyme* of historical consciousness that Europe could evoke, but every gesture of recoiling from its difference – from Brontë's Protestantism of refusal, to the happy self-regard of Thackeray's tourists, to the crisis of non-recognition undergone by Dorothea – is an implicit acknowledgment that something in European experience (or, the experience of Europe) must be resisted. Despite its occasionally cosmopolitan willingness to take on the continent, much of Victorian literature is nonetheless an effort to hold in abeyance the Other across the Channel.

Victorian empire

PABLO MUKHERJEE

In Catherine Spence's novel, *Gathered In* (1881–2) a group of Australians stop to pay their respects at Elizabeth Barrett Browning's grave in Florence. Marvelling at how the poet's reputation attracted people from the 'Australian wilds' to 'the busy centre of old civilization', the hero Kenneth suggests that 'genius is the strongest link to bind the world together'. Edith, the heroine, replies that Australians should be grateful to Britain, more than anything else, for producing English literature – a benign force that binds all English-speaking people together. Kenneth goes on: 'We are nearer to England for all practical purposes ... in Melbourne than the American colonies ever were, and I feel sure that its literature takes a very strong hold on the colonial mind.'[1] This idea of a globalized English literature is found, amongst other places, in the preface of a West Indian novel, *Creoleana* (1842). After claiming that he was not able to judge the general merit of West Indian literature, the author, J. Orderson, says that Barbadian authors had nonetheless contributed lavishly to its making, and moreover, 'there are some of her children, who should not be considered as mere drones in the republic of letters; but rather as having contributed to enlarge the hive and dilate the comb'.[2] Australia, Barbados, Florence – the physical distance between these places is apparently annulled by the power of English literature. And although Orderson uses Goethe's idea of the 'world republic of letters' to make a specific claim for the idea of a West Indian literature, Catherine Spence's Australians make clear that what we have here is not so much a republic, but an empire. A global empire of English literature, written in places as remote from each other as Barbados and Australia, but whose prime meridian, so to speak, is the 'old country' – England.

---

1 Catherine Helen Spence, *Gathered In* (Sydney University Press, 1977), chapter 56, p. 281.
2 J. W. Orderson, *Creoleana* (London: Saunders and Otley, 1842), pp. v–vi.

This literature is a force – a force as effective as military hardware, as expansive as capital, as elaborate as diplomacy – that binds and knits, in turn, both the reality and idea of Victorian England and the world.

But if English literature connects the extremities of the earth, it can also raise the spectre of an altogether more disturbing proximity that disputes the celebratory accounts of global English civilization and empire. Writing in 1890, just after the explorer Henry Morton Stanley had published his bestselling account of travels in central Africa, William Booth started his exploration of the condition of English urban 'underclasses' with a simple question and a statement – 'As there is a darkest Africa, is there also not a darkest England? Civilisation, which can breed its own barbarians, does it not also breed its own pygmies?'[3] And not just pygmies. As he surveys London, Booth sees all the features of Stanley's 'darkest Africa' exactly reproduced in London – the slave traders (pub owners!), violated 'negresses' (pretty orphan girls), slavery (sweat shops), two varieties of savages (factory workers). This, indeed, is a different kind of globalization – a world empire of suffering, perhaps – that binds the Congolese tribes and East End workers (but also, as we shall see, Indian peasants, Scottish Highlanders, Australian aborigines, West Indian plantation workers, and Canadian loggers) together in a system of destitution and death. Global expansion and global destruction, universal celebration and universal mourning, a paramount sense of achievement and a simultaneous sense of loss – these are some of the core structural elements of Victorian literature and Victorian empire. The understanding of one requires an understanding of the other.

Materialities

In 1862, people flocked to the world exhibition at London's South Kensington, where they could see, amongst other marvels, seven thousand exhibits from India alone, and numerous further items from thirty other colonies.[4] Sixteen years later, the singer and performer G. H. Macdermott was giving five performances a night in front of heaving crowds (at four different venues) of the hit song 'By Jingo', written by G. W. Hunt in response to the Russo-Turkish crisis that drew England into a bitter eastern European

---

3 'General' Booth, *In Darkest England and the Way Out* (London: International Headquarters of the Salvation Army, 1890), p. 1.
4 John M. Mackenzie, 'Empire and Metropolitan Cultures', in Andrew Porter (ed.), *The Oxford History of the British Empire, vol. 3* (Oxford and New York: Oxford University Press, 1999), p. 282.

war.[5] Elizabeth Thompson's paintings, *Calling the Roll After an Engagement*, based on the events of the same conflict, and her *Quatre-Bras*, depicting a stirring scene from the battle of Waterloo fought over half a century ago, drew long queues at exhibitions and forced John Ruskin to revise his opinions about female painters ('I had always said that no woman could paint') and concede that Thompson provided 'the first fine Pre-Raphaelite picture of battle we have had'.[6] From 1869 onwards, thousands of readers snapped up copies of the *Illustrated London News* and its rival paper, the *Graphic*, to admire the illustrations by Frederic Villiers and Melton Prior of the numerous wars that engaged British forces across the world.[7] The *Boy's* and *Girl's Own* papers (first published in 1879 and 1880 respectively), packed with stirring tales of global and local adventures of English heroes and heroines for the consumption of children and teenagers, sold 200,000 copies every week.[8] By the end of the century, the arch-imperialist and business tycoon Cecil Rhodes cast a sardonic eye on the British political scene – 'They are tumbling over each other, Liberals and Conservatives, to show which side are the greatest and most enthusiastic imperialists.'[9] In other words, it seems that the everyday life of the British people, certainly from the 1860s, was saturated with events that constantly reminded them of their particular relationship to the world, a relationship defined primarily by imperial possessions and competition with rival European powers.

Yet, the reach and scope of empire in Victorian Britain has been a matter of long and intense debate (especially amongst historians and economists). P. J. Cain, for example, concludes that empire was of relatively modest economic and political significance to British everyday life in the nineteenth century, since by his calculations it contributed, for example, 22.4 per cent of £152 million worth of imports in 1854, and between 1865 and 1914 attracted

5 Penny Summerfield, 'Patriotism and empire: Music-Hall Entertainment 1870–1914', in John M. Mackenzie (ed.), *Imperialism and Popular Culture* (Manchester and New York: Manchester University Press, 1986), p. 26.
6 John Ruskin, *Notes on Some of the Principal Pictures Exhibited in the Rooms of the Royal Academy* (1875), in *The Works of John Ruskin*, ed. E. T. Cook and Alexander Wedderburn, 39 vols. (London: George Allen, 1903–12), vol. XIV, p. 308. For a discussion of Ruskin's opinion on British popular art of the period, see John Springhall, ' "Up Guards and at Them!": British Imperialism and Popular Art, 1880–1914', in Mackenzie, *Imperialism and Popular Culture*, p. 66.
7 Springhall, ' "Up Guards" ', p. 51.
8 Mackenzie, 'Empire and Metropolitan Cultures', p. 289.
9 Cecil Rhodes, speech in Cape Town, 18 July 1899, in 'Vindex' [John Stuart Verschoyle], *Cecil Rhodes: His Political Life and Speeches, 1881–1900* (London: Chapman and Hall, 1900), p. 642.

just under half of British overseas financial investments.[10] Yet, Cain is working with a particularly narrow notion of 'empire', one that includes India and the 'white settlements' such as Canada, Australia, and South Africa, but excludes all the 'dependent' territories acquired through a constant process of war and diplomatic treaties. Moreover, Cain locates Europe and USA outside the conceptual boundaries of empire, whereas, as the subjects of Thompson's paintings and 'By Jingo' show, British interaction with these territories and peoples was also understood through a prism that can be called imperial. For a Victorian Briton, Russia, France, Turkey, Germany, even the USA, were all, at various times, rival empires. Marlow, Joseph Conrad's narrator in *Heart of Darkness* (1899), looks at a map of Africa that is coloured according to the possessions of jostling European nations. Not only was contemporary Europe imperial, but even to think themselves as Europeans, Victorians had to think themselves as successors, specifically, of Greek and Roman *empires*, as H. Rider Haggard's immensely popular novels *King Solomon's Mines* (1885) and *She* (1887), testify. Then, there was the matter of areas such as China, Latin America, and Turkey, that required, according to Lord Palmerston, 'a dressing every eight to ten years to keep them in order' and saw British military and political interventions in 1839–42 (China), 1845 (Argentina), 1857 (Peru), 1863 (Chile), 1839 and 1853–6 (on behalf of Turkey against Egypt and Russia).[11] These interventions can hardly be called anything but 'imperial'. In economic and political terms, then, it may make more sense to see a nineteenth-century world system divided between a west European 'core' dominated by Victorian Britain, and a 'periphery' consisting of 'capitalist neo-Europes' and 'tropical colonies'. The peripheries provided the core with food, metals, and labour and then absorbed the goods produced by the countries of the industrialized core. This process simultaneously 'developed' the European core and 'underdeveloped' the rest of the globe. B. R. Tomlinson shows how the total manufacturing output of European 'core' countries went up from 34.1 per cent of the world share in 1830, to 62 per cent in 1880 and 63 per cent in 1900, whereas over the same period the share of the 'tropical' peripheries went from 63.3 per cent to 23.3 per cent, and finally to 13.4 per cent.[12]

---

10 P. J. Cain, 'Economics and Empire: The Metropolitan Context', in Porter, *British Empire*, pp. 42–50.

11 Martin Lynn, 'British Policy, Trade, and Informal Empire in Mid-Nineteenth Century', in Porter, *British Empire*, pp. 110–12.

12 B. R. Tomlinson, 'Economics and Empire: The Periphery and the Imperial Economy', in Porter, *British Empire*, pp. 65–71.

Victorian empire, then, cannot simply be conceived of as the territories and wealth directly commanded by Britain. Rather, it emerges as a dominant element of a global system that drew all parts of the earth into a close network of exploitation, extraction, profit, power, loss, and devastation. There are scarcely any areas of Victorian British life that were not touched by this relationship, although the charge of it varied throughout the century. Victorian literature in English, therefore, absorbed, produced, reproduced, and refracted this world imperial condition. And, although here we will be looking at English literature primarily written in Victorian Britain, the white settlements, and to some extent, India, the patterns that emerge should draw our attention to the fact that this literature was, like Britain's empire, global in its reach.

Networks

In 1820, the voyages from the English port of Southampton to the imperial outpost of Calcutta, in eastern India, took anything between five to eight months, one way. By 1855, the same trip took a little over a month, usually no more than fifty days. The traditional route around the southern tip of Africa, which took in 11,380 miles of often dreary sailing, was now cut down to a more manageable 7,710 miles, thanks to the building of the Suez Canal (opened 1869) and the standardization of the steam engines on ships. Calcutta, relatively speaking, suddenly seemed no longer located in the realms of the fabled east, but in territories of more mundane dimensions. Other technological feats contributed to this radical shrinking of time and space in the Victorian world. In India alone, a thousand miles of railway track had been laid by 1860, and by early 1870, more than five thousand miles of the vast country were criss-crossed by these iron veins along which flowed arms, goods, people that energized the empire. Overhead wires sang alongside the railway lines with the 480,000 telegrams written in the single year of 1869. Comparable processes of the development of this 'informational empire' could be seen in similar 'public works' projects undertaken in Canada, Africa, and Australia.[13] And of course, all these marvels could be found in abundant concentration in Britain itself.

Little wonder then, that images of wires, tracks, trains, cables crop up repeatedly in Victorian literature. George Eliot used the web as a central,

13 Robert Kubicek, 'British Expansion, Empire and Technological Change', in Porter, *British Empire*, pp. 251–60.

guiding metaphor in *Middlemarch* (1871), and a key scene of the novel superbly captures the ambivalence people felt towards the railways, an agent both of change and destruction as well as unstoppable progress. Similar ambivalence about the railways can be found throughout Victorian and, indeed, European literature in the nineteenth century. Dickens fuses the train with thoughts of death in *Dombey and Son* (1846–8), in Tolstoy's *Anna Karenina* (1877) it is a vehicle both of desire and suicide, and Zola's *La Bête Humaine* (1877) depends on it for an examination of lust and murder. This literary ambivalence towards the railways brings into view a crucial component of the Victorian *zeitgeist*. A world empire depended on a smooth flow of information, arms and armies, goods, settlers, and administration. Yet, the space–time alteration brought about by the technologies that now materially bound different societies ushered in a revolution in the senses about proximity, belonging, and difference. The Australian aboriginal peoples, Canadian trappers, Chinese labourers in Hong Kong, Zulu warriors, and village cricketers from Kent, were all thrown together by a global web or net of wires, cables, ships, and railways. But could this mean that they were all the children of empire in the same way? Let us consider two kinds of network that dominated Victorian thoughts and actions – biological and technological.

Blood

At the climax of Rider Haggard's bestseller *She* (1887), the horrified group of English adventurers watch as the 'celestially beautiful' and 'pure Arabic' Ayesha begins shrinking – 'smaller she grew and smaller still, till she was no larger than a baboon. Now the skin was puckered into a million wrinkles, and on the shapeless face was the stamp of unutterable age ... no larger than a big monkey ... it was the *same* woman.'[14] More than Ayesha's death, it is the thought of her being at the same time 'racially' pure (therefore supremely desirable) as well as a degenerate (African) animal that provides the titillating thrust of Rider Haggard's prose. In becoming a baboon, of course, Ayesha joins Rider Haggard's Gagool from his previous best-seller *King Solomon's Mines* (1885), to form a benighted sisterhood of fictional African women who are each desired, feared, and loathed to the extent that they can hardly be called women, or even human, any more – 'there is Gagaoola, if she was a woman and not a

14 H. Rider Haggard, *She* (Oxford University Press, 1991), chapter 26, p. 294.

fiend. But she was a hundred at least, and therefore not marriageable, so I don't count her.'[15] Victorian narrators gaze at African men, too, with a highly similar mixture of desire and loathing. Ignosi's splendid physique is lovingly described in *King Solomon's Mines*, and his true identity as a Kukuana king is revealed as he stands naked in front of the admiring explorers. But this, the perfect African body, is balanced by loathsome descriptions of Twala, Ignosi's evil twin, who is finally slain by Sir Henry. If Victorian networks had made whole new objects of desire available to men of the British ruling classes, it also invigorated categories such as 'race' in order to differentiate between the desired subjects and those (men) who were empowered to desire.

The notion of a racial difference, coded in blood, hardened even as the physical distance between people vanished. Waldo, the unworldly boy growing up in Olive Schreiner's African farm, perfectly demonstrates this tension between the sense of being linked to the world, to other forms of life, and the dread that fuels the need to distinguish one's own self from these other forms. Living in the isolated vast expanse of the southern African veldts, Waldo likes to feel 'strange life' beating against him, as he imagines being with a medieval monk, little Malay boys, Hindu philosophers, and 'kaffir' witch doctors. At the same moment, the sight of a native southern African man going to fetch his food elicits thoughts about racial difference and decay – 'Will his race melt away in the heat of collision with a higher? Are the men of the future to see his bones only in museums – a vestige of one link that spanned between the dog and the white man?'[16] Upon 'discovering' the pagan tribes of north-west Afghanistan, Daniel Dravot, the 'man who would be king' of Rudyard Kipling's short story of that name (1888) cries, 'These men aren't niggers; they're English! Look at their eyes – look at their mouth ... They're the Lost Tribes, or something like it, and they've grown to be English.'[17] Yet, this imagined link, rather than facilitating the dream of empire, turns it into a ghastly nightmare. Upon discovering that those who they had thought to be gods were mortals like them, the tribesmen kill Dravot and maim his companion Carnehan, who comes back to Bombay clutching Dravot's severed head, having lost his own mind in the process. In the Canadian writer

---

15 H. Rider Haggard, *King Solomon's Mines* (Oxford University Press, 2006), chapter 1, p. 10.
16 'Ralph Iron' (Olive Schreiner), *The Story of an African Farm* (Oxford University Press, 1992), Part II, chapter 8, p. 195.
17 Rudyard Kipling, 'The Man Who Would be King' (1888), in *Collected Stories*, ed. Robert Gottlieb (London: Everyman, 1994), pp. 243–4.

James de Mille's fantasy novel, *A Strange Manuscript found in a Copper Cylinder* (1888), Adam More discovers a part-'Caucasian', part-'Semitic' tribe living in the Antarctic, but any celebration of the discovery of this kinship is premature, as the tribe practises a death-cult, and intend to sacrifice and eat the horrified More, who then contrives to escape with (obviously) the help of a beautiful local woman.

All these lost tribes, shrinking women, cannibal men, and 'degenerate' aboriginals signal a fundamental contradiction of life in the Victorian empire. The unprecedented expansion of global networks brought with it a sense of kinship between people living at the 'core' of England and those living in the 'peripheries' of Africa, Asia, Latin America, and even Scotland and southern Europe. Yet, the material reality of the mode in which these networks were established, that of conquest and exploitation, meant that this kinship could not in any sense be admitted as being equal. A hierarchic category of difference had to be established: one that could justify the extent of global inequality and suffering. The racist and racial theorist James Froude admitted that there is no congenital difference in the capacities between white and non-white 'races', but he thought the difference lay in 'the centuries of training and discipline which have given us [that is, British people] the start in the race'.[18] Henry Morton Stanley thought a pygmy of the central Congo was to him far more venerable than any other wonder of the world, but only because she or he represented 'the oldest types of primeval man ... eternally exiled by their vice, to live the life of human beasts in morass and fen and jungle wild'.[19] Mary Kingsley wrote of the pleasures and dangers of pursuing the African mind – 'Stalking the wild West African idea is one of the most charming pursuits in the world ... I must warn you also that your own mind requires protection when you send it stalking the savage idea through the tangled forests, the dark caves, the swamps and fogs of the Ethiopian intellect.'[20] One of the things that makes Conrad's *Heart of Darkness* such a significant novel is precisely the meticulous exposure of the logic of the hierarchical categorizing of life forms and space in Kurtz's injunction – 'exterminate all the brutes!'[21]

18 James Anthony Froude, *The English in the West Indies* (London: Longman, Green & Co., 1888), p. 124.
19 Henry M. Stanley, *In Darkest Africa*, 2 vols. (London: S. Low, Marston, Searle and Rivington, 1890), vol. II, pp. 40–1.
20 Mary Kingsley, *Travels in West Africa* (London: Everyman, 1987), pp. 160–6.
21 Joseph Conrad, *Heart of Darkness* (London: Penguin, 2007), p. 62.

Iron

What distinguished the 'higher' from the 'lower', in the Victorian hierarchy of human kinship, was their ability to make and build things. Civilized Europeans killed with Henry-Martini rifles and Gatling machine guns, as the numerous passages in Henry Stanley's African travelogues attest, while savages had spears, and at best, outdated blunderbusses. Manchester, London, Edinburgh, Paris, Vienna – the lines and planning of these cities were said to be distinctively modern and progressive, as opposed to the haphazard and jumbled mass of Delhi, Constantinople, Peking – seats of decayed and degenerated societies. Indeed, some of the 'neo-Europes' claimed to be the true seats of modernity, having outstripped even the European cores in the race of material progress. In *The Recollections of Geoffrey Hamlyn* (1859), Henry Kingsley's Scottish hero Kenneth is shocked at the dismissive tones adopted by his Australian relatives towards the venerable city of Edinburgh in their eulogies for Melbourne. A little later in the book, a disguised European aristocrat compares the decay of Venice to the making of Melbourne in epic terms – 'I have seen what but a small moiety of the world . . . has never seen before . . . I have seen Melbourne.'[22] Gazing at Quebec, French and Swedish aristocrats in the Canadian William Kirby's historical thriller *The Golden Dog* (1877) see 'old France transplanted, transfigured . . . the glory of North America as the motherland is the glory of Europe'.[23]

Whether in the 'new' or 'old' Europe, cities, guns, factories, ships, railways, roads were all thought to stand for a specifically 'core' European modernity. Since they not only bound the world in an iron network, but also distributed unequal power, the rest of the world was seen as either imperfectly modern, or as hopelessly primitive. The peoples of these regions of the world had to be made to follow the tracks of modernity in a dutiful fashion, but always at a respectful distance, or they would either face Kurtzian extermination or obliteration as beings dwelling outside the space and time curvature of the 'contemporary', or they would be expected to co-operate in assimilation – that is, adopting the habits and values of dominant Western culture. So, where these networks brought forward evidence of radically different trajectories of the 'modern', these had to be

---

22 Henry Kingsley, *The Recollections of Geoffrey Hamlyn* (St Lucia: University of Queensland Press, 1996), p. 281.
23 William Kirby, *The Golden Dog* (New York and Montreal: Lovell, Adam, and Wesson, 1877), p. 14.

accommodated, however uneasily, into Victorian fictions. The ruins of an African city in Zimbabwe, the social and political organization of native Canadian tribes, the metal work of western and southern African tribes, the military organizational capacity of Sudanese tribesmen, religious practices of Saudi Arabians and Afghan mountain tribes, Indian cotton-weavers – the historical evidence of the non-European origin of these 'civilizational' activities were transformed in the Victorian imagination as being either *actually* European or the fossilized remains of a previous stage of human evolution. When James de Mille's sailors discover a copper cylinder at sea they are puzzled by its workmanship and debate whether it is Chinese or Moroccan. It turns out to be the handiwork of a tribe that has built an urban civilization in the Antarctic ice: 'Here in all directions there were unmistakable signs of human life – the outlines of populous cities and busy towns and hamlets; roads winding far away along the plain . . . and mighty works of industry in the shape of massive structures, terraced slopes, long rows of arches, ponderous pyramids, and battlemented walls.'[24] But Antarctic aboriginals cannot be allowed to have such civilized attributes, and it is soon revealed that the tribe was originally from the Mediterranean, and were 'part-Caucasian' and 'part-semitic'. Similarly, Rider Haggard's adventurers in *King Solomon's Mines* marvel at the intricate metalwork of the chain mail worn by the royal warriors of Kukuanaland, but duly discover that the Africans cannot make it: the armour was handed to them by ancient Phoenician traders. And his Amhaggars, the secret tribe of *She*, are powerful precisely because they are ruled by Ayesha, whose genealogy is linked to that of the ancient Greeks. The Canadian explorer Alexander Ross is struck by the 'grand and imposing' sight of a native Canadian tribal gathering on the plains, where a town-sized wigwam camp has sprung up from nothing, throbbing with business and pleasure. Yet rather than being a mark of civic ingenuity, he interprets this as a view of 'life without disguise; the feelings, the passions, the propensities, as they ebb and flow in the savage breast'.[25] And for Richard Burton, the oriental city invokes not modernity, but its dead and ghostly counterpart: 'Not a line is straight, the tall dead walls of the Mosques slope over their massy buttresses . . . Briefly, the whole view is so strange, so fantastic, so ghostly, that it seems preposterous to imagine that in

---

24 James de Mille, *A Strange Manuscript found in a Copper Cylinder* (London: Chatto & Windus, 1888), p. 54.
25 Alexander Ross, *The Fur Hunters of the Far West: A Narrative of Adventures in the Oregon and Rocky Mountains*, 2 vols. (London: Smith, Elder & Co., 1855), vol. 1, p. 21.

such places human beings like ourselves can be born, and live through life, and carry out the command "increase and multiply"'.[26] Things that dispute the norms of Victorian modernity can only be imagined either as being a lesser version of it, or as belonging to the realm of the savage and the dead.

Possessions

Even as the Victorians' sense of connection with the world was enhanced by modern capitalism and empire, the very essence of these systems ensured a simultaneous enhancement in their sense of entitlement and possession. It became difficult, if not impossible, to look at countries, peoples, societies, and environments, as anything other than property. For Charles Dilke, giving India up would not only be a crushing blow to British prosperity, but would unleash the 'domino-effect' of the growth of 'separatist feelings' in Canada, South Africa, Australia, and the rest of the British empire.[27] In a letter written in 1841, Lord Palmerston neatly captured the motor that drove the relentless global expansion:

> The rivalship of European manufacturers is fast excluding our production from the markets of Europe and we must unremittingly endeavour to find in other parts of the world new vents for the produce of our industry ... Abyssinia, Arabia, the countries on the Indus, and the new markets in China, will at no distant period give a most important extension to the range of our foreign commerce.[28]

Tennyson expressed the same sentiments more poetically as he imagined an aged *Ulysses* (1842) – 'It little profits that an idle king, / By this still hearth, among these barren crags, / Match'd with an aged wife, I mete and dole / Unequal laws unto a savage race, / That hoard, and sleep, and feed, and know not me.'[29] The hearth, the existing wealth of a nation, the comforts of familiarity, can no longer be seen as enough – they are of 'little profit' and synonymous with cursed idleness. Instead, like Palmerston dreaming about China, Arabia, Abyssinia, and India, Ulysses too, must move forever on – 'Tho' much is taken, much abides; and tho' / We are not now that strength

---

26 Richard F. Burton, *Personal Narrative of a Pilgrimage to al-Madinah and Meccah* (New York: Dover, 1964), p. 89.

27 Charles Dilke, *Problems of Greater Britain*, 2 vols. (London and New York: Macmillan, 1890), vol. II, p. 3.

28 Lynn, 'British Policy', p. 106.

29 Alfred Tennyson, 'Ulysses,' in *The Poems of Tennyson*, ed. Christopher Ricks, 3 vols. (Longman: Harlow, 1987), vol. I, p. 615, lines 1–5.

which in old days / Moved earth and heaven, that which we are, we are,– / One equal temper of heroic hearts, / Made weak by time and fate, but strong in will / To strive, to seek, to find, and not to yield.'[30]

The very essence of the new lands that the Victorians found themselves in was thought to rest in their capacity to yield in a quite different sense. Alexander Ross waxed eloquent about the fruitfulness of Canada in dedicating his book to his patron Sir George Simpson – the country was already sending scholars to British universities, it bore a network of churches that increased the numbers of the faithful amongst the native tribes, and 'two hundred importers from England, with capital almost exclusively of colonial creation' had been created. Moreover, the native tribes excelled, in his eyes, as labour force, being even better than the coal-heavers of Lancashire, the Liverpool dockers, west African porters, and other peoples who formed the 'sinews of empire'.[31] In addition to these people of the new lands, the land itself was imagined as giving itself up to the embrace of the Victorians. In Australian poet Charles Harpur's popular *The Creek of the Four Graves* (1883), the archetypal settler goes forth to tame the wilderness into 'wider pastures for his fast / Increasing flocks and herds'. But as darkness falls, the wilderness grows ever stranger, with the forest echoing with eerie voices, till with a diabolical yell of rage, 'Yea, beings in their dread inherited hate / Awful, vengeful as hell's worst fiends, are come / In vengeance! For behold from the long grass / And nearer brakes arise the bounding forms / of painted savages.' If the trope of an enemy (usually painted savages) who contest the possession of the land is familiar, the resolution of Harpur's poem is less so. Pursued by the native Australians, the pioneer takes shelter in a cave on a rock face beneath a knot of trees. The savages cannot find him – 'They marvelled; passing strange to them it seemed; / Some old mysterious fables of their race, / That brooded o'er the valley and the creek, / Returned upon their minds, and fear-struck all / And silent, they withdrew.'[32] The land itself – its caves and nooks and crannies and trees and the myths that surround them – protects the settler against its original inhabitants, thereby also blessing his pursuit of widening his pastures, presumably on a more convenient occasion.

---

30 *Ibid.*, p. 620, lines 65–70. 31 Ross, *Fur Hunters*, p. iv.
32 Donovan Clarke (ed.), *Charles Harpur* (Sydney and London: Angus and Robertson, 1963), p. 10.

Sometimes, Victorians saw in the land what appeared to be the universal drama of colonization. Mary Kingsley found in the astonishing generative capacities of the west African mangrove forests an entire 'natural' history of empire – the pioneer dwarf roots struggling to establish themselves on the hostile tidal mud flats, and in their eventual deaths paving the way for the secondary roots to conquer the territory.[33] By and large, the urge to convert what was thought of as wilderness and forests to more 'civilized' and profitable landscapes made the former, just as much as their inhabitants, appear as enemies who must be understood and then conquered. 'Naturalists' who catalogue the unfamiliar landscape, even as 'pioneers' shoot the native animals and humans, populate Victorian literature. Often, they are fused into the single figure of the adventurer who is a man of wisdom as well as a man of blood – Rider Haggard's explorers, Richard Burton, Conrad's Kurtz, Henry Morton Stanley. Indeed, Stanley's account of his African travels is as notable for his slaughter of 'hostile' tribes as it is for the militant terms he uses to describe his progress – hacking, chopping, outflanking, and charging the trees – indeed, the whole eco-system of the central Congo. When he comes across animals, Stanley spends loving pages describing how he killed them. When he stumbles on human beings, he kidnaps them for 'measurement'. Looking at a woman thus captured, Stanley writes 'She was as plump as a thanksgiving Turkey or a Christmas goose; her breasts glistened with the sheen of old ivory, and as she stood with clasped hands drooping below – though her body was nude – she was the very picture of young modesty.'[34] A human body is seen in terms both of food (turkey, goose) and goods (ivory). To look at the 'wilderness' and its people, is also to capture, kill, measure, possess, and consume.

Yet, as Conrad's Marlow dryly suggests, the conquest of the earth, 'which mostly means the taking it away from those who have a different complexion or slightly flatter nose than ourselves', was not a pretty thing if one looked into it too much. Endemic in Victorian writing was also the nagging feeling that there was something drastically wrong with the mode of this sense of entitlement, with how the earth became possession. Not many writers possessed Stanley's pious ability to celebrate the enslavement and slaughter of fellow human beings. By the end of

---

33 Kingsley, *Travels in West Africa*, p. 26.   34 Stanley, *In Darkest Africa*, vol. II, p. 44.

the century, Conrad could present Marlow's observation of the effects of European possession of Africa on Africans in painfully direct terms:

> I could see every rib, the joints of their limbs were like knots in a rope; each had an iron collar on his neck ... They were dying slowly – it was very clear. They were not enemies, they were not criminals, they were nothing earthly now, – nothing but black shadows of disease and starvation, lying confusedly in the greenish gloom.[35]

Rudyard Kipling matches the insight of Conrad when he describes how two English men bind and torture an Indian leper to extract information from him:

> I understood then how men and women and little children can endure to see a witch burnt alive ... though the Silver Man had no face, you could see horrible feelings passing through the slab that took its place, exactly as waves of heat play across red-hot iron – gun barrels for instance. Strickland shaded his eyes with his hands for a moment, and we got to work. This part is not to be printed.[36]

When Henry Kingsley's muscular Christian Australian settler rhapsodizes about the 'greatest colony of the greatest race in the world' he is interrupted by the worldly European doctor who reminds him that his claims were made at the expense of the Irish, Jews, Germans, Chinese, and the 'blackfellow', whose claims are always ignored.[37]

This historical awareness of their possessions being contested and their wealth being dependent on absolute force, helped fuse the trope of treasure (or wealth) with guilt and trauma in the writing of the Victorians. In their most successful imaginative acts, writers saw such treasure or wealth as a disruptive force in domestic Britain, exposing the structures of inequity that lay at the core of their contemporary society. Before David Balfour can inherit the riches that he has been denied by his uncle in Robert L. Stevenson's *Kidnapped* (1886), he briefly becomes a white slave on a Scottish ship, is rescued by a flamboyant Jacobite who opens his eyes to the English devastation of the Scottish highlands, and witnesses the poverty amongst the once independent clans there. Likewise, in his *Treasure Island* (1884), the exciting narrative of Jim Hawkins's hunt for

---

35 Conrad, *Heart of Darkness*, pp. 63–5.
36 Kipling, 'The Mark of the Beast' (1890), in *Collected Stories*, p. 304.
37 Kingsley, *Travels in West Africa*, p. 442.

treasure is simultaneously an exposure of the brutality of English navy and marine life that sustained the global empire. As Jim acknowledges when he finds the treasure – 'How many it had cost in the amassing, what blood and sorrow, what good ships scuttled on the deep ... what shame and lies and cruelty, perhaps no man alive could tell.'[38]

Perhaps the most sustained, and amongst the most remarkable Victorian treatments of guilt, imperial wealth, and domestic inequities can be found in Wilkie Collins's *The Moonstone* (1868). The novel begins with the account of an English officer murdering and then stealing a priceless jewel in the famous siege of Srirangapatnam, fortress of the Indian ruler, Tipu Sultan. The main action consists of the recovery of this diamond by three 'avenging' Indians from the English descendants of the officer. This story of theft, detection, and recovery of the jewel is told in a way that exposes the oppressive class and gender relations of Victorian Britain. The female servant of the grand country manor, suspected of the theft because of her past, and suffering from an unrequited love for the hero, Franklin Blake, commits suicide (triggering a *J'accuse*-style monologue from her friend that fuses an utopic vision of workers' rebellion with that of a feminist 'sisterhood' in an extraordinary manner). Franklin Blake's moral weakness is exposed further by the silent sufferings of the heroine, Rachel, who thinks Frank is guilty of stealing the jewel (he has removed it while sleepwalking under the influence of opium). The 'real' thief turns out to be Godfrey Ablewhite, the hypocritical 'Christian' hero who is tracked down and murdered by the Indians. And the key character who scientifically proves Franklin's (relative) innocence is Ezra Jennings, a dying 'half-caste' medical student who has long suffered from British racism. This bare outline can do little justice to the narrative sophistication and human comedy with which Collins exposes the networks that bind imperial possessions and domestic inequities. The process that converted the entire world into commodities to be extracted and possessed was also necessarily at work at the heart of Victorian Britain. Sitting by the quicksands, Rosanna Spearman, the doomed servant, thinks she sees hundreds of suffocating people struggling under the undulating surface. Although the Indians manage to achieve some justice by heroically rescuing their property, the beginning and the end of the book suggest that the cycle of historical despoliation is hardly about to end.

---

38 Robert Louis Stevenson, *Treasure Island* (London: Penguin, 1999), chapter 33, p. 185.

Deaths

Writing to her sister about her journey through north and central India in the late 1830s, Emily Eden exclaimed 'You cannot conceive of the horrible sights we see, particularly children; perfect skeletons in many cases, their bones through their skin, without a rag of clothing, and are utterly unlike human creatures ... I am sure there is no sort of violent atrocity I should not commit for food, with a starving baby.'[39] She was passing through one of the many districts in India that would be repeatedly hit by famine throughout the Victorian period. The conquest of the earth did not, by any means, only mean shooting to kill. It also involved condemning millions to the agony of slow death by starvation and disease in the name of trade, modernization, and progress. The conversion of the forests into pastures and trade routes in Asia and Africa, and the de-industrialization of hand-powered manufacturing bases there, destroyed flexible social welfare networks that had been built over centuries.[40] During times of droughts and other environmental disasters – such as those caused by El Niño cycles – the iron laws of the modern market, where profit was infinitely more valuable than welfare, condemned global millions to unspeakable deaths. In Victorian India alone, between 1876 and 1902, anything between 12 and 30 million people died of hunger. Globally, there may have been between 50 to 60 million untimely deaths.[41] The English journalist William Digby, travelling in India half a century after Emily Eden, was in no doubt that the 'unnecessary deaths of millions of Indians' would be the most notable monument of the British empire.[42] For was it not curious, he enquired, that the Victorian imperial administration ensured that most of India's rice and wheat surplus had been exported to London between 1875 and 1878, while Indians died in their millions in their own land? Was it not telling that railway lines and telegraphs – those icons of progress – instead of speeding relief to the victims, contributed instead to hoarding and price hikes that in fact sealed the victims' fates? Was it not illuminating that, faced with deaths on an almost unimaginable scale, the official representative of the 'higher' form of civilization – the imperial Viceroy Lord Lytton – issued strict orders against

---

39 Emily Eden, *Up the Country* (London and St Ives: Virago, 1983), p. 65.
40 Tomlinson, 'Economics and Empire', p. 65.
41 Mike Davis, *Late Victorian Holocausts: El Niño Famines and the Making of the Third World* (London and New York: Verso, 2001), p. 7.
42 William Digby, *'Prosperous' British India: A Revelation from Official Records* (London: Unwin, 1901), p. 122.

any government intervention to reduce the price of food and denounced 'humanitarian hysterics'?[43] But contrary to accusations of incompetence and even 'latent' insanity, Lytton seems to have understood, like Kurtz, the essence of capital and empire. The wealth of the 'core' European nations must necessarily depend on the extermination of the brutes.

Victorian literature responded in various ways to this globalization of death. One was to see death as the essence of other, less civilized societies. James de Mille's Antarctic tribe displays all the attributes of progress – cities, ships, weapons, and even forms of air travel. But, 'with them death is the highest blessing. They all love death and seek after it. To die for another is immortal glory.'[44] Likewise, Rider Haggard's Kukuanas in *King Solomon's Mines* and his Amhaggars in *She* both indulge in ritual celebrations involving mass slaughter, cannibal rites, and mummification. The power of Ayesha, in *She*, lies in the fact that she has found a way to go beyond the human biological life-cycle into a much longer geological duration – 'Nature hath her animating spirit as well as man, who is Nature's child, and he who can find that spirit, and let it breathe upon him, shall live with her life.' But her pronouncement 'naught really dies' is shown to be horribly wrong, as instead of semi-eternal life, the fountain of fire turns her body into a pageant of evolutionary degeneration.[45] In the wasted lands of Asia, Africa, but also Ireland and Transylvania – Victorian imagination, in attempting to shy away from the glare of historical causes, would find death arising from *within* the native societies. Ghost stories would be whispered, the Gothic mode became rampant.

Yet, the feeling that death was not all *their* business, that it might somehow be *ours* as well, haunted Victorians. In 'Gone' (1876), the Australian poet Adam Lindsay Gordon seeks courage from the fate of 'he whose bones in yon desert bleach'd' and urges all to accept the sufferings of the living as inevitable and inconsequential in the face of the certainty of death: 'No tears are needed – our cheeks are dry, / We have none to waste upon living woe; / Shall we sigh for one who has ceased to sigh / Having gone, my friends, where we all must go?'[46] This contemplation of mortality is transformed into an individual longing for death by Tennyson in 'Tithonus' (1842) where, held captive by the immortal goddess, the legendary Greek

---

43 Davis, *Late Victorian Holocausts*, p. 31.   44 De Mille, *Strange Manuscript*, p. 100.
45 Haggard, *She*, chapter 13, pp. 152, 154.
46 Adam Lindsay Gordon, 'Gone', in *Sea Spray and Smoke Drift* (London and Melbourne, 1911), p. 19, lines 52–6.

looks with longing at all-pervasive death – 'The woods decay, the woods decay and fall, / The vapors weep their burthen to the ground, / Man comes and tills the field and lies beneath, / And after many a summer dies the swan.'[47]

A distinctive Victorian move was to extend this heightened consciousness of the inevitable, even impending, death of the individual, to that of human history, and more specifically, to imperial history. Victorian writing is full of melancholic notes on the passing of human imperial civilizations. Tennyson's dying King Arthur offers the consoling thought that the cataclysmic dying of eras is a part of the divine plan – 'The old order changeth, yielding place to new, / And God fulfils himself in many ways, / Lest one good custom should corrupt the world.'[48] Others were less sanguine. Looking at the Thames gleaming in the evening light, Conrad's Marlow is reminded of the 'darkness' that once pervaded England. Here, human individual and historical mortality cannot be distinguished – 'We live in a flicker – may it last as long as the old earth keeps rolling! But darkness was here yesterday.'[49] The fear that England would be doomed, in the cycle of historical life and death, to darkness once again could never really be kept at bay. The sight of the dying Indian masses triggers a dystopic fantasy in Emily Eden: 'An odd world certainly! Perhaps two thousand years hence, when the art of steam has been forgotten ... some black Governor-General of England will be marching through its southern provinces, and will go and look at some ruins, and doubt whether London ever was a large town, and will feed some white-looking skeletons.'[50] Eden is not capable of documenting the culpability of the Victorian imperial system for the mass deaths she was witnessing (she was travelling with her brother, the viceroy). But she could transform historical guilt and fear into a fantastic vision of the future death of imperial Britain in a world ruled by Asians and Africans. Olive Schreiner's Waldo, too, is haunted by visions of universal death. 'He saw before him a long stream of people, a great dark multitude, that moved in one direction ... He thought of how that stream had rolled on through all long ages of the past – how the Greeks and Romans had gone over; the countless millions of China and India, they were going over now.'[51] Yet, Waldo is well aware that the disappearance of human societies, unlike the

---

47 Tennyson, 'Tithonus' (1859), in *Poems*, vol. II, p. 607, lines 1–4.
48 Tennyson, 'Morte D'Arthur' (1845), in *Poems*, vol. III., p. 7, lines 240–2.
49 Conrad, *Heart of Darkness*, p. 50.   50 Eden, *Up the Country*, pp. 66–7.
51 Schreiner, *African Farm*, Part I, chapter I, p. 37.

death of stars, is triggered by historical forces. Meditating on the cave drawings by ancient southern African people, he marvels at the aesthetic powers of these so-called 'primitives'. Where are they now? – 'the Boers have shot them all, so we never see a little yellow face peeping out among the stones ... And the wild bucks have gone, and those days, and we are here. But we will be gone soon, and only the stones will lie on here.'[52] Waldo, like Walter Benjamin's Angel of History, can only look at the debris of humanity piling up: 'civilization', 'progress' and other categories offer up their bare flesh and bone – 'there is no justice. The ox dies in the yoke beneath his master's whip ... The back man is shot like a dog, and it all goes well with the shooter. The innocent are accused, and the accuser triumphs.'[53] Haunted by the globalized production of death, writers of the Victorian empire could not wipe visions of apocalypse from their eyes.

Readings

We began by invoking networks, webs, and confluences to suggest that the binding of Britain (and within Britain, of the 'provinces' to London) to the world through the twin thrusts of capital and empire was the central feature of Victorian England. We have detected, through a rapid montage of patterns that appear in novels, letters, poetry, and travelogues what Raymond Williams termed the 'structures of feeling' that underpin the contradictions and resolutions that Victorian literature offered. Can we draw some general conclusions as to the relationship between Victorian empire and Victorian literature?

First, if we accept that Victorian empire was a process of globalization, then we have to stretch the category of 'Victorian English literature' beyond its conventionally understood boundaries. It makes no sense to treat Australian, Canadian, Indian, African, Scottish, and Caribbean texts from the period as not Victorian, given that they constantly reflected on their literary, material, and ideological relationship with England (even when these claim and achieve successful breakage with 'English' models). These texts were largely published by English publishing companies, circulated through the imperial communication networks, and reacted to the cultural, political, and material norms of a London-centric England. This is not a claim for the derivative nature of all Victorian English writing, but a suggestion that we

---

52 *Ibid.*, Part i, chapter 2, p. 50.   53 *Ibid.*, Part ii, chapter i, section vii, p. 149.

read this writing as a system of world or global English – a system that was unevenly developed, just as capital and empire forced an uneven development of the world. We must always pay scrupulous attention to the 'local' historical, material, and aesthetic specificities of texts produced in the disparate parts of the world. But we must also, together with Dickens, Eliot, Tennyson, Kipling, read Marcus Clarke, Olive Schreiner, Flora Annie Steele, Charles Harpur, and Catherine Spence to grasp the true extent of Victorian writing.

Second, this globally networked nature of Victorian English literature obliges us to read single texts through multiple lenses. Edward Said's reading of Jane Austen's *Mansfield Park* (1814) scandalized scholars with its suggestion that the history and literature of British plantations in Antigua was central to our understanding of the 'domestic' story of Fanny Price.[54] The normative reading of Austen's novel treats the references to the Bertram estates in Antigua either as casual asides or sees Said's analysis as a malicious attempt to portray Austen's novel as having a pro-slavery bias.[55] Yet, Said's concern is not to pass judgments on Austen's views on slavery (he dismisses such critical tack as 'silly' and hails the novel as a serious and sophisticated one), but to show how she 'synchronizes domestic with international authority' by exposing the connections between imperial property and notions of law, propriety, civility.[56] In fact, Victorian literature is distinguished by such sophisticated awareness between 'domestic' and 'international' networks. Charles Dickens's Dombey's stifling and brooding patriarchal authority is explicitly linked to his empire of global trade, and what makes Pip's life intolerable in *Great Expectations* is precisely the knowledge that his gentlemanly aspirations depend on Australian wealth channelled back to England by an escaped convict. When George Eliot's Dorothea breaks down and weeps in front of the majestic Roman ruins and paintings in Italy, she is overwhelmed not only by the misery of her new marriage but by the crushing historical awareness of the majesty and passing of the great ancient European empires and the lessons this transience holds for the 'new Rome' – Britain. It is possible to read Arthur Morrison's bestselling *A Child of the Jago* (1896) as an exposé of the criminalization and sufferings of a precise neighbourhood in London's East End. But this reading becomes infinitely

---

54 Edward Said, *Culture and Imperialism* (London: Vintage, 1994), pp. 100–16.
55 See, for example, Susan Fraiman, 'Jane Austen and Edward Said: Gender, Culture and Imperialism', *Critical Inquiry* 21 (1995), pp. 805–21, and Gabrielle D. V. White, *Jane Austen in the Context of Abolition* (New York: Palgrave, 2006).
56 Said, *Culture and Imperialism*, p. 104.

richer when we see how precisely Morrison echoes General Booth's sentiments by reproducing exact features of Stanley's 'darkest Africa' in his London. Morrison's 'Jago' is shrouded with an equatorial darkness and heat, is populated by warring, barely human tribes (the Ranns and the Learys), features tropes of cannibalism (Sally Green), has a muscular missionary trying to spread civilization (Rev. Henry Sturt), and a savage hero (Dicky) who is innately good but is finally overwhelmed by the forces arrayed against him.[57] No longer, like Conrad's Marlow, can we hold on to the fragile hope that darkness belonged to yesterday. It is already visible today. Empire has brought Africa to London, and London to Africa, and an intertextual alertness to the different verbal and ideological currents that are played upon by Morrison allows us to find these displacements as we read. Finally, 'globalized' English literature invites us to read Victorian English together with, as well as against, literature in other languages. Although the remit of this particular volume emphasizes the *English* Novel, poetry, drama, and travel-writing, each major Victorian literary form had its rich counterparts throughout the 'formal' and 'informal empires'. A reading of Thackeray and Dickens becomes richer when read in relation to the Brazilian novelist Machado de Assis, or the Bengali Bankim Chattopadhyay. The debate about the aesthetic traditions and modernity of Tennyson, the Brownings, and the Pre-Raphaelites can be seen in a new light when these resurface in the Chinese poetry of Huang Tsun-Hsien and Liang Chi-Chao. The accounts of their travels given by Burton, Stanley, Eden, and Kingsley slant differently when angled through the portrait of Victorian England given by the Arab writer Muhammad al-Muwaylihi. Empire brought 'world' and 'English' literature together in creative tension with one another. Only when we read them in tandem with one another can we gain a full sense of the complexity and force of the historical currents that mark the intersection of literature with the constantly shifting human, political, ecological, and cultural power dynamics of Victorian empire.

57 Arthur Morrison, *A Child of the Jago* (London: Methuen & Co., 1896).

Writing about America

DEIRDRE DAVID

These people speak our language, use our prayers, read
our books, and ruled by our laws, dress themselves in our image,
are warm with our blood ... They are our sons and daughters, the
source of our greatest pride, and as we grow old they should be the
staff of our age.
(Anthony Trollope, *North America*, 1862[1])

On 22 March 1775, Edmund Burke rose in the House of Commons with the aim
of restoring 'the former unsuspecting confidence of the colonies in the mother
country': the occasion for his speech was a debate on the wisdom of restricting
American trade with England.[2] In a graphic deployment of the familiar metaphor of nation as body, Burke describes England as a fertile but exhausted
mother being fed by her American colonies, and to those fellow members of the
House who charge America with having unnaturally drawn life from the
colonial mother, responds that in 1775 she sustains the nation that was once
the selfless protector of her dependent outposts; now is the time for a grateful
England to treat those colonies as political allies not as commercial competitors.
Whereas at the beginning of the eighteenth century, the American colonies
imported corn and grain from England, now the New World feeds the Old, and
England should remember that she would have faced a 'desolating famine, if this
child of your old age, with a true filial piety, with a Roman charity, had not put
the full breast of its youthful exuberance to the mouth of the exhausted parent'.[3]

Given the long-standing ubiquity in British literature of metaphors of the
body and colonization – one thinks, for instance, of Donne's 'To His Mistris

---

1 Anthony Trollope, *North America*, 2 vols. (London: Dawsons of Pall Mall, 1868), vol. 1,
p. 357.
2 Edmund Burke, 'Speech on Moving His Resolutions for Conciliation with the
Colonies', 22 March 1775, in *The Works of the Right Honorable Edmund Burke*, 9 vols.
(Boston: Little Brown and Company, 1889), vol. II, pp. 101–86: p. 106.
3 *Ibid.*, p. 116.

Going to Bed' in which the speaker celebrates his lover's body as 'O my America! my new-found-land, / My kingdome, safeliest when with one man man'd, / My Myne of precious stones, My Empirie, / How blest am I in this discovering thee!'[4] – it is hardly surprising that Burke fuses body and family when advancing his American argument for collaboration in place of confrontation. From early Puritan celebrations of escape from the paternal grip of a corrupt society, through eighteenth-century travel writing that promises colonial wealth to vigorous young men who leave the mother-country, to the Victorian responses to America that are the subject of this chapter, one finds an abundance of family metaphors. But with the ending of the Revolutionary War and the emergence of a post-colonial nation, English writing about America becomes problematized in ways it had not been before: it confronts the discursive challenge of negotiating an obvious yet complex affiliation between the imperial nation and the lost colonies. Amanda Claybaugh, for example, has observed that the many books published in the first half of the nineteenth century dealing with America 'did much to set the terms for the period's articulation of national differences. Through their description of American manners, they established an array of still-familiar oppositions: American openness and British reserve, American energy and British leisure, American merchants and British gentlemen.' Claybaugh goes on to note that these books also 'threw into relief the many connections ... In particular, they illuminated a shared Anglo-American culture of social reform.'[5]

Writing about America emerges as a post-colonial difficulty, not from the familiar perspective of the once-colonized but from that of the former colonizer: where the 'real language problem' for the post-colonial writer, in the words of the poet Jumpy Joshi in Salman Rushdie's *The Satanic Verses*, is to find a way 'to bend it, shape it, how to let it be our freedom, how to repossess its poisoned wells',[6] the challenge for the Victorian writer was to fathom the appropriate imagery for celebrating and/or critiquing a nation so similar to England in terms of race, language, and culture. Family metaphors gain a certain enduring utility in this negotiation of similarity and difference. Early Victorian writers construct narratives of a juvenile

---

4 John Donne, Elegie xix, 'To His Mistris Going to Bed', in *John Donne: Complete Poetry and Selected Prose*, ed. John Hayward (London: The Nonesuch Press, 1967), lines 27–30, pp. 96–7.
5 Amanda Claybaugh, 'Towards a New Transatlanticism: Dickens in the United States', *Victorian Studies* 48:3 (2006), pp. 439–60: p. 439.
6 Salman Rushdie, *The Satanic Verses* (New York: Viking, 1989), p. 281.

nation, culturally raw, morally unformed; those representing America in the middle of the century favour images of a bustling, rowdy country; by the 1880s, the high Victorian preoccupation with social analysis gives way to celebration of a nation definitively grown apart from England – exotically distinct, fascinatingly 'other', and compellingly wild. At the end of the Victorian period, the family metaphor is as exhausted as Burke's colonial mother.

Fired by pride and curiosity, Victorian travellers to America who routinely lambasted uncouth table manners, the use of spittoons, and the absence of an artistic culture, could not resort to images of continental raciness or 'native' barbarity to explain what they saw as shambling democracy and crude social mores. America was 'other', and yet not. As Lawrence Buell observes, during the nineteenth century America 'remained for many foreign commentators (especially the British), albeit diminishingly, the unvoiced "other" – with the predictable connotations of exoticism, barbarism, and unstructuredness'.[7] As a consequence, many of these writers construct narratives of a rambunctious nation forgetful of its English origins and manners; Christopher Mulvey notes that many English people crossed the Atlantic with their minds set against finding 'a gentleman in the former colonies'.[8] Others, with more ambiguous responses, indict both the mother-country and the child-colony for creating and perpetuating vulgarity and materialism: Thomas Hamilton, one of those gentleman-travellers bent on finding no gentlemen like himself in America, first ironically praises England for her 'motherly care' in bleeding her colonies to replenish 'her own parental exchequer', and then indicts her for failing to provide them with proper cultural training. Hamilton warns of anarchy if the former colonies continue to be ruled by 'the despotism of the mob'.[9] Rebecca Gratz, one of Philadelphia's prominent social figures, took strong exception to Hamilton's views and wrote to her sister on 28 October 1833 'I have been reading Hamilton's "Men and Manners" and am quite provoked that he should have lent his talents to such an unfair purpose as that of misrepresenting America for political views – because it seems as if no English traveller can speak the truth of us.'[10] In 1864, strongly criticizing

7 Lawrence Buell, 'American Literary Emergence as Postcolonial Phenomenon', *American Literary History* 4:3 (1992), pp. 411–42: p. 417.
8 Christopher Mulvey, *Transatlantic Manners: Social Patterns in Nineteenth-Century Anglo-American Travel Literature* (Cambridge University Press, 1990), p. 24.
9 Thomas Hamilton, *Men and Manners in America* (Edinburgh and London: William Blackwood and Sons, 1843; New York: Johnson Reprint, 1968), p. 174.
10 *The Letters of Rebecca Gratz* (Philadelphia: Jewish Publication Society of America, 1929), p. 186.

the writing of figures such as Hamilton about America, Henry Tuckerman declared that 'the more refined tone of his work is somewhat marred by the same flippancy and affectation of superior taste, which give such a cockney pertness to so many of his countrymen's written observations when this country is the theme'.[11]

Early post-colonial admirers of America also advanced a comforting similarity to Burke's exhausted mother-country. For William Cobbett, writing in 1819, America was a grand place, full of the appealing descendants of Englishmen, Irishmen, and Scotsmen: 'blindfold an Englishman and convey him to New York, unbind his eyes, and he will think himself in an English city'.[12] Later Victorians even elaborate an image of the post-colonial nation so deeply attached to its former colonizer that it longs for reunion: Marianne Finch, an Englishwoman travelling in America in the 1850s, declares that Americans speak of England 'with a kind of filial tenderness, and yearn after her as if she were a mother from whom they had been separated in childhood'.[13] And that intrepid adventurer, Isabella Bird, records a toast to 'Old England' made in her presence that vows 'the educated youth of America' looks upon her 'as upon a venerated mother'.[14] Given the establishment of the American travel narrative in the literary marketplace by the 1850s, Bird arrived with well-rehearsed notions of what to expect, yet at the end of her stay she declared that an 'entire revolution has been effected in my way of looking at things since I landed on the shores of the New World'.[15] Where other travellers had emphasized moral and cultural differences (almost always to the detriment of America), Bird saw remarkable similarities: Edinburgh and Boston are more alike than Boston and Chicago, the 'artisans' of English manufacturing towns have more in common with the New England descendants of Puritans than with 'the reckless inhabitants of the newly-settled territories west of the Mississippi'.[16]

---

11 Henry T. Tuckermann, *America and Her Commentators: With a Critical Sketch of Travel in the United States* (1864; New York: Augustus M. Kelley, 1970), p. 223.

12 William Cobbett, *A Year's Residence in the United States of America: Treating of the Face of the Country, the Climate, the Soil, the Products, the Mode of Cultivating the Land, the Prices of Land, of Labour, of Food, of Raiment: of the Expenses of Housekeeping and of the Usual Manner of Living; of the Manners and Customs of the People; and of the Institutions of the Country, Civil, Political and Religious* (1818; Carbondale: Southern Illinois University Press, 1964), p. 231.

13 Marianne Finch, *An Englishwoman's Experience in America* (1853; New York: Negro Universities Press, 1969), p. 169.

14 Isabella Lucy Bird, *The Englishwoman in America* (1856; Madison: University of Wisconsin Press, 1966), pp. 446–7.

15 *Ibid.*, p. 323.   16 *Ibid.*, p. 322.

Arriving in America influenced by the textual construction of an alien nation, Bird left convinced of indelible affiliations rooted in race, language, and culture.

Whether, then, voicing their disgust or admiration, English writers frequently resort to family images. And whether recording their impressions in the travel narratives that dominate the first quarter of the nineteenth century, or making their American experience the subject of the longer works of social analysis that emerge in the mid-Victorian period, or recounting their American travels (often to the West) in the form of memoirs, letters, or published lectures, at the end of the century, English writers always engage, consciously or not, with the discursive challenge of how to represent a post-colonial nation that was both reassuringly English and alarmingly something else.

The great political experiment

In 1819, Washington Irving declared that

> it has been the peculiar lot of our country, to be visited by the worst kind of English travellers ... it has been left to the broken down tradesman, the scheming adventurer, the wandering mechanic, the Manchester and Birmingham agent, to be [England's] oracles respecting America ... where one of the greatest political experiments in the history of the world is now performing, and which presents the most profound and momentous studies for the statesman and the philosopher.[17]

Elaborating Irving's observation, Jane Mesick argues that before 1812 America was 'unfortunate in the type of travellers' who arrived in the new nation: raw with wounded pride or disappointed in their expectations, they tended to see only chaos and cultural crudeness.[18] Even the most sympathetic of post-Revolutionary War travellers who set the rhetorical stage for the Victorians who came after them, rarely understood themselves to be witnesses to 'one of the greatest political experiments' in the history of the world. To be sure, some arrived with idealistic expectations, but most were armed with defensive disgust and disdain.

---

17 Washington Irving, 'English Writers on America', in *The Legend of Sleepy Hollow and Other Stories* (Harmondsworth: Penguin Classics, 1999), p. 43.
18 See Jane Louise Mesick, *The English Traveller in America, 1785–1835* (New York: Columbia University Press, 1922), p. 270.

The contradiction between a promise of individual liberty and the practice of slavery, the treatment of America's indigenous peoples, and the condition of her women, proved predictable targets for early Victorian writers such as Frances Wright and Basil Hall, and, most sensationally, Frances Trollope.[19] In particular regard to slavery, Christopher Mulvey argues that

> British travellers, whether or not they were aware of it and for the most part they were aware of it, were entering here as elsewhere in their commentary upon American morality and manners into a discourse that had at all points been fully worked over by the Americans themselves ... This was certainly the case on the moral and philosophical discussion of slavery.[20]

Trollope's *Domestic Manners of the Americans*, one of the fiercest critiques in the some two hundred books on America published by English people between 1836 and 1860, took direct aim at slavery and her book did not endear her to American readers, something she forthrightly anticipated in its afterword: 'I suspect that what I have written will make it evident I do not like America ... I do not like them. I do not like their principles, I do not like their manners, I do not like their opinions.'[21] Despite the fact that most of her travel in America, in the late 1820s and early 1830s, was in 'Western communities', where, observed a mid-century American commentator on English attitudes, 'neither manners nor culture, economy nor character had attained any well-organized or harmonious development',[22] she criticizes *all* Americans for gobbling their food, spitting on the hems of women's dresses, and betraying the ideal of individual freedom through slavery and the displacement of 'Red Indians' from their lands: 'You will see them with one hand hoisting the cap of liberty, and with the other flogging their slaves. You will see them one hour lecturing the mob on the indefeasible rights of man, and the next driving from their homes the children of the soil, whom they have bound themselves to protect by the most solemn treaties.'[23] In contrast to Trollope, who came to America some twelve years later than

19 See, for example, Frances Wright, *Views of Society and Manners in America* (1821; Cambridge, MA: Belknap Press of Harvard University Press, 1963) and Basil Hall, *Travels in America, in the Years 1827 and 1828* (London: Simpkin and Marshall, 1830).

20 Mulvey, *Transatlantic Manners*, pp. 47–8.

21 Frances Trollope, *Domestic Manners of the Americans* (New York: Alfred Knopf, 1949), p. 404.

22 Tuckermann, *America and Her Commentators*, p. 226.

23 Trollope, *Domestic Manners*, p. 222.

she, Frances Wright found many things about America quite pleasing: boarding-houses, for example, were fine places to mix easily with the 'natives' and observe 'the tone of national manners', an experience she found inoffensive rather then repellent.[24]

Trollope declared that American women were 'guarded by a seven-fold shield of habitual insignificance' and that all the enjoyments of American men are found 'in the absence of women': it is only from the clergy that they receive the 'attention which is dearly valued by every female heart throughout the world'.[25] The lamentable subordination of American women may be traced to the fact that although American men may have inherited the spirit of independence stoutly fought for by their fathers, they have not inherited the ability to become scholars and gentlemen: the mother-country, through desire to profit from her metaphorical children, so alienated them that they fatally rejected the benign influence of English civilization. In a negotiation of blame for both countries, Trollope indicts both mother and child: for the taxation of tea, England lost her colonies, and for truculent intransigence, America forfeited the possibility of sharing in 'her mother's grace and glory'.[26]

One of the most industrious and prolific travellers to America, the journalist Harriet Martineau, arrived in 1834, eager to turn her impressions into a didactic narrative. One of a large group of transatlantic reformers who, as Amanda Claybaugh observes, crossed and recrossed the Atlantic, 'paying visits to one another, going on lecture tours, and attending Anglo-American conventions against slavery and for temperance or world peace',[27] Martineau aimed to revise the narratives of other English visitors: her *Society in America* (1837) is notable for its analysis of the social panorama. Always interested in the intersection of American morality and institutions, she dissected virtually everything she saw in Jacksonian America – from Shaker women in Hancock, Massachusetts (a spectacle 'too shocking for ridicule') to enslaved men in South Carolina.[28]

Her remedy for the transatlantic Woman Question was simple and direct: women must be educated, freed by adequately compensated employment

24 Wright, *Views of Society*, p. 12.   25 Trollope, *Domestic Manners*, pp. 69, 75.
26 *Ibid.*, pp. 405–6.   27 Claybaugh, 'Towards a New Transatlanticism', p. 439.
28 Harriet Martineau, *Society in America*, 3 vols. (London: Saunders and Otley, 1837), vol. I, pp. 313–14. In his *Diary in America*, Captain Marryat refers frequently to Martineau's *Society in America*, usually to her detriment. See Captain Frederick Marryat, *Diary in America*, ed. Jules Zanger (1839; Bloomington: Indiana University Press, 1960).

from dependence on their families, and accorded fair participation in determining the laws that govern their lives. Arriving in America armed with
her understanding of its democratic principles, she was appalled by a dis-
crepancy between that understanding and the actual condition of women,
as Trollope had been before her. Less emotionally affronted than Trollope,
however, Martineau was disappointed that American women were not
more like herself: well educated, intellectually ambitious, and financially
independent. Her attack on slavery is similarly grounded in contradiction as
she punctuates arguments anchored in the economic inefficiency of owning
a labourer rather than purchasing his labour power with the graphic
accounts of violence that were to be more sensationally deployed by
Dickens in his chapter on slavery in *American Notes* (to be discussed later
in this chapter). Relying upon her abolitionist credentials as representative
of an abolitionist nation (Britain abolished slavery in the West Indies on
1 August 1834), Martineau announces that the moral gap between a doctrine
of independence and the enslavement of human beings is uneconomical,
pernicious, and absurd; she advances specious arguments in favour of
slavery in order to demolish them, ridiculing, for example, the slave owner's
claim that 'an endearing relation' exists between master and slave. For
Martineau, as long as slaves remain property, rather than being liberated
to the economic freedom of selling their labour power, and as long as
women remain uneducated, rather than being released to the social freedom
of rejecting marriage for financial security, both slave owners and husbands
end up with a very poor bargain. Uneducated American women and lazy
American slaves are cheap but worthless commodities.

When the English actress Fanny Kemble arrived in America in 1832 on an
acting tour with her father, she quickly began keeping a journal, later to be
published in 1835 under her married name, Frances Anne Butler. The *Journal*
generously documents Kemble's American pleasures – among them, the
glorious scenery along the Hudson River and the 'unmingled good will, and
cordial, real kindness' with which she was received; it also unabashedly
advertises her unhappiness with the 'peculiarities' of the country in which,
as things turned out, she was to spend roughly one third of the rest of her
life. As a glamorous young actress whose adulation was surpassed only by
that heaped on Dickens in the 1840s, she packs her *Journal* with sprightly
anecdotes of actors so terrified they became mute when she stepped on
stage and of politicians practised in the arts of flirtation; but she peppers her
praise with controversial commentary on the transatlantic working classes,
the raw nature of American culture, and the unhappy state of American

women. Despite the charismatic personality that distinguished her from those more austere English women travellers who preceded her (Trollope and Martineau), she alarmed readers on both sides of the Atlantic.

Kemble admired the confidence of the American worker, grounded, she believed, in his importance to American business as it developed the material resources of the nation. She was less positive about American artistic culture, or rather the lack of it: 'Where are all the picture-galleries – the sculpture – the works of art and science – the countless wonders of human ingenuity and skill?' By the time Kemble's *Journal* was published in 1835, Americans were accustomed to a denigration of their literature and visual art and to distaste for their manners, but her criticism of the sex customarily treated with exaggerated deference caused great offence. Where Trollope and Martineau had tended to generalize about the subordination of women, Kemble goes into gritty details: she was appalled by the way American women behaved so aggressively when together and distressed by their acquiescence in being treated as 'comparative ciphers' when in male company;[29] she was revolted by their sugary diet and their practice of stuffing children with pastries; and she found their disinclination to exercise dispiriting. Physically fearless throughout her life, Kemble's behaviour when she arrived at Niagara Falls in 1831 suggests her temperamental difference from a number of other English visitors.

Almost all nineteenth-century visitors to North America journeyed to Niagara and gazing at the falls was a particularly Victorian experience, as Rupert Brooke wryly noted in 1913: he begged the friend to whom he recounted his feelings not to tell anyone he had stared at 'the thing' and had the 'purest Nineteenth-Century grandiose thoughts, about the Destiny of Man, the Irresistibility of Fate, the Doom of Nations, and the fact that Death awaits us All'.[30] For Martineau, however, Niagara had prompted musings on her own position as analytical observer. In 1837, she stood in a 'thunder cavern' and untroubled by the wet whirlwind, the foaming flood, and the thunderous sound of water falling on the rocks, she decided she was watching 'world-making'. Unlike visitors who trembled at the sight of the sublime, Martineau thought the whole thing 'like the systems of the sky . . . one of the hands of Nature's clock'.[31] When Kemble arrived at Niagara, she

29 Frances Anne Butler, *The Journal of Frances Anne Butler*, 2 vols. (London: John Murray, 1835), vol. I, pp. 99–101, 202.
30 Rupert Brooke to A. F. Scholfield, July–August 1913, in *The Letters of Rupert Brooke*, chosen and ed. Geoffrey Keynes (London: Faber & Faber, 1967), p. 491.
31 Martineau, *Society in America*, vol. I, p. 211.

rushed through the garden of the hotel, sprang down a narrow footpath, and stood on the 'brink of the abyss' – as unafraid at this moment as she was to become later when confronting her husband about slavery.[32]

Kemble's most significant writing about America is to be found in the journal she kept when she visited her husband's rice and cotton plantations in Georgia, places of 'material beauty and moral degradation'.[33] In graphic detail, she records the almost infernal living and working conditions of the Butler slaves and her desperation as she listened, in her role as plantation mistress, to pleas from the female slaves for alleviation of their burdens. A fervent abolitionist before she arrived in Georgia, Kemble realized at the end of her four-month visit that all she could achieve was small improvements in conditions on the plantation: in part, she accommodates herself to this realization through a strategy of colonial distance – she figures herself always as an 'Englishwoman' in a barbaric place. Unable to publish her Georgian journal because of threats from her husband to deny access to her children if she did so, it was not until 1863 that she released it in the hope of swaying England from its support for the south, which was grounded primarily, of course, in the need for a steady supply of cotton. Kemble's eyewitness testimony is unique in all Victorian writing about American slavery, although the institution itself was, of course, an obligatory topic for any writer fashioning a response to American society.

Dickens to Trollope

When Charles Dickens sailed for America on the steamship *Britannia* in 1842, like others before him he expected to visit prisons, hospitals, asylums, workhouses, and orphanages, and he had prepared himself for the experience by reading Trollope and Martineau. By the early 1840s, English writing about America had settled into its defining characteristics: critique of American manners, morals, and politics; a journey to principal cities such as Boston, New York, and Washington DC, and visits to such natural wonders as the prairies of the West and Niagara Falls. Amanda Claybaugh notes that the itinerary also often included institutions of reform: the poor houses of Boston, the asylums of Long Island, and the prisons of Philadelphia.[34]

---

32 Butler, *Journal*, vol. II, pp. 286–7.
33 Frances Anne Kemble, *Journal of a Residence on a Georgian Plantation in 1838–1839* (1863; Athens: University of Georgia Press, 1984), p. 226.
34 Claybaugh, 'Towards a New Transatlanticism', p. 446.

Moreover, by the 1840s this writing began to figure America less as an immature nation than as a robust country, its identity shaped not quite so much by affiliation with England as by its seemingly endless geographical and commercial expansion. Dickens's *American Notes* show that he deviated little from the conventional itinerary, although his vivid expression of disgust with almost all things American is uniquely his own: political life consisted of 'despicable trickery at elections; under-handed tamperings with public officers; cowardly attacks upon opponents';[35] newspapers went in for 'pimpering and pandering for all degrees of vicious taste, and gorging with coined lies the most voracious maw'.[36] Like Kemble before him, he was struck by the instructive difference between the English and American working classes, although his American example was hardly the norm: he based his views on a day-long visit to the famous cluster of woollen, cotton, and carpet factories in Lowell, Massachusetts. The factory girls are warmly and sensibly dressed; they work in spaces where the windows are full of plants; they subscribe to circulating libraries and there are pianos in the boarding-houses. Declaring it would be unjust to make comparisons with the English workers, Dickens nevertheless asks his readers to consider the difference between Lowell and 'those great haunts of misery' to be found in English factory towns, places that inspired, of course, his creation of Coketown in *Hard Times* (1854).[37]

Dickens's chapter on slavery is the most impassioned in *American Notes*. Adopting the persuasive strategy of merely reprinting advertisements for 'runaway' slaves who may be identified by having iron bars on their legs, brand marks on their cheeks, and whip marks on their backs, he asks how English people cannot cry shame on those 'who notch the ears of men and women, cut pleasant posies in the shrinking flesh, learn to write with pens of red-hot iron on the human face'.[38] Better, Dickens thunders, to wipe out the history of the new nation and return the land to its indigenous peoples: 'restore the forest and the Indian village; in lieu of stars and stripes, let some poor feather flutter in the breeze; replace the streets and squares with wigwams; and though the death-song of a hundred haughty warriors fill the air, it will be music to the shriek of one unhappy slave'.[39] On a steamboat from Cincinnati to Louisville, Dickens encountered one such

---

35 Charles Dickens, *American Notes and Pictures from Italy* (Oxford University Press, 1970), p. 120.
36 *Ibid.*, p. 88.   37 *Ibid.*, p. 70.   38 *Ibid.*, p. 242.   39 *Ibid.*, p. 243.

'haughty warrior', a figure who stirred his sympathy for those peoples who trustingly put their marks upon treaties and were regularly betrayed; he was remarkably handsome, 'with long black hair, an aquiline nose, broad cheek-bones, a sunburnt complexion, and a very bright, keen, dark, and piercing eye ... as stately and complete a gentleman of Nature's making, as ever I beheld'.[40]

This steamboat journey also took Dickens to the 'dismal Cairo' situated at the junction of the Ohio and Mississippi rivers on flat, low, and marshy ground, 'a breeding-place of fever, ague, and death; vaunted in England as a mine of Golden Hope, and speculated in, on the faith of monstrous repre-sentations, to many people's ruin'.[41] Here, the wishful fantasy of America is assaulted by reality and the dream of wealth is brought up against fever and death. Here is where Martin Chuzzlewit – a figure representative of the entry of American experience into the Victorian novel – bent on making his fortune at the geographical heart of the vast new nation, wakes up to find himself in 'Eden', an anti-Paradise, where a 'fetid vapour, hot and sickening as the breath of an oven, rose up from the earth'.[42] After *Martin Chuzzlewit*, references to America began to appear regularly in the Victorian novel: in Elizabeth Gaskell's *North and South* (1848), for example, the industrial north feels the economic fluctuations in the cotton trade.

Dickens's despair over America abated somewhat, however, and when he made his second visit to America from November 1868 to April 1869, his ill health exacerbated by the New England winter, he declared himself 'astounded' by the amazing changes in American life – changes in the rise of huge cities, changes in the 'graces and amenities' of life, changes in the Press. He resolved that his 'testimony' to the 'unsurpassable politeness, delicacy, sweet temper, hospitality, consideration' shown to him by Americans should be permanently recorded in the form of the appending of a copy of his speech to all editions of *American Notes*.[43]

When Frances Trollope's son Anthony Trollope travelled to America, first in 1859 for a brief stop-over in New York on his way back to England from the West Indies, and then in August 1861, he replaced what he saw as her undisciplined female attack on the lost colonies with his more temper-ate male analysis. In his *Autobiography*, he argues that the faults of his

---

40 *Ibid.*, pp. 166–7.   41 *Ibid.*, p. 171.
42 Charles Dickens, *Martin Chuzzlewit* (London: Oxford University Press, 1968), chapter 23, p. 381.
43 Dickens, *American Notes*, p. 254.

mother's book may be traced to the gender of the writer: 'No observer was certainly ever less qualified to judge of the prospects or even of the happiness of a young people ... Whatever she saw she judged, as most women do, from her own standing-point.'[44] Although Trollope admitted that his mother wrote vividly, he believed she lacked the intellectual power to analyse the political system that produced the social absurdities she found so abominable. This work of intellectual analysis (undertaken notably well by Harriet Martineau, incidentally) 'is fitter for a man than for a woman'.[45]

Elaborating Burke's family metaphor, Trollope initiates the analysis he believed most women were incapable of undertaking with a description of maternal England at the outbreak of the Revolutionary War. After England 'suffers those pangs which Nature calls upon mothers to endure', the former colonies are first gendered male: this is the time 'when the son stands alone by his own strength' and he is the 'most successful child that ever yet has gone off from a successful parent and taken its own path into the world'.[46] As this miraculous child matures, however, 'he' becomes a 'she', and Trollope develops a transatlantic fantasy in which America is a dutiful daughter armed with the lessons of her responsible mother: 'She is to go forth, and do as she best may in the world under that teaching which her old home has given her.'[47] This sentimentalized daughter is the instructive opposite of a character in the novel Trollope wrote after returning from America: Wallachia Petrie in He Knew He Was Right (1869). Having asserted that most American women are 'hard, dry, and melancholy', Trollope then assigns these qualities to his fictional character, an abolitionist and a 'poetess' who so terrifies Charles Glascock, English heir to a title and a fortune, that he wonders about the wisdom of proposing to Caroline Spalding since Wallachia is her close friend: 'There were certain forms of the American female so dreadful that no wise man would wilfully come in contact with them. Miss Petrie's ferocity was distressing to him, but her eloquence and enthusiasm were worse even than her ferocity.' As John Hall observes, Wallachia Petrie 'has some successors in Trollope's fiction'. Hall points to characters associated with the 'Female Disabilities Institute' in Is He Popenjoy? (1874–75), to Elias Gotobed, the American Senator who is the title figure of Trollope's 1877 novel, and to

---

44 Anthony Trollope, An Autobiography (1883; Harmondsworth: Penguin Books, 1993), pp. 21–2.
45 Trollope, North America, vol. I, p. 2.   46 Ibid., p. 100.   47 Ibid., p. 106.

Isabel Boncassen, the American heiress in *The Duke's Children*, the last of the Palliser novels, published in 1880.[48]

Aiming to correct his mother's imprecise analyses and to countenance her sympathy for oppressed American women, Trollope still follows her lead by taking aim at the by-now familiar targets of corrupt government and hypocrisy in regard to slavery. The American lower classes tended to 'tread on his corns' and make his daily life 'unpleasant', although he concedes respect for their intelligence and industry; the difficulty for Trollope was his distaste for any government based on the establishment of equality since he thought it 'the vilest' form to which man can descend. In contrast to Anthony Trollope, Barbara Bodichon declared in October 1857 (she was visiting New Orleans): 'Until I came to America I hardly felt the strange want of rational liberty in England. How came Franklin and Washington to dare to try this huge experiment?'[49] Figuring the American nation in somatic terms, Trollope wonders whether she has 'the thews and muscles' to carry a national debt, manage a dangerously unstable economy, and create a proper trade balance with her allies. Eventually reassured by the fact that Americans have 'got our blood in their veins', Trollope anticipates they will pull through with the model of English financial fortitude and daring in front of them. Connected to England by ties of blood, by commercial relations, by a community of literature which will 'require centuries to obliterate', America will triumph. Where it will fail, though, is in eliminating slavery since the founding fathers failed to provide means for the gradual extinction of the institution: in the meantime, even though 'negroes' were brought to America 'under compulsion', Trollope declares they have 'multiplied in the western world and have there become a race happier ... than their still untamed kinsmen in Africa'.[50]

The beyond

In 1873 Isabella Bird arrived in America, for the second time, determined to cross the Rocky Mountains on horseback. Her narrative of this three-month adventure provides a remarkable account of a part of America, which

48 Trollope, *North America*, vol. 1, p. 153; Anthony Trollope, *He Knew He Was Right* (Oxford University Press, 2009), chapter 66, p. 530; N. John Hall, *Trollope* (Oxford: Clarendon Press, 1991), pp. 343, 423, 465.
49 Barbara Leigh Bodichon, *An American Diary 1857–1858*, ed. Joseph W. Reed, Jr. (London: Routledge and Kegan Paul, 1972), p. 72.
50 Trollope, *North America*, vol. 1, p. 62.

although well travelled by settlers and visitors, had received little attention in Victorian writing. A story of survival in the bitter cold of the Rockies, of being deprived of her English comforts, and of her friendship with 'Rocky Mountain Jim', *A Lady's Life in the Rocky Mountains* vividly registers the challenge of being in a world where, as Bird puts it, 'Everything suggests a beyond.'[51] But despite the suggestion of a 'beyond', Bird's narrative addresses a number of the themes that were dominant in the 'before', in her 1854 *An Englishwoman in America* and in the mid-Victorian writing that precedes the story of her Rocky Mountain trek: the condition of the lower classes, the position of women, and the prospects for the American Indian. And Bird regresses in another sense: it is as if the West becomes a new locus of a freshly colonized America as she describes bleak Colorado and 'savage' Indians; as Fanny Kemble positioned herself as a civilized 'Englishwoman' in the barbaric south, so Isabella Bird becomes a superior and judgmental figure.

A 'hard greed, and the exclusive pursuit of gain', Bird believes, 'are eating up family love and life throughout the west'.[52] Drawing her example from visits to lower-class English immigrants eking out a living in Colorado, people who hate England 'with a bitter, personal hatred', and whose ability to live almost entirely without comfort and ease is 'only possible to people of British stock',[53] Bird frames her views with English attitudes carried across the Atlantic: they suggest the necessarily contrapuntal nature of much Victorian writing about America. When she meets an English doctor and his wife, she knows from the woman's accent that she is 'a lady'; her 'refined, courteous, graceful English manner' reassures Bird and they spend the evening doing needlework as the doctor reads Tennyson aloud.[54] A strikingly handsome plains scout and trapper, Rocky Mountain Jim, initially frightens Bird with his appearance, an image of what can happen to a refined Englishman in the rough and ready west, but when he begins to speak, she forgets his reputation 'for his manner was that of a chivalrous gentleman, his accent refined, and his language easy and elegant'.[55]

Bird's descriptions of the indigenous people she saw on a train heading up into the Colorado mountains show that the disgust of English writers with slavery did not always extend to sympathy for displaced peoples whose land has been taken from them and whose trust in American decency has been

51 Isabella Bird, *A Lady's Life in the Rocky Mountains*, 4th edn. (London: John Murray, 1881), p. 33.
52 *Ibid.*, p. 53.   53 *Ibid.*, pp. 51, 57.   54 *Ibid.*, p. 57.   55 *Ibid.*, p. 92.

constantly betrayed by the tearing-up of treaties. Bird displays none of Dickens's romanticizing of the Choctaw chief into a noble figure. For her, the Indians are entirely barbaric, beyond the reach of the influences of European civilization: the first four cars of the train are 'clustered over' with 'perfect savages, without any aptitude for even aboriginal civilization'; hideously filthy, carrying bows and arrows, and reputedly living on grasshoppers, they are 'a most impressive incongruity in the midst of the tokens of an omnipotent civilization'.[56] Bird declares unambiguously that the 'Indian problem' will never be solved until the Indian is extinct: treated so cruelly that white Americans are to them the incarnation of 'devilry', and reduced to a 'degraded pauperism' by their friends, they have no future.[57]

After the 1870s, Victorian writing about America enlarged its scope as steamboat and railroad travel led to new territory and to encounters with new ethnic groups. Apart from discussing 'Negroes' or 'Indians', English writers had until this time mainly concerned themselves with European peoples, which explains, in part, the pervasive interest in affiliations of language, customs, and physical appearance. But when the late Victorian writer encounters new landscapes and peoples, the problematical issue of similarity and difference fades away, and with it, the handy family metaphors. For Robert Louis Stevenson, travelling in California in the 1880s, the scenery around Monterey seems somewhat like Scotland, yet the boats in the harbour are 'of a strange outlandish design', the streets smell of the burning of joss-sticks, and one sees men guiding their pencils from right to left as they write home with news of Monterey 'to the Celestial empire'.[58] California is a place of constant transformation: 'All things in this new land are moving farther on: the wine-vats and the miner's blasting tools but picket for a night, like Bedouin pavilions; and tomorrow, to fresh woods! This stir of change and these perpetual echoes of the moving footfall haunt the land.'[59]

In March 1889, a twenty-three-year-old Rudyard Kipling left Calcutta for San Francisco, despatched by the Anglo-Indian newspaper *The Pioneer* with the assignment of sending reports back to the Anglo-Indian community. Travelling in an opposite direction from most who traversed the continent, he went from west to east – through Montana, Utah, Omaha, and Chicago, to his final destination in New York. Not intended for

---

56 *Ibid.*, pp. 4–5.   57 *Ibid.*, p. 215.
58 Robert Louis Stevenson, 'The Old Pacific Capital', in *The Lantern-Bearers and Other Essays* (New York: Farrar Straus Giroux, 1988), p. 129.
59 Robert Louis Stevenson, *The Silverado Squatters* (London: Chatto and Windus, 1883), p. 46.

American publication, Kipling's reports capture the closing moments of the push west, the manners of vulgar American tourists in Yellowstone, and the sight of rivers of pig and cattle blood in the Chicago slaughterhouses – a nightmarish city, a huge wilderness of 'terrible streets' full of 'terrible people, who talked money through their noses'. This is an America brashly detached from the mother-country, the former colonies grown to brawny adulthood. How 'to take in even one-thousandth of this huge, roaring, many sided continent?'[60] is the question Kipling asks himself.

What Kipling loves most about the American west is American women – these are not the hard, dry, and melancholy creatures who so bothered Anthony Trollope: they are clever, they can talk, they can think, and the most desirable of the many with whom he flirted as he made his way east, was a 'very trim young maiden – who had just stepped out of one of Mr James's novels'. As their party makes its way through Yellowstone, from 'her very resolute little mouth'[61] he receives a lecture on American literature while the other tourists tout the wonders of American enterprise and opportunity. In many ways, *American Notes* reads as an elegy for the quickly disappearing timbered landscape and the romanticized world of the cowboy. Kipling asserts that America must change its pattern of seldom attempting 'to put back anything that it has taken from Nature's shelves. It grabs all it can and moves on';[62] he tells of a cavalry captain regaling him with gory tales of Indian warfare: 'of ambush, firing on the rear-guard, heat that split the skull better than any tomahawk, cold that wrinkled the very liver'. When Kipling encounters 'real cowboys, not the Buffalo Bill article',[63] they are unwashed, picturesque ruffians, destined, he predicts, to go under as soon as the country is settled.

Admitting that its government is 'provisional', its law 'the notion of the moment', and its railways 'made of hairpins and matchsticks', Kipling declares Americans to be 'the biggest, finest, and best people on the surface of the globe!'[64] America sets an example for England in her fervent patriotism: where the average Englishman regards his country 'as an abstraction to supply him with policemen and fire-brigades',[65] Americans, despite an obsession

60 Rudyard Kipling, *American Notes: Rudyard Kipling's West*, ed. Arrell Morgan Gibson (Norman: University of Oklahoma Press, 1981), p. 141. Kipling's *Notes* were never intended for American publication and were pirated and published in America in 1891 (obviously without his permission). In 1899, Kipling copyrighted the letters and published them with his collected works, *From Sea to Sea*.
61 Kipling, *American Notes*, p. 106.   62 *Ibid.*, pp. 150–1.   63 *Ibid.*, p. 99.
64 *Ibid.*, p. 124.   65 *Ibid.*, p. 152.

with money and a heedless devastation of the land, have created a dazzling nation that bears little resemblance to the mother-country from which the child-colonies separated themselves a century before. Kipling predicts a future for the west unlike anything imagined by the founding fathers: a society dominated by the 'Anglo-American-German-Jew' who with English lungs above Teuton feet will be 'the finest writer, poet, and dramatist . . . By virtue of his Jew blood – just a little, little drop – he'll be a musician and a painter too.'[66] With no mention of little drops of 'Jew blood', Matthew Arnold also pays tribute to Kipling's Teutonic Americans. On his lecture tour in the early 1880s, Arnold displaces a century of family metaphors that figure America as England's offspring, by saluting her citizens for having come 'of the best parentage which a modern nation can have . . . You are fifty millions sprung from this excellent Germanic stock, having passed through this excellent Puritan discipline, and set in this enviable and unbounded country.'[67]

In January 1882, Oscar Wilde arrived in New York to begin a lecture tour promoted by the American representatives of Richard D'Oyly Carte; since Wilde was generally understood to be the model for Bunthorne in *Patience* and since a New York production of *Patience* had opened in September 1881, Wilde seemed an appealing figure to represent Gilbert and Sullivan in America. During his tour he delivered two principal lectures, the first on 'The English Renaissance' and the second on 'Decorative Art in America'. In many ways more engaging than the lectures, however, are the letters he wrote home to English friends, and the American character Hester Worsley in *A Woman of No Importance*, written some nine years after his return and first performed in April 1893. Similarly to Charles Kingsley, who lectured in America in 1874, Wilde chronicles the financial details of his tour, but unlike Kingsley, his interest in America was not a moral or religious one. Kingsley's earnest sensibility is notably absent from Wilde's delight in the florid exuberance of America, even as he wittily ridicules its manners.[68]

Where Dickens wrote indignantly about American slavery, and where Martineau and Kemble lamented the cipher-like separation of the sexes in America, Wilde found everything he saw a subject for amused ridicule.

---

66 *Ibid.*, pp. 124–5.

67 Matthew Arnold, *Discourses in America* (London: Macmillan and Co., 1885), p. 71.

68 For Kingsley's letters, see *Charles Kingsley's American Notes: Letters from a Lecture Tour 1874*, ed. Robert Bernard Martin (Princeton: Princeton University Library, 1958). Martin makes the interesting point, incidentally, that English writers and lecturers who criticized America were often the recipients of 'an equal amount of abuse': newspaper accounts of Kingsley's lectures were 'frequently condescending, sometimes forthrightly rude' (p. 9).

As Peter Conrad observes, Wilde dissociated himself entirely 'from the Victorian concern about the composition of American society'.[69] Americans were merely dull, the big cities aesthetically distasteful, American marriage an opportunity for satire. Where Dickens's interest in American prisons was grounded in a concern with penal reform (the Eastern Penitentiary prison outside Philadelphia was run on a dreadful system of 'rigid, strict, and hopeless solitary confinement. I believe it, in its effects, to be cruel and wrong'[70]), Wilde's only interest in a prison outside Lincoln, Nebraska was the appearance of the prisoners – 'Poor odd types of humanity in hideous striped dresses making bricks in the sun.'[71] Wilde, however, seems to have had Dickens's success in America always in mind: when not likening the reception accorded him to that which greeted 'The Royal Boy' (a popular contemporary nickname for the Prince of Wales), he gleefully records audiences 'larger and more wonderful than even Dickens had . . . nothing like it since Dickens, they tell me'.[72] Everything offers amusement: in the 'middle of coyotes and canons', he announces that the miners were 'big-booted, red-shirted, yellow-bearded and delightful ruffians'; in the Rocky Mountain town of Leadville he speaks to an audience composed entirely of miners, 'their make-up excellent, red shirts and blonde beards . . . I spoke to them of the early Florentines, and they slept as though no crime had ever stained the ravines of their mountain home. I described to them pictures of Botticelli, and the name, which seemed to them like a new drink, roused them from their dreams.'[73]

As Anthony Trollope did in *He Knew He Was Right*, Wilde translates his views of American women (and American life) into literary characterization and plotting. In *A Woman of No Importance*, the young American woman Hester Worsley is of little dramatic interest since she seems merely a spokesperson for moral criticism of the English upper class, yet Wilde endows her with a sincerity notably free of the acerbic commentary found in his letters. Defending America, she declares, 'We are trying to build up life . . . on a better, truer, purer basis than life rests on here . . . You shut out from our society the gentle and the good. You laugh at the simple and the pure . . . your English society seems to me shallow, selfish, foolish.'[74]

69 Peter Conrad, *Imagining America* (New York: Oxford University Press, 1980), p. 63.
70 Dickens, *American Notes*, p. 99.
71 *The Letters of Oscar Wilde*, ed. Rupert Hart-Davis (New York: Harcourt, Brace and World Inc., 1962), p. 115.
72 *Ibid.*, pp. 86–7.   73 *Ibid.*, p. 111.
74 Oscar Wilde, *A Woman of No Importance*, in *The Importance of Being Earnest And Other Plays*, ed. Peter Raby (New York: Oxford University Press, 1995), Act III, line 263.

Needless to say, everything in America that was simple and pure Wilde treated as material for amused derision, yet in Hester Worsley he seems, for a moment at least, to abandon his cynicism. As most critics note, *A Woman of No Importance* is very much a woman's play: its plot hinges on the abandonment of a pregnant young woman by an aristocratic cad, his discovery that he has a son, and the eventual decision of mother and son, together with Hester Worsley, to reject the father's rather belated offer of marriage: the son will marry Hester and English ruling-class superficiality is trounced by American wealth and moral sincerity (Hester is the heiress to a rather large dry-goods fortune). If Anthony Trollope decried the melancholic hardness of American women, Wilde celebrates their moral courage, especially when it is backed up by a fortune.

Burke began the complex nineteenth-century narrative of England and America with a shining composition of grateful child nurturing the mother country: after the Revolutionary War, the lost colonies become a brash new nation, whose similarity to and difference from England becomes a post-colonial difficulty for Victorian writers, a difficulty that is negotiated, in part, through the deployment of family metaphors. But by the 1880s, America has already herself become the colonizer and Britain has begun her long imperial decline – political developments implicitly acknowledged and stoutly countered by Tennyson in a poem that salutes the opening of the Indian and Colonial Exhibition. The fourth stanza reads as follows:

> Britain fought her sons of yore –
> Britain fail'd; and never more,
> Careless of our growing kin,
> Shall we sin our father's sin,
> Men that in that narrower day –
> Unprophetic rulers they –
> Drove from out the mother's nest
> That young eagle of the West
> To forage for herself alone:
> Britons, hold your own![75]

Tennyson transforms Burke's nurturing child into a foraging 'young eagle of the West' driven from the mother's nest by those of Burke's opponents who fought her colonial 'sons'. Now, Britons must hold on to their 'own', those

---

75 Alfred Tennyson, 'Opening of the Indian and Colonial Exhibition by the Queen, Written at the Request of the Prince of Wales', in *The Poems of Tennyson*, ed. Christopher Ricks 3 vols. (Harlow: Longman, 1987), vol. III, pp. 147–8, lines 21–30.

hard-won imperial possessions accrued during Victoria's long reign. It is Oscar Wilde, though, who seems to have the last Victorian word in the deployment of family metaphors to figure the century-long complex affiliation between England and America: in *A Woman of No Importance*, the former colonies become again the nurturing offspring since it is Hester Worsley's money and moral rectitude that will literally and metaphorically sustain and invigorate the impecunious and faltering mother.

PART VI

*

VICTORIAN AFTERLIVES

32

1900 and the *début de siècle*: poetry, drama, fiction

JOSEPH BRISTOW

The last book that the eighty-nine-year-old novelist Rebecca West published during her long and distinguished career was *1900*: a beautifully illustrated account of the most decisive cultural and political events that occurred not only in Britain but also across the globe during this pivotal year. Amid her wide-ranging discussion of such dispersed phenomena as the Second Anglo-Boer War, the Boxer Rebellion, the tidal wave that swept the Texas coast, and the evident decline in Queen Victoria's health, West – who took her professional name from Henrik Ibsen's forthright heroine in *Rosmersholm* (1886) – turns her attention to the unsettled literary climate in England at the turn of the century. Her inquiries for the most part focus less on drama and poetry and more on fiction: the genre in which she would firmly establish her reputation, some years after she started contributing her frequently irreverent articles – ones that did not hesitate to attack established figures such as George Bernard Shaw, Mary Augusta Ward, and H. G. Wells – to the *Clarion* (a socialist newspaper founded by Robert Blatchford in 1891) and the *Freewoman* (a sexually progressive feminist journal published in 1911 and 1912). 'In Great Britain', West writes, 'the literature of 1900 did little to dispel the curious preoccupation of the time. Fiction was the thing and it had developed along perilous lines.'[1] The problem, she claims, lay with the legacy of Charles Dickens, although she did not blame him for creating 'a multitude of characters who were bright with the colours of life and spoke with living tongues'. According to West, it was Dickens's followers who lacked his genius for enabling 'readers to participate in the joys and enjoyable terrors of real life without paying the usual penalties of experience'. In her view, far too many of the novels that populated the lists of publishers served up

---

1 Rebecca West, *1900* (London: Weidenfeld and Nicolson, 1982), p. 120.

this 'staple literary diet' to a largely unthinking readership, and – as a troubling result – 'it spoiled their palates'.[2]

The problem, as West sees it, lay in the fact that some precious talents had not lived long enough to transform the world of fiction. In this context, the first writer who comes to mind is Robert Louis Stevenson, whose untimely death from a cerebral haemorrhage in 1894 occurred when this immensely hard-working but physically delicate writer was only forty-four. By the turn of the century, Stevenson enjoyed an illustrious reputation. Six years after his death, readers who had long enjoyed his popular romances, such as *Treasure Island* (1883) and *Strange Case of Dr Jekyll and Mr Hyde* (1886), could read his endearing letters to family members and close friends, as well as consult several admiring book-length studies of a packed career that took him all the way from his native Scotland to Samoa: the unsettled nation where he tried, during the final phase of his short life, to make peaceful interventions into the colonial conflicts that troubled the population. In 1900, the American novelist Henry James – who sixteen years earlier had engaged with Stevenson in an important debate about the respective qualities of romance and realism – concluded that the ailing Scottish writer finally managed in the South Seas 'to turn his life into the fairy tale of achieving ... such a happy physical consciousness'.[3] 'He lived to the topmost pulse', James observes,[4] and so – on the basis of what readers now knew of a life story that appeared almost as adventurous as Stevenson's popular narratives – the memory of this great author had 'passed ineffaceably into happy legend'.[5]

Stevenson's legendary loss, in West's eyes, proved all the more regrettable when she considers the belligerent author whose unavoidable presence in 1900 attracted greater national attention than anyone else. Aged thirty-five, Rudyard Kipling was the Anglo-Indian son of artistically inclined parents who had links, on his mother's side, with the Pre-Raphaelites. Raised in Lahore, where his father served as keeper of the local museum, Kipling was removed at an early age to England, where he received his education, initially at a lodging-house run by a mean-minded couple in Southsea, and then at a military boys' school in North Devon. On returning to India at the

---

2 *Ibid.*

3 Henry James, 'The Letters of Robert Louis Stevenson', *North American Review* 170 (1900), p. 68. James and Stevenson developed a friendship after Stevenson published 'A Humble Remonstrance', *Longman's Magazine* 5 (1884), pp. 139–47; this essay is a reply to James, 'The Art of Fiction', *Longman's Magazine* 4 (1884), pp. 502–21.

4 James, 'Letters', p. 62.   5 *Ibid.*, p. 77.

age of sixteen, he began his adult life as a journalist. Soon his poems and stories of colonial life emerged in the *Civil and Military Gazette*, and by his early twenties he had published two accomplished volumes, *Departmental Ditties and Other Verses* (1886) and *Plain Tales from the Hills* (1886). Once he arrived at London in late 1889, Kipling was fêted by almost everyone he met. A member of the Savile Club (to which Stevenson had belonged), Kipling came into close contact with leading literary figures such as the popular novelist Walter Besant, the literary critic Edmund Gosse, and the historian of myth and legend Andrew Lang.

When Kipling's poems featuring the regular foot-soldier, 'Tommy Atkins', began to appear in W. E. Henley's *Scots Observer* in 1890, Kipling's reputation soared. It did so because enthusiastic readers of these lively works, collected as *Barrack-Room Ballads* (1892), thought they embodied the authentic spirit of empire. In his rough-edged Cockney, the irrepressible Tommy voices his demanding experiences of military life in a raucous tone that imitates some of the most renowned performances made famous on the music-hall stage. Time and again, this working-class persona bellows at the top of his voice to let the nation know that ordinary combatants 'aren't no thin red 'eroes, nor we aren't no blackguards too'.[6] More to the point, Kipling's boisterous ballads successfully impressed their military realism on a large late-Victorian readership because they displayed great metrical virtuosity. Kipling, though few critics have observed this important fact, modelled many of his poems on the entrancing rhythms that Algernon Charles Swinburne made infamous in his early controversial volumes of poetry, *Poems and Ballads* (1866) and *Songs before Sunrise* (1871).[7] To be sure, Swinburne addressed erotic subject matter and anti-monarchical sentiments that belonged to an entirely different sensibility from the imperialist 'beast of the age' that for West 'assailed' Kipling's vibrant imagination.[8] But no matter how much Tommy condescends to the 'pore benighted heathen' that he has defeated in Sudan,[9] it remains the case that what Kipling absorbed from Swinburne was a finely honed talent for outspokenness that could leave a lasting impression on those he chose to browbeat. In 1898, for example, when Kipling urged

---

6 Rudyard Kipling, 'Tommy', in *Rudyard Kipling's Verse: Inclusive Edition* (Garden City, NY: Doubleday, Page, 1921), p. 454.
7 One of the few critics to recognize Kipling's debts to Swinburne is Jacqueline S. Bratton, 'Kipling's Magic Art', in Harold Orel (ed.), *Critical Essays on Rudyard Kipling* (Boston: G.K. Hall, 1989), pp. 45–65.
8 West, *1900*, p. 122.   9 Kipling, 'Fuzzy-Wuzzy', in *Verse*, p. 456.

Theodore Roosevelt to 'Take up the White Man's Burden'[10] in the name of extending American rule over the Spanish-controlled Philippines, the presumptuousness with which Kipling adopted this memorable phrase certainly struck the future president as 'poor poetry'. Yet, in his role as Assistant Secretary of the Navy, Roosevelt, who advocated war against Spain, could not help but admire Kipling's bullying 'expansionist view'.[11]

Even if some readers found Kipling's loud tone and coarse subject matter in poor taste, it was hard for them to ignore the craftsmanship of his writings. Hence Oscar Wilde's grudging admiration for the 'superb flashes of vulgarity' that he glimpsed in *Plain Tales*.[12] By 1901, when Kipling's reputation was at its peak, he published *Kim*: the novel that West regards as his 'greatest work'.[13] Set in India, Kipling's narrative focuses on a figure that had long been dear to Victorian readers: the abandoned orphan, whose precarious plight Dickens in particular had made an object of heart-wrenching interest in *Oliver Twist* (1838) and *Great Expectations* (1861). Young Kimball O'Hara, 'a poor white of the very poorest', is the offspring of a drunken sergeant serving in the Mavericks and an Irish mother who served as nursemaid to a military officer.[14] At the start of Kipling's story, the boy has been left in the care of an Indian woman, whose negligence has been such that the boy lives like a street urchin. The child's fortunes transform when he encounters a kindly Buddhist lama, and the friendship they develop ensures that the boy has close contact with native traditions. At the same time, his father's regiment tracks Kim down and arranges for him to be sent to an Anglo-Indian school, where his formal education makes him into an adept imperial subject. Meanwhile, during his vacations Kim spends time with the lama, who has generously paid his tuition fees. As a consequence, Kim turns out to be a unique cultural hybrid that the colonial authorities can exploit in the name of playing the 'Great Game': the political manoeuvring involved in outwitting Britain's imperial enemy, Russia, on India's northern border. In his subsequent role as a secret

---

10 Kipling, 'Take up the White Man's Burden', in *Verse*, p. 371.
11 Theodore Roosevelt, 'To Henry Cabot Lodge', 12 January 1899, *Letters*, ed. Elting E. Morison, with John M. Blum and John J. Buckley, 8 vols. (Cambridge, MA: Harvard University Press, 1951–4), vol. II, p. 909.
12 Oscar Wilde, 'The Critic as Artist: With Some Remarks upon the Importance of Discussing Everything – A Dialogue: Part II', in Oscar Wilde, *Criticism: Historical Criticism, Intentions, the Soul of Man*, ed. Josephine M. Guy, in *The Complete Works of Oscar Wilde*, 4 vols. to date (Oxford University Press, 2000–present), vol. IV, p. 200.
13 West, 1900, p. 122.
14 Rudyard Kipling, *Kim* (Peterborough, ONT: Broadview, 2005), p. 53.

service agent, the teenage Kim pursues the 'Great Game' while he travels with the lama along a lengthy route that leads ultimately to the Himalayas. Although the lama believes that Kim is simply keeping him company as he pursues a spiritual journey to a holy River of the Arrow, the truth is that Kim follows the Grand Trunk Road under the discreet guidance of the native spymaster Huree Babu, who successfully foils the plans of two spies to mount an invasion into British colonial territory.

Yet to think of Kipling purely as an unquestioning imperialist is mistaken, especially when he contends that the future of empire lies not in the hands of the authorities based in London but in a resilient orphan who has never visited Britain. Throughout his writings, Kipling assumed that the noble, ever-expanding mission of empire largely remained in the custody of those native-born colonial subjects where the transplanted 'white man' should reign supreme. By the time imperial forces had suffered serious losses during the Anglo-Boer War, Kipling did not hesitate to criticize the complacency of the introspective 'Island' (as he belittlingly termed Britain) that gave the empire its marching orders. In 'The Islanders' (1902), his uninhibited poetic voice attacks 'the flannelled fools at the wicket':[15] the privately educated men whose unworldly upbringing had led them to believe that conducting warfare is similar to playing a game of field sports. Even if patriotic fervour was at its height during the 'Khaki Election' that shot the Conservatives to power in 1900, Kipling focused on differing kinds of British self-interestedness: the middle classes who sensed that war 'will minish our trade'; the 'master of many a shire' who preferred pursuing 'red deer horn' to fighting the enemy; and the 'workmen' who never bent beneath a dictatorial 'mandate ... to strike no more'.[16] By making these blunt observations, Kipling was putting pressure on a point that he had already emphasized in earlier poems such as 'Et Dona Ferentes' (1896). In this objectionable work, which takes its title from Virgil's *Aeneid*, his speaker delights in the moment when military conflict at last awakens the admirable 'Island-Devil' that lurks not so far beneath the 'Measured speech and ordered action' of the British imperial rulers: 'the hard pent rage ate inward, till some idiot went too far ... /"Let 'em have it!" and they had it, and the same was merry war'.[17] Such aggressive lines show the lengths to which Kipling would go to inflame liberal fair-mindedness. Yet it took decades before the British education

15 Kipling, 'The Islanders', in *Verse*, p. 349.   16 *Ibid.*, p. 350.
17 Kipling, 'Et Dona Ferentes', in *Verse*, p. 332.

system looked critically at Kipling's provocations, and for years poems of this type remained a staple of the high school curriculum.

Kipling's dazzling success as the self-appointed bard of empire could not, in West's eyes, contrast more starkly with the depressing fate suffered by Wilde, who in a state of self-imposed exile died of meningitis in a shabby quarter of Paris towards the end of 1900. Five years earlier, Wilde's meteoric career plunged when his ill-judged libel suit against the Marquess of Queensberry foundered at the Old Bailey. The insulting visiting-card that Queensberry left at Wilde's club, the Albermarle, on 18 February 1895, had a somewhat illegible scrawl on it. Most readers assume that the wording is supposed to read 'Oscar Wilde, posing as sodomite', though the word 'sodomite' is misspelled.[18] Wilde interpreted this statement as a libel, and took out a suit because of it. At the end of a trial filled with sensational disclosures, the public learned that Queensberry was probably right to have accused Wilde of 'posing as a sodomite'. This unruly aristocrat's grudge against the gifted Irish writer – whose reputation as a dramatist was unrivalled at the time – stemmed from the fact that his youngest son, Lord Alfred Douglas, had for several years been intimate with Wilde. Moreover, Queensberry's henchmen had garnered sufficient information to conclude that Wilde and Douglas were consorting with young homosexual men, some of whom were involved in brothels of the kind that became public knowledge through the Cleveland Street affair of 1889–90, a scandal that arose when the police discovered a male brothel on Cleveland Street, in the West End of London. In the summer of 1889, a police constable was in the process of investigating a theft from the Central Telegraph Office when he learned that a fifteen-year-old employee had fourteen shillings in his possession. When asked where he had procured these funds, the boy divulged the fact that he had been working at the nearby brothel. The investigation led to the questioning of Lord Arthur Somerset, who subsequently fled the country.[19] Once Wilde's prosecution collapsed, the Home Secretary, H. H. Asquith, ordered that Wilde (and not, it is worth noting, Douglas) should be arrested on charges of committing acts of 'gross

18 Richard Ellmann discusses the wording of the card in *Oscar Wilde* (New York: Knopf, 1988), p. 438.
19 The press named two other high-ranking men, Henry Fitzroy, Earl of Euston, and Prince Victor Albert, in reports of the case that led to the imprisonment of two men, Henry Newlove and George Veck, under the provisions of the eleventh section of the Criminal Law Amendment Act (1885) – the ruling under which Wilde was convicted in 1895. The most detailed recent account of the scandal is Morris B. Kaplan, *Sodom on the Thames: Sex, Love, and Scandal in Wilde Times* (Ithaca, NY: Cornell University Press, 2005), pp. 166–223.

indecency'. In the last week of May 1895, the shamed author was committed to two years in solitary confinement with hard labour: the maximum sentence under the terms of an 1885 law that banned all sexually intimate relations between men, even in private.

In the autobiographical document published (in a carefully edited version) as *De Profundis* in 1905, readers learned that Wilde's imprisonment proved so humiliating that it almost broke his spirit. Nonetheless, the literary skill with which Wilde represented the brutality of his incarceration inspired practically everyone who read this moving work, which he completed toward the end of his sentence, to think about the rough justice that the law had meted out against him. Within a matter of months, *De Profundis* had been reprinted numerous times, and it ensured that Wilde's name – no matter how much he had been vilified in public – could not be ignored. In any case, by 1898 (the year after his release) Wilde had already drawn attention to the horrors of his incarceration with *The Ballad of Reading Gaol*, whose one hundred and nine stanzas mount a thoughtful protest against an antiquated prison system in desperate need of reform. Even if Wilde felt he could not at first publish this poem under his own name (the earliest editions used the number of his prison cell, 'C.3.3.', instead), towards the end of his life his identity as the author of what became a best-selling work was plain for everyone to see. Sadly, even though Wilde's widely circulated *Ballad* went through some seven editions by 1899, he died in poverty and obscurity, tended by two loyal friends who were seeking to defray his considerable debts.

The posthumous success of *De Profundis* put Wilde's insolvent estate back in order, and with it came a measure of respectability. By 1908, the appearance of an authoritative fourteen-volume edition of his *Collected Works* also assisted in the slow but sure recovery of his reputation. Although the Lord Chamberlain still censored Wilde's experimental French-language drama, *Salomé* (1892), because it broke the law by representing biblical characters on stage, it remained the case that increasing numbers of people in the early twentieth century had come to appreciate the power of Wilde's play through Richard Strauss's operatic version. Strauss's *Salome* enjoyed its first British performance at Covent Garden, if not without interference from the Lord Chamberlain's office, in 1910. What is more, Wilde's four witty society comedies, which first excited the London stage with *Lady Windermere's Fan* (1892), came back into production in 1901, and they have remained popular with audiences ever since. It did, however, take another thirty years before the first public production of Wilde's *Salomé* was permitted in Britain.

As West observes, it is ironic to think that Wilde suffered such a harsh sentence when another author whose 'idea of romance was linked with the young male and not with the female'[20] became associated with the most admirable kinds of national sentiment. The writer in question is A. E. Housman, who arranged for a copy of his anonymously published collection of poems, *A Shropshire Lad* (1896), to be sent to Wilde after his release. (Echoes of Housman's finely modulated stanzas can be heard in Wilde's *Ballad*.[21]) 'The grace of the verses', West writes, 'was indisputable; but, granted the subject matter, it seems odd that the British reading public immediately took it to its heart.'[22] Certainly, Housman's fame grew so much that by World War I copies of the much-reprinted *Shropshire Lad* were handed to British soldiers as a token of national pride. Yet, as West suggests, it can appear strange that the male homoeroticism implicit in parts of Housman's collection failed to arouse consternation when Wilde's imprisonment gave such public visibility to what Douglas, in a noteworthy poem, called 'the Love that dare not speak its name'.[23] But, then, Housman's succinct stanzas incorporate his fascination with same-sex desire in a proudly English, and therefore unthreatening, pastoral. Even if Housman admitted that he had never visited Shropshire, he evoked the rural beauty of this Midlands county through ordinary personae whose economical phrasing and modulated rhythms sounded sincere without becoming banal: 'Loveliest of trees, the cherry now / Is hung with bloom along the bough.'[24] These famous lines come from an exquisite lyric in which the twenty-year-old speaker dwells on the fact that he will most probably witness the cherry's glorious springtime blooms for another fifty years. Yet such a thought

20 West, 1900, p. 127.
21 Echoes of both poem 'IX' and poem 'XLVII' in *A Shropshire Lad* can be heard in Wilde's *Ballad*. The first lyric addresses a hanging in a jail, while the second explores the crucifixion of Jesus Christ. Both the need to abolish capital punishment and the importance of Christian forgiveness are central to Wilde's poem. I discuss the relations between Housman's and Wilde's respective works in '"All Men Kill the Thing They Love": Romance, Realism, and *The Ballad of Reading Gaol*,' in Philip E. Smith (ed.), *Approaches to Teaching Oscar Wilde* (New York: MLA, 2008), pp. 230–47.
22 West, 1900, p. 127.
23 The phrase 'The Love that dare not speak its name' first appeared in Alfred Douglas's poem, 'Two Loves', in John Francis Bloxam's magazine, *The Chameleon* (1894); the poem is reprinted in Brian Reade (ed.), *Sexual Heretics: Male Homosexuality in English Literature from 1850 to 1900* (London: Routledge and Kegan Paul, 1970), p. 162. The poem had been used as part of the evidence against Wilde in his trial, although Douglas's authorship was not mentioned.
24 A. E. Housman, poem 'II,' *A Shropshire Lad*, in *The Poems of A. E. Housman*, ed. Archie Burnett (Oxford: Clarendon Press, 1997), p. 4.

encourages the young man to reflect on the transience of human life: 'Fifty springs are little room', he concludes.[25] Accordingly, he decides to 'see the cherry hung with snow',[26] just so he can enjoy to the full its beauty in every season before he dies.

The gentle elegiac tone that we hear in these lines characterizes the tender mood of *A Shropshire Lad*, in which many poems address the depart-ure of a loved one. Yet the manner in which Housman's male speakers contemplate bereavement can at times touch on emotions that relate more to their desire for intimacy with other men than with women. This point surfaces in the poem that opens with the question, 'Is my team ploughing?' – a moving lyric that takes the form of a dialogue between, on the one hand, the spirit of a farmhand who looks down from the spheres upon his former wife, and, on the other hand, the male friend who has taken his place in her bed. The deceased wants to know whether his mortal pal has 'found ... sleep in / A better bed than' the one he has in heaven. Housman's concise three-beat lines provide the following endearing answer

> Yes, lad, I lie easy,
>   I lie as lads would choose;
> I cheer a dead man's sweetheart,
>   Never ask me whose.[27]

Noticeably, the woman whose bed in which the two men have lain at different times never intervenes in their exchange, which miraculously spans mortal and immortal worlds. Instead, Housman's poem concentrates on the two lads' fond concern with each other's welfare, and in the end – as we see in this stanza – the one who remains on earth declares that the close bond between his heavenly brother rests on the fact that they have, one after another, shared the same 'sweetheart'. Obliquely but tantaliz-ingly, the lyric implies that for one man to 'lie easy' with a woman he needs to assure his departed chum that all is well in the bedroom. The discretion with which he offers such assurance ('Never ask me whose') more than probably discouraged Housman's readers from thinking that there was anything risqué in these affections. In all likelihood, West implies, the 'chastity of Housman's language'[28] meant that the considerate sentiments of his poetry distracted attention away from its underlying

25 *Ibid.* 26 *Ibid.*, p. 5. 27 *Ibid.*, p. 29. 28 West, 1900, p. 127.

homoeroticism, and so it seldom crossed the minds of his thousands of readers that such finely controlled works even hinted at impropriety.

All in all, West's perspective on the literature of 1900 is fairly jaded. She recoils from the hostility that Thomas Hardy experienced in the press when he depicted, with compassion and discretion, the sexual assault and subsequent bearing of an illegitimate child in *Tess of the d'Urbervilles* (1892), and she deplores the fact that – even though Hardy wrote just as 'chastely' as Housman[29] – the critical attacks on the agnosticism of *Jude the Obscure* (1896) deterred him from composing any further novels (although he completed his revisions to *The Well-Beloved* (1897), a work that he started writing before *Jude*). In 1900, it seems, the reading public was altogether more interested in works by writers of adventure stories (such as Anthony Hope) and authors of thrillers (such as Henry Seton Merriman). Granted, there existed a thriving periodical literature, including the *Saturday Review*, to which Max Beerbohm – later renowned for his elegant radio broadcasts – contributed satirical cartoons and lively theatre reviews. Similarly, popular journals such as the 'immortal' *Strand* presented the exploits of Arthur Conan Doyle's consummate detective, Sherlock Holmes, to a very large reading public.[30] Moreover, the 'dignified specialist publications' such as the *Art Journal* and the *Connoisseur* contained high quality articles.[31] All the same, to West, with the hindsight of more than eighty years, the literary world of 1900 looked somewhat 'chaotic'.[32]

1900: the literary turn of the century

In many respects, West's assessment is reasonably fair. If we turn to the second edition of *Annals of English Literature* (1961), then it becomes evident that very few works that appeared in 1900 have joined the evolving canon. Joseph Conrad's great novel, *Lord Jim*, which focuses on the well-intentioned but misguided exploits of a chief mate carrying Muslim pilgrims across the Indian Ocean, is perhaps the best-known novel to emerge during this year. The fictional narrative that probably caused the greatest controversy at the time was Laurence Housman's anonymously issued *Englishwoman's Love-Letters*, a risk-taking sequence of eighty-one passionate epistles that touches on incestuous desire. For some reason, this highly erotic work of fiction has not received much attention since. (Then again, comparatively little has

29 *Ibid.*   30 *Ibid.*   31 *Ibid.*   32 *Ibid.*

been written on Laurence Housman's substantial achievements in book illustration, the essay, fiction, drama, and poetry. The brother of A. E. Housman, he became a noted suffrage and homophile campaigner.) Mary Augusta Ward maintained immense popularity with her ninth novel, *Eleanor* (staged, three years later, as a play), while Marie Corelli – who outsold all other contemporary novelists – published her twenty-first volume of fiction, *Boy*. The careers of both of these prolific writers (who were equally hostile to the gathering campaigns for the franchise) have been treated to thoughtful biographical research, though neither could be considered a major influence on literary tradition.[33] Noticeably, West omits the fact that the author whom she subjected to fierce criticism in the *Freewoman*, and who soon after became the father of her son, brought out one of his earliest humorous excursions into the humdrum lives of the lower middle classes. H. G. Wells's *Love and Mr Lewisham* helped shift his well-established reputation as a writer of compelling scientific romances – such as *The Island of Doctor Moreau* (1896) – to that of a social realist who had great skill in putting misplaced cultural aspirations under satirical scrutiny, as we can see in *Kipps: The Story of a Simple Soul* (1905) and *The History of Mr Polly* (1910).

In some ways, Wells's turn-of-the-century fiction was revisiting for Fabian socialist purposes the cultural terrain that the conservative-minded George Gissing – arguably the greatest late-Victorian literary analyst of the *petite bourgeoisie* – had explored in an imposing body of naturalist fiction, including *In the Year of Jubilee* (1894). Among the last works that Gissing published during his industrious but impecunious career was *The Private Papers of Henry Ryecroft* (1903): a fine meditation, embodied in the persona of an imaginary author, on many cultural topics, including the business of writing. In his first-person narrative, Ryecroft on occasion looks at the ways in which leading Victorian novelists coped with 'the processes of "literary" manufacture and the ups and downs of the "literary" market': a tough business that Gissing had already explored, with his characteristic mordant wit, in what is arguably his greatest novel, *New Grub Street* (1891).[34] Ryecroft singles out Anthony Trollope ('an admirable writer of the pedestrian school'),[35] Charlotte Brontë (whose 'pinched life ... would have been

---

33 John Sutherland, *Mrs Humphry Ward: Eminent Victorian, Pre-Eminent Edwardian* (Oxford: Clarendon Press, 1990), and Brian Masters, *Now Barabbas Was a Rotter: The Extraordinary Life of Marie Corelli* (London: Hamish Hamilton, 1978).
34 George Gissing, *The Private Papers of Henry Ryecroft* (London: Archibald Constable, 1903), p. 213.
35 *Ibid.*

brightened had' she received 'but ... one third of what ... the publisher gained by her books'),[36] and Charles Dickens (whose impressive career reveals that 'no long work of prose fiction was ever brought into existence save by methodical labour').[37] Gissing, as Ryecroft's comments show, cherished no illusions about the hard graft that went into producing works prized for their literary distinction.

In the sphere of poetry, W. B. Yeats, a comparatively little-known Irish writer in his mid-thirties, published one of his early allegorical verse-dramas, *The Shadowy Waters*, which was produced in Dublin four years later. Altogether more famous at the time (though promptly forgotten after his death in 1915), Stephen Phillips won astonishing plaudits for his verse-drama, *Herod*, which ran for eighty performances at Her Majesty's Theatre, as well as the volume containing his long poem in blank verse, *Marpessa*, which had previously been included in his prize-winning *Poems* (1897). (The influential weekly review, the *Academy*, had bestowed a hundred guineas on Phillips for the latter volume. Yet leading critic Arthur Symons, who had stood at the forefront of literary Decadence in Britain, rightly thought *Poems* 'neither original as poetry nor genuine as drama', finding many of the contents to be derivative of Alfred Tennyson's early works.[38]) Meanwhile, William Ernest Henley – whose jingoistic verses included in his *Song of the Sword* (1892) rivalled Kipling's in their imperial pugnacity – issued *For England's Sake: Verses and Songs in Time of War*, which features a somewhat ineptly worded 'Health unto Her Majesty', in which the last line of each stanza concludes with the following toast: 'Here's to our sovereign – you, Ma'am, you!'[39]

At the time of the second trial that Wilde endured in 1895, Henley delighted in the fact that 'the Bugger' Wilde was 'at Bay'.[40] Henley had already, with the aid of his editorial assistant, Charles Whibley, used the *Scots Observer* as a forum for discussing the putatively immoral nature of Wilde's novel, *The Picture of Dorian Gray*.[41] Yet it is altogether too easy to view Henley solely as an imperialist zealot, as well as a homophobe who

---

36 *Ibid.*   37 *Ibid.*, p. 216.
38 [Arthur Symons], 'Mr Stephen Phillips', *Quarterly Review* 195 (1903), p. 498.
39 William Ernest Henley, 'A Health unto Her Majesty', in *The Works of William Ernest Henley*, 5 vols. (London: Macmillan, 1926), vol. 1, p. 237.
40 'To Charles Whibley', 13 April 1895, in *The Selected Letters of W. E. Henley*, ed. Damian Atkinson (Aldershot: Ashgate, 1999), p. 245.
41 During the summer of 1890, the controversy around Wilde's novel prompted Henley's journal to host a three-month debate about immorality in art; the various contributions to this discussion are brought together in Stuart Mason (ed.), *Oscar Wilde – Art and Morality: A Record of the Discussion which Followed the Publication of 'Dorian Gray'*, 2nd edn (London: Frank Palmer, 1912).

taunted Wilde and subsequently relished the Irish writer's imprisonment. His long career as a writer and editor, which began in 1875 with the appearance of his autobiographical sequence of experimental poems, 'In Hospital', played a crucial role in providing editorial support for a generation of younger male writers whom Beerbohm wittily nicknamed the 'Regatta'. The most eminent of this group of protégés was J. M. Barrie, who enjoyed success with his plays as early as 1892, although his greatest popularity arose from *Peter Pan* (1904): a remarkable piece of theatrical innovation (involving the illusion of aerial flight) that developed from his sequence of children's stories, *The Little White Bird, or Adventures in Kensington Gardens* (1902). But it was not only the 'Regatta' that Henley promoted. In the early 1890s, he also accepted for publication one of the more sensitive sections of Hardy's *Tess of the d'Urbervilles*, and from 1894 to 1897 – when he edited the *New Review* – he published such noted works as Conrad's *The Nigger of the 'Narcissus'* (1897), James's *What Maisie Knew* (1897), and Wells's *The Time Machine* (1895).

The stage, by comparison, shows similar unevenness in quality and innovation. Arthur Wing Pinero, whose long career as a playwright began in the mid 1870s, had for more than a decade responded to contemporary calls to produce a more serious form of drama in light of the 'Ibsenism' (as George Bernard Shaw styled it) that shocked London theatregoers from the late 1880s onward. In 1899, he saw his well-made society comedy, *The Gay Lord Quex*, enjoy an exceptionally good run of three hundred performances in the West End. (The play was subsequently adapted for film in 1920.) Pinero's subject matter addressed the behaviour of the aristocratic libertine whose stylish improprieties, such as we witness in the behaviour of Wilde's theatrical dandies, had preoccupied the London stage since the Restoration. Predictably, Pinero marries off the protagonist, who confidently declares that he used to believe 'that a man's whole duty to woman – meaning his mistresses – . . . is liberally discharged when he has made settlement on her, or stuck her into his will!'[42] No matter how much he tried to make his dramas more socially engaged than those of his predecessors, Pinero's best plays from the 1890s and 1900s remain caught within conventional morality that dictates, for example, that the sexually promiscuous protagonist of *The Second Mrs Tanqueray* (1893) must ultimately commit suicide, while the politicized New Woman who strives to live in a 'Free Union' with her lover

42 Arthur Wing Pinero, *The Gay Lord Quex: A Comedy in Four Acts* (London: William Heinemann, 1903), p. 33.

in *The Notorious Mrs Ebbsmith* (1895) must in the end maim herself (by retrieving, with heavy-handed symbolism, a Bible from the flames).

Increasingly prominent, though by no means popular, in the theatrical world was George Bernard Shaw, initially as a very informed reviewer of the London stage. Although the texts of many of his plays had been published by 1900, few of them had been performed because of the hostile Lord Chamberlain's office. Both Laurence Housman and Harley Granville-Barker would have their plays banned because they offended the state censor: the Lord Chamberlain's office refused to license Laurence Housman's nativity play, *Bethlehem*, for public performance because it represented the Holy Family on stage. Housman's play was produced privately, and ran for three weeks in London in late 1902. Barker's political drama, *Waste*, which touched on abortion and depicts an adulterous affair, was banned in 1907; the Stage Society produced the play privately later in the year. *Waste* finally received a license for public performance in 1920. At the turn of the century, however, Shaw had probably suffered more censorship than any other dramatist. The appearance of *Three Plays for Puritans* in 1901 was typical of Shaw's predicament. Although all of the works in this volume dated from the mid to late 1890s, only one of them – *Captain Brassbound's Conversion* – had been produced in London prior to publication, and, even then, there were only two nights when one could have attended the play, which the Stage Society mounted for a select audience. Of the two remaining dramas, *The Devil's Disciple*, which puts American Puritanism under sharp scrutiny, had to wait until 1907 before it appeared at the Savoy Theatre. Similarly, *Caesar and Cleopatra* – the third work attacking puritanical morality – was only available to London audiences in the same year at the same venue. It took until 1904, when Granville-Barker and John Vedrenne began their renowned three-year management of the Court Theatre, that Shaw had exactly the kind of forum, with a largely sympathetic audience, in which his socialist dramas could thrive. His major successes at the Court, especially *John Bull's Other Island* (1904) and *Major Barbara* (1905), tackled controversial material, including an unflinching depiction of a defrocked priest in the former play, and a thoughtful critique of the Salvation Army in the latter.

Even in the early 1900s, however, some commentators thought Shaw's socially engaged dramas unstageable, given the rhetorical weight they placed on polemical subject matter. Shaw's plays nonetheless drew theatre-goers who were at last responding to the critic William Archer's long-standing demands for the serious development of a 'New Drama' and 'Free Drama' that was emancipated from the strictures of the Lord Chamberlain's office.[43] When World War One broke out, Shaw – by then well into his sixties – was arguably the most established playwright of his time, as the sensational reception of his comedy of class exploitation, *Pygmalion* (1914), plainly reveals. Born in the 1850s, Shaw eventually became the belated literary figurehead who could at last celebrate the fact that in drama he had always been well ahead of his time. For the younger generation born in the 1870s and 1880s, however, the literary turn of the century largely meant that their careers developed at a point when some of the contradictions that West identified were beginning to unravel, along paths that pointed the way towards recognizably modern types of writing.

After 1900: the literary *début de siècle*

To speak of the start of the twentieth century as the *début de siècle* is by no means as conventional as labelling the 1890s the *fin de siècle*.[44] The reason is that during the 1890s the century's *fin* was widely touted in literary culture, especially in relation to contentious discussions of literary Decadence and cultural degeneration. It was almost as if the bohemian culture linked with Decadent literary journals such as Henry Harland's *Yellow Book* (1894–97) and Aubrey Beardsley and Arthur Symons's *Savoy* (1896) cherished the cultural decay of the stuffy moralizing that by that time seemed synonymous with Her Majesty's long reign. Succeeding generations, however, were not always willing to repudiate the idea that they could make sense of their era by referring to the monarch on the throne. Once Edward VII succeeded his mother in 1901, it was not uncommon for the new generation to refer to itself as Edwardian, in a manner that followed the convention, dating from the mid 1870s, where mid and late nineteenth-century individuals alluded to their era as Victorian. The same would be true of later writers, such as Virginia Woolf, who had no hesitation in calling her peers Georgians. It was not just the fact that George V's long reign began in 1910 that inclined Woolf towards using this term. She associated the label with a generation of literary authors who had to move forward because their Edwardian

---

43 In the 1890s, Archer was arguably the most vocal advocate for both a socially engaged drama and an end to the Lord Chamberlain's regulation of the theatres. Among his many important essays on these topics is 'The Free Stage and the New Drama', *Fortnightly Review* n.s. 50 (1891), pp. 663–72.

44 In adopting the term *début de siècle*, I am following Bruce Clarke's usage in *Dora Marsden and Early Modernism: Gender, Individualism, Science* (Ann Arbor: University of Michigan Press, 1996), p. 22.

forebears 'had made a pretty poor show'.[45] Yet when we reflect on the fact that literary historians habitually think of Woolf as a Modernist who took explicit steps to break with tradition, we can see that the terms that have been used to periodize the 1900s and 1910s are somewhat arbitrary. Moreover, each term carries with it certain assumptions about the political mood, subject matter, and style of the writing. Nonetheless, all three of these terms – Edwardian, Georgian, and Modernist – point to moments and movements that mark out several literary-historical debuts, all of which come into clearer focus when we turn, in the first instance, to poetry.

One of the most innovative poets who eventually came to notice in the 1910s was Charlotte Mew (1869–1928), who temporarily made her mark with an extraordinary short story in the *Yellow Book* ('Passed') before slipping for some time into comparative obscurity. Mew's faltering career as poet, which involved several false starts, began with two highly conventional sonnets on Queen Victoria's death, which appeared in the ailing magazine, *Temple Bar* (1866–1905): a journal that belonged to a group of mid-Victorian periodicals that at one time catered to the aspiring middle classes' literary tastes. Even if, in its declining years, this journal gave space to important emergent authors such as E. M. Forster (one of his earliest stories, 'Albergo Empedocle', appeared there in 1903), many of its contents appeared outmoded, and Mew's poems were no exception. 'Let Thy Spirit Reign', Mew's poetic voice declares in honour of the queen, 'For England is not England without Thee'.[46]

Such writing is so staid that one would hardly imagine that by 1912 Mew would publish her astonishing dramatic monologue, 'The Farmer's Bride', in the *Nation*, and the staggering transformation in Mew's work points to larger shifts in the form and content that poetry would take in the 1910s. In this striking poem, a distraught West Country farmer recounts the story of his unhappy union with a 'maid, / Too young maybe', who 'turned afraid / Of love' once they were wed. Accordingly, he tells us, she fled. 'We chased her', he adds, recalling that he and his pals 'caught her, fetched her home at

45 On 21 May 1922, Woolf wrote to Janet Case: 'But don't you agree with me that the Edwardians, from 1895 to 1914, made a pretty poor show. By the Edwardians, I mean Shaw, Wells, Galsworthy, the Webbs, Arnold Bennett. We Georgians have our work cut out for us, you see. There is not a single living writer (English) I respect.' *The Letters of Virginia Woolf*, ed. Nigel Nicolson and Joanne Trautmann, 6 vols. (New York: Harcourt Brace Jovanovich, 1975–80), vol. II, p. 529.

46 Charlotte Mew, 'V.R.I.', in *Collected Poems and Prose*, ed. Val Warner (Manchester: Carcanet, 1981), p. 59. I elaborate some of my points about Mew's poetry in 'Charlotte Mew's Aftereffects', *Modernism/Modernity* 16:2 (2009), pp. 255–80.

last, / And turned the key upon her, fast'. Now that she remains in domestic captivity, his young wife 'does the work around the house', although she keeps silent: *'I've* hardly heard her speak at all.'[47] In no respect can the farmer take any pleasure in his spouse, since 'She sleeps up in the attic there.' At the end of his speech, he divulges his frustrated yearning for his young bride's beauty: 'O! my God! The down, / The soft young down of her, the brown, / The brown of her – her eyes, her hair, her hair!'[48] These memorable lines display Mew's skill in weaving internal rhymes into rhythmically entrancing phrases that communicate the farmer's longing for intimacy with a woman whom he has gone to lengths to imprison. Yet what proves so powerful in 'The Farmer's Bride' is that the long vowels of 'her eyes, her hair, her hair!' do more than simply articulate the farmer's endless craving for her body.

Mew's fine poem shows that the farmer's longing, no matter how poignant it may sound, deserves never to be reciprocated because it underlies his desire to coerce his terrified spouse to his will. Moreover, the fact that the poem appeared in a left-leaning journal that gave staunch support to the intense campaigns for women's suffrage says much about Mew's depiction of a scene that reminds us of the oppressive legal situation that married women occupied for most of the Victorian era. Prior to 1882, under English law, a married woman was treated as her husband's chattel. In 1912, it would have been difficult for readers of the *Nation* to ignore the fact that disenfranchised women were no longer going to 'work about the house . . . / . . . like a mouse'.[49] For two years, suffragists had been on hunger strike in jail, and the surging violence (including arson attacks) linked with obtaining the vote, had grown more intense than ever before.

A number of readers were so struck by 'The Farmer's Bride' that they contacted Mew, and, within the next few years, she moved in various circles associated with the literary socialite Catherine Dawson Scott (later founder of International P.E.N.), the novelist May Sinclair, and the young Alida Klemantaski, who assisted Harold Monro, the publisher whose Poetry Bookshop hosted noteworthy poetry readings and issued many significant volumes of modern poetry, including Ezra Pound's anthology, *Des Imagistes* (1914). These encounters led to the publication of one of Mew's poems in the *Egoist* (1914–19), the journal linked most closely with Imagism. It was in

---

47 Mew, 'The Farmer's Bride', in *Poems and Prose*, p. 1.   48 *Ibid.*, p. 2.
49 *Ibid.*, p. 1.

the *Egoist* that Imagist poet H. D. reviewed Mew's first book, *The Farmer's Bride*, which Monro brought out in 1916. H. D. claims that Mew 'has grown a new bloom from [Robert] Browning's sowing, has followed a master without imitating him'.[50] Such comments show that in developing the dramatic monologue Mew was in part continuing a tradition that had its clear origins in the earliest Victorian poetry dating from the 1830s. Yet Mew's habitual interest in irregular meters and mixed rhyme schemes discloses her dissatisfaction with fixed forms.

Many of Mew's finest poems, such as 'In Nunhead Cemetery', 'The Forest Road', and 'Madeleine in Church', exploit exceptionally long lines that appear determined to resist syntactical closure. At the same time, these remarkable writings address experiences that are so traumatic that her personae yearn for their lives to come to an end. As the sexually ambiguous speaker in 'The Forest Road' comes to the close of his (or her) reflections on the terrible loss of a lover, the monologue reaches this startling climax:

> Then you lie there
> Dear and wild heart behind this quivering snow
> With two red stains on it: and I will strike and tear
> Mine out, and scatter it to yours.[51]

More often than not, Mew's speakers urge their own deaths, making visceral appeals to mortifying the human body, in a devastating style that positions her work within a growing modern literature of trauma.

Unfortunately, even though Mew attracted a small number of keen supporters (Conrad Aiken, Louis Untermeyer, and Virginia Woolf expressed enthusiasm for her poetry), her reputation went into decline soon after she took her life, by drinking disinfectant, at the age of fifty-eight. In the obituaries, much was made of her personal unhappiness. Moreover, she never found a firm foothold in the literary culture of her time. In 1915, for example, Mew came to blows with Sinclair, who had begun to act as Mew's mentor, if not unofficial agent, by circulating the poems of this newfound friend to various literary figures, including Pound. Besides the fact that Mew embarrassed herself by passionately declaring her love for Sinclair (a feminist who remained, on principle, celibate), the poet's unwillingness to follow the novelist's increasing embrace of emergent Modernism appears to have

---

50 H. D., Review of Mew, *The Farmer's Bride*, *Egoist* (September 1916), p. 135.
51 Mew, 'The Forest Road', in *Poetry and Prose*, p. 22.

created sufficient tension to end their alliance. Mew did, however, cherish the company of Thomas Hardy and Florence Hardy, who, through mutual contacts, welcomed her into their home. Hardy, whose own reputation as a poet developed belatedly after *Wessex Poems and Other Verses* appeared in 1898, took particular pleasure in Mew's 'Fin de Fête', which appeared in the *Sphere*, an illustrated weekly, in 1923. In this haunting lyric, Mew's speaker addresses a departed loved one, after a day's pleasure at a local fair: 'So you and I should have slept', the poetic voice states, just before bedtime. But no sooner has this speaker given voice to a profound sense of isolation ('Oh, what a lonely head!') than he or she – the sex remains unclear – glimpses the spirit of the departed in 'the shadow of waving bough / In the moonlight over your bed'.[52] At its greatest, Mew's poetry acknowledges the undying power of intimate desire in the face of irremediable loss.

Much younger than Mew, Rupert Brooke, born in 1887, also came into contact with the Poetry Bookshop, first in October 1912 when he defended Lascelles Abercrombie in Monro's *Poetry Review* from Pound's attacks, and then two months later when he went to buy a copy of his friend Edward Marsh's anthology, *Georgian Poetry 1911–1912*, in which the work of a group of up-and-coming male writers – including William H. Davies, Wilfrid Gibson, James Elroy Flecker, D. H. Lawrence, John Masefield, and Walter de la Mare – reached a very broad audience. He belonged to a generation that was certainly attempting to distance itself from its Victorian poetic inheritance by injecting an anti-poetic realism in its work, although early Modernists such as Pound seldom spared the Georgians' lack of formal innovation from searing criticism. By 1915, soon after Brooke died during his military service in the Aegean, his famous war sonnet, 'The Soldier', appeared in the third of Marsh's anthologies, which sold more than 19,000 copies. Very quickly, Brooke became a household name, largely because the Dean of St Paul's and Winston Churchill held him up as an icon of noble sacrifice that the nation had to make in such bloodbaths as the Battle of Gallipoli. While Brooke did not die in action (his death was caused by septicaemia arising from a bug-bite), he gained a reputation as a heroic warrior on the basis of the patriotic sentiments that he enshrined in 'The Soldier': 'If I should die, think only this of me: / That there's some corner of a foreign field / That is for ever England.'[53] That Brooke was also exceedingly good-looking (a fact that he never ceased to manipulate in his busy social life),

52 Mew, 'Fin de Fête', in *Poetry and Prose*, p. 40.
53 Rupert Brooke, 'The Soldier,' *New Numbers* 1:4 (1914) p. 169, reprinted in *The Poems of Rupert Brooke: A Centenary Edition*, ed. Timothy Rogers (Ealing: Black Swan, 1987), p. 133.

as well as a fellow of King's College Cambridge, elevated him as the most legendary son of a nation that was experiencing a wartime death-toll like no other ever known in human history. As a consequence, his *Collected Poems* (1918), featuring Marsh's adulatory memoir, went into numerous editions, and several of his best-known works – especially 'The Old Vicarage, Grantchester' – presented him as the ultimate celebrant of Englishness.

By the middle of the twentieth century, however, a number of documents surfaced that threw light on the unseemly aspects of Brooke's career, and his consecrated image as a blond-haired, blue-eyed English god transformed into that of a sexist, anti-Semitic, and homophobic individual, who relented his early involvement with the bohemian generation that the painter Vanessa Stephen styled as 'neo-pagans'. This grouping formed part of the milieu that would become, by the 1910s, associated with Bloomsbury (particularly James Strachey, Lytton Strachey, and Virginia Woolf). Brooke's revealing letters throw into sharp relief the struggles he went through as he sought to fend off the types of Decadent poetry to which his earliest mentor, St John Lucas, introduced him while he was a student at Rugby School. As a teenager, Brooke became an avid reader of 1890s poets such as Ernest Dowson, he eagerly consumed Wilde's *De Profundis*, and he immersed himself in French Symbolist writers, including Paul Verlaine. Later, he looked to maverick late-Victorian poets such as John Davidson as beacons of a spirited life-force that would help him break away from the puritan upbringing that had at times stifled him. Yet the evident problems that Brooke encountered when he tried to locate himself in literary history were paralleled by other difficulties in his life. To begin with, his gravitation away from Fabian socialism to Churchill's conservatism shows how hard it was for him to establish a political standpoint of his own. Furthermore, he was to some degree undecided whether his sexuality was oriented more towards the same than the opposite sex. Similarly, his early hostility to feminism emerged at a time when he became intimate with women with professional aspirations (one of them, the Bedales schoolgirl Noel Olivier, became a distinguished pediatrician). Brooke's struggles were symptomatic of a gifted mind acutely sensitive to the most contentious social and political upheavals of his time.

Many kinds of uncertainty are recognizable throughout Brooke's early poetry, which strives to break certain taboos while remaining unable to create formal innovations. In his largely regular lyrics, he could and did cause discomfort, most notably to his publisher, Martin Secker, who had qualms about Brooke's diction before publishing *Poems* (at the poet's expense) in 1911. Secker's misgivings were evident to the reviewer who found 'swagger and brutality'[54] in Brooke's sonnet, 'A Channel Passage', which recalls the 'cold gorge' that 'rose' in his throat and led to his 'sea-sick ... / Retchings'.[55] In a similar vein, 'Dead Men's Love' struck a different commentator as 'disgusting', no doubt because this lyric focuses on a 'damned successful Poet' who cannot face up to the fact that he and his beloved (whose 'limbs ... / ... had served love well') were 'Dust'. Not only that, those limbs had a repulsively 'filthy smell'.[56] This lyric, which suggests that traditional poetic idealizations of love should be dead and buried, forms part of a larger canon of Brooke's poems that endeavour (but mostly fail) to devise a fresh literary idiom for talking frankly about sexual intimacy. Brooke balked at the poetic conventions that he knew well from his close acquaintance with Renaissance literature (he was a scholar of John Webster's dramas, as well as a highly knowledgeable reader of John Donne's poetry and sermons). By 1913, as we can see in 'The Way that Lovers Use', his speaker states that the time-honoured lyric rendering of courtship has become clichéd, if not downright mechanical:

> The way that lovers use is this:
> They bow, catch hands, with never a word,
> And their lips meet, and they do kiss
> – So I have heard.[57]

As these deliberately flat lines suggest, it is not only that poetry has turned the rituals of intimacy into a series of impersonal gestures. The truth is that the lyric representation of sexual love also has no immediacy – since it is now faintly overheard, located at a far distance from direct experience.

Even if it remains impossible to regard Brooke as an avant-garde writer, it is worth observing that he was informed about decisive transformations in European art, as his thoughtful writings on German Expressionism reveal. In 1912, Brooke provided the following definition of '*Die Expressionisten*': 'It recognizes what is, roughly, the main reason of this modern art – a very sensible one – namely, that the *chief* object of a good picture is to convey the

---

54 [Anon.] review of Rupert Brooke, *Poems*, *Times Literary Supplement* (29 August 1912), p. 337.
55 Brooke, 'A Channel Passage', in *Poems*, p. 53.
56 Brooke, 'Dead Men's Love', in *Poems*, p. 72. Brooke quotes from the review of his *Poems* (1911) in an unspecified 'Oxford magazine' in a letter to Edward Marsh, 25 November 1912, in *The Letters of Rupert Brooke*, ed. Geoffrey Keynes (London: Faber and Faber, 1968), p. 409.
57 Brooke, 'The Way that Lovers Use', in *Poems*, p. 103.

expression of an emotion of the artist and *not*, as some people have been supposing, his impression of something he sees.'[58] His contacts also kept him abreast of important cultural developments in Britain. In 1910, for example, his schooldays friend James Strachey, who later edited the major English translation of Sigmund Freud's works, told him that he had just discovered the identity of the author of *Chains* (1909): an innovative play that had a single performance at the Court Theatre before reopening the following year for fourteen performances at the Duke of York's. The dramatist, much to Strachey's surprise, turned out to be the shorthand typist who worked for his cousin, St Loe Strachey, editor of the *Spectator*. 'She'd kept it dark', James Strachey remarks, 'for fear of St Loe being shocked & angry.'[59] As it turned out, the editor was 'delighted'. Yet the fact that Elizabeth Baker feared her boss's wrath says much about the somewhat intimidated position that women playwrights occupied in London's theatrical world. Although it would be untrue to assert that female dramatists had no place in Victorian theatre, their near invisibility points to the restrictive sexual politics of the nineteenth-century stage. Arguably, the most memorable plays that women wrote in the Victorian period were of the closet variety. (Some of the most sexually polemical writings of poets Augusta Webster and Michael Field were closet dramas not designed for stage production. These writings follow in a tradition that Joanna Baillie established in the Romantic era.) Soon after the turn of the century, with the shift towards a more socially engaged style of theatre and women's increasing demands for the franchise, there arose professional opportunities for women not just to produce typewritten copies of men's play-texts but also compose some of their own. It is no accident that Baker belonged to a newly developed cadre of office workers who were rapidly transforming the nature of secretarial employment from a traditionally male to an increasingly female occupation.

As its title suggests, *Chains* relates to the experience of feeling enslaved to oppressive authorities, and Baker draws this sense of human bondage into focus by writing about lives whose daily rituals and disappointments she knew well. Like Gissing and Wells before her, Baker portrays the tiresome

---

58 Rupert Brooke, 'The Post-Impressionist Exhibition at the Grafton Galleries', *Cambridge Review* 2 [1912] pp. 125–6 and 158–9, reprinted in *The Prose of Rupert Brooke*, ed. Christopher Hassall (London: Sidgwick and Jackson, 1956), p. 184.

59 James Strachey, 'To Rupert Brooke', 10 February 1910, in *Friends and Apostles: The Correspondence of Rupert Brooke and James Strachey, 1905–1914*, ed. Keith Hale (New Haven: Yale University Press, 1998), p. 102.

existence of the respectable lower middle classes. Charley, the male protagonist, commutes from his modest home at 55 Acacia Avenue to his office on
the recently opened Hammersmith and City line on the London Underground. The stage directions tell us that Charley *'is an ordinary specimen of
the city clerk, dressed in correct frock-coat, dark trousers, carefully creased, much
cuff, and a high collar'*. Moreover, he dons a *'silk hat'* that is part of a detested
'uniform' that he would like to 'pitch ... into the river'.[60] Together with his
spouse, a timid housewife named Lily, they have a lodger (comically named
Tennant) who reads the *Daily Mirror*: the pictorial daily newspaper that
magnate Alfred Harmsworth founded in 1903. In the first scene, the audience
hears Tennant singing Battison Haynes's popular ditty about Irish emigration
to America. Not surprisingly, he soon announces that he plans on leaving
England for the colonies. This was a topic that Kipling had praised in poems
such as 'Chant-Pagan', in which his working-class soldier (in the mould of
Tommy Atkins) wonders, after spending time serving in the Anglo-Boer war,
whether he 'can ever take on / With awful old England again', now that he
stands in awe of 'valleys as big as a shire' and "igh inexpressible skies.'[61] [G]oing
farming' in Australia strikes Tennant as altogether preferable to the prospect
of maintaining a 'good situation', where he works as a clerk (as Charley
observes) from '[n]ine to six, with an hour for lunch and tea thrown in'.[62]

The action of *Chains* pivots on Charley's agitated decision to follow
Tennant's plan by turning away from the 'beastly business of quill-driving'[63]
and make a 'fair start'[64] in a world where he can cultivate far more than just
the vegetables that he tends in his suburban garden. Charley's resolve,
however, throws his marriage into crisis because he declares that he would
have to leave Lily behind until he becomes properly settled abroad.
Towards the end of the play, his discontent with the workplace extends to
his annoyance with the obligations that come with marriage. He boldly tells
his father-in-law: 'marriage shouldn't tie a man up as if he was a slave'.[65]
Assuredly, he does not wish to injure Lily's feelings. He stresses that he has
no desire to desert her for ever. But it is clear that what he hates most
about his lowly occupation is the way it emasculates him. 'We're not men,
we're machines', he says of his fellow clerks who labour in the City of
London.[66] This is a powerful sentiment familiar from Victorian novels such

---

60 Elizabeth Baker, *Chains*, in Linda Fitzsimmons and Viv Gardner (eds.), *New Woman
   Plays* (London: Methuen, 1991), p. 87.
61 Kipling, 'Chant-Pagan', in *Verse*, p. 525.   62 Baker, *Chains*, p. 92.
63 *Ibid.*, p. 104.   64 *Ibid.*, p. 119.   65 *Ibid.*, p. 120.   66 *Ibid.*

as Dickens's *Hard Times* (1854) and Modernist films such as Charlie Chaplin's *Modern Times* (1936). What is unique in Baker's play is that it explores these frustrations neither in the factory nor on the assembly-line but in the respectable lower middle-class parlour. In the end, Charley loses faith in the idea of escaping when he learns that Lily is pregnant. There is, however, more of a glimmer of hope in the distinctly modern character of Maggie (Lily's sister), who insists that women must rise to the occasion in changing their humdrum lives. The men, she says, 'want stirring up – and it's the women who've got to do the stirring'.[67] That is why she urges Charley to embark on his adventures. Since she has given up her job as a shop-girl and broken off her engagement, Maggie welcomes the opportunity no longer to 'be safe' and for the first time not be 'afraid of risk'.[68] Even though *Chains* concludes with Charley throwing his map of the world into the fire and picking up his detested silk hat, it remains the case that Maggie is the figure that is ready to face an unpredictable future – one that she expects will become increasingly enabling for women of her class.

Baker's *Chains* joins with the ranks of several remarkable dramas whose social realism had proved almost impossible to present on the Victorian stage. Other women writers, such as Elizabeth Robins in *Votes for Women!* (1907), used drama to look daringly, from a feminist standpoint, at the problems of patriarchal authoritarianism. Equally critical of men's dominance, Githa Sowerby's accomplished *Rutherford and Son* (1912) focuses on a northern industrial world that had in previous years largely been the preserve of fiction and poetry. Her fine play compares well with powerful social-realist plays such as Galsworthy's *Strife* (1909), which confirmed his growing reputation as a writer of just the kind of serious drama that Archer praised in Shaw's and Barker's productions at the Court. In *Strife*, the liberal-minded Galsworthy sets out to show that the entrenched positions that union leaders and employers adopt in a painful industrial dispute have damaging personal consequences. There is no question that Galsworthy's Edwardian dramas, such as *The Silver Box* (1906) (on class conflict) and *Justice* (1910) (on prison reform), belong to an increasingly politicized British theatre that by the mid twentieth century would show little hesitation in approaching volatile subject matter in face of the Lord Chamberlain's prescriptions. (In 1968 the Theatres Act abolished the state censor.)

67 *Ibid.*, p. 124.   68 *Ibid.*, p. 128.

If Galsworthy is typical of his generation in producing dramas that confront present political conflicts unapologetically, then he is equally representative as a writer who turned to the novel as a genre that could trace the more prominent cultural and social shifts that had taken place since the end of Victoria's reign. In the same year that he attracted Archer's attention with *The Silver Box*, Galsworthy published *A Man of Property* (1906), his distinguished Naturalist novel about the upper-crust Forsyte family that he would revisit in the two other chronicles that comprise *The Forsyte Saga* (1922), as well as in other stories, such as *Two Forsyte Interludes* (1927), which he continued to write to the end of his career. Galsworthy's 1906 novel opens twenty years earlier, at a rather stuffy party in London where 'an upper middle-class family in full plumage' provides 'so clear a reproduction of society in miniature'.[69] His aim is to explore various members of this tightly knit patriarchal clan, which has risen from humble agricultural roots in Dorset to an arrogant property-owning dynasty. The family has so little 'foresight' that it believes that the capital it commands renders it invincible. Galsworthy's interest lies mainly in showing how challenges to the ironically named Forsytes' unbending sense of authority emerge in the shape of outsiders.

For the most part, the less privileged individuals whom the Forsytes either marry or employ become casualties of the family's ruthless self-interest. The violence that the Forsytes embody becomes obvious in an episode when a 'coster . . . taking his girl for a Sunday airing' in a 'shallopy chariot' tries to show off by racing next to Swithin Forsyte's phaeton. Like some grisly tyrant spawned in ancient Rome, Swithin not only 'laid his whip-lash across the mare's flank' but also 'raised his whip to lash the costermonger'. Racing faster, the wheels of the two carriages collide. Since Swithin is determined to maintain his superiority, he ensures that 'the lighter vehicle skidded, and was overturned'. One of the passengers in the phaeton is Irene, unhappily married to a Forsyte, who asks: 'Are we going to have an accident, Uncle Swithin?'[70] It is a pointed enquiry because Irene will be subjected to an attempted marital rape, and she will soon learn that the family's persecution of her lover – the struggling architect Philip Bossinney – has literally thrown him, panicking, under a bus. Bossiney's death means that Irene cannot escape from the family's clutches, and the novel

69 John Galsworthy, *The Man of Property*, in *The Forsyte Saga* (Oxford University Press, 1995), chapter 1, p. 15.
70 *Ibid.*, chapter 3, p. 129.

concludes, chillingly, with her return to the family home 'like an animal wounded to death'.[71] (Galsworthy's phrasing bears noticeable similarities to Mew's 'Farmer's Bride'.) Later in *The Forsyte Saga*, Galsworthy follows Irene's success in separating from Soames, and, some years after, her successful marriage to another member of the family: a man who openly declares that he is a feminist. Yet it is important to observe that the social realism that Galsworthy devised to advance his liberal critique of the hidebound Victorian age hardly impressed his Modernist contemporaries. In the opening issue of *Blast*, a magazine that put literary writings alongside polemical manifestos on the state of the arts, Wyndham Lewis set 'Galsworthy' near the head of a boldly typewritten list of cultural figures that he believed should be, metaphorically at least, destroyed.[72] For Lewis, it seems, Galsworthy's outmoded style obscured the crucial substance of this writer's fiction. (Among the other culprits that Lewis wished to defame on the same page are St Loe Strachey, Marie Corelli, and William Archer.)

By the 1910s several authors had joined with Galsworthy in using the novel to chronicle the palpable shifts that British society had undergone since the later part of the Victorian period. Novels such as Samuel Butler's *The Way of All Flesh* (1903), Netta Syrett's *The Victorians: The Development of a Modern Woman* (1915), W. Somerset Maugham's *Of Human Bondage* (1916), and May Sinclair's *Mary Olivier* (1919) serve to indicate the transforming possibilities for men and women who refuse to conform to parental strictures and expectations. The same is true of Edmund Gosse's great autobiography, *Father and Son* (1907), which recounts his growth as a literary man who had to break from his parents' unswerving commitment to the Plymouth Brethren. Virginia Woolf's most commercially successful novel, *The Years* (1937), belongs to this tradition, as does Rebecca West's *The Fountain Overflows* (1956): a *roman-à-clef* that tells the story of an unusual middle-class family through the eyes of Rose Aubrey, who bears close resemblances to the Cicily Fairfield (Rebecca West's birth name) who was ten years old when Queen Victoria died. At the end of this fine work, which begins in 1900 and concludes when Rose receives a scholarship to attend music college, West's protagonist can finally assert: 'I was a musician in my own right . . . I was a human being and liked my kind.'[73] At roughly the same age as Rose, Fairfield attended the Royal College of Dramatic Art, after which

71 *Ibid.*, chapter 9, p. 294.   72 Wyndham Lewis, 'Blast,' in *Blast* 1 (1914), p. 21.
73 Rebecca West, *The Fountain Overflows* (New York: Viking Press, 1956), p. 435.

she started a career in which she played the part of Ibsen's Rebecca West: an identity that, through an act of remarkable self-reinvention, she made her own.

West remained the youngest member of a literary generation whose coming of age during the *début de siècle* involved constant sparring with a Victorian literary heritage that she not only knew well but could also dissect with scathing wit. In a noteworthy review, she observes that Victorian writing began with figures such as Dickens and Browning who 'dragged' the English language 'through the mud', and it ended with a group of *fin-de-siècle* stylists such as Wilde who refused to eat 'peas with their knives'. Unfortunately, even if Wilde's circle helped to improve people's manners, they 'had no new gospel to preach'.[74] Already, by 1912, West knew that the gulf between her Victorian literary inheritance and her modern authorial identity was impossible to breach. Perhaps that is why, as her last book *1900* shows, the end-point of the nineteenth century exerted such pressure on her imagination, from the *début de siècle* until the end of her eighty-nine years.

74 Rebecca West, review of J. M. Kennedy, *English Literature, 1880–1902* [1912], *Freewoman*, 25 July 1912, p. 187.

The future of Victorian literature

JAY CLAYTON

In May 2008 Victorian science fiction came to life as installation art in London and New York. Two enormous drills burst upwards through piers on the South Bank and in Brooklyn, the bits still rotating from the stupendous effort supposedly required to dig a transatlantic tunnel. Michel Verne, son of Jules Verne, published a story in *The Strand Magazine* in 1895 about a tunnel beneath the Atlantic. More than a century later, the artist Paul St George imagined the completion of such a tunnel and the construction of a Telectroscope, another Victorian technological fantasy, a never perfected machine that could transmit images along a telegraph wire. The artist installed a 37-foot long, 11-foot tall, brass and wood viewing tube in each of the cities and connected them via a video conferencing link, so that spectators, for a small fee, could wave and dance and scrawl messages to their counterparts across the pond. The massive faux-Victorian viewing tubes were only the tangible manifestations of a more elaborate fiction. On an accompanying website and blog, the artist tells the story of his (imaginary) great-grandfather, Alexander Stanhope St George, who began construction of the 3,460 mile tunnel in the 1890s but was forced to abandon the dig because of a series of disastrous mishaps.[1] Lost from history, the project lay dormant until Paul St George 'rediscovered' his fictitious great-grandfather's plans and set out to complete both the transatlantic tunnel and the Telectroscope.

Quaint, captivating, tongue-in-cheek, yet oddly inspirational in its invocation of an age of heroic aspirations and grand engineering, the installation nicely captures twenty-first century attitudes towards Victorian culture. How did we grow so nostalgic for clunky nineteenth-century machinery? When did commercialism, irony, and simulation get reconciled with childlike

---

1 The official website is 'The Telectroscope, 22 May–15 June 2008', www.tiscali.co.uk/telectroscope, and the blog is 'Do You Believe in the Telectroscope,' www.telectroscope.net.

pleasure and utopian dreams? And how do all of these attitudes comport with today's generally critical perspective on Victorian colonialism, racial attitudes, gender assumptions, and class inequalities? By way of concluding this history of the Victorian period, this chapter will offer some answers to these questions, as well as speculations about future developments.

The twentieth century began with a backlash against the Victorian age. So the usual story runs, and with good reason. As the previous chapter indicates, writers as various as Virginia Woolf, Rebecca West, Samuel Butler, and Edmund Gosse staked out their own turf by repudiating the supposedly staid manners, stuffy interiors, and sexual repressiveness of the previous century. James Joyce's parody of Dickens in chapter 14 of *Ulysses* was only one of many literary, journalistic, and popular illustrations to mock Victorian authors as sentimental storytellers of hearth and home, sententious sages, or blustering jingoists. Scholarship in recent decades has revealed how much more complicated Joyce's engagements were with his immediate predecessors, including his own ambivalent debt to Dickens, but he was hardly unique.[2] Ezra Pound invoked the names of remote Provençal poets rather than let on how much his early dramatic monologues owed to Robert Browning, and T. S. Eliot pointed to Dante, the Metaphysical poets, and the classical authors of Greece and Rome as the tradition that had nurtured his individual talent rather than acknowledge his debt to Victorian verse.

Literary critics in the early decades of the twentieth century often followed suit. Advocates of Modernism in the novel contrasted its formal experimentation and self-referentiality with what they regarded as the improbable plots, naive realism, and mawkish happy endings of Victorian fiction. Critics of poetry too, such as I. A. Richards and William Empson in England and the New Critics in America, developed influential methods of close reading around many of the same poets that Eliot celebrated, while adding Eliot himself and William Butler Yeats to the pantheon. F. R. Leavis, an advocate of moral 'seriousness' in the novel, celebrated the achievements of a select 'great tradition' of Victorian novelists, but he followed Eliot

---

2 For Joyce's debt to Dickens, see Jay Clayton, 'Londublin: Dickens's London in Joyce's Dublin', *Novel* 28 (1995), pp. 327–42; Ira B. Nadel, ' "Nightplots": *Our Mutual Friend* and *Finnegans Wake*', in William Baker and Ira B. Nadel Baker (eds.), *Redefining the Modern: Essays on Literature and Society in Honor of Joseph Wiesenfarth* (Madison, NJ: Fairleigh Dickinson University Press, 2004), pp. 75–88; and Paul K. Saint-Amour, ' "Christmas yet to come": Hospitality, Futurity, the *Carol*, and *The Dead*', *Representations* 98 (2007), pp. 93–117.

in attacking Victorian poetry.[3] By the time Edmund Wilson wrote his revisionary essay 'Dickens: The Two Scrooges' (1939), he declared it was bold to suggest that a popular Victorian novelist was worthy of critical attention. Like his peers, Dickens had come to be viewed by other critics as 'one of those Victorian scarecrows with ludicrous Freudian flaws – so infantile, pretentious, and hypocritical as to deserve only a perfunctory sneer'.[4]

For a critic with impeccable Modernist credentials like Wilson to take Dickens seriously went a long way toward jump-starting the re-evaluation of Victorian fiction that followed World War II. Lionel Trilling's influential 1953 article on *Little Dorrit* worked to the same end by focusing attention on late Dickens, where the intricate patterns of symbolism made the novelist seem a worthy predecessor of Kafka and other modern writers.[5] In the post-war years, the rehabilitation of Victorian literature was largely shaped by its institutionalization in the university curriculum and academic criticism. In England, the influential cultural critic Raymond Williams, and social historians such as E. P. Thompson and Asa Briggs, brought renewed attention to the radical legacy of Victorian culture. Williams's method of analysing the 'structure of feeling' of a particular historical moment was influential at the time and on later attempts to relate collective experience to cultural expression, especially among members of the Birmingham School of Cultural Studies.[6]

Academic formalists in the post-war years also began to apply methods fashioned in response to the demands of a Modernist canon to Victorian novels. Hence it became possible to study intricate textual patterns of symbolism

---

3 See F. R. Leavis, *The Great Tradition: George Eliot, Henry James, Joseph Conrad* (New York: G. W. Stewart: 1948) and *New Bearings in English Poetry: A Study of the Contemporary Situation* (Ann Arbor: University of Michigan Press, 1960). For Richards's and Empson's positions, see I. A. Richards, *Practical Criticism: A Study of Literary Judgment* (London: K. Paul, Trench, Trubner, 1929) and William Empson, *Seven Types of Ambiguity* (London: Chatto and Windus, 1930). Cleanth Brooks's *Modern Poetry and the Tradition* (Chapel Hill: University of North Carolina Press, 1939) is representative of the New Critics' attitudes towards Victorian poetry.

4 Edmund Wilson, *The Wound and the Bow: Seven Studies in Literature* (New York: Oxford University Press, 1965), p. 3.

5 Lionel Trilling, 'Little Dorrit', *Kenyon Review* 15 (1953), pp. 577–90.

6 See Raymond Williams, *Culture and Society: 1780–1950* (London: Chatto & Windus, 1958) and *The Long Revolution: An Analysis of the Democratic, Industrial, and Cultural Changes Transforming Our Society* (New York: Columbia University Press, 1961). His concept of 'structure of feeling' may be found in *The Long Revolution*, p. 48. Asa Briggs, *Victorian People: A Reassessment of Persons and Themes 1851–67* (University of Chicago Press, 1955) and E. P. Thompson, *The Making of the English Working Class* (New York: Vintage Books, 1963) were important contributions to radical social history in the post-war years.

in late Dickens, ambiguity in *Wuthering Heights*, form in *Middlemarch*, imagery in *Jude the Obscure*, and impressionism in *Heart of Darkness*.[7] The success of these New Critical readings of Victorian novels in the fifties paved the way for a phenomenon that we now take for granted – the application of each new critical method to the (widening) canon of nineteenth-century fiction. Between the mid 1950s and the 1990s, one wave after another of literary theory was illustrated through – and in some cases, developed by – readings of Victorian novels. Important critical work on Victorian fiction played a role in the promulgation of Anglo-American versions of phenomenology (J. Hillis Miller), structuralism (Frank Kermode), deconstruction (Hillis Miller again; Cynthia Chase), reader response (Wolfgang Iser), Marxism (Raymond Williams; Terry Eagleton; Fredric Jameson), psychoanalytic criticism (Peter Brooks; Shoshanna Felman), Bakhtinian criticism (Bakhtin himself; Peter K. Garrett), feminism (Elaine Showalter; Sandra Gilbert and Susan Gubar; Mary Poovey), post-colonial studies (Gayatri Spivak), new historicism (Catherine Gallagher; D. A. Miller), and queer theory (Eve Sedgwick). The analysis of Victorian fiction aided in establishing each of these methods as an approved discourse in the academy, a possible form of knowledge in the institution of literary studies.

The study of Victorian poetry had less effect on emerging critical movements. Although the Romantic poets underwent a critical revival in the sixties and seventies at the hands of influential scholars such as Northrop Frye, Harold Bloom, and M. H. Abrams, then played major roles in post-structuralist theory through the agency of Paul de Man and in new historicism through the efforts of Alan Liu, David Simpson, and Marjorie Levinson, Victorian poets usually did not receive this kind of attention from literary theorists. There were few ground-breaking theoretical works devoted to the Victorian poets until the 1990s, when cultural studies and gender approaches began to explore the role of Victorian poetry in shaping social attitudes.[8]

---

7 See, respectively, Trilling, 'Little Dorrit'; Dorothy van Ghent, 'On *Wuthering Heights*', in *The English Novel: Form and Function* (New York: Harper and Row, 1961), pp. 153–70; Barbara Hardy, *The Novels of George Eliot: A Study in Form* (New York: Oxford University Press, 1959); Frederick P. W. McDowell, 'The Symbolical Use of Imagery and Contrast in *Jude the Obscure*', *Modern Fiction Studies* 6 (1960), pp. 233–50; and Marvin Mudrick, 'The Originality of Conrad', *Hudson Review* 11 (1958), pp. 545–53.
8 There were exceptions, of course, such as J. Hillis Miller's phenomenological study *The Disappearance of God; Five Nineteenth-Century Writers* (Cambridge, MA: Harvard University Press, 1963), Alan Sinfield's cultural-materialist *The Language of Tennyson's 'In Memoriam'* (New York: Barnes & Noble, 1971), and Margaret Homans's Post-structuralist and feminist *Women Writers and Poetic Identity: Dorothy Wordsworth, Emily Brontë, and Emily Dickinson* (Princeton University Press, 1980). Theoretical work on Victorian poetry in the 1990s was stimulated by Margaret Reynolds's edition of Elizabeth Barrett

If this account of backlash in the first half of the twentieth century and recuperation in the second represents a common – and largely accurate – story about the reputation of Victorian literature in the twentieth century, it nonetheless leaves out a great deal. It leaves out the continuing appeal of Victorian fiction within popular culture. The very sentimentality, faith in progress, and love of country that led literary arbiters of taste to reject the values of the previous age still moved ordinary readers, while the apparently strait-laced morality enshrined the old chestnuts as bedtime reading in the nursery and edifying texts for schools. Inconsistency proved no impediment. Distaste for Victorian prudishness or stilted manners co-existed easily with a longing for a safer, more secure world. If anything, contradictions only multiplied the pleasures of denouncing hypocrisy while fantasizing about a time of refinement and decorum.

This contradictory structure of feeling, to use Raymond Williams's term, has persisted throughout the twentieth century. Dickens serves as the prime example. The nostalgic character of Dickens's presence is especially visible around Christmas time, when productions of *A Christmas Carol* become a staple of radio, television, movies, musicals, and amateur theatricals. Such nostalgia for a simpler life is by no means incompatible with commercial exploitation. Scrooge is a familiar figure in magazine and television commercials, such as the Canadian Tire jingle that runs 'Spend like Santa, Save like Scrooge'. The annual 'Charles Dickens Victorian Christmas' at the Mt. Hope Victorian Estate and Winery, near Hershey, Pennsylvania features a visit by the great novelist himself. But Christmas is not the only holiday season when Dickens may turn up. There is an entire theme park called Dickens World in Chatham, Kent, but the commercialization of Dickens has been an immense success for the export market too. From the mid nineteenth century onwards, the commodification of this novelist has been an important feature of transatlantic culture.[9] Dickens merchandise can be found on street corners and in malls all across the American continent. Philadelphia has a pub called the Dickens Inn, and right around the corner is another one called The Artful Dodger (this latter name turns up in Saskatoon, Saskatchewan too). There is a well-established dating service

---

Browning's *Aurora Leigh* (Athens: Ohio University Press, 1990) and included Isobel Armstrong's *Victorian Poetry: Poetry, Poetics, and Politics* (London: Routledge, 1993) and Yopie Prins's *Victorian Sappho* (Princeton University Press, 1999).

9 For an analysis of Dickens's presence in commodity culture, see Jay Clayton, 'Is Pip Postmodern? Or, Dickens at the Turn of the Millennium', in *Charles Dickens in Cyberspace: The Afterlife of the Nineteenth Century in Postmodern Culture* (Oxford University Press, 2003).

called Great Expectations and a chain of maternity stores with the same name. Bad puns seem irresistible. In the Richmond, Virginia area, there is a candle shop called Great Waxpectations; in Winnipeg, a dessert restaurant called Baked Expectations; in Brooklyn, a beauty salon called Great Hair-Spectations; in Manhattan, a wine tasting called Grape Expectations; and on *Saturday Night Live*, a skit called 'Great Expectorations'.

Early in the twentieth century the ubiquity of Victoriana in popular culture reinforced the notion that serious readers should look elsewhere for literary qualities. This split between low and high culture in regard to Victorian literature was just part of a larger fragmentation of the market, a segmenting of the reading public that can be traced back to publishing practices in the previous age but that reached its apogee in the twentieth century. Andreas Huyssen has called this split 'the great divide', and it was remarked upon by commentators throughout the century.[10] Jürgen Habermas, Michael Walzer, Anthony Giddens, and numerous other social theorists have identified the split as part of a trend within modernity towards differentiation in all aspects of life. Increasing specialization in the economic, administrative, social, and cultural spheres was one of the most prominent features of the twentieth century, and remains with us today.

Given the split between elite and popular culture, it is not surprising that a narrative of backlash followed by recuperation in the literary sphere has seemed adequate for most literary histories that dealt with the twentieth century's response to Victorian literature. To understand twenty-first century developments, however – to grasp the appeal of the Telectroscope, for example – one needs to attend to a wide range of cultural developments, not just those in literary and academic circles.

Let me pick up the narrative in the World War II years. At a moment in history when British national identity was under siege, an impressive set of film-makers turned to Victorian fiction for material. Beginning with William Wyler's *Wuthering Heights* (1939) and continuing through a version of *Jane Eyre* (1944) starring Orson Welles, to David Lean's two Dickensian masterpieces, *Great Expectations* (1946) and *Oliver Twist* (1948), acclaimed films drew on precisely the popular loyalty that Victorian fiction inspired to construct stories of hope, perseverance, and mutual support for troubled times. The voiceover with which *Jane Eyre* begins nicely illustrates the parallel audiences were invited to draw with their own time: 'My name is

---

10 Andreas Huyssen, *After the Great Divide: Modernism, Mass Culture, Postmodernism* (Bloomington: Indiana University Press, 1986).

Jane Eyre ... I was born in 1820, a harsh time of change in England.'[11] Throughout the century, Victorian fiction spoke to the cinema public in this way – there were scores of movies made from these four novels alone – and each generation of film-makers fashioned the Victorian classics to their own ends. Dianne Sadoff has shown how the century-long vogue for Victorian 'heritage films' gave us very different Brontë and Dickens films in the 1940s from those of the 1990s; how James Whale's *Frankenstein* (1931) and Tod Browning's *Dracula* (1931) exploited Depression-era fears, while horror movies of the 1950s used the same originals to explore homosexual panic, and the lavish productions of the 1990s indulged a taste for the pleasures of consumption; or, finally, how a wave of Henry James adaptations in the 1970s explored the hypocrisy of society while another wave at the turn of the millennium laid bare their latent sexual content.[12]

Film was the dominant popular genre for much of the twentieth century, but its commercial character made it hard for critics in the post-war years to think of it as anything but a vehicle of exploitation and manipulation. The industrial mode of its production and distribution, the power of its advertising and publicity machines, the taint of its association with propaganda in both World War II and the Cold War, the dominance of Hollywood, the eagerness of other media such as newspapers, radio, and television to promote the star system – all these factors and more led intellectuals to criticize film as a form of 'mass culture', not popular expression. The most influential formulation of this position came from the Frankfurt School theorists Max Horkheimer and Theodor Adorno, who employed the phrase 'the culture industry' to describe the alliance between creativity and capital that they feared led to fascism and other modern forms of domination.[13] The reconceptualization of low culture as a mode of *mass* rather than *popular* experience depended on a historical narrative of its own, one elaborated most thoroughly in the Marxist tradition, in which the popular cultures of earlier epochs were seen as organic expressions of the people, but those of the twentieth century were regarded as centralized modes of distraction controlled from on high.

---

11 *Jane Eyre*, dir. Robert Stevenson (Twentieth Century Fox, 1944).
12 Dianne Sadoff, *Victorian Vogue: British Novels on Screen* (Minneapolis: University of Minnesota Press, 2009).
13 Max Horkheimer and Theodor W. Adorno, *Dialectic of Enlightenment: Philosophical Fragments*, ed. Gunzelin Schmid Noerr, trans. Edmund Jephcott (1947; Stanford University Press, 2002), pp. 94–136.

This critique of low culture from the Left reinforced the more established line of attack from both proponents of Modernism and conservative critics in the Arnoldian tradition (figures who sometimes overlapped). The combination gave a political as well as a moral urgency to maintaining the barrier between high literature and mass entertainment. Not until the social upheavals of the 1960s did the great divide between these two cultural formations begin to be reconfigured.

In the 1960s the growth of the counter-culture undermined this barrier like so many others. Fuelled by the anti-establishment impulses of the decade, the first stirrings of the Post-modern movement attempted to suture the stylistic experiments of Joyce, Woolf, and Pound to pop-culture subject matter drawn from TV, the Western, detective fiction, porn flicks, newspapers, and kitsch. Post-modern arts channelled the radical desublimation of energies that Herbert Marcuse championed, and they flaunted their pleasure in incorporating the detritus of mass culture. Debates over the definition of this protean term 'Post-modernism' abound, and an adequate account of even its early years would have to distinguish among impulses in fiction (Barth, Heller, Pynchon, Vonnegut, Barthelme), poetry (Olsen, Duncan and the Black Mountain group; O'Hara, Ashbery and the New York school), non-fiction (New Journalists such as Mailer and Capote), the graphic arts (Andy Warhol's pop-art), architecture (Venturi's strip-mall chic), and theatre (absurdist comedy). Yet in the context of a discussion of Victorian literature, we do not have to explore the intricacies of Post-modernism in the 1960s because none of this artistic ferment affected the way in which nineteenth-century literature was understood. Despite the crumbling of distinctions between low and high culture, attitudes towards the Victorian era remained split along the same faultlines – scepticism and critique, in some quarters, and popular affection in others.

Take a quintessentially Post-modern literary form, the genre Linda Hutcheon named 'historiographic metafiction'.[14] Novels in this vein turned the genre of historical fiction into self-reflexive meditations on the fictional nature of all history. John Fowles's *The French Lieutenant's Woman* (1969), which was set in the nineteenth century and imitated Victorian prose style, staged its own literariness by encouraging readers to choose among three possible endings. The novel incorporated analyses of class conditions and

14 Linda Hutcheon, *A Poetics of Postmodernism: History, Theory, Fiction* (New York: Routledge, 1988). See also Amy J. Elias, *Sublime Desire: History and Post-1960s Fiction* (Baltimore: Johns Hopkins University Press, 2001).

sexual norms, as well as digressions on Darwin, Dickens, and Arnold. All of these gestures served to deconstruct the Victorian narrative conventions that the novel simultaneously employed. Jean Rhys's *Wide Sargasso Sea* (1966), a novel that re-imagined the life of Bertha Mason, the madwoman imprisoned in the attic in *Jane Eyre*, similarly questioned the racial and gender assumptions of Brontë's original story. A landmark work of post-colonial resistance, Rhys's story explored the repressed subtext of a Victorian classic still revered by twentieth-century popular culture.

In academic circles the social forces that were responsible for the growth of the counter-culture in the 1960s contributed to an enormous expansion of the canon of Victorian literature. These forces might be loosely grouped under the heading of identity politics, particularly in the areas of race, class, gender, sexuality, and post-colonial movements. They helped facilitate the entry into the curriculum of an array of previously neglected Victorian texts: novels and poetry by women writers, periodical writing, books by working-class writers, underground erotic novels, like *My Secret Life* and *The Pearl*,[15] sensation fiction, New Woman fiction from the end of the century, and Victorian science fiction and utopian fables, like Edward Bulwer Lytton's *The Coming Race* (1871), Samuel Butler's *Erewhon* (1872), and William Morris's *News from Nowhere* (1890). Yet the expansion of the academic canon had little effect on popular perceptions of the Victorians. The trend may have inflamed conservative intellectuals like Allan Bloom, but it did not alter prevailing stereotypes of nineteenth-century society. Elegant manners and teasing romance were the qualities of Victorian life that Hollywood still put on display in Peter Bogdanovich's adaptation of *Daisy Miller* (1974).

The impact of new social movements on universities in the 1960s was augmented by the advent of continental literary theory. Post-modern theorists challenged the validity of grand meta-narratives, the autonomy of the literary work, and the authority of the author. These interventions, familiar now to every student of recent literary theory, transformed long-standing practices in Victorian studies of relating works of literature to a social context, now renamed an intertextual web of connections. Additionally, the institutionalization of programmes in women's (and later gender)

15 For studies of Victorian erotic literature, see Steven Marcus, *The Other Victorians: A Study of Sexuality and Pornography in Mid-Nineteenth-Century England* (New York: Basic Books, 1966) and Ellen Bayuk Rosenman, *Unauthorized Pleasures: Accounts of Victorian Erotic Experience* (Ithaca, NY: Cornell University Press, 2003).

studies, African American and Black and Asian studies, and courses in gay, lesbian, and queer studies, post-colonial studies, and cultural studies trained successive generations of students in interdisciplinary methods that loosened the definition of the literary. The end result was a conception of Victorian literature in the academy that scarcely resembled the narrow shelf of works featured in the first half of the twentieth century.

Post-modern responses to Victorian literature – whether in 1960s metafiction or academic literary criticism of the 1970–80s – paradoxically enhanced the prestige of the era by subjecting it to powerful critiques. Nothing could contrast more with the popular relationship to these works, which remained embedded in a structure of feeling involving sentimentality, nostalgia, class hierarchy, and the romance of colonialism. Witness the enduring appeal of BBC adaptations during this period, which also became the staple of America's *Masterpiece Theater*, premiering in 1971 after a decade of anti-establishment turmoil. These adaptations offered relief from the counter-culture under the mantle of cultural seriousness. With versions of Dickens, George Eliot, the Brontës, Trollope, Collins, Gaskell, Hardy, Conan Doyle, and numerous other Victorian novelists, as well as historical period pieces and biographies, television adaptations have kept alive the image of Victorian England that Modernists rebelled against, New Critics rendered ambiguous, and Post-modernists undermined.

In the arena of public life, a similarly stable conception of Victorian values remained current on both sides of the Atlantic until even more recently. It hardly mattered whether one was conservative or liberal – the cultural politics of admiring the Victorians in public forums conformed to a recognizable pattern. During the culture wars of the 1980–90s, politicians such as the British Prime Minister Margaret Thatcher and the US Speaker of the House Newt Gingrich extolled 'Victorian virtues' of hard work, traditional mores, and family values. Neo-conservative intellectuals did the same. Gertrude Himmelfarb, a respected historian of Victorian society, produced several volumes of cultural commentary that held up the nineteenth century as an admonishment to our wayward times.[16] William Bennett, head of the US National Endowment for the Humanities under Ronald Reagan, became wealthy by promoting his conception of Victorian virtue in anthologies, tapes, calendars, and illustrated children's tales. Ethical in tone and intent, neo-conservative Victorianism produced a powerful narrative of cultural

---

16 See Gertrude Himmelfarb, *The De-Moralization of Society: From Victorian Virtues to Modern Values* (New York: Knopf, 1995) and *On Looking into the Abyss: Untimely Thoughts on Culture and Society* (New York: Knopf, 1994).

decay. It relied on popular nostalgia for a vanished past to fuel a call for a return to once cherished ideals.

Liberal admirers of Victorianism in public debates followed a different but related pattern. Rather than a story of decline, they invoked a universal conception of culture as a repository of timeless truths, which retained their importance regardless of the historical period. The liberal position uses culture as a touchstone with which to measure out praise or blame impartially to both yesterday and today. Matthew Arnold is its tutelary spirit, and notable exponents during the 1980–90s included Eugene Goodheart and Martha Nussbaum.[17] The latter employed Dickens's *Hard Times* to instruct public policy experts – whether nineteenth-century utilitarians or twentieth-century cost-benefit analysts – in the importance of imagination and love. Nussbaum's *Poetic Justice* (1995) conducted a sustained debate with the ideas of Richard Posner, a prominent jurist and leader of the Law and Economics movement, over her contention that reading Dickens could help policy-makers more than abstract economic formulas because his novels treated problems in terms of fundamental views about human freedom that have 'universal significance'.[18] In the same year Oscar Hijuelos's well-reviewed novel *Mr Ives' Christmas* (1995) celebrated Dickens in much the same liberal spirit, turning to *A Christmas Carol* for insights into the consequences of urban poverty, no matter what its time period.

Despite their opposed agendas, the liberal view of Victorian literature was the mirror image of the neo-conservative one. Both relied on the popular understanding of the Victorian period, not the sceptical stance of Post-modernism. In politics, even longer than in other domains, the popular response to the Victorians remained distinct from that of high culture, even as the latter has become more capacious and socially inclusive. For most of the twentieth century, the popular structure of feeling has served the purposes of both a liberal and a neo-conservative stance towards the past, and it has survived in the face of rejection by high Modernism, recuperation on formalist terms following World War II, Post-modern attempts to abolish the split between high and low culture, and academic efforts to renovate the canon.

---

17 See Eugene Goodheart, *The Skeptic Disposition in Contemporary Criticism* (Princeton University Press, 1984) and *The Reign of Ideology* (New York: Columbia University Press, 1997); Martha C. Nussbaum, *Poetic Justice: The Literary Imagination and Public Life* (Boston: Beacon Press, 1995).

18 Nussbaum, *Poetic Justice*, p. 8.

With the coming of the twenty-first century, has anything changed? Surprisingly enough, I think something has. The old popular response does not seem to explain the public appeal of Victorianism in our times. Neither does the Post-modern posture of sceptical critique. If the Telectroscope may be taken as a sign, however whimsical, the meaning of the Victorian is shifting. Reflect again on the reactions this artwork evokes. Delight in quaint, oversized technology, especially since one knows the marvel relies on digitalization and satellite communications; fascination with grand ambitions, especially when doomed to failure, because acknowledging the likelihood of defeat upfront allows the renewal of utopian dreams without naivety; the temptation to abandon oneself to childlike enjoyments – clowning around, pulling faces for the camera – and to watching children bestow a more earnest attention on this imposing machine; the willingness to pay money for a simulation, a patent fabrication, and having paid for the privilege, to sustain the fiction that it is real; the many delicious indulgences irony affords and the benefit of being in on the joke; and finally, an awareness of the problems of colonialism, racism, misogyny, and class prejudice inherent in the age one is visiting courtesy of this elaborately staged piece of art. Together these responses form a distinctive set of affects, intellectual perspectives, beliefs, aspirations, and desires. They suggest the outline of a twenty-first century structure of feeling, which stands in contrast to most of the twentieth-century attitudes towards Victorian culture considered here.

The casual visitor to the installation might miss the project's critical dimension. Viewed as a tourist attraction, the Telectroscope seems like another example of what Fredric Jameson complained about in his book *Postmodernism*: the tendency to substitute an 'indiscriminate appetite for dead styles and fashions' for the ability to engage in genuine historical thought. Surrounded by crowds of spectators enjoying a brief outing on the docks, the exhibition does seem to betray some of the very symptoms that led Jameson to diagnose contemporary culture as 'irredeemably historicist, in the bad sense': commercialism, marketing, retro fashion, the past as style not substance.[19] But the temporary installation is part of a larger intermediated fiction, accessible through its website and blog, which uses simulated maps, architectural drawings, doctored historical photographs, video, and the written word to tell a story about the artist's imaginary great-grandfather, the pioneer who supposedly initiated the project.

19 Fredric Jameson, *Postmodernism, or, the Cultural Logic of Late Capitalism* (Durham, NC: Duke University Press, 1991), p. 287.

The virtual, multimedia, and networked aspects of the production are integral to what is distinctive about twenty-first century responses to the past: even the most casual spectators grasp the analogy between our global digital communications environment and Victorian networks of technology and conquest.

According to the website, the artist's great-grandfather Alexander Stanhope St George, was a colonial subject – the Creole product of a Sierra Leonian mother and a British father, one of three children out of seven to survive to adulthood in mid nineteenth-century London. (The artist characterizes himself as 'cultural diversity personified with German Jewish, Sierra Leonian, French and Manchester Jewish ancestry').[20] Driven to better himself, like his hero the great Victorian engineer Isambard Kingdom Brunel, who completed the first tunnel under the Thames, Alexander determined to 'make my name through my own endeavour alone'.[21] The website includes a famous photo of Brunel, standing in front of the anchor of his steamship the *Great Eastern* just before its launch. The photo has been doctored by the addition of a section supposedly torn off the original, showing the young Alexander posed by the great man. Dressed in working-class clothes, the boy dramatizes the distance I. K. Brunel has risen from his father Marc Brunel's humble origins, while the racialized features of the boy's face remind viewers that mid-Victorian London was then, as it is now, an ethnically diverse world capital. Alexander's determination, however, came at a cost to his wife and newborn child, whom he abandoned for his dream, and the workers, many of whom died in the tunnelling operation. Less skilled labourers, drafted to continue the project, ultimately mutinied against their working conditions. Disappointment, the shame of failure, and confinement in an insane asylum were Alexander's only reward.[22]

The racial and class issues that subtend this tragedy of overweening ambition give a critical edge to the Telectroscope installation. The powerful drill that smashed upwards through the docks on the exhibit's first day and the massive mechanism itself take on a more intimidating aspect in the

20 Paul St George, 'The Artist', www.tiscali.co.uk/telectroscope/cn/the_artist/index.php.
21 Paul St George, 'Story: The Inventor,' www.tiscali.co.uk/telectroscope/cn/the_artist/index.php. St George's choice of Brunel accords with his countrymen's contemporary interest in Victorian culture. A BBC poll to determine 'The Greatest Britons' ranked I. K. Brunel number two of all time, trailing only Winston Churchill. http://news.bbc.co.uk/2/hi/entertainment/2341661.stm.
22 Paul St George, 'Story: A Tragic End', www.tiscali.co.uk/telectroscope/cn/the_artist/index.php.

context of a Victorian tale of monomania, relentless ambition, an abandoned wife and child, mistreatment of labourers, and work-site insurrection. Unlike the academic and the Post-modern critiques of Victorian literature, this critical edge is not isolated from popular affect and desires. At least a rough grasp of the historical and intellectual contexts of the exhibit is an inextricable part of what makes it fun.

The synthesis of ironic insight and amusement that characterizes the Telectroscope takes its inspiration from the popular genre of steampunk, which originated in the science fiction of the 1990s. A variant of the cyberpunk movement pioneered by William Gibson and Bruce Sterling in the 1980s, steampunk exported hacker culture and a *noir* style to the Victorian past. When they first came on the scene, both cyberpunk and steampunk were examples of the kind of subcultural movements Raymond Williams and the Birmingham School of Cultural Studies explored. Williams was prescient in understanding subcultures as popular 'resources for hope', which nurtured local communities of feeling and practice.[23] What seems different in the twenty-first century is the way globalization and the Internet have enabled subcultural structures of feeling to expand rapidly beyond the boundaries of the local. Steampunk has spread well beyond the genre of science fiction to become an international cultural phenomenon. It has its own magazines, anime films such as *Steamboy* (2004), role-playing games, comics and graphic novels such as *The League of Extraordinary Gentlemen* (1999–onwards), films such as *Van Helsing* (2004) and the *Golden Compass* (2007), clothing lines, and fashion accessories. Home and office furniture can be 'modded' with Victorian fittings, resembling the polished brass and wood used in the Telectroscope. From a subcultural lifestyle, steampunk has emerged to become mainstream enough to be featured in the Style section of the *New York Times* or at the Burning Man Festival in Nevada's Black Rock Desert, where for two years running the artist group Kinetic Steam Works exhibited a functioning steam engine.

The novel character of twenty-first century responses to the Victorian past can be explored in more depth by turning to literature. A remarkable series of novels and plays dealing with the Victorian age have been published in recent years. Although many of them came out in the 1990s and should be labelled 'late-twentieth century' or perhaps 'proto-twenty-first century', I will group them together as twenty-first century texts to highlight

---

23 The phrase comes from the title of Raymond Williams, *Resources of Hope: Culture, Democracy, Socialism* (London: Verso, 1989).

what the new century may hold in store. Something about the Victorian period has excited contemporary writers in unprecedented ways. The flood of books is impressive not only in quantity but quality – it includes some of the most celebrated works of our time and has garnered the Booker Prize, two Pulitzers, and two National Book Awards, as well as many short-listings for those honours. Merely to list the most notable of these works is to register a surprising conjunction: A. S. Byatt's *Possession* (1990) and *Angels and Insects* (1992); Charles Johnson's *Middle Passage* (1990); William Gibson and Bruce Sterling's *The Difference Engine* (1991); Caryl Phillips's *Cambridge* (1991) and *Crossing the River* (1993); Susan Sontag's *The Volcano Lover* (1992); Victoria Glendinning's *Electricity* (1995); Margaret Atwood's *Alias Grace* (1996); Andrea Barrett's *Ship Fever* (1996), *The Voyage of the Narwhal* (1998), and *Servants of the Map* (2002); Steven Millhauser's *Martin Dressler* (1997); Peter Carey's *Jack Maggs* (1998); Simon Mawer's *Mendel's Dwarf* (1998); Roger McDonald's *Mr Darwin's Shooter* (1998); Sarah Waters's *Tipping the Velvet* (1998), *Affinity* (1999), and *Fingersmith* (2002); Thomas Mallon's *Two Moons* (2000); Matthew Kneale's *English Passengers* (2000); Jasper Fforde's *The Eyre Affair* (2002); Daniel Mason's *The Piano Tuner* (2002); Michel Faber's *The Crimson Petal and the White* (2002); Edward P. Jones's *The Known World* (2003); David Mitchell's *Cloud Atlas* (2004); Colm Tóibín's *The Master* (2004); Julian Barnes's *Arthur & George* (2005); Michael Cunningham's *Specimen Days* (2005); Emma Darwin's *The Mathematics of Love* (2006); and Lloyd Jones's *Mister Pip* (2006).

What has prompted this outpouring of twenty-first century literature dealing with the Victorian age? I can think of a number of factors, all of which have to do with a sense of relationship between then and now. This emphasis on connection, on relation within the context of great, sometimes overwhelming historical change, is new. The twentieth-century response to Victorian literature emphasized difference, whether it was the difference of rebellion in high Modernism or the difference that fosters nostalgia in popular culture. In the twenty-first century the pleasure is in seeing the parallels.

Let me begin with geography. One may notice the list includes Anglophone authors whose cultural heritage circles the globe – the United Kingdom, Africa, Canada, the United States, the Caribbean, New Zealand, and Japan. Queen Victoria's empire touched these cultures too, something that fascinates contemporary novelists. Charles Johnson, Edward P. Jones, and Caryl Phillips take the Atlantic triangle formed by the slave trade – England to Africa to the Americas – as an inevitable context for their stories.

But their novels do not 'write back to the empire' in the fashion of Jean Rhys and other post-colonial authors of the 1960s. Instead, they confront their own implication in global structures of power, structures that are illuminated by juxtaposition with those of the earlier age. Lloyd Jones's *Mr Pip*, a tale that explores the conflicting meanings *Great Expectations* came to hold for a village on a Pacific island during a bloody civil war, traces a similarly tangled network of racial, cultural, and economic guilt and atonement. David Mitchell does something comparable in *Cloud Atlas*, a novel with six narratives nesting inside one another as in a Russian doll. The sections set in the Pacific during the nineteenth century echo H. G. Wells's *The Island of Dr Moreau* (later alluded to by name) and foreshadow a post-apocalyptic future on an island that once was Hawaii to parallel past, present, and future forms of slavery. To these examples, one could add the novels by Roger McDonald and Daniel Mason, as well as Andrea Barrett's story 'Birds with No Feet', each of which puts Victorian adventures in the Pacific and South Asia in dialogue with globalization today.[24] Like the Atlantic novels, the aim is not to indict the past but to implicate both past and present in a historical relationship that has relevance for the twenty-first century.

A similar intention lies behind one of the salient structural features of many texts, the two-generation plot, which alternates between a contemporary group of characters, often scientists or artists, and characters from the Victorian era. The device is so common that it could be said to constitute a sub-genre within twenty-first century literature. Among the best examples of this structure is A. S. Byatt's *Possession*, which alternates the story of two contemporary scholars, hunting for evidence of an affair between two Victorian writers, and the nineteenth-century pair of lovers themselves. Andrea Barrett's *Ship Fever*, a short story collection that juxtaposes the lives of Victorian naturalists – Darwin, Wallace, and Mendel – with those of scientists today, employs this structure both within some of the individual stories and across the collection as a whole. 'The Behavior of the Hawkweeds' encapsulates Barrett's technique in miniature. The story moves fluently back and forth in time between a lonely woman in the present married to a genetics professor at a New England college, her immigrant grandfather who once knew Gregor Mendel, and Mendel himself, who worked in isolation on a discovery that no one would notice until the next century. What

---

24 Andrea Barrett's story 'Birds with no Feet' appeared in her National Book Award winning collection, *Ship Fever* (New York: Norton, 1996), pp. 103–22.

unites the three is a letter that Mendel gave to the woman's grandfather, and which she in turn shared with her husband. Mendel's letter is like a genetic trait passed down through time, but the letter itself is less important than the stories the characters tell one another about its transmission. These stories, more than the inheritance itself, bind the present to the past in ways that both damage and redeem. Stories prove as tenacious as genetics in connecting us across time.[25]

A third group of works violates the conventions of historical fiction by openly displaying anachronisms. Charles Johnson's *Middle Passage* is flagrant in the way it mentions developments like dime novels and spacemen before their time and injects rhetoric about minorities, systematic discrimination, and standards of excellence from recent affirmative action debates into conversations aboard a slave ship in 1830. The anachronisms in Susan Sontag's *The Volcano Lover* are structural: the early nineteenth-century story is interrupted at intervals by references to the twentieth-century author who is writing the tale. Jasper Fforde's hilarious fiction about a world in which people can transport themselves into Victorian novels and change their plots, features anachronism as simply another counterfactual given. Finally, Gibson and Sterling's alternative history *The Difference Engine*, which imagines how society would be changed if Charles Babbage had brought his computer into production, presents the Victorian era as a full-blown information order, complete with massive databases, photo-IDs, credit cards, and international data transmission via telegraph. Often regarded as the pre-eminent example of steampunk, this novel is thus a crucial predecessor of the Telectroscope.

Like the novels above, the Telectroscope works to alter spectators' relationship to time and space. Setting both a two-generation plot and conscious anachronism in a transatlantic context, the artwork has a proleptic power. By casting us back in time, it reaches forward to reveal features of our own day that are often obscured by the wonders of instantaneous communication. Peering into a massive tube and seeing other visitors peering back 'in real time', as they say, one is touched by an unreal temporality. This experience possesses a haptic dimension. One has to go down to the docks and gesture with one's body or scrawl messages on a white board to establish communication with the other end. If one merely sought to make contact with someone across the Atlantic, one could flick

---

25 See Barrett, 'The Behavior of the Hawkweeds', in *ibid.*, pp. 11–33.

on a webcam and dial the phone. Instead, the physical nature of the performance, the size and materiality of the installation, enforce a different kind of relationship.

Alexander Stanhope St George aspired to create a 'device for the suppression of absence',[26] but his optical machine could never have achieved such a goal. The silence from the other end of the tunnel brings that home powerfully. Art cannot suppress absence either. Contemporary novels about the Victorian age impress that point more than any other. However vividly one brings the time of the Victorians into one's life, they remain absent, like silent moving figures on the far side of a sea. What comes through, however, is a sense of relationship. It is not history that this twenty-first century art explores but the nature of historical relationships. That is what such dislocating temporal effects convey. Machines from another time, parallel narratives, two-generation plots, and compelling anachronisms do not suppress absence but make it meaningful.

26 Paul St George, 'Story: The Idea,' www.tiscali.co.uk/telectroscope/cn/the_artist/index.php.

Select bibliography

Chapter 1: Publishing and the materiality of the book

Briggs, Asa and Peter Burke, *A Social History of the Media, from Gutenberg to the Internet* (London: Polity Press, 2002)

Eliot, Simon and Jonathan Rose (eds.), *A Companion to the History of the Book* (Oxford and New York: Blackwell Publishing, 2007)

Erickson, Lee, *The Economy of Literary Form: English Literature and the Industrialization of Publishing, 1800–1850* (Baltimore and London: Johns Hopkins University Press, 1996)

Feather, J., *A History of British Publishing*, 2nd edn (London and New York: Routledge, 2006)

Finkelstein, David, *The House of Blackwood: Author–Publisher Relations in the Victorian Era* (Philadelphia: Pennsylvania State University Press, 2002)

Finkelstein, David and Alistair McCleery, *An Introduction to Book History* (London and New York: Routledge, 2005)

(eds.), *The Book History Reader*, 2nd revised edn (London and New York: Routledge, 2006)

Gillies, Mary Ann, *The Professional Literary Agent in Britain, 1880–1920* (University of Toronto Press, 2007)

Griest, Guinevere L., *Mudie's Circulating Library and the Victorian Novel* (Bloomington and London: Indiana University Press, 1970)

Hepburn, James, *The Author's Empty Purse and the Rise of the Literary Agent* (London: Oxford University Press, 1968)

Keating, Peter, *The Haunted Study: A Social History of the English Novel, 1875–1914* (London: Secker & Warburg, 1989)

Patten, Robert L., *Charles Dickens and His Publishers* (Oxford University Press, 1978)

Raven, James, *The Business of Books: Booksellers and the English Book Trade* (New Haven and London: Yale University Press, 2007)

Secord, James A., *Victorian Sensation: The Extraordinary Publication, Reception, and Secret Authorship of Vestiges of the Natural History of Creation* (University of Chicago Press, 2000)

Seville, Catherine, *The Internationalisation of Copyright Law: Books, Buccaneers and the Black Flag in the Nineteenth Century* (Cambridge University Press, 2006)

Chapter 2: Victorian reading

Altick, Richard, *The English Common Reader: A Social History of the Mass Reading Public, 1800–1900* (University of Chicago Press, 1957)

Brantlinger, Patrick, *The Reading Lesson: The Threat of Mass Literacy in Nineteenth-Century Britain* (Bloomington: University of Indiana Press, 1998)

Cavallo, Guglielmo and Roger Chartier (eds.), *A History of Reading in the West* (Cambridge: Polity Press, 1999)

Eliot, Simon, 'The Business of Victorian Publishing', in Deirdre David (ed.), *The Cambridge Companion to the Victorian Novel* (Cambridge University Press, 2001), pp. 37–60

Flint, Kate, *The Woman Reader, 1837–1914* (Oxford: Clarendon Press, 1993)

Jordan, John O. and Robert L. Patten (eds.), *Literature in the Marketplace: Nineteenth-Century British Reading and Publishing Practices* (Cambridge University Press, 1995), pp. 165–94

Mitch, David, *The Rise of Popular Literacy in Victorian England* (Philadelphia: University of Pennsylvania Press, 1992)

Rose, Jonathan, *The Intellectual Life of the British Working Classes* (New Haven and London: Yale University Press, 2003)

Sutherland, John, *Victorian Fiction: Writers, Publishers, Readers* (Basingstoke: Palgrave, 2006)

St Clair, William, *The Reading Nation in the Romantic Period* (Cambridge University Press, 2004)

Vincent, David, *Literacy and Popular Culture: England 1750–1914* (Cambridge University Press, 1989)

Chapter 3: Periodicals and reviewing

Beetham, Margaret, *A Magazine of Her Own? Domesticity and Desire in the Woman's Magazine, 1800–1914* (London and New York: Routledge, 1996)

Brake, Laurel, *Subjugated Knowledges: Journalism, Gender and Literature in the Nineteenth Century* (Houndmills, Basingstoke: Macmillan, 1994)

Brake, Laurel, Bill Bell, and David Finkelstein (eds.), *Nineteenth-Century Media and the Construction of Identities* (Houndmills, Basingstoke: Palgrave, 2000)

Brake, Laurel and Julie F. Codell, (eds.), *Encounters in the Victorian Press: Editors, Authors, Readers* (Houndmills, Basingstoke: Palgrave Macmillan, 2005)

Brake, Laurel and Marysa Demoor (eds.), *Dictionary of Nineteenth-Century Journalism in Great Britain and Ireland* (Gent: Academia Press; London: The British Library, 2009)

Demoor, Marysa, *Their Fair Share: Women, Power and Criticism in the Athenaeum, from Millicent Garrett Fawcett to Katherine Mansfield, 1870–1920* (Aldershot: Ashgate, 2000)

Fraser, Hilary, Stephanie Green, and Judith Johnston, *Gender and the Victorian Periodical* (Cambridge University Press, 2003)

King, Andrew, *The London Journal, 1845–83: Periodicals, Production and Gender* (Aldershot: Ashgate, 2004)

King, Andrew and John Plunkett (eds.), *Victorian Print Media: A Reader* (Oxford and New York: Oxford University Press, 2005)

Mussell, James, *Science, Time and Space in the Late Nineteenth-Century Periodical Press* (Aldershot: Ashgate, 2007)

Onslow, Barbara, *Women of the Press in Nineteenth-Century Britain* (Houndmills, Basingstoke: Macmillan, 2000)

Shattock, Joanne, *Politics and Reviewers: The Edinburgh and the Quarterly in the Early Victorian Age* (London: Leicester University Press, 1989)

Shattock, Joanne and Michael Wolff (eds.), *The Victorian Press: Samplings and Soundings* (London: Leicester University Press, 1982)

Sinnema, Peter W., *Dynamics of the Pictured Page: Representing the Nation in the Illustrated London News* (Aldershot: Ashgate, 1998)

Vann, J. Don, and Rosemary T. VanArsdel (eds.), *Victorian Periodicals and Victorian Society* (University of Toronto Press, 1994)

Research tools

Houghton, Walter E. *et al.* (eds.), *The Wellesley Index to Victorian Periodicals 1824–1900*, 5 vols. (Toronto and London: University of Toronto Press and Routledge & Kegan Paul, 1965–88)

Wolff, Michael, John S. North, and Dorothy Deering, *The Waterloo Directory of Victorian Periodicals 1824–1900* (Waterloo: Wilfred Laurier Press, 1976)

Chapter 4: The expansion of Britain

Armstrong, Isobel, *Victorian Poetry: Poetics and Politics* (London: Routledge, 1993)

Ashton, Rosemary, *142 Strand: A Radical Address in Victorian London* (London: Chatto and Windus, 2006)

Brantlinger, Patrick, *Rule of Darkness: British Literature and Imperialism* (Ithaca, NY: Cornell University Press, 1995)

Brantlinger, Patrick and William B. Thesing (eds.), *A Companion to the Victorian Novel* (Oxford: Blackwell, 2002)

Brooks, Chris, *Signs for the Times: Symbolic Realism in the Mid-Victorian World* (London: George Allen and Unwin, 1984)

Burrow, John, *A Liberal Descent: Victorian Historians and the English Past* (Cambridge University Press, 1981)

Chadwick, Owen, *The Victorian Church*, 2 vols. vol. I, 1829–1859; vol. II, 1860–1901 (London: A&C Black, 1966)

Dooley, Allan C., *Author and Printer in Victorian England* (Charlottesville: University Press of Virginia, 1992)

Gallagher, Catherine, *The Industrial Reformation of English Fiction: Social Discourse and Narrative Form* (Chicago and London: Chicago University Press, 1985)

Goodlad, Lauren, M. E., *Victorian Literature and the Victorian State: Character and Governance in a Liberal Society* (Baltimore and London: Johns Hopkins University Press, 2003)

Hoppen, K. Theodore, *The Mid-Victorian Generation: 1846–1886*, New Oxford History of England (Oxford: Oxford University Press, 1998)

Poovey, Mary, *Uneven Development: The Ideological Work of Gender in Mid-Victorian England* (Chicago and London: Chicago University Press, 1988)

Ruse, Michael, *The Darwinian Revolution: Science Red in Tooth and Claw*, 2nd edn (Chicago and London: University of Chicago Press, 1999)

Shattock, Joanne and Michael Wolff (eds.), *The Victorian Periodical Press: Samplings and Soundings* (Leicester University Press, 1982)

Young, Paul, *Globalization and the Great Exhibition: The Victorian New World Order* (London: Palgrave, 2008)

Chapter 5: High Victorianism

Briggs, Asa, *The Making of Modern England, 1783–1867: The Age of Improvement* (New York: Harper and Row, 1965)

Burn, W. L., *The Age of Equipoise: A Study of the Mid-Victorian Generation* (New York: Norton, 1965)

Evans, Eric J., *The Forging of the Modern State: Early Industrial Britain, 1783–1870*, 3rd edn (Harlow: Longman, 2001)

Hall, Catherine, Keith McClelland, and Jane Rendall, *Defining the Victorian Nation: Class, Race, Gender and the Reform Act of 1867* (Cambridge University Press, 2000)

Hobsbawm, Eric, *The Age of Capital 1848–1875* (New York: Vintage, 1996)

Parry, J. P., *The Rise and Fall of Liberal Government in Victorian Britain* (New Haven: Yale University Press, 1993)

Perkin, Harold, *The Origins of Modern English Society 1780–1880* (London: Routledge and Kegan Paul, 1969)

Vernon, James, *Politics and the People: A Study in English Political Culture, c. 1815–1867* (Cambridge University Press, 1993)

Young, G. M., *Portrait of an Age: Victorian England.* 2nd edn, 2 vols. (London: Oxford University Press, 1960)

Chapter 6: The *fin de siècle*

Anderson, Amanda, *The Powers of Distance: Cosmopolitanism and the Cultivation of Detachment* (Princeton University Press, 2001)

Anderson, Amanda and Joseph Valente (eds.), *Disciplinarity at the Fin de Siècle* (Princeton University Press, 2002)

Arata, Stephen, *Fictions of Loss in the Victorian Fin de Siècle: Identity and Empire* (Cambridge University Press, 1996)

Brantlinger, Patrick, *The Reading Lesson: The Threat of Mass Literacy in Nineteenth-Century British Fiction* (Bloomington: Indiana University Press, 1998)

Dowling, Linda, *Language and Decadence in the Victorian Fin de Siècle* (Princeton University Press, 1986)

Feldman, Jessica, *Victorian Modernism: Pragmatism and the Varieties of Aesthetic Experience* (Cambridge University Press, 2002)

Felski, Rita, *The Gender of Modernity* (Cambridge, MA: Harvard University Press, 1995)

Flint, Kate, *The Woman Reader 1837–1914* (Oxford: Clarendon Press, 1993)

Frankel, Nicholas, *Masking the Text: Essays on Literature & Mediation in the 1890s* (High Wycombe, Bucks: Rivendale Press, 2009)

Gagnier, Regenia, *The Insatiability of Human Wants: Economics and Aesthetics in Market Society* (University of Chicago Press, 2000)

Helsinger, Elizabeth, *Poetry and the Pre-Raphaelite Arts: Dante Gabriel Rossetti and William Morris* (New Haven: Yale University Press, 2008)

Ledger, Sally and Scott McCracken (eds.), *Cultural Politics at the Fin de Siècle* (Cambridge University Press, 1995)

Marshall, Gail (ed.), *The Cambridge Companion to the Fin de Siècle* (Cambridge University Press, 2007)

McClintock, Anne, *Imperial Leather: Race, Gender, and Sexuality in the Colonial Contest* (New York: Routledge, 1995)

Prins, Yopie, *Victorian Sappho* (Princeton University Press, 1999)

Psomiades, Kathy Alexis, *Beauty's Body: Femininity and Representation in British Aestheticism* (Stanford University Press, 1997)

Showalter, Elaine, *Sexual Anarchy: Gender and Culture at the Fin de Siècle* (New York: Viking, 1990)

Chapter 7: Lyric and the lyrical

Bernstein, Charles (ed.), *Close Listening: Poetry and the Performed Word* (Oxford University Press, 1998)

Blasing, Mutlu Konuk, *Lyric Poetry: The Pain and the Pleasure of Words* (Princeton University Press, 2007)

Brewster, Scott, *Lyric* (London: Routledge, 2009)

Culler, Jonathan, 'Why Lyric?' *PMLA* 123:1 (2008), pp. 201–6

Dubrow, Heather, *The Challenges of Orpheus: Lyric Poetry and Early Modern England* (Baltimore: Johns Hopkins University Press, 2008)

Frye, Northrop, 'Approaching the Lyric', in Chariva Hosek and Patricia Parker (eds.), *Lyric Poetry: Beyond New Criticism* (Ithaca and London: Cornell University Press, 1985), pp. 31–7

Griffiths, Eric, *The Printed Voice of Victorian Poetry* (Oxford: Clarendon Press, 1989)

Holden, Jonathan, *The Rhetoric of the Contemporary Lyric* (Bloomington: Indiana University Press, 1980)

Hollander, John, *The Work of Poetry* (New York: Columbia University Press, 1997)

Leighton, Angela, *On Form: Poetry, Aestheticism, and the Legacy of a Word* (Oxford University Press, 2007)

Palgrave, Francis Turner, *The Golden Treasury: Of the Best Songs and Lyrical Poems in the English Language, 1861*, ed. Christopher Ricks (London: Penguin, 1991)

Rogers, William Elford, *The Three Genres and the Interpretation of Lyric* (Princeton University Press, 1983)

Rowlinson, Matthew, 'Lyric', in Richard Cronin, Alison Chapman and Antony H.Harrison (eds.), *A Companion to Victorian Poetry* (Oxford: Blackwell, 2002)

Stewart, Susan, *Poetry and the Fate of the Senses* (Chicago and London: Chicago University Press, 2002)

Tucker, Herbert F., 'Dramatic Monologue and the Overhearing of Lyric', in Frye *et al.*, *Lyric Poetry: Beyond New Criticism*, pp. 226–43.

Vendler, Helen, *Invisible Listeners: Lyric Intimacy in Herbert, Whitman, and Ashbery* (Princeton University Press, 2005)

Chapter 8: Epic

Bakhtin, M. M., *The Dialogic Imagination: Four Essays* (Austin: University of Texas Press, 1981)

Barczewski, Stephanie L., *Myth and National Identity in Nineteenth-Century Britain: The Legends of King Arthur and Robin Hood* (Oxford University Press, 2000)

Crawford, Robert, *The Modern Poet: Poetry, Academia, and Knowledge since the 1750s* (Oxford University Press, 2001)

Curran, Stuart, *Poetic Form and British Romanticism* (New York: Oxford University Press, 1986)

Dentith, Simon, *Epic and Empire in Nineteenth-Century Britain* (Cambridge University Press, 2006)

Downes, Jeremy M., *Recursive Desire: Rereading Epic Tradition* (Tuscaloosa and London: University of Alabama Press, 1997)

Foerster, Donald M., *The Fortunes of Epic Poetry: A Study in English and American Criticism 1750–1950* (Washington DC: Catholic University of America Press, 1962)

Gibson, Mary Ellis, *Epic Reinvented: Ezra Pound and the Victorians* (Ithaca, NY and London: Cornell University Press, 1995)

Griffiths, F. T., and S. J. Rabinowitz, *Novel Epics: Gogol, Dostoevsky, and National Narrative* (Evanston, IL: Northwestern University Press, 1990)

Graham, Colin, *Ideologies of Epic: Nation, Empire, and Victorian Epic Poetry* (Manchester University Press, 1998)

Jenkyns, Richard, *The Victorians and Ancient Greece* (Cambridge, MA: Harvard University Press, 1980)

Lucas, John, *England and Englishness: Ideas of Nationhood in English Poetry* (London: Hogarth Press, 1990)

Lukács, György, *The Historical Novel*, trans. Hannah and Stanley Mitchell (1937; London: Merlin Press, 1962)

　The Theory of the Novel: A Historical-Philosophical Essay on the Forms of Great Epic Literature, trans. Anna Bostock (1920; London: Merlin Press, 1971)

Merchant, Paul, *The Epic* (London: Methuen, 1971)

Moretti, Franco, *Modern Epic: The World-System from Goethe to Garcia Marquez*, trans. Quintin Hoare (London: Verso, 1996)

Mori, Masaki, *Epic Grandeur: Toward a Comparative Poetics of the Epic* (Albany NY: SUNY Press, 1997)

Oberhelman, Steven M., Van Kelly, and Richard J. Golsan (eds.), *Epic and Epoch: Essays on the Interpretation and History of a Genre* (Lubbock: Texas Tech University Press, 1994)

Quint, David, *Epic and Empire: Politics and Generic Form from Virgil to Milton* (Princeton University Press, 1993)

Rajan, Balachandra, *The Form of the Unfinished: English Poetics from Spenser to Pound* (Princeton University Press, 1985)

Reynolds, Matthew, *The Realms of Verse: English Poetry in a Time of Nation-Building* (Oxford University Press, 2001)

Roberts, Adam, *Romantic and Victorian Long Poems: A Guide* (Aldershot: Ashgate, 1999)

Scholes, Robert E. and Robert Kellogg, *The Nature of Narrative* (New York: Oxford University Press, 1964)

Shaffer, Elinor S., *'Kubla Khan' and The Fall of Jerusalem: The Mythological School in Biblical Criticism and Secular Literature 1770–1880* (Cambridge University Press, 1975)

Tillyard, E. M. W., *The Epic Strain in the English Novel* (London: Chatto and Windus, 1958)

Trumpener, Katie, *Bardic Nationalism: The Romantic Novel and the British Empire* (Princeton University Press, 1997)

Tucker, Herbert F., *Epic: Britain's Heroic Muse 1790–1910* (New York: Oxford University Press, 2008)

Chapter 9: Melodrama

Booth, Michael R., *English Melodrama* (London: Herbert Jenkins, 1965)

  Victorian Spectacular Theatre, 1850–1910 (London: Routledge & Kegan Paul, 1981)

Branscombe, Peter, 'Melodrama', in *The New Grove Dictionary of Music and Musicians*, vol. xii, ed. Stanley Sadie (London: Macmillan, 1980), pp. 116–18

Bratton, Jacky, Jim Cook, and Christine Gledhill (eds.), *Melodrama: Stage Picture Screen* (London: British Film Institute Publishing, 1994)

Brewster, Ben and Lea Jacobs, *Theatre to Cinema: Stage Pictorialism and the Early Feature Film* (Oxford University Press, 1997)

Brooks, Peter, *The Melodramatic Imagination: Balzac, Henry James, Melodrama, and the Mode of Excess* (1976; New Haven: Yale University Press, 2nd edn., with new preface, 1995)

Gledhill, Christine (ed.), *Home is Where the Heart Is: Studies in Melodrama and the Woman's Film* (London: British Film Institute Publishing, 1987)

Hadley, Elaine, *Melodramatic Tactics: Theatricalized Dissent in the English Marketplace, 1800–1885* (Stanford University Press, 1995)

Hays, Michael and Anastasia Nicolopolou (eds.), *Melodrama: The Cultural Emergence of a Genre* (New York: St Martin's Press, 1996)

Mayer, David and Matthew Scott, *'Four Bars of Agit': Incidental Music for Victorian and Edwardian Melodrama* (London: Samuel French and the Theatre Museum, V&A, 1983)

Meisel, Martin, *Realizations: Narrative, Pictorial and Theatrical Arts in Nineteenth-Century England* (Princeton University Press, 1983)

  'Scattered Chiaroscuro: Melodrama as a Matter of Seeing', in Bratton, Cook, and Gledhill, *Melodrama*, pp. 65–81

Moody, Jane, *Illegitimate Theatre in London, 1770–1840* (Cambridge University Press, 2000)

Nicoll, Allardyce, *A History of English Drama, 1660–1900*, vols. iv and v (Cambridge University Press, 1967)

Powell, Kerry (ed.), *The Cambridge Companion to Victorian and Edwardian Theatre* (Cambridge University Press, 2004)

Rahill, Frank, *The World of Melodrama* (University Park: Pennsylvania State University Press, 1967)

Shepherd, Simon and Peter Womack, *English Drama: A Cultural History* (Oxford: Blackwell, 1996)

Smith, James L., *Melodrama* (London: Methuen & Co, 1973)

Vardac, A. Nicholas, *Stage to Screen: Theatrical Method from Garrick to Griffith* (Cambridge, MA: Harvard University Press, 1949)

Chapter 10: Sensation

Bown, Nicola, Carolyn Burdett, and Pamela Thurschwell (eds.), *The Victorian Supernatural* (Cambridge University Press, 2004)

Brantlinger, Patrick, 'Imperial Gothic: Atavism and the Occult in the British Adventure Novel 1880–1914', in *Rule of Darkness: British Literature and Imperialism 1830–1914* (Ithaca, NY: Cornell University Press, 1988), pp. 227–53

'What is Sensational about the "Sensation Novel"?', *Nineteenth-Century Fiction*, 37:1 (1982), pp. 1–28

Briggs, Julia, *Night Visitors: The Rise and Fall of the Ghost Story* (London: Faber, 1977)

Cvetkovich, Ann, *Mixed Feelings: Feminism, Mass Culture, and Victorian Sensationalism* (New Brunswick, NJ: Rutgers University Press, 1992)

Diamond, Michael, *Victorian Sensation: Or, the Spectacular, the Shocking and the Scandalous in Nineteenth-Century Britain* (London: Anthem, 2003)

Hughes, Winifred, *The Maniac in the Cellar* (Princeton University Press, 1980)

Hurley, Kelly, *The Gothic Body: Sexuality, Materialism, and Degeneration at the Fin de Siècle* (Cambridge University Press, 1996)

Levine, Caroline, *The Serious Pleasures of Suspense: Victorian Realism and Narrative Doubt* (Charlottesville: University Press of Virginia, 2003)

Malchow, H. M., *Gothic Images of Race in Nineteenth-Century Britain* (Berkeley and Los Angeles: University of California Press, 1996)

Mighall, Robert, *A Geography of Victorian Gothic Fiction: Mapping History's Nightmares* (Oxford University Press, 1999)

Miller, D. A., *The Novel and the Police* (Berkeley and Los Angeles: University of California Press, 1988)

Punter, David, *The Literature of Terror: A History of Gothic Fictions from 1765 to the Present Day* (London and New York: Longman, 1980)

Pykett, Lyn, *The Improper Feminine: The Women's Sensation Novel and the New Woman Writing* (London: Routledge, 1992)

Taylor, Jenny Bourne, *In the Secret Theatre of Home: Wilkie Collins, Sensation Narrative and Nineteenth-Century Psychology* (London and New York: Routledge, 1988)

Thomas, Ronald R., *Detective Fiction and the Rise of Forensic Science* (Cambridge University Press, 1999)

Chapter 11: Autobiography

Amigoni, David, *Victorian Biography: Intellectuals and the Ordering of Discourse* (New York: St Martin's Press, 1993)

Amigoni, David (ed.), *Life Writing and Victorian Culture* (Aldershot and Burlington, VT: Ashgate, 2006)

Broughton, Trev, *Men of Letters, Writing Lives: Masculinity and Literary Auto/biography in the Late-Victorian Period* (London and New York: Routledge, 1999)

Cockshut, A. O. J., *The Art of Autobiography in 19th & 20th century England* (New Haven: Yale University Press, 1984)

Codell, Julie, *The Victorian Artist: Artists' Lifewritings in Britain, ca. 1870–1910* (Cambridge University Press, 2003)

Corbett, Mary Jean, *Representing Femininity: Middle-Class Subjectivity in Victorian and Edwardian Women's Autobiographies* (New York: Oxford University Press, 1992)

Danahay, Martin A., *A Community of One: Masculine Autobiography and Autonomy in Nineteenth-Century Britain* (Albany: State University of New York Press, 1993)

Fleishman, Avrom, *Figures of Autobiography: The Language of Self-writing in Victorian and Modern England* (Berkeley: University of California Press, 1983)

Fuchs, Miriam and Craig Howes (eds.), *Teaching Life Writing Texts* (New York: Modern Language Association of America, 2008)

Gagnier, Regenia, *Subjectivities: A History of Self-Representation in Britain, 1832–1920* (Oxford University Press, 1991)

Landow, George P. (ed.), *Approaches to Victorian Autobiography* (Athens: Ohio University Press, 1979)

Machann, Clinton, *The Genre of Autobiography in Victorian Literature* (Ann Arbor: University of Michigan Press, 1994)

MacKay, Carol Hanbery, *Creative Negativity: Four Victorian Exemplars of the Female Quest* (Stanford University Press, 2001)

Newey, Vincent and Philip Shaw (eds.), *Mortal Pages, Literary Lives: Studies in Nineteenth-century Autobiography* (Aldershot: Scolar Press; Brookfield, VT: Ashgate, 1996)

Olney, James, *Metaphors of Self: The Meaning of Autobiography* (Princeton University Press, 1972)

Peterson, Linda H., *Traditions of Victorian Women's Autobiography: The Poetics and Politics of Life Writing* (Charlottesville: University Press of Virginia, 1999)

Victorian Autobiography: The Tradition of Self-Interpretation (New Haven: Yale University Press, 1986)

Sanders, Valerie, *The Private Lives of Victorian Women: Autobiography in Nineteenth-Century England* (Hemel Hempstead and New York: Harvester Wheatsheaf, 1989)

Chapter 12: Comic and Satirical

Altick, Richard D., *Punch: the Lively Youth of a British Institution 1841–1851* (Columbus: Ohio State University Press, 1997)

Barreca, Regina (ed.), *The Penguin Book of Women's Humor* (Harmondsworth: Penguin, 1996)

Bergson, Henri, 'Laughter: an Essay on the Meaning of the Comic', in Wylie Sypher (ed.), *Comedy* (Baltimore: Johns Hopkins University Press, 1980)

Dyer, Gary, *British Satire and the Politics of Style 1789–1832* (Cambridge University Press, 1997)

Freud, Sigmund, 'Humour', in *The Pelican Freud Library, Volume 14: Art and Literature* (Harmondsworth: Penguin, 1985)

The Pelican Freud Library, Volume 6: Jokes and their Relation to the Unconscious (Harmondsworth: Penguin, 1991)

Gatrell, Vic, *City of Laughter: Sex and Satire in Eighteenth-Century London* (London: Atlantic, 2006)

Gillooly, Eileen, *Smile of Discontent: Humor, Gender, and Nineteenth-Century British Fiction* (University of Chicago, 1999)

Henkle, Roger B., *Comedy and Culture: England 1820–1900* (Princeton University Press, 1980)

Jones, Steven E., 'Nineteenth-Century Satiric Poetry' in Ruben Quintano (ed.), *A Companion to Satire* (Oxford: Blackwell, 2007), pp. 340–60

Kincaid, James R., *Dickens and the Rhetoric of Laughter* (Oxford: Clarendon Press, 1971)

Lecercle, Jean-Jacques, *Philosophy of Nonsense: The Intuitions of Victorian Nonsense Literature* (London: Routledge, 1994)

Martin, Robert Bernard, *The Triumph of Wit: A Study of Victorian Comic Theory* (Oxford: Clarendon Press, 1974)

Meredith, George, 'An Essay on Comedy', in Wylie Sypher (ed.), *Comedy* (Baltimore: Johns Hopkins University Press, 1980)

Muir, Frank (ed.), *The Oxford Book of Humorous Prose* (Oxford University Press, 1992)

Palmeri, Frank, 'Cruikshank, Thackeray, and the Victorian Eclipse of Satire', *Studies in English Literature 1500–1900* 44:4 (2004), pp. 753–77

'Narrative Satire in the Nineteenth Century' in Ruben Quintano (ed.), *A Companion to Satire* (Oxford: Blackwell, 2007), pp. 361–76

Pearsall, Ronald, *Collapse of Stout Party: Victorian Wit and Humour* (London: Weidenfeld and Nicholson, 1975)

Slater, Michael, *Douglas Jerrold 1803–1857* (London: Duckworth, 2002)

Sutherland, John, *The Longman Companion to Victorian Fiction* (London: Longman, 1988)

Tave, Stuart, *The Amiable Humorist: A Study in the Comic Theory and Criticism of the Eighteenth and Early Nineteenth Centuries* (University of Chicago Press, 1960)

Wagner-Lawlor, Jennifer A. (ed.), *The Victorian Comic Spirit: New Perspectives* (Aldershot: Ashgate, 2000)

Chapter 13: Innovation and experiment

Armstrong, Isobel, *The Radical Aesthetic* (Oxford: Wiley-Blackwell, 2000)

Brantlinger, Patrick and William B. Thesing (eds.), *A Companion to the Victorian Novel* (Oxford: Blackwell, 2002)

Bristow, Joseph (ed.), *The Cambridge Companion to Victorian Poetry* (Cambridge University Press, 2000)

Cronin, Richard, Alison Chapman, and Antony Harrison (eds.), *A Companion to Victorian Poetry* (Oxford: Blackwell, 2002)

Felluga, Dino, 'The Critic's New Clothes: *Sartor Resartus* and "Cold Carnival" ', *Criticism* 37 (1995), pp. 583–99

Forrest-Thomson, Veronica, *Poetic Artifice. A Theory of Twentieth-century Poetry* (New York: St Martin's Press, 1978)

Frankel, Nicholas, *Masking the Text. Essays on Literature and Mediation in the 1890s* (High Wycombe: Rivendale Press, 2009)

Langbaum, Robert, *The Poetry of Experience. The Dramatic Monologue in Modern Literary Tradition* (London: Chatto and Windus, 1957)

Latane, David E. Jr., *Browning's Sordello and the Aesthetics of Difficulty. ELS* Monographs no. 40 (Victoria, BC: University of Victoria Press, 1987)

Lecercle, Jean-Jacques, *Philosophy of Nonsense: The Intuitions of Victorian Nonsense* (London: Routledge, 1994)

Levine, George, *The Boundaries of Fiction. Carlyle, Macaulay, Newman* (Princeton University Press, 1968)

Malcolm, Noel, *The Origins of English Nonsense* (HarperCollins: London, 1997)

Maxwell, Richard (ed.), *The Victorian Illustrated Book* (Charlottesville: University Press of Virginia, 2002)

Patten, Robert, *Charles Dickens and his Publishers* (Oxford: Clarendon Press, 1978)

Saintsbury, George, *A History of English Prosody*. Vol. III, From Blake to Mr. Swinburne (London: Macmillan and Co. Ltd., 1910)

Stevenson, Richard, *The Experimental Impulse in George Meredith's Fiction* (Lewisburg, PA: Bucknell University Press, 2004)

Stewart, Susan, *Nonsense. Aspects of Intertextuality in Folklore and Literature* (Baltimore: Johns Hopkins University Press, 1989)

Storey, Graham, 'Hopkins as a Mannerist', *Studies in the Literary Imagination* 21 (1988), pp. 77–90

Tucker, Herbert, *Tennyson and the Doom of Romanticism* (Cambridge, MA: Harvard University Press, 1988)

Chapter 14: Writing for children

Banerjee, Jacqueline, *Through the Northern Gate: Childhood and Growing up in British Fiction, 1719–1900* (New York: Peter Lang, 1996)

Boone, Troy, *The Youth of Darkest England: Working-Class Children at the Heart of Victorian Empire* (New York: Routledge, 2005)

Bratton, J. S., *The Impact of Victorian Children's Fiction* (London: Croom Helm, 1981)

Bristow, Joseph, *Empire Boys: Adventures in a Man's World* (London: HarperCollins, 1991)

Carpenter, Humphrey, *Secret Gardens: A Study of the Golden Age of Children's Literature* (Boston: Houghton Mifflin, 1985)

Carpenter, Kevin, *Penny Dreadfuls and Comics: English Periodicals for Children from Victorian Times to the Present Day* (London: Victoria and Albert Museum, 1983)

Castle, Kathryn, *Britannia's Children: Reading Colonialism through Children's Books and Magazines* (Manchester University Press, 1996)

Clark, Beverly Lyon, *Regendering the School Story: Sassy Sissies and Tattling Tomboys* (New York: Garland, 1996)

Cunningham, Hugh, *The Children of the Poor: Representations of Childhood since the Seventeenth Century* (Oxford: Basil Blackwell, 1991)

Cutt, Margaret Nancy, *Ministering Angels: A Study of Nineteenth-Century Evangelical Religious Writing for Children* (Wormley, Herts: Five Owls, 1979)

Darton, F. J. Harvey, *Children's Books in England: Five Centuries of Social Life*, 3rd edn (Cambridge University Press, 1982)

Denisoff, Dennis (ed.), *Nineteenth-Century Childhood and the Rise of Consumer Culture.* (Burlington, VT: Ashgate, 2007)

Dixon, Diana, 'Children and the Press, 1866–1914', in Michael Harris and Alan Lee (eds.), *The Press in English Society from the Seventeenth to Nineteenth Centuries* (Rutherford, NJ: Fairleigh Dickinson University Press, 1986), pp. 133–48

'From Instruction to Amusement: Attitudes of Authority in Children's Periodicals before 1914', *Victorian Periodicals Review* 19 (1986), pp. 63–7

Drotner, Kirsten, *English Children and Their Magazines, 1751–1945* (New Haven: Yale University Press, 1988)

Gubar, Marah, *Artful Dodgers: Reconceiving the Golden Age of Children's Literature* (New York: Oxford University Press, 2009)

Knoepflmacher, U. C., *Ventures into Childland: Victorians, Fairy Tales, and Femininity* (University of Chicago Press, 1998)

Kooistra, Lorraine Janzen, 'Poetry in the Victorian Marketplace: The Illustrated *Princess* as a Christmas Gift Book', *Victorian Poetry* 45:1 (2007), pp. 49–76

Jackson, Rosemary, *Fantasy: The Literature of Subversion* (New York: Methuen, 1981)

MacDonald, Robert H., 'Reproducing the Middle-Class Boy: From Purity to Patriotism in the Boys' Magazines, 1892–1914', *Journal of Contemporary History* 24 (1989), pp. 519–39
'Signs from the Imperial Quarter: Illustrations in *Chums*, 1892–1914', *Children's Literature* 16 (1988), pp. 31–55

MacKenzie, John M., 'Imperialism and Juvenile Literature', in *Propaganda and Empire: The Manipulation of British Public Opinion, 1880–1960* (Manchester University Press, 1984), pp. 198–226

Manlove, Colin N., *The Fantasy Literature of England* (Houndsmill, Basingstoke: Macmillan, 1999)

McGavran, James Holt, Jr. (ed.), *Romanticism and Children's Literature in Nineteenth-Century England* (Athens: University of Georgia Press, 1991)

Musgrave, P. W., *From Brown to Bunter: The Life and Death of the School Story* (London: Routledge, 1985)

Nelson, Claudia, *Boys Will Be Girls: The Feminine Ethic and British Children's Fiction, 1857–1917* (New Brunswick, NJ: Rutgers University Press, 1991)

Prickett, Stephen, *Victorian Fantasy* (Hassocks: Harvester Wheatsheaf, 1979)

Quigly, Isabel, *The Heirs of Tom Brown: The English School Story* (London: Chatto & Windus, 1982)

Reynolds, Kimberley, *Girls Only? Gender and Popular Children's Fiction in Britain, 1880–1910* (New York: Harvester Wheatsheaf, 1990)

Richards, Jeffrey, *Imperialism and Juvenile Literature* (Manchester University Press, 1989)

Richards, Jeffrey (ed.), *Happiest Days: The Public Schools in English Fiction* (Manchester University Press, 1988)

Silver, Carole G., *Strange and Secret Peoples: Fairies and Victorian Consciousness* (New York: Oxford University Press, 1999)

Chapter 15: Education

Anderson, Robert, *British Universities: Past and Present* (London: Hambledon Continuum, 2006)

Bamford, T. W., *The Rise of the Public Schools* (London: Nelson, 1967)

Birch, Dinah, *Our Victorian Education* (Oxford: Blackwell, 2007)

Copelman, Dina, *London's Women Teachers: Gender, Class and Feminism, 1870–1930* (London: Routledge and Kegan Paul, 1996)

De Bellaigue, Christina, *Educating Women: Schooling and Identity in England and France, 1800–1867* (Oxford University Press, 2007)
'Teaching as a Profession for Women', *Historical Journal* 44 (2001), pp. 963–88

Dyhouse, C., *Girls Growing Up in Late Victorian and Edwardian England* (London: Routledge and Kegan Paul, 1981)

Fletcher, Pauline and Patrick Scott, *Culture and Education in Victorian England* (London: Bucknell University Press, 1990)

Gargano, Elizabeth, *Reading Victorian Schoolrooms: Childhood and Education in Nineteenth-Century Fiction* (New York and London: Routledge, 2008)

Harrison, J. F. C., *Learning and Living* (London: Routledge and Kegan Paul, 1961)

Hilton, Mary, 'Revisioning Romanticism: Towards a Women's History of Progressive Thought 1780–1850', *History of Education* 30 (2001), pp. 471–87

Hilton, Mary and Pamela Hirsch (eds.), *Practical Visionaries: Women, Education, and Social Progress, 1790–1930* (Harlow: Longman, 2000)

Hughes, Kathryn, *The Victorian Governess* (London and Rio Grande: The Hambledon Press, 1993)

Hurt, John, *Education in Evolution* (London: Hart-Davis, 1971)

Lecaros, Cecilia Wadsö, *The Victorian Governess Novel* (Lund University Press, 2001)

Martin, Jane, *Women and the Politics of Schooling in Victorian and Edwardian England* (London and New York: Leicester University Press, 1999)

Pedersen, Joyce Sanders, *The Reform of Girls' Secondary Education in Victorian England: A Study of Elites and Educational Change* (London and New York: Garland, 1987)

    'Schoolmistresses and Headmistresses: Elites and Education in Nineteenth-Century England', *Journal of British Studies* 15 (1975), pp. 135–62

Peterson, M. Jeanne, 'The Victorian Governess: Status Incongruence in Family and Society', in Martha Vicinus (ed.) *Suffer and Be Still: Women in the Victorian Age* (Bloomington: Indiana University Press, 1973)

Poovey, Mary, *Uneven Developments: The Ideological Work of Gender in Mid-Victorian England* (London: Virago, 1989)

Roach, John, *A History of Secondary Education in England, 1800–1870* (London: Longman, 1986)

Rothblatt, Sheldon, *The Revolution of the Dons: Cambridge and Society in Victorian England* (London: Faber, 1968)

Shuttleworth, Sally, *The Mind of the Child: Child Development in Literature, Science and Medicine, 1840–1900* (Oxford University Press, 2010)

Smith, John, ' "Merely a Growing Dilemma of Etiquette?": The Deepening Gulf between the Victorian Clergyman and Victorian Schoolteacher', *History of Education* 33 (2004), pp. 157–76

Smithser, Neil, *Social Paralysis and Social Change: British Working-Class Education in the Nineteenth Century* (Berkeley: University of California Press, 1991)

Stephens, W. B., *Education in Britain, 1750–1914* (New York: St Martin's Press, 1998)

Sutherland, Gillian, *Elementary Education in the Nineteenth Century* (London: Historical Association, 1971)

Thormählen, Marianne, *The Brontës and Education* (Cambridge University Press, 2007)

Vincent, David, *Literacy and Popular Culture: England 1750–1914* (Cambridge University Press, 1989)

Wardle, David, *English Popular Education 1780–1975* (Cambridge University Press, 1976)

Chapter 16: Spirituality

Bown, Nicola, Carolyn Burdett, and Pamela Thurschwell (eds.), *The Victorian Supernatural* (Cambridge University Press, 2004)

Chadwick, Owen, *The Victorian Church*, 2 vols. (London: A.& C.Black, 1966)

Cheyette, Brian, *Constructions of the Jew in English Literature and Society: Racial Interpretations, 1875–1945* (Cambridge University Press, 1993)

Cunningham, Valentine, *Everywhere Spoken Against: Dissent in the Victorian Novel* (Oxford: Clarendon Press, 1975)

Dixon, Joy, *Divine Feminine: Theosophy and Feminism in England* (Baltimore and London: Johns Hopkins University Press, 2001)

Jasper, David and T. R. Wright (eds.), *The Critical Spirit and the Will to Believe: Essays in Nineteenth-Century Literature and Religion* (London and Basingstoke: Macmillan, 1989)

Knight, Mark and Emma Mason, *Nineteenth-Century Religion and Literature: An Introduction* (Oxford University Press, 2006)

Krueger, Christine, *The Reader's Repentance: Women Preachers, Women Writers, and Nineteenth-Century Social Discourse* (Chicago and London: University of Chicago Press, 1992)

Marsh, Joss, *Word Crimes: Blasphemy, Culture, and Literature in Nineteenth-Century England* (Chicago University Press, 1998)

Nixon, Jude V. (ed.), *Victorian Religious Discourse: New Directions in Criticism* (New York and Basingstoke, Palgrave Macmillan, 2004)

Parsons, Gerald, James R. Moore, and John Wolffe, *Religion in Victorian Britain*, 5 vols. (Manchester University Press, 1988–97)

Watson, J. R., *The English Hymn: A Critical and Historical Study* (Oxford: Clarendon Press, 1997)

Winter, Alison, *Mesmerized: Powers of Mind in Victorian Britain* (Chicago and London: University of Chicago Press, 1998)

Chapter 17: Material

Bailkin, Jordana, *The Culture of Property: The Crisis of Liberalism in Modern Britain* (University of Chicago Press, 2004)

Bizup, Joseph, *Manufacturing Culture: Vindications of Early Victorian Industry* (Charlottesville: University of Virginia Press, 2003)

Brake, Laurel, *Print in Transition, 1850–1910: Studies in Media and Book History* (New York: St Martin's Press, 2000)

Buzard, James, Joseph W. Childers, and Eileen Gillooly (eds.), *Victorian Prism: Refractions of the Crystal Palace* (Charlottesville: University of Virginia Press, 2007)

Cohen, Deborah, *Household Gods: The British and their Possessions* (New Haven: Yale University Press, 2006)

Coombes, Annie, *Reinventing Africa: Museums, Material Culture and the Popular Imagination in Late Victorian and Edwardian England* (New Haven: Yale University Press, 1994)

Freedgood, Elaine, *The Ideas in Things. Fugitive Meaning in the Victorian Novel* (University of Chicago Press, 2006)

(ed.), *Factory Production in Nineteenth-Century Britain* (Oxford University Press, 2003)

Kriegel, Lara, *Grand Designs: Labor, Empire, and the Museum in Victorian Culture* (Durham, NC: Duke University Press, 2007)

Lindner, Christoph, *Fictions of Commodity Culture: From the Victorian to the Postmodern* (Aldershot: Ashgate, 2003)

Novak, Daniel A., *Realism, Photography, and Nineteenth-Century Fiction* (Cambridge University Press, 2005)

Plotz, John, *Portable Property: Victorian Culture on the Move* (Princeton University Press, 2008)

Rappaport, Erika, *Shopping for Pleasure: Women in the Making of London's West End* (Princeton University Press, 2000)

Chapter 18: Economics and finance

Brantlinger, Patrick, *Fictions of State: Culture and Credit in Britain, 1694–1994* (Ithaca, NY: Cornell University Press, 1996)

Crosby, Christina, 'Financial', in Herbert F. Tucker (ed.), *A Companion to Victorian Literature and Culture* (Oxford: Blackwell, 1999), pp. 225–43

Finkelstein, David, *The House of Blackwood: Author–Publisher Relations in the Victorian Era* (University Park: Pennsylvania State University Press, 2002)

Gagnier, Regenia, *The Insatiability of Human Wants: Economics and Aesthetics in Market Society* (University of Chicago Press, 2000)

Gallagher, Catherine, *The Body Economic: Life, Death, and Sensation in Political Economy and the Victorian Novel* (Princeton University Press, 2006)

Klaver, Claudia C., *A/Moral Economics: Classical Political Economy & Cultural Authority in Nineteenth-Century England* (Columbus: Ohio State University Press, 2003)

Poovey, Mary, 'Forgotten Writers, Neglected Histories: Charles Reade and the Nineteenth-Century Transformation of the British Literary Field', *ELH* 71 (2004), pp. 433–53

'Introduction', *The Financial System in Nineteenth-Century Britain* (New York: Oxford University Press, 2002), pp. 1–33

Robb, George, *White-Collar Crime in Modern England: Financial Fraud and Business Morality 1845–1929* (Cambridge University Press, 1992)

Shell, Marc, *The Economy of Literature* (Baltimore: Johns Hopkins University Press, 1978)

Sutherland, J. A., *Victorian Novelists and Publishers* (University of Chicago Press, 1976)

Woodmansee, Martha and Mark Osteen (eds.), *The New Economic Criticism: Studies at the Intersection of Literature and Economics* (London: Routledge, 1999)

Chapter 19: History

Buckley, Jerome H., 'The Four Faces of Victorian Time', in C. A. Patrides (ed.), *Aspects of Time* (Manchester University Press, 1976)

Bullen, J. B., *The Myth of the Renaissance in Nineteenth-Century Writing* (Oxford: Clarendon Press, 1994)

Burrow, J. W., *A Liberal Descent: Victorian Historians and the English Past* (Cambridge University Press, 1981)

Chandler, Alice, *A Dream of Order: The Medieval Ideal in Nineteenth-Century Literature* (London: Routledge & Kegan Paul, 1971)

Fleishman, Avrom, *The English Historical Novel: Walter Scott to Virginia Woolf* (Baltimore and London: Johns Hopkins University Press, 1971)

Fraser, Hilary, *The Victorians and Renaissance Italy* (Oxford: Blackwell Publishing, 1992)

Girouard, Mark, *The Return to Camelot: Chivalry and the English Gentleman* (New Haven and London: Yale University Press, 1981)

Gooch, G. P., *History and Historians in the Nineteenth Century* (London: Longmans, Green & Co., 1913)

Hale, J. R. (ed.), *The Evolution of British Historiography from Bacon to Namier* (London: Macmillan, 1967)

Hill, Rosemary, *God's Architect: Pugin and the Building of Romantic Britain* (London: Allen Lane, 2007)

Hobsbawm, Eric, and Terence Ranger (eds.), *The Invention of Tradition* (Cambridge University Press, 1983)

Kaplan, Fred, *Thomas Carlyle: A Bibliography* (Cambridge University Press, 1983)

Marriott, Sir John, *English History in English Fiction* (London and Glasgow: Blackie and Son, 1940)

Masson, David, *British Novelists and their Styles: Being a Critical Sketch of the History of British Prose Fiction* (Cambridge: Macmillan & Co., 1859)

Sanders, Andrew, ' "Utter Indifference"? The Anglo-Saxons in the Nineteenth-Century Novel', in Donald Scragg and Carole Weinberg (eds.), *Literary Appropriations of the Anglo-Saxons from the Thirteenth to the Twentieth Century* (Cambridge University Press, 2000), pp. 157–73

'Victorian Romance: Romance and Mystery', in Corinne Sanders (ed.), *A Companion to Romance; From Classical to Contemporary* (Oxford: Blackwell Publishing, 2004), pp. 375–88

Chapter 20: Sexuality

Anderson, Amanda, *Tainted Souls and Painted Faces: The Rhetoric of Fallenness in Victorian Culture* (Ithaca, NY: Cornell University Press, 1993)

Ardis, Ann, *New Women, New Novels: Feminism and Early Modernism* (New Brunswick, NJ: Rutgers University Press, 1990)

Armstrong, Nancy, *Desire and Domestic Fiction: A Political History of the Novel* (Oxford University Press, 1987)

Cohen, Ed, *Talk on the Wilde Side* (New York: Routledge, 1992)

Cominos, Peter, 'Late-Victorian Sexual Respectability and the Social System', *International Review of Social History* 8 (1963), pp. 18–48, 216–50

Foucault, Michel, *The History of Sexuality. Vol. 1. An Introduction*, trans. Richard Hurley (New York: Vintage, 1978)

Houghton, Walter, *The Victorian Frame of Mind, 1830–1870* (New Haven: Yale University Press, 1957)

Levine, Philippa (ed.), *Gender and Empire* (Oxford University Press, 2004)

Marcus, Sharon, *Between Women: Friendship, Desire, and Marriage in Victorian England* (Princeton University Press, 2007)

McClintock, Anne, *Imperial Leather: Race, Gender, and Sexuality in the Colonial Contest* (New York: Routledge, 1995)

Poovey, Mary, *Uneven Developments: The Ideological Work of Gender in Mid-Victorian England* (University of Chicago Press, 1988)

Sedgwick, Eve Kosofsky, *Between Men: English Literature and Male Homosocial Desire* (New York: Columbia University Press, 1985)

Epistemology of the Closet (Berkeley: University of California Press, 1990)

Showalter, Elaine, *Sexual Anarchy: Gender and Culture at the Fin de Siècle* (New York: Viking Penguin, 1990)

Walkowitz, Judith, *City of Dreadful Delight: Narratives of Sexual Danger in Late-Victorian London* (University of Chicago Press, 1992)

   Prostitution and Victorian Society: Women, Class, and the State (Cambridge University Press, 1980)

Chapter 21: Aesthetics

Armstrong, Isobel (ed.), *Victorian Scrutinies: Reviews of Poetry 1830–1870* (London: Athlone Press, 1972)

Ashton, Rosemary, *The German Idea: Four English Writers and the Reception of German Thoughts, 1800–1860* (Cambridge University Press, 1980)

Bashford, Christina, 'Learning to Listen: Audiences for Chamber Music in Early-Victorian London', *Journal of Victorian Culture* 4 (1999), pp. 25–51

Beardsley, Monroe C., *Aesthetics from Classical Greece to the Present: A Short History* (Tuscaloosa: University of Alabama Press, 1966)

Bosanquet, Bernard, *History of Aesthetic* (London: Allen and Unwin, 1892)

Brett, David, *On Decoration* (Cambridge: Lutterworth, 1992)

Byerly, Alison, ' "The Language of the Soul": George Eliot and Music', *Nineteenth-Century Literature* 44:1 (1989), pp. 1–17

   Realism, Representation, and the Arts in Victorian Literature (Cambridge University Press, 1997)

Christ, Carol. T. and John O. Jordan (eds.), *Victorian Literature and the Victorian Visual Imagination* (Berkeley: University of California Press, 1995)

Cohen, Deborah, *Household Gods: The British and Their Possessions* (New Haven: Yale University Press, 2006)

Correa, Delia da Sousa, *George Eliot, Music, and Victorian Culture* (Basingstoke: Palgrave Macmillan, 2003)

Crary, Jonathan, *Suspensions of Perception: Attention, Spectacle, and Modern Culture* (Cambridge, MA: October/MIT Press, 1999)

   Techniques of the Observer: On Vision and Modernity in the Nineteenth Century (Cambridge, MA: October/MIT Press, 1994)

Dale, Catherine, *Music Analysis in Britain in the Nineteenth and Early Twentieth Centuries* (Aldershot: Ashgate, 2005)

Dickerson, Vanessa D. (ed.), *Keeping the Victorian House: A Collection of Essays* (New York: Garland, 1995)

Dowling, Linda, *The Vulgarization of Art: The Victorians and Aesthetic Democracy* (Charlottesville: University of Virginia Press, 1996)

Eagleton, Terry, *The Ideology of the Aesthetic* (Oxford: Basil Blackwell, 1990)

Feldman, Jessica R., *Victorian Modernism: Pragmatism and the Varieties of Aesthetic Experience* (Cambridge University Press, 2002)

Ferry, Luc, *Homo Aestheticus: The Invention of Taste in the Democratic Age*, trans. Robert de Loaiza (University of Chicago Press, 1993)

Flint, Kate, *The Victorians and the Visual Imagination* (Cambridge University Press, 2000)

Freedman, Jonathan, *Professions of Taste: Henry James, British Aestheticism, and Commodity Culture* (Stanford University Press, 1990)

Gagnier, Regenia, *Idylls of the Marketplace: Oscar Wilde and the Victorian Public* (Stanford University Press, 1986)

Gilbert, Katharine Everett and Helmut Kuhn, *A History of Aesthetics* (Bloomington: Indiana University Press, 1953)

Gillett, Paula, *Worlds of Art: Painters in Victorian Society* (New Brunswick, NJ: Rutgers University Press, 1990)

Helsinger, Elizabeth, *Poetry and the Pre-Raphaelite Arts: Dante Gabriel Rossetti and William Morris* (New Haven: Yale University Press, 2008)

Ruskin and the Art of the Beholder (Cambridge, MA: Harvard University Press, 1982)

Kramer, Lawrence, *Music and Poetry: The Nineteenth Century and After* (Berkeley: University of California Press, 1984)

Landow, George P., *The Aesthetic and Critical Theories of John Ruskin* (Princeton University Press, 1971)

Leighton, Angela, *On Form: Poetry, Aestheticism, and the Legacy of a Word* (Oxford University Press, 2007)

Lippman, Edward A. (ed.), *Musical Aesthetics: A Historical Reader. Vol. II, The Nineteenth Century* (Stuyvesant, NY: Pendragon Press, 1988)

Logan, Thad, *The Victorian Parlor* (Cambridge University Press, 2001)

Lubbock, Jules, *The Tyranny of Taste: The Politics of Architecture and Design in Britain, 1550–1960* (New Haven: Yale University Press, 1995)

Macleod, Dianne Sachko, *Art and the Victorian Middle Class: Money and the Making of Cultural Identity* (Cambridge University Press, 1996)

McGann, Jerome, *Rossetti and the Game That Must Be Lost* (New Haven: Yale University Press, 2000)

Meisel, Martin, *Realizations: Narrative, Pictorial, and Theatrical Arts in Nineteenth-Century England* (Princeton University Press, 1983)

Musgrave, Michael (ed.), *George Grove, Music and Victorian Culture* (Basingstoke: Palgrave Macmillan, 2003)

Picker, John M., *Victorian Soundscapes* (New York: Oxford University Press, 2003)

Prettejohn, Elizabeth, *Art for Art's Sake: Aestheticism in Victorian Painting* (New Haven: Yale University Press, 2007)

Psomiades, Kathy Alexis, *Beauty's Body: Femininity and Representation in British Aestheticism* (Stanford University Press, 1997)

Schaffer, Talia, *The Forgotten Female Aesthetes: Literary Culture in Late Victorian England* (Charlottesville: University of Virginia Press, 1999)

Schaffer, Talia and Kathy Psomiades (eds.), *Women and British Aestheticism* (Charlottesville: University of Virginia Press, 1984)

Scott, Derek B., *The Singing Bourgeois: Songs of the Victorian Drawing Room and Parlour* (Milton Keynes: Open University Press, 1989)

Siegel, Jonah, *Desire and Excess: The Nineteenth-Century Culture of Art* (Princeton University Press, 2000)

Haunted Museum: Longing, Travel and the Art-Romance Tradition (Princeton University Press, 2005)

Solie, Ruth A., *Music In Other Words: Victorian Conversations* (Berkeley: University of California Press, 2004)

Stein, Richard, *The Ritual of Interpretation: the Fine Arts as Literature in Ruskin, Rossetti, and Pater* (Cambridge, MA: Harvard University Press, 1975)

Temperley, Nicholas (ed.), *Music in Britain: The Romantic Age, 1800–1914* (London: Athlone, 1981)

Weber, William, *Music and the Middle Class: The Social Structure of Concert Life in London, Paris, and Vienna between 1830 and 1848* (New York: Holmes & Meier, 1975)

Weliver, Phyllis, *The Musical Crowd in English Fiction, 1840–1910: Class, Culture and Nation* (Basingstoke: Palgrave Macmillan, 2006)

(ed.), *The Figure of Music in Nineteenth-Century British Poetry* (Aldershot: Ashgate, 2005)

Williams, Carolyn, *Transfigured World: Walter Pater's Aesthetic Historicism* (Ithaca, NY: Cornell University Press, 1989)

Winn, James Anderson, *Unsuspected Eloquence: A History of the Relations between Poetry and Music* (New Haven: Yale University Press, 1981)

Woodmansee, Martha, *The Author, Art, and the Market* (New York: Columbia University Press, 1994)

Chapter 22: Science and literature

Amigoni, David, *Colonies, Cults and Evolution* (Cambridge University Press, 2007)

Beer, Gillian, *Darwin's Plots: Evolutionary Narrative in Darwin, George Eliot, and Nineteenth Century Fiction*, 3rd edn (Cambridge University Press, 2009)

Open Fields: Science in Cultural Encounter (Oxford University Press, 1996)

Bown, Nicola, Carolyn Burdett, and Pamela Thurschwell (eds.), *The Victorian Supernatural* (Cambridge University Press, 2004)

Brown, Daniel, *Hopkins and Idealism: Philosophy, Physics, Poetry* (Oxford: Clarendon Press, 1997)

Caldwell, Janis, *Literature and Medicine in Nineteenth-Century Britain: from Mary Shelley to George Eliot* (Cambridge University Press, 2004)

Clayton, Jay, *Charles Dickens in Cyberspace: the Afterlife of the Nineteenth Century in Postmodern Culture* (Oxford University Press, 2003)

Jenkins, Alice, *Space and the 'March of Mind': Literature and the Physical Sciences in Britain 1815–1850* (Oxford University Press, 2007)

Levine, George, *Darwin and the Novelists: Patterns of Science in Victorian Fiction* (Cambridge, MA: Harvard University Press, 1988)

Dying to Know: Scientific Epistemology and Narrative in Victorian England (University of Chicago Press, 2002)

O'Connor, Ralph, *The Earth on Show: Fossils and the Poetics of Popular Science, 1802–1856* (University of Chicago Press, 2007)

Otis, Laura, *Membranes: Metaphors of Invasion in Nineteenth-Century Literature, Science and Politics* (Baltimore: Johns Hopkins University Press, 1999)

(ed.), *Literature and Science in the Nineteenth Century: an Anthology* (Oxford University Press, 2002)

Paradis, James (ed.), *Samuel Butler: Victorian Against the Grain* (Toronto University Press, 2007)

Radford, Andrew, *Thomas Hardy and the Survivals of Time* (Aldershot: Ashgate, 2003)

Richardson, Angelique, *Love and Eugenics in the Late Nineteenth Century: Rational Reproduction and the New Woman* (Oxford University Press, 2003)

Shuttleworth, Sally, *Charlotte Brontë and Victorian Psychology* (Cambridge University Press, 1996)

George Eliot and Nineteenth-Century Science: the Make-believe of a Beginning (Cambridge University Press, 1984)

Smith, Jonathan, *Fact and Feeling: Baconian Science and the Nineteenth-Century Literary Imagination* (Madison: University of Wisconsin Press, 1994)

Taylor, Jenny Bourne, and Sally Shuttleworth (eds.), *Embodied Selves: An Anthology of Psychological Texts, 1830–1890* (Oxford University Press, 1998)

Thurschwell, Pamela, *Literature, Technology, and Magical Thinking, 1880–1920* (Cambridge University Press, 2001)

Chapter 23: Subjectivity, psychology, and the imagination

Armstrong, Isobel, *Victorian Poetry: Poetry, Poetics and Politics* (London: Routledge, 1993)

Bynum, William F., Roy Porter, and Michael Shepherd (eds.), *The Anatomy of Madness: Essays in the History of Psychiatry*. I. *People and Ideas*. II. *Institutions and Society*. III. *The Asylum and its Psychiatry* (London: Tavistock Publications and Routledge, 1985–8)

Campbell, Matthew, Jacqueline M. Labbe, and Sally Shuttleworth (eds.), *Memory and Memorials 1789–1914: Literary and Cultural Perspectives* (London: Routledge, 2000)

Chase, Karen, *Eros and Psyche: The Representation of Personality in Charlotte Brontë, Charles Dickens, and George Eliot* (New York: Methuen, 1984)

Dames, Nicholas, *Amnesiac Selves: Nostalgia, Forgetting, and British Fiction 1810–1870* (Oxford University Press, 2001)

Danziger, Kurt, *Naming the Mind: How Psychology Found its Language* (London: Sage, 1997)

Davis, Michael, *George Eliot and Nineteenth-Century Psychology: Exploring the Unmapped Country* (Aldershot: Ashgate, 2006)

Dixon, Thomas, *From Passions to Emotions: The Creation of a Secular Psychological Category* (Cambridge University Press, 2003)

Faas, Ekbert, *Retreat into the Mind: Victorian Poetry and the Rise of Psychiatry* (Princeton University Press, 1988)

Foucault, Michel, *Madness and Civilization: a History of Insanity in the Age of Reason*, trans. Richard Howard (1967; London: Routledge, 2001)

Humphrey, Nicholas, *A History of the Mind* (New York: Simon and Schuster, 1992)

Jacyna, L. S., 'The Physiology of Mind, the Unity of Nature, and the Moral Order in Victorian Thought', *British Journal for the History of Science* 14:2 (1981), pp. 109–32

Kearns, Michael S., *Metaphors of Mind in Fiction and Psychology* (Lexington: University Press of Kentucky, 1987)

Luckhurst, Roger, *The Invention of Telepathy 1870–1901* (Oxford University Press, 2002)

Mason, Michael York, '*Middlemarch* and Science: Problems of Life and Mind', *Review of English Studies* n.s. 22:86 (1971), pp. 151–69

Matus, Jill, *Shock, Memory and the Unconscious in Victorian Fiction* (Cambridge University Press, 2009)

'Victorian Framings of the Mind: Recent Work on Mid-Nineteenth-Century Theories of the Unconscious, Memory, and Emotion', *Literature Compass* 4:4 (2007), pp. 1257–76

Reid, Julia, *Robert Louis Stevenson, Science, and the Fin de Siècle* (Basingstoke: Palgrave Macmillan, 2006)

Rylance, Rick, *Victorian Psychology and British Culture 1850–1880* (Oxford University Press, 2000)

Scull, Andrew, *Museums of Madness: The Social Organization of Insanity in Nineteenth-Century England* (London: Allen Lane, 1979)

Showalter, Elaine, *The Female Malady: Women, Madness and English Culture, 1830–1980* (1985; London: Virago, 1987)

Shuttleworth, Sally, *Charlotte Brontë and Victorian Psychology* (1996; Cambridge University Press, 2004)

Small, Helen, *Love's Madness: Medicine, The Novel and Female Insanity, 1800–1865* (Oxford: Clarendon Press, 1996)

Smith, Roger, *The Fontana History of the Human Sciences* (London: Fontana, 1997)

'The Physiology of the Will: Mind, Body, and Psychology in the Periodical Literature, 1855–1875', in Geoffrey Cantor and Sally Shuttleworth (eds.), *Science Serialized: Representations of the Sciences in Nineteenth-Century Periodicals* (Cambridge, MA: MIT Press, 2004), pp. 81–110

Taylor, Jenny Bourne, *In the Secret Theatre of Home: Wilkie Collins, Sensation Narrative, and Nineteenth-Century Psychology* (London: Routledge, 1988)

'Obscure Recesses: Locating the Victorian Unconscious', in J. B. Bullen (ed.), *Writing and Victorianism* (London: Longman, 1997), pp. 137–79

Taylor, Jenny Bourne and Sally Shuttleworth (eds.), *Embodied Selves: An Anthology of Psychological Texts 1830–1890* (Oxford: Clarendon Press, 1998)

Vrettos, Athena, 'Dickens and the Psychology of Repetition', *Victorian Studies* 42:3 (1999/2000), pp. 399–426

Winter, Alison, *Mesmerized: Powers of Mind in Victorian Britain* (University of Chicago Press, 1998)

Young, Robert M., *Mind, Brain and Adaptation in the Nineteenth Century: Cerebral Localization and its Biological Context from Gall to Ferrier* (Oxford: Clarendon Press, 1970)

Chapter 24: Cityscapes

Benjamin, Walter, *Charles Baudelaire: A Lyric Poet in the Era of High Capitalism*, trans. Harry Zohn (London: New Left Books, 1973)

Bernstein, Carol L., *The Celebration of Scandal: Toward the Sublime in Victorian Urban Fiction* (University Park: Pennsylvania State University Press, 1991)

Briggs, Asa, *Victorian Cities* (New York: Harper and Row, 1970)

Dyos, H. J., *Exploring the Urban Past: Essays in Urban History*, ed. David Cannadine and David Reeder (Cambridge University Press, 1982)

Dyos, H. J., and Michael Wolff (eds.), *The Victorian City: Images and Realities*. 2 vols. (London: Routledge and Kegan Paul, 1973)

Feldman, Jessica, *Gender on the Divide: The Dandy in Modernist Literature* (Ithaca, NY: Cornell University Press, 1993)

Gallagher, Catherine, *The Industrial Reformation of English Fiction, 1832–1867* (University of Chicago Press, 1985)

Hunt, Tristram, *Building Jerusalem: The Rise and Fall of the Victorian City* (New York: Henry Holt, 2005)

Keating. P. J., *The Working Classes in Victorian Fiction* (New York: Barnes and Noble, 1971)

Marcus, Steven, *Engels, Manchester, and the Working Class* (New York: Random House, 1974)

Nead, Lynda, *Victorian Babylon: People, Streets, and Images of the Nineteenth-Century City* (New Haven: Yale University Press, 2000)

Nord, Deborah Epstein, *Walking the Victorian Streets: Women, Representation, and the City* (Ithaca, NY: Cornell University Press, 1995)

Olsen, Donald J., *The Growth of Victorian London* (London: B. T. Batsford, 1976)

Pike, David L., *Subterranean Cities: The World Beneath Paris and London, 1800–1945* (Ithaca, NY: Cornell University Press, 2005)

Stallybrass, Peter and Allon White, *The Politics and Poetics of Transgression* (Ithaca, NY: Cornell University Press, 1986)

Vicinus, Martha, *The Industrial Muse: A Study of Nineteenth-Century British Working-Class Culture* (New York: Barnes and Noble, 1974)

Walkowitz, Judith, *City of Dreadful Delight: Narratives of Sexual Danger in Late-Victorian London* (University of Chicago Press, 1992)

Williams, Raymond, *The Country and the City* (London: Chatto and Windus, 1973)

Chapter 25: The Rural scene: Victorian literature and the natural world

Crary, Jonathan, *Techniques of the Observer: On Vision and Modernity in the Nineteenth Century* (Cambridge, MA: MIT Press, 1990)

Ebbatson, Roger, *An Imaginary England: Nation, Landscape and Literature, 1840–1920* (Aldershot: Ashgate, 2004)

Flint, Kate, *The Victorians and the Visual Imagination* (Cambridge University Press, 2000)

Helsinger, Elizabeth K., *Rural Scenes and National Representation: Britain, 1815–1850* (Princeton University Press, 1997)

Heringman, Noah (ed.), *Romantic Science: The Literary Forms of Natural History* (Albany, NY: SUNY Press, 2003)

Hunter, Shelagh, *Victorian Idyllic Fiction: Pastoral Strategies* (London: Macmillan, 1984)

Jager, Colin, *The Book of God: Secularization and Design in the Romantic Era* (Philadelphia: University of Pennsylvania Press, 2006)

King, Amy, 'Reorienting the Scientific Frontier: Victorian Tide Pools and Literary Realism', *Victorian Studies* 47 (2005), pp. 153–63

MacLean, Gerald, Donna Landry, and Joseph P. Ward (eds.), *The Country and the City Revisited: England and the Politics of Culture, 1550–1850* (Cambridge University Press, 1999)

Wallace, Anne D., *Walking, Literature, and English Culture: the Origins and Uses of Peripatetic in the Nineteenth Century* (Oxford: Clarendon Press, 1993)

Wheeler, Michael (ed.), *Ruskin and Environment: The Storm Cloud of the Nineteenth Century* (Manchester University Press, 1995)

Williams, Raymond, *The Country and the City* (London: Chatto & Windus, 1973)

Young, Robert, *Darwin's Metaphor: Nature's Place in Victorian Culture* (Cambridge University Press, 1985)

Chapter 26: 'The annihilation of space and time': literature and technology

Anderson, Benedict, *Imagined Communities: Reflections on the Origin and Spread of Nationalism* (1983; London and New York: Verso, 2006)

Appadurai, Arjun (ed.), *The Social Life of Things: Commodities in Cultural Perspective* (Cambridge University Press, 1986)

Armstrong, Nancy, *Fiction in the Age of Photography: The Legacy of British Realism* (Cambridge, MA: Harvard University Press, 1999)

Benjamin, Walter, 'The Work of Art in the Age of Mechanical Reproduction' in *Illuminations*, trans. Harry Zohn (London: Fontana, 1973), pp. 219–53

Crary, Jonathan, *Techniques of the Observer: On Vision and Modernity in the Nineteenth Century* (Cambridge, MA and London: MIT Press, 1990)

Daly, Nicholas, *Literature, Technology, and Modernity, 1860–2000* (Cambridge University Press, 2004)

Gallagher, Catherine, *The Industrial Reformation of English Fiction, 1832–1867* (University of Chicago Press, 1985)

Kern, Stephen, *The Culture of Time and Space, 1880–1918* (Cambridge, MA: Harvard University Press, 2003)

Kittler, Friedrich A., *Discourse Networks, 1800/1900*, trans. Michael Metteer and Chris Cullens (1985; Stanford University Press, 1992)

Latour, Bruno, *We Have Never Been Modern*, trans. Catherine Porter (1991; Cambridge, MA: Harvard University Press, 1993)

Novak, Daniel A., *Realism, Photography, and Nineteenth-Century Fiction* (Cambridge University Press, 2008)

Schivelbusch, Wolfgang, *The Railway Journey: The Industrialization of Time and Space in the Nineteenth Century* (1977; Berkeley: University of California Press, 1986)

Seltzer, Mark, *Bodies and Machines* (New York and London: Routledge, 1992)

Thomas, Ronald, *Detective Fiction and the Rise of Forensic Science* (Cambridge University Press, 1999)

Thurschwell, Pamela, *Literature, Technology and Magical Thinking, 1880–1920* (Cambridge University Press, 2001)

Williams, Rosalind, *Notes on the Underground: An Essay on Technology, Society, and the Imagination* (Cambridge, MA and London: MIT Press, 1990)

Chapter 27: Space of the nineteenth-century novel

Bachelard, Gaston, *The Poetics of Space*, trans. Maria Jolas (1958; Boston: Beacon Press, 1969)

Casey, Edward S., *The Fate of Place. A Philosophical History* (Berkeley and London: University of California Press, 1997)

Harvey, David, *Spaces of Capital, Towards a Critical Geography* (London and New York: Routledge, 2001)

Lefebvre, Henri, *The Production of Space*, trans. Donald Nicholson-Smith (1974; Oxford: Blackwell, 1991)

Michie, Helena and Ronald R. Thomas (eds.), *Nineteenth-Century Geographies* (New Brunswick, NJ: Rutgers University Press, 2002)

Moretti, Franco, *Atlas of the European Novel 1800–1900* (London: Verso, 1998)

Rose, Gillian, *Feminism and Geography* (Minneapolis: University of Minnesota Press, 1993)

Chapter 28: National and regional literatures

Buzard, James, *Disorienting Fiction: The Autoethnographic Work of Nineteenth-Century British Novels* (Princeton University Press, 2005)

Cairns, David and Shaun Richards, *Writing Ireland: Colonialism, Nationalism, and Culture* (Manchester University Press, 1988)

Charnell-White, Cathryn, *Bardic Circles: National, Regional and Personal Identity in the Bardic Vision of Iolo Morganwg* (Cardiff: University of Wales Press, 2007)

Corbett, Mary Jean, *Allegories of Union in Irish and English Writing, 1790–1870* (Cambridge University Press, 2000)

Davis, Leith, Ian Duncan, and Janet Sorensen (eds.), *Scotland and the Borders of Romanticism* (Cambridge University Press, 2004)

Duncan, Ian, 'The Provincial or Regional Novel', in Patrick Brantlinger and William B. Thesing (eds.), *A Companion to the Victorian Novel* (Malden, MA: Blackwell, 2005), pp. 318–35

  Scott's Shadow: The Novel in Romantic Edinburgh (Princeton University Press, 2007)

Duff, David and Catherine Jones (eds.), *Scotland, Ireland, and the Romantic Aesthetic* (Lewisburg, PA: Bucknell University Press, 2008)

Fegan, Melissa, *Literature and the Irish Famine 1845–1919* (New York: Oxford University Press, 2002)

Fielding, Penny, *Scotland and the Fictions of Geography: North Britain, 1760–1830* (Cambridge University Press, 2008)

Hall, Catherine, Keith McLelland, and Jane Rendall, *Defining the Victorian Nation: Class, Race, Gender and the Reform Act of 1867* (Cambridge University Press, 2000)

Helsinger, Elizabeth, *Rural Scenes and National Representations* (Princeton University Press, 1997)

Kumar, Krishan, *The Making of English National Identity* (Cambridge University Press, 2003)

Kiberd, Declan, *Irish Classics* (Cambridge, MA: Harvard University Press, 2001)

Jenkins, Geraint H. (ed.), *The Welsh Language and Its Social Domains 1801–1911* (Cardiff: University of Wales Press, 2000)

Lloyd, David, *Anomalous States: Irish Writing and the Post-Colonial Moment* (Dublin: Lilliput Press, 1993)

Martin, Maureen M., *The Mighty Scot: Nation, Gender, and the Nineteenth-Century Mystique of Scottish Masculinity* (Albany: State University of New York Press, 2009)

McNeil, Kenneth, *Scotland, Britain, Empire: Writing the Highlands, 1760–1860* (Athens: Ohio State University Press, 2007)

Morash, Christopher, *Writing the Irish Famine* (New York: Clarendon Press, 1995)

O'Connell, Helen, *Ireland and the Fiction of Improvement* (New York: Oxford University Press, 2006)

Poovey, Mary, *Making a Social Body: British Cultural Formations, 1830–1864* (University of Chicago Press, 1995)

Samuel, Raphael (ed.), *Patriotism: the Making and Unmaking of British National Identity*, Vol III, *National Fictions* (London: Routledge, 1989)

Trumpener, Katie, *Bardic Nationalism: The Romantic Novel and the British Empire* (Princeton University Press, 1997)

Williams, Raymond, *The Country and the City* (London: Chatto and Windus, 1973)

Chapter 29: Britain and Europe

Ashton, Rosemary, *The German Idea: Four English Writers and the Reception of German Thought, 1800–1860* (Cambridge University Press, 1980)

Buzard, James, *The Beaten Track: European Tourism, Literature, and the Ways to 'Culture', 1800–1918* (Oxford University Press, 1993)

   Disorienting Fiction: The Autoethnographic Work of Nineteenth-Century British Novels (Princeton University Press, 2005)

Casanova, Pascale, *The World Republic of Letters*, trans. M. B. DeBevoise (1999; Cambridge, MA: Harvard University Press, 2004)

Clements, Patricia, *Baudelaire and the English Tradition* (Princeton University Press, 1985)

Cohen, Margaret and Carolyn Dever (eds.), *The Literary Channel: The Inter-National Invention of the Novel* (Princeton University Press, 2002)

Devonshire, M. G., *The English Novel in France, 1830–1870* (London: University of London Press, 1929)

France, Peter and Kenneth Haynes (eds.), *The Oxford History of Literary Translation in English, vol. IV* (Oxford University Press, 2006)

Hurst, Isobel, *Victorian Women Writers and the Classics: The Feminine of Homer* (Oxford University Press, 2006)

Marcus, Sharon, 'Same Difference? Transnationalism, Comparative Literature, and Victorian Studies', *Victorian Studies* 45:4 (2003), pp. 677–86

Maxwell, Richard, *The Mysteries of Paris and London* (Charlottesville: University of Virginia Press, 1992)

Moretti, Franco, *Atlas of the European Novel, 1800–1900* (London: Verso, 1998)

Pemble, John, *The Mediterranean Passion: Victorians and Edwardians in the South* (Oxford University Press, 1987)

Prins, Yopie, *Victorian Sappho* (Princeton University Press, 1999)

Rignall, John, 'Europe in the Victorian Novel', in Francis O'Gorman (ed.), *A Concise Companion to the Victorian Novel* (Oxford: Blackwell, 2005)

   George Eliot and Europe (Aldershot: Scolar, 1997)

Starkie, Enid, *From Gautier to Eliot: The Influence of France on English Literature, 1851–1939* (London: Hutchinson, 1960)

Thomson, Patricia, *George Sand and the Victorians: Her Influence and Reputation in Nineteenth-Century England* (London: Macmillan, 1977)

Turton, Glyn, *Turgenev and the Context of English Literature, 1850–1900* (London: Routledge, 1992)

Varouxakis, Georgios, *Victorian Political Thought on France and the French* (Basingstoke: Palgrave, 2002)

Chapter 30: Victorian empire

Ahmad, Aijaz, 'The Politics of Literary Postcoloniality', *Race and Class* 36.3 (1995), pp. 1–20

Anderson, Benedict, *Imagined Communities: Reflections on the Origin and Spread of Nationalism* (London and New York: Verso, 1991)

Appiah, Kwame Anthony, 'Is the Post- in Postmodernism the Post- in Postcolonial?', *Critical Inquiry* 17 (1991), pp. 336–51

Arac, Jonathan and Harriet Ritvo (eds.), *Macropolitics of Nineteenth-Century Literature: Nationalism, Exoticism, Imperialism* (Philadelphia: University of Pennsylvania Press, 1991)

Beinart, William and Lotte Hughes, *Environment and Empire* (Oxford University Press, 2007)

Bhabha, Homi K., *The Location of Culture* (London and New York: Verso, 1994)

Blaut, J. M., *The Colonizer's Model of the World: Geographical Diffusionism and Eurocentric History* (New York and London: Guildford, 1993)

Boehmer, Elleke, *Empire, the National, and the Postcolonial: Resistance in Interaction* (Oxford and New York: Oxford University Press, 2002)

Brennan, Timothy, 'The National Longing for Form', in Homi K. Bhabha (ed.), *Nation and Narration* (London and New York: Routledge, 1990), pp. 44–70

Cain, P. J. and A. G. Hopkins, *British Imperialism: Crisis and Deconstruction 1914–1990* (London and New York: Longman, 1993)

Césaire, Aimé, *Discourse on Colonialism*, trans. Joan Pinkham (1950; New York and London: Monthly Review Press, 1970)

Chatterjee, Partha, *Nationalist Thought and the Colonial World: A Derivative Discourse* (Minneapolis: University of Minnesota Press, 1986)

Chaturvedi, Vinayak (ed.), *Mapping Subaltern Studies and the Postcolonial* (London and New York: Verso, 2000)

Dirlik, Arif, *The Postcolonial Aura: Third World Criticism in the Age of Global Capitalism* (Boulder, Co: Westview Press, 1997)

Fabian, Johannes, *Time and the Other: How Anthropology Makes its Objects* (New York: Columbia University Press, 1983)

Fanon, Frantz, *The Wretched of the Earth*, trans. Constance Farrington (1961; New York: Grove Press, 1968)

Guha, Ranajit and Gayatri Chakravorty Spivak (eds.), *Selected Subaltern Studies* (New York and London: Oxford University Press, 1988)

Hall, Catherine, *Civilising Subjects: Metropolis and Colony in the English Imagination 1830–1867* (University of Chicago Press, 2002)

Hobsbawm, Eric, *The Age of Empire: 1875–1914* (London: Cardinal; New York: Pantheon, 1987)

Huggan, Graham, *The Postcolonial Exotic: Marketing the Margins* (London and New York: Routledge, 2001)

Hulme, Peter, *Colonial Encounters: Europe and the Native Caribbean 1492–1797* (London and New York: Routledge, 1989)

Jameson, Fredric, 'Third World Literature in the Era of Multinational Capitalism', *Social Text* 15 (1986), pp. 65–88

Kiernan, V. G., *The Lords of Human Kind: European Attitudes to the Outside World in the Imperial Age* (London: Weidenfeld and Nicholson, 1969)

Lazarus, Neil, *Nationalism and Cultural Practice in the Postcolonial World* (Cambridge University Press, 1999)

Levine, Philippa, *Gender and Empire* (Oxford University Press, 2004)

McClintock, Anne, *Imperial Leather: Race, Gender and Sexuality in the Colonial Contest* (London and New York: Routledge, 1995)

Mohanty, Chandra Talpade, 'Under Western Eyes: Feminist Scholarship and Colonial Discourse', in Chandra Talpade Mohanty, Ann Russo, and Lordes Torres (eds.), *Third World Women and the Politics of Feminism* (Bloomington: Indiana University Press, 1991), pp. 51–81

Parry, Benita, *Delusions and Discoveries: Studies on India in the British Imagination* (London and New York: Verso, 1998)

Pratt, Mary Louise, *Imperial Eyes: Travel Writing and Transculturation* (London: Routledge, 1992)

Richards, Thomas, *The Imperial Archive: Knowledge and the Fantasy of Empire* (London and New York: Verso, 1993)

Rodney, Walter, *How Europe Underdeveloped Africa* (London: Bogle L'Ouverture Publications, 1972)

Said, Edward, *Culture and Imperialism* (1993; London: Vintage, 1994)

  Orientalism (New York: Random House, 1978)

Spivak, Gayatri Chakravorty, 'Can the Subaltern Speak?' in Cary Nelson and Lawrence Grossberg (eds.), *Marxism and the Interpretation of Culture* (Urbana: University of Illinois Press, 1988), pp. 271–313

  'Three Women's Texts and a Critique of Imperialism', *Critical Inquiry* 12:1 (1985), pp. 243–61

Viswanathan, Gauri, *Masks of Conquest: Literary Study and British Rule in India* (New York: Columbia University Press; London: Faber and Faber, 1989)

Chapter 31: Writing about America

Buell, Lawrence, 'American Literary Emergence as Postcolonial Phenomenon', *American Literary History* 4 (1992), pp. 411–42

Butler, Leslie, *Critical Americans: Victorian Intellectuals and Transatlantic Liberal Reform* (Chapel Hill: University of North Carolina Press, 2007)

Claybaugh, Amanda, *The Novel of Purpose: Literature and Social Reform in the Anglo-American World* (Ithaca, NY: Cornell University Press, 2007)

Conrad, Peter, *Imagining America* (New York: Oxford University Press, 1980)

Fender, Stephen, *Sea Changes: British Emigration & American Literature* (Cambridge and New York: Cambridge University Press, 1992)

Flint, Kate, *The Transatlantic Indian 1776–1930* (Princeton University Press, 2009)

Frankel, Robert, *Observing America: The Commentary of British Visitors to the United States, 1890–1950* (Madison: University of Wisconsin Press, 2007)

Giles, Paul, *Atlantic Republic. The American Tradition in English Literature* (New York: Oxford University Press, 2007)

Transatlantic Insurrections: British Culture and the Formation of American Literature, 1730–1860 (Philadelphia: University of Pennsylvania Press, 2001)

Virtual Americas: Transnational Fictions and the Transatlantic Imaginary (Durham, NC: Duke University Press, 2002)

Gilroy, Paul, *The Black Atlantic: Modernity and Double-Consciousness* (Cambridge, MA: Harvard University Press, 1993)

McFadden, Margaret, *Golden Cables of Sympathy: The Transatlantic Sources of Nineteenth-Century Feminism* (Lexington: University Press of Kentucky, 1999)

Manning, Susan, *Fragments of Union: Making Connections in Scottish and American Writing* (Basingstoke and New York: Palgrave, 2002)

Mulvey, Christopher, *Anglo-American Landscapes: A Study of Nineteenth-Century Anglo-American Travel Literature* (Cambridge University Press, 1983)

Transatlantic Manners: Social Patterns in Nineteenth-Century Anglo-American Travel Literature (Cambridge University Press, 1990)

Tamarkin, Elisa, *Anglophilia: Deference, Devotion, and Antebellum America* (University of Chicago Press, 2008)

Tennenhouse, Leonard, *The Importance of Feeling English: American Literature and the British Diaspora, 1750–1850* (Princeton University Press, 2007)

Weisbuch, Robert, *Atlantic Double-Cross* (Chicago and London: University of Chicago Press, 1986)

Chapter 32: 1900 and the *début de siècle*: poetry, drama, fiction

Bristow, Joseph, 'Charlotte Mew's Aftereffects', *Modernism/Modernity*, 16:2 (2009), pp. 255–80

(ed.), *The Fin-de-Siècle Poem: English Literary Culture and the 1890s* (Athens: Ohio University Press, 2005)

Chothia, Jean, *English Drama of the Early Modern Period, 1890–1940* (Harlow: Longman, 1996)

Hibberd, Dominic, *Harold Monro: Poet of the New Age* (Basingstoke: Palgrave, 2001)

Hynes, Samuel, *The Edwardian Turn of Mind* (Princeton University Press, 1968)

Kemp, Sandra, Charlotte Mitchell, and David Trotter, *Edwardian Fiction: An Oxford Companion* (Oxford University Press, 1997)

Nicholls, Peter, *Modernisms: A Literary Guide* (Basingstoke: Macmillan, 1995)

Perkins, David, *A History of Modern Poetry: from the 1890s to the High Modernist Mode* (Cambridge, MA: Harvard University Press, 1976)

Trotter, David, *The English Novel in History, 1895–1920* (London: Routledge, 1993)

Wilson, A. N., *After the Victorians: The Decline of Britain in the World* (London: Hutchinson, 2005)

Chapter 33: The future of Victorian Literature

Clayton, Jay, *Charles Dickens in Cyberspace: The Afterlife of the Nineteenth Century in Postmodern Culture* (Oxford University Press, 2003)

Elias, Amy J., *Sublime Desire: History and Post-1960s Fiction* (Baltimore: Johns Hopkins University Press, 2001)

Heilmann, Ann and Mark Llewellyn, *Neo-Victorianism: The Victorians in the Twenty-First Century, 1999–2009* (Basingstoke: Palgrave Macmillan, 2010)

Hutcheon, Linda, *A Poetics of Postmodernism: History, Theory, Fiction* (New York: Routledge, 1988)

Joyce, Simon, *The Victorians in the Rearview Mirror* (Athens: Ohio University Press, 2007)

Kaplan, Cora, *Victoriana: Histories, Fictions, Criticism* (New York: Columbia University Press, 2007)

Krueger, Christine L., *Functions of Victorian Culture at the Present Time* (Athens: Ohio University Press, 2002)

Kucich, John and Dianne F. Sadoff, *Victorian Afterlife: Postmodern Culture Rewrites the Nineteenth-Century* (Minneapolis: University of Minnesota Press, 2000)

Pulham, Patricia and Rosario Arias (eds.), *Haunting and Spectrality in Neo-Victorian Fiction* (Basingstoke: Palgrave Macmillan, 2009)

Sadoff, Dianne, *Victorian Vogue: British Novels on Screen* (Minneapolis: University of Minnesota Press, 2009)

Taylor, Miles and Michael Wolff (eds.), *The Victorians Since 1901: Histories, Representations and Revisions* (Manchester University Press, 2004)

Index

1851 Census, 80
1870 Education Act, 332

Abbott, Edwin
    Flatland, 548
actresses
    life-writing of, 254
Adams, Lindsay, 657
aesthetes
    female, 137
aesthetics
    definition of, 444
Ainsworth, W. Harrison, 176, 201, 222, 416,
        514
    Jack Sheppard, 43
    Rookwood, 222
Alcott, Louisa May, 355
All the Year Round, 65, 71, 499
Allen, Grant, 137
    Physiological Aesthetics, 136
    The Evolutionist at Large, 485
    The Type-Writer Girl, 443
Andersen, Hans Christian, 316
anonymity, 67
Anstruther-Thomson, Kit, 137
Archer, William, 698
Arnold, Matthew, 35, 47, 91, 102, 103, 109, 180,
        181, 299, 307, 346–7, 353, 360,
        367, 460, 462, 464, 505, 507,
        632, 722
    and the present, 108
    function of criticism, 73–4
    Hellenic values, 114
    Jewishness, 679
    literature and religion, 353
    on aesthetics, 448–9, 452
    on America, 679
    on Celtic national character, 614–15
    on culture, 74

    on English national character, 615
    on function of poet, 458
    on Hellenism, 367, 638
    on literary criticism, 76
    on role of poet, 448, 503–4
    on William Shakespeare, 302
    on William Wordsworth, 296
    poetic tradition, 125
    WORKS
    Culture and Anarchy, 111
    Empedocles on Etna, 504
    'Function of Criticism at the Present
        Time', 90
    'The Scholar-Gipsy', 539
    'Thyrsis', 441
    'Tristram and Iseult', 417
Arnold, Thomas, 338–9, 340, 341, 417
    The Christian Life, 338
'art for art's sake', 450
artists
    life-writing of, 253
Arts and Crafts movement, 18, 307, 381, 450
Associated Booksellers, 33
Atherstone, Edwin, 186
attentiveness, 63
Austin, Alfred, 73, 190
    on sensation fiction, 44
Australia, 25, 595, 641, 644
authors
    and life-writing, 257
Aytoun, William Edmonstoune
    Firmilian, 181

Babbage, Charles, 374
Bagehot, Walter, 60, 61, 105, 108, 185,
        389, 393
    on Robert Browning, 461
Bailey, Philip James
    Festus, 175

Bain, Alexander, 485, 494
Baker, Elizabeth
   Chains, 706, 708
Bakhtin, Mikhail, 575
ballad opera, 195
ballads
   Irish, 619
Ballantyne, Robert Michael, 541, 546
   Under the Waves, 547
Banim, John and Michael, 605
banks and banking, 388–9
Barham, Richard
   Ingoldsby Legends, 22
Barrie, James Matthew, 697
Bartmann, Sarah, 425
Baudelaire, Charles, 126, 128, 129, 145, 310,
      526, 632
   Les Fleurs du Mal, 127, 632
   'The Painter of Modern Life', 61
Beardsley, Aubrey
   illustrations to *Salome*, 295
Bede, Cuthbert (Edward Bradley)
   *The Adventures of Mr Verdant
      Green*, 336
Beerbohm, Max, 694
   as comic writer, 286
Beeton, Isabella, 321
Belloc, Hilaire
   Bad Child's Book of Beasts, 313
Benjamin, Walter, 554
Bennett, Arnold, 67, 126, 142
   Clayhanger, 11
   on reading, 36
Besant, Annie, 249
   Autobiography, 249
Besant, Walter, 30
   *All Sorts and Conditions of
      Men*, 524
Bickersteth, Edward Henry
   Yesterday, To-Day, and For Ever, 186
bigamy, 436
Bird, Isabella
   and America, 666, 675–7
Blackmore, Richard Doddridge, 417, 613
   Clara Vaughan, 239, 240
Blake, William, 451
Blavatsky, Madame, 356
Blessington, Marguerite
   The Governess, 342
Blind, Mathilde, 189
   The Ascent of Man, 485
   'The Message', 432, 433
   'The Russian Student's Tale', 428

board schools, 332
Bodichon, Barbara
   on America, 675
book illustration, 17–19
Booth, Charles
   *Life and Labour of the People
      in London*, 525
Booth, William, 642
Borrow, George, 613
Bosanquet, Bernard
   History of Aesthetic, 140
Boucicault, Dion, 199, 201
   and Irish drama, 617–18
   WORKS
   After Dark, 201, 210, 561
   Black Ey'd Susan, 211
   The Corsican Brothers, 212–13
   The Octoroon, 202, 207–8, 211
Bowman, Anne
   The Boy Voyagers, 321
Boy's Own Paper, 324, 643
boys' magazines, 323
Braddon, Mary Elizabeth, 65, 499, 562
   Aurora Floyd, 227
   John Marchmont's Legacy, 227
   Lady Audley's Secret, 227, 228, 229, 461,
      463, 499, 561
   The Doctor's Wife, 231
Bradlaugh, Charles, 144
Bridgwater Treatises, 477
British and Foreign Bible Society, 35
British Association for the Advancement of
      Science, 473
Brontë, Anne
   Agnes Grey, 263, 541
   The Tenant of Wildfell Hall, 362, 463
Brontë, Charlotte, 257, 507, 695
   and fairy tale, 315
   autobiographical fiction, 263
   on Great Exhibition, 375
   on John Ruskin, 414, 446
   WORKS
   Jane Eyre, 195, 247, 263, 324, 342, 362,
      371, 372, 381, 427, 434, 454,
      509, 588, 720
   Shirley, 518
   Villette, 98–100, 263, 278–9, 362, 442, 454,
      461, 516, 588, 622
Brontë, Emily, 451, 549
   poems, 161–2, 362
   Wuthering Heights, 233, 278, 425, 461,
      537, 539, 581, 582–3, 587,
      715, 717

Brooke, Catherine Louisa, 240
Brooke, Rupert, 704–6
  Englishness, 703–4
  on Niagara Falls, 670
Broughton, Rhoda, 45, 229
  Cometh Up as a Flower, 431
Browne, Jane Euphemia ('Aunt Effie')
  'Little Rain-drops', 313
Browning, Elizabeth Barrett
  on L. E. L., 299
  WORKS
  Aurora Leigh, 183–4, 255, 423, 636
  Casa Guidi Windows, 636
  'Sonnets from the Portuguese', 439
  'The Cry of the Children', 566
Browning, Robert, 91, 158–9, 301,
          351–2, 445, 449, 459,
          461, 713
  comedy in poetry, 268
  dramatic monologues, 90
  influence on Modernist poetry, 702
  style, 302
  WORKS
  'By the Fireside', 439
  'Childe Roland to the Dark Tower
    Came', 159
  'Christmas Eve', 361
  'Fra Lippo Lippi', 161, 447
  'James Lee's Wife', 112
  'My Last Duchess', 159, 431
  Paracelsus, 174
  Sordello, 175, 296–7
  Strafford, 174, 419
  The Ring and the Book, 92, 111, 186, 187,
    268, 460
Buchanan, Robert, 189
Buckle, H. T.
  History of Civilization, 182–3
Buckley, Julia,
  The Governess, 342
Burnett, Frances Hodgson
  Little Lord Fauntleroy, 321
Burton, Richard, 260, 650
  travel writing, 260
Butler, Samuel
  Erewhon, 284, 483–4
  The Way of all Flesh, 250, 266, 284–5,
    359, 369
Byron, George Gordon, 301

Caine, Hall, 134
Caird, Mona, 438
Caldecott, Randolph, 326, 327, 328

Calverley, Charles Stuart
  parody of Browning's *The Ring and the
    Book*, 268
Canada, 84
Carleton, William
  The Black Prophet, 619
  Traits and Stories of Irish Peasantry, 617
Carlyle, Thomas, 2, 61, 100, 107, 120, 353, 407,
          485, 495, 518, 555, 611, 624
  as historian, 410–13
  influence on Charles Dickens, 420
  influence on George Meredith, 309
  influence on John Ruskin, 446
  on democracy, 118
  on humour, 270
  on industrialism, 410–13
  on mechanization, 85
  on race, 101
  on reviewing, 59–60
  on Robert Browning's *Sordello*, 296–7
  on value of autobiography, 243
  WORKS
  Chartism, 517, 518
  Frederick the Great, 179
  On Heroes and Hero-Worship, 254
  'On History', 85
  Past and Present, 265, 359
  Sartor Resartus, 243, 270, 289–92, 357, 537
  'Signs of the Times', 79, 566
  The French Revolution, 172–3, 174
Carpenter, Edward, 538
Carpenter, William Benjamin, 497, 499
Carroll, Lewis, 169, 306
  'Hiawatha's Photographing', 281
  Alice in Wonderland, 312, 435, 473, 482
  and parody, 281
  Through the Looking-Glass, 312
Chadwick, Edwin
  *Report on the Sanitary Condition of the
    Labouring Population*, 518
Chalmers, Thomas, 391
Chambers, Robert
  *Vestiges of the Natural History
    of Creation*, 476
Charlesworth, Maria Louisa
  Ministering Children, 315
Chartism, 519, 608
Children's Friend, 324
cinema, 218, 564
circulating libraries, 20, 37, 50
Clare, John, 296, 604
Clifford, William Kingdon, 485
Clough, Anne Jemima, 341–3

Clough, Arthur Hugh, 341, 350
  and religion, 346, 365
  WORKS
  Amours de Voyage, 180, 636
  Dipsychus, 181
  'Easter Day, Naples 1849', 366
  Long-Vacation Pastoral, 179
  The Bothie of Toper-na-fuosich, 179, 610
  'The Latest Decalogue', 267
Cobbe, Frances Power, 108, 429, 497
  Life, 257
Cobbett, William, 604
  on America, 665
Coleridge, Samuel Taylor
  on William Wordsworth's poetry,
    295–6
Coleridge, Sara
  Pretty Lessons in Verse, 312
Collins, Charles Allston
  Convent Thoughts, 544
Collins, Wilkie, 11, 32
  periodical publication, on, 71
  sensationalism, 230
  WORKS
  Antonina, 420
  Armadale, 229, 230
  Man and Wife, 227
  The Law and the Lady, 240
  The Moonstone, 230, 239, 499, 655
  The Woman in White, 229, 426, 427,
    435, 463, 499, 587
Collins, William, 499
colonial publishing, 25–6
commodity culture, 376–7
commodity fetishism, 382
Conrad, Joseph, 32, 129, 190, 653
  Heart of Darkness, 644, 648, 654, 658, 661
  Lord Jim, 694
Cooper, James Fenimore
  adapted for stage, 216
Cooper, Thomas
  Purgatory of Suicides, 177
Cope, Charles West, 419
copyright, 28–30, 34, 69, 85, 196
Corelli, Marie
  Boy, 695
Cornhill Magazine, 58
Craik, Dinah Mulock
  Bread Upon the Waters, 342
  Olive, 462, 463
Craik, George, 54
Crane, Walter, 323, 326
Crimean War, 87, 259

Croker, Bithia Mary, 233
Cromie, Robert
  A Plunge into Space, 547
Cross, Victoria (Annie Sophie Cory), 438
Cruikshank, George, 18, 115, 201, 274, 316,
    461, 513
Cullwick, Hannah, 441
Cushman, Charlotte, 440, 442

Dale, Thomas
  development of English literature
    studies, 343
Dallas, Eneas Sweetland, 114, 497, 504
  Poetics, 451
Daly, Augustin
  Under the Gaslight, 201, 210, 561
dandy, 145, 376, 377, 527
Darwin, Charles, 86, 87–9, 111, 260, 350,
    467, 477, 486, 539
  Autobiography, 249
  *Expression of the Emotions in Man and
    Animals*, 494
  Journal of Researches, 85, 88
  On the Origin of Species, 82, 386, 478–9,
    480, 548
  The Descent of Man, 117
  Voyage of the Beagle, 260
Darwin, Erasmus, 250
Davis, Elizabeth
  Autobiography, 259
de Mille, James
  Strange Manuscript, 648
De Quincey, Thomas, 402, 403, 511
  *Confessions of an English Opium
    Eater*, 262
De Vere, Aubrey
  'The Year of Sorrow Ireland 1849', 619
death
  culture of, 387
decadence, 130
degeneration, 500
detective fiction, 379
detectives, fictional, 238–41
Dickens, Charles, 2, 5, 18, 21, 52, 60, 71, 81, 93,
    94, 96, 100, 110, 112, 120, 176,
    193, 216, 220, 221, 224, 225,
    239, 242, 262, 263, 265, 266,
    267, 269, 270, 271, 272, 273,
    274, 275, 277, 278, 283, 289,
    294, 297, 314, 315, 317, 337,
    338, 354, 360, 376, 377, 384, 385,
    393, 395, 397, 413, 423, 433,
    461, 462, 507, 508, 514, 515,

518, 520, 531, 551, 553, 555,
558, 570, 579, 582, 584, 594,
598, 623, 625, 630, 631, 633,
660, 663, 669, 672, 680, 685,
688, 696, 708, 713, 714, 716,
721, 722, 740, 748, 749,
750, 757
and America, 673
and detectives, 239
and sensation, 225
illustrations to, 18
influence of popular theatre on, 216
memories of childhood, 262–3
on execution of Marie and Frederick
 Manning, 220–1, 242
on melodrama, 193
WORKS
A Christmas Carol, 233
A Tale of Two Cities, 181, 222, 273, 420
American Notes, 672–3, 677
Barnaby Rudge, 176
Bleak House, 217, 221, 224, 225, 266,
 274, 358, 384, 395–7, 435, 454,
 463, 520–1, 522, 585, 586
David Copperfield, 262, 263, 421, 423,
 428, 432
Dombey and Son, 262, 271, 345, 377,
 426, 551, 588, 594–7,
 646, 660
Great Expectations, 43, 51, 119, 122,
 247, 380, 384, 570, 579,
 660, 727
Hard Times, 224, 394, 395–7, 516, 518, 519,
 555, 558–9, 569, 722
Little Dorrit, 262, 397, 426, 442, 522, 523,
 570, 623, 625
Martin Chuzzlewit, 266, 673
'Mugby Junction', 553
Nicholas Nickleby, 272–3
Oliver Twist, 18, 176, 224, 273, 425, 514
Our Mutual Friend, 43, 51, 110, 111, 225,
 293–4, 395–7, 399, 514, 520,
 524, 531
Pickwick Papers, 71, 176, 270–1, 507
'The Haunted Man', 433
'The Mudfog Papers', 570
The Mystery of Edwin Drood, 463
The Old Curiosity Shop, 93–4, 95, 534
'The Signal-Man', 233
Dickinson, Emily, 168
Diderot, Denis, 197
Digby, William, 656
Dilke, Charles, 651

Disraeli, Benjamin, 46, 350, 514, 617
 on Manchester, 517
 WORKS
 Endymion, 30
 Revolutionary Epick, 174
 Sybil, 418, 518, 519, 608
 Tancred, 476
Dixon, Ella Hepworth
 My Flirtations, 285
Dixon, Richard Watson, 190
Dobell, Sydney, 502
Dodd, George
 Days at the Factories, 373–4
Dodd, William, 251
Doughty, Charles M.
 The Dawn in Britain, 191
Doyle, Arthur Conan, 32, 239–40, 241, 332,
 379, 526, 563–4, 694
 Micah Clarke, 417
dramatic monologue, 301–3, 459
Du Maurier, George
 Trilby, 368, 369, 426, 432, 464
Dunlop, John
 Oliver Cromwell, 174

Eden, Emily, 656, 658
 Up the Country, 258
Edgeworth, Maria
 Castle Rackrent, 606
 Ennui, 607
Education Act 1870, 40, 69
Edward VII
 death of, 2
Edwardian
 as term, 699–700
Egan, Pierce, 515
Egerton, George (Mary Chavelita Dunne
 Bright), 438
Eliot, George, 67, 96–8, 278, 349, 536
 and Edith Simcox, 440
 and melodrama, 216
 and music, 448
 and sensation, 226
 as reviewer, 73
 on Charles Darwin, 479
 on German humour, 269
 on Ruskin, 415
 review of Wilhelm Riehl, 95
 translations, 365
 WORKS
 Adam Bede, 97, 358, 359, 421, 428
 Daniel Deronda, 190, 349, 368, 394, 426,
  497, 509, 523, 524, 605

Eliot, George (cont.)
  Felix Holt, 519
  Middlemarch, 97–8, 117, 120, 122, 217, 280,
        359, 380, 383, 386, 397, 400,
        427, 454, 463, 479, 497, 498,
        551, 555, 588, 612, 646, 660
  Romola, 30, 113, 182, 420
  Scenes of Clerical Life, 362
  Silas Marner, 397–9, 535
  The Mill on the Floss, 97, 98, 247, 263,
        279, 344–5, 434, 463, 497, 535,
        589–94, 597, 612
  The Spanish Gypsy, 186, 187, 190
Eliot, T. S., 305, 370
  on lyric, 154–5, 166
  The Waste Land, 530
Elliotson, John, 499
Elliott, Ebenezer
  Village Patriarch, 177
Ellis, Havelock, 139, 422
  'A Note on Paul Bourget', 131
Ellis, Sarah Stickney, 321
  Sons of the Soil, 177
entropy, 474
Esquirol, Etienne
  Treatise on Insanity, 490
Ewing, Juliana
  Story of a Short Life, 315

fairy tales, 177, 315–17, 327, 555
Faraday, Michael, 469, 473
Farrar, Frederic
  Eric, or Little by Little, 319, 337
Ferguson, Samuel
  Congal, 620
Ferrier, James, 491
Ferrier, Susan
  Marriage, 607
fetishism, 382–3
'Field, Michael' (Katherine Bradley and
        Edith Cooper), 439, 706
  'Cyclamen', 546
financial journalism, 391, 392–3
Finch, Marianne
  on America, 665
Fitchett, John
  King Alfred, 178
Fitzball, Edward, 199, 200
Fitzgerald, Edward
  'Rubáiyát of Omar Khayyám', 366
Flaubert, Gustave, 554
  Madame Bovary, 624
Fleshly School of Poetry, 434

Forrest, Frank, 251
Forrester, Andrew
  The Female Detective, 240
Forster, Edward Morgan, 11, 700
Forster, John, 31, 262
Foucault, Michel
  History of Sexuality, 423–4
Fox, William Johnson, 447, 503
  on Tennyson's poetry, 451
frame poems, 459
Frazer, James George, 190
  The Golden Bough, 475
Freeman, Edward Augustus
  History of the Norman Conquest, 189
Freud, Sigmund
  'The Uncanny', 234
Frith, William Powell
  The Railway Station, 553
Frost, Robert
  on lyric, 155
Froude, James Anthony, 360
  racial theory, 648
  translator of Goethe, 624
  WORKS
  History of England, 182, 415
  The Nemesis of Faith, 248, 365

Gallienne, Richard Le
  'A Ballad of London', 527
Galsworthy, John, 708–10
  Justice, 708
  Strife, 708
  The Silver Box, 708
Galt, John, 605
Galton, Francis
  Memories of my Life, 250
Garnett, Edward, 27
Gaskell, Elizabeth, 226, 380, 518, 536
  and realism, 95
  on omnibus reading, 553
  WORKS
  Cousin Phillis, 557
  Cranford, 280, 553
  Life of Charlotte Brontë, 257, 263
  Mary Barton, 94, 224, 372–3, 428, 518,
        519, 560, 608
  'My Lady Ludlow', 550
  North and South, 95, 98, 224, 358, 454,
        516, 519, 534–5, 558, 569,
        585, 609, 673
  Sylvia's Lovers, 182, 421
  Wives and Daughters, 422
Gaspey, Thomas, 222

Georgian
   as term, 700
ghost stories, 232, 233–5, 351
Gibbon, Edward, 335
   Decline and Fall of the Roman Empire,
      89, 420
gift annuals, 17, 22, 300, 313, 554
Gilbert, William Schwenck, and Arthur
      Sullivan
   comic operas, 283–4
Girl's Own Paper, 324, 643
girls' education, 342–3
girls' magazines, 323
Gissing, George, 141, 480, 524, 529, 530, 624,
      695–6
   Born in Exile, 336
   New Grub Street, 43, 141, 638, 695
   The Nether World, 535
   The Odd Women, 529
   The Private Papers of Henry Ryecroft, 695
   Workers in the Dawn, 141
Godwin, William, 223
Gosse, Edmund, 710
   Father and Son, 250, 360, 481
Gosse, Philip Henry, 481–2
Gothic Revival, 375
governesses, 342, 371
Grand, Sarah
   The Heavenly Twins, 429, 587
Granville-Barker, Harley, 698
   Waste, 698
Graphic, 643
Gratz, Rebecca
   on Thomas Hamilton, 664
Great Exhibition, 79, 84, 100, 101, 105, 373,
      375–6, 456, 520
   Catalogue, 79, 100–1
Green, John Richard
   Short History of the English People, 189
Greenaway, Kate, 323, 326, 327
   Marigold Garden, 313
Greenwood, James, 42
Greg, Percy
   Across the Zodiac, 547
Greg, William Rathbone, 38
Gregory, Augusta, 618
Griffin, Gerald
   The Collegians, 616
Grossmith, George and Weedon
   Diary of a Nobody, 142, 276, 282, 283
Grote, George
   History of Greece, 177
grotesque, 460–1

Grundy, Sydney
   The New Woman, 428
Guild of Literature and Art, 65
Gurney, Edmund, 448

Haggard, Rider, 32, 190, 644
   and romance fiction, 134
   WORKS
   King Solomon's Mines, 540, 646–7, 650, 657
   She, 146, 233, 646, 650, 657
Haines, J. T., 200
Hale, William White, 248, 263
Hall, Anna Maria
   Stories of the Governess, 342
Hall, Basil, 667
Hallam, Arthur, 156, 296, 297–8, 386, 539
   and Alfred Tennyson, 441
   on Tennyson's poetry, 297–8, 307,
      447, 451
   poetic criticism, 91
Hamilton, Thomas
   on America, 664
handmade items, 380
Hanslick, Eduouard, 448
Hardy, Thomas, 47, 287, 423, 501, 537, 613
   and photography, 568
   and religion, 358
   and sensationalism, 230
   on circulating libraries, 52
   poetry, 703
   WORKS
   A Laodicean, 138, 567
   Far from the Madding Crowd, 46, 121, 365
   Jude the Obscure, 52, 232, 346, 368–9, 423,
      579, 580–1, 694
   Tess of the d'Urbervilles, 138, 428, 480,
      501, 560, 581, 614, 694, 697
   The Dynasts, 192
   The Return of the Native, 368, 501
   The Well-Beloved, 463, 694
Harpur, Charles
   The Creek of the Four Graves, 652
Haweis, Hugh
   Music and Morals, 448
Hawker, Robert Stephen
   Quest of the Sangraal, 417
Hayes, Alice, 246
   A Legacy, or Widow's Mite, 246
Hazlitt, William, 23, 73
Helmholtz, Hermann von, 448, 474
Helps, Arthur, 34
Hemans, Felicia, 299
   'Casabianca', 312

Hemyng, Bracebridge, 515
Henley, William Ernest, 696
   'In Hospital', 697
Henty, George Alfred, 321, 323, 541
Hill, Rowland, 47, 49
Holcroft, Thomas
   A Tale of Mystery, 198, 215
Home, Daniel D., 351
Hood, Thomas, 275–6, 316
   'Dream of Eugene Aram', 223
   'The Song of the Shirt', 378, 566–7
Hope, Anthony, 694
Hopkins, Gerard Manley, 129–33, 136, 169–71,
      297, 363, 364, 441
   and 'sprung rhythm', 306
   and the natural world, 542–3
   metrical innovation, 306
   WORKS
   'Binsey Poplars', 542
   'Hurrahing in Harvest', 445
   'Spelt from Sibyl's Leaves', 170–1, 474
   'That Nature is a Heraclitean
      Fire', 133
   'The Leaden Echo and the Golden
      Echo', 542
   'The Windhover', 130
Horne, Richard Henry
   Orion, 177
House, Humphry
   Dickens World, 5
Household Words, 45, 65, 71, 94, 100, 239, 499,
      516, 556
Housman, A. E., 165, 166, 171, 694
   homosexuality and, 692–4
   nostalgia in, 539
Housman, Laurence, 694–5, 698
   Bethlehem, 698
   Englishwoman's Love-Letters, 694
How, William (Bishop of Wakefield), 369
Howitt, Mary
   Autobiography, 257
   Our Cousins in Ohio, 259
Hudson, William Henry
   A Crystal Age, 548
Hughes, Thomas
   Tom Brown at Oxford, 340
   Tom Brown's Schooldays, 319–20, 339
Hugo, Victor, 451
Hume, Fergus
   The Mystery of a Hansom Cab, 239
Hunt, George William, 642
Hunt, James Leigh, 73
Hutton, Richard Holt, 73, 76, 365

Huxley, Thomas Henry, 133, 469, 471, 473,
      474, 485
   Man's Place in Nature, 475
Huysmans, Joris-Karl, 145
hymns, 169

Ibsen, Henrik, 216
Illustrated London News, 19, 61, 63, 83, 643
   'Supplement' on the Great Exhibition,
      100
illustration, 58, 63–4, 222
   for children's books, 325–7
India, 86, 116, 258, 377, 406, 425, 595, 644,
      645, 656
   literary consumption, 26
Indian Rebellion 1857, 106
Ingelow, Jean, 186
Ireland
   and national identity, 601–2, 603
   and national literature, 621
Irish nationalism, 107
Irving, Washington
   on English travellers in America, 666

James, George Payne Rainsford, 176
James, Henry, 126, 451
   and melodrama, 216
   and the telegraph, 571
   film adaptation, 718, 720
   on sensation fiction, 436
   on Wilkie Collins, 226
   WORKS
   'In the Cage', 570
   The Portrait of a Lady, 570–1
   The Princess Casamassima, 585
   'The Turn of the Screw', 233
James, Montague Rhodes, 235
James, William, 356, 497
Jefferies, Richard, 613
   After London, 482, 483, 537
   Bevis, 539, 541
Jerome, Jerome K.
   Three Men in a Boat, 282–3
Jerrold, Douglas, 200
   as comic writer, 276
   WORKS
   Black Ey'd Susan, 202, 204, 207, 216
   The Rent Day, 210
Jevons, W. Stanley, 389
   Theory of Political Economy, 392
Jewishness, 364
Jewsbury, Geraldine, 27, 431
Jewsbury, Maria Jane, 53

Johnston, Ellen, 251, 252
Jones, Ernest
    'Song of the Low', 267
Jowett, Benjamin, 367
Joyce, James, 369
    A Portrait of the Artist as a Young Man,
       146–7, 154
    Ulysses, 713

Kailyard school, 599, 613
Kant, Immanuel
    on space, 576–8
Kay, James
    *Moral and Physical Condition of the
       Working Classes*, 518
Keary, Annie, 320
    Castle Daly, 618
Keble, John, 352, 353, 363
    The Christian Year, 355
Kelmscott Press, 18
Kemble, Fanny (Frances Anne Butler)
    on America, 669–70
    on slavery, 670–1
Kemble, John Mitchell
    Saxons in England, 182
Kingsley, Charles, 86, 87, 248, 363
    and Charles Darwin, 483
    lectures on Alexandria, 89, 547
    WORKS
    Alton Locke, 224
    Hereward the Wake, 416
    Hypatia, 420
    The Water-Babies, 483, 540, 547
    Two Years Ago, 548
    Westward Ho!, 417
    Yeast, 536
Kingsley, Henry
    Recollections of Geoffrey Hamlyn, 649, 654
Kingsley, Mary, 261, 383, 648, 653
    travels in Africa, 260
Kingston, William Henry Giles, 323
Kipling, Rudyard, 32, 190, 686–90
    and supernatural, 233
    on America, 677–9
    WORKS
    'Et Dona Ferentes', 689
    Kim, 603, 686–9
    Stalky & Co., 320, 324, 344
    'The Islanders', 689
    'The Man Who Would Be King', 647, 654
Kirby, William
    The Golden Dog, 649
Koenig presses, 15

Landon, Letitia Elizabeth, 298–300, 441
Lang, Andrew
    and fairy tale, 316
Lawrence, David Herbert
    The Rainbow, 11
Lear, Edward, 169, 280, 306, 327
    'The Courtship of the Yonghy-Bonghy-
       Bo', 308
Lee, Vernon, 137, 139, 441, 451, 464
    on aesthetics, 452
Lee-Hamilton, Eugene and Annie, 542
Le Fanu, Sheridan, 233, 499
    WORKS
    and locked-room mystery, 239
    Carmilla, 237
    Uncle Silas, 499
Lessing, Gotthold Ephraim, 197
Lever, Charles, 603
Levy, Amy
    poetic diction, 435
    WORKS
    'Ballade of an Omnibus', 529
    'Epitaph', 386–7
    'The ballad of religion and marriage',
       268
    The Romance of a Shop, 463, 529
Lewes, George Henry, 73, 230, 479, 497, 498
    on English authorship, 254
    on Jane Austen, 612
Lewis, Leopold
    The Bells, 199, 202, 213–14, 218
Lewis, Wyndham, 710
    on Mudie's Circulating Library, 51
liberalism, 115
Liddon, Henry Parry, 363
Linton, Eliza Lynn, 52
    Autobiography of Christopher Kirkland,
       257, 263
    'Girl of the Period', 67, 431
    My Literary Life, 257
    Theodora Desanges, 484
Linton, William James
    Bob Thin, 177
literacy, 38–41, 49
literary agents, 31–2
Lombroso, Cesare, 500
London Journal, 58
Longfellow, Henry Wadsworth
    Hiawatha, 281
Lover, Samuel
    Irish Evenings, 617
Lyell, Charles, 548
    Principles of Geology, 386, 478

Lytton, Edward Bulwer, 176, 178, 222, 416,
        420, 514, 636
    Paul Clifford, 223
    Rienzi, 420
    The Coming Race, 483

Macaulay, Thomas Babington, 26, 85,
        407–10, 415
    History of England, 182
    Lays of Ancient Rome, 178
MacDonald, George, 316
    At the Back of the North Wind, 317
Machen, Arthur, 132, 142
    The Hills of Dreams, 142
Mackay, Charles
    'The Days that are Gone', 554
magazine publication, 24
Malthus, Thomas Robert, 391
Mangan, James Clarence
    'Soul and Country', 619
    'The Warning Voice', 619
Mann, Horace, 358
Manning, Marie and Frederick, 221–2
    execution, 220–1
Mansel, Henry Longueville, 499
    on sensation fiction, 436
Marryat, Frederick, 176
    The Children of the New Forest, 419
Marsh, Richard
    The Beetle, 142
Marshall, Alfred, 392
Martineau, Harriet, 48, 246–7, 351, 674
    on America, 261, 668–9
    on Niagara Falls, 670
    WORKS
    Autobiography, 249, 255, 256, 257
    History of the Peace, 83
    Illustrations of Political Economy, 391, 516
Martineau, Robert
    The Last Day in the Old Home, 589
Martyn, Edward, 618
Marx, Eleanor, 624
Marx, Karl, 16, 113, 145, 266, 381, 382, 419
    Das Capital, 392
Masson, David, 504
Maudsley, Henry
    on gender difference, 230
Maurice, Frederick Denison, 365
Maxwell, James Clerk, 468, 470
    as poet, 472
Mayhew, Henry, 79–82, 93, 224, 252,
        514–15, 525
    London Labour and London Poor, 95

McCulloch, John R., 391
Meade, Elizabeth
    A World of Girls, 337
Meade, L. T. (Elizabeth Thomasina
        Meade Smith), 320
Mearns, Andrew
    Bitter Cry of Outcast London, 524
Mechanics' Institutes, 76, 334, 454, 490
Meredith, George, 137, 297
    on comedy, 267, 282
    style, 302, 309–10
    WORKS
    Modern Love, 442
    The Egoist, 282
    Vittoria, 636
Meredith, Owen
    Chronicles and Characters, 189
    King Poppy, 190
Merriman, Henry Seton, 694
mesmerism, 249, 351, 490
Mew, Charlotte, 700–3
    'Passed', 528
    'The Farmer's Bride', 700–1
    'The Forest Road', 702
microscope, 81
Mill, James, 494
Mill, John Stuart, 391
    on literature, 505
    on lyric, 153
    on marriage, 425
    on poetry, 459
    on reading, 43
    on Thomas Carlyle's style, 289
    relationship with Harriet
        Taylor, 440
    WORKS
    Autobiography, 246, 440
    On Liberty, 427, 605
    The Subjection of Women, 118
    'What Is Poetry', 451
missionary literature, 259
Mitford, Mary Russell, 605
Molesworth, Mary Louisa
    Carrots, 314
Montgomery, Florence
    Misunderstood, 316
Moodie, Susannah, 259
    Roughing it in the Bush, 258
Moore, George, 52, 480, 616, 624
    and suburbia, 142
More, Hannah, 246
Morley, Henry
    'Ground in the Mill', 224

Morris, William, 140, 143, 187–8, 370, 381–2,
    450, 456
  and William Butler Yeats, 191
  as poet, 304
  WORKS
  Earthly Paradise, 110
  News from Nowhere, 128, 419, 482, 530,
    538, 551
  Sigurd the Volsung, 191
  The Defence of Guinevere, 417, 434, 459
Morrison, Arthur, 524
  A Child of the Jago, 143, 530, 660
Moxon, Edward, 18, 22
Mudie's Circulating Library, 22, 23, 50–2,
    54, 368, 393, 623
Müller, Max, 317
Mulock, Dinah
  John Halifax, Gentleman, 83
Munby, Arthur, 441
muscular Christianity, 340
museums, 62, 143

Naden, Constance
  The New Orthodoxy, 485–6
Napier, General Sir Charles
  William the Conqueror, 416
National Gallery, 455
Nesbit, E. (Edith Bland), 315, 324
New Journalism, 41–2, 43
New Woman, 429, 431, 437
Newgate fiction, 43, 222–3, 514
Newman, Francis, 248, 365
  Phases of Faith, 247, 354
Newman, John Henry, 86, 87, 111, 248,
    340, 354, 359, 362, 363, 364,
    365, 628
  Oxford Movement and, 340
  WORKS
  Apologia pro vita sua, 114, 247
  Callista, 181, 420
  'Lead, kindly Light', 169
  Loss and Gain, 247, 263, 336
Newton, John, 246
Nietszche, Friedrich, 287
Nightingale, Florence, 259
nonsense poetry, 169
Nordau, Max, 500
  Degeneration, 236
Norton, Caroline, 429
nostalgia, 109, 111, 112, 113, 121, 261,
    534, 716
Noyes, Alfred
  Drake, An English Epic, 191

O'Flanagan, James Roderick, 227
Obscene Publications Act 1857, 436
Oliphant, Laurence, 393
Oliphant, Margaret, 263, 351, 393, 612
  as woman writer, 256
  on Englishness, 612
  on literature, 403
  on sensation fiction, 230
  on Wilkie Collins, 232
  WORKS
  Hester, 397, 430, 431
  John Drayton, 556, 565
  Miss Marjoribanks, 381
Orderson, J. W.
  Creoleana, 641
Osborne, Sidney Godolphin, 537
Oxford Movement, 244, 248, 354, 363, 419

Paley, William
  Natural Theology, 534
Palgrave, Francis, 152, 156
  The Golden Treasury, 22, 151
Palmerston, Lord (Henry John Temple), 651
pantomime, 195, 198
Parkes, Fanny
  Wanderings of a Pilgrim, 258
Pater, Walter, 108, 114–15, 118, 126, 129, 132,
    134–6, 137, 140, 293, 296, 304,
    368, 441, 450, 451–2, 453, 464,
    505, 636
  and Dante Gabriel Rossetti, 125, 303
  WORKS
  Marius the Epicurean, 420, 452
  Studies in the History of the Renaissance,
    112, 114, 163–4, 165,
    452, 464
Patmore, Coventry, 297
  and metrical theory, 451
  on English poetry, 306
  on role of poet, 448
Peacock, Thomas Love
  Gryll Grange, 274
Penny Illustrated Paper, 63
periodical press, 56–76
periodicals for children, 322–5
Pfeiffer, Emily
  and evolution, 476–7
Phillips, Stephen
  Herod, 696
  Marpessa, 696
phonograph, 457, 484, 564
photography, 64, 90, 206, 218, 326, 457, 554
  and fiction, 568

Pinero, Arthur Wing, 216, 697–8
   The Notorious Mrs Ebbsmith, 698
   The Second Mrs Tanqueray, 697
Pitt, George Dibdin
   The String of Pearls, 201
Pixérécourt, Guilbert de, 196
Planché, James
   The Vampire, or, The Bride of the Isles, 212
playwrights, 113
Poe, Edgar Allan, 238
Poetry Bookshop, 701
poetry publication, 22
political economy, 390, 391–2
Pollok, Robert
   The Course of Time, 173
postal system, 46, 47–9, 571
Potter, Beatrix, 327, 328
Pound, Ezra, 152, 713
Pre-Raphaelite Brotherhood, 73, 96, 297, 307,
      449–50, 460
Pre-Raphaelitism, 326, 543
Prest, Thomas Peckett, 222
Prince, Mary, 259
prostitution, 160, 425, 428, 431, 432–3, 515, 516,
      527, 528
pseudonyms, 67
public libraries, 37–8
Public Libraries Act 1850, 334
Publishers Association, 33
publishers' readers, 26–8
Pugin, Augustus Welby, 412, 418
   Contrasts, 517
   influence on John Ruskin, 446
Punch, 45, 72, 265, 276, 378, 514, 515
   on Newgate Fiction, 223
   on sensation fiction, 562
Pusey, Edward Bouverie, 363
Pygmalion and Galatea, myth of, 197

Queen Victoria, 1, 685
   death, 700
   *Leaves from the Journal of Our Life
      in the Highlands*, 609
Queen's Volunteer Rifle Corps, 102–4,
      109, 121–2

Rackham, Arthur, 327
Ragged School Union, 337
railway, 2, 15, 46, 47, 58, 70, 96, 201, 231, 233,
      364, 405, 510, 552, 555, 561, 571,
      594, 646, 656, 678
   1840s boom, 88, 390, 392
   accidents, 42

and class distinctions, 120
bookstalls, 7, 20, 22, 23, 24–5
   in India, 645
   libraries, 51
   reading, 45, 70
   timetables, 226, 238
   underground, 551
Rathbone, Hannah Mary
   Childhood, 317
Reade, Charles, 403
   Gold, 393
   Hard Cash, 225, 499
   It's Never Too Late to Mend, 225
   Put Yourself in His Place, 225
   The Cloister and the Hearth, 181, 225, 417
Reade, John Edmund, 174
Reed, Talbot Baines
   Fifth Form at St Dominic's, 337
Reynolds, George William MacArthur, 514
Rhodes, Cecil, 643
Ricardo, David, 391
Riehl, Wilhelm
   Natural History of German Life, 95, 97
Robertson, Thomas William, 209, 216
Robertson, Tom
   Caste, 116, 120
Robins, Elizabeth
   Votes for Women!, 708
Robinson, W. Heath, 327
Rogers, Henry, 248
Roman Catholicism, 86
Ros, Amanda M.
   comic writer, 286
Ross, Alexander, 650, 652
Rossetti, Christina, 112, 316, 359
   and love, 439
   and religion, 363, 441
   WORKS
      'Goblin Market', 306, 307, 434, 441
      'In the Bleak Mid-Winter', 169
      Sing-Song, 314
      'Song', 167–8
      'The Convent Threshold', 160
Rossetti, Dante Gabriel, 125, 296, 297, 303–5,
      445, 450, 464, 545
   as translator, 303–4
   WORKS
      'Chimes', 308
      'Hand and Soul', 292
      'Jenny', 302–3, 432, 433, 459
      'The Blessed Damozel', 434
      The House of Life, 112
      'The Woodspurge', 544–5

rotary press, 16, 70
Royal Institution, 473
royalty payments, 31
Ruskin, John, 130, 131, 140–1, 145, 153, 154, 156,
　　　　168, 310, 343, 363, 374–5, 381, 392,
　　　　449, 450, 452, 457, 462, 464, 485,
　　　　540, 549, 555, 556, 568, 586, 627
　and fairy tale, 316
　and nature, 518, 538–9, 540, 544
　and noise pollution, 551
　and the aesthetic, 445–7
　and the grotesque, 461
　and the picturesque, 462
　and women painters, 643
　WORKS
　Fors Clavigera, 120, 123
　Praeterita, 261–2, 355
　Sesame and Lilies, 34, 111
　The King of the Golden River, 314, 317
　The Stones of Venice, 183, 407, 413–15,
　　　　518, 636, 637
　Unto This Last, 114, 116

Said, Edward
　on Jane Austen, 660
Sappho, 435, 451
Schreiner, Olive
　The Story of an African Farm, 355, 647,
　　　　658–9
Scotland
　and national identity, 601
Scott, Walter, 16, 21, 174, 176, 294, 416, 419,
　　　　546, 598, 601, 606, 609, 615,
　　　　616, 619, 625
　view of Macaulay, 409
　WORKS
　Ivanhoe, 406, 608
　Minstrelsy of the Scottish Border, 177
　Redgauntlet, 607
　Waverley, 421
Scrope, William
　on Scottishness, 609
Seacole, Mary
　*The Wonderful Adventures of
　　　　Mrs Seacole*, 259
seamstress, 378
secularization, 250
Seeley, John Robert, 97
　Expansion of England, 82, 84, 85
sentimental drama, 195, 196
serialisation of fiction, 20–1, 23
Sewell, Anna
　Black Beauty, 314

Sewell, Elizabeth Missing, 347–8
Seymour, Robert
　illustrator of *Pickwick Papers*, 293, 294
Shaftesbury, Lord (Anthony Ashley-
　　　　Cooper), 337, 338, 447
Sharp, Evelyn, 320
Shaw, Bernard, 698–9
　John Bull's Other Island, 698
　Major Barbara, 698
　The Devil's Disciple, 698
Shaw, Flora, 320
Shelley, Mary
　Frankenstein, 581, 583–4
Shelley, Percy Bysshe, 152, 451
Sherwood, Mrs Henry, 311
　History of the Fairchild Family, 355
Shorthouse, Joseph Henry
　John Inglesant, 419
Simcox, Edith
　and George Eliot, 440
Simmel, Georg, 584
Sims, George Robert, 240
　The Lights O'London, 217
Sinclair, Catherine
　Holiday House, 327
Sinclair, May, 702
slavery, 259
　British travellers in America on, 667
Smiles, Samuel
　Self-Help, 88, 253, 335, 427
Smith, Adam, 391, 392, 447
Smith, Alexander, 502, 504
Smith, Charles Manby
　The Working Man's Way in the World,
　　　　252–3
socialism, 107
Society for Promoting Christian
　　　　Knowledge, 35
Society for the Diffusion of Useful
　　　　Knowledge, 42
Society of Authors, 30, 33, 65
Somerville, Alexander
　The Autobiography of a Working Man, 251
Somerville, Edith, 541
Soulsby, Lucy, 36
Southey, Robert
　Joan of Arc, 172, 173, 174
Sowerby, Githa
　Rutherford and Son, 708
Spasmodic poets, 180, 502
Speke, John, 260
Spence, Catherine
　Gathered In, 641

Spencer, Herbert, 133, 477, 494, 495, 502
 on music, 448
spiritualism, 351
sportsmen
 life-writing of, 260
Stanley, Henry Morton, 642, 648, 649,
   653, 661
Stead, William Thomas, 42
steam press, 15, 19, 46, 70, 84, 556
steampunk, 725
Stebbins, Emma, 440, 442
Stedman, Clarence
 Victorian Poets, 89
Stephen, Fitzjames, 56
Stephen, Leslie, 66
stereoscope, 457
Sterling, John, 296
 on Thomas Carlyle, 291
Stevenson, Robert Louis, 127, 419, 500, 507
 on California, 677
 WORKS
  Kidnapped, 610, 654
  'Olalla', 500
  The Master of Ballantrae, 610
  Strange Case of Dr Jekyll and Mr Hyde,
   146, 236, 500,
   525–6, 610
  Treasure Island, 322, 654
Stewart, Dugald, 505, 506
Stoker, Bram
 Dracula, 142, 146, 229, 237–8, 436, 526,
   564–5, 587, 614, 636
Strachey, James, 706
Strachey, Lytton
 Eminent Victorians, 11, 360, 423
Strand Magazine, 563
Stretton, Hesba (Sarah Smith)
 Jessica's First Prayer, 315
Strickland, Samuel
 Twenty-Seven Years in Canada, 258
Stubbs, William
 Constitutional History of England, 189
Sturm und Drang, 195
Stutfield, Hugh, 437
suburbia, 142–3, 380
Sully, James, 444, 506
Sunday schools, 332, 341
supernatural, 221
Surtees, Robert Smith, 271–2, 541
 Jorrocks' Jaunts and Jollities, 270
Swinburne, Algernon, 124, 126, 127, 184, 296,
   304–5, 306, 308, 367, 450–1,
   462, 464, 505, 632

and Kipling, Rudyard, 687
and parody, 269, 292–3
on Blake, 126
on William Blake, 124, 126, 129
WORKS
 'A Forsaken Garden', 548
 'Anactoria', 435
 'By the North Sea', 308
 'Hertha', 305
 'The Garden of Proserpine', 134
 'The Triumph of Time', 434
 Tristram of Lyonesse, 191
Symonds, John Addington, 422, 441
Symons, Arthur, 129, 144, 527–8, 696
 The Symbolist Movement in Literature, 164
Synge, John Millington, 598, 620
Syrett, Netta, 438

Talfourd, Thomas Noon
 Ion, 174
Taunton Commission, 333
Taylor, Harriet, 440
Taylor, Henry
 Philip van Artevelde, 174
Taylor, Philip Meadows
 The Story of my Life, 254
Taylor, Tom
 The Ticket-of-Leave Man, 201
telegraph, 561, 571, 645, 656
telegraph boys, 437
temperance, 316
temperance melodramas, 200
Tennyson, Alfred, 89, 91, 92, 113, 126, 151, 158, 161,
   268, 298, 299, 301, 303, 651–2
 and Arthur Hallam, 441
 and epic, 179
 and parody, 269
 and religion, 350
 Becket, 417
 dramatic monologues, 301
 on America, 681
 WORKS
  'English Idyls', 458
  Enoch Arden, 116, 120
  Harold, 416
  Idylls of the King, 116, 123, 178, 185, 186,
   187, 417, 620, 658
  In Memoriam, 89, 298, 306, 357, 366, 386,
   441, 477–8
  Locksley Hall, 551
  'Mariana', 156–8, 162
  Maud, 92, 181, 298, 393, 459, 568
  'Oriana', 307

Poems, Chiefly Lyrical, 2, 156–8
Queen Mary, 417
'Riflemen Form!', 103, 104, 122
'The Brook', 472
'The Higher Pantheism', 269
'The Kraken', 547
'The Lady of Shalott', 460, 535
The Princess, 179, 298, 313
'The Two Voices', 357, 496
'Tithonus', 658
'Ulysses', 93
'Vastness', 547
Thackeray, William Makepeace, 65, 181, 266,
        276, 278, 292, 316, 376–7, 406,
        410, 461, 462, 508, 514
    and fairy tale, 315
    as comic writer, 278
    on John Forster, 31
    on Newgate fiction, 223
    on travellers to Europe, 633–4
    WORKS
    Catherine, A Story, 223
    De Juventute, 405–6
    The History of Henry Esmond, 417
    Vanity Fair, 179, 272, 277–8, 361–2,
        421, 426, 585, 587, 588, 629
The Germ, 292, 449
Theosophical Society, 356
thermodynamics, 474
Thierry, Augustin
    *Histoire de la conquête d'Angleterre par les
        Normands*, 406
Thompson, Elizabeth, 643
Thomson, James
    City of Dreadful Night, 367, 462, 530–1
three-decker novel, 16, 21–2, 30
Timperley, Charles
    'To the Steam Press', 557
Tonna, Charlotte Elizabeth
    Personal Recollections, 257
Traill, Catherine Parr
    Backwoods of Canada, 258
Tristan, Flora, 516
Trollope, Anthony, 695
    and America, 673–5
    and fox hunting, 272, 541
    Barsetshire novels, 612
    Can You Forgive Her?, 395, 400–2
    comic writing, 280
    on copyright, 29
    on fiction writing, 347
    on reading, 44
    'A Ride Across Palestine', 436

WORKS
Autobiography, 255
Barchester Towers, 588
He Knew He Was Right, 429, 430, 431,
        432, 442, 674
Is He Popenjoy?, 674
La Vendée, 179
Phineas Redux, 621
The American Senator, 674
The Duke's Children, 675
The Eustace Diamonds, 185, 379
The Fixed Period, 280
The Last Chronicle of Barset, 185
The Prime Minister, 425
The Small House at Allington, 587
The Way We Live Now, 30, 116, 397,
        522, 523
Trollope, Frances, 667
    and comic fiction, 271
    on America, 668
    on Americans, 667
    on slavery, 667
Tucker, Charlotte ('A.L.O.E.')
    The Light in the Robber's Cave, 322
Tuckerman, Henry, 665
Tylor, Edward Burnett, 383
    Primitive Culture, 383
Tyndall, John, 133, 135, 470,
        473, 485

Vaizey, Mrs George de Horne
        (Jessie Bell), 320
vampire, 237–8, 614
Verne, Jules, 547
Verne, Michel, 712
Vernon, Lee, 137
Victorian
    connotations of term, 288
    definition of term, 4, 11, 659–60
'Victorian values', 722
Vizetelly, Henry, 437, 468

Wales
    cultural identity, 600–1
Wallace, Alfred Russel, 86, 88
    The Wonderful Century, 1
Ward, Mary Augusta
    Eleanor, 695
    Robert Elsmere, 72, 248, 368
Warren, Samuel, 19
Watts, Isaac, 312
Webster, Augusta, 706
    'A Castaway', 428

Wells, Herbert George, 142, 190, 559
  Scientific training, 468
  WORKS
    Love and Mr Lewisham, 695
    The First Men in the Moon, 547
    The Food of the Gods, 466–7, 468
    The Island of Dr Moreau, 237, 467, 540, 727
    The Time Machine, 237, 475, 525, 565
Welsh
  national identity, 604
West, Rebecca, 710–11
  1900, 685–6, 694
Whatley, Richard, 391
Whistler, James McNeill, 450, 457
Whitman, Walt, 451, 473–4
Whymper, Edward, 541
Wilde, Oscar, 35, 73, 126, 136, 144, 146, 296,
          300, 426, 438, 441, 450, 451,
          529, 690–2, 697, 704, 711
  aesthetic criticism, 464, 505
  and comedy, 286
  and fairy tales, 317
  and homosexuality, 437
  and journalism, 61
  and the United States, 679–81, 682
  on American society, 679
  on Robert Browning, 158, 301–2
  on Rudyard Kipling, 688
  on the American West, 680
  WORKS
    A Woman of No Importance, 679,
      680, 682
    'Impressions du Matin', 527
    Salomé, 295, 691
    'Symphony in Yellow', 527
    The Ballad of Reading Gaol, 691
    'The Critic as Artist', 74–5, 76
    'The Decay of Lying', 477, 484
    The Importance of Being Earnest,
      266, 437
    The Picture of Dorian Gray, 146, 236
    'The Soul of Man Under Socialism',
      144–5
Williams, Raymond, 104–5, 458, 511, 515, 659,
      714, 725
Wiseman, Cardinal Nicholas
  Fabiola, 420

Woman's World, 61
women
  readers, 36, 37, 44, 230–1
Wood, Ellen (Mrs Henry), 229, 499
  East Lynne, 227, 228, 349
Woolf, Virginia, 2, 699, 713
  on Charlotte Mew, 702
  on George Meredith, 309
  on Victorian poetry, 438
  Women and London, 529
  WORKS
    Orlando, 11
    The Years, 529, 710
Wordsworth, William, 246, 296, 301, 347,
      470, 598
  on childhood, 312
  The Prelude, 180, 255, 511
Working Men's Colleges, 76
working men's clubs, 20
World War I, 3
Wright, Frances, 667
  on America, 668

Yeats, William Butler, 124, 128, 713
  and Ireland, 618, 620
  and Walter Pater, 164, 464
  on beauty and imagination, 134
  on William Blake, 124
  WORKS
    Celtic Twilight, 620
    The Shadowy Waters, 696
    The Wanderings of Oisin, 191
Yelverton bigamy-divorce trial, 227
Yonge, Charlotte Mary, 323
  Countess Kate, 319
  The Clever Woman of the Family, 116
  The Daisy Chain, 345
  The Heir of Redclyffe, 355, 363
  The Trial, 103
  Unknown to History, 417

Zola, Emile, 141, 437
  on experimental method, 468
  WORKS
    Germinal, 468
    La Bête Humaine, 646
    La Terre, 468